ODBC 3.5 DEVELOPER'S GUIDE

ODBC 3.5 Developer's Guide

Roger E. Sanders

McGraw-Hill
New York • San Francisco • Washington, D.C. • Auckland
Bogotá • Caracas • Lisbon • London • Madrid • Mexico City
Milan • Montreal • New Delhi • San Juan • Singapore
Sydney • Tokyo • Toronto

Library of Congress Cataloging-in-Publication Data

Sanders, Roger E.
　　ODBC 3.5 developer's guide / Roger Sanders.
　　　　p.　　cm.
　　Includes bibliographical references and index.
　　ISBN 0-07-058087-1
　　1. Relational databases.　2. Database design.　3. Microsoft ODBC.
　4. Application software—Development.　I. Title.
　QA76.9.D3S253723　1998
　005.75'6—dc21　　　　　　　　　　　　　　　　　98-24785
　　　　　　　　　　　　　　　　　　　　　　　　　　　CIP

McGraw-Hill

A Division of The McGraw-Hill Companies

1 2 3 4 5 6 7 8 9 0　1FGR/1FGR　9 0 3 2 1 0 9 8

P/N 134226-5
PART OF ISBN 0-07-058087-1

*The sponsoring editor for this book was Simon Yates and the production
supervisor was Tina Cameron. It was set in Century Schoolbook by Douglas &
Gayle Limited.*

Printed and bound by Quebecor / Fairfield.

McGraw-Hill books are available at special quantity discounts to use as
premiums and sales promotions, or for use in corporate training programs.
For more information, please write to Director of Special Sales, McGraw-Hill,
11 West 19th Street, New York, NY 10011. Or contact your local bookstore.

This book is printed on recycled, acid-free paper containing a minimum of 50%
recycled de-inked fiber.

DEDICATION

To my "second father" and mentor, Marek; to my father-in-law, Tom; and to my father, Allen.

ACKNOWLEDGMENTS

A project of this magnitude requires both a great deal of time and the support of many different people. I would like to express my gratitude to the following people for their contributions:

Thomas Cox–Microsoft Corporation

Thomas provided me with information about Version 3.5, and he reviewed portions of the manuscript for content and accuracy. He also helped me track down the people and the resources I needed to produce this book.

F. Mitchell Hughes–Microsoft Corporation

Mitchell was my key contact at Microsoft. Among other things, he made sure I received a beta copy of the ODBC 3.5 SDK and the ODBC 3.5 on-line documentation.

Kristen Sanders

My daughter Kristen helped me check ODBC 2.0, 3.0, and 3.5 SQL-STATEs during the development of Appendix B.

I would also like to thank my editor, Simon Yates, and the rest of the staff at McGraw-Hill for their help and support.

Most of all, I would like to thank my wife, Beth, for all her help and encouragement, and for once again overlooking the things that did not get done while I worked on this book.

CONTENTS

Contents

Contents

FOREWORD

In the spring of 1993, I was a contract programmer on a client-server development project for a Fortune 500 company. One of the major obstacles of that project is that we had no idea how it was going to be deployed: our early prototypes were running on XDB, IT was running DB2, R&D was a Sybase shop, and rumor had it that we were all converting to Oracle in six months. After researching the issue for some months, we crossed our fingers and committed to a newly fledged product called ODBC 1.0.

Despite some initial problems getting a stable set of drivers together, and despite the dire warnings of industry naysayers, we pressed on. When we demonstrated a second-generation prototype that could run against five unique DBMS servers, selected by the user at run-time, it was clear that this was a product that would change data access permanently.

My early exposure to ODBC led to a job writing ODBC drivers for Q+E Software, (later acquired by Intersolv,) and eventually my acceptance of the ODBC test lead position at Microsoft.

Over the years, as ODBC has grown, changed, and finally aligned with X/Open SQL CLI; there are two things that would have made my life much easier: drivers that were guaranteed to match the specification and a comprehensive reference to all versions and flavors of ODBC. While the first area has slowly matured, there has been little progress on the second – until now.

Roger Sanders has composed an indispensable tool for anyone who is learning, writing, maintaining, or reverse engineering ODBC code. The ability to easily compare conformance and behavioral differences between versions of the API is unique and extremely valuable. This book is clearly organized, concisely written, and extremely thorough. Details such as listing the pre-requisites of each API entry are a great benefit.

In addition to its value as a reference, this work also provides a wonderful tutorial. Roger has presented the key ODBC programming concepts in a clear and logical manner – the discussion of column-wise vs. row-wise binding is a gem. The exhaustive set of sample programs is also a fantastic resource.

As ODBC completes the transition from a grand concept to a mature technology, this volume will serve as a trusted companion for the ODBC programmer.

Thomas W. Cox
Sr. Systems Developer
SAS Institute Inc
twcox@pagesz.net

INTRODUCTION

Ten years ago, the idea that you could develop an application to access a database and, without modifying the program code, use that same application to access other databases was unthinkable. Then in 1991 Microsoft Corporation developed a callable SQL interface known as *Open Database Connectivity (ODBC)* for the Microsoft Windows operating system. Since then, ODBC has made interoperable database access not only possible, but commonplace.

Since its introduction, ODBC has gone through three major revisions. The latest version, Version 3.5, has just been released. This book is designed to provide you with a conceptual overview of ODBC, as well as a comprehensive reference that covers all versions of ODBC, along with the international standards upon which ODBC is based.

Why I Wrote This Book

While I was writing the section on IBM's Call Level Interface (CLI) for my first book, *The Developer's Handbook to DB2 for Common Servers,* I used the *Microsoft ODBC 2.0 Software Programmer's Reference and SDK Guide* to help identify similarities and differences between IBM CLI and ODBC 2.0. I noticed that this book provided several large example programs that incorporated several ODBC Application Programming Interface (API) function calls. Although this is a common approach used in many programming references, I have always preferred small example programs that illustrate a single concept over large example programs that illustrate many concepts—I would rather combine concepts in my own application (once I understand them) than to extract concepts individually from someone else's application as I am trying to learn them. This is the approach I used to explain application development with IBM's CLI and as I wrote that section, I began to think that a book that presented ODBC application development in a similar manner might make learning ODBC easier.

When ODBC 3.0 came out, I noticed that little had changed in the documentation format. In fact, because ODBC 3.x applications work differently with ODBC 2.0 drivers, and because ODBC 2.0 is *not* covered in the ODBC 3.x documentation, the new documentation is insufficient for developers using older ODBC drivers. The new documentation also assumes that the reader has a least some level of knowledge about and experience using ODBC. It became clear that a book was needed that someone with no prior knowledge of ODBC could understand, and that documented, compared, and contrasted each version of ODBC, along with the international standards on which ODBC is based.

Who Is This Book For

This book is for anyone who is interested in developing Open Database Connectivity (ODBC) applications. It written for both the beginner and for the advanced user that wants a comprehensive reference covering all versions, including the latest (version 3.5).

To get the most out of this book, you should have a working knowledge of the C++ programming language. An understanding of relational database concepts and structured query language (SQL) is also helpful, although not crucial, because an overview of these topics is provided in the book.

How This Book Is Organized

This book is divided into two major parts. Part 1 introduces basic ODBC fundamentals. This section contains six chapters designed to introduce you to ODBC and provide you with information about how ODBC provides applications with many of the features available in most relational database management systems (without applying the restrictions that come with using RDBMS-specific features).

Chapter 1 provides some of the history behind the development of ODBC, including: the introduction of the relational database model, the development of SQL and the various ways it can be used in applications, the Call Level Interface (CLI), why ODBC was created, and how ODBC has aligned itself with the latest industry standards. This chapter also defines what ODBC is, and what ODBC is not. The chapter concludes with a discussion on the advantages and disadvantages of using ODBC as opposed to embedded SQL.

Chapter 2 introduces ODBC architecture by providing a general description of client/server architecture as it relates to data access. This is followed by a comprehensive introduction to the four main components of ODBC architecture (applications, drivers, the ODBC Driver Manager, and data sources) and a brief look at how they work together.

Chapter 3 takes a close look at the two specific mechanisms ODBC uses to provide and maintain data consistency while working with various data sources: transactions and concurrency control. This chapter also describes the transaction isolation levels and concurrency control types that ODBC uses to maintain data integrity.

Chapter 4 examines the SQL syntax and grammar recognized and used by ODBC. This chapter describes the basic SQL statements used for data manipulation and data definition, along with the special clauses and predicates that can be used with them, and the escape sequences used by ODBC to process data source specific SQL statements. This chapter also describes the various ways that SQL statements can be constructed in an ODBC application.

Chapter 5 introduces the major components used in almost all ODBC applications to interact with data sources. This chapter introduces the concept of *handles* and explains how they are used. The chapter also describes how data buffers and length/indicator buffers are used to transfer data between ODBC applications and drivers or data sources.

Chapter 6 examines the basic processing path all ODBC applications follow and describes the three main tasks that almost all ODBC applications perform. This chapter also describes the steps required to convert ODBC source code files into executable programs.

Part 2 contains information about each ODBC API function that can be used in an application. This section is designed to be a detailed ODBC function reference; the nine chapters in this section group the ODBC API functions according to their functionality.

Chapter 7 describes the steps an ODBC application must take to initialize the ODBC environment and establish a connection to a data source or driver. This chapter also contains a detailed reference section covering each ODBC API function that can be used to initialize the ODBC environment and establish a connection to a data source or driver. Each API function described in this chapter is accompanied by a Visual C++ example that illustrates how to code the API in an application program.

Chapter 8 shows how an ODBC application can obtain detailed information about, and to a lesser extent control, the capabilities of a particular data source or driver with which it is working. This chapter also contains a detailed reference section that covers each ODBC API function that can be used to obtain information about or control a data source or driver's capabilities. Each API function described in this chapter is accompanied by a Visual C++ example that illustrates how to code the API in an application program.

Chapter 9 describes the process used by an ODBC application to prepare and execute an SQL statement. This chapter also contains a detailed reference section that covers each ODBC API function that can be used to prepare, associate application variables to (bind), and submit SQL statements for execution. Each API function described in this chapter is accompanied by a Visual C++ example that illustrates how to code the API in an application program.

Chapter 10 examines the *metadata* used to describe a result data set, and shows how an application can use this metadata to retrieve (fetch) results produced when an SQL statement that produces a result data set (such as a **SELECT SQL** statement) is executed. This chapter also contains a detailed reference section that covers each ODBC API function that can be used to obtain result data set metadata, associate application variables to (bind) columns in a result data set, and perform basic data retrieval operations. Each API function described in this chapter is accompanied by a Visual C++ example that illustrates how to code the API in an application program.

Chapter 11 introduces the *extended* cursors (that is, block cursors and scrollable cursors) used by ODBC to perform advanced data retrieval operations. This chapter also contains a detailed reference section covering each ODBC API function that can be used to perform advanced data retrieval operations, using ODBC's extended cursor set. Each API function described in this chapter is accompanied by a Visual C++ example that illustrates how to code the API in an application program.

Chapter 12 describes the methods an ODBC application can use to modify data in a data source as well as to determine how many rows were actually affected by a insert, update, or delete operation. This chapter also contains a detailed reference section that covers each ODBC API function that can be used to insert, update, and delete rows of data in a data source. Each API function described in this chapter is accompanied by a Visual C++ example that illustrates how to code the API in an application program.

Chapter 13 introduces the concept of descriptors. Although they have been "behind the scenes" for quite some time, with version 3.0, descriptors were brought out of hiding. This chapter is designed to introduce ODBC descriptors and show how they can be used to streamline application processing. This chapter also contains a detailed reference section that covers each ODBC API function that can be used to retrieve information from, modify, and copy descriptor records. Each API function described in this chapter is accompanied by a Visual C++ example that illustrates how to code the API in an application program.

Chapter 14 describes the mechanisms used by ODBC to report the success or failure of an ODBC API function call to the calling application. This chapter also contains a detailed reference section that covers each ODBC

API function that can be used to retrieve error/warning information from a diagnostic record and return it to an application. Each API function described in this chapter is accompanied by a Visual C++ example that illustrates how to code the API in an application program.

Chapter 15 describes the system catalog of a data source and explains how the information stored in it can be used by an application. This chapter also contains a detailed reference section that covers each ODBC API function that can be used to retrieve information from the system catalog of a specified data source. Each API function described in this chapter is accompanied by a Visual C++ example that illustrates how to code the API in an application program.

Syntax Conventions Used In This Book

SQL statement syntax is presented throughout this book to show the basic format to use when coding a particular SQL statement. The following conventions are used wherever SQL statement syntax is presented:

- [*parameter*]   Parameters shown inside brackets are required parameters and must be specified.

- <*parameter*>   Parameters shown inside angle brackets are optional parameters and do not have to be specified.

- *parameter* | *parameter*   Parameters, or other items separated by vertical bars indicate that you must select one item from the list of items presented.

- *parameter*,...   If a parameter is followed by a comma and three periods (ellipsis), then multiple instances of that parameter can be included in the statement.

The following examples illustrate these syntax conventions:

- Example 1:

  ```
  CONNECT TO [server-name] <connection-mode> <USER
  [authorization-ID] USING [password]
  ```

  In this example, both *connection-mode* and **USER** *[authorization-ID]* **USING** *[password]* are optional parameters, as indicated by the angle brackets. The *server-name*, *authorization-ID*, and *password* parameters are required, as indicated by the brackets. However, *authorization-ID*, and *password* are only required parameters if the `USER [authorization-ID] USING [password]` option is specified.

■ Example 2:

`RELEASE [server-name | CURRENT | ALL <SQL> ]`

In this example, either *server-name*, `CURRENT`, or `ALL <SQL>` can be specified, as indicated by the vertical bar. One of these items must be specified, as indicated by the brackets. If `ALL` is selected, `SQL` can be added (that is, `ALL SQL`), however it is not required, as indicated by the angle brackets.

■ Example 3:

`CREATE <UNIQUE> INDEX [index-name] ON [table-name] ( [column-name <ASC | DESC>,...] )`

In this example, *index-name*, *table-name*, and at least one *column-name* must be specified, as indicated by the brackets. `UNIQUE`, `ASC`, and `DESC` are options, as indicated by the angle brackets. Either `ASC`, or `DESC` can be specified as an option, but not both (as indicated by the vertical bar). More than one `column-name <ASC | DESC>` option can be specified, as indicated by the `...` that follows the `column-name <ASC | DESC>` option.

API Conformance

A header similar to the one shown below is provided with each ODBC API function call:

COMPATABILITY					
X/OPEN 95 CLI	ISO/IEC 92 CLI	ODBC 1.0	ODBC 2.0	ODBC 3.0	ODBC 3.5
☒	☑	☑	☑	☐	☐

API CONFORMANCE LEVEL	**CORE**

Each standards specification that the ODBC API function conforms to will be checked ✓; if the API conformed to an earlier version of a particular standard specification but is no longer supported by that specification, the box under the specification will contain an ✗ .

A Word About ODBC 3.5 Unicode Support

Unicode is a method of software character encoding that treats all characters as having a fixed width of two bytes. This method is used as an alternative to the ANSI character encoding method that is normally used by Windows, which because characters are treated as having a fixed width of one byte, is limited to 256 characters. Because Unicode can represent over 65,000 characters, it accommodates many languages whose characters are not represented in ANSI encoding.

Unicode does not require the use of codepages, which ANSI uses to accommodate a limited set of languages and it is an improvement over the Double-Byte Character Set (DBCS), which uses a mixture of 8-bit and 16-bit characters and requires the use of codepages.

One of the major differences between ODBC 3.0 and ODBC 3.5 is that the ODBC 3.5 Driver Manager is Unicode-enabled. This means that when using ODBC 3.5, the Driver Manager maps function string arguments and string data to either Unicode or ANSI characters, as required by the application and/or driver. This also means that the ODBC 3.5 Driver Manager supports the use of a Unicode driver with both a Unicode application and an ANSI application; the use of an ANSI driver with an ANSI application; and that it provides limited Unicode-to-ANSI mapping for a Unicode application that is working with an ANSI driver.

I have tried to document cases where Unicode support has an affect or imposes a limitation on an ODBC API function being used; however, for the sake of saving space, I have not gone into great detail about Unicode application development. If you are developing applications that need to provide full Unicode support, consult the ODBC 3.5 On-Line Help for more information.

You can find out more information about the Unicode standard, by visiting the web site :http://www.cam.spyglass.com/unicode.html.

About the Examples

The example programs provided are an essential part of this book, therefore, it is imperative that they are accurate. To make the use of each ODBC API function call clear, I included only the required overhead in each example, and I provided very limited error checking. I have also tried to design the example programs so that they verify that the ODBC API function call being demonstrated actually executed as expected. For instance, an example program illustrating statement attribute modification might retrieve and display a record before and after the modification to verify that the ODBC API function used to modify the data worked correctly.

I compiled and tested all the examples in this book with Visual C++ 5.0, running against a Microsoft Access or Microsoft SQL Server database. Appendix D shows the steps used to create the Microsoft Access database test environment and the steps used to reproduce and test all of the examples provided in this book.

A Word About ODBC API Parameter And Return Code Data Types

As you examine the ODBC API Syntax conventions and examples provided, you may notice that in many cases the Syntax section may indicate that a parameter in an API function call is one data type and the actual data type used in the example program is another. For example, the Syntax section for the **SQLConnect()** function shows that the first parameter has the data type SQLHDBC, but the data type used for the first parameter in the **SQLConnect()** function call shown in example CH7EX1.CPP is SQLHANDLE. You may also notice that some ODBC API functions have a return code data type of SQLRETURN while others (ODBC 2.0 and earlier only) have a return code data type of RETCODE.

Although at first glance these differences may appear to be errors, they are not. An examination of the header file SQLTYPES.H will show that many data types that appear to be different are actually the same. For example, the following excerpt from the SQLTYPES.H header file shows that although different data types exist for environment, connection, statement, and descriptor handles, they are all really the same.

```
/*-----------------------------------------------------------------*/
** SQLTYPES.H - This file defines the types used in ODBC          */
**                                                                 */
** (C) Copyright 1995-1996 By Microsoft Corp.                      */
**                                                                 */
**      Created 04/10/95 for 2.50 specification                    */
**      Updated 12/11/95 for 3.00 specification                    */
/*-----------------------------------------------------------------*/

. . .
/* generic data structures */
#if (ODBCVER >= 0x0300)
#if defined(WIN32)
```

```
typedef void*                    SQLHANDLE;
#else
typedef SQLINTEGER               SQLHANDLE;
#endif  /* defined(WIN32) */
typedef SQLHANDLE                SQLHENV;
typedef SQLHANDLE                SQLHDBC;
typedef SQLHANDLE                SQLHSTMT;
typedef SQLHANDLE                SQLHDESC;
#else
#if defined(WIN32)
typedef void*                    SQLHENV;
typedef void*                    SQLHDBC;
typedef void*                    SQLHSTMT;
#else
typedef SQLINTEGER               SQLHENV;
typedef SQLINTEGER               SQLHDBC;
typedef SQLINTEGER               SQLHSTMT;
#endif  /* defined(WIN32) */
#endif  /* ODBCVER >= 0x0300 */
. . .
```

Feedback and Source Code on the Diskette

I have tried to make sure that all the information and examples provided in this book are accurate; however, I am not perfect. If you happen to find a problem with some of the information in this book or with one of the example programs, please send me the correction so I can make the appropriate changes in future printings. In addition, I would welcome any comments you might have about this book. The best way to communicate with me is via e-mail at r-**bsanders@mindspring.com**.

As mentioned earlier, all the example programs provided in this book have been tested for accuracy. Thus, if you type them in exactly as they appear in the book, they should compile and execute successfully. To help you avoid all that typing, electronic copies of these programs have been provided on the diskette accompanying this book.

Limits of Liability and Warranty Disclaimer

Both the publisher and I have used our best efforts in preparing the material in this book. These efforts include obtaining technical information from Microsoft Corporation as well as developing and testing the example programs to determine their effectiveness and accuracy. We make no warranty of any kind, expressed or implied, with regard to the documentation and example programs provided in this book. We shall not be liable in any event for incidental or consequential damages in connection with or arising out of the furnishing, performance, or use of either this documentation or these example programs.

1

Introduction to ODBC

ODBC, an acronym for Open Database Connectivity, is a standardized set of *application programming interface* (API) function calls that can be used to access data stored in both relational and non-relational *database management systems* (DBMSs). The first part of this chapter provides some of the history behind the development of ODBC, including:

- The introduction of the relational database model
- The development of *Structured Query Language* (SQL) and the various ways it can be used in applications
- The Call Level Interface (CLI).
- Why ODBC was created and how it has aligned itself with the latest CLI standards.

This is followed by an explanation of what ODBC is (and what it is not). Finally, the advantages and disadvantages of using ODBC as opposed to embedded SQL are discussed.

The History of SQL and ODBC

In order to understand why ODBC was developed, it is important to look at how data processing has evolved over the last twenty-five years. The first significant event in data processing that eventually led to the development of ODBC was the introduction of the relational database model. That's where we will begin our discussion.

The Relational Database

Most database management systems available today are based on the *relational database* model. The first relational database model was introduced in the early 1970's at the IBM San Jose Research Center by Mr. E. F. Codd. This model is designed around a set of powerful mathematical concepts known as *Relational Algebra* and it is based on the following operations:

SELECTION—This operation selects a record or records from a table based on a specified condition.

PROJECTION—This operation returns a column or columns from a table based on some condition.

JOIN—This operation allows you to paste two or more tables together. Each table must have a common column before a JOIN can work.

UNION—This operation combines two like tables to produce a set of all records found in both tables. Each table must have compatible columns before a UNION can work. In other words, each field in the first table must match each field in the second table. Essentially, a UNION of two tables is the same as the mathematical addition of two tables.

DIFFERENCE—This operation tells you what records are unique to one table when two tables are compared. Again, each table must have identical columns before a DIFFERENCE can work. Essentially, a DIFFERENCE of two tables is the same as the mathematical subtraction of two tables.

INTERSECTION—This operation tells you what records are common to two or more tables when they are compared. This operation involves performing the UNION and DIFFERENCE operations twice.

PRODUCT—This operation combines two dissimilar tables to produce a set of all records found in both tables. Essentially, a PRODUCT of two tables is the same as the mathematical multiplication of two tables. The PRODUCT operation can often produce unwanted side effects, requiring you to use the PROJECTION operation to clean them up.

As you can see, in a relational database data is perceived to exist in one or more two-dimensional tables. These tables are made up of rows and columns, where each record (row) is divided into fields (columns) containing individual pieces of information. Although data is not actually stored this way, visualizing it as a collection of two-dimensional tables makes it easier to describe data needs in easy-to-understand terms. Figure 1–1 illustrates how data appears to be stored in a relational DBMS.

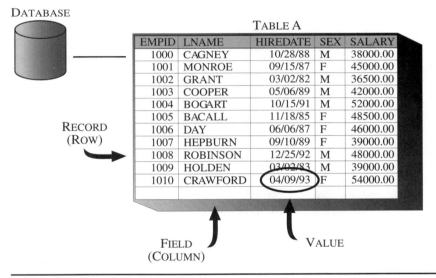

DATABASE

TABLE A

RECORD (ROW)

EMPID	LNAME	HIREDATE	SEX	SALARY
1000	CAGNEY	10/28/88	M	38000.00
1001	MONROE	09/15/87	F	45000.00
1002	GRANT	03/02/82	M	36500.00
1003	COOPER	05/06/89	M	42000.00
1004	BOGART	10/15/91	M	52000.00
1005	BACALL	11/18/85	F	48500.00
1006	DAY	06/06/87	F	46000.00
1007	HEPBURN	09/10/89	F	39000.00
1008	ROBINSON	12/25/92	M	48000.00
1009	HOLDEN	03/02/83	M	39000.00
1010	CRAWFORD	04/09/93	F	54000.00

FIELD (COLUMN)

VALUE

Figure 1–1 *Data in a relational database management system can be visualized as residing in a two dimensional table.*

Structured Query Language

A relational database provides users with the ability to store, access, and modify data in an organized and efficient way. However, gaining access to the data stored in relational databases has not always been easy. Originally, the only way to retrieve data stored in a relational database was by executing one or more custom programs written in a high-level programming language (usually COBOL). Although these programs could be written to present a relatively friendly interface to a non-technical user, access to the data itself required the services of a knowledgeable programmer. Consequently, casual access to data stored in a relational database was not practical.

Users were not entirely happy with this situation—although they had an excellent way to store data, getting access to it often required convincing a DBMS programmer to write special software. For example, if a company's sales department wanted to see the total sales for the previous month, and if it wanted this information ranked by each salesperson's length of service in the company, it had two choices: the department could either use an existing program that allowed the information in the database to be accessed in exactly this manner, or it had to ask a programmer to create such a program. Many times this proved to be more work than it was worth, and it was an expensive solution for one-time, or ad-hoc, inquiries. As more and more users wanted easy access to their data, this problem grew larger and larger.

Providing users with the ability to access their data on an ad-hoc basis required giving them a language with which to express their requests. Many query languages (so named because a single request to a database is defined as a query) were developed for this purpose but one of them, *Structured Query Language*, invented at IBM in the 1970s, became the most popular one in use. Structured Query Language, more commonly known by its acronym, SQL, became an *American National Standards Institute* (ANSI) standard in 1986 and an *International Organization for Standardization* (ISO) standard in 1987. It is used today in many database management systems. Initially, SQL was defined as a language that was to be separate from all other programming languages. However, in 1989, the original standard specifications were modified and the following methods of interfacing SQL with other programming languages were defined:

- Direct Invocation—Specified that SQL statements can be invoked directly from an application program

- Embedded SQL—Specified that SQL statements can be embedded directly within the source code of an application program. The 1989 standards specification defined embedded SQL statements for the COBOL, FORTRAN, PL/1, and Pascal programming languages.

- Module Language—Specified a programmatic access to SQL procedures stored in compiled program modules. These SQL procedures can be called from a conventional program in the same manner a subroutine or external function would be called. Like conventional subroutines or external functions, SQL procedures can use parameter passing to obtain values from and return values to the calling program.

In 1992, ANSI modified the standards specification again, and the newest (and latest) SQL specification, known as SQL-92, was released. The SQL-92 specification included several new items:

- Additional data types, including date and time
- Support for dynamic SQL
- Scrollable cursors
- Full outer-join support
- Definitions for connections to database environments (to address the needs of client/server architectures)

The SQL-92 specification has become the international standard for SQL and, consequently, it has had the greatest impact on the development of ODBC.

EMBEDDED SQL Because SQL is non-procedural by design, it is not an actual programming language; therefore, most database applications are built by combining the decision and sequence control of a high-level programming language with the data storage, manipulation, and retrieval capabilities of SQL. This is the central idea behind embedded SQL: SQL statements to be sent to a DBMS are embedded directly in the source code file of an application program. Because an embedded SQL program contains a mixture of SQL and high-level programming language statements, it cannot be submitted directly to a compiler designed exclusively for the high-level language being used. Instead, embedded SQL programs must be compiled through a multistep process.

Two types of SQL can be used in an application program—*static SQL* and *dynamic SQL*—and each have their own advantages and disadvantages.

STATIC SQL A *static SQL* statement is an SQL statement that is hard-coded in an application program when the source code file is written. Because static SQL statements reside in the source code itself, the application knows all SQL statement formats in advance. Unfortunately, high-level programming language compilers cannot interpret SQL; therefore, all source code files containing static SQL statements must be processed by an SQL precompiler before they can be compiled. Likewise, DBMSs cannot work directly with high-level programming language variables. Instead, they work with *host variables* that are defined in a special place (so the SQL precompiler can recognize them) within an embedded SQL source code file. The SQL precompiler translates all SQL statements in a source code file to the appropriate host language function calls and converts the actual SQL statements into host language comments. The

SQL precompiler also evaluates the declared data types of all host variables defined and determines which data conversion methods need to be used when data is moved to and from the database. Additionally, the SQL precompiler performs error checking on each coded SQL statement and ensures that appropriate host variable data types are used for their respective table column values.

Static SQL has the advantage of executing quickly, because its operational form already exists as an access plan in the database. The trade-off is that all static SQL statements must be prepared before the application program can be executed—they cannot be modified at application run time. Additionally, when static SQL statements are used in an application their operational packages must be "bound" to each database the application will work with before they can be executed.

NOTE: *Because static SQL applications require prior knowledge of database, table, schema, and field names, changes made to these objects after the application is developed could produce undesirable results.*

DYNAMIC SQL Although static SQL statements are easy to use, their functionality is limited because their format must be known in advance by the precompiler and because they can only work with host variables. *Dynamic SQL* statements do not have precoded fixed formats, so the data objects they use can change each time the statement is executed. This is useful for an application in which the format and the syntax of the SQL statements to be used are not known when the source code is written. Dynamic SQL statements do not have to be precompiled and bound to the database they will access (although the overhead required to use dynamic SQL statements sometimes has to be precompiled and bound to the database). Instead, they are compiled along with the high-level language source code in which they are embedded to create an executable program and all "binding" takes place at application run time. Dynamic SQL statements also enable the optimizer to see the real values of arguments, so they are not confined to the use of host variables.

Because the actual creation of dynamic SQL statements is based on the flow of programming logic at application run time, they are more powerful than static SQL statements. Unfortunately, dynamic SQL statements are also more complicated to use and implement. Additionally, because the optimized access plans for dynamic SQL statements are generated at application run time rather than at compile time, most dynamic SQL statements execute slower than their static SQL counterparts.

NOTE: *Because dynamic SQL statements use the most current database information available during execution, sometimes they can execute faster than equivalent static SQL statements, particularly when the database has been modified since the application was last precompiled. If source code files containing static SQL are re-precompiled after a database is modified (and after the database information is updated), static SQL statements always execute faster than their dynamic SQL statement counterparts.*

HOW SQL IS PROCESSED BY A DATABASE   Regardless of the type of SQL used in an application program (static or dynamic), it is important to understand how SQL statements are processed by the DBMS when it receives them.

In order to process an SQL statement, a DBMS must perform the following steps:

1. The DBMS parses the SQL statement (that is, it breaks the statement up into individual words, called tokens, and makes sure that it has a valid verb and valid clauses, etc.). Syntax errors and misspellings may also be detected in this step.

2. The DBMS validates the statement by checking it against the system catalog. Do all the tables named in the statement exist in the database? Do all the columns exist, and are the column names unambiguous? Does the user have the required authorization to execute the statement? Certain semantic errors can also be detected in this step.

3. The DBMS generates an access plan for the statement. The access plan is a binary representation of the steps required to actually perform the work requested by the SQL statement; it is the DBMS equivalent of executable code.

4. The DBMS optimizes the access plan. Can an index be used to speed a search? Should the DBMS first apply a search condition to one table and then join it to another, or should it begin with the join and use the search condition afterward? Can a sequential search through a table be avoided or reduced to a subset of the table? After exploring the various ways to carry out the access plan, the DBMS chooses the one that it will use.

5. The DBMS executes the statement by running the access plan.

Figure 1–2 shows the steps involved in processing an SQL statement.

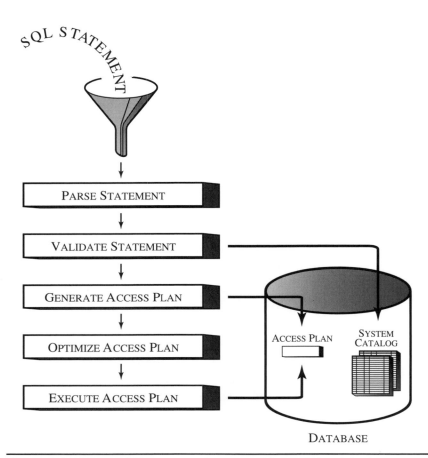

Figure 1–2 *How an SQL statement is processed by a relational database management system.*

The amount of database access required and the amount of time needed to execute each step varies. Parsing an SQL statement does not require access to the database and typically can be done very quickly. Optimization, on the other hand, is a very CPU-intensive process and requires exclusive access to the system catalog/tables. For a complex, multitable query, the optimizer may explore thousands of different ways of carrying out the same query. However, the cost of executing such queries inefficiently is usually so high that the time spent in optimization is more than regained in increased query execution speed. This is even more significant if the same optimized access plan can be used over and over to perform repetitive query tasks.

PROCEDURES AND MODULES SQL statements do not have to be embedded directly within a source code file in order to be sent to a DBMS for processing. They can also be placed in procedures, which can then be called from another source code file. These procedures generally contain a single SQL statement and data is passed to and from the statement through one or more procedure (function) arguments. SQL procedures are typically stored in modules (which can be thought of as object or function libraries) that can be linked to application code. However, the the manner in which procedures in a module and an application are actually linked together is implementation-dependent. For example, the procedures could be compiled into object code and linked directly to the application code, they could be compiled and stored in the DBMS (as stored procedures), and calls to access plan identifiers could be placed in the application code, or they could be linked and interpreted at application run time (for example, as Dynamic Link Libraries).

The main advantage of using modules and procedures as opposed to embedding SQL statements in an application source code file is that this approach cleanly separates SQL statements from high-level programming languages. This separation makes application development easier because only the modules containing SQL statements have to be precompiled. Also, in theory, this approach should enable you to make changes to one part of an application without having to change the other—the two parts only need to be relinked to produce a modified application.

The Call Level Interface (CLI)

At first, companies installed and used a single DBMS and all database access was done either through the front end of the installed system or through applications written (using embedded SQL) to work exclusively with that system. However, as the use of computers grew and more computer hardware and software became available, companies began to acquire several different DBMSs. This situation became even more complex with the introduction of the *Personal Computer* (PC); PCs brought in a whole new set of tools for querying, analyzing, and displaying data, as well as a number of inexpensive, easy-to-use DBMSs. Seemingly overnight, a single corporation could find itself with data scattered across a myriad of hardware (PCs, servers, and mini-computers), stored in a variety of incompatible databases, and accessed by a vast number of tools, few of which could get at every piece of the company's data.

To make matters worse, before developers could even begin to try to re-solve these issues, along came *client/server* computing. Client/server com-puting revolved around the idea to use inexpensive PCs (the clients) to provide a graphical front end to the data and mini-computers and main-frame computers (the servers) to host the DBMS where their computing power and central location could be used to provide quick, coordinated data access. This new paradigm raised a serious question: "How could the front-end software be connected to the back-end databases?

Similar problems faced *independent software vendors* (ISVs) that were writing and marketing "database-centric" applications. Because of the dif-ferences in DBMSs, vendors were usually forced to write one version of the application (or to write DBMS-specific code) for each DBMS they wanted to access. This often meant a huge amount of resources were spent writing and maintaining data-access routines, rather than writing the ap-plications themselves. Applications were often sold not on their quality but on whether they could access data in a specific DBMS.

Although the standardization of SQL helped to reduce the amount of DBMS-specific differences both sets of developers faced, what they needed most was a way to access data in any DBMS: the former group needed a way to merge data from different DBMSs in a single application, while the latter group needed a way to write a single application that could interact with any DBMS available. In short, both groups needed *interoperability*.

At the same time that ANSI was working on the SQL-92 standards specification, the X/Open Company and a consortium of leading software and hardware database vendors known as the *SQL Access Group* (SAG) (which is now a part of the X/Open Company) jointly developed a stan-dard specification for a callable SQL interface. This interface, referred to as the *X/Open Call-Level Interface* (or X/Open CLI), focused on using function calls to invoke dynamic SQL statements instead of blending SQL with another programming language.

NOTE: *DBMSs that support embedded SQL already have some type of call-level interface. When embedded SQL is processed by an SQL precompiler, each SQL statement found is converted into a corresponding function call. However, these function calls are undocumented and they were never intended to be used directly by programmers.*

In 1995, X/Open modified the original CLI standards specification and the newer specification became an ISO/IEC standard shortly afterwards.

The goal of the X/Open CLI interface was to increase the portability of database applications by allowing them to become independent of any one

DBMS's programming interface. CLI is similar to dynamic SQL (in fact CLI supports the dynamic SQL described in the SAG and X/Open SQL CAE specification) in that SQL statements are passed to the DBMS for processing at runtime, but it differs from embedded SQL as a whole in that there are no embedded SQL statements and no precompiler is required. CLI is especially useful in client/server architectures; the application program residing on one computer (the client) can make CLI function calls that can be sent across a network to a DBMS residing on another computer (the server) for processing.

The ODBC Interface

In 1991, Microsoft Corporation developed a callable SQL interface, known as *Open Database Connectivity* (ODBC), for the Microsoft Windows operating system. Earlier versions of the ODBC interface were modeled directly from a preliminary draft of the original X/Open CLI interface and from the SAG SQL CAE specification. This interface contained all the functions in the CLI specifications of the X/Open draft as well as some additional functions that were needed by many applications. The ODBC interface defined an operating environment where a database specific library, or *driver*, is required for each data source supporting it. A driver implements the functions in the ODBC API and it is dynamically loaded (based on the database name provided with the connection request) at application run time by an ODBC *Driver Manager*. When the application is executed, the ODBC Driver Manager receives its ODBC API function calls and routes them to the appropriate data source-specific driver. Figure 1–3 shows an example of how applications interact with a data source via the ODBC Driver Manager and a data source driver.

By using drivers, an application can be linked directly to a single ODBC driver library rather than to several data source-specific libraries. To use a different driver, the application does not need to be recompiled or relinked; instead it simply loads the new driver and calls the ODBC API functions stored there. If the application needs to access multiple data sources simultaneously, it simply loads multiple drivers. The actual format of an ODBC driver is operating system-specific. For example, on the Windows 95 and Windows NT operating system, drivers are treated as *dynamic link libraries* (DLLs).

ODBC 3.X AND STANDARD CLI Although earlier versions of ODBC were based on preliminary drafts of the X/Open and ISO/IEC CLI specifications, they did not fully meet the standards specifications finalized in

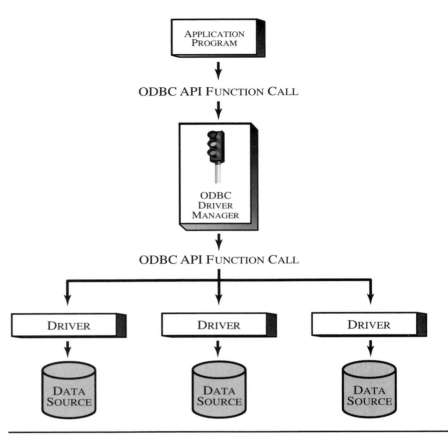

Figure 1–3 How ODBC application programs interact with various data sources via an ODBC Driver Manager and data source-specific drivers.

1995. One of the most significant changes in versions 3.x of ODBC is its alignment with the following CLI specifications standards:

■ The X/Open CAE Specification "Data Management: SQL Call-Level Interface (CLI)"

■ ISO/IEC 9075-3:1995 (E) Call-Level Interface (SQL/CLI)

NOTE: *ODBC 3.0 and 3.5's features are a superset of each of these standards. The Call Level Interface specifications defined in these standards and in ODBC are continually evolving in a cooperative manner in order to produce new functionality that provides application developers with additional capabilities.*

As a result of this alignment, an application written to the X/Open and ISO CLI specifications will work with an ODBC 3.x driver or a CLI standards-compliant driver when it:

1. Is compiled with ODBC 3.x header files
2. Is linked with ODBC 3.x libraries
3. Gains access to the appropriate driver through the ODBC 3.x Driver Manager

Likewise, a driver written to the X/Open and ISO CLI specifications will work with an ODBC 3.x application or a CLI standards-compliant application when it is

1. Compiled with ODBC 3.x header files.
2. Linked with ODBC 3.x libraries

and when the ODBC 3.x application gains access to it through the ODBC 3.x Driver Manager.

Additionally, the Core interface conformance level encompasses all the features in the ISO CLI standards and all the non-optional features in the X/Open CLI standards. Because all ODBC 3.x drivers are required to support the features in the Core interface conformance level, an ODBC 3.x driver supports all the features used by a CLI standards-compliant application. Likewise, an ODBC 3.x application that only uses the features in ISO CLI and/or the non-optional features of the X/Open CLI works with any CLI standards-compliant driver. Driver interface conformance levels are discussed in detail in Chapter 2.

NOTE: *Although ODBC 3.x is closely aligned with the latest Call-Level Interface (CLI) specifications standards, it is important to note that the API naming conventions used by ODBC differ from the naming conventions used in the specifications standards: ODBC begins the name of each of its APIs with the letters "SQL"; the X/Open and ISO/IEC specifications standards do not. For example, the ODBC API function* **SQLAllocHandle()** *is named* **AllocHandle()** *in the X/Open and ISO/IEC specifications standards.*

What ODBC 3.x Is (and Is Not)

Many misconceptions about ODBC exist in the computing world. To the end user, it may be just another computer acronym. To the application developer, it is a library of data-access API routines. To many others, it is the cure-all to any database access problem.

First and foremost, ODBC is a specification for a set of data access call-level interface APIs. This set of APIs remains the same regardless of the data source, operating system, or high-level programming language used (although many functions work with "C language data types," ODBC APIs are language-independent). The ODBC 3.x API set contains all the functions defined in the 1995 X/Open and ISO/IEC CLI standards specifications, along with additional functions commonly needed by developers of screen-based database applications (for example, scrollable cursors).

In addition to specifying a standard call-level interface, ODBC also defines a standard SQL grammar based on the X/Open SQL CAE specification. Differences between the two grammars are minor and primarily are due to the differences between the SQL grammar required by embedded SQL (X/Open) and the SQL grammar required by CLI (ODBC). There are also some extensions to the ODBC SQL grammar to support commonly available language features not covered by the X/Open grammar.

Although ODBC API functions are called from within an application, the functions themselves are actually implemented by data source-specific drivers. This allows applications to access data in a data source-independent manner. The use of drivers also provides the ability to access multiple data sources simultaneously, however the code needed to do this can be quite complex.

ODBC itself supports a significant number of DBMS features—more than are provided by most DBMSs—but it does not require drivers to provide the same level of support. Instead, drivers are only required to implement a subset of those features. Drivers can implement any or all of the remaining features if they are supported by the underlying data source, or if the driver chooses to emulate them. However, every driver must support two special ODBC API functions that can return general information to an application about a driver's capabilities, as well as a list of ODBC functions the driver supports. Thus, ODBC applications can be written to exploit the features of a single data source supported by a driver, to use only the features used by all data sources, or to check for support of a particular feature and use it accordingly. ODBC does not require applications to be written with "the lowest common denominator" of functionality in mind.

Because ODBC defines a common interface for all the data source features it supports, ODBC applications contain feature-specific code, not data source-specific code, and they can use any data source-specific driver supporting those features. One advantage of this is that applications do not need to be updated when the features supported by a data source are enhanced; instead, when updated drivers are installed, an application can automatically use the new features because its code is feature-specific, not driver- or DBMS-specific.

It is important to understand that ODBC is designed to utilize database capabilities, not supplement them. Therefore, application writers should not expect the use of ODBC to suddenly transform a simple data source into a full-featured, relational database engine. Additionally, applications using ODBC are responsible for providing any cross-database functionality needed. For example, ODBC is not a heterogeneous join engine, nor is it a distributed transaction processor. However, because ODBC is data source-independent, it can be used to build such cross-database tools.

Advantages and Drawbacks of Using ODBC Instead of Embedded SQL

It was mentioned earlier that database applications using embedded SQL usually require a precompiler to convert SQL statements into high-level language source code that can then be compiled, bound to a database, and executed. Normally, SQL precompilers are designed specifically for the database product they are packaged with. This means that precompilers essentially tie embedded SQL applications to a single database product (the one they are shipped with). Therefore, in order for an embedded SQL application to work with other database products, it may have to be modified first and it will always have to be rebuilt using other database SQL precompilers. Additionally, if the other database product uses access plans (packages), the embedded SQL application will also have to be bound to the new database(s).

In contrast, database applications that use ODBC do not require precompilation or binding. Instead, they use a standardized set of API function calls to execute dynamic SQL statements (and related services) at application run time. Because ODBC applications do not require precompilation, they do not have to be recompiled or rebound in order to work with other database products. This means that once an ODBC application has been written and successfully compiled, it can immediately be run against other database products that support ODBC (and if ODBC 3.x is used—against products supporting Standard CLI). ODBC API function calls and embedded SQL statements also differ in the following ways:

- ODBC API function calls do not require the explicit declaration of host variables. Instead, any variable defined in an ODBC application source code file can be used to send or retrieve data to and from any data source.

- ODBC API function calls do not require the explicit declaration of cursors. Instead, cursors are automatically generated as they are needed.

- Use of the OPEN SQL statement is unnecessary in ODBC applications. Because cursors are automatically generated for ODBC API function calls that need them, they are also automatically opened whenever a multiple row SELECT SQL statement is executed.

- Unlike embedded SQL, ODBC API function calls allow the use of parameter markers in SQL statements.

- ODBC API function calls manage SQL statement-related information for the application by using *statement handle*s that treat this data as an abstract object. Statement handles eliminate the need to use database product-specific data structures, such as SQLCA and SQLDA. *Environment handles* and *connection handles* are also provided to ODBC applications so they can reference global variables and connection specific information.

- ODBC has the ability to support two or more concurrent transactions on different database server connections. ODBC can also support two or more connections to the same database server at the same time.

Despite these differences between ODBC function calls and embedded SQL statements, there is an important common concept between the two. Applications using ODBC can execute any SQL statement that can be dynamically prepared in embedded SQL. This is guaranteed because an ODBC application passes all of its SQL statements directly to the data source for dynamic execution instead of attempting to execute them itself.

NOTE: *ODBC can also accept some SQL statements that cannot be dynamically prepared in embedded SQL, such as compound SQL statements. In addition, ODBC can process any SQL statement that can be dynamically prepared by the DBMS product that the application is running against. This is because some DBMS products may support SQL statements that other DBMS products do not.*

By allowing the data source to execute all SQL statements, the portability of ODBC applications is guaranteed. This is not always the case with embedded SQL statements because the way in which SQL statements are dynamically prepared can vary with each relational database product. Also, since COMMIT and ROLLBACK SQL statements can be dynamically prepared by some database products but cannot be dynamically prepared by others, they are not used in ODBC applications. Instead, ODBC applications use a special API function call to perform ROLLBACK and COMMIT operations. This ensures that ODBC applications can successfully end their transactions, regardless of what database product is being used.

As with almost everything else in life, there are tradeoffs for the portability that ODBC provides. For one thing, ODBC applications cannot take advantage of the API calls offered by a specific data source and remain portable. Data source-specific APIs can be called from an ODBC application; however, the ODBC application may no longer execute on other database platforms without first being modified, recompiled, or both. Another disadvantage of ODBC can be seen in the performance comparison between dynamic and static SQL. Dynamic SQL is prepared at runtime, while static SQL is written directly in the source code file and prepared when the source code file is precompiled. Since preparing SQL statements requires additional processing time, static SQL is usually more efficient than dynamic SQL. Moreover, since ODBC is essentially another layer on top of dynamic SQL, performance may be reduced even further (tests conducted by Intersolv and Microsoft have shown a 2% to 5% reduction in performance; however, this may be insignificant compared to performance increases that can be gained with optimum network configurations). If optimum performance is a major issue, then using ODBC may not be an option.

NOTE: *Applications can take advantage of both ODBC and embedded SQL by creating static SQL stored procedures and invoking them from within an ODBC application. It is also possible to write key modules with embedded SQL and link them to ODBC applications. This approach, however, complicates the application design and should only be considered if static SQL stored procedures, for some reason, cannot be used.*

SUMMARY

Data processing has undergone several major changes in the last 25 years. Most of these changes have, in one way or another, influenced the development of the Call Level Interface and ODBC. ODBC (acronym for *Open Database Connectivity*) is Microsoft Corporation's standardized *Application Programming Interface* (API) that can be used to access data stored in both relational and non-relational database management systems. ODBC provides an alternative to *Structured Query Language* (SQL) and it can be used to perform essentially equivalent operations against any data source that has a corresponding ODBC driver.

The important difference between embedded SQL statements and ODBC API function calls lies in how the actual SQL statements are invoked. With embedded SQL, an application prepares and executes SQL for a single DBMS. With ODBC, an application uses procedure calls at application run time to perform SQL operations. In order for a dynamic SQL application to work with a different database management system, the application would have to be precompiled and recompiled for that database management system. Since ODBC applications do not have to be precompiled, they can be executed against a variety of data sources without undergoing any alteration.

Typically, an application using embedded SQL will execute faster than an equivalent ODBC application. However, if ODBC is used instead of SQL in an application program, data stored in a variety of personal computer, minicomputer, and mainframe DBMSs can be accessed and manipulated, regardless of the data storage format, and programming interface used.

ODBC Architecture

As mentioned in Chapter 1, ODBC was primarily designed to exploit client/server architectures. Because of this, the underlying architecture of ODBC is based on the client/server model. To lay the groundwork for the discussion of ODBC architecture, this chapter starts out with a general description of client/server architecture as it relates to data access. This is followed by a comprehensive introduction to the four main components of ODBC—applications, drivers, the Driver Manager, and data sources—as well as a brief look at how they work together.

The Client/Server Model

Client/server architecture focuses on breaking an application into two separate parts, putting those parts on two different machines, and having them communicate with each other as the application executes. This allows the DBMS intelligence to reside on a minicomputer or mainframe (the server) where computing power and centralized control can be used to provide quick, coordinated data access while the application logic resides on one or more PCs (the client) so that it can make effective use of all the resources the PC has to offer without causing a bottleneck at the server. This concept uses the resources of both the clients and the servers to their fullest potential. On the surface, it appears that a client/server system only has two main components: the client and the server. However, another important component exists that must not be overlooked: the data protocol that provides the communication layer between the client and the server. In addition to these three major components, several other subcomponents complete the client/server architecture.

Figure 2–1 illustrates the three major components of client/server architecture, along with some of their subcomponents.

As we examine the roles these three major components play, we will look at some of the smaller subcomponents stored within them and discuss the tasks they perform. By the way, if you're curious about where ODBC fits in Figure 2–1, it replaces the Database API subcomponent of the Client.

The Role of the Client

In a client/server system, application logic resides and runs on the client. This application logic is responsible for managing the information displayed on the screen, processing user input, and interacting with the server. Unlike other applications, a client/server application does not use file *input/output* (I/O) primitives to communicate with data sources. Instead, it uses an entirely different programming mechanism—the Database API. Although alternatives exist, the Database API is typically a combination of SQL and some type of programming interface (such as CLI) that sends SQL statements to a data source for processing. The Database API provides a much higher level of abstraction than simple file I/O primitives.

Just below the Database API, (in our simplified representation of client/server architecture) is the network/communications interface. This subcomponent works with the network transport layer to actually transmit data to and receive data from the server workstation. The network/

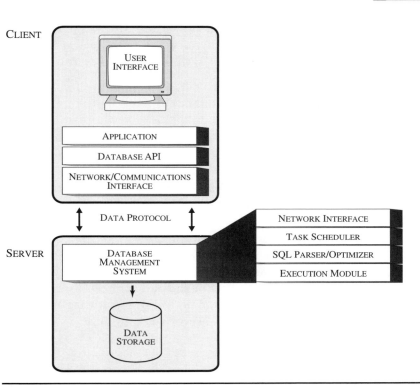

Figure 2–1 *The three major components in client/server architecture, along with some of their subcomponents.*

communications interface is another abstraction layer that hides from the client/server application logic the details of the particular network software being used (for example, Novell NetWare, TCP/IP, or SNA). Although some important differences exist (for example, the network programming interface's ability to cancel requests in progress and to deal with issues related to asynchronous processing), the core of the network/communications interface looks remarkably like simple file I/O primitives.

The Role of the Server

In a client/server system, the DBMS resides and runs on the server. The DBMS interacts with one or more clients by means of a network/communications interface similar to the network/communications interface subcomponent used on the client. In addition to the network/communications interface, the DBMS also contains several other subcomponents, such as a task scheduler, and an SQL parser/optimizer that allow it to process requests it receives from the client/server application on the client workstation. The DBMS controls all access to its data.

Data Protocol

In a client/server system, the data protocol component describes the form of the information exchanged between the client and the server. Information is sent to and returned from the server by means of a programming interface that looks very similar to simple file I/O (that is, it opens a connection to the server, writes to the server, reads from the server, and closes the connection). Actual information exchanged between the client and the server includes things like SQL strings, result data sets from queries, and error messages; all of which are typically encoded in a very terse format in order to reduce the actual number of bytes sent across the network. The flow of the data protocol is made possible by all the other underlying layers of networking software and hardware existing on both the client and the server workstations.

The Components of ODBC Architecture

ODBC was designed around the client/server architecture model. ODBC was also designed with the assumption that a programming interface that can send and receive the data protocol of an SQL-supporting data source will function and perform just like the native (SQL precompiler generated) API for that data source. Because of this assumption, ODBC is not limited to client/server DBMSs; instead, ODBC's overall architecture is flexible enough to work with desktop databases and file-oriented data stores such as spreadsheets and ASCII text files.

Unlike the client/server architecture model, ODBC's architecture consists of four major components.

■ Applications—Applications are responsible for interacting with the user and for calling ODBC functions to submit SQL statements to and retrieve results from one or more data sources.

■ Drivers—Drivers process ODBC function calls, submit SQL requests to specific data sources, and return results to applications. Drivers are also responsible for interacting with software that is needed to access a specific data source (for example, the software that interfaces to underlying networks or file systems).

■ The Driver Manager—The Driver Manager loads and calls one or more drivers on behalf of an application.

■ Data Sources—Data sources consist of sets of data and their associated environments, which include operating system, DBMS, and network platform used (if any) to access the DBMS that an application wants to access. The term data source is used rather loosely to describe any set of data that has a supporting ODBC driver.

Figure 2–2 shows how these four components work with both file-oriented and client/server DBMS data sources. Notice how in ODBC architecture, the Database API component of client/server architecture (shown in Figure 2–1) has been divided into two components—the ODBC Driver and the ODBC Driver Manager.

Applications

Applications are executable programs that call ODBC API functions to access data in one or more data sources. Because the majority of data access work is done with SQL, applications usually use ODBC API function calls to submit SQL statements to data sources and to retrieve the results (if any) generated when those statements are executed. In addition to calling ODBC API functions, applications perform all other work external to the ODBC interface.

Although many kinds of applications exist, most can be classified as one of the following types:

■ Generic

■ Vertical

■ Custom

GENERIC APPLICATIONS   Generic applications, often referred to as shrink-wrapped applications or off-the-shelf applications, are designed to work with a variety of different data sources. Examples include a spreadsheet or statistics package that uses ODBC to import data for further analysis, and a word processing package that uses ODBC to obtain a mailing list

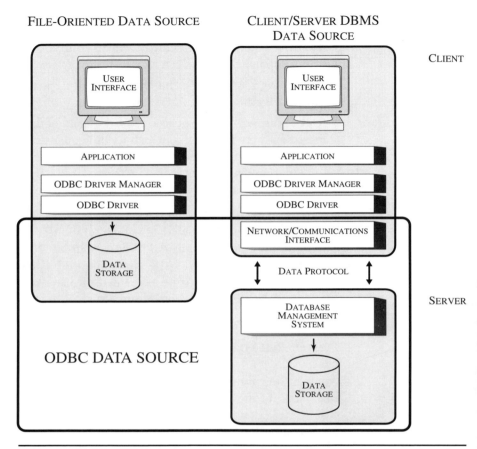

Figure 2–2 How the four components of ODBC architecture recognize and work with file-oriented and client/server DBMS data sources.

from a database. The one thing all generic applications have in common is that they are highly interoperable among data sources and/or DBMS products and they tend to use ODBC in a relatively generic manner.

Interactive application development environments (IDEs), such as PowerBuilder, Microsoft Visual Basic, and Microsoft Visual C++ make up an important subcategory of generic applications. Even though applications constructed with these IDEs may only work with a single data source, the IDE itself needs to be able to work with many different data sources.

VERTICAL APPLICATIONS   Vertical applications are usually designed to perform a single type of task and to work with a database schema (a logical grouping of database objects) controlled by the application developer. An example would be an order entry package using ODBC to store data in dBASE for small businesses and in Oracle for large corporations. Vertical applications use ODBC in a manner in which they are not tied to any one specific data source, although they might be tied to a limited number of data sources that provide similar functionality (typically, a vertical application works with a single data source). Thus, vertical applications can be sold independently from data source/DBMS products. Vertical applications are usually interoperable when they are developed but are sometimes modified to include non-interoperable code once a particular data source product is chosen.

CUSTOM APPLICATIONS   Custom applications are designed to perform a specific task, usually within a single company. An application in a large company that gathers sales data from several divisions (each of which uses a different data source) and creates a single report would be an example of a custom application. ODBC is often used in developing custom applications because it provides a common programming interface. Application developers only need to learn one interface instead of several. Because custom applications are generally written to work with specific data sources and drivers, they are not interoperable.

Drivers

Drivers are libraries that implement the functions in the ODBC API for a specific data source. Each driver is customized for a specific data source, therefore they are not interchangeable (that is, a driver for Oracle cannot be used to access data in a dBASE database). Because drivers are customized for a single data source, they typically limit their implementation of the ODBC API to the capabilities of the underlying data source for which they are written. For example, if a data source does not support outer joins, then neither does its driver. The one major exception to this occurs in drivers for data sources without standalone database engines, such as Xbase. Drivers for these types of data sources must implement all ODBC API functions that support at least a minimal amount of SQL.

Drivers provide applications with the ability to access a variety of data sources. However, because the ODBC API functions supported by each driver can vary, an application needs to have some idea of which functions are supported by the driver it is working with (and which are not). Fortunately, every driver must support two ODBC APIs that allow an application to determine, at run time, the ODBC API capabilities and the SQL grammar constructs it (and consequently the underlying data source) supports.

NOTE: *Applications designed to work with a single driver or with a small, known set of drivers can be written so that they only use the ODBC APIs and SQL grammar constructs provided by that driver or set of drivers.*

Drivers are responsible for performing the following tasks:

- Connecting to and disconnecting from the data source.
- Checking for function errors not checked by the Driver Manager.
- Initiating transactions.
- Submitting SQL statements to the data source for execution. If necessary, the driver converts ODBC SQL to data source-specific SQL before it submits it to the data source for processing. Often, this conversion is limited to replacing escape sequences with the appropriate data source-specific SQL.
- Sending data to and retrieving data from the data source, including converting data types as specified by the application.
- Mapping data source-specific errors to ODBC SQLSTATEs.

DRIVER CONFORMANCE LEVELS   When the ANSI group created the SQL-92 standard, they understood that each DBMS supports a different set of SQL functionality and syntax. Because of this, the SQL-92 standard defines three distinct levels of SQL functionality: *Entry*, *Intermediate*, and *Full*. The ODBC standard goes one step further by defining conformance levels for drivers in two areas: the ODBC API and the ODBC SQL grammar (including ODBC SQL data types). Conformance levels make up the highest category of driver capability partitioning in ODBC.

The whole concept of conformance levels was incorporated into ODBC for the following reasons:

- To provide the ability for applications and drivers to implement portions of the ODBC API, specific to their needs, without having to implement complete functionality. Not only does this reduce development time for drivers, it allows simpler, smaller drivers to be developed. It also provides a clear migration path for providing greater levels of functionality in later releases of drivers and applications.

▪ To align ODBC with current CLI standards so that the distinction between truly standard and extension portions the ODBC API would be readily apparent. The SQL standard itself has maintained conformance levels since its first release in 1986. There were two levels then; with SQL-92 (the current standard) there are three.

▪ To help achieve interoperability. At lower conformance levels, an application has less work to do to operate with multiple data sources; the drawback is that the lower conformance levels provide less functionality. Higher conformance levels provide an application with greater power. However, programming for higher conformance levels requires an application to be more complex.

Conformance levels make an application programmer's job easier by defining a standard set of functionality that both the driver developer and application developer can rely on. By definition, if a driver claims to conform to a specific API or SQL conformance level, it must support all the functionality defined by that conformance level. If the data source associated with a driver does not provide some of the functionality defined for a conformance level, the driver must either provide the missing functionality itself or claim to conform to a lower conformance level. However, the converse is not true—if a driver provides all the functionality defined by one conformance level and some of the functionality of the next conformance level, the driver does not have to provide the missing functionality. In addition, if a driver supports all the functionality defined for a higher conformance level, it must provide all the functionality defined by all lower conformance levels. Applications can determine the exact functionality provided by a driver by calling three ODBC API functions at run time, that all drivers, regardless of their conformance level, must support.

API CONFORMANCE LEVELS API conformance levels are used to categorize the sets of ODBC API function calls a driver supports. To simplify API (or interface) conformance specification, ODBC defines three API conformance levels: *Core*, *Level 1*, and *Level 2*. Unfortunately, interface conformance levels do not always neatly divide into support for specific lists of ODBC API functions. That's because some functions can provide more or less functionality, depending on how they are used.

NOTE: *The ODBC interface conformance levels in Version 3.x have different requirements than the ODBC interface conformance levels of the same name in Version 2.0 or earlier. In particular, all the features implied by ODBC 2.0 interface conformance Level 1 are now part of the Core interface conformance level. Consequently, many ODBC drivers may now only report Core level interface conformance.*

CORE FUNCTIONALITY The Core interface conformance level provides all the basic functionality an application needs in order to work with a data source. Core level functionality was designed so that driver developers who only wanted to use the standard ODBC API set would have a clearly defined subset to do just that. The standard ODBC API subset defined for Core level conformance provides all the functionality defined in the ISO/IEC CLI specification and all the non-optional functionality defined in the 1992 X/Open CLI specification. A Core level interface conformant ODBC driver allows an application to do the following:

- Allocate and free all types of handles.
- Close cursors, release bound columns, and reset all parameter marker buffers.
- Bind result data set columns to application variables.
- Handle dynamic parameters, including arrays of parameters, but only in the input direction.
- Specify a bind offset.
- Perform data-at-execution sequences.
- Manage cursors and cursor names.
- Gain access to the description (metadata) of result data sets.
- Query the data dictionary. (The driver is not required to support multi-part names of database tables and views. However, certain features of the SQL-92 specification, such as column qualification and names of indexes, are syntactically comparable to multi-part names.)
- Manage data sources and connections.
- Obtain information about drivers, no matter which ODBC level they support.
- Prepare and execute SQL statements using the dynamic SQL model of the SQL-92 standard (that is, prepare and execute a statement, optionally supplying parameter values at run time).

- Fetch a single row, or multiple rows of data from a result data set —in the forward direction only.

- Retrieve data, in parts, from an unbound column of a result data set.

- Obtain the current values of all environment, connection, and SQL statement attributes, set all attributes to their default values, and set certain attributes to non-default values.

- Manipulate certain fields of descriptor records.

- Obtain information from diagnostic record fields.

- Detect driver capabilities.

- Detect the result of any text substitutions made to an SQL statement before it is sent to the data source.

- Commit a transaction.

- Cancel the data-at-execution dialog and, in multithread environments, cancel an ODBC function executing in another thread. Core level interface conformance does not mandate support for asynchronous execution of functions nor the ability to cancel an ODBC function that is executing asynchronously. Neither the platform nor the ODBC driver needs to be multithreaded for the driver to conduct independent activities at the same time. However, in multithread environments, the ODBC driver must be thread-safe. Serialization of requests from the application is a conformant way to implement this specification, even though it may create serious performance problems.

- Obtain row-identifying column information for any table in the data source.

NOTE: *All ODBC drivers must provide at least Core level interface conformance.*

LEVEL 1 FUNCTIONALITY The Level 1 interface conformance level provides functionality that allows application developers to build a wider variety of full-featured applications than is possible with Core level functionality. It includes all the Core interface conformance level functionality plus additional features usually available in *On-Line Transaction Processing* (OLTP) relational DBMSs. In addition to the functionality provided by a Core interface conformant driver, a Level 1 interface conformant driver allows an application to do the following:

- Specify the schema of database tables and views (using two-part naming conventions).

- Invoke true asynchronous execution of ODBC functions where applicable. On a given connection, ODBC functions can either be all synchronous or all asynchronous.

- Use scrollable cursors and thereby obtain access to a result data set in directions other than forward-only.

- Obtain primary keys of tables.

- Use stored procedures (through the ODBC escape sequence for procedure calls) and query the data dictionary for information about stored procedures. (The process by which procedures are created and stored on the data source is outside the scope of this book.)

- Connect to a data source by interactively browsing a list of available servers.

- Use ODBC functions instead of SQL statements to perform certain database operations.

- Gain access to the contents of multiple result data sets generated by batch SQL submissions and stored procedures.

- Delimit transactions spanning several ODBC functions, with true atomicity.

- Roll back a transaction.

LEVEL 2 FUNCTIONALITY The Level 2 interface conformance level provides all the functionality that Microsoft could think of to provide a rich, robust set of data access. In addition to the functionality provided by a Level 1 interface conformant driver, a Level 2 interface conformant driver allows an application to do all the following:

- Use three-part naming conventions for database tables and views.

- Describe dynamic parameters.

- Use input parameters, output parameters, input/output parameters, and result values of stored procedures.

- Use bookmarks, including retrieving bookmarks, retrieving data from a result data set (fetching) based on a bookmark, and performing update by, delete by, and fetch by bookmark operations.

- Retrieve advanced information about the data dictionary.

- Use ODBC functions instead of SQL statements to perform additional database operations.

- Enable asynchronous execution of ODBC functions for specified individual SQL statements.

- Obtain automatic update row-identifying column information for any table in the data source.

- Change cursor concurrency states from read-only to other locked states.

- The ability to time out login requests and SQL queries.

- The ability to change the default isolation level; that is, the ability to execute transactions with the serializable level of isolation.

SQL CONFORMANCE LEVELS As mentioned earlier, the SQL-92 standard outlines three levels of SQL functionality: *Entry, Intermediate,* and *Full.* Rather than use these three levels, ODBC defines its own set of SQL grammar conformance levels: *Minimum, Core,* and *Extended.*

One of the most confusing issues with regard to ODBC drivers is the SQL conformance levels they support. Many people believe that because ODBC defines its own three levels of SQL grammar support, only the SQL statements defined in each level can be passed to the data source. This is not true. The main purpose for defining SQL conformance levels was merely to provide a guideline for interoperability—not to put a constraint on what applications can and cannot use or on what drivers must prevent from reaching the data source. A second purpose was to provide some level of assurance that if a driver indicated it supported a particular SQL conformance level, developers could indeed count on everything in that level being available for use. Because ODBC SQL grammar conformance levels are guidelines rather than restrictions, applications are free to send any SQL statement to a data source, even if the statement is not described within the ODBC SQL conformance level the driver claims to be conformant to. Drivers can support additional SQL statements and, in fact, they may provide all the functionality defined by the SQL-92 Entry, Intermediate, and/or Full SQL functionality level. If a driver claims to conform to a specific ODBC SQL conformance level, it must support all the functionality defined by that conformance level. Drivers can support additional features defined for any of the higher levels; however, a driver does not provide all the functionality defined for a conformance level, it must claim to conform to a lower conformance level.

MINIMUM SQL GRAMMAR SUPPORT The Minimum SQL grammar conformance level provides the barest essentials needed to write ODBC applications. The purpose of the Minimum SQL conformance level is twofold:

- To provide a least common denominator subset of the SQL-92 Entry SQL functionality level so that applications can interoperate with a minimum amount of effort as long as the limitations on SQL functionality are not too constraining.

- To provide a target SQL grammar for driver writers who want to create drivers to access flat files and files supporting Indexed Sequential Access Methods (ISAM).

Consequently, the Minimum SQL grammar conformance level provides limited SQL functionality because it only supports the following SQL constructs:

- Simple Data Definition Language (DDL) statements: **CREATE TABLE** and **DROP TABLE** statements.

- Simple Data Manipulation Language (DML) statements: **SELECT**, **INSERT**, searched **UPDATE**, and searched **DELETE** statements.

- Simple expressions.

- Character data types: **CHAR**, **VARCHAR**, and **LONG VARCHAR**.

CORE SQL GRAMMAR SUPPORT The Core SQL grammar conformance level provides nearly all the functionality defined in the 1992 SAG and X/Open SQL CAE specification. Most of the SQL functionality in this specification was taken directly from the ISO/IEC standard for SQL. The only differences are some limits and restrictions specified by X/Open to facilitate the creation of portable applications and some extensions (such as index creation) not covered by the ISO/IEC standard. In addition to the functionality provided by the Minimum SQL grammar conformance level, the Core SQL grammar conformance level supports the following:

- More Data Definition Language (DDL) statements: **ALTER TABLE**, **CREATE/DROP INDEX**, **CREATE/DROP VIEW**, and **GRANT/REVOKE** statements.

- Full **SELECT** statement functionality, including subqueries and result data set functions: **SUM()**, **MAX()**, **MIN()**, **AVG()**, and **COUNT()**.

- More data types: **DECIMAL**, **NUMERIC**, **SMALLINT**, **INTEGER**, **REAL**, **FLOAT**, and **DOUBLE PRECISION**.

EXTENDED SQL GRAMMAR SUPPORT The Extended SQL grammar conformance level provides support for all SQL extensions unique to ODBC. This SQL grammar conformance level is essentially a convenient category for advanced SQL features and data types that many data sources support but for which there is no equivalent in the SQL 1992 SAG and X/Open SQL CAE specification. In addition to the functionality provided by both the Minimum and the Core SQL grammar conformance levels, the Extended SQL grammar conformance level supports the following:

- More Data Manipulation Language (DML) statements: positioned **UPDATE**, positioned **DELETE**, **SELECT FOR UPDATE** statements, **UNION** clauses, and outer joins.

- More expressions: date, time, and timestamp literals and scalar functions such as **ROUND()** and **SUBSTRING()**.

- More data types: **BIT, TINYINT, BIGINT, BINARY, VARBINARY, LONG VARBINARY, DATE, TIME**, and **TIMESTAMP**.

- Stored procedure calls.

- Batch SQL execution.

NOTE: *Most SQL DBMS vendors supported Core SQL when ODBC 1.0 shipped in the fall of 1992. However, by the time the first ODBC 2.0 developer's conference occurred in September 1993, Microsoft had received strong feedback that most flat file and ISAM driver writers were trying to provide Core SQL grammar support. Because they could provide Core SQL grammar support for everything except positioned UPDATEs, positioned DELETEs, SELECT FOR UPDATEs, and UNION clauses, they wanted these constructs moved to the next SQL conformance level so that more drivers could claim to conform to the Core SQL conformance level. Consequently, in ODBC 2.0, these four constructs were moved from the Core SQL grammar level to the Extended SQL grammar level. This means that if you are developing an application that checks SQL conformance levels to determine whether any of these four constructs are supported, it also has to check the version number of the ODBC driver being used.*

Although ODBC defines SQL syntax that adheres to the SQL-92 standard, drivers are required to translate ODBC SQL syntax into the syntax recognized by the data source they support. Unfortunately, some data sources support SQL syntax for which there is no equivalent in ODBC. To prevent driver developers from having to build a complete SQL parser to handle this type of SQL syntax, ODBC provides a method known as an *escape sequence* that allows these translations to be done with simple string scanning routines. An escape sequence is nothing more than a pair of curly braces ({ }) surrounding an SQL statement and a preceding one-

or two-character token identifying the type of SQL statement that is coded within the braces. Escape sequences are often used with date and time literals, outer joins, scalar functions (that is, numeric, string, date, time, system, and conversion functions), and stored procedure invocation. Escape sequences are covered in greater detail in Chapter 4.

TYPES OF DRIVERS   Regardless of the ODBC interface conformance level and SQL grammar conformance level an ODBC driver supports, all ODBC drivers can be classified as one of the following types:

- One-tier driver
- Two-tier driver
- Three-tier driver

ONE-TIER DRIVERS   In ODBC, a one-tier driver is a driver that accesses a desktop database file, an ISAM supported file, or a flat file. One-tier drivers are typically found on systems in which the data source and the driver are physically located on the same machine; hence only one machine, or "tier," is used. The major characteristic distinguishing a one-tier driver from any other type of driver is that the one-tier driver itself does all the SQL processing. That's because the data source the driver communicates with is not an SQL database engine—the native programming interface to the data source consists of file I/O or ISAM function calls. This means that the driver itself becomes the SQL database engine; the driver parses, optimizes, and executes all SQL statements passed to it by an application. Because the capabilities of one-tier drivers are usually limited to file-oriented operations, they typically only implement the subset of ODBC SQL functionality defined by the Minimum SQL conformance level.

When processing SQL statements from applications, file I/O drivers do not perform any of the optimizations typically found in relational DBMSs because there are no indexes. Instead, they must always search an entire file when looking for data. ISAM drivers, on the other hand, can perform very good optimization, because, as the term implies, ISAM systems have indexes, which can dramatically improve performance over the file I/O system. Figure 2–3 illustrates how one-tier drivers communicate with file and ISAM data sources.

Drivers for ASCII text files and for spreadsheet files such as Lotus 1-2-3 and Microsoft Excel are examples of one-tier drivers that use file I/O operations to communicate with a data source. Drivers for dBASE, Paradox, and Microsoft Access are examples of one-tier drivers that use ISAM programming interfaces to communicate with a data source.

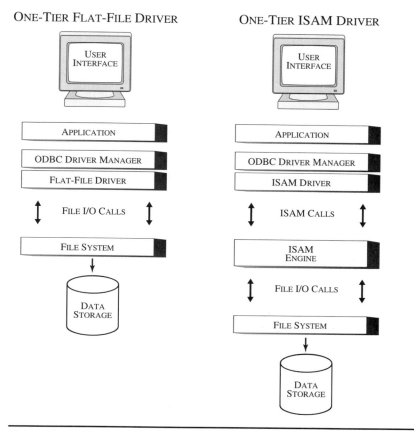

Figure 2–3 One-tier driver architecture.

TWO-TIER DRIVERS A two-tier driver is a driver that accesses any data source that supports SQL. Two-tier drivers are typically found on client/server systems; however, they can also be found on systems in which both the data source and the driver are physically located on the same machine. Instead of doing all the SQL processing like one-tier drivers do, two-tier drivers only process ODBC-specific function calls; all SQL statements are passed to the data source for processing. Two-tier drivers work with the data source they support in a client/server relationship. The driver (acting as a client) sends and receives data protocol or maps to the data source's native Database API, but it doesn't directly access the data. The data source (acting as a server) receives SQL requests from the driver, executes them, and sends the results back. A driver that uses the data source's underlying data protocol merely acts as a conduit between an application and the data source. A driver that maps to a data source's native Database API acts as both a conduit and as a translator: it must convert the ODBC API function calls to native Database APIs before it sends them to the data source for processing. Drivers that translate ODBC API function calls to native Database API calls are usually slower than drivers that use data protocol. Figure 2–4 illustrates how two-tier drivers communicate with a data source that supports SQL.

Examples of two-tier drivers include drivers for Microsoft SQL Server (which directly manipulates the data protocol) and drivers for Oracle (which map to Oracle's native Database API—OCI).

THREE-TIER DRIVERS (AND BEYOND)   From the application's point of view, three-tier drivers are not much different from two-tier drivers. The main difference is that, instead of connecting directly to the data source, the

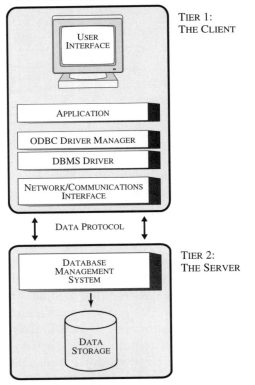

TWO-TIER DBMS DRIVER

TIER 1:
THE CLIENT

USER INTERFACE

APPLICATION

ODBC DRIVER MANAGER

DBMS DRIVER

NETWORK/COMMUNICATIONS INTERFACE

DATA PROTOCOL

TIER 2:
THE SERVER

DATABASE MANAGEMENT SYSTEM

DATA STORAGE

Figure 2–4   Two-tier driver architecture

three-tier driver, connects to a server that acts as a *gateway* to another server that hosts the target data source. A gateway is a piece of software that causes one machine or data source to look like another. The gateway can and usually does connect to multiple servers; each server may contain one or more data sources.

In client/server systems using ODBC-based applications to access data in multiple data sources, three-tier drivers move a lot of the complexity from the application on the client to the DBMS on the server. This can be a tremendous help in simplifying the installation, configuration, and administration of drivers—all clients use a single driver to connect to the gateway, and the gateway routes all requests to the appropriate data source-specific driver on the appropriate server.

The nature of three-tier drivers makes it easy to create any number of tiers in a system. For example, an application could talk to a gateway that talks to another gateway rather than to the target data source, effectively making the system a four-tier configuration. This is not common practice, however, because most performance gains are achieved by off-loading clients to a network server, which can usually be boosted in capacity to meet the needs of more clients without having to add another gateway machine to the configuration. Figure 2–5 illustrates how three-tier drivers communicate with data sources via a gateway.

NOTE: *Although the one-tier, two-tier, and three-tier models provide a good framework for understanding the different types of drivers, some drivers do not fit neatly into any of these categories. For example, consider a system in which a driver is used to access dBASE files on a network file server. Two machines are involved here, but because the interface between the driver and the data source is file I/O, the driver is a one-tier driver. However, if multiple users will be using this system for shared file access, the driver and the application need to know when the data will be accessed concurrently by multiple users on the file server. The driver can no longer assume that it will only be processing local file I/O. This consideration makes the driver not purely one-tier, although it is certainly not two-tier as described above.*

Another case that does not fit perfectly into the model is a client/server DBMS configured to run on one machine. In this case the client software and the server software are running on the same physical hardware but in logically separate processes. Because the data access is separated into another program or DLL apart from the driver itself, the driver used is still a two-tier driver as far as ODBC is concerned.

THREE-TIER GATEWAY DRIVER

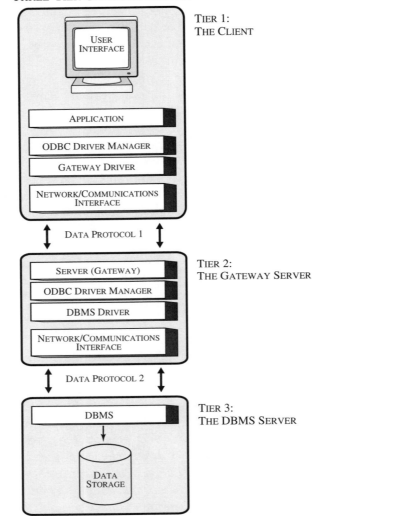

Figure 2–5   Three-tier driver architecture

The Driver Manager

The Driver Manager is a special library that manages communication between applications and drivers. Applications call ODBC API functions in the Driver Manager, and the Driver Manager is responsible for routing the calls to the appropriate driver. When an application tries to connect to a data source, the Driver Manager determines which driver is required, loads it (assuming it is not already loaded), stores the address of each of the driver's API function calls in memory, and calls the connection API function in the driver (which causes the driver to initialize itself and to establish a connection to its underlying data source). From that point on, the Driver Manager simply examines each function call made by the application and, using the driver's API function addresses stored in memory, calls the corresponding API function in the driver (unless it is a function call the Driver Manager itself processes, as is the case when the application asks for the name of a driver). When an application disconnects from a data source, the Driver Manager calls the disconnect API function in the driver (which causes the driver to terminate the connection to its underlying data source) and unloads the corresponding driver from memory, provided the driver is not being used by any other application. If more than one application is using a driver, the driver is not unloaded from memory until the last application using it no longer needs it.

In addition to loading and unloading drivers, the Driver Manager also performs some rudimentary error checking to ensure that ODBC API functions are being called in the right order and that ODBC API function arguments contain valid values. This error checking relieves driver developers from a burdensome task because most of the robust error checking that drivers have traditionally been responsible for is enforced by the Driver Manager.

It would be reasonable to think that applications could interact directly with drivers without having to go through the Driver Manager, and, in fact, ODBC could have been designed that way. However, consider what would happen if that were the case. Unless an application was linked directly to a particular driver, it would have to build a table of pointers to the API functions in the driver being used and call each of those API functions by pointer. If the application needed to work with multiple drivers at the same time, yet another level of complexity would be added to the equation—the application would first have to set an API function pointer to point to the correct API function in the correct driver, and then call the API function through that pointer. The Driver Manager solves this problem by providing a single place from which to call each ODBC API function. Because the Driver Manager is either statically linked to an application or dynamically loaded by an application at run time, all ODBC API functions are called by name in the Driver Manager, rather than by pointer in each driver used.

Data Sources

A *data source* is simply the source of the data. It can be a flat-file, a particular database in a DBMS, or even a spreadsheet file. For example, a data source might be an Oracle DBMS running on Windows NT, accessed by Novell Netware; an IBM DB2 DBMS running on MVS, accessed through a gateway; a collection of dBASE files in a server directory; or a local Microsoft Access database file.

In ODBC, the term *data source* refers to the actual location of the data as well as all the technical information needed to access the data: the driver name, network address, network software, and so on. Specifically, the term data source is used in ODBC for two purposes:

- As a conceptual term defining the kind of data the end user wants to access (for example, "Payroll," "Sales," or "Personnel"). In practice, the data source includes the DBMS software running on a physical machine with some operating system on some hardware platform and the networking software required to access the machine (if appropriate).

- As the actual name an end user or a system administrator assigns via an ODBC utility to describe a particular collection of software components (such as an ODBC driver, a network library, a server name or address, a DBMS, etc.). For example, when an ODBC driver is installed on an end user's machine, the ODBC installation routine guides the user through the process of creating a data source name for the driver and the target location that identifies where the data the driver will access resides (that is, the directory name on a local machine or the network address of a server).

TYPES OF DATA SOURCES   There are two types of data sources in ODBC: machine data sources and file data sources. Although both types contain similar information about the actual location of data and the technical information needed to get to it, they differ how they store this information. Because of this difference, they are used in a somewhat different manner.

Machine data sources are stored on the system with a user-defined name and all the information the Driver Manager and driver need to connect to the actual data source.

With file data sources, all the information the Driver Manager and driver need to connect to the actual data source are stored in a flat file with the .DSN extension. File data sources do not have user-defined data source names like machine data sources do, and they are not registered to any one user or workstation. Because of this, connection information can be used repeatedly by a single user or it can be shared among several users.

The connection process is streamlined with a file data source because the .DSN file contains the connection string that would otherwise have to be built for a call to an ODBC API connect function. Another advantage of using file data sources is that .DSN files can be copied to any workstation; thus, identical data sources can be used by many workstations as long as they all have the appropriate driver installed. Also, if a .DSN file is placed on a network, it can be used simultaneously by multiple applications.

Although a file data source can be shared by multiple applications it can also be unshareable. This is accomplished by placing an unshareable .DSN file on a single machine, and having it contain connection information for a machine data source. Unshareable file data sources exist mainly to provide a simple way to convert machine data sources to file data sources so that applications can be designed to work solely with file data sources. When the Driver Manager is sent the information in an unshareable file data source, it connects as necessary to the machine data source that the .DSN file refers to.

Both machine data sources and file data sources can be categorized as either User or System data sources: a user data source is only visible to a specific user, and can only be used on the current machine while a system data source is visible to all users on a machine (including users accessing the machine via network services).

SUMMARY

ODBC architecture was designed around the client/server computing model—the idea that inexpensive PCs (the clients) could be used to provide a front end to data while mini-computers and mainframe computers (the servers) could be used to host the DBMS. ODBC was also designed around the assumption that any programming interface that can send and receive the data protocol of any SQL-supporting data source will function and perform just like the native (SQL precompiler generated) API for that data source. Somewhat like client/server architecture, ODBC's architecture is comprised of four main components.

- Applications
- Drivers
- The Driver Manager
- Data Sources

Applications are executable programs that call ODBC API functions to access data in one or more data sources. Most applications fall into one of the following categories:

- Generic—Applications designed to work with a variety of different data sources.
- Vertical—Applications designed to perform a single type of task and work with a database schema controlled by the application developer.
- Custom—Applications designed to perform a specific task within a single company.

Drivers are libraries that implement the functions in the ODBC API set for a specific data source. ODBC defines conformance levels for drivers in two areas: the ODBC API and the ODBC SQL grammar (including ODBC SQL data types). API conformance levels are used to categorize the sets of ODBC API function calls supported by a driver. ODBC defines the following three API conformance levels:

- Core—Provides all the basic functionality an application needs in order to work with a data source.
- Level 1—Provides functionality that allows application developers to build a wider variety of full-featured applications than is possible with the Core level functionality.
- Level 2—Provides all the functionality Microsoft could think of to provide a rich, robust set of data access.

ODBC defines the following three SQL grammar conformance levels:

- Minimum—Provides the barest essentials needed to write ODBC applications.
- Core—Provides nearly all the functionality defined in the 1992 SAG and X/Open SQL CAE specification.
- Extended—Provides support for SQL extensions unique to ODBC.

If a driver supports all the functionality defined for a higher conformance level, it must provide all the functionality defined by all lower conformance levels. Regardless of the ODBC interface conformance level and SQL grammar conformance level an ODBC driver supports, all ODBC drivers can be classified as one of the following types:

- One-tier—A driver that accesses a desktop database file, an ISAM supported file, or a flat file.

- Two-tier—A driver that accesses a data source that supports SQL.

- Three-tier—A driver that connects to a server that acts as a gateway to another server that hosts the target data source.

The Driver Manager is a special library that manages communication between applications and drivers. Applications call ODBC API functions in the Driver Manager, and the Driver Manager is responsible for routing the call to the appropriate driver.

Data sources are simply the source of the data and all relevant information needed to access it. A data source can be a flat-file, a particular database in a relational DBMS, or even a spreadsheet file. Two types of data sources exist in ODBC:

- Machine—Data sources stored on the system under a user-defined name and all the information the Driver Manager and driver need to connect to the actual data source driver.

- File—Data sources whose connection information is stored in a special .DSN file that the Driver Manager uses to connect to the actual data source driver.

3

Transactions and Concurrency Control

ODBC uses two specific mechanisms, transactions and concurrency control, to provide and maintain data consistency while working with various data sources. This chapter is designed to introduce you to the concepts of database consistency and to the two mechanisms ODBC uses to enforce it. The first part of this chapter defines data consistency and lists some of the requirements a database management system must provide in order to ensure that data integrity is always maintained. This is followed by a close look at the heart of all data manipulation, the transaction, and at the various ways a transaction can be terminated. Finally, the transaction isolation levels and concurrency control types that ODBC uses to maintain data integrity are discussed.

What Is Data Consistency?

The best way to define data consistency is by example. Suppose your company owns a chain of restaurants and you have a database designed to keep track of supplies stored in each of those restaurants. To facilitate the supplies purchasing process, your database contains an inventory table for each restaurant in the chain and, whenever supplies are received or used by a restaurant, the inventory table for that restaurant is updated. Now, suppose some bottles of ketchup are physically moved from one restaurant to another. The ketchup bottle count value in the donating restaurant's table needs to be lowered and the ketchup bottle count value in the receiving restaurant's table needs to be raised in order to accurately represent this inventory move. If a user lowers the ketchup bottle count from the donating restaurant's inventory table but fails to raise the ketchup bottle count in the receiving restaurant's inventory table, your data has become inconsistent because the total ketchup bottle count for the entire chain of restaurants is now incorrect.

Data can become inconsistent if a user fails to make all necessary changes (as in the previous example), if the system crashes while the user is in the middle of making changes, or if an application accessing data stops prematurely for some reason. Inconsistency can also occur when several users are accessing the same data at the same time. For example, one user might read another user's changes before the data has been properly updated and take some inappropriate action or make an incorrect change based on the premature data values read.

In order to properly maintain data consistency, solutions must be provided for the following questions:

- How can you maintain generic consistency of data, if you do not know what each individual data owner/user wants?
- How can you keep a single application from accidentally destroying data consistency?
- How can you ensure that multiple applications accessing the same data at the same time will not destroy data consistency?

ODBC provides solutions for these questions through transaction support and concurrency control.

Transactions

A *transaction*, or a *unit of work*, is a recoverable sequence of one or more SQL operations grouped together as a single unit within an application process. The initiation and termination of a transaction define the points of data consistency within an application process; either all SQL operations within a transaction are applied to the data source, or the effects of all SQL operations within a transaction are completely "undone".

Transactions and commitment control are relational database concepts that have been around for quite some time. They provide the capability to commit or recover from pending changes made to a database in order to enforce data consistency and integrity. With embedded SQL applications, transactions are automatically initiated when the application process is started. With ODBC, transactions are implicitly started whenever an ODBC application begins working with a data source. If a data source requires explicit transaction initiation, its driver must explicitly initiate one (if no current transaction exists) whenever an application using it executes an SQL statement requiring a transaction.

Regardless of how transactions are initiated, they are terminated when they are either committed or rolled back. When a transaction is committed, all changes made to the data source since the transaction was initiated are made permanent. When a transaction is rolled back, all changes made to the data source since the transaction was initiated are removed and the data in the data source is returned to the state it was in before the transaction began. In either case, the data source is guaranteed to be in a consistent state at the completion of each transaction.

A commit or roll back operation affects only the data changes made within the transaction they end. As long as data changes remain uncommitted, other application processes are usually unable to see them, and they can be removed with the roll back operation. However, once data changes are committed, they become accessible to other application processes, and they can no longer be removed by a roll back operation.

Transaction Commit Modes

The ODBC interface provides two modes of transaction processing that determine how and when transactions are committed (or, if possible, rolled back). They are:

- Auto-commit mode
- Manual-commit mode

AUTO-COMMIT MODE In auto-commit mode, every operation performed on a data source (that is, each SQL statement processed) is treated as an individual transaction that is automatically terminated (with a commit operation) as soon as it is complete. Because SQL statements are committed immediately after they are executed, data changes they make cannot be undone with a roll back operation. Auto-commit mode is suitable for many real-world transactions that contain only one SQL statement.

If a data source does not use transactions, auto-commit mode is the only commit mode available to an ODBC application. If a data source uses transactions, but does not support auto-commit mode, its driver can emulate auto-commit mode by manually committing each SQL statement as soon as it is executed.

MANUAL-COMMIT MODE If a group of SQL statements are executed together in auto-commit mode, the data source determines when they are to be committed. Each SQL statement can be committed as soon as it is executed, or all SQL statements in the group can be treated as a single transaction, in which case the transaction is committed as soon as the last statement in the group is executed. Some data sources support both of these behaviors (in which case a way may be provided for selecting one or the other). If an error occurs before all the SQL statements in the group have been executed, it is usually up to the data source to determine whether the SQL statements in the group that have already been executed are to be committed or rolled back.

In manual-commit mode, the application decides when and how groups of SQL statements are to be committed (or rolled back). This is the normal transaction commit mode used by most relational databases. In addition, this transaction commit mode should be used by interoperable applications with a need or a desire to process multiple SQL statements as a single transaction. Switching from manual-commit mode to auto-commit mode automatically causes any open transactions on the specified connection to be committed.

Transaction Support

The degree of transaction support available for an application is defined by each driver (and its underlying data source). Single-user databases that don't need to manage multiple updates to its data typically do not provide transaction support. In this case, the driver won't provide transaction support either. Some databases only support transactions for Data Manipulation Language (DML) SQL statements; restrictions or special transaction semantics control/limit the use of Data Definition Language (DDL) SQL statements. In this case, the driver may provide transaction support for multiple, simultaneous updates to tables but not for adding new tables and/or changing the definition of existing tables.

An application can query a driver to find out whether it supports transactions, and if so, the level of support it provides. If a particular driver does not support transactions, and if the application has the ability to lock and unlock data (using data source specific APIs—not ODBC APIs), transaction support can be achieved by having the application lock and unlock rows of data (or tables), as needed.

Transaction Isolation

So far, we have only looked at transactions from a single-user data source point-of-view. With single-user data sources, each transaction occurs serially and does not have to contend with interference from other transactions. However, with multi-user data sources, transactions can occur simultaneously, and each transaction has the potential to interfere with another one. Transactions that have the potential of interfering with one another are said to be *interleaved*, or parallel, transactions. Transactions that run isolated from each other are said to be *serializable*, which means that the results of running them simultaneously are the same as the results of running them one right after another (serially). Ideally, all transactions should be serializable.

So why is it important that transactions be serializable? Consider the following problem: Suppose a salesman is entering orders on a database system at the same time a clerk is sending out bills. Now suppose the salesman enters an order from Company X but does not commit it (the salesman is still talking to the representative from Company X). While the salesman is on the phone, the clerk queries the database for a list of all outstanding orders, sees the order for Company X, and sends them a bill. Now suppose the representative from Company X decides to cancel the order; the salesman rolls back the transaction because the representative changed his mind and the order information was never committed. A week later, Company X gets a bill for a part they never ordered. If the salesman's transaction and the clerk's transaction had been isolated from each other (serialized), this problem would never have occurred. Either the salesman's transaction would have finished before the clerk's transaction started, or the clerk's transaction would have finished before the salesman's transaction started; in either case Company X would not have received a bill.

When transactions are not isolated from each other in multi-user environments, the following three types of events (or phenomenon) can occur:

- Dirty Reads. Occurs when a transaction reads data that has not yet been committed. For example: Transaction 1 changes a row of data and Transaction 2 reads the changed row before Transaction 1 commits the change. If Transaction 1 rolls back the change, Transaction 2 will have read data that is considered never to have existed.

- Nonrepeatable Reads. Occurs when a transaction reads the same row of data twice but gets different data values each time. For example: Transaction 1 reads a row of data, and Transaction 2 changes or deletes that row and commits the change. If Transaction 1 attempts to reread the row, it retrieves different data values (if the row was updated) or discovers that the row no longer exists (if the row was deleted).

- Phantoms. Occurs when a row of data matches a search criteria but initially is not seen. For example: Transaction 1 reads a set of rows that satisfy some search criteria and Transaction 2 inserts a new row matching Transaction 1's search criteria. If Transaction 1 re-executes the query statement that produced the original set of rows, a different set of rows will be retrieved.

Transaction Isolation Levels

ODBC defines four levels of transaction isolation that can prevent all, some, or none of these events from occurring. These four transaction isolation levels (as defined by SQL-92) are, in order from least to most isolated:

- Read Uncommitted
- Read Committed
- Repeatable Read
- Serializable

Table 3–1 shows these four transaction isolation levels as well as the types of events that can occur when each one is used.

Table 3–1 Transaction isolation levels supported by ODBC and the phenomenon that can occur when each is used.

ODBC Transaction Isolation Level	Dirty Reads	Nonrepeatable Reads	Phantoms
Read Uncommitted	Yes	Yes	Yes
Read Committed	No	Yes	Yes
Repeatable Read	No	No	Yes
Serializable	No	No	No

Adapted from *Microsoft ODBC 3.0 Programmer's Reference, Volume 1, and SDK Guide*, page 249.

NOTE: *Most relational DBMSs use more complex isolation levels than these to increase transaction isolation and concurrency. When this is the case, the transaction isolation levels provided by ODBC do not dictate how the DBMS isolates multiple transactions from each other.*

READ UNCOMMITTED The *Read Uncommitted* isolation level allows a transaction to access uncommitted changes made by other transactions (either in this application or others). A transaction using the Read Uncommitted isolation level cannot lock other transactions out of the row of data it is reading; therefore, transactions are not isolated from each other. If the Read Uncommitted isolation level is being used by a transaction that is working with a data source that supports other transaction isolation levels, the data source ignores the mechanism it uses to implement those levels.

To keep from adversely affecting other transactions, the Read Uncommitted level is typically only used by read-only transactions.

READ COMMITTED The *Read Committed* isolation level allows a transaction to acquire a read lock (if it only reads the data) or a write lock (if it updates or deletes data) on the current row of data with which it is working. This means that the row of data being used by the transaction cannot be changed or removed by other transactions until the lock is terminated. Read locks are released when the transaction moves off the current row; write locks are held until the transaction is committed or rolled back.

Transactions using the Read Committed isolation level wait until rows of data that are write-locked by other transactions are unlocked before they acquire their own locks; this prevents them from reading "dirty" data.

REPEATABLE READ   The *Repeatable Read* isolation level allows a transaction to acquire read locks on all rows of data it returns to an application and write locks on all rows of data it inserts, updates, or deletes. By using the Repeatable Read isolation level, **SELECT** SQL statements issued multiple times within the same transaction always yield the same result. A transaction using the Repeatable Read isolation level can retrieve and manipulate the same rows of data as many times as needed until it completes. However, no other transaction can insert, update, or delete a row of data that would affect the result table being accessed, until the isolating transaction releases its locks; that is, until the isolating transaction is either committed or rolled back.

Transactions using the Repeatable Read isolation level wait until rows of data write-locked by other transactions are unlocked before they acquire their own locks; this prevents them from reading "dirty" data. In addition, because other transactions cannot update or delete rows of data that are locked by a transaction using the Repeatable Read isolation level, nonrepeatable read situations are avoided.

SERIALIZABLE   The *Serializable* isolation level allows a transaction to acquire read locks (if it only reads rows of data) or write locks (if it inserts, updates, or deletes rows of data) for the entire range of data that it affects. For example, if a transaction using the Serializable isolation level executes the SQL statement **SELECT * FROM ORDERS**, the range is the entire **ORDERS** table; therefore, the transaction acquires a read lock for the entire table and no new rows can be inserted until the transaction releases the lock. If a transaction using the Serializable isolation level executes the SQL statement **DELETE FROM ORDERS WHERE STATUS = CLOSED**, the range is all rows with a status of **CLOSED**; therefore, the transaction acquires write locks for all rows in the **ORDERS** table with a status of **CLOSED** and does not allow any rows to be inserted or updated in such a way that the resulting row has a status of **CLOSED**. No other transaction can insert, update, or delete a row of data that would affect the range of affected data until the isolating transaction releases its locks; that is, when the isolating transaction is either committed or rolled back.

Transactions using the Serializable isolation level wait until rows of data that are write-locked by other transactions are unlocked before they acquire their own locks; this prevents them from reading "dirty" data. In addition, because other transactions cannot update or delete rows of data that are locked by a transaction using the Serializable isolation level, nonrepeatable read situations are avoided. Furthermore, because no other transaction can insert rows into the range of rows that are locked by a transaction using the Serializable isolation level, phantoms are prevented.

NOTE: *Transaction isolation levels do not affect a transaction's ability to see its own changes—transactions can always see changes they make. For example, suppose a transaction contains two* **UPDATE** *statements, the first of which raises by ten percent the pay of all employees and the second of which sets to the minimum amount the pay of any employees below a minimum amount. Because both* **UPDATE** *statements are executed in the same transaction, the second* **UPDATE** *statement can see the results of the first.*

Selecting the Appropriate Transaction Isolation Level

Higher levels of transaction isolation offer the most protection for data integrity. Serializable transactions are guaranteed to be unaffected by other transactions and therefore are guaranteed to provide the highest level of data integrity. However, higher levels of transaction isolation can reduce application performance because the chances the application will have to wait for locks on data to be released are increased. In the following cases, an application may choose to use a lower level of transaction isolation in order to increase overall performance:

- When it can be guaranteed that no other transactions will exist that might interfere with the application's transactions. For example, one person in a small company maintains dBASE files containing personnel data on their computer and these files are not shared with other users. This situation only occurs in limited circumstances.

- When speed is more critical than accuracy and any errors that can occur are likely to be small. For example, suppose that a company makes many small sales, and that large sales are rare. A transaction that estimates the total value of all open sales might safely use the Read Uncommitted isolation level. Although the transaction might include orders that are in the process of being opened or closed that could subsequently be rolled back, these would tend to cancel each other out and the transaction would execute much faster because it is not blocked each time it encounters such an order.

ODBC applications have the ability to set the transaction isolation level for a particular transaction. Before doing so, it is usually a good idea to query the driver being used to find out what transaction isolation levels the underlying data source supports and what the default isolation level is. If the underlying data source does not support the desired isolation level, the application can usually select the next highest level.

Concurrency Control

Another issue that must be addressed in multi-user database system environments is the ability of two transactions to simultaneously use the same data (*concurrency*). When higher transaction isolation levels are used, concurrency is usually reduced. This is because transaction isolation is accomplished by acquiring locks and, as more rows of data are locked fewer transactions can be completed without having to wait for one or more locks to be released. While reduced concurrency is generally accepted as a trade-off for using the higher transaction isolation levels needed to maintain data integrity, it can become an issue in interactive applications that perform large amounts of read/write activity. However, as long as multiple transactions are accessing data in read-only mode, concurrency should be a minor issue.

Types of Concurrency Control

To solve the problem of reduced concurrency with high transaction isolation levels, ODBC allows an application to specify the type of concurrency control to use. Valid concurrency control types are:

- Read-Only
- Locking
- Optimistic

READ-ONLY   Read-Only concurrency control only allows a transaction to read data. Transactions using read-only concurrency control are not allowed to update or delete data. Although a data source might lock rows to enforce Repeatable Read and Serializable isolation levels, it can use read locks instead of write locks if Read-Only concurrency control is specified. This increases overall concurrency because other transactions can at least read data. If no concurrency control type is specified for a transaction, this is the default concurrency control type used.

LOCKING   Locking concurrency control allows a transaction to use the lowest level of locking necessary to make sure it can update or delete rows of data in a result data set. With Locking concurrency control, rows of data are locked as they are retrieved (*fetched*) so that they cannot be modified by other transactions. This usually results in very low concurrency levels, especially when the Repeatable Read and/or Serializable transaction isolation levels are used.

When Locking concurrency control is used, Update locks are the preferred locks to use because they don't prevent other transactions from reading the locked data. Because some data sources do not expose such a lock to applications, an application can perform a "dummy update" (by setting one column equal to itself) on rows before they are retrieved to acquire an exclusive lock on the row of data (or on the page containing the row of data).

OPTIMISTIC Optimistic concurrency control allows a transaction to avoid using locks until just before a row of data is to be updated or deleted. Optimistic concurrency derives its name from the "optimistic" assumption that collisions between transactions rarely occur. This is the opposite of Locking, or "pessimistic" concurrency control, in which the application developer believes that collisions between transactions are commonplace.

In optimistic concurrency, a row of data is left unlocked until just before it is updated or deleted. At that point, the row of data is reread and checked to see if it has changed since it was last read. To determine whether a row of data has been changed, the current version of the data is compared to a previously cached version. This comparison can be based on a special row-versioning column (such as a timestamp column) or on the values of all the columns in the row. If the latter method is used, columns containing *binary large objects* (BLOBs) are usually excluded due to their size and the assumption that they are not the only differentiating column for a row of data.

 If the comparison shows that the row of data has not been changed by another transaction, the current transaction increases concurrency control to Locking (to acquire a write lock on the row) and executes an **UPDATE** or **DELETE** SQL statement with a **WHERE** clause that specifies the version or values the row had the last time the transaction read it. If the comparison shows that the row of data has been changed, the **UPDATE** or **DELETE** operation automatically fails and must be tried again. If the **WHERE** clause does not uniquely identify the row of data, other rows might also be updated or deleted.

Optimistic concurrency can be implemented either by the data source or by the application. In either case, applications should use a low transaction isolation level such as Read Committed whenever Optimistic concurrency control is used; using a higher transaction isolation level cancels out the increased concurrency gained by using Optimistic concurrency control. Optimistic concurrency control provides more concurrency than Locking concurrency control, but it is also more expensive (in terms of performance) if a collision occurs. A collision is said to have occurred when another transaction updates or deletes a row of data between the time it was last read by the current transaction and the time it is updated or deleted. Optimistic concurrency control is called "optimistic" because it works best when collisions are infrequent.

The Relationship of Concurrency Control to Isolation Levels

It is important to point out that although ODBC provides a way for an application to specify both the desired transaction isolation level and the concurrency control type used, it isn't always clear which options make sense and which don't.

For example, if a data source supports the Serializable transaction isolation level and the application uses that level, it would be silly for the application to also use any concurrency control other than Read-Only. Why? Because when the application tells the data source that it wants to be completely isolated from other transactions, there is no reason for it to further specify either Locking or Optimistic concurrency control; the data source automatically provides the proper concurrency control.

Application programmers should follow similar reasoning when using the other transaction isolation levels and concurrency control options. Does setting the transaction isolation level to Repeatable Read and then using either Locking or Optimistic concurrency control make sense? Yes, but only if the application will be re-executing the same query and needs to be aware of new rows that might appear in the result data set.

Concurrency control types are most often used by applications that specify low transaction isolation levels such as Read Committed or Read Uncommitted. In effect, applications combining concurrency control types and transaction isolation levels in this manner are indicating that they want to have the benefit of higher concurrency in exchange for the increased risks of encountering dirty reads, nonrepeatable reads and phantom phenomenon. ODBC was designed in such a way that it lets the application developer make the choice.

SUMMARY

A transaction is a recoverable sequence of SQL operations grouped as a single unit. The initiation and termination of a transaction define the points of data consistency within an application process; either all SQL operations within a transaction are applied to the data source (committed), or the effects of all SQL operations within a transaction are completely "undone" (rolled back).

ODBC provides the following modes of transaction processing that determine how and when transactions are to be committed (or, if possible, rolled back):

■ Auto-commit mode

■ Manual-commit mode

In auto-commit mode, each SQL statement processed is treated as an individual transaction that is committed right after it is executed. In manual-commit mode, transactions must be explicitly committed or rolled back.

In a multi-user database system, transactions can occur simultaneously, and each transaction has the potential to interfere with another one. When transactions are not isolated from each other in multi-user environments, the following three types of events can occur:

■ Dirty Reads

■ Nonrepeatable Reads

■ Phantoms

ODBC defines four levels of transaction isolation that can prevent all, some, or none of these events from occurring. They are:

■ Read Uncommitted

■ Read Committed

■ Repeatable Read

■ Serializable

Higher levels of transaction isolation offer the most protection for the integrity of database data. However, higher levels of transaction isolation can also reduce application performance.

Concurrency is another issue that must be addressed in a multi-user database system environment. When higher transaction isolation levels are used, concurrency is usually reduced. To solve this problem, ODBC allows an application to use any of the following levels of concurrency control:

- Read-Only
- Locking
- Optimistic

Concurrency control types are most often used by applications that specify low transaction isolation levels such as Read Committed or Read Uncommitted.

4

SQL Statements and ODBC

Many people wrongly believe that ODBC is a replacement for SQL. Instead, ODBC applications perform almost all data retrieval and manipulation by submitting SQL statements to data sources for processing. This chapter is designed to introduce you to the SQL syntax and grammar recognized by ODBC. The first part of this chapter describes the basic SQL statements that are used for data manipulation and data definition, along with the special clauses and predicates that can be used with them. This is followed by a close look at data source-specific SQL statements and the escape sequences used by ODBC to process them. Next, the various ways SQL statements can be constructed in an ODBC application is described. Finally, techniques that can be used to construct interoperable SQL statements are discussed.

This chapter is not designed to teach you how to write complex and clever SQL data manipulation statements. It is instead designed to present ODBC's 'version' of the SQL statements typically used in an ODBC application and to point out where they might differ from other implementations.

Types of SQL Statements

Because SQL's primary function is to support the definition, manipulation, and control of data in a relational database, most SQL statements fall under one of the following classifications:

- Data Manipulation Language (DML) Statements
- Data Definition Language (DDL) Statements
- Data Control Statements

Data manipulation language (DML) statements are used to retrieve data from, add data to, and otherwise manipulate data in a relational database. *Data definition language* (DDL) statements are used to define the data objects (that is, tables, views, indexes, and so on) that make up a relational database. *Data control* statements control the execution of DML and DDL SQL statements to ensure that data stored in a relational database remains consistent and secure in a multi-user environment. Of these three, data manipulation language statements are used the most in ODBC application, followed by data definition language statements.

Data Manipulation Language (DML) Statements

Four basic SQL statements can be used for data manipulation in an ODBC application. They are:

- The **SELECT** statement
- The **INSERT** statement
- The **UPDATE** statement
- The **DELETE** statement

THE SELECT SQL STATEMENT AND ITS CLAUSES Eventually, almost every database application needs to retrieve specific data from the data source it is interacting with. In both embedded SQL and ODBC applications, the **SELECT** SQL statement is used to perform all data retrieval operations. When a **SELECT** statement is sent to a data source for processing, the data source gathers or *selects* the data that meets the precise specifications defined by the **SELECT** statement and returns it to the application.

In an embedded SQL application, data retrieved by a **SELECT** statement can be moved directly into a result data set (which is then accessed by a cursor that the application defines) or into one or more application host variables. However, in an ODBC application, data retrieved by a **SELECT** statement is not actually moved directly into the application. Instead, data is moved into a special storage buffer and other ODBC API functions are responsible for moving it from the storage buffer to the application.

Because the **SELECT** statement is the primary SQL statement used to retrieve data, it can be the most complex, and the most complicated SQL statement used—six different clauses can be used with a **SELECT** statement and each of these clauses has its own set of predicates. Although some commercial implementations of SQL may support other SQL statement clauses, only the following **SELECT** statement clauses are recognized by ODBC:

- **FROM**
- **WHERE**
- **GROUP BY**
- **HAVING**
- **UNION**
- **ORDER BY**

THE FROM CLAUSE   The **FROM** clause is used in conjunction with a table reference list to tell the data source which table(s) to retrieve data from. The syntax for the simplest form of a **SELECT** SQL statement which, by design, must always contain a **FROM** clause is:

```
SELECT [item_list] FROM [table_list]
```

Column names (specified alone or with an alias), literals, expressions, ODBC scalar functions, or data source-specific functions can usually be included in the *item_list*; whether a particular element can be used is dependent on the data source driver's SQL conformance level. The *table_list* can contain table names, table names with correlation names (that is, user-created aliases to be used as a more meaningful qualifier to column names elsewhere in the query or in a subquery), or an outer join specification that specifies the table names and condition to use for an outer join.

OUTER JOINS   Outer join specifications are included in the ODBC SQL grammar because they are used quite often, especially with relational DBMSs. The basic idea behind an outer join is as follows: Suppose Table A and Table B are joined by an ordinary (inner) join. Any row in either Table A or Table B that doesn't match a row in the other table (under the rules of the join condition) is left out of the result data set. By contrast, if Table A and Table B are joined by an outer join, any row in either Table A or Table B not containing a matching row in the other table is included in the result data set (exactly once) and columns in that row that would have contained matching values from the other table are empty. Thus, an outer join adds nonmatching rows to a result data set where an inner join would exclude them. A *left* outer join of Table A with Table B preserves nonmatching rows from Table A, a *right* outer join of Table A with Table B preserves nonmatching rows from Table B, and a *full* outer join preserves nonmatching rows from both Table A and Table B.

The syntax for the simplest form of a **SELECT** SQL statement using an outer join is:

```
SELECT [item_list] FROM {oj [table_reference_1] [LEFT |
    RIGHT | FULL] OUTER JOIN [table_reference_2 |
    outer_join] ON [join_condition] }
```

NOTE: *{ oj } is the ODBC escape sequence for outer joins. Escape sequences are discussed later in this chapter.*

THE WHERE CLAUSE   The **WHERE** clause is used to tell the data source how to search one or more tables for specific data. The **WHERE** clause is always followed by a search condition containing one or more predicates defining how the data source is to choose the information contained in the result data set produced. Six types of **WHERE** clause predicates are supported by ODBC. They are:

▓ Relational Predicates (Comparisons)

▓ **BETWEEN**

▓ **LIKE**

▓ **IN**

▓ **EXISTS**

▓ **NULL**

RELATIONAL PREDICATES The relational predicates (otherwise known as comparisons) are the operators that can be used to define a comparison relationship between two values. The following comparison operators are recognized by ODBC:

- < (Less than)
- > (Greater than)
- <= (Less than or equal to)
- >= (Greater than or equal to)
- = (Equal to)
- <> (Not equal to)

> **NOTE:** *Although many data sources allow the use of the NOT keyword and/or the NOT operator (!) as comparison operators (for example NOT = or !=), neither are supported by ODBC's SQL grammar.*

Relational predicates are used to include or exclude rows from the final result data set produced. Therefore, they are typically used to specify a condition in which the value of a column is less than, greater than, equal to, or not equal to a specified literal value. For example, the SQL statement

```
SELECT LastName FROM Employees WHERE Salary > 50000
```

produces a result data set containing the last name of all employees whose salary is greater than $50,000.

It is up to the application to ensure that the data type of the comparison column and the data type of the literal, or other value being checked, are compatible. If necessary, scalar functions can be embedded in the **SELECT** statement to make this happen.

THE BETWEEN PREDICATE The **BETWEEN** predicate is used to define a comparison relationship in which a value is checked to see whether it falls within a range of values. For example, the SQL statement

```
SELECT LastName FROM Employees WHERE EmpID BETWEEN 100 AND
    120
```

produces a result data set containing the last name of all employees whose employee number is greater than or equal to 100 and less than or equal to 120.

If the **NOT** negation operator is applied to the **BETWEEN** predicate, a value is checked to see whether it falls outside a range of values. For example, the SQL statement

```
SELECT LastName FROM Employees WHERE EmpID NOT BETWEEN 100
       AND 120
```

produces a result data set containing the last name of all employees whose employee number is less than 100 and greater than 120.

THE LIKE PREDICATE The **LIKE** predicate is used to define a comparison relationship in which a character value is checked to see whether it contains a prescribed pattern. The prescribed pattern is any arbitrary character string. Characters in the pattern string are interpreted as follows:

■ The underscore character (_) is treated as a wild card that stands for any single character.

■ The percent character (%) is treated as a wild card that stands for any sequence of characters.

■ All other characters are treated as regular characters (that is, they stand for themselves).

For example, the SQL statement

```
SELECT LastName, FirstName FROM Employees WHERE LastName
       LIKE "La%"
```

produces a result data set containing the last name and first name of all employees whose last name begins with the letters "La" (for example, Larson, Layton, Lawson, and so on).

When using wild card characters, care must be taken to ensure that they are placed in the appropriate location in the pattern string. Note in the preceding example, only records for employees whose last name begins with the characters "La" would be returned. If the pattern specified had been "%La%", records for employees whose last name contains the characters "La" (anywhere in the name) would have been returned.

Likewise, you must also be careful about using upper- and lowercase letters in pattern strings. If the data source processing the **SELECT** statement is configured to sort in a case-sensitive manner, the characters used in a pattern string must match the case used to store the data in the column being searched.

NOTE: *Although the* **LIKE** *predicate can be an appealingly easy method to use to search for needed data, it should be used with caution. In most relational database management systems, processing a* **LIKE** *predicate is the slowest type*

of operation that can be performed, and it can be extremely resource-intensive. This is why LIKE predicates should only be used when there is no other way to locate the data needed.

THE IN PREDICATE The **IN** predicate is used to define a comparison relationship in which a value is checked to see whether it matches a value in a finite list of values. **IN** predicates come in two different formats: one simple and the other quite complex.

In its simplest form, the **IN** predicate can compare a value against a finite set of literal values. For example, the SQL statement

```
SELECT LastName FROM Customers WHERE State IN ("CA", "NY",
    "IL")
```

produces a result data set containing the last name of all customers living in California, New York, and Illinois.

In its more complex form, the **IN** predicate can compare a value against a finite set of values generated by a subquery. For example, the SQL statement

```
SELECT CustID FROM Customers WHERE State IN (SELECT State
    FROM Regions WHERE RegionID = 1)
```

produces a result data set containing the customer ID of all customers living in any state considered part of Region 1. In this example, the subquery `SELECT State FROM Regions WHERE RegionID = 1` produces a list of all states found in the territory the company has identified as "Region 1". Then the outer or main query checks each state value in the customers table to see if it exists in the set of state values returned from the subquery.

THE EXISTS PREDICATE The **EXISTS** predicate is used to determine whether a particular row of data exists in a table. The **EXISTS** predicate is always followed by a subquery; therefore, it returns a TRUE or FALSE value indicating whether a particular row of data is found in the result data set generated by the subquery. For example, the SQL statement

```
SELECT CompanyName FROM Suppliers WHERE EXISTS (SELECT *
    FROM AcountsPayable WHERE AmtDue > 10000 AND
    AcountsPayable.CustID = Suppliers.CustID)
```

produces a result data set containing the name of all supplier companies owed $10,000 or more.

EXISTS predicates are often ANDed with other conditions to determine final row selection.

THE NULL PREDICATE The **NULL** predicate is used to determine whether a particular column in a row of data contains a value. For example, the SQL statement

```
SELECT EmpID FROM Employees WHERE MiddleInitial IS NULL
```

produces a result data set containing the employee IDs of all employees whose record does not contain a value for the MiddleInitial column.

> **NOTE:** **NULL** *and zero (0) or blank (" ") are not the same.* **NULL** *is a special marker used to represent missing information. On the other hand, zero or blank (empty string) are actual values that can be placed in a column to indicate a specific value (or lack thereof). Some data sources do not recognize* **NULL** *values while others allow the user to decide whether each individual column in a table supports* **NULL** *values. Before writing SQL statements that check for* **NULL** *values, make sure the data source supports them and that the* **NULL** *value is valid for the column(s) specified.*

THE GROUP BY CLAUSE The **GROUP BY** clause is used to organize the rows of data in a result data set by the values contained in the column(s) specified. The **GROUP BY** clause is also used to specify on what column to break for control breaks when using aggregate functions such as **SUM()** and **AVG()**. For example, the SQL statement

```
SELECT DeptName, SUM(SalesAmt) FROM Departments D,
     SalesHistory S WHERE D.DeptID = S.DeptID GROUP BY
     DeptName
```

produces a result data set containing one row for each department with rows in the sales history table. Each row in the result data set produced contains the department name and the total sales amount for that department.

A common mistake often made with this type of query is the addition of other non-aggregate columns to the **GROUP BY** clause. Because grouping is performed by combining all the non-aggregate columns together into a single, concatenated key and breaking whenever that key value changes, extraneous columns can cause unexpected breaks.

> **NOTE:** *Some data sources do not allow non-aggregate columns to be specified in the* **GROUP BY** *clause.*

THE HAVING CLAUSE   The **HAVING** clause is used to apply further selection criteria to columns referenced in a **GROUP BY** clause. The **HAVING** clause uses the same syntax as the **WHERE** clause, except that it refers to grouped data rather than raw data. Like the **WHERE** clause, the **HAVING** clause is commonly used to tell the data source how to search one or more tables for specific data. For example, if a **HAVING** clause were added to the previous example like this:

```
SELECT DeptName, SUM(SalesAmt) FROM Departments D,
     SalesHistory S WHERE D.DeptID = S.DeptID GROUP BY
     DeptName HAVING SUM(SalesAmt) > 1000000
```

the result data set produced would contain one row for each department with rows in the sales history table whose total sales amount exceeds one million dollars.

THE UNION CLAUSE   The **UNION** clause is used to combine two separate and individual result data sets to produce one single result data set. In order for two result data sets to be combined with a **UNION** clause, they both must have the same number of columns and each of those columns must have the exact same data types assigned to them.

For example, suppose a company keeps employee information in a special table that is archived at the end of each year. Just before the table is archived, a new table is created, and the records for all employees still employed by the company are copied to it. Throughout the year, as new employees are hired, they are added to the new table. To obtain a list of all employees employed by the company in 1996 and 1997, each archived table would have to be queried, and the results would have to be combined. This operation could be performed by using the **UNION** clause in an SQL statement. For example:

```
SELECT LastName, EmpID FROM Employees96 UNION SELECT
     LastName, EmpID FROM Employees97
```

When executed, this SQL statement produces a result data set containing the last name and the employee ID of all employees that worked for the company in 1996 and 1997.

By default, when two result data sets are combined, all duplicate rows are removed. However, all rows of data in each result data set (including duplicates) are copied to the combined result data if the keyword **ALL** follows the **UNION** clause (for example: **UNION ALL**).

THE ORDER BY CLAUSE   The **ORDER BY** clause is used to sort and order the rows of data in a result data set by the values contained in the column(s) specified. Multiple columns can be used for ordering, and each column used can be ordered in either ascending or descending order; if the keyword **ASC** follows the column name, ascending order is used; if the keyword **DESC** follows the column name, descending order is used. When more than one column is specified for the **ORDER BY** clause, the result data set produced is sorted by the first column specified (the primary sort), then the sorted data is sorted again by the next column specified, and so on. For example, the SQL statement

```
SELECT LastName, FirstName, DeptID FROM Employees ORDER BY
       DeptID ASC, LastName ASC
```

produces a result data set containing employee last names, first names, and department IDs ordered by department ID and employee last name (the department IDs would be in ascending order and the employee last names associated with a each department would be in ascending alphabetical order).

If a column in the result data set is a summary column or a result column that cannot be specified by name, an integer value corresponding to the column number can be used in place of a column name. When integer values are used, the first or leftmost column in the result data set is treated as column 1, the next is column 2, and so on. Although integer values are primarily used in the **ORDER BY** clause to specify columns that cannot be specified by name, they can be used in place of almost any column name. For example, the previous SQL statement could also have been coded as:

```
SELECT LastName, FirstName, DeptID FROM Employees ORDER BY
       3 ASC, 1 ASC
```

THE INSERT STATEMENT   In some cases, a database application may need to add specific data to the data source it is interacting with. In both embedded SQL and ODBC applications, the **INSERT** SQL statement is used to add one or more rows of data to a data source. The **INSERT** statement is easier to use than the **SELECT** statement because it does not have as many optional clauses and predicates.

The syntax for the simplest form of an **INSERT** SQL statement is:

```
INSERT INTO [table_name] < ( [columns_list] ) > VALUES (
       [values_list] )
```

If values are provided for all columns in the table (in the *values_list*), column names do not have to be provided. However, if the number of values in the *values_list* does not match the number of columns in the table or if values in the *values_list* are to be placed in specific columns in the table, column names must be explicitly stated (in the *columns_list*). Depending on how a table was defined, NULL or some predefined default value may be inserted into columns for which no corresponding value is provided.

Literal values for columns can be hardcoded directly into an **INSERT** statement or they can be placed in variables to be populated at application run time. The **INSERT** statement expects values to be provided at run time if dynamic parameter markers (question marks) are coded into the **VALUES** clause in place of literal values. The following is an example of such an **INSERT** statement:

```
INSERT INTO Employees VALUES (?, ?, ?, ?, ?)
```

The **INSERT** statement can also contain a subselect in place of literal values in the **VALUES** clause. This format of the **INSERT** statement creates a type of "cut and paste" action in which values are retrieved from one table and inserted into another.

THE UPDATE STATEMENT   Sometimes, a database application may need to change data that already exists in the data source with which it is interacting. In both embedded SQL and ODBC applications, the **UPDATE** SQL statement is used to change specific data values in a data source. An **UPDATE** statement can change the value of one, many, or all the columns in a row of data. However, some data sources, do not allow primary key values for a table to be changed with the **UPDATE** statement. In these instances, you must delete the existing row and insert the new modified row.

Like the **INSERT** statement, the **UPDATE** statement is easier to use than the **SELECT** statement even though it optionally uses the **WHERE** clause and its predicates.

The syntax for the simplest form of an **UPDATE** SQL statement is:

```
UPDATE [table_name] SET [column] = [value] <WHERE
    [where_condition] >
```

In the ODBC, the **UPDATE** statement must always contain a **WHERE** clause unless it is a positioned **UPDATE** statement (see Chapter 12 for more information on performing positioned updates).

THE DELETE STATEMENT   Occasionally, a database application may need to remove existing data from the data source it is interacting with. In both embedded SQL and ODBC applications, the **DELETE** SQL statement is used to remove one or more rows of data from a data source. The syntax for the simplest form of a **DELETE** SQL statement is:

```
DELETE FROM [table_name] <WHERE [where_condition] >
```

Omitting the **WHERE** clause in a **DELETE** statement causes the delete operation to be applied to all rows in the specified table. Therefore, it is important to always provide a **WHERE** clause with a **DELETE** statement unless you explicitly want to erase all data stored in a table.

Data Definition Language (DDL) Statements

In addition to the data manipulation language statements described previously, ODBC also supports the following data definition language statements:

- **ALTER TABLE**
- **CALL**
- **CREATE INDEX**
- **CREATE TABLE**
- **CREATE VIEW**
- **DROP INDEX**
- **DROP TABLE**
- **DROP VIEW**
- **GRANT**
- **REVOKE**

Although some of these statements are almost self-explanatory, (for example the **DROP TABLE** statement), others can be quite complex. Additionally, almost all data definition language statements are data source specific. For example, the **CREATE TABLE** statement does not use the standard ODBC data types; instead, it uses data source-specific data types. Because of this, the syntax is not provided for data definition language statements and they are not discussed in detail.

Escape Sequences

When the X/Open Company and the SQL Access Group developed the 1992 SQL CAE specification, they recognized that some data sources would need a way to process exceptions and additions to the standard SQL language. Thus, the SQL CAE specification defines a special "escape clause" method that can be used to send SQL language extensions directly to the data source.

A number of SQL language features, such as outer joins and scalar function calls, are implemented by almost every DBMS. Unfortunately, the SQL syntax for these features are usually data source-specific—even when standard SQL syntaxes have been defined for them by the various SQL standards specifications. Because of this, ODBC provides several pre-defined escape sequences that provide applications with a standardized SQL grammar that can be used to invoke these features. ODBC escape sequences use the "escape clause" method defined in the 1992 SQL CAE specification to send data source-specific SQL grammar to a data source (via the driver) for processing.

In ODBC 2.0 and earlier, the standard syntax for an escape sequence was:

```
-(*vendor(vendor_name), product(product_name) extension *)-
```

To make application development easier, the following shorthand syntax could be used instead of the longer version:

```
{extension}
```

In ODBC 3.x, the longer form of the escape sequence is no longer supported and the shorthand form is used exclusively.

ODBC escape sequences are recognized and parsed by drivers. When a driver receives an escape sequence, it replaces it with the appropriate data source-specific SQL grammar before sending it to the data source for processing. Usually, drivers only support the escape sequences that can be mapped to the underlying data source's SQL language features (that is, if a data source does not support a particular feature, neither will its driver).

ODBC provides escape sequences (and corresponding standardized SQL syntax) for the following SQL language features:

- Date, time, and timestamp literals
- Datetime interval literals
- Scalar functions such as numeric, string, and data type conversion functions

- **LIKE** predicate escape characters
- Outer joins
- Stored procedure calls

Date, Time, and Timestamp Literals

The ODBC escape sequence for date, time, and timestamp literals is

```
{literal_type 'value'}
```

where *literal_type* is one of the values shown in Table 4–1 and value is a valid date, time, or timestamp value specified using the appropriate value in Table 4–1.

Table 4–1   ODBC Date, Time, and Timestamp Escape Sequence Literals and Formats

Data Type	*literal_type* Value	*value* Format
Date	d	yyyy-mm-dd
Time	t	hh:mm:ss[1]
Timestamp	ts	yyyy-mm-dd hh:mm:ss[.f...][1]

Adapted from *Microsoft ODBC 3.0 Programmer's Reference, Volume 1, and SDK Guide*, page 130.

[1] The number of digits to the right of the decimal point in a time or timestamp literal containing a seconds component is dependent on the seconds precision supported by the descriptor.

If the data source supports date, time, or timestamp data types, its driver must support the corresponding ODBC escape sequence. In drivers supporting ODBC, the data, time, and timestamp literals escape sequence may also support the datetime literals defined in the ANSI SQL-92 specification, which are different from the ODBC escape sequences.

Datetime Interval Literals

The ODBC escape sequence for a datetime interval literal is:

```
{interval < + | - > 'value' < interval_qualifier >}
```

where *value* is the value to be converted and *interval_qualifier* is either a single datetime field or a value composed of two datetime fields, in the form:

```
<leadingfield> to <trailingfield>
```

For example, the ODBC escape sequence:

```
{interval '163-11' YEAR(3) to Month}
```

specifies an interval of 163 years and 11 months. The interval leading precision is 3.

All interval literals begin with the word **"interval"**. This keyword, along with the opening brace, is sufficient to indicate that it is an interval literal. If the data source supports a date/time interval data type, its driver must also support the corresponding ODBC escape sequence. Data sources drivers can also support the datetime literals defined in the ANSI SQL92 specification, which are different from the ODBC escape sequences for datetime interval literals.

Scalar Function Calls

The ODBC escape sequence for calling a scalar function is:

```
{fn scalar_function}
```

where *scalar_function* is one of the functions listed in Appendix A.

Scalar functions return a value for each row in a database table. For example, the **ABS()** (absolute value) scalar function takes a numeric column as an argument and returns the absolute value of each value in that column.

For maximum interoperability, applications should use the **CONVERT()** scalar function to make sure the output of a scalar function is the required data type. The **CONVERT()** function converts data from one SQL data type to another. The syntax of the **CONVERT()** function is:

```
CONVERT(value_exp, data_type)
```

where *value_exp* is a column name, the result of another scalar function, or a literal value, and *data_type* is a keyword that matches a valid SQL data type identifier.

NOTE: *An application can mix calls to scalar functions that use native SQL syntax and calls to scalar functions that use ODBC syntax. However, whenever possible, interoperable applications should avoid using scalar functions that use native SQL syntax.*

LIKE Predicate Escape Character

The ODBC escape sequence that defines the LIKE predicate escape character is:

```
{escape 'escape_character'}
```

where *escape_character* is any character that is supported by the data source.

In a LIKE predicate, the percent sign character (%) and the underscore character (_) are used as wildcard characters. In order to use an actual percent sign or underscore character in a LIKE predicate, it must be preceded by an escape character that has been previously defined with the LIKE predicate escape character ODBC escape sequence.

Outer Joins

The ODBC escape sequence that defines an outer join is:

```
{oj outer_join}
```

where *outer_ join* is an outer join statement in the following format:

```
table_reference [LEFT | RIGHT | FULL] OUTER JOIN
        [table_reference | outer_join] ON search_condition
```

where *table_reference* specifies a table name, *outer_ join* specifies a secondary outer join, and *search_condition* specifies the join condition between the table references. An outer join request must appear after the FROM clause of a SELECT statement and before the WHERE clause (if one exists). ODBC supports SQL-92 left, right, and full outer join syntax.

Stored Procedure Calls

The ODBC escape sequence for calling a stored procedure is:

```
{<?=> call procedure_name < (<parameter, ...> ) >}
```

where *procedure_name* specifies the name of a stored procedure and *parameter* specifies one or more stored procedure parameters values.

A stored procedure is an executable object (usually containing one or more precompiled SQL statements) stored in the data source. A stored procedure can have zero or more parameters and it can also return a value as indicated by the optional parameter marker **"?="** at the beginning of the escape sequence syntax. If the parameter is an input or an input/output parameter, its value can be either a literal value or a parameter marker (interoperable applications should always use parameter markers). If a parameter is an output parameter, its value must always be a parameter marker.

If an input or input/output parameter is omitted, the stored procedure uses the default value of the parameter. If an input/output parameter is omitted or if a literal value is supplied for the parameter, the driver discards the output value. Similarly, if the parameter marker for the return value of a procedure is omitted, the driver discards the return value. Finally, if an application specifies a return value parameter for a stored procedure that does not return a value, the driver sets the value of the length/indicator buffer bound to the parameter to **SQL_NULL_DATA**.

Input and input/output parameters can be omitted from stored procedure calls. If a stored procedure is called without parentheses (that is, **{call procedure_name}**), the driver calls the procedure without sending it any parameter values. If a stored procedure is called with parentheses but without any parameters (that is **{call procedure_name ()}**), the driver instructs the data source to use the default value for the first parameter; all other parameters are ignored.

NOTE: *If a stored procedure does not have parameters and if it is called with parenthesis (that is,* **{call procedure_name ()}** *), the procedure fails.*

Constructing SQL Statements

In an ODBC application, SQL statements can be constructed in one of three ways: they can be hard-coded during application development; they can be dynamically constructed at application run time; or they can be entered directly by the user at application run time. Although applications generally use only one of these methods, any combination can be used.

Hard-Coded SQL Statements

Applications designed to perform one or more fixed tasks usually contain hard-coded SQL statements. There are several advantages to using this approach:

▪ Hard-coded SQL statements can be prototyped and tested before the application is written.

▪ Hard-coded SQL statements are simple to implement.

▪ Hard-coded SQL statements simplify the application.

Hard-coded SQL statements become more dynamic when they contain parameter markers instead of literal values. Additionally, it is usually easier to construct a parameterized SQL statement because the data values it uses can be sent to the DBMS in their native types, such as integers and floating point numbers, instead of having to be converted into strings.

If a hard-coded SQL statement is to be executed repeatedly, it can be prepared for even greater efficiency. Additionally, if parameterized SQL statements are prepared, they can be treated as if they were multiple statements—just by changing the parameter values each time the statements are executed. In this case, the SQL statement only has to be re-executed; there is no need to rebuild (reprepare) it.

Another way to use hard-coded SQL statements is to put them in special stored procedures. Because stored procedures are constructed at application development time and stored on the data source, the SQL statements in them do not have to be prepared at application run time. The drawback with using this method is that the syntax for creating stored procedures is usually data source specific; therefore, stored procedures must be constructed separately for each data source that an application using them will run against.

Run-Time-Constructed (Dynamic) SQL Statements

Applications designed to perform ad-hoc analysis usually build their SQL statements at application run time. The same is true for most interactive development environments (IDEs) such as Visual BASIC and Visual C++. However, the SQL statements IDEs construct are typically hard-coded in the application the IDE is being used to develop, where they can be optimized and tested.

Applications that build their SQL statements at run time provide tremendous flexibility to the user. Unfortunately, constructing and using SQL statements at application run time is vastly more complex than using hard-coded SQL statements. Furthermore, testing such applications can be difficult because they can construct an arbitrary number of SQL statements. Another disadvantage of this approach is that it takes far more processing time to dynamically construct and execute an SQL statement than it does to use a hard-coded SQL statement. Fortunately, this is rarely a concern because such applications tend to be very user interface intensive and the time the application spends constructing SQL statements is generally small compared to the time the user spends entering information.

User-Supplied SQL Statements

Some applications designed to perform ad-hoc analysis allow the user to enter SQL statements directly into the application. This approach simplifies application coding because the user is responsible for building the SQL statement, and the data source is responsible for checking the statement's validity. Because writing a graphical user interface that adequately exposes the intricacies of SQL is a difficult task, simply asking the user to enter SQL statement text may be a preferable alternative. However, this requires the user to be knowledgeable about both SQL and the underlying schema of the data source being queried.

Interoperable SQL

SQL statements can be constructed so that they are either interoperable or data source-specific. Generic applications designed to work with a variety of data sources must use interoperable SQL statements whereas custom applications designed to exploit the capabilities of one (or possibly two) data source(s) can use data source-specific SQL. Vertical applications usually fall somewhere in between, demanding a certain level of data source-specific functionality, but otherwise using interoperable SQL statements.

A number of things can determine whether an SQL statement is interoperable, by design:

- SQL grammar used
- Catalog and schema usage
- Catalog name position
- Identifier case
- Escape sequences used

- Literal prefixes and suffixes
- Parameter markers in procedure calls
- DDL statements used

Choosing an SQL Grammar

Before constructing SQL statements in an ODBC application, you must first decide on which grammar to use. In addition to the grammars available from the various standards bodies, such as X/Open, ANSI, and ISO/IEC, virtually every DBMS vendor defines their own grammar, each of which varies slightly from one of the standard grammars.

The SQL grammar chosen affects how the driver processes all SQL statements—a driver must always convert SQL-92 SQL statements and ODBC-defined escape sequences to data source-specific SQL. Because most SQL grammars are based on one or more of the various standards specifications, most drivers do little or no work to meet this requirement. Typically, when a driver encounters SQL grammar it does not recognize, it assumes the grammar is data source-specific and passes the unrecognized SQL statement, without modification, to the data source for execution.

Thus, there are really two choices of grammar to use: the ODBC SQL-92 grammar (and the ODBC escape sequences) or a data source-specific grammar. Of the two, only the SQL-92 grammar is interoperable; therefore, all interoperable applications should use it. Applications that are not interoperable can use the SQL-92 grammar, a data source-specific grammar, or a combination of the two. Data source-specific grammars have two advantages over the SQL-92 grammar: they can exploit any features the data source provides that aren't covered by SQL-92 and they can be executed faster (marginally) because the driver does not have to modify them.

Even if the ODBC SQL-92 grammar is used, there are other obstacles that must be overcome to ensure that an application is interoperable. For example, what does an application do if it wants to use a feature, such as an outer join, which may not be supported by all data sources it will interact with? At this point, the application writer must make some decisions about what language features are required and what features are optional. Generally, if a particular feature is required by an application and a driver does not support it, the application refuses to run with that driver. However, if the feature is optional, the application can often work around it.

Catalog and Schema Usage

The ability to support catalog and schema names as object name identifiers varies from data source to data source. Data sources may or may not support catalog and schema names in one or more of the following types of SQL statements:

- Data Manipulation Language (DML) statements
- Stored procedure calls
- Table definition statements
- Index definition statements
- Authorization privilege definition statements

Therefore, interoperable applications should limit their usage of catalog and schema names, especially when working with these types of SQL statements.

Catalog Name Position

The position of a catalog name in an identifier and how it is separated from the rest of the identifier varies from data source to data source. When quoting identifiers containing more than one part, interoperable applications must be careful to quote each part separately and to avoid quoting the character that separates the identifiers.

Quoted Identifiers

In an SQL statement, identifiers that contain special characters or match keywords must be enclosed in identifier quote characters—identifiers enclosed in such characters are known as quoted identifiers (or as delimited identifiers in SQL-92). The primary reason for quoting identifiers is to make the SQL statement containing them parseable. Such identifiers are driver (and therefore data source) specific. To be safe, interoperable applications should make sure that all identifiers, except those used for pseudo-columns, are quoted.

Identifier Case

In SQL statements and catalog function arguments, identifiers and quoted identifiers can be either case sensitive or case insensitive. How identifiers are stored in the system catalog is relevant only for display purposes, such as when an application displays the results of a catalog function; it does not change the case sensitivity of identifiers. Therefore, interoperable applications usually do not have to be concerned about identifier case sensitivity.

Escape Sequences

You saw earlier in this chapter that ODBC defines escape sequences for date, time, and timestamp literals, datetime interval literals, scalar function calls, **LIKE** predicate escape characters, outer joins, and stored procedure calls. In addition to these escape sequences, data sources often support other extensions to the standard SQL syntax. Interoperable applications should avoid using data source-specific extensions; the ODBC escape sequences should be used instead.

Literal Prefixes and Suffixes

In an SQL statement, a literal is a character representation of an actual data value. Literals for some data types require special prefixes and suffixes. Interoperable applications should use the values returned in the **LITERAL_PREFIX** and **LITERAL_SUFFIX** columns in the result data set created by the **SQLGetTypeInfo()** ODBC API function call for all data types except date, time, and timestamps. For date, time, timestamp, and datetime interval literals, interoperable applications should use the escape sequences discussed earlier.

Parameter Markers in Procedure Calls

When calling stored procedures that accept parameter values, interoperable applications should always use parameter markers instead of literal values.

DDL Statements

DDL SQL statements can vary tremendously among data sources. As mentioned earlier in this chapter, ODBC only defines SQL statements for the most common data definition language operations. All other DDL statements are data source specific; therefore, interoperable applications should avoid using data definition language SQL statements. In general, this is not a problem, because such operations tend to be highly data source specific and are best left to the proprietary database administration software shipped with the data source or the setup program shipped with the driver.

Another problem with using DDL statements is that the data type names they use also vary tremendously among data sources. Rather than defining standard data type names and forcing drivers to convert them to DBMS-specific names, drivers can provide the data source-specific data type names to applications. If an interoperable application cannot avoid using DDL statements, it should use these names in all SQL statements that create and alter tables.

SUMMARY

ODBC applications perform almost all their data retrieval and manipulation by submitting SQL statements to a specific data source for processing. Because the primary function of SQL is to support the definition, manipulation, and control of data in a relational database, most SQL statements fall into one of the following classifications:

- Data Manipulation Language (DML) Statements
- Data Definition Language (DDL) Statements
- Data Control Statements

Data manipulation language statements are used to retrieve data from, add data to, and manipulate data stored in a relational database. Data definition language statements are used to define the data objects (that is, tables, views, indexes, and so on) that make up a relational database. Data control statements control the execution of DML and DDL SQL statements to ensure that a relational database remains consistent and secure in a multi-user environment.

ODBC recognizes four basic data manipulation language SQL statements. They are:

- The **SELECT** statement
- The **INSERT** statement
- The **UPDATE** statement
- The **DELETE** statement

Different clauses can be used with a **SELECT** statement and each clause has its own set of predicates. The following **SELECT** statement clauses are recognized by ODBC:

▓ **FROM**

▓ **WHERE**

▓ **GROUP BY**

▓ **HAVING**

▓ **UNION**

▓ **ORDER BY**

In addition to these six clauses, six types of **WHERE** clause predicates are also supported by ODBC. They are:

▓ Relational Predicates (Comparisons)

▓ **BETWEEN**

▓ **LIKE**

▓ **IN**

▓ **EXISTS**

▓ **NULL**

In addition to the DML statements described previously, ODBC also supports the following DDL statements:

▓ **ALTER TABLE**

▓ **CALL**

▓ **CREATE INDEX**

▓ **CREATE TABLE**

▓ **CREATE VIEW**

▓ **DROP INDEX**

▓ **DROP TABLE**

▓ **DROP VIEW**

▓ **GRANT**

▓ **REVOKE**

A number of SQL language features, such as outer joins and scalar function calls, are implemented by almost every DBMS. Unfortunately, the SQL syntax for these features is usually data source specific. Because of this, ODBC provides a set of escape sequences that provide a standardized SQL grammar for invoking the following SQL language features:

- Date, time, and timestamp literals
- Datetime interval literals
- Scalar functions such as numeric, string, and data type conversion functions
- **LIKE** predicate escape characters
- Outer joins
- Stored procedure calls

SQL statements can be constructed in ODBC applications in one of three ways:

- they can be hard-coded during application development
- they can be dynamically constructed at application run time
- they can be entered directly by the user at application run time

Applications designed to perform a fixed task usually contain hard-coded SQL statements. Applications designed to perform ad-hoc analysis usually build their SQL statements at application run time. However, some applications designed to perform ad-hoc analysis allow the user to enter SQL statements directly into the application. This approach simplifies application development because the application relies on the user to build the SQL statement and on the data source to check the statement's validity.

SQL statements can be either interoperable or data source specific, depending on how they are coded. A number of things can determine whether an SQL statement is interoperable:

- SQL grammar used
- Catalog and schema usage
- Catalog name position
- Identifier case
- Escape sequences used
- Literal prefixes and suffixes
- Parameter markers in procedure calls
- DDL statements

5

Components ODBC Uses to Interact with Applications

ODBC uses a set of special components to help applications communicate with one or more data sources. This chapter is designed to introduce you to the major components that can be found in almost all ODBC applications. The first part of this chapter introduces the concept of handles and describes how they are used to access and/or update information about the environment, a connection to a data source, an SQL statement, and a descriptor. This is followed by a short discussion about environment, connection, and SQL statement handle states and state transitions. Next, the data buffers and length/indicator buffers used with many ODBC API functions, are described. Finally, the C and SQL data types used by ODBC are discussed along with information about how one data type is converted to the other.

Handles

One of the first fundamental issues that CLI and ODBC designers had to address was how to allow applications to access multiple data sources simultaneously, yet free them from having to allocate and manage global variables and/or data structures (such as the SQLCA and SQLDA data structures used with embedded SQL) for each data source used. Their solution was to use (with some modifications) the handle concept that was already being used by the Microsoft Windows operating system. In Windows, a *handle* is simply an application pointer variable that refers to a data object the operating system uses to store context information. In a Windows application, handles are used to access data structures for which only Windows knows the details. The same is true with ODBC: applications never look "inside" a handle nor can they directly manipulate the data stored in the storage area the handle points to (this concept is known as *information hiding*).

In Windows, handles are always managed by the operating system; consequently, the underlying data structure for each handle is defined and managed by Windows and its format is never changed. The developers of ODBC wanted to provide a way for driver developers to define their own data structures, yet be able to use the handle concept to keep their data structures private. Their solution was to define special ODBC API allocation functions for each handle used (in ODBC 3.x these individual API functions have been replaced by a single function that does the same job). The ODBC API allocation function(s) enable a driver to attach its own private data structure to each handle used; therefore applications always use the same kind of handle and the driver manipulates it accordingly. This approach has another benefit; the Driver Manager can use its own set of handles to manage each driver loaded and to provide the necessary mappings between applications and drivers.

The handle concept also makes it easier for application developers to obtain and process error information when an ODBC API function call fails. Without handles, it would be very difficult to return error information to applications; ODBC would have to either return all error information as an API function return code value, or it would have to store error information in a local or global memory storage area that could only be accessed by the application. Either of these two approaches would add complexity to ODBC application development, and this complexity would increase each time a new thread was used. The handle approach in a multithreaded environment always makes it clear to both the application and the Driver Manager where context and error information should be stored. Additionally, when an error occurs, there is never a question about what the application is supposed to do—it should pass the handle used in the API function that generated the error to the appropriate ODBC error handling function.

The context information kept in handles can also be used to expose additional features supported by a driver, such as synchronous cancel. Synchronous cancel enables an application to start executing an SQL statement on one thread and cancel its execution on another thread. Again, handles make this type of functionality possible because the handle used to execute the SQL statement in one thread can be used in any other thread to cancel it—the handle lets the Driver Manager know that both actions are to be performed for the same SQL statement.

NOTE: *Although an application allocates only one set of handles; two sets of handles are actually used. One set is allocated within the Driver Manager by the application and is used to communicate between the application and the Driver Manager. The other set is allocated by the driver and is used to communicate between the Driver Manager and the driver. Each set of handles is only meaningful to the ODBC component it belongs to; that is, only the Driver Manager can interpret Driver Manager handles and only a driver can interpret its own driver handles. This allows each driver to have its own data structure for each handle without requiring that the Driver Manager and application understand the structure's format and contents. When an application passes a handle to the Driver Manager in an ODBC API function call, the Driver Manager doesn't pass it along to the driver; instead, the Driver Manager uses it to find the corresponding driver handle. The handle allocated by the driver is the actual handle that gets passed with the API function call.*

ODBC uses the following four types of handles:

- Environment handles
- Connection handles
- Statement handles
- Descriptor handles

The Environment Handle

An *environment handle* is a pointer to a data storage area containing ODBC specific information that is global in nature. This information includes:

■ The current state of the environment.

■ The current value of each environment attribute.

■ The handle for each connection data storage area currently allocated within the environment.

■ The number of connections currently available in the environment and their current state ("Connected" or "Disconnected").

■ Diagnostic information about the current environment.

Every application program that intends to use ODBC must begin by allocating an environment handle. Usually only one environment handle can be allocated per application and it must be allocated before any other handles are allocated. All other handles (that is, all connection, statement, and descriptor handles for an application) are managed within the context of an environment handle.

In addition to being an application's global placeholder for all other handles and for context information, the environment handle is used in a limited number of ODBC API functions for the following purposes:

■ To pass any errors occuring at the environment level (such as an attempt to free the environment handle while connections are still active or an attempt to use an invalid environment handle during connection handle allocation) to the appropriate ODBC error handling function.

■ To serve as the context handle for the ODBC API function that enumerates the data sources that are currently installed (**SQLDataSources()**).

■ To serve as the context handle for the ODBC API function that enumerates the drivers currently installed (**SQLDrivers()**).

■ To manage transactions when the **SQLEndTran()** function or the **SQLTransact()** function is used to commit or roll back all open transactions on all connections (rather than have an application commit or roll back outstanding transactions on each connection, the environment handle can be used to force the Driver Manager to commit or rollback outstanding transactions on all connections).

The Connection Handle

A *connection handle* is a pointer to a data structure that contains information about a data source connection being managed by the ODBC Driver Manager. This information includes:

- The current state of the connection.
- The current value of each connection attribute.
- The handle for each SQL statement data storage area currently allocated within the connection.
- The handle for each descriptor data storage area currently allocated within the connection.
- Diagnostic information about the connection.

From the data source driver's perspective, a connection handle is used to keep track of a network connection to a server or, alternately, to keep track of directory and local data file information. From the Driver Manager's perspective, a connection handle is used to identify which driver to load/use and which data source to use with a particular driver.

When a connection handle is allocated, the Driver Manager stores it inside the data storage area the environment handle points to. Because multiple connection handles can be allocated, the Driver Manager maintains a list of all connection handles associated with an environment handle. Each time a new connection handle is allocated, it is added to the list; once a connection handle is allocated, it can be used to establish a connection to a data source. ODBC does not prevent an application from making multiple, simultaneous connections to one or more data sources if the driver supports them. Thus, in a particular ODBC environment, multiple connection handles might point to a variety of drivers and data sources, the same driver and a variety of data sources, or the same driver and data source.

When a connection is made to a data source via a connection handle, the appropriate driver is loaded into memory, an array of pointers to the ODBC API functions in that driver are stored in the connection handle, and the data source is made available to the application. At this point the connection handle is said to be in an "Active" or a "Connected" state to distinguish it from a connection handle that is in an "Allocated" state. Thereafter, each time an ODBC API function is called with the connection handle specified as an argument, the Driver Manager looks up the corresponding API function entry point in the array of function pointers stored in the connection handle and routes the call to the appropriate function in the driver.

In addition to storing connection information and establishing connections to data sources, connection handles are also used in a number of ODBC API functions for the following purposes:

- To terminate (break) a connection to a data source.
- To pass any errors occuring at the connection level (such as the failure to load a driver, the failure to connect to the server across

the network, a network communication error, an attempt to use a connection already in use, and so on), to the appropriate ODBC error handling function.

■ To set connection options such as time-outs, transaction isolation levels, and so on.

■ As the main transaction management handle. The context of a transaction is determined by the connection handle; that is, the set of all SQL statements associated with a connection handle constitutes the scope of a transaction.

■ As an argument of the ODBC API informational functions that return information about a driver, a data source, and/or a connection associated with a connection handle.

■ To return SQL strings to an application with all escape sequences and/or clauses translated to data source-specific syntax.

The Statement Handle

A *statement handle* is a pointer to a data structure containing information about a single SQL statement. This information includes:

■ The current state of the SQL statement.

■ The current value of each SQL statement attribute.

■ The addresses of all application variables bound to the SQL statement's parameter markers.

■ The addresses of all application variables bound to columns in the SQL statement's result data set.

■ Diagnostic information about the SQL statement.

The statement handle is the real workhorse of ODBC. It is used to process all SQL statements contained in an application; both application-defined SQL statements and the SQL statements performed behind the scenes when an ODBC API data source catalog query function is called. Notably, statement handles are used in ODBC API function calls to bind parameter markers and result data set columns to application variables, prepare and execute SQL statements, retrieve metadata about result data sets, retrieve (fetch) results from result data sets, and retrieve diagnostic information.

Each SQL statement used in an application must have its own statement handle and each statement handle used can only be associated with one connection handle. However, multiple statement handles can be associated with a single connection handle. When an ODBC API function is called with a statement handle specified as an argument, the ODBC Driver Manager uses the connection handle stored within the statement handle to route the function call to the appropriate data source driver. Drivers then use the statement handle to obtain information they need to execute the SQL statement for the application and to store result data sets created (if any) after the statement is executed.

The Descriptor Handle

A *descriptor handle* is a pointer to a data storage area containing a collection of metadata that describes either the parameters of an SQL statement or the columns of a result data set, as seen by the application or driver.

Four types of descriptors are recognized by ODBC 3.x:

- Application Parameter Descriptors (APD)—Contains information about the application variables (buffers) bound to the parameter markers used in an SQL statement, such as their addresses, lengths, and C data types.

- Implementation Parameter Descriptors (IPD)—Contains information about the parameters used in an SQL statement, such as their SQL data types, lengths, and nullability.

- Application Row Descriptors (ARD)—Contains information about the application variables (buffers) bound to the columns in a result data set, such as their addresses, lengths, and C data types.

- Implementation Row Descriptors (IRD)—Contains information about the columns in a result data set, such as their SQL data types, lengths, and nullability.

Four descriptor handles (one for each type of descriptor described) are automatically allocated when a statement handle is allocated. These descriptor handles remain associated with the statement handle that allocated them for the life of that handle.

ODBC 3.x applications can explicitly allocate additional descriptor handles for a specific connection handle. Once allocated, these descriptor handles can be associated with one or more statement handles that are associated with the same connection handle to fulfill the role of an APD or ARD descriptor.

Most operations in ODBC can be performed without the use of explicitly defined descriptor handles. However, explicitly defined descriptor handles can provide a convenient shortcut for some ODBC operations. For example, suppose an application wants to insert data stored in two different sets of buffers into a particular data source. To use the first set of buffers, the application has to bind each buffer to a parameter marker in an **INSERT** statement, and then execute the statement. To use the second set of buffers, it has to repeat this entire process with the second set of buffers. Alternately, the application could set up the bindings to the first set of buffers in one explicitly defined descriptor handle and to the second set of buffers in another explicitly defined descriptor handle. To switch between the sets of bindings, the application simply modifies the attributes of the SQL statement's handle, and associates the correct descriptor handle (as the APD descriptor) with the SQL statement just before it is executed.

State Transitions

ODBC defines discrete states for each environment, connection, and SQL statement. For example, an environment has three possible states:

- **Unallocated**—No environment handle is allocated.
- **Allocated**—An environment is allocated but no connection handles are allocated.
- **Connection**—An environment handle and one or more connection handles are allocated.

A connection has seven possible states:

- **No Environment**—No environment handle or connection handle is allocated.
- **Unallocated**—An environment handle is allocated but no connection handle is allocated.
- **Allocated**—An environment handle and a connection handle is allocated.
- **Need Data**—Connection function needs data.
- **Connected**—Connected to a data source.
- **Statement**—Connected to a data source and a statement handle has been allocated.

- **Transaction**—Connected to a data source and a transaction is in progress.

And a statement has thirteen states:

- **Unallocated**—No statement handle is allocated.
- **Allocated**—A statement handle is allocated.
- **No Results**—A statement has been prepared and no result data set will be created.
- **Results**—A statement has been prepared and a result data set will be created, however it may be empty.
- **Executed**—A statement has been executed and no result data set was created.
- **Opened**—A statement has been executed and a result data set was created, however it may be empty. The cursor has been opened and it is positioned before the first row of data in the result data set.
- **SQLFetch**—The cursor has been positioned by `SQLFetch()` or `SQLFetchScroll()`.
- **SQLExtendedFetch**—The cursor has been positioned by `SQLExtendedFetch()`.
- **Need Data**—A function needs data and `SQLParamData()` has not been called.
- **Must Put**—A function needs data and `SQLPutData()` has not been called.
- **Can Put**—A function needs data and `SQLPutData()` has been called.
- **Still Executing**—A statement is still executing. A statement is left in this state after a function that was executed asynchronously returns the value `SQL_STILL_EXECUTING`. A statement is temporarily put in this state while any function that uses a statement handle as an argument is executing.
- **Async Canceled**—Asynchronous execution has been canceled.

An environment, a connection, or a statement moves from one state to another whenever an application calls an ODBC API function with the handle specified as an argument. This movement is known as *state transition*. For example, allocating an environment handle with the ODBC API function `SQLAllocHandle()` or `SQLAllocEnv()` moves the environment from the "Unallocated" state to the "Allocated" state. Freeing it with the ODBC API function **SQLFreeHandle()** or **SQLFreeEnv()** moves the environment from the "Allocated" state back to the "Unallocated" state.

Some ODBC API functions do not affect states at all (for example, the functions that retrieve environment, connection, and statement attributes). Other ODBC API functions only affect the state of a single item (for example, the function that disconnects from a data source can change a connection from the "Connected" state to the "Allocated" state. Other ODBC API functions, however, affect the state of more than one item (for example, the functions that allocate a connection handle, change both a connection from the "Unallocated" state to the "Allocated" state and the environment from the "Allocated" state to the "Connection" state).

Because ODBC defines a limited number of legal state transitions for environments, connections, and statements, most ODBC API functions must be called in a certain order. For example, an application must call the ODBC API function that executes an SQL statement that generates a result data set before it can call the ODBC API function that retrieves data from the result data set created. If an application calls an ODBC API function out of order, the function returns a state transition error— SQLSTATE **HY**010 (Function sequence error). Some state transitions are inherent in the design of ODBC. For example, it is not possible to allocate a connection handle without first allocating an environment handle, because the ODBC API function that allocates a connection handle requires an environment handle as one of its arguments. Other state transitions are enforced either by the Driver Manager or by drivers.

From the application's point of view, state transitions are generally straightforward because well-written applications tend to call ODBC API functions in their proper order.

Buffers

A *buffer* is any portion of application memory (either stack or heap) used to pass data between an application and a data source (via a driver). *Input buffers* are used to pass data from the application to the data source and *output buffers* are used to return data from the data source to the application.

NOTE: *If an ODBC API function returns* **SQL_ERROR**, *the contents of any output buffers that would have been filled by that function are undefined.*

To make ODBC interoperable with various high-level programming languages, most buffers used have an indeterminate data type. The addresses of these buffers appear as arguments of type **SQLPOINTER** in most ODBC API function references and the buffers themselves generally come in pairs; one is the actual data buffer and the other is a length/indicator buffer. The data buffer in this pair is used to pass the data itself, while the length/indicator buffer is used to pass either the length of the data stored in the data buffer or a special predefined value that provides information about the data stored in the data buffer (for example, **SQL_NULL_DATA**, is an indicator value that indicates the data is NULL). The length of the actual data in a data buffer is usually different from the length (or size) of the data buffer itself. Figure 5–1 shows the relationship between a data buffer and the length/indicator buffer.

NOTE: The length of both the data buffer and the data it contains is measured in bytes, as opposed to characters. This distinction is unimportant for applications using ANSI strings because bytes and characters are essentially the same size. This distinction becomes more important for applications using character systems in which bytes and characters are different sizes. An example of such a character system is the double-byte character system (DBCS) used throughout most of Asia.

A length/indicator buffer must be provided any time the data buffer contains variable-length data, such as character or binary data. If the data buffer contains fixed-length data, such as an integer or a data structure, a length/indicator buffer is only needed if one or more special indicator values are to be passed to an ODBC API function; the length of the data in the data buffer is already known. In fact, if an application uses a length/indicator buffer with fixed-length data, the driver ignores any length values passed in it.

When a data buffer is used to represent a driver-defined descriptor record field, a diagnostic record field, or an environment, connection, or

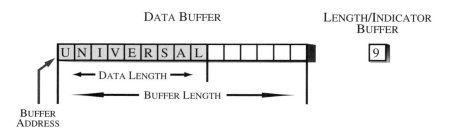

Figure 5–1 *The relationship between a data buffer and its corresponding length/indicator buffer.*

statement attribute, the application should inform the Driver Manager about the nature of the data in the buffer by setting the length argument in any ODBC API function call that sets/retrieves field or attribute values as follows:

- If the ODBC API function argument that the value for the field or attribute is (or is to be) stored in is a pointer to a character string, the length argument should contain either the length of the string or **SQL_NTS** (indicating that the string is null-terminated).

- If the ODBC API function argument that the value for the field or attribute is (or is to be) stored in is a pointer to a binary buffer, the length argument should contain the result of the **SQL_LEN_BINARY_ATTR(*length*)** macro.

- If the ODBC API function argument that the value for the field or attribute is (or is to be) stored in is a pointer to a value other than a character string or a binary string, the length argument should contain the value **SQL_IS_POINTER**.

- If the ODBC API function argument that the value for the field or attribute is (or is to be) stored in contains a fixed-length value, the length argument should contain either **SQL_IS_INTEGER**, **SQL_IS_UINTEGER**, **SQL_SMALLINT**, or **SQL_USMALLINT**.

Deferred Buffers

A *deferred buffer* is a buffer whose contents are used at some point after it is specified in an ODBC API function call. For example, when a buffer is bound to a parameter marker in an SQL statement with an ODBC API function call, the driver saves information about the buffer itself—but it does not examine the buffer's contents. Later, when the application executes the SQL statement, the driver retrieves the information it saved about the buffer and uses it to retrieve a value from the buffer and send it to the data source. Thus, the input of data in the buffer is deferred.

Both input and output buffers can be deferred. Table 5–1 summarizes the common uses of deferred buffers, and the ODBC API functions that specify and use them.

Allocating and Freeing Buffers

All buffers are allocated and freed by the application— stack buffers are allocated when they are declared, heap buffers are allocated by calling the

Table 5–1   Deferred Buffer Usage

Buffer Use	Type	Specified With	Used by
Sending data for input parameters	Deferred input	SQLBindParameter( )	SQLExecute( ) SQLExecDirect()
Sending data to insert or update a row in a result data set	Deferred input	SQLBindCol( )	SQLSetPos( )
Returning data for output and input/ output parameters	Deferred output	SQLBindParameter( )	SQLExecute( ) SQLExecDirect( )
Returning data from a result data set	Deferred output	SQLBindCol( )	SQLFetch( ) SQLFetchScroll( ) SQLExtendedFetch( ) SQLSetPos( ) SQLBulkOperations( )

Adapted from *Microsoft ODBC 3.0 Programmer's Reference, Volume 1, and SDK Guide*, page 59.

appropriate high-level language memory allocation function. If a buffer is not going to be used as a deferred buffer, it only needs to exist for the duration of the call to the ODBC API function that references it. On the other hand, because deferred buffers are specified in one ODBC API function call and used in another, they must exist from the time they are specified in the first ODBC API function call until they are either used or unspecified by another ODBC API function call. The same is true for deferred length/indicator buffers. An application programming error can occur if a deferred buffer is freed while the driver still expects it to exist. Such errors are easily made if a deferred buffer is declared or allocated locally within an application-specific function; by design, the buffer is freed when application control leaves the function.

Describing Data Buffers

Data buffers are described to ODBC API functions by three pieces of information.

■ Data Type—The C data type of the buffer.

■ Address—The physical memory address of the data buffer.

■ Length (in bytes)—The length or size, in bytes, of the data buffer.

Often one, two, or even all three of these pieces of information about a buffer are passed to a driver as ODBC API function arguments.

DATA BUFFER TYPE   The C data type of a buffer is automatically specified by an application written in C or C++ when it is declared or when memory for it is allocated. In the case of generic memory—that is, memory pointed to by a pointer of type void—the C data type is provided when the memory is typecast by the application.

Regardless of how a buffer's C data type is specified, a driver discovers buffer data types in one of two ways:

■ Buffer Data Type Arguments—Some ODBC API functions with an argument for a data buffer also have an argument for an associated C data type. This is usually the case for buffers used to transfer parameter marker and result data set values between an application and a data source.

■ Predefined Data Types—Some ODBC API functions automatically assume that a data buffer is a specific C data type. This is usually the case for buffers used to retrieve options or attributes from a data source. In this case, the application is responsible for declaring or allocating a buffer of the appropriate C data type.

DATA BUFFER ADDRESS   An address is automatically assigned to a buffer when it is declared or when memory for it is allocated (provided the memory allocation was successful). All ODBC API functions that work with buffers have an argument that is used to specify the buffer's address. Unless it is strictly prohibited by the ODBC API function, a buffer's address can be a NULL pointer value. If a NULL pointer buffer address is specified for an input argument, the driver ignores the information stored in the buffer. If a NULL pointer buffer address is specified for an output argument, the driver does not return a value to that buffer. In both cases, the driver ignores any corresponding buffer C data type and length/indicator arguments.

DATA BUFFER LENGTH   The length of a buffer is specified when it is declared or when memory for it is allocated (in applications written in C or C++). ODBC API functions that work with buffers often have an argument that is used to specify the buffer's length in bytes. Data buffer lengths are only required for output buffers—the driver uses them to avoid writing past the end of the buffer. However, the driver only checks a data buffer's length when it is writing variable-length data, such as character or binary data, to the buffer. If the driver is writing fixed length data, such as integer or data structure data to the buffer it ignores the value in the data buffer length argument and assumes that the buffer is large enough to hold the data. Therefore, it is important for an application to declare/allocate a buffer that is large enough when working with fixed-length data.

A driver always returns the number of bytes (not the number of characters) written to the buffer in the buffer length argument if the buffer-length argument is associated with an output buffer argument that receives a string value. If the data buffer is not large enough to hold the string value returned, the string is truncated and the length returned in the buffer length argument is the maximum byte length needed to store the complete string value. For ANSI characters, that length is always twice the actual number of characters in the string, because the buffer could contain DBCS characters. Fixed-length data is never truncated.

Using Length/Indicator Buffers

I mentioned earlier that the length/indicator buffer is used to pass either the byte length of the data in the data buffer or a special indicator value to the data source. Depending on the ODBC API function used, a length/indicator buffer is defined to be either an **SQLINTEGER** or an **SQLSMALLINT** data type. Because it is a fixed-length buffer, only one argument is needed to describe it. If the data buffer the length/indicator buffer refers to is a non-deferred input buffer, this argument contains the byte length of the data itself or an indicator value. If the data buffer the length/indicator buffer refers to is a deferred input buffer, a non-deferred output buffer, or an output buffer, this argument contains the address of the length/indicator buffer.

Unless it is specifically prohibited, the value specified in a length/indicator buffer ODBC API function argument can be 0 (if a non-deferred input buffer is used) or a NULL pointer (if a output or deferred input buffer is used). If either value is specified for an input buffer, the driver ignores the byte length of the data. If either value is specified for an output buffer, the driver does not return the byte length of the data written to the buffer nor an indicator value.

The following length/indicator values are valid:

■ 0—Ignore (input)/don't return (output) the byte length of the data in the corresponding data buffer.

- n, where n > 0—The size, in bytes of the data in the corresponding data buffer.

- **SQL_NTS**—A null-terminated string is in the corresponding data buffer; this is a convenient way for C/C++ programmers to pass strings without having to calculate their byte length. This value is legal only when the data buffer is an input buffer.

- **SQL_NULL_DATA**—The data in the corresponding data buffer is a NULL data value and should be ignored. This value is only legal for SQL data sent to or retrieved from the driver.

- **SQL_DATA_AT_EXEC**—The corresponding data buffer does not contain any data. Instead, the data is sent by calling the **SQLPutData()** ODBC API function after an SQL statement is executed, or when either the **SQLBulkOperations()** or **SQLSetPos()** ODBC API functions are called. This value is legal only for SQL data sent to the driver.

- Result of the **SQL_LEN_DATA_AT_EXEC(length)** macro—Similar to **SQL_DATA_AT_EXEC**.

- **SQL_NO_TOTAL**—The driver cannot determine the number of bytes of long data still available to be returned in the corresponding output buffer. This value is only legal for SQL data retrieved from the driver.

- **SQL_DEFAULT_PARAM**—A stored procedure is to use the default value for a parameter instead of the value in the corresponding data buffer.

- **SQL_COLUMN_IGNORE**—The **SQLBulkOperations()** or **SQLSetPos()** ODBC API functions are to ignore the value in the corresponding data buffer. When updating a row of data by a call to either of these functions, the column value is not changed. When inserting a new row of data by a call to either of these functions, the column value is set to its default value or, if the column does not have a default, to NULL.

Data Length, Buffer Length, and Truncation

It is important to realize that the data length stored in a length/indicator buffer is the byte length of the data as it is (or as it will be) stored in the corresponding data buffer, not as it is (or as it will be) stored in the data source. This distinction is important because often data stored as one data type in a data buffer is stored as a different data type in the data source. Thus, for data being sent to the data source, the byte length specifies the size of the data before it is converted to the data source's data type. For data being returned from the data source, the byte length value specifies the size of the data after it has been converted to the data buffer's data type and before any truncation is done.

For fixed-length data, such as an integer or a data structure, the byte length of the data is always the size of the data type of the buffer. For variable-length data, such as character or binary data, it is important to recognize that the byte length of the data is separate and often different from the byte length of the buffer. For example, suppose an application allocates 20 bytes for a character data buffer. Now suppose the driver has 10 bytes of character data to return; it returns those 10 bytes in the data buffer and sets the length/indicator buffer to 10. The byte length of the data is 10, and the byte length of the buffer is 20. Now suppose the driver has 30 bytes of character data to return; it truncates the data to 20 bytes, returns those 20 bytes in the data buffer, sets the length/indicator buffer to 60 (because of DBCS), and returns **SQL_SUCCESS_WITH_INFO**. The byte length of the data is 60 (the DBCS length before truncation), and the byte length of the buffer is still 20.

Whenever data is truncated, a diagnostic record containing detailed information about the truncation is created. Because it takes time for the driver to create this diagnostic record and for the application to process it, data truncation can reduce overall performance. In most cases data truncation can be avoided simply by allocating data buffers that are large enough. Although this may not always be possible, especially when working with long data. When data truncation occurs, the application can sometimes allocate a larger buffer and retrieve (fetch) the data again; however, this approach will not work in all cases and should usually be avoided.

A Word about Character Data and C/C++ Strings

If an application terminates strings with the null character, as is the standard practice in C and C++, then the length/indicator buffer can contain either the length (in bytes) of the string (excluding the null-terminator) or the value **SQL_NTS** (to indicate that the data is a null-terminated string). The length/indicator buffer can also contain the value 0 to specify a zero-length string, which is different from a NULL value. When null-terminated strings are used to hold character data, the null-termination character is not considered to be part of the data and therefore it is not counted as part of the string's byte length. When the value **SQL_NTS** is used, the driver attempts to determine the length of the string by locating the position of the null-termination character.

When character data is returned from a data source to an application, it is always null-terminated. This practice allows application developers to choose whether they want to handle character data as strings or as character arrays. If an output buffer is not large enough to hold all the character data returned, the driver truncates it to the byte length of the buffer minus the number of bytes needed for the null-termination character (usually 1 byte), null-terminates the truncated data, and stores it in the appropriate data buffer. This means that applications must take into account the space needed for the null-termination character when allocating memory for output buffers that receive character data from a data source. For example, a 51-byte output buffer is needed to hold 50 bytes of character data.

Special care must be taken by both the application and driver when sending or receiving long character data in parts. In these situations, if the data is passed as a series of null-terminated strings, the null-termination characters on all strings except the last one must be stripped off before the data can be reassembled.

NOTE: *Because character data can be stored in a non-null-terminated array with its byte length stored in a length/indicator buffer, it is possible to embed NULL characters within character data. However, the behavior of ODBC API functions when this type of data is used is undefined and how the data will be handled is driver-specific. Interoperable applications should always treat character data that contains embedded null characters as binary data.*

Data Types

When ODBC was originally designed, a set of data types had to be defined so that no information would be lost between applications and data sources. To provide interoperability, these data types had to be defined in such a way that data source-specific information wouldn't have to be encoded in application logic. Specifically, ODBC had to provide a precise definition of the type of data being placed into application memory buffers; otherwise the data wouldn't have any meaning.

Other characteristics of the data, however, did not have to be defined so precisely. For example, the maximum length of character data types varies widely, but there is no reason to enforce a length limit in ODBC as long as an application can determine the limits from the driver. However, this means that if an application copies data from one data source to another, it can't assume that the length limits of the two data sources are the same.

In order to build robustness and reliability into ODBC, Microsoft carefully reviewed the SQL-92 standard and the top ten (in terms of market share) database products and compiled a list of data types, including type names, length limits, and all behavioral characteristics. Then, using this list, they created a second list of C data types to which every data type on the first list could be mapped without losing information. Ultimately, this led to the development of two sets of data types for ODBC: SQL data types, which are used in the data source, and C data types, which are used in applications. ODBC supports the SQL type/C type distinction by providing a set of SQL data type names that begin with the prefix **SQL_** and a similar set of C data type names that begin with the prefix **SQL_C_**.

SQL Data Type Identifiers

ODBC defines type identifiers for and describes the general characteristics of several SQL data types that might be mapped to a corresponding data type within a data source. However, each data source defines its own SQL data types and each one may or may not have a corresponding ODBC SQL type identifier; the driver determines how each data source-specific data type is mapped to an ODBC SQL type identifier.

For example, **SQL_CHAR** is the ODBC SQL type identifier for a character column with a fixed length: typically between 1 and 254 characters. These characteristics correspond to the **CHAR** data type found in many SQL data sources. Thus, when an application discovers that the ODBC SQL type identifier for a column is **SQL_CHAR**, it can assume it is dealing with a column that has a **CHAR** data type. However, the byte length of the column should still be checked—the application should not assume that its length is between 1 and 254 characters.

ODBC defines a wide variety of SQL type identifiers; however, a driver is not required to use/support all of them. Typically, a driver only uses/supports the ODBC SQL identifiers it needs to expose the SQL data types supported by the underlying data source. If an underlying data source supports SQL data types to which there is no corresponding ODBC SQL type identifier, the driver can define additional ODBC SQL type identifiers or it can try to map the data source SQL data type to the next closest one.

C Data Type Identifiers

ODBC also defines type identifiers for the C data types that might be mapped to a corresponding data type in a data source. Among other things, these type identifiers are used to describe the application variables and/or buffers that are bound to SQL statement parameter markers and result data set columns. For example, suppose an application wants to retrieve data from a result data set column in character format. First, it declares a variable with the **SQLCHAR** * data type, then it binds this variable to the result data set column with a C data type identifier of **SQL_C_CHAR**.

ODBC also defines a default C data type mapping for each SQL data type identifier. For example, a 2-byte **INTEGER** data type in a data source is, by default, mapped to a 2-byte integer in an application. To use the default mapping, an application simply specifies **SQL_C_DEFAULT** as the C data type identifier. Interoperable applications should never rely on default mapping.

NOTE: In ODBC 1.0, all integer C data types were defined as signed. Unsigned C data types and their corresponding type identifiers were added in ODBC 2.0. Because of this, applications need to be particularly careful with integer data types when dealing with ODBC 1.0 version drivers.

Data Type Conversions

Data can be converted from one data type to another at any of the following times:

- When data is transferred from one application variable to another (C to C)
- When data in an application variable is sent to an SQL statement parameter (C to SQL)
- When data in a result data set column is returned in an application variable (SQL to C)
- When data is transferred from one data source column to another (SQL to SQL)

When an application binds a variable to a parameter marker in an SQL statement or to a column in a result data set, it implicitly specifies a data type conversion between an SQL data type and the C data type of the application variable. For example, suppose a column in a result data set contains integer data. If the application binds an integer variable to the column, it implicitly specifies that no conversion is necessary; if however, the application binds a character variable to the column, it implicitly specifies that the data is to be converted from an integer to a character.

ODBC contains an internal set of rules defining how data is converted between each SQL and C data type. Basically, all reasonable conversions, such as character to integer and integer to float, are supported; ill-defined conversions, such as float to date, are not. By design, drivers are required to support all C data type conversions for each SQL data type they support.

ODBC also defines a scalar function for converting data from one SQL data type to another. This scalar function (**CONVERT()**) is mapped by the driver to any underlying scalar function(s) designed to perform conversions in the data source. Because these are data source-specific functions, ODBC does not define how these types of conversions are to work or which conversions must be supported.

SUMMARY

A handle is simply an application pointer variable that refers to a data object in which ODBC can store context information. ODBC uses four types of handles:

- Environment handles
- Connection handles
- Statement handles
- Descriptor handles

An environment handle is a pointer to a data storage area containing ODBC specific information that is global in nature. Every application program using ODBC must begin by allocating an environment handle and only one environment handle can be allocated per application. An environment handle must be allocated before any other handle is allocated.

A connection handle is a pointer to a data structure containing information about a data source connection being managed by the ODBC Driver Manager. From the data source driver's perspective, a connection handle is used to keep track of a network connection to a server or alternately to keep track of directory and local data file information. From the

Driver Manager's perspective, a connection handle is used to identify which driver to use and which data source to use with that driver.

A statement handle is a pointer to a data structure containing information about a single SQL statement. The statement handle is the real workhorse of ODBC. It is used to process all SQL statements contained in an application. Each SQL statement must have its own statement handle and each statement handle used can only be associated with one connection handle.

A descriptor handle is a pointer to a data storage area containing a collection of metadata describing either the parameters of an SQL statement or the columns of a result data set, as seen by the application or driver.

There are four types of descriptors that ODBC 3.x recognizes.

▨ Application Parameter Descriptor (APD)

▨ Implementation Parameter Descriptor (IPD)

▨ Application Row Descriptor (ARD)

▨ Implementation Row Descriptor (IRD)

One descriptor handle is automatically allocated for each type of descriptor described, when a statement handle is allocated. In addition to these descriptor handles, ODBC 3.x applications can explicitly allocate descriptor handles for a specific connection.

ODBC defines three discrete states for each environment, seven discrete states for each connection, and thirteen discrete states for each SQL statement. An environment, connection, or statement moves from one state to another when an application calls ODBC API functions with its handle as an argument. This movement is known as state transition.

A buffer is any portion of application memory (either stack or heap) used to pass data between an application and a data source. Input buffers are used to pass data from the application to the data source and output buffers are used to return data from the data source to the application. A deferred buffer is a buffer whose contents are used at some point after it is specified in an ODBC API function call. All buffers are allocated and freed by the application.

Data buffers are described to ODBC API functions by three pieces of information.

▨ The C data type of the buffer.

▨ The physical memory address of the buffer.

▨ The length or size of the buffer in bytes.

Length/indicator buffers are often used to pass either the byte length of the data in a data buffer or a special indicator to the data source. The following lengths/indicators are valid length/indicator values:

- 0
- n, where n > 0
- `SQL_NTS`
- `SQL_NULL_DATA`
- `SQL_DATA_AT_EXEC`
- Result of the `SQL_LEN_DATA_AT_EXEC(length)` macro
- `SQL_NO_TOTAL`
- `SQL_DEFAULT_PARAM`
- `SQL_COLUMN_IGNORE`

Two sets of data types are used by ODBC: SQL data types and C data types. ODBC defines type identifiers for and describes the general characteristics of the SQL data types that might be mapped to a corresponding data type in a data source. ODBC also defines type identifiers for the C data types that might be mapped to a corresponding data type in a data source. Among other things, these type identifiers are used to describe the application variables/buffers that are bound to SQL statement parameters and result data set columns.

Data can be converted from one data type to another at any of the following times:

- When data is transferred from one application variable to another (C to C)
- When data in an application variable is sent to an SQL statement parameter (C to SQL)
- When data in a result data set column is returned in an application variable (SQL to C)
- When data is transferred from one data source column to another (SQL to SQL)

6

Basic Steps Used to Create an ODBC Application

This chapter is designed to introduce you to the basic processing path ODBC applications follow and to the steps required to convert ODBC source code files into executable programs. This chapter begins by describing the three main tasks almost all ODBC applications perform. This is followed by a brief discussion about how a high-level programming language compiler and linker are used to convert ODBC application source code files to an executable program.

Parts of an ODBC Application Program

Application programs written for ODBC are organized so that they perform three distinct tasks.

- Initialization
- Transaction Processing
- Termination

One or more ODBC API function calls may be required to perform each of these tasks and, as mentioned in Chapter 5, many of these ODBC API functions must also be called in the appropriate order or an error condition occurs. As well as the three distinct tasks listed; there are also general tasks, such as error handling, that can be incorporated throughout an ODBC application's source code file(s).

The Initialization Task

In the initialization task, the Driver Manager is loaded and resources needed by the transaction processing task are allocated and initialized. At a minimum, an ODBC application must allocate one environment data storage area and at least one connection data storage area. Once these data storage areas have been allocated and their corresponding handles initialized, one or both handle(s) are passed to the Driver Manager (as arguments) whenever an ODBC API function call is made. During the initialization task, an application also tells the Driver Manager which ODBC specification it plans to follow.

ALLOCATING RESOURCES The **SQLAllocHandle()** function must always be the first function called in the initialization task and it must be called with the **SQL_HANDLE_ENV** option specified (**SQLAllocEnv()** can also be used if working with earlier releases of ODBC). Once an environment storage area is established, the **SQLAllocHandle()** function must then be called with the **SQL_HANDLE_DBC** option specified to establish a communications area for the data source connection that will soon be established (**SQLAllocConnect()** can also be used if working with earlier releases of ODBC). If an application intends to connect concurrently to more than one data source (or to connect concurrently multiple times to the same data source), it must call the **SQLAllocHandle()** (or the **SQLAllocConnect()**) function for each connection it plans to establish. The handles returned from these calls are then used with the **SQLConnect()**, **SQLDriverConnect()**, or the **SQLBrowseConnect()** function to establish the desired data source connections. Figure 6–1 illustrates how a connection data storage area is allocated during the initialization task of an application, and how its handle is then passed to the Driver Manager with subsequent ODBC API function calls.

The use of separate connection handles ensures that multi-threaded applications can use one connection per thread without encountering concurrency problems.

Declaring the Application's ODBC Version

A special set of ODBC API function calls can be used to control the attributes associated with an environment and/or a connection. Some of these attributes must be set before a connection to a data source is made while others can only be set afterwards.

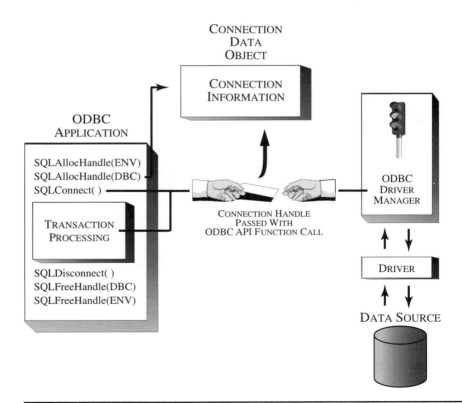

Figure 6–1 *How ODBC connection handles are established and used.*

Before an application allocates a connection handle, it must set the **SQL_ATTR_ODBC_VERSION** environment attribute to either **SQL_OV_ODBC3** or **SQL_OV_ODBC2**. This attribute tells the Driver Manager that the application follows either the ODBC 3.x or the ODBC 2.0 or earlier specification when using the following items:

■ SQLSTATEs—Many SQLSTATE values are different between versions.

■ Date, Time, and Timestamp Type identifiers—Date, Time, and Timestamp SQL and C data type identifiers are different between versions.

■ The *CatalogName* argument in **SQLTables()**—In ODBC 2.0, if the wild card characters (**%** and **_**) are used in the *CatalogName* argument of the **SQLTables()** ODBC API function, they are treated literally. In ODBC 3.x, they are treated as wild cards. Thus, an application that follows the ODBC 2.0 specification cannot use wild cards with this argument.

The ODBC 3.x Driver Manager and ODBC 3.x drivers check the version of the ODBC specification to which an application is written and respond accordingly.

NOTE: Applications that follow the ODBC 3.x specification must use conditional code to avoid using functionality that exists only in ODBC 3.x when working with ODBC 2.0 or earlier drivers. ODBC 2.0 or earlier drivers do not support ODBC 3.x functionality because the application declares that it follows the ODBC 3.x specification. Furthermore, ODBC 3.x drivers do not cease to support ODBC 3.x functionality because the application declares that it follows the ODBC 2.0 or earlier specification.

The Driver Manager's Role During the Initialization Task

When applications call ODBC API functions, they are actually calling Driver Manager functions with the same name as the ODBC API functions in a data source driver. Usually, when an ODBC API function in the Driver Manager is called, some simple checks are performed, and the function call is passed to the driver for processing. The connection process is handled differently.

When an application calls the `SQLAllocHandle()` function with either the `SQL_HANDLE_ENV` or the `SQL_HANDLE_DBC` option specified (or the `SQLAllocEnv()` and `SQLAllocConnect()` function), the appropriate handles are only allocated in the Driver Manager. At this point, the Driver Manager cannot call the corresponding function in the driver because it does not know which driver to use. Similarly, if the application uses the handle of an unconnected connection in ODBC API function calls used to retrieve and/or specify connection attributes (for example, to declare the application's ODBC level), only the Driver Manager can process the calls. Because no driver has been loaded, the Driver Manager retrieves/stores attribute values from/to its own connection handle. If an application tries to retrieve the value for an attribute that has not been set, or an attribute that ODBC does not define a default value for, SQLSTATE **08**003 (Connection not open) is returned.

Once the application calls the `SQLConnect()`, `SQLDriverConnect()`, or the `SQLBrowseConnect()` function, the Driver Manager first determines which driver to use, then it determines whether a driver is currently loaded for the connection specified.

If no driver is loaded for the connection, the Driver Manager checks to see whether the specified driver is loaded on another connection handle in the same environment. If not, the Driver Manager loads the driver for the connection and calls the `SQLAllocHandle()` function in the driver with the `SQL_HANDLE_ENV` option specified (or the `SQLAllocEnv()` function). Then the Driver Manager calls the `SQLAllocHandle()` function in the driver with the `SQL_HANDLE_DBC` option specified (or the `SQLAllocConnect()` function).

If the application sets any connection attributes before the driver was loaded, the Driver Manager calls the `SQLSetConnectAttr()` (or the `SQLSetConnectOption()`) function in the driver to set them. Finally, the Driver Manager calls the connection function in the driver.

If the specified driver has already been loaded for the connection, the Driver Manager only calls the connection function in the driver. In this case, the driver must make sure that all connection attributes (options) for the connection maintain their current settings.

If a different driver is loaded for the connection, the Driver Manager calls the `SQLFreeHandle()` function in the driver with the `SQL_HANDLE_DBC` option specified (or the `SQLFreeConnect()` function) to terminate the connection and free the allocated connection handle. If there are no other connections using the driver, the Driver Manager calls the `SQLFreeHandle()` function in the driver with the `SQL_HANDLE_ENV` option specified (or the `SQLFreeEnv()` function) to free the environment. Then it unloads the driver.

The Driver Manager then performs the same operations performed when a driver is not loaded for the connection.

The Transaction Processing Task

The transaction processing task follows the initialization task and makes up the bulk of an ODBC application. This is where the SQL statements that query and/or modify data are passed to the Driver Manager (which forwards them to the data source via the data source driver) by various ODBC API function calls. In the transaction processing task, an application performs the following five steps, in the order shown:

1. Allocates statement handles.

2. Prepares and executes SQL statements.

3. Processes the results.

4. Commits or rolls back the transaction.

5. Frees statement handles.

Figure 6–2 illustrates these five steps and identifies the ODBC 3.x API function calls that are used to perform them.

ALLOCATING STATEMENT HANDLES   As mentioned in Chapter 5, a statement handle refers to a data object containing information about a single SQL statement. This information includes the SQL statement text, any dynamic SQL statement arguments, cursor information, bindings for dynamic SQL statement parameter marker arguments and result data set columns, result values, and status information. Statement handles are allocated by calling the **SQLAllocHandle()** function with the **SQL_HANDLE_STMT** option specified (or the **SQLAllocStmt()** function). A statement handle must be allocated for an SQL statement before that statement can be executed. Also, each statement handle allocated must be associated with a specific data source connection handle.

PREPARING AND EXECUTING SQL STATEMENTS   Once a statement handle has been allocated, there are two methods that can be used to specify and execute an actual SQL statement:

■ Prepare then Execute—This method separates the preparation of the SQL statement from its actual execution and is typically used when an SQL statement is executed repeatedly (usually with different parameter values) or when the application needs information about the columns in the result data set produced before the SQL statement can be executed.

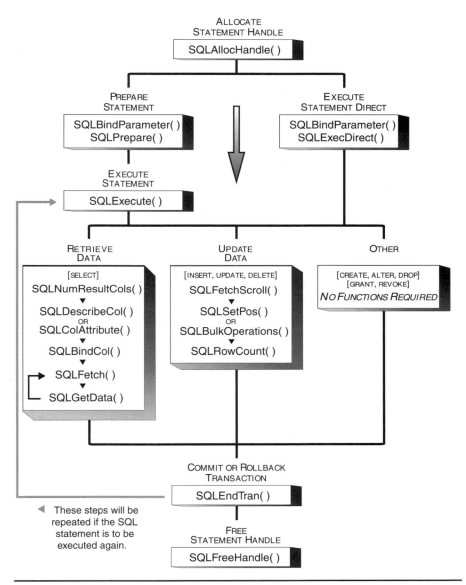

Figure 6–2 *The typical order of ODBC API function calls in the transaction processing task.*

▨ Execute Direct—This method combines the prepare step and the execute step into a single step and is usually used when an SQL statement is executed only once or when the application does not need additional information about the columns in the result data set produced before the SQL statement can be executed.

Both of these preparation and execution methods enable the use of parameter markers in place of expressions in an SQL statement. Parameter markers are represented by the question mark (?) character and they indicate the position in the SQL statement where the contents of application variables are to be substituted when the SQL statement is prepared and executed. Parameter markers are referenced sequentially, from left to right, starting at number one. When an application variable is associated with a parameter marker in an SQL statement, it is said to be "bound" to that parameter marker. Binding is carried out by calling the **SQLBindParameter()** function. Once a parameter marker is bound to an application variable, the information about that variable remains in effect until it is overridden, or until the application unbinds it or frees it's corresponding statement handle. The C data type of the application variable being bound should be the same as the SQL data type required by the SQL statement, whenever possible. If you bind a variable of a C data type that is different from the SQL data type required by the SQL statement to a parameter marker, the Driver Manager automatically attempts to convert the contents of the bound variable to the required data type.

No data is read from a bound variable until the actual SQL statement is executed. By using bound variables, an application can execute the same SQL statement many times and receive different results, simply by modifying the contents of the bound parameter variables.

PROCESSING THE RESULTS   After the SQL statement has been prepared and executed, the results of the execution must be retrieved and processed. SQL statement execution result information is obtained from the data storage areas to which the connection and statement handles point. If the SQL statement was not a **SELECT** statement, then the only additional processing required after the SQL statement has been executed is the regular check of the ODBC API function return code to ensure that no error occurred. If, however, the SQL statement was a **SELECT** statement, the following steps are generally needed in order to retrieve each row data in the result data set produced:

1. Determine the structure (i.e. the number of columns, column data types, and data lengths) of the result data set.

2. Bind application variables to the columns in the result data set (optional).

3. Repeatedly fetch the next row of data from the result data set into the bound application variables. Values for columns that were not

bound to application variables in Step 2 can be retrieved by calling the **SQLGetData()** function after each successful fetch.

The first step analyzes the prepared or executed SQL statement to determine the structure of the result data set produced. If the SQL statement was hard coded into the application, this step isn't necessary because the structure of the result data set is already known. If, however, the SQL statement was generated at runtime (that is, entered by a user), then the application needs to query the result data set in order to obtain this information. Result data set structure information can be obtained by calling the **SQLNumResultsCol()**, the **SQLDescribeCol()**, the **SQLColAttribute()** and/or the **SQLColAttributes()** function immediately after the SQL statement has been either prepared or executed.

The second step binds application variables to columns in the result data set, so that the application program can retrieve data directly into them. Columns in a result data set are bound to application variables in a manner similar to the way that application variables are bound to SQL statement parameter markers. However, this time the variables are used as output arguments and data is written to them whenever the **SQLFetch()** function call is used. Because the **SQLGetData()** function call can also be used to retrieve data, application variable binding is optional.

The third step actually retrieves the data stored in the result data set by repeatedly calling the **SQLFetch()** function until no more data exists. If any application variables have been bound to columns in the result data set, their values will automatically be updated each time **SQLFetch()** is called. The **SQLGetData()** function call can be used to retrieve data from any columns that were not previously bound. This ODBC API function call is also useful for retrieving variable length column data in smaller pieces which cannot be done when bound application variables are used. All column data in the result data set can be retrieved by using any combination of these two methods. If any data conversion is necessary, it occurs automatically when the **SQLFetch()** function is called (if bound variables are used), or it can be can be indicated when the **SQLGetData()** function call is invoked. While performing these steps, the application should always check the return code each time an ODBC API function call is made to ensure that no errors have occurred.

If the SQL statement specified was a positioned **UPDATE** or **DELETE** statement, it is necessary to use a cursor (a moveable pointer to a row within a result data set). Unlike embedded SQL, where cursor names are used to retrieve, update, or delete rows, in ODBC a cursor name is needed only for positioned **UPDATE** and **DELETE** SQL statements because they reference a cursor by name. A cursor name is automatically generated, if appropriate, when the **SQLAllocStmt()** function call is executed.

ENDING THE TRANSACTION (ROLLBACK OR COMMIT)   Transactions allow a group of SQL statements to be processed as a single operation. This means that all SQL statements within the operation are guaranteed to be completed (committed) or undone (rolled back), as if they were a single SQL statement. ODBC applications can contain multiple data source connections, and each connection to a data source constitutes a separate transaction boundary. Figure 6–3 shows the two transaction boundaries that would exist in an ODBC application that communicates with two separate databases.

As mentioned previously, ODBC applications can be configured to run in either auto-commit or manual-commit mode. In auto-commit mode, each SQL statement is treated as a complete transaction, and it is automatically committed if the SQL statement was successfully executed. For non-query SQL statements, this commit takes place immediately after the statement is executed. For query SQL statements, this commit takes place immediately after the cursor being used is closed (remember: ODBC function calls automatically declare and open a cursor if it is needed). In manual-commit mode, transactions are started implicitly the first time the application accesses the data source (that is, the first occurrence of any ODBC function call that returns a result data set). Transactions are ended when the **SQLEndTrans()** function is called (or the **SQLTransact()** function). This ODBC function call is used to either rollback or commit the changes made to the database by the current transaction. Therefore, all SQL statements executed between the time the data source was first accessed and the time the **SQLEndTrans()** function call is made are treated as a single transaction.

The auto-commit mode is the default commit mode and is usually sufficient for very simple ODBC applications. However, larger applications, particularly applications that need to perform updates, should switch to manual-commit mode as soon as the data source connection is established.

All transactions must be ended before the connection to the data source is terminated (that is, before the **SQLDisconnect()** function is called). However, it is not a good idea to wait this long before you commit or rollback a transaction because of the concurrency and locking problems that can arise. Likewise, it is not always a good idea to use the auto-commit mode or to call the **SQLEndTrans()** function after each SQL statement is

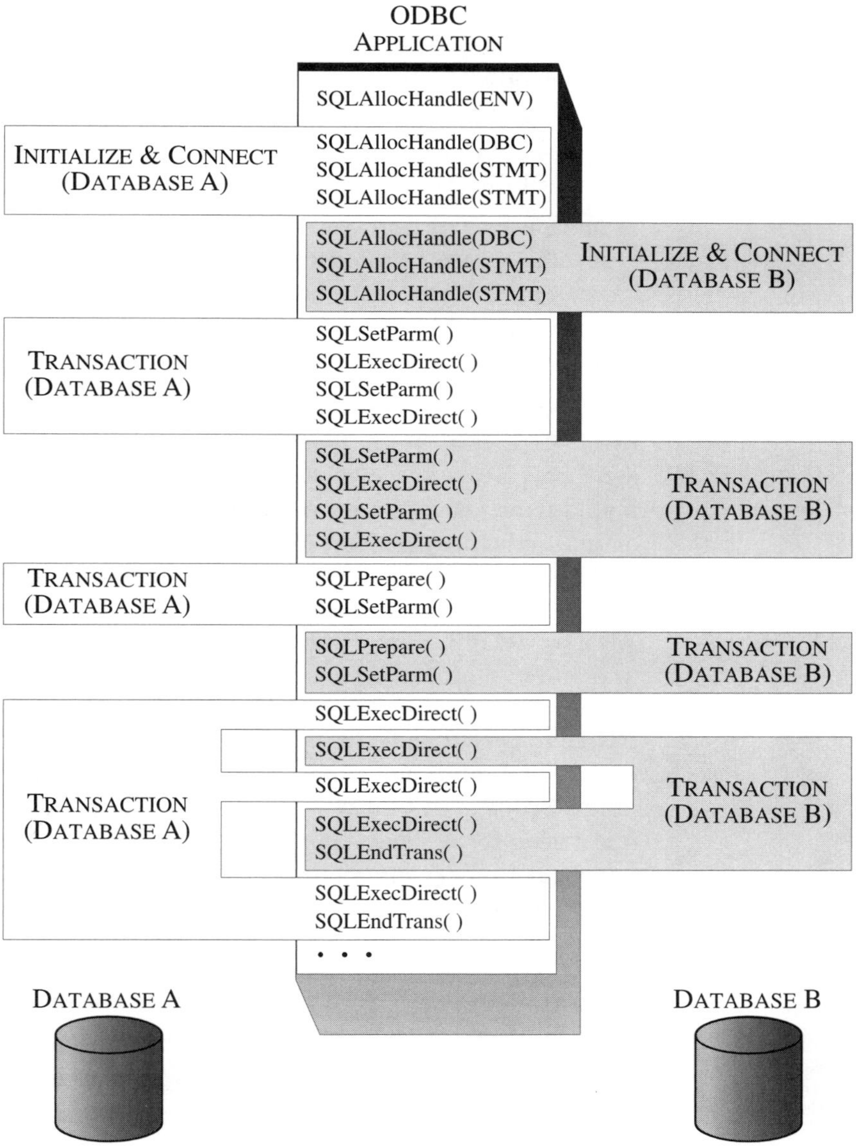

ODBC
APPLICATION

	SQLAllocHandle(ENV)
INITIALIZE & CONNECT (DATABASE A)	SQLAllocHandle(DBC) SQLAllocHandle(STMT) SQLAllocHandle(STMT)
	SQLAllocHandle(DBC) SQLAllocHandle(STMT) SQLAllocHandle(STMT) — INITIALIZE & CONNECT (DATABASE B)
TRANSACTION (DATABASE A)	SQLSetParm( ) SQLExecDirect( ) SQLSetParm( ) SQLExecDirect( )
	SQLSetParm( ) SQLExecDirect( ) SQLSetParm( ) SQLExecDirect( ) — TRANSACTION (DATABASE B)
TRANSACTION (DATABASE A)	SQLPrepare( ) SQLSetParm( )
	SQLPrepare( ) SQLSetParm( ) — TRANSACTION (DATABASE B)
TRANSACTION (DATABASE A)	SQLExecDirect( ) SQLExecDirect( ) SQLExecDirect( ) — TRANSACTION (DATABASE B) SQLExecDirect( ) SQLEndTrans( ) SQLExecDirect( ) SQLEndTrans( )

• • •

DATABASE A

DATABASE B

Figure 6–3 *Transaction boundaries in an ODBC application that works with two different databases simultaneously.*

executed, because this increases overhead and reduces application performance. When trying to decide the best time to end a transaction, consider the following:

■ Only the current transaction can be committed or rolled back; therefore, all dependent SQL statements should be kept within the same transaction.

■ Various table and row locks can be held by the current transaction. Ending the current transaction releases these locks and allows other applications access to the data.

■ Once a transaction has successfully been committed or rolled back, it is fully recoverable from the system log files. Any transaction open at the time of a system failure or application program trap is not recoverable. Therefore, transactions should be ended, as soon as is reasonably possible.

When defining transaction boundaries, keep in mind that all resources associated with the transaction, except those associated with a held cursor, are released. However, prepared SQL statements, cursor names, bound parameters, and column bindings are maintained from one transaction to the next. This means that once an SQL statement has been prepared, it does not need to be re-prepared, even after a commit or roll back occurs, as long as it remains associated with the same statement handle. Also, by default, cursors are preserved after a transaction is committed, and emptied after a transaction is rolled back.

FREEING SQL STATEMENT HANDLES   After the results of an executed SQL statement have been processed, the SQL statement handle data storage area that was allocated when the transaction processing began needs to be freed. SQL statement handles are freed by calling the **SQLFreeHandle()** function with the **SQL_HANDLE_STMT** option specified (or the **SQLFreeStmt()** function). When used, this ODBC API function call performs one or more of the following tasks:

■ Unbinds all previously bound column application variables.

■ Unbinds all previously bound parameter application variables.

■ Closes any open cursors and discards their results.

■ Drops the SQL statement handle, and releases all associated resources.

NOTE: If an SQL statement handle is not dropped, it can be used to process another SQL statement. However, when an SQL statement handle is reused, any cached access plan for the SQL statement associated with that handle will be discarded.

The Termination Task

The termination task takes place just before the ODBC application terminates. This is where all data source connections are ended and all resources allocated by the initialization task are freed and returned to the operating system. Usually, these resources consist of an environment data storage area and one or more connection data storage areas. After all existing database connections are terminated with the **SQLDisconnect()** function, their corresponding connection data storage areas are freed by calling the **SQLFreeHandle()** function with the **SQL_HANDLE_DBC** option specified (or the **SQLFreeConnect()** function). When all connection data storage areas are freed, the environment data storage area is freed by calling the **SQLFreeHandle()** function with the **SQL_HANDLE_ENV** option specified (or the **SQLFreeEnv()** function). Once the termination task has completed, the application can return control to the operating system.

The Driver Manager's Role during the Termination Task

When the application calls the **SQLDisconnect()** function, the Driver Manager calls the corresponding **SQLDisconnect()** function in the driver. However, it leaves the driver loaded in case the application decides to reconnect to it later.

When the application calls the **SQLFreeHandle()** function with the **SQL_HANDLE_DBC** option specified (or the **SQLFreeConnect()** function), the Driver Manager calls the corresponding **SQLFreeHandle()** (or **SQLFreeConnect()**) function in the driver. If the driver is no longer being used by any other connections, the Driver Manager then calls the **SQLFreeHandle()** function in the driver with the **SQL_HANDLE_ENV** option specified (or the **SQLFreeEnv()** function) and unloads the driver.

Creating Executable Applications

Once ODBC source code files have been written, the next step is to convert them into an executable application program. This conversion process involves the following steps:

1. Compiling the source code files to create object modules.
2. Linking the object modules to create an executable program.

After an application source code file has been written, it must be compiled by a high-level language compiler (such as Visual C++, Visual Basic, and so on). The high-level language compiler converts the source code file into an object module the linker uses to create the executable program. Once the source file has been compiled without errors, the resulting object module is used as input to the linker. The linker combines specified object modules and high-level language libraries to produce an executable application (provided no errors or unresolved external references occur). For Windows operating systems, this executable application can be either an *executable load module* (.EXE) or a *dynamic link library* (.DLL). Figure 6–4, illustrates this source code file to executable application conversion process.

Running, Testing, and Debugging ODBC Applications

Once your application program has been successfully compiled and linked, you can run the program and determine whether it performs as expected. You should be able to run your ODBC application program just like you would run any other application program on your particular operating system. If problems occur, you can use the following to help test and debug your code:

- When compiling and linking, specify the proper compiler and linker options, so that the executable program produced can be used with a symbolic debugger (usually provided with the high-level language compiler).

- Make full use of the **SQLGetDiagRec()**, **SQLGetDiagField()** or **SQLError()** ODBC API function calls. Display all diagnostic error messages and return codes generated, whenever an ODBC API function call fails.

SUMMARY

The goal of this chapter was to provide you with an overview of how ODBC application source code files are structured and to describe the processes involved in converting ODBC application source code files into executable application programs.

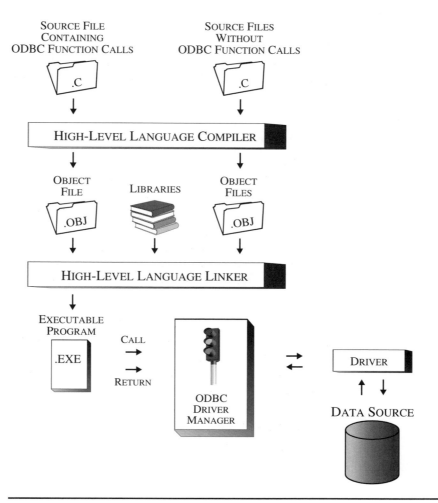

Figure 6–4 *Process used to convert ODBC source code files to executable application programs.*

Application programs written for ODBC are organized so that they perform three distinct tasks.

- Initialization
- Transaction Processing
- Termination

In the initialization task, the Driver Manager is loaded and all resources needed by the transaction processing task are allocated and initialized. At a minimum, an ODBC application must allocate one environment data storage area and at least one connection data storage area within the initialization task.

Before an application allocates a connection handle, it must tell the Driver Manager which ODBC specification it plans to follow. This is done by setting an environment attribute.

The transaction processing task follows the initialization task and makes up the bulk of an ODBC application. In the transaction processing task, an application performs the following five steps, in the order shown:

1. Allocates statement handles.

2. Prepares and executes SQL statements.

3. Processes the results.

4. Commits or rolls back the transaction.

5. Frees statement handles.

There are two methods that can be used to specify and execute an actual SQL statement.

■ Prepare then Execute.

■ Execute Direct

The termination task takes place just before the ODBC application terminates. This is where all data source connections are ended and all resources allocated by the initialization task are freed and returned to the operating system.

Once ODBC source code files have been written, the next step is to convert them into an executable application program. This conversion process involves the following steps:

1. Compiling the source code files to create object modules.

2. Linking the object modules to create an executable program.

Initializing ODBC and Connecting to a Data Source or Driver

ODBC provides several API functions that are used to initialize the ODBC environment and establish a connection to a data source or driver. This chapter is designed to introduce you to these API functions. The first part of this chapter introduces the environment and connection handle allocation functions and describes how they are used to initialize the ODBC Driver Manager. This is followed by a detailed discussion about the data source/driver connection functions available. Next, the functions used to free environment and connection handles previously allocated are described. Finally, a detailed reference section covering each ODBC API function that can be used to initialize the ODBC environment and establish a connection to a data source or driver is provided.

Initializing the ODBC Environment

Before an ODBC application can access data in any data source, it must connect to that data source, either directly or indirectly through a corresponding ODBC driver. An application connects to a data source or driver by sending a connection request to the ODBC Driver Manager. However, before the Driver Manager can process any type of requests, it must first be loaded and initialized by the application. How an application physically loads the Driver Manager is operating system-dependent; on the Windows NT Server, Windows NT Workstation, or Windows 95 operating system, an application can either statically link directly to the ODBC Driver Manager library at compile time or it can dynamically load and link to the Driver Manager Dynamic Link Library (DLL) at application run time. Once the Driver Manager is loaded, an application initializes it by allocating memory for one environment and one or more connection handles.

Allocating an Environment Handle

Regardless of how the ODBC Driver Manager is loaded, an application must initialize it by allocating an environment handle. To do this an application:

1. Creates (declares) an environment handle variable.

   and

2. Calls either the **SQLAllocHandle()** function (ODBC 3.x drivers) or the **SQLAllocEnv()** function (ODBC 2.0 or earlier drivers) and passes it the address of the environment handle variable.

When either of these functions are called, the ODBC Driver Manager allocates a structure in which to store information about the environment and stores the handle to this structure in the environment handle variable specified. Although only one call is made to either the **SQLAllocHandle()** or the **SQLAllocEnv()** functions, two levels of these functions are actually used; the first resides in the ODBC Driver Manager and the second can be found in each data source driver. However, until the appropriate driver is actually loaded, the Driver Manager doesn't know which driver-level **SQLAllocHandle()** or **SQLAllocEnv()** function to use. Therefore, it delays calling the driver-level **SQLAllocHandle()** or **SQLAllocEnv()** function until the **SQLConnect()**, **SQLDriverConnect()** or **SQLBrowseConnect()**

function is called to establish a connection to a data source. When either of these functions is called, the Driver Manager loads the appropriate driver; then it calls the driver-level **SQLAllocHandle()** or **SQLAllocEnv()** function. For more information about how the Driver Manager interacts with a data source driver before and during the connection process, refer to "The Driver Manager's Role During the Initialization Task" in Chapter 6.

Allocating a Connection Handle

After an application allocates an environment handle, it must allocate a connection handle before it can connect to a specific data source or driver. To do this it:

1. Creates (declares) a connection handle variable.

   and

2. Calls either the **SQLAllocHandle()** function (ODBC 3.x drivers) or the **SQLAllocConnect()** function (ODBC 2.0 or earlier drivers) and passes it the previously allocated environment handle along with the address of the connection handle variable.

When either of these functions are called, the ODBC Driver Manager allocates a structure in which to store information about the connection in the environment handle specified, and stores the handle to this structure in the connection handle variable specified. As with the **SQLAllocHandle()** function and the **SQLAllocEnv()** function, two levels of the **SQLAllocConnect()** function are used; the first resides in the ODBC Driver Manager and the second can be found in each data source driver. Again, because the Driver Manager has not yet loaded the appropriate driver, it delays calling the driver-level **SQLAllocHandle()** or **SQLAllocConnect()** function until the application establishes a connection to a data source.

It is important to realize that allocating a connection handle is not the same as physically loading a driver—a driver is never loaded until a connection function is called. Thus, after an application allocates a connection handle, the only ODBC API functions it can legitimately call before connecting to a data source or driver are

▓ **SQLGetConnectAttr()**—ODBC 3.x

▓ **SQLSetConnectAttr()**—ODBC 3.x

- `SQLGetConnectOption()`—ODBC 2.0 or earlier
- `SQLSetConnectOption()`—ODBC 2.0 or earlier
- `SQLGetInfo()` with the `SQL_ODBC_VER` option specified.

If any other ODBC API functions are called, SQLSTATE **08**003 (Connection not open) is returned.

Connecting to a Data Source or Driver

Once a connection handle has been allocated and its attributes/options have been set, an application can use it to connect to a data source or driver. Three different ODBC API functions can be used to establish a connection. They are:

- `SQLConnect()`
- `SQLDriverConnect()`
- `SQLBrowseConnect()`

Applications can use any combination of these functions to connect to any number of data sources and drivers—at the same time if necessary. Additionally, an application's connections can consist of a variety of drivers and data sources, a single driver and a variety of data sources, or even multiple connections to the same driver and data source.

NOTE: *Some drivers limit the number of active connections they support. An application can call the* `SQLGetInfo()` *function with the* `SQL_MAX_DRIVER_CONNECTIONS` *option specified to determine how many active connections a particular driver supports.*

Connecting with `SQLConnect()`

The simplest ODBC API connection function available, `SQLConnect()`, assumes that the only information needed to establish a connection is a data source name and, optionally, a user (authorization) ID and password. This function works well for applications that need to connect to data sources that may or may not require a user ID and/or password. It also works well for applications that want to control their own connection interface or that have no user interface at all. Such applications can either hardcode the necessary connection information directly into the **SQLConnect()** function call, or they can prompt the user for the data source name, user ID, and password and pass the information gathered to the **SQLConnect()** function. The **SQLConnect()** function is the only connection function supported by both the X/Open 95 and the ISO/IEC 92 CLI standards.

Connecting with **SQLDriverConnect()**

The **SQLConnect()** function assumes that any information other than data source name, user ID, and password needed to establish a connection to a data source is stored in the ODBC section of the system information storage area (either the [ODBC] section of the ODBC.INI file or the ODBC subkey in the system registry). However, storing additional connection information in the system information storage area can sometimes produce undesirable side effects. For example, suppose a driver needs one user ID/password to log into a server workstation and a different user ID/password to log into a relational DBMS residing on the server. Because the **SQLConnect()** function accepts only one user ID and password, the second user ID and password would have to be stored in the system information storage area. This has the potential to cause a breach in security, particularly if the password stored in the system information storage area is not encrypted.

The **SQLDriverConnect()** function eliminates this problem by allowing an application to send connection information to the driver via a connection string, as opposed to storing it in the information storage area. This connection string is simply a series of keyword/value pairs, separated by semicolons, that contains information used to establish the connection. Using the previous example, a custom program that always uses the "Payroll" data source might prompt the user for user IDs and passwords and build the following connection string to pass to the driver with the **SQLDriverConnect()** function:

    DSN=Payroll;UID=Sanders;PWD=Cat;UIDDBMS=Sanders;PWDDBMS=Dog;

where:

the Data Source Name (**DSN**) keyword specifies the data source name, the **UID** and **PWD** keywords specify the user ID and password for the server, and the **UIDDBMS** and **PWDDBMS** keywords specify the user ID and password for the relational DBMS on the server (the final semicolon is optional).

When called, the **SQLDriverConnect()** function parses this string; uses the "Payroll" data source name to retrieve additional connection information from the system (for example, the server address); and logs in to the server and DBMS using the specified user IDs and passwords.

All keyword-value pairs specified in a connection string must adhere to the following syntax rules:

- The keywords and their values can not contain the **[] {} () , ; ? * = !** or **@** characters.

- Because of the registry grammar, keywords and data source names cannot contain the backslash (\) character.

- The value of the **DSN** keyword cannot consist only of blanks, and cannot contain leading blanks.

- Spaces are not allowed around the equal sign (=) in the keyword-value pair.

PROMPTING THE USER FOR CONNECTION INFORMATION

If an application using the **SQLConnect()** function needs to prompt the user for connection information, such as a user ID and password, it must provide and process its own user interface. While this allows an application to control its look and feel, it may force the application to use driver-specific code. Particularly, when the application needs to prompt the user for driver-specific connection information. Unfortunately, using driver-specific code can keep generic applications from executing. Generic applications are designed to work with any and all drivers, including drivers that do not exist when the application is written. Applications using the **SQLDriverConnect()** function can eliminate this problem by letting the driver prompt the user for any connection information needed—having the driver prompt for information it needs keeps driver-specific information out of the application.

The **SQLDriverConnect()** function can also be used to prompt the user for a data source. When the **SQLDriverConnect()** function receives an empty connection string, the ODBC 3.0 Driver Manager displays the dialog box shown in Figure 7–1.

This dialog prompts the user to select a data source from a list of data sources recognized by ODBC. Note that the user can select the "New" button to add a new data source "on the fly" if the desired data source does not appear in the list. Once the user selects a data source from the list, the Driver Manager constructs a connection string specifying that data source and passes it to the appropriate driver. The driver can then prompt the user for any additional information it needs.

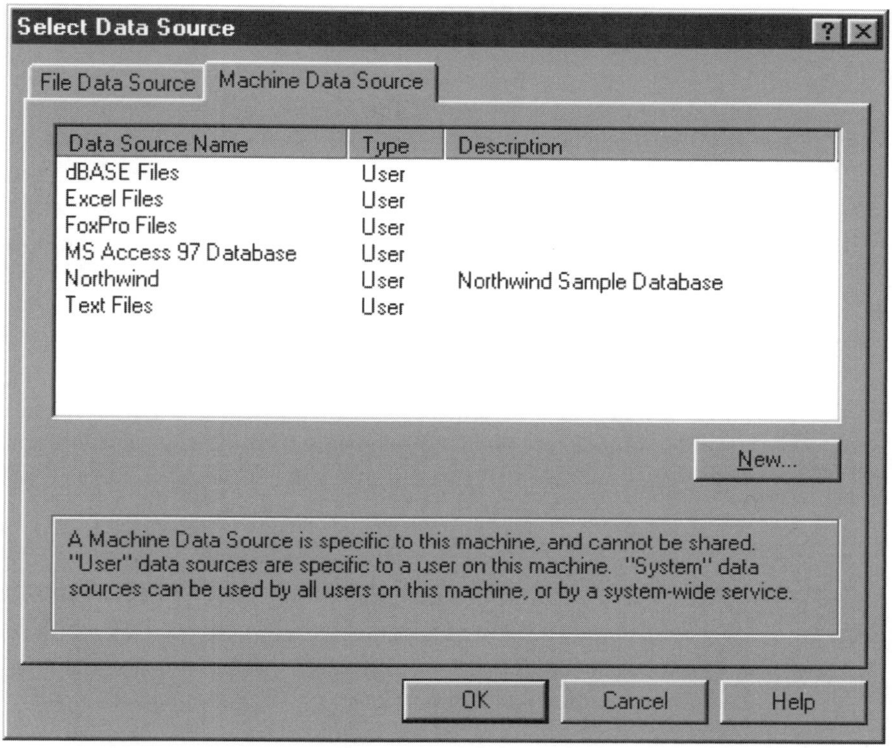

Figure 7–1 *The ODBC 3.0 connection information dialog used by SQLDriverConnect( ) to obtain connection information from a user.*

Depending on how the **SQLDriverConnect()** function is used, an application can let ODBC prompt the user for everything needed to establish a connection, it can provide the name of a data source and let ODBC prompt the user for any additional connection information needed, or it can provide everything needed to establish a connection without having ODBC to prompt the user for anything.

CONNECTING USING FILE DATA SOURCES Applications that repeatedly build the same connection string to connect to a specific data source can streamline the connection process by using a file data source. With file data sources, all the information needed to establish a connection is stored in a special file, that has a .DSN extension. File data sources are usually created by the **SQLDriverConnect()** function; if **SQLDriverConnect()** is called with a connection string containing the **SAVEFILE** keyword/value pair, the ODBC Driver Manager saves the output connection string created by the function call to a .DSN file. The .DSN file generated will contain a driver name (or another data source name in the case of an unshareable file data source), and optionally, one or more keyword/value pairs that were used to establish the connection. The minimum information a shareable .DSN file can have is the **DRIVER=DriverName** keyword/value pair while an unshareable .DSN file can only contain the **DSN=DataSourceName** keyword/value pair. In either case, once a .DSN file has been created, it can be used repeatedly by a single application or it can be shared among several applications as long as the appropriate driver is installed.

When the **SQLDriverConnect()** function is called with the **FILEDSN** keyword/value pair specified in the connection string, the Driver Manager uses the contents of the specified .DSN file to build the actual connection string that will be used to establish the connection. The Driver Manager then attempts to establish a connection to the appropriate data source using this connection string.

NOTE: *The actual connection string used by the* **SQLDriverConnect()** *function is the union of the keyword/value pairs stored in the .DSN file and any keyword/value pairs that were specified in the connection string that contained the* **FILEDSN** *keyword/value pair. If a keyword/value pair in the .DSN file conflict with a keyword/value pair used in the connection string, the Driver Manager determines which of the two keyword/value pairs should be used.*

CONNECTING DIRECTLY TO DRIVERS Although most applications connect to a specific data source, some applications want or need to connect directly to a driver. To do this, an application specifies the **DRIVER=DriverName** keyword/value pair in the connection string used with the **SQLDriverConnect()** function in place of the **DSN=DataSourceName** keyword/value pair. The value assigned to the **DRIVER** keyword is the description of the driver as returned by the **SQLDrivers()** function. For example, suppose a driver has the description "Paradox Driver" and requires the name of a directory containing the data files. To connect to this driver, an application could use either of the following connection strings:

```
DRIVER={Paradox Driver};Directory=C:\MYDATA;
```

or

```
DRIVER={Paradox Driver};
```

With the first string, the driver does not need any additional information. With the second string, the driver needs to prompt for the name of the directory containing the data files. Conceptually, when an application connects directly to a driver, a temporary data source is created at run time.

Connecting with **SQLBrowseConnect()**

Like the **SQLDriverConnect()** function, the **SQLBrowseConnect()** function uses a connection string to send connection information to a driver. However, unlike the **SQLDriverConnect()** function, the **SQLBrowseConnect()** function can be used to construct a complete connection string at application run time. This difference enables an application to do two things:

- Build its own dialog boxes to prompt a user for connection information, thereby retaining control over its "look and feel."
- Search (browse) the system for data sources that can be used by a particular driver, possibly in several steps. For example, an application might first browse the network for servers and after choosing a server browse the server for databases that are accessible by a specific driver.

Here's how the **SQLBrowseConnect()** function is typically used:

1. An application calls the **SQLBrowseConnect()** function and passes it a connection string, known as the browse request connection string, containing a keyword/value pair that specifies a particular driver or data source to use.

2. The driver returns a connection string, known as the browse result connection string, containing keywords, possible values (if the keyword accepts a discrete set of values) for each keyword, and a user-friendly name for each keyword to the calling application.

3. The application displays a dialog box listing the user-friendly names and prompts the user for specific keyword values (using the information returned in the browse result connection string).

4. After the user has provided the appropriate information, the application builds a new browse request connection string using the keywords obtained from the browse result connection string and the values provided by the user. This connection string is then returned to the driver with another call to the **SQLBrowseConnect()** function.

5. If enough information was provided to establish a connection, a connection is made to the data source and the connection string

used is returned to the application. If not, a new browse result connection string is returned to the application and steps 3 and 4 are repeated.

Because connection strings are passed back and forth between an application and a driver, the driver can provide several levels of browsing by returning a new browse result connection string each time the application returns the old one (see step 5). For example, the first time an application calls the **SQLBrowseConnect()** function, the driver might return keywords that prompt the user for a server name. When the application returns the server name to the driver with a second **SQLBrowseConnect()** call, the driver might return keywords that prompt the user for a database name. The browsing process would be complete after the application returned the database name to the driver with another **SQLBrowseConnect()** function call.

Each time the **SQLBrowseConnect()** function returns a new browse result connection string, **SQL_NEED_DATA** is returned as the return code. This lets the application know that the connection process is not complete. Until the **SQLBrowseConnect()** function returns **SQL_SUCCESS**, the connection is in a "Need Data" state and its handle cannot be used for any other purposes (for example, to set a connection attribute). An application can terminate the connection browsing process at any time by calling the **SQLDisconnect()** function.

Connecting to a Default Data Source

A driver may select a predefined data source, called the default data source, in certain cases where a data source name is not explicitly specified by an application such as:

- When the **SQLConnect()** function is called with the **DSN** (data source name) parameter set to a zero-length string, a NULL pointer, or "DEFAULT."

- When the **SQLDriverConnect()** function is called with a connection string containing either the keyword/value pair **DSN=DEFAULT** or the **DSN** keyword and a data source not stored in the system information storage area.

In either case, when a default data source is specified, how it will be used is driver-dependant. In some cases, use of the default data source may involve administrative action and may depend on the user.

Connection Pooling

The whole connection process adds a certain amount of processing requirements to an application. Thus, applications that repeatedly connect and disconnect from a data source (for example, some Internet applications) and middle-tier applications that connect to a data source over a network can require a significant amount of overhead. With these types of applications, connection pooling can be used to provide significant performance gains and reduce application overhead. When connection pooling is enabled, each time a new connection is established, it is placed in a common *pool* and any application can use or reuse it without having to perform the complete connection process. Each connection in a connection pool can be used repeatedly by multiple applications.

Connection pooling is enabled by setting the **SQL_ATTR_CONNECTION_POOLING** environment attribute to **SQL_CP_ONE_PER_DRIVER** (which specifies a maximum of one pool per driver) or **SQL_CP_ONE_PER_HENV** (which specifies a maximum of one pool per environment) before an environment handle is allocated (the **SQLSetEnvAttr()** function is used to set the **SQL_ATTR_CONNECTION_POOLING** attribute). If the **SQL_CP_ONE_PER_DRIVER** environment attribute is set to **SQL_CP_ONE_PER_DRIVER**, a single connection pool is supported for each driver, and it is not possible to share connections between environments. If an application works with many drivers and few environments, this may be more efficient. If the **SQL_CP_ONE_PER_DRIVER** environment attribute is set to **SQL_CP_ONE_PER_HENV**, a single connection pool is supported for each environment, and it is possible to share connections between environments. If an application works with many environments and few drivers, this may be more efficient. If the **SQL_CP_ONE_PER_DRIVER** environment attribute is set to **SQL_CP_OFF**, connection pooling is disabled.

When an environment handle is allocated after connection pooling has been enabled, the environment (known as a *shared environment*) the environment handle refers to can be used by all applications that use one or more of the connections in the pool. By allowing an environment and its associated connections to be used (shared) by multiple components in a single process, standalone components that are part of the same process can interact with each other without being aware of each other's existence.

The actual shared environment to be used by all applications is not determined until a connection handle is allocated. At that time, the Driver Manager attempts to find an existing shared environment that matches the environment attributes set by the application. If no such environment exists, one is created with a reference count (maintained by the Driver Manager) of 1, and its handle is returned to the application. If, however, a matching shared environment is found, the environment handle is returned to the application, and its reference count is incremented by 1.

When connection pooling is used, the pool is automatically maintained by the ODBC Driver Manager. Each time an application calls **SQLConnect()** or **SQLDriverConnect()**, the Driver Manager attempts to find an existing connection in the pool matching the criteria specified. This criteria includes the connection options passed to the **SQLConnect()** function (the data source name, user ID, and password), the keyword/value pairs specified in the connection string used with the **SQLDriverConnect()** function, and any connection attributes set since the connection handle was allocated. The Driver Manager checks this criteria against the corresponding connection keywords and attributes of each connection in the pool and, if a match is found, that connection is used. However, if a match is not found, a new connection is created. When an application calls the **SQLDisconnect()** function, the connection is returned to the connection pool, and made available for reuse. The actual size of the pool grows dynamically as resource allocations are requested, and it shrinks as resource allocations are freed due to inactivity timeout—if a connection is inactive for a period of time (it has not been used in an ODBC API function call), it is removed from the pool. The size of the pool is limited only by memory constraints and any limits imposed by the server.

NOTE: *Connection pooling can be used by an ODBC application exhibiting ODBC 2.0 behavior as long as the application can call the* **SQLSetEnvAttr()** *function. When using connection pooling, the application must not execute SQL statements that change the database or the context of the database, such as changing the database name, which changes the catalog used by a data source.*

Disconnecting from a Data Source or Driver

When an application has finished using a data source or driver, it can call the **SQLDisconnect()** function to free any SQL statements handles allocated for the connection and terminate the connection. Once a connection to a data source or driver is terminated, the connection handle associated with the connection can be reused to either connect to a different data source/driver or to reconnect to the same data source/driver. However, when deciding whether to remain connected or to disconnect and reconnect later, the relative costs of each option must be weighed because both connecting to a data source and remaining connected can be relatively costly depending on the connection medium being used. To properly evaluate the tradeoffs, assumptions sometimes have to be made about the likelihood of performing further operations on the same data source and about the time frame in which further operations will be performed.

Freeing Environment and Connection Handles

When an application has finished using a connection to a particular data source or driver, it can call either the **SQLFreeHandle()** function (ODBC 3.x drivers) or the **SQLFreeConnect()** function (ODBC 2.0 or earlier drivers) to free the connection handle associated with the connection. When a connection handle is freed, the memory used to store the structure that contained information about the connection is released and the handle can no longer be used.

When an application has finished using ODBC, it can call either the **SQLFreeHandle()** function (ODBC 3.x) or the **SQLFreeEnv()** function (ODBC 2.0 or earlier) to free the environment handle that was first allocated during the initialization process. When an environment handle is freed, the memory used to store the structure containing information about the environment is released and ODBC API functions can no longer be used. All connection handles associated with an environment handle must be freed before the environment handle itself can be freed.

It is an application programming error to use any freed handle in a call to an ODBC API function; doing so has undefined, but probably fatal, consequences.

The ODBC Initialization and Data Source/Driver Connection Control Functions

Table 7–1 lists the ODBC API functions used to allocate or free resources and establish connections to specified data sources and/or drivers.

Each of these functions are described in detail in the remaining portion of this chapter.

Table 7–1   The ODBC Initialization and Data Source/Driver Connection Control Functions

Function Name	Description
SQLAllocHandle( )	Allocates an environment, connection, SQL statement, or descriptor handle and its associated resources.
SQLAllocEnv( )	Allocates an environment handle and its associated resources.
SQLAllocConnect( )	Allocates a data source connection handle and its associated resources.
SQLConnect( )	Establishes a connection to a specified data source using a specific user ID and password.
SQLDriverConnect( )	Establishes a connection to a specified data source or driver using a connection string, or optionally requests that the ODBC Driver Manager and/or driver display the ODBC connection dialog so that the end user can provide connection infomation.
SQLBrowseConnect( )	Returns successive levels of connection attributes and corresponding valid values to an application. When all connection attributes have been specified, a connection to the data source is established.
SQLDisconnect( )	Closes a data source connection.
SQLFreeHandle( )	Releases an environment, connection, SQL statement or descriptor handle and its associated resources.
SQLFreeConnect( )	Releases a data source connection handle and its associated resources.
SQLFreeEnv( )	Releases an environment handle and its associated resources.

SQLAllocHandle

COMPATABILITY					
X/OPEN 95 CLI	ISO/IEC 92 CLI	ODBC 1.0	ODBC 2.0	ODBC 3.0	ODBC 3.5
☑	☑	☐	☐	☑	☑

API CONFORMANCE LEVEL **CORE**

Purpose The **SQLAllocHandle()** function is used to allocate memory for an environment, connection, SQL statement, or descriptor handle.

Syntax

```
SQLRETURN  SQLAllocHandle    (SQLSMALLINT   HandleType,
                              SQLHANDLE     InputHandle,
                              SQLHANDLE     *OutputHandle);
```

Parameters

HandleType Specifies the type of handle to allocate memory for. This parameter must be set to one of the following values:

- **SQL_HANDLE_ENV** Allocate memory for an environment handle.
- **SQL_HANDLE_DBC** Allocate memory for a connection handle.
- **SQL_HANDLE_STMT** Allocate memory for an SQL statement handle.
- **SQL_HANDLES_DESC** Allocate memory for a descriptor handle.

InputHandle Specifies the existing handle in whose context the environment, connection, statement, or descriptor handle is to be allocated. If *HandleType* is set to **SQL_HANDLE_ENV**, this parameter must be set to **SQL_NULL_HANDLE**; otherwise, if *HandleType* is set to **SQL_HANDLE_DBC**, this parameter must contain a previously allocated environment handle, and if *HandleType* is set to **SQL_HANDLE_STMT** or **SQL_**

HANDLE_DESC, this parameter must contain a previously allocated connection handle.

OutputHandle   A pointer to a location in memory where this function is to store the starting address of the allocated handle's information storage buffer (data structure).

Description   The **SQLAllocHandle()** function is used to allocate handles (and their associated resources) for environments, connections, SQL statements, and descriptors.

To allocate an environment handle, an application calls this function with the *HandleType* parameter set to **SQL_HANDLE_ENV** and the *InputHandle* parameter set to **SQL_NULL_HANDLE**. During execution, the ODBC Driver Manager (and later the driver) allocates memory for the environment information storage buffer and passes the starting address of that buffer (the environment handle) back to the application in the *OutputHandle* parameter. The environment handle returned by this function can then be passed to all subsequent ODBC API function calls requiring an environment handle as an input parameter; the handle is used by other ODBC API functions to reference global information related to the environment, including information about available connection handles and information about whether a specific connection handle is active.

To allocate a connection handle, an application calls this function with the *HandleType* parameter set to **SQL_HANDLE_DBC** and the *InputHandle* parameter set to a previously allocated environment handle. During execution, the ODBC Driver Manager (and later the driver) allocates memory for the connection information storage buffer and passes the starting address of that buffer (the connection handle) back to the application in the *OutputHandle* parameter. The connection handle returned by this function can then be passed to all subsequent ODBC API function calls requiring a connection handle as an input parameter; the handle is used by other ODBC API functions to reference information related to a specific data source connection, including general status information, the current transaction state, and connection error information.

To allocate a SQL statement handle, an application calls this function with the *HandleType* parameter set to **SQL_HANDLE_STMT** and the *InputHandle* parameter set to a previously allocated connection handle. During execution, the ODBC Driver Manager (and later the driver) allocates memory for the SQL statement information storage buffer and passes the starting address of the buffer (the SQL statement handle) back to the application in the *OutputHandle* parameter. The SQL statement handle returned by this function can then be passed to all subsequent ODBC API function calls that require a statement handle as an input parameter; the handle is used by other ODBC API functions to reference information related to a specific SQL statement, including cursor information, result data set information, status information for SQL statement processing, and statement processing error information.

To allocate a descriptor handle, an application calls this function with the *HandleType* parameter set to **SQL_HANDLE_DESC** and the *InputHandle* parameter set to a previously allocated connection handle. During execution, the ODBC Driver Manager (and later the driver) explicitly allocates memory for a descriptor information storage buffer and passes the starting address of the buffer (the descriptor handle) back to the application in the *OutputHandle* parameter. An application can direct a driver to use an explicitly allocated application descriptor in place of an automatically allocated one when processing SQL statements for a specific data source connection by calling the **SQLSetStmtAttr()** function with the **SQL_ATTR_APP_ROW_DESC** or **SQL_ATTR_APP_PARAM_DESC** attribute and the descriptor handle returned by this function specified.

NOTE: *In ODBC 3.x, this function replaces the ODBC 2.0 functions* **SQLAllocEnv()** *(for allocating environment handles),* **SQLAllocConnect()** *(for allocating connection handles), and* **SQLAllocStmt()** *(for allocating SQL statement handles).*

Return Codes SQL_SUCCESS, SQL_SUCCESS_WITH_INFO, SQL_INVALID_HANDLE, or SQL_ERROR

SQLSTATEs Two levels of the **SQLAllocHandle()** function are used—one resides in the ODBC Driver Manager and the other resides in the data source driver. The Driver Manager does not call the driver-level **SQLAllocHandle()** function to allocate environment and connection handles until the application calls the **SQLConnect()**, **SQLDriverConnect()**, or **SQLBrowseConnect()** function. If an error occurs in the driver-level **SQLAllocHandle()** function, the Driver Manager-level **SQLConnect**, **SQLDriverConnect**, or **SQLBrowseConnect** function returns **SQL_ERROR** and an appropriate SQLSTATE value.

If this function returns **SQL_SUCCESS_WITH_INFO** or **SQL_ERROR**, one of the following SQLSTATE values may be obtained by calling the **SQLGetDiagRec()** function:

01000, **08**003*, **HY**000, **HY**001*, **HY**009*, **HY**010*, **HY**013, **HY**014, **HY**092*, **HYC**00, **HYT**01, or **IM**001*

* Returned by the ODBC Driver Manager.

Unless noted otherwise, each of these SQLSTATE values are returned by the data source driver. Refer to Appendix B for detailed information about each SQLSTATE value that can be returned by the ODBC Driver Manager or by a data source driver.

Comments

■ Environment handle allocation occurs both within the Driver Manager and within each driver used by the application. If an error occurs when this function is called with the *HandleType* parameter set to **SQL_HANDLE_ENV**, the error value returned is dependent on the level (Driver Manager or driver) at which the error occurred.

■ If the Driver Manager cannot allocate memory for the handle pointer stored in the *OutputHandle* parameter (or if a NULL pointer is specified for the *OutputHandle* parameter) when this function is called with the *HandleType* parameter set to **SQL_HANDLE_ENV**, the Driver Manager sets the *OutputHandle* parameter to **SQL_NULL_HENV** (unless a NULL pointer was specified) and **SQL_ERROR** is returned. In this case, because there is no handle with which to associate additional diagnostic information, the **SQLGetDiagRec()** function cannot be used to obtain additional information about why the error occurred. (If the driver has additional diagnostic information, it puts the information on a skeletal handle that it allocates and the Driver Manager reads error information from the diagnostic structure associated with this handle.)

■ The Driver Manager does not call the driver-level **SQLAllocHandle()** function to allocate an environment handle until the **SQLConnect()**, **SQLDriverConnect()**, or **SQLBrowseConnect()** function is called. If an error occurs in the driver-level **SQLAllocHandle()** function, the Driver Manager-level **SQLConnect()**, **SQLDriverConnect()**, or **SQLBrowseConnect()** function returns **SQL_ERROR** and the diagnostic record contains SQLSTATE **IM**004, along with a driver-specific SQLSTATE value.

■ If **SQL_ERROR** is returned by this function when a handle other than an environment handle is allocated, the values **SQL_NULL_HDBC**, **SQL_NULL_HSTMT**, or **SQL_NULL_HDESC** are stored in the *OutputHandle* parameter, depending on the value stored in the *HandleType* parameter (provided the *OutputHandle* parameter did not refer to a null pointer when this function was called).

■ More than one environment, connection, or statement handle at a time can be allocated by an application, but only if multiple allocations are supported by the driver being used (drivers may impose limits on the number of one or more types of handles that can be allocated at one time). ODBC does not limit the number of environment, connection, statement, or descriptor handles that can be allocated at any one time.

■ Because many implementations support only one environment handle, interoperable applications should only allocate one environment handle.

■ If an existing environment, connection, statement, or descriptor handle (an environment, connection, statement, or descriptor handle allocated by a previous call to this function) is specified in the *OutputHandle* parameter, the address of the information storage buffer (data structure) the environment, connection, statement, or descriptor handle points to is overwritten when this function executes. Consequently, memory used by the information storage buffer (data structure) the environment, connection, statement, or descriptor handle originally pointed to can no longer be freed because its starting address is no longer available. Programming errors of this type cannot be detected by ODBC; therefore, no associated return code or SQLSTATE is generated when this kind of error occurs.

■ This function does not set the **SQL_ATTR_ODBC_VERSION** environment attribute when it is used to allocate an environment handle. Instead, an explicit call to the **SQLSetEnvAttr()** function must be made.

■ For some standards-compliant applications, this function is mapped to the function **SQLAllocHandleStd()** at compile time. The difference between this function and the **SQLAllocHandleStd()** function is that the **SQLAllocHandleStd()** function sets the **SQL_ATTR_ODBC_VERSION** environment attribute to **SQL_OV_ODBC3** when it is called with the *HandleType* parameter set to **SQL_HANDLE_ENV**. This is done because standards-compliant applications are always ODBC 3.x applications. Moreover, the standards do not require that the application version be registered. Otherwise, **SQLAllocHandle()** and **SQLAllocHandleStd()** are identical.

■ Descriptors were introduced in ODBC 3.0 and they are not supported by ODBC 2.0 (or earlier) drivers. Therefore, when working with an ODBC 2.0 or earlier driver, this function can not be used to allocate a descriptor handle.

■ When a statement handle is allocated, a set of four descriptor handles are implicitly allocated.

■ An implementation descriptor handle cannot be explicitly allocated by this function.

■ Applications can use the same environment, connection, statement, or descriptor handle in several different threads on operating systems that support multiple threads.

■ When the Driver Manager processes this function with the *HandleType* parameter set to **SQL_HANDLE_ENV** and the *InputHandle* parameter set to **SQL_NULL_HANDLE**, it checks the **Trace** keyword in the ODBC section of the system information storage area (either the [ODBC] section of ODBC.INI file or the ODBC subkey in the registry) and, if its value is set to 1, the Driver Manager enables tracing for the current application on a computer running Windows 95, Windows NT Server, or Windows NT Workstation. If tracing is enabled, tracing begins when an environment handle is allocated, and ends when an environment handle is freed.

Prerequisites   The **SQL_ATTR_ODBC_VERSION** environment attribute must be set before this function is used to allocate a connection handle.

Restrictions   If an existing handle is to be specified in the *OutputHandle* parameter, the **SQLFreeHandle()** function must first be used to free it before this function is used to reallocate it. Overwriting ODBC handles without freeing them first may lead to inconsistent behavior or errors within drivers.

See Also   **SQLFreeHandle(), SQLAllocEnv(), SQLAllocConnect(), SQLGetEnvAttr(), SQLSetEnvAttr()**

Example   The following Visual C++ program illustrates how to allocate an environment handle and a connection handle and how to establish a connection to a data source.

```
/*————————————————————————————————————————————— */
/* NAME:     CH7EX1.CPP                                     */
/* PURPOSE: Illustrate How To Use The Following ODBC API Function  */
/*          In A C++ Program:                               */
/*                                                          */
/*               SQLAllocHandle()                           */
/*               SQLConnect()                               */
/*               SQLDisconnect()                            */
/*               SQLFreeHandle()                            */
/*                                                          */
```

```
/* OTHER ODBC APIs SHOWN:                                           */
/*        SQLSetEnvAttr()                                           */
/*                                                                  */
/*────────────────────────────────────────────────────────────── */

// Include The Appropriate Header Files
#include <windows.h>
#include <sql.h>
#include <sqlext.h>
#include <iostream.h>

// Define The ODBC_Class Class
class ODBC_Class
{
    // Attributes
    public:
        SQLHANDLE      EnvHandle;
        SQLHANDLE      ConHandle;
        SQLRETURN      rc;

    // Operations
    public:
        ODBC_Class();                            // Constructor
        ~ODBC_Class();                           // Destructor
};

// Define The Class Constructor
ODBC_Class::ODBC_Class()
{
    // Initialize The Return Code Variable
    rc = SQL_SUCCESS;

    // Allocate An Environment Handle
    rc = SQLAllocHandle(SQL_HANDLE_ENV, SQL_NULL_HANDLE, &EnvHandle);

    // Set The ODBC Application Version To 3.x
    if (rc == SQL_SUCCESS)
        rc = SQLSetEnvAttr(EnvHandle, SQL_ATTR_ODBC_VERSION,
                (SQLPOINTER) SQL_OV_ODBC3, SQL_IS_UINTEGER);

    // Allocate A Connection Handle
    if (rc == SQL_SUCCESS)
        rc = SQLAllocHandle(SQL_HANDLE_DBC, EnvHandle, &ConHandle);
}

// Define The Class Destructor
ODBC_Class::~ODBC_Class()
{
    // Free The Connection Handle
    if (ConHandle != NULL)
        SQLFreeHandle(SQL_HANDLE_DBC, ConHandle);
```

```
        // Free The Environment Handle
        if (EnvHandle != NULL)
            SQLFreeHandle(SQL_HANDLE_ENV, EnvHandle);
}

/*————————————————————————————————————————————————*/
/* The Main Function                               */
/*————————————————————————————————————————————————*/
int main()
{
    // Declare The Local Memory Variables
    SQLRETURN   rc = SQL_SUCCESS;
    SQLCHAR     DBName[10] = "Northwind";

    // Create An Instance Of The ODBC_Class Class
    ODBC_Class  Example;

    // Connect To The Northwind Sample Database - If Successful,
    // Display An Appropriate Message
    if (Example.ConHandle != NULL)
    {
        rc = SQLConnect(Example.ConHandle, DBName, SQL_NTS,
                   (SQLCHAR *) "", SQL_NTS, (SQLCHAR *) "", SQL_NTS);

        if (rc == SQL_SUCCESS || rc == SQL_SUCCESS_WITH_INFO)
            cout << "Connected to Northwind database." << endl;

        // Disconnect From The Northwind Sample Database
        rc = SQLDisconnect(Example.ConHandle);
    }

    // Return To The Operating System
    return(rc);
}
```

SQLAllocEnv

COMPATABILITY					
X/OPEN 95 CLI	ISO/IEC 92 CLI	ODBC 1.0	ODBC 2.0	ODBC 3.0	ODBC 3.5
☒	☑	☑	☑	☐	☐

API CONFORMANCE LEVEL   **CORE**

Purpose   The **SQLAllocEnv()** function is used to allocate memory for an environment handle.

Syntax   RETCODE   SQLAllocEnv   (HENV FAR *EnvironmentHandle);

Parameters   *EnvironmentHandle*   A pointer to a memory location where this function is to store the starting address of the allocated environment handle's information storage buffer (data structure).

Description   The **SQLAllocEnv()** function is used to allocate memory for an environment handle (and its associated resources) and to initialize the ODBC call-level interface so that it can be used by an application. The environment handle returned by this function can be used by other ODBC API functions to reference global information related to the environment, including information about available connection handles and information about whether or not a specific connection handle is active. An application working with an ODBC 2.0 (or earlier) driver must call this function before it calls any other ODBC API function; the resulting environment handle must be passed to all subsequent ODBC API function calls requiring an environment handle as an input parameter.

NOTE: *In ODBC 3.x, this function has been replaced by the* **SQLAllocHandle()** *function.*

Return Codes   SQL_SUCCESS or SQL_ERROR

SQLSTATEs   If this function fails, SQLSTATE values cannot be returned by the **SQLError()** function because no valid environment handle exists with which to associate additional diagnostic information.

Two levels of the **SQLAllocEnv()** function are used—one resides in the ODBC Driver Manager and the other is in the data source driver. The Driver Manager does not call the driver-level **SQLAllocEnv()** function to allocate an environment handle until the application calls the **SQLConnect()**, **SQLDriverConnect()**, or **SQLBrowseConnect()** function. If an error occurs in the driver-level **SQLAllocEnv()** function, the Driver Manager-level **SQLConnect()**, **SQLDriverConnect()**, or **SQLBrowseConnect()** function returns **SQL_ERROR**. A subsequent call to the **SQLError()** function with the environment handle specified as an input parameter (and the connection handle and statement handle parameters set to **SQL_NULL_HDBC** and **SQL_NULL_HSTMT**, respectively) produces SQLSTATE **IM**004, followed by SQLSTATE **S1**000 or a driver-specific SQLSTATE value ranging from **S1**000 to **S19ZZ**.

Comments

▨ An application should never have more than one environment handle active at any given time.

▨ If an existing environment handle (an environment handle allocated by a previous call to this function) is specified in the *EnvironmentHandle* parameter, the address of the information storage buffer (data structure) the environment handle points to is overwritten when this function executes. Consequently, memory used by the information storage buffer (data structure) the environment handle originally pointed to can no longer be freed because its starting address is no longer available. Programming errors of this type can not be detected by ODBC; therefore, no associated return code or SQLSTATE is generated when this kind of error occurs.

▨ If the **SQL_ERROR** return code is returned by this function and if *EnvironmentHandle* is equal to **SQL_NULL_HENV**, the calling application can assume that a memory allocation error occurred.

▨ If the **SQL_ERROR** return code is returned by this function and if *EnvironmentHandle* is not equal to **SQL_NULL_HENV**, then the environment handle is a restricted handle, and it can only be used as an input parameter for the **SQLFreeEnv()** function.

▨ Applications can use the same environment handle in several different threads on operating systems that support multiple threads.

▨ When the Driver Manager processes this function, it checks the **Trace** keyword in the ODBC section of the system information storage area (either the [ODBC] section of ODBC.INI file or the ODBC subkey in the registry), and if its value is set to 1, the

Driver Manager enables tracing for the current application on a computer running Windows 95, Windows NT Server, or Windows NT Workstation. If tracing is enabled, tracing begins when the environment handle is allocated and ends when the environment handle is freed.

Prerequisites There are no prerequisites for using this function call.

Restrictions An application should never call this function when a current, valid environment handle already exists.

See Also `SQLFreeEnv()`, `SQLAllocHandle()`, `SQLGetEnvAttr()`, `SQLSetEnvAttr()`

Example The following Visual C++ program illustrates how to allocate an environment handle and a connection handle and how to establish a connection to a data source.

```
/*─────────────────────────────────────────────────────────── */
/* NAME:     CH7EX2.CPP                                        */
/* PURPOSE: Illustrate How To Use The Following ODBC API Functions */
/*          In A C++ Program:                                  */
/*                                                             */
/*              SQLAllocEnv()                                  */
/*              SQLAllocConnect()                              */
/*              SQLConnect()                                   */
/*              SQLDisconnect()                                */
/*              SQLFreeConnect()                               */
/*              SQLFreeEnv()                                   */
/*                                                             */
/*─────────────────────────────────────────────────────────── */

// Include The Appropriate Header Files
#include <windows.h>
#include <sql.h>
#include <sqlext.h>
#include <iostream.h>

// Define The ODBC_Class Class
class ODBC_Class
{
    // Attributes
    public:
        HENV      EnvHandle;
        HDBC      ConHandle;
        RETCODE   rc;

    // Operations
    public:
        ODBC_Class();                            // Constructor
```

```
        ~ODBC_Class();                              // Destructor
};

// Define The Class Constructor
ODBC_Class::ODBC_Class()
{
    // Initialize The Return Code Variable
    rc = SQL_SUCCESS;

    // Allocate An Environment Handle
    rc = SQLAllocEnv(&EnvHandle);

    // Allocate A Connection Handle
    if (rc == SQL_SUCCESS)
        rc = SQLAllocConnect(EnvHandle, &ConHandle);
}

// Define The Class Destructor
ODBC_Class::~ODBC_Class()
{
    // Free The Connection Handle
    if (ConHandle != NULL)
        SQLFreeConnect(ConHandle);

    // Free The Environment Handle
    if (EnvHandle != NULL)
        SQLFreeEnv(EnvHandle);
}

/*————————————————————————————————————————————*/
/* The Main Function                                          */
/*————————————————————————————————————————————*/
int main()
{
    // Declare The Local Memory Variables
    RETCODE    rc = SQL_SUCCESS;
    SQLCHAR    DBName[10] = "Northwind";

    // Create An Instance Of The ODBC_Class Class
    ODBC_Class   Example;

    // Connect To The Northwind Sample Database - If Successful,
    // Display An Appropriate Message
    if (Example.ConHandle != NULL)
    {
        rc = SQLConnect(Example.ConHandle, DBName, SQL_NTS,
                (SQLCHAR *) "", SQL_NTS, (SQLCHAR *) "", SQL_NTS);

        if (rc == SQL_SUCCESS || rc == SQL_SUCCESS_WITH_INFO)
            cout << "Connected to Northwind database." << endl;

        // Disconnect From The Northwind Sample Database
        rc = SQLDisconnect(Example.ConHandle);
    }
```

```
// Return To The Operating System
return(rc);
}
```

SQLAllocConnect

COMPATABILITY					
X/OPEN 95 CLI	ISO/IEC 92 CLI	ODBC 1.0	ODBC 2.0	ODBC 3.0	ODBC 3.5
✗	✓	✓	✓	☐	☐

API CONFORMANCE LEVEL   **CORE**

Purpose   The **SQLAllocConnect()** function is used to allocate memory for a connection handle (within a specified environment).

Syntax
```
RETCODE   SQLAllocConnect   (HENV        EnvironmentHandle,
                             HDBC FAR    *ConnectionHandle);
```

Parameters

EnvironmentHandle	An environment handle that refers to a previously allocated environment information storage buffer (data structure).
ConnectionHandle	A pointer to a location in memory where this function is to store the starting address of the allocated connection handle's information storage buffer (data structure).

Description   The **SQLAllocConnect()** function is used to allocate memory for a connection handle (and its associated resources) within a specified environment. The connection handle returned by this function can be used by other ODBC API functions to reference information related to a specific data source connection, including general status information, the current transaction state, and error information. An application working with an ODBC 2.0 (or earlier) driver must call this function before it calls any other ODBC API function that requires a connection handle as an input parameter.

NOTE: *In ODBC 3.x, this function has been replaced by the* **SQLAllocHandle()** *function.*

Return Codes   SQL_SUCCESS, SQL_SUCCESS_WITH_INFO, SQL_INVALID_HANDLE, or SQL_ERROR

SQLSTATEs   Two levels of the SQLAllocConnect() function are used—one resides in the ODBC Driver Manager and the other is in the data source driver. The Driver Manager does not call the driver-level SQLAllocConnect() function to allocate a connection handle until the application calls the SQLConnect(), SQLDriverConnect(), or SQLBrowseConnect() function. If an error occurs in the driver-level SQLAllocConnect() function, the Driver Manager-level SQLConnect(), SQLDriverConnect(), or SQLBrowseConnect() function returns SQL_SUCCESS_WITH_INFO or SQL_ERROR and a subsequent call to the SQLError() function with the connection handle and statement handle parameters set to SQL_NULL_HDBC and SQL_NULL_HSTMT, respectively will produce one or more of the following SQLSTATE values:

01000, **S1**000, **S1**001*, or **S1**009*

* Returned by the ODBC Driver Manager.

Unless noted otherwise, each of these SQLSTATE values are returned by the data source driver. Refer to Appendix B for detailed information about each SQLSTATE value that can be returned by the ODBC Driver Manager or by a data source driver.

Comments   ▨ If an existing connection handle (a connection handle that was allocated by a previous call to this function) is specified in the *ConnectionHandle* parameter, the address of the information storage buffer (data structure) the connection handle points to is overwritten when this function executes. Consequently, memory used by the information storage buffer (data structure) the connection handle originally pointed to can no longer be freed because its starting address is no longer available. Programming errors of this type cannot be detected by ODBC; therefore, no associated return code or SQLSTATE is generated when this kind of error occurs.

▨ Applications can use the same connection handle in several different threads on operating systems that support multiple threads.

Prerequisites   The SQLAllocEnv() function must be called before this function is called.

Restrictions   There are no restrictions associated with this function call.

See Also   `SQLFreeConnect(), SQLAllocHandle(), SQLAllocEnv(),`
`SQLConnect(), SQLDriverConnect(), SQLBrowseConnect(),`
`SQLGetConnectAttr(), SQLSetConnectAttr(), SQLGetConnectOption(),`
`SQLSetConnectOption()`

Example   See the example provided for the `SQLAllocEnv()` function on page 147.

SQLConnect

COMPATABILITY					
X/OPEN 95 CLI	ISO/IEC 92 CLI	ODBC 1.0	ODBC 2.0	ODBC 3.0	ODBC 3.5
✓	✓	✓	✓	✓	✓

API CONFORMANCE LEVEL   **CORE**

Purpose   The `SQLConnect()` function is used to establish a connection to a specified driver and its underlying data source.

Syntax

SQLRETURN	SQLConnect	(SQLHDBC	*ConnectionHandle,*
		SQLCHAR	**DSName,*
		SQLSMALLINT	*DSNameSize,*
		SQLCHAR	**UserID,*
		SQLSMALLINT	*UserIDSize,*
		SQLCHAR	**Password,*
		SQLSMALLINT	*PasswordSize);*

Parameters

ConnectionHandle   A data source connection handle that refers to a previously allocated connection information storage buffer (data structure).

DSName   A pointer to a location in memory where the name of the data source to connect to is stored.

DSNameSize   The length of the data source name value stored in the *DSName* parameter.

UserID   A pointer to a location in memory where the user's authorization name (user identifier) is stored.

UserIDSize   The length of the user authorization name value stored in the *UserID* parameter.

Password   A pointer to a location in memory where the password for the specified authorization name is stored.

PasswordSize   The length of the password value stored in the *Password* parameter.

Description   The **SQLConnect()** function is used to establish a connection to a specified driver and its underlying data source. When using this function, an application must supply the name of a target data source and optionally, a user ID (authorization name) and a corresponding password (authorization string). When a connection to the target data source is established, the connection handle specified with this function call can be used to reference all information about the connection, including status, transaction state, and error information.

The value specified in the *DSName* parameter controls how the ODBC Driver Manager and a driver work together to establish a connection to a data source:

▨ If the *DSName* parameter contains a valid data source name, the Driver Manager locates the corresponding data source specification in the system information storage area (either the [ODBC] section of ODBC.INI file or the ODBC subkey in the registry) and connects to the associated driver. The Driver Manager then passes the values specified for the *DSName*, *DSNameSize*, *UserID*, *UserIDSize*, *Password*, and *PasswordSize* parameters directly to the driver.

▨ If the *DSName* parameter contains an invalid data source name or a NULL pointer, the Driver Manager locates the default data source specification in the system information storage area and connects to the associated driver. The Driver Manager then passes the values specified for the *UserID*, *UserIDSize*, *Password*, and *PasswordSize* parameters directly to the driver; "DEFAULT" and 7 are passed in place of the values specified for the *DSName* and *DSNameSize* parameters, respectively.

▨ If the *DSName* parameter contains the value "DEFAULT" the Driver Manager locates the default data source specification in the system information storage area and connects to the associated driver. The Driver Manager then passes the values specified for the *DSName, DSNameSize, UserID, UserIDSize, Password,* and *PasswordSize* parameters directly to the driver.

■ If the *DSName* parameter contains an invalid data source name or a NULL pointer, and if a default data source specification does not exist, the Driver Manager returns **SQL_ERROR** and SQLSTATE **IM**002 (Data source name not found and no default driver specified) to the calling application.

■ After the Driver Manager establishes a connection to a driver, the driver locates its corresponding data source specification in the system information storage area. This specification can contain driver-specific information and can be used to provide additional required connection information not provided by the **SQLConnect()** function parameters.

Return Codes   **SQL_SUCCESS**, **SQL_SUCCESS_WITH_INFO**, **SQL_INVALID_HANDLE**, or **SQL_ERROR**

SQLSTATE   If this function returns **SQL_SUCCESS_WITH_INFO** or **SQL_ERROR**, one of the following SQLSTATE values may be obtained by calling the **SQLGetDiagRec()** function (ODBC 3.x driver) or the **SQLError()** function (ODBC 2.0 or earlier driver):

ODBC 3.X
01000, **01**S02, **08**001, **08**002*, **08**004, **08**S01, **28**000, **HY**000, **HY**001*, **HY**013, **HY**090*, **HYT**00, **HYT**01, **IM**001*, **IM**002*, **IM**003*, **IM**004*, **IM**005*, **IM**006, **IM**009, or **IM**010*

ODBC 2.0 OR EARLIER
01000, **08**001, **08**002*, **08**004, **08**S01, **28**000, **IM**001*, **IM**002*, **IM**003*, **IM**004*, **IM**005*, **IM**006*, **IM**009, **S1**000, **S1**001*, **S1**090*, or **S1**T00
* Returned by the ODBC Driver Manager.

Unless noted otherwise, each of these SQLSTATE values are returned by the data source driver. Refer to Appendix B for detailed information about each SQLSTATE value that can be returned by the ODBC Driver Manager or by a data source driver.

Comments   ■ The input length parameters (that is, *DSNameSize*, *UserIDSize*, and *PasswordSize*) can be set to either the actual length of their associated data values (not including a null-terminating character) or to the value **SQL_NTS** to indicate that the associated data is a null-terminated string.

■ The length of the data source name specified in the *DSName* parameter must not exceed 128 characters.

▦ If the *DSName* parameter contains the value "DEFAULT," the *UserIDSize* parameter and the *PasswordSize* parameter must be set to 0.

▦ A list of available data sources an application can connect to can be obtained by calling the **SQLDataSources()** function.

▦ An application can connect to more than one data source at the same time, however only one connection can be current at one time.

▦ If a default translation library has been defined for the specified data source (in the system information storage area), the driver automatically connects to it. A different translation library can be loaded by calling the **SQLSetConnectAttr()** function with the **SQL_ATTR_TRANSLATE_LIB** attribute specified (ODBC 3.x driver) or the **SQLSetConnectOption()** function with the **SQL_TRANSLATE_LIB** option specified (ODBC 2.0 or earlier driver). A translation option within the loaded library can be changed by calling the **SQLSetConnectAttr()** function with the **SQL_ATTR_TRANSLATE_OPTION** attribute specified (ODBC 3.x driver) or the **SQLSetConnectOption()** function with the **SQL_TRANSLATE_OPTION** option specified (ODBC 2.0 or earlier driver).

Prerequisites A connection handle must be allocated with the **SQLAllocHandle()** function (ODBC 3.x driver) or the **SQLAllocConnect()** function (ODBC 2.0 or earlier driver) before this function is called.

Restrictions There are no restrictions associated with this function call.

See Also SQLAllocHandle(), SQLAllocConnect(), SQLDriverConnect(), SQLBrowseConnect(), SQLDisconnect(), SQLDrivers(), SQLDataSources(), SQLGetConnectAttr(), SQLSetConnectAttr(), SQLGetConnectOption(), SQLSetConnectOption()

Example See the examples provided for the **SQLAllocHandle()** function on page 138 and the **SQLAllocEnv()** function on page 147.

SQLDriverConnect

COMPATABILITY					
X/OPEN 95 CLI	ISO/IEC 92 CLI	ODBC 1.0	ODBC 2.0	ODBC 3.0	ODBC 3.5
☐	☐	✓	✓	✓	✓

API CONFORMANCE LEVEL   **CORE***

*IN ODBC 2.0, THIS FUNCTION WAS A LEVEL 1 API CONFORMANCE LEVEL FUNCTION

Purpose

The SQLDriverConnect() function is used to establish a connection to a specified data source that requires additional information not provided by the SQLConnect() function OR to allow a data source driver to prompt the user for required connection information.

Syntax

```
SQLRETURN SQLDriverConnect  (SQLHDBC         ConnectionHandle,
                             SQLHWND         WindowHandle,
                             SQLCHAR         *ConnectIn,
                             SQLSMALLINT     ConnectInSize,
                             SQLCHARU        *ConnectOut,
                             SQLSMALLINT     ConnectOutMaxSize,
                             SQLSMALLINT     *ConnectOutSize,
                             SQLUSMALLINT    DriverCompletion);
```

Parameters

ConnectionHandle   A data source connection handle that refers to a previously allocated connection information storage buffer (data structure).

WindowHandle   The platform dependent window handle used for displaying the ODBC connection information dialog if additional prompting is necessary in order to obtain all mandatory connection information (on Windows, this is the parent Windows handle). If this parameter contains a NULL pointer, the ODBC connection dialog is not displayed.

ConnectIn   A pointer to a location in memory where a full, partial, or empty (NULL pointer) connection string is stored. This connection string is used to pass one or more values needed to establish a connection to a data source to a driver for processing.

ConnectInSize

The length of the connection string value stored in the *ConnectIn* parameter.

ConnectOut

A pointer to a location in memory where this function is to store the complete connection string used to connect to the data source—provided a connection was successfully established.

ConnectOutMaxSize

The maximum size of the memory storage buffer where this function is to store the complete data source connection string used to connect to the data source.

ConnectOutSize

A pointer to a location in memory where this function is to store the actual number of bytes written to the complete data source connection string memory storage buffer (*ConnectOut*).

DriverCompletion

Specifies when the ODBC Driver Manager or driver is to display the ODBC connection information dialog used to prompt the user for additional connection information. This parameter must be set to one of the following values:

▪ **SQL_DRIVER_PROMPT**
The ODBC connection information dialog is always displayed. Information from both the connection string and the data source specification in the system information storage area (either the [ODBC] section of ODBC.INI file or the ODBC subkey in the registry) is used for initial values, which can be overridden or supplemented by data input via the ODBC connection dialog.

- **SQL_DRIVER_COMPLETE**

  The ODBC connection information dialog is displayed only if there is not enough information in the connection string provided to establish a connection to the specified data source. Information from the connection string is used as initial values, which can be overridden or supplemented by data input via the ODBC connection dialog.

- **SQL_DRIVER_COMPLETE_REQUIRED**

  The ODBC connection information dialog is displayed only if there is not enough mandatory information in the connection string provided to establish a connection to the specified data source. Information from the connection string is used as initial values, which can be overridden or supplemented by data input via the ODBC connection dialog. The end user is only prompted for mandatory information; controls for information that is not required to connect to the specified data source are disabled.

- **SQL_DRIVER_NOPROMPT**

  The ODBC connection information dialog is not displayed and the user is not prompted for connection information. The ODBC Driver Manager attempts to establish a connection to the specified data source, using the connection string provided. If there is not enough information in the connection string to establish a connection to the specified data source, **SQL_ERROR** is returned.

Description   The `SQLDriverConnect()` function is used as an alternative to the `SQLConnect()` function to establish a connection to a specified data source. Both functions are used to establish a connection to a specific data source, but the `SQLDriverConnect()` function provides the following additional capabilities:

- It allows an application to establish a connection to a data source by using a connection string containing the data source name, one or more user IDs, one or more corresponding passwords, and any other information that is needed by the data source.

- It allows an application to establish a connection to a data source by using a partial connection string or no additional information; in which case, the ODBC Driver Manager and the driver can each prompt the user for additional connection information.

- It allows an application to establish a connection to a data source that is not defined in the system information storage area. If the application supplies a partial connection string, the driver can prompt the user for any required connection information.

- It allows an application to establish a connection to a file data source by using a connection string constructed from the information stored in a .DSN (file data source) file.

Once a connection is established by the `SQLDriverConnect()` function, the complete connection string used to connect to the data source is returned to the calling application. The application can store this string and use it later if it needs to make subsequent connections to the same data source (for a given user ID).

Return Codes   `SQL_SUCCESS`, `SQL_SUCCESS_WITH_INFO`, `SQL_NO_DATA`, `SQL_NO_DATA_FOUND` (ODBC 2.0 or earlier driver), `SQL_INVALID_HANDLE`, or `SQL_ERROR`

SQLSTATEs   If this function returns `SQL_SUCCESS_WITH_INFO` or `SQL_ERROR`, one of the following SQLSTATE values may be obtained by calling the `SQLGetDiagRec()` function (ODBC 3.x driver) or the `SQLError()` function (ODBC 2.0 or earlier driver):

ODBC 3.X
01000, 01004, 01S00, 01S02, 01S08, 01S09*, 08001, 08002*, 08004, 08S01, 28000, HY000, HY001, HY013, HY090*, HY092*, HY110*, HYC00, HYT00, HYT01, IM001*, IM002*, IM003*, IM004*, IM005*, IM006*, IM007, IM008, IM009, IM010*, IM011*, IM012*, IM014*, or IM015*

ODBC 2.0 OR EARLIER
01000, **01**004, **01**S00, **08**001, **08**002*, **08**004, **08**S01, **28**000, **IM**001*,
IM002*, **IM**003*, **IM**004*, **IM**005*, **IM**006*, **IM**007, **IM**008*, **IM**009,
IM010*, **IM**011*, **IM**012*, **S1**000, **S1**001, **S1**090*, **S1**110*, or **S1**T00
* Returned by the ODBC Driver Manager.

Unless noted otherwise, each of these SQLSTATE values are returned by the data source driver. Refer to Appendix B for detailed information about each SQLSTATE value that can be returned by the ODBC Driver Manager or by a data source driver.

Comments

▨ Applications should allocate at least 1,024 bytes of memory for the buffer in which this function is to store the complete connection string used to connect to the data source (*ConnectOut*).

▨ If the complete connection string used is a Unicode string, the *ConnectOutMaxSize* parameter must contain an even number.

▨ If the complete connection string's actual length is greater than or equal to the maximum string size value specified in the *ConnectOutMaxSize* parameter, the complete connection string is truncated to *ConnectOutMaxSize*–1 (the length of a null-termination character) characters.

▨ The connection string stored in the *ConnectIn* parameter must have the following format:

```
keyword=attribute; ...
```

or

```
DRIVER=<[>attribute<]>; ...
```

The **keyword=attribute** combination can be any of the following:

▨ **DSN=Data Source Name**—Specifies the name of a data source, as returned by the **SQLDataSources()** function or the data sources child-dialog of the ODBC connection information dialog.

▨ **UID=User ID**—Specifies the user ID (authorization name) of the user attempting to establish the connection.

▨ **PWD=Password**—Specifies the password corresponding to the user ID (authorization name) specified. If a password is not required for the specified user ID, an empty password string should be used (**PWD=;**).

- **FILEDSN=.DSN_File Name**—Specifies the name of a .DSN file that should be used to build the connection string needed to connect to a file data source. This file contains a set of keywords and their corresponding attribute values.

- **DRIVER=Driver Name**—Specifies the name of a driver, as returned by the **SQLDrivers()** function.

- **SAVEFILE=.DSN File_Name**—Specifies the name of a .DSN file in which all **keyword=attribute** combinations are used to make the current, successful connection to a data source are to be saved.

The connection string may also include any number of driver-defined keywords and their corresponding attribute values.

- Attribute values containing the characters [] {} () , ; ? * = ! and @ should be avoided.

- Data source names cannot contain leading spaces (blanks) or the backslash (\ ) character. Likewise, data source names can not consist only of spaces.

- Applications do not have to add braces ([ ]) around the attribute value provided for the **DRIVER** keyword unless the attribute value itself contains a semicolon (;), in which case the braces are required.

- The **DRIVER** keyword was introduced in ODBC 2.0 and it is not supported by ODBC 1.0 drivers.

- The **FILEDSN** and **SAVEFILE** keywords were introduced in ODBC 3.0 and are not supported by ODBC 2.0 or earlier drivers.

- If any **keyword=attribute** combination is repeated in the connection string, the driver uses the attribute value associated with the first occurrence of the keyword.

- The **DSN** keyword and the **DRIVER** keyword are mutually exclusive; if both are used in the same connection string, the ODBC Driver Manager and the driver use whichever keyword appears first—the keyword appearing second is ignored.

- The **DSN** keyword and the **FILEDSN** keyword are mutually exclusive; if both are used in the same connection string, the ODBC Driver Manager and the driver use whichever keyword appears first—the keyword appearing second is ignored.

- The default directory used for loading or saving a .DSN file is a combination of the path specified by the CommonFileDir registry key stored in HKEY_LOCAL_MACHINE\SOFTWARE\Microsoft\ Windows\CurrentVersion and ODBC\DataSources. (For example:

if the CommonFileDir registry key contained the value C:\Program Files\Common Files, the default directory would be C:\Program Files\Common Files\ODBC\Data Sources.)

- If any keyword is used in conjunction with the **FILEDSN** keyword, the attribute value assigned to the keyword in the connection string is used instead of the attribute value assigned to the same keyword in the .DSN file specified.

- The **SAVEFILE** keyword must be used in conjunction with the **DRIVER** keyword, the **FILEDSN** keyword, or both. Otherwise, **SQL_SUCCESS_WITH_INFO** and SQLSTATE **01S09** (Invalid keyword.) will be returned. Also, the **SAVEFILE** keyword must appear before the **DRIVER** keyword in the connection string, or the results will be undefined.

- An application can connect to more than one data source at the same time, however only one connection can be current at one time.

- If a default translation library has been defined for the specified data source (in the system information storage area), the driver automatically connects to it. A different translation library can be loaded by calling the **SQLSetConnectAttr()** function with the **SQL_ATTR_TRANSLATE_LIB** attribute specified (ODBC 3.x driver) or the **SQLSetConnectOption()** function with the **SQL_TRANSLATE_LIB** option specified (ODBC 2.0 or earlier driver). A translation option within the loaded library can be changed by calling the **SQLSetConnectAttr()** function with the **SQL_ATTR_TRANSLATE_OPTION** attribute specified (ODBC 3.x driver) or the **SQLSetConnectOption()** function with the **SQL_TRANSLATE_OPTION** option specified (ODBC 2.0 or earlier driver).

- The **PWD** keyword and its corresponding attribute value is not stored in a .DSN file.

- The following restrictions apply when this function is used to connect to a pooled connection:

  - No connection pooling processing is performed when the **SAVEFILE** keyword is specified in the connection string.

  - If connection pooling is enabled, this function can only be called with the *DriverCompletion* parameter set to **SQL_DRIVER_NOPROMPT**; if the *DriverCompletion* parameter is set to any other value, **SQL_ERROR** and SQLSTATE **HY**110 (Invalid driver completion) is returned.

Prerequisites   A connection handle must be allocated with the `SQLAllocHandle()` function (ODBC 3.x driver) or the `SQLAllocConnect()` function (ODBC 2.0 or earlier driver) before this function is called.

Restrictions   There are no restrictions associated with this function call.

See Also   `SQLAllocHandle()`, `SQLAllocConnect()`, `SQLConnect()`, `SQLBrowseConnect()`, `SQLDisconnect()`

Example   The following Visual C++ program illustrates how to establish a connection to a data source using the `SQLDriverConnect()` function.

```
/*-----------------------------------------------------------------*/
/* NAME:     CH7EX3.CPP                                            */
/* PURPOSE: Illustrate How To Use The Following ODBC API Function */
/*          In A C++ Program:                                     */
/*                                                                */
/*              SQLDriverConnect()                                */
/*                                                                */
/* OTHER ODBC APIs SHOWN:                                         */
/*          SQLAllocHandle()         SQLSetEnvAttr()              */
/*          SQLDisconnect()          SQLFreeHandle()              */
/*                                                                */
/*-----------------------------------------------------------------*/

// Include The Appropriate Header Files
#include <windows.h>
#include <sql.h>
#include <sqlext.h>
#include <iostream.h>

// Define The ODBC_Class Class
class ODBC_Class
{
    // Attributes
    public:
        SQLHANDLE      EnvHandle;
        SQLHANDLE      ConHandle;
        SQLRETURN      rc;

    // Operations
    public:
        ODBC_Class();                              // Constructor
        ~ODBC_Class();                             // Destructor
};

// Define The Class Constructor
ODBC_Class::ODBC_Class()
```

```
{
    // Initialize The Return Code Variable
    rc = SQL_SUCCESS;

    // Allocate An Environment Handle
    rc = SQLAllocHandle(SQL_HANDLE_ENV, SQL_NULL_HANDLE, &EnvHandle);

    // Set The ODBC Application Version To 3.x
    if (rc == SQL_SUCCESS)
        rc = SQLSetEnvAttr(EnvHandle, SQL_ATTR_ODBC_VERSION,
                    (SQLPOINTER) SQL_OV_ODBC3, SQL_IS_UINTEGER);

    // Allocate A Connection Handle
    if (rc == SQL_SUCCESS)
        rc = SQLAllocHandle(SQL_HANDLE_DBC, EnvHandle, &ConHandle);
}

// Define The Class Destructor
ODBC_Class::~ODBC_Class()
{
    // Free The Connection Handle
    if (ConHandle != NULL)
        SQLFreeHandle(SQL_HANDLE_DBC, ConHandle);

    // Free The Environment Handle
    if (EnvHandle != NULL)
        SQLFreeHandle(SQL_HANDLE_ENV, EnvHandle);
}

/*————————————————————————————————————————————*/
/* The Main Function                                          */
/*————————————————————————————————————————————*/
int main()
{
    // Declare The Local Memory Variables
    SQLRETURN    rc = SQL_SUCCESS;
    SQLCHAR      ConnectIn[30];

    // Create An Instance Of The ODBC_Class Class
    ODBC_Class   Example;

    // Build A Connection String
    strcpy((char*) ConnectIn, "DSN=Northwind;UID=\"\";PWD=\"\";");

    // Connect To The Northwind Sample Database - If Successful,
    // Display An Appropriate Message
    if (Example.ConHandle != NULL)
    {
```

```
    rc = SQLDriverConnect(Example.ConHandle, NULL, ConnectIn,
             SQL_NTS, NULL, 0, NULL, SQL_DRIVER_NOPROMPT);

    if (rc == SQL_SUCCESS || rc == SQL_SUCCESS_WITH_INFO)
        cout << "Connected to Northwind database." << endl;

    // Disconnect From The Northwind Sample Database
    rc = SQLDisconnect(Example.ConHandle);
}

// Return To The Operating System
return(rc);
}
```

SQLBrowseConsnect

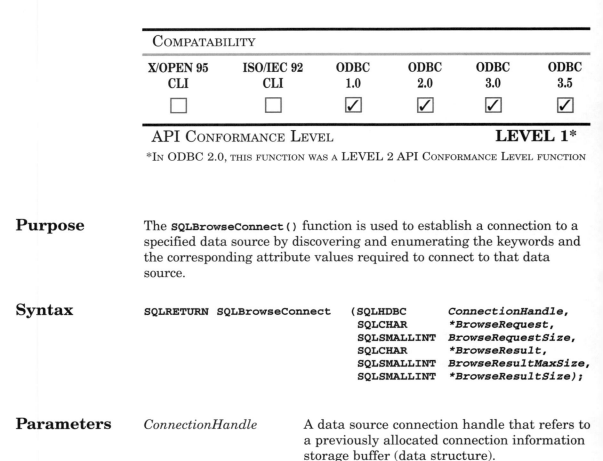

COMPATABILITY					
X/OPEN 95 CLI	ISO/IEC 92 CLI	ODBC 1.0	ODBC 2.0	ODBC 3.0	ODBC 3.5
☐	☐	☑	☑	☑	☑

API CONFORMANCE LEVEL   **LEVEL 1***

*IN ODBC 2.0, THIS FUNCTION WAS A LEVEL 2 API CONFORMANCE LEVEL FUNCTION

Purpose   The SQLBrowseConnect() function is used to establish a connection to a specified data source by discovering and enumerating the keywords and the corresponding attribute values required to connect to that data source.

Syntax
```
SQLRETURN SQLBrowseConnect   (SQLHDBC      ConnectionHandle,
                              SQLCHAR      *BrowseRequest,
                              SQLSMALLINT  BrowseRequestSize,
                              SQLCHAR      *BrowseResult,
                              SQLSMALLINT  BrowseResultMaxSize,
                              SQLSMALLINT  *BrowseResultSize);
```

Parameters   *ConnectionHandle*   A data source connection handle that refers to a previously allocated connection information storage buffer (data structure).

BrowseRequest	A pointer to a location in memory where a browse request connection string is stored. This string is used to pass one or more values needed for a connection request to the specified data source for processing.
BrowseRequestSize	The length of the browse request connection string value stored in the *BrowseRequest* parameter.
BrowseResult	A pointer to a location in memory where this function is to store the browse result connection string—provided additional information is needed in order to establish a connection to the specified data source.
BrowseResultMaxSize	The maximum size of the memory storage buffer where this function is to store the browse result connection string.
BrowseResultSize	A pointer to a location in memory where this function is to store the actual number of bytes written to the browse result connection string memory storage buffer (*BrowseResult*).

Description

The **SQLBrowseConnect()** function is used to establish a connection to a specified data source by discovering and enumerating the keywords and their corresponding attribute values that are required to connect to that data source.

The first time the **SQLBrowseConnect()** function is called, the browse request connection string specified in the *BrowseRequest* parameter must contain either the **DSN** keyword or the **DRIVER** keyword along with a corresponding attribute value. Depending upon which of these keywords is stored in the browse request connection string, the following takes place:

- If the browse request connection string contains the **DSN** keyword, the Driver Manager tries to locate a corresponding data source specification in the system information storage area (either the [ODBC] section of ODBC.INI file or the ODBC subkey in the registry).

- If the Driver Manager finds the corresponding data source specification, it loads the associated driver; the driver can then retrieve information about the data source from the system information storage area.

■ If the Driver Manager cannot find the corresponding data source specification in the system information storage area, it locates the default data source specification and loads the associated driver; the driver can retrieve information about the default data source from the system information storage area. "DEFAULT" is passed to the driver as the attribute value for the **DSN** keyword.

■ If the Driver Manager cannot find the corresponding data source specification and if there is no default data source specification, the Driver Manager returns **SQL_ERROR** with SQLSTATE **IM**002 (Data source name not found and no default driver specified) to the calling application.

■ If the browse request connection string contains the **DRIVER** keyword, the Driver Manager loads the specified driver without attempting to locate a data source in the system information storage area.

After the appropriate driver is loaded, an attempt to connect to its underlying data source is made. If additional connection attributes are required (but were not provided in the browse request connection string), the driver returns **SQL_NEED_DATA** to the application and a connection string identifying the next connection attribute (or set of attributes) needed is stored in the browse result connection string memory storage buffer (*BrowseResult*).

The application uses the contents of the browse result connection string returned to build the browse request connection string for the next call to the **SQLBrowseConnect()** function. All mandatory attributes (those not preceded by an asterisk) identified in the browse result connection string must be included in the next **SQLBrowseConnect()** function call. When all connection attributes have been enumerated, the driver returns **SQL_SUCCESS**, a connection to the data source is established and the complete connection string used to connect to the data source is returned to the calling application. The application can store this string and use it later if it needs to make subsequent connections to the same data source (for a given user ID)—the complete connection string can be used with the **SQLDriverConnect()** function to establish another connection, however it cannot be used in another call to the **SQLBrowseConnect()** function. If **SQLBrowseConnect()** is called after it returns **SQL_SUCCESS**, the entire sequence of calls must be repeated.

Return Codes   SQL_SUCCESS, SQL_SUCCESS_WITH_INFO, SQL_NEED_DATA, SQL_INVALID_HANDLE, or SQL_ERROR

SQLSTATEs

If this function returns **SQL_SUCCESS_WITH_INFO**, **SQL_NEED_DATA**, or **SQL_ERROR**, one of the following SQLSTATE values may be obtained by calling the **SQLGetDiagRec()** function (ODBC 3.x driver) or the **SQLError()** function (ODBC 2.0 or earlier driver):

ODBC 3.X
01000, **01**004, **01**S00, **01**S02, **08**001, **08**002*, **08**004, **08**S01, **28**000, **HY**000, **HY**001*, **HY**013, **HY**090*, **HYT**00, **HYT**01, **IM**001*, **IM**002*, **IM**003*, **IM**004*, **IM**005*, **IM**006*, **IM**009, **IM**010*, **IM**011*, or **IM**012*

ODBC 2.0 OR EARLIER
01000, **01**004, **01**S00, **08**001, **08**002*, **08**004, **08**S01, **28**000, **IM**001*, **IM**002*, **IM**003*, **IM**004*, **IM**005*, **IM**006*, **IM**009, **IM**010*, **IM**011*, **IM**012*, **S1**000, **S1**001*, **S1**090*, or **S1**T00
* Returned by the ODBC Driver Manager.

Unless noted otherwise, each of these SQLSTATE values are returned by the data source driver. Refer to Appendix B for detailed information about each SQLSTATE value that can be returned by the ODBC Driver Manager or by a data source driver.

Comments

▪ Applications should allocate at least 1,024 bytes of memory for the buffer in which this function is to store the browse result connection string and the complete connection string used to connect to the data source (*BrowseResult*).

▪ If the browse result/complete connection string's actual length is greater than or equal to the maximum string size value specified in the *BrowseResultMaxSize* parameter, the browse result/complete connection string is truncated to *BrowseResultMaxSize*–1 (the length of a null-termination character) characters.

▪ The browse request connection string stored in the *BrowseRequest* parameter must have the following format:

    keyword=attribute; ...

or

    DRIVER=<[>attribute<]>; ...

The **keyword=attribute** combination can be any of the following:

▪ **DSN=Data Source Name**—Specifies the name of a data source, as returned by the **SQLDataSources()** function or the data sources child-dialog of the ODBC connection dialog.

▪ **UID=User ID**—Specifies the user ID (authorization name) of the user attempting to establish the connection.

▣ **PWD=Password**—Specifies the password that corresponds to the user ID (authorization name) specified. If a password is not required for the specified user ID, an empty password string should be used (**PWD=;**).

▣ **DRIVER=Driver Name**—Specifies the name of a driver, as returned by the **SQLDrivers()** function.

The browse request connection string may also include any number of driver-defined keywords and their corresponding attribute values.

▣ The **DRIVER** keyword was introduced in ODBC 2.0 and it is not supported by ODBC 1.0 drivers.

▣ If any **keyword=attribute** combination is repeated in the browse request connection string, the driver uses the attribute value associated with the first occurrence of the keyword.

▣ The **DSN** keyword and the **DRIVER** keyword are mutually exclusive; if both are used in the same browse request connection string, the ODBC Driver Manager and the driver use whichever keyword appears first—the keyword that appears second is ignored.

▣ The browse result connection string stored in the *BrowseResult* parameter should be used according to the following semantic rules:

▣ If an asterisk (*) precedes a **keyword=attribute** combination, the attribute is optional and may be omitted in the next **SQLBrowseConnect()** function call.

▣ A driver-defined keyword names the kind of attribute for which an attribute value may be supplied (for example, **HOST**, **SERVER**, **DATABASE**, **DBMS**).

▣ ODBC-defined keywords and driver-defined keywords include a localized (user-friendly) version of the keyword (for example, "Host," "Server," "Database Name," "Database Management System"). However, the keyword itself, not the description, must be used in the browse request string that is passed back to the driver.

▣ An attribute value list may be included with ODBC-defined keywords and driver-defined keywords. An attribute value list is an enumeration of actual values that are valid for the corresponding attribute keyword (for example, it may be a list of server names or database names). Attribute value lists are enclosed in curly braces ({ }).

▣ If an attribute keyword is followed by a single question mark (?), a single value corresponds to the attribute keyword.

▣ Each call to **SQLBrowseConnect()** returns only the attribute information needed to satisfy the next level of the connection process. The driver associates connection state information with the connection handle so that the context can always be determined on each function call.

■ Attribute values containing the characters [] {} () , ; ? * = ! and @ should be avoided.

■ Data source names cannot contain leading spaces (blanks) or the backslash (\ ) character. Likewise, data source names can not consist only of spaces.

■ Applications using ODBC 3.x drivers do not have to add braces ([ ]) around the attribute value provided for the **DRIVER** keyword unless the attribute itself contains a semicolon (;), in which case the braces are required. Applications using ODBC 2.0 drivers are required to add braces around the attribute value provided for the **DRIVER** keyword.

■ This function does not support connection pooling—If **SQLBrowseConnect()** is called while connection pooling is enabled, **SQL_ERROR** and SQLSTATE **HY**000 (General error) is returned.

■ An application cannot use the contents of previous browse result connection strings to build the current browse request connection string. That is, it cannot specify different values for attributes that were set in previous levels.

■ This function also returns **SQL_NEED_DATA** if recoverable, nonfatal errors occurred during the browse process (for example, if an invalid password or attribute keyword was supplied by the application). When **SQL_NEED_DATA** is returned and the browse result connection string is unchanged, an error has occurred and the application can call the **SQLGetDiagRec()** function (ODBC 3.x drivers) or the **SQLError()** function (ODBC 2.0 or earlier drivers) to return SQLSTATE information about browse-time errors. This permits an application to correct the attribute value and continue the browse connect.

■ An application can terminate the browse process at any time by calling the **SQLDisconnect()** function.

■ If this function returns **SQL_ERROR**, outstanding connections are terminated and the connection handle specified is returned to the "Unconnected" state.

Prerequisites   A connection handle must be allocated with the `SQLAllocHandle()`
                    function (ODBC 3.x driver) or the `SQLAllocConnect()` function (ODBC
                    2.0 or earlier driver) before this function is called.

Restrictions   There are no restrictions associated with this function call.

See Also   `SQLAllocHandle()`, `SQLAllocConnect()`, `SQLConnect()`,
                    `SQLDriverConnect()`, `SQLDisconnect()`

Example   The following Visual C++ program illustrates how to establish a
                    connection to a data source using the `SQLBrowseConnect()` function.

```
/*————————————————————————————————————————————————————*/
/* NAME:     CH7EX4.CPP                                                  */
/* PURPOSE: Illustrate How To Use The Following ODBC API Function */
/*          In A C++ Program:                                            */
/*                                                                       */
/*               SQLBrowseConnect()                                      */
/*                                                                       */
/* OTHER ODBC APIs SHOWN:                                                */
/*          SQLAllocHandle()        SQLSetEnvAttr()                      */
/*          SQLDisconnect()         SQLFreeHandle()                      */
/*                                                                       */
/*————————————————————————————————————————————————————*/

// Include The Appropriate Header Files
#include <windows.h>
#include <sql.h>
#include <sqlext.h>
#include <iostream.h>

// Define The ODBC_Class Class
class ODBC_Class
{
    // Attributes
    public:
        SQLHANDLE       EnvHandle;
        SQLHANDLE       ConHandle;
        SQLRETURN       rc;

    // Operations
    public:
        ODBC_Class();                               // Constructor
        ~ODBC_Class();                              // Destructor
};

// Define The Class Constructor
ODBC_Class::ODBC_Class()
{
    // Initialize The Return Code Variable
    rc = SQL_SUCCESS;
```

```
    // Allocate An Environment Handle
    rc = SQLAllocHandle(SQL_HANDLE_ENV, SQL_NULL_HANDLE, &EnvHandle);

    // Set The ODBC Application Version To 3.x
    if (rc == SQL_SUCCESS)
        rc = SQLSetEnvAttr(EnvHandle, SQL_ATTR_ODBC_VERSION,
                (SQLPOINTER) SQL_OV_ODBC3, SQL_IS_UINTEGER);

    // Allocate A Connection Handle
    if (rc == SQL_SUCCESS)
        rc = SQLAllocHandle(SQL_HANDLE_DBC, EnvHandle, &ConHandle);
}

// Define The Class Destructor
ODBC_Class::~ODBC_Class()
{
    // Free The Connection Handle
    if (ConHandle != NULL)
        SQLFreeHandle(SQL_HANDLE_DBC, ConHandle);

    // Free The Environment Handle
    if (EnvHandle != NULL)
        SQLFreeHandle(SQL_HANDLE_ENV, EnvHandle);
}

/*———————————————————————————————————————————————————— */
/* The Main Function                                     */
/*———————————————————————————————————————————————————— */
int main()
{
    // Declare The Local Memory Variables
    SQLRETURN      rc = SQL_NEED_DATA;
    SQLCHAR        BrowseRequest[1024];
    SQLCHAR        BrowseResult[1024];
    SQLSMALLINT    BrowseResultLen;

    // Create An Instance Of The ODBC_Class Class
    ODBC_Class     Example;

    // Build The Initial Connection String
    strcpy((char *) BrowseRequest, "DRIVER={SQL Server};");

    // Connect To The SQL Server Sample Database - If Successful,
    // Display An Appropriate Message
    if (Example.ConHandle != NULL)
    {
        while (rc == SQL_NEED_DATA)
        {
            // Initiate The Browse Connect Request
            rc = SQLBrowseConnect(Example.ConHandle, BrowseRequest,
                    SQL_NTS, BrowseResult, sizeof(BrowseResult),
                    &BrowseResultLen);

            // If More Connection Information Is Needed ..
            if (rc == SQL_NEED_DATA)
```

```
                    {
                         // Display The Next Request
                         cout << BrowseResult << endl << endl;

                         /*─────────────────────────────────────*/
                         /* The First Time Through This Loop, The Following */
                         /* Might Be Displayed:                  */
                         /*                                      */
                         /*   SERVER:Server={server1,server2,server3}; */
                         /*   UID:Login ID=?;PWD:Password=?;*APP:AppName=?; */
                         /*   *WSID:WorkStation ID=?;            */
                         /*                                      */
                         /* The Second Time Through, The Following Might Be */
                         /* Displayed:                           */
                         /*                                      */
                         /*   *DATABASE:Database={master,model,SAMPLE}; */
                         /*   *LANGUAGE:Language={us_english,Francais}; */
                         /*                                      */
                         /*─────────────────────────────────────*/

                         // Prompt The User For The Next Portion Of The
                         // Connection String
                         cin >> BrowseRequest;

                         /*─────────────────────────────────────*/
                         /* The First Time Through This Loop, The User */
                         /* Response Might Be:                   */
                         /*                                      */
                         /*   SERVER=server1;UID=userid;PWD=password; */
                         /*                                      */
                         /* The Second Time Through, The User Response */
                         /* Might Be:                            */
                         /*                                      */
                         /*   DATABASE=SAMPLE;                   */
                         /*                                      */
                         /*─────────────────────────────────────*/
                    }
               }

          // If Successful, Print A Success Message And The Connection
          // String Used
          if (rc == SQL_SUCCESS || rc == SQL_SUCCESS_WITH_INFO)
          {
               cout << "Connected to SQL Server Database." << endl << endl;
               cout << "Connection String Used : " << BrowseResult << endl;
          }

          // Disconnect From The SQL Server Sample Database
          rc = SQLDisconnect(Example.ConHandle);
     }

     // Return To The Operating System
     return(rc);
}
```

SQLDisconnect

COMPATABILITY

X/OPEN 95 CLI	ISO/IEC 92 CLI	ODBC 1.0	ODBC 2.0	ODBC 3.0	ODBC 3.5
✓	✓	✓	✓	✓	✓

API CONFORMANCE LEVEL   **CORE**

Purpose   The SQLDisconnect() function is used to close the data source connection associated with a specific connection handle.

Syntax   SQLRETURN   SQLDisconnect   (SQLHDBC   *ConnectionHandle*);

Parameters *ConnectionHandle*   A data source connection handle that refers to a previously allocated connection information storage buffer (data structure).

Description The SQLDisconnect() function is used to close the data source connection associated with a specific connection handle. If an application calls the SQLDisconnect() function before it has freed all SQL statement handles associated with the specified connection handle, the driver automatically frees them, along with any descriptor handles that were implicitly or explicitly allocated for the connection, after it successfully disconnects from the data source, provided none of the SQL statements associated with the connection are still executing asynchronously. When this function is called, the connection handle itself remains valid and the SQLConnect(), SQLDriverConnect(), or SQLBrowseConnect() function can be called again to establish a connection to another data source or to reestablish a connection to the same data source.

Return Codes SQL_SUCCESS, SQL_SUCCESS_WITH_INFO, SQL_INVALID_HANDLE, or SQL_ERROR

SQLSTATE   If this function returns SQL_SUCCESS_WITH_INFO or SQL_ERROR, one of the following SQLSTATE values may be obtained by calling the SQLGetDiagRec() function (ODBC 3.x driver) or the SQLError() function (ODBC 2.0 or earlier driver):

ODBC 3.X

01000, **01**002, **08**003*, **25**000, **HY**000, **HY**001, **HY**010*, **HY**013, **HYT**01, or **IM**001*

ODBC 2.0 OR EARLIER

01000, **01**002, **08**003*, **25**000, **IM**001*, **S1**000, **S1**001, or **S1**010*

* Returned by the ODBC Driver Manager.

Unless noted otherwise, each of these SQLSTATE values are returned by the data source driver. Refer to Appendix B for detailed information about each SQLSTATE value that can be returned by the ODBC Driver Manager or by a data source driver.

Comments

▨ If this function is called while one or more SQL statements associated with the specified connection handle are still executing asynchronously, **SQL_ERROR** is returned along with SQLSTATE **HY**010 (ODBC 3.x driver) or SQLSTATE **S1**010 (ODBC 2.0 or earlier driver).

▨ If this function is called while there is an incomplete transaction associated with the specified connection handle, **SQL_ERROR** is returned along with SQLSTATE **25**000 (all drivers) and the transaction remains unchanged and open. An incomplete transaction is a transaction that has not been committed or rolled back.

▨ If this function is called after the **SQLBrowseConnect()** function returns **SQL_NEED_DATA** and before it returns a different return code, the browse connect process is terminated and the connection is returned to the "Unconnected" state.

▨ If connection pooling is enabled and this function is called to terminate a connection that is part of a shared environment, the connection is returned to the connection pool and remains available to other components that are using the same shared environment.

Prerequisites

All outstanding transactions associated with the specified data source connection must be terminated with the **SQLEndTran()** function (ODBC 3.x driver) or the **SQLTransact()** function (ODBC 2.0 or earlier driver) before this function is called.

Restrictions

There are no restrictions associated with this function call.

See Also   `SQLConnect()`, `SQLDriverConnect()`, `SQLBrowseConnect()`, `SQLEndTran()`, `SQLTransact()`

Example   See the examples provided for the `SQLConnect()` function, on page 153, the `SQLDriverConnect()` function on page 156, and the `SQLBrowseConnect()` function on page 165.

SQLFreeHandle

COMPATABILITY

X/OPEN 95 CLI	ISO/IEC 92 CLI	ODBC 1.0	ODBC 2.0	ODBC 3.0	ODBC 3.5
☑	☑	☐	☐	☑	☑

API CONFORMANCE LEVEL   **CORE**

Purpose   The `SQLFreeHandle()` function is used to release an environment, connection, statement, or descriptor handle and free all memory associated with it.

Syntax
```
SQLRETURN   SQLFreeHandle   (SQLSMALLINT   HandleType,
                             SQLHANDLE     Handle);
```

Parameters   *HandleType*   Specifies the type of handle that the memory to be freed is associated with. This parameter must contain one of the following values:

▨ `SQL_HANDLE_ENV`   Free memory associated with an environment handle.

▨ `SQL_HANDLE_DBC`   Free memory associated with a connection handle.

▨ `SQL_HANDLE_STMT`   Free memory associated with an SQL statement handle.

■ **SQL_HANDLES_DESC** Free memory associated with a descriptor handle.

Handle An environment, connection, statement, or descriptor handle that refers to a previously allocated environment, connection, statement, or descriptor information storage buffer (data structure).

Description The **SQLFreeHandle()** function is used to release an environment, connection, statement, or descriptor handle and free memory associated with it.

To free an environment handle, an application calls this function with the *HandleType* parameter set to **SQL_HANDLE_ENV** and the *Handle* parameter set to a previously allocated environment handle.

To free a connection handle, an application calls this function with the *HandleType* parameter set to **SQL_HANDLE_DBC** and the *Handle* parameter set to a previously allocated connection handle.

To free a SQL statement handle, an application calls this function with the *HandleType* parameter set to **SQL_HANDLE_STMT** and the *Handle* parameter set to a previously allocated SQL statement handle.

To free a descriptor handle, an application calls this function with the *HandleType* parameter set to **SQL_HANDLE_DESC** and the *Handle* parameter set to a previously allocated descriptor handle.

*NOTE: In ODBC 3.x, this function replaces the ODBC 2.0 functions **SQLFreeEnv()** (for freeing environment handles), **SQLFreeConnect()** (for freeing connection handles), and **SQLFreeStmt()** (for freeing SQL statement handles with the **SQL_DROP** option specified).*

Return Codes SQL_SUCCESS, SQL_INVALID_HANDLE, or SQL_ERROR

SQLSTATEs If this function returns **SQL_ERROR**, one of the following SQLSTATE values may be obtained by calling the **SQLGetDiagRec()** function:

HY000, **HY**001, **HY**010*, **HY**013, **HY**017*, **HYT**01, or **IM**001*

* Returned by the ODBC Driver Manager.

Unless noted otherwise, each of these SQLSTATE values are returned by the data source driver. Refer to Appendix B for detailed information about each SQLSTATE value that can be returned by the ODBC Driver Manager or by a data source driver.

Comments

- Descriptors were introduced in ODBC 3.0, and they are not supported by ODBC 2.0 (or earlier) drivers. Therefore, when working with an ODBC 2.0 (or earlier) driver, this function cannot be used to free a descriptor handle.

- The Driver Manager does not check the validity of a handle when it is used in an ODBC API function call. Therefore, an application should not use a handle once it has been freed.

- If **SQL_ERROR** is returned when this function is called, the handle that was supposed to be freed remains valid.

- If a shared environment is being used, the application calling this function to free an environment handle no longer has access to the environment once this function is executed. However, the environment's resources are not necessarily freed at that time. In a shared environment, each time this function is called to free an environment handle, the environment reference count maintained by the Driver Manager is decremented by 1. As long as the reference count does not equal 0, the shared environment is not freed because it is still being used by another component. However, when the reference count equals 0, the shared environment's resources are freed.

- When an application frees a connection handle, all SQL statements and descriptors that are open on the specified connection are dropped.

- When an application frees an SQL statement handle that has results pending, the pending results are discarded.

- When an application frees an SQL statement handle, the driver automatically frees all implicitly allocated descriptors associated with that handle.

- When an application frees an explicitly allocated descriptor handle, memory being referenced by a pointer field of a result data set's column attribute (that is, the **SQL_DESC_DATA_PTR**, **SQL_DESC_INDICATOR_PTR**, and **SQL_DESC_OCTET_LENGTH_PTR** fields) is not released. Otherwise, all memory allocated by the driver for column attribute fields of a result data set is freed when the descriptor handle is freed.

- When an explicitly allocated descriptor handle is freed, all statements the freed handle had been associated with revert to their respective implicitly allocated descriptor handles.

- When the Driver Manager processes this function with the *HandleType* parameter set to **SQL_HANDLE_ENV** and the *Handle* parameter set to **SQL_NULL_HANDLE**, it checks the TraceAutoStop keyword in the ODBC section of the system information storage area (either the [ODBC] section of ODBC.INI file or the ODBC subkey in the registry) and, if its value is set to 1, the Driver Manager disables tracing for all applications on a computer running Windows 95, Windows NT Server, or Windows NT Workstation and it sets the value of the **Trace** keyword in the ODBC section of the system information storage area to 0.

Prerequisites   An application must free all connection handles associated with an environment handle before this function is called to free an environment handle. Otherwise, **SQL_ERROR** is returned and the environment handle and any active connection handles associated with it remain valid.

The **SQLDisconnect()** function must be called to terminate any connection that might be associated with the connection handle specified before this function is called to free a connection handle. Otherwise, **SQL_ERROR** is returned and the connection handle remains valid.

Restrictions   This function cannot be used to free an implicitly allocated descriptor.

See Also   SQLAllocHandle(), SQLAllocEnv(), SQLAllocConnect(), SQLFreeEnv(), SQLFreeConnect()

Example   See the example provided for the **SQLAllocHandle()** function on page <<insert final page number here>>.

SQLFreeConnect

COMPATABILITY					
X/OPEN 95 CLI	ISO/IEC 92 CLI	ODBC 1.0	ODBC 2.0	ODBC 3.0	ODBC 3.5
✗	✓	✓	✓	☐	☐

API CONFORMANCE LEVEL   **CORE**

Purpose   The **SQLFreeConnect()** function is used to release a data source connection handle and free all memory associated with it.

Syntax   RETCODE SQLFreeConnect   (HDBC   *ConnectionHandle*);

Parameters   *ConnectionHandle*   A data source connection handle that refers to a previously allocated connection information storage buffer (data structure).

Description   The SQLFreeConnect() function is used to invalidate and free a specified data source connection handle. Whenever a data source connection handle is freed, all resources associated with that connection handle are also freed. When an application frees a connection handle, all SQL statements that are open on a specified connection are dropped.

> **NOTE:**   *In ODBC 3.x, this function has been replaced by the* SQLFreeHandle() *function.*

Return Codes   SQL_SUCCESS, SQL_SUCCESS_WITH_INFO, SQL_INVALID_HANDLE, or SQL_ERROR

SQLSTATEs   If this function returns SQL_SUCCESS_WITH_INFO or SQL_ERROR, one of the following SQLSTATE values may be obtained by calling the SQLError() function:

01000, **08**S01, **S1**000, or **S1**010*

* Returned by the ODBC Driver Manager.

Unless noted otherwise, each of these SQLSTATE values are returned by the data source driver. Refer to Appendix B for detailed information about each SQLSTATE value that can be returned by the ODBC Driver Manager or by a data source driver.

Comments   ▦ If this function is called while a data source connection still exists for the connection handle specified, SQL_ERROR is returned and the specified connection handle remains valid.

Prerequisites   The SQLDisconnect() function must be called to terminate any connection that might be associated with the connection handle specified before this function is called.

Restrictions   There are no restrictions associated with this function call.

See Also   SQLDisconnect(), SQLFreeHandle()

Example   See the example provided for the **SQLAllocEnv()** function on page 147.

SQLFreeEnv

COMPATABILITY

X/OPEN 95 CLI	ISO/IEC 92 CLI	ODBC 1.0	ODBC 2.0	ODBC 3.0	ODBC 3.5
☒	☑	☑	☑	☐	☐

API CONFORMANCE LEVEL   **CORE**

Purpose   The **SQLFreeEnv()** function is used to release an environment handle and free all memory associated with it.

Syntax   RETCODE   SQLFreeEnv   (HENV   *EnvironmentHandle*);

Parameters   *EnvironmentHandle*   An environment handle that refers to a previously allocated environment information storage buffer (data structure).

Description   The **SQLFreeEnv()** function is used to invalidate and free an environment handle. When an environment handle is freed, all resources associated with that environment handle are also freed. This function call is the last ODBC API function call that an application working with an ODBC 2.0 (or earlier) driver should make before it terminates and returns control to the operating system.

NOTE: In ODBC 3.x, this function has been replaced by the **SQLFreeHandle()** *function.*

Return Codes   SQL_SUCCESS, SQL_SUCCESS_WITH_INFO, SQL_INVALID_HANDLE, or SQL_ERROR

SQLSTATEs   If this function returns **SQL_SUCCESS_WITH_INFO** or **SQL_ERROR**, one of the following SQLSTATE values may be obtained by calling the **SQLError()** function.

01000, **S1**000, or **S1**010*

* Returned by the ODBC Driver Manager.

Unless noted otherwise, each of these SQLSTATE values are returned by the data source driver. Refer to Appendix B for detailed information about each SQLSTATE value that can be returned by the ODBC Driver Manager or by a data source driver.

Comments   ■ If this function is called while an active connection handle exists for the environment handle specified, **SQL_ERROR** is returned and the environment handle and all active connection handles associated with it remain valid.

■ When the Driver Manager processes this function, it checks the TraceAutoStop keyword in the ODBC section of the system information storage area (either the [ODBC] section of ODBC.INI file or the ODBC subkey in the registry), and if its value is set to 1, the Driver Manager disables tracing for the all applications on a computer running Windows 95, Windows NT Server, or Windows NT Workstation and it sets the value of the **Trace** keyword in the ODBC section of the system information storage area to 0.

Prerequisites   The **SQLFreeConnect()** function must be called (one or more times) to free every active connection handle associated with the environment handle specified before this function is called.

Restrictions   There are no restrictions associated with this function call.

See Also   **SQLFreeHandle()**, **SQLFreeConnect()**

Example   See the example provided for the **SQLAllocEnv()** function on page 147.

8

Determining and Controlling Data Source and Driver Capabilities

All data sources and drivers are not created equal. Because of this, ODBC provides several API functions that can be used to obtain detailed information about, and to a lesser extent, control the capabilities of a particular data source or driver. This chapter is designed to introduce you to these API functions. The first part of this chapter introduces the set of functions that can be used to determine what data sources and drivers are available. This is followed by a brief discussion about the functions that can be used to determine exactly what functionality a data source or driver provides (and what functionality it doesn't provide).

Next, the functions used to obtain or change the values of different driver attributes (options) that control environment, connection, and SQL statement processing are described. Finally, a detailed reference section covering each ODBC API function that can be used to obtain information about or control a data source or driver's capabilities is provided.

Finding Out What Data Sources and/or Drivers Are Available

When an application is designed to work with only one or two specific data sources or drivers, information about those data source(s) or driver(s) is usually hard-coded directly into the application. This is often the case with custom and vertical applications—these types of applications typically only work with one or two data sources of which a predefined schema is already known. Applications that are more generic in design often allow the user to select and use a data source or driver at run time. This type of application usually provides the user with a list of available data sources and/or drivers and allows them to select the ones they want to work with—whether the list contains data sources, drivers, or both often depends on how the application is designed.

A list of available data sources can be obtained in one of two ways.

1. An application can call the **SQLDriverConnect()** function with a connection string that contains the DSN keyword and no associated value. In this case the ODBC Driver Manager connection information dialog is displayed along with a list of available data source names.

2. An application can call the **SQLDataSources()** function to retrieve a list of available data source names (and corresponding descriptions) one at a time. This function is implemented by the ODBC Driver Manager; therefore, it can be called before any drivers are loaded.

An application can call the **SQLDrivers()** function to retrieve a list of available drivers, one at a time. The **SQLDrivers()** function also returns a list of file extensions each file-based driver recognizes (for example, a dBASE ODBC driver would recognize the .DBF extension) along with information that indicates whether the files are treated as tables or as databases. Because this function is also implemented by the Driver Manager, it can be called before any drivers are loaded.

Applications that work with file-based drivers may choose to allow the user to select a file name as opposed to a data source name—because users often know that their data is stored in a particular file, it is easier for them to choose a file instead of a corresponding (and possibly unknown) data source name. Using this approach, an application can construct a dialog box that prompts the user to choose a file from a list of files that is generated using the extensions returned by the **SQLDrivers()** function. Then, after a user has selected a file, the application can connect directly to the driver by calling the **SQLDriverConnect()** function with a connection string that contains the **DRIVER=DriverName** keyword/value pair.

Obtaining Information About a Data Source or Driver

Because an ODBC application can connect to a variety of data sources and drivers, it needs to be able to obtain information about the data source or driver it is connected to. By design, all drivers must provide three specific ODBC API functions that provide information about the capabilities of the driver itself and the capabilities of the driver's underlying data source. By knowing the capabilities and limitations of a particular data source or driver, an application can adjust its behavior accordingly without having to incorporate tremendous amounts of conditional code that evaluates every available data source.

The first of these three functions, the **SQLGetInfo()** function, can be used to obtain information about the various characteristics of a data source or driver. Of the three functions, this one is probably the most powerful—over 165 different pieces of information can be obtained (for example, a data source or driver's API and SQL grammar conformance levels, the driver's version number, and functionality capabilities (such as the ability to support transactions), just to name a few).

The second of these functions, the **SQLGetFunctions()** function, tells an application whether a particular ODBC API function is supported by a data source or driver. An application can use this function to find out whether a particular ODBC API function is supported, or it can tell this function to return a list of all ODBC API functions available, along with flags that indicate specifying whether each function in the list is supported.

The last function, the **SQLGetTypeInfo()** function, provides an application with information about the native data types used by the data source associated with a driver. When this function is called, the driver builds a result data set of which each row describes a single data type recognized by the underlying data source. If the underlying data source does not support user-defined data types, the driver usually keeps the native data type information in a data structure that is returned to the application when the **SQLGetTypeInfo()** function is called. However, if the underlying data source uses an extensible data type system (that is, it supports user-defined data types), the driver must query the underlying data source before it can return native data types to the calling application.

Retrieving and Setting Driver Attributes (Options)

All the information returned about a data source or driver by the **SQLGetInfo()**, **SQLGetFunctions()**, and **SQLGetTypeInfo()** functions is static—that is it can not be changed by an application. Most drivers also contain dynamic information about their capabilities, which can be changed to meet an application's needs. Each individual piece of dynamic driver information is classified as one of the following:

- An Environment attribute
- A Connection attribute (option)
- An SQL statement attribute (option)

These classifications are used to identify the behavior that each piece of dynamic information affects.

Environment Attributes

Environment attributes (or options) affect the behavior of ODBC API functions that operate under a specified environment. An application can retrieve the value of an environment attribute at any time by calling the **SQLGetEnvAttr()** function and it can set an environment attribute by calling the **SQLSetEnvAttr()** function. Environment attributes can be changed as long as no connection handle has been allocated for the environment.

DECLARING THE APPLICATION'S ODBC VERSION   An application is not required to set most environment attributes because all attributes have a default value. However, an application must always set the **SQL_ATTR_ODBC_VERSION** environment attribute immediately after an environment handle is allocated. This attribute tells the ODBC Driver Manager that the application follows either the ODBC 3.x specification or the ODBC 2.0 (or earlier) specification when using the following items:

■ SQLSTATEs—Many SQLSTATE values are different between ODBC 2.0 and ODBC 3.x. Also, more SQLSTATEs can be returned for API functions that are working with ODBC 3.x drivers.

■ Date, Time, and Timestamp Type Identifiers—Date, Time, and Timestamp SQL and C data type identifiers are different between ODBC 2.0 and ODBC 3.x. Table 8–1 shows the date, time, and timestamp data type identifiers for both versions.

■ *CatalogName* argument in the **SQLTables()** function—In ODBC 2.0, wild card characters ('%' and '_') used in the *CatalogName* argument of the **SQLTables()** ODBC API function are treated

Table 8–1   *The Date, Time, and Timestamp Type Identifiers Used by ODBC 2.0 and ODBC 3.x*

ODBC 2.0	OCBC 3.x
SQL Type Identifiers	
SQL_DATE	SQL_TYPE_DATE
SQL_TIME	SQL_TYPE_TIME
SQL_TIMESTAMP	SQL_TYPE_TIMESTAMP
C Type Identifiers	
SQL_C_DATE	SQL_C_TYPE_DATE
SQL_C_TIME	SQL_C_TYPE_TIME
SQL_C_TIMESTAMP	SQL_C_TYPE_TIMESTAMP

Adapted from table on page 92 of *Microsoft ODBC 3.0 Software Development Kit & Programmer's Reference.*

literally. In ODBC 3.x, they are treated as wild cards. Thus, an application that follows the ODBC 2.0 specification cannot use these characters as wild card characters in the *CatalogName* argument of the **SQLTables()** function.

The ODBC 3.x Driver Manager and ODBC 3.x drivers check the version of the ODBC specification to which an application is written and respond accordingly. For example, if an application following the ODBC 2.0 specification calls the **SQLExecute()** function before calling the **SQLPrepare()** function, the ODBC 3.x Driver Manager returns SQLSTATE **S1**010 (Function sequence error). If same application follows the ODBC 3.x specification, the Driver Manager returns SQLSTATE **HY**010 (Function sequence error).

Connection Attributes

Connection attributes (or options) affect the behavior of data source and driver connections. An application can retrieve the value of a connection attribute at any time by calling either the **SQLGetConnectAttr()** function (ODBC 3.x) or the **SQLGetConnectOption()** function (ODBC 2.0 or earlier), and it can set a connection attribute by calling either the **SQLSetConnectAttr()** function (ODBC 3.x) or the **SQLSetConnectOption()** function (ODBC 2.0 or earlier). If the **SQLSetConnectAttr()** function or the **SQLSetConnectOption()** is called before a driver is loaded, the ODBC Driver Manager stores the attributes in its connection structure and sets them in the driver during the connection process. An application is not required to set any connection attribute—all connection attributes have default values, some of which are driver specific.

Timing becomes a very important element when setting connection attributes because:

- some connection attributes can be set any time after the connection handle is allocated.

- some connection attributes can be set after the connection handle is allocated, but not after the actual connection to the data source is established.

- some connection attributes can only be set after the connection handle is allocated and the connection to the data source is established.

- some connection attributes can only be set after the connection handle is allocated and the connection to the data source is established and only when there are no outstanding transactions or open cursors on the connection.

For example, the login timeout (**SQL_ATTR_LOGIN_TIMEOUT**) attribute applies to the connection process and is effective only if it is set before a connection is established. Likewise, the attribute that specifies whether the ODBC cursor library is to be used (**SQL_ATTR_ODBC_CURSORS**) must be set before a connection is established. That's because the ODBC cursor library resides between the Driver Manager and the driver; therefore, it must be loaded before the driver.

The **SQLSetConnectAttr()** function and the **SQLSetConnectOption()** function can also be used to set statement attributes (options) for all statement handles currently associated with a data source connection, as well as for all future statement handles to be allocated under the same connection handle.

SQL Statement Attributes

SQL statement attributes (or options) affect the behavior of ODBC API functions executed using a specific SQL statement handle. An application can retrieve the value of an SQL statement attribute at any time by calling either the **SQLGetStmtAttr()** function (ODBC 3.x) or the **SQLGetStmtOption()** function (ODBC 2.0 or earlier) and it can set an SQL statement attribute by calling either the **SQLSetStmtAttr()** function (ODBC 3.x) or the **SQLSetStmtOption()** function (ODBC 2.0 or earlier). As with connection attributes, timing becomes a very important element when setting SQL statement attributes:

■ The **SQL_ATTR_CONCURRENCY, SQL_ATTR_CURSOR_TYPE, SQL_ATTR_SIMULATE_CURSOR**, and **SQL_ATTR_USE_BOOKMARKS** statement attributes must be set before the SQL statement associated with the statement handle is executed.

■ The **SQL_ATTR_ASYNC_ENABLE** and **SQL_ATTR_NOSCAN** statement attributes can be set at any time but are not applied until the SQL statement associated with the statement handle is used again.

■ The **SQL_ATTR_MAX_LENGTH, SQL_ATTR_MAX_ROWS**, and **SQL_ATTR_ QUERY_TIMEOUT** statement attributes can be set at any time, but it is driver-specific whether they are applied before the SQL statement associated with the statement handle is used again.

■ All other statement attributes can be set at any time.

An application is not required to set any SQL statement attribute because all attributes have a default value.

NOTE: *In ODBC 2.0 and earlier, some SQL statement attributes could be set at the connection level. However, this was changed in ODBC 3.0—ODBC 3.x applications should never set SQL statement attributes at the connection level. The only exception to this rule are the* **SQL_ATTR_METADATA_ID** *and* **SQL_ATTR_ ASYNC_ENABLE** *attributes, which are both connection attributes and statement attributes, and can be set at either the connection level or the statement level.*

The ODBC Data Source/Driver Information and Attribute Control Functions

Table 8–2 lists the ODBC API functions used to obtain information about available data sources and drivers and to set environment, connection, and SQL statement processing attributes (options).

Each of these functions are described, in detail, in the remaining portion of this chapter.

Table 8–2 The ODBC Data Source/Driver Information and Attribute Control Functions

Function Name	Description
SQLDataSources()	Generates a list of data sources to which an application can connect.
SQLDrivers()	Generates a list of drivers to which an application can connect.
SQLGetInfo()	Retrieves information about a specific driver and its underlying data source.
SQLGetFunctions()	Retrieves information about whether a specific ODBC API function is supported by a driver (and its underlying data source).
SQLGetTypeInfo()	Retrieves information about the native data types supported by a data source.
SQLGetEnvAttr()	Retrieves the current value of a specific environment attribute (option).

Table 8–2 The ODBC Data Source/Driver Information and Attribute Control Functions (Continued)

Function Name	Description
SQLSetEnvAttr()	Changes the value of a specific environment attribute (option).
SQLGetConnectAttr()	Retrieves the current value of a specific data source connection attribute (option).
SQLSetConnectAttr()	Changes the value of a specific data source connection attribute (option).
SQLGetConnectOption()	Retrieves the current value of a specific data source connection attribute (option).
SQLSetConnectOption()	Changes the value of a specific data source connection attribute (option).
SQLGetStmtAttr()	Retrieves the current value of a specific SQL statement attribute (option).
SQLSetStmtAttr()	Changes the value of a specific SQL statement attribute (option).
SQLGetStmtOption()	Retrieves the current value of a specific SQL statement attribute (option).
SQLSetStmtOption()	Changes the value of a specific SQL statement attribute (option).

SQLDataSources

COMPATABILITY

X/OPEN 95 CLI	ISO/IEC 92 CLI	ODBC 1.0	ODBC 2.0	ODBC 3.0	ODBC 3.5
✓	✓	✓	✓	✓	✓

API CONFORMANCE LEVEL   **CORE***

*IN ODBC 2.0, THIS FUNCTION WAS A LEVEL 2 API CONFORMANCE LEVEL FUNCTION

Purpose
The `SQLDataSources()` function is used to obtain information about one or more data sources that are available for an application to connect to.

Syntax

```
SQLRETURN   SQLDataSources   (SQLHENV          EnvironmentHandle,
                              SQLUSMALLINT     Selection,
                              SQLCHAR          *DSName,
                              SQLSMALLINT      DSNameMaxSize,
                              SQLSMALLINT      *DSNameSize,
                              SQLCHAR          *Description,
                              SQLSMALLINT      DescriptionMaxSize,
                              SQLSMALLINT      *DescriptionSize);
```

Parameters

EnvironmentHandle   An environment handle that refers to a previously allocated environment information storage buffer (data structure).

Selection   Specifies which data source, among a list of data sources, this function is to retrieve information for. This parameter must be set to one of the following values:

▨ **SQL_FETCH_FIRST**
Retrieve information about the first user and/or system data source in the list.

▨ **SQL_FETCH_NEXT**
Retrieve information about the next user and/or system data source in the list.

■ **SQL_FETCH_FIRST_USER**
Retrieve information about the first user data source in the list.

■ **SQL_FETCH_FIRST_SYSTEM**
Retrieve information about the first system data source in the list.

DSName	A pointer to a location in memory where this function is to store the data source name retrieved.
DSNameMaxSize	The maximum size of the memory storage buffer where this function is to store the data source name retrieved.
DSNameSize	A pointer to a location in memory where this function is to store the actual number of bytes written to the data source name memory storage buffer (*DSName*).
Description	A pointer to a location in memory where this function is to store the description of the driver that is associated with the data source name retrieved.
DescriptionMaxSize	The maximum size of the memory storage buffer where this function is to store the data source description retrieved.
DescriptionSize	A pointer to a location in memory where this function is to store the actual number of bytes written to the driver description memory storage buffer (*Description*).

Description   The **SQLDataSources()** function is used to produce a list of data source (database) names that an application can connect to. The ODBC Driver Manager retrieves this information from the system information storage area (either the [ODBC] section of the ODBC.INI file or the ODBC subkey in the registry). Because this function is implemented in the ODBC Driver Manager, it is supported for all drivers regardless of the driver's standards compliance level. However, each driver determines how a particular data source name is mapped to an actual data source.

Return Codes `SQL_SUCCESS`, `SQL_SUCCESS_WITH_INFO`, `SQL_NO_DATA`, `SQL_NO_DATA_FOUND` (ODBC 2.0 or earlier driver), `SQL_INVALID_HANDLE`, or `SQL_ERROR`

SQLSTATEs If this function returns `SQL_SUCCESS_WITH_INFO` or `SQL_ERROR`, one of the following SQLSTATE values may be obtained by calling the `SQLGetDiagRec()` function (ODBC 3.x driver) or the `SQLError()` function (ODBC 2.0 or earlier driver):

ODBC 3.X
01000*, **01**004*, **HY**000*, **HY**001*, **HY**013, **HY**090*, or **HY**103*

ODBC 2.0 OR EARLIER
01000*, **01**004*, **S1**000*, **S1**001*, **S1**090*, or **S1**103*

* Returned by the ODBC Driver Manager.

Unless noted otherwise, each of these SQLSTATE values are returned by the data source driver. Refer to Appendix B for detailed information about each SQLSTATE value that can be returned by the ODBC Driver Manager or by a data source driver.

Comments ▣ If the server name string's actual length is greater than or equal to the maximum string size value specified in the *DSNameMaxSize* parameter, the server name string is truncated to *DSNameMaxSize*–1 (the length of a NULL-termination character) characters.

▣ If the driver description string's actual length is greater than or equal to the maximum string size value specified in the *DescriptionMaxSize* parameter, the description is truncated to *DescriptionMaxSize*–1 (the length of a NULL-termination character) characters.

▣ When this function is called with the *Selection* parameter set to `SQL_FETCH_FIRST`, subsequent calls to this function with the *Selection* parameter set to `SQL_FETCH_NEXT` return both user and system data source names.

▣ When this function is called with the *Selection* parameter set to `SQL_FETCH_FIRST_USER`, all subsequent calls to this function with the *Selection* parameter set to `SQL_FETCH_NEXT` return only user data source names.

▣ When this function is called with the *Selection* parameter set to `SQL_FETCH_FIRST_SYSTEM,` all subsequent calls to this function with the *Selection* parameter set to **SQL_FETCH_NEXT** return only system data source names.

■ If the *Selection* parameter is set to **SQL_FETCH_NEXT**, the first time this function is called the first data source name found is returned.

■ This function is usually called before a connection to a data source is established.

■ An application can call this function multiple times to retrieve all data source names available.

■ If this function is called when there are no more data source names to be retrieved, **SQL_NO_DATA** (ODBC 3.x drivers) or **SQL_NO_DATA_FOUND** (ODBC 2.0 or earlier drivers) is returned by the ODBC Driver Manager. If this function is called with the *Selection* parameter set to **SQL_FETCH_NEXT** immediately after it returns **SQL_NO_DATA** or **SQL_NO_DATA_FOUND**, the first data source name in the list will be returned.

■ The *Selection* parameter values **SQL_FETCH_FIRST_USER** and **SQL_FETCH_FIRST_SYSTEM** are not recognized by X/Open 95- and ISO/IEC 92-compliant drivers.

■ The list of data sources returned by this function may not contain all the data sources an application can connect to. Furthermore, there is no guarantee that an application can successfully connect to a data source that is returned by this function; for example, a data source may require authentication information the application does not provide.

Prerequisites

There are no prerequisites for using this function call.

Restrictions

There are no restrictions associated with this function call.

See Also

SQLDrivers(), **SQLConnect()**, **SQLDriverConnect()**, **SQLBrowseConnect()**

Example

The following Visual C++ program illustrates how the **SQLDataSources()** function can be used to produce a list of data sources that an application can connect to.

```
/*------------------------------------------------------------------*/
/* NAME:      CH8EX1.CPP                                            */
/* PURPOSE: Illustrate How To Use The Following ODBC API Function   */
/*          In A C++ Program:                                       */
/*                                                                  */
/*              SQLDataSources()                                    */
```

```
/*                                                                      */
/*  OTHER ODBC APIs SHOWN:                                              */
/*          SQLAllocHandle()              SQLSetEnvAttr()               */
/*          SQLFreeHandle()                                             */
/*                                                                      */
/*─────────────────────────────────────────────────────────────────────*/

// Include The Appropriate Header Files
#include <windows.h>
#include <sql.h>
#include <sqlext.h>
#include <iostream.h>

// Define The ODBC_Class Class
class ODBC_Class
{
    // Attributes
    public:
        SQLHANDLE    EnvHandle;
        SQLRETURN    rc;

    // Operations
    public:
        ODBC_Class();                                  // Constructor
        ~ODBC_Class();                                 // Destructor
        SQLRETURN    ShowDataSources();
};

// Define The Class Constructor
ODBC_Class::ODBC_Class()
{
    // Initialize The Return Code Variable
    rc = SQL_SUCCESS;

    // Allocate An Environment Handle
    rc = SQLAllocHandle(SQL_HANDLE_ENV, SQL_NULL_HANDLE, &EnvHandle);

    // Set The ODBC Application Version To 3.x
    if (rc == SQL_SUCCESS)
        rc = SQLSetEnvAttr(EnvHandle, SQL_ATTR_ODBC_VERSION,
                (SQLPOINTER) SQL_OV_ODBC3, SQL_IS_UINTEGER);
}

// Define The Class Destructor
ODBC_Class::~ODBC_Class()
{
    // Free The Environment Handle
    if (EnvHandle != NULL)
        SQLFreeHandle(SQL_HANDLE_ENV, EnvHandle);
}

// Define The ShowDataSources() Member Function
SQLRETURN ODBC_Class::ShowDataSources()
{
```

```
    // Declare The Local Memory Variables
    SQLCHAR        DataSource[31];
    SQLCHAR        Description[255];
    SQLSMALLINT    DS_Size;
    SQLSMALLINT    DescSize;

    // Print The Information Header
    cout.setf(ios::left);
    cout.width(24);
    cout << "Data Source" << "Description (Comment)" << endl;
    for (int i = 0; i < 60; i++)
        cout << "-";
    cout << endl;

    // List All ODBC Data Sources Available
    while (rc != SQL_NO_DATA)
    {
        // Retrieve A Data Source Name
        rc = SQLDataSources(EnvHandle, SQL_FETCH_NEXT, DataSource,
                sizeof(DataSource), &DS_Size, Description,
                sizeof(Description), &DescSize);

        // Print The Data Source Name Retrieved
        if (rc != SQL_NO_DATA)
        {
            cout.setf(ios::left);
            cout.width(24);
            cout << DataSource << Description << endl;
        }
    }

    // Return The ODBC API Return Code To The Calling Function
    if (rc == SQL_NO_DATA)
        rc = SQL_SUCCESS;
    return(rc);
}

/*------------------------------------------------------------*/
/* The Main Function                                          */
/*------------------------------------------------------------*/
int main()
{
    // Declare The Local Memory Variables
    SQLRETURN   rc = SQL_SUCCESS;

    // Create An Instance Of The ODBC_Class Class
    ODBC_Class  Example;

    // List The Data Sources That Are Available To The Application
    rc = Example.ShowDataSources();

    // Return To The Operating System
    return(rc);
}
```

SQLDrivers

COMPATABILITY

X/OPEN 95 CLI	ISO/IEC 92 CLI	ODBC 1.0	ODBC 2.0	ODBC 3.0	ODBC 3.5
☐	☐	☑	☑	☑	☑

API CONFORMANCE LEVEL   CORE*

*IN ODBC 2.0, THIS FUNCTION WAS A LEVEL 2 API CONFORMANCE LEVEL FUNCTION

Purpose   The **SQLDrivers()** function is used to obtain information about one or more drivers that are available for an application to connect to.

Syntax

```
SQLRETURN SQLDrivers    (SQLHENV        EnvironmentHandle,
                         SQLUSMALLINT   Selection,
                         SQLCHAR        *Description,
                         SQLSMALLINT    DescriptionMaxSize,
                         SQLSMALLINT    *DescriptionSize,
                         SQLCHAR        *Attributes,
                         SQLSMALLINT    AttributesMaxSize,
                         SQLSMALLINT    *AttributesSize);
```

Parameters

EnvironmentHandle   An environment handle that refers to a previously allocated environment information storage buffer (data structure).

Selection   Specifies which driver, from a list of drivers, this function is to retrieve information for. This parameter must be set to one of the following values:

■ **SQL_FETCH_FIRST**
Retrieve information about the first driver in the list.

■ **SQL_FETCH_NEXT**
Retrieve information about the next driver in the list.

Description   A pointer to a location in memory where this function is to store the driver description information retrieved.

DescriptionMaxSize	The maximum size of the memory storage buffer where this function is to store the driver description retrieved.
DescriptionSize	A pointer to a location in memory where this function is to store the actual number of bytes written to the driver description memory storage buffer (*Description*).
Attributes	A pointer to a location in memory where this function is to store the driver attribute information retrieved.
AttributesMaxSize	The maximum size of the memory storage buffer where this function is to store the driver attribute information retrieved.
AttributesSize	A pointer to a location in memory where this function is to store the actual number of bytes written to the driver attributes memory storage buffer (*Attributes*).

Description

The **SQLDrivers()** function is used to obtain information about one or more drivers sources that an application can connect to. Along with the description of a particular driver, this function returns additional information about the driver in a list of keyword/value pairs. All keywords listed in the system information storage area (either the [ODBC] section of the ODBC.INI file or the ODBC subkey in the registry) for drivers is returned **for all drivers**, except for the **CreateDSN** keyword, which is used to prompt creation of data sources, and therefore is optional. Each keyword/value pair is terminated with a NULL byte, and the entire list is terminated with a NULL byte (that is, two NULL bytes mark the end of the list). For example, a file-based driver using C syntax might return the following list of attributes (**\0** represents a NULL character):

```
FileUsage=1\0FileExtns=*.dbf\0\0
```

Because **SQLDrivers()** is implemented in the ODBC Driver Manager, it is supported for all drivers regardless of the driver's standards compliance level.

Return Codes

SQL_SUCCESS, SQL_SUCCESS_WITH_INFO, SQL_NO_DATA, SQL_NO_DATA_FOUND (ODBC 2.0 or earlier driver), SQL_INVALID_HANDLE, or SQL_ERROR

SQLSTATEs

If this function returns **SQL_SUCCESS_WITH_INFO** or **SQL_ERROR**, one of the following SQLSTATE values may be obtained by calling the **SQLGetDiagRec()** function (ODBC 3.x driver) or the **SQLError()** function (ODBC 2.0 or earlier driver):

ODBC 3.X DRIVER
01000*, **01**004*, **HY**000, **HY**001*, **HY**013, **HY**090*, or **HY**103*

ODBC 2.0 OR EARLIER DRIVER
01000*, **01**004*, **S1**000*, **S1**001*, **S1**090*, or **S1**103*

* Returned by the ODBC Driver Manager.

Unless noted otherwise, each of these SQLSTATE values are returned by the data source driver. Refer to Appendix B for detailed information about each SQLSTATE value that can be returned by the ODBC Driver Manager or by a data source driver.

Comments

- If the driver description string's actual length is greater than or equal to the maximum string size value specified in the *DescriptionMaxSize* parameter, the description is truncated to *DescriptionMaxSize*–1 (the length of a NULL-termination character) characters.

- If the driver attributes string's actual length is greater than or equal to the maximum string size value specified in the *AttributesMaxSize* parameter, the attributes string is truncated to *AttributesMaxSize*–1 (the length of a NULL-termination character) characters and **SQL_SUCCESS_WITH_INFO**, along with SQLSTATE **01**004 (Data Truncated) is returned.

- If the driver attributes string is a Unicode string, the *AttributesMaxSize* parameter must contain an even number.

- Driver attribute keywords and their corresponding values are added to the system information storage area when a driver is installed.

- When this function is called with the Selection parameter set to **SQL_FETCH_FIRST**, subsequent calls to this function with the *Selection* parameter set to **SQL_FETCH_NEXT** returns all driver names.

- If the *Selection* parameter is set to **SQL_FETCH_NEXT** the first time this function is called, the first driver name found is returned.

- An application can call this function multiple times to retrieve information about all drivers available.

- If this function is called when there is no more driver information to be retrieved, **SQL_NO_DATA** (ODBC 3.x drivers) or **SQL_NO_DATA_**

FOUND (ODBC 2.0 or earlier drivers) is returned by the ODBC Driver Manager. If this function is called with the *Selection* parameter set to SQL_FETCH_NEXT immediately after it returns SQL_NO_DATA or SQL_NO_DATA_FOUND, it returns information about the first driver found will be returned.

Prerequisites   There are no prerequisites for using this function call.

Restrictions   There are no restrictions associated with this function call.

See Also   SQLDataSources(), SQLConnect(), SQLDriverConnect(), SQLBrowseConnect()

Example   The following Visual C++ program illustrates how the SQLDrivers() function can be used to produce a list of drivers that an application can connect to.

```
/*———————————————————————————————————*/
/* NAME:     CH8EX2.CPP                                    */
/* PURPOSE: Illustrate How To Use The Following ODBC API Function */
/*          In A C++ Program:                              */
/*                                                         */
/*               SQLDrivers()                              */
/*                                                         */
/* OTHER ODBC APIs SHOWN:                                  */
/*          SQLAllocHandle()           SQLSetEnvAttr()     */
/*          SQLFreeHandle()                                */
/*                                                         */
/*———————————————————————————————————*/

// Include The Appropriate Header Files
#include <windows.h>
#include <sql.h>
#include <sqlext.h>
#include <iostream.h>

// Define The ODBC_Class Class
class ODBC_Class
{
    // Attributes
    public:
        SQLHANDLE   EnvHandle;
        SQLRETURN   rc;

    // Operations
    public:
        ODBC_Class();                   // Constructor
        ~ODBC_Class();                  // Destructor
```

```
        SQLRETURN   ShowDrivers();
};

// Define The Class Constructor
ODBC_Class::ODBC_Class()
{
    // Initialize The Return Code Variable
    rc = SQL_SUCCESS;

    // Allocate An Environment Handle
    rc = SQLAllocHandle(SQL_HANDLE_ENV, SQL_NULL_HANDLE, &EnvHandle);

    // Set The ODBC Application Version To 3.x
    if (rc == SQL_SUCCESS)
        rc = SQLSetEnvAttr(EnvHandle, SQL_ATTR_ODBC_VERSION,
                (SQLPOINTER) SQL_OV_ODBC3, SQL_IS_UINTEGER);
}

// Define The Class Destructor
ODBC_Class::~ODBC_Class()
{
    // Free The Environment Handle
    if (EnvHandle != NULL)
        SQLFreeHandle(SQL_HANDLE_ENV, EnvHandle);
}

// Define The ShowDrivers() Member Function
SQLRETURN ODBC_Class::ShowDrivers()
{
    // Declare The Local Memory Variables
    SQLCHAR       DriverDesc[255];
    SQLCHAR       Attributes[255];
    SQLSMALLINT   DescSize;
    SQLSMALLINT   AttrSize;
    int           i, j;
    SQLCHAR       Value[50];

    // List All ODBC Data Sources Available
    while (rc != SQL_NO_DATA)
    {
        // Retrieve Information About A Driver
        rc = SQLDrivers(EnvHandle, SQL_FETCH_NEXT, DriverDesc,
                sizeof(DriverDesc), &DescSize, Attributes,
                sizeof(Attributes), &AttrSize);

        // Print The Driver Description
        if (rc != SQL_NO_DATA)
            cout << <DriverDesc << endl << <endl;

        // Parse And Print The Driver Attributes
        if (rc != SQL_NO_DATA)
            for (i = 0, j = 0; i << AttrSize; i++, j++)
            {
                Value[j] = Attributes[i];
```

```
            if (Attributes[i] == '\0')
            {
                cout << "  " << Value << endl;
                j = 0;
            }
        }
    cout << endl;
    }

    // Return The ODBC API Return Code To The Calling Function
    if (rc == SQL_NO_DATA)
        rc = SQL_SUCCESS;
    return(rc);
}

/*—————————————————————————————————————————————*/
/* The Main Function                                              */
/*—————————————————————————————————————————————*/
int main()
{
    // Declare The Local Memory Variables
    SQLRETURN  rc = SQL_SUCCESS;

    // Create An Instance Of The ODBC_Class Class
    ODBC_Class  Example;

    // List The Drivers That Are Available To The Application
    rc = Example.ShowDrivers();

    // Return To The Operating System
    return(rc);
}
```

SQLGetInfo

COMPATABILITY					
X/OPEN 95 CLI	ISO/IEC 92 CLI	ODBC 1.0	ODBC 2.0	ODBC 3.0	ODBC 3.5
✓	✓	✓	✓	✓	✓

API CONFORMANCE LEVEL	CORE*

*IN ODBC 2.0, THIS FUNCTION WAS A LEVEL 1 API CONFORMANCE LEVEL FUNCTION

Purpose   The **SQLGetInfo()** function is used to retrieve general information about the driver (and its underlying data source) an application is currently connected to.

Syntax

```
SQLRETURN SQLGetInfo   (SQLHDBC        ConnectionHandle,
                        SQLUSMALLINT   InfoType,
                        SQLPOINTER     InfoValue,
                        SQLSMALLINT    InfoValueMaxSize,
                        SQLSMALLINT    *InfoValueSize);
```

Parameters   *ConnectionHandle*   A data source connection handle that refers to a previously allocated connection information storage buffer (data structure).

InfoType   A value that identifies the type of data source information to be retrieved. This parameter must be set to one of the values shown in Appendix C.

InfoValue   A pointer to a location in memory where this function is to store the information retrieved from the driver/data source. Depending on the type of information being retrieved, the following can be returned:

- an **SQLUSMALLINT** value
- an **SQLUINTEGER** bitmask
- an **SQLUINTEGER** flag
- an **SQLUINTEGER** binary value
- a NULL-terminated character string

InfoValueMaxSize   The maximum size of the memory storage buffer where this function is to store the driver/data source information retrieved.

InfoValueSize   A pointer to a location in memory where this function is to store the actual number of bytes written to the driver/data source information memory storage buffer (*InfoValue*). If the value returned in the driver/data source information memory storage buffer is not a NULL-terminated string, or if a NULL pointer is specified in the *InfoValue* parameter, this parameter is ignored.

Description   The **SQLGetInfo()** function is used to retrieve general information about the driver and data source an application is currently connected to. Appendix C alphabetically lists each value that can be specified for the *InfoType* parameter along with a description of the information returned for that value when this function is executed.

To take advantage of different data sources, more information type values may be defined in future releases of ODBC. In fact, a range of information types (0 to 999) has been reserved by ODBC to allow for future expansion. In addition, ODBC driver developers are required to reserve values for their own driver-specific use from X/Open.

Return Code   **SQL_SUCCESS, SQL_SUCCESS_WITH_INFO, SQL_INVALID_HANDLE,** or **SQL_ERROR**

SQLSTATEs   If this function returns **SQL_SUCCESS_WITH_INFO** or **SQL_ERROR**, one of the following SQLSTATE values may be obtained by calling the **SQLGetDiagRec()** function (ODBC 3.x driver) or the **SQLError()** function (ODBC 2.0 or earlier driver):

ODBC 3.X
01000, **01**004, **08**003*, **08**S01, **HY**000, **HY**001, **HY**013, **HY**024*, **HY**090*, **HY**096, **HY**C00, **HY**T01 or **IM**001*

ODBC 2.0 OR EARLIER
01000, **01**004, **08**003*, **22**003, **IM**001*, **S1**000, **S1**001, **S1**009*, **S1**090*, **S1**096*, **S1**C00, or **S1**T00

* Returned by the ODBC Driver Manager.

Unless noted otherwise, each of these SQLSTATE values are returned by the data source driver. Refer to Appendix B for detailed information about each SQLSTATE value that can be returned by the ODBC Driver Manager or by a data source driver.

Comments   ■ If **SQL_DRIVER_HDESC** or **SQL_DRIVER_HSTMT** is specified in the *InfoType* parameter, the *InfoValue* parameter is treated as both an input and an output parameter for this function. (See the **SQL_DRIVER_HDESC** and/or the **SQL_DRIVER_HSTMT** description in Appendix C for more information.)

■ If the value returned for the information type specified in the *InfoType* parameter is a string, and if that string's actual length is greater than or equal to the maximum string size value specified in the *InfoValueMaxSize* parameter, the value will be truncated to *InfoValueMaxSize–1* (the length of a NULL-termination character) characters.

■ If the value returned for the information type specified in the *InfoType* parameter is a Unicode string, the *InfoValueMaxSize* parameter must contain an even number.

■ If the value returned to the *InfoValue* buffer is not a character string, or if *InfoValue* is a NULL pointer, the *InfoValueMaxSize* parameter is ignored. In this case, the driver assumes that the size of *InfoValue* is **SQLUSMALLINT** or **SQLUINTEGER**, based on the *InfoType* specified.

■ If an information type specified in the *InfoType* parameter is in the range reserved for use by ODBC but is not defined by the version of ODBC the driver being used supports, this function returns SQLSTATE **HY**096 (Invalid argument value). To determine what version of ODBC a driver conforms to, an application can call this function with the **SQL_DRIVER_ODBC_VER** information type specified.

■ If an information type specified in the *InfoType* parameter is in the range reserved for driver-specific use but is not supported by the driver being used, this function returns SQLSTATE **HYC**00 (Optional feature not implemented).

Prerequisites   There are no prerequisites for using this function call.

Restrictions   All calls to this function require an open connection, except when the *InfoType* parameter is set to **SQL_ODBC_VER** (which returns the version of the ODBC Driver Manager).

See Also   `SQLGetFunctions()`, `SQLGetTypeInfo()`, `SQLGetConnectAttr()`, `SQLGetStmtAttr()`

Example   The following Visual C++ program illustrates how the `SQLGetInfo()` function can be used to obtain information about the data source that an application is connected to.

```
/*------------------------------------------------------------*/
/* NAME:     CH8EX3.CPP                                        */
/* PURPOSE: Illustrate How To Use The Following ODBC API Function */
/*          In A C++ Program:                                 */
/*                                                            */
/*              SQLGetInfo()                                  */
/*                                                            */
/* OTHER ODBC APIs SHOWN:                                     */
/*          SQLAllocHandle()          SQLSetEnvAttr()         */
/*          SQLConnect()              SQLDisconnect()         */
/*          SQLFreeHandle()                                   */
/*                                                            */
/*------------------------------------------------------------*/

// Include The Appropriate Header Files
```

```cpp
#include <windows.h>
#include <sql.h>
#include <sqlext.h>
#include <iostream.h>

// Define The ODBC_Class Class
class ODBC_Class
{
    // Attributes
    public:
        SQLHANDLE   EnvHandle;
        SQLHANDLE   ConHandle;
        SQLRETURN   rc;

    // Operations
    public:
        ODBC_Class();                               // Constructor
        ~ODBC_Class();                              // Destructor
        SQLRETURN   ShowConnectionInfo();
};

// Define The Class Constructor
ODBC_Class::ODBC_Class()
{
    // Initialize The Return Code Variable
    rc = SQL_SUCCESS;

    // Allocate An Environment Handle
    rc = SQLAllocHandle(SQL_HANDLE_ENV, SQL_NULL_HANDLE, &EnvHandle);

    // Set The ODBC Application Version To 3.x
    if (rc == SQL_SUCCESS)
        rc = SQLSetEnvAttr(EnvHandle, SQL_ATTR_ODBC_VERSION,
                (SQLPOINTER) SQL_OV_ODBC3, SQL_IS_UINTEGER);

    // Allocate A Connection Handle
    if (rc == SQL_SUCCESS)
        rc = SQLAllocHandle(SQL_HANDLE_DBC, EnvHandle, &ConHandle);
}

// Define The Class Destructor
ODBC_Class::~ODBC_Class()
{
    // Free The Connection Handle
    if (ConHandle != NULL)
        SQLFreeHandle(SQL_HANDLE_DBC, ConHandle);

    // Free The Environment Handle
    if (EnvHandle != NULL)
        SQLFreeHandle(SQL_HANDLE_ENV, EnvHandle);
}

// Define The ShowConnectionInfo() Member Function
SQLRETURN ODBC_Class::ShowConnectionInfo(void)
{
```

```cpp
    // Declare The Local Memory Variables
    SQLCHAR       Buffer[255];
    SQLSMALLINT   InfoSize;

    // Obtain And Display Information About The Current Connection
    rc = SQLGetInfo(ConHandle, SQL_DATABASE_NAME,
              (SQLPOINTER) &Buffer, sizeof(Buffer), &InfoSize);
    if (rc == SQL_SUCCESS)
        cout << "Database Name : " << Buffer << endl;

    rc = SQLGetInfo(ConHandle, SQL_DRIVER_NAME,
              (SQLPOINTER) &Buffer, sizeof(Buffer), &InfoSize);
    if (rc == SQL_SUCCESS)
        cout << "Driver Name   : " << Buffer << endl;

    // Return The ODBC API Return Code To The Calling Function
    return(rc);
}

/*————————————————————————————————————————————————*/
/* The Main Function                                              */
/*————————————————————————————————————————————————*/
int main()
{
    // Declare The Local Memory Variables
    SQLRETURN  rc = SQL_SUCCESS;
    SQLCHAR    DBName[10] = "Northwind";

    // Create An Instance Of The ODBC_Class Class
    ODBC_Class  Example;

    // Connect To The Northwind Sample Database
    if (Example.ConHandle != NULL)
    {
        rc = SQLConnect(Example.ConHandle, DBName, SQL_NTS,
                  (SQLCHAR *) "", SQL_NTS, (SQLCHAR *) "", SQL_NTS);

        // Obtain And Display Information About The Current
        // Connection
        if (rc == SQL_SUCCESS || rc == SQL_SUCCESS_WITH_INFO)
            rc = Example.ShowConnectionInfo();

        // Disconnect From The Northwind Database
        rc = SQLDisconnect(Example.ConHandle);
    }

    // Return To The Operating System
    return(rc);
}
```

SQLGetFunctions

COMPATABILITY					
X/OPEN 95 CLI	ISO/IEC 92 CLI	ODBC 1.0	ODBC 2.0	ODBC 3.0	ODBC 3.5
✓	✓	✓	✓	✓	✓

API CONFORMANCE LEVEL   **CORE***

*IN ODBC 2.0, THIS FUNCTION WAS A LEVEL 1 API CONFORMANCE LEVEL FUNCTION

Purpose

The `SQLGetFunctions()` function is used to determine whether a specific ODBC API function is supported by the driver an application is currently connected to.

Syntax

```
SQLRETURN SQLGetFunctions    (SQLHDBC        ConnectionHandle,
                              QLUSMALLINT    Function,
                              SQLUSMALLINT   *Supported);
```

Parameters

ConnectionHandle   A data source connection handle that refers to a previously allocated connection information storage buffer (data structure).

Function   A value that identifies the ODBC API function of interest. This parameter must be set to one of the values shown in Table 8–3.

Supported   A pointer to a location in memory where this function is to store the value **SQL_TRUE** or **SQL_FALSE** depending on whether the specified function is supported by the driver the application is currently connected to. In some cases this is a single value; in other cases it can be an array of **SQL_TRUE** and/or **SQL_FALSE** values.

Description

The `SQLGetFunctions()` function is used to determine whether a specific ODBC API function is supported by the driver an application is currently connected to. This information allows an application to adapt to varying levels of ODBC API function support as it connects to different drivers and executes against various data sources. Table 8–3 alphabetically lists each value that can be specified for the *Function* parameter, along with information about the types of drivers that are able to recognize that particular value.

Table 8–3   ODBC API Function Values

Function Value	Recognized By
SQL_API_SQLALLOCCONNECT	ODBC 2.0 (or earlier) drivers only
SQL_API_SQLALLOCENV	ODBC 2.0 (or earlier) drivers only
SQL_API_SQLALLOCHANDLE	ODBC 3.x drivers only
SQL_API_SQLALLOCSTMT	ODBC 2.0 (or earlier) drivers only
SQL_API_SQLBINDCOL	All drivers
SQL_API_SQLBINDPARAMETER	All drivers
SQL_API_SQLBROWSECONNECT	All drivers
SQL_API_SQLBULKOPERATIONS	ODBC 3.x drivers only
SQL_API_SQLCANCEL	All drivers
SQL_API_SQLCLOSECURSOR	ODBC 3.x drivers only
SQL_API_SQLCOLATTRIBUTE	ODBC 3.x drivers only
SQL_API_SQLCOLATTRIBUTES	ODBC 2.0 (or earlier) drivers only
SQL_API_SQLCOLUMNPRIVILEGES	All drivers
SQL_API_SQLCOLUMNS	All drivers
SQL_API_SQLCONNECT	All drivers
SQL_API_SQLCOPYDESC	ODBC 3.x drivers only
SQL_API_SQLDATASOURCES	All drivers
SQL_API_SQLBESCRIBECOL	All drivers
SQL_API_SQLDESCRIBEPARAM	All drivers
SQL_API_SQLDISCONNECT	All drivers
SQL_API_SQLDRIVERCONNECT	All drivers
SQL_API_SQLDRIVERS	All drivers
SQL_API_SQLENDTRAN	ODBC 3.x drivers only
SQL_API_SQLERROR	ODBC 2.0 (or earlier) drivers only
SQL_API_SQLEXECDIRECT	All drivers
SQL_API_SQLEXECUTE	All drivers
SQL_API_SQLEXTENDEDFETCH	ODBC 2.0 (or earlier) drivers only
SQL_API_SQLFETCH	All drivers
SQL_API_SQLFETCHSCROLL	ODBC 3.x drivers only
SQL_API_SQLFOREIGNKEYS	All drivers
SQL_API_SQLFREECONNECT	ODBC 2.0 (or earlier) drivers only

Table 8–3 ODBC API Function Values (Continued)

Function Value	Recognized By
SQL_API_SQLFREEENV	ODBC 2.0 (or earlier) drivers only
SQL_API_SQLFREEHANDLE	ODBC 3.x drivers only
SQL_API_SQLFREESTMT	All drivers
SQL_API_SQLGETCONNECTATTR	ODBC 3.x drivers only
SQL_API_SQLGETCONNECTOPTION	ODBC 2.0 (or earlier) drivers only
SQL_API_SQLGETCURSORNAME	All drivers
SQL_API_SQLGETDATA	All drivers
SQL_API_SQLGETDESCFIELD	ODBC 3.x drivers only
SQL_API_SQLGETDESCREC	ODBC 3.x drivers only
SQL_API_SQLGETDIAGFIELD	ODBC 3.x drivers only
SQL_API_SQLGETDIAGREC	ODBC 3.x drivers only
SQL_API_SQLGETENVATTR	ODBC 3.x drivers only
SQL_API_SQLGETFUNCTIONS	All drivers
SQL_API_SQLGETINFO	All drivers
SQL_API_SQLGETSTMTATTR	ODBC 3.x drivers only
SQL_API_SQLGETSTMTOPTION	ODBC 2.0 (or earlier) drivers only
SQL_API_SQLGETTYPEINFO	All drivers
SQL_API_SQLMORERESULTS	All drivers
SQL_API_SQLNATIVESQL	All drivers
SQL_API_SQLNUMPARAMS	All drivers
SQL_API_SQLNUMRESULTCOLS	All drivers
SQL_API_SQLPARAMDATA	All drivers
SQL_API_SQLPARAMOPTIONS	ODBC 2.0 (or earlier) drivers only
SQL_API_SQLPREPARE	All drivers
SQL_API_SQLPRIMARYKEYS	All drivers
SQL_API_SQLPROCEDURECOLUMNS	All drivers
SQL_API_SQLPROCEDURES	All drivers
SQL_API_SQLPUTDATA	All drivers
SQL_API_SQLROWCOUNT	All drivers
SQL_API_SQLSETCONNECTATTR	ODBC 3.x drivers only
SQL_API_SQLSETCONNECTOPTION	ODBC 2.0 (or earlier) drivers only

Table 8–3 ODBC API Function Values (Continued)

Function Value	Recognized By
SQL_API_SQLSETCURSORNAME	All drivers
SQL_API_SQLSETDESCFIELD	ODBC 3.x drivers only
SQL_API_SQLSETDESCREC	ODBC 3.x drivers only
SQL_API_SQLSETENVATTR	ODBC 3.x drivers only
SQL_API_SQLSETPARAM	ODBC 2.0 (or earlier) drivers only
SQL_API_SQLSETPOS	All drivers
SQL_API_SQLSETSCROLLOPTIONS	ODBC 2.0 (or earlier) drivers only
SQL_API_SQLSETSTMTATTR	ODBC 3.x drivers only
SQL_API_SQLSETSTMTOPTION	ODBC 2.0 (or earlier) drivers only
SQL_API_SQLSPECIALCOLUMNS	All drivers
SQL_API_SQLSTATISTICS	All drivers
SQL_API_SQLTABLEPRIVILEGES	All drivers
SQL_API_SQLTABLES	All drivers
SQL_API_SQLTRANSACT	ODBC 2.0 (or earlier) drivers only
SQL_API_ALL_FUNCTIONS	ODBC 2.0 (or earlier) applications/drivers only
SQL_API_ODBC3_ALL_FUNCTIONS	ODBC 3.x applications only

This function is implemented in the ODBC Driver Manager; however, it can also be implemented in a driver—if a driver implements this function, the ODBC Driver Manager calls the function in the driver. Otherwise, it executes its own **SQLGetFunctions()** function.

NOTE: *The ODB Driver Manager will map an ANSI function to the corresponding Unicode function if the Unicode function exists, and it will map a Unicode function to the corresponding ANSI function if the ANSI function exists.*

Return Codes **SQL_SUCCESS**, **SQL_SUCCESS_WITH_INFO**, **SQL_INVALID_HANDLE**, or **SQL_ERROR**

SQLSTATEs   If this function returns **SQL_SUCCESS_WITH_INFO** or **SQL_ERROR**, one of the following SQLSTATE values may be obtained by calling the **SQLGetDiagRec()** function (ODBC 3.x driver) or the **SQLError()** function (ODBC 2.0 or earlier driver):

ODBC 3.X
01000, **08**S01, **HY**000, **HY**001, **HY**010*, **HY**013, **HY**095*, **HYT**01

ODBC 2.0 OR EARLIER
01000, **S1**000, **S1**001, **S1**010*, or **S1**095*

* Returned by the ODBC Driver Manager.

Unless noted otherwise, each of these SQLSTATE values are returned by the data source driver. Refer to Appendix B for detailed information about each SQLSTATE value that can be returned by the ODBC Driver Manager or by a data source driver.

Comments   ▨ If the value specified in the *Function* parameter is **SQL_API_ODBC3_ ALL_FUNCTIONS**, the *Supported* parameter points to a **SQLSMALLINT** array of **SQL_API_ODBC3_ALL_FUNCTIONS_SIZE** elements. The Driver Manager treats this array as a 4,000-bit bitmap that can be used to determine whether an ODBC 3.5 or earlier function is supported. In this case, the **SQL_FUNC_EXISTS()** macro can be called to determine specific function support. An ODBC 3.x application can call **SQLGetFunctions()** with **SQL_API_ODBC3_ALL_FUNCTIONS** specified against both an ODBC 3.x and an ODBC 2.0 driver.

▨ If the value specified in the *Function* parameter is **SQL_API_ALL_ FUNCTIONS**, *Supported* parameter points to an **SQLUSMALLINT** array of 100 elements. The array is indexed by the **#define** values that are used by the *Function* parameter to identify each ODBC function; some elements of the array are unused and reserved for future use. Each element in this array contains **SQL_TRUE** if it identifies an ODBC 2.0 or earlier function that is supported by the driver and **SQL_FALSE** if it identifies an ODBC 2.0 or earlier function that is not supported by the driver or if it doesn't identify an ODBC function.

▨ Both arrays returned in the *Supported* parameter use zero-based indexing.

▨ This function always returns that the **SQLGetFunctions()**, **SQLDataSources()**, and **SQLDrivers()** functions are supported. That's because these three functions are implemented in the ODBC Driver Manager.

■ If this function is called with `SQL_API_ODBC3_ALL_FUNCTIONS` specified in the *Function* parameter, the `SQL_FUNC_EXISTS` (*Supported, Function*) macro can be used to determine whether a specific ODBC 3.x or earlier function is supported. An application calls the `SQL_FUNC_EXISTS()` macro with the *Supported* argument set to the memory location specified in the *Supported* parameter in the previous `SQLGetFunctions()` call, and with the *Function* argument set to the appropriate function value (See Table 8–3). The `SQL_FUNC_EXISTS()` macro returns `SQL_TRUE` if the function is supported and `SQL_FALSE` if it is not.

■ When working with an ODBC 2.0 driver, the ODBC 3.x Driver Manager returns `SQL_TRUE` for the `SQLAllocHandle()` and `SQLFreeHandle()` functions because `SQLAllocHandle()` is mapped to `SQLAllocEnv()`, `SQLAllocConnect()`, or `SQLAllocStmt()`, and `SQLFreeHandle()` is mapped to `SQLFreeEnv()`, `SQLFreeConnect()`, or `SQLFreeStmt()`. However, `SQLAllocHandle()` or `SQLFreeHandle()` function calls with the *HandleType* parameter set to `SQL_HANDLE_DESC` is not supported, even though `SQL_TRUE` is returned for both of these functions. That's because there is no ODBC 2.0 function to map to in this case.

Prerequisites   A connection to a data source or driver must exist before this function is called.

Restrictions   There are no restrictions associated with this function call.

See Also   `SQLGetInfo()`, `SQLGetTypeInfo()`, `SQLGetConnectAttr()`, `SQLGetStmtAttr()`

Example   The following Visual C++ program illustrates how the `SQLGetFunctions()` function can be used to determine whether or not a specific ODBC API function is supported by the data source that an application is connected to.

```
/*----------------------------------------------------------------*/
/* NAME:     CH8EX4.CPP                                           */
/* PURPOSE: Illustrate How To Use The Following ODBC API Function */
/*          In A C++ Program:                                     */
/*                                                                */
/*               SQLGetFunctions()                                */
/*                                                                */
/* OTHER ODBC APIs SHOWN:                                         */
/*          SQLAllocHandle()            SQLSetEnvAttr()           */
```

```
/*               SQLConnect()              SQLDisconnect()              */
/*               SQLFreeHandle()                                        */
/*                                                                      */
/*--------------------------------------------------------------------*/

// Include The Appropriate Header Files
#include <windows.h>
#include <sql.h>
#include <sqlext.h>
#include <iostream.h>

// Define The ODBC_Class Class
class ODBC_Class
{
    // Attributes
    public:
        SQLHANDLE    EnvHandle;
        SQLHANDLE    ConHandle;
        SQLRETURN    rc;

    // Operations
    public:
        ODBC_Class();                          // Constructor
        ~ODBC_Class();                         // Destructor
};

// Define The Class Constructor
ODBC_Class::ODBC_Class()
{
    // Initialize The Return Code Variable
    rc = SQL_SUCCESS;

    // Allocate An Environment Handle
    rc = SQLAllocHandle(SQL_HANDLE_ENV, SQL_NULL_HANDLE, &EnvHandle);

    // Set The ODBC Application Version To 3.x
    if (rc == SQL_SUCCESS)
        rc = SQLSetEnvAttr(EnvHandle, SQL_ATTR_ODBC_VERSION,
                  (SQLPOINTER) SQL_OV_ODBC3, SQL_IS_UINTEGER);

    // Allocate A Connection Handle
    if (rc == SQL_SUCCESS)
        rc = SQLAllocHandle(SQL_HANDLE_DBC, EnvHandle, &ConHandle);
}

// Define The Class Destructor
ODBC_Class::~ODBC_Class()
{
    // Free The Connection Handle
    if (ConHandle != NULL)
        SQLFreeHandle(SQL_HANDLE_DBC, ConHandle);
```

```cpp
    // Free The Environment Handle
    if (EnvHandle != NULL)
        SQLFreeHandle(SQL_HANDLE_ENV, EnvHandle);
}

/*————————————————————————————————————————————— */
/* The Main Function                             */
/*————————————————————————————————————————————— */
int main()
{
    // Declare The Local Memory Variables
    SQLRETURN       rc = SQL_SUCCESS;
    SQLCHAR         DBName[10] = "Northwind";
    SQLUSMALLINT    Supported;

    // Create An Instance Of The ODBC_Class Class
    ODBC_Class   Example;

    // Connect To The Northwind Sample Database
    if (Example.ConHandle != NULL)
    {
        rc = SQLConnect(Example.ConHandle, DBName, SQL_NTS,
                  (SQLCHAR *) "", SQL_NTS, (SQLCHAR *) "", SQL_NTS);

        // Determine Whether Or Not The Current Data Source Supports
        // The SQLBrowseConnect() Function
        if (rc != SQL_SUCCESS || rc != SQL_SUCCESS_WITH_INFO)
        {
            rc = SQLGetFunctions(Example.ConHandle,
                      SQL_API_SQLBROWSECONNECT, &Supported);

            // Retrieve And Display The Results
            if (rc == SQL_SUCCESS || rc == SQL_SUCCESS_WITH_INFO)
            {
                cout << "SQLBrowseConnect() is ";
                if (Supported == TRUE)
                    cout << "supported ";
                else
                    cout << "not supported ";
                cout << "by the current data source." << endl;
            }
        }

        // Disconnect From The Northwind Sample Database
        rc = SQLDisconnect(Example.ConHandle);
    }

    // Return To The Operating System
    return(rc);
}
```

SQLGetTypeInfo

Compatability

X/OPEN 95 CLI	ISO/IEC 92 CLI	ODBC 1.0	ODBC 2.0	ODBC 3.0	ODBC 3.5
✓	✓	✓	✓	✓	✓

API Conformance Level   **CORE***

*In ODBC 2.0, this function was a LEVEL 1 API Conformance Level function

Purpose

The `SQLGetTypeInfo()` function is used to retrieve information about the data types supported by the data source an application is currently connected to.

Syntax

```
SQLRETURN SQLGetTypeInfo    (SQLHSTMT      StatementHandle,
                             SQLSMALLINT   SQLDataType);
```

Parameters

StatementHandle   An SQL statement handle that refers to a previously allocated SQL statement information storage buffer (data structure).

SQLDataType   The SQL data type that information is to be retrieved for. This parameter must be set to a data source-specific data type or to one of the following values:

- `SQL_CHAR`
- `SQL_VARCHAR`
- `SQL_LONGVARCHAR`
- `SQL_DECIMAL`
- `SQL_NUMERIC`
- `SQL_SMALLINT`
- `SQL_INTEGER`
- `SQL_REAL`
- `SQL_FLOAT`
- `SQL_DOUBLE`
- `SQL_BIT`

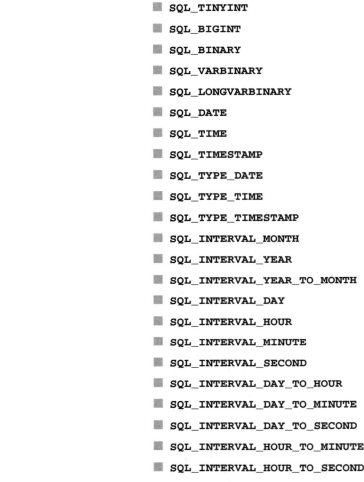

- SQL_TINYINT
- SQL_BIGINT
- SQL_BINARY
- SQL_VARBINARY
- SQL_LONGVARBINARY
- SQL_DATE
- SQL_TIME
- SQL_TIMESTAMP
- SQL_TYPE_DATE
- SQL_TYPE_TIME
- SQL_TYPE_TIMESTAMP
- SQL_INTERVAL_MONTH
- SQL_INTERVAL_YEAR
- SQL_INTERVAL_YEAR_TO_MONTH
- SQL_INTERVAL_DAY
- SQL_INTERVAL_HOUR
- SQL_INTERVAL_MINUTE
- SQL_INTERVAL_SECOND
- SQL_INTERVAL_DAY_TO_HOUR
- SQL_INTERVAL_DAY_TO_MINUTE
- SQL_INTERVAL_DAY_TO_SECOND
- SQL_INTERVAL_HOUR_TO_MINUTE
- SQL_INTERVAL_HOUR_TO_SECOND
- SQL_INTERVAL_MINUTE_TO_SECOND
- SQL_INTERVAL_YEAR_TO_MONTH
- SQL_ALL_TYPES

NOTE: *The* **SQL_ALL_TYPES** *value causes information about all SQL data types to be returned.*

Description   The **SQLGetTypeInfo()** function is used to retrieve information about the data types supported by the data source that an application is currently connected to. The information returned by this function is placed in a result data set and can be processed by using the same functions that are used to process a result data set generated by an SQL query. Table 8–4 describes this result data set.

One or more driver-defined columns may be added to this result data set. When that is the case, applications should gain access to each driver-specific column by counting down from column 19 (**INTERVAL_PRECISION**) of the result data set rather than by specifying an explicit ordinal position.

Table 8–4   *Result Data Set Returned By* **SQLGetTypeInfo()**

Column Number	Column Name	Data Type	Description
1	**TYPE_NAME** (ODBC2.0)	**VARCHAR**(128) **NOT NULL**	The data source-specific character representation of the SQL data type identified in the **DATA_TYPE** column. Valid values for this column include:
			CHAR, VARCHAR, LONG VARCHAR, WCHAR, VARWCHAR, LONGWVARCHAR, DECIMAL, NUMERIC, SMALLINT, INTEGER, REAL, FLOAT, DOUBLE PRECISION, BIT, TINYINT, BIGINT, BINARY, VARBINARY, LONG VARBINARY, DATE, TIME, TIMESTAMP, INTERVAL MONTH, INTERVAL YEAR, INTERVAL YEAR TO MONTH, INTERVAL DAY, INTERVAL HOUR, INTERVAL MINUTE, INTERVAL SECOND, INTERVAL DAY TO HOUR, INTERVAL DAY TO MINUTE, INTERVAL DAY TO SECOND, INTERVAL HOUR TO MINUTE, INTERVAL HOUR TO SECOND, INTERVAL MINUTE TO SECOND, GUID
2	**DATA_TYPE** (ODBC 2.0)	**SMALLINT** **NOT NULL**	An ODBC or driver-specific SQL data type that is supported by the data source. Valid values for this column include:
			SQL_CHAR, SQL_VARCHAR, SQL_LONGVARCHAR, SQL_WCHAR, SQL_WVARCHAR, SQL_WLONGVARCHAR, SQL_DECIMAL, SQL_NUMERIC, SQL_SMALLINT, SQL_INTEGER, SQL_REAL, SQL_FLOAT, SQL_DOUBLE, SQL_BIT, SQL_TINYINT, SQL_BIGINT, SQL_BINARY, SQL_VARBINARY, SQL_LONGVARBINARY, SQL_TYPE_DATE, SQL_TYPE_TIME, SQL_TYPE_TIMESTAMP, SQL_INTERVAL_MONTH, SQL_INTERVAL_YEAR, SQL_INTERVAL_YEAR_TO_MONTH, SQL_INTERVAL_DAY,SQL_INTERVAL_HOUR, SQL_INTERVAL_MINUTE, SQL_INTERVAL_SECOND, SQL_INTERVAL_DAY_TO_HOUR, SQL_INTERVAL_DAY_TO_MINUTE, SQL_INTERVAL_DAY_TO_SECOND,

Table 8–4 Result Data Set Returned By **SQLGEtTypeInfo()** (Continued)

Column Number	Column Name	Data Type	Description
			SQL_INTERVAL_HOUR_TO_MINUTE, SQL_INTERVAL_HOUR_TO_SECOND, SQL_INTERVAL_MINUTE_TO_SECOND, SQL_GUID
			For datetime and interval data types, this column contains the concise data type (such as **SQL_TYPE_DATE** or **SQL_INTERVAL_YEAR_TO_MONTH**, rather than the non-concise data type such as **SQL_DATETIME** or **SQL_INTERVAL**) (ODBC 3.x applications only).
			NOTE: SQL data types returned for ODBC 3.x, ODBC 2.0, and ODBC 1.0 applications may be different.
3	**COLUMN_SIZE**[1] (ODBC 2.0)	**INTEGER**	The maximum number of bytes needed to display the column data in character form.
			For numeric data types, this is either the total number of digits, or the total number of bits allowed in the column, depending on the value in the **NUM_PREC_RADIX** column.
			For character or binary string data types, this is the size of the string (string length), in bytes.
			For date, time, and timestamp data types, this is the total number of characters required to display the value when it is converted to a character string.
			For interval data types, this is the total number of characters in the character representation of the interval literal (as defined by the interval leading precision value).
4	**LITERAL_PREFIX** (ODBC 2.0)	**VARCHAR**(128)	One or more characters used as a prefix for a literal representation of the SQL data type identified in the **DATA_TYPE** column. For example, a single quotation mark (') might be used for character data types, or '0x' might be used for binary data types.
			For data types where a literal prefix is not applicable, this column is set to NULL.
5	**LITERAL_SUFFIX** (ODBC 2.0)	**VARCHAR**(128)	One or more characters used as a suffix to terminate a literal representation of the SQL data type identified in the **DATA_TYPE** column.

Table 8–4 Result Data Set Returned By **SQLGetTypeInfo()** (Continued)

Column Number	Column Name	Data Type	Description
			For example, a single quotation mark (') might be used for character data types.
			For data types in which a literal prefix is not applicable, this column is set to NULL.
6	**CREATE_PARAMS** (ODBC 2.0)	**VARCHAR**(128)	A list of keywords, separated by commas, corresponding to each parameter an application may specify in parentheses when using the name returned in the **TYPE_NAME** column as a data type in SQL (for example, **LENGTH**, **PRECISION**, **SCALE**, etc.). The keywords appear in the list in the order required by the SQL syntax. For example, **CREATE_PARAMS** for **DECIMAL** would be **"PRECISION, SCALE"**; **CREATE_PARAMS** for **VARCHAR** would be **"LENGTH"**. If no parameters are specified for the data type are returned (for example: **INTEGER**), this column is set to NULL.
			The driver supplies the **CREATE_PARAMS** text in the language of the country where it is used.
			Note: The intent of **CREATE_PARAMS** is to enable an application to customize the interface for a Data Definition Language (DDL) builder. An application using this column should expect to only to be able to determine the number of arguments required to define the data type.
7	**NULLABLE** (ODBC 2.0)	**SMALLINT NOT NULL**	Indicates whether the data type accepts a NULL value. Valid values for this column are:
			SQL_NO_NULLS: The data type does not accept NULL values.
			SQL_NULLABLE: The data type accepts NULL values.
			SQL_NULLABLE_UNKNOWN: It is not known whether the data type accepts NULL values.
8	**CASE_SENSITIVE** (ODBC 2.0)	**SMALLINT NOT NULL**	Indicates whether the data type can be treated as case sensitive for collation and comparison purposes. Valid values for this column are:
			SQL_TRUE: The data type is a character data type and is case-sensitive.
			SQL_FALSE: The data type is a character data type that is not case- sensitive, the data type is not a character data type.

Table 8–4   Result Data Set Returned By **SQLGetTypeInfo()**   (Continued)

Column Number	Column Name	Data Type	Description
9	**SEARCHABLE** (ODBC 2.0)	**SMALLINT NOT NULL**	Indicates how the data type is used in an SQL **WHERE** clause. Valid values for this column are:
			SQL_SEARCHABLE: The data type can be used with any comparison operators in a **WHERE** clause.
			SQL_PRED_CHAR (ODBC 3.x): The data type can only be used in a **WHERE** clause **LIKE** predicate.
			SQL_LIKE_ONLY (ODBC 2.0): The data type can only be used in a **WHERE** clause **LIKE** predicate.
			SQL_PRED_BASIC (ODBC 3.x): The data type can be used with all comparison operators in a **WHERE** clause except a **LIKE** predicate.
			SQL_ALL_EXCEPT_LIKE (ODBC 2.0): The data type can be used with all comparison operators in a **WHERE** clause except a **LIKE** predicate.
			SQL_PRED_NONE (ODBC 3.x): The data type can not be used in a **WHERE** clause.
			SQL_UNSEARCHABLE (ODBC 2.0): The data type can not be used in a **WHERE** clause.
10	**UNSIGNED_ ATTRIBUTE** (ODBC 2.0)	**SMALLINT**	Indicates whether the data type is unsigned. Valid values for this column are:
			SQL_TRUE: The data type is unsigned.
			SQL_FALSE: The data type is signed.
			NULL: This attribute is not applicable to the data type or the data type is not numeric.
11	**FIXED_PREC_ SCALE**[2] (ODBC 2.0)	**SMALLINT NOT NULL**	Indicates whether the data type is an exact numeric data type that always has the same precision and scale (that is, the same width and number of decimal places). Valid values for this column are:
			SQL_TRUE: The data type has a predefined fixed precision and scale.
			SQL_FALSE: The data type does not have a predefined fixed precision and scale.

Table 8–4 Result Data Set Returned By **SQLGetTypeInfo()** (Continued)

Column Number	Column Name	Data Type	Description
12	AUTO_UNIQUE_ VALUE[3] (ODBC 2.0)	SMALLINT	Indicates whether a column of this data type is automatically set to a unique value whenever a new row is inserted. Valid values for this column are:
			SQL_TRUE: The data type is auto-incrementing.
			SQL_FALSE: The data type is not auto-incrementing.
			NULL: This attribute is not applicable to the data type or the data type is not numeric.
			An application can insert values into a column that has this attribute, but typically it cannot update the values in the column. When an INSERT operation is performed on an auto-increment column, a unique value is inserted into the column. The increment used is data-source specific—an application should not assume that an auto-increment column starts at any particular point or increments by any particular value.
13	LOCAL_TYPE_NAME (ODBC 2.0)	VARCHAR(128)	Character representation of any localized (native language) name for the data type that is different from the regular data type name stored in the **TYPE_NAME** column.
			If there is no localized name for the data type, this column is set to NULL.
			This column is intended to be used for display purposes only. The character set of the string is locale-dependent and usually defaults to the character set used by the data source.
14	MINIMUM_SCALE (ODBC 2.0)	INTEGER	The minimum scale value of the SQL data type. If the data type has a fixed scale, both the **MINIMUM_SCALE** column and the **MAXIMUM_ SCALE** column contain the same value. For example, an **SQL_TYPE_TIMESTAMP** data type might have a fixed scale for fractional seconds.
			This column is set to NULL for data types where scale is not applicable.
15	MAXIMUM_SCALE (ODBC 2.0)	INTEGER	The maximum scale value of the SQL data type. If the maximum scale is not defined separately in the data source, but is defined instead to be the same as the maximum length of the column, then this column contains the same value as the **COLUMN_SIZE** column.
			This column is set to NULL for data types where scale is not applicable.

Table 8–4   Result Data Set Returned By **SQLGetTypeInfo()**   (Continued)

Column Number	Column Name	Data Type	Description
16	**SQL_DATA_TYPE** (ODBC 3.0)	**SMALLINT NOT NULL**	The SQL data type of the column identified in the **COLUMN_NAME** column, as it would appear in the **SQL_DESC_TYPE** field of an implementation row descriptor record. This can be an ODBC SQL data type or a driver-specific SQL data type.
			This column usually contains the same value as the **DATA_TYPE** column, with the following exception:
			For datetime and interval data types, this column contains the non-concise data type (such as **SQL_DATETIME** or **SQL_INTERVAL**), rather than the concise data type (such as **SQL_TYPE_DATE** or **SQL_INTERVAL_YEAR_TO_MONTH**). If this column contains **SQL_DATETIME** or **SQL_INTERVAL**, the specific data type can be obtained from the **SQL_DATETIME_SUB** column.
			NOTE: SQL data types returned for ODBC 3.x, ODBC 2.0, and ODBC 1.0 applications may be different.
17	**DATETIME_SUB** (ODBC 3.0)	**SMALLINT**	The subtype code for datetime and interval data types. For datetime or interval data types, the **DATA_TYPE** field in the result data set contains **SQL_DATETIME** or **SQL_INTERVAL**, respectively, and the **SQL_DATETIME_SUB** field contains the subcode for the specific datetime or interval data type. For all other data types, this column is set to NULL.
18	**NUM_PREC_RADIX** (ODBC 3.0)	**SMALLINT**	The radix value of the data type.
			For approximate numeric data types, this column contains the value **2** and the **COLUMN_SIZE** column contains the number of bits allowed in the column.
			For exact numeric data types, this column contains the value **10**, and the **COLUMN_SIZE** column contains the number of decimal digits allowed for the column.
			For numeric data types, this column can contain either **10** or **2**.
			For data types where radix is not applicable, this column is set to NULL.
19	**INTERVAL_ PRECISION** (ODBC 3.0)	**SMALLINT**	For interval data types this column contains the interval leading precision value. For all other data types, this column is set to NULL.

(The information above was adapted from the table on pages 821–826 of *Microsoft ODBC 3.0 Software Development Kit & Programmer's Reference*.)

[1] In ODBC 2.0 and earlier, this column was named **PRECISION**.

[2] In ODBC 2.0 and earlier, this column was named **MONEY**.

[3] In ODBC 2.0 and earlier, this column was named **AUTO_INCREMENT**.

NOTE: *Depending on the driver being used,* `SQLGetTypeInfo()` *may or may not return information for all valid data types. However, an application can use any valid data type regardless of whether it is returned in the result data set produced by this function.*

The data types returned by `SQLGetTypeInfo()` are the SQL-specific data types supported by the data source. These data types are intended to be used in Data Definition Language (DDL) statements.

Return Codes   `SQL_SUCCESS`, `SQL_SUCCESS_WITH_INFO`, `SQL_STILL_EXECUTING`, `SQL_INVALID_HANDLE`, or `SQL_ERROR`

SQLSTATEs   If this function returns `SQL_SUCCESS_WITH_INFO` or `SQL_ERROR`, one of the following SQLSTATE values may be obtained by calling the `SQLGetDiagRec()` function (ODBC 3.x driver) or the `SQLError()` function (ODBC 2.0 or earlier driver):

ODBC 3.X
01000, **01**S02, **08**S01, **24**000, **40**001, **40**003, **HY**000, **HY**001, **HY**004, **HY**008, **HY**010*, **HY**013, **HYC**00, **HYT**00, **HYT**01, or **IM**001*

ODBC 2.0 OR EARLIER
01000, **08**S01, **24**000*, **IM**001*, **S1**000, **S1**001, **S1**004*, **S1**008, **S1**010*, **S1C**00, or **S1T**00
* Returned by the ODBC Driver Manager.

Unless noted otherwise, each of these SQLSTATE values are returned by the data source driver. Refer to Appendix B for detailed information about each SQLSTATE value that can be returned by the ODBC Driver Manager or by a data source driver.

Comments   ■ Applications must use the type names returned in the `TYPE_NAME` column of the result data set produced by this function in `ALTER TABLE` and `CREATE TABLE` SQL statements.

■ One or more rows in the result data set produced by this function can contain the same value in the `DATA_TYPE` column.

■ If there is more than one name by which a data type can be specified, the result data set produced by this function may contain one row for each name. For example, for the data type `SQL_VARCHAR`, there might be one row for `VARCHAR` and one row for `CHARACTER VARYING`.

▨ The result data set returned by this function is ordered first by **DATA_TYPE**, and then by how closely the each data type maps to the corresponding ODBC SQL data type.

▨ Data types defined by the data source take precedence over user-defined data types. For example, suppose a data source defined **INTEGER** and **COUNTER** data types, where **COUNTER** is auto-incrementing, and a user-defined data type **WHOLENUM** has also been defined. These would be returned in the order **INTEGER**, **WHOLENUM**, and **COUNTER**, because **WHOLENUM** maps closely to the ODBC SQL data type **SQL_INTEGER**, while the auto-incrementing data type, even though supported by the data source, does not map closely to an ODBC SQL data type.

▨ Drivers can return information about data types other than those returned in the result data set produced by this function. For example, in creating the result data set for a catalog function, the driver might use a data type not supported by the data source.

Prerequisites   A connection to a driver/data source must exist before this function is called.

Restrictions   There are no restrictions associated with this function call.

See Also   SQLGetInfo(), SQLGetStmtAttr(), SQLBindCol(), SQLColAttribute(), SQLColAttributes(), SQLFetch(), SQLFetchScroll(), SQLExtendedFtech(), SQLCancel()

Example   The following Visual C++ program illustrates how the SQLGetTypeInfo() function can be used to obtain information about a specific data type.

```
/*------------------------------------------------------------*/
/* NAME:      CH8EX5.CPP                                       */
/* PURPOSE: Illustrate How To Use The Following ODBC API Function */
/*          In A C++ Program:                                 */
/*                                                            */
/*              SQLGetTypeInfo()                              */
/*                                                            */
/* OTHER ODBC APIs SHOWN:                                     */
/*          SQLAllocHandle()          SQLSetEnvAttr()         */
/*          SQLConnect()              SQLBindCol()            */
/*          SQLFetch()                SQLDisconnect()         */
/*          SQLFreeHandle()                                   */
/*                                                            */
/*------------------------------------------------------------*/

// Include The Appropriate Header Files
#include <windows.h>
```

```cpp
#include <sql.h>
#include <sqlext.h>
#include <iostream.h>

// Define The ODBC_Class Class
class ODBC_Class
{
    // Attributes
    public:
        SQLHANDLE   EnvHandle;
        SQLHANDLE   ConHandle;
        SQLHANDLE   StmtHandle;
        SQLRETURN   rc;

    // Operations
    public:
        ODBC_Class();                                  // Constructor
        ~ODBC_Class();                                 // Destructor
        SQLRETURN   ShowTypeInfo(SQLSMALLINT DataType);
};

// Define The Class Constructor
ODBC_Class::ODBC_Class()
{
    // Initialize The Return Code Variable
    rc = SQL_SUCCESS;

    // Allocate An Environment Handle
    rc = SQLAllocHandle(SQL_HANDLE_ENV, SQL_NULL_HANDLE, &EnvHandle);

    // Set The ODBC Application Version To 3.x
    if (rc == SQL_SUCCESS)
        rc = SQLSetEnvAttr(EnvHandle, SQL_ATTR_ODBC_VERSION,
                (SQLPOINTER) SQL_OV_ODBC3, SQL_IS_UINTEGER);

    // Allocate A Connection Handle
    if (rc == SQL_SUCCESS)
        rc = SQLAllocHandle(SQL_HANDLE_DBC, EnvHandle, &ConHandle);
}

// Define The Class Destructor
ODBC_Class::~ODBC_Class()
{
    // Free The Connection Handle
    if (ConHandle != NULL)
        SQLFreeHandle(SQL_HANDLE_DBC, ConHandle);

    // Free The Environment Handle
    if (EnvHandle != NULL)
        SQLFreeHandle(SQL_HANDLE_ENV, EnvHandle);
}

// Define The ShowTypeInfo() Member Function
SQLRETURN ODBC_Class::ShowTypeInfo(SQLSMALLINT DataType)
{
```

```
// Declare The Local Memory Variables
SQLCHAR        TypeName[129];
SQLSMALLINT  ColumnSize;

// Allocate An SQL Statement Handle
rc = SQLAllocHandle(SQL_HANDLE_STMT, ConHandle, &StmtHandle);

// Retrieve Information About The Specified Data Type
if (rc == SQL_SUCCESS)
{
    rc = SQLGetTypeInfo(StmtHandle, DataType);
    if (rc == SQL_SUCCESS)
    {
        // Bind Columns In The Result Data Set Returned To
        // Application Variables
        rc = SQLBindCol(StmtHandle, 1, SQL_C_CHAR,
                (SQLPOINTER) &TypeName, sizeof(TypeName), NULL);

        rc = SQLBindCol(StmtHandle, 3, SQL_C_DEFAULT,
                (SQLPOINTER) &ColumnSize, sizeof(ColumnSize),
                NULL);

        // Retrieve And Display The Results
        SQLFetch(StmtHandle);
        cout << "SQL Data Type                : SQL_CHAR" << endl;
        cout << "Data-Source Data Type Name : ";
        cout << TypeName << endl;
        cout << "Column Size Supported        : ";
        cout << ColumnSize << endl;
    }

    // Free The SQL Statement Handle
    if (StmtHandle != NULL)
        SQLFreeHandle(SQL_HANDLE_STMT, StmtHandle);
}

// Return The ODBC API Return Code To The Calling Function
return(rc);
}

/*─────────────────────────────────────────────────────────────── */
/* The Main Function                                               */
/*─────────────────────────────────────────────────────────────── */
int main()
{
    // Declare The Local Memory Variables
    SQLRETURN  rc = SQL_SUCCESS;
    SQLCHAR    DBName[10] = "Northwind";

    // Create An Instance Of The ODBC_Class Class
    ODBC_Class  Example;

    // Connect To The Northwind Sample Database
    if (Example.ConHandle != NULL)
    {
```

```
        rc = SQLConnect(Example.ConHandle, DBName, SQL_NTS,
                (SQLCHAR *) "", SQL_NTS, (SQLCHAR *) "", SQL_NTS);

        // Call The ShowTypeInfo() Member Function
        if (rc == SQL_SUCCESS || rc == SQL_SUCCESS_WITH_INFO)
            Example.ShowTypeInfo(SQL_CHAR);

        // Disconnect From The Northwind Sample Database
        rc = SQLDisconnect(Example.ConHandle);
    }

    // Return To The Operating System
    return(rc);
}
```

SQLGetEnvAttr

COMPATABILITY					
X/OPEN 95 CLI	ISO/IEC 92 CLI	ODBC 1.0	ODBC 2.0	ODBC 3.0	ODBC 3.5
✓	✓	☐	☐	✓	✓

API CONFORMANCE LEVEL   **CORE**

Purpose   The SQLGetEnvAttr() function is used to retrieve the current setting of a specified environment attribute.

Syntax
```
SQLRETURN SQLGetEnvAttr    (SQLHENV      EnvironmentHandle,
                            SQLINTEGER   Attribute,
                            SQLPOINTER   Value,
                            SQLINTEGER   ValueMaxSize,
                            SQLINTEGER   *StringLength);
```

Parameters   *EnvironmentHandle*   An environment handle that refers to a previously allocated environment information storage buffer (data structure).

Attribute   The environment attribute whose value is to be retrieved. This parameter must be set to one of the following values:

- **SQL_ATTR_CONNECTION_POOLING**
- **SQL_ATTR_CP_MATCH**
- **SQL_ATTR_ODBC_VERSION**
- **SQL_ATTR_OUTPUT_NTS**

Value	A pointer to a location in memory where this function is to store the current value of the specified environment attribute.
ValueMaxSize	The maximum size of the memory storage buffer where this function is to store the current value of the specified environment attribute. If the attribute value retrieved is not a character string value, this parameter is ignored.
StringLength	A pointer to a location in memory where this function returns the actual number of bytes written to the attribute value memory storage buffer (*Value*). If the attribute value retrieved is not a character string value, this parameter is ignored.

Description

The **SQLGetEnvAttr()** function is used to retrieve the current setting of a specified environment attribute. This function can be called at any time after an environment handle is allocated, as long as that environment handle has not been freed. Table 8–5 alphabetically lists each value that can be specified for the *Attribute* parameter, along with a description of the information returned for that value when this function is executed.

All environment attributes successfully set by an application for a specified environment persist until the environment handle is freed with the **SQLFreeHandle()** function (ODBC 3.x driver) or the **SQLFreeEnv()** function (ODBC 2.0 or earlier driver). Because more than one environment handle can be allocated simultaneously in ODBC 3.x, environment attribute settings on one environment are not affected when another environment is allocated.

Return Codes

SQL_SUCCESS, **SQL_SUCCESS_WITH_INFO**, **SQL_NO_DATA**, **SQL_INVALID_HANDLE**, or **SQL_ERROR**

SQLSTATEs

If this function returns **SQL_SUCCESS_WITH_INFO** or **SQL_ERROR**, one of the following SQLSTATE values may be obtained by calling the **SQLGetDiagRec()** function:

01000, **01**004, **HY**000, **HY**001, **HY**013, **HY**092, **HY**C00, or **IM**001*

* Returned by the ODBC Driver Manager.

Table 8–5 *Environment Attributes*

Attribute	Data Type	Description
SQL_ATTR_CONNECTION_POOLING (ODBC 3.0)	32-bit **SQLUINTEGER**	Enables or disables connection pooling at the environment level.

Valid values for this attribute are:

SQL_CP_OFF: Connection pooling is turned off. This is the default value for this attribute.

SQL_CP_ONE_PER_DRIVER: A single connection pool is supported for each driver (that is, every connection in a pool is associated with one driver).

SQL_CP_ONE_PER_HENV: A single connection pool is supported for each environment (that is, every connection in a pool is associated with one environment).

Connection pooling is enabled by setting the **SQL_ATTR_CONNECTION_POOLING** attribute to **SQL_CP_ONE_PER_DRIVER** or **SQL_CP_ONE_PER_HENV**. This call must be made before the application allocates the shared environment for which connection pooling is to be enabled. The environment handle in the call to **SQLSetEnvAttr()** is set to NULL, which makes **SQL_ATTR_CONNECTION_POOLING** a process-level attribute. After connection pooling is enabled, the application then allocates an implicit shared environment by calling the **SQLAllocHandle()** function with the *InputHandle* parameter set to **SQL_HANDLE_ENV**.

After connection pooling has been enabled and a shared environment has been selected for an application, the **SQL_ATTR_CONNECTION_POOLING** attribute cannot be changed for that environment because a NULL environment handle was used to set this attribute initially.

If this attribute is set while connection pooling is already enabled on a shared environment, the attribute only affects subsequent shared environment allocations. |

Table 8–5 Environment Attributes (Continued)

Attribute	Data Type	Description
SQL_ATTR_CP_MATCH (ODBC 3.0)	32-bit **SQLUINTEGER**	Determines how a connection is chosen from a connection pool. When **SQLConnect()** or **SQLDriverConnect()** is called, in order to determine which connection is to be reused from the pool, the ODBC Driver Manager attempts to match the connection options specified in the call and the connection attributes set by the application to the keywords and connection attributes of the connections in the pool. The value of this attribute determines the level of precision used to match the two. Valid values for this attribute are:
		SQL_CP_STRICT_MATCH: Only connections exactly matching the connection options in the call and the connection attributes set by the application are reused. This is the default value for this attribute.
		SQL_CP_RELAXED_MATCH: Connections with matching connection string keywords can be used. Keywords must match, but not all connection attributes must match.
SQL_ATTR_ODBC_VERSION (ODBC 3.0)	32-bit **INTEGER**	Determines whether certain functionality exhibits ODBC 2.0 behavior or ODBC 3.x behavior. Valid values for this attribute are:
		SQL_OV_ODBC3: The ODBC Driver Manager and driver exhibit the following ODBC 3.x behavior:
		The driver returns and expects ODBC 3.x codes for date, time, and timestamp.
		The driver returns ODBC 3.x SQLSTATE codes when **SQLError()**, **SQLGetDiagField()**, or **SQLGetDiagRec()** are called.
		The *CatalogName* parameter in the **SQLTables()** function accepts a search pattern.

Table 8–5 Environment Attributes (Continued)

Attribute	Data Type	Description
		SQL_OV_ODBC2: The ODBC Driver Manager and driver exhibit the following ODBC 2.0 (and earlier) behavior:
		The driver returns and expects ODBC 2.0 codes for date, time, and timestamp.
		The driver returns ODBC 2.0 SQLSTATE codes when **SQLError()**, **SQLGetDiagField()**, or **SQLGetDiagRec()** are called.
		The *CatalogName* parameter in the **SQLTables()** function does not accept a search pattern.
		An application must set this environment attribute before calling any function requiring a valid environment handle as an input parameter, or the call returns SQLSTATE **HY**010 (Function sequence error).
		The **SQL_OV_ODBC2** value is especially useful for an ODBC 2.0 application working with an ODBC 3.x driver.
SQL_ATTR_OUTPUT_NTS (ODBC 3.0)	32-bit **INTEGER**	Determines how the driver returns string data. Valid values for this attribute are:
		SQL_TRUE: The driver appends a NULL-terminator character to string data before it is returned. This is the default value for this attribute.
		SQL_FALSE: The driver does not append a NULL-terminator character to string data before it is returned.
		At this time only **SQL_TRUE** is supported. An attempt to set this attribute to **SQL_FALSE** returns **SQL_ERROR** and SQLSTATE **HYC**00 (Optional feature not implemented).

(The preceding information was adapted from the table on pages 945–947 of *Microsoft ODBC 3.0 Software Development Kit & Programmer's Reference*.)

Unless noted otherwise, each of these SQLSTATE values are returned by the data source driver. Refer to Appendix B for detailed information about each SQLSTATE value that can be returned by the ODBC Driver Manager or by a data source driver.

Comments

■ If the *Value* parameter contains a NULL pointer, no length is returned in the *StringLength* parameter.

■ If an attribute that returns a string value is specified in the *Attribute* parameter, the *Value* parameter must contain a pointer to a buffer in which this function can return the string.

■ If an attribute that returns a string value is specified in the *Attribute* parameter, and if that string value's actual length is greater than or equal to the maximum string size value specified in the *ValueMaxSize* parameter, the value is truncated to *ValueMaxSize*–1 (the length of a NULL-termination character) characters.

■ There are no driver-specific environment attributes.

■ The **SQL_ATTR_OUTPUT_NTS** environment attribute is supported by all standards-compliant applications. Therefore, the ODBC 3.x Driver Manager returns **SQL_TRUE** for this attribute. Likewise, the **SQL_ATTR_OUTPUT_NTS** environment attribute can only be set to **SQL_TRUE** by the **SQLSetEnvAttr()** function.

Prerequisites   An environment handle must be allocated before this function is called.

Restrictions   There are no restrictions associated with this function call.

See Also   SQLSetEnvAttr(), SQLGetConnectAttr(), SQLSetConnectAttr(), SQLGetConnectOption(), SQLSetConnectOption(), SQLGetStmtAttr(), SQLSetStmtAttr(), SQLGetStmtOption(), SQLSetStmtOption()

Example   The following Visual C++ program illustrates how to retrieve and change the current value of an environment attribute.

```
/*————————————————————————————————————————————————— */
/* NAME:     CH8EX6.CPP                                         */
/* PURPOSE: Illustrate How To Use The Following ODBC API Functions */
/*          In A C++ Program:                                   */
/*                                                              */
/*               SQLGetEnvAttr()                                */
/*               SQLSetEnvAttr()                                */
```

```
/*                                                                   */
/* OTHER ODBC APIs SHOWN:                                            */
/*          SQLAllocHandle()          SQLFreeHandle()                */
/*                                                                   */
/*──────────────────────────────────────────────────────────────────*/

// Include The Appropriate Header Files
#include <windows.h>
#include <sql.h>
#include <sqlext.h>
#include <iostream.h>

// Define The ODBC_Class Class
class ODBC_Class
{
    // Attributes
    public:
        SQLHANDLE     EnvHandle;
        SQLRETURN     rc;
        SQLINTEGER    CPValue;

    // Operations
    public:
        ODBC_Class();                              // Constructor
        ~ODBC_Class();                             // Destructor
        SQLRETURN  GetConnPoolingValue();
        SQLRETURN  SetConnPoolingValue(SQLINTEGER CPValue);
};

// Define The Class Constructor
ODBC_Class::ODBC_Class()
{
    // Initialize The Return Code Variable
    rc = SQL_SUCCESS;

    // Allocate An Environment Handle
    rc = SQLAllocHandle(SQL_HANDLE_ENV, SQL_NULL_HANDLE, &EnvHandle);

    // Set The ODBC Application Version To 3.x
    if (rc == SQL_SUCCESS)
        rc = SQLSetEnvAttr(EnvHandle, SQL_ATTR_ODBC_VERSION,
                (SQLPOINTER) SQL_OV_ODBC3, SQL_IS_UINTEGER);
}

// Define The Class Destructor
ODBC_Class::~ODBC_Class()
{
    // Free The Environment Handle
    if (EnvHandle != NULL)
        SQLFreeHandle(SQL_HANDLE_ENV, EnvHandle);
}

// Define The GetConnPoolingValue() Member Function
SQLRETURN ODBC_Class::GetConnPoolingValue(void)
{
```

```
    // Declare The Local Memory Variables
    SQLINTEGER   ValueLength;

    // Determine Whether Or Not Connection Pooling Is Enabled
    rc = SQLGetEnvAttr(EnvHandle, SQL_ATTR_CONNECTION_POOLING,
            (SQLPOINTER) &CPValue, SQL_IS_UINTEGER, &ValueLength);

    // Display The Information Retrieved
    if (rc == SQL_SUCCESS)
    {
        if (CPValue == SQL_CP_OFF)
            cout << "Connection Pooling is disabled.";
        else
            cout << "Connection Pooling is enabled.";
        cout << endl;
    }

    // Return The ODBC API Return Code To The Calling Function
    return(rc);
}

// Define The SetConnPoolingValue() Member Function
SQLRETURN ODBC_Class::SetConnPoolingValue(SQLINTEGER CPValue)
{
    // Set The Connection Pooling Environment Attribute
    rc = SQLSetEnvAttr(EnvHandle, SQL_ATTR_CONNECTION_POOLING,
            (SQLPOINTER) CPValue, SQL_IS_UINTEGER);

    // Return The ODBC API Return Code To The Calling Function
    return(rc);
}

/*------------------------------------------------------------------*/
/* The Main Function                                                */
/*------------------------------------------------------------------*/
int main()
{
    // Declare The Local Memory Variables
    SQLRETURN   rc = SQL_SUCCESS;

    // Create An Instance Of The ODBC_Class Class
    ODBC_Class   Example;

    // Determine Whether Or Not Connection Pooling Is Enabled
    rc = Example.GetConnPoolingValue();

    // Tell The Driver Use Connection Pooling For Each Environment
    rc = Example.SetConnPoolingValue(SQL_CP_ONE_PER_HENV);

    // Determine Whether Or Not Connection Pooling Was Turned On
    rc = Example.GetConnPoolingValue();

    // Return To The Operating System
    return(rc);
}
```

SQLSetEnvAttr

COMPATABILITY					
X/OPEN 95 CLI	ISO/IEC 92 CLI	ODBC 1.0	ODBC 2.0	ODBC 3.0	ODBC 3.5
☑	☑	☐	☐	☑	☑

API CONFORMANCE LEVEL	CORE

Purpose   The **SQLSetEnvAttr()** function is used to modify the current value of a specified environment attribute.

Syntax
```
SQLRETURN SQLSetEnvAttr     (SQLHENV      EnvironmentHandle,
                             SQLINTEGER   Attribute,
                             SQLPOINTER   Value,
                             SQLINTEGER   StringLength);
```

Parameters

EnvironmentHandle   An environment handle that refers to a previously allocated environment information storage buffer (data structure).

Attribute   The environment attribute whose value is to be modified. This parameter must be set to one of the following values:

- **SQL_ATTR_CONNECTION_POOLING**
- **SQL_ATTR_CP_MATCH**
- **SQL_ATTR_ODBC_VERSION**
- **SQL_ATTR_OUTPUT_NTS**

Value   A pointer to a location in memory where the new value for the environment attribute is stored. Depending on the environment attribute being set, this pointer can reference either a 32-bit integer value, or a NULL-terminated character string.

StringLength   The length of the environment attribute value stored in the *Value* parameter. If the attribute value is a 32-bit integer value, this parameter is ignored.

Description   The `SQLSetEnvAttr()` function is used to modify the current value of a specified environment attribute. Refer to the `SQLGetEnvAttr()` function for more information about each environment attribute available.

All environment attributes successfully set by an application for the specified environment persist until the environment handle is freed with the `SQLFreeHandle()` function (ODBC 3.x driver) or the `SQLFreeEnv()` function (ODBC 2.0 or earlier driver). Because more than one environment handle can be allocated simultaneously in ODBC 3.x, environment attribute settings on one environment are not affected when another environment is allocated. Once an environment attribute is set, that attribute's value affects all data source connections that exist or become allocated under the specified environment.

Return Codes   `SQL_SUCCESS`, `SQL_SUCCESS_WITH_INFO`, `SQL_INVALID_HANDLE`, or `SQL_ERROR`

SQLSTATEs   If this function returns `SQL_SUCCESS_WITH_INFO` or `SQL_ERROR`, one of the following SQLSTATE values may be obtained by calling the `SQLGetDiagRec()` function:

01000, **01**S02, **HY**000, **HY**001, **HY**009, **HY**010*, **HY**013, **HY**024, **HY**090, **HY**092*, or **HYC**00*

* Returned by the ODBC Driver Manager.

Unless noted otherwise, each of these SQLSTATE values is returned by the data source driver. Refer to Appendix B for detailed information about each SQLSTATE value that can be returned by the ODBC Driver Manager or by a data source driver.

Comments   ▦ There are no driver-specific environment attributes.

▦ Connection attributes cannot be set by this function.

▦ This function can be called more than once to set any environment attribute; if this function is called more than once with the same attribute specified, the value for that attribute is overridden.

▦ An application using pooled connections should always evaluate, and if necessary, set the `SQL_ATTR_CP_MATCH` attribute. This attribute determines how a requested connection is matched to a pooled connection when pooled connections are used. If the `SQL_ATTR_CP_MATCH` environment attribute is set to `SQL_CP_STRICT_MATCH`, the match must be exact for a connection in the pool to be used. If the `SQL_ATTR_CP_MATCH` environment attribute is set to `SQL_CP_RELAXED_MATCH`, the connection options specified in the call to **SQLConnect()** must match, but not all the connection attributes must match.

Prerequisites An environment handle must be allocated before this function is called.

Restrictions An application can only call this function if no connection handle has been allocated on the environment.

See Also SQLGetEnvAttr(), SQLGetConnectAttr(), SQLSetConnectAttr(), SQLGetConnectOption(), SQLSetConnectOption(), SQLGetStmtAttr(), SQLSetStmtAttr(), SQLGetStmtOption(), SQLSetStmtOption()

Example See the example provided for the **SQLGetEnvAttr()** function, on page 231.

SQLGetConnectAttr

COMPATABILITY

X/OPEN 95 CLI	ISO/IEC 92 CLI	ODBC 1.0	ODBC 2.0	ODBC 3.0	ODBC 3.5
☑	☑	☐	☐	☑	☑

API CONFORMANCE LEVEL   **CORE**

Purpose The **SQLGetConnectAttr()** function is used to retrieve the current setting of a specified connection attribute.

Syntax
```
SQLRETURN SQLGetConnectAttr  (SQLHDBC     ConnectionHandle,
                              SQLINTEGER  Attribute,
                              SQLPOINTER  Value,
                              SQLINTEGER  ValueMaxSize,
                              SQLINTEGER  *StringLength);
```

Parameters
ConnectionHandle   A data source connection handle that refers to a previously allocated connection information storage buffer (data structure).

Attribute   The connection attribute whose value is to be retrieved. This parameter must be set to one of the following values:

- `SQL_ATTR_ACCESS_MODE`
- `SQL_ATTR_ASYNC_ENABLE`
- `SQL_ATTR_AUTO_IPD`
- `SQL_ATTR_AUTOCOMMIT`
- `SQL_ATTR_CONNECTION_TIMEOUT`
- `SQL_ATTR_CURRENT_CATALOG`
- `SQL_ATTR_LOGIN_TIMEOUT`
- `SQL_ATTR_METADATA_ID`
- `SQL_ATTR_ODBC_CURSORS`
- `SQL_ATTR_PACKET_SIZE`
- `SQL_ATTR_QUIET_MODE`
- `SQL_ATTR_TRACE`
- `SQL_ATTR_TRACEFILE`
- `SQL_ATTR_TRANSLATE_LIB`
- `SQL_ATTR_TRANSLATE_OPTION`
- `SQL_ATTR_TXN_ISOLATION`

Value

A pointer to a location in memory where this function is to store the current value of the specified connection attribute.

ValueMaxSize

The size of the memory storage buffer where this function is to store the current value of the specified connection attribute. If an ODBC-defined attribute is to be retrieved and if the attribute value is a 32-bit integer value, this parameter is ignored. If a driver-defined attribute is to be retrieved, this parameter may be set as follows:

- If the value of the specified connection attribute is a character string, this parameter may be set to the actual length of the string or to `SQL_NTS`.
- If the value of the specified connection attribute is a binary string, this parameter may be set to the result of the

SQL_LEN_BINARY_ATTR(*length*) macro. Usually, this macro places a negative value in this parameter.

■ If the value of the specified connection attribute is anything other than a character string or binary string, this parameter may be set to **SQL_IS_POINTER**.

■ If the value of the specified connection attribute is a fixed-length data type, this parameter may be set to **SQL_IS_INTEGER** or **SQL_IS_UINTEGER**, as appropriate.

StringLength   A pointer to a location in memory where this function is to store the actual number of bytes written to the attribute value memory storage buffer (*Value*). If the attribute value retrieved is not a character string value, this parameter is ignored.

Description   The **SQLGetConnectAttr()** function is used to retrieve the current setting of a specified connection attribute. This function can be called at any time after a connection handle is allocated, as long as that connection handle has not been freed. Table 8–6 lists alphabetically each value that can be specified for the *Attribute* parameter, along with a description of the information returned for that value when this function is executed.

To take advantage of different data sources, more connection attributes may be defined in future releases of ODBC. In fact, a range of connection attributes (0 to 999) has been reserved by ODBC to allow for future expansion. In addition, ODBC driver developers are required to reserve values for their own driver-specific use from X/Open.

NOTE: *In ODBC 3.x, this function replaces the ODBC 2.0 function* **SQLGetConnectOption()**.

Return Codes   **SQL_SUCCESS, SQL_SUCCESS_WITH_INFO, SQL_NO_DATA, SQL_INVALID_HANDLE,** or **SQL_ERROR**

Table 8-6   Connection Attributes( )

Attribute	Data Type	Description
SQL_ATTR_ACCESS_MODE (ODBC 1.0)	**SQLUINTEGER**	Specifies the type of SQL requests that can be made to the connected data source. Valid values for this attribute are:
		SQL_MODE_READ_ONLY: Indicates that the connection is not required to support SQL statements causing updates to occur. This mode can be used to optimize locking strategies, transaction management, or other areas as appropriate to the driver or data source.
		SQL_MODE_READ_WRITE: Indicates that the connection is required to support SQL statements causing updates to occur. This is the default value for this attribute.
		Note: When this attribute is set to **SQL_MODE_READ_ONLY**, the driver is not required to prevent the submission of SQL statements that cause updates to occur from reaching the driver. The behavior of the driver and data source when asked to process such SQL statements with a read-only connection is implementation-defined.
SQL_ATTR_ASYNC_ENABLE (ODBC 3.0)	**SQLUINTEGER**	Specifies whether an ODBC API function called by an SQL statement on the specified connection is executed asynchronously. Valid values for this attribute are:
		SQL_ASYNC_ENABLE_OFF: All future statement handles allocated on this connection cannot be executed asynchronously. This is the default value for this attribute.
		SQL_ASYNC_ENABLE_ON: All future statement handles allocated on this connection can be executed asynchronously. It is driver-defined whether this setting also enables asynchronous execution for existing statement handles associated with the connection. An error is returned if asynchronous execution is enabled while there is an active statement on the connection.
		This attribute can be set as long as the **SQLGetInfo()** function returns **SQL_AM_CONNECTION** or **SQL_AM_STATEMENT** when it is called with the **SQL_ASYNC_MODE** option specified.
		After a function has been called asynchronously, only the original function, **SQLAllocHandle()**, **SQLCancel()**, **SQLGetDiagField()**, or **SQLGetDiagRec()** can be called on the statement handle or the connection handle associated with the

Table 8–6   Connection Attributes( ) (Continued)

Attribute	Data Type	Description
		statement handle, until the original function returns a code other than **SQL_STILL_EXECUTING**. Any other function called on the statement handle or the connection handle associated with the statement handle returns **SQL_ERROR** with an SQLSTATE of **HY**010 (Function sequence error). Functions can be called on other statement handles.
		In general, applications should execute ODBC API functions asynchronously only on single-thread operating systems. On multithread operating systems, applications should execute ODBC API functions on separate threads, rather than executing them asynchronously on the same thread.
		The following functions can be executed asynchronously:
		SQLBulkOperations(), SQLColAttribute(), SQLColumnPrivileges(), SQLColumns(), SQLCopyDesc(), SQLDescribeCol(), SQLDescribeParam(), SQLExecDirect(), SQLExecute(), SQLFetch(), SQLFetchScroll(), SQLForeignKeys(), SQLGetData(), SQLGetDescField(),[1] SQLGetDescRec(),[1] SQLGetDiagField(), SQLGetDiagRec(), SQLGetTypeInfo(), SQLMoreResults(), SQLNumParams(), SQLNumResultCols(), SQLParamData(), SQLPrepare(), SQLPrimaryKeys(), SQLProcedureColumns(), SQLProcedures(), SQLPutData(), SQLSetPos(), SQLSpecialColumns(), SQLStatistics(), SQLTablePrivileges(), SQLTables()
SQL_ATTR_AUTO_IPD (ODBC 3.0)	SQLUINTEGER	Specifies whether automatic population of the implementation parameter descriptor (IPD) after a **SQLPrepare()** function call is supported. Valid values for this attribute are:
		SQL_TRUE: Automatic population of the IPD after a call to **SQLPrepare()** is supported by the driver.
		SQL_FALSE: Automatic population of the IPD after a call to **SQLPrepare()** is not supported by the driver.
		This connection attribute is a read-only attribute; its value can be retrieved by the **SQLGetConnectAttr()** function, but it cannot be set by the **SQLSetConnectAttr()** function.

Table 8-6 Connection Attributes( ) (Continued)

Attribute	Data Type	Description
		If the **SQL_ATTR_AUTO_IPD** connection attribute is set to **SQL_TRUE**, the statement attribute **SQL_ATTR_ENABLE_AUTO_IPD** can be set to **SQL_TRUE** or **SQL_FALSE** (to turn automatic population of the IPD on or off).
		If the **SQL_ATTR_AUTO_IPD** connection attribute is set to **SQL_FALSE**, the statement attribute **SQL_ATTR_ENABLE_AUTO_IPD** can only be set to **SQL_FALSE**.
		The default value of the **SQL_ATTR_AUTO_IPD** connection attribute is the same as the value of the **SQL_ATTR_AUTO_IPD** statement attribute.
		Servers that don't support prepared statements cannot populate the IPD automatically.
SQL_ATTR_AUTOCOMMIT (ODBC 1.0)	**SQLUINTEGER**	Specifies whether to use auto-commit or manual-commit mode. Valid values for this attribute are:
		SQL_AUTOCOMMIT_OFF: The driver uses manual-commit mode, and the application must explicitly commit or roll back transactions with the **SQLEndTran( )** function.
		SQL_AUTOCOMMIT_ON: The driver uses auto-commit mode, therefore each SQL statement is committed immediately after it is executed. This is the default value for this attribute.
		Any open transactions on the connection are automatically committed when the **SQL_ATTR_ AUTOCOMMIT** connection attribute is set to **SQL_AUTOCOMMIT_ON** (to change from manual-commit mode to auto-commit mode).
		Note: Some data sources delete the access plans and close the cursors for all SQL statements on a connection each time an SQL statement is committed; auto-commit mode can cause this to happen after each non-query statement is executed, or when the cursor associated with a query is closed.
		When a batch of statements are executed in auto-commit mode, two things are possible:
		1. The entire batch can be treated as an auto-commitable unit, or
		2. Each statement in the batch is treated as an auto-commitable unit.

Table 8–6 *Connection Attributes( ) (Continued)*

Attribute	Data Type	Description
		It is driver-defined whether a batch is treated as an auto-commitable unit, or whether each individual statement within the batch is auto-commitable. Some data sources may support both these behaviors and may provide a way of choosing one or the other.
SQL_ATTR_CONNECTION_ TIMEOUT (ODBC 3.0)	**SQLUINTEGER**	Specifies the number of seconds to wait for any request on the connection to complete before returning control to the application. The driver should return SQLSTATE **HYT**00 (Timeout expired) anytime it is possible to timeout in a situation not associated with query execution or login. If the value for this attribute is **0**, the timeout is disabled and an application waits indefinitely for a request to be completed.
SQL_ATTR_CURRENT_ CATALOG (ODBC 2.0)	Character string	Specifies the name of the catalog to be used by the data source. For example, in SQL Server, the catalog is a database, so the driver sends a **USE** *database* SQL statement to the data source where *database* is the database name stored in this attribute. For a single-tier driver, the catalog might be a directory, so the driver changes its current directory to the directory specified.
SQL_ATTR_LOGIN_ TIMEOUT (ODBC 1.0)	**SQLUINTEGER**	Specifies the number of seconds to wait for a login request to complete before returning control to the application. The default value for this attribute is driver-dependent. If the value for this attribute is **0**, the timeout is disabled and an application will wait indefinitely for a connection. If the timeout value specified exceeds the maximum login timeout value recognized by the data source, the driver substitutes that value and returns SQLSTATE **01**S02 (Option value changed).
SQL_ATTR_METADATA_ID (ODBC 3.0)	**SQLUINTEGER**	Specifies how the string parameters of catalog functions are treated. Valid values for this attribute are: **SQL_TRUE**: The string parameters of catalog functions are treated as identifiers. The case is not significant. For non-delimited strings, the driver removes any trailing spaces, and the string is folded to uppercase. For delimited strings, the driver removes any leading or trailing spaces, and takes whatever is between the delimiters literally. If one of these parameters contains a NULL pointer, the function returns **SQL_ERROR** and SQLSTATE **HY**009 (Invalid use of NULL pointer).

Table 8–6 *Connection Attributes( ) (Continued)*

Attribute	Data Type	Description
		SQL_FALSE: The string parameters of catalog functions are not treated as identifiers. The case is significant. They can contain a string search pattern or not, depending on the argument. This is the default value for this attribute.
		The *TableType* parameter of the **SQLTables()** function, which takes a list of values, is not affected by this attribute.
		The **SQL_ATTR_METADATA_ID** can also be set on the SQL statement level. (It is the only connection attribute that is also a statement attribute.)
SQL_ATTR_ODBC_CURSORS (ODBC 2.0)	SQUINTEGER	Specifies how the ODBC Driver Manager uses the ODBC cursor library. Valid values for this attribute are:
		SQL_CUR_USE_IF_NEEDED: The Driver Manager uses the ODBC cursor library only if it is needed. If the driver supports the **SQL_FETCH_PRIOR** option of the **SQLFetchScroll()** function, the Driver Manager uses the scrolling capabilities of the driver. Otherwise, it uses the ODBC cursor library.
		SQL_CUR_USE_ODBC: The Driver Manager uses the ODBC cursor library.
		SQL_CUR_USE_DRIVER: The Driver Manager uses the scrolling capabilities of the driver. This is the default value for this attribute.
SQL_ATTR_PACKET_SIZE (ODBC 2.0)	SQLUINTEGER	Specifies the network packet size (in bytes).
		If the packet size specified size exceeds the maximum packet size or is smaller than the minimum packet size recognized by the driver, the driver substitutes that value and returns SQLSTATE **01**S02 (Option value changed).
		If the application attempts to set the packet size after a connection has already been made, the driver returns SQLSTATE **HY**011 (Attribute cannot be set now).
		Note: Many data sources either do not support this option or can only return the network packet size (they can't change it).
SQL_ATTR_QUIET_MODE (ODBC 2.0)	32-bit window handle (**HWND**)	Specifies the platform-specific parent window handle to use when displaying child dialogs. If the window handle is a NULL pointer, the driver does not

Table 8–6 Connection Attributes( ) (Continued)

Attribute	Data Type	Description
		display any dialogs. If the window handle is not a null pointer, it should be the parent window handle of the application—this is the default value for this attribute. Note: The **SQL_ATTR_QUIET_MODE** connection attribute does not apply to the dialogs displayed by the **SQLDriverConnect()** function.
SQL_ATTR_TRACE (ODBC 1.0)	**SQLUINTEGER**	Specifies whether the ODBC Driver Manager is to perform tracing. Valid values for this attribute are: **SQL_OPT_TRACE_OFF**: The ODBC Driver Manager is not to write each ODBC function call to the trace file. This is the default value for this attribute. **SQL_OPT_TRACE_ON**: The ODBC Driver Manager is to write each ODBC function call to the trace file. An application specifies a trace file with the **SQL_ATTR_TRACEFILE** connection attribute. If the trace file specified already exists, the Driver Manager appends records to it. Otherwise, a new file is created. If tracing is on and no trace file has been specified, the Driver Manager writes to the file SQL.LOG in the root directory. An application can set the variable **ODBCSharedTraceFlag** to enable tracing dynamically. Tracing is then turned on for all ODBC applications currently running; if an application turns tracing off, it is turned off only for that application. If the **Trace** keyword in the system information storage area (registry) is set to **1** when an application allocates an environment handle, tracing is enabled for all handles that are allocated later by the application. Calling **SQLSetConnectAttr()** to turn tracing on or off does not require that the specified connection handle be valid, and does not return **SQL_ERROR** if a NULL connection handle is specified. This attribute applies to all connections. Note: When tracing is on, the Driver Manager can return SQLSTATE **IM**013 (Trace file error) from any function.
SQL_ATTR_TRACEFILE (ODBC 1.0)	Null-terminated character string	Specifies the name of the trace file to use when tracing is turned on. The default value for this attribute is specified with the **TraceFile** keyname in the system information storage area.

Table 8-6 Connection Attributes( ) (Continued)

Attribute	Data Type	Description
		Calling **SQLSetConnectAttr()** to specify a trace file name does not require that the specified connection handle be valid, and does not return **SQL_ERROR** if a NULL connection handle is specified. This attribute applies to all connections
SQL_ATTR_TRANSLATE_LIB (ODBC 1.0)	Null-terminated character string	Specifies the name of a library containing the functions **SQLDriverToDataSource()** and **SQLDataSourceToDriver()** that the driver accesses to perform tasks such as character set translation. This attribute can only be set if the driver has connected to the data source. This attribute's setting will persist across connections.
SQL_ATTR_TRANSLATE_ OPTION (ODBC 1.0)	32-bit integer	Specifies a value that is passed to the translation library. This attribute can only be specified if the driver has connected to the data source.
SQL_ATTR_TXN_ISOLATION (ODBC 1.0)	32-bit bitmask	Specifies the transaction isolation level to use for the current connection. An application must call **SQLEndTran** to commit or roll back all open transactions on a connection, before calling the **SQLSetConnectAttr()** function with this attribute specified. The valid values for the *Value* parameter can be determined by calling the **SQLGetInfo()** function with the *InfoType* parameters set to **SQL_TXN_ISOLATION_OPTIONS**.

(The information above was adapted from the table on pages 945–947 *of Microsoft ODBC 3.0 Software Development Kit & Programmer's Reference*.)

SQLSTATEs If this function returns **SQL_SUCCESS_WITH_INFO** or **SQL_ERROR**, one of the following SQLSTATE values may be obtained by calling the **SQLGetDiagRec()** function:

01000, **01**004, **08**003*, **08**S01, **HY**000, **HY**001, **HY**010*, **HY**013, **HY**090*, **HY**092, **HYC**00, **HYT**01, or **IM**001*

* Returned by the ODBC Driver Manager.

Unless noted otherwise, each of these SQLSTATE values are returned by the data source driver. Refer to Appendix B for detailed information about each SQLSTATE value that can be returned by the ODBC Driver Manager or by a data source driver.

Comments ▪ If the *Value* parameter contains a NULL pointer, no length is returned in the *StringLength* parameter.

■ If an attribute that returns a string value is specified in the *Attribute* parameter, and if that string value's actual length is greater than or equal to the maximum string size value specified in the *ValueMaxSize* parameter, the value is truncated to *ValueMaxSize*-1 (the length of a NULL-termination character) characters.

■ If an attribute that returns a string value is specified in the *Attribute* parameter, the *Value* parameter must contain a pointer to a buffer in which this function can return the string.

■ If the value returned for the attribute specified in the *Attribute* parameter is a Unicode string, the *ValueMaxSize* parameter must contain an even number.

■ An application may or may not have to establish a connection to a data source before calling this function, depending on the attribute value being retrieved.

■ If this function is called and an attribute that does not have a value is specified, **SQL_NO_DATA** is returned. An attributes value can be either a default value or a value that was set by a prior call to **SQLSetConnectAttr()**.

■ If **SQL_ATTR_TRACE** or **SQL_ATTR_TRACEFILE** is specified in the *Attribute* parameter, the connection handle specified in the *ConnectionHandle* parameter does not have to be valid since these attributes apply to all connections.

■ While an application can set SQL statement attributes with the **SQLSetConnectAttr()** function, an application cannot use this function to retrieve SQL statement attribute values; the **SQLGetStmtAttr()** function must be used instead.

■ The value of the **SQL_ATTR_AUTO_IPD** connection attribute can be returned by this function, but it cannot be set by the **SQLSetConnectAttr()** function.

Prerequisites   A connection handle must be allocated before this function is called.

Restrictions   There are no restrictions associated with this function call.

See Also   SQLSetConnectAttr(), SQLGetConnectOption(),
SQLSetConnectOption(), SQLGetEnvAttr(), SQLSetEnvAttr(),
SQLGetStmtAttr(), SQLSetStmtAttr(), SQLGetStmtOption(),
SQLSetStmtOption()

Example   The following Visual C++ program illustrates how to retrieve and change the current value of a connection attribute.

```
/*-----------------------------------------------------------------*/
/* NAME:       CH8EX7.CPP                                          */
/* PURPOSE: Illustrate How To Use The Following ODBC API Functions */
/*          In A C++ Program:                                      */
/*                                                                 */
/*               SQLGetConnectAttr()                               */
/*               SQLSetConnectAttr()                               */
/*                                                                 */
/* OTHER ODBC APIs SHOWN:                                          */
/*          SQLAllocHandle()          SQLSetEnvAttr()              */
/*          SQLConnect()              SQLDisconnect()              */
/*          SQLFreeHandle()                                        */
/*                                                                 */
/*-----------------------------------------------------------------*/

// Include The Appropriate Header Files
#include <windows.h>
#include <sql.h>
#include <sqlext.h>
#include <iostream.h>

// Define The ODBC_Class Class
class ODBC_Class
{
    // Attributes
    public:
        SQLHANDLE     EnvHandle;
        SQLHANDLE     ConHandle;
        SQLRETURN     rc;
        SQLUINTEGER   ACValue;

    // Operations
    public:
        ODBC_Class();                                // Constructor
        ~ODBC_Class();                               // Destructor
        SQLRETURN   GetAutoCommitValue();
        SQLRETURN   SetAutoCommitValue(SQLUINTEGER ACValue);
};

// Define The Class Constructor
ODBC_Class::ODBC_Class()
{
    // Initialize The Return Code Variable
    rc = SQL_SUCCESS;

    // Allocate An Environment Handle
    rc = SQLAllocHandle(SQL_HANDLE_ENV, SQL_NULL_HANDLE, &EnvHandle);

    // Set The ODBC Application Version To 3.x
    if (rc == SQL_SUCCESS)
        rc = SQLSetEnvAttr(EnvHandle, SQL_ATTR_ODBC_VERSION,
                (SQLPOINTER) SQL_OV_ODBC3, SQL_IS_UINTEGER);

    // Allocate A Connection Handle
```

```cpp
    if (rc == SQL_SUCCESS)
        rc = SQLAllocHandle(SQL_HANDLE_DBC, EnvHandle, &ConHandle);
}

// Define The Class Destructor
ODBC_Class::~ODBC_Class()
{
    // Free The Connection Handle
    if (ConHandle != NULL)
        SQLFreeHandle(SQL_HANDLE_DBC, ConHandle);

    // Free The Environment Handle
    if (EnvHandle != NULL)
        SQLFreeHandle(SQL_HANDLE_ENV, EnvHandle);
}

// Define The GetAutoCommitValue() Member Function
SQLRETURN ODBC_Class::GetAutoCommitValue(void)
{
    // Declare The Local Memory Variables
    SQLINTEGER  ValueLength;

    // Determine Whether Or Not The Driver Is In Auto-Commit Mode
    rc = SQLGetConnectAttr(ConHandle, SQL_ATTR_AUTOCOMMIT,
            (SQLPOINTER) &ACValue, SQL_IS_UINTEGER, &ValueLength);

    // Display The Information Retrieved
    if (rc == SQL_SUCCESS)
    {
        if (ACValue == SQL_AUTOCOMMIT_ON)
            cout << "The driver is in auto-commit mode.";
        else
            cout << "The driver is in manual-commit node.";
        cout << endl;
    }

    // Return The ODBC API Return Code To The Calling Function
    return(rc);
}

// Define The SetAutoCommitValue() Member Function
SQLRETURN ODBC_Class::SetAutoCommitValue(SQLUINTEGER ACValue)
{
    // Set The Auto-Commit Connection Attribute
    rc = SQLSetConnectAttr(ConHandle, SQL_ATTR_AUTOCOMMIT,
            (SQLPOINTER) ACValue, SQL_IS_UINTEGER);

    // Return The ODBC API Return Code To The Calling Function
    return(rc);
}

/*———————————————————————————————————————— */
/* The Main Function                        */
/*———————————————————————————————————————— */
int main()
```

```
{
    // Declare The Local Memory Variables
    SQLRETURN   rc = SQL_SUCCESS;
    SQLCHAR     DBName[10] = "Northwind";

    // Create An Instance Of The ODBC_Class Class
    ODBC_Class   Example;

    // Connect To The Northwind Sample Database
    if (Example.ConHandle != NULL)
    {
        rc = SQLConnect(Example.ConHandle, DBName, SQL_NTS,
                (SQLCHAR *) "", SQL_NTS, (SQLCHAR *) "", SQL_NTS);

        // Determine Whether Or Not The Driver Is In Auto-Commit Mode
        rc = Example.GetAutoCommitValue();

        // Tell The Driver To Use Manual-Commit Mode
        rc = Example.SetAutoCommitValue(SQL_AUTOCOMMIT_OFF);

        // Determine Whether Or Not The Driver Is Now Using
        // Manual-Commit Mode
        rc = Example.GetAutoCommitValue();

        // Disconnect From The Northwind Sample Database
        rc = SQLDisconnect(Example.ConHandle);
    }

    // Return To The Operating System
    return(rc);
}
```

SQLSetConnectAttr

COMPATABILITY

X/OPEN 95 CLI	ISO/IEC 92 CLI	ODBC 1.0	ODBC 2.0	ODBC 3.0	ODBC 3.5
✓	✓	☐	☐	✓	✓

API CONFORMANCE LEVEL   **CORE**

Purpose   The SQLSetConnectAttr() function is used to modify the current value of a specified connection attribute.

Syntax

```
SQLRETURN SQLGetConnectAttr (SQLHDBC      ConnectionHandle,
                             SQLINTEGER   Attribute,
                             SQLPOINTER   Value,
                             SQLINTEGER   StringLength);
```

Parameters

ConnectionHandle   A data source connection handle that refers to a previously allocated connection information storage buffer (data structure).

Attribute   The connection attribute whose value is to be modified. This parameter must be set to one of the following values:

- **SQL_ATTR_ACCESS_MODE**
- **SQL_ATTR_ASYNC_ENABLE**
- **SQL_ATTR_AUTO_IPD**
- **SQL_ATTR_AUTOCOMMIT**
- **SQL_ATTR_CONNECTION_TIMEOUT**
- **SQL_ATTR_CURRENT_CATALOG**
- **SQL_ATTR_LOGIN_TIMEOUT**
- **SQL_ATTR_METADATA_ID**
- **SQL_ATTR_ODBC_CURSORS**
- **SQL_ATTR_PACKET_SIZE**
- **SQL_ATTR_QUIET_MODE**
- **SQL_ATTR_TRACE**
- **SQL_ATTR_TRACEFILE**
- **SQL_ATTR_TRANSLATE_LIB**
- **SQL_ATTR_TRANSLATE_OPTION**
- **SQL_ATTR_TXN_ISOLATION**

Value   A pointer to a location in memory where the new value for the connection attribute is stored. Depending on the connection attribute being set, this pointer can reference either a 32-bit integer value, or a NULL-terminated character string.

StringLength   The length of the connection attribute value stored in the *Value* parameter. If an ODBC-defined attribute value is to be set and if the attribute value is a 32-bit integer value, this parameter is ignored. If a driver-defined attribute value is to be set, this parameter must be set as follows:

- If the value of the specified connection attribute is a character string, this parameter should be set to the actual length of the string or to **SQL_NTS**.
- If the value of the specified connection attribute is a binary string, this parameter should be set to the result of the **SQL_LEN_BINARY_ATTR(*length*)** macro. Usually, this macro places a negative value in this parameter.
- If the value of the specified connection attribute is anything other than a character string or binary string, this parameter should be set to **SQL_IS_ POINTER**.
- If the value of the specified connection attribute is a fixed-length data type, this parameter should be set to **SQL_IS_INTEGER** or **SQL_IS_UINTEGER**, as appropriate.

Description   The **SQLSetConnectAttr()** function is used to modify the current value of a specified connection attribute. Refer to the **SQLGetConnectAttr()** function for more information about each connection attribute available.

All connection and statement attributes successfully set by an application for a specified connection handle persist until the connection handle is freed with the **SQLFreeHandle()** function (ODBC 3.x driver) or the **SQLFreeConnect()** function (ODBC 2.0 or earlier driver). If an application calls this function before connecting to a data source, the attribute persists even if the **SQLSetConnectAttr()** driver function fails when the application attempts to connect to the data source. Furthermore, if an application sets a driver-specific attribute, the attribute persists even if the application connects to a different driver using the same connection handle.

An application can call this function at any time between the time the connection handle is allocated and freed, however, some connection attributes can only be set before a connection has been made, while others can only be set after a connection has been made. Table 8–7 identifies when each connection attribute can be set.

NOTE: In ODBC 3.x, this function replaces the ODBC 2.0 function `SQLSetConnectOption()`.

Table 8-7 When connection attributes can be set

Attribute	Set Before Connection	Set After Connection
SQL_ATTR_ACCESS_MODE	Yes	Yes[1]
SQL_ATTR_ASYNC_ENABLE	Yes	Yes[2]
SQL_ATTR_AUTO_IPD	Yes	Yes
SQL_ATTR_AUTOCOMMIT	Yes	Yes
SQL_ATTR_CONNECTION_TIMEOUT	Yes	Yes
SQL_ATTR_CURRENT_CATALOG	Yes	Yes[1]
SQL_ATTR_LOGIN_TIMEOUT	Yes	No
SQL_ATTR_METADATA_ID	Yes	Yes
SQL_ATTR_ODBC_CURSORS	Yes	No
SQL_ATTR_PACKET_SIZE	Yes	No
SQL_ATTR_QUIET_MODE	Yes	Yes
SQL_ATTR_TRACE	Yes	Yes
SQL_ATTR_TRACEFILE	Yes	Yes
SQL_ATTR_TRANSLATE_LIB	No	Yes
SQL_ATTR_TRANSLATE_OPTION	No	Yes
SQL_ATTR_TXN_ISOLATION	Yes	Yes[3]

(Adapted from table on pages 896–897 of *Microsoft ODBC 3.0 Software Development Kit & Programmer's Reference.)*

[1]**SQL_ATTR_ACCESS_MODE** and **SQL_ATTR_CURRENT_CATALOG** can be set before or after connecting, depending on the driver. However, interoperable applications should set them before connecting because some drivers do not support changing these after connecting.

[2]**SQL_ATTR_ASYNC_ENABLE** must be set before there is an active statement.

[3]**SQL_ATTR_TXN_ISOLATION** can only be set if there are no open transactions on the connection.

Return Codes `SQL_SUCCESS`, `SQL_SUCCESS_WITH_INFO`, `SQL_INVALID_HANDLE`, or `SQL_ERROR`

SQLSTATEs If this function returns `SQL_SUCCESS_WITH_INFO` or `SQL_ERROR`, one of the following SQLSTATE values may be obtained by calling the `SQLGetDiagRec()` function:

01000, **01**S02, **08**002, **08**003*, **08**S01, **24**000, **3D**000, **HY**000, **HY**001, **HY**009, **HY**010*, **HY**011, **HY**013, **HY**024, **HY**090*, **HY**092*, **HYC**00, **HYT**01, **IM**001*, or **IM**009

* Returned by the ODBC Driver Manager.

Unless noted otherwise, each of these SQLSTATE values are returned by the data source driver. Refer to Appendix B for detailed information about each SQLSTATE value that can be returned by the ODBC Driver Manager or by a data source driver.

Comments
- If a driver-specific value is specified in the *Attribute* parameter, a signed integer value may be stored in the memory location refered to by the *Value* parameter.
- In ODBC 3.x, statement attributes cannot be set at the connection level. This does not include the `SQL_ATTR_METADATA_ID` and `SQL_ATTR_ASYNC_ENABLE` attributes, because both are connection and statement attributes and can be set at either the connection level or the statement level.
- ODBC 3.x applications should never use the `SQLSetConnectOption()` function to set SQL statement attributes at the connection level.
- Some connection attributes support substitution of a similar value if the data source does not support the value specified in the *Value* parameter. In such cases, the driver returns `SQL_SUCCESS_WITH_INFO` and SQLSTATE **01**S02 (Option value changed). For example, if *Attribute* is `SQL_ATTR_PACKET_SIZE` and if the value specified in *Value* parameter exceeds the maximum packet size, the driver substitutes the maximum size. An application can call the `SQLGetConnectAttr()` function after setting a connection attribute to determine whether a substitution occurred, and if so, to obtain the substituted value.
- The *StringLength* parameter is ignored if the length is defined by the attribute itself, which is the case for all attributes introduced in ODBC 2.0 or earlier.

Prerequisites A connection handle must be allocated before this function is called.

Restrictions There are no restrictions associated with this function call.

See Also SQLGetConnectAttr(), SQLGetConnectOption(),
SQLSetConnectOption(), SQLGetEnvAttr(), SQLSetEnvAttr(),
SQLGetStmtAttr(), SQLSetStmtAttr(), SQLGetStmtOption(),
SQLSetStmtOption()

Example See the example provided for the **SQLGetConnectAttr()** function, on page 241.

SQLGetConnectOption

COMPATABILITY

X/OPEN 95 CLI	ISO/IEC 92 CLI	ODBC 1.0	ODBC 2.0	ODBC 3.0	ODBC 3.5
☒	☐	☑	☑	☐	☐

API CONFORMANCE LEVEL **LEVEL 1**

Purpose The **SQLGetConnectOption()** function is used to retrieve the current setting of a specified connection option (attribute).

Syntax
```
RETCODE SQLGetConnectOption     (HDBC     ConnectionHandle,
                                 UWORD    Option,
                                 PTR      Value);
```

Parameters *ConnectionHandle*   A data source connection handle that refers to a previously allocated connection information storage buffer (data structure).

Option   The connection option (attribute) whose value is to be retrieved. This parameter must be set to one of the following values:

▪ **SQL_ACCESS_MODE**

▪ **SQL_AUTOCOMMIT**

▪ **SQL_CURRENT_QUALIFIER**

- **SQL_LOGIN_TIMEOUT**
- **SQL_ODBC_CURSORS**
- **SQL_OPT_TRACE**
- **SQL_OPT_TRACEFILE**
- **SQL_PACKET_SIZE**
- **SQL_QUIET_MODE**
- **SQL_TRANSLATE_DLL**
- **SQL_TRANSLATE_OPTION**
- **SQL_TXN_ISOLATION**

Value   A pointer to a location in memory where this function is to store the current value of the connection option (attribute) specified. Depending on the connection option value being retrieved, this pointer can reference either a 32-bit integer value, or a NULL-terminated character string.

Description   The **SQLGetConnectOption()** function is used to retrieve the current setting of a specified connection option (attribute). Table 8–8 lists alphabetically each value that can be specified for the *Option* parameter, along with a description of the information returned for that value when this function is executed.

To take advantage of different data sources, more connection options may be defined in future releases of ODBC. In fact, a range of connection options (0 to 999) has been reserved by ODBC to allow for future expansion. In addition, ODBC driver developers are required to reserve values for their own driver-specific use from X/Open.

NOTE: *In ODBC 3.x, this function has been replaced by the* **SQLGetConnectAttr()** *function.*

Return Codes   **SQL_SUCCESS, SQL_SUCCESS_WITH_INFO, SQL_NO_DATA_FOUND, SQL_INVALID_HANDLE,** or **SQL_ERROR**

Table 8–8 Connection Options

Option	Data Type	Description
SQL_ACCESS_MODE (ODBC 1.0)	32-bit integer	Specifies the type of SQL requests that can be made to the connected data source. Valid values for this option are:
		SQL_MODE_READ_ONLY: Indicates that the connection is not required to support SQL statements that cause updates. This mode can be used to optimize locking strategies, transaction management, or other areas as appropriate to the driver or data source.
		SQL_MODE_READ_WRITE: Indicates that the connection is required to support SQL statements that cause updates. This is the default value for this option.
		Note: When this option is set to **SQL_MODE_READ_ ONLY**, the driver is not required to prevent the submission of SQL statements that cause updates to occur from reaching the driver. The behavior of the driver and data source when asked to process such SQL statements with a read-only connection is implementation-defined.
SQL_AUTOCOMMIT (ODBC 1.0)	32-bit integer	Specifies whether to use auto-commit or manual-commit mode. Valid values for this option are:
		SQL_AUTOCOMMIT_OFF: The driver uses manual-commit mode, and the application must explicitly commit or roll back transactions with the **SQLTransact()** function.
		SQL_AUTOCOMMIT_ON: The driver uses auto-commit mode; therefore each SQL statement is committed immediately after it is executed. This is the default value for this option.
		Any open transactions on the connection are automatically committed when the **SQL_AUTOCOMMIT** connection option is set to **SQL_AUTOCOMMIT_ON** (to change from manual-commit mode to auto-commit mode).
		Note: Some data sources delete the access plans and close the cursors for all SQL statements on a connection each time an SQL statement is committed; auto-commit mode can cause this to happen after each non-query statement is executed, or when the cursor associated with a query is closed.

Table 8–8   Connection Options (Continued)

Option	Data Type	Description
SQL_CURRENT_QUALIFIER (ODBC 2.0)	Null-terminated character string	Specifies the name of the qualifier to be used by the data source. For example, in SQL Server, the qualifier is a database, so the driver sends a **USE** *database* SQL statement to the data source, where *database* is the database name stored in this option. For a single-tier driver, the qualifier might be a directory, in which case the driver changes its current directory to the directory specified.
SQL_LOGIN_TIMEOUT (ODBC 1.0)	32-bit integer	Specifies the number of seconds to wait for a login request to complete before returning control to the application. The default value for this option is driver-dependent. If the value for this option is **0**, the timeout is disabled and an application will wait indefinitely for a connection. If the timeout value specified exceeds the maximum login timeout value recognized by the data source, the driver substitutes that value and returns SQLSTATE **01S02** (Option value changed).
SQL_ODBC_CURSORS (ODBC 2.0)	32-bit bitmask	Specifies how the ODBC Driver Manager uses the ODBC cursor library. Valid values for this option are: **SQL_CUR_USE_IF_NEEDED**: The Driver Manager uses the ODBC cursor library only if it is needed. If the driver supports the **SQL_FETCH_PRIOR** option of the **SQLExtendedFetch()** function, the Driver Manager uses the scrolling capabilities of the driver. Otherwise, it uses the ODBC cursor library. **SQL_CUR_USE_ODBC**: The Driver Manager uses the ODBC cursor library. **SQL_CUR_USE_DRIVER**: The Driver Manager uses the scrolling capabilities of the driver. This is the default value for this option.
SQL_TRACE (ODBC 1.0)	32-bit integer	Specifies whether the ODBC Driver Manager is to perform tracing. Valid values for this option are: **SQL_OPT_TRACE_OFF**: The ODBC Driver Manager is not to write each ODBC function call to the trace file. This is the default value for this option. **SQL_OPT_TRACE_ON**: The ODBC Driver Manager is to write each ODBC function call to the trace file.

Table 8-8   Connection Options (Continued)

Option	Data Type	Description
		An application specifies a trace file with the **SQL_OPT_TRACEFILE** connection option. If the trace file specified already exists, the Driver Manager appends records to it. Otherwise, a new file is created. If tracing is on and no trace file has been specified, the Driver Manager writes to the file SQL.LOG in the root directory.
		In Windows and WOW, the Driver Manager writes to the trace file each time any application calls an ODBC API function. In Windows NT, the Driver Manager only writes to the trace file when the application that turned tracing on calls an ODBC API function. If the **Trace** keyword in the system information storage area (either the [ODBC] section of the ODBC.INI file or the ODBC subkey in the registry) is set to **1** when an application allocates an environment handle, tracing is enabled. In Windows and WOW, tracing is enabled for all applications; on Windows NT, tracing is only enabled for the application that turned tracing on.
		Note: When tracing is on, the Driver Manager can return SQLSTATE **IM**013 (Trace file error) from any function.
SQL_OPT_TRACEFILE (ODBC 1.0)	Null-terminating character string	Specifies the name of the trace file to use when tracing is turned on. The default value for this option is specified with the **TraceFile** keyname in the system information storage area.
SQL_PACKET_SIZE (ODBC 2.0)	32-bit integer	Specifies the network packet size (in bytes).
		If the packet size specified exceeds the maximum packet size or is smaller than the minimum packet size recognized by the driver, the driver substitutes that value and returns SQLSTATE **01**S02 (Option value changed).
		Note: Many data sources either do not support this option or can only return the network packet size (they can't change it).
SQL_QUIET_MODE (ODBC 2.0)	32-bit window handle (**HWND**)	Specifies the platform-specific parent window handle to use when displaying child dialogs. If the window handle is a NULL pointer, the driver does not display any dialogs. If the window handle is not a NULL pointer, it should be the parent window handle of the application—this is the default value for this option.
		Note: The **SQL_QUIET_MODE** connection option does not apply to the dialog displayed by the **SQLDriverConnect()** function.

Table 8-8 Connection Options (Continued)

Option	Data Type	Description
SQL_TRANSLATE_DLL (ODBC 1.0)	Null-terminated character string	Specifies the name of a library containing the functions **SQLDriverToDataSource()** and **SQLDataSourceToDriver()** that the driver accesses to perform tasks such as character set translation. This option can only be set if the driver has connected to the data source. This option's setting will persist across connections.
SQL_TRANSLATE_ OPTION (ODBC 1.0)	32-bit integer	Specifies a value that is to be passed to the translation library. This option can only be specified if the driver has connected to the data source.
SQL_ATTR_TXN_ ISOLATION (ODBC 1.0)	32-bit bitmask	Specifies the transaction isolation level to use for the current connection. The following terms are used to define transaction isolation levels:

Dirty Read: Transaction 1 changes a row. Transaction 2 reads the changed row before Transaction 1 commits the change. If Transaction 1 rolls back the change, Transaction 2 will have read a row that is considered to have never existed.

Nonrepeatable Read: Transaction 1 reads a row. Transaction 2 updates or deletes that row and commits this change. If Transaction 1 attempts to reread the row, it will receive different row values or discover that the row has been deleted.

Phantom: Transaction 1 reads a set of rows that satisfy search criteria. Transaction 2 generates one or more rows (either through inserts or updates) that match the search criteria. If Transaction 1 re-executes the statement that reads the rows, it receives a different set of rows.

If the data source supports transactions, the driver returns one of the following bitmasks:

SQL_TXN_READ_UNCOMMITTED:
Dirty reads, nonrepeatable reads, and phantoms are possible.

SQL_TXN_READ_COMMITTED:
Dirty reads are not possible. Nonrepeatable reads and phantoms are possible.

SQL_TXN_REPEATABLE_READ:
Dirty reads and nonrepeatable reads are not possible.

SQL_TXN_SERIALIZABLE:
Transactions are serializable. Serializable transactions do not allow dirty reads, nonrepeatable reads, or phantoms.

Table 8-8 Connection Options (Continued)

Option	Data Type	Description
		SQL_TXN_VERSIONING: Transactions are serializable, but higher concurrency is possible than with **SQL_TXN_SERIALIZABLE**. Versioning transactions do not allow dirty reads, nonrepeatable reads, or phantoms.
		Typically, **SQL_TXN_SERIALIZABLE** is implemented by using locking protocols that reduce concurrency and **SQL_TXN_VERSIONING** is implemented by using a non-locking protocol such as record versioning.
		An application must call **SQLTransact()** to commit or roll back all open transactions on a connection, before calling the **SQLSetConnectOption()** function with this option specified. Valid values for this option can be determined by calling the **SQLGetInfo()** function with the *InfoType* parameter set to **SQL_TXN_ISOLATION_OPTIONS**.

(Adapted from the table on pages 454–457 of *Microsoft ODBC 2.0 Programmer's Reference and SDK Guide*.)

SQLSTATEs

If this function returns **SQL_SUCCESS_WITH_INFO** or **SQL_ERROR**, one of the following SQLSTATE values may be obtained by calling the **SQLError()** function:

01000, **08**003*, **IM**001*, **S1**000, **S1**001, **S1**010*, **S1**092*, or **S1C00**

* Returned by the ODBC Driver Manager.

Unless noted otherwise, each of these SQLSTATE values are returned by the data source driver. Refer to Appendix B for detailed information about each SQLSTATE value that can be returned by the ODBC Driver Manager or by a data source driver.

Comments

■ If an option that returns a string value is specified in the *Option* parameter, the *Value* parameter must contain a pointer to a buffer in which this function can return the string.

■ The maximum length a string value can be (excluding the NULL termination character) is **SQL_MAX_OPTION_STRING_LENGTH** bytes.

■ An application may or may not have to establish a connection to a data source before calling this function, depending on the option value being retrieved.

■ If this function is called and an option that does not have a value is specified, **SQL_NO_DATA_FOUND** is returned. An option's value can be either a default value or a value set by a prior call to **SQLSetConnectOption()**.

■ While an application can set SQL statement options with the **SQLSetConnectOption()** function, an application cannot use this function to retrieve SQL statement option values; the **SQLGetStmtOption()** function must be used to retrieve the current values of SQL statement options.

Prerequisites   A connection handle must be allocated before this function is called.

Restrictions   There are no restrictions associated with this function call.

See Also   SQLSetConnectOption(), SQLGetConnectAttr(), SQLSetConnectAttr(), SQLGetEnvAttr(), SQLSetEnvAttr(), SQLGetStmtAttr(), SQLSetStmtAttr(), SQLGetStmtOption(), SQLSetStmtOption()

Example   The following Visual C++ program illustrates how to retrieve and change the current value of a connection option (attribute).

```
/*--------------------------------------------------------------*/
/* NAME:      CH8EX8.CPP                                         */
/* PURPOSE: Illustrate How To Use The Following ODBC API Functions */
/*          In A C++ Program:                                    */
/*                                                               */
/*               SQLGetConnectOption()                           */
/*               SQLSetConnectOption()                           */
/*                                                               */
/* OTHER ODBC APIs SHOWN:                                        */
/*          SQLAllocEnv()              SQLAllocConnect()          */
/*          SQLConnect()               SQLDisconnect()            */
/*          SQLFreeConnect()           SQLFreeEnv()               */
/*                                                               */
/*--------------------------------------------------------------*/

// Include The Appropriate Header Files
#include <windows.h>
#include <sql.h>
#include <sqlext.h>
#include <iostream.h>

// Define The ODBC_Class Class
class ODBC_Class
{
    // Attributes
    public:
        HENV           EnvHandle;
```

```
        HDBC              ConHandle;
        RETCODE           rc;
        UDWORD            ACValue;

    // Operations
    public:
        ODBC_Class();                              // Constructor
        ~ODBC_Class();                             // Destructor
        RETCODE   GetAutoCommitValue();
        RETCODE   SetAutoCommitValue(UDWORD ACValue);
};

// Define The Class Constructor
ODBC_Class::ODBC_Class()
{
    // Initialize The Return Code Variable
    rc = SQL_SUCCESS;

    // Allocate An Environment Handle
    rc = SQLAllocEnv(&EnvHandle);

    // Allocate A Connection Handle
    if (rc == SQL_SUCCESS)
        rc = SQLAllocConnect(EnvHandle, &ConHandle);
}

// Define The Class Destructor
ODBC_Class::~ODBC_Class()
{
    // Free The Connection Handle
    if (ConHandle != NULL)
        SQLFreeConnect(ConHandle);

    // Free The Environment Handle
    if (EnvHandle != NULL)
        SQLFreeEnv(EnvHandle);
}

// Define The GetAutoCommitValue() Member Function
RETCODE ODBC_Class::GetAutoCommitValue(void)
{
    // Determine Whether Or Not The Driver Is In Auto-Commit Mode
    rc = SQLGetConnectOption(ConHandle, SQL_AUTOCOMMIT,
            (PTR) &ACValue);

    // Display The Information Retrieved
    if (rc == SQL_SUCCESS)
    {
        if (ACValue == SQL_AUTOCOMMIT_ON)
            cout << "The driver is in auto-commit mode.";
        else
            cout << "The driver is in manual-commit node.";
        cout << endl;
    }
```

```
    // Return The ODBC API Return Code To The Calling Function
    return(rc);
}

// Define The SetAutoCommitValue() Member Function
RETCODE ODBC_Class::SetAutoCommitValue(UDWORD ACValue)
{
    // Set The Auto-Commit Connection Attribute
    rc = SQLSetConnectOption(ConHandle, SQL_AUTOCOMMIT,
            (UDWORD) ACValue);

    // Return The ODBC API Return Code To The Calling Function
    return(rc);
}

/*————————————————————————————————————————————————————————————— */
/* The Main Function                                             */
/*————————————————————————————————————————————————————————————— */
int main()
{
    // Declare The Local Memory Variables
    RETCODE   rc = SQL_SUCCESS;
    SQLCHAR   DBName[10] = "Northwind";

    // Create An Instance Of The ODBC_Class Class
    ODBC_Class   Example;

    // Connect To The Northwind Sample Database
    if (Example.ConHandle != NULL)
    {
        rc = SQLConnect(Example.ConHandle, DBName, SQL_NTS,
                (SQLCHAR *) "", SQL_NTS, (SQLCHAR *) "", SQL_NTS);

        // Determine Whether Or Not The Driver Is In Auto-Commit Mode
        rc = Example.GetAutoCommitValue();

        // Tell The Driver To Use Manual-Commit Mode
        rc = Example.SetAutoCommitValue(SQL_AUTOCOMMIT_OFF);

        // Determine Whether Or Not The Driver Is Now Using
        // Manual-Commit Mode
        rc = Example.GetAutoCommitValue();

        // Disconnect From The Northwind Sample Database
        rc = SQLDisconnect(Example.ConHandle);
    }

    // Return To The Operating System
    return(rc);
}
```

SQLSetConnectOption

COMPATABILITY

X/OPEN 95 CLI	ISO/IEC 92 CLI	ODBC 1.0	ODBC 2.0	ODBC 3.0	ODBC 3.5
☒	☐	☑	☑	☐	☐

API CONFORMANCE LEVEL   **LEVEL 1**

Purpose   The **SQLSetConnectOption()** function is used to modify the current value of a specified connection option (attribute).

Syntax
```
RETCODE SQLSetConnectOption    (HDBC      ConnectionHandle,
                                UWORD     Option,
                                UDWORD    Value);
```

Parameters

ConnectionHandle	A data source connection handle that refers to a previously allocated connection information storage buffer (data structure).
Option	The connection option (attribute) whose value is to be modified. This parameter must be set to one of the following values:

- **SQL_ACCESS_MODE**
- **SQL_AUTOCOMMIT**
- **SQL_CURRENT_QUALIFIER**
- **SQL_LOGIN_TIMEOUT**
- **SQL_ODBC_CURSORS**
- **SQL_OPT_TRACE**
- **SQL_OPT_TRACEFILE**
- **SQL_PACKET_SIZE**
- **SQL_QUIET_MODE**
- **SQL_TRANSLATE_DLL**
- **SQL_TRANSLATE_OPTION**
- **SQL_TXN_ISOLATION**

Value	The new value for the connection option

(attribute) specified. Depending on the connection option (attribute) being set, this is a 32-bit integer value or a NULL-terminated character string.

Description The **SQLSetConnectOption()** function is used to modify the current value of a specified connection option (attribute). This function can also be used to specify SQL statement options for all statement handles that exist for the current connection, as well as for all future SQL statement handles that may be allocated for this connection. Refer to the **SQLGetConnectOption()** function for more information about each connection option available.

All connection and statement options successfully set by an application for the specified connection handle persist until the connection handle is freed with the **SQLFreeConnect()** function. If an application calls this function before connecting to a data source, the option persists even if the **SQLSetConnectAttr()** driver function fails when the application attempts to connect to the data source. Furthermore, if an application sets a driver-specific option, the option persists even if the application connects to a different driver using the same connection handle.

NOTE: *In ODBC 3.x, this function has been replaced by the* **SQLSetConnectAttr()** *function.*

DATA TRANSLATION Data translation is performed for all data flowing between the driver and the data source. The translation option (set with the **SQL_TRANSLATE_OPTION** option) can be any 32-bit value—its meaning is dependent on the translation DLL being used. A new option can be set at any time; however, new options are not be applied until the next exchange of data following the call to **SQLSetConnectOption()** function occurs. A default translation DLL may be specified for a data source in the system information storage area (either the [ODBC] section of the ODBC.INI file or the ODBC subkey in the system registry). If so, the default translation DLL is loaded by the driver at connection time. A translation option (**SQL_TRANSLATE_OPTION**) may be specified in the data source specification as well.

An application can call this function with the **SQL_TRANSLATE_DLL** option specified to change the translation DLL for a connection after a connection to the data source has been established. The driver attempts to load the specified DLL and, if the attempt fails, **SQL_ERROR** and SQLSTATE **IM**009 (Unable to load translation DLL) is returned.

If no translation DLL is specified in the system information storage area, or by calling this function, the driver does not attempt to translate data and any value provided for the translation option is ignored.

Return Codes SQL_SUCCESS, SQL_SUCCESS_WITH_INFO, SQL_INVALID_HANDLE, or SQL_ERROR

SQLSTATEs If this function returns SQL_SUCCESS_WITH_INFO or SQL_ERROR, one of the following SQLSTATE values may be obtained by calling the SQLError() function:

01000, **01**S02, **08**002, **08**003, **08**S01, **IM**001*, **IM**009, **S1**000, **S1**001, **S1**009, **S1**010*, **S1**011, **S1**092*, or **S1**C00

* Returned by the ODBC Driver Manager.

Unless noted otherwise, each of these SQLSTATE values are returned by the data source driver. Refer to Appendix B for detailed information about each SQLSTATE value that can be returned by the ODBC Driver Manager or by a data source driver.

When the value specified in the *Option* parameter is an SQL statement option, this function can return any SQLSTATE value that can be returned by the SQLSetStmtOption() function.

Comments ▪ An application can call this function to set an SQL statement option. When this occurs, the driver sets the statement option for any statement handles associated with the specified connection handle and establishes the statement option as a default for any statement handles later allocated for that connection handle.

▪ Some connection options support substitution of a similar value if the data source does not support the value specified in the *Value* parameter. In such cases, the driver returns SQL_SUCCESS_WITH_INFO and SQLSTATE **01**S02 (Option value changed). For example, if the *Option* parameter is set to SQL_PACKET_SIZE and the value specified in the *Value* parameter exceeds the maximum packet size, the driver substitutes the maximum size. An application can call the SQLGetConnectOption() function (for connection options) or the SQLGetStmtOption() function (for statement options) after setting a connection or statement option to determine whether a substitution occurred, and if so, to obtain the substituted value.

▪ The maximum length a string value can be (excluding the NULL-termination character) is SQL_MAX_OPTION_STRING_LENGTH bytes.

Prerequisites A connection handle must be allocated before this function is called.

Restrictions   There are no restrictions associated with this function call.

See Also   SQLGetConnectOption(), SQLGetConnectAttr(),
SQLSetConnectAttr(), SQLGetEnvAttr(), SQLSetEnvAttr(),
SQLGetStmtAttr(), SQLSetStmtAttr(), SQLGetStmtOption(),
SQLSetStmtOption()

Example   See the example provided for the SQLGetConnectOption() function, on
page 259.

SQLGetStmtAttr

COMPATABILITY

X/OPEN 95 CLI	ISO/IEC 92 CLI	ODBC 1.0	ODBC 2.0	ODBC 3.0	ODBC 3.5
☑	☑	☐	☐	☑	☑

API CONFORMANCE LEVEL   **CORE**

Purpose   The SQLGetStmtAttr() function is used to retrieve the current setting of
a specified SQL statement attribute.

Syntax   SQLRETURN SQLGetStmtAttr   (SQLHSTMT   *StatementHandle*,
                                      SQLINTEGER   *Attribute*,
                                      SQLPOINTER   *Value*,
                                      SQLINTEGER   *ValueMaxSize*,
                                      SQLINTEGER   **StringLength*);

Parameters   *StatementHandle*   An SQL statement handle that refers to a
                                     previously allocated SQL statement information
                                     storage buffer (data structure).

            Attribute   The SQL statement attribute whose value is to be
                          retrieved. This parameter must be set to one of the
                          following values:

            ▪ SQL_ATTR_APP_PARAM_DESC

            ▪ SQL_ATTR_APP_ROW_DESC

            ▪ SQL_ATTR_ASYNC_ENABLE

            ▪ SQL_ATTR_CONCURRENCY

- SQL_ATTR_CURSOR_SCROLLABLE
- SQL_ATTR_CURSOR_SENSITIVITY
- SQL_ATTR_CURSOR_TYPE
- SQL_ATTR_ENABLE_AUTO_IPD
- SQL_ATTR_FETCH_BOOKMARK_PTR
- SQL_ATTR_IMP_PARAM_DESC
- SQL_ATTR_IMP_ROW_DESC
- SQL_ATTR_KEYSET_SIZE
- SQL_ATTR_MAX_LENGTH
- SQL_ATTR_MAX_ROWS
- SQL_ATTR_METADATA_ID
- SQL_ATTR_NOSCAN
- SQL_ATTR_PARAM_BIND_OFFSET_PTR
- SQL_ATTR_PARAM_BIND_TYPE
- SQL_ATTR_PARAM_OPERATION_PTR
- SQL_ATTR_PARAM_STATUS_PTR
- SQL_ATTR_PARAMS_PROCESSED_PTR
- SQL_ATTR_PARAMSET_SIZE
- SQL_ATTR_QUERY_TIMEOUT
- SQL_ATTR_RETRIEVE_DATA
- SQL_ATTR_ROW_ARRAY_SIZE
- SQL_ATTR_ATTR_ROW_BIND_OFFSET_PTR
- SQL_ATTR_ROW_BIND_TYPE
- SQL_ATTR_ROW_NUMBER
- SQL_ATTR_ROW_OPERATION_PTR
- SQL_ATTR_ROW_STATUS_PTR
- SQL_ATTR_ROWS_FETCHED_PTR
- SQL_ATTR_SIMULATE_CURSOR
- SQL_ATTR_USE_BOOKMARKS

Value	A pointer to a location in memory where this function is to store the current value of the specified SQL statement attribute.
ValueMaxSize	The size of the memory storage buffer where this function is to store the current value of the

specified SQL statement attribute. If an ODBC-defined attribute is to be retrieved and if the attribute value is a 32-bit integer value, this parameter is ignored. If a driver-defined attribute is to be retrieved, this parameter may be set as follows:

■ If the value of the specified SQL statement attribute is a character string, this parameter may be set to the actual length of the string or to **SQL_NTS**.

■ If the value of the specified SQL statement attribute is a binary string, this parameter may be set to the result of the **SQL_LEN_BINARY_ATTR** *(length)* macro. Usually, this macro places a negative value in this parameter.

■ If the value of the specified SQL statement attribute is anything other than a character string or binary string, this parameter may be set to **SQL_IS_POINTER**.

■ If the value of the specified SQL statement attribute is a fixed-length data type, this parameter may be set to **SQL_IS_INTEGER** or **SQL_IS_UINTEGER**, as appropriate.

StringLength   A pointer to a location in memory where this function is to store the actual number of bytes written to the attribute value memory storage buffer *(Value)*. If the attribute value retrieved is not a character string value, this parameter ignored.

Description   The **SQLGetStmtAttr()** function is used to retrieve the current setting of a specified SQL statement attribute. Table 8–9 lists alphabetically each value that can be specified for the *Attribute* parameter, along with a description of the information returned for that value when this function is executed.

Table 8–9 *SQL Statement Attributes*

Attribute	Data Type	Description
SQL_ATTR_APP_PARAM_DESC (ODBC 3.0)	Descriptor handle	Specifies the application parameter descriptor (APD) that is to be used with the specified SQL statement handle by subsequent calls to **SQLExecute()** and **SQLExecDirect()**. Initially, this attribute contains the handle of the APD descriptor that was implicitly allocated when the statement handle was allocated. If this attribute is set to **SQL_NULL_DESC**, any explicitly allocated APD descriptor handle associated with the statement handle is dissociated from it, and this attribute is reset to its initial value (that is, it will contain the handle of the APD descriptor that was implicitly allocated APD and assigned to the statement handle. This attribute cannot contain a handle to a descriptor that was implicitly allocated for another statement handle or the handle of another descriptor that was implicitly set on the same statement; implicitly allocated descriptor handles cannot be associated with more than one statement at a time.
SQL_ATTR_APP_ROW_DESC (ODBC 3.0)	Descriptor handle	Specifies the application row descriptor (ARD) that is to be used with the specified SQL statement handle by subsequent calls to **SQLBulkOperations()**, **SQLFetch()**, **SQLFetchScroll()**, or **SQLSetPos()**. Initially, this attribute contains the handle of the ARD descriptor that was implicitly allocated when the statement handle was allocated. If this attribute is set to **SQL_NULL_DESC**, any explicitly allocated ARD descriptor handle associated with the statement handle is dissociated from it, and this attribute is reset to its initial value (that is, it will contain the handle of the ARD descriptor that was implicitly allocated ARD and assigned to the statement handle.) This attribute cannot contain a handle to a descriptor that was implicitly allocated for another statement handle or the handle of another descriptor that was implicitly set on the same statement; implicitly allocated descriptor handles cannot be associated with more than one statement at a time.
SQL_ATTR_ASYNC_ENABLE (ODBC 1.0)	**SQLUINTEGER**	Specifies whether an ODBC API function called with the specified statement handle is executed asynchronously. Valid values for this attribute are: **SQL_ASYNC_ENABLE_OFF**: A function called with the specified SQL statement handle is not executed asynchronously. This is the default value for this attribute.

Table 8–9   *SQL Statement Attributes (Continued)*

Attribute	Data Type	Description
		SQL_ASYNC_ENABLE_ON: A function called with the specified SQL statement handle is executed asynchronously. After a function has been called asynchronously, only the original function, **SQLCancel()**, **SQLGetDiagRec()**, **SQLError()**, or **SQLGetDiagField()**, can be called on the statement handle, and only the original function, **SQLAllocHandle()**, **SQLAllocStmt()**, **SQLGetDiagRec()**, **SQLError()**, **SQLGetDiagField()**, or **SQLGetFunctions()** can be called on the connection handle associated with the statement handle until the original function returns a code other than **SQL_STILL_EXECUTING**. Any other function called on the statement handle or the connection handle associated with the statement handle returns **SQL_ERROR** and SQLSTATE **HY**010 (Function sequence error). Functions can be called on other statement handles. In general, applications should only execute ODBC API functions asynchronously on single-thread operating systems. On multithread operating systems, applications should execute ODBC API functions on separate threads, rather than executing them asynchronously on the same thread. The following functions can be executed asynchronously:

SQLBulkOperations()	**SQLColAttribute()**
SQLColumnPrivileges()	**SQLColumns()**
SQLCopyDesc()	**SQLDescribeCol()**
SQLDescribeParam()	**SQLExecDirect()**
SQLExecute()	**SQLFetch()**
SQLFetchScroll()	**SQLForeignKeys()**
SQLGetData()	**SQLGetDescField()**[1]
SQLGetDescRec()[1]	**SQLGetDiagField()**
SQLGetDiagRec()	**SQLGetTypeInfo()**
SQLMoreResults()	**SQLNumParams()**
SQLNumResultCols()	**SQLParamData()**
SQLPrepare()	**SQLPrimaryKeys()**
SQLProcedureColumns()	**SQLProcedures()**
SQLPutData()	**SQLSetPos()**,
SQLSpecialColumns()	**SQLStatistics()**
SQLTablePrivileges()	**SQLTables()**

The statement attribute **SQL_ATTR_ASYNC_ENABLE** may already be set for drivers that provide statement level asynchronous-execution support. If so, its initial

Table 8–9 *SQL Statement Attributes (Continued)*

Attribute	Data Type	Description
		value is the same as the value of the connection level **SQL_ATTR_ASYNC_ENABLE** attribute at the time the statement handle was allocated.
		This attribute is a read-only attribute for drivers with connection-level, asynchronous execution support and its initial value is the same as the value of the connection level **SQL_ATTR_ASYNC_ENABLE** attribute at the time the statement handle was allocated.
SQL_ATTR_CONCURRENCY (ODBC 2.0)	**SQLUINTEGER**	Specifies the cursor concurrency level to use. Valid values for this attribute are:
		SQL_CONCUR_READ_ONLY: Cursors are read-only. No updates are allowed. This is the default value for this attribute.
		SQL_CONCUR_LOCK: Cursors use the lowest level of locking sufficient to ensure that the row can be updated.
		SQL_CONCUR_ROWVER: Cursors use optimistic concurrency control, comparing row versions.
		SQL_CONCUR_VALUES: Cursors use optimistic concurrency control, comparing values.
		This attribute cannot be specified for a cursor that is already open.
		If the **SQL_ATTR_CURSOR_TYPE** attribute is changed to a cursor type value that doesn't support the current value of the **SQL_ATTR_CONCURRENCY** attribute, the **SQL_ATTR_CONCURRENCY** attribute is changed and a warning is issued the next time the **SQLExecDirect()** or the **SQLPrepare()** function is called.
		If the driver supports the **SELECT FOR UPDATE** SQL statement, and if such a statement is executed while the **SQL_ATTR_CONCURRENCY** attribute is set to **SQL_CONCUR_READ_ONLY**, **SQL_ERROR** is returned.
		If the **SQL_ATTR_CONCURRENCY** attribute is changed to a value the driver supports for some values of the **SQL_ATTR_CURSOR_TYPE** attribute, but not for the current value of the **SQL_ATTR_CURSOR_TYPE** attribute, the value of the **SQL_ATTR_CURSOR_TYPE** attribute is changed and SQLSTATE **01S02** (Option value changed) is returned the next time the **SQLExecDirect()** or the **SQLPrepare()** function is called.

Table 8–9   SQL Statement Attributes (Continued)

Attribute	Data Type	Description
		If the specified concurrency value is not supported by the data source, the driver substitutes a different concurrency value and SQLSTATE **01**S02 (Option value changed) is returned. The driver substitutes **SQL_CONCUR_ROWVER** for **SQL_CONCUR_VALUES**, and vice versa. The driver substitutes, in order, **SQL_CONCUR_ROWVER** or **SQL_CONCUR_VALUES** for **SQL_CONCUR_LOCK**. The validity of the substituted value is not checked until execution time.
SQL_ATTR_CURSOR_SCROLLABLE (ODBC 3.0)	**SQLUINTEGER**	Specifies the level of cursor support that the application requires. Valid values for this attribute are: **SQL_NONSCROLLABLE**: Scrollable cursors are not required on the statement handle. The only value that can be specified for the *FetchOrientation* parameter of the **SQLFetchScroll()** function, is **SQL_FETCH_NEXT**. This is the default value for this attribute. **SQL_SCROLLABLE**: Scrollable cursors are required on the statement handle. Any valid value can be specified for the *FetchOrientation* parameter of the **SQLFetchScroll()** function. When this attribute is changed, all subsequent calls to **SQLExecute()** and **SQLExecDirect()** are affected.
SQL_ATTR_CURSOR_SENSITIVITY (ODBC 3.0)	**SQLUINTEGER**	Specifies whether one cursor on the statement handle can see changes made to a result data set by another cursor on the same statement handle. Valid values for this attribute are: **SQL_INSENSITIVE**: All cursors on the statement handle see a result data set without reflecting any changes made to it by any other cursor. Insensitive cursors are read-only. This corresponds to a static cursor with a read-only concurrency. **SQL_SENSITIVE**: All cursors on the statement handle can see all changes made to a result data set by another cursor. **SQL_UNSPECIFIED**: What the cursor type is, and whether cursors on the statement handle can see changes made to a result set by another cursor is unspecified. Cursors on the statement handle may make visible none, some, or all such changes made to a result data set. This is the default value for this attribute.

Table 8–9   *SQL Statement Attributes (Continued)*

Attribute	Data Type	Description
		When this attribute is changed, all subsequent calls to **SQLExecute()** and **SQLExecDirect()** are affected.
SQL_ATTR_CURSOR_ TYPE (ODBC 2.0)	**SQLUINTEGER**	Specifies the cursor type. Valid values for this attribute are:
		SQL_CURSOR_FORWARD_ONLY: The cursor can only scroll forward. This is the default value for this attribute.
		SQL_CURSOR_STATIC: The data in the result set is static, therefore the cursor is static.
		SQL_CURSOR_KEYSET_DRIVEN: The cursor is a keyset cursor; the driver saves and uses the keys for the number of rows specified in the **SQL_ATTR_KEYSET_SIZE** statement attribute.
		SQL_CURSOR_DYNAMIC: The cursor is a dynamic (block) cursor; the driver only saves and uses the keys for the rows in the rowset.
		This attribute cannot be specified after the SQL statement associated with the statement handle specified has been prepared.
		If the specified cursor type is not supported by the data source, the driver substitutes a different cursor type and returns SQLSTATE **01**S02 (Option value changed). The driver substitutes, in order, a keyset-driven or static cursor for a dynamic (block) cursor. The driver substitutes a static cursor for a keyset-driven cursor.
SQL_ATTR_ENABLE_ AUTO_IPD (ODBC 3.0)	**SQLUINTEGER**	Specifies whether automatic population of implementation parameter descriptors (IPD) is to be performed after **SQLPrepare()** executes. Valid values for this attribute are:
		SQL_TRUE: The IPD descriptor is to be populated automatically after **SQLPrepare()** is called.
		SQL_FALSE: The IPD descriptor is not to be populated automatically after **SQLPrepare()** is called.
		The default value of this attribute is the same as the value of the **SQL_ATTR_AUTO_IPD** connection attribute
		If the **SQL_ATTR_AUTO_IPD** connection attribute is set to **SQL_FALSE**, this attribute can only be set to **SQL_FALSE**.

Table 8–9 SQL Statement Attributes (Continued)

Attribute	Data Type	Description
SQL_ATTR_FETCH_ BOOKMARK_PTR (ODBC 3.0)	Pointer	Stores a pointer to a binary bookmark value. When the **SQLFetchScroll()** function is called with the *FetchOrientation* parameter set to **SQL_FETCH_ BOOKMARK**, the driver retrieves the bookmark value from this attribute. The default value for this attribute is a NULL pointer.
		The bookmark value stored in this attribute is not used for **SQL_UPDATE_BY_BOOKMARK**, **SQL_DELTE_BY_ BOOKMARK**, or **SQL_FETCH_BY_BOOKMARK** operations (refer to the **SQLBulkOperations()** function), which use bookmarks cached in rowset buffers.
SQL_ATTR_IMP_PARAM_ DESC (ODBC 3.0)	Descriptor handle	Identifies the implementation parameter descriptor (IPD) that was implicitly allocated when the statement handle was initially allocated. This attribute can be retrieved by the **SQLGetStmtAttr()** function, but it can not be set by the **SQLSetStmtAttr()** function.
SQL_ATTR_IMP_ROW_ DESC (ODBC 3.0)	Descriptor handle	Identifies the implementation row descriptor (IRD) that was implicitly allocated when the statement handle was initially allocated. This attribute can be retrieved by the **SQLGetStmtAttr()** function, but it can not be set by the **SQLSetStmtAttr()** function.
SQL_ATTR_KEYSET_SIZE (ODBC 2.0)	**SQLUINTEGER**	Specifies the number of rows to be in the keyset of a keyset-driven cursor. If the keyset size is **0** (the default value for this attribute), the cursor is fully keyset-driven. If the keyset size is greater than **0**, the cursor is a mixed cursor (keyset-driven within the keyset and dynamic outside of the keyset).
		If the specified keyset size exceeds the maximum keyset size allowed, the driver substitutes that size and returns SQLSTATE **01**S02 (Option value changed).
		SQLFetch() or **SQLFetchScroll()** returns an error if the keyset size is greater than 0 and less than the rowset size.
SQL_ATTR_MAX_LENGTH (ODBC 1.0)	**SQLUINTEGER**	Specifies the maximum amount of data that the driver will return from a character or binary column.
		If this attribute is set to **0** (which is the default value for this attribute), the driver attempts to return all available data.
		If the maximum length specified is smaller than the length of the data available, the data is truncated by the **SQLFetch()** or **SQLGetData()** function and **SQL_SUCCESS** is returned.

Table 8–9 *SQL Statement Attributes (Continued)*

Attribute	Data Type	Description
		If the maximum length specified is less than the minimum amount of data the data source can return, or greater than the maximum amount of data the data source can return, the driver substitutes the appropriate value and returns SQLSTATE **01**S02 (Option value changed).
		This attribute can be set while a cursor is open; however, the setting may not take effect immediately, in which case the driver returns SQLSTATE **01**S02 (Option value changed), and the attribute is reset to its original value.
		This attribute is intended to reduce network traffic and should only be supported when the data source (as opposed to the driver) in a multiple-tier driver can implement it. This mechanism should not be used by applications to truncate data.
SQL_ATTR_MAX_ROWS (ODBC 1.0)	**SQLUINTEGER**	Specifies the maximum number of rows to return to the application for a **SELECT** SQL statement. Conceptually, this attribute's value is applied when a result data set is created and limits the result data set to the specified number of rows. If the number of rows in the result data set is larger that the number of rows specified, the result data set is truncated.
		If this attribute is set to **0** (which is the default value for this attribute), the driver returns all rows available.
		The value of this attribute applies to all result data sets associated with the statement handle, including the result data sets returned by the catalog functions.
		This attribute is intended to reduce network traffic. It is driver-defined whether this attribute applies to SQL statements other than **SELECT** SQL statements (such as catalog functions).
		This attribute can be set while a cursor is open; however, the setting may not take effect immediately, in which case the driver returns SQLSTATE **01**S02 (Option value changed), and the attribute is reset to its original value.
SQL_ATTR_METADATA_ID (ODBC 3.0)	**SQLUINTEGER**	Specifies how the string parameters (arguments) of catalog functions are to be treated. Valid values for this attribute are:

Table 8–9 *SQL Statement Attributes (Continued)*

Attribute	Data Type	Description
		SQL_TRUE: The string parameters of catalog functions are treated as identifiers. For non-delimited strings, the driver removes any trailing spaces, and the string is folded to upper case. For delimited strings, the driver removes any leading or trailing spaces, and takes literally whatever is between the delimiters. Case is insignificant. If one of these arguments is set to a NULL pointer, the catalog function returns **SQL_ERROR** and SQLSTATE **HY**009 (Invalid use of NULL pointer). **SQL_FALSE**: The string parameters of catalog functions are not treated as identifiers (that is, string parameters can contain either a simple string or a string search pattern, depending on the parameter. Case is significant. This is the default value for this attribute. The *TableType* parameter of the **SQLTables()** function, which takes a list of values, is not affected by this attribute. This attribute can also be set at the connection level. (This attribute and the **SQL_ATTR_ASYNC_ENABLE** attribute are the only statement attributes that are also connection attributes.)
SQL_ATTR_NOSCAN (ODBC 1.0)	SQLUINTEGER	Specifies whether the driver is to scan SQL statements for ODBC escape sequences. Valid values for this attribute are: **SQL_NOSCAN_OFF**: The driver is to scan SQL statements for ODBC escape sequences. This is the default value for this attribute. **SQL_NOSCAN_ON**: The driver is to send the SQL statement directly to the data source without scanning for ODBC escape sequences.
SQL_ATTR_PARAM_BIND_OFFSET_PTR (ODBC 3.0)	SQLUINTEGER pointer	Specifies an offset to be added to pointers to change the binding of dynamic parameters. If this attribute contains a vaild pointer, the driver dereferences the pointer, adds the dereferenced value to each of the deferred fields in the descriptor record (**SQL_DESC_DATA_PTR**, **SQL_DESC_INDICATOR_PTR**, and **SQL_DESC_OCTET_LENGTH_PTR**), and uses the new pointer values when binding. By default, this attribute contains a NULL pointer. The bind offset is always added directly to the **SQL_DESC_DATA_PTR**, **SQL_DESC_INDICATOR_PTR**, and **SQL_DESC_OCTET_LENGTH_PTR** descriptor record fields. If the offset is changed to a different

Table 8–9 *SQL Statement Attributes (Continued)*

Attribute	Data Type	Description
		value, the new value is added directly to the value in the descriptor field (earlier offset values are ignored). This statement attribute corresponds to the **SQL_DESC_BIND_OFFSET_PTR** field of the application parameter descriptor header record.
SQL_ATTR_PARAM_BIND_TYPE (ODBC 3.0)	**SQLUINTEGER**	Specifies the binding orientation to be used for dynamic parameters. By default, this attribute is set to **SQL_PARAM_BIND_BY_COLUMN** to specify column-wise binding. To select row-wise binding, this attribute is set to the length of the structure (or the instance of a buffer) that is bound to a set of dynamic parameters. This length must include space for all the bound parameters and any padding of the structure or buffer to ensure that when the address of a bound parameter is incremented with the specified length, the result points to the beginning of the same parameter in the next set of parameter values. By using the **sizeof()** operator in ANSI C, this behavior is guaranteed. This statement attribute corresponds to the **SQL_DESC_BIND_TYPE** field of the application parameter descriptor header record.
SQL_ATTR_PARAM_OPERATION_PTR (ODBC 3.0)	**SQLUSMALLINT** pointer	Contains a pointer to an array of parameter operation values that can be set by the application to indicate whether a set of parameter values are to be used or ignored when **SQLExecute()** or **SQLExecDirect()** is called. Each element in this array can contain the following values: **SQL_PARAM_PROCEED**: The set of parameter values are to be used by the **SQLExecute()** or **SQLExecDirect()** function call. **SQL_PARAM_IGNORE**: The set of parameter values are not to be used by the **SQLExecute()** or **SQLExecDirect()** function call. If no elements in the array are set, all sets of parameter values are used by **SQLExecute()** or **SQLExecDirect()** function calls. If this statement attribute contains a NULL pointer, all sets of parameter values are used by **SQLExecute()** or **SQLExecDirect()** function calls, however, no parameter status values are returned by the driver. This attribute can be set at any time, but the new value is not used until the next time **SQLExecute()** or **SQLExecDirect()** is called.

Table 8–9 *SQL Statement Attributes (Continued)*

Attribute	Data Type	Description
		This statement attribute corresponds to the **SQL_DESC_ARRAY_STATUS_PTR** field of the application parameter descriptor header record.
SQL_ATTR_PARAM_ STATUS_PTR (ODBC 3.0)	**SQLUSMALLINT** pointer	Contains a pointer to an array of parameter status values that will contain status information about each set of parameter values used after **SQLExecute()** or **SQLExecDirect()** has been executed. This statement attribute is only required if the **SQL_ATTR_ PARAMSET_SIZE** attribute contains a value greater than **1**.
		An application must allocate an array of **SQLUSMALLINT** values with as many elements as there are parameter values, and store a pointer to the array in this attribute. When **SQLExecute()** or **SQLExecDirect()** is called, the driver populates the specified array; If this attribute contains a NULL pointer (the default), no status values are generated and the array is not populated.
		Each element in the array can contain the following values:
		SQL_PARAM_SUCCESS: The SQL statement was successfully executed using the set of parameter values.
		SQL_PARAM_SUCCESS_WITH_INFO: The SQL statement was successfully executed using the set of parameter values; however, warning information was generated and is available in one or more diagnostic records.
		SQL_PARAM_ERROR: An error occurred while processing the SQL statement using the set of parameter values. Additional error information is available in one or more diagnostic records.
		SQL_PARAM_UNUSED: The set of parameter values was not used, possibly because some previous set of parameter values caused an error that aborted further processing, or because **SQL_PARAM_IGNORE** was set for the set of parameter values in the specified array.
		SQL_PARAM_DIAG_UNAVAILABLE: Diagnostic information is not available. For example, when the driver treats arrays of parameter values as a monolithic unit, error information is not generated.
		If a call to **SQLExecute()** or **SQLExecDirect()** did not return **SQL_SUCCESS** or **SQL_SUCCESS_ WITH_INFO**, the contents of the array pointed to by this attribute are undefined.

Table 8–9 SQL Statement Attributes (Continued)

Attribute	Data Type	Description
		This attribute can be set at any time, but the new value is not used until the next time **SQLFetch()** or **SQLFetchScroll()** is called.
		This statement attribute corresponds to the **SQL_DESC_ARRAY_STATUS_PTR** field of the implementation parameter descriptor header record.
SQL_ATTR_PARAMS_PROCESSED_PTR (ODBC 3.0)	**SQLUINTEGER** pointer	Contains a pointer to a buffer that contains the number of sets of parameter values that have already been processed (including parameter value sets that caused an error to occur).
		If this attribute contains a NULL pointer, no number is returned by a call to **SQLExecute()** or **SQLExecDirect()**.
		If the call to **SQLExecute()** or **SQLExecDirect()** that fills in the buffer pointed to by this attribute does not return **SQL_SUCCESS** or **SQL_SUCCESS_WITH_INFO**, the contents of the buffer are undefined.
		This statement attribute corresponds to the **SQL_DESC_ROWS_PROCESSED_PTR** field of the implementation parameter descriptor header record.
SQL_ATTR_PARAMSET_SIZE (ODBC 3.0)	**SQLUINTEGER**	Specifies the number of values available for each parameter marker.
		By default, the value for this attribute is **1**. If this attribute contains a value greater than **1**, the **SQL_DESC_DATA_PTR**, **SQL_DESC_INDICATOR_PTR**, and **SQL_DESC_OCTET_LENGTH_PTR** fields of each parameter/column descriptor record contain pointers to arrays (APD or ARD descriptors only). The cardinality of each array is equal to the value of this attribute.
		This statement attribute corresponds to the **SQL_DESC_ARRAY_SIZE** field of the application parameter descriptor header record.
SQL_ATTR_QUERY_TIMEOUT (ODBC 1.0)	**SQLUINTEGER**	Specifies the number of seconds to wait for an SQL statement to execute before returning control to the application. If this attribute is equal to **0** (the default value for this attribute), then there is no time out. If the specified timeout exceeds the maximum timeout supported by the data source or is smaller than the minimum timeout supported by the data source, the driver substitutes the timeout value and returns SQLSTATE **01**S02 (Option value changed). The query timeout specified in this statement attribute is valid in both synchronous and asynchronous modes.

Table 8–9 SQL Statement Attributes (Continued)

Attribute	Data Type	Description
		Note that an application does not have to call **SQLCloseCursor()** to reuse a **SELECT** SQL statement if the statement timed out.
SQL_ATTR_RETRIEVE_DATA (ODBC 2.0)	**SQLUINTEGER**	Specifies whether the **SQLFetchScroll()**, and in ODBC 3.x, **SQLFetch()** functions are to retrieve data after they position the cursor. Valid values for this attribute are:
		SQL_RD_ON: **SQLFetchScroll()** and **SQLFetch()** retrieve data after they position the cursor to the specified location. This is the default value for this attribute.
		SQL_RD_OFF: **SQLFetchScroll()** and **SQLFetch()** do not retrieve data after they position the cursor.
		By setting this attribute to **SQL_RD_OFF**, an application can either verify whether a row exists or retrieve a bookmark for a row without incurring the overhead of retrieving data.
		This attribute can be set while a cursor is open; however, the setting may not take effect immediately, in which case the driver will return SQLSTATE 01S02 (Option value changed), and the attribute is reset to its original value.
SQL_ATTR_ROW_ARRAY_SIZE (ODBC 3.0)	**SQLUINTEGER**	Specifies the number of rows returned by each call to **SQLFetch()** or **SQLFetchScroll()** (number of rows in the rowset). This is also the number of rows in a bookmark array that are used in a bulk bookmark operation performed by the **SQLBulkOperations()** function. By default, the value for this attribute is **1**. If the specified rowset size exceeds the maximum rowset size supported by the data source, the driver substitutes that value and returns SQLSTATE 01S02 (Option value changed).
		This statement attribute corresponds to the **SQL_DESC_ARRAY_SIZE** field of the application row descriptor header record.
SQL_ATTR_ROW_BIND_OFFSET_PTR (ODBC 3.0)	**SQLUINTEGER** pointer	Contains a pointer to an offset that is to be added to pointers to change the binding of column data. By default, this attribute contains a NULL pointer. If this attribute contains a pointer to a binding offset, instead of a NULL pointer, the driver dereferences the pointer and adds the dereferenced value to each deferred field

Table 8–9 SQL Statement Attributes (Continued)

Attribute	Data Type	Description
		that has a non-NULL value in the **SQL_DESC_DATA_ PTR**, **SQL_DESC_INDICATOR_PTR**, and **SQL_DESC_ OCTET_LENGTH_PTR** fields of the application row descriptor and uses the new pointer values when binding.
		This statement attribute corresponds to the **SQL_DESC_BIND_OFFSET_PTR** field of the application row descriptor header record.
SQL_ATTR_ROW_BIND_ TYPE (ODBC 1.0)	SQLUINTEGER	Specifies the binding orientation to use when the **SQLFetch()** or **SQLFetchScroll()** function is called.
		By default, this attribute is set to **SQL_BIND_BY_ COLUMN** and column-wise binding is used. Row-wise binding is specified by setting this attribute to the length of a structure or an instance of a buffer into which all result data set columns are bound. If a length is specified, it must include space for all the bound columns and any padding of the structure or buffer to ensure that when the address of a bound column is incremented with the specified length, the result points to the beginning of the same column in the next row. By using the **sizeof()** operator in ANSI C, this behavior is guaranteed.
		This statement attribute corresponds to the **SQL_DESC_BIND_TYPE** field of the application row descriptor header record.
SQL_ATTR_ROW_NUMBER (ODBC 2.0)	SQLUINTEGER	Identifies the number of the current row in the entire result data set. If the number of the current row cannot be determined or if there is no current row, this attribute contains the number **0**.
		This attribute can be retrieved by the **SQLGetStmtAttr()** function, but it can not be set by the **SQLSetStmtAttr()** function.
SQL_ATTR_ROW_ OPERATION_PTR (ODBC 3.0)	SQLUSMALLINT pointer	Contains a pointer to an array of row operation values that can be set by the application to indicate whether or not the row is to be ignored by the **SQLSetPos()** function (rows cannot be ignored by using this array with the **SQLBulkOperations()** function). Each element in the array can contain the following values:

Table 8–9 *SQL Statement Attributes (Continued)*

Attribute	Data Type	Description
		SQL_ROW_PROCEED: The row is included in the bulk operation performed by the **SQLSetPos()** function. (This setting does not guarantee the operation will occur on the row. If the row has the status **SQL_ROW_ERROR** in the IRD row status array, the driver may not be able to perform the operation on the row.)
		SQL_ROW_IGNORE: The row is excluded from the bulk operation performed by the **SQLSetPos()** function.
		If no elements in the array are set, or if this attribute contains a NULL pointer, all rows are included in the bulk operation performed by the **SQLSetPos()** function.
		If this attribute contains a NULL pointer, the driver does not return row status values.
		If an element in the array is set to **SQL_ROW_IGNORE**, the value in the row status array for the ignored row is not changed
		This attribute can be set at any time, but the new value is not used until the next time **SQLSetPos()** is called.
		This statement attribute corresponds to the **SQL_DESC_ARRAY_STATUS_PTR** field of the application row descriptor header record.
SQL_ATTR_ROW_STATUS_PTR (ODBC 3.0)	**SQLUSMALLINT** pointer	Contains a pointer to an array of row status values that will contain status information after the **SQLBulkOperations()**, **SQLFetch()**, **SQLFetchScroll()**, or **SQLSetPos()** function has been executed.
		An application must allocate an array of **SQLUSMALLINT** values with as many elements as there are rows in the rowset and store a pointer to the array in this attribute. When the **SQLBulkOperations()**, **SQLFetch()**, **SQLFetchScroll()**, or **SQLSetPos()** function is called, the driver populates the specified array; If this attribute contains a NULL pointer (the default), no status values are generated and the array is not populated. Each element in the array can contain the following values:
		SQL_ROW_SUCCESS: The row was successfully fetched and has not been changed since it was last fetched.
		SQL_ROW_SUCCESS_WITH_INFO: The row was successfully fetched and has not been changed since it was last fetched. However, a warning was returned about the row.

Table 8–9 *SQL Statement Attributes (Continued)*

Attribute	Data Type	Description
		SQL_ROW_ERROR: An error occurred while fetching the row. **SQL_ROW_UPDATED**: The row was successfully fetched and has been changed since it was last fetched. If the row is fetched again, its status is **SQL_ROW_SUCCESS**. **SQL_ROW_DELETED**: The row has been deleted since it was last fetched. **SQL_ROW_ADDED**: The row was inserted by the **SQLBulkOperations()** function. If the row is fetched again, its status is **SQL_ROW_SUCCESS**. **SQL_ROW_NOROW**: The rowset overlapped the end of the result data set and no row was returned that corresponded to an element of the row status array. If a call to **SQLBulkOperations()**, **SQLFetch()**, **SQLFetchScroll()**, or **SQLSetPos()** did not return **SQL_SUCCESS** or **SQL_SUCCESS_WITH_INFO**, the contents of the array referenced by this attribute are undefined. This attribute can be set at any time, but the new value is not used until the next time **SQLBulkOperations()**, **SQLFetch()**, **SQLFetchScroll()**, or **SQLSetPos()** is called. This statement attribute corresponds to the **SQL_DESC_ARRAY_STATUS_PTR** field of the implementation row descriptor header record.
SQL_ATTR_ROWS_FETCHED_PTR (ODBC 2.0)	**SQLUINTEGER** pointer	Contains a pointer to a buffer containing the number of rows fetched by **SQLFetch()** or **SQLFetchScroll()** or the number of rows affected (including rows that returned errors) by a bulk operation performed by **SQLBulkOperations()** or **SQLSetPos()**. If this attribute contains a NULL pointer, no value is returned. The value stored in this attribute is only valid if a call to **SQLFetch()**, **SQLFetchScroll()**, **SQLBulkOperations()** or **SQLSetPos()** returned **SQL_SUCCESS** or **SQL_SUCCESS_WITH_INFO**. If **SQL_SUCCESS** or **SQL_SUCCESS_WITH_INFO** was not returned, the contents of the buffer pointed to by this attribute are undefined unless **SQL_NO_DATA** was returned, in which case the number **0** was also returned.

Table 8–9 SQL Statement Attributes (Continued)

Attribute	Data Type	Description
		This statement attribute corresponds to the **SQL_DESC_ROWS_PROCESSED_PTR** field of the implementation row descriptor header record.
SQL_ATTR_SIMULATE_CURSOR (ODBC 2.0)	**SQLUINTEGER**	Specifies whether drivers that simulate positioned **UPDATE** and **DELETE** SQL statements guarantee that such statements only affect one row. To simulate positioned **UPDATE** and **DELETE** statements, most drivers construct a searched **UPDATE** or **DELETE** SQL statement containing a **WHERE** clause that specifies the each column's value in the current row. Unless these columns make up a unique key, such a statement may affect more than one row. To guarantee that such statements affect only one row, the driver determines the columns in a unique key and adds these columns to the result data set. If an application guarantees that the columns in the result data set make up a unique key, the driver is not required to do so. This may reduce overall execution time.

Valid values for this attribute are:

SQL_SC_NON_UNIQUE:
The driver does not guarantee that simulated positioned **UPDATE** or **DELETE** SQL statements will affect only one row; it is the application's responsibility to do so. If a positioned **UPDATE** or **DELETE** SQL statement affects more than one row, **SQLExecute()**, **SQLExecDirect()**, or **SQLSetPos()** returns SQLSTATE **01**001 (Cursor operation conflict).

SQL_SC_TRY_UNIQUE:
The driver attempts to guarantee that simulated positioned **UPDATE** or **DELETE** SQL statements affect only one row. The driver always executes such statements even if they might affect more than one row, such as when there is no unique key. If a positioned **UPDATE** or **DELETE** SQL statement affects more than one row, **SQLExecute()**, **SQLExecDirect()**, or **SQLSetPos()** returns SQLSTATE **01**001 (Cursor operation conflict).

SQL_SC_UNIQUE:
The driver guarantees that simulated positioned **UPDATE** or **DELETE** SQL statements affect only one row. If the driver cannot guarantee this for a given statement, **SQLExecDirect()** or **SQLPrepare()** returns an error.

If the data source provides native SQL support for positioned **UPDATE** and **DELETE** SQL statements, and the driver does not simulate cursors, **SQL_SUCCESS** is returned when an application sets this attribute to **SQL_SC_UNIQUE** and **SQL_SUCCESS_WITH_INFO** is returned if an application tries to set this attribute to anything else.

Table 8–9 *SQL Statement Attributes (Continued)*

Attribute	Data Type	Description
		If the data source provides the **SQL_SC_TRY_UNIQUE** level of support, and the driver does not, **SQL_SUCCESS** is returned when an application sets this attribute to **SQL_SC_TRY_UNIQUE** and **SQL_SUCCESS_WITH_INFO** is returned when an application sets this attribute to **SQL_SC_NON_UNIQUE**.
		If the cursor simulation type specified is not supported by the data source, the driver substitutes a different simulation type and returns SQLSTATE **01**S02 (Option value changed).
		The driver substitutes, in order, the **SQL_SC_TRY_UNIQUE** or the **SQL_SC_NON_UNIQUE** cursor simulation type for the **SQL_SC_UNIQUE** cursor simulation type. The driver substitutes the **SQL_SC_NON_UNIQUE** cursor simulation type for the **SQL_SC_TRY_UNIQUE** cursor simulation type.
SQL_ATTR_USE_BOOKMARKS (ODBC 2.0)	**SQLUINTEGER**	Specifies whether an application uses bookmarks with a cursor. Valid values for this attribute are:
		SQL_UB_OFF: An application uses bookmarks with a cursor. This is the default value for this attribute.
		SQL_UB_VARIABLE : An application uses bookmarks with a cursor, and the driver provides variable-length bookmarks if they are supported. (ODBC 3.x)
		SQL_UB_ON: An application uses bookmarks with a cursor .(ODBC 2.0 or earlier)
		ODBC 3.x applications should always use variable-length bookmarks even when working with ODBC 2.0 drivers (which only support 4-byte, fixed-length bookmarks). This is because a fixed-length bookmark is just a special case of a variable-length bookmark..
		When working with an ODBC 2.0 driver, the ODBC Driver Manager maps **SQL_UB_VARIABLE** to **SQL_UB_ON**.
		To use bookmarks with a cursor, the application must specify this attribute with the **SQL_UB_VARIABLE** value before opening the cursor.

(Adapted from the table on pages 978– 992 of *Microsoft ODBC 3.0 Software Development Kit & Programmer's Reference*.)

[1]These functions can be called asynchronously only if the descriptor associated with the SQL statement handle is an implementation parameter (IPD) or implementation row (IRD) descriptor; and not an application descriptor.

may be defined in future releases of ODBC. In fact, a range of information types (0 to 999) has been reserved by ODBC to allow for future expansion. In addition, ODBC driver developers are required to reserve values for their own driver-specific use from X/Open.

NOTE: *In ODBC 3.x, this function replaces the ODBC 2.0 function* `SQLGetStmtOption()`.

Return Codes   `SQL_SUCCESS`, `SQL_SUCCESS_WITH_INFO`, `SQL_INVALID_HANDLE`, or `SQL_ERROR`

SQLSTATEs   If this function returns `SQL_SUCCESS_WITH_INFO` or `SQL_ERROR`, one of the following SQLSTATE values may be obtained by calling the `SQLGetDiagRec()` function:

01000, **01**004, **24**000, **HY**000, **HY**001, **HY**010*, **HY**013, **HY**090*, **HY**092, **HY**109, **HYC**00, **HYT**01, or **IM**001*

* Returned by the ODBC Driver Manager.

Unless noted otherwise, each of these SQLSTATE values are returned by the data source driver. Refer to Appendix B for detailed information about each SQLSTATE value that can be returned by the ODBC Driver Manager or by a data source driver.

Comments
- If the *Value* parameter contains a NULL pointer, no length is returned in the *StringLength* parameter.
- If an attribute that returns a string value is specified in the *Attribute* parameter, and if that string value's actual length is greater than or equal to the maximum string size value specified in the *ValueMaxSize* parameter, the value is truncated to *ValueMaxSize*-1 (the length of a NULL-termination character) characters and NULL terminated by the driver.
- If an attribute that returns a string value is specified in the *Attribute* parameter, the *Value* parameter must contain a pointer to a buffer in which this function can return the string.
- If the value returned for the attribute specified in the *Attribute* parameter is a Unicode string, the *ValueMaxSize* parameter must contain an even number.
- The `SQL_ATTR_IMP_PARAM_DESC`, `SQL_ATTR_ROW_NUMBER`, and `SQL_ATTR_IMP_ROW_DESC`, statement attributes are read-only; therefore, they can be retrieved by this function, but they can not be set by the `SQLSetStmtAttr()` function.

Prerequisites   An SQL statement handle must be allocated before this function is called.

Restrictions   There are no restrictions associated with this function call.

See Also   SQLSetStmtAttr(), SQLGetStmtOption(), SQLSetStmtOption(),
SQLGetEnvAttr(), SQLSetEnvAttr(), SQLGetConnectAttr(),
SQLSetConnectAttr(), SQLGetConnectOption(),
SQLSetConnectOption()

Example   The following Visual C++ program illustrates how to retrieve and change
the current value of an SQL statement attribute.

```
/*------------------------------------------------------------------*/
/* NAME:      CH8EX9.CPP                                            */
/* PURPOSE: Illustrate How To Use The Following ODBC API Functions  */
/*          In A C++ Program:                                       */
/*                                                                  */
/*                SQLGetStmtAttr()                                  */
/*                SQLSetStmtAttr()                                  */
/*                                                                  */
/* OTHER ODBC APIs SHOWN:                                           */
/*          SQLAllocHandle()          SQLSetEnvAttr()               */
/*          SQLConnect()              SQLDisconnect()               */
/*          SQLFreeHandle()                                         */
/*                                                                  */
/*------------------------------------------------------------------*/

// Include The Appropriate Header Files
#include <windows.h>
#include <sql.h>
#include <sqlext.h>
#include <iostream.h>

// Define The ODBC_Class Class
class ODBC_Class
{
    // Attributes
    public:
        SQLHANDLE      EnvHandle;
        SQLHANDLE      ConHandle;
        SQLHANDLE      StmtHandle;
        SQLRETURN      rc;
        SQLUINTEGER    MaxRows;

    // Operations
    public:
        ODBC_Class();                                // Constructor
        ~ODBC_Class();                               // Destructor
        SQLRETURN   GetMaxRowsValue();
        SQLRETURN   SetMaxRowsValue(SQLUINTEGER MaxRows);
};

// Define The Class Constructor
ODBC_Class::ODBC_Class()
```

```
{
    // Initialize The Return Code Variable
    rc = SQL_SUCCESS;

    // Allocate An Environment Handle
    rc = SQLAllocHandle(SQL_HANDLE_ENV, SQL_NULL_HANDLE, &EnvHandle);

    // Set The ODBC Application Version To 3.x
    if (rc == SQL_SUCCESS)
        rc = SQLSetEnvAttr(EnvHandle, SQL_ATTR_ODBC_VERSION,
                 (SQLPOINTER) SQL_OV_ODBC3, SQL_IS_UINTEGER);

    // Allocate A Connection Handle
    if (rc == SQL_SUCCESS)
        rc = SQLAllocHandle(SQL_HANDLE_DBC, EnvHandle, &ConHandle);
}

// Define The Class Destructor
ODBC_Class::~ODBC_Class()
{
    // Free The Connection Handle
    if (ConHandle != NULL)
        SQLFreeHandle(SQL_HANDLE_DBC, ConHandle);

    // Free The Environment Handle
    if (EnvHandle != NULL)
        SQLFreeHandle(SQL_HANDLE_ENV, EnvHandle);
}

// Define The GetMaxRowsValue() Member Function
SQLRETURN ODBC_Class::GetMaxRowsValue(void)
{
    // Declare The Local Memory Variables
    SQLINTEGER   ValueLength;

    // Determine The Number Of Rows The Driver Will Return For A
    // SELECT SQL Statement
    rc = SQLGetStmtAttr(StmtHandle, SQL_ATTR_MAX_ROWS,
             (SQLPOINTER) &MaxRows, SQL_IS_UINTEGER, &ValueLength);

    // Display The Information Retrieved
    if (rc == SQL_SUCCESS)
    {
        cout << "Maximum number of rows to return : ";
        cout << MaxRows << endl;
    }

    // Return The ODBC API Return Code To The Calling Function
    return(rc);
}

// Define The SetMaxRowsValue() Member Function
SQLRETURN ODBC_Class::SetMaxRowsValue(SQLUINTEGER MaxRows)
{
    // Specify The Number Of Rows That The Driver Is To Return For A
    // SELECT SQL Statement
```

```
    rc = SQLSetStmtAttr(StmtHandle, SQL_ATTR_MAX_ROWS,
            (SQLPOINTER) MaxRows, SQL_IS_UINTEGER);

    // Return The ODBC API Return Code To The Calling Function
    return(rc);
}

/*────────────────────────────────────────────────────────────*/
/* The Main Function                                          */
/*────────────────────────────────────────────────────────────*/
int main()
{
    // Declare The Local Memory Variables
    SQLRETURN   rc = SQL_SUCCESS;
    SQLCHAR     DBName[10] = "Northwind";

    // Create An Instance Of The ODBC_Class Class
    ODBC_Class  Example;

    // Connect To The Northwind Sample Database
    if (Example.ConHandle != NULL)
    {
        rc = SQLConnect(Example.ConHandle, DBName, SQL_NTS,
                (SQLCHAR *) "", SQL_NTS, (SQLCHAR *) "", SQL_NTS);

        // Allocate An SQL Statement Handle
        rc = SQLAllocHandle(SQL_HANDLE_STMT, Example.ConHandle,
                &Example.StmtHandle);

        if (rc == SQL_SUCCESS)
        {
            // Determine The Number Of Rows The Driver Will Return
            // For A SELECT SQL Statement
            rc = Example.GetMaxRowsValue();

            // Tell The Driver To Return Up To 25 Rows For A
            // SELECT SQL Statement
            rc = Example.SetMaxRowsValue(25);

            // Determine Whether Or Not The Driver Will Now Return
            // Up To 25 Rows For A SELECT SQL Statement
            rc = Example.GetMaxRowsValue();

            // Free The SQL Statement Handle
            if (Example.StmtHandle != NULL)
                SQLFreeHandle(SQL_HANDLE_STMT, Example.StmtHandle);
        }

        // Disconnect From The Northwind Sample Database
        rc = SQLDisconnect(Example.ConHandle);
    }

    // Return To The Operating System
    return(rc);
}
```

SQLSetStmtAttr

COMPATABILITY					
X/OPEN 95 CLI	ISO/IEC 92 CLI	ODBC 1.0	ODBC 2.0	ODBC 3.0	ODBC 3.5
✓	✓	☐	☐	✓	✓

API CONFORMANCE LEVEL **CORE**

Purpose The `SQLSetStmtAttr()` function is used to modify the current value of a specified SQL statement attribute.

Syntax
```
SQLRETURN  SQLSetStmtAttr  (SQLHSTMT     StatementHandle,
                            SQLINTEGER   Attribute,
                            SQLPOINTER   Value,
                            SQLINTEGER   StringLength);
```

Parameters

StatementHandle   An SQL statement handle that refers to a previously allocated SQL statement information storage buffer (data structure).

Attribute   The SQL statement attribute whose value is to be modified. This parameter must be set to one of the following values:

- SQL_ATTR_APP_PARAM_DESC
- SQL_ATTR_APP_ROW_DESC
- SQL_ATTR_ASYNC_ENABLE
- SQL_ATTR_CONCURRENCY
- SQL_ATTR_CURSOR_SCROLLABLE
- SQL_ATTR_CURSOR_SENSITIVITY
- SQL_ATTR_CURSOR_TYPE
- SQL_ATTR_ENABLE_AUTO_IPD
- SQL_ATTR_FETCH_BOOKMARK_PTR
- SQL_ATTR_IMP_PARAM_DESC
- SQL_ATTR_IMP_ROW_DESC
- SQL_ATTR_KEYSET_SIZE
- SQL_ATTR_MAX_LENGTH

- **SQL_ATTR_MAX_ROWS**
- **SQL_ATTR_METADATA_ID**
- **SQL_ATTR_NOSCAN**
- **SQL_ATTR_PARAM_BIND_OFFSET_PTR**
- **SQL_ATTR_PARAM_BIND_TYPE**
- **SQL_ATTR_PARAM_OPERATION_PTR**
- **SQL_ATTR_PARAM_STATUS_PTR**
- **SQL_ATTR_PARAMS_PROCESSED_PTR**
- **SQL_ATTR_PARAMSET_SIZE**
- **SQL_ATTR_QUERY_TIMEOUT**
- **SQL_ATTR_RETRIEVE_DATA**
- **SQL_ATTR_ROW_ARRAY_SIZE**
- **SQL_ATTR_ATTR_ROW_BIND_OFFSET_PTR**
- **SQL_ATTR_ROW_BIND_TYPE**
- **SQL_ATTR_ROW_NUMBER**
- **SQL_ATTR_ROW_OPERATION_PTR**
- **SQL_ATTR_ROW_STATUS_PTR**
- **SQL_ATTR_ROWS_FETCHED_PTR**
- **SQL_ATTR_SIMULATE_CURSOR**
- **SQL_ATTR_USE_BOOKMARKS**

Value

A pointer to a location in memory where the new value for the SQL statement attribute is stored. Depending on the SQL statement attribute being set, this pointer can reference either a 32-bit integer value or a NULL-terminated character string.

StringLength

The length of the SQL statement attribute value stored in the *Value* parameter. If an ODBC-defined attribute value is to be set and if the attribute value is a 32-bit integer value, this parameter is ignored. If a driver-defined attribute value is to be set, this parameter must be set as follows:

- If the value of the specified SQL statement attribute is a character string, this parameter should be set to the actual length of the string or to **SQL_NTS**.

■ If the value of the specified SQL statement attribute is a binary string, this parameter should be set to the result of the **SQL_LEN_BINARY_ATTR**(*length*) macro. Usually, this macro places a negative value in this parameter.

■ If the value of the specified SQL statement attribute is anything other than a character string or binary string, this parameter should be set to **SQL_IS_POINTER**.

■ If the value of the specified SQL statement attribute is a fixed-length data type, this parameter should be set to **SQL_IS_INTEGER** or **SQL_IS_UINTEGER**, as appropriate.

Description

The **SQLSetStmtAttr()** function is used to modify the current value of a specified SQL statement attribute. Refer to the **SQLGetStmtAttr()** function for more information about each statement attribute available.

Each statement handle's statement attributes remain in effect until they are changed by another call to **SQLSetStmtAttr()** or until the statement handle is freed with the **SQLFreeHandle()** function (ODBC 3.x driver) or the **SQLFreeStmt()** function (ODBC 2.0 or earlier driver). Calling the **SQLFreeStmt()** function with the **SQL_CLOSE**, **SQL_UNBIND**, or **SQL_RESET_PARAMS** option specified does not cause statement attributes to be reset.

Many statement attributes correspond to a descriptor's header field—setting these attributes actually results in the setting of the descriptor fields. Setting fields by calling **SQLSetStmtAttr()**, rather than **SQLSetDescField()**, has the advantage of not having to obtain a descriptor handle before a field can be set.

Setting attributes for one SQL statement can affect other SQL statements. Especially when the Application Parameter Descriptor (APD) or the Application Row Descriptor (ARD) associated with the statement handle is explicitly allocated and associated with other statement handles. Because **SQLSetStmtAttr()** modifies the APD or ARD, the modifications apply to all statements with which these descriptors are associated. If this is not the desired behavior, the application should disassociate the descriptor from the other statements (by calling **SQLSetStmtAttr()** to set the **SQL_ATTR_APP_ROW_DESC** or **SQL_ATTR_APP_PARAM_DESC** field to a different descriptor handle) before calling **SQLSetStmtAttr()** again.

When a descriptor field is set as a result of the corresponding statement attribute being set, the field is only set for the applicable descriptors that are currently associated with the statement handle specified in the *StatementHandle* parameter, and the attribute setting does not affect any descriptors that may be associated with that statement handle in the future. Likewise, when a descriptor field that is also a statement attribute is set by a calling the **SQLSetDescField()** function, the corresponding statement attribute is also set.

Table 8–10 shows the statement attributes that correspond to descriptor header fields.

NOTE: *In ODBC 3.x, this function replaces the ODBC 2.0 function* **SQLSetStmtOption()**.

Return Codes   SQL_SUCCESS, SQL_SUCCESS_WITH_INFO, SQL_INVALID_HANDLE, or SQL_ERROR

Table 8–10   Statement Attributes that Correspond to Descriptor Header Record Fields

Statement Attribute	Descriptor Header Record Field	Descriptor Type
SQL_ATTR_PARAM_BIND_OFFSET_PTR	SQL_DESC_BIND_OFFSET_PTR	APD
SQL_ATTR_PARAM_BIND_TYPE	SQL_DESC_BIND_TYPE	APD
SQL_ATTR_PARAM_OPERATION_PTR	SQL_DESC_ARRAY_STATUS_PTR	APD
SQL_ATTR_PARAM_STATUS_PTR	SQL_DESC_ARRAY_STATUS_PTR	IPD
SQL_ATTR_PARAMS_PROCESSED_PTR	SQL_DESC_ROWS_PROCESSED_PTR	IPD
SQL_ATTR_PARAMSET_SIZE	SQL_DESC_ARRAY_SIZE	APD
SQL_ATTR_ROW_ARRAY_SIZE	SQL_DESC_ARRAY_SIZE	ARD
SQL_ATTR_ROW_BIND_OFFSET_PTR	SQL_DESC_BIND_OFFSET_PTR	ARD
SQL_ATTR_ROW_BIND_TYPE	SQL_DESC_BIND_TYPE	ARD
SQL_ATTR_ROW_OPERATION_PTR	SQL_DESC_ARRAY_STATUS_PTR	ARD
SQL_ATTR_ROW_STATUS_PTR	SQL_DESC_ARRAY_STATUS_PTR	IRD
SQL_ATTR_ROWS_FETCHED_PTR	SQL_DESC_ROWS_PROCESSED_PTR	IRD

(Adapted from the table on page 977 of *Microsoft ODBC 3.0 Software Development Kit & Programmer's Reference.*)

SQLSTATEs

If this function returns **SQL_SUCCESS_WITH_INFO** or **SQL_ERROR**, one of the following SQLSTATE values may be obtained by calling the **SQLGetDiagRec()** function:

01000, **01**S02, **08**S01, **24**000, **HY**000, **HY**001, **HY**009, **HY**010*, **HY**011, **HY**013, **HY**017*, **HY**024, **HY**090*, **HY**092*, **HY**C00, **HY**T01, or **IM**001*

* Returned by the ODBC Driver Manager.

Unless noted otherwise, each of these SQLSTATE values is returned by the data source driver. Refer to Appendix B for detailed information about each SQLSTATE value that can be returned by the ODBC Driver Manager or by a data source driver.

Comments

- If a driver-specific value is specified in the *Attribute* parameter, an signed integer value may be stored in the memory location referred to by the *Value* parameter.
- In ODBC 3.x, connection attributes cannot be set at the statement level. This does not include the **SQL_ATTR_METADATA_ID** and **SQL_ATTR_ASYNC_ENABLE** attributes, because both are connection and statement attributes and can be set at either the connection level or the statement level.
- ODBC 3.x applications should never use the **SQLSetStmtOption()** function to set connection attributes at the statement level.
- Some statement attributes support substitution of a similar value if the data source does not support the value specified in the *Value* parameter. In such cases, the driver returns **SQL_SUCCESS_WITH_INFO** and SQLSTATE **01**S02 (Option value changed). For example, if *Attribute* is **SQL_ATTR_CONCURRENCY**, *Value* is **SQL_CONCUR_ROWVER**, and the data source does not support this, the driver substitutes **SQL_CONCUR_VALUES** and returns **SQL_SUCCESS_WITH_INFO**. An application can call the **SQLGetStmtAttr()** function after setting a statement attribute to determine whether or not a substitution occurred, and if so, to obtain the substituted value.

Prerequisites

An SQL statement handle must be allocated before this function is called.

Restrictions

There are no restrictions associated with this function call.

See Also

SQLGetStmtAttr(), SQLGetStmtOption(), SQLSetStmtOption(), SQLGetEnvAttr(), SQLSetEnvAttr(), SQLGetConnectAttr(), SQLSetConnectAttr(), SQLGetConnectOption(), SQLSetConnectOption()

Example   See the example provided for the **SQLGetStmtAttr()** function, on page 272.

SQLGetStmtOption

COMPATABILITY					
X/OPEN 95 CLI	ISO/IEC 92 CLI	ODBC 1.0	ODBC 2.0	ODBC 3.0	ODBC 3.5
☒	☐	☑	☑	☐	☐

API CONFORMANCE LEVEL   **LEVEL 1**

Purpose   The **SQLGetStmtOption()** function is used to retrieve the current setting of a specified SQL statement option (attribute).

Syntax

```
SQLRETURN   SQLGetStmtOption        (HSTMT      StatementHandle,
                                     UWORD      Option,
                                     PTR        Value);
```

Parameters   *StatementHandle*   An SQL statement handle that refers to a previously allocated SQL statement information storage buffer (data structure).

Option   The SQL statement option (attribute) whose value is to be retrieved. This parameter must be set to one of the following values:

- SQL_ASYNC_ENABLE
- SQL_BIND_TYPE
- SQL_CONCURRENCY
- SQL_CURSOR_TYPE
- SQL_KEYSET_SIZE
- SQL_MAX_LENGTH
- SQL_MAX_ROWS
- SQL_NOSCAN
- SQL_QUERY_TIMEOUT
- SQL_RETRIEVE_DATA

- SQL_ROWSET_SIZE
- SQL_SIMULATE_CURSOR
- SQL_USE_BOOKMARKS

Value   A pointer to a location in memory where this function is to store the current value of the SQL statement option (attribute) specified. Depending on the SQL statement option value being retrieved, this pointer can reference either a 32-bit integer value, or a null-terminated character string.

Description   The **SQLGetStmtOption()** function is used to retrieve the current setting of a specified SQL statement option (attribute). Table 8–11 alphabetically lists each value that can be specified for the *Option* parameter, along with a description of the information returned for that value when this function is executed.

NOTE: In ODBC 3.x, this function has been replaced by the **SQLGetStmtAttr()** *function.*

Return Codes   SQL_SUCCESS, SQL_SUCCESS_WITH_INFO, SQL_INVALID_HANDLE, or SQL_ERROR

SQLSTATEs   If this function returns **SQL_SUCCESS_WITH_INFO** or **SQL_ERROR**, one of the following SQLSTATE values may be obtained by calling the **SQLError()** function:

01000, **24**000, **IM**001*, **S1**000, **S1**001, **S1**010*, **S1**011, **S1**092*, **S1**109, or **S1**C00

* Returned by the ODBC Driver Manager.

Unless noted otherwise, each of these SQLSTATE values is returned by the data source driver. Refer to Appendix B for detailed information about each SQLSTATE value that can be returned by the ODBC Driver Manager or by a data source driver.

Table 8–11 SQL Statement Options

Option	Data Type	Description
SQL_ASYNC_ENABLE (ODBC 1.0)	32-bit integer	Specifies whether an ODBC API function called with the specified SQL statement handle is executed asynchronously: **SQL_ASYNC_ENABLE_OFF**: A function called with the specified SQL statement handle will not be executed asynchronously. This is the default value for this option. **SQL_ASYNC_ENABLE_ON**: A function called with the specified SQL statement handle will be executed asynchronously. After a function has been called asynchronously, only the original function, **SQLCancel()**, **SQLAllocStmt()**, **SQLError()**, or **SQLGetFunctions()**, can be called on the statement handle or on the connection handle associated with the statement handle until the original function returns a code other than **SQL_STILL_EXECUTING**. Any other function called on the statement handle or the connection handle associated with the statement handle returns **SQL_ERROR** and SQLSTATE S1010 (Function sequence error). Functions can be called on other statement handles. In general, applications should only execute ODBC API functions asynchronously on single-thread operating systems. On multithread operating systems, applications should execute ODBC API functions on separate threads, rather than executing them asynchronously on the same thread. The following functions can be executed asynchronously:

SQLColAttributes()		SQLColumnPrivileges()
SQLColumns()		SQLDescribeCol()
SQLDescribeParam()		SQLExecDirect()
SQLExecute()		SQLExtendedFetch()
SQLFetch1()		SQLForeignKeys()
SQLGetData()		SQLGetTypeInfo()
SQLMoreResults()		SQLNumParams()
SQLNumResultCols()		SQLParamData()
SQLPrepare()		SQLPrimaryKeys()
SQLProcedureColumns()		SQLProcedures()
SQLPutData()		SQLSetPos()
SQLSpecialColumns()		SQLStatistics()
SQLTablePrivileges()		SQLTables()

Option	Data Type	Description
SQL_BIND_TYPE (ODBC 1.0)	32-bit integer	Specifies the binding orientation to use when the **SQLExtendedFetch()** function is called. By default, this option is set to **SQL_BIND_BY_COLUMN** and column-wise binding is used. Row-wise binding is specified by setting this option to the length of a structure or an instance of a buffer into which all result data set

Table 8–11   SQL Statement Options (Continued)

Option	Data Type	Description
		columns are bound. If a length is specified, it must include space for all the bound columns and any padding of the structure or buffer to ensure that when a bound column address is incremented with the specified length, the result points to the beginning of the same column in the next row. By using the **sizeof()** operator in ANSI C, this behavior is guaranteed.
SQL_CONCURRENCY (ODBC 2.0)	32-bit integer	Specifies the cursor concurrency level to use. Valid values for this option are:
		SQL_CONCUR_READ_ONLY: Cursora are read-only. No updates are allowed. This is the default value for this option.
		SQL_CONCUR_LOCK: Cursors use the lowest level of locking sufficient to ensure that the row can be updated.
		SQL_CONCUR_ROWVER: Cursors use optimistic concurrency control, comparing row versions.
		SQL_CONCUR_VALUES: Cursors use optimistic concurrency control, comparing values.
		This option cannot be specified for a cursor that is already open.
		This option can be set via the *Concurrency* parameter of the **SQLSetScrollOptions()** function.
		If the specified concurrency value is not supported by the data source, the driver substitutes a different concurrency value and SQLSTATE **01S02** (Option value changed) is returned. The driver substitutes **SQL_CONCUR_ROWVER** for **SQL_CONCUR_VALUES**, and vice versa. The driver substitutes, in order, **SQL_CONCUR_ROWVER** or **SQL_CONCUR_VALUES** for **SQL_CONCUR_LOCK**. The validity of the substituted value is not checked until execution time.
SQL_CURSOR_TYPE (ODBC 2.0)	32-bit integer	Specifies the cursor type. Valid values for this option are:
		SQL_CURSOR_FORWARD_ONLY: The cursor can only scroll forward. This is the default value for this option.
		SQL_CURSOR_STATIC: The data in the result set is static, therefore the cursor is static.
		SQL_CURSOR_KEYSET_DRIVEN: The cursor is a keyset cursor; the driver saves and uses the keys for the number of rows specified in the **SQL_KEYSET_SIZE** statement option.

Table 8–11   SQL Statement Options (Continued)

Option	Data Type	Description
		SQL_CURSOR_DYNAMIC: The cursor is a dynamic (block) cursor; the driver saves and uses the keys only for the rows in the rowset.
		This option cannot be specified after the SQL statement associated with the statement handle specified has been prepared.
		If the specified cursor type is not supported by the data source, the driver substitutes a different cursor type and returns SQLSTATE **01**S02 (Option value changed). The driver substitutes, in order, a keyset-driven or static cursor for a dynamic (block) cursor. The driver substitutes a static cursor for a keyset-driven cursor.
SQL_KEYSET_SIZE (ODBC 2.0)	32-bit integer	Specifies the number of rows to be in the keyset of a keyset-driven cursor. If the keyset size is **0** (the default value for this option), the cursor is fully keyset-driven. If the keyset size is greater than **0**, the cursor is a mixed cursor (keyset-driven within the keyset and dynamic outside of the keyset).
		If the specified keyset size exceeds the maximum keyset size allowed, the driver substitutes that size and returns SQLSTATE **01**S02 (Option value changed).
		SQLExtendedFetch() returns an error if the keyset size is greater than **0** and less than the rowset size.
SQL_MAX_LENGTH (ODBC 1.0)	32-bit integer	Specifies the maximum amount of data that the driver will return from a character or binary column.
		If this option is set to **0** (which is the default value for this option), the driver attempts to return all available data.
		If the maximum length specified is smaller than the length of the data available, the data is truncated by the **SQLFetch()** or **SQLGetData()** function (**SQL_ SUCCESS** is returned).
		If the maximum length specified is less than the minimum amount of data the data source can return, or greater than the maximum amount of data the data source can return, the driver substitutes the appropriate value and returns SQLSTATE **01**S02 (Option value changed).
		This option can be set while a cursor is open; however, the setting may not take effect immediately, in which case the driver returns SQLSTATE **01**S02 (Option value changed), and the option is reset to its original value.

Table 8–11   SQL Statement Options (Continued)

Option	Data Type	Description
		This option is intended to reduce network traffic and should only be supported when the data source (as opposed to the driver) in a multiple-tier driver can implement it. This mechanism should not be used by applications to truncate data.
SQL_MAX_ROWS (ODBC 1.0)	32-bit integer	Specifies the maximum number of rows to return to the application for a **SELECT** SQL statement. Conceptually, this option's value is applied when a result data set is created and limits the result data set to the specified number of rows. If the number of rows in the result data set is larger that the number of rows specified, the result data set is truncated.
		If this option is set to **0** (which is the default value for this option), the driver returns all rows available.
		The value of this option applies to all result data sets associated with the statement handle, including the result data sets returned by the catalog functions.
		This option is intended to reduce network traffic. It is driver-defined whether this option applies to SQL statements other than **SELECT** SQL statements (such as catalog functions).
		This option can be set while a cursor is open; however, the setting may not take effect immediately, in which case the driver returns SQLSTATE **01S02** (Option value changed), and the option is reset to its original value.
SQL_NOSCAN (ODBC 1.0)	32-bit integer	Specifies whether the driver is to scan SQL statements for ODBC escape sequences. Valid values for this option are:
		SQL_NOSCAN_OFF: The driver is to scan SQL statements for ODBC escape sequences. This is the default value for this option.
		SQL_NOSCAN_ON: The driver is to send the SQL statement directly to the data source without scanning for ODBC escape sequences.
SQL_QUERY_TIMEOUT (ODBC 1.0)	32-bit integer	Specifies the number of seconds to wait for an SQL statement to execute before returning control to the application. If this option is equal to **0** (the default value for this option), then there is no time out. If the specified timeout exceeds the maximum timeout supported by the data source or is smaller than the minimum timeout supported by the data source, the driver substitutes that timeout value and returns **SQL**SQLSTATE **01S02** (Option value changed).

Table 8–11 SQL Statement Options (Continued)

Option	Data Type	Description
		Note that an application does not have to call **SQLFreeStmt()** with the **SQL_CLOSE** option specified to reuse a **SELECT** SQL statement if the statement timed out.
SQL_RETRIEVE_DATA (ODBC 2.0)	32-bit integer	Specifies whether the **SQLExtendedFetch()** function is to retrieve data after it positions the cursor. Valid values for this option are:
		SQL_RD_ON: **SQLExtendedFetch()** retrieves data after it positions the cursor. This is the default value for this option.
		SQL_RD_OFF: **SQLExtendedFetch()** does not retrieve data after it positions the cursor.
		By setting this option to **SQL_RD_OFF**, an application can verify whether a row exists or retrieve a bookmark for a row without incurring the overhead of retrieving data.
SQL_ROWSET_SIZE (ODBC 2.0)	32-bit integer	Specifies the number of rows that are to be returned by each call to **SQLExtendedFetch()** (the number of rows in the rowset). By default, the value for this option is 1. If the specified rowset size exceeds the maximum rowset size supported by the data source, the driver substitutes that value and returns SQLSTATE **01S02** (Option value changed).
		This option can be set while a cursor is open; it can also be set via the *RowSet* parameter of the **SQLSetScrollOptions()** function.
SQL_SIMULATE_CURSOR (ODBC 2.0)	32-bit integer	Specifies whether drivers that simulate positioned **UPDATE** and **DELETE** SQL statements guarantee that such statements only affect one row. To simulate positioned **UPDATE** and **DELETE** SQL statements, most drivers construct a searched **UPDATE** or **DELETE** statement containing a **WHERE** clause that specifies the value of each column in the current row. Unless these columns make up a unique key, such a statement may affect more than one row. To guarantee that such SQL statements affect only one row, the driver determines the columns in a unique key and adds these columns to the result data set. If an application guarantees that the columns in the result data set make up a unique key, the driver is not required to do so. This may reduce overall execution time.

Table 8–11   SQL Statement Options (Continued)

Option	Data Type	Description
		Valid values for this option are:

SQL_SC_NON_UNIQUE:
The driver does not guarantee that simulated positioned **UPDATE** or **DELETE** SQL statements affect only one row; it is the application's responsibility to do so. If a positioned **UPDATE** or **DELETE** SQL statement affects more than one row, **SQLExecute()** or **SQLExecDirect()** returns SQLSTATE **01**001 (Cursor operation conflict).

SQL_SC_TRY_UNIQUE:
The driver attempts to guarantee that simulated positioned **UPDATE** or **DELETE** SQL statements affect only one row. The driver always executes such statements, even if they might affect more than one row, such as when there is no unique key. If a positioned **UPDATE** or **DELETE** statement affects more than one row, **SQLExecute()** or **SQLExecDirect()** returns SQLSTATE **01**001 (Cursor operation conflict).

SQL_SC_UNIQUE:
The driver guarantees that simulated positioned **UPDATE** or **DELETE** SQL statements affect only one row. If the driver cannot guarantee this for a given statement, **SQLExecDirect()** or **SQLPrepare()** returns an error.

If the data source provides native SQL support for positioned **UPDATE** and **DELETE** SQL statements, and the driver does not simulate cursors, **SQL_SUCCESS** is returned when an application sets this option to **SQL_SC_UNIQUE** and **SQL_SUCCESS_WITH_INFO** is returned if an application tries to set this option to anything else.

If the data source provides the **SQL_SC_TRY_UNIQUE** level of support, and the driver does not, **SQL_SUCCESS** is returned when an application sets this option to **SQL_SC_TRY_UNIQUE** and **SQL_SUCCESS_WITH_INFO** is returned when an application sets this option to **SQL_SC_NON_UNIQUE**.

If the cursor simulation type specified is not supported by the data source, the driver substitutes a different simulation type and returns SQLSTATE **01**S02 (Option value changed).

The driver substitutes, in order, the **SQL_SC_TRY_UNIQUE** or the **SQL_SC_NON_UNIQUE** cursor simulation type for the **SQL_SC_UNIQUE** cursor simulation type. The driver substitutes the **SQL_SC_NON_UNIQUE** cursor simulation type for the **SQL_SC_TRY_UNIQUE** cursor simu-

Table 8–11 SQL Statement Options (Continued)

lation type.

Option	Data Type	Description
SQL_USE_BOOKMARKS (ODBC 2.0)	32-bit integer	Specifies whether an application uses bookmarks with a cursor. Valid values for this option are:
		SQL_UB_OFF: An application does not use bookmarks with a cursor. This is the default value for this option.
		SQL_UB_ON: An application uses bookmarks with a cursor.
		To use bookmarks with a cursor, an application must set this option before the cursor is opened.

Comments
- If an option that returns a string value is specified in the *Option* parameter, the *Value* parameter must contain a pointer to a buffer in which this function can return the string.
- The maximum length that a string value can be (excluding the NULL-termination character) is **SQL_MAX_OPTION_STRING_LENGTH** bytes.
- The **SQL_GET_BOOKMARK** and **SQL_ROW_NUMBER** statement options are read-only; their values can be retrieved by this function, but their values can not be set by the **SQLSetStmtOption()** function.

Prerequisites An SQL statement handle must be allocated before this function is called.

Restrictions There are no restrictions associated with this function call.

See Also **SQLSetStmtOption()**, **SQLGetStmtAttr()**, **SQLSetStmtAttr()**, **SQLGetEnvAttr()**, **SQLSetEnvAttr()**, **SQLGetConnectAttr()**, **SQLSetConnectAttr()**, **SQLGetConnectOption()**, **SQLSetConnectOption()**

Example The following Visual C++ program illustrates how to retrieve and change the current value of an SQL statement option (attribute).

```
/*-------------------------------------------------------------*/
/* NAME:     CH8EX10.CPP                                       */
/* PURPOSE:  Illustrate How To Use The Following ODBC API Functions */
/*           In A C++ Program:                                 */
/*                                                             */
/*                SQLGetStmtOption()                           */
```

```
/*                  SQLSetStmtOption()                                      */
/*                                                                          */
/*  OTHER ODBC APIs SHOWN:                                                  */
/*              SQLAllocEnv()              SQLAllocConnect()                 */
/*              SQLConnect()               SQLAllocStmt()                    */
/*              SQLFreeStmt()              SQLDisconnect()                   */
/*              SQLFreeConnect()           SQLFreeEnv()                      */
/*                                                                          */
/*————————————————————————————————————————————————————————————*/


// Include The Appropriate Header Files
#include <windows.h>
#include <sql.h>
#include <sqlext.h>
#include <iostream.h>

// Define The ODBC_Class Class
class ODBC_Class
{
    // Attributes
    public:
        HENV        EnvHandle;
        HDBC        ConHandle;
        HSTMT       StmtHandle;
        RETCODE     rc;
        UDWORD      MaxRows;

    // Operations
    public:
        ODBC_Class();                                  // Constructor
        ~ODBC_Class();                                 // Destructor
        RETCODE     GetMaxRowsValue();
        RETCODE     SetMaxRowsValue(UDWORD MaxRows);
};

// Define The Class Constructor
ODBC_Class::ODBC_Class()
{
    // Initialize The Return Code Variable
    rc = SQL_SUCCESS;

    // Allocate An Environment Handle
    rc = SQLAllocEnv(&EnvHandle);

    // Allocate A Connection Handle
    if (rc == SQL_SUCCESS)
        rc = SQLAllocConnect(EnvHandle, &ConHandle);
}

// Define The Class Destructor
ODBC_Class::~ODBC_Class()
{
    // Free The Connection Handle
    if (ConHandle != NULL)
```

```
            SQLFreeConnect(ConHandle);

    // Free The Environment Handle
    if (EnvHandle != NULL)
        SQLFreeEnv(EnvHandle);
}

// Define The GetMaxRowsValue() Member Function
RETCODE ODBC_Class::GetMaxRowsValue(void)
{
    // Determine The Number Of Rows The Driver Will Return For A
    // SELECT SQL Statement
    rc = SQLGetStmtOption(StmtHandle, SQL_MAX_ROWS,
                (PTR) &MaxRows);

    // Display The Information Retrieved
    if (rc == SQL_SUCCESS)
    {
        cout << "Maximum number of rows to return : ";
        cout << MaxRows << endl;
    }

    // Return The ODBC API Return Code To The Calling Function
    return(rc);
}

// Define The SetMaxRowsValue() Member Function
RETCODE ODBC_Class::SetMaxRowsValue(UDWORD MaxRows)
{
    // Specify The Number Of Rows That The Driver Is To Return For A
    // SELECT SQL Statement
    rc = SQLSetStmtOption(StmtHandle, SQL_MAX_ROWS,
                (UDWORD) MaxRows);

    // Return The ODBC API Return Code To The Calling Function
    return(rc);
}

/*-------------------------------------------------------------*/
/* The Main Function                                           */
/*-------------------------------------------------------------*/
int main()
{
    // Declare The Local Memory Variables
    RETCODE   rc = SQL_SUCCESS;
    SQLCHAR   DBName[10] = "Northwind";

    // Create An Instance Of The ODBC_Class Class
    ODBC_Class   Example;

    // Connect To The Northwind Sample Database
    if (Example.ConHandle != NULL)
    {
```

```
rc = SQLConnect(Example.ConHandle, DBName, SQL_NTS,
        (SQLCHAR *) "", SQL_NTS, (SQLCHAR *) "", SQL_NTS);

// Allocate An SQL Statement Handle
rc = SQLAllocStmt(Example.ConHandle, &Example.StmtHandle);
if (rc == SQL_SUCCESS)
{
    // Determine The Number Of Rows The Driver Will Return
    // For A SELECT SQL Statement
    rc = Example.GetMaxRowsValue();

    // Tell The Driver To Return Up To 25 Rows For A
    // SELECT SQL Statement
    rc = Example.SetMaxRowsValue(25);

    // Determine Whether Or Not The Driver Will Now Return
    // Up To 25 Rows For A SELECT SQL Statement
    rc = Example.GetMaxRowsValue();

    // Free The SQL Statement Handle
    if (Example.StmtHandle != NULL)
        SQLFreeStmt(Example.StmtHandle, SQL_DROP);
}

// Disconnect From The Northwind Sample Database
rc = SQLDisconnect(Example.ConHandle);
}

// Return To The Operating System
return(rc);
}
```

SQLSetStmtOption

COMPATABILITY

X/OPEN 95 CLI	ISO/IEC 92 CLI	ODBC 1.0	ODBC 2.0	ODBC 3.0	ODBC 3.5
☒	☐	☑	☑	☐	☐

API CONFORMANCE LEVEL   **LEVEL 1**

Purpose   The `SQLSetStmtOption()` function is used to modify the current value of a specified SQL statement option (attribute).

Syntax
```
SQLRETURN   SQLSetStmtOption   (HSTMT     StatementHandle,
                                UWORD     Option,
                                UDWORD    Value);
```

Parameters

StatementHandle An SQL statement handle that refers to a previously allocated SQL statement information storage buffer (data structure).

Option The SQL statement option (attribute) whose value is to be modified. This parameter must be set to one of the following values:

- **SQL_ASYNC_ENABLE**
- **SQL_BIND_TYPE**
- **SQL_CONCURRENCY**
- **SQL_CURSOR_TYPE**
- **SQL_KEYSET_SIZE**
- **SQL_MAX_LENGTH**
- **SQL_MAX_ROWS**
- **SQL_NOSCAN**
- **SQL_QUERY_TIMEOUT**
- **SQL_RETRIEVE_DATA**
- **SQL_ROWSET_SIZE**
- **SQL_SIMULATE_CURSOR**
- **SQL_USE_BOOKMARKS**

Value The new value for the SQL statement option (attribute) specified. Depending on the SQL statement option (attribute) being set, this is a 32-bit integer value or a NULL-terminated character string.

Description The **SQLSetStmtOption()** function is used to modify the current value of a specified SQL statement option. Refer to the **SQLGetStmtOption()** function for more information about each SQL statement option available.

A statement's options remain in effect until they are changed by another call to **SQLSetStmtOption()** or until the statement handle is freed with the **SQLFreeStmt()** function (with the **SQL_DROP** option specified. Calling the **SQLFreeStmt()** function with the **SQL_CLOSE**, **SQL_UNBIND**, or **SQL_RESET_PARAMS** option specified does not cause statement options to be reset.

NOTE: *In ODBC 3.x, this function has been replaced by the* **SQLSetStmtAttr()** *function.*

Return Codes SQL_SUCCESS, SQL_SUCCESS_WITH_INFO, SQL_INVALID_HANDLE, or SQL_ERROR

SQLSTATEs If this function returns SQL_SUCCESS_WITH_INFO or SQL_ERROR, one of the following SQLSTATE values may be obtained by calling the SQLError() function:

01000, 01S02, 08S01, 24000, IM001*, S1000, S1001, S1009, S1010*, S1011, S1092*, or S1C00

* Returned by the ODBC Driver Manager.

Unless noted otherwise, each of these SQLSTATE values is returned by the data source driver. Refer to Appendix B for detailed information about each SQLSTATE value that can be returned by the ODBC Driver Manager or by a data source driver.

Comment ▨ Some statement options support substitution of a similar value if the data source does not support the value specified in the *Value* parameter. In such cases, the driver returns SQL_SUCCESS_WITH_INFO and SQLSTATE 01S02 (Option value changed). For example, if the *Option* parameter is set to SQL_ATTR_CONCURRENCY, the *Value* parameter is set to SQL_CONCUR_ROWVER, and the data source does not support this option setting. The driver substitutes SQL_CONCUR_VALUES and returns SQL_SUCCESS_WITH_INFO. An application can call the SQLGetStmtOption() function after setting a statement option to determine whether a substitution occurred, and if so, to obtain the substituted value.

▨ The maximum length that a string value can be (excluding the NULL-termination character) is SQL_MAX_OPTION_STRING_LENGTH bytes.

▨ To set an option for all statements associated with a specific connection handle, an application should call the SQLSetConnectOption() function.

Prerequisites An SQL statement handle must be allocated before this function is called.

Restrictions There are no restrictions associated with this function call.

See Also SQLGetStmtOption(), SQLGetStmtAttr(), SQLSetStmtAttr(), SQLGetEnvAttr(), SQLSetEnvAttr(), SQLGetConnectAttr(), SQLSetConnectAttr(), SQLGetConnectOption(), SQLSetConnectOption()

Examples See the example provided for the SQLGetStmtOption() function, on page 301.

9

Preparing and Executing SQL Statements

ODBC applications perform most of their data retrieval and data manipulation operations by submitting SQL statements to a data source for processing. This chapter is designed to introduce you to the set of API functions that are used to prepare and execute SQL statements. The first part of this chapter introduces the functions used to prepare an SQL statement for execution. This is followed by a discussion about the functions used to associate application variables and buffers to parameter markers coded in SQL statement syntax. Next, the functions used to submit SQL statements to the data source for processing are described. Then, the functions used to send large data values to the data source and to terminate transactions are discussed. Finally, a detailed reference section covering each ODBC API function that can be used to prepare, associate application variables to, and submit SQL statements for execution is provided.

Allocating an SQL Statement Handle

Just as a handle is used to access and modify an application's environment, a handle is used to submit an SQL statement to a data source for processing and to access the results. Thus, before an SQL statement can be prepared and executed, a statement handle must first be allocated. To do this an application:

1. Creates (declares) an SQL statement handle variable.

and

2. Calls either the **SQLAllocHandle()** function (ODBC 3.x drivers) or the **SQLAllocStmt()** function (ODBC 2.0 or earlier drivers) with the statement handle variable address specified.

When either of these functions is called, the ODBC Driver Manager allocates a structure in the connection handle specified in which to store information about the SQL statement, and stores the handle to this structure in the SQL statement handle variable specified. As with the **SQLAllocHandle()**, the **SQLAllocEnv()** function, and the **SQLAllocConnect()** function, two levels of the **SQLAllocStmt()** function are used—the first resides in the ODBC Driver Manager and the second can be found in each data source driver. When an application calls either of these functions, the Driver Manager allocates its own structure and calls the corresponding function in the driver.

For many drivers, allocating statement handles is an expensive task. Therefore, it is usually more efficient for an application to use an existing SQL statement handle repeatedly than to free existing statement handles when they are no longer needed and allocate new ones. Reusing statement handles also allows an application to stay under the limitation some drivers place on the number of statements that can be "Active" at one time. The exact definition of "Active" is driver-specific, but it often refers to any SQL statement that has been prepared or executed and still has results available. For example, after an **INSERT** SQL statement has been prepared, it is generally considered to be "Active;" after a **SELECT** SQL statement has been executed and the cursor is still open, it is generally considered to be "Active;" but after a **CREATE TABLE** SQL statement has been executed, it is generally considered to be "Inactive."

When result data sets are created on statement handles, applications must be careful to close the cursor and destroy the result data set associated with the statement handle before it is reused.

Using SQL Statement Parameter Markers

Literal values can be, and often are, hard-coded directly into SQL statements. For example, suppose you want to add a record to a table named Parts that has columns named PartID, Description, and Price. You could do this by preparing and executing the following SQL statement:

```
INSERT INTO Parts (PartID, Description, Price) VALUES
(2100, 'Drive shaft', 50.00)
```

Although this SQL statement correctly inserts a new record in the Parts table, its use is limited because it can only insert one specific record into the table. Therefore, this approach would not be a good solution for a data entry application that might need to insert several different records into the Parts table. An alternative approach is to construct one or more SQL statements at application run time using the specific values that need to be inserted into the table. Although this approach provides more flexibility, it is not the best solution because of the complexity required to construct and execute multiple SQL statements at run time. The best approach to this type of problem is to construct an SQL statement so that it contains parameter markers in place of literal values. For example, our previous SQL statement could be constructed like this:

```
INSERT INTO Parts (PartID, Description, Price) VALUES (?,
?, ?)
```

When SQL statements are coded in this manner, each parameter marker used must be associated with, or *bound* to an application variable. Once all parameter markers have been bound, an application can simply set/change the values of each bound variable and execute the SQL statement. If the SQL statement is to be executed multiple times, the process can be made even more efficient by preparing and executing the statement in separate steps.

Parameter markers provide the flexibility gained by constructing SQL statements at run time while eliminating most of the added complexity (particularly the additional coding needed to convert numerical data values to and from text). For example, suppose the PartID column of the Parts table described in the previous examples was defined to hold integer data. If an SQL statement designed to insert new records is constructed at application run time (without parameter markers), the application must convert the Part ID to text (to build the SQL statement) and the data source must convert it back to an integer (to store it in the column). By using a parameter marker, the application could send the Part ID to the driver (and to its underlying data source) as an integer, thereby saving one or more data conversions. For long data values this becomes critical because the text forms of such values often exceed the maximum length allowed for an SQL statement.

Parameter markers are only allowed in certain places in SQL statements. For example, they cannot be used in the list of columns to be returned by a **SELECT** SQL statement, nor can they be used as the operand of a binary operator such as the equals sign (=). In general, parameter markers are legal if they are used in Data Manipulation Language (DML) statements; parameter markers are not legal when used in DDL statements.

Binding Parameters to Application Variables

As mentioned earlier, each parameter marker in an SQL statement must be associated with, or bound to, an application variable before the statement is executed. When an application binds a variable to a parameter marker in an SQL statement, it describes the variable (that is, memory address, C data type, and so on) to the driver. It also describes the parameter itself (that is, the SQL data type, precision, etc.). The driver stores this information in the structure it maintains for the SQL statement (referred to by the statement handle) and uses the information to retrieve the value from the variable and send it to the data source when the SQL statement is executed.

The **SQLBindParameter()** function is used to bind parameter markers in an SQL statement to application variables, one parameter marker at a time. Each time this function is called the application specifies:

■ The parameter marker number. Parameters are numbered in increasing order as they appear from left to right in the SQL statement, beginning with the number 1. While it is legal to specify a parameter marker number higher than the actual number of parameter markers in the SQL statement, additional parameter marker values are ignored when the SQL statement is executed.

- The parameter marker type (that is, input, output, or input/output). Except for parameter markers used in stored procedure calls, all parameter markers are treated as input parameters.

- The C data type, memory address, and size (length), in bytes, of the application variable being bound to the parameter marker. The driver must be able to convert the data from the C data type specified to the SQL data type used by the data source or an error will occur.

- The SQL data type, precision, and scale of the parameter marker itself.

- Optionally, the memory address of a length/indicator variable. This variable is used to provide the byte length of binary or character data, specify that the data is NULL, or specify that the data is long and will be sent with the **SQLPutData()** function.

Parameter markers can be bound to application variables in any order.

NOTE: *In ODBC 1.0, parameter markers were bound to application variables with the* **SQLSetParam()** *function. The ODBC Driver Manager is responsible for mapping calls between* **SQLSetParam()** *and* **SQLBindParameter()***, depending on the versions of ODBC being used by both the application and the driver.*

Application variables can be bound to parameter markers in an SQL statement any time before the statement is sent to the data source for execution. Once an application variable is bound to a parameter marker, it remains bound until one of the following occurs:

- A different application variable is bound to the same parameter marker.

- All parameter markers are unbound. This is done by calling the **SQLFreeStmt()** function with the **SQL_RESET_PARAMS** option specified.

- The statement handle associated with the SQL statement containing the parameter marker is released (freed).

To bind a parameter marker to a different variable, an application simply rebinds the parameter marker with the new variable; the previous binding is automatically released. However, if a parameter marker is rebound after an SQL statement has been executed, the new binding does not take effect until the SQL statement is re-executed. Applications must ensure that variables are not freed until after they are unbound.

Binding Parameters by Name

Some DBMSs allow an application to specify a stored procedure's parameters by name, instead of by position, when the procedure is invoked. In ODBC, these parameters are referred to as *named parameters*, and they can only be used in SQL statements that call stored procedures; otherwise, named parameters are not supported by ODBC.

The **SQLBindParameter()** function is typically used to bind named parameters to application variables; however when this function is used, the parameter being bound must be identified by the **SQL_DESC_NAME** field of the implementation parameter descriptor (IPD) record associated with the SQL statement that's calling the stored procedure—not by its position in the SQL statement. Because named parameters are identified by IPD descriptor records, the **SQLSetDescField()** and **SQLSetDescRec()** functions can also be used to perform the binding process. Regardless of how a named parameter is bound, the **SQL_DESC_NAME** field of its corresponding IPD descriptor record must be set to **SQL_NAMED**. That's because the driver checks the value of the **SQL_DESC_UNNAMED** field of IPD descriptor records to determine whether or not named parameters are being used.

The main difference between named parameters and unnamed parameters lies in the relationship between the IPD descriptor record number, the position number of the parameter marker in the stored procedure call, and the parameter itself. When unnamed parameters are used, the first parameter marker is always related to the first parameter record in the IPD descriptor which, in turn, is related to the first parameter specified in the stored procedure call. When named parameters are used, the first parameter marker is still related to the first parameter record of the IPD descriptor, but the relationship between the record number of the descriptor and the parameter specified in the procedure call no longer exists. Therefore, named parameters do not use the mapping of the descriptor record number to the procedure parameter position; this mapping is replaced by the mapping of the descriptor record name to the procedure parameter name. In addition, the order in which the parameter appears in the procedure call is not important, and the parameter's record number is ignored.

NOTE: *If automatic population of the IPD is enabled, the driver populates the descriptor such that the order of the parameter descriptor records correspond to the order the parameters appear in the procedure definition, even if named parameters are used.*

Named parameters and unnamed parameters cannot be mixed; if one named parameter is used, all remaining parameters must be named parameters. If an SQL statement contains one or more unnamed parameters, all named parameters must be treated as unnamed parameters.

Binding Parameters to Arrays

ODBC 3.x applications can extend the flexibility that parameters provide by specifying multiple values (stored in arrays) for each parameter used in an SQL statement. For example, by using an array of values with a parameterized **INSERT** SQL statement, an application can insert several rows of data into a data source *with a single function call* (provided the data source supports the use of parameter value arrays). Because only a limited number of DBMSs have the ability to execute SQL statements whose parameters have been bound to arrays, drivers often emulate this support by executing the SQL statement multiple times—once for each value (or set of values) in the array. However, before an application attempts to use parameter value arrays, it must ensure that the driver being used supports them.

There are several advantages to using arrays of parameter values. First, network traffic is reduced because the data for many SQL statements can be sent in a single packet. Second, some data sources can execute SQL statements using arrays faster than they can execute an equivalent amount of separate SQL statements. Finally, when data is stored in an array, as is often the case for screen data, all the rows in a particular column can be bound to a parameter with a single function call and multiple rows can be updated by executing a single SQL statement.

An application binds parameters to arrays in the same manner that it binds parameters to other application variables—by calling the **SQLBindParameter()** function. The only difference is that the addresses specified in the **SQLBindParameter()** call reference arrays instead of variables. However, before binding parameters to arrays, an application must decide which of the following binding styles it will use:

■ *Column-wise binding* An array is bound to each parameter in the SQL statement This is called column-wise binding because a column of values is bound to one parameter in the statement.

■ *Row-wise binding* A data structure that holds a single data value for each parameter in the SQL statement is defined and each element of the first structure in an array of these structures is bound to each parameter in the SQL statement. This is called row-wise binding because a row of values is bound to all parameters in the statement.

Whether to use column-wise binding or row-wise binding is largely a matter of preference. Column-wise binding is the default binding style used; applications can change from column-wise binding to row-wise binding by setting the **SQL_ATTR_PARAM_BIND_TYPE** statement attribute. Depending on how the processor being used accesses memory, row-wise binding might execute faster. However, any performance difference is likely to be negligible except in cases where very large numbers of rows of parameter values are used.

COLUMN-WISE BINDING When column-wise binding is used, two arrays are bound to each parameter in an SQL statement for which data values are to be provided. The first array holds the data values used by the statement and the second array holds length/indicator values corresponding to the data values stored in the first array. Both arrays contain as many elements as are needed to store the values for the parameter. If several parameters in an SQL statement are to be bound to arrays, all the arrays must contain the same number of elements. Figure 9–1 illustrates how column-wise binding works.

ROW-WISE BINDING When row-wise binding is used, a data structure that holds a single data value and a corresponding length/indicator value for each parameter in an SQL statement for which data values are to be provided is defined by the application (elements can be placed in this structure in any order). Then, the application sets the **SQL_ATTR_PARAM_ BIND_TYPE** statement attribute to the size of this data structure to notify the driver that row-wise binding is being used. The application then allocates an array of these data structures that contains as many elements as are needed to store the values for the parameter. Finally, the address of each element in the first structure of this array is bound to each parameter in the SQL statement.

Figure 9–2 illustrates how row-wise binding works.

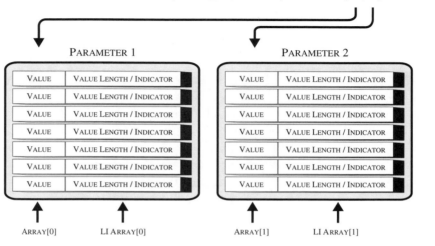

Figure 9–1 Column-wise parameter binding

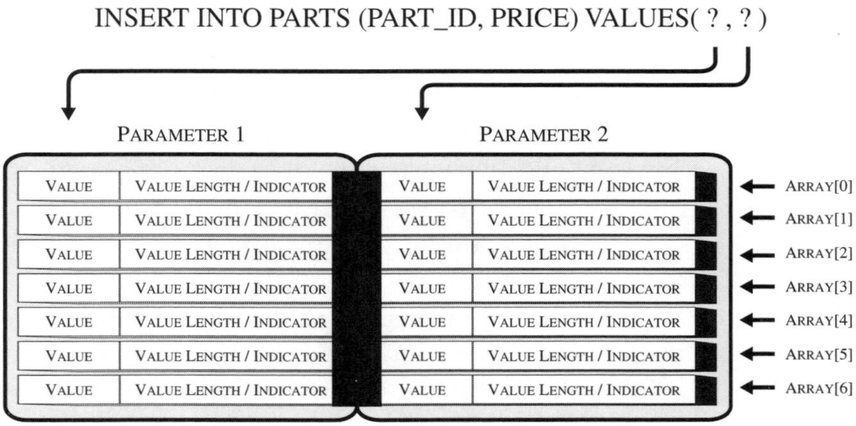

Figure 9–2 Row-wise parameter binding

During execution, the driver calculates the address of the data for a particular row and column by solving the equation:

```
Address = Bound Address + ((Row Number - 1) * Structure
Size) + Offset
```

where rows are numbered from 1 to the size of the array, and the offset, if any, is the value stored in the **SQL_ATTR_PARAM_BIND_OFFSET_PTR** statement attribute.

Setting Parameter Values

To set the value of a parameter that has been (or that will be) bound to an application variable, an application simply assigns a value to the variable. When application variables are set is not important, as long they are set sometime before the SQL statement to which they are bound is executed. Thus, an application can set the value of a variable before or after it is bound to a parameter and it can change the value as many times as it wants. Each time the SQL statement is executed, the driver simply retrieves the current value of each variable bound to the statement and sends it to the data source.

If a length/indicator variable was bound to a parameter (when the application variable was bound), it must be set to one of the following values before the SQL statement is executed:

■ The actual length, in bytes, of the data value stored in the bound application variable. The driver only checks this length if the application variable contains character or binary data.

■ **SQL_NTS** (A NULL-terminated string is stored in the bound application variable).

■ **SQL_NULL_DATA** (A NULL value is stored in the bound application variable. In this case, the driver ignores the value of the bound variable).

■ **SQL_DATA_AT_EXEC** or the result of the **SQL_LEN_DATA_AT_EXEC(length)** macro (The value stored in the bound application variable is to be sent to the data source by the **SQLPutData()** function).

How a driver actually processes parameter values when SQL statements containing them are executed is driver dependent. In most cases, the driver sends the value directly to the data source (if necessary, the driver converts the value from its C data type and byte length to the appropriate SQL data type, precision, and scale before sending it to the data source). In other cases, the driver converts the value to text and inserts it into the SQL statement before sending the statement to the data source.

Setting Arrays of Parameter Values

When using arrays of values, the setup is a bit more involved. If column-wise binding was used, the application assigns a value to each element of the array containing parameter values, just as it would set a single application variable. Then, the application sets each element of the corresponding length/indicator array using the same rules that apply for setting bound length/indicator variables. If row-wise binding is used, the application assigns a value to each parameter value element of each structure in the array. Then, it sets each length/indicator element of each structure in the array.

Once the appropriate values have been stored in all bound arrays, the application must then tell the driver how many elements are in the arrays. The application must also provide the driver with the address of a variable in which it can return information about the number of elements (sets of parameter values) it processes. Finally, the application must also provide the driver with the address of a variable in which it can return status information about each element (sets of parameter values) it processes. In ODBC 2.0 and earlier applications, this is done by calling the **SQLParamOptions()** function. In ODBC 3.x applications, this is done by setting the **SQL_ATTR_PARAMSET_SIZE**, **SQL_ATTR_PARAMS_PROCESSED_PTR**, and the **SQL_ATTR_PARAM_STATUS_PTR** statement attributes with the **SQLSetStmtAttr()** function.

ODBC 3.x applications can also use the **SQL_ATTR_PARAM_OPERATION_PTR** statement attribute to ignore one or more rows of parameter values—if an element of the array stored in this attribute is set to **SQL_PARAM_IGNORE**, the set of parameter values corresponding to that element is excluded from SQLExecute or **SQLExecDirect()** function calls. The array stored in the **SQL_ATTR_PARAM_OPERATION_PTR** attribute is allocated and set by the application and read by the driver.

Changing Parameter Bindings (and Values) with Offsets

ODBC 3.x applications can specify that an offset be added to a bound parameter's address and to the corresponding length/indicator buffer address when SQLExecute or **SQLExecDirect()** is called. This feature allows an application to change parameter bindings (and values) without calling the **SQLBindParameter()** function to rebind previously bound parameters. When offsets are used, the original bindings represent a *template* of how the application buffers are laid out—the application can move this template to different areas of memory simply by changing the offset. New offsets can be specified at any time; each time an offset is specified, it is added to the originally bound buffer address. This means that offset additions are not cumulative—each offset cancels the previous offset used. It goes with out saying that the sum of the address and the offset must always be a valid address (either or both the offset and the address to which the offset is added, can be invalid, as long as the sum of the two is a valid address).

NOTE: *Binding offsets are not supported by ODBC 2.0 and earlier drivers.*

Executing SQL Statements

With ODBC, there are four ways to execute SQL statements. Each depends on when the SQL statement is prepared by the data source and who defined it. The four methods available are:

- *Direct execution* The SQL statement is prepared and executed in a single step at application run time. The SQL statement is defined by the application.

- *Prepared execution* The SQL statement is prepared and executed in two separate steps at application run time. With this approach, the SQL statement can be prepared once and executed multiple times. The SQL statement is defined by the application.

- *Stored procedures* One or more SQL statements are compiled at development time and stored in the data source as a procedure that can be executed later. A stored procedure can be executed one or more times at application run time. The application can obtain information about available stored procedures by using the ODBC catalog function **SQLProcedures()**. The SQL statements used in a stored procedure are usually defined by a separate application.

- *Catalog functions* The application can call an ODBC API function that returns a predefined result data set. Catalog functions usually submit a predefined SQL statement or call a stored procedure created specifically for this purpose. A catalog function can be executed one or more times at application run time.

Direct Execution

The direct execution method is the simplest method to use to execute an SQL statement. When an SQL statement is executed using this method, the data source compiles it into an access plan and immediately executes that plan. The major drawback of using this method is that the SQL statement must be parsed and compiled each time it is executed. In addition, an application cannot retrieve information about the result data set created by the statement (if any) until after the statement is executed (this restriction is removed if the statement is prepared and executed in two separate steps). For these reasons, the direct execution method works best for SQL statements that are only going to be executed once.

EXECUTING SQL STATEMENTS WITH THE DIRECT EXECUTION METHOD To execute an SQL statement using the direct execution method, an application:

1. Binds any parameter markers that were coded in the SQL statement to application variables.
2. Sets the values of all bound variables.
3. Calls the **SQLExecDirect()** function with the SQL statement specified.

When the **SQLExecDirect()** function is called, the driver:

1. Modifies the SQL statement to use the data source's SQL grammar (this includes replacing any escape sequences that may have been used with the appropriate SQL grammar unless the **SQL_ATTR_NOSCAN** statement attribute has been set).
2. Retrieves the current values of the variables bound to parameter markers in the statement and converts them as necessary.
3. Sends the statement, along with the converted parameter values to the data source for processing.
4. Returns any errors detected (including sequencing or state errors, syntactic errors, and semantic errors) to the application that called the **SQLExecDirect()** function.

Prepared Execution

If an SQL statement is to be executed more than once, prepared execution is a much more efficient method to use. With prepared execution, an

SQL statement is compiled (prepared) to produce an access plan in one step and executed in another. Because the access plan is created in a separate step it can be executed one or more times—either immediately after the statement is prepared, or sometime later in the program.

Prepared execution is faster than direct execution for statements that are to be executed more than once, primarily because the statement only has to be parsed and compiled once; whereas statements executed directly must be parsed and compiled each time they are executed. Prepared execution can also provide a reduction in network traffic because the driver can send an access plan identifier to the data source each time the statement is executed (provided the data source supports access plan identifiers) as opposed to sending an entire SQL statement. Another advantage of prepared execution is that it provides an application the ability to retrieve information about the result data set that will be generated (if any) any time after the statement is prepared.

NOTE: *Returning information about result data sets produced (metadata) for prepared, unexecuted statements is expensive for some drivers and should be avoided by interoperable applications whenever possible.*

Direct execution should be used instead of prepared execution when an SQL statement is only going to be executed once; in this case prepared execution is slightly slower than direct execution because an additional ODBC function call is required. Prepared execution is commonly used by vertical and custom applications to repeatedly execute the same, parameterized SQL statement.

NOTE: *Some data sources automatically delete access plans that have been created for prepared execution each time a transaction is terminated (either by explicitly calling the* **SQLEndTran()** *or* **SQLTransact()** *function or by running in autocommit mode). Applications working with these data sources should either run in manual commit mode or use direct execution.*

EXECUTING SQL STATEMENTS WITH THE PREPARED EXECUTION METHOD To execute an SQL statement using the prepared execution method, an application:

1. Binds application variables to any parameter markers that were coded in the statement.
2. Calls the **SQLPrepare()** function with the SQL statement specified.

3. Sets the values of all bound variables. This step can also be performed before the SQL statement is prepared.

4. Calls the **SQLExecute()** function with the prepared SQL statement specified.

5. Repeats steps 2 and 3 as necessary.

When the **SQLPrepare()** function is called, the driver:

1. Modifies the SQL statement to use the data source's SQL grammar (this includes replacing any escape sequences that may have been used with the appropriate SQL grammar unless the **SQL_ATTR_NOSCAN** statement attribute has been set).

2. Sends the statement to the data source for preparation.

3. Stores the returned access plan identifier for later execution (if the preparation succeeded) or returns any errors detected (if the preparation failed) to the application that called the **SQLPrepare()** function.

NOTE: *Some drivers do not return errors at this point; instead, they wait to return errors when the statement is executed or when catalog functions are called. Thus,* **SQLPrepare()** *might appear to have succeeded when in fact it has failed.*

When the **SQLExecute()** function is called, the driver:

1. Retrieves the current values of the variables bound to parameter markers in the statement and converts them as necessary.

2. Sends the access plan identifier along with the converted parameter values to the data source for execution.

3. Returns any errors detected to the application that called the **SQLExecute()** function. These are generally run-time errors such as SQLSTATE **24000** (Invalid cursor state). However, some drivers return syntactic and semantic errors at this point.

If the data source does not support prepared execution, the driver usually tries to emulate it as much as possible. For example, the driver might do nothing when the **SQLPrepare()** function is called, then perform direct execution of the statement when the **SQLExecute()** function is called. If the driver cannot emulate prepared execution, it stores the statement when **SQLPrepare()** is called and submits it for execution when

`SQLExecute()` is called. Because emulated prepared execution is not perfect, `SQLExecute()` can return any errors normally returned by `SQLPrepare()`.

Stored Procedures

A stored procedure is an executable object that is stored in the data source. It generally consists of one or more precompiled SQL statements. There are a number of advantages to using stored procedures—all are based on the fact that using stored procedures moves SQL statement processing from the application to the data source. These advantages include:

- Increased performance. Stored procedures are usually the fastest way to execute SQL statements. Like prepared execution, the SQL statement(s) used are compiled and executed in two separate steps. However, with stored procedures, SQL statements are parsed and compiled when the application is developed and executed at application run time.

- Adherence to business rules. A business rule is simply a rule about the way in which a company does business. For example, only someone with the title *Sales Person* might be allowed to add new sales orders. Incorporating business rules in stored procedures allows individual companies to customize vertical applications by rewriting the procedures called by an application. For example, an order entry application might call the procedure `InsertOrder()` with a fixed number of parameters; exactly how `InsertOrder()` is implemented can and may vary from company to company.

- Replaceability. Because business rules can be incorporated into stored procedures, procedures can be replaced without affecting the application(s) that use them. For example, if a business rule changes after a company has bought and installed an application, the company can change the stored procedure that implements that rule. From the application's standpoint, nothing has changed; it still calls a particular procedure to accomplish a particular task.

- Interoperable applications can use DBMS-specific SQL. Stored procedures provide a way for applications to exploit DBMS-specific SQL and still remain interoperable.

- Stored procedures survive transactions. As noted earlier, the access plans for all prepared statements on a connection are deleted when a transaction is committed or rolled back by some data sources. SQL statements in stored procedures survive all transactions because they are permanently stored in the data source (whether the procedures survive in a prepared, partially prepared, or unprepared state is DBMS-specific).

■ Separate development. Stored procedures can be developed separately from the rest of the application. In large corporations, this might provide a way to further exploit the skills of highly specialized programmers; application programmers can write user interface code and database programmers can write stored procedures.

Stored procedures are generally used by vertical and custom applications. Because procedures are generally written to perform a specific task in the context of a particular application, there is little reason to use them in generic applications. Furthermore, generic applications should not construct procedures at application run time in hopes of increasing SQL statement execution performance; not only is this approach likely to be slower than prepared or direct execution, it also requires the use of DBMS- specific SQL statements, which limit the application's interoperability.

Unfortunately, there are also a few disadvantages to using stored procedures:

■ Procedures must be written and compiled for each DBMS the application expects to work with. While this is not a problem for custom applications, it can significantly increase development and maintenance time for vertical applications designed to work with several different DBMSs.

■ Many DBMSs do not provide support for stored procedures. Again, this is most likely to be a problem for vertical applications designed to work with a number of DBMSs.

■ ODBC does not define a standard grammar for creating procedures. This means that although applications can call procedures interoperably, they cannot create them interoperably.

EXECUTING STORED PROCEDURES To execute a stored procedure, an application:

1. Binds any parameter markers that were coded in the SQL statement to application variables.

2. Sets the values of all bound variables.

3. Calls the **SQLExecDirect()** function with the SQL statement specified. This statement can use the escape sequence defined by ODBC or DBMS-specific syntax to call a stored procedure; statements that use DBMS-specific syntax are not interoperable.

When the **SQLExecDirect()** function is called, the driver:

1. Retrieves the current values of the variables that were bound to parameter markers in the statement and converts them as necessary.

2. Calls the procedure stored in the data source and sends it the converted parameter values for processing. How the stored procedure is actually called is driver-specific. For example, the driver might modify the SQL statement to use the data source's SQL grammar and submit this statement for execution, or it might call the procedure directly using a Remote Procedure Call (RPC) mechanism that is defined in the data stream protocol of the DBMS.

3. Returns the values of output and input/output parameters, and/or the procedure return code value to the application that called the stored procedure (if the procedure executed successfully). Note that these values might not be available until after all other results (row counts and result data sets) generated by the procedure have been processed.

Catalog Functions

Because the ODBC catalog functions create result data sets, they are similar to other result data set-generating SQL statements. In fact, the ODBC catalog functions are often implemented by executing predefined SQL statements or by calling predefined stored procedures that are shipped with the driver or the DBMS. Almost anything that applies to SQL statements that create result data sets also applies to the ODBC catalog functions. For example, the **SQL_ATTR_MAX_ROWS** statement attribute limits the number of rows returned by a catalog function, just as it limits the number of rows returned by a **SELECT** SQL statement.

To execute any of the catalog functions, an application simply calls the appropriate function. Refer to Chapter 15 for more information about the ODBC catalog functions.

Working with Batches of SQL Statements

Although SQL statements are typically processed one at a time, occasionally two or more SQL statements need to be handled as a single unit, otherwise referred to as a *batch*. This is often more efficient than submitting statements separately, because network traffic can often be reduced and the data source can sometimes optimize the execution of a batch of SQL statements in ways that it can't optimize the execution of individual statements. In most batch implementations, the entire set of SQL statements are executed before any results are returned to the calling application. In other implementations, an ODBC API function (**SQLMoreResults()**) must be called to trigger the execution of the next statement in the batch.

ODBC supports the following types of batches:

- Explicit batches. An explicit batch contains two or more SQL statements separated by semicolons (**;**). Note that no semicolon follows the last statement in the list.

- Stored Procedures. If a stored procedure contains more than one SQL statement, it is considered to contain a batch of SQL statements.

- Arrays of parameter values. Arrays of parameter values can be used with a parameterized SQL statement as an effective way to perform batch operations. For example, arrays of parameter values can be used with an **INSERT** SQL statement to insert multiple rows of data into a table while executing only a single SQL statement.

SQL statements can be loosely divided into the following five categories:

- Result data set-generating statements. These are SQL statements that generate a result data set. For example, the **SELECT** SQL statement is a result data set-generating statement.

- Row count-generating statements. These are SQL statements that generate a count of affected rows. For example, **INSERT**, **UPDATE**, and **DELETE** are row-count-generating statements.

- Data Definition Language (DDL) statements. These are SQL statements that modify the structure of the database. For example, **CREATE TABLE** and **DROP INDEX** are DDL statements.

■ Context-changing statements. These are SQL statements that change the context of a database. For example, in SQL Server, **USE** and **SET** are context-changing statements.

■ Administrative statements. These are SQL statements that are used to perform administrative tasks for a database. For example, **GRANT** and **REVOKE** are administrative statements.

SQL statements in the first two categories are collectively known as result-generating statements. SQL statements in the latter three categories are collectively known as result-free statements. ODBC only supports batches containing result-generating statements because the semantics of result-free statements can vary greatly from data source to data source.

When an error occurs while a batch of SQL statements is being executed, one of four things can happen; which one happens is data source-specific and may depend on the statements included in the batch:

■ No statements in the batch are executed.

■ No statements in the batch are executed and the current transaction is rolled back.

■ All the statements in the batch that were processed before the error was generated are executed.

■ All of the statements in the batch except the statement that caused the error are executed.

In the first two cases, **SQLExecute()** and **SQLExecDirect()** return **SQL_ERROR**. In the latter two cases, **SQLExecute()** and **SQLExecDirect()** may return **SQL_SUCCESS_WITH_INFO** or **SQL_SUCCESS**, depending on the driver's implementation. In all cases, diagnostic information can be retrieved by calling **SQLGetDiagRec()**, **SQLError()**, or **SQLGetDiagField()**. However, the nature and depth of the information returned by these functions is data source-specific. Furthermore, it is unlikely that the information returned will identify the statement that generated the error.

Sending Long (Large) Data Values to the Data Source

When an application variable is bound to a parameter marker in an SQL statement, the driver automatically retrieves the data value from the variable and sends it to the data source when the statement is executed.

This handles most situations provided the value to be sent to the data source does not exceed a predefined size (usually 254 characters or bytes). However, in some cases, larger data values need to be sent. For example, an application may want to store a long text document or a large graphic image in a DBMS that is capable of storing this kind of data. Because such data would typically be stored in a file, rather than in a single buffer, and because the driver might not be designed to work with data values that exceed a predefined size, the data would have to be sent to the data source in several small pieces, rather than as a whole.

The process of breaking large data values into smaller parts and sending them to a data source is known as a *data-at-execution sequence* and parameter markers that serve as placeholders for large data values are known as *data-at-execution parameters.*

To initiate a data-at-execution sequence, an application:

1. Binds any data-at-execution parameter markers coded in the SQL statement to both application variables and corresponding length/indicator variables.

2. Stores in each bound variable a meaningful value that will be used later to identify the data value to be sent to the data source in parts. For example, this value might be the name or handle of a file containing data (the value stored in the bound variable is not used by the driver).

3. Stores **SQL_DATA_AT_EXEC**, or the result of the **SQL_LEN_DATA_ AT_EXEC(*length*)**, macro in each bound length/indicator buffer. The **SQL_LEN_DATA_AT_EXEC(*length*)** is used when the data source that is to receive the data needs to know how many bytes of data will be sent so it can pre-allocate space. Both of these values indicate to the driver that the data for the parameter will be sent with the **SQLPutData()** function.

4. Calls the **SQLExecute()** or the **SQLExecDirect()** function with the SQL statement specified.

When the **SQLExecute()** or the **SQLExecDirect()** function is called, the driver:

1. Discovers that a length/indicator buffer contains the value **SQL_DATA_AT_EXEC** or the result of the **SQL_LEN_DATA_AT_ EXEC(*length*)** macro.

2. Returns **SQL_NEED_DATA** to the application that called the **SQLExecute()** or the **SQLExecDirect()** function.

When the application receives the **SQL_NEED_DATA** return code, it then:

1. Calls **SQLParamData()** to retrieve the address of the application variable bound to the data-at-execution parameter and to start the data-at-execution sequence.

2. Calls the **SQLPutData()** function to send the parameter data to the driver/data source. If the data is too large to fit into a single buffer, as is usually the case with long data, the **SQLPutData()** function is called repeatedly (to send the data in parts) until all the data has been sent to the data source; it is up to the driver and data source to reassemble the data as it is received.

3. Calls the **SQLParamData()** function again to indicate that all data has been sent for the parameter.

When the **SQLParamData()** function is called to indicate that all data has been sent for the parameter, the driver:

1. Returns **SQL_NEED_DATA** and the value identifying the next parameter to the application that called the **SQLParamData()** function if another data-at-execution parameter exists. Each time **SQL_NEED_DATA** is returned to the application, the same steps are repeated to send the appropriate parameter data to the data source.

or

2. Returns **SQL_SUCCESS** or **SQL_SUCCESS_WITH_INFO** along with any return value or diagnostic value that **SQLExecute()** or **SQLExecDirect()** can return to the function that called the **SQLParamData()** function (provided no other data-at-execution parameter exists).

After the **SQLExecute()** or **SQLExecDirect()** function returns **SQL_NEED_DATA** and before all data has been sent for the last data-at-execution parameter in the SQL statement, the statement is in the "Need Data" state and only the **SQLPutData()**, **SQLParamData()**, **SQLCancel()**, **SQLGetDiagRec()**, **SQLError()**, and **SQLGetDiagField()** functions can be called. If the **SQLCancel()** function is called while the SQL statement is in the "Need Data" state, all statement processing is terminated and the statement is returned to its previous state.

NOTE: *An application can send any type of data value to the data source at SQL statement execution time with the* **SQLPutData()** *function. However, if the data is small enough to fit in a single buffer, there is generally no reason to use the* **SQLPutData()** *function—it is much easier to bind an application variable to the SQL statement and let the driver retrieve the data from the variable when the statement is executed.*

When both arrays of parameter values and data-at-execution parameters are used in the same SQL statement, you need to be aware of a couple of problems that can occur. First, if an array of parameter values is bound to a data-at-execution parameter, the **SQLParamData()** function does not automatically extract and return an element of this array to the application. Instead, it returns the scalar value the application supplied. This means that the value returned by the **SQLParamData()** is insufficient for specifying the parameter for which the application needs to send data; the current row number must also be taken into consideration.

When only some of the elements of a parameter array are data-at-execution parameters, the application must provide the address of an array containing elements for all the parameters when the **SQLBindParameter()** function is called. This array is interpreted normally for the parameters that are not data-at-execution parameters. However, for the data-at-execution parameters, the value the **SQLParamData()** function provides to the application, which usually could be used to identify the data being requested, is always the address of the array—not the address of an element in the array.

Asynchronous Execution

By default, all drivers execute ODBC functions synchronously; that is, an application calls a function and the driver does not return control to the application until that function has finished executing. However, some functions can be executed asynchronously; that is, an application calls a function and the driver, after performing some minimal processing, returns control to the application. The application can then call other functions while the first function is still executing.

Asynchronous execution is primarily supported for functions that, for the most part, are executed on the data source, such as the functions that prepare and execute SQL statements and retrieve (fetch) data. Refer to the **SQL_ATTR_ASYNC_ENABLE** attribute in Table 8-9 for a list of ODBC API functions that can be executed asynchronously. Asynchronous execution is most useful when the function being executed takes a considerable amount of time to complete (for example, when a complex SQL query statement is executed against a large database).

Asynchronous execution is controlled on either a per-statement basis or on a per-connection basis, depending on the data source being used. In other words, an application does not specify that a particular function is to be executed asynchronously; instead, it specifies that all functions executed on a particular statement or connection handle are to be executed asynchronously. Applications can call the **SQLGetInfo()** function with the **SQL_ASYNC_MODE** information type specified to find out which method is supported by the data source being used: **SQL_AM_CONNECTION** is returned if connection-level asynchronous execution is supported; **SQL_AM_STATEMENT** is returned if statement-level asynchronous execution is supported. Asynchronous execution can be enabled or disabled by setting the **SQL_ATTR_ASYNC_ENABLE** attribute of the appropriate connection or statement handle to **SQL_ASYNC_ENABLE_ON** or **SQL_ASYNC_ENABLE_OFF**, respectively.

NOTE: *Asynchronous execution can only be enabled when there are no active statements on either the connection or the statement handle. If asynchronous execution is enabled while an active statement exists, an error is generated.*

When an application executes a function after asynchronous processing has been enabled, the driver performs a minimal amount of processing (such as checking arguments for errors), hands the rest of the processing off to the data source, and returns **SQL_STILL_EXECUTING** along with control, to the application. The application is then free to perform other tasks. The application must also poll the driver at regular intervals to determine whether or not the function has finished executing (by calling the function with the same arguments that were originally used). As long as the function is executing, **SQL_STILL_EXECUTING** is returned by the driver. When the function completes execution, the code that would have been returned if the function had been executed synchronously (such as **SQL_SUCCESS**, **SQL_ERROR**, or **SQL_NEED_DATA**) is returned by the driver.

When the application polls the driver to determine whether a function is still executing, it must use the same statement handle that was used when the function was first called. That's because asynchronous execution is tracked on a per-statement handle basis. The application must also supply valid values for the other function parameters to get past error checking in the ODBC Driver Manager. However, after the driver checks the statement handle and determines that the statement is executing asynchronously, it ignores all other parameters.

While a function is being executed asynchronously, the application can call functions on other statement handles, and it can call functions on any connection handle other than the one that the asynchronous function's statement handle is associated with. The application can only call the same function (to poll the driver), **SQLCancel()**, **SQLGetDiagRec()**, **SQLError()**, and **SQLGetDiagField()**, on the statement handle on which the asynchronous function is running—

SQLGetDiagRec() and SQLGetDiagField() can be called to return diagnostic header information, but not diagnostic record information. The application can only call the SQLAllocHandle() (to allocate a statement handle), SQLAllocStmt(), SQLGetDiagRec(), SQLGetDiagField(), or SQLGetFunctions() function on the connection handle associated with the statement handle that the asynchronous function is running on.

After the driver returns SQL_STILL_EXECUTING and before it returns a return code indicating the function has completed execution, the SQLCancel() function can be called to try to terminate the function's execution. Unfortunately, when SQLCancel() is called, there is no guarantee that function execution was actually canceled (for example, if the function finished execution before SQLCancel() was called execution would not be canceled). In this case, the return code returned by SQLCancel() doesn't help—it indicates whether SQLCancel() successfully attempted to cancel the function, not whether the function was actually canceled. The only way an application can determine whether the asynchronous function's processing was canceled is by polling the driver (that is, calling the function again). If the function was canceled, the driver returns SQL_ERROR and SQLSTATE HY008 (Operation canceled). Otherwise, the driver returns a different code (for example, SQL_STILL_EXECUTING, SQL_SUCCESS, or SQL_ERROR with a different SQLSTATE) to indicate that the function was not canceled.

NOTE: *In general, applications should only execute functions asynchronously on single-threaded operating systems. On multithread operating systems, functions should be executed synchronously on separate threads, rather than asynchronously on the same thread. No functionality is lost if drivers that operate only on multithread operating systems do not support asynchronous execution.*

Committing and Rolling Back Transactions

It was discussed earlier that ODBC applications can execute in two different modes: auto-commit and manual-commit mode. In auto-commit mode, each SQL statement is treated as a complete transaction that is automatically committed when the SQL statement is processed. In manual-commit mode, when an application submits an SQL statement to the driver/data source for processing and no transaction is open, the driver implicitly starts a transaction and it is up to the application to terminate it (either by committing it or by rolling it back). To commit or roll back a transaction while operating in manual-commit mode, an application calls either the **SQLEndTran()** function (ODBC 3.x drivers) or the **SQLTransact()** function (ODBC 2.0 and earlier drivers).

The ODBC Driver Manager does not call these function when the application is running in auto-commit mode; instead it returns **SQL_SUCCESS** even if the application attempts to roll back the transaction. Drivers for DBMSs that support transactions typically implement this function by executing a **COMMIT** or a **ROLLBACK** SQL statement. Because drivers for DBMSs that do not support transactions only recognize the auto-commit mode, these functions have no effect.

Freeing SQL Statement Handles

When an application has finished working with a particular SQL statement, it can call either the **SQLFreeHandle()** function (ODBC 3.x drivers) or the **SQLFreeStmt()** function (ODBC 2.0 or earlier drivers) to free the statement handle associated with the SQL statement. When a statement handle is freed, the memory used to store the structure containing information about the SQL statement is released and the handle can no longer be used.

NOTE: *When the* **SQLDisconnect()** *function is called, all statement handles associated with the specified connection are automatically freed*

Often, it is more efficient to reuse statement handles, rather than free them and allocate new ones. However, before executing a new SQL statement on an existing statement handle, an application should ensure that the current statement settings (that is, statement attributes, parameter bindings, and result data set bindings) are appropriate. Generally, all parameter and result data set bindings associated with the old SQL statement need to be unbound before new parameter and result data set bindings are established for the new SQL statement.

It is an application programming error to use any freed handle in a call to an ODBC API function; doing so has undefined but probably fatal consequences.

The SQL Statement Processing Functions

Table 9–1 lists the ODBC API functions used to prepare and submit SQL statements to a data source for processing.

Each of these functions are described in detail in the remainder of this chapter.

Table 9–1 The ODBC Statement Processing Functions

Function Name	Description
SQLAllocStmt()	Allocates an SQL statement handle and its associated resources.
SQLPrepare()	Prepares an SQL statement for execution.
SQLBindParameter()	Assigns data storage for a parameter marker in an SQL statement.
SQLSetParm()	Assigns data storage for a parameter marker in an SQL statement.
SQLParamOptions()	Specifies an array of multiple values for parameter markers.
SQLNumParams()	Retrieves the number of parameter markers used in an SQL statement.
SQLDescribeParam()	Retrieves information about a specific parameter marker in an SQL statement.
SQLExecute()	Executes a prepared SQL statement.
SQLExecDirect()	Prepares and executes an SQL statement immediately.
SQLNativeSql()	Retrieves the text of an SQL statement after it has been translated by the data source driver.
SQLParamData()	Used in conjunction with the **SQLPutData()** function to process data-at-execution parameters (that is, to support long data processing).
SQLPutData()	Used in conjunction with the **SQLParamData()** function to send part or all of a data value associated with a parameter marker from the application to the data source (used to process long data values).
SQLCancel()	Cancels SQL statement processing.
SQLTransact()	Rolls back or commits the current transaction.
SQLTransact()	Rolls back or commits the current transaction.
SQLFreeStmt()	Ends SQL statement processing, closes the associated cursor, discards pending result data, and, optionally, frees all resources associated with a statement handle.

SQLAllocStmt

COMPATABILITY

X/OPEN 95 CLI	ISO/IEC 92 CLI	ODBC 1.0	ODBC 2.0	ODBC 3.0	ODBC 3.5
✗	✓	✓	✓	☐	☐

API CONFORMANCE LEVEL   **CORE**

Purpose   The `SQLAllocStmt()` function is used to allocate memory for an SQL statement handle and to associate an SQL statement handle with a specific data source connection.

Syntax
```
RETCODE   SQLAllocStmt   (HDBC       ConnectionHandle,
                          HSTMT FAR  *StatementHandle);
```

Parameters   *ConnectionHandle*   A data source connection handle that refers to a previously allocated connection information storage buffer (data structure).

StatementHandle   A pointer to a location in memory where this function is to store the starting address of the allocated SQL statement handle's information storage buffer (data structure).

Description   The `SQLAllocStmt()` function is used to allocate memory for an SQL statement handle and to associate an SQL statement handle with a specific data-source connection. ODBC uses SQL statement handles to reference information associated with an SQL statement. This information includes descriptor information, attribute values, result data set values, cursor information, and status information for the SQL statement being processed. Each SQL statement must have its own statement handle; however, statement handles can be reused by different SQL statements.

NOTE: *In ODBC 3.x, this function has been replaced by the* `SQLAllocHandle()` *function.*

ReturnCodes SQL_SUCCESS, SQL_SUCCESS_WITH_INFO, SQL_INVALID_HANDLE, or SQL_ERROR

SQLSTATEs If this function returns SQL_SUCCESS_WITH_INFO or SQL_ERROR, one of the following SQLSTATE values may be obtained by calling the SQLError() function:

01000, **08**003*, **IM**001*, **S1**000, **S1**001*, or **S1**009*

*Returned by the ODBC Driver Manager.

Unless noted otherwise, each of these SQLSTATE values is returned by the data source driver. Refer to Appendix B for detailed information about each SQLSTATE value that can be returned by the ODBC Driver Manager or by a data source driver.

Comments ■ If an existing statement handle (a statement handle allocated by a previous call to this function) is specified in the *StatementHandle* parameter, the information storage buffer (data structure) address the statement handle points to is overwritten when this function executes. Consequently, memory used by the information storage buffer (data structure) the statement handle originally pointed to can no longer be freed because its starting address is no longer available. Programming errors of this type can not be detected by ODBC; therefore, no associated return code or SQLSTATE is generated when this kind of error occurs.

■ Applications can use the same statement handle in several different threads on operating systems that support multiple threads.

Prerequisites The SQLConnect() function, the SQLDriverConnect(), or the SQLBrowseConnect() function must be executed before this function is called.

Restrictions There are no restrictions associated with this function call.

See Also SQLFreeStmt(), SQLAllocHandle(), SQLAllocConnect(), SQLConnect(), SQLDriverConnect(), SQLBrowseConnect(), SQLGetStmtAttr(), SQLSetStmtAttr(), SQLGetStmtOption(), SQLSetStmtOption()

Example   The following Visual C++ program illustrates how to allocate and free an SQL statement handle.

```
/*────────────────────────────────────────────────────────────────*/
/* NAME:     CH9EX1.CPP                                            */
/* PURPOSE: Illustrate How To Use The Following ODBC API Functions */
/*          In A C++ Program:                                      */
/*                                                                 */
/*              SQLAllocStmt()                                     */
/*              SQLFreeStmt()                                      */
/*                                                                 */
/* OTHER ODBC APIs SHOWN:                                          */
/*        SQLAllocEnv()        SQLAllocConnect()                   */
/*          SQLConnect()       SQLExecDirect()                     */
/*          SQLBindCol()       SQLFetch()                          */
/*          SQLDisconnect()    SQLFreeConnect()                    */
/*          SQLFreeEnv()                                           */
/*                                                                 */
/*────────────────────────────────────────────────────────────────*/

// Include The Appropriate Header Files
#include <windows.h>
#include <sql.h>
#include <sqlext.h>
#include <iostream.h>

// Define The ODBC_Class Class
class ODBC_Class
{
    // Attributes
    public:
        HENV     EnvHandle;
        HDBC     ConHandle;
        HSTMT    StmtHandle;
        RETCODE  rc;

    // Operations
    public:
        ODBC_Class();                              // Constructor
        ~ODBC_Class();                             // Destructor
        RETCODE  ShowResults();
};

// Define The Class Constructor
ODBC_Class::ODBC_Class()
{
    // Initialize The Return Code Variable
    rc = SQL_SUCCESS;

    // Allocate An Environment Handle
    rc = SQLAllocEnv(&EnvHandle);
```

```
    // Allocate A Connection Handle
    if (rc == SQL_SUCCESS)
        rc = SQLAllocConnect(EnvHandle, &ConHandle);
}

// Define The Class Destructor
ODBC_Class::~ODBC_Class()
{
    // Free The Connection Handle
    if (ConHandle != NULL)
        SQLFreeConnect(ConHandle);

    // Free The Environment Handle
    if (EnvHandle != NULL)
        SQLFreeEnv(EnvHandle);
}

// Define The ShowResults() Member Function
RETCODE ODBC_Class::ShowResults(void)
{
    // Declare The Local Memory Variables
    SQLCHAR   LastName[50];
    SQLCHAR   FirstName[50];

    // Bind The Columns In The Result Data Set Returned To
    // Application Variables
    rc = SQLBindCol(StmtHandle, 1, SQL_C_CHAR, (SQLPOINTER)
            LastName, sizeof(LastName), NULL);

    rc = SQLBindCol(StmtHandle, 2, SQL_C_CHAR, (SQLPOINTER)
            FirstName, sizeof(FirstName), NULL);

    // Display A Header
    cout << "Employees :" << endl << endl;

    // While There Are Records In The Result Data Set Generated,
    // Retrieve And Display Them
    while (rc != SQL_NO_DATA_FOUND)
    {
        rc = SQLFetch(StmtHandle);
        if (rc != SQL_NO_DATA_FOUND)
            cout << FirstName << " " << LastName << endl;
    }

    // Return The ODBC API Return Code To The Calling Function
    return(rc);
}

/*─────────────────────────────────────────────────────────────*/
/* The Main Function                                            */
/*─────────────────────────────────────────────────────────────*/
int main()
{
    // Declare The Local Memory Variables
```

```
RETCODE   rc = SQL_SUCCESS;
SQLCHAR   DBName[10] = "Northwind";
SQLCHAR   SQLStmt[255];

// Create An Instance Of The ODBC_Class Class
ODBC_Class   Example;

// Connect To The Northwind Sample Database
if (Example.ConHandle != NULL)
{
    rc = SQLConnect(Example.ConHandle, DBName, SQL_NTS,
            (SQLCHAR *) "", SQL_NTS, (SQLCHAR *) "", SQL_NTS);

    // Allocate An SQL Statement Handle
    rc = SQLAllocStmt(Example.ConHandle, &Example.StmtHandle);
    if (rc == SQL_SUCCESS)
    {
        // Define A SELECT SQL Statement
        strcpy((char *) SQLStmt, "SELECT Employees.LastName, ");
        strcat((char *) SQLStmt, "Employees.FirstName FROM ");
        strcat((char *) SQLStmt, "Employees");

        // Prepare And Execute The SQL Statement
        rc = SQLExecDirect(Example.StmtHandle, SQLStmt, SQL_NTS);

        // Display The Results Of The SQL Query
        if (rc == SQL_SUCCESS)
            Example.ShowResults();

        // Free The SQL Statement Handle
        if (Example.StmtHandle != NULL)
            SQLFreeStmt(Example.StmtHandle, SQL_DROP);
    }

    // Disconnect From The Northwind Sample Database
    rc = SQLDisconnect(Example.ConHandle);
}

// Return To The Operating System
return(rc);
}
```

SQLPrepare

COMPATABILITY

X/OPEN 95 CLI	ISO/IEC 92 CLI	ODBC 1.0	ODBC 2.0	ODBC 3.0	ODBC 3.5
✓	✓	✓	✓	✓	✓

API CONFORMANCE LEVEL   **CORE**

Purpose

The **SQLPrepare()** function is used to send an SQL statement to a data source so it can be prepared (compiled) for execution.

Syntax

```
SQLRETURN   SQLPrepare   (SQLHSTMT      StatementHandle,
                          SQLCHAR       *SQLString,
                          SQLINTEGER    SQLStringSize);
```

Parameters

StatementHandle   An SQL statement handle that refers to a previously allocated SQL statement information storage buffer (data structure).

SQLString   A pointer to a location in memory where the SQL statement string to be prepared is stored.

SQLStringSize   The length of the SQL statement string stored in the *SQLString* parameter.

Description

The **SQLPrepare()** function is used to send an SQL statement (associated with an SQL statement handle) to a data source so it can be prepared (compiled) for execution. Once an SQL statement has been prepared, it can be submitted to the data source for execution or the statement handle associated with the prepared statement can be used to obtain information about the format of the result data set that will be produced (if any) when the prepared statement is executed.

SQL statements that have been prepared can be executed multiple times by the **SQLExecute()** function without having to be re-prepared; provided the statement handle associated with the prepared SQL statement is not freed by the **SQLFreeHandle()** function (ODBC 3.x drivers) or the **SQLFreeStmt()** function (ODBC 2.0 and earlier drivers) or modified by a **SQLPrepare()**, **SQLExecDirect()**, or catalog function (**SQLColumns()**, **SQLTables()**, and so on) function call.

Return Codes `SQL_SUCCESS`, `SQL_SUCCESS_WITH_INFO`, `SQL_STILL_EXECUTING`, `SQL_INVALID_HANDLE`, or `SQL_ERROR`

SQLSTATEs If this function returns `SQL_SUCCESS_WITH_INFO` or `SQL_ERROR`, one of the following SQLSTATE values may be obtained by calling the `SQLGetDiagRec()` function (ODBC 3.x driver) or the `SQLError()` function (ODBC 2.0 or earlier driver):

ODBC 3.X
01000, 01S02, 08S01, 21S01, 21S02, 22018, 22019, 22025, 24000*, 34000, 3D000, 3F000, 42000, 42S01, 42S02, 42S11, 42S12, 42S21, 42S22, HY000, HY001, HY008, HY009*, HY010*, HY013, HY090*, HYC00, HYT00, HYT01, or IM001*

ODBC 2.0 OR EARLIER
01000, 08S01, 21S01, 21S02, 22005, 24000*, 34000, 37000, 42000, IM001*, S0001, S0002, S0011, S0012, S0021, S0022, S1000, S1001, S1008, S1009*, S1010*, S1090*, or S1T00

*Returned by the ODBC Driver Manager.

Unless noted otherwise, each of these SQLSTATE values is returned by the data source driver. Refer to Appendix B for detailed information about each SQLSTATE value that can be returned by the ODBC Driver Manager or by a data source driver.

Comments
- The driver may modify the SQL statement specified to match the SQL grammar used by the data source before it submits the statement to the data source for preparation. The driver also replaces most escape sequences used with the appropriate SQL syntax.
- Some drivers cannot return syntax errors or access violations when this function is called; instead, syntax errors or access violations are only returned when subsequent related functions (such as `SQLNumResultCols()`, `SQLDescribeCol()`, `SQLColAttribute()`, and `SQLExecute()`) are called. Therefore, applications must be designed in such a way that delayed error reporting by the `SQLPrepare()` function does not create problems.
- Depending on the capabilities of the driver and its underlying data source, parameter information (such as data types) is checked either when the SQL statement is prepared (if all parameters have been bound), or when the statement is executed (if all parameters have not been bound).

■ For maximum interoperability, an application should unbind all parameters that applied to an old SQL statement before preparing a new SQL statement on the same statement handle. This prevents errors caused by old parameter information being applied to the new SQL statement from occurring.

■ For some implementations, it may be more efficient to call the **SQLDescribeCol()** or the **SQLDescribeParam()** function after an SQL statement has been executed (with the **SQLExecute()** or **SQLExecDirect()** function) rather than after the SQL statement has been prepared (with this function).

■ Some data sources automatically delete access plans been created for prepared execution each time a transaction is terminated (either by explicitly calling the **SQLEndTran()** or **SQLTransact()** function or by running in autocommit mode).

■ If an open cursor exists on the statement handle specified when this function is called, **SQL_ERROR** and SQLSTATE **24**000 (Invalid cursor state) will be returned.

Prerequisites   There are no prerequisites for using this function call.

Restrictions   If an application uses this function to prepare and the **SQLExecute()** function to submit a **COMMIT** or **ROLLBACK** SQL statement, the application will no longer be interoperable. Because the **COMMIT** and/or **ROLLBACK** SQL statement is not supported by all DBMSs, use of these SQL statements should be avoided.

See Also   SQLAllocHandle(), SQLAllocStmt(), SQLBindParameter(), SQLSetParam(), SQLBindCol(), SQLExecute(), SQLExecDirect(), SQLCancel(), SQLEndTran(), SQLTransact()

Example   The following Visual C++ program illustrates how to use the **SQLPrepare()** function to send an SQL statement to the data source so it can be prepared for processing .

```
/*------------------------------------------------------------*/
/* NAME:     CH9EX2.CPP                                        */
/* PURPOSE: Illustrate How To Use The Following ODBC API Functions */
/*          In A C++ Program:                                  */
/*                                                             */
/*              SQLPrepare()                                   */
/*              SQLExecute()                                   */
/*                                                             */
/* OTHER ODBC APIs SHOWN:                                      */
/*              SQLAllocHandle()      SQLSetEnvAttr()          */
```

```
/*              SQLConnect()          SQLDisconnect()                      */
/*              SQLBindCol()          SQLFetch()                           */
/*              SQLFreeHandle()                                            */
/*                                                                         */
/*-------------------------------------------------------------------------*/

// Include The Appropriate Header Files
#include <windows.h>
#include <sql.h>
#include <sqlext.h>
#include <iostream.h>

// Define The ODBC_Class Class
class ODBC_Class
{
    // Attributes
    public:
        SQLHANDLE    EnvHandle;
        SQLHANDLE    ConHandle;
        SQLHANDLE    StmtHandle;
        SQLRETURN    rc;

    // Operations
    public:
        ODBC_Class();                              // Constructor
        ~ODBC_Class();                             // Destructor
        SQLRETURN ShowResults();
};

// Define The Class Constructor
ODBC_Class::ODBC_Class()
{
    // Initialize The Return Code Variable
    rc = SQL_SUCCESS;

    // Allocate An Environment Handle
    rc = SQLAllocHandle(SQL_HANDLE_ENV, SQL_NULL_HANDLE, &EnvHandle);

    // Set The ODBC Application Version To 3.x
    if (rc == SQL_SUCCESS)
        rc = SQLSetEnvAttr(EnvHandle, SQL_ATTR_ODBC_VERSION,
                (SQLPOINTER) SQL_OV_ODBC3, SQL_IS_UINTEGER);

    // Allocate A Connection Handle
    if (rc == SQL_SUCCESS)
        rc = SQLAllocHandle(SQL_HANDLE_DBC, EnvHandle, &ConHandle);
}

// Define The Class Destructor
ODBC_Class::~ODBC_Class()
{
```

```
    // Free The Connection Handle
    if (ConHandle != NULL)
        SQLFreeHandle(SQL_HANDLE_DBC, ConHandle);

    // Free The Environment Handle
    if (EnvHandle != NULL)
        SQLFreeHandle(SQL_HANDLE_ENV, EnvHandle);
}

// Define The ShowResults() Member Function
SQLRETURN ODBC_Class::ShowResults(void)
{
    // Declare The Local Memory Variables
    SQLCHAR    LastName[50];
    SQLCHAR    FirstName[50];

    // Bind The Columns In The Result Data Set Returned To
    // Application Variables
    rc = SQLBindCol(StmtHandle, 1, SQL_C_CHAR, (SQLPOINTER)
            LastName, sizeof(LastName), NULL);

    rc = SQLBindCol(StmtHandle, 2, SQL_C_CHAR, (SQLPOINTER)
            FirstName, sizeof(FirstName), NULL);

    // Display A Header
    cout << "Employees :" << endl << endl;

    // While There Are Records In The Result Data Set Generated,
    // Retrieve And Display Them
    while (rc != SQL_NO_DATA)
    {
        rc = SQLFetch(StmtHandle);
        if (rc != SQL_NO_DATA)
            cout << FirstName << " " << LastName << endl;
    }

    // Return The ODBC API Return Code To The Calling Function
    return(rc);
}

/*-----------------------------------------------------------*/
/* The Main Function                                         */
/*-----------------------------------------------------------*/
int main()
{
    // Declare The Local Memory Variables
    SQLRETURN    rc = SQL_SUCCESS;
    SQLCHAR      DBName[10] = "Northwind";
    SQLCHAR      SQLStmt[255];

    // Create An Instance Of The ODBC_Class Class
    ODBC_Class   Example;
```

```c
// Connect To The Northwind Sample Database
if (Example.ConHandle != NULL)
{
    rc = SQLConnect(Example.ConHandle, DBName, SQL_NTS,
            (SQLCHAR *) "", SQL_NTS, (SQLCHAR *) "", SQL_NTS);

    // Allocate An SQL Statement Handle
    rc = SQLAllocHandle(SQL_HANDLE_STMT, Example.ConHandle,
            &Example.StmtHandle);
    if (rc == SQL_SUCCESS)
    {
        // Define A SELECT SQL Statement
        strcpy((char *) SQLStmt, "SELECT Employees.LastName, ");
        strcat((char *) SQLStmt, "Employees.FirstName FROM ");
        strcat((char *) SQLStmt, "Employees");

        // Prepare The SQL Statement
        rc = SQLPrepare(Example.StmtHandle, SQLStmt, SQL_NTS);

        // Execute The SQL Statement
        rc = SQLExecute(Example.StmtHandle);

        // Display The Results Of The SQL Query
        if (rc == SQL_SUCCESS)
            Example.ShowResults();

        // Free The SQL Statement Handle
        if (Example.StmtHandle != NULL)
            SQLFreeHandle(SQL_HANDLE_STMT, Example.StmtHandle);
    }

    // Disconnect From The Northwind Sample Database
    rc = SQLDisconnect(Example.ConHandle);
}

// Return To The Operating System
return(rc);
}
```

SQLBindParameter

COMPATABILITY

X/OPEN 95* CLI	ISO/IEC 92* CLI	ODBC 1.0	ODBC 2.0	ODBC 3.0	ODBC 3.5
✓	✓	☐	✓	✓	✓

API CONFORMANCE LEVEL   CORE**

*IN X/OPEN 95 AND ISO/IEC 92, THIS FUNCTION IS CALLED BINDPARAM

**IN ODBC 2.0, THIS FUNCTION WAS A LEVEL 1 API CONFORMANCE LEVEL
  FUNCTION

Purpose   The `SQLBindParameter()` function is used to associate (bind) parameter markers in an SQL statement with application variables.

Syntax

```
SQLRETURN SQLBindParameter  (SQLHSTMT      StatementHandle,
                             SQLUSMALLINT  ParamMarkerNum,
                             SQLSMALLINT   ParameterType,
                             SQLSMALLINT   CDataType,
                             SQLSMALLINT   SQLDataType,
                             SQLUINTEGER   ValueSize,
                             SQLSMALLINT   Decimals,
                             SQLPOINTER    Value,
                             SQLINTEGER    ValueBufferSize,
                             SQLINTEGER    *ValueSize_Indicator);
```

Parameters   *StatementHandle*

An SQL statement handle that refers to a previously allocated SQL statement information storage buffer (data structure).

ParamMarkerNum

Specifies the parameter marker's location in the SQL statement text. Parameter markers are numbered sequentially from left to right, starting with 1, as they appear in the SQL statement.

ParameterType

Specifies the type of parameter marker being bound. This parameter must be set to one of the following values:

■ **SQL_PARAM_INPUT**
Specifies that the parameter marker is associated with an SQL statement other than a stored procedure call or that the

parameter marker is associated with an input parameter of a called stored procedure.

▪ **SQL_PARAM_OUTPUT**
Specifies that the parameter marker is associated with an output parameter of a called stored procedure or with the return value of a called stored procedure.

▪ **SQL_PARAM_INPUT_OUTPUT**
Specifies that the parameter marker is associated with an input/output parameter of a called stored procedure.

CDataType

The C language data type of the parameter being bound. This parameter must be set to one of the following values:

▪ **SQL_C_CHAR**

▪ **SQL_C_SSHORT**

▪ **SQL_C_USHORT**

▪ **SQL_C_SLONG**

▪ **SQL_C_ULONG**

▪ **SQL_C_FLOAT**

▪ **SQL_C_DOUBLE**

▪ **SQL_C_BIT**

▪ **SQL_C_STINYINT**

▪ **SQL_C_UTINYINT**

▪ **SQL_C_SBIGINT**

▪ **SQL_C_UBIGINT**

▪ **SQL_C_BINARY**

▪ **SQL_C_BOOKMARK**

▪ **SQL_C_VAR_BOOKMARK**

▪ **SQL_C_DATE**

▪ **SQL_C_TIME**

▪ **SQL_C_TIMESTAMP**

▪ **SQL_C_TYPE_DATE**

▪ **SQL_C_TYPE_TIME**

▪ **SQL_C_TYPE_TIMESTAMP**

- **SQL_C_NUMERIC**
- **SQL_C_DEFAULT**

NOTE: *The* **SQL_C_DEFAULT** *value causes data to be transferred from its default C data type to the SQL data type specified.*

SQLDataType The SQL data type of the parameter being bound. This parameter must be set to one of the following values:

- **SQL_CHAR**
- **SQL_VARCHAR**
- **SQL_LONGVARCHAR**
- **SQL_DECIMAL**
- **SQL_NUMERIC**
- **SQL_SMALLINT**
- **SQL_INTEGER**
- **SQL_REAL**
- **SQL_FLOAT**
- **SQL_DOUBLE**
- **SQL_BIT**
- **SQL_TINYINT**
- **SQL_BIGINT**
- **SQL_BINARY**
- **SQL_VARBINARY**
- **SQL_LONGVARBINARY**
- **SQL_DATE**
- **SQL_TIME**
- **SQL_TIMESTAMP**
- **SQL_TYPE_DATE**
- **SQL_TYPE_TIME**
- **SQL_TYPE_TIMESTAMP**
- **SQL_INTERVAL_MONTH**
- **SQL_INTERVAL_YEAR**
- **SQL_INTERVAL_YEAR_TO_MONTH**

- ▓ `SQL_INTERVAL_DAY`
- ▓ `SQL_INTERVAL_HOUR`
- ▓ `SQL_INTERVAL_MINUTE`
- ▓ `SQL_INTERVAL_SECOND`
- ▓ `SQL_INTERVAL_DAY_TO_HOUR`
- ▓ `SQL_INTERVAL_DAY_TO_MINUTE`
- ▓ `SQL_INTERVAL_DAY_TO_SECOND`
- ▓ `SQL_INTERVAL_HOUR_TO_MINUTE`
- ▓ `SQL_INTERVAL_HOUR_TO_SECOND`
- ▓ `SQL_INTERVAL_MINUTE_TO_SECOND`
- ▓ `SQL_INTERVAL_YEAR_TO_MONTH`

ValueSize	The total number of bytes of data to be sent to the data source for the specified parameter marker OR the size of the maximum number of digits used by the data type (precision) of the column or parameter (if the *SQLDataType* parameter is set to `SQL_DECIMAL`, `SQL_NUMERIC`, `SQL_FLOAT`, `SQL_REAL`, or `SQL_DOUBLE`).
Decimals	The number of digits to the right of the decimal point if the *SQLDataType* parameter is set to `SQL_DECIMAL`, `SQL_NUMERIC`, `SQL_TIME`, `SQL_TIMESTAMP`, `SQL_TYPE_TIME`, `SQL_TYPE_TIMESTAMP`, `SQL_INTERVAL_SECOND`, `SQL_INTERVAL_DAY_TO_SECOND`, `SQL_INTERVAL_HOUR_TO_SECOND`, or `SQL_INTERVAL_MINUTE_TO_SECOND`.
Value	A pointer to a location in memory where the value associated with the parameter marker is stored.
ValueBufferSize	The size of the memory storage buffer used to store the value associated with the parameter marker.
ValueSize_Indicator	A pointer to a location in memory where either the size of the data value associated with the parameter marker or a special indicator value associated with the parameter marker is stored. This parameter can be set to one of the following indicator values:

- ■ **SQL_NTS**
  The data value associated with the parameter marker is a NULL-terminated string.

- ■ **SQL_NULL_DATA**
  The data value associated with the parameter marker is a NULL value

- ■ **SQL_DEFAULT_PARAM**
  A stored procedure is to use the default data value defined for the parameter associated with the parameter marker.

- ■ **SQL_DATA_AT_EXEC**
  The data value associated with the parameter marker will be sent to the data source with the **SQLPutData()** function.

- ■ The result of the **SQL_LEN_DATA_AT_EXEC(length)** macro.
  This indicates that the data value associated with the parameter marker will be sent to the data source with the **SQLPutData()** function.

Description   The **SQLBindParameter()** function is used to associate (bind) parameter markers in an SQL statement to application variables. A parameter marker is represented by a question mark character (?) in an SQL statement and is used to indicate a position in the statement where an application supplied value is to be substituted when that statement is executed. When parameter markers are bound to application variables, data is transferred from the application to the appropriate data source when either the **SQLExecute()** or the **SQLExecDirect()** function is called. If necessary, data conversion occurs as the data is transferred.

The **SQLBindParameter()** function essentially extends the capability of the **SQLSetParam()** function (provided in ODBC 1.0) by providing a method for:

- ■ Specifying whether a parameter marker is an input, an output, or an input/output parameter marker; this information ensures that data values associated with parameter markers in SQL statements that invoke stored procedures are handled correctly.

- ■ Specifying an array of values for a parameter marker.

NOTE: *In ODBC 2.0 and later, this function replaces the ODBC 1.0 function* **SQLSetParam()**.

Return Codes   SQL_SUCCESS, SQL_SUCCESS_WITH_INFO, SQL_INVALID_HANDLE, or
SQL_ERROR

SQLSTATEs   If this function returns **SQL_SUCCESS_WITH_INFO** or **SQL_ERROR**, one
of the following SQLSTATE values may be obtained by calling the
SQLGetDiagRec() function (ODBC 3.x driver) or the **SQLError()** function
(ODBC 2.0 driver):

ODBC 3.X
01000, **07**006, **07**009*, **HY**000, **HY**001, **HY**003, **HY**004, **HY**009*,
HY010*, **HY**013, **HY**021, **HY**090*, **HY**104, **HY**105*, **HY**C00, **HY**T01, or
IM001*

ODBC 2.0
01000, **07**006, **IM**001*, **S1**000, **S1**001, **S1**003*, **S1**004*, **S1**009*, **S1**010*,
S1090*, **S1**093*, **S1**094, **S1**104, **S1**105*, or **S1**C00

*Returned by the ODBC Driver Manager.

Unless noted otherwise, each of these SQLSTATE values is returned
by the data source driver. Refer to Appendix B for detailed information
about each SQLSTATE value that can be returned by the ODBC Driver
Manager or by a data source driver.

Comments   ■ An application calls this function repeatedly to bind each parameter
marker used in an SQL statement. All bindings remain in effect
until the parameter markers are rebound, the **SQLFreeStmt()**
function is called with the **SQL_RESET_PARAMS** option specified, or the
SQLSetDescField() function is used to set the **SQL_DESC_COUNT** field
of the application parameter descriptor (APD) header record to **0**.

■ A variable must be bound to each parameter marker specified in
an SQL statement before that statement can be executed. When
this function is executed, the variables specified in both the *Value*
and the *ValueSize_Indicator* parameters are treated as deferred
arguments. However, their storage locations must be valid and
they must contain data values when the SQL statement they are
bound to is executed.

■ If the value specified in the *ParameterNumber* parameter is
greater than the value of the **SQL_DESC_COUNT** field of the
application parameter descriptor (APD) header record, the value of
the **SQL_DESC_COUNT** field is changed to the value specified.

- Parameter markers in SQL statements that do not call stored procedures (for example **SELECT** and **INSERT** statements) are treated as input parameters; therefore, the *ParameterType* parameter should be set to **SQL_PARAM_INPUT** when binding to parameter markers in these types of statements.

- The **SQLProcedureColumns()** function can be used to determine the parameter type (input, output, input/output) of a stored procedure parameter; if an application cannot determine the parameter type for a stored procedure parameter, the *ParameterType* parameter should be set to **SQL_PARAM_INPUT**.

- If the *ParameterType* parameter is set to **SQL_PARAM_INPUT** and the stored procedure's parameter is an output or an input/output parameter, the value that would have been returned for the parameter is discarded by the driver.

- When an SQL statement that has been bound to application variables is executed, each bound application variable must contain a valid value or the corresponding length/indicator variable must contain **SQL_NULL_DATA**, **SQL_DATA_AT_EXEC**, or the result of the **SQL_LEN_DATA_AT_EXEC(*length*)** macro.

- If the *CDataType* parameter contains one of the datetime data types, the **SQL_DESC_TYPE** field of the APD descriptor record for the parameter is set to **SQL_DATETIME**, the **SQL_DESC_CONCISE_TYPE** field is set to the concise datetime C data type, and the **SQL_DESC_DATETIME_INTERVAL_CODE** field is set to the appropriate subcode for the specific datetime C data type.

- If the *CDataType* parameter contains one of the interval data types, the **SQL_DESC_TYPE** field of the parameter's APD descriptor record is set to **SQL_INTERVAL**, the **SQL_DESC_CONCISE_TYPE** field is set to the concise interval C data type, and the **SQL_DESC_DATETIME_INTERVAL_CODE** field is set to the appropriate interval subcode. By default, the **SQL_DESC_DATETIME_INTERVAL_PRECISION** field of the parameter's descriptor APD record is set to **2** and the **SQL_DESC_PRECISION** field is set to **6**. If either default value is not appropriate, the application should explicitly set the descriptor fields to the appropriate value (by calling either the **SQLSetDescField()** or the **SQLSetDescRec()** function).

- If the *CDataType* parameter contains a numeric data type, the **SQL_DESC_PRECISION** field of the parameter's APD record is set to the driver-defined precision and the **SQL_DESC_SCALE** field is set to **0**. If either default value is inappropriate, the application should explicitly set the descriptor fields to the appropriate value (by calling either the `SQLSetDescField()` or the `SQLSetDescRec()` function).

▪ If the *SQLDataType* parameter contains a datetime data type, the `SQL_DESC_TYPE` field of the parameter's (IPD) descriptor record is set to `SQL_DATETIME`, the `SQL_DESC_CONCISE_TYPE` field is set to the concise datetime SQL data type, and the `SQL_DESC_DATETIME_ INTERVAL_CODE` field is set to the appropriate subcode for the specific datetime SQL data type.

▪ If the *SQLDataType* parameter contains one of the interval data types, the `SQL_DESC_TYPE` field of the parameter's IPD descriptor record is set to `SQL_INTERVAL`, the `SQL_DESC_CONCISE_TYPE` field is set to the concise interval SQL data type, and the `SQL_DESC_ DATETIME_INTERVAL_CODE` field is set to the appropriate interval subcode. By default, the `SQL_DESC_DATETIME_INTERVAL_PRECISION` field of the parameter's IPD descriptor record is set to the interval leading precision, and the `SQL_DESC_PRECISION` field is set to the interval seconds precision, if applicable. If either default value is inappropriate, the application should explicitly set the descriptor fields to the appropriate value (by calling either the `SQLSetDescField()` or the `SQLSetDescRec()` function).

▪ If the *SQLDataType* parameter contains a numeric data type, the `SQL_DESC_PRECISION` field of the parameter's IPD descriptor record is set to the driver-defined precision and the `SQL_DESC_ SCALE` field is set to `0`. If either default value is not appropriate, the application should explicitly set the descriptor fields to the appropriate value (by calling either the `SQLSetDescField()` or the `SQLSetDescRec()` function).

▪ If the *SQLDataType* parameter is set to `SQL_CHAR`, `SQL_VARCHAR`, `SQL_LONGVARCHAR`, `SQL_BINARY`, `SQL_VARBINARY`, `SQL_ LONGVARBINARY`, or one of the concise SQL datetime or interval data types, the `SQL_DESC_LENGTH` field of the parameter's IPD descriptor record is set to the value stored in the *ValueSize* parameter.

▪ If the *SQLDataType* parameter is set to `SQL_DECIMAL`, `SQL_ NUMERIC`, `SQL_FLOAT`, `SQL_REAL`, or `SQL_DOUBLE`, the `SQL_DESC_ PRECISION` field of the parameter's IPD descriptor record is set to the value stored in the *ValueSize* parameter.

▪ If the *SQLDataType* parameter is set to `SQL_TYPE_TIME`, `SQL_ TYPE_TIMESTAMP`, `SQL_INTERVAL`, `SQL_NUMERIC`, or `SQL_DECIMAL`, the `SQL_DESC_PRECISION` field of the parameter's IPD descriptor record is set to the value stored in the *Decimals* parameter. For all other data types, the value stored in the *Decimals* parameter is ignored.

- The C data type specified in the *CDataType* parameter must be compatible with the SQL data type specified in the *SQLDataType* parameter, or an error will occur.

- A NULL pointer can be stored in the *Value* parameter, provided the corresponding *ValueSize_Indicator* parameter is set to **SQL_NULL_DATA** or **SQL_DATA_AT_EXEC**. (This applies only to input or input/output parameters.)

- If a NULL pointer is not stored in the *Value* parameter, and if the corresponding *ValueSize_Indicator* parameter does not contain **SQL_NTS, SQL_NULL_DATA, SQL_DATA_AT_EXEC, SQL_DEFAULT_PARAM**, a value greater than or equal to **0**, or a value less than or equal to the result of the **SQL_LEN_DATA_AT_EXEC(*length*)** macro), SQLSTATE **HY**090 (Invalid string or buffer length) is returned.

- An application can pass a parameter's value to the data source by either placing the value in the *Value* buffer or by making one or more calls to the **SQLPutData()** function. If the second option is used, the associated parameter is treated as a data-at-execution parameter. If a data-at-execution parameter is specified (by setting the *ValueSize_Indicator* parameter to **SQL_DATA_AT_EXEC** or to the result of the **SQL_LEN_DATA_AT_EXEC(*length*)** macro), an application-defined, 32-bit value associated with the parameter can be stored in the *Value* parameter. For example, the value might be a token such as a parameter number, a pointer to data, or a pointer to a structure the application used to bind input parameter values. This value is returned to the application by a subsequent **SQLParamData()** function call (which initiates a data-at-execution sequence) and can be used to identify the data-at-execution parameter.

- A parameter can be bound to a Unicode C data type, even if the underlying driver does not support Unicode data.

- If the *ParameterType* parameter is set to **SQL_PARAM_INPUT_OUTPUT** or **SQL_PARAM_OUTPUT**, the *Value* parameter must contain a pointer to a buffer where the output value can be stored.

- If a stored procedure returns one or more result data sets/row counts, the buffer in which the output value can be stored (stored in the *Value* parameter) is not guaranteed to be set until all result data sets/row counts have been processed. This means that the values of a stored procedure's output parameters and return values are unavailable until the **SQLMoreResults()** function returns **SQL_NO_DATA**. If the cursor for the statement handle associated with a stored procedure is closed, these values are discarded.

■ If a stored procedure returns one or more result data sets/row counts, the buffer in which the length/indicator value can be stored (stored in the *ValueSize_Indicator* parameter) is not guaranteed to be set until all result data sets/row counts have been processed. This means that the values of a stored procedure's output parameters and return values are unavailable until the **SQLMoreResults()** function returns **SQL_NO_DATA**. If the cursor for the statement handle associated with the stored procedure is closed, these values are discarded.

■ If the value of the **SQL_ATTR_PARAMSET_SIZE** statement attribute is greater than **1**, the *Value* parameter must point to an array.

■ If the value of the **SQL_ATTR_PARAMSET_SIZE** statement attribute is greater than **1**, the *ValueSize_Indicator* parameter must point to an array of **SQLINTEGER** values.

■ If the *Value* parameter points to an array, the *ValueBufferSize* parameter should be set to the length of a single element in the array. This value is used to determine the location of values in the array, both with input and with output parameters.

■ If the *ParameterType* parameter is set to **SQL_PARAM_INPUT_OUTPUT**, and if a character data type is specified in the *CDataType* parameter, and if the size of the data to be returned to the application is greater than or equal to the memory storage buffer size value specified in the *ValueBufferSize* parameter, the data is truncated to *ValueBufferSize*-1 (the length of a NULL-termination character) and NULL-terminated by the driver.

■ If the *ParameterType* parameter is set to **SQL_PARAM_INPUT_OUTPUT**, and if a binary data type is specified in the *CDataType* parameter, and if the size of the data to be returned to the application is greater than or equal to the memory storage buffer size value specified in the *ValueBufferSize* parameter, the data will be truncated to *ValueBufferSize* bytes.

■ If the *ParameterType* parameter is set to **SQL_PARAM_INPUT_OUTPUT** and if a data type other than a character or binary data type is specified in the *CDataType* parameter, the value stored in the *ValueBufferSize* parameter is ignored.

■ If the *ParameterType* parameter is set to **SQL_PARAM_INPUT** and if a NULL pointer is stored in the *ValueSize_Indicator* parameter, the driver assumes that all parameter values are non-NULL and that all character and binary data is NULL-terminated.

- If the *ParameterType* parameter is set to **SQL_PARAM_OUTPUT** and if a NULL pointer is stored in both the *Value* and the *ValueSize_Indicator* parameters, the driver discards the output value.

- A NULL pointer should never be stored in the *ValueSize_Indicator* parameter when the data type of the parameter is **SQL_C_BINARY**. To ensure that a driver does not accidentally truncate **SQL_C_BINARY** data, the *ValueSize_Indicator* parameter should always contain a pointer to a valid length value.

- If the *ParameterType* parameter is set to **SQL_PARAM_OUTPUT** or **SQL_PARAM_INPUT_OUTPUT**, the *ValueSize_Indicator* parameter should point to a buffer in which the driver can return **SQL_NULL_DATA**, the number of bytes of data available in the *Value* parameter (excluding the NULL-termination byte of character data), or **SQL_NO_TOTAL** (if the number of bytes of data available in the *Value* parameter cannot be determined).

- The value specified in the *ParameterType* parameter is stored in the **SQL_DESC_PARAMETER_TYPE** field of the corresponding IPD record.

- The **SQL_DESC_DATA_PTR** field of the APD descriptor record for the parameter is set to the value stored in the *Value* parameter.

- The **SQL_DESC_OCTET_LENGTH** field of the parameter's APD descriptor record is set to the value stored in the *ValueBufferSize* parameter.

- The **SQL_DESC_OCTET_LENGTH** field and the **SQL_DESC_INDICATOR_PTR** field of the parameter's APD descriptor record is set to the value stored in the *ValueSize_Indicator* parameter.

- Because the values stored in the variables referenced by the *Value* and *ValueSize_Indicator* parameters are not verified until the SQL statement is executed, data content or format errors are not detected or reported until either the **SQLExecute()** or the **SQLExecDirect()** function is called.

- When an ODBC 1.0 application calls the **SQLSetParam()** function in an ODBC 2.0 driver, the ODBC Driver Manager converts the call to an **SQLBindParameter()** function call in which the *ParameterType* parameter is set to **SQL_PARAM_INPUT_OUTPUT**.

- When an ODBC 1.0 application calls the **SQLSetParam()** function in an ODBC 3.x driver, the ODBC Driver Manager converts the call to an **SQLBindParameter()** function call in which the *ValueBufferSize* parameter is set to **SQL_SETPARAM_VALUE_MAX**.

Prerequisites   The **SQLPrepare()** function should be called to prepare the SQL statement for execution before this function is called whenever attributes for the result data set columns that may be produced when the SQL statement is executed are not already known.

Restrictions Applications using ODBC 1.0 drivers must use the **SQLSetParam()** function instead of this function.

See Also SQLPrepare(), SQLExecute(), SQLExecDirect(), SQLParamData(), SQLParamOptions(), SQLPutData()

Example The following Visual C++ program illustrates how to use the **SQLBindParameter()** function to associate (bind) a local memory variable to a parameter marker in an SQL statement.

```
/*-----------------------------------------------------------------------*/
/* NAME:     CH9EX3.CPP                                                   */
/* PURPOSE: Illustrate How To Use The Following ODBC API Function         */
/*          In A C++ Program:                                             */
/*                                                                        */
/*                SQLBindParameter()                                      */
/*                                                                        */
/* OTHER ODBC APIs SHOWN:                                                 */
/*          SQLAllocHandle()        SQLSetEnvAttr()                       */
/*          SQLConnect()            SQLDisconnect()                       */
/*          SQLPrepare()            SQLExecute()                          */
/*          SQLBindCol()            SQLFetch()                            */
/*          SQLFreeHandle()                                               */
/*                                                                        */
/*-----------------------------------------------------------------------*/

// Include The Appropriate Header Files
#include <windows.h>
#include <sql.h>
#include <sqlext.h>
#include <iostream.h>

// Define The ODBC_Class Class
class ODBC_Class
{
    // Attributes
    public:
        SQLHANDLE    EnvHandle;
        SQLHANDLE    ConHandle;
        SQLHANDLE    StmtHandle;
        SQLRETURN    rc;

    // Operations
    public:
```

```
            ODBC_Class();                          // Constructor
            ~ODBC_Class();                         // Destructor
            SQLRETURN ShowResults();
};

// Define The Class Constructor
ODBC_Class::ODBC_Class()
{
    // Initialize The Return Code Variable
    rc = SQL_SUCCESS;

    // Allocate An Environment Handle
    rc = SQLAllocHandle(SQL_HANDLE_ENV, SQL_NULL_HANDLE, &EnvHandle);

    // Set The ODBC Application Version To 3.x
    if (rc == SQL_SUCCESS)
        rc = SQLSetEnvAttr(EnvHandle, SQL_ATTR_ODBC_VERSION,
                (SQLPOINTER) SQL_OV_ODBC3, SQL_IS_UINTEGER);

    // Allocate A Connection Handle
    if (rc == SQL_SUCCESS)
        rc = SQLAllocHandle(SQL_HANDLE_DBC, EnvHandle, &ConHandle);
}

// Define The Class Destructor
ODBC_Class::~ODBC_Class()
{
    // Free The Connection Handle
    if (ConHandle != NULL)
        SQLFreeHandle(SQL_HANDLE_DBC, ConHandle);

    // Free The Environment Handle
    if (EnvHandle != NULL)
        SQLFreeHandle(SQL_HANDLE_ENV, EnvHandle);
}

// Define The ShowResults() Member Function
SQLRETURN ODBC_Class::ShowResults(void)
{
    // Declare The Local Memory Variables
    SQLCHAR   ProductName[50];

    // Bind The Column In The Result Data Set Returned To An
    // Application Variable
    rc = SQLBindCol(StmtHandle, 1, SQL_C_CHAR, (SQLPOINTER)
            ProductName, sizeof(ProductName), NULL);

    // Display A Header
    cout << "Product Name :" << endl << endl;

    // While There Are Records In The Result Data Set Generated,
```

```
    // Retrieve And Display Them
    while (rc != SQL_NO_DATA)
    {
        rc = SQLFetch(StmtHandle);
        if (rc != SQL_NO_DATA)
            cout << ProductName << endl;
    }

    // Return The ODBC API Return Code To The Calling Function
    return(rc);
}

/*————————————————————————————————————————————————————————*/
/* The Main Function                                        */
/*————————————————————————————————————————————————————————*/
int main()
{
    // Declare The Local Memory Variables
    SQLRETURN     rc = SQL_SUCCESS;
    SQLCHAR       DBName[10] = "Northwind";
    SQLCHAR       SQLStmt[255];
    SQLSMALLINT   InStock;

    // Create An Instance Of The ODBC_Class Class
    ODBC_Class   Example;

    // Connect To The Northwind Sample Database
    if (Example.ConHandle != NULL)
    {
        rc = SQLConnect(Example.ConHandle, DBName, SQL_NTS,
                (SQLCHAR *) "", SQL_NTS, (SQLCHAR *) "", SQL_NTS);

        // Allocate An SQL Statement Handle
        rc = SQLAllocHandle(SQL_HANDLE_STMT, Example.ConHandle,
                &Example.StmtHandle);
        if (rc == SQL_SUCCESS)
        {
            // Define A SELECT SQL Statement That Uses A Parameter
            // Marker
            strcpy((char *) SQLStmt, "SELECT Products.ProductName ");
            strcat((char *) SQLStmt, "FROM Products WHERE ");
            strcat((char *) SQLStmt, "Products.UnitsInStock > ?");

            // Prepare The SQL Statement
            rc = SQLPrepare(Example.StmtHandle, SQLStmt, SQL_NTS);

            // Bind The Parameter Marker In The SQL Statement To A
            // Local Application Variable
            rc = SQLBindParameter(Example.StmtHandle, 1,
                    SQL_PARAM_INPUT, SQL_C_SHORT, SQL_SMALLINT, 0,
                    0, (SQLPOINTER) &InStock, 0, NULL);
```

```
                    // Populate The "Bound" Application Variable
                    InStock = 25;

                    /*————————————————————————————————————————————————*/
                    /* Note: Normally, A Bound Application Variable Would    */
                    /* Be Populated By The User, Via A User Interface        */
                    /*————————————————————————————————————————————————*/

                    // Execute The SQL Statement
                    rc = SQLExecute(Example.StmtHandle);

                    // Display The Results Of The SQL Query
                    if (rc == SQL_SUCCESS)
                        Example.ShowResults();

                    // Free The SQL Statement Handle
                    if (Example.StmtHandle != NULL)
                        SQLFreeHandle(SQL_HANDLE_STMT, Example.StmtHandle);
            }

            // Disconnect From The Northwind Sample Database
            rc = SQLDisconnect(Example.ConHandle);
    }

    // Return To The Operating System
    return(rc);
}
```

COLUMN-WISE BINDING The following Visual C++ program illustrates how to use the **SQLBindParameter()** function to bind parameter markers in an SQL statement to arrays— using column-wise binding.

```
/*————————————————————————————————————————————————————————————*/
/* NAME:     CH9EX3A.CPP                                        */
/* PURPOSE: Illustrate How To Use The SQLBindParameter() ODBC API */
/*          Function To Bind Parameters In An SQL Statement To  */
/*          Application Arrays Using Column-Wise Binding.       */
/*                                                              */
/* OTHER ODBC APIs SHOWN:                                       */
/*              SQLAllocHandle()        SQLSetEnvAttr()         */
/*              SQLDriverConnect()      SQLSetStmtAttr()        */
/*              SQLPrepare()            SQLExecute()            */
/*              SQLDisconnect()         SQLFreeHandle()         */
/*                                                              */
/*————————————————————————————————————————————————————————————*/

// Include The Appropriate Header Files
#include <windows.h>
#include <sql.h>
#include <sqlext.h>
#include <iostream.h>
```

```
// Define The ODBC_Class Class
class ODBC_Class
{
    // Attributes
    public:
        SQLHANDLE   EnvHandle;
        SQLHANDLE   ConHandle;
        SQLHANDLE   StmtHandle;
        SQLRETURN   rc;

    // Operations
    public:
        ODBC_Class();                          // Constructor
        ~ODBC_Class();                         // Destructor
        SQLRETURN InsertRows();
};

// Define The Class Constructor
ODBC_Class::ODBC_Class()
{
    // Initialize The Return Code Variable
    rc = SQL_SUCCESS;

    // Allocate An Environment Handle
    rc = SQLAllocHandle(SQL_HANDLE_ENV, SQL_NULL_HANDLE, &EnvHandle);

    // Set The ODBC Application Version To 3.x
    if (rc == SQL_SUCCESS)
        rc = SQLSetEnvAttr(EnvHandle, SQL_ATTR_ODBC_VERSION,
                    (SQLPOINTER) SQL_OV_ODBC3, SQL_IS_UINTEGER);

    // Allocate A Connection Handle
    if (rc == SQL_SUCCESS)
        rc = SQLAllocHandle(SQL_HANDLE_DBC, EnvHandle, &ConHandle);
}

// Define The Class Destructor
ODBC_Class::~ODBC_Class()
{
    // Free The Connection Handle
    if (ConHandle != NULL)
        SQLFreeHandle(SQL_HANDLE_DBC, ConHandle);

    // Free The Environment Handle
    if (EnvHandle != NULL)
        SQLFreeHandle(SQL_HANDLE_ENV, EnvHandle);
}

// Define The InsertRows() Member Function
SQLRETURN ODBC_Class::InsertRows(void)
{
    // Declare The Local Memory Variables
    SQLRETURN    rc;
    SQLCHAR      SQLStmt[255];
    SQLUINTEGER  ArraySize = 3;
```

```
SQLINTEGER      OrderNumArray[3];
SQLSMALLINT     StockNumArray[3];
SQLCHAR         ShipToArray[3][7];
SQLINTEGER      ShipToLI_Array[3];
SQLINTEGER      TakenByArray[3];
SQLCHAR         SpecInstrArray[3][20];
SQLINTEGER      SpecInstrLI_Array[3];

// Initialize The Input Array Variables
OrderNumArray[0] = 97;
OrderNumArray[1] = 98;
OrderNumArray[2] = 99;

StockNumArray[0] = 70;
StockNumArray[1] = 90;
StockNumArray[2] = 100;

strcpy((char *) ShipToArray[0], "123456");
strcpy((char *) ShipToArray[1], "123456");
strcpy((char *) ShipToArray[2], "123456");

ShipToLI_Array[0] = SQL_NTS;
ShipToLI_Array[1] = SQL_NTS;
ShipToLI_Array[2] = SQL_NTS;

TakenByArray[0] = 123;
TakenByArray[1] = 124;
TakenByArray[2] = 125;

strcpy((char *) SpecInstrArray[0], "Payable in 30 days.");
strcpy((char *) SpecInstrArray[1], "Payable in 60 days.");
strcpy((char *) SpecInstrArray[2], "Payable in 90 days.");

SpecInstrLI_Array[0] = SQL_NTS;
SpecInstrLI_Array[1] = SQL_NTS;
SpecInstrLI_Array[2] = SQL_NTS;

// Allocate An SQL Statement Handle
rc = SQLAllocHandle(SQL_HANDLE_STMT, ConHandle, &StmtHandle);
if (rc == SQL_SUCCESS)
{
    // set The SQL_ATTR_ROW_BIND_TYPE Statement Attribute To Tell
    // The Driver To Use Column-Wise Binding.
    rc = SQLSetStmtAttr(StmtHandle, SQL_ATTR_PARAM_BIND_TYPE,
            SQL_PARAM_BIND_BY_COLUMN, 0);

    // Tell The Driver That There Are 3 Values For Each Parameter
    // (By Setting The SQL_ATTR_PARAMSET_SIZE Statement
    // Attribute)
    rc = SQLSetStmtAttr(StmtHandle, SQL_ATTR_PARAMSET_SIZE,
            (SQLPOINTER) ArraySize, 0);

    // Define An INSERT SQL Statement That Uses Parameter
    // Markers
```

```
        strcpy((char *) SQLStmt, "INSERT INTO ORDERS ");
        strcat((char *) SQLStmt, "(ORDERNUM, STOCKNUM, SHIPTO, ");
        strcat((char *) SQLStmt, "TAKENBY, SPECINSTR) VALUES ");
        strcat((char *) SQLStmt, "(?, ?, ?, ?, ?)");

        // Prepare The SQL Statement
        rc = SQLPrepare(StmtHandle, SQLStmt, SQL_NTS);

        // Bind The Parameter Markers To Local Arrays
        rc = SQLBindParameter(StmtHandle, 1, SQL_PARAM_INPUT,
                SQL_C_DEFAULT, SQL_INTEGER, 0, 0, OrderNumArray, 0,
                NULL);

        rc = SQLBindParameter(StmtHandle, 2, SQL_PARAM_INPUT,
                SQL_C_SHORT, SQL_SMALLINT, 0, 0, StockNumArray, 0,
                NULL);

        rc = SQLBindParameter(StmtHandle, 3, SQL_PARAM_INPUT,
                SQL_C_CHAR, SQL_CHAR, 7, 0, ShipToArray, 7,
                ShipToLI_Array);

        rc = SQLBindParameter(StmtHandle, 4, SQL_PARAM_INPUT,
                SQL_C_DEFAULT, SQL_INTEGER, 0, 0, TakenByArray, 0,
                NULL);

        rc = SQLBindParameter(StmtHandle, 5, SQL_PARAM_INPUT,
                SQL_C_CHAR, SQL_CHAR, 20, 0, SpecInstrArray, 20,
                SpecInstrLI_Array);

        // Execute The SQL Statement
        rc = SQLExecute(StmtHandle);

        // Free The SQL Statement Handle
        if (StmtHandle != NULL)
            SQLFreeHandle(SQL_HANDLE_STMT, StmtHandle);
    }

    // Return The ODBC API Return Code To The Calling Function
    return(rc);
}


/*------------------------------------------------------------------*/
/* The Main Function                                                */
/*------------------------------------------------------------------*/
int main()
{
    // Declare The Local Memory Variables
    SQLRETURN  rc = SQL_SUCCESS;
    SQLCHAR    ConnectIn[40];

    // Create An Instance Of The ODBC_Class Class
    ODBC_Class  Example;

    // Build A Connection String
```

```
        strcpy((char *) ConnectIn,
            "DSN=SQLServer;UID=userid;PWD=password;");

        // Connect To The SQL Server Sample Database
        if (Example.ConHandle != NULL)
        {
            rc = SQLDriverConnect(Example.ConHandle, NULL, ConnectIn,
                    SQL_NTS, NULL, 0, NULL, SQL_DRIVER_NOPROMPT);

            // Insert 3 Row Of Data Into The ORDERS Table In The SAMPLE
            // Database
            rc = Example.InsertRows();

            // If The Rows Were Added, Print A Message Saying So
            if (rc == SQL_SUCCESS)
            {
                cout << "3 rows have been added to the ORDERS table.";
                cout << endl;
            }

            // Disconnect From The SQL Server Sample Database
            rc = SQLDisconnect(Example.ConHandle);
        }

        // Return To The Operating System
        return(rc);
}
```

ROW-WISE BINDING The following Visual C++ program illustrates how to use the `SQLBindParameter()` function to bind parameter markers in an SQL statement to arrays—using row-wise binding.

```
/*————————————————————————————————————————————————*/
/* NAME:     CH9EX3B.CPP                                     */
/* PURPOSE: Illustrate How To Use The SQLBindParameter() ODBC API   */
/*          Function To Bind Parameters In An SQL Statement To   */
/*          Application Arrays Using Row-Wise Binding.       */
/*                                                           */
/* OTHER ODBC APIs SHOWN:                                    */
/*          SQLAllocHandle()       SQLSetEnvAttr()           */
/*          SQLDriverConnect()     SQLSetStmtAttr()          */
/*          SQLPrepare()           SQLExecute()              */
/*          SQLDisconnect()        SQLFreeHandle()           */
/*                                                           */
/*————————————————————————————————————————————————*/

// Include The Appropriate Header Files
#include <windows.h>
#include <sql.h>
#include <sqlext.h>
#include <iostream.h>

// Define The ODBC_Class Class
```

```
class ODBC_Class
{
    // Attributes
    public:
        SQLHANDLE    EnvHandle;
        SQLHANDLE    ConHandle;
        SQLHANDLE    StmtHandle;
        SQLRETURN    rc;

    // Operations
    public:
        ODBC_Class();                         // Constructor
        ~ODBC_Class();                        // Destructor
        SQLRETURN InsertRows();
};

// Define The Class Constructor
ODBC_Class::ODBC_Class()
{
    // Initialize The Return Code Variable
    rc = SQL_SUCCESS;

    // Allocate An Environment Handle
    rc = SQLAllocHandle(SQL_HANDLE_ENV, SQL_NULL_HANDLE, &EnvHandle);

    // Set The ODBC Application Version To 3.x
    if (rc == SQL_SUCCESS)
        rc = SQLSetEnvAttr(EnvHandle, SQL_ATTR_ODBC_VERSION,
                (SQLPOINTER) SQL_OV_ODBC3, SQL_IS_UINTEGER);

    // Allocate A Connection Handle
    if (rc == SQL_SUCCESS)
        rc = SQLAllocHandle(SQL_HANDLE_DBC, EnvHandle, &ConHandle);
}

// Define The Class Destructor
ODBC_Class::~ODBC_Class()
{
    // Free The Connection Handle
    if (ConHandle != NULL)
        SQLFreeHandle(SQL_HANDLE_DBC, ConHandle);

    // Free The Environment Handle
    if (EnvHandle != NULL)
        SQLFreeHandle(SQL_HANDLE_ENV, EnvHandle);
}

// Define The InsertRows() Member Function
SQLRETURN ODBC_Class::InsertRows(void)
{
    // Declare The Local Memory Variables
    SQLRETURN     rc;
    SQLCHAR       SQLStmt[255];
    SQLUINTEGER   ArraySize = 3;
```

```
// Define The ORDER_INFO Structure And Allocate An Array
// Of 3 Structures
typedef struct {
    SQLUINTEGER OrderNum;
    SQLINTEGER  OrderNum_LI;
    SQLUINTEGER StockNum;
    SQLINTEGER  StockNum_LI;
    SQLCHAR     ShipTo[7];
    SQLINTEGER  ShipTo_LI;
    SQLUINTEGER TakenBy;
    SQLINTEGER  TakenBy_LI;
    SQLCHAR     SpecInstr[20];
    SQLINTEGER  SpecInstr_LI;
} ORDER_INFO;

ORDER_INFO OrderInfoArray[3];

// Initialize The Input Structure Array
OrderInfoArray[0].OrderNum = 97;
OrderInfoArray[0].OrderNum_LI = 0;
OrderInfoArray[0].StockNum = 70;
OrderInfoArray[0].StockNum_LI = 0;
strcpy((char *) OrderInfoArray[0].ShipTo, "123456");
OrderInfoArray[0].ShipTo_LI = SQL_NTS;
OrderInfoArray[0].TakenBy = 123;
OrderInfoArray[0].TakenBy_LI = 0;
strcpy((char *) OrderInfoArray[0].SpecInstr, "Payable in 30 days.");
OrderInfoArray[0].SpecInstr_LI = SQL_NTS;

OrderInfoArray[1].OrderNum = 98;
OrderInfoArray[1].OrderNum_LI = 0;
OrderInfoArray[1].StockNum = 90;
OrderInfoArray[1].StockNum_LI = 0;
strcpy((char *) OrderInfoArray[1].ShipTo, "123456");
OrderInfoArray[1].ShipTo_LI = SQL_NTS;
OrderInfoArray[1].TakenBy = 124;
OrderInfoArray[1].TakenBy_LI = 0;
strcpy((char *) OrderInfoArray[1].SpecInstr, "Payable in 60 days.");
OrderInfoArray[1].SpecInstr_LI = SQL_NTS;

OrderInfoArray[2].OrderNum = 99;
OrderInfoArray[2].OrderNum_LI = 0;
OrderInfoArray[2].StockNum = 100;
OrderInfoArray[2].StockNum_LI = 0;
strcpy((char *) OrderInfoArray[2].ShipTo, "123456");
OrderInfoArray[2].ShipTo_LI = SQL_NTS;
OrderInfoArray[2].TakenBy = 125;
OrderInfoArray[2].TakenBy_LI = 0;
strcpy((char *) OrderInfoArray[2].SpecInstr, "Payable in 90 days.");
OrderInfoArray[2].SpecInstr_LI = SQL_NTS;

// Allocate An SQL Statement Handle
rc = SQLAllocHandle(SQL_HANDLE_STMT, ConHandle, &StmtHandle);
if (rc == SQL_SUCCESS)
{
```

```c
// Store The Size Of The ORDER_INFO Structure In The
// SQL_ATTR_PARAM_BIND_TYPE Statement Attribute - This Tells
// The Driver To Use Row-Wise Binding.
rc = SQLSetStmtAttr(StmtHandle, SQL_ATTR_PARAM_BIND_TYPE,
        (SQLPOINTER) sizeof(ORDER_INFO), 0);

// Tell The Driver That There Are 3 Values For Each Parameter
// (By Setting The SQL_ATTR_PARAMSET_SIZE Statement
// Attribute)
rc = SQLSetStmtAttr(StmtHandle, SQL_ATTR_PARAMSET_SIZE,
        (SQLPOINTER) ArraySize, 0);

// Define An INSERT SQL Statement That Uses Parameter
// Markers
strcpy((char *) SQLStmt, "INSERT INTO ORDERS ");
strcat((char *) SQLStmt, "(ORDERNUM, STOCKNUM, SHIPTO, ");
strcat((char *) SQLStmt, "TAKENBY, SPECINSTR) VALUES ");
strcat((char *) SQLStmt, "(?, ?, ?, ?, ?)");

// Prepare The SQL Statement
rc = SQLPrepare(StmtHandle, SQLStmt, SQL_NTS);

// Bind The Parameter Markers To Local Variables
rc = SQLBindParameter(StmtHandle, 1, SQL_PARAM_INPUT,
        SQL_C_ULONG, SQL_INTEGER, 0, 0,
        &OrderInfoArray[0].OrderNum, 0,
        &OrderInfoArray[0].OrderNum_LI);

rc = SQLBindParameter(StmtHandle, 2, SQL_PARAM_INPUT,
        SQL_C_SHORT, SQL_SMALLINT, 0, 0,
        &OrderInfoArray[0].StockNum, 0,
        &OrderInfoArray[0].StockNum_LI);

rc = SQLBindParameter(StmtHandle, 3, SQL_PARAM_INPUT,
        SQL_C_CHAR, SQL_CHAR, 7, 0,
        OrderInfoArray[0].ShipTo, 7,
        &OrderInfoArray[0].ShipTo_LI);

rc = SQLBindParameter(StmtHandle, 4, SQL_PARAM_INPUT,
        SQL_C_ULONG, SQL_INTEGER, 0, 0,
        &OrderInfoArray[0].TakenBy, 0,
        &OrderInfoArray[0].TakenBy_LI);

rc = SQLBindParameter(StmtHandle, 5, SQL_PARAM_INPUT,
        SQL_C_CHAR, SQL_CHAR, 20, 0,
        OrderInfoArray[0].SpecInstr, 20,
        &OrderInfoArray[0].SpecInstr_LI);

// Execute The SQL Statement
rc = SQLExecDirect(StmtHandle, SQLStmt, SQL_NTS);
```

```
            // Free The SQL Statement Handle
            if (StmtHandle != NULL)
                SQLFreeHandle(SQL_HANDLE_STMT, StmtHandle);
    }

    // Return The ODBC API Return Code To The Calling Function
    return(rc);
}

/*————————————————————————————————————————————————*/
/* The Main Function                                              */
/*————————————————————————————————————————————————*/
int main()
{
    // Declare The Local Memory Variables
    SQLRETURN   rc = SQL_SUCCESS;
    SQLCHAR     ConnectIn[40];

    // Create An Instance Of The ODBC_Class Class
    ODBC_Class  Example;

    // Build A Connection String
    strcpy((char *) ConnectIn,
        "DSN=SQLServer;UID=userid;PWD=password;");

    // Connect To The SQL Server Sample Database
    if (Example.ConHandle != NULL)
    {
        rc = SQLDriverConnect(Example.ConHandle, NULL, ConnectIn,
                SQL_NTS, NULL, 0, NULL, SQL_DRIVER_NOPROMPT);

        // Insert 3 Row Of Data Into The ORDERS Table In The SAMPLE
        // Database
        rc = Example.InsertRows();

        // If The Rows Were Added, Print A Message Saying So
        if (rc == SQL_SUCCESS)
        {
            cout << "3 rows have been added to the ORDERS table.";
            cout << endl;
        }

        // Disconnect From The SQL Server Sample Database
        rc = SQLDisconnect(Example.ConHandle);
    }

    // Return To The Operating System
    return(rc);
}
```

SQLSetParam

COMPATABILITY					
X/OPEN 95 CLI	**ISO/IEC 92 CLI**	**ODBC 1.0**	**ODBC 2.0**	**ODBC 3.0**	**ODBC 3.5**
☒	☐	☑	☐	☐	☐

API CONFORMANCE LEVEL   **CORE**

Purpose

The **SQLSetParam()** function is used to associate (bind) parameter markers in an SQL statement with application variables.

Syntax

```
RETCODE   SQLSetParam (HSTMT       StatementHandle,
                       UWORD       ParamMarkerNum,
                       SWORD       CDataType,
                       SWORD       SQLDataType,
                       SWORD       Precision,
                       SUDWORD     Scale,
                       PTR         Value,
                       SDWORD FAR  *ValueSize);
```

Parameters

StatementHandle   An SQL statement handle that refers to a previously allocated SQL statement information storage buffer (data structure).

ParamMarkerNum   Specifies the parameter marker's location in the SQL statement text. Parameter markers are numbered sequentially from left to right, starting with 1, as they appear in the SQL statement.

CDataType   The C language data type of the parameter being bound. This parameter must be set to one of the following values:

- SQL_C_CHAR
- SQL_C_SHORT
- SQL_C_LONG
- SQL_C_FLOAT
- SQL_C_DOUBLE
- SQL_C_BIT

- SQL_C_TINYINT
- SQL_C_BINARY
- SQL_C_BOOKMARK
- SQL_C_DATE
- SQL_C_TIME
- SQL_C_TIMESTAMP
- SQL_C_DEFAULT

NOTE: *The* SQL_C_DEFAULT *value causes data to be transferred from its default C data type to the SQL data type specified.*

SQLDataType	The SQL data type of the parameter being bound. This parameter must be set to one of the following values:

- SQL_CHAR
- SQL_VARCHAR
- SQL_LONGVARCHAR
- SQL_DECIMAL
- SQL_NUMERIC
- SQL_SMALLINT
- SQL_INTEGER
- SQL_REAL
- SQL_FLOAT
- SQL_DOUBLE
- SQL_BIT
- SQL_TINYINT
- SQL_BIGINT
- SQL_BINARY
- SQL_VARBINARY
- SQL_LONGVARBINARY
- SQL_DATE
- SQL_TIME
- SQL_TIMESTAMP

Precision	The total number of bytes of data to be sent to the data source for the specified parameter marker OR the maximum decimal precision of the number (if the *SQLDataType* parameter value is **SQL_DECIMAL** or **SQL_NUMERIC**).
Scale	The number of digits to the right of the decimal point if the *SQLDataType* parameter value is **SQL_DECIMAL**, **SQL_NUMERIC**, or **SQL_TIMESTAMP**.
Value	A pointer to a location in memory where the value associated with the parameter marker is stored.
ValueSize	A pointer to a location in memory where the size of the data value associated with the parameter marker is stored.

Description   The **SQLSetParam()** function is used to associate (bind) parameter markers in an SQL statement with application variables. A parameter marker is represented by a question mark character (?) in an SQL statement and is used to indicate a position in the statement where an application supplied value is to be substituted when the statement is executed. When parameter markers are bound to application variables, data is transferred from the application to the appropiate data source when either the **SQLExecute()** or the **SQLExecDirect()** function is called. If necessary, data conversion occurs as the data is transferred.

NOTE: *In ODBC 2.0 and later, this function has been replaced by the* **SQLBindParameter()** *function.*

Return Codes   SQL_SUCCESS, SQL_SUCCESS_WITH_INFO, SQL_INVALID_HANDLE, or SQL_ERROR

SQLSTATES   If this function returns **SQL_SUCCESS_WITH_INFO** or **SQL_ERROR**, one of the following SQLSTATE values may be obtained by calling the **SQLError()** function:

01000, **07**006, **IM**001*, **S1**000, **S1**001, **S1**003*, **S1**004*, **S1**009*, **S1**010*, **S1**090*, **S1**093*, **S1**094, **S1**104, **S1**105*, or **S1**C00

*Returned by the ODBC Driver Manager.

Unless noted otherwise, each of these SQLSTATE values is returned by the data source driver. Refer to Appendix B for detailed information about each SQLSTATE value that can be returned by the ODBC Driver Manager or by a data source driver.

Comments

■ An application calls this function repeatedly to bind each parameter marker used in an SQL statement. All bindings remain in effect until the parameter markers are rebound or until the **SQLFreeStmt()** function is called with the **SQL_DROP** or **SQL_RESET_PARAMS** option specified.

■ A variable must be bound to each parameter marker specified in an SQL statement before that statement can be executed. When this function is executed, the variables specified in both the *Value* and the *ValueSize* parameters are treated as deferred arguments. However, their storage locations must be valid and they must contain data values when the SQL statement they are bound to is executed (the *Value* parameter's storage location does not have to have a valid value if the *ValueSize* parameter is set to **SQL_NULL_DATA** or **SQL_DATA_AT_EXEC**).

■ A NULL pointer can be stored in the *Value* parameter provided the corresponding *ValueSize* parameter is set to **SQL_NULL_DATA** or **SQL_DATA_AT_EXEC**.

■ If the *CDataType* parameter is set to **SQL_C_CHAR**, the value stored in the *ValueSize* parameter must be the exact length of the data string to be passed to the data source if the data string is not NULL-terminated (length is determined by counting the number of characters in the string). The *ValueSize* parameter can contain either a NULL pointer or the value **SQL_NTS** (if the actual data string is null-terminated).

■ If the *SQLDataType* parameter contains a binary or character data type, the *Precision* parameter must specify the length, in bytes, of the data value.

■ If the *CDataType* parameter is set to **SQL_C_TIMESTAMP**, the value stored in the Precision parameter can be from 16 to 26 and is interpreted as the length of characters needed to display the timestamp value in character format.

■ If the *SQLDataType* parameter is set to **SQL_TIMESTAMP**, the *Scale* parameter represents the number of digits to the right of the decimal point in the character representation of the timestamp value (for example, the *Scale* parameter value for 1996-05-15 12:35:18.002 would be 3).

- The C data type specified in the *CDataType* parameter must be compatible with the SQL data type specified in the *SQLDataType* parameter, or an error will occur.

- To specify a NULL value for a bound parameter, assign the value **SQL_NULL_DATA** to the *ValueSize* parameter.

- An application can pass a parameter's value to the data source by either placing the value in the *Value* buffer or by making one or more calls to the **SQLPutData()** function. If the second option is used, the associated parameter is treated as a data-at-execution parameter. If a data-at-execution parameter is specified (by setting the *ValueSize* parameter to **SQL_DATA_AT_EXEC**), an application-defined, 32-bit value associated with the parameter can be stored in the *Value* parameter. For example, the value might be a token such as a parameter number, a pointer to data, or a pointer to a structure the application used to bind input parameter values. This value is returned to the application by a subsequent **SQLParamData()** function call (which initiates a data-at-execution sequence) and can be used to identify the data-at-execution parameter.

- After the SQL statement has been executed, and the results have been processed, an application may wish to reuse the SQL statement handle to execute a different SQL statement. If the parameter marker specifications are different (number of parameters, length, or data type has changed) the **SQLFreeStmt()** function should be called with the **SQL_RESET_PARAMS** option specified to reset or clear the current parameter bindings.

- Because the values stored in the variables referenced by the *Value* and *ValueSize* parameters are not verified until the SQL statement is executed, data content or format errors are not detected or reported until either the **SQLExecute()** or the **SQLExecDirect()** function is called.

- How an application sends an array of character or binary parameter values to the driver are driver-defined.

- When an ODBC 1.0 application calls the **SQLSetParam()** function in an ODBC 2.0 or later driver, the ODBC Driver Manager converts the call to an **SQLBindParameter()** function call in which the *ParameterType* parameter is set to **SQL_PARAM_INPUT_OUTPUT** and the *ValueBufferSize* parameter is set to **SQL_SETPARAM_VALUE_MAX**.

Prerequisites The `SQLPrepare()` function should be called to prepare the SQL statement for execution before this function is called, unless attributes for the columns in the result data set that may be produced when the statement is executed are already known.

Restrictions This function cannot be used to bind application variables to parameter markers in an SQL statement that calls a stored procedure.

This function must not be used to bind an array of application variables to a parameter marker when the `SQLParamOptions()` function has been used to specify multiple input parameter values.

See Also `SQLBindParameter()`, `SQLPrepare()`, `SQLExecute()`, `SQLExecDirect()`, `SQLParamOptions()`, `SQLPutData()`

Example The following Visual C++ program illustrates how to use the `SQLSetParam()` function to associate (bind) a local memory variable to a parameter marker in an SQL statement.

```
/*-----------------------------------------------------------------*/
/* NAME:      CH9EX4.CPP                                            */
/* PURPOSE: Illustrate How To Use The Following ODBC API Function   */
/*          In A C++ Program:                                       */
/*                                                                  */
/*                SQLSetParam()                                     */
/*                                                                  */
/* OTHER ODBC APIs SHOWN:                                           */
/*            SQLAllocEnv()          SQLAllocConnect()              */
/*            SQLAllocStmt()         SQLConnect()                   */
/*            SQLPrepare()           SQLExecute()                   */
/*            SQLBindCol()           SQLFetch()                     */
/*            SQLFreeStmt()          SQLDisconnect()                */
/*            SQLFreeConnect()       SQLFreeEnv()                   */
/*                                                                  */
/*-----------------------------------------------------------------*/

// Include The Appropriate Header Files
#include <windows.h>
#include <sql.h>
#include <sqlext.h>
#include <iostream.h>

// Define The ODBC_Class Class
class ODBC_Class
{
    // Attributes
    public:
        HENV        EnvHandle;
        HDBC        ConHandle;
```

```
        HSTMT       StmtHandle;
        RETCODE   rc;

    // Operations
    public:
        ODBC_Class();                         // Constructor
        ~ODBC_Class();                        // Destructor
        RETCODE   ShowResults();
};

// Define The Class Constructor
ODBC_Class::ODBC_Class()
{
    // Initialize The Return Code Variable
    rc = SQL_SUCCESS;

    // Allocate An Environment Handle
    rc = SQLAllocEnv(&EnvHandle);

    // Allocate A Connection Handle
    if (rc == SQL_SUCCESS)
        rc = SQLAllocConnect(EnvHandle, &ConHandle);
}

// Define The Class Destructor
ODBC_Class::~ODBC_Class()
{
    // Free The Connection Handle
    if (ConHandle != NULL)
        SQLFreeConnect(ConHandle);

    // Free The Environment Handle
    if (EnvHandle != NULL)
        SQLFreeEnv(EnvHandle);
}

// Define The ShowResults() Member Function
RETCODE ODBC_Class::ShowResults(void)
{
    // Declare The Local Memory Variables
    SQLCHAR  ProductName[50];

    // Bind The Columns In The Result Data Set Returned To
    // Application Variables
    rc = SQLBindCol(StmtHandle, 1, SQL_C_CHAR, (SQLPOINTER)
            ProductName, sizeof(ProductName), NULL);

    // Display A Header
    cout << "Product Name :" << endl << endl;

    // While There Are Records In The Result Data Set Generated,
    // Retrieve And Display Them
    while (rc != SQL_NO_DATA_FOUND)
    {
```

```
        rc = SQLFetch(StmtHandle);
        if (rc != SQL_NO_DATA_FOUND)
            cout << ProductName << endl;
    }

    // Return The ODBC API Return Code To The Calling Function
    return(rc);
}

/*------------------------------------------------------------------*/
/* The Main Function                                                */
/*------------------------------------------------------------------*/
int main()
{
    // Declare The Local Memory Variables
    RETCODE        rc = SQL_SUCCESS;
    SQLCHAR        DBName[10] = "Northwind";
    SQLCHAR        SQLStmt[255];
    SQLSMALLINT    InStock;

    // Create An Instance Of The ODBC_Class Class
    ODBC_Class  Example;

    // Connect To The Northwind Sample Database
    if (Example.ConHandle != NULL)
    {
        rc = SQLConnect(Example.ConHandle, DBName, SQL_NTS,
                (SQLCHAR *) "", SQL_NTS, (SQLCHAR *) "", SQL_NTS);

        // Allocate An SQL Statement Handle
        rc = SQLAllocStmt(Example.ConHandle, &Example.StmtHandle);
        if (rc == SQL_SUCCESS)
        {
            // Define A SELECT SQL Statement That Uses A Parameter
            // Marker
            strcpy((char *) SQLStmt, "SELECT Products.ProductName ");
            strcat((char *) SQLStmt, "FROM Products WHERE ");
            strcat((char *) SQLStmt, "Products.UnitsInStock > ?");

            // Prepare The SQL Statement
            rc = SQLPrepare(Example.StmtHandle, SQLStmt, SQL_NTS);

            // Bind The Parameter Marker In The SQL Statement To A
            // Local Application Variable
            rc = SQLSetParam(Example.StmtHandle, 1, SQL_C_SHORT,
                    SQL_SMALLINT, 0, 0, (SQLPOINTER) &InStock,
                    NULL);

            // Populate The "Bound" Application Variable
            InStock = 25;

            /*------------------------------------------------------*/
            /* Note: Normally, A Bound Application Variable Would   */
            /* Be Populated By The User, Via A User Interface       */
            /*------------------------------------------------------*/
```

```
        // Execute The SQL Statement
        rc = SQLExecute(Example.StmtHandle);

        // Display The Results Of The SQL Query
        if (rc == SQL_SUCCESS)
            Example.ShowResults();

        // Free The SQL Statement Handle
        if (Example.StmtHandle != NULL)
            SQLFreeStmt(Example.StmtHandle, SQL_DROP);
    }

    // Disconnect From The Northwind Sample Database
    rc = SQLDisconnect(Example.ConHandle);
}

// Return To The Operating System
return(rc);
}
```

SQLParamOptions

COMPATABILITY

X/OPEN 95 CLI	ISO/IEC 92 CLI	ODBC 1.0	ODBC 2.0	ODBC 3.0	ODBC 3.5
☐	☐	☑	☑	☐	☐

API CONFORMANCE LEVEL   **LEVEL 2**

Purpos

The SQLParamOptions() function is used to specify multiple values for each parameter marker assigned to an application variable by the SQLBindParameter() function.

Syntax

```
RETCODE  SQLParamOptions  (HSTMT          StatementHandle,
                           UDWORD         NumRows,
                           UDWORD FAR     *RowIndex);
```

Parameters

StatementHandle   An SQL statement handle that refers to a previously allocated SQL statement information storage buffer (data structure).

NumRows	The number of values (rows) provided for each parameter marker.
RowIndex	A pointer to a location in memory where the value for the parameter array index (current row number) is stored.

Description

The **SQLParamOptions()** function is used to specify multiple values for each parameter marker assigned to an application variable by the **SQLBindParameter()** function. Each time the SQL statement containing parameter markers is executed, the *RowIndex* parameter specifies which set of values in the array of values to use in place of the parameter markers.

The ability to specify multiple values for a set of parameters is useful for bulk inserts and other work requiring the data source to process the same SQL statement multiple times with different parameter values. For example, an application can specify three sets of values for each parameter marker used in an **INSERT** SQL statement and then execute the **INSERT** statement once (that is, with a single set of **SQLPrepare()**, **SQLBindParameter()**, and **SQLExecute()** function calls) to perform three separate insert operations

NOTE: *In ODBC 3.x, this function has been replaced by calls to the* **SQLSetStmtAttr()** *function.*

Return Codes

SQL_SUCCESS, SQL_SUCCESS_WITH_INFO, SQL_INVALID_HANDLE, or **SQL_ERROR**

SQLSTATEs

If this function returns **SQL_SUCCESS_WITH_INFO** or **SQL_ERROR**, one of the following SQLSTATE values may be obtained by calling the **SQLError()** function:

01000, **IM**001*, **S1**000, **S1**001, **S1**010*, or **S1**107*

*Returned by the ODBC Driver Manager.

Unless noted otherwise, each of these SQLSTATE values is returned by the data source driver. Refer to Appendix B for detailed information about each SQLSTATE value that can be returned by the ODBC Driver Manager or by a data source driver.

Comments

■ As a statement executes, the driver stores to the number of the current row of parameter values in the *RowNum* parameter; the first row is row 1, the next row is row 2, and so on. The contents of the *RowNum* parameter can be used as follows:

- When **SQLParamData()** returns **SQL_NEED_DATA** for data-at-execution parameters, the application can access the value stored in the *RowNum* parameter to determine which row of parameters is being executed.

- When **SQLExecute()** or **SQLExecDirect()** function returns an error, the application can access the value stored in the *RowNum* parameter in order to find out which row of parameter values generated the error.

- When the **SQLExecute()**, **SQLExecDirect()**, **SQLParamData()**, or **SQLPutData()** function is successfully executed, the value stored in the *RowNum* parameter is the total number of parameter value rows processed.

Prerequisites   There are no prerequisites for using this function call.

Restrictions   There are no restrictions associated with this function call.

See Also   SQLBindParameter(), SQLMoreResults(), SQLSetStmtOption()

Example   The following Visual C++ program illustrates how to use the SQLParamOptions() function to tell the driver that multiple values will be supplied for each bound parameter.

```
/*----------------------------------------------------------------*/
/* NAME:     CH9EX5.CPP                                           */
/* PURPOSE: Illustrate How To Use The Following ODBC API Function */
/*          In A C++ Program:                                     */
/*                                                                */
/*               SQLParamOptions()                                */
/*                                                                */
/* OTHER ODBC APIs SHOWN:                                         */
/*          SQLAllocEnv()            SQLAllocConnect()            */
/*          SQLDriverConnect()       SQLAllocStmt()               */
/*          SQLPrepare()             SQLExecute()                 */
/*          SQLBindParameter()       SQLFreeStmt()                */
/*          SQLDisconnect()          SQLFreeConnect()             */
/*          SQLFreeEnv()                                          */
/*                                                                */
/*----------------------------------------------------------------*/

// Include The Appropriate Header Files
#include <windows.h>
```

```cpp
#include <sql.h>
#include <sqlext.h>
#include <iostream.h>

// Define The ODBC_Class Class
class ODBC_Class
{
    // Attributes
    public:
        HENV        EnvHandle;
        HDBC        ConHandle;
        HSTMT       StmtHandle;
        RETCODE     rc;

    // Operations
    public:
        ODBC_Class();                               // Constructor
        ~ODBC_Class();                              // Destructor
        RETCODE     InsertRows();
};

// Define The Class Constructor
ODBC_Class::ODBC_Class()
{
    // Initialize The Return Code Variable
    rc = SQL_SUCCESS;

    // Allocate An Environment Handle
    rc = SQLAllocEnv(&EnvHandle);

    // Allocate A Connection Handle
    if (rc == SQL_SUCCESS)
        rc = SQLAllocConnect(EnvHandle, &ConHandle);
}

// Define The Class Destructor
ODBC_Class::~ODBC_Class()
{
    // Free The Connection Handle
    if (ConHandle != NULL)
        SQLFreeConnect(ConHandle);

    // Free The Environment Handle
    if (EnvHandle != NULL)
        SQLFreeEnv(EnvHandle);
}

// Define The InsertRows() Member Function
RETCODE ODBC_Class::InsertRows(void)
{
    // Declare The Local Memory Variables
    SQLCHAR         SQLStmt[255];
    SQLINTEGER      OrderNumArray[3];
```

```
SQLSMALLINT   StockNumArray[3];
SQLCHAR       ShipToArray[3][7];
SQLINTEGER    TakenByArray[3];
SQLCHAR       SpecInstrArray[3][20];

// Initialize The Input Arrays
OrderNumArray[0] = 97;
OrderNumArray[1] = 98;
OrderNumArray[2] = 99;

StockNumArray[0] = 70;
StockNumArray[1] = 90;
StockNumArray[2] = 100;

strcpy((char *) ShipToArray[0], "123456");
strcpy((char *) ShipToArray[1], "123456");
strcpy((char *) ShipToArray[2], "123456");

TakenByArray[0] = 123;
TakenByArray[1] = 124;
TakenByArray[2] = 125;

strcpy((char *) SpecInstrArray[0], "Payable in 30 days.");
strcpy((char *) SpecInstrArray[1], "Payable in 60 days.");
strcpy((char *) SpecInstrArray[2], "Payable in 90 days.");

// Define An INSERT SQL Statement That Uses Parameter
// Markers
strcpy((char *) SQLStmt, "INSERT INTO ORDERS ");
strcat((char *) SQLStmt, "(ORDERNUM, STOCKNUM, SHIPTO, ");
strcat((char *) SQLStmt, "TAKENBY, SPECINSTR) VALUES ");
strcat((char *) SQLStmt, "(?, ?, ?, ?, ?)");

// Allocate An SQL Statement Handle
rc = SQLAllocStmt(ConHandle, &StmtHandle);
if (rc == SQL_SUCCESS)
{
    // Prepare The SQL Statement
    rc = SQLPrepare(StmtHandle, SQLStmt, SQL_NTS);

    // Tell ODBC That Three Values Will Be Provided For Each
    // Parameter Marker In The SQL Statement
    rc = SQLParamOptions(StmtHandle, 3, NULL);

    // Bind The Parameter Markers To Local Variables
    rc = SQLBindParameter(StmtHandle, 1, SQL_PARAM_INPUT,
            SQL_C_DEFAULT, SQL_INTEGER, 0, 0, OrderNumArray, 0,
            NULL);

    rc = SQLBindParameter(StmtHandle, 2, SQL_PARAM_INPUT,
            SQL_C_SHORT, SQL_SMALLINT, 0, 0, StockNumArray, 0,
            NULL);
```

```
    rc = SQLBindParameter(StmtHandle, 3, SQL_PARAM_INPUT,
            SQL_C_CHAR, SQL_CHAR, 7, 0, ShipToArray, 7, NULL);

    rc = SQLBindParameter(StmtHandle, 4, SQL_PARAM_INPUT,
            SQL_C_DEFAULT, SQL_INTEGER, 0, 0, TakenByArray, 0,
            NULL);

    rc = SQLBindParameter(StmtHandle, 5, SQL_PARAM_INPUT,
            SQL_C_CHAR, SQL_CHAR, 20, 0, SpecInstrArray, 20,
            NULL);

    // Execute The SQL Statement
    rc = SQLExecute(StmtHandle);

    // Free The SQL Statement Handle
    if (StmtHandle != NULL)
        SQLFreeStmt(StmtHandle, SQL_DROP);
    }

    // Return The ODBC API Return Code To The Calling Function
    return(rc);
}

/*-------------------------------------------------------------*/
/* The Main Function                                           */
/*-------------------------------------------------------------*/
int main()
{
    // Declare The Local Memory Variables
    RETCODE   rc = SQL_SUCCESS;
    SQLCHAR   ConnectIn[40];

    // Create An Instance Of The ODBC_Class Class
    ODBC_Class   Example;

    // Build A Connection String
    strcpy((char *) ConnectIn,
        "DSN=SQLServer;UID=userid;PWD=password;");

    // Connect To The SQL Server Sample Database
    if (Example.ConHandle != NULL)
    {
        rc = SQLDriverConnect(Example.ConHandle, NULL, ConnectIn,
                SQL_NTS, NULL, 0, NULL, SQL_DRIVER_NOPROMPT);

        // Insert 3 Row Of Data Into The ORDERS Table In The SAMPLE
        // Database
        rc = Example.InsertRows();

        // If The Rows Were Added, Print A Message Saying So
        if (rc == SQL_SUCCESS)
        {
            cout << "3 rows have been added to the ORDERS table.";
```

```
        cout << endl;
    }

    // Disconnect From The SQL Server Sample Database
    rc = SQLDisconnect(Example.ConHandle);
}

// Return To The Operating System
return(rc);
}
```

SQLNumParams

COMPATABILITY

X/OPEN 95 CLI	ISO/IEC 92 CLI	ODBC 1.0	ODBC 2.0	ODBC 3.0	ODBC 3.5
☐	☐	✓	✓	✓	✓

API CONFORMANCE LEVEL   **CORE***

*IN ODBC 2.0, THIS FUNCTION WAS A LEVEL 2 API CONFORMANCE LEVEL FUNCTION

Purpose   The SQLNumParams() function is used to retrieve the number of parameter markers used in a specified SQL statement.

Syntax

```
SQLRETURN SQLNumParams  (SQLHSTMT        StatementHandle,
                         SQLSMALLINT     *PMarkerNumber);
```

Parameters   *StatementHandle*   An SQL statement handle that refers to a previously allocated SQL statement information storage buffer (data structure).

PMarkerNumber   A pointer to a location in memory where this function is to store the number of parameter markers found in the SQL statement associated with the statement handle specified.

Description   The SQLNumParams() function is used to retrieve the number of parameter markers used in a specified SQL statement. This function is typically used to determine how many **SQLBindParameter()** function calls are needed to associate (bind) application variables to the SQL statement associated with an SQL statement handle.

Return Codes   SQL_SUCCESS, SQL_SUCCESS_WITH_INFO, SQL_STILL_EXECUTING, SQL_INVALID_HANDLE, or SQL_ERROR

SQLSTATEs   If this function returns **SQL_SUCCESS_WITH_INFO** or **SQL_ERROR**, one of the following SQLSTATE values may be obtained by calling the **SQLGetDiagRec()** function (ODBC 3.x driver) or the **SQLError()** function (ODBC 2.0 or earlier driver):

ODBC 3.X
01000, **08**S01, **HY**000, **HY**001, **HY**008, **HY**010*, **HY**013, **HYT**01, or **IM**001*

ODBC 2.0 OR EARLIER
01000, **IM**001*, **S1**000, **S1**001, **S1**008, **S1**010*, or **S1T**00

*Returned by the ODBC Driver Manager.

Unless noted otherwise, each of these SQLSTATE values is returned by the data source driver. Refer to Appendix B for detailed information about each SQLSTATE value that can be returned by the ODBC Driver Manager or by a data source driver.

Comments   ▪ If the SQL statement associated with the statement handle specified in the *StatementHandle* parameter does not contain parameter markers, this function returns **0** to the *PMarkerNumber* parameter.

▪ The **SQL_DESC_COUNT** field of the SQL statement handle's IPD descriptor header record contains the value that this function returns to the *PMarkerNumber* parameter.

Prerequisites   The **SQLPrepare()** function must be called to prepare the SQL statement for executing before this function is called.

Restrictions   There are no restrictions associated with this function call.

See Also   SQLPrepare(), SQLDescribeParam(), SQLBindParameter()

Example   The following Visual C++ program illustrates how to use the **SQLNumParams()** function to determine how many parameter markers were coded in an SQL statement.

```
/*───────────────────────────────────────────────────────────*/
/* NAME:     CH9EX6.CPP                                        */
/* PURPOSE: Illustrate How To Use The Following ODBC API Function */
/*          In A C++ Program:                                  */
/*                                                             */
/*              SQLNumParams()                                 */
/*                                                             */
/* OTHER ODBC APIs SHOWN:                                      */
/*          SQLAllocHandle()          SQLSetEnvAttr()          */
/*          SQLConnect()              SQLPrepare()             */
/*          SQLDisconnect()           SQLFreeHandle()          */
/*                                                             */
/*───────────────────────────────────────────────────────────*/

// Include The Appropriate Header Files
#include <windows.h>
#include <sql.h>
#include <sqlext.h>
#include <iostream.h>

// Define The ODBC_Class Class
class ODBC_Class
{
    // Attributes
    public:
        SQLHANDLE    EnvHandle;
        SQLHANDLE    ConHandle;
        SQLHANDLE    StmtHandle;
        SQLRETURN    rc;

    // Operations
    public:
        ODBC_Class();                        // Constructor
        ~ODBC_Class();                       // Destructor
};

// Define The Class Constructor
ODBC_Class::ODBC_Class()
{
    // Initialize The Return Code Variable
    rc = SQL_SUCCESS;

    // Allocate An Environment Handle
    rc = SQLAllocHandle(SQL_HANDLE_ENV, SQL_NULL_HANDLE, &EnvHandle);

    // Set The ODBC Application Version To 3.x
    if (rc == SQL_SUCCESS)
        rc = SQLSetEnvAttr(EnvHandle, SQL_ATTR_ODBC_VERSION,
                (SQLPOINTER) SQL_OV_ODBC3, SQL_IS_UINTEGER);
```

```cpp
    // Allocate A Connection Handle
    if (rc == SQL_SUCCESS)
        rc = SQLAllocHandle(SQL_HANDLE_DBC, EnvHandle, &ConHandle);
}

// Define The Class Destructor
ODBC_Class::~ODBC_Class()
{
    // Free The Connection Handle
    if (ConHandle != NULL)
        SQLFreeHandle(SQL_HANDLE_DBC, ConHandle);

    // Free The Environment Handle
    if (EnvHandle != NULL)
        SQLFreeHandle(SQL_HANDLE_ENV, EnvHandle);
}

/*-----------------------------------------------------------------*/
/* The Main Function                                               */
/*-----------------------------------------------------------------*/
int main()
{
    // Declare The Local Memory Variables
    SQLRETURN     rc = SQL_SUCCESS;
    SQLCHAR       DBName[10] = "Northwind";
    SQLCHAR       SQLStmt[255];
    SQLSMALLINT   NumParams;

    // Create An Instance Of The ODBC_Class Class
    ODBC_Class  Example;

    // Connect To The Northwind Sample Database
    if (Example.ConHandle != NULL)
    {
        rc = SQLConnect(Example.ConHandle, DBName, SQL_NTS,
                (SQLCHAR *) "", SQL_NTS, (SQLCHAR *) "", SQL_NTS);

        // Allocate An SQL Statement Handle
        rc = SQLAllocHandle(SQL_HANDLE_STMT, Example.ConHandle,
                &Example.StmtHandle);
        if (rc == SQL_SUCCESS)
        {
            // Define An INSERT SQL Statement That Uses Parameter
            // Markers
            strcpy((char *) SQLStmt, "INSERT INTO Shippers ");
            strcat((char *) SQLStmt, "(ShipperID, CompanyName, ");
            strcat((char *) SQLStmt, "Phone) VALUES (?, ?, ?)");

            // Prepare The SQL Statement
            rc = SQLPrepare(Example.StmtHandle, SQLStmt, SQL_NTS);

            // Obtain And Display The Number Of Parameter Markers
            // Found In The SQL Statement
            rc = SQLNumParams(Example.StmtHandle, &NumParams);
```

```
        if (rc == SQL_SUCCESS)
        {
            cout << "Number of parameter markers found : ";
            cout << NumParams << endl;
        }

        // Free The SQL Statement Handle
        if (Example.StmtHandle != NULL)
            SQLFreeHandle(SQL_HANDLE_STMT, Example.StmtHandle);
    }

    // Disconnect From The Northwind Sample Database
    rc = SQLDisconnect(Example.ConHandle);
}

// Return To The Operating System
return(rc);
}
```

SQLDescribeParam

COMPATABILITY

X/OPEN 95 CLI	ISO/IEC 92 CLI	ODBC 1.0	ODBC 2.0	ODBC 3.0	ODBC 3.5
☐	☐	☑	☑	☑	☑

API CONFORMANCE LEVEL   **LEVEL 2**

Purpose   The `SQLDescribeParam()` function is used to retrieve information about a column or expression with which a specified parameter marker in a prepared SQL statement is associated.

Syntax
```
SQLRETURN SQLDescribeParam    (SQLHSTMT        StatementHandle,
                               SQLUSMALLINT    ParamMarkerNum,
                               SQLSMALLINT     *SQLDataType,
                               SQLUINTEGER     *ValueSize,
                               SQLSMALLINT     *Decimals,
                               SQLSMALLINT     *Nullable);
```

Parameters   *StatementHandle*   An SQL statement handle that refers to a previously allocated SQL statement information storage buffer (data structure).

ParamMarkerNum	Specifies the parameter marker's location in the SQL statement text. Parameter markers are as numbered sequentially from left to right, starting with 1, as they appear in the SQL statement.
SQLDataType	A pointer to a location in memory where this function is to store the SQL data type associated with the specified parameter.
ValueSize	A pointer to a location in memory where this function is to store either the number of bytes of data expected by the data source for the specified parameter OR the size of the maximum number of digits used by the data type (precision) of the column or expression with which the specified parameter marker is associated.
Decimals	A pointer to a location in memory where this function is to store the number of digits expected to be to the right of the decimal point in the column or expression with which the specified parameter marker is associated.
Nullable	A pointer to a location in memory where this function is to store information about whether the column or expression with which the specified parameter marker is associated can accept NULL values. After this function executes, the memory location this parameter points to will contain one of the following values:

- **SQL_NO_NULLS**
  The column or expression with which the specified parameter marker is associated does not allow NULL values.

- **SQL_NULLABLE**
  The column or expression with which the specified parameter marker is associated allows NULL values.

- **SQL_NULLABLE_UNKNOWN**
  Whether the column or expression with which the specified parameter marker is associated allows NULL values cannot be determined by the driver.

Description   The **SQLDescribeParam()** function is used to retrieve information about a column or expression with which a specified parameter marker in a prepared SQL statement is associated.

Return Codes   **SQL_SUCCESS**, **SQL_SUCCESS_WITH_INFO**, **SQL_STILL_EXECUTING**, **SQL_INVALID_HANDLE**, or **SQL_ERROR**

SQLSTATE   If this function returns **SQL_SUCCESS_WITH_INFO** or **SQL_ERROR**, one of the following SQLSTATE values may be obtained by calling the **SQLGetDiagRec()** function (ODBC 3.x driver) or the **SQLError()** function (ODBC 2.0 or earlier driver):

ODBC 3.X
01000, **07**009*, **08**S01, **21**S01, **HY**000, **HY**001, **HY**008, **HY**010*, **HY**013, **HY**T01, or **IM**001*

ODBC 2.0 OR EARLIER
01000, **IM**001*, **S1**000, **S1**001, **S1**008, **S1**010*, **S1**093*, or **S1**T00

*Returned by the ODBC Driver Manager.

Unless noted otherwise, each of these SQLSTATE values is returned by the data source driver. Refer to Appendix B for detailed information about each SQLSTATE value that can be returned by the ODBC Driver Manager or by a data source driver.

Comments   ◼ The information returned by this function is also available in the IPD descriptor associated with the statement handle specified.

◼ The **SQL_DESC_CONCISE_TYPE** field of the SQL statement handle's IPD descriptor parameter record contains the value this function returns to the *SQLDataType* parameter. If the data type cannot be determined, **SQL_UNKNOWN_TYPE** is returned.

◼ In ODBC 3.x, **SQL_TYPE_DATE**, **SQL_TYPE_TIME**, or **SQL_TYPE_TIMESTAMP** is returned in the *SQLDataType* parameter for date, time, or timestamp data, respectively. In ODBC 2.0, **SQL_DATE**, **SQL_TIME**, or **SQL_TIMESTAMP** is returned. The ODBC Driver Manager performs the required mappings when an ODBC 2.0 application is working with an ODBC 3.x driver, or when an ODBC 3.x application is working with an ODBC 2.0 or earlier driver.

- The **SQL_DESC_NULLABLE** field of the SQL statement handle's IPD descriptor parameter record contains the value this function returns to the *Nullable* parameter.

- The *ParamMarkerNum* parameter can be set to **0** to describe the bookmark column.

- When the *ParamMarkerNum* parameter is equal to **0** (for a bookmark column), **SQL_BINARY** is returned in the *SQLDataType* parameter for variable-length bookmarks. (**SQL_INTEGER** is returned if bookmarks are being used by an ODBC 3.x application working with an ODBC 2.0 or earlier driver, or by an ODBC 2.0 application working with an ODBC 3.x driver.)

- This function does not return parameter type (i.e. input, input/output, or output) information for parameters used in SQL statements that call stored procedures. That's because parameters used in SQL statements other than those that call stored procedures are treated as input parameters. An application must call the **SQLProcedureColumns()** function to determine the parameter type of each parameter used in an SQL statement that calls a stored procedure.

Prerequisites   There are no prerequisites for using this function call.

Restrictions   There are no restrictions associated with this function call.

See Also   SQLAllocHandle(), SQLAllocConnect(), SQLFreeEnv(),
SQLFreeHandle(), SQLGetEnvAttr(), SQLSetEnvAttr()

Example   The following Visual C++ program illustrates how to use the **SQLDescribeParam()** function to obtain information about a bound parameter.

```
/*-----------------------------------------------------------------*/
/* NAME:     CH9EX7.CPP                                            */
/* PURPOSE: Illustrate How To Use The Following ODBC API Function  */
/*          In A C++ Program:                                      */
/*                                                                 */
/*              SQLDescribeParam()                                 */
/*                                                                 */
/* OTHER ODBC APIs SHOWN:                                          */
/*          SQLAllocHandle()        SQLSetEnvAttr()                */
/*          SQLDriverConnect()      SQLPrepare()                   */
```

```
/*              SQLDisconnect()      SQLFreeHandle()                */
/*                                                                 */
/*───────────────────────────────────────────────────────────────*/

// Include The Appropriate Header Files
#include <windows.h>
#include <sql.h>
#include <sqlext.h>
#include <iostream.h>

// Define The ODBC_Class Class
class ODBC_Class
{
    // Attributes
    public:
        SQLHANDLE    EnvHandle;
        SQLHANDLE    ConHandle;
        SQLHANDLE    StmtHandle;
        SQLRETURN    rc;

    // Operations
    public:
        ODBC_Class();                           // Constructor
        ~ODBC_Class();                          // Destructor
};

// Define The Class Constructor
ODBC_Class::ODBC_Class()
{
    // Initialize The Return Code Variable
    rc = SQL_SUCCESS;

    // Allocate An Environment Handle
    rc = SQLAllocHandle(SQL_HANDLE_ENV, SQL_NULL_HANDLE, &EnvHandle);

    // Set The ODBC Application Version To 3.x
    if (rc == SQL_SUCCESS)
        rc = SQLSetEnvAttr(EnvHandle, SQL_ATTR_ODBC_VERSION,
                (SQLPOINTER) SQL_OV_ODBC3, SQL_IS_UINTEGER);

    // Allocate A Connection Handle
    if (rc == SQL_SUCCESS)
        rc = SQLAllocHandle(SQL_HANDLE_DBC, EnvHandle, &ConHandle);
}

// Define The Class Destructor
ODBC_Class::~ODBC_Class()
{
    // Free The Connection Handle
    if (ConHandle != NULL)
        SQLFreeHandle(SQL_HANDLE_DBC, ConHandle);

    // Free The Environment Handle
```

```
    if (EnvHandle != NULL)
        SQLFreeHandle(SQL_HANDLE_ENV, EnvHandle);
}

/*————————————————————————————————————————*/
/* The Main Function                         */
/*————————————————————————————————————————*/
int main()
{
    // Declare The Local Memory Variables
    SQLRETURN      rc = SQL_SUCCESS;
    SQLCHAR        ConnectIn[40];
    SQLCHAR        SQLStmt[255];
    SQLSMALLINT    DataType;
    SQLUINTEGER    ColSize;
    SQLSMALLINT    Decimals;
    SQLSMALLINT    Nullable;

    // Create An Instance Of The ODBC_Class Class
    ODBC_Class    Example;

    // Build A Connection String
    strcpy((char *) ConnectIn,
        "DSN=SQLServer;UID=userid;PWD=password;");

    // Connect To The SQL Server Sample Database
    if (Example.ConHandle != NULL)
    {
        rc = SQLDriverConnect(Example.ConHandle, NULL, ConnectIn,
                SQL_NTS, NULL, 0, NULL, SQL_DRIVER_NOPROMPT);

        // Allocate An SQL Statement Handle
        rc = SQLAllocHandle(SQL_HANDLE_STMT, Example.ConHandle,
                &Example.StmtHandle);
        if (rc == SQL_SUCCESS)
        {
            // Define An INSERT SQL Statement That Uses Parameter
            // Markers
            strcpy((char *) SQLStmt, "INSERT INTO ORDERS ");
            strcat((char *) SQLStmt, "(ORDERNUM, STOCKNUM, ");
            strcat((char *) SQLStmt, "SPECINSTR) VALUES (?, ?, ?)");

            // Prepare The SQL Statement
            rc = SQLPrepare(Example.StmtHandle, SQLStmt, SQL_NTS);

            // Obtain And Display Information About The First
            // Parameter Marker Found In The SQL Statement
            rc = SQLDescribeParam(Example.StmtHandle, 1, &DataType,
                    &ColSize, &Decimals, &Nullable);

            if (rc == SQL_SUCCESS)
```

```
        {
            cout << "Parameter 1 : " << endl << endl;
            cout << "Data Type   : " << DataType << endl;
            cout << "Column Size : " << ColSize << endl;
            cout << "Decimals    : " << Decimals << endl;
            cout << "Nullable    : " << Nullable << endl;
        }

        // Free The SQL Statement Handle
        if (Example.StmtHandle != NULL)
            SQLFreeHandle(SQL_HANDLE_STMT, Example.StmtHandle);
    }

    // Disconnect From The SQL Server Sample Database
    rc = SQLDisconnect(Example.ConHandle);
}

// Return To The Operating System
return(rc);
}
```

SQLExecute

COMPATABILITY

X/OPEN 95 CLI	ISO/IEC 92 CLI	ODBC 1.0	ODBC 2.0	ODBC 3.0	ODBC 3.5
✓	✓	✓	✓	✓	✓

API CONFORMANCE LEVEL   **CORE**

Purpose   The SQLExecute() function is used to execute an SQL statement that has been successfully prepared (by the SQLPrepare() function) using the current values of any parameter marker variables that have been bound to the SQL statement.

Syntax   SQLRETURN   SQLExecute (SQLHSTMT   StatementHandle);

Parameters *StatementHandle*   An SQL statement handle that refers to a previously allocated SQL statement information storage buffer (data structure).

Description   The **SQLExecute()** function is used to execute a specified SQL statement that has been successfully prepared by the **SQLPrepare()** function. The prepared SQL statement string may contain one or more parameter markers—a parameter marker is represented by a question mark character (?) in an SQL statement and is used to indicate a position in the statement where an application supplied value is to be substituted when this function is called. When the prepared SQL statement is executed, the current values of the application variables that have been bound to the parameter markers coded in the SQL statement are used to replace the parameter markers themselves.

Once the results from an **SQLExecute()** function call have been processed, the prepared SQL statement can be executed again, with new (or with the same) parameter marker values specified.

Return Codes   SQL_SUCCESS, SQL_SUCCESS_WITH_INFO, SQL_NEED_DATA, SQL_STILL_EXECUTING, SQL_NO_DATA, SQL_INVALID_HANDLE, or SQL_ERROR

SQLSTATEs   If this function returns **SQL_SUCCESS_WITH_INFO** or **SQL_ERROR**, one of the following SQLSTATE values may be obtained by calling the **SQLGetDiagRec()** function (ODBC 3.x driver) or the **SQLError()** function (ODBC 2.0 or earlier driver):

ODBC 3.X
01000, **01**001, **01**003, **01**004, **01**006, **01**007, **01**S02, **01**S07, **07**002, **07**006, **07**S01, **08**S01, **21**S02, **22**001, **22**002, **22**003, **22**007, **22**008, **22**012, **22**015, **22**018, **22**019, **22**025, **23**000, **24**000, **40**001, **40**003, **42**000, **44**000, **HY**000, **HY**001, **HY**008, **HY**010*, **HY**013, **HY**090, **HY**105, **HY**109, **HY**C00, **HYT**00, **HYT**01, or **IM**001*

ODBC 2.0 OR EARLIER
01000, **01**004, **01**006, **01**S03, **01**S04, **07**001, **08**S01, **22**003, **22**005, **22**008, **22**012, **23**000, **24**000*, **40**001, **42**000, **IM**001*, **S1**000, **S1**001, **S1**008, **S1**010*, **S1**090, **S1**109, **S1**C00, or **S1**T00

*Returned by the ODBC Driver Manager.

Unless noted otherwise, each of these SQLSTATE values are returned by the data source driver. Refer to Appendix B for detailed information about each SQLSTATE value that can be returned by the ODBC Driver Manager or by a data source driver.

SQLExecute() can return any SQLSTATE that can be returned by **SQLPrepare()** depending upon when the data source evaluates the SQL statement associated with the statement handle.

Comments

■ An application must call the `SQLCloseCursor()` function before re-executing a **SELECT** SQL statement.

■ If an application is running in manual-commit mode, and if a transaction has not already been initiated when this function is called, the driver initiates a transaction before it sends the SQL statement to the data source for processing.

■ If an application uses this function to execute a prepared **COMMIT** or **ROLLBACK** SQL statement, the application is no longer interoperable. Because the **COMMIT** and/or the **ROLLBACK** SQL statement is not supported by all DBMSs, use of these SQL statements should be avoided.

■ If the SQL statement being executed contains one or more data-at-execution parameters, **SQL_NEED_DATA** is returned to the calling application and the application is responsible for sending the appropriate data value to the data source (using the `SQLParamData()` and `SQLPutData()` functions).

■ If the SQL statement being executed is a searched **UPDATE** statement or a searched **DELETE** statement that does not affect rows in the data source, **SQL_NO_DATA** is returned to the calling application.

■ If the SQL statement being executed contains at least one parameter marker and if the value of the **SQL_ATTR_PARAMSET_SIZE** statement attribute is greater than **1**, the parameter marker points to an array of parameter values and the SQL statement is executed once using each value in the array.

■ If the SQL statement being executed is a query that cannot support bookmarks and if bookmarks are enabled, the driver attempts, by changing an attribute value, to change the environment to one that supports bookmarks. If this occurs, SQLSTATE 01S02 (Option value changed) is returned to the calling application.

■ When connection pooling is enabled, an application must not execute SQL statements that change the database or the context of the database.

Prerequisites

The `SQLPrepare()` function must be called to prepare the SQL statement for execution and all parameter markers coded in the SQL statement must be bound to application variables before this function is called.

Restrictions   There are no restrictions associated with this function call.

See Also   SQLBindParameter(), SQLSetParam(), SQLPrepare(), SQLExecDirect(),
                   SQLParamData(), SQLPutData()

Example   See the example provided for the SQLPrepare() function on page 347.

SQLExecDirect

COMPATABILITY

X/OPEN 95 CLI	ISO/IEC 92 CLI	ODBC 1.0	ODBC 2.0	ODBC 3.0	ODBC 3.5
✓	✓	✓	✓	✓	✓

API CONFORMANCE LEVEL   **CORE**

Purpose   The SQLExecDirect() function is used to prepare and execute a
                   preparable SQL statement, using the current values of any parameter
                   marker variables that have been bound to the SQL statement.

Syntax
```
SQLRETURN   SQLExecDirect   (SQLHSTMT      StatementHandle,
                             SQLCHAR       *SQLString,
                             SQLINTEGER    SQLStringSize);
```

Parameters   *StatementHandle*   An SQL statement handle that refers
                                        to a previously allocated SQL statement
                                        information storage buffer (data structure).

                   SQLString   A pointer to a location in memory where the
                                        SQL statement to be prepared and executed is
                                        stored.

                   SQLStringSize   The length of the SQL statement stored in the
                                        SQLString parameter.

Description   The SQLExecDirect() function is used to prepare and execute a
                   preparable SQL statement using the current values of any parameter
                   marker variables that have been bound to the SQL statement.
                   SQLExecDirect() is the fastest way to submit an SQL statement that is

to be executed only once to the data source. Because the SQL statement is both prepared and executed in the same step, the specified SQL statement must be reprepared each time it is executed.

The SQL statement string to be prepared and executed may contain one or more parameter markers—a parameter marker is represented by a question mark character (?) in an SQL statement and is used to indicate a position in the statement where an application supplied value is to be substituted when this function is called. When the SQL statement is executed, the current values of the application variables bound to the parameter markers coded in the SQL statement are used to replace the parameter markers themselves.

Return Codes   SQL_SUCCESS, SQL_SUCCESS_WITH_INFO, SQL_NEED_DATA, SQL_STILL_EXECUTING, SQL_NO_DATA, SQL_INVALID_HANDLE, or SQL_ERROR

SQLSTATEs   If this function returns SQL_SUCCESS_WITH_INFO or SQL_ERROR, one of the following SQLSTATE values may be obtained by calling the SQLGetDiagRec() function (ODBC 3.x driver) or the SQLError() function (ODBC 2.0 or earlier driver):

ODBC 3.X
01000, 01001, 01003, 01004, 01006, 01007, 01S02, 01S07, 07002, 07006, 07S01, 08S01, 21S01, 21S02, 22001, 22002, 22003, 22007, 22008, 22012, 22015, 22018, 22019, 22025, 23000, 24000, 34000, 3D000, 3F000, 40001, 40003, 42000, 42S01, 42S02, 42S11, 42S12, 42S21, 42S22, 44000, HY000, HY001, HY008, HY009*, HY010*, HY013, HY090*, HY105, HY109, HYC00, HYT00, HYT01, or IM001*

ODBC 2.0 OR EARLIER
01000, 01004, 01006, 01S03, 01S04, 07001, 08S01, 21S01, 21S02, 22003, 22005, 22008, 22012, 23000, 24000*, 34000, 37000, 40001, 42000, IM001*, S0001, S0002, S0011, S0012, S0021, S0022, S1000, S1001, S1008, S1009*, S1010*, S1090*, S1109, S1C00, or S1T00

* Returned by the ODBC Driver Manager.

Unless noted otherwise, each of these SQLSTATE values are returned by the data source driver. Refer to Appendix B for detailed information about each SQLSTATE value that can be returned by the ODBC Driver Manager or by a data source driver.

Comments   ■ The data source the SQL statement is passed to for processing must be able to dynamically prepare and execute SQL statements.

- If an application is running in manual-commit mode, and if a transaction has not already been initiated when this function is called, the driver initiates a transaction before it sends the SQL statement to the data source for processing.

- If an application uses this function to execute a prepared **COMMIT** or **ROLLBACK** SQL statement, the application is no longer interoperable. Because the **COMMIT** and/or **ROLLBACK** SQL statement is not supported by all DBMSs, use of these SQL statements should be avoided.

- If the SQL statement being executed contains one or more data-at-execution parameters, **SQL_NEED_DATA** is returned to the calling application and the application is responsible for sending the appropriate data value to the data source (using the **SQLParamData()** and **SQLPutData()** functions).

- If the SQL statement being executed is a searched **UPDATE** statement or a searched **DELETE** statement that does not affect rows in the data source, **SQL_NO_DATA** is returned to the calling application.

- If the SQL statement being executed contains at least one parameter marker and if the value of the **SQL_ATTR_PARAMSET_SIZE** statement attribute is greater than **1**, the parameter marker points to an array of parameter values and the SQL statement is executed once using each value in the array.

- If the SQL statement being executed is a query that cannot support bookmarks, and if bookmarks are enabled, the driver attempts, by changing an attribute value, to change the environment to one that supports bookmarks. If this occurs, SQLSTATE **01**S02 (Option value changed) is returned to the calling application.

- When connection pooling is enabled, an application must not execute SQL statements that change the database or the context of the database.

Prerequisites   There are no prerequisites for using this function call.

Restrictions   There are no restrictions associated with this function call.

See Also   **SQLBindParameter()**, **SQLSetParam()**, **SQLPrepare()**, **SQLExecute()**, **SQLParamData()**, **SQLPutData()**

Example   The following Visual C++ program illustrates how to use the
SQLExecDirect() function to prepare and execute an SQL statement in
a single step.

```
/*----------------------------------------------------------------*/
/* NAME:     CH9EX8.CPP                                           */
/* PURPOSE: Illustrate How To Use The Following ODBC API Function */
/*          In A C++ Program:                                     */
/*                                                                */
/*               SQLExecDirect()                                  */
/*                                                                */
/* OTHER ODBC APIs SHOWN:                                         */
/*          SQLAllocHandle()          SQLSetEnvAttr()             */
/*          SQLConnect()              SQLBindCol()                */
/*          SQLFetch()                SQLDisconnect()             */
/*          SQLFreeHandle()                                       */
/*                                                                */
/*----------------------------------------------------------------*/

// Include The Appropriate Header Files
#include <windows.h>
#include <sql.h>
#include <sqlext.h>
#include <iostream.h>

// Define The ODBC_Class Class
class ODBC_Class
{
    // Attributes
    public:
        SQLHANDLE    EnvHandle;
        SQLHANDLE    ConHandle;
        SQLHANDLE    StmtHandle;
        SQLRETURN    rc;

    // Operations
    public:
        ODBC_Class();                         // Constructor
        ~ODBC_Class();                        // Destructor
        SQLRETURN ShowResults();
};

// Define The Class Constructor
ODBC_Class::ODBC_Class()
{
    // Initialize The Return Code Variable
    rc = SQL_SUCCESS;

    // Allocate An Environment Handle
    rc = SQLAllocHandle(SQL_HANDLE_ENV, SQL_NULL_HANDLE, &EnvHandle);

    // Set The ODBC Application Version To 3.x
    if (rc == SQL_SUCCESS)
```

```
        rc = SQLSetEnvAttr(EnvHandle, SQL_ATTR_ODBC_VERSION,
                    (SQLPOINTER) SQL_OV_ODBC3, SQL_IS_UINTEGER);

    // Allocate A Connection Handle
    if (rc == SQL_SUCCESS)
        rc = SQLAllocHandle(SQL_HANDLE_DBC, EnvHandle, &ConHandle);
}

// Define The Class Destructor
ODBC_Class::~ODBC_Class()
{
    // Free The Connection Handle
    if (ConHandle != NULL)
        SQLFreeHandle(SQL_HANDLE_DBC, ConHandle);

    // Free The Environment Handle
    if (EnvHandle != NULL)
        SQLFreeHandle(SQL_HANDLE_ENV, EnvHandle);
}

// Define The ShowResults() Member Function
SQLRETURN ODBC_Class::ShowResults(void)
{
    // Declare The Local Memory Variables
    SQLCHAR   LastName[50];
    SQLCHAR   FirstName[50];

    // Bind The Columns In The Result Data Set Returned To
    // Application Variables
    rc = SQLBindCol(StmtHandle, 1, SQL_C_CHAR, (SQLPOINTER)
            LastName, sizeof(LastName), NULL);

    rc = SQLBindCol(StmtHandle, 2, SQL_C_CHAR, (SQLPOINTER)
            FirstName, sizeof(FirstName), NULL);

    // Display A Header
    cout << "Employees :" << endl << endl;

    // While There Are Records In The Result Data Set Generated,
    // Retrieve And Display Them
    while (rc != SQL_NO_DATA)
    {
        rc = SQLFetch(StmtHandle);
        if (rc != SQL_NO_DATA)
            cout << FirstName << " " << LastName << endl;
    }

    // Return The ODBC API Return Code To The Calling Function
    return(rc);
}

/*------------------------------------------------------------*/
/* The Main Function                                          */
/*------------------------------------------------------------*/
int main()
```

```
{
    // Declare The Local Memory Variables
    SQLRETURN    rc = SQL_SUCCESS;
    SQLCHAR      DBName[10] = "Northwind";
    SQLCHAR      SQLStmt[255];

    // Create An Instance Of The ODBC_Class Class
    ODBC_Class   Example;

    // Connect To The Northwind Sample Database
    if (Example.ConHandle != NULL)
    {
        rc = SQLConnect(Example.ConHandle, DBName, SQL_NTS,
                (SQLCHAR *) "", SQL_NTS, (SQLCHAR *) "", SQL_NTS);

        // Allocate An SQL Statement Handle
        rc = SQLAllocHandle(SQL_HANDLE_STMT, Example.ConHandle,
                &Example.StmtHandle);
        if (rc == SQL_SUCCESS)
        {
            // Define A SELECT SQL Statement
            strcpy((char *) SQLStmt, "SELECT Employees.LastName, ");
            strcat((char *) SQLStmt, "Employees.FirstName FROM ");
            strcat((char *) SQLStmt, "Employees");

            // Prepare And Execute The SQL Statement
            rc = SQLExecDirect(Example.StmtHandle, SQLStmt, SQL_NTS);

            // Display The Results Of The SQL Query
            if (rc == SQL_SUCCESS)
                Example.ShowResults();

            // Free The SQL Statement Handle
            if (Example.StmtHandle != NULL)
                SQLFreeHandle(SQL_HANDLE_STMT, Example.StmtHandle);
        }

        // Disconnect From The Northwind Sample Database
        rc = SQLDisconnect(Example.ConHandle);
    }

    // Return To The Operating System
    return(rc);
}
```

SQLNativeSql

COMPATABILITY					
X/OPEN 95 CLI	ISO/IEC 92 CLI	ODBC 1.0	ODBC 2.0	ODBC 3.0	ODBC 3.5
☐	☐	✓	✓	✓	✓

API CONFORMANCE LEVEL	CORE*

*IN ODBC 2.0, THIS FUNCTION WAS A LEVEL 2 API CONFORMANCE LEVEL FUNCTION

Purpose   The **SQLNativeSql()** function is used to display an SQL statement string as it will be seen by the data source (after it is modified by the driver).

Syntax

```
SQLRETURN SQLNativeSql (SQLHDBC       ConnectionHandle,
                        SQLCHAR       *SQLStringIn,
                        SQLINTEGER    SQLStringInSize,
                        SQLCHAR       *SQLStringOut,
                        SQLINTEGER    SQLStringOutMaxSize,
                        SQLINTEGER    *SQLStringOutSize);
```

Parameters

ConnectionHandle	A data source connection handle that refers to a previously allocated connection information storage buffer (data structure).
SQLStringIn	A pointer to a location in memory where the SQL statement string to be translated is stored.
SQLStringInSize	The length of the SQL statement string stored in the *SQLStringIn* parameter.
SQLStringOut	A pointer to a location in memory where this function is to store the translated SQL statement string (the SQL statement string that will be seen by the data source).
SQLStringOutMaxSize	The maximum size of the memory storage buffer where this function is to store the translated SQL statement string.
SQLStringOutSize	A pointer to a location in memory where this function is to store the actual number of bytes

written to the translated SQL statement string memory storage buffer (*SQLStringOut*).

Description

The `SQLNativeSql()` function is used to display an SQL statement string as it will be seen by the data source (after it is modified by the driver). Primarily, this function is used to show how ODBC escape sequences are translated by a driver. Escape sequences are used extensively by ODBC to define various SQL extensions.

The following are examples of what `SQLNativeSql()` might return for an input SQL string containing the scalar function CONVERT. Assume that the column EmpID is of type **INTEGER** in the data source:

```
SELECT { fn CONVERT (EmpID, SQL_SMALLINT) } FROM Employee
```

A driver for Microsoft SQL Server might return the following translated SQL string:

```
SELECT convert (smallint, EmpID) FROM Employee
```

A driver for ORACLE Server might return the following translated SQL string:

```
SELECT to_number (EmpID) FROM Employee
```

A driver for Ingress might return the following translated SQL string:

```
SELECT int2 (EmpID) FROM Employee
```

Return Codes

SQL_SUCCESS, SQL_SUCCESS_WITH_INFO, SQL_INVALID_HANDLE, or SQL_ERROR

SQLSTATEs

If this function returns **SQL_SUCCESS_WITH_INFO** or **SQL_ERROR**, one of the following SQLSTATE values may be obtained by calling the `SQLGetDiagRec()` function (ODBC 3.x driver) or the `SQLError()` function (ODBC 2.0 or earlier driver):

ODBC 3.X
01000, **01**004, **08**003, **08**S01, **22**007, **24**000, **HY**000, **HY**001, **HY**009*, **HY**013, **HY**090*, **HY**109, **HY**T01, or **IM**001*

ODBC 2.0 OR EARLIER
01000, **01**004, **08**003, **37**000, **IM**001*, **S1**000, **S1**001, **S1**009*, or **S1**090*

*Returned by the ODBC Driver Manager.

Unless noted otherwise, each of these SQLSTATE values are returned by the data source driver. Refer to Appendix B for detailed information about each SQLSTATE value that can be returned by the ODBC Driver Manager or by a data source driver.

Comments

■ This function does not execute the SQL statement stored in the *SQLStringIn* parameter.

■ If the translated SQL statement string's actual length is greater than or equal to the maximum string size value specified in the *StringOutMaxSize* parameter, it is truncated to *StringOutMaxSize–1* (the length of a NULL-termination character) characters.

■ If the translated SQL statement string to be returned in the *SQLStringOut* parameter is a Unicode string, the *SQLStringOutMaxSize* parameter must contain an even number.

Prerequisites   There are no prerequisites for using this function call.

Restrictions   There are no restrictions associated with this function call.

See Also   The information on ODBC escape sequences in Chapter 4.

Example   The following Visual C++ program illustrates how to use the `SQLExecDirect()` function to show how an SQL statement will be converted by a driver before it is sent to the underlying data source for processing.

```
/*-----------------------------------------------------------------*/
/* NAME:     CH9EX9.CPP                                            */
/* PURPOSE: Illustrate How To Use The Following ODBC API Function  */
/*          In A C++ Program:                                      */
/*                                                                 */
/*             SQLNativeSql()                                      */
/*                                                                 */
/* OTHER ODBC APIs SHOWN:                                          */
/*          SQLAllocHandle()        SQLSetEnvAttr()                */
/*          SQLConnect()            SQLDisconnect()                */
/*          SQLFreeHandle()                                        */
/*                                                                 */
/*-----------------------------------------------------------------*/

// Include The Appropriate Header Files
#include <windows.h>
#include <sql.h>
#include <sqlext.h>
```

```
#include <iostream.h>

// Define The ODBC_Class Class
class ODBC_Class
{
    // Attributes
    public:
        SQLHANDLE    EnvHandle;
        SQLHANDLE    ConHandle;
        SQLHANDLE    StmtHandle;
        SQLRETURN    rc;

    // Operations
    public:
        ODBC_Class();                           // Constructor
        ~ODBC_Class();                          // Destructor
};

// Define The Class Constructor
ODBC_Class::ODBC_Class()
{
    // Initialize The Return Code Variable
    rc = SQL_SUCCESS;

    // Allocate An Environment Handle
    rc = SQLAllocHandle(SQL_HANDLE_ENV, SQL_NULL_HANDLE, &EnvHandle);

    // Set The ODBC Application Version To 3.x
    if (rc == SQL_SUCCESS)
        rc = SQLSetEnvAttr(EnvHandle, SQL_ATTR_ODBC_VERSION,
                (SQLPOINTER) SQL_OV_ODBC3, SQL_IS_UINTEGER);

    // Allocate A Connection Handle
    if (rc == SQL_SUCCESS)
        rc = SQLAllocHandle(SQL_HANDLE_DBC, EnvHandle, &ConHandle);
}

// Define The Class Destructor
ODBC_Class::~ODBC_Class()
{
    // Free The Connection Handle
    if (ConHandle != NULL)
        SQLFreeHandle(SQL_HANDLE_DBC, ConHandle);

    // Free The Environment Handle
    if (EnvHandle != NULL)
        SQLFreeHandle(SQL_HANDLE_ENV, EnvHandle);
}
```

```
/*———————————————————————————————————————————————————*/
/* The Main Function                                    */
/*———————————————————————————————————————————————————*/
int main()
{
    // Declare The Local Memory Variables
    SQLRETURN     rc = SQL_SUCCESS;
    SQLCHAR       DBName[10] = "Northwind";
    SQLCHAR       SQLStmt[255];
    SQLCHAR       TranslatedStmt[255];
    SQLINTEGER    StmtLen;

    // Create An Instance Of The ODBC_Class Class
    ODBC_Class  Example;

    // Connect To The Northwind Sample Database
    if (Example.ConHandle != NULL)
    {
        rc = SQLConnect(Example.ConHandle, DBName, SQL_NTS,
                (SQLCHAR *) "", SQL_NTS, (SQLCHAR *) "", SQL_NTS);

        // Define A SELECT SQL Statement That Contains An ODBC
        // Scalar Function And An Escape Sequence
        strcpy((char *) SQLStmt, "SELECT {fn CONVERT (EmployeeID, ");
        strcat((char *) SQLStmt, "SQL_SMALLINT) } FROM Employees ");

        // Obtain And Display The Translated SQL Statement
        rc = SQLNativeSql(Example.ConHandle, SQLStmt, SQL_NTS,
                TranslatedStmt, sizeof(TranslatedStmt), &StmtLen);
        if (rc == SQL_SUCCESS)
        {
            cout << "Original Statement :" << endl << endl;
            cout << "    " << SQLStmt << endl << endl;
            cout << "Translated Statement :" <<endl << endl;
            cout << "    " << TranslatedStmt << endl;
        }

        // Disconnect From The Northwind Sample Database
        rc = SQLDisconnect(Example.ConHandle);
    }

    // Return To The Operating System
    return(rc);
}
```

SQLParamData

COMPATABILITY

X/OPEN 95 CLI	ISO/IEC 92 CLI	ODBC 1.0	ODBC 2.0	ODBC 3.0	ODBC 3.5
✓	✓	✓	✓	✓	✓

API CONFORMANCE LEVEL   **CORE***

*IN ODBC 2.0, THIS FUNCTION WAS A LEVEL 1 API CONFORMANCE LEVEL FUNCTION

Purpose

The **SQLParamData()** function is used in conjunction with the **SQLPutData()** function to send data for data-at-execution parameters to the appropriate data source when an SQL statement is executed OR to send data for data-at-execution columns to the appropriate data source when **SQLBulkOperations()** or **SQLSetPos()** is used to add or update a row of data.

Syntax

```
SQLRETURN   SQLParamData   (SQLHSTMT      StatementHandle,
                            SQLPOINTER    *Value);
```

Parameters

StatementHandle   An SQL statement handle that refers to a previously allocated SQL statement information storage buffer (data structure).

Value   A pointer to a location in memory where the actual value associated with a bound parameter or column is stored. This will be the same location in memory that was specified in either the **SQLBindParameter()** function (ODBC 2.0 or later), the **SQLSetParam()** function (ODBC 1.0), or the **SQLBindCol()** function.

Description

The **SQLParamData()** function is used in conjunction with the **SQLPutData()** function to send data for data-at-execution parameters to the appropriate data source when an SQL statement is executed OR to send data for data-at-execution columns to the appropriate data source when **SQLBulkOperations()** or **SQLSetPos()** is used to add or update a row of data.

Data-at-execution parameters and columns are bound to application variables at the same time other parameters or columns are bound to application variables; however, with data-at-execution parameters and columns the value **SQL_DATA_AT_EXEC**, instead of the data value size, is specified during the binding process. When an application calls **SQLExecute()**, **SQLExecDirect()** (to execute the SQL statement), **SQLBulkOperations()**, or **SQLSetPos()** (to add/update a row of data), the driver returns **SQL_NEED_DATA** when it encounters a data-at-execution parameter or column. The application then calls this function to determine which data it should send. If the driver is waiting for parameter data, the value placed in the rowset buffer when the parameter was bound is returned. If the driver is waiting for column data, the address of the row where the data can be found is returned. In either case, the application uses this information to retrieve the data that is to be sent to the driver.

Once the application knows what data to send, it calls the **SQLPutData()** function repeatedly until all the data-at-execution data for the parameter or column has been sent to the driver. After all data has been sent, the application calls this function again to inform the driver that all the requested data has been sent and to advance to the next data-at-execution parameter or column. If no more data-at-execution parameters or columns exist, the driver returns **SQL_SUCCESS** or **SQL_SUCCESS_WITH_INFO** to the application and the SQL statement is executed or the **SQLBulkOperations()** or **SQLSetPos()** function call is processed.

Return Codes

SQL_SUCCESS, **SQL_SUCCESS_WITH_INFO**, **SQL_NEED_DATA**, **SQL_NO_DATA**, **SQL_STILL_EXECUTING**, **SQL_INVALID_HANDLE**, or **SQL_ERROR**

SQLSTATEs

If this function returns **SQL_SUCCESS_WITH_INFO** or **SQL_ERROR**, one of the following SQLSTATE values may be obtained by calling the **SQLGetDiagRec()** function (ODBC 3.x driver) or the **SQLError()** function (ODBC 2.0 or earlier driver):

ODBC 3.X
01000, **07**006, **08**S01, **22**026, **40**001, **40**003, **HY**000, **HY**001, **HY**008, **HY**010*, **HY**013, **HYT**01, or **IM**001*

ODBC 2.0 OR EARLIER
01000, **08**S01, **22**026, **IM**001*, **S1**000, **S1**001, **S1**008, **S1**010*, or **S1T**00

*Returned by the ODBC Driver Manager.

Unless noted otherwise, each of these SQLSTATE values are returned by the data source driver. Refer to Appendix B for detailed information about each SQLSTATE value that can be returned by the ODBC Driver Manager or by a data source driver.

If this function is called to send data for a data-at-execution parameter in an SQL statement, it can return any SQLSTATE that can be returned by the function called to execute the statement (**SQLExecute()** or **SQLExecDirect()**). If this function is called to send data for a data-at-execution column in the data source, it can return any SQLSTATE that can be returned by the function called to do the add/update operation (**SQLBulkOperations()** or **SQLSetPos()**).

Comments
■ If the SQL statement being executed is a searched **UPDATE** statement or a searched **DELETE** statement that does not affect rows in the data source, **SQL_NO_DATA** is returned to the calling application if this function is called.

■ The information returned by this function is also available in the **SQL_DESC_DATA_PTR** field of the IPD descriptor parameter record associated with the statement handle specified.

Prerequisites   There are no prerequisites for using this function call.

Restrictions   There are no restrictions associated with this function call.

See Also   SQLPutData(), SQLCancel(), SQLBindParameter(), SQLSetParm(), SQLBindCol(), SQLExecute(), SQLExecDirect(), SQLBulkOperations(), SQLSetPos()

Example   The following Visual C++ program illustrates how to use the **SQLParamData()** and **SQLPutData()** functions to send long data values to a data source.

```
/*------------------------------------------------------------------*/
/* NAME:     CH9EX10.CPP                                            */
/* PURPOSE: Illustrate How To Use The Following ODBC API Functions  */
/*          In A C++ Program:                                       */
/*                                                                  */
/*              SQLParamData()                                      */
/*              SQLPutData()                                        */
/*              SQLCancel()                                         */
/*                                                                  */
/* OTHER ODBC APIs SHOWN:                                           */
```

```
/*              SQLAllocHandle()          SQLSetEnvAttr()                */
/*              SQLDriverConnect()        SQLPrepare()                   */
/*              SQLBindParameter()        SQLExecute()                   */
/*              SQLDisconnect()           SQLFreeHandle()                */
/*                                                                      */
/*----------------------------------------------------------------------*/

// Include The Appropriate Header Files
#include <windows.h>
#include <sql.h>
#include <sqlext.h>
#include <iostream.h>
#include <fstream.h>

// Define The ODBC_Class Class
class ODBC_Class
{
    // Attributes
    public:
        SQLHANDLE   EnvHandle;
        SQLHANDLE   ConHandle;
        SQLHANDLE   StmtHandle;
        SQLRETURN   rc;

    // Operations
    public:
        ODBC_Class();                           // Constructor
        ~ODBC_Class();                          // Destructor
        SQLRETURN SendLongData();
};

// Define The Class Constructor
ODBC_Class::ODBC_Class()
{
    // Initialize The Return Code Variable
    rc = SQL_SUCCESS;

    // Allocate An Environment Handle
    rc = SQLAllocHandle(SQL_HANDLE_ENV, SQL_NULL_HANDLE, &EnvHandle);

    // Set The ODBC Application Version To 3.x
    if (rc == SQL_SUCCESS)
        rc = SQLSetEnvAttr(EnvHandle, SQL_ATTR_ODBC_VERSION,
                (SQLPOINTER) SQL_OV_ODBC3, SQL_IS_UINTEGER);

    // Allocate A Connection Handle
    if (rc == SQL_SUCCESS)
        rc = SQLAllocHandle(SQL_HANDLE_DBC, EnvHandle, &ConHandle);
}

// Define The Class Destructor
ODBC_Class::~ODBC_Class()
{
    // Free The Connection Handle
    if (ConHandle != NULL)
```

```
        SQLFreeHandle(SQL_HANDLE_DBC, ConHandle);

    // Free The Environment Handle
    if (EnvHandle != NULL)
        SQLFreeHandle(SQL_HANDLE_ENV, EnvHandle);
}

// Define The SendLongData() Member Function
SQLRETURN ODBC_Class::SendLongData(void)
{
    // Declare The Local Memory Variables
    ifstream      InFile;
    SQLPOINTER    Value;
    SQLCHAR       Buffer[15];
    SQLCHAR       InputParam[] = "Special Instructions";
    size_t        NumBytes = 0;
    size_t        DataSize = 0;

    // Open An External Data File - If An Error Occurs, Call
    // The SQLCancel() Function To Terminate The Data-At-Execution
    // Sequence And Exit
    InFile.open("SPECINFO.TXT", ios::in | ios::nocreate);
    if (InFile.fail())
    {
        rc = SQLCancel(StmtHandle);
        return(SQL_ERROR);
    }

    // Start The Data-At-Execution Sequence By Calling
    // SQLParamData()
    rc = SQLParamData(StmtHandle, (SQLPOINTER *) &Value);

    // Examine The Contents Of Value (Returned By SQLParamData())
    // To Determine Which Data-At-Execution Parameter Currently
    // Needs Data
    if (strcmp((const char *) Value, (const char *) InputParam) == 0
        && rc ==   SQL_NEED_DATA)
    {
        // As Long As Data Is Available For The Parameter, Retrieve
        // Part Of It From The External Data File And Send It To The
        // Data Source
        while (InFile.get(Buffer, sizeof(Buffer)))
        {
            NumBytes = strlen((const char *) Buffer);
            rc = SQLPutData(StmtHandle, (SQLPOINTER) Buffer,
                    SQL_NTS);
            DataSize = DataSize + NumBytes;

            // If The Amount Of Data Retrieved Exceeds The Size Of
            // The Column (Which Is 200 Bytes), Call The SQLCancel()
            // Function To Terminate The Data-At-Execution
            // Sequence And Exit
            if (DataSize > 200)
            {
```

```
                rc = SQLCancel(StmtHandle);
                return(SQL_ERROR);
            }
        }

        // Call SQLParamData() Again To Terminate The
        // Data-At-Execution Sequence
        rc = SQLParamData(StmtHandle, (SQLPOINTER *) &Value);

        // Display A Message Telling How Many Bytes Of Data Were Sent
        if (rc == SQL_SUCCESS || rc == SQL_SUCCESS_WITH_INFO)
        {
            cout << "Successfully inserted " << DataSize ;
            cout << " bytes of data into the database." << endl;
        }
    }

    // Close The External Data File
    InFile.close();

    // Return The ODBC API Return Code To The Calling Function
    return(rc);
}

/*————————————————————————————————————————————————*/
/* The Main Function                                         */
/*————————————————————————————————————————————————*/
int main()
{
    // Declare The Local Memory Variables
    SQLRETURN    rc = SQL_SUCCESS;
    SQLCHAR      ConnectIn[40];
    SQLCHAR      SQLStmt[255];
    SQLCHAR      InputParam[25] = "Special Instructions";
    SQLINTEGER   Indicator = SQL_DATA_AT_EXEC;

    // Create An Instance Of The ODBC_Class Class
    ODBC_Class  Example;

    // Build A Connection String
    strcpy((char *) ConnectIn,
        "DSN=SQLServer;UID=userid;PWD=password;");

    // Connect To The SQL Server Sample Database
    if (Example.ConHandle != NULL)
    {
        rc = SQLDriverConnect(Example.ConHandle, NULL, ConnectIn,
                SQL_NTS, NULL, 0, NULL, SQL_DRIVER_NOPROMPT);

        // Allocate An SQL Statement Handle
        rc = SQLAllocHandle(SQL_HANDLE_STMT, Example.ConHandle,
                &Example.StmtHandle);
        if (rc == SQL_SUCCESS)
```

```
        {
            // Define An INSERT SQL Statement That Contains A
            // Data-At-Execution Parameter
            strcpy((char *) SQLStmt, "INSERT INTO ORDERS ");
            strcat((char *) SQLStmt, "(ORDERNUM, STOCKNUM, SHIPTO,");
            strcat((char *) SQLStmt, " TAKENBY, SPECINSTR) VALUES ");
            strcat((char *) SQLStmt, "(99, 100, '123456', 123, ?)");

            // Prepare The SQL Statement
            rc = SQLPrepare(Example.StmtHandle, SQLStmt, SQL_NTS);

            // Bind The Parameter Marker In The SQL Statement To A
            // Local Application Variable - This Parameter Will Use
            // SQLParamData() And SQLPutData() To Send Data In Pieces
            // (Note: The Column Size Is 200 Characters)
            rc = SQLBindParameter(Example.StmtHandle, 1,
                        SQL_PARAM_INPUT, SQL_C_DEFAULT, SQL_CHAR, 200,
                        0, (SQLPOINTER) InputParam, 25, &Indicator);

            // Execute The SQL Statement
            rc = SQLExecute(Example.StmtHandle);

            // The Return Code SQL_NEED_DATA Should Be Returned,
            // Indicating That SQLParamData() And SQLPutData() Need
            // To Be Called
            if (rc == SQL_NEED_DATA)
                rc = Example.SendLongData();

            // Free The SQL Statement Handle
            if (Example.StmtHandle != NULL)
                SQLFreeHandle(SQL_HANDLE_STMT, Example.StmtHandle);
        }

        // Disconnect From The Northwind Sample Database
        rc = SQLDisconnect(Example.ConHandle);
    }

    // Return To The Operating System
    return(rc);
}
```

SQLPutData

COMPATABILITY

X/OPEN 95 CLI	ISO/IEC 92 CLI	ODBC 1.0	ODBC 2.0	ODBC 3.0	ODBC 3.5
✓	✓	✓	✓	✓	✓

API CONFORMANCE LEVEL   CORE*

*IN ODBC 2.0, THIS FUNCTION WAS A LEVEL 1 API CONFORMANCE LEVEL FUNCTION

Purpose

The **SQLPutData()** function is used in conjunction with the **SQLParamData()** function to send data for data-at-execution parameters to the appropriate data source when an SQL statement is executed OR to send data for data-at-execution columns to the appropriate data source when **SQLBulkOperations()** or **SQLSetPos()** is used to add or update a row of data.

Syntax

```
SQLRETURN  SQLPutData  (SQLHSTMT     StatementHandle,
                        SQLPOINTER   Value,
                        SQLINTEGER   ValueSize_Indicator);
```

Parameters

StatementHandle   An SQL statement handle that refers to a previously allocated SQL statement information storage buffer (data structure).

Value   A pointer to a location in memory where the data value (or a portion of the data value) for the parameter marker or column that was specified in either the **SQLBindParameter()** function (ODBC 2.0 or later), the **SQLSetParam()** function (ODBC 1.0), or the **SQLBindCol()** function is stored.

ValueSize_Indicator   Either the number of bytes of data to be sent to the data source when this function is executed OR one of the following special indicator values:

■ **SQL_NTS**
The data value is a NULL-terminated string.

▢ **SQL_NULL_DATA**
The data value is a NULL value.

▢ **SQL_DEFAULT_PARAM**
A stored procedure is to use the appropriate default data value.

Description   The **SQLPutData()** function is used in conjunction with the **SQLParamData()** function to send data for data-at-execution parameters to the appropriate data source when an SQL statement is executed OR to send data for data-at-execution columns to the appropriate data source when **SQLBulkOperations()** or **SQLSetPos()** is used to add or update a row of data.

Data-at-execution parameters and columns are bound to application variables at the same time other parameters or columns are bound to application variables; however, with data-at-execution parameters and columns the value **SQL_DATA_AT_EXEC**, instead of the data value size, is specified during the binding process. When an application calls **SQLExecute()**, **SQLExecDirect()** (to execute the SQL statement), **SQLBulkOperations()**, or **SQLSetPos()** (to add/update a row of data), the driver returns **SQL_NEED_DATA** when it encounters a data-at-execution parameter or column. The application then calls the **SQLParamData()** function to determine which data it should send. If the driver is waiting for parameter data, the value placed in the rowset buffer when the parameter was bound is returned. If the driver is waiting for column data, the address of the row where the data can be found is returned. In either case, the application uses this information to retrieve the data that is to be sent to the driver.

Once the application knows what data to send, it calls this function repeatedly until all the data-at-execution data for the parameter or column has been sent to the driver. After all data has been sent, the application calls the **SQLParamData()** function again to inform the driver that all the requested data has been sent and to advance to the next data-at-execution parameter or column. If no more data-at-execution parameters or columns exist, the driver returns **SQL_SUCCESS** or **SQL_SUCCESS_WITH_INFO** to the application and the SQL statement is executed or the **SQLBulkOperations()** or **SQLSetPos()** function call is processed.

Return Codes   **SQL_SUCCESS**, **SQL_SUCCESS_WITH_INFO**, **SQL_STILL_EXECUTING**, **SQL_INVALID_HANDLE**, or **SQL_ERROR**

SQLSTATEs   If this function returns **SQL_SUCCESS_WITH_INFO** or **SQL_ERROR**, one of the following SQLSTATE values may be obtained by calling the **SQLGetDiagRec()** function (ODBC 3.x driver) or the **SQLError()** function (ODBC 2.0 or earlier driver):

ODBC 3.X
01000, **01**004, **07**006, **07**S01, **08**S01, **22**001, **22**003, **22**007, **22**008, **22**012, **22**015, **22**018, **HY**000, **HY**001, **HY**008, **HY**009*, **HY**010*, **HY**013, **HY**019, **HY**020, **HY**090, **HYT**01, or **IM**001*

ODBC 2.0 OR EARLIER
01000, **01**004, **08**S01, **22**001, **22**003, **22**005, **22**008, **IM**001*, **S1**000, **S1**001, **S1**008, **S1**009*, **S1**010*, **S1**090, or **S1T**00

*Returned by the ODBC Driver Manager.

Unless noted otherwise, each of these SQLSTATE values are returned by the data source driver. Refer to Appendix B for detailed information about each SQLSTATE value that can be returned by the ODBC Driver Manager or by a data source driver.

NOTE: Some of these SQLSTATEs may be reported on the final **SQLParamData()** *function call rather than when the* **SQLPutData()** *function is called.*

If this function is called to send data for a data-at-execution parameter in an SQL statement, it can return any SQLSTATE that can be returned by the function called to execute the statement (**SQLExecute()** or **SQLExecDirect()**). If this function is called to send data for a data-at-execution column in the data source, it can return any SQLSTATE that can be returned by the function called to do the add/update operation (**SQLBulkOperations()** or **SQLSetPos()**).

Comments   ▓ The value stored in the *ValueSize_Indicator* parameter is ignored unless:

   ▓ The C data type of the parameter or column is **SQL_C_CHAR** or **SQL_C_BINARY**.

   ▓ The C data type of the parameter or column is **SQL_C_DEFAULT** and the default C data type for the specified SQL data type is **SQL_C_CHAR** or **SQL_C_BINARY**.

■ The value is **SQL_NTS**, **SQL_NULL_DATA**, or **SQL_DEFAULT_PARAM**.

■ The amount of data sent to the data source by this function can vary for a given parameter or column.

■ A data-at-execution parameter or column can be bound to a Unicode C data type, even if the underlying driver does not support Unicode data.

Prerequisites The **SQLParamData()** function must be executed before this function is called.

Restrictions This function can be called multiple times to send large data values to the data source in several small pieces—but only when sending character or binary data to a column with a character, binary, or data source-specific data type. If this function is called multiple times under any other conditions, **SQL_ERROR** and SQLSTATE **HY**019 (Non-character and non-binary data sent in pieces) are returned.

See Also SQLParamData(), SSQLCancel(), QLBindParameter(), SQLSetParam(), SQLBindCol(), SQLExecute(), SQLExecDirect(), SQLBulkOperations(), SQLSetPos()

Example See the example provided for the **SQLParamData()** function on page 414.

SQLCancel

COMPATABILITY					
X/OPEN 95 CLI	ISO/IEC 92 CLI	ODBC 1.0	ODBC 2.0	ODBC 3.0	ODBC 3.5
✓	✓	✓	✓	✓	✓

API CONFORMANCE LEVEL   **CORE**

Purpose The **SQLCancel()** function is used to terminate SQL statement processing.

Syntax SQLRETURN SQLCancel (SQLHSTMT   *StatementHandle*);

Parameters *StatementHandle*   An SQL statement handle that refers to a previously allocated SQL statement information storage buffer (data structure).

Description The **SQLCancel()** function is used to terminate SQL statement processing. Specifically, the this function is used to end the following:

- A function running asynchronously for an SQL statement.
- A *data-at-execution* sequence.
- A function running on another thread.

CANCELING ASYNCHRONOUS PROCESSING When an application executes a function asynchronously, the driver performs a minimal amount of processing (such as checking arguments for errors), hands the rest of the processing to the data source, and returns control to the application, along with the **SQL_STILL_EXECUTING** return code. The application is then free to perform other tasks; however it must poll the driver at regular intervals, by calling the function with the same arguments that were originally used, to determine when the asynchronous function is finished.

After the driver returns **SQL_STILL_EXECUTING** and before it returns a return code indicating the function has completed execution, the **SQLCancel()** function can be called to try to terminate the function's execution. Unfortunately, when **SQLCancel()** is called, there is no guarantee that function execution was actually canceled; the return code returned by **SQLCancel()** only indicates whether **SQLCancel()** successfully attempted to cancel the function. The only way an application can determine whether the asynchronous function's processing was canceled is by polling the driver after **SQLCancel()** is called. If the function was canceled, the driver returns **SQL_ERROR** and SQLSTATE **HY**008 (Operation canceled).

CANCELING A DATA-AT-EXECUTION SEQUENCE *Data-at-execution* parameters and columns are bound to application variables at the same time other parameters or columns are bound to application variables; however, with data-at-execution parameter and columns the value **SQL_DATA_AT_EXEC**, instead of the data value size, is specified during the binding process. When an application calls **SQLExecute()**, **SQLExecDirect()** (to execute the SQL statement), **SQLBulkOperations()**, or **SQLSetPos()** (to add/update a row of data), the driver returns **SQL_NEED_DATA** when it encounters a data-at-execution parameter or column. The application then calls the **SQLParamData()** function to determine which data it should send.

Once the application knows what data to send, it calls the **SQLPutData()** function repeatedly until all the data-at-execution data for the parameter or column has been sent to the driver. After all data has been sent, the application calls the **SQLParamData()** function again to inform the driver that all the requested data has been sent and to advance to the next data-at-execution parameter or column. If no more data-at-execution parameters or columns exist, the driver returns **SQL_SUCCESS** or **SQL_SUCCESS_WITH_INFO** to the application and the SQL statement is executed or the **SQLBulkOperations()** or **SQLSetPos()** function call is processed.

After the driver returns **SQL_NEED_DATA**, and before data has been sent for all data-at-execution parameters or columns, the **SQLCancel()** function can be called to terminate the data-at-execution sequence. After the data-at-execution sequence has been canceled, the **SQLExecute()**, **SQLExecDirect()**, **SQLBulkOperations()** or **SQLSetPos()** function can be called again; canceling a data-at-execution sequence has no effect on the SQL statement, the cursor state, or the current cursor position.

CANCELING FUNCTIONS IN MULTITHREAD APPLICATIONS

In a multithread application, an application can call an ODBC API function synchronously on another thread. An application can terminate a function running on a separate thread by calling **SQLCancel()** with the same statement handle that was used to invoke the target function. How the function is canceled depends on the driver and the operating system. As with asynchronous functions, the **SQLCancel()** function's return code only indicates whether the driver processed the request successfully. If the function is indeed canceled, it returns **SQL_ERROR** and SQLSTATE **HY**008 (Operation canceled).

If an SQL statement is being executed by the function that **SQLCancel()** is attempting to terminate, it's possible for both the SQL statement and the cancel operation to execute successfully and return **SQL_SUCCESS**. In this case, the ODBC Driver Manager assumes that any cursor opened by the SQL statement during execution was closed by the cancel operation. The result of this is that the application is no longer able to use the cursor.

Return Codes SQL_SUCCESS, SQL_SUCCESS_WITH_INFO, SQL_INVALID_HANDLE, or SQL_ERROR

SQLSTATEs If this function returns **SQL_SUCCESS_WITH_INFO** or **SQL_ERROR**, one of the following SQLSTATE values may be obtained by calling the **SQLGetDiagRec()** function (ODBC 3.x driver) or the **SQLError()** function (ODBC 2.0 or earlier driver):

ODBC 3.X
01000, **HY**000, **HY**001, **HY**013, **HY**018, **HYT**01, or **IM**001*

ODBC 2.0 OR EARLIER
01000, **70**100, **IM**001*, **S1**000, or **S1**001

*Returned by the ODBC Driver Manager.

Unless noted otherwise, each of these SQLSTATE values are returned by the data source driver. Refer to Appendix B for detailed information about each SQLSTATE value that can be returned by the ODBC Driver Manager or by a data source driver.

Comments

■ In ODBC 2.0, if an application calls **SQLCancel()** when no processing is being done on the statement, handle specific **SQLCancel()** has the same effect as **SQLFreeStmt()** with the **SQL_CLOSE** option specified; this behavior is defined only for completeness, and applications should call **SQLFreeStmt()** or **SQLCloseCursor()** to close cursors. In ODBC 3.x, this is not the case; a call to **SQLCancel()** when no processing is being done on the statement handle has no effect at all. To close a cursor, an application should call **SQLCloseCursor()**, not **SQLCancel()**.

■ When this function is called, diagnostic records are returned for a function running asynchronously on the statement handle specified or for a function on the statement handle specified that needs data; diagnostic records are not returned, however, for a function running on a statement handle on another thread.

Prerequisites   There are no prerequisites for using this function call.

Restrictions   There are no restrictions associated with this function call.

See Also   **SQLPutData()**, **SQLParamData()**, **SQLExecute()**, **SQLExecDirect()**

Example   See the example provided for the **SQLParamData()** function on page 414.

SQLEndTran

COMPATABILITY

X/OPEN 95 CLI	ISO/IEC 92 CLI	ODBC 1.0	ODBC 2.0	ODBC 3.0	ODBC 3.5
✓	✓	☐	☐	✓	✓

API CONFORMANCE LEVEL	CORE

Purpose   The `SQLEndTran()` function is used to request a commit or a rollback operation for all active transactions associated with a specific environment or connection handle.

Syntax

```
SQLRETURN   SQLEndTran   (SQLSMALLINT    HandleType,
                          SQLHANDLE      Handle,
                          SQLSMALLINT    Action);
```

Parameters   *HandleType*

Specifies which type of handle to request a commit or rollback operation for. This parameter must be set to one of the following values:

▪ **SQL_HANDLE_ENV**
This value requests a commit or rollback operation for an environment handle.

▪ **SQL_HANDLE_DBC**
This value requests a commit or rollback operation for a connection handle.

Handle

The environment or connection handle whose transaction(s) are to be terminated.

Action

The action to use to terminate the current transaction. This parameter must be set to one of the following values:

▪ **SQL_COMMIT**
Terminate the current transaction and make all changes made to the data source by that transaction permanent.

■ **SQL_ROLLBACK**
Terminate the current transaction and back out (remove) all changes made to the data source by that transaction.

Description   The **SQLEndTran()** function is used to request a commit or a rollback operation for all active transactions associated with a specific connection handle. This function can also request that a commit or rollback operation be performed for all active transactions found on all connections associated with a specific environment handle. When this function is called, all changes made to the data source (via the specified connection or environment handle) since the connection was established or since the last call to the **SQLEndTran()** function was made (whichever is the most recent) are either committed or rolled back.

A transaction ends when the application calls this function—all active transactions associated with a data source connection must be ended before the connection to the data source can be terminated.

NOTE: *In ODBC 3.x, this function replaces the ODBC 2.0 function* **SQLTransact()**.

Return Codes   **SQL_SUCCESS, SQL_SUCCESS_WITH_INFO, SQL_INVALID_HANDLE**, or **SQL_ERROR**

SQLSTATEs   If this function returns **SQL_ERROR**, one of the following SQLSTATE values may be obtained by calling the **SQLGetDiagRec()** function:

01000, **08**003*, **08**007, **25S01**, **25S02**, **25S03**, **40001**, **40002**, **HY**000, **HY**001, **HY**010*, **HY**012*, **HY**013, **HY**092*, **HYC**00, **HYT01**, or **IM**001*

*Returned by the ODBC Driver Manager.

Unless noted otherwise, each of these SQLSTATE values are returned by the data source driver. Refer to Appendix B for detailed information about each SQLSTATE value that can be returned by the ODBC Driver Manager or by a data source driver.

Comments   ■ This function cannot be used to commit or roll back transactions on a shared environment. If this function is called with either a shared environment handle or a shared environment's connection handle specified in the *Handle* parameter, **SQL_ERROR** and SQLSTATE **HY**092 (Invalid attribute/option identifier) will be returned.

■ If a valid environment handle is specified in the *Handle* parameter, the ODBC Driver Manager attempts to commit or roll back each active transaction found on all connection handles that are in the "Connected" state by calling the **SQLTransact()** function in the driver associated with each connection handle. The Driver Manager only returns **SQL_SUCCESS** if it receives **SQL_SUCCESS** from the driver associated with each connection handle found. If the Driver Manager receives **SQL_ERROR** from one or more connection handles, it returns **SQL_ERROR** to the application. The **SQLGetDiagRec()** function can then be called on each connection handle to determine which connection(s) failed during the commit or rollback operation.

■ The ODBC Driver Manager does not simulate a global transaction across all connection handles and, therefore, does not use two-phase commit protocols. (A two-phase commit is generally used to commit transactions that are spread across multiple data sources. In its first phase, the data sources are polled to determine to whether they can commit their part of the transaction. In the second phase, the transaction is actually committed on all data sources. If any data sources reply in the first phase that they cannot commit the transaction, the second phase does not occur.)

■ If the *Action* parameter is set to **SQL_COMMIT**, this function issues a commit request for all active operations on all statement handles associated with an affected connection handle.

■ If the *Action* parameter is set to **SQL_ROLLBACK**, this function issues a rollback request for all active operations on all statement handles associated with an affected connection handle.

■ If no transactions are active when this function is called, **SQL_SUCCESS** is returned (indicating that there is no work to be committed or rolled back) and the drivers/data sources being used are not affected—provided the drivers and/or data sources being used support transactions.

■ An application can call the **SQLGetInfo()** function with the **SQL_CURSOR_COMMIT_BEHAVIOR** and **SQL_CURSOR_ROLLBACK_BEHAVIOR** information type values specified to determine how transaction operations affect cursor behavior. If either of these information types return **SQL_CB_DELETE**, all open cursors on all statement handles associated with the connection handle are closed and deleted (and pending results are discarded) when this function is executed—SQL statement handles are left in the "Allocated" (unprepared) state and the application can either reuse them or free them.

- If the **SQL_CURSOR_COMMIT_BEHAVIOR** or **SQL_CURSOR_ROLLBACK_BEHAVIOR** information types return **SQL_CB_CLOSE**, all open cursors on all statement handles associated with the connection handle are closed and SQL statement handles are left in the "Prepared" state; the application can execute the SQL statement associated with the statement handle by calling the **SQLExecute()** function without calling the **SQLPrepare()** function first.

- If the **SQL_CURSOR_COMMIT_BEHAVIOR** or **SQL_CURSOR_ROLLBACK_BEHAVIOR** information types return **SQL_CB_PRESERVE**, open cursors associated with the connection handle are not affected by this function—cursors remain where they were before this function was called.

- Drivers and data sources that do not support transactions are effectively always in autocommit mode. In this case, if this function is called with the *Action* parameter set to **SQL_COMMIT**, **SQL_SUCCESS** is returned; if this function is called with the *Action* parameter set to **SQL_ROLLBACK**, **SQL_ERROR** and SQLSTATE **HYC00** (Driver not capable) is returned, indicating that a rollback operation can not be performed.

- If the *HandleType* parameter is set to **SQL_HANDLE_ENV**, and a valid environment handle is specified in the *Handle* parameter, the ODBC Driver Manager calls the **SQLEndTran()** function in each ODBC 3.x driver associated with the environment (the *Handle* parameter of each driver-specific **SQLEndTran()** function will be set to the driver's environment handle before the function is called). The driver attempts to commit or roll back transactions in the "Connected" state on all connections in the environment. However, it is important to realize that neither the driver(s) nor the Driver Manager performs a two-phase commit on the connections in the environment; this is merely a programming convenience to simultaneously call the **SQLEndTran()** function for all connections in the environment. Inactive connections do not affect the transaction.

- If the *HandleType* parameter is set to **SQL_HANDLE_ENV** and a valid environment handle is specified in the *Handle* parameter, and there are multiple connections in a "Connected" state in the specified environment, the ODBC Driver Manager calls the **SQLTransact()** function in each ODBC 2.0 driver once for each connection that is in a "Connected" state in that environment (the *ConnectionHandle* parameter of each driver-specific **SQLTransact()** function will be set to the driver's connection handle before the function is called). The driver attempts to commit or roll back transactions in the "Connected" state. Inactive connections do not affect the transaction.

Prerequisites   There are no prerequisites for using this function call.

Restrictions   There are no restrictions associated with this function call.

See Also   `SQLSetStmtOption()`, `SQLGetInfo()`, `SQLFreeStmt()`, `SQLFreeHandle()`

Example   The following Visual C++ program illustrates how to use the `SQLEndTran()` function to terminate a transaction.

```
/*---------------------------------------------------------------------*/
/* NAME:      CH9EX11.CPP                                              */
/* PURPOSE: Illustrate How To Use The Following ODBC API Function      */
/*          In A C++ Program:                                          */
/*                                                                     */
/*                 SQLEndTran()                                        */
/*                                                                     */
/* OTHER ODBC APIs SHOWN:                                              */
/*          SQLAllocHandle()        SQLSetEnvAttr()                    */
/*          SQLConnect()            SQLSetConnectAttr()                */
/*          SQLExecDirect()         SQLBindCol()                       */
/*          SQLFetch()              SQLDisconnect()                    */
/*          SQLFreeHandle()                                            */
/*                                                                     */
/*---------------------------------------------------------------------*/

// Include The Appropriate Header Files
#include <windows.h>
#include <sql.h>
#include <sqlext.h>
#include <iostream.h>

// Define The ODBC_Class Class
class ODBC_Class
{
    // Attributes
    public:
        SQLHANDLE    EnvHandle;
        SQLHANDLE    ConHandle;
        SQLHANDLE    StmtHandle;
        SQLRETURN    rc;

    // Operations
    public:
        ODBC_Class();                          // Constructor
        ~ODBC_Class();                         // Destructor
```

```
            SQLRETURN ShowResults();
};

// Define The Class Constructor
ODBC_Class::ODBC_Class()
{
    // Initialize The Return Code Variable
    rc = SQL_SUCCESS;

    // Allocate An Environment Handle
    rc = SQLAllocHandle(SQL_HANDLE_ENV, SQL_NULL_HANDLE, &EnvHandle);

    // Set The ODBC Application Version To 3.x
    if (rc == SQL_SUCCESS)
        rc = SQLSetEnvAttr(EnvHandle, SQL_ATTR_ODBC_VERSION,
                    (SQLPOINTER) SQL_OV_ODBC3, SQL_IS_UINTEGER);

    // Allocate A Connection Handle
    if (rc == SQL_SUCCESS)
        rc = SQLAllocHandle(SQL_HANDLE_DBC, EnvHandle, &ConHandle);
}

// Define The Class Destructor
ODBC_Class::~ODBC_Class()
{
    // Free The Connection Handle
    if (ConHandle != NULL)
        SQLFreeHandle(SQL_HANDLE_DBC, ConHandle);

    // Free The Environment Handle
    if (EnvHandle != NULL)
        SQLFreeHandle(SQL_HANDLE_ENV, EnvHandle);
}

// Define The ShowResults() Member Function
SQLRETURN ODBC_Class::ShowResults(void)
{
    // Declare The Local Memory Variables
    SQLCHAR   LastName[50];
    SQLCHAR   FirstName[50];

    // Bind The Columns In The Result Data Set Returned To
    // Application Variables
    rc = SQLBindCol(StmtHandle, 1, SQL_C_CHAR, (SQLPOINTER)
            LastName, sizeof(LastName), NULL);

    rc = SQLBindCol(StmtHandle, 2, SQL_C_CHAR, (SQLPOINTER)
            FirstName, sizeof(FirstName), NULL);

    // Display A Header
    cout << "Employees :" << endl << endl;

    // While There Are Records In The Result Data Set Generated,
    // Retrieve And Display Them
    while (rc != SQL_NO_DATA)
```

```
    {
        rc = SQLFetch(StmtHandle);
        if (rc != SQL_NO_DATA)
            cout << FirstName << " " << LastName << endl;
    }

    // Return The ODBC API Return Code To The Calling Function
    return(rc);
}

/*-----------------------------------------------------------*/
/* The Main Function                                         */
/*-----------------------------------------------------------*/
int main()
{
    // Declare The Local Memory Variables
    SQLRETURN   rc = SQL_SUCCESS;
    SQLCHAR     DBName[10] = "Northwind";
    SQLCHAR     SQLStmt[255];

    // Create An Instance Of The ODBC_Class Class
    ODBC_Class   Example;

    // Connect To The Northwind Sample Database
    if (Example.ConHandle != NULL)
    {
        rc = SQLConnect(Example.ConHandle, DBName, SQL_NTS,
                (SQLCHAR *) "", SQL_NTS, (SQLCHAR *) "", SQL_NTS);

        // Allocate An SQL Statement Handle
        rc = SQLAllocHandle(SQL_HANDLE_STMT, Example.ConHandle,
                &Example.StmtHandle);
        if (rc == SQL_SUCCESS)
        {
            // Turn Manual-Commit Mode On
            rc = SQLSetConnectAttr(Example.ConHandle,
                    SQL_ATTR_AUTOCOMMIT,
                    (SQLPOINTER) SQL_AUTOCOMMIT_OFF,
                    SQL_IS_UINTEGER);

            // Define A SELECT SQL Statement
            strcpy((char *) SQLStmt, "SELECT Employees.LastName, ");
            strcat((char *) SQLStmt, "Employees.FirstName FROM ");
            strcat((char *) SQLStmt, "Employees");

            // Prepare And Execute The SQL Statement
            rc = SQLExecDirect(Example.StmtHandle, SQLStmt, SQL_NTS);

            // Display The Results Of The SQL Query
            if (rc == SQL_SUCCESS)
                Example.ShowResults();

            // Commit The Transaction
```

```
        rc = SQLEndTran(SQL_HANDLE_DBC, Example.ConHandle, SQL_COMMIT);

        // Free The SQL Statement Handle
        if (Example.StmtHandle != NULL)
            SQLFreeHandle(SQL_HANDLE_STMT, Example.StmtHandle);
    }

    // Disconnect From The Northwind Sample Database
    rc = SQLDisconnect(Example.ConHandle);
}

// Return To The Operating System
return(rc);
}
```

SQLTransact

COMPATABILITY

X/OPEN 95 CLI	ISO/IEC 92 CLI	ODBC 1.0	ODBC 2.0	ODBC 3.0	ODBC 3.5
☒	☐	✓	✓	☐	☐

API CONFORMANCE LEVEL   **CORE**

Purpose   The **SQLTransact()** function is used to request a commit or a rollback operation for all active transactions associated with a specific environment or connection handle.

Syntax
```
SQLRETURN    SQLTransact    (HENV      EnvironmentHandle,
                             HDBC      ConnectionHandle,
                             UWORD     Action);
```

Parameters   *EnvironmentHandle*   An environment handle that refers to a previously allocated environment information storage buffer (data structure).

                 ConnectionHandle   A data source connection handle that refers to a previously allocated connection information storage buffer (data structure).

Action   The action to use to terminate the current
                            transaction. This parameter must be set to
                            one of the following values:

▨ **SQL_COMMIT**
Terminate the current transaction and
make all changes made to the data
source by that transaction permanent.

▨ **SQL_ROLLBACK**
Terminate the current transaction and
back out (remove) all changes made to
the data source by that transaction.

Description   The **SQLTransact()** function is used to request a commit or a rollback
operation for all active transactions associated with a specific connection
handle. This function can also request that a commit or rollback operation
be performed for all active transactions found on all connections
associated with a specific environment handle. When this function is
called, all changes made to the data source (via the specified connection
or environment handle) since the connection was established or since the
last call to the **SQLTransact()** function was made (whichever is the most
recent) are either committed or rolled back.

A transaction ends when the application calls this function. All active
transactions associated with a data source connection, must be ended before the connection to the data source can be terminated.

NOTE: *In ODBC 3.x, this function has been replaced by the* **SQLEndTran()**
function.

Return Codes   SQL_SUCCESS, SQL_SUCCESS_WITH_INFO, SQL_INVALID_HANDLE, or
SQL_ERROR

SQLSTATEs   If this function returns **SQL_SUCCESS_WITH_INFO** or **SQL_ERROR**, one of the
following SQLSTATE values may be obtained by calling the **SQLError()**
function:

01000, **08**003*, **08**007, **IM**001*, **S1**000, **S1**001, **S1**010*, **S1**012*, or **S1**C00

*Returned by the ODBC Driver Manager.

Unless noted otherwise, each of these SQLSTATE values are returned
by the data source driver. Refer to Appendix B for detailed information

about each SQLSTATE value that can be returned by the ODBC Driver Manager or by a data source driver.

Comments

■ If the *ConnectionHandle* parameter contains the value **SQL_NULL_ HDBC**, the *EnvironmentHandle* parameter must contain the environment handle with which the connection is associated.

■ If the *ConnectionHandle* parameter contains the value **SQL_NULL_ HDBC**, and the *EnvironmentHandle* parameter contains a valid environment handle, the ODBC Driver Manager attempts to commit or roll back transactions on all connection handles that are in the "Connected" state by calling the **SQLTransact()** function in the driver associated with each connection handle. The Driver Manager only returns **SQL_SUCCESS** if it receives **SQL_SUCCESS** from the driver associated with each connection handle found. If the Driver Manager receives **SQL_ERROR** from one or more connection handles, it returns **SQL_ERROR** to the application. The **SQLError()** function can then be called on each connection handle to determine which connection(s) failed during the commit or rollback operation.

■ If the *ConnectionHandle* parameter contains the value **SQL_NULL_ HDBC**, and the *EnvironmentHandle* parameter contains a valid environment handle, a commit or rollback operation is performed on each active transaction found on each open connection in the environment. In this case, **SQL_SUCCESS** is only returned to the application if **SQL_SUCCESS** is returned by all affected connections. If the commit or rollback operation fails for one or more of the open connections, **SQL_ERROR** is returned to the calling application. The **SQLError()** function will then need to be called on each connection handle in the environment to determine which connection(s) failed during the commit or rollback operation.

■ The ODBC Driver Manager does not simulate a global transaction across all connection handles and, therefore, does not use two-phase commit protocols.

■ If the *ConnectionHandle* parameter contains a valid connection handle, the *EnvironmentHandle* parameter is ignored and the ODBC Driver Manager calls the **SQLTransact()** function in the driver for the specified connection handle.

■ If the *ConnectionHandle* parameter contains the value **SQL_NULL_ HDBC** and if the *EnvironmentHandle* parameter contains the value **SQL_NULL_HENV**, **SQL_INVALID_HANDLE** is returned when this function is executed.

■ If the *Action* parameter is set to **SQL_COMMIT**, this function issues a commit request for all active operations on all statement handles associated with an affected connection handle.

■ If the *Action* parameter is set to **SQL_ROLLBACK**, this function issues a rollback request for all active operations on all statement handles associated with an affected connection handle.

■ If no transactions are active when this function is called, **SQL_SUCCESS** is returned (indicating that there is no work to be committed or rolled back) and the drivers/data sources being used are not affected—provided the drivers and/or data sources being used support transactions.

■ An application can call the **SQLGetInfo()** function with the **SQL_CURSOR_COMMIT_BEHAVIOR** and **SQL_CURSOR_ROLLBACK_BEHAVIOR** information type values specified to determine how transaction operations affect cursor behavior. If either of these information types return **SQL_CB_DELETE**, all open cursors on all statement handles associated with the connection handle are closed and deleted (and pending results are discarded) when this function is executed—SQL statement handles are left in the "Allocated" (unprepared) state and the application can either reuse them or free them.

■ If the **SQL_CURSOR_COMMIT_BEHAVIOR** or **SQL_CURSOR_ROLLBACK_BEHAVIOR** information types return **SQL_CB_CLOSE**, all open cursors on all statement handles associated with the connection handle are closed and SQL statement handles are left in the "Prepared" state; the application can execute the SQL statement associated with the statement handle by calling the **SQLExecute()** function without calling the **SQLPrepare()** function first.

■ If the **SQL_CURSOR_COMMIT_BEHAVIOR** or **SQL_CURSOR_ROLLBACK_BEHAVIOR** information types return **SQL_CB_PRESERVE**, open cursors associated with the connection handle are not affected by this function—cursors remain where they were before this function was called.

■ Drivers and data sources that do not support transactions are effectively always in autocommit mode. In this case, if this function is called with the *Action* parameter set to **SQL_COMMIT**, **SQL_SUCCESS** is returned; if this function is called with the *Action* parameter set to **SQL_ROLLBACK**, **SQL_ERROR** and SQLSTATE **S1C00** (Driver not capable) are returned, indicating that a rollback operation can not be performed.

Prerequisites   There are no prerequisites for using this function call.

Restrictions   There are no restrictions associated with this function call.

See Also   `SQLSetStmtOption()`, `SQLGetInfo()`, `SQLFreeStmt()`, `SQLFreeHandle()`

Example   The following Visual C++ program illustrates how to use the `SQLTransact()` function to terminate a transaction.

```
/*-------------------------------------------------------------------*/
/* NAME:     CH9EX12.CPP                                            */
/* PURPOSE: Illustrate How To Use The Following ODBC API Function   */
/*          In A C++ Program:                                       */
/*                                                                  */
/*              SQLTransact()                                       */
/*                                                                  */
/* OTHER ODBC APIs SHOWN:                                           */
/*          SQLAllocEnv()           SQLAllocConnect()               */
/*          SQLConnect()            SQLSetConnectOption()           */
/*          SQLAllocStmt()          SQLExecDirect()                 */
/*          SQLBindCol()            SQLFetch()                      */
/*          SQLDisconnect()         SQLFreeStmt()                   */
/*          SQLFreeConnect()        SQLFreeEnv()                    */
/*                                                                  */
/*-------------------------------------------------------------------*/

// Include The Appropriate Header Files
#include <windows.h>
#include <sql.h>
#include <sqlext.h>
#include <iostream.h>

// Define The ODBC_Class Class
class ODBC_Class
{
    // Attributes
    public:
        HENV        EnvHandle;
        HDBC        ConHandle;
        HSTMT       StmtHandle;
        RETCODE     rc;

    // Operations
    public:
        ODBC_Class();                           // Constructor
        ~ODBC_Class();                          // Destructor
        RETCODE     ShowResults();
};

// Define The Class Constructor
```

```
ODBC_Class::ODBC_Class()
{
    // Initialize The Return Code Variable
    rc = SQL_SUCCESS;

    // Allocate An Environment Handle
    rc = SQLAllocEnv(&EnvHandle);

    // Allocate A Connection Handle
    if (rc == SQL_SUCCESS)
        rc = SQLAllocConnect(EnvHandle, &ConHandle);
}

// Define The Class Destructor
ODBC_Class::~ODBC_Class()
{
    // Free The Connection Handle
    if (ConHandle != NULL)
        SQLFreeConnect(ConHandle);

    // Free The Environment Handle
    if (EnvHandle != NULL)
        SQLFreeEnv(EnvHandle);
}

// Define The ShowResults() Member Function
RETCODE ODBC_Class::ShowResults(void)
{
    // Declare The Local Memory Variables
    SQLCHAR  ProductName[50];

    // Bind The Columns In The Result Data Set Returned To
    // Application Variables
    rc = SQLBindCol(StmtHandle, 1, SQL_C_CHAR, (SQLPOINTER)
            ProductName, sizeof(ProductName), NULL);

    // Display A Header
    cout << "Product Name :" << endl << endl;

    // While There Are Records In The Result Data Set Generated,
    // Retrieve And Display Them
    while (rc != SQL_NO_DATA_FOUND)
    {
        rc = SQLFetch(StmtHandle);
        if (rc != SQL_NO_DATA_FOUND)
            cout << ProductName << endl;
    }

    // Return The ODBC API Return Code To The Calling Function
    return(rc);
}

/*------------------------------------------------------------*/
/* The Main Function                                          */
/*------------------------------------------------------------*/
```

```
int main()
{
    // Declare The Local Memory Variables
    RETCODE   rc = SQL_SUCCESS;
    SQLCHAR   DBName[10] = "Northwind";
    SQLCHAR   SQLStmt[255];

    // Create An Instance Of The ODBC_Class Class
    ODBC_Class   Example;

    // Connect To The Northwind Sample Database
    if (Example.ConHandle != NULL)
    {
        rc = SQLConnect(Example.ConHandle, DBName, SQL_NTS,
                (SQLCHAR *) "", SQL_NTS, (SQLCHAR *) "", SQL_NTS);

        // Allocate An SQL Statement Handle
        rc = SQLAllocStmt(Example.ConHandle, &Example.StmtHandle);
        if (rc == SQL_SUCCESS)
        {
            // Turn Manual-Commit Mode On
            rc = SQLSetConnectOption(Example.ConHandle,
                    SQL_AUTOCOMMIT, (UDWORD) SQL_AUTOCOMMIT_OFF);

            // Define A SELECT SQL Statement
            strcpy((char *) SQLStmt, "SELECT Employees.LastName, ");
            strcat((char *) SQLStmt, "Employees.FirstName FROM ");
            strcat((char *) SQLStmt, "Employees");

            // Prepare And Execute The SQL Statement
            SQLExecDirect(Example.StmtHandle, SQLStmt, SQL_NTS);

            // Display The Results Of The SQL Query
            if (rc == SQL_SUCCESS)
                Example.ShowResults();

            // Commit The Transaction
            rc = SQLTransact(Example.EnvHandle, Example.ConHandle,
                    SQL_COMMIT);

            // Free The SQL Statement Handle
            if (Example.StmtHandle != NULL)
                SQLFreeStmt(Example.StmtHandle, SQL_DROP);
        }

        // Disconnect From The Northwind Sample Database
        rc = SQLDisconnect(Example.ConHandle);
    }

    // Return To The Operating System
    return(rc);
}
```

SQLFreeStmt

COMPATABILITY					
X/OPEN 95 CLI	ISO/IEC 92 CLI	ODBC 1.0	ODBC 2.0	ODBC 3.0	ODBC 3.5
☒	☑	☑	☑	☐	☐

API CONFORMANCE LEVEL **CORE**

Purpose   The **SQLFreeStmt()** function is used to stop all processing associated with a specific SQL statement handle, discard all pending results, close any open cursors, and free all memory associated with a statement handle.

Syntax   SQLRETURN SQLFreeStmt (HSTMT   *StatementHandle,*
                                    UWORD   *Option);*

Parameters   *StatementHandle*   An SQL statement handle that refers to a previously allocated SQL statement information storage buffer (data structure).

Option   The method to use when freeing the SQL statement handle. This parameter must be set to one of the following values:

■ **SQL_CLOSE**
Close all cursors associated with the SQL statement handle and discard any pending results. In this case, the SQL statement handle itself is not destroyed.

■ **SQL_DROP**
Close all cursors associated with the SQL statement handle, discard any pending results, and free all resources associated with the SQL statement handle. In this case, the SQL statement handle is destroyed and must be re-allocated before it can be used again.

■ **SQL_UNBIND**
Unbind (release) all column buffers currently bound to the SQL statement handle.

■ **SQL_RESET_PARAMS**
Release all parameter marker buffer bound to the SQL statement handle.

Description

The **SQLFreeStmt()** function invalidates and frees or re-initializes an SQL statement handle. When this function is invoked one or more of the following take place:

■ All processing being done by the SQL statement associated with the SQL statement handle is stopped.

■ All open cursors associated with the SQL statement handle are closed.

■ All parameter bindings are reset.

■ All result data set columns that have been bound to application variables are unbound.

■ All ODBC resources associated with the SQL statement handle are freed and the SQL statement handle is deleted (dropped).

This function should be called for each SQL statement handle created with the **SQLAllocStmt()** function when all processing associated with that SQL statement handle has been completed.

NOTE: *In ODBC 3.x, this function has been replaced by the* **SQLFreeHandle()** *function.*

Return Codes   SQL_SUCCESS, SQL_SUCCESS_WITH_INFO, SQL_INVALID_HANDLE, or SQL_ERROR

SQLSTATEs

If this function returns **SQL_SUCCESS_WITH_INFO** or **SQL_ERROR**, one of the following SQLSTATE values may be obtained by calling the **SQLError()** function:

01000, **IM**001*, **S1**000, **S1**001, **S1**010*, or **S1**092*

*Returned by the ODBC Driver Manager.

Unless noted otherwise, each of these SQLSTATE values are returned by the data source driver. Refer to Appendix B for detailed information about each SQLSTATE value that can be returned by the ODBC Driver Manager or by a data source driver.

Comments

■ An application can call this function to terminate processing of a **SELECT** SQL statement without freeing the statement handle.

■ The **SQL_DROP** option frees all resources allocated by the **SQLAllocStmt()** function.

Prerequisites

There are no prerequisites for using this function call.

Restrictions

There are no restrictions associated with this function call.

See Also

SQLEndTran(), **SQLAllocStmt()**, **SQLAllocHandle()**, **SQLCancel()**

Example

See the example provided for the **SQLAllocStmt()** function on page 342.

10

Retrieving Results (Basic)

When **SELECT** SQL statements, stored procedures containing **SELECT** SQL statements, or an ODBC catalog function is submitted to a data source for execution, a conceptual table, known as a *result data set* is created and populated with all data from the data source that matches the selection criteria specified. The process of retrieving rows of data from a result data set and returning them to an application, in tabular form, is called *fetching*. This chapter is designed to introduce you to the basic set of API functions used to fetch data from a result data set.

This chapter begins by examining the *metadata* that is used to describe a result data set. This is followed by an introduction to the functions used to retrieve metadata information and return it to an application. Next, the process of associating (binding) application variables and buffers to columns in a result data set is described. Then, the basic *cursor* is introduced, along with the functions used to retrieve and set the name of the cursor associated with a result data set. This is followed by an introduction to the function used to fetch a row of data from a result data set and return results to all *bound* variables. Next, the function used to obtain data values from *unbound* columns in a result data set is discussed. Finally, a detailed reference section covering each ODBC API function that can be used to obtain result data set metadata and perform basic data retrieval is provided.

Was A Result Data Set Created ?

When an application contains hard-coded SQL statements, the application developer usually knows whether one or more of the SQL statements used will generate a result data set. However, when an application constructs SQL statements at run time, the developer does not always know when a result data set will be created. This is particularly true if the application provides a way for users to enter and execute customized SQL statements. It is also true when an application constructs an SQL statement at run time that calls a stored procedure.

In both cases, an application can call the **SQLNumResultCols()** function to determine whether a result data set was produced when an SQL statement was executed; if the **SQLNumResultCols()** function returns **0**, no result data set was produced. If a result data set was produced, the **SQLNumResultCols()** function returns the number of columns that exist in the result data set created to the calling application.

Result Data Set Metadata

Before data in a result data set can be returned to an application, the characteristics of that result data set must be known. These characteristics are stored as *metadata*, which is simply data that describes other data. Result data set metadata contains detailed information about the result data set, including the number of columns in the result data set, the data types of each of those columns, their names, precision, nullability, and so on. Inter-operable applications should always check the metadata of result data set columns. That's because the metadata for a column in a result data set might differ from the metadata returned for the same column by a catalog function. Even data types can be different because the data source might alter the data type when it creates the result data set.

Applications need the information stored in metadata to perform most result data set operations. For example, an application needs to know the data type of a column in order to bind a variable of the appropriate data type to that column. How metadata is obtained for a result data set is dependent on application design:

- Vertical applications work with predefined tables and perform predefined operations on those tables. Because the result data set metadata for such applications is defined before the application is written and is controlled by the application developer, it can be hard-coded into the application. For example, if a column is defined as a 4-byte integer in the data source, the application can always bind a 4-byte integer to that column. When metadata is hard-coded in the application, a change to the tables used by the application generally implies a change to the application code. This is rarely a problem because such changes are generally made as part of a new release of the application.

- Like vertical applications, custom applications generally work with predefined tables and perform predefined operations on those tables. Again, because the result data set metadata for such applications is defined before the application is written, it is often hard-coded directly into the application.

- Generic applications, especially applications that enable the user to specify ad-hoc queries, rarely know the metadata of the result data sets they create. Because the result data set metadata is not known in advance, it must be obtained at application run time.

All applications, regardless of how they are designed, can hard-code the metadata for result data sets returned by ODBC catalog functions.

Obtaining Metadata Information

Three functions, **SQLDescribeCol()**, **SQLColAttribute()** (ODBC 3.x drivers), and **SQLColAttributes()** (ODBC 2.0 or earlier drivers) can be used to obtain metadata for a result data set. The **SQLDescribeCol()** function returns five commonly used pieces of information about a column in a result data set (the column's name, data type, precision, scale, and nullability); the **SQLColAttribute()** and **SQLColAttributes()** functions only return a specific metadata value. However, when called multiple times, **SQLColAttribute()** or **SQLColAttributes()** can return a much richer selection of metadata values, including the column's case sensitivity, display size, updatability, and the ability to be used in an SQL statement **WHERE** clause. In addition, **SQLColAttribute()** and **SQLColAttributes()** can obtain driver-specific metadata; that is, a column's driver-specific C and SQL data types, descriptor types, information types, diagnostic types, and attributes.

Many applications, especially ones that only display data, only need the metadata returned by the **SQLDescribeCol()** function. Other applications, particularly applications that update data, need the additional metadata that can be returned by the **SQLColAttribute()** or **SQLColAttributes()** function. Often, applications call the **SQLDescribeCol()** function to obtain basic metadata information, and follow it with one or more **SQLColAttribute()** (ODBC 3.x drivers) or **SQLColAttributes()** (ODBC 2.0 or earlier drivers) function calls to retrieve additional specific metadata information.

An application can retrieve result set metadata at any time after an SQL statement has been prepared or executed and before the cursor referencing the result data set is closed. However, very few applications actually need to acquire result data set metadata before an SQL statement is executed. In fact, it is good programming practice to wait until an SQL statement has been executed before trying to retrieve result data set metadata. The main reason for this is that some data sources cannot return metadata for prepared statements, and emulation of this operation by the driver is often a slow process.

Retrieving metadata from the data source is often an expensive process. Because of this, applications should only request the metadata they absolutely need.

Binding Result Data Set Columns

Just as application variables and/or memory buffers can be bound to parameter markers used in SQL statements, application variables and/or buffers can be bound to the columns of a result data set. Conceptually, the process is the same. When an application binds a variable to a column in the result data set, it describes that variable (its address, data type, etc.) to the driver. The driver stores this information in the structure it maintains for the statement handle and uses the information to retrieve the value from the column when a row of data is fetched, or when a positioned insert, update, or delete operation is performed.

An application can bind variables to as many or as few result data set columns as it wants (in fact, data can be retrieved from a result data set with no binding at all). Which result data set columns are bound and which columns are not is application dependent. For example, an application designed to generate a report would probably create a result data set containing all the columns used in the report and then bind application variables to and retrieve the data for all columns in the result data set. On the other hand, an application designed to display a screen full of data might allow the user to decide which information to display; such an application would most likely create a result data set containing all columns the user might want to display, then only bind application variables to and retrieve the data for columns in the result data set that were chosen by the user.

Because column bindings are just records containing information about an application variable or buffer associated with a result data set, and because they are independent of the result data set, they can be created in any order. For example, suppose an application binds application variables to the columns of the result data set generated by the following SQL statement:

```
SELECT * FROM Orders
```

If the application then executes the SQL statement:

```
SELECT * FROM Customers
```

using the same SQL statement handle, the column bindings for the first result data set remain in effect because those are the bindings that were stored in the data structure associated with the statement handle.

NOTE: *In most cases, this is poor programming practice and should be avoided. Applications should call the* **SQLFreeStmt()** *function with the* **SQL_UNBIND** *option specified to remove all column bindings associated with a statement handle before reusing that statement handle with a new SQL statement.*

Using SQLBindCol()

The SQLBindCol() function is used to bind application variables and/or buffers to columns in a result data set, one column at a time. Each time this function is called, the application specifies:

- The column number. Columns are numbered in increasing order in the result data set as they appear from left to right beginning with the number 1. If a bookmark column is included in the result data set, column number 0 is the bookmark column. If a column number higher than the actual number of columns in the result data set is specified, an error occurs; however, this kind of error will not be detected until the result data set is created, so it is returned by SQLFetch(), not SQLBindCol().

- The C data type, memory address, and size (length), in bytes, of the application variable being bound to the result data set column. The driver must be able to convert the data from the SQL data type used by the data source to the C data type specified (fetch operations) or from the C data type specified to the SQL data type used by the data source (positioned insert, update, and delete operations); otherwise, an error will occur. Again, this kind of error might not be detected until the result data set is created, so it is returned by SQLFetch(), not SQLBindCol().

- Optionally, the memory address of a length/indicator variable. This optional variable is used to obtain/set the byte length of binary or character data, or to determine/specify whether the data is NULL.

Once an application variable is bound to a column in a result data set, it remains bound until one of the following occurs:

- A different application variable is bound to the same column.
- The column is unbound. This is done by calling the SQLBindCol() function with a NULL pointer specified as the variable's address.
- All columns are unbound. This is done by calling the SQLFreeStmt() function with the SQL_UNBIND option specified.
- The statement handle associated with the SQL statement containing the parameter marker is released (freed).

The actual use of bound application variables is deferred; that is, they are bound to result data set columns with the SQLBindCol() function, but the driver accesses them from other functions—namely SQLFetch(),

`SQLFetchScroll()`, `SQLExtendedFetch()`, `SQLBulkOperations()`, or `SQLSetPos()`. Therefore, applications must ensure that bound variables remain valid (are not freed) as long as the binding remains in effect.

To bind a column to a different variable, an application simply rebinds the column with the new variable; the previous binding is automatically released. However, the new binding does not take effect until the next row of data is fetched—new bindings are not applied to rows that have already been fetched. For example, suppose an application binds the columns in a result data set to application variables and calls `SQLFetch()`. The driver automatically returns the data found in the first row of the result data set to the bound variables. Now suppose the application binds the columns to a different set of application variables. The driver does not place the data for the just-fetched row into the newly bound buffers. Instead, it waits until `SQLFetch()` is called again; then it returns the data found in the next row of the result data set to the newly bound variables.

Changing Parameter Bindings (And Values) With Offsets

ODBC 3.x applications can specify that an offset be added to a bound variable's address and to the corresponding length/indicator buffer address when `SQLFetch()`, `SQLFetchScroll()`, `SQLExtendedFetch()`, `SQLBulkOperations()`, or `SQLSetPos()` is called. This feature allows an application to change column bindings (and values) without calling the `SQLBindCol()` function to rebind previously bound result data set columns. When offsets are used, the original bindings represent a *template* of how the application buffers are laid out—the application can move this "template" to different areas of memory simply by changing the offset. New offsets can be specified at any time; each time an offset is specified, it is added to the originally bound buffer address. This means that offset additions are not cumulative—each offset specified cancels the previous offset used. It goes with out saying that the sum of the address and the offset must always be a valid address (either or both the offset and the address to which the offset is added, can be invalid, as long as the sum of the two is a valid address).

 NOTE: *Binding offsets are not supported by ODBC 2.0 and earlier drivers.*

Binding Columns to Arrays

In addition to using offsets to change column bindings, columns can also be bound to arrays. Because this type of binding is typically used in more advanced data retrieval operations, it is not discussed here. Instead, this information is presented in Chapter 11, "Results Retrieval (Advanced)".

Fetching Data

An application fetches (retrieves) rows from a result data set by using a *cursor*. The name cursor, as it applies to databases, probably originated from the blinking cursor found on a computer screen. Just as that cursor indicates the current position on the screen and identifies where typed words will appear next, a database cursor indicates the current position in the result data set and identifies what row of data will be returned to an application next.

The cursor model used in ODBC is based on the cursor model used in embedded SQL. However, one notable difference between these two models exists in how cursors are declared and opened. In embedded SQL, a cursor must be explicitly declared and opened before it can be used. In ODBC, a cursor is implicitly defined and opened whenever an SQL statement that creates a result data set is executed. In both cases, when a cursor is opened, it is positioned just before the first row of data in the result data set. Likewise, a cursor must be closed after an application has finished using it.

Unlike the cursors that are typically used in embedded SQL, ODBC cursors can have different characteristics. The most common type of cursor, known as a forward-only cursor, can only move forward through a result data set. Forward-only cursors provide a fast mechanism for making a single pass through a result data set. However, if an application using a forward-only cursor needs to return to a row that was fetched earlier, it must close and reopen the cursor, then re-fetch rows, starting from the beginning of the result data set, until it reaches the required row. Applications can get around this limitation by reading the result data set once and storing the fetched data locally (usually in an array or a linked list). However, this approach only works well with small amounts of data. A better solution is to use a scrollable-cursor, which provides random access to a result data set. Because the forward-only cursor is the default cursor type used in ODBC, the remainder of this chapter focuses on this cursor type. Scrollable cursors are discussed, in detail, in Chapter 11.

Naming Cursors

Whenever a cursor is implicitly created by ODBC, the data source generates and assigns it a unique name. Applications can retrieve this name by calling the **SQLGetCursorName()** function, or they can assign a unique name to the cursor by calling **SQLSetCursorName()** function before executing an SQL statement that creates a result data set (cursors are created and named when an SQL statement is prepared). For most fetch operations, the name of the cursor associated with a result data set is unimportant; cursor names are typically used in conjunction with positioned **UPDATE** and **DELETE** operations.

Using SQLFetch()

The **SQLFetch()** function is used to retrieve (fetch) a row of data from a result data set. When called, **SQLFetch()** advances the cursor to the next row in the result data set and returns the data for all columns that were bound to application variables by the **SQLBindCol()** function. If no columns were bound, **SQLFetch()** advances the cursor without returning any data. **SQLFetch()** can be used with any kind of cursor; however, it only moves a cursor in the forward-only direction.

Exactly how **SQLFetch()** is implemented is driver specific. Generally, when **SQLFetch()** is called, the driver performs the following tasks for each bound column in a row:

1. Sets the length/indicator variable to **SQL_NULL_DATA** and proceeds to the next column if the data is NULL. If the data is NULL and no length/indicator buffer was bound, SQLSTATE **22**002 (Indicator variable required but not supplied) is returned and the driver proceeds to the next row. If the data for the column is not NULL, the driver proceeds to step 2.

2. If the **SQL_ATTR_MAX_LENGTH** statement attribute is set to a nonzero value and the column contains character or binary data, it truncates the data to **SQL_ATTR_MAX_LENGTH** bytes.

NOTE: *The* **SQL_ATTR_MAX_LENGTH** *statement attribute is intended to reduce network traffic. It is generally implemented by the data source, which truncates the data before returning it across the network.*

3. Converts the data to the C data type specified for the bound application variable.

4. If the data was converted to a variable-length data type, such as a character or binary data type, the driver determines whether the length of the data exceeds the size of the bound variable/buffer. If the length of character data (including the NULL-termination character) exceeds the size of the bound variable/buffer, the driver truncates the data to the size of the bound variable/buffer–1 and NULL-terminates the data. If the length of binary data exceeds the size of the bound variable/buffer, the driver truncates it to the size of the bound variable/buffer. (The size of the bound variable/buffer is specified with the **SQLBindCol()** function).

Data truncation tends to be rare, because the size a buffer needs to be to hold the entire data value can be obtained from the result data set metadata before the buffer is bound to a column.

The driver never truncates data converted to fixed-length data types; it always assumes that the length of the data buffer is the size of the C data type specified.

5. Stores the converted (and possibly truncated) data in the bound application variable/buffer.

6. Stores the length of the data in the bound length/indicator variable. For character or binary data, this is the length of the data after conversion and before truncation. If the driver cannot determine the length of the data after conversion, as is sometimes the case with long data, it sets the length to **SQL_NO_TOTAL**. If data was truncated due to the value of the **SQL_ATTR_MAX_LENGTH** statement attribute, the value of this attribute (as opposed to the actual length) is stored in the bound length/indicator variable. For all other data types, this is the length of the data after conversion; that is, it is the size of the C data type the data was converted to. If no length/indicator variable was bound to the column, the driver discards the data length value.

7. Returns **SQL_SUCCESS** to the calling application if the data was successfully transferred to the bound application variable/buffer.

Returns **SQL_SUCCESS_WITH_INFO** and SQLSTATE **01**S07 (Fractional truncation) if the data was truncated during conversion without a loss of significant digits (for example, if the real number 1.234 is truncated to 1 when converted to an integer).

Returns **SQL_SUCCESS_WITH_INFO** and SQLSTATE **01**004 (Data truncated) if the data was truncated because the length of the bound variable/buffer was too small (for example, if the string "abcdef" were to be returned to a 4-byte buffer).

Returns **SQL_SUCCESS** if data was truncated to the length specified in the **SQL_ATTR_MAX_LENGTH** statement attribute.

Returns **SQL_ERROR** (if the rowset size is 1) or **SQL_SUCCESS_WITH_ INFO** (if the rowset size is greater than 1) and SQLSTATE **22**003 (Numeric value out of range) if data was truncated during conversion with a loss of significant digits (for example, if an **SQL_INTEGER** value greater than 100,000 were converted to an **SQL_C_TINYINT**). In this case, the application can continue fetching rows, but all data for the current row will be lost.

Returns **SQL_NO_DATA** (ODBC 3.x drivers) or **SQL_NO_DATA_FOUND** (ODBC 2.0 or earlier drivers) if the cursor has reached the end of the result data set.

Keeping Track of the Number of Rows Fetched

A *rows fetched* buffer can be used to keep track of the number of rows fetched, including those rows for which no data was returned because an error occurred during the fetch operation. This buffer must be allocated by the application, and when its address is stored in the **SQL_ATTR_ROWS_FETCHED_ PTR** statement attribute, its contents are updated each time **SQLFetch()** (and **SQLFetchScroll()**) is called. If the **SQL_ATTR_ROWS_FETCHED_PTR** statement attribute contains a NULL pointer, neither of these functions returns the number of rows fetched. The contents of the rows fetched buffer is undefined if **SQLFetch()** or **SQLFetchScroll()** does not return **SQL_SUCCESS** or **SQL_ SUCCESS_WITH_INFO**, except when **SQL_NO_DATA** (ODBC 3.x drivers) or **SQL_NO_DATA_FOUND** (ODBC 2.0 or earlier drivers) is returned, in which case the value in the rows fetched buffer is set to **0**.

If a rows fetched buffer is specified, an application can often examine its contents to determine the row number for the current row in the result data set. If a rows fetched buffer is not used, an application can obtain the same information by calling the **SQLGetStmtAttr()** function with the **SQL_ATTR_ROW_NUMBER** attribute specified.

Closing the Cursor

Often, developers assume that when the **SQLFetch()** function returns **SQL_NO_DATA** (ODBC 3.x drivers) or **SQL_NO_DATA_FOUND** (ODBC 2.0 or earlier drivers), the associated cursor is automatically closed. However, this is not the case—although cursors are implicitly created and opened when SQL statements that create a result data set are executed, they must be explicitly closed. Even cursors for empty result data sets (result data sets created when an SQL statement that returned no rows was executed successfully) must be explicitly closed. In ODBC 3.x, the `SQLCloseCursor()` function is used to explicitly close an open cursor. In ODBC 2.0 or earlier, the `SQLFreeStmt()`, can be used to explicity close an open cursor.

With a few drivers, when a transaction is committed or rolled back either by explicitly calling `SQLEndTran()` (ODBC 3.x drivers) or `SQLTransact()` (ODBC 2.0 or earlier drivers), or by operating in autocommit mode, all cursors on all statement handles associated with the connection handle being used are automatically closed. However, this is considered to be an exception, rather than the rule—with all other drivers, the application itself is responsible for closing cursors when they are no longer needed.

> **NOTE:** As long as a cursor remains open, the statement handle the cursor is associated with cannot be used for most other operations (for example, executing other SQL statements).

Getting Long Data

Each time a row is fetched from a result data set, the driver automatically stores the data for bound columns in the appropriate application variables/buffers. What happens to the data stored in unbound columns is driver specific; most drivers either retrieve the data and discard it or never retrieve it at all.

Applications can retrieve data from unbound columns by calling the `SQLGetData()` function. The `SQLGetData()` function is commonly used to retrieve large data values, which often exceed a predefined size (usually 254 characters or bytes). Because such data often cannot be stored in a single buffer, it is retrieved in parts from the driver by the `SQLGetData()` function after all other data in the row has been fetched. With respect to a single column, `SQLGetData()` behaves in the same manner as `SQLFetch()`: It retrieves the data for a column, converts it to the application variable's data type (if appropriate), and stores the converted value in that variable. It also returns the byte length of the data in the length/indicator buffer provided.

> **NOTE:** An application can retrieve any type of data value from a result data set with the `SQLGetData()` function. However, if the data is small enough to fit in a single buffer, there is generally no reason to use the `SQLGetData()` function —it is much easier to bind an application variable to the result data set column and let the driver store the data in the variable when the `SQLFetch()` function is called.

To retrieve large data from an unbound column, an application:

1. Calls **SQLFetch()**, **SQLFetchScroll()** (ODBC 3.x drivers), or **SQLExtendedFetch()** (ODBC 2.0 or earlier drivers) to position the cursor on a row of data in the result data set. Any of these functions automatically retrieves data for all bound columns and stores it in the appropriate application variables/buffers.

2. Calls the **SQLGetData()** function. **SQLGetData()** has the same arguments as **SQLBindCol()**: a statement handle, a column number, the C data type, address, and byte length of an application variable, and the address of a length/indicator buffer. Both **SQLGetData()** and **SQLBindCol()** perform essentially the same task: Each describe an application variable to the driver and specify that the data for a particular column should be returned in that variable. The major differences are that the **SQLGetData()** function is called after a row is fetched (and is sometimes called late binding for this reason), and that the binding specified by the **SQLGetData()** function only lasts for the duration of the call.

When the **SQLGetData()** function is called, the driver:

1. Returns **SQL_NO_DATA** (ODBC 3.x drivers) or **SQL_NO_DATA_FOUND** (ODBC 2.0 or earlier drivers) if it has already returned all the data for the column.

2. Sets the length/indicator variable to **SQL_NULL_DATA** if the data is NULL. If the data is NULL and no length/indicator buffer was bound, SQLSTATE **22**002 (indicator variable required but not supplied) is returned and the driver proceeds to the next row. If the data for the column is not NULL, the driver proceeds to step 3.

3. If the **SQL_ATTR_MAX_LENGTH** statement attribute is set to a nonzero value and the column contains character or binary data and **SQLGetData()** has not been called previously for the column, it truncates the data to **SQL_ATTR_MAX_LENGTH** bytes.

NOTE: *The* **SQL_ATTR_MAX_LENGTH** *statement attribute is intended to reduce network traffic. It is generally implemented by the data source, which truncates the data before returning it across the network.*

---

4. Converts the data to the C data type specified for the application variable. The data is given the default precision and scale for that data type. If the C data type is **SQL_ARD_TYPE**, the data type in the **SQL_DESC_CONCISE_TYPE** field of the *application row descriptor*

(ARD) is used and the data is given the precision and scale stored in the SQL_DESC_DATETIME_INTERVAL_PRECISION, SQL_DESC_ PRECISION, and SQL_DESC_SCALE fields of the ARD descriptor, depending upon the data type in the SQL_DESC_CONCISE_TYPE field.

5. If the data was converted to a variable-length data type, such as a character or binary data type, the driver determines whether the length of the data exceeds the size of the variable/buffer. If the length of character data (including the NULL-termination character) exceeds the size of the variable/buffer, the driver truncates the data to the size of the variable/buffer–1 and NULL-terminates the data. If the length of binary data exceeds the size of the variable/buffer, the driver truncates it to the size of the variable/buffer.

   Data truncation tends to be rare, because the size a buffer needs to be in order to hold the entire data value can be obtained from the result data set metadata before the buffer is used.

   The driver never truncates data converted to fixed-length data types; it always assumes that the length of the data buffer is the size of the C data type specified.

6. Stores the converted (and possibly truncated) data in the application variable/buffer.

7. Stores the length of the data in the length/indicator variable. For character or binary data, this is the length of the data after conversion and before truncation. If the driver cannot determine the length of the data after conversion, as is sometimes the case with long data, it sets the length to SQL_NO_TOTAL. (The last call to SQLGetData() for a particular column must always return the length of the data, not 0 or SQL_NO_TOTAL.) If data was truncated due to the value of the SQL_ATTR_MAX_LENGTH statement attribute, the value of this attribute (as opposed to the actual length) is stored in the length/indicator variable. For all other data types, this is the length of the data after conversion; that is, it is the size of the C data type that the data was converted to.

   When SQLGetData() is called multiple times in succession for the same column, this is the length of the data available at the start of each call; that is, the value returned in the length/indicator buffer decreases with each SQLGetData() call by the number of bytes returned in the previous call.

8. Returns **SQL_SUCCESS** if all the data in the column has been retrieved.

Returns **SQL_SUCCESS_WITH_INFO** and SQLSTATE **01**S07 (Fractional truncation) if the data was truncated during conversion without a loss of significant digits (for example, if the real number 1.234 is truncated to 1 when converted to an integer).

Returns **SQL_SUCCESS_WITH_INFO** and SQLSTATE **01**004 (Data truncated) if the data was truncated because the length of the variable/buffer was too small (for example, if the string "abcdef" were to be returned to a 4-byte buffer).

Returns **SQL_SUCCESS** if data was truncated to the length specified in the **SQL_ATTR_MAX_LENGTH** statement attribute.

Returns **SQL_NO_DATA** (ODBC 3.x drivers) or **SQL_NO_DATA_FOUND** (ODBC 2.0 or earlier drivers) if there is no more data to return.

Each time **SQL_SUCCESS_WITH_INFO** is returned to the application, **SQLGetData()** is called again (with the same column specified) to retrieve another part of or the remainder of the data stored in the column.

When large data values are retrieved in parts, the application is responsible for putting the parts together. Often, this is done by a simple concatenation of the parts of the data. However, because each part is NULL-terminated, the application must remove all but the last NULL-termination character when concatenating the parts.

Variable-length bookmarks can also be returned, in parts, by **SQLGetData()**. As with other data, a call to **SQLGetData()** to return variable-length bookmarks in parts returns **SQL_SUCCESS_WITH_INFO** and SQLSTATE **01**004 (String data, right truncated) when there is more data to be returned. This is different from the case where a variable-length bookmark is truncated by a call to **SQLFetch()** or **SQLFetchScroll()**, which returns **SQL_ERROR** and SQLSTATE **22**001 (String data, right truncated).

There are a number of restrictions that must be taken into consideration when using the **SQLGetData()** function. In general, columns accessed with **SQLGetData()**:

■ Must be accessed in order of increasing column number (because of how the columns of a result data set are read from the data source).

■ Cannot be bound to application variables.

■ Must have a higher column number than the last bound column. For example, if the last bound column is column 3, it is an error to call **SQLGetData()** for column 2. For this reason, applications should always place long data columns at the end of select lists.

■ Cannot be used if **SQLFetch()**, **SQLFetchScroll()** (ODBC 3.x driver), or **SQLExtendedFetch()** (ODBC 2.0 or earlier driver) was called to retrieve more than one row.

NOTE: *Some drivers do not enforce all these restrictions. Interoperable applications should either assume they exist or determine which restrictions are not enforced by calling the* **SQLGetInfo()** *function with the* **SQL_GETDATA_ EXTENSIONS** *information type specified.*

Controlling Result Data Set Size

An application can reduce network traffic in DBMS-based drivers by limiting the number of rows returned in a result data set. This is done by setting the **SQL_ATTR_MAX_ROWS** statement attribute before executing an SQL statement that creates a result data set. If an application does not need all the data usually returned in a character or binary column, network traffic can be further reduced by setting the **SQL_ATTR_MAX_LENGTH** statement attribute before executing the statement. This restricts the number of bytes of data returned for any character or binary column. For example, suppose a column contains long text documents. If an application that browses the table containing this column only needs to display the first page of each document, the **SQL_ATTR_MAX_LENGTH** statement attribute can be used to limit the amount of data returned for a column to a single page. An application can also let the driver truncate character or binary data, by binding a small buffer to the column.

The Basic SQL Results Retrieval Functions

Table 10–1 lists the ODBC API functions used to perform the basic process of retrieving rows of data from a result data set.

Each of these functions are described, in detail, in the remaining portion of this chapter.

Table 10–1 The ODBC Basic Results Retrieval Functions

Function Name	Description
SQLDescribeCol()	Describes a column in a result data set.
SQLNumResultCols()	Retrieves and returns the number of columns in a result data set.
SQLColAttribute()	Retrieves information about a column in a result data set.
SQLColAttributes()	Retrieves information about a column in a result data set.
SQLBindCol()	Assigns data storage for a column in a result data set.
SQLGetCursorName()	Retrieves the cursor name for a cursor associated with an SQL statement handle.
SQLSetCursorName()	Specifies a cursor name for a cursor associated with an SQL statement handle.
SQLFetch()	Retrieves a single row of data from a result data set and returns it to bound application variables.
SQLCloseCursor()	Closes a cursor that has been opened on an SQL statement handle.
SQLGetData()	Retrieves data from a single column (in the current row) of a result data set.

SQLNumResultCols

COMPATABILITY

X/OPEN 95 CLI	ISO/IEC 92 CLI	ODBC 1.0	ODBC 2.0	ODBC 3.0	ODBC 3.5
✓	✓	✓	✓	✓	✓

API CONFORMANCE LEVEL   **CORE**

Purpose   The `SQLNumResultCols()` function is used to determine the number of columns that exist in a result data set.

Syntax
```
SQLRETURN    SQLNumResultCols  (SQLHSTMT      StatementHandle,
                                SQLSMALLINT   *NumColumns);
```

Parameters

StatementHandle   An SQL statement handle that refers to a previously allocated SQL statement information storage buffer (data structure).

NumColumns   A pointer to a location in memory where this function is to store the number of columns found in the result data set associated with the specified SQL statement handle.

Description   The `SQLNumResultCols()` function is used to determine the number of columns that exist in a result data set. If the last SQL statement or ODBC API function executed (using the specified SQL statement handle) did not produce a result data set, the value 0 is returned in the *NumColumns* parameter (to indicate there is no result data set) when this function is executed.

An application can call this function any time after an SQL statement is prepared or executed. However, because some data sources cannot easily describe result data sets that will be created by examining prepared SQL statements, performance can suffer if this function is called after a statement is prepared, but before it is actually executed.

> **NOTE:** *A result data set can be empty. This is different from a result data set not being created at all. Other than the fact that it has no rows of data in it, an empty result data set is like any other result data set. Thus, an application can retrieve metadata for, attempt to fetch rows from, and must close the cursor associated with an empty result data set.*

Return Codes SQL_SUCCESS, SQL_SUCCESS_WITH_INFO, SQL_STILL_EXECUTING, SQL_INVALID_HANDLE, or SQL_ERROR

SQLSTATEs If this function returns SQL_SUCCESS_WITH_INFO or SQL_ERROR, one of the following SQLSTATE values may be obtained by calling the SQLGetDiagRec() function (ODBC 3.x driver) or the SQLError() function (ODBC 2.0 or earlier driver):

ODBC 3.X
01000, 08S01, **HY**000, **HY**001, **HY**008, **HY**010*, **HY**013, **HYT**01, or **IM**001*

ODBC 2.0 OR EARLIER
01000, **IM**001*, **S1**000, **S1**001, **S1**008, **S1**010*, or **S1T**00

*Returned by the ODBC Driver Manager.

Unless noted otherwise, each of these SQLSTATE values is returned by the data source driver. Refer to Appendix B for detailed information about each SQLSTATE value that can be returned by the ODBC Driver Manager or by a data source driver.

SQLNumResultCols() can return any SQLSTATE that can be returned by SQLPrepare() or SQLExecute() when called after SQLPrepare() and before SQLExecute() depending upon when the data source evaluates the SQL statement associated with the statement handle specified.

Comments
- The value returned to the *NumColumns* parameter does not include the bookmark column (if the result data set contains a bound bookmark column).
- If the SQL statement associated with *StatementHandle* does not produce a result data set, 0 is returned in the *NumColumns* parameter.
- The SQL_DESC_COUNT field of the IRD descriptor header record associated with the SQL statement handle specified contains the value that this function returns to the *NumColumns* parameter.

Prerequisites　　The `SQLPrepare()` function or the `SQLExecDirect()` function must be called before this function is called.

Restrictions　　This function can only be called successfully if the SQL statement is in the "Prepared," "Executed," or "Positioned" state.

See Also　　　　`SQLBindCol()`, `SQLDescribeCol()`, `SQLColAttribute()`,
`SQLColAttributes()`, `SQLPrepare()`, `SQLExecute()`, `SQLExecDirect()`,
`SQLGetData()`

Example　　　　The following Visual C++ program illustrates how to use the
`SQLNumResultCols()` function to determine how many columns
exist in a result data set.

```
/*————————————————————————————————————————————————————————————————*/
/* NAME:     CH10EX1.CPP                                           */
/* PURPOSE:  Illustrate How To Use The Following ODBC API Function */
/*           In A C++ Program:                                     */
/*                                                                 */
/*                SQLNumResultCols()                               */
/*                                                                 */
/* OTHER ODBC APIs SHOWN:                                          */
/*           SQLAllocHandle()          SQLSetEnvAttr()             */
/*           SQLConnect()              SQLExecDirect()             */
/*           SQLDisconnect()           SQLFreeHandle()             */
/*                                                                 */
/*————————————————————————————————————————————————————————————————*/

// Include The Appropriate Header Files
#include <windows.h>
#include <sql.h>
#include <sqlext.h>
#include <iostream.h>

// Define The ODBC_Class Class
class ODBC_Class
{
    // Attributes
    public:
        SQLHANDLE    EnvHandle;
        SQLHANDLE    ConHandle;
        SQLHANDLE    StmtHandle;
        SQLRETURN    rc;

    // Operations
    public:
        ODBC_Class();                          // Constructor
        ~ODBC_Class();                         // Destructor
};
```

```
// Define The Class Constructor
ODBC_Class::ODBC_Class()
{
    // Initialize The Return Code Variable
    rc = SQL_SUCCESS;

    // Allocate An Environment Handle
    rc = SQLAllocHandle(SQL_HANDLE_ENV, SQL_NULL_HANDLE, &EnvHandle);

    // Set The ODBC Application Version To 3.x
    if (rc == SQL_SUCCESS)
        rc = SQLSetEnvAttr(EnvHandle, SQL_ATTR_ODBC_VERSION,
                    (SQLPOINTER) SQL_OV_ODBC3, SQL_IS_UINTEGER);

    // Allocate A Connection Handle
    if (rc == SQL_SUCCESS)
        rc = SQLAllocHandle(SQL_HANDLE_DBC, EnvHandle, &ConHandle);
}

// Define The Class Destructor
ODBC_Class::~ODBC_Class()
{
    // Free The Connection Handle
    if (ConHandle != NULL)
        SQLFreeHandle(SQL_HANDLE_DBC, ConHandle);

    // Free The Environment Handle
    if (EnvHandle != NULL)
        SQLFreeHandle(SQL_HANDLE_ENV, EnvHandle);
}

/*-----------------------------------------------------------------*/
/* The Main Function                                               */
/*-----------------------------------------------------------------*/
int main()
{
    // Declare The Local Memory Variables
    SQLRETURN      rc = SQL_SUCCESS;
    SQLCHAR        DBName[10] = "Northwind";
    SQLCHAR        SQLStmt[255];
    SQLSMALLINT    NumCols;

    // Create An Instance Of The ODBC_Class Class
    ODBC_Class   Example;

    // Connect To The Northwind Sample Database
    if (Example.ConHandle != NULL)
    {
        rc = SQLConnect(Example.ConHandle, DBName, SQL_NTS,
                (SQLCHAR *) "", SQL_NTS, (SQLCHAR *) "", SQL_NTS);

        // Allocate An SQL Statement Handle
        rc = SQLAllocHandle(SQL_HANDLE_STMT, Example.ConHandle,
                &Example.StmtHandle);
        if (rc == SQL_SUCCESS)
```

```
{
    // Define A SELECT SQL Statement
    strcpy((char *) SQLStmt, "SELECT * FROM Customers");

    // Prepare And Execute The SQL Statement
    rc = SQLExecDirect(Example.StmtHandle, SQLStmt, SQL_NTS);

    // Find Out How Many Columns Exist In The Result Data Set
    // Produced By The SQL Query (Display The Result)
    if (rc == SQL_SUCCESS)
    {
        rc = SQLNumResultCols(Example.StmtHandle, &NumCols);

        cout << "Number Of Columns In The Result Data Set: ";
        cout << NumCols << endl;
    }

    // Free The SQL Statement Handle
    if (Example.StmtHandle != NULL)
        SQLFreeHandle(SQL_HANDLE_STMT, Example.StmtHandle);
}

    // Disconnect From The Northwind Sample Database
    rc = SQLDisconnect(Example.ConHandle);
}

// Return To The Operating System
return(rc);
}
```

SQLDescribeCol

COMPATABILITY

X/OPEN 95 CLI	ISO/IEC 92 CLI	ODBC 1.0	ODBC 2.0	ODBC 3.0	ODBC 3.5
✓	✓	✓	✓	✓	✓

API CONFORMANCE LEVEL   **CORE**

Purpose   The SQLDescribeCol() function is used to retrieve basic result data set metadata information (specifically, column name, SQL data type, column size, decimal precision, and nullability) for a specified column in a result data set.

Syntax

```
SQLRETURN   SQLDescribeCol   (SQLHSTMT        StatementHandle,
                              SQLUSMALLINT    ColumnNumber,
                              SQLCHAR         *ColumnName,
                              SQLSMALLINT     ColNameMaxSize,
                              SQLSMALLINT     *ColNameSize,
                              SQLSMALLINT     *SQLDataType,
                              SQLUINTEGER     *ColumnSize,
                              SQLSMALLINT     *Decimals,
                              SQLSMALLINT     *Nullable);
```

Parameters

StatementHandle	An SQL statement handle that refers to a previously allocated SQL statement information storage buffer (data structure).
ColumnNumber	Specifies the column's location in the result data set. Columns are numbered sequentially from left to right, starting with 1, as they appear in the result data set.
ColumnName	A pointer to a location in memory where this function is to store the name of the specified column.
ColNameMaxSize	The maximum size of the memory storage buffer where this function is to store the column name retrieved.
ColNameSize	A pointer to a location in memory where this function is to store the actual number of bytes written to the column name memory storage buffer (*ColumnName*).
SQLDataType	A pointer to a location in memory where this function is to store the SQL data type of the specified column. The following SQL data types are supported:

- SQL_CHAR

- SQL_VARCHAR

- SQL_LONGVARCHAR

- SQL_DECIMAL

- SQL_NUMERIC

- SQL_SMALLINT

- SQL_INTEGER

- SQL_REAL

- SQL_FLOAT

- SQL_DOUBLE
- SQL_BIT
- SQL_TINYINT
- SQL_BIGINT
- SQL_BINARY
- SQL_VARBINARY
- SQL_LONGVARBINARY
- SQL_DATE
- SQL_TIME
- SQL_TIMESTAMP
- SQL_TYPE_DATE
- SQL_TYPE_TIME
- SQL_TYPE_TIMESTAMP
- SQL_INTERVAL_MONTH
- SQL_INTERVAL_YEAR
- SQL_INTERVAL_YEAR_TO_MONTH
- SQL_INTERVAL_DAY
- SQL_INTERVAL_HOUR
- SQL_INTERVAL_MINUTE
- SQL_INTERVAL_SECOND
- SQL_INTERVAL_DAY_TO_HOUR
- SQL_INTERVAL_DAY_TO_MINUTE
- SQL_INTERVAL_DAY_TO_SECOND
- SQL_INTERVAL_HOUR_TO_MINUTE
- SQL_INTERVAL_HOUR_TO_SECOND
- SQL_INTERVAL_MINUTE_TO_SECOND
- SQL_INTERVAL_YEAR_TO_MONTH

ColumnSize	A pointer to a location in memory where this function is to store the maximum length, in bytes, of the column as it is defined in the data source.
Decimals	A pointer to a location in memory where this function is to store the number of digits to the right of the decimal point for columns that

have one of the following SQL data types
(*SQLDataType*):

- **SQL_DECIMAL**

- **SQL_NUMERIC**

- **SQL_TIME**

- **SQL_TIMESTAMP**

- **SQL_TYPE_TIME**

- **SQL_TYPE_TIMESTAMP**

- **SQL_INTERVAL_SECOND**

- **SQL_INTERVAL_DAY_TO_SECOND**

- **SQL_INTERVAL_HOUR_TO_SECOND**

- **SQL_INTERVAL_MINUTE_TO_SECOND**

Nullable   A pointer to a location in memory where this
function is to store information about whether
the column accepts/allows NULL values. The
following values are supported:

- **SQL_NO_NULLS**
  The specified column does not allow
  NULL values.

- **SQL_NULLABLE**
  The specified column allows NULL values.

- **SQL_NULLABLE_UNKNOWN**
  Whether the specified column allows
  NULL values cannot be determined by
  the driver.

Description   The **SQLDescribeCol()** function is used to retrieve basic result data set
metadata information (specifically, column name, SQL data type, column
size, decimal precision, and nullability) for a specified column in a result
data set. If the basic result data set metadata for a column in a result data
set is not known in advance, this function the **SQLColAttribute()**
function (ODBC 3.x drivers) or the **SQLColAttributes()** function (ODBC
2.0 or earlier drivers) can be called to obtain the metadata so that an
appropriate application variable can be bound to it.

An application can call this function any time after an SQL statement
is prepared or executed. However, because some data sources cannot easily describe result data sets that will be created by examining prepared
SQL statements, performance can suffer if this function is called after a
statement is prepared, but before it is actually executed.

Return Codes SQL_SUCCESS, SQL_SUCCESS_WITH_INFO, SQL_STILL_EXECUTING, SQL_INVALID_HANDLE, or SQL_ERROR

SQLSTATEs If this function returns **SQL_SUCCESS_WITH_INFO** or **SQL_ERROR**, one of the following SQLSTATE values may be obtained by calling the **SQLGetDiagRec()** function (ODBC 3.x driver) or the **SQLError()** function (ODBC 2.0 or earlier driver):

ODBC 3.X
01000, **01**004, **07**005, **07**009*, **08**S01, **HY**000, **HY**001, **HY**008, **HY**010*, **HY**013, **HY**090*, **HY**T01, or **IM**001*

ODBC 2.0 OR EARLIER
01000, **01**004, **24**000, **IM**001*, **S1**000, **S1**001, **S1**002*, **S1**008, **S1**010*, **S1**090*, or **S1**T00

*Returned by the ODBC Driver Manager.

Unless noted otherwise, each of these SQLSTATE values are returned by the data source driver. Refer to Appendix B for detailed information about each SQLSTATE value that can be returned by the ODBC Driver Manager or by a data source driver.

SQLDescribeCol() can return any SQLSTATE that can be returned by **SQLPrepare()** or **SQLExecute()** when called after **SQLPrepare()** and before **SQLExecute()** depending on when the data source evaluates the SQL statement associated with the statement handle specified.

Comments
- If the *ColumnNumber* parameter is set to **0**, metadata for the bookmark column is returned.
- When the *ColumnNumber* parameter is set to **0** (for a bookmark column), **SQL_BINARY** is returned in the *SQLDataType* parameter for variable-length bookmarks. (**SQL_INTEGER** is returned if bookmarks are being used by an ODBC 3.x application working with an ODBC 2.0 or earlier driver, or by an ODBC 2.0 application working with an ODBC 3.x driver.)
- If the column name string's actual length is greater than or equal to the maximum string size value specified in the *ColNameMaxSize* parameter, the server name string is truncated to *ColNameMaxSize*–1 (the length of a NULL-termination character) characters.
- If the column name string is a Unicode string, the *ColNameMaxSize* parameter must contain an even number.

- If the column is an expression, the *ColumnName* parameter will contain either an empty string or a driver-defined name.
- If the data type for a column cannot be determined, the driver returns **SQL_UNKNOWN_TYPE** to the *SQLDataType* parameter.
- If the number of decimal digits for a column cannot be determined or is not applicable, the driver returns **0** to the *Decimals* parameter.
- The **SQL_DESC_NAME** field of the IRD descriptor column record for the SQL statement handle contains the value that this function returns to the *ColumnName* parameter.
- The **SQL_DESC_CONCISE_TYPE** field of the IRD descriptor column record for the SQL statement handle contains the value that this function returns to the *SQLDataType* parameter.
- The **SQL_DESC_NULLABLE** field of the IRD descriptor column record for the SQL statement handle contains the value that this function returns to the *Nullable* parameter.
- In ODBC 3.x, **SQL_TYPE_DATE**, **SQL_TYPE_TIME**, or **SQL_TYPE_TIMESTAMP** is returned in the *SQLDataType* parameter for date, time, or timestamp data, respectively. In ODBC 2.0, **SQL_DATE**, **SQL_TIME**, or **SQL_TIMESTAMP** is returned. The ODBC Driver Manager performs the required mappings when an ODBC 2.0 application is working with an ODBC 3.x driver, or when an ODBC 3.x application is working with an ODBC 2.0 or earlier driver.
- All versions of ODBC can return **SQL_NULLABLE_UNKNOWN** to the *Nullable* parameter; however, because the X/Open and SQL Access Group Call Level Interface specifications do include this value, ODBC applications working with CLI standards-compliant drivers cannot expect it to be returned.

Prerequisites   The **SQLPrepare()** function or the **SQLExecDirect()** function must be executed before this function is called.

Restrictions   This function can only be called successfully if the SQL statement is in the "Prepared," "Executed," or "Positioned" state.

See Also   **SQLColAttribute()**, **SQLColAttributes()**, **SQLPrepare()**, **SQLExecute()**, **SQLExecDirect()**, **SQLNumResultCols()**

Example   The following Visual C++ program illustrates how to use the **SQLDescribeCol()** function to obtain general information about a column in a result data set.

```
/*---------------------------------------------------------------*/
/* NAME:      CH10EX2.CPP                                         */
/* PURPOSE: Illustrate How To Use The Following ODBC API Function */
/*          In A C++ Program:                                     */
/*                                                                */
/*              SQLDescribeCol()                                  */
/*                                                                */
/* OTHER ODBC APIs SHOWN:                                         */
/*          SQLAllocHandle()          SQLSetEnvAttr()             */
/*          SQLConnect()              SQLExecDirect()             */
/*          SQLNumResultCols()        SQLDisconnect()             */
/*          SQLFreeHandle()                                       */
/*                                                                */
/*---------------------------------------------------------------*/

// Include The Appropriate Header Files
#include <windows.h>
#include <sql.h>
#include <sqlext.h>
#include <iostream.h>

// Define The ODBC_Class Class
class ODBC_Class
{
    // Attributes
    public:
        SQLHANDLE    EnvHandle;
        SQLHANDLE    ConHandle;
        SQLHANDLE    StmtHandle;
        SQLRETURN    rc;

    // Operations
    public:
        ODBC_Class();                        // Constructor
        ~ODBC_Class();                       // Destructor
        SQLRETURN ShowColInfo();
};

// Define The Class Constructor
ODBC_Class::ODBC_Class()
{
    // Initialize The Return Code Variable
    rc = SQL_SUCCESS;

    // Allocate An Environment Handle
    rc = SQLAllocHandle(SQL_HANDLE_ENV, SQL_NULL_HANDLE, &EnvHandle);

    // Set The ODBC Application Version To 3.x
    if (rc == SQL_SUCCESS)
        rc = SQLSetEnvAttr(EnvHandle, SQL_ATTR_ODBC_VERSION,
                (SQLPOINTER) SQL_OV_ODBC3, SQL_IS_UINTEGER);

    // Allocate A Connection Handle
    if (rc == SQL_SUCCESS)
```

```
            rc = SQLAllocHandle(SQL_HANDLE_DBC, EnvHandle, &ConHandle);
}

// Define The Class Destructor
ODBC_Class::~ODBC_Class()
{
    // Free The Connection Handle
    if (ConHandle != NULL)
        SQLFreeHandle(SQL_HANDLE_DBC, ConHandle);

    // Free The Environment Handle
    if (EnvHandle != NULL)
        SQLFreeHandle(SQL_HANDLE_ENV, EnvHandle);
}

// Define The ShowColInfo() Member Function
SQLRETURN ODBC_Class::ShowColInfo(void)
{
    // Declare The Local Memory Variables
    SQLSMALLINT    NumCols;
    SQLCHAR        ColName[50];
    SQLSMALLINT    ColNameLen;
    SQLSMALLINT    ColType;
    SQLUINTEGER    ColSize;
    SQLSMALLINT    Scale;
    SQLSMALLINT    Nullable;

    // Find Out How Many Columns Exist In The Result Data Set
    rc = SQLNumResultCols(StmtHandle, &NumCols);
    if (rc == SQL_SUCCESS)
    {
        // Display A Header
        cout << "Column Names :" << endl << endl;

        // Obtain And Display The Name Of Each Column
        for (int i = 1; i <= (int) NumCols; i++)
        {
            rc = SQLDescribeCol(StmtHandle, i, ColName,
                    sizeof(ColName), &ColNameLen, &ColType,
                    &ColSize, &Scale, &Nullable);

            if (rc == SQL_SUCCESS)
                cout << ColName << endl;
        }
    }

    // Return The ODBC API Return Code To The Calling Function
    return(rc);
}

/*————————————————————————————————————————————————————————*/
/* The Main Function                                      */
/*————————————————————————————————————————————————————————*/
```

```
int main()
{
    // Declare The Local Memory Variables
    SQLRETURN    rc = SQL_SUCCESS;
    SQLCHAR      DBName[10] = "Northwind";
    SQLCHAR      SQLStmt[255];

    // Create An Instance Of The ODBC_Class Class
    ODBC_Class  Example;

    // Connect To The Northwind Sample Database
    if (Example.ConHandle != NULL)
    {
        rc = SQLConnect(Example.ConHandle, DBName, SQL_NTS,
                (SQLCHAR *) "", SQL_NTS, (SQLCHAR *) "", SQL_NTS);

        // Allocate An SQL Statement Handle
        rc = SQLAllocHandle(SQL_HANDLE_STMT, Example.ConHandle,
                &Example.StmtHandle);
        if (rc == SQL_SUCCESS)
        {
            // Define A SELECT SQL Statement
            strcpy((char *) SQLStmt, "SELECT * FROM ");
            strcat((char *) SQLStmt, "[Order Details] WHERE ");
            strcat((char *) SQLStmt, "Quantity < 20");

            // Prepare And Execute The SQL Statement
            rc = SQLExecDirect(Example.StmtHandle, SQLStmt, SQL_NTS);

            // Display Information About The Columns In The Result
            // Data Set Produced By The SQL Query
            if (rc == SQL_SUCCESS)
                Example.ShowColInfo();

            // Free The SQL Statement Handle
            if (Example.StmtHandle != NULL)
                SQLFreeHandle(SQL_HANDLE_STMT, Example.StmtHandle);
        }

        // Disconnect From The Northwind Sample Database
        rc = SQLDisconnect(Example.ConHandle);
    }

    // Return To The Operating System
    return(rc);
}
```

SQLColAttribute

COMPATABILITY

X/OPEN 95 CLI	ISO/IEC 92 CLI	ODBC 1.0	ODBC 2.0	ODBC 3.0	ODBC 3.5
✗	✓	☐	☐	✓	✓

API CONFORMANCE LEVEL   **CORE**

Purpose

The **SQLColAttribute()** function is used to retrieve descriptor information (for example, column name, data type, column size, decimal precision, and nullability) for a specified column in a result data set.

Syntax

```
SQLRETURN   SQLColAttribute   (SQLHSTMT       StatementHandle,
                               SQLUSMALLINT   ColumnNumber,
                               SQLUSMALLINT   Attribute,
                               SQLPOINTER     CharacterValue,
                               SQLSMALLINT    CharValueMaxSize,
                               SQLSMALLINT    *CharValueSize,
                               SQLPOINTER     NumericValue);
```

Parameters

StatementHandle   An SQL statement handle that refers to a previously allocated SQL statement information storage buffer (data structure).

ColumnNumber   Specifies the column's location in the result data set. Columns are numbered sequentially from left to right, starting with 1, as they appear in the result data set.

Attribute   Specifies the column attribute for which information is to be retrieved. This parameter must be set to one of the following values:

▓ **SQL_DESC_AUTO_UNIQUE_VALUE**

▓ **SQL_DESC_BASE_COLUMN_NAME**

▓ **SQL_DESC_BASE_TABLE_NAME**

▓ **SQL_DESC_CASE_SENSITIVE**

▓ **SQL_DESC_CATALOG_NAME**

▓ **SQL_DESC_CONCISE_TYPE**

- **SQL_DESC_COUNT**
- **SQL_DESC_DISPLAY_SIZE**
- **SQL_DESC_FIXED_PREC_SCALE**
- **SQL_DESC_LABEL**
- **SQL_DESC_LENGTH**
- **SQL_DESC_LITERAL_PREFIX**
- **SQL_DESC_LITERAL_SUFFIX**
- **SQL_DESC_LOCAL_TYPE_NAME**
- **SQL_DESC_NAME**
- **SQL_DESC_NULLABLE**
- **SQL_DESC_NUM_PREX_RADIX**
- **SQL_DESC_OCTET_LENGTH**
- **SQL_DESC_PRECISION**
- **SQL_DESC_SCALE**
- **SQL_DESC_SCHEMA_NAME**
- **SQL_DESC_SEARCHABLE**
- **SQL_DESC_TABLE_NAME**
- **SQL_DESC_TYPE**
- **SQL_DESC_TYPE_NAME**
- **SQL_DESC_UNNAMED**
- **SQL_DESC_UNSIGNED**
- **SQL_DESC_UPDATABLE**

CharacterValue A pointer to a location in memory where this function is to store the current value of the specified attribute (if the attribute value is a character value).

CharValueMaxSize The size of the memory storage buffer where this function is to store the current value of the specified attribute (descriptor field). If an ODBC-defined attribute is to be retrieved, and if the attribute value is a 32-bit integer value, this parameter is ignored. If a driver-defined field is to be retrieved, this parameter may be set as follows:

- If the value of the specified attribute (descriptor field) is a character string, this parameter may be set to the actual length of the string or to **SQL_NTS**.

- If the value of the specified attribute (descriptor field) is a binary string, this parameter may be set to the result of the **SQL_LEN_BINARY_ATTR(length)** macro. Usually, this macro places a negative value in this parameter.

- If the value of the specified attribute (descriptor field) is anything other than a character string or binary string, this parameter may be set to **SQL_IS_POINTER**.

- If the value of the specified attribute (descriptor field) is a fixed-length data type, this parameter may be set to **SQL_IS_INTEGER**, **SQL_IS_UINTEGER**, **SQL_SMALLINT**, or **SQLUSMALLINT**, as appropriate.

CharValueSize   A pointer to a location in memory where this function is to store the actual number of bytes written to the attribute (descriptor field) character value memory storage buffer (*CharacterValue*). If the attribute (descriptor field) value retrieved is not a character string value, this parameter ignored.

NumberValue   A pointer to a location in memory where this function is to store the current value of the specified attribute (if the attribute value is a numeric value).

Description   The **SQLColAttribute()** function is used to retrieve descriptor information (for example, column name, data type, column size, decimal precision, and nullability) for a specified column in a result data set. Table 10–2 lists alphabetically each value that can be specified for the *Attribute* parameter, along with a description of the information returned for that value when this function is executed.

If the various attributes about a result data set column are not known, this function (or the **SQLDescribeCol()** function) can be called after an

SQL query statement has been prepared or executed, to determine the attributes of a column before binding it to an application variable.

To take advantage of different data sources, more column attributes may be defined in future releases of ODBC. In fact, a range of column attributes (0 to 999) has been reserved by ODBC to allow for future expansion. In addition, ODBC driver developers are required to reserve values for their own driver-specific use from X/Open.

NOTE: *In ODBC 3.x, this function replaces the ODBC 2.0 function* `SQLColAttributes()`.

Return Codes   `SQL_SUCCESS`, `SQL_SUCCESS_WITH_INFO`, `SQL_STILL_EXECUTING`, `SQL_INVALID_HANDLE`, or `SQL_ERROR`

SQLSTATEs   If this function returns `SQL_SUCCESS_WITH_INFO` or `SQL_ERROR`, one of the following SQLSTATE values may be obtained by calling the `SQLGetDiagRec()` function:

01000, **01**004, **07**005, **07**009*, **HY**000, **HY**001, **HY**008, **HY**010*, **HY**013, **HY**090*, **HY**091, **HY**C00, **HYT**01, or **IM**001*

*Returned by the ODBC Driver Manager.

Unless noted otherwise, each of these SQLSTATE values are returned by the data source driver. Refer to Appendix B for detailed information about each SQLSTATE value that can be returned by the ODBC Driver Manager or by a data source driver.

`SQLColAttribute()` can return any SQLSTATE that can be returned by `SQLPrepare()` or `SQLExecute()` when called after `SQLPrepare()` and before `SQLExecute()` depending on when the data source evaluates the SQL statement associated with the statement handle specified.

Comments
■ Attributes for columns can be retrieved in any order.

■ When the *ColumnNumber* parameter is set to **0** (for a bookmark column), all attributes except `SQL_DESC_TYPE` and `SQL_DESC_OCTET_LENGTH` return undefined values.

■ For character data, if the number of bytes of data available for the specified attribute is greater than or equal to the maximum string size value specified in the *CharValueMaxSize* parameter, the attribute string value is truncated to *CharValueMaxSize–1* (the

Table 10–2   *Column Attribute (Descriptor) Information Returned By* **SQLColAttribute()**

Attribute	Data Type	Description
SQL_DESC_AUTO_ UNIQUE_VALUE (ODBC 1.0)	32-bit integer	Indicates whether the column's data type is an auto increment data type. Valid values for this attribute are: **SQL_TRUE**: The column's data type is an auto increment data type. **SQL_FALSE**: The column's data type is not an auto increment data type or the column does not contain numeric data. This attribute is only valid for columns containing numeric data types. Values can be inserted into auto increment data type columns; however, existing auto increment data type column values cannot be updated. When data is inserted into an auto-increment data type column, a unique value (determined by adding a predefined increment value to the last value used) is inserted into the column. The actual increment value used to construct the new unique value is not defined; instead it is data-source-specific. Thus, an application should not assume that an auto-increment column starts at any particular point or increments by any particular value.
SQL_DESC_BASE_ COLUMN_NAME (ODBC 3.0)	Character string	Identifies the name assigned to the base column corresponding to the column in the result data set. If the base column is unnamed (as in the case when a column in a result data set corresponds to an expression), an empty string (" ") is returned for this attribute. This information is obtained from the **SQL_DESC_BASE_COLUMN_ NAME** field (a read-only field) of the IRD descriptor record.
SQL_DESC_BASE_ TABLE_NAME (ODBC 3.0)	Character string	Identifies the name of the base table containing the column. If the base table name cannot be determined, an empty string (" ") is returned for this attribute. This information is obtained from the **SQL_DESC_BASE_TABLE_ NAME** field (a read-only field) of the IRD descriptor record.
SQL_DESC_CASE_ SENSITIVE (ODBC 1.0)	32-bit integer	Indicates whether the column's data type is treated as case sensitive for collations and comparisons. Valid values for this attribute are: **SQL_TRUE**: The column's data type is treated as case sensitive for collations and comparisons. **SQL_FALSE**: The column's data type is either not a character data type or is not treated as case sensitive for collations and comparisons.

Table 10–2 Continued

Attribute	Data Type	Description
SQL_DESC_ CATALOG_NAME (ODBC 2.0)	Character string	Identifies the catalog (qualifier) of the table containing the column. If a data source does not support catalogs (qualifiers) or if the catalog name cannot be determined, an empty string (" ") is returned for this attribute. If the column is an expression or part of a view, the value returned for this attribute is implementation-defined.
SQL_DESC_ CONCISE_TYPE (ODBC 3.0)	32-bit integer	Identifies the concise data type (such as **SQL_TYPE_DATE** or **SQL_INTERVAL_YEAR_TO_MONTH**) for datetime and interval data types. This information is obtained from the **SQL_DESC_CONCISE_TYPE** field of the IRD descriptor record.
SQL_DESC_COUNT (ODBC 1.0)	32-bit integer	Identifies the number of columns that are available in the result data set. If there are no columns in the result data set, **0** is returned by this attribute. This information is obtained from the **SQL_DESC_COUNT** field or the IRD descriptor header record.
SQL_DESC_ DISPLAY_SIZE (ODBC 1.0)	32-bit integer	Identifies the maximum number of characters needed to display data from the column.
SQL_DESC_FIXED_ PREC_SCALE (ODBC 1.0)	32-bit integer	Indicates whether the column has a fixed precision scale. Valid values for this attribute are: **SQL_TRUE:** The column has a fixed precision and non-zero scale that are data-source specific. **SQL_FALSE:** The column does not have a fixed precision and non-zero scale that are data-source specific.
SQL_DESC_LABEL (ODBC 2.0)	Character string	Identifies the label assigned to the column. If a column does not have a label, the column name is stored in this attribute. If the column is unlabeled and unnamed, an empty string (" ") is returned for this attribute.
SQL_DESC_LENGTH (ODBC 3.0)	32-bit integer	Identifies the total number of bytes of data associated with the column. This is the length, in bytes, of the data transferred when the **SQLFetch()** or **SQLGetData()** function is called for this column (provided **SQL_C_DEFAULT** is specified as the column's C data type). If the column contains fixed length character or binary string data, the actual length of the column (minus the size of the NULL termination character) is returned. If the column contains variable length character or binary string data, the maximum column length is returned. If the column contains numeric data, the length returned may be different from the size of the data stored in the data source.

Table 10–2 *Continued*

Attribute	Data Type	Description
		This information is obtained from the IRD record's **SQL_DESC_LENGTH** field of the IRD descriptor record.
SQL_DESC_ LITERAL_PREFIX (ODBC 3.0)	Character string	Identifies one or more characters used as a prefix for a literal representation of the SQL data type used by the column. For example, a single quotation mark (') might be used for character data types, or '0x' might be used for binary data types. If a literal prefix is not applicable for the data type used, an empty string (" ") is returned for this attribute.
SQL_DESC_ LITERAL_SUFFIX (ODBC 3.0)	Character string	Identifies one or more characters used as a suffix for a literal representation of the SQL data type used by the column. For example, a single quotation mark (') might be used for character data types. If a literal suffix is not applicable for the data type used, an empty string (" ") is returned for this attribute.
SQL_DESC_LOCAL_ TYPE_NAME (ODBC 3.0)	Character string	Contains a character representation of any localized (native language) name for the data type used by the column that is different from the regular data type name used. If there is no localized name for the data type used, an empty string (" ") is returned for this attribute. This column is intended to be used for display purposes only. The string's character set is locale-dependent and usually defaults to the character set used by the data source.
SQL_DESC_NAME (ODBC 3.0)	Character string	Identifies the name or alias assigned to the column—if a column alias does not apply, the column name is returned for this attribute. If the column is unnamed, an empty string (" ") is returned for this attribute. The driver sets the **SQL_DESC_UNNAMED** attribute to **SQL_NAMED** if it populates this attribute; it sets the **SQL_DESC_UNNAMED** attribute to **SQL_UNNAMED** if it stores an empty string (" ") in this attribute. This information is obtained from the **SQL_DESC_NAME** field of the IRD descriptor header record.
SQL_DESC_ NULLABLE (ODBC 3.0)	32-bit integer	Indicates whether the column can contain NULL values. Valid values for this attribute are: **SQL_NULLABLE:** The column can contain NULL values. **SQL_NO_NULLS:** The column cannot contain NULL values. **SQL_NULLABLE_UNKNOWN:** Whether the column can contain NULL values is not known. This information is obtained from the **SQL_DESC_NULLABLE** field of the IRD descriptor record.

Table 10–2 Continued

Attribute	Data Type	Description
SQL_DESC_NUM_ PREX_RADIX (ODBC 3.0)	32-bit integer	Identifies the radix value of the data type used by the column. For approximate numeric data types, this attribute contains the value **2**, and the **SQL_DESC_PRECISION** attribute contains the number of bits allowed. For exact numeric data types, this attribute contains the value **10**, and the **SQL_DESC_PRECISION** attribute contains the number of decimal digits allowed. For numeric data types, this attribute can contain either **10** or **2**. For data types where radix is not applicable, this attribute is set to **0**.
SQL_DESC_ OCTET_LENGTH (ODBC 3.0)	32-bit integer	Identifies the length, in octets (bytes), of character string or binary data types. For fixed-length character types, this is the actual length in bytes. For variable-length character or binary types, this is the maximum length, in bytes. In either case, length values returned for character strings always include the NULL-termination character. This information is obtained from the **SQL_DESC_OCTECT_LENGTH** field of the IRD descriptor record.
SQL_DESC_ PRECISION (ODBC 3.0)	32-bit integer	Identifies the maximum number of bytes needed to display the column data in character form. For exact data types, this attribute contains the number of digits. For approximate numeric data types, this attribute contains the number of bits in the mantissa (binary precision). For **SQL_TYPE_TIME**, **SQL_TYPE_TIMESTAMP**, or **SQL_INTERVAL_ SECOND** data types, this attribute contains the numbers of digits in the fractional seconds component of the value. This information is obtained from the **SQL_DESC_PRECISION** field of the IRD descriptor record.
SQL_DESC_SCALE (ODBC 3.0)	32-bit integer	Identifies the scale defined for **DECIMAL** and **NUMERIC** data types. This field is undefined for all other data types. This information is obtained from the **SQL_DESC_ SCALE** field of the IRD descriptor record.

Table 10–2 *Continued*

Attribute	Data Type	Description
SQL_DESC_ SCHEMA_NAME (ODBC 2.0)	Character string	Identifies the schema (owner) of the table containing the column. If a data source does not support schemas (owners), or if the schema name cannot be determined, an empty string (" ") is returned for this attribute. If the column is an expression or part of a view, the value stored in this attribute is implementation defined.
SQL_DESC_ SEARCHABLE (ODBC 1.0)	32-bit integer	Indicates how the column data type is used in a **WHERE** clause. Valid values for this attribute are: **SQL_PRED_NONE:** The column cannot be used in a **WHERE** clause. (ODBC 3.x) **SQL_UNSEARCHEABLE:** The column cannot be used in a **WHERE** clause. (ODBC 2.0.) **SQL_PRED_CHAR:** The column can be used in a **WHERE** clause, but only with the **LIKE** predicate. (ODBC 3.x) **SQL_LIKE_ONLY:** The column can be used in a **WHERE** clause, but only with the **LIKE** predicate. (ODBC 2.0) **SQL_PRED_BASIC:** The column can be used in a **WHERE** clause with all the comparison operators except **LIKE**. (ODBC 3.x) **SQL_ALL_EXCEPT_LIKE:** The column can be used in a **WHERE** clause with all the comparison operators except **LIKE**. (ODBC 2.0) **SQL_PRED_SEARCHABLE:** The column can be used in a **WHERE** clause with any comparison operator. (ODBC 3.x) **SQL_SEARCHABLE:** The column can be used in a **WHERE** clause with any comparison operator. (ODBC 2.0) Columns with **SQL_LONGVARCHAR** and **SQL_LONGVARBINARY** data types usually have an **SQL_DESC_SEARCHABLE** attribute of **SQL_PRED_CHAR**.
SQL_DESC_ TABLE_NAME (ODBC 2.0)	Character string	Identifies the name of the table containing the column. If the table name cannot be determined, an empty string (" ") is returned for this attribute. If the column is an expression or part of a view, the value stored in this attribute is implementation defined.
SQL_DESC_TYPE (ODBC 1.0)	32-bit integer	Identifies the concise SQL data type for the data type (other than datetime and interval data types) used by the column. For the datetime and interval data types, this field specifies the verbose data type, which is **SQL_DATETIME** or **SQL_INTERVAL**, respectively.

Table 10–2 *Continued*

Attribute	Data Type	Description
		If the column is a bookmark column (column number 0), this attribute contains **SQL_BINARY** if the bookmark is a variable-length bookmark, and **SQL_INTEGER** if the bookmark is a fixed-length bookmark.
		This information is obtained from the **SQL_DESC_TYPE** field of the IRD descriptor record.
SQL_DESC_TYPE_NAME (ODBC 1.0)	Character string	Identifies the data source-specific character representation of the SQL data type used by the column. Valid values for this column include:

CHAR	VARCHAR
LONG VARCHAR	DECIMAL
NUMERIC	SMALLINT
INTEGER	REAL
FLOAT	DOUBLE PRECISION
BIT	TINYINT
BIGINT	BINARY
VARBINARY	LONG VARBINARY
DATE	TIME
TIMESTAMP	

Attribute	Data Type	Description
		If the data source-specific SQL data type name cannot be determined, an empty string is returned for this attribute.
SQL_DESC_UNNAMED (ODBC 3.0)	32-bit integer	Indicates whether a column in a result data set has an alias or a name. Valid values for this attribute are:
		SQL_NAMED: The **SQL_DESC_NAME** attribute contains a column alias, or if a column alias does not apply, a column name.
		SQL_UNNAMED: The **SQL_DESC_NAME** attribute does not contain a column alias or a column name.
		This attribute is set by the driver when the **SQL_DESC_NAME** attribute is set.
		This information is obtained from the **SQL_DESC_UNNAMED** field of the IRD descriptor record.
SQL_DESC_UNSIGNED (ODBC 1.0)	32-bit integer	Indicates whether the column data type is a signed or an unsigned data type. Valid values for this attribute are:
		TRUE: The column's data type is an unsigned data type.
		FALSE: The column's data type is a signed data type.

Table 10–2 *Continued*

Attribute	Data Type	Description
SQL_DESC_ UPDATABLE (ODBC 1.0)	32-bit integer	Indicates whether the column data type is an updateable data type. Valid values for this attribute are:
		SQL_ATTR_READONLY: The column data type is read-only (this value is returned if the column was generated by a catalog function call).
		SQL_ATTR_WRITE: The column data type is updatable.
		SQL_ATTR_READWRITE_UNKNOWN: Whether the column data type is updateable is not known.
		This attribute describes the ability to update the column in the result data set, not the column in the base table. The ability to update the base column on which the result data set column is based may be different from the value of this attribute. Whether a column is updatable can be based on the data type, user privileges, and the definition of the result data set itself.

(Adapted from the table on pages 521–527 of *Microsoft ODBC 3.0 Software Development Kit & Programmer's Reference*.)

length of a NULL-termination character) characters and is NULL-terminated by the driver. The *CharValueMaxSize* parameter is ignored for all other types of data; the driver assumes that the size of the data is 32 bits.

■ If the value returned for the attribute specified in the *Attribute* parameter is a Unicode string, the *CharValueMaxSize* must contain an even number.

■ This function either returns a character string value (in the *CharacterValue* parameter) or an 32-bit signed integer value (in the *NumericValue* parameter). When information is returned in the *NumericValue* parameter, the *CharacterValue*, *CharValueMaxSize*, and *CharValueSize* parameters are ignored. When information is returned in the *CharacterValue* parameter, the *NumericValue* parameter is ignored.

■ When mapping **SQLColAttributes()** to **SQLColAttribute()** (when an ODBC 2.0 application is working with an ODBC 3.x driver) or when mapping **SQLColAttribute()** to **SQLColAttributes()** (when an ODBC 3.x application is working with an ODBC 2.0 driver) the ODBC Driver Manager passes the value specified in the *Attribute* parameter through, maps it to a new value, or returns an error, as follows:

■ If the **#define** value of the ODBC 2.0 attribute is the same as the **#define** value of the ODBC 3.x attribute, the value specified in the *Attribute* parameter is passed through.

If the **#define** value of the ODBC 2.0 attribute is different from the **#define** value of the ODBC 3.x attribute, as is the case with the **COUNT**, **NAME**, and **NULLABLE** values, the value specified in the *Attribute* parameter is mapped to the corresponding value. For example, **SQL_COLUMN_COUNT** is mapped to **SQL_DESC_COUNT**, and **SQL_DESC_COUNT** is mapped to **SQL_COLUMN_COUNT**, depending on the direction of the mapping.

If the attribute is a new value in ODBC 3.x for which there was no corresponding value in ODBC 2.0, it is not mapped when an ODBC 3.x application uses it in a call to **SQLColAttribute()** with an ODBC 2.0 driver, and SQLSTATE **HY**091 (Invalid descriptor field identifier) is returned.

The **#define** values of the ODBC 2.0 attributes **SQL_COLUMN_LENGTH**, **SQL_COLUMN_PRECISION**, and **SQL_COLUMN_SCALE** are different from the **#define** values of the ODBC 3.x attributes **SQL_DESC_PRECISION**, **SQL_DESC_SCALE**, and **SQL_DESC_LENGTH**. These values are different because precision, scale, and length are defined differently in ODBC 3.x than in ODBC 2.0. If an ODBC 3.x driver does not support both the ODBC 3.x values and the ODBC 2.0 values, **SQL_ERROR** is returned.

NOTE: *The prefix used to define attribute values in ODBC 3.x is different from that used in ODBC 2.0. The ODBC 3.x prefix is* **SQL_DESC**; *the ODBC 2.0 prefix is* **SQL_COLUMN**.

■ This function is a more extensible alternative to the **SQLDescribeCol()** function; **SQLDescribeCol()** returns a fixed set of column metadata information based on the ANSI-89 SQL standards—**SQLColAttribute()** allows access to the more extensive set of column metadata (IRD descriptor information) defined in the ANSI SQL-92 standard and/or in DBMS vendor extensions.

■ Because the information returned by this function is stored in the IRD descriptor record associated with the column specified, this information can also be obtained by calling the **SQLGetDescField()** function with the appropriate IRD descriptor handle specified.

Prerequisites   The `SQLPrepare()` function or the `SQLExecDirect()` function must be called before this function is called. For performance reasons, an application should wait until an SQL statement has been executed before calling this function.

Restrictions   There are no restrictions associated with this function call.

See Also   `SQLColAttributes()`, `SQLDescribeCol()`, `SQLGetDescField()`, `SQLGetDescField()`

Example   The following Visual C++ program illustrates how to use the `SQLColAttribute()` function to obtain specific information about a column in a result data set.

```
/*-------------------------------------------------------------------*/
/* NAME:      CH10EX3.CPP                                            */
/* PURPOSE: Illustrate How To Use The Following ODBC API Function    */
/*          In A C++ Program:                                        */
/*                                                                   */
/*                  SQLColAttribute()                                */
/*                                                                   */
/* OTHER ODBC APIs SHOWN:                                            */
/*          SQLAllocHandle()        SQLSetEnvAttr()                  */
/*          SQLConnect()            SQLExecDirect()                  */
/*          SQLNumResultCols()      SQLDisconnect()                  */
/*          SQLFreeHandle()                                          */
/*                                                                   */
/*-------------------------------------------------------------------*/

// Include The Appropriate Header Files
#include <windows.h>
#include <sql.h>
#include <sqlext.h>
#include <iostream.h>

// Define The ODBC_Class Class
class ODBC_Class
{
    // Attributes
    public:
        SQLHANDLE   EnvHandle;
        SQLHANDLE   ConHandle;
        SQLHANDLE   StmtHandle;
        SQLRETURN   rc;

    // Operations
    public:
        ODBC_Class();                           // Constructor
        ~ODBC_Class();                          // Destructor
        SQLRETURN ShowColInfo();
};
```

```
// Define The Class Constructor
ODBC_Class::ODBC_Class()
{
    // Initialize The Return Code Variable
    rc = SQL_SUCCESS;

    // Allocate An Environment Handle
    rc = SQLAllocHandle(SQL_HANDLE_ENV, SQL_NULL_HANDLE, &EnvHandle);

    // Set The ODBC Application Version To 3.x
    if (rc == SQL_SUCCESS)
        rc = SQLSetEnvAttr(EnvHandle, SQL_ATTR_ODBC_VERSION,
                    (SQLPOINTER) SQL_OV_ODBC3, SQL_IS_UINTEGER);

    // Allocate A Connection Handle
    if (rc == SQL_SUCCESS)
        rc = SQLAllocHandle(SQL_HANDLE_DBC, EnvHandle, &ConHandle);
}

// Define The Class Destructor
ODBC_Class::~ODBC_Class()
{
    // Free The Connection Handle
    if (ConHandle != NULL)
        SQLFreeHandle(SQL_HANDLE_DBC, ConHandle);

    // Free The Environment Handle
    if (EnvHandle != NULL)
        SQLFreeHandle(SQL_HANDLE_ENV, EnvHandle);
}

// Define The ShowColInfo() Member Function
SQLRETURN ODBC_Class::ShowColInfo(void)
{
    // Declare The Local Memory Variables
    SQLSMALLINT  NumCols;
    SQLCHAR      TypeName[50];
    SQLSMALLINT  TypeNameLen;

    // Find Out How Many Columns Exist In The Result Data Set
    rc = SQLNumResultCols(StmtHandle, &NumCols);
    if (rc == SQL_SUCCESS)
    {
        // Display A Header
        cout << "Column Data Types :" << endl << endl;

        // Obtain And Display The Name Of Each Column
        for (int i = 1; i <= (int) NumCols; i++)
        {
            rc = SQLColAttribute(StmtHandle, i, SQL_DESC_TYPE_NAME,
                    TypeName, sizeof(TypeName), &TypeNameLen, NULL);

            if (rc == SQL_SUCCESS)
                cout << "Column " << i << " : " << TypeName << endl;
        }
```

```
    }

    // Return The ODBC API Return Code To The Calling Function
    return(rc);
}

/*------------------------------------------------------------------*/
/* The Main Function                                                */
/*------------------------------------------------------------------*/
int main()
{
    // Declare The Local Memory Variables
    SQLRETURN    rc = SQL_SUCCESS;
    SQLCHAR      DBName[10] = "Northwind";
    SQLCHAR      SQLStmt[255];

    // Create An Instance Of The ODBC_Class Class
    ODBC_Class   Example;

    // Connect To The Northwind Sample Database
    if (Example.ConHandle != NULL)
    {
        rc = SQLConnect(Example.ConHandle, DBName, SQL_NTS,
                  (SQLCHAR *) "", SQL_NTS, (SQLCHAR *) "", SQL_NTS);

        // Allocate An SQL Statement Handle
        rc = SQLAllocHandle(SQL_HANDLE_STMT, Example.ConHandle,
                  &Example.StmtHandle);
        if (rc == SQL_SUCCESS)
        {
            // Define A SELECT SQL Statement
            strcpy((char *) SQLStmt, "SELECT * FROM ");
            strcat((char *) SQLStmt, "[Order Details] WHERE ");
            strcat((char *) SQLStmt, "Quantity < 20");

            // Prepare And Execute The SQL Statement
            rc = SQLExecDirect(Example.StmtHandle, SQLStmt, SQL_NTS);

            // Display Information About The Columns In The Result
            // Data Set Produced By The SQL Query
            if (rc == SQL_SUCCESS)
                Example.ShowColInfo();

            // Free The SQL Statement Handle
            if (Example.StmtHandle != NULL)
                SQLFreeHandle(SQL_HANDLE_STMT, Example.StmtHandle);
        }

        // Disconnect From The Northwind Sample Database
        rc = SQLDisconnect(Example.ConHandle);
    }

    // Return To The Operating System
    return(rc);
}
```

SQLColAttributes

COMPATABILITY

X/OPEN 95 CLI	ISO/IEC 92 CLI	ODBC 1.0	ODBC 2.0	ODBC 3.0	ODBC 3.5
☐	☐	✓	✓	☐	☐

API CONFORMANCE LEVEL **CORE**

Purpose

The **SQLColAttributes()** function is used to retrieve descriptor information (for example, column name, data type, column size, decimal precision, and nullability) for a specified column in a result data set.

Syntax

```
SQLRETURN   SQLColAttributes  (HSTMT       StatementHandle,
                               UWORD       ColumnNumber,
                               UWORD       Attribute,
                               PTR         CharacterValue,
                               SWORD       CharValueMaxSize,
                               SWORD FAR   *CharValueSize,
                               SWORD FAR   *NumericValue);
```

Parameters

StatementHandle   An SQL statement handle that refers to a previously allocated SQL statement information storage buffer (data structure).

ColumnNumber   Specifies the column's location in the result data set. Columns are numbered sequentially from left to right, starting with 1, as they appear in the result data set.

Attribute   The column attribute for which information is to be retrieved. This parameter must be set to one of the following values:

- **SQL_COLUMN_AUTO_INCREMENT**
- **SQL_COLUMN_CASE_SENSITIVE**
- **SQL_COLUMN_COUNT**
- **SQL_COLUMN_DISPLAY_SIZE**
- **SQL_COLUMN_LABEL**
- **SQL_COLUMN_LENGTH**

- **SQL_COLUMN_MONEY**
- **SQL_COLUMN_NAME**
- **SQL_COLUMN_NULLABLE**
- **SQL_COLUMN_OWNER_NAME**
- **SQL_COLUMN_PRECISION**
- **SQL_COLUMN_QUALIFIER_NAME**
- **SQL_COLUMN_SCALE**
- **SQL_COLUMN_SEARCHABLE**
- **SQL_COLUMN_TABLE_NAME**
- **SQL_COLUMN_TYPE**
- **SQL_COLUMN_TYPE_NAME**
- **SQL_COLUMN_UNSIGNED**
- **SQL_COLUMN_UPDATABLE**

CharacterValue	A pointer to a location in memory where this function is to store the current value of the specified attribute (if the attribute value is a character value).
CharValueMaxSize	The size of the memory storage buffer where this function is to store the current value of the specified attribute.
CharValueSize	A pointer to a location in memory where this function is to store the actual number of bytes written to the attribute character value memory storage buffer (*CharacterValue*). If the attribute value retrieved is not a character string value, this parameter is ignored.
NumberValue	A pointer to a location in memory where this function is to store the current value of the specified attribute (if the attribute value is a numeric value).

Description   The **SQLColAttributes()** function is used to retrieve descriptor information (for example, column name, data type, column size, decimal precision, and nullability) for a specified column in a result data set. Table 10–3 lists alphabetically each value that can be specified for the *Attribute* para-meter, along with a description of the information returned for that value when this function is executed.

Table 10–3 Column Attributes( )

Attribute	Data Type	Description
SQL_COLUMN_ AUTO_INCREMENT (ODBC 1.0)	32-bit integer	Indicates whether the column's data type is an auto increment data type. Valid values for this attribute are: **TRUE**: The column's data type is an auto increment data type. **FALSE**: The column's data type is not an auto increment data type or the column does not contain numeric data. This attribute is only valid for columns containing numeric data types. Values can be inserted into auto increment data type columns; however, existing auto increment data type column values cannot be updated.
SQL_COLUMN_ CASE_SENSITIVE (ODBC 1.0)	32-bit integer	Indicates whether the column's data type is treated as case sensitive for collations and comparisons. Valid values for this attribute are: **TRUE**: The column's data type is treated as case sensitive for collations and comparisons. **FALSE**: The column's data type is not treated as case sensitive for collations and comparisons.
SQL_COLUMN_ COUNT (ODBC 1.0)	32-bit integer	Identifies the number of columns that are available in the result data set. If there are no columns in the result data set, **0** is returned for this attribute.
SQL_COLUMN_ DISPLAY_SIZE (ODBC 1.0)	32-bit integer	Identifies the maximum number of characters needed to display data from the column.
SQL_COLUMN_ LABEL (ODBC 2.0)	Character string	Identifies the label assigned to the column. If the column is unlabeled and unnamed, an empty string (" ") is returned for this attribute.
SQL_COLUMN_ LENGTH (ODBC 1.0)	32-bit integer	Identifies the total number of data bytes associated with the column. This is the length, in bytes, of the data transferred when the **SQLFetch()** or **SQLGetData()** function is called for this column (provided **SQL_C_DEFAULT** is specified as the C data type of the column). If the column contains fixed length character or binary string data, the actual length of the column (minus the size of the NULL termination character) is returned. If the column contains variable length character or binary string data, the maximum length of the column is returned. If the column contains numeric data, the length returned may be different from the size of the data stored in the data source.

Table 10–3 *Continued*

Attribute	Data Type	Description
SQL_COLUMN_ MONEY (ODBC 1.0)	32-bit integer	Indicates whether the column data type is a money data type. Valid values for this attribute are: **TRUE:** The column's data type is a money data type. **FALSE:** The column's data type is not a money data type.
SQL_COLUMN_ NAME (ODBC 1.0)	Character string	Identifies the name assigned to the column. If the column is unnamed, an empty string (" ") is returned for this attribute. If the column was derived from an expression, the column name stored in this attribute is data source product-specific.
SQL_COLUMN_ NULLABLE (ODBC 1.0)	32-bit integer	Indicates whether the column can contain NULL values. Valid values for this attribute are: **SQL_NO_NULLS:** The column cannot contain NULL values. **SQL_NULLABLE:** The column can contain NULL values.
SQL_COLUMN_ OWNER_NAME (ODBC 2.0)	Character string	Identifies the owner (schema) of the table containing the column. If a data source does not support owners (schemas) or if the owner name cannot be determined, an empty string (" ") is returned for this attribute. If the column is an expression or part of a view, the value stored in this attribute is implementation-defined.
SQL_COLUMN_ PRECISION (ODBC 1.0)	32-bit integer	Identifies the maximum number of bytes needed to display the column data in character form. For numeric data types, this attribute contains either the total number of digits or the total number of bits allowed in the column.
SQL_COLUMN_ QUALIFIER_NAME (ODBC 2.0)	Character string	Identifies the qualifier (catalog) of the table containing the column. If a data source does not support qualifiers (catalogs) or if the qualifier name cannot be determined, an empty string (" ") is returned for this attribute. If the column is an expression or part of a view, the value stored in this attribute is implementation-defined.
SQL_COLUMN_ SCALE (ODBC 1.0)	32-bit integer	Identifies the total number of significant digits to the right of the decimal point. For columns with time or timestamp data types, this attribute contains the number of digits in the fractional seconds component. For columns with data types where decimal digits are not applicable, this attribute is set to NULL. For columns with any other data type, this attribute contains the decimal digits of the column on the data source.

Table 10-3 Continued

Attribute	Data Type	Description
SQL_COLUMN_ SEARCHABLE (ODBC 1.0)	32-bit integer	Indicates how the column data type is used in a **WHERE** clause. Valid values for this attribute are: **SQL_SEARCHABLE:** The column can be used in a **WHERE** clause with any comparison operators. (ODBC 3.x) **SQL_LIKE_ONLY:** The column can be used in a **WHERE** clause but only with the **LIKE** predicate. **SQL_ALL_EXCEPT_LIKE:** The column can be used in a **WHERE** clause with all comparison operators except **LIKE**. **SQL_UNSEARCHABLE:** The column cannot be used in a **WHERE** clause. Columns with **SQL_LONGVARCHAR** and **SQL_LONGVARBINARY** data types usually have an **SQL_COLUMN_SEARCHABLE** attribute of **SQL_LIKE_ONLY**.
SQL_COLUMN_ TABLE_NAME (ODBC 2.0)	Character string	Identifies the name of the table containing the column. If the table name cannot be determined, an empty string (" ") is returned for this attribute.
SQL_COLUMN_TYPE (ODBC 1.0)	32-bit integer	Identifies the ODBC or driver-specific SQL data type of the column. Valid values for this column include: SQL_CHAR SQL_VARCHAR SQL_LONGVARCHAR SQL_DECIMAL SQL_NUMERIC SQL_SMALLINT SQL_INTEGER SQL_REAL SQL_FLOAT SQL_DOUBLE SQL_BIT SQL_TINYINT SQL_BIGINT SQL_BINARY SQL_VARBINARY SQL_LONGVARBINARY SQL_TYPE_DATE SQL_TYPE_TIME SQL_TYPE_TIMESTAMP
SQL_COLUMN_ TYPE_NAME (ODBC 1.0)	Character string	Identifies the data source-specific character representation of the SQL data type name identified in the **SQL_COLUMN_TYPE** attribute. Valid values for this column include: CHAR VARCHAR LONG VARCHAR DECIMAL NUMERIC SMALLINT INTEGER REAL FLOAT DOUBLE PRECISION BIT TINYINT BIGINT BINARY VARBINARY LONG VARBINARY DATE TIME TIMESTAMP

Table 10–3 *Continued*

Attribute	Data Type	Description
SQL_COLUMN_ UNSIGNED (ODBC 1.0)	32-bit integer	Indicates whether the column data type is a signed or an unsigned data type. Valid values for this attribute are: **TRUE**: The column's data type is an unsigned data type. **FALSE**: The column's data type is a signed data type.
SQL_COLUMN_ UPDATABLE (ODBC 1.0)	32-bit integer	Indicates whether the column data type is an updateable data type. Valid values for this attribute are: **SQL_ATTR_READONLY**: The column data type is read-only (this value is returned if the column was generated by a catalog function call). **SQL_ATTR_WRITE**: The column data type is updatable. **SQL_ATTR_READWRITE_UNKNOWN**: Whether the column data type is updateable is not known.

(Adapted from the table on pages 238–241 of *Microsoft ODBC 2.0 Programmers Reference and SDK Guide*.)

If the various attributes about a result data set column (such as, data type and length) are not known, this function (or the **SQLDescribeCol()** function) can be called after an SQL query statement has been prepared or executed, to determine the attributes of a column before binding it to an application variable.

To take advantage of different data sources, more column attributes may be defined in future releases of ODBC. In fact, a range of column attributes (0 to 999) has been reserved by ODBC to allow for future expansion. In addition, ODBC driver developers are required to reserve values for their own driver-specific use from X/Open.

NOTE: *In ODBC 3.x, this function has been replaced by the* **SQLColAttribute()** *function.*

Return Codes SQL_SUCCESS, SQL_SUCCESS_WITH_INFO, SQL_STILL_EXECUTING, SQL_INVALID_HANDLE, or SQL_ERROR

SQLSTATEs If this function returns **SQL_SUCCESS_WITH_INFO** or **SQL_ERROR**, one of the following SQLSTATE values may be obtained by calling the **SQLError()** function:

01000, **01**004, **24**000, **IM**001*, **S**1000, **S**1001, **S**1002*, **S**1008, **S**1010*, **S**1090*, **S**1091*, **S**1C00, or **S**1T00

*Returned by the ODBC Driver Manager.

Unless noted otherwise, each of these SQLSTATE values are returned by the data source driver. Refer to Appendix B for detailed information about each SQLSTATE value that can be returned by the ODBC Driver Manager or by a data source driver.

SQLColAttributes() can return any SQLSTATE that can be returned by **SQLPrepare()** or **SQLExecute()** when called after **SQLPrepare()** and before **SQLExecute()** depending on when the data source evaluates the SQL statement associated with the statement handle specified.

Comments
▨ This function returns either a character string value (in the *CharacterValue* parameter) or a 32-bit signed integer value (in the *NumericValue* parameter). When information is returned in the *NumericValue* parameter, the *CharacterValue, CharValueMaxSize,* and *CharValueSize* parameters are ignored. When information is returned in the *CharacterValue* parameter, the *NumericValue* parameter is ignored.

▨ This function is a more extensible alternative to the **SQLDescribeCol()** function; **SQLDescribeCol()** returns a fixed set of column metadata information based on the ANSI-89 SQL standards—**SQLColAttributes()** allows access to the more extensive set of column metadata descriptor information defined in the ANSI SQL-92 standard and/or in DBMS vendor extensions.

Prerequisites
The **SQLPrepare()** function or the **SQLExecDirect()** function must be called before this function is called.

Restrictions
This function cannot be used to return information about the bookmark column (column 0).

See Also
SQLDescribeCol(), SQLSetColAttribute()

Example
The following Visual C++ program illustrates how to use the **SQLColAttribute()** function to obtain specific information about a column in a result data set.

```
/*------------------------------------------------------------------------*/
/* NAME:     CH10EX4.CPP                                                   */
/* PURPOSE: Illustrate How To Use The Following ODBC API Function          */
/*          In A C++ Program:                                              */
/*                                                                         */
/*             SQLColAttributes()                                          */
/*                                                                         */
/* OTHER ODBC APIs SHOWN:                                                  */
/*          SQLAllocEnv()              SQLAllocConnect()                    */
/*          SQLAllocStmt()             SQLConnect()                         */
/*          SQLExecDirect()            SQLNumResultCols()                   */
/*          SQLDisconnect()            SQLFreeStmt()                        */
/*          SQLFreeConnect()           SQLFreeEnv()                         */
/*                                                                         */
/*------------------------------------------------------------------------*/

// Include The Appropriate Header Files
#include <windows.h>
#include <sql.h>
#include <sqlext.h>
#include <iostream.h>

// Define The ODBC_Class Class
class ODBC_Class
{
    // Attributes
    public:
        HENV      EnvHandle;
        HDBC      ConHandle;
        HSTMT     StmtHandle;
        RETCODE   rc;

    // Operations
    public:
        ODBC_Class();                        // Constructor
        ~ODBC_Class();                       // Destructor
        RETCODE   ShowColInfo();
};

// Define The Class Constructor
ODBC_Class::ODBC_Class()
{
    // Initialize The Return Code Variable
    rc = SQL_SUCCESS;

    // Allocate An Environment Handle
    rc = SQLAllocEnv(&EnvHandle);

    // Allocate A Connection Handle
    if (rc == SQL_SUCCESS)
        rc = SQLAllocConnect(EnvHandle, &ConHandle);
}

// Define The Class Destructor
ODBC_Class::~ODBC_Class()
```

```
{
    // Free The Connection Handle
    if (ConHandle != NULL)
        SQLFreeConnect(ConHandle);

    // Free The Environment Handle
    if (EnvHandle != NULL)
        SQLFreeEnv(EnvHandle);
}

// Define The ShowColInfo() Member Function
SQLRETURN ODBC_Class::ShowColInfo(void)
{
    // Declare The Local Memory Variables
    SQLSMALLINT  NumCols;
    SQLCHAR      TypeName[50];
    SQLSMALLINT  TypeNameLen;

    // Find Out How Many Columns Exist In The Result Data Set
    rc = SQLNumResultCols(StmtHandle, &NumCols);
    if (rc == SQL_SUCCESS)
    {
        // Display A Header
        cout << "Column Data Types :" << endl << endl;

        // Obtain And Display The Name Of Each Column
        for (int i = 1; i <= (int) NumCols; i++)
        {
            rc = SQLColAttributes(StmtHandle, i, SQL_COLUMN_TYPE_NAME,
                    TypeName, sizeof(TypeName), &TypeNameLen, NULL);

            if (rc == SQL_SUCCESS)
                cout << "Column " << i << " : " << TypeName << endl;
        }
    }

    // Return The ODBC API Return Code To The Calling Function
    return(rc);
}

/*----------------------------------------------------------------------*/
/* The Main Function                                                    */
/*----------------------------------------------------------------------*/
int main()
{
    // Declare The Local Memory Variables
    RETCODE  rc = SQL_SUCCESS;
    SQLCHAR  DBName[10] = "Northwind";
    SQLCHAR  SQLStmt[255];

    // Create An Instance Of The ODBC_Class Class
    ODBC_Class  Example;

    // Connect To The Northwind Sample Database
    if (Example.ConHandle != NULL)
    {
```

```
rc = SQLConnect(Example.ConHandle, DBName, SQL_NTS,
        (SQLCHAR *) "", SQL_NTS, (SQLCHAR *) "", SQL_NTS);

// Allocate An SQL Statement Handle
rc = SQLAllocStmt(Example.ConHandle, &Example.StmtHandle);
if (rc == SQL_SUCCESS)
{
    // Define A SELECT SQL Statement
    strcpy((char *) SQLStmt, "SELECT * FROM ");
    strcat((char *) SQLStmt, "[Order Details] WHERE ");
    strcat((char *) SQLStmt, "Quantity < 20");

    // Prepare And Execute The SQL Statement
    rc = SQLExecDirect(Example.StmtHandle, SQLStmt, SQL_NTS);

    // Display Information About The Columns In The Result
    // Data Set Produced By The SQL Query
    if (rc == SQL_SUCCESS)
        Example.ShowColInfo();

    // Free The SQL Statement Handle
    if (Example.StmtHandle != NULL)
        SQLFreeStmt(Example.StmtHandle, SQL_DROP);
}

// Disconnect From The Northwind Sample Database
rc = SQLDisconnect(Example.ConHandle);
}

// Return To The Operating System
return(rc);
}
```

SQLBindCol

COMPATABILITY					
X/OPEN 95 CLI	ISO/IEC 92 CLI	ODBC 1.0	ODBC 2.0	ODBC 3.0	ODBC 3.5
✓	✓	✓	✓	✓	✓

API CONFORMANCE LEVEL   **CORE**

Purpose   The **SQLBindCol()** function is used to associate (bind) columns in a result data set with application variables.

Syntax

```
SQLRETURN  SQLBindCol  (SQLHSTMT        StatementHandle,
                        SQLUSMALLINT    ColumnNumber,
                        SQLSMALLINT     CDataType,
                        SQLPOINTER      Value,
                        SQLINTEGER      ValueMaxSize,
                        SQLINTEGER      *ValueSize_Indicator);
```

Parameters

StatementHandle	An SQL statement handle that refers to a previously allocated SQL statement information storage buffer (data structure).
ColumnNumber	Specifies the column's location in the result data set. Columns are numbered sequentially from left to right, starting with 1, as they appear in the result data set.
CDataType	The C language data type of the value memory storage buffer (*Value*) being bound. This parameter must be set to one of the following values:

- SQL_C_CHAR
- SQL_C_SSHORT
- SQL_C_USHORT
- SQL_C_SLONG
- SQL_C_ULONG
- SQL_C_FLOAT
- SQL_C_DOUBLE
- SQL_C_BIT
- SQL_C_STINYINT
- SQL_C_UTINYINT
- SQL_C_SBIGINT
- SQL_C_UBIGINT
- SQL_C_BINARY
- SQL_C_BOOKMARK
- SQL_C_VAR_BOOKMARK
- SQL_C_DATE
- SQL_C_TIME
- SQL_C_TIMESTAMP
- SQL_C_TYPE_DATE

- **SQL_C_TYPE_TIME**
- **SQL_C_TYPE_TIMESTAMP**
- **SQL_C_NUMERIC**

Value A pointer to a location in memory where the driver is to store column data (or an array of column data) when it is retrieved (fetched) from the result data set or where the application is to store column data that is to be written to a data source with a positioned **UPDATE** or **DELETE** operation.

ValueMaxSize The maximum size of the memory storage buffer where the driver is to store the column data retrieved.

ValueSize_Indicator A pointer to a location in memory where the driver is to store (or retrieve) either the size of the data value associated with the column or a special indicator value associated with the column data.

Any of the following indicator values can be returned to this memory location by the driver (for fetch operations):

- **SQL_NO_TOTAL**
  The size of the column data value is unknown.

- **SQL_NULL_DATA**
  The data value associated with the column is NULL.

The application can store any of the following indicator values in this memory location (for positioned **INSERT**, **UPDATE**, and **DELETE** operations):

- **SQL_NTS**
  The data value associated with the column is a NULL-terminated string.

- **SQL_NULL_DATA**
  The data value associated with the column is NULL.

- **SQL_COLUMN_IGNORE**
  The data value associated with the column is to be ignored.

■ **SQL_DATA_AT_EXEC**
The data value associated with the column is to be sent to the data source with the **SQLGetData()** function.

■ The result of the **SQL_LEN_DATA_AT_ EXEC(*length*)** macro
The data value associated with the column is to be sent to the data source with the **SQLGetData()** function.

Description   The **SQLBindCol()** function is used to associate (bind) columns in a result data set to application variables and, optionally, length/indicator variables. When columns in a result data set are bound to application variables, data is transferred from the data source to the appropriate application variable/buffer when the **SQLFetch()**, **SQLFetchScroll()** (ODBC 3.x drivers), **SQLExtendedFetch()** (ODBC 2.0 or earlier drivers), or **SQLSetPos()** function is called. Conversely, data is transferred from bound application variable/buffers to the data source when the **SQLBulkOperations()** or **SQLSetPos()** function is called to update or insert a row of data. If necessary, data conversion occurs as the data is transferred.

Return Codes   **SQL_SUCCESS, SQL_SUCCESS_WITH_INFO, SQL_INVALID_HANDLE**, or **SQL_ERROR**

SQLSTATEs   If this function returns **SQL_SUCCESS_WITH_INFO** or **SQL_ERROR**, one of the following SQLSTATE values may be obtained by calling the **SQLGetDiagRec()** function (ODBC 3.x driver) or the **SQLError()** function (ODBC 2.0 or earlier driver):

ODBC 3.X
01000, **07**006*, **07**009, **HY**000, **HY**001, **HY**003, **HY**010*, **HY**013, **HY**090*, **HY**C00, **HY**T01, or **IM**001*

ODBC 2.0 OR EARLIER
01000, **IM**001*, **S1**000, **S1**001, **S1**002, **S1**003*, **S1**009, **S1**010*, **S1**090*, or **S1**C00

*Returned by the ODBC Driver Manager.

Unless noted otherwise, each of these SQLSTATE values are returned by the data source driver. Refer to Appendix B for detailed information about each SQLSTATE value that can be returned by the ODBC Driver Manager or by a data source driver.

Comments

▨ Columns are numbered in increasing column order as they appear in the result data set, starting at 0, where column 0 is the bookmark column. If bookmarks are not used (that is, if the **SQL_ATTR_USE_BOOKMARKS** SQL statement attribute is set to **SQL_UB_OFF**) column numbers start at 1.

▨ When data is retrieved from a result data set by **SQLFetch()**, **SQLFetchScroll()**, **SQLExtendedFetch()**, or **SQLSetPos()**, the driver converts the data to the C data type specified in the *CDataType* parameter. When data is sent to the data source by **SQLBulkOperations()** or **SQLSetPos()**, the driver converts the data from this C data type.

▨ If an interval data type is stored in the *CDataType* parameter, the default interval leading precision (**2**) and the default interval seconds precision (**6**), as set in the ARD descriptor's **SQL_DESC_DATETIME_INTERVAL_PRECISION** and **SQL_DESC_PRECISION** fields, respectively, are used for data conversion.

▨ If a numeric data type (**SQL_C_NUMERIC**) is stored in the *CDataType* parameter, the default precision (driver-defined) and default scale (**0**), as set in the ARD descriptor's **SQL_DESC_PRECISION** and **SQL_DESC_SCALE** fields, are used for data conversion. If the default precision or scale is not appropriate, an application should explicitly set the appropriate descriptor field by calling **SQLSetDescField()** or **SQLSetDescRec()**.

▨ If a NULL pointer is stored in the *Value* parameter, the driver unbinds any application variable/buffer currently bound to the column specified. An application can unbind the application variable currently bound to a column, without unbinding the corresponding length/indicator buffer (if a NULL pointer is stored in the *Value* parameter and a valid value is stored in the *ValueSize_Indicator* parameter).

▨ An application can unbind all bound columns by calling **SQLFreeStmt()** with the **SQL_UNBIND** option specified.

▨ When the driver returns fixed-length data such as integer or date structure data to an application variable it assumes the buffer is large enough to hold the data. Therefore, it is important for the application to use a variable or allocate a buffer that is large enough to hold the fixed-length data stored in the column; otherwise the driver will write past the end of the buffer.

▨ When a value less than **0** is stored in the *ValueMaxSize* parameter, SQLSTATE **HY**090 (Invalid string or buffer length) is returned. This is not the case when **0** is stored in the *ValueMaxSize* parameter; however, if a character data type is specified in the *CDataType* parameter, an application should not store **0** in the *ValueMaxSize* parameter because ISO CLI-compliant drivers return SQLSTATE **HY**090 (Invalid string or buffer length) when this condition is encountered.

■ If the indicator buffer and the length buffer are separate buffers, the indicator buffer can only return **SQL_NULL_DATA**, while the length buffer can return all other values specified.

■ If a NULL pointer is stored in the *ValueSize_Indicator* parameter, no length or indicator value is used.

■ If no length/indicator variable is bound to a column, **SQL_ERROR** is returned if a NULL value is found in the column when data is fetched.

■ Although it is not required, it is strongly recommended that an application set the **SQL_ATTR_USE_BOOKMARKS** statement attribute before binding an application variable to column 0.

■ In ODBC 2.0, applications, set the *CDataType* parameter to **SQL_C_DATE**, **SQL_C_TIME**, or **SQL_C_TIMESTAMP** to indicate that the data is to be returned to a date, time, or timestamp structure. In ODBC 3.x, applications set the *CDataType* parameter to **SQL_C_TYPE_DATE**, **SQL_C_TYPE_TIME**, or **SQL_C_TYPE_TIMESTAMP**. The Driver Manager makes appropriate mappings, if necessary, based on the application and driver version.

Prerequisites   There are no prerequisites for using this function call.

Restrictions   There are no restrictions associated with this function call.

See Also   SQLFetch(), SQLExtendedFetch(), SQLGetData()

Example   The following Visual C++ program illustrates how to use the SQLBindCol() function to associate (bind) a local memory variable to a column in a result data set.

```
/*---------------------------------------------------------------------*/
/* NAME:     CH10EX5.CPP                                               */
/* PURPOSE:  Illustrate How To Use The Following ODBC API Functions    */
/*           In A C++ Program:                                         */
/*                                                                     */
/*               SQLBindCol()                                          */
/*               SQLFetch()                                            */
/*                                                                     */
```

```
/* OTHER ODBC APIs SHOWN:                                       */
/*            SQLAllocHandle()        SQLSetEnvAttr()           */
/*            SQLConnect()            SQLExecDirect()           */
/*            SQLDisconnect()         SQLFreeHandle()           */
/*                                                             */
/*———————————————————————————————————————————————————————————*/

// Include The Appropriate Header Files
#include <windows.h>
#include <sql.h>
#include <sqlext.h>
#include <iostream.h>

// Define The ODBC_Class Class
class ODBC_Class
{
    // Attributes
    public:
        SQLHANDLE   EnvHandle;
        SQLHANDLE   ConHandle;
        SQLHANDLE   StmtHandle;
        SQLRETURN   rc;

    // Operations
    public:
        ODBC_Class();                          // Constructor
        ~ODBC_Class();                         // Destructor
        SQLRETURN ShowResults();
};

// Define The Class Constructor
ODBC_Class::ODBC_Class()
{
    // Initialize The Return Code Variable
    rc = SQL_SUCCESS;

    // Allocate An Environment Handle
    rc = SQLAllocHandle(SQL_HANDLE_ENV, SQL_NULL_HANDLE, &EnvHandle);

    // Set The ODBC Application Version To 3.x
    if (rc == SQL_SUCCESS)
        rc = SQLSetEnvAttr(EnvHandle, SQL_ATTR_ODBC_VERSION,
                 (SQLPOINTER) SQL_OV_ODBC3, SQL_IS_UINTEGER);

    // Allocate A Connection Handle
    if (rc == SQL_SUCCESS)
        rc = SQLAllocHandle(SQL_HANDLE_DBC, EnvHandle, &ConHandle);
}

// Define The Class Destructor
ODBC_Class::~ODBC_Class()
{
    // Free The Connection Handle
    if (ConHandle != NULL)
        SQLFreeHandle(SQL_HANDLE_DBC, ConHandle);
```

```
        // Free The Environment Handle
        if (EnvHandle != NULL)
            SQLFreeHandle(SQL_HANDLE_ENV, EnvHandle);
}


// Define The ShowResults() Member Function
SQLRETURN ODBC_Class::ShowResults(void)
{
        // Declare The Local Memory Variables
        SQLCHAR    LastName[50];
        SQLCHAR    FirstName[50];

        // Bind The Columns In The Result Data Set Returned To
        // Application Variables
        rc = SQLBindCol(StmtHandle, 1, SQL_C_CHAR, (SQLPOINTER) LastName,
                    sizeof(LastName), NULL);

        rc = SQLBindCol(StmtHandle, 2, SQL_C_CHAR, (SQLPOINTER) FirstName,
                    sizeof(FirstName), NULL);

        // Display A Header
        cout << "Employees :" << endl << endl;

        // While There Are Records In The Result Data Set Generated,
        // Retrieve And Display Them
        while (rc != SQL_NO_DATA)
        {
            rc = SQLFetch(StmtHandle);
            if (rc != SQL_NO_DATA)
                cout << FirstName << " " << LastName << endl;
        }

        // Return The ODBC API Return Code To The Calling Function
        return(rc);
}

/*————————————————————————————————————————————————*/
/* The Main Function                                               */
/*————————————————————————————————————————————————*/
int main()
{
        // Declare The Local Memory Variables
        SQLRETURN  rc = SQL_SUCCESS;
        SQLCHAR    DBName[10] = "Northwind";
        SQLCHAR    SQLStmt[255];

        // Create An Instance Of The ODBC_Class Class
        ODBC_Class  Example;

        // Connect To The Northwind Sample Database
        if (Example.ConHandle != NULL)
        {
            rc = SQLConnect(Example.ConHandle, DBName, SQL_NTS,
                    (SQLCHAR *) "", SQL_NTS, (SQLCHAR *) "", SQL_NTS);
```

```
        // Allocate An SQL Statement Handle
        rc = SQLAllocHandle(SQL_HANDLE_STMT, Example.ConHandle,
                &Example.StmtHandle);
        if (rc == SQL_SUCCESS)
        {
            // Define A SELECT SQL Statement
            strcpy((char *) SQLStmt, "SELECT Employees.LastName, ");
            strcat((char *) SQLStmt, "Employees.FirstName FROM ");
            strcat((char *) SQLStmt, "Employees");

            // Prepare And Execute The SQL Statement
            rc = SQLExecDirect(Example.StmtHandle, SQLStmt, SQL_NTS);

            // Display The Results Of The SQL Query
            if (rc == SQL_SUCCESS)
                Example.ShowResults();

            // Free The SQL Statement Handle
            if (Example.StmtHandle != NULL)
                SQLFreeHandle(SQL_HANDLE_STMT, Example.StmtHandle);
        }

        // Disconnect From The Northwind Sample Database
        rc = SQLDisconnect(Example.ConHandle);
    }

    // Return To The Operating System
    return(rc);
}
```

SQLGetCursorName

COMPATABILITY					
X/OPEN 95 CLI	ISO/IEC 92 CLI	ODBC 1.0	ODBC 2.0	ODBC 3.0	ODBC 3.5
✓	✓	✓	✓	✓	✓

API CONFORMANCE LEVEL   **CORE**

Purpose

The SQLGetCursorName() function is used to retrieve the name of the cursor associated with a specific SQL statement handle.

Syntax

```
SQLRETURN  SQLGetCursorName  (SQLHSTMT      StatementHandle,
                              SQLCHAR       *CursorName,
                              SQLSMALLINT   CursorNameMaxSize,
                              SQLSMALLINT   *CursorNameSize);
```

Parameters

StatementHandle	An SQL statement handle that refers to a previously allocated SQL statement information storage buffer (data structure).
CursorName	A pointer to a location in memory where this function is to store the cursor name retrieved.
CursorNameMaxSize	The maximum size of the memory storage buffer where this function is to store the cursor name retrieved.
CursorNameSize	A pointer to a location in memory where this function is to store the actual number of bytes written to the cursor name memory storage buffer (*CursorName*).

Description

The **SQLGetCursorName()** function is used to retrieve the name of the cursor associated with a specific SQL statement handle. When this function is executed, the cursor name internally generated by ODBC is returned unless that cursor name was explicitly renamed by the **SQLSetCursorName()** function; in which case, the new cursor name is returned.

Cursor names are only used in positioned **UPDATE** and **DELETE** statements (for example, **UPDATE [table-name]** ... **WHERE CURRENT OF [cursor-name]**).

Return Codes

SQL_SUCCESS, **SQL_SUCCESS_WITH_INFO**, **SQL_INVALID_HANDLE**, or **SQL_ERROR**

SQLSTATEs

If this function returns **SQL_SUCCESS_WITH_INFO** or **SQL_ERROR**, one of the following SQLSTATE values may be obtained by calling the **SQLGetDiagRec()** function (ODBC 3.x driver) or the **SQLError()** function (ODBC 2.0 or earlier driver):

ODBC 3.X
01000, **01**004, **HY**000, **HY**001, **HY**010*, **HY**013, **HY**015*, **HY**090*, **HYT**01, or **IM**001*

ODBC 2.0 OR EARLIER
01000, **01**004, **IM**001*, **S1**000, **S1**001, **S1**010*, **S1**015*, or **S1**090*

*Returned by the ODBC Driver Manager.

Unless noted otherwise, each of these SQLSTATE values are returned by the data source driver. Refer to Appendix B for detailed information about each SQLSTATE value that can be returned by the ODBC Driver Manager or by a data source driver.

Comments

■ If the cursor name string's actual length is greater than or equal to the maximum string size value specified in the *CursorNameMaxSize* parameter, it is truncated to *CursorNameMaxSize*–1 (the length of a NULL-termination character) characters.

■ If the name assigned to the cursor is a Unicode string, the *CursorNameMaxSize* parameter must contain an even number.

■ If the application does not call **SQLSetCursorName()** to define a cursor name, the driver automatically generates a name. This name begins with the letters "SQL_CUR" (or the letters "SQLCUR" if an X/Open 95 or ISO/IEC 92 compliant driver is being used) and does not exceed **SQL_MAX_ID_LENGTH** (**18**) characters in length.

■ With ODBC 2.0 applications, if no cursor is open and if no cursor name has been set by the application, SQLSTATE **S1**015 (No cursor name available) is returned when this function is called. With ODBC 3.x applications, the driver always returns the cursor name regardless of when this function is called and regardless of whether the name was created explicitly (by the application) or implicitly (by ODBC).

■ The **SQLSetCursorName()** function can be used to rename a cursor associated with an SQL statement handle, provided the cursor is in the "Allocated" or "Prepared" state.

■ A cursor name set either explicitly or implicitly remains set until the SQL statement handle that the cursor is associated with is freed.

Prerequisites   There are no prerequisites for using this function call.

Restrictions   There are no restrictions associated with this function call.

See Also   SQLSetCursorName(), SQLPrepare(), SQLExecute(), SQLExecDirect(), SQLFetch(), SQLCloseCursor()

Example   The following Visual C++ program illustrates how to use the **SQLGetCursorName()** function to obtain the system-generated name of a cursor.

```
/*------------------------------------------------------------------*/
/* NAME:     CH10EX6.CPP                                            */
/* PURPOSE: Illustrate How To Use The Following ODBC API Function   */
/*          In A C++ Program:                                       */
/*                                                                  */
/*               SQLGetCursorName()                                 */
/*                                                                  */
/* OTHER ODBC APIs SHOWN:                                           */
/*          SQLAllocHandle()          SQLSetEnvAttr()               */
/*          SQLConnect()              SQLExecDirect()               */
/*          SQLDisconnect()           SQLFreeHandle()               */
/*                                                                  */
/*------------------------------------------------------------------*/
```

```
// Include The Appropriate Header Files
#include <windows.h>
#include <sql.h>
#include <sqlext.h>
#include <iostream.h>

// Define The ODBC_Class Class
class ODBC_Class
{
    // Attributes
    public:
        SQLHANDLE   EnvHandle;
        SQLHANDLE   ConHandle;
        SQLHANDLE   StmtHandle;
        SQLRETURN   rc;

    // Operations
    public:
        ODBC_Class();                       // Constructor
        ~ODBC_Class();                      // Destructor
};

// Define The Class Constructor
ODBC_Class::ODBC_Class()
{
    // Initialize The Return Code Variable
    rc = SQL_SUCCESS;

    // Allocate An Environment Handle
    rc = SQLAllocHandle(SQL_HANDLE_ENV, SQL_NULL_HANDLE, &EnvHandle);

    // Set The ODBC Application Version To 3.x
    if (rc == SQL_SUCCESS)
        rc = SQLSetEnvAttr(EnvHandle, SQL_ATTR_ODBC_VERSION,
                (SQLPOINTER) SQL_OV_ODBC3, SQL_IS_UINTEGER);

    // Allocate A Connection Handle
    if (rc == SQL_SUCCESS)
        rc = SQLAllocHandle(SQL_HANDLE_DBC, EnvHandle, &ConHandle);
}

// Define The Class Destructor
ODBC_Class::~ODBC_Class()
{
    // Free The Connection Handle
    if (ConHandle != NULL)
        SQLFreeHandle(SQL_HANDLE_DBC, ConHandle);

    // Free The Environment Handle
    if (EnvHandle != NULL)
        SQLFreeHandle(SQL_HANDLE_ENV, EnvHandle);
}
```

```
/*————————————————————————————————————————————————————————*/
/* The Main Function                                        */
/*————————————————————————————————————————————————————————*/
int main()
{
    // Declare The Local Memory Variables
    SQLRETURN      rc = SQL_SUCCESS;
    SQLCHAR        DBName[10] = "Northwind";
    SQLCHAR        SQLStmt[255];
    SQLCHAR        CursorName[80];
    SQLSMALLINT    CNameSize;

    // Create An Instance Of The ODBC_Class Class
    ODBC_Class  Example;

    // Connect To The Northwind Sample Database
    if (Example.ConHandle != NULL)
    {
        rc = SQLConnect(Example.ConHandle, DBName, SQL_NTS,
                (SQLCHAR *) "", SQL_NTS, (SQLCHAR *) "", SQL_NTS);

        // Allocate An SQL Statement Handle
        rc = SQLAllocHandle(SQL_HANDLE_STMT, Example.ConHandle,
                &Example.StmtHandle);
        if (rc == SQL_SUCCESS)
        {
            // Define A SELECT SQL Statement
            strcpy((char *) SQLStmt, "SELECT Employees.LastName, ");
            strcat((char *) SQLStmt, "Employees.FirstName FROM ");
            strcat((char *) SQLStmt, "Employees");

            // Prepare And Execute The SQL Statement
            rc = SQLExecDirect(Example.StmtHandle, SQLStmt, SQL_NTS);

            // Retrieve And Display The ODBC-Generated Cursor Name
            if (rc == SQL_SUCCESS)
            {
                rc = SQLGetCursorName(Example.StmtHandle, CursorName,
                        sizeof(CursorName), &CNameSize);

                cout << "ODBC-Generated Cursor Name : ";
                cout << CursorName << endl << endl;
            }

            // Free The SQL Statement Handle
            if (Example.StmtHandle != NULL)
                SQLFreeHandle(SQL_HANDLE_STMT, Example.StmtHandle);
        }

        // Disconnect From The Northwind Sample Database
        rc = SQLDisconnect(Example.ConHandle);
    }
```

```
// Return To The Operating System
return(rc);
}
```

SQLSetCursorName

COMPATABILITY

X/OPEN 95 CLI	ISO/IEC 92 CLI	ODBC 1.0	ODBC 2.0	ODBC 3.0	ODBC 3.5
✓	✓	✓	✓	✓	✓

API CONFORMANCE LEVEL   **CORE**

Purpose

The **SQLSetCursorName()** function is used to assign a user-defined name to a cursor that is associated with an active SQL statement handle.

Syntax

```
SQLRETURN    SQLSetCursorName    (SQLHSTMT       StatementHandle,
                                  SQLCHAR        *CursorName,
                                  SQLSMALLINT    ursorNameSize);
```

Parameters

StatementHandle		An SQL statement handle that refers to a previously allocated SQL statement information storage buffer (data structure).
CursorName		A pointer to a location in memory where the user-defined cursor name is stored.
CursorNameSize		The length of the cursor name specified in the *CursorName* parameter.

Description

The **SQLSetCursorName()** function is used to assign a user-defined name to a cursor that is associated with an active SQL statement handle. Usually, an ODBC driver generates and uses an internally generated cursor name whenever a SQL query statement is either prepared or executed directly. This function enables an application to replace this internally generated cursor name with a user-defined name. This user-defined cursor name can then be used in place of the internally generated cursor name in positioned **UPDATE** and positioned **DELETE** SQL statements. Once assigned, a user-defined cursor name remains associated with the SQL statement handle specified until the SQL statement handle is deleted or until the cursor is renamed by another **SQLSetCursorName()** function call.

Return Codes **SQL_SUCCESS**, **SQL_SUCCESS_WITH_INFO**, **SQL_INVALID_HANDLE**, or **SQL_ERROR**

SQLSTATEs If this function returns **SQL_SUCCESS_WITH_INFO** or **SQL_ERROR**, one of the following SQLSTATE values may be obtained by calling the **SQLGetDiagRec()** function (ODBC 3.x driver) or the **SQLError()** function (ODBC 2.0 or earlier driver):

ODBC 3.X
01000, **01**004, **24**000, **34**000, **3C**000, **HY**000, **HY**001, **HY**009*, **HY**010*, **HY**013, **HY**090*, **HYT**01, or **IM**001*

ODBC 2.0 OR EARLIER
01000, **24**000, **34**000, **3C**000, **IM**001*, **S1**000, **S1**001, **S1**009*, **S1**010*, or **S1**090*

*Returned by the ODBC Driver Manager.

Unless noted otherwise, each of these SQLSTATE values are returned by the data source driver. Refer to Appendix B for detailed information about each SQLSTATE value that can be returned by the ODBC Driver Manager or by a data source driver.

Comments

■ For efficient processing, the cursor name specified should not include any leading or trailing spaces. Also, if the cursor name includes a delimited identifier, the delimiter should be positioned as the first character in the cursor name.

■ All cursor names within a connection must be unique. The maximum length of a cursor name is defined by the driver. For maximum interoperability, it is recommended that applications limit cursor names to 18 characters.

■ With ODBC 3.x applications, if a cursor name is a quoted identifier, it is treated in a case-sensitive manner, and can contain characters that SQL syntax usually would not permit or would treat specially, such as blanks or reserved keywords. If a cursor name is to be treated in a case-sensitive manner, it must be passed as a quoted identifier.

■ If the SQL statement being executed is a **SELECT** SQL statement, and if the application called **SQLSetCursorName()** to associate a cursor name with the statement, then the driver uses the cursor

name specified. Otherwise, the driver generates a cursor name
that begins with the letters "SQL_CUR" (or the letters "SQLCUR"
if and X/Open 95 or ISO/IEC 92 compliant driver is being used)
and does not exceed **SQL_MAX_ID_LENGTH** (**18**) characters in length.

- A cursor name that is set either explicitly or implicitly remains set
  until the SQL statement handle that the cursor is associated with
  is freed.

Prerequisites There are no prerequisites for using this function call.

Restrictions This function can only rename a cursor associated with an SQL statement handle that is in the "Allocated" or "Prepared" state.

See Also SQLSetCursorName(), SQLPrepare(), SQLExecute(), SQLExecDirect(), SQLFetch(), SQLCloseCursor()

Example The following Visual C++ program illustrates how to use the SQLSetCursorName() function to assign a user-defined name to a cursor.

```
/*------------------------------------------------------------------*/
/* NAME:     CH10EX7.CPP                                            */
/* PURPOSE: Illustrate How To Use The Following ODBC API Function   */
/*          In A C++ Program:                                       */
/*                                                                  */
/*                SQLSetCursorName                                  */
/*                                                                  */
/* OTHER ODBC APIs SHOWN:                                           */
/*          SQLAllocHandle()          SQLSetEnvAttr()               */
/*          SQLConnect()              SQLPrepare()                  */
/*          SQLExecute()              SQLGetCursorName()            */
/*          SQLDisconnect()           SQLFreeHandle()               */
/*                                                                  */
/*------------------------------------------------------------------*/

// Include The Appropriate Header Files
#include <windows.h>
#include <sql.h>
#include <sqlext.h>
#include <iostream.h>

// Define The ODBC_Class Class
class ODBC_Class
{
    // Attributes
    public:
        SQLHANDLE    EnvHandle;
        SQLHANDLE    ConHandle;
        SQLHANDLE    StmtHandle;
        SQLRETURN    rc;
```

```
    // Operations
    public:
        ODBC_Class();                              // Constructor
        ~ODBC_Class();                             // Destructor
};

// Define The Class Constructor
ODBC_Class::ODBC_Class()
{
    // Initialize The Return Code Variable
    rc = SQL_SUCCESS;

    // Allocate An Environment Handle
    rc = SQLAllocHandle(SQL_HANDLE_ENV, SQL_NULL_HANDLE, &EnvHandle);

    // Set The ODBC Application Version To 3.x
    if (rc == SQL_SUCCESS)
        rc = SQLSetEnvAttr(EnvHandle, SQL_ATTR_ODBC_VERSION,
                (SQLPOINTER) SQL_OV_ODBC3, SQL_IS_UINTEGER);

    // Allocate A Connection Handle
    if (rc == SQL_SUCCESS)
        rc = SQLAllocHandle(SQL_HANDLE_DBC, EnvHandle, &ConHandle);
}

// Define The Class Destructor
ODBC_Class::~ODBC_Class()
{
    // Free The Connection Handle
    if (ConHandle != NULL)
        SQLFreeHandle(SQL_HANDLE_DBC, ConHandle);

    // Free The Environment Handle
    if (EnvHandle != NULL)
        SQLFreeHandle(SQL_HANDLE_ENV, EnvHandle);
}

/*-------------------------------------------------------------------*/
/* The Main Function                                                 */
/*-------------------------------------------------------------------*/
int main()
{
    // Declare The Local Memory Variables
    SQLRETURN    rc = SQL_SUCCESS;
    SQLCHAR      DBName[10] = "Northwind";
    SQLCHAR      SQLStmt[255];
    SQLCHAR      CursorName[80];
    SQLSMALLINT  CNameSize;

    // Create An Instance Of The ODBC_Class Class
    ODBC_Class  Example;

    // Connect To The Northwind Sample Database
    if (Example.ConHandle != NULL)
    {
```

```
    rc = SQLConnect(Example.ConHandle, DBName, SQL_NTS,
            (SQLCHAR *) "", SQL_NTS, (SQLCHAR *) "", SQL_NTS);

    // Allocate An SQL Statement Handle
    rc = SQLAllocHandle(SQL_HANDLE_STMT, Example.ConHandle,
            &Example.StmtHandle);
    if (rc == SQL_SUCCESS)
    {
        // Define A SELECT SQL Statement
        strcpy((char *) SQLStmt, "SELECT Employees.LastName, ");
        strcat((char *) SQLStmt, "Employees.FirstName FROM ");
        strcat((char *) SQLStmt, "Employees");

        // Prepare The SQL Statement
        rc = SQLPrepare(Example.StmtHandle, SQLStmt, SQL_NTS);

        // Set The Cursor Name
        rc = SQLSetCursorName(Example.StmtHandle, (SQLCHAR *)
                "EMP_CURSOR", SQL_NTS);

        // Execute The SQL Statement
        rc = SQLExecute(Example.StmtHandle);

        // Retrieve And Display The New Cursor Name
        if (rc == SQL_SUCCESS)
        {
            rc = SQLGetCursorName(Example.StmtHandle, CursorName,
                    sizeof(CursorName), &CNameSize);

            cout << "User-Defined Cursor Name : ";
            cout << CursorName << endl;
        }

        // Free The SQL Statement Handle
        if (Example.StmtHandle != NULL)
            SQLFreeHandle(SQL_HANDLE_STMT, Example.StmtHandle);
    }

    // Disconnect From The Northwind Sample Database
    rc = SQLDisconnect(Example.ConHandle);
}

// Return To The Operating System
return(rc);
}
```

SQLFetch

COMPATABILITY

X/OPEN 95 CLI	ISO/IEC 92 CLI	ODBC 1.0	ODBC 2.0	ODBC 3.0	ODBC 3.5
✓	✓	✓	✓	✓	✓

API CONFORMANCE LEVEL **CORE**

Purpose

The **SQLFetch()** function is used to advance a cursor to the next row of data in a result data set and to retrieve data from any bound columns that exist for that row into their associated application variables.

Syntax

```
SQLRETURN   SQLFetch   (SQLHSTMT     StatementHandle);
```

Parameters

StatementHandle   An SQL statement handle that refers to a previously allocated SQL statement information storage buffer (data structure).

Description

The **SQLFetch()** function is used to advance a cursor to the next row of data in a result data set and to retrieve data from any bound columns that exist for that row into their associated application variables. This function can only be called while a result data set exists (that is, after an SQL statement that creates a result set is executed and before the cursor associated with that result data set is closed). If the application has specified a pointer to a row status array or an application variable/buffer in which to return the number of rows fetched, **SQLFetch()** returns this information as well.

When the **SQLFetch()** function is called, the appropriate data transfer is performed along with any data conversion that was specified when the columns were bound. Data in unbound columns can also be retrieved individually after the **SQLFetch()** function executes by calling the **SQLGetData()** function.

Return Codes

SQL_SUCCESS, SQL_SUCCESS_WITH_INFO, SQL_NO_DATA, SQL_NO_DATA_FOUND (ODBC 2.0 or earlier drivers), **SQL_STILL_EXECUTING, SQL_INVALID_HANDLE,** or **SQL_ERROR**

For all those SQLSTATEs that can return **SQL_SUCCESS_WITH_INFO** or **SQL_ERROR** (except **01**xxx SQLSTATEs), **SQL_SUCCESS_WITH_INFO** is returned if an error occurs on one or more, but not all, rows of a multi-row operation, and **SQL_ERROR** is returned if an error occurs on a single-row operation.

SQLSTATEs

If this function returns **SQL_SUCCESS_WITH_INFO** or **SQL_ERROR**, one of the following SQLSTATE values may be obtained by calling the **SQLGetDiagRec()** function (ODBC 3.x driver) or the **SQLError()** function (ODBC 2.0 or earlier driver):

ODBC 3.X
01000, 01004, 01S01, 01S07, 07006, 07009, 08S01, 22001, 22002, 22003, 22007, 22012, 22015, 22018, 24000, 40001, 40003, HY000, HY001, HY008, HY010*, HY013, HY090, HY107, HYC00, HYT01, or IM001*

ODBC 2.0 OR EARLIER
01000, 01004, 07006, 08S01, 22003, 22012, 24000, 40001, IM001*, S1000, S1001, S1002, S1008, S1010*, S1C00, or S1T00

*Returned by the ODBC Driver Manager.

Unless noted otherwise, each of these SQLSTATE values are returned by the data source driver. Refer to Appendix B for detailed information about each SQLSTATE value that can be returned by the ODBC Driver Manager or by a data source driver.

Comments

■ Calls to **SQLFetch()** can be mixed with calls to **SQLFetchScroll()** but cannot be mixed with calls to **SQLExtendedFetch()**.

■ If an ODBC 3.x application works with an ODBC 2.0 driver, the Driver Manager maps **SQLFetch()** calls to **SQLExtendedFetch()** if the ODBC 2.0 driver supports **SQLExtendedFetch()**, or to **SQLFetch()** (which can only fetch a single row) if the ODBC 2.x driver does not support **SQLExtendedFetch()**.

■ When a result data set is first created, the cursor is positioned before the start of the first row in the result data set.

■ In ODBC 3.x, **SQLFetch()** fetches the next rowset. This is equivalent to calling **SQLFetchScroll()** with the **SQL_FETCH_NEXT** orientation specified.

■ The contents of all bound application variables/buffers and their corresponding length/indicator variables are undefined if this function does not return **SQL_SUCCESS** or **SQL_SUCCESS_WITH_INFO**.

Prerequisites This function can only be called after a result data set has been generated for the SQL statement handle specified. A result data set can be generated either by executing an SQL query, by calling the **SQLGetTypeInfo()** function, or by calling any ODBC catalog function described in Chapter 15.

Restrictions There are no restrictions associated with this function call.

See Also **SQLExtendedFetch()**, **SQLFetchScroll()**, **SQLBindCol()**, **SQLExecute()**, **SQLExecDirect()**, **SQLGetData()**

Example See the example provided for the **SQLBindCol()** function on page 499.

SQLCloseCursor

COMPATABILITY

X/OPEN 95 CLI	ISO/IEC 92 CLI	ODBC 1.0	ODBC 2.0	ODBC 3.0	ODBC 3.5
✓	✓	☐	☐	✓	✓

API CONFORMANCE LEVEL   **CORE**

Purpose The **SQLCloseCursor()** function is used to close a cursor that has been opened on an SQL statement handle.

Syntax SQLRETURN   SQLCloseCursor   (SQLHSTMT   *StatementHandle*);

Parameters *StatementHandle*   An SQL statement handle that refers to a previously allocated SQL statement information storage buffer (data structure).

Description The **SQLCloseCursor()** function is used to close a cursor that has been opened on an SQL statement handle. If a cursor is closed while it contains results that are pending, those results are discarded.

Return Codes SQL_SUCCESS, SQL_SUCCESS_WITH_INFO, SQL_INVALID_HANDLE, or SQL_ERROR

SQLSTATEs

If this function returns **SQL_SUCCESS_WITH_INFO** or **SQL_ERROR**, one of the following SQLSTATE values may be obtained by calling the **SQLGetDiagRec()** function:

01000, **24**000, **HY**000, **HY**001, **HY**010*, **HY**013, **HY**T01, or **IM**001*

*Returned by the ODBC Driver Manager.

Unless noted otherwise, each of these SQLSTATE values are returned by the data source driver. Refer to Appendix B for detailed information about each SQLSTATE value that can be returned by the ODBC Driver Manager or by a data source driver.

Comments

■ If this function is called when no cursor is open, **SQL_ERROR** is returned, along with SQLSTATE **24**000 (Invalid cursor state).

■ Calling this function is equivalent to calling the **SQLFreeStmt()** function with the **SQL_CLOSE** option specified with one exception; the **SQLFreeStmt()** function does not return an error if it is called when no cursor is open.

■ If an ODBC 3.x application working with an ODBC 2.0 driver calls this function when no cursor is open, an error is not returned, because the ODBC Driver Manager maps the **SQLCloseCursor()** function to the **SQLFreeStmt()** function with the **SQL_CLOSE** option specified.

Prerequisites

There are no prerequisites for using this function call.

Restrictions

There are no restrictions associated with this function call.

See Also

SQLGetCursorName(), **SQLSetCursorName()**, **SQLFetch()**

Example

The following Visual C++ program illustrates how to use the **SQLCloseCursor()** function to close a cursor and discard remaining results.

```
/*------------------------------------------------------------------*/
/* NAME:     CH10EX8.CPP                                            */
/* PURPOSE: Illustrate How To Use The Following ODBC API Function   */
/*          In A C++ Program:                                       */
/*                                                                  */
/*               SQLCloseCursor()                                   */
/*                                                                  */
/* OTHER ODBC APIs SHOWN:                                           */
/*          SQLAllocHandle()        SQLSetEnvAttr()                 */
```

```
/*              SQLConnect()            SQLExecDirect()                    */
/*              SQLBindCol()            SQLFetch()                         */
/*              SQLDisconnect()         SQLFreeHandle()                    */
/*                                                                         */
/*———————————————————————————————————————————————————————————————————————*/

// Include The Appropriate Header Files
#include <windows.h>
#include <sql.h>
#include <sqlext.h>
#include <iostream.h>

// Define The ODBC_Class Class
class ODBC_Class
{
    // Attributes
    public:
        SQLHANDLE    EnvHandle;
        SQLHANDLE    ConHandle;
        SQLHANDLE    StmtHandle;
        SQLRETURN    rc;

    // Operations
    public:
        ODBC_Class();                       // Constructor
        ~ODBC_Class();                      // Destructor
        SQLRETURN ShowResults();
};

// Define The Class Constructor
ODBC_Class::ODBC_Class()
{
    // Initialize The Return Code Variable
    rc = SQL_SUCCESS;

    // Allocate An Environment Handle
    rc = SQLAllocHandle(SQL_HANDLE_ENV, SQL_NULL_HANDLE, &EnvHandle);

    // Set The ODBC Application Version To 3.x
    if (rc == SQL_SUCCESS)
       rc = SQLSetEnvAttr(EnvHandle, SQL_ATTR_ODBC_VERSION,
                (SQLPOINTER) SQL_OV_ODBC3, SQL_IS_UINTEGER);

    // Allocate A Connection Handle
    if (rc == SQL_SUCCESS)
        rc = SQLAllocHandle(SQL_HANDLE_DBC, EnvHandle, &ConHandle);
}

// Define The Class Destructor
ODBC_Class::~ODBC_Class()
{
    // Free The Connection Handle
    if (ConHandle != NULL)
        SQLFreeHandle(SQL_HANDLE_DBC, ConHandle);
```

```
    // Free The Environment Handle
    if (EnvHandle != NULL)
        SQLFreeHandle(SQL_HANDLE_ENV, EnvHandle);
}


// Define The ShowResults() Member Function
SQLRETURN ODBC_Class::ShowResults(void)
{
    // Declare The Local Memory Variables
    SQLINTEGER   OrderID;
    SQLCHAR      ShipName[41];
    int          Counter = 0;

    // Bind The Columns In The Result Data Set Returned To
    // Application Variables
    rc = SQLBindCol(StmtHandle, 1, SQL_C_ULONG, (SQLPOINTER)
            &OrderID, sizeof(SQLINTEGER), NULL);

    rc = SQLBindCol(StmtHandle, 2, SQL_C_CHAR, (SQLPOINTER)
            ShipName, sizeof(ShipName), NULL);

    // Display A Header
    cout.setf(ios::left);
    cout.width(10);
    cout << "Order ID" << "Shipper" << endl << endl;

    // While There Are Records In The Result Data Set Generated,
    // Retrieve And Display Them
    while (rc != SQL_NO_DATA)
    {
        rc = SQLFetch(StmtHandle);
        if (rc != SQL_NO_DATA)
        {
            cout.setf(ios::left);
            cout.width(10);
            cout << OrderID << ShipName << endl;
        }

        // Increment The Loop Counter - Stop When The First
        // 20 Records Have Been Displayed
        Counter++;
        if (Counter == 20)
        {
            rc = SQLCloseCursor(StmtHandle);
            break;
        }
    }

    // Return The ODBC API Return Code To The Calling Function
    return(rc);
}
```

```
/*————————————————————————————————————————————*/
/* The Main Function                            */
/*————————————————————————————————————————————*/
int main()
{
    // Declare The Local Memory Variables
    SQLRETURN  rc = SQL_SUCCESS;
    SQLCHAR    DBName[10] = "Northwind";
    SQLCHAR    SQLStmt[255];

    // Create An Instance Of The ODBC_Class Class
    ODBC_Class  Example;

    // Connect To The Northwind Sample Database
    if (Example.ConHandle != NULL)
    {
        rc = SQLConnect(Example.ConHandle, DBName, SQL_NTS,
                (SQLCHAR *) "", SQL_NTS, (SQLCHAR *) "", SQL_NTS);

        // Allocate An SQL Statement Handle
        rc = SQLAllocHandle(SQL_HANDLE_STMT, Example.ConHandle,
                &Example.StmtHandle);
        if (rc == SQL_SUCCESS)
        {
            // Define A SELECT SQL Statement
            strcpy((char *) SQLStmt, "SELECT Orders.OrderID, ");
            strcat((char *) SQLStmt, "Orders.ShipName FROM Orders ");
            strcat((char *) SQLStmt, "WHERE Orders.ShipCountry = ");
            strcat((char *) SQLStmt, "'USA'");

            // Prepare And Execute The SQL Statement
            SQLExecDirect(Example.StmtHandle, SQLStmt, SQL_NTS);

            // Display The First 20 Records Returned by The SQL Query
            if (rc == SQL_SUCCESS)
                Example.ShowResults();

            // Free The SQL Statement Handle
            if (Example.StmtHandle != NULL)
                SQLFreeHandle(SQL_HANDLE_STMT, Example.StmtHandle);
        }

        // Disconnect From The Northwind Sample Database
        rc = SQLDisconnect(Example.ConHandle);
    }

    // Return To The Operating System
    return(rc);
}
```

SQLGetData

COMPATABILITY

X/OPEN 95 CLI	ISO/IEC 92 CLI	ODBC 1.0	ODBC 2.0	ODBC 3.0	ODBC 3.5
☑	☑	☑	☑	☑	☑

API CONFORMANCE LEVEL   **CORE***

*IN ODBC 2.0, THIS FUNCTION WAS A LEVEL 1 API CONFORMANCE LEVEL FUNCTION

Purpose The **SQLGetData()** function is used to retrieve data for a single unbound column in the current row of a result data set.

Syntax

```
SQLRETURN   SQLGetData   (SQLHSTMT         StatementHandle,
                          SQLUSMALLINT     ColumnNumber,
                          SQLSMALLINT      CDataType,
                          SQLPOINTER       Value,
                          SQLINTEGER       ValueMaxSize,
                          SQLINTEGER       *ValueSize_Indicator);
```

Parameters

StatementHandle   An SQL statement handle that refers to a previously allocated SQL statement information storage buffer (data structure).

ColumnNumber   Specifies the column's location in the result data set. Columns are numbered sequentially from left to right, starting with 1, as they appear in the result data set.

CDataType   The C language data type of the value memory storage buffer (*Value*) that the column data being retrieved is to be stored in. This parameter must be set to one of the following values:

▨ **SQL_C_CHAR**

▨ **SQL_C_SSHORT**

▨ **SQL_C_USHORT**

▨ **SQL_C_SLONG**

▨ **SQL_C_ULONG**

▨ **SQL_C_FLOAT**

- SQL_C_DOUBLE
- SQL_C_BIT
- SQL_C_STINYINT
- SQL_C_UTINYINT
- SQL_C_SBIGINT
- SQL_C_UBIGINT
- SQL_C_BINARY
- SQL_C_BOOKMARK
- SQL_C_VAR_BOOKMARK
- SQL_C_DATE
- SQL_C_TIME
- SQL_C_TIMESTAMP
- SQL_C_TYPE_DATE
- SQL_C_TYPE_TIME
- SQL_C_TYPE_TIMESTAMP
- SQL_C_NUMERIC
- SQL_ARD_TYPE
- SQL_C_DEFAULT

NOTE: *The* **SQL_ARD_TYPE** *value causes the driver to use the C data type specified in the* **SQL_DESC_CONCISE_TYPE** *field of the ARD descriptor record for the column. If this field contains the value* **SQL_C_DEFAULT**, *the driver selects the appropriate C data type to use based on the SQL data type of the column in the data source.*

Value	A pointer to a location in memory where this function is to store column data when it is retrieved from the result data set.
ValueMaxSize	The maximum size of the memory storage buffer where this function is to store the column data retrieved.
ValueSize_Indicator	A pointer to a location in memory where this function is to store either the size of the data value associated with the column or a special indicator value associated with the column data. Any of the following indicator values can be stored in this memory location:

SQL_NO_TOTAL:
The size of the column data value is unknown.

SQL_NULL_DATA:
The data value associated with the column is NULL.

Description

The **SQLGetData()** function is used to retrieve data for a single unbound column in the current row of a result data set. This function is an alternative to the **SQLBindCol()** function and can be used to transfer data directly into application variables (either whole, or in parts) once the cursor has been positioned on a row of data. The **SQLGetData()** function is commonly used to retrieve large data values, which often exceed a predefined size (usually 254 characters or bytes). Because such data often cannot be stored in a single buffer, it is retrieved from the driver in parts with the **SQLGetData()** function after all other data in the row has been fetched. With respect to a single column, **SQLGetData()** behaves in the same manner as **SQLFetch()**: It retrieves the data for a column, converts it to the data type of the application variable (if appropriate), and stores the converted value in that variable. It also returns the byte length of the data in the length/indicator buffer.

Return Codes

SQL_SUCCESS, SQL_SUCCESS_WITH_INFO, SQL_NO_DATA, SQL_NO_DATA_FOUND (ODBC 2.0 or earlier driver), SQL_STILL_EXECUTING, SQL_INVALID_HANDLE, or SQL_ERROR

SQLSTATEs

If this function returns **SQL_SUCCESS_WITH_INFO** or **SQL_ERROR**, one of the following SQLSTATE values may be obtained by calling the **SQLGetDiagRec()** function (ODBC 3.x driver) or the **SQLError()** function (ODBC 2.0 or earlier driver):

ODBC 3.X
01000, **01**004, **01**S07, **07**006, **07**009*, **08**S01, **22**002, **22**003, **22**007, **22**012, **22**015, **22**018, **24**000*, **HY**000, **HY**001, **HY**003*, **HY**008, **HY**010*, **HY**013, **HY**090*, **HY**109, **HY**C00, **HY**T01, or **IM**001*

ODBC 2.0 OR EARLIER
01000, **01**004, **07**006, **08**S01, **22**003, **22**005, **22**008, **24**000*, **IM**001*, **S1**000, **S1**001, **S1**002, **S1**003*, **S1**008, **S1**009*, **S1**010*, **S1**090*, **S1**109, **S1**C00, or **S1**T00

*Returned by the ODBC Driver Manager.

Unless noted otherwise, each of these SQLSTATE values are returned by the data source driver. Refer to Appendix B for detailed information about each SQLSTATE value that can be returned by the ODBC Driver Manager or by a data source driver.

Comments

■ Columns are numbered in increasing column order as they appear in the result data set, starting at 0, where column 0 is the bookmark column. If bookmarks are not used (that is, if the **SQL_ATTR_USE_BOOKMARKS** SQL statement attribute is set to **SQL_UB_OFF**) column numbers start at 1.

■ This function can only be called after one or more rows have been fetched from the result data set by **SQLFetch()**, **SQLFetchScroll()** (ODBC 3.x drivers), or **SQLExtendedFetch()** (ODBC 2.0 or earlier drivers).

■ It is possible to bind some columns in a row and call **SQLGetData()** for others, although this is subject to some restrictions.

■ When the driver returns fixed-length data such as integer or date structure data to an application variable, it assumes the buffer is large enough to hold the data. Therefore, it is important for the application to use a variable or allocate a buffer large enough to hold the fixed-length data stored in the column; otherwise the driver will write past the end of the buffer.

■ When a value less than **0** is stored in the *ValueMaxSize* parameter, SQLSTATE **HY**090 (Invalid string or buffer length) is returned. This is not the case when **0** is stored in the *ValueMaxSize* parameter; however, if a character data type is specified in the *CDataType* parameter, an application should not store **0** in the *ValueMaxSize* parameter because ISO CLI-compliant drivers return QLSTATE **HY**090 (Invalid string or buffer length) when this condition is encountered.

■ If a NULL pointer is stored in the *Value* parameter, the value stored in the *ValueMaxSize* parameter is ignored by the driver.

■ If a NULL pointer is stored in the *ValueSize_Indicator* parameter, no length or indicator value is used.

■ If no length/indicator variable is used, **SQL_ERROR** is returned if a NULL value is found in a column when data is fetched.

■ This function cannot be used to retrieve the bookmark value for a row just inserted by the **SQLBulkOperations()** function, because the cursor is not positioned on the new row. An application can retrieve the bookmark for such a row by binding column 0 to an application variable before calling **SQLBulkOperations()** to add the new row, in which case **SQLBulkOperations()** returns the bookmark in the bound buffer. The **SQLFetchScroll()** function can then be called with **SQL_FETCH_BOOKMARK** option specified to reposition the cursor on that row.

▦ If an interval data type is stored in the *CDataType* parameter, the default interval leading precision (**2**) and the default interval seconds precision (**6**), as set in the ARD descriptor's **SQL_DESC_ DATETIME_INTERVAL_PRECISION** and **SQL_DESC_PRECISION** fields, respectively, are used for the data conversion.

▦ If a numeric data type (**SQL_C_NUMERIC**) is stored in the *CDataType* parameter, the default precision (driver-defined) and default scale (**0**), as set in the ARD descriptor's **SQL_DESC_PRECISION** and **SQL_DESC_ SCALE** fields, are used for data conversion. If the default precision or scale is not appropriate, an application should explicitly set the appropriate descriptor field by calling **SQLSetDescField()** or **SQLSetDescRec()** to set the **SQL_DESC_CONCISE_TYPE** field to **SQL_C_NUMERIC**, and call **SQLGetData()** with **SQL_ARD_TYPE** specified in the *CDataType* parameter, which causes the precision and scale values in the descriptor record fields to be used.

▦ In ODBC 2.0, applications, set the *CDataType* parameter to **SQL_C_DATE**, **SQL_C_TIME**, or **SQL_C_TIMESTAMP** to indicate that the data is to be returned to a date, time, or timestamp structure. In ODBC 3.x, applications set the *CDataType* parameter to **SQL_C_TYPE_DATE**, **SQL_C_TYPE_TIME**, or **SQL_C_TYPE_TIMESTAMP**. The Driver Manager makes appropriate mappings, if necessary, based on the application and driver version.

Prerequisites   The **SQLFetch()** function must be called before this function is called. If the **SQLFetch()** call fails, this function should not be called.

Restrictions   If the driver does not support extensions to **SQLGetData()**, this function can only return data for unbound columns that have a position number that is greater than that of the last bound column. Furthermore, within each row of data, the value specified in the *ColumnNumber* parameter in each call to **SQLGetData()** must be greater than or equal to the value specified in the *ColumnNumber* parameter of the previous call; that is, data must be retrieved in increasing column number order. Finally, if no extensions are supported, **SQLGetData()** cannot be called if the rowset size is greater than 1. Drivers can relax any of these restrictions; an application can call the **SQLGetInfo()** function to determine which of these restrictions are enforced and which are relaxed.

There are two exceptions to these restrictions and a driver's ability to relax them. First, **SQLGetData()** should never be called for a forward-only cursor when the rowset size is greater than **1**. Second, if a driver supports bookmarks, it must always support the ability to call **SQLGetData()** for column 0, even if it does not allow applications to call **SQLGetData()** for other columns that are physically located in the result data set before the last bound column. (When an application is working with an ODBC 2.0 driver, **SQLGetData()** successfully returns a bookmark when called with 0 specified in the *ColumnNumber* parameter after a call to **SQLFetch()**, because **SQLFetch()** is mapped by the ODBC 3.x Driver Manager to **SQLExtendedFetch()** with an orientation of **SQL_FETCH_NEXT** specified, and **SQLGetData()** is mapped to **SQLGetStmtOption()** with the option **SQL_GET_BOOKMARK** specified.)

See Also   SQLBindCol(), SQLFetch(), SQLExtendedFetch(), SQLGetStmtOption()

Example   The following Visual C++ program illustrates how to use the **SQLGetData()** function to retrieve data from an unbound column of a result data set.

```
/*------------------------------------------------------------------*/
/* NAME:      CH10EX9.CPP                                           */
/* PURPOSE: Illustrate How To Use The Following ODBC API Function   */
/*           In A C++ Program:                                      */
/*                                                                  */
/*              SQLGetData()                                        */
/*                                                                  */
/* OTHER ODBC APIs SHOWN:                                           */
/*           SQLAllocHandle()        SQLSetEnvAttr()                */
/*           SQLConnect()            SQLExecDirect()                */
/*           SQLBindCol()            SQLFetch()                     */
/*           SQLDisconnect()         SQLFreeHandle()                */
/*                                                                  */
/*------------------------------------------------------------------*/

// Include The Appropriate Header Files
#include <windows.h>
#include <sql.h>
#include <sqlext.h>
#include <iostream.h>

// Define The ODBC_Class Class
class ODBC_Class
{
    // Attributes
    public:
```

```
        SQLHANDLE    EnvHandle;
        SQLHANDLE    ConHandle;
        SQLHANDLE    StmtHandle;
        SQLRETURN    rc;

    // Operations
    public:
        ODBC_Class();                              // Constructor
        ~ODBC_Class();                             // Destructor
        SQLRETURN ShowResults();
};

// Define The Class Constructor
ODBC_Class::ODBC_Class()
{
    // Initialize The Return Code Variable
    rc = SQL_SUCCESS;

    // Allocate An Environment Handle
    rc = SQLAllocHandle(SQL_HANDLE_ENV, SQL_NULL_HANDLE, &EnvHandle);

    // Set The ODBC Application Version To 3.x
    if (rc == SQL_SUCCESS)
        rc = SQLSetEnvAttr(EnvHandle, SQL_ATTR_ODBC_VERSION,
                (SQLPOINTER) SQL_OV_ODBC3, SQL_IS_UINTEGER);

    // Allocate A Connection Handle
    if (rc == SQL_SUCCESS)
        rc = SQLAllocHandle(SQL_HANDLE_DBC, EnvHandle, &ConHandle);
}

// Define The Class Destructor
ODBC_Class::~ODBC_Class()
{
    // Free The Connection Handle
    if (ConHandle != NULL)
        SQLFreeHandle(SQL_HANDLE_DBC, ConHandle);

    // Free The Environment Handle
    if (EnvHandle != NULL)
        SQLFreeHandle(SQL_HANDLE_ENV, EnvHandle);
}

// Define The ShowResults() Member Function
SQLRETURN ODBC_Class::ShowResults(void)
{
    // Declare The Local Memory Variables
    SQLINTEGER   OrderID;
    SQLCHAR      ShipName[41];

    // Bind The First Column In The Result Data Set Returned To
    // An Application Variable
    rc = SQLBindCol(StmtHandle, 1, SQL_C_ULONG, (SQLPOINTER)
            &OrderID, sizeof(SQLINTEGER), NULL);
```

```cpp
    // Display A Header
    cout.setf(ios::left);
    cout.width(10);
    cout << "Order ID" << "Shipper" << endl << endl;

    // While There Are Records In The Result Data Set Generated,
    // Retrieve And Display Them
    while (rc != SQL_NO_DATA)
    {
        rc = SQLFetch(StmtHandle);
        if (rc != SQL_NO_DATA)
        {

            // Retrieve The Value In The Second Column Of The Result
            // Data Set (Stored In The Current Row)
            rc = SQLGetData(StmtHandle, 2, SQL_C_CHAR, (SQLPOINTER)
                    ShipName, sizeof(ShipName), NULL);

            if (rc != SQL_NO_DATA)
            {
                cout.setf(ios::left);
                cout.width(10);
                cout << OrderID << ShipName << endl;
            }
        }
    }

    // Return The ODBC API Return Code To The Calling Function
    return(rc);
}

/*------------------------------------------------------------------*/
/* The Main Function                                                */
/*------------------------------------------------------------------*/
int main()
{
    // Declare The Local Memory Variables
    SQLRETURN   rc = SQL_SUCCESS;
    SQLCHAR     DBName[10] = "Northwind";
    SQLCHAR     SQLStmt[255];

    // Create An Instance Of The ODBC_Class Class
    ODBC_Class  Example;

    // Connect To The Northwind Sample Database
    if (Example.ConHandle != NULL)
    {
        rc = SQLConnect(Example.ConHandle, DBName, SQL_NTS,
                (SQLCHAR *) "", SQL_NTS, (SQLCHAR *) "", SQL_NTS);

        // Allocate An SQL Statement Handle
        rc = SQLAllocHandle(SQL_HANDLE_STMT, Example.ConHandle,
                &Example.StmtHandle);
        if (rc == SQL_SUCCESS)
```

```
    {
        // Define A SELECT SQL Statement
        strcpy((char *) SQLStmt, "SELECT Orders.OrderID, ");
        strcat((char *) SQLStmt, "Orders.ShipName FROM Orders ");
        strcat((char *) SQLStmt, "WHERE Orders.ShipCountry = ");
        strcat((char *) SQLStmt, "'USA'");

        // Prepare And Execute The SQL Statement
        rc = SQLExecDirect(Example.StmtHandle, SQLStmt, SQL_NTS);

        // Display The Results Of The SQL Query
        if (rc == SQL_SUCCESS)
            Example.ShowResults();

        // Free The SQL Statement Handle
        if (Example.StmtHandle != NULL)
            SQLFreeHandle(SQL_HANDLE_STMT, Example.StmtHandle);
    }

    // Disconnect From The Northwind Sample Database
    rc = SQLDisconnect(Example.ConHandle);
}

// Return To The Operating System
return(rc);
}
```

11

Retrieving Results (Advanced)

The last chapter introduced the basic set of ODBC API functions that are used to fetch (retrieve) data from a result data set. This chapter continues this discussion by introducing you to the advanced set of ODBC API functions that can be used to fetch data. It begins by describing the two types of attributes used in ODBC extended cursors. This is followed by a discussion about block cursors and how application variables can be bound to columns in a result data set when block cursors are used. Then, scrollable cursors are described and the four types of scrollable cursors available to ODBC applications are introduced. Next, bookmarks are discussed and how bookmark data can be stored and retrieved is explained. This is followed by a brief discussion about multiple results. Finally, a detailed reference section covering each ODBC API function used to perform advanced data retrieval is provided.

ODBC Extended Cursors

Most DBMSs provide a simple model for retrieving data from result data sets created in response to a query. In this model, rows of data are returned to an application, one at a time, in the order specified by the query, until the end of the result data set is reached. You saw in the last chapter that the mechanism used to implement this simple model is the forward-only cursor.

Early in the development of ODBC (in fact, before the term ODBC was invented), Rick Vicik of Microsoft took a collection of ideas and proposals for cursor management and pioneered the design of a more advanced cursor model for client/server architectures. This model, which became the foundation upon which cursors in ODBC and several other products are based, contains several *extended* cursors that are designed to overcome many of the limitations imposed by the simple forward-only cursor found in most DBMSs.

The extended cursors used in ODBC are defined in terms of two broad types of attributes (*block* and *scrollable*), and they can contain components of either or both.

Block Cursors

In the client/server environment, many applications spend a significant amount of time retrieving data from the database. Part of this time is spent actually bringing the data across the network and part of it is spent on network overhead (for example, a call made by a driver to request a row of data). Often, the time spent on network overhead can be reduced by using block (otherwise referred to as "fat") cursors, which can return more than one row at a time.

The rows returned when data is fetched with a block cursor are known as a *rowset*. It is important not to confuse a rowset with a result data set. The result data set is maintained at the data source, while the rowset is maintained in application buffers. Also, while the result data set is fixed, the rowset is not—it changes position and contents each time a new set of rows are fetched.

Just as a traditional SQL forward-only cursor points to the current row, a block cursor points to the current rowset—when a block cursor first returns a rowset, the current row is the first row of that rowset. If an application wants to perform operations that operate on a single row (that is, make calls to **SQLGetData()**, perform positioned updates, and posi-

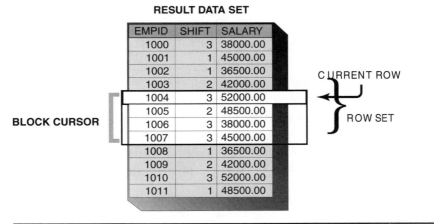

RESULT DATA SET

EMPID	SHIFT	SALARY
1000	3	38000.00
1001	1	45000.00
1002	1	36500.00
1003	2	42000.00
1004	3	52000.00
1005	2	48500.00
1006	3	38000.00
1007	3	45000.00
1008	1	36500.00
1009	2	42000.00
1010	3	52000.00
1011	1	48500.00

BLOCK CURSOR

CURRENT ROW

ROW SET

Figure 11–1   *Components of a Block Cursor.*

tioned deletes, etc.) it must indicate which row in the rowset is to be treated as the current row. Figure 11–1 shows the relationship of a block cursor, a result data set, a rowset, and a current row in a rowset.

Whether a cursor is a block cursor is independent of whether it is scrollable.

Binding Columns for use with Block Cursors

Because block cursors return multiple rows of data, applications that use them must bind an array of variables/buffers to each column in the result data set. Collectively, these arrays are sometimes referred to as *rowset buffers*. An application binds columns to arrays in the same manner that it binds columns to other application variables: by calling the **SQLBindCol()** function. The only difference is that the addresses specified in the **SQLBindCol()** function call reference arrays instead of variables. However, before binding columns to arrays, an application must decide which of the following binding styles it will use:

■ Column-wise binding   One or more arrays are bound to each column in the result data set for which data is to be returned. This is called column-wise binding because each array (or set of arrays) is associated with a single column in the result data set.

■ Row-wise binding   A data structure that holds a single data value for each column in a row is defined, and each element of the first structure in an array of these structures is bound to each column in the result data set for which data is to be returned. This is called row-wise binding because each data structure contains the data for a single row in the result data set.

Whether to use column-wise binding or row-wise binding is largely a matter of preference. Column-wise binding is the default binding style used; applications can change from column-wise binding to row-wise binding by setting the **SQL_ATTR_ROW_BIND_TYPE** statement attribute (ODBC 3.x drivers) or the **SQL_BIND_TYPE** statement option (ODBC 2.0 or earlier driver). Row-wise binding might correspond more closely to the application's data layout, in which case it could provide better performance.

COLUMN-WISE BINDING   When column-wise binding is used, one, two, and in some cases, three arrays are bound to each column in a result data set for which data values are to be returned. The first array holds the data values that will be retrieved from the column and the second array holds length/indicator values that correspond to the data values returned in the first array. With ODBC 3.x, length values and indicator values are returned in separate arrays if the **SQL_DESC_INDICATOR_PTR** and **SQL_DESC_OCTET_LENGTH_PTR** descriptor fields contain different array address values; in this case, a third array is bound to the column. Each array contains as many elements as there are rows in the rowset.

An application informs the driver that it is using column-wise binding by setting the **SQL_ATTR_ROW_BIND_TYPE** statement attribute (ODBC 3.x drivers) or the **SQL_ROW_BIND_TYPE** statement option (ODBC 2.0 or earlier driver). The driver then returns the data for each row in the rowset in successive elements of each array. Figure 11–2 shows how column-wise binding works (in this illustration, length values and indicator values are returned in the same array).

ROW-WISE BINDING   When row-wise binding is used, a data structure containing one, two, or in some cases, three elements for each column in a result data set for which data values are to be returned is defined by the application (elements can be placed in this structure in any order). The first element holds the data values to be retrieved from the column and the second element holds length/indicator values that correspond to the data values returned in the first element. With ODBC 3.x, length values and indicator values are returned in separate elements if the **SQL_DESC_INDICATOR_PTR** and **SQL_DESC_OCTET_LENGTH_PTR** descriptor fields contain different structure element address values; if this is the case, the structure must also contain a third element for each column. The application then allocates an array of these structures that contains as many elements as there are rows in the rowset. Next, the application in-

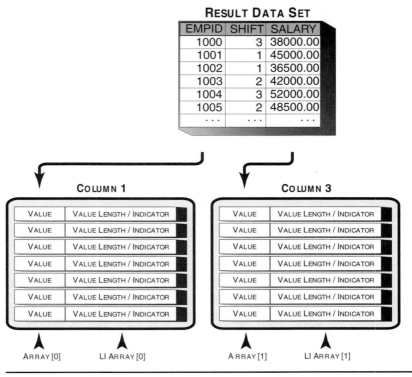

Figure 11–2   *Column-Wise Result Data Set Column Binding.*

forms the driver that it is using row-wise binding by storing the size of the data structure used in the **SQL_ATTR_ROW_BIND_TYPE** statement attribute (ODBC 3.x drivers) or the **SQL_ROW_BIND_TYPE** statement option (ODBC 2.0 or earlier driver). Finally, the address of each element in the first structure of the allocated array is bound to the appropriate column in the result data set.

Figure 11–3 shows how row-wise binding works.

During execution, the driver calculates the data address for a particular row and column by solving the equation:

```
Address = Bound Address + ((Row Number - 1) * Structure
Size)
```

where rows are numbered from 1 to the size of the rowset. (One is subtracted from the row number because array indexing in C/C++ is zero-based.)

Generally, the data structure definition only contains elements for the columns to be bound. However, the data structure can also contain elements that are not related to result data set columns.

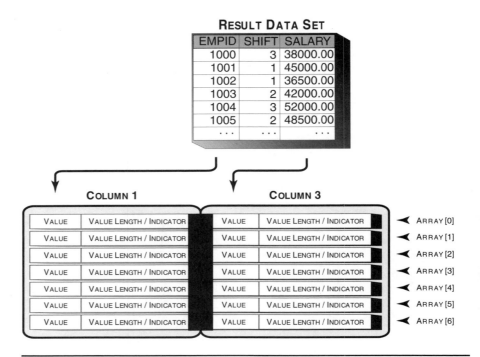

Figure 11–3 Row-Wise Result Data Set Column Binding.

Using Block Cursors

To use block cursors, an application simply sets the rowset size, binds the rowset buffers (as described in the previous section), optionally sets up a *rows fetched* and a *row status* array, and calls an ODBC API fetch function that provides block cursor support. In ODBC 2.0 and earlier, block cursor support is provided by the **SQLExtendedFetch()** function call. In ODBC 3.x, block cursor support is provided by the **SQLFetch()** and **SQLScrollFetch()** functions; SQLExtendedFetch() is no longer used.

NOTE: *In ODBC 2.0 or earlier drivers,* **SQLFetch()** *only supports single-row, forward-only cursors. Therefore, when an ODBC 3.x application calls* **SQLFetch()** *in an ODBC 2.0 or earlier driver, the driver returns a single row of data unless it also supports* **SQLExtendedFetch()** *(in which case the* **SQLFetch()** *function call is mapped to an* **SQLExtendedFetch()** *function call).*

Setting the Rowset Size

Screen-based applications often set the rowset size to match the number of rows that will be displayed on the screen; if the user resizes the screen, the application changes the rowset size accordingly. Other applications tend to set the rowset size to match the largest number of rows the application can reasonably handle—with larger rowsets, network overhead is sometimes reduced. Exactly how large such a rowset can be depends on the size of each row in the result data set and the amount of memory available.

In ODBC 1.0, rowset size is set by calling the **SQLSetScrollOptions()** function, in ODBC 2.0, rowset size is controlled by the value stored in the **SQL_ROWSET_SIZE** statement option, and in ODBC 3.x, rowset size is controlled by the value stored in the **SQL_ATTR_ROW_ARRAY_SIZE** statement attribute. An application can change the rowset size or bind new rowset buffers (by calling **SQLBindCol()** or by specifying a binding offset) before or after rows have been fetched. However, the implications of changing the rowset size once rows have been fetched depends largely on the function being used:

■ **SQLFetch()** (ODBC 3.x only), **SQLFetchScroll()**, and **SQLExtendedFetch()** use the rowset size in effect at the time they are called. Note, however, that when **SQLFetchScroll()** is called with the **SQL_FETCH_NEXT** fetch orientation specified, the cursor is incremented based on the rowset size of the previous fetch, then a new rowset is fetched, based on the current rowset size.

■ **SQLSetPos()** uses the rowset size that was in effect during the preceding call to **SQLFetch()** or **SQLFetchScroll()**. That's because **SQLSetPos()** operates on a rowset that has already been set. **SQLSetPos()** picks up the new rowset size if **SQLBulkOperations()** is called after the rowset size is changed.

■ **SQLBulkOperations()** uses the rowset size that's in effect at the time it is called, because it performs on a table operations that are independent of any fetched rowset.

Using a Rows Fetched Buffer

A *rows fetched* buffer is often used to tell an application how many rows were fetched (including those rows for which no data was returned because an error occurred while they were being fetched) when a block cursor is used. In ODBC 2.0 or earlier applications, the address of this buffer is specified in an **SQLExtendedFetch()** function parameter. In ODBC 3.x applications, this buffer's address is specified with the **SQL_ATTR_ROWS_FETCHED_PTR** statement attribute. In both versions, the rows fetched buffer must be allocated by the application; it is automatically populated by the driver when a block cursor is used. If a rows fetched buffer is used, an application must make sure that its address remains valid as long as the block cursor associated with it remains open.

NOTE: *If a rows fetched buffer is used in an ODBC 3.x application, the* **SQL_ATTR_ROW_NUMBER** *statement attribute contains the number of the current row in the result data set. ODBC 3.x applications can call the* **SQLGetStmtAttr()** *function to retrieve this value.*

Using a Row Status Array

In addition to data, **SQLFetch()** (ODBC 3.x drivers), **SQLFetchScroll()**, and **SQLExtendedFetch()** can return status information about each row in the rowset to a *row status* array. This array is allocated by the application and must have as many elements as there are rows in the rowset. In ODBC 2.0 or earlier applications, the address of this buffer is specified in an **SQLExtendedFetch()** function parameter. In ODBC 3.x applications, the address of this buffer is specified with the **SQL_ATTR_ROW_STATUS_PTR** statement attribute. Values that describe the status of each row in the rowset and that indicate when that status has changed since it was last fetched are stored in this array whenever **SQLFetch()** (ODBC 3.x drivers), **SQLFetchScroll()**, **SQLExtendedFetch()**, **SQLBulkOperations()**, and **SQLSetPos()** are executed. Table 11-1 lists the values that can be returned for each element in a row status array.

The contents of the row status array are undefined if **SQLFetch()** (ODBC 3.x drivers), **SQLFetchScroll()**, or **SQLExtendedFetch()** does not return **SQL_SUCCESS** or **SQL_SUCCESS_WITH_INFO**.

SQLGetData() and Block Cursors

Because **SQLGetData()** is designed to retrieve data from a single column within a single row, it cannot be used to populate an array with data from multiple rows. The reason for this is that the primary use of **SQLGetData()** is to fetch long data in parts and there is little or no reason to do this for more than one row at a time. Therefore, in order to use **SQLGetData()** with

Table 11–1 Row Status Values

Row Status	Description
SQL_ROW_SUCCESS	The row was successfully fetched and it has not been changed since it was last fetched.
SQL_ROW_SUCCESS_WITH_INFO	The row was successfully fetched and it has not been changed since it was last fetched. However, a warning was generated about the row.
SQL_ROW_ERROR	An error occurred while fetching the row.
SQL_ROW_UPDATED	The row was successfully fetched and it has been updated since it was last fetched. If the row is fetched again, or refreshed by SQLSetPos(), its status will be changed to the new status. Some drivers cannot detect changes to data, and therefore cannot return this value.
SQL_ROW_DELETED	The row has been deleted since it was last fetched.
SQL_ROW_ADDED	The row was inserted by SQLBulkOperations(). If the row is fetched again, or is refreshed by SQLSetPos(), its status is SQL_ROW_SUCCESS. This value is not set by SQLFetch() or SQLFetchScroll().
SQL_ROW_NOROW	The rowset overlapped the end of the result set and no row was returned that corresponded to this element of the row status array.

(Adapted from the table on page 198 of *Microsoft ODBC 3.0 Software Development Kit & Programmer's Reference*.)

a block cursor, an application must first position the cursor on a single row within the rowset returned. This positioning can be done by calling SQLSetPos() with the SQL_POSITION operation specified.

Scrollable Cursors

Interactive applications, especially those written for personal computers, often need to provide a way for a user to scroll through data in a result data set, by using the arrow keys, the PgUp or PgDn key, or the scroll bar and a mouse. For such applications, returning to a previously fetched row can be a problem. One possible solution is to close and reopen the cursor, then fetch rows until the cursor reaches the required row. Another possibility is to read the result data set once, and store it locally in order to implement scrolling in the application. Both methods only work well with small result data sets, and the latter method is difficult to implement. A better solution is to use a cursor that can move forward *and* backward in the result data set. A cursor that provides the ability to move forward and backward within a result data set is called a *scrollable cursor*.

The ability to move backward in a result data set raises an important question: Should the cursor detect changes made to rows previously fetched? In other words, should it detect updated, deleted, and newly inserted rows? This question arises because the definition of a result data set (that is, the set of rows matching certain criteria) does not state when rows are checked to see if they match that criteria, nor does it state whether rows must contain the same data each time they are fetched. The former omission makes it possible for scrollable cursors to detect whether rows have been inserted or deleted, while the latter makes it possible for them to detect updated data.

To cover the needs of different applications, ODBC defines the following four different types of scrollable cursors:

- Static
- Dynamic
- Keyset-driven
- Mixed

Each of these cursors vary both in their expense and in their ability to detect changes made to the result data set: Static cursors detect few or no changes but are relatively cheap to implement. Dynamic cursors detect all changes but are expensive to implement. Keyset-driven and mixed cursors lie somewhere in between, detecting most changes but at less expense than dynamic cursors.

Static Cursors

A *static cursor* is a cursor in which the result data set appears to be static. That's because static cursors do not usually detect changes made to the result data set after the cursor is opened. For example, suppose a static cursor fetches a row of data from a result data set. Now suppose another application then updates that row. If the static cursor refetches the row, it does not see the changes made by the other application. Static cursors never detect inserts, updates, and deletes made by other applications; however, static cursors may detect their own inserts, updates, and deletes, although they are not required to do so. This type of cursor is most useful for read-only applications that do not need the most up-to-date data available or for applications in which multiple users never need to modify data concurrently.

Static cursors are commonly implemented by locking the rows in the result data set or by making a copy, or snapshot, of the result data set. While locking rows is relatively easy to do, the drawback of this approach is that it significantly reduces transaction concurrency. Making a copy or a snapshot of a result data set allows greater concurrency and provides the cursor with a way to keep track of its own inserts, updates, and deletes by modifying the copy. However, a copy is more expensive to make and can differ from the underlying data as that data is changed by other applications.

Dynamic Cursors

Dynamic cursors can detect changes made to the result data set after the cursor is opened. For example, suppose a dynamic cursor fetches two rows of data from a result data set. Now suppose another application then updates one of those rows and deletes the other one. If the dynamic cursor attempts to refetch the rows, it returns the new values for the updated row and does not return the deleted row.

Dynamic cursors detect their own inserts, updates, and deletes as well as inserts, updates, and deletes made by other applications. (This is subject to the isolation level of the transaction, as defined by the **SQL_ATTR_TXN_ISOLATION** connection attribute.)

Keyset-Driven Cursors

A *keyset-driven cursor* is a cursor that lies somewhere between a static and a dynamic cursor in its ability to detect changes. Like static cursors, keyset-driven cursors do not always detect changes to the set of rows in the result data set or to the order in which rows are returned. Like dynamic cursors, keyset-driven cursors are able to detect changes to row values in the result data set (dependent upon the transaction isolation level being used). The advantage of using this type of cursor is that it enables access to the most up-to-date values and it allows an application to fetch rows based on absolute position within a result data set.

When a keyset-driven cursor is opened, it saves *keys* (unique row identifiers) for the entire result data set. A key can be a row ID (if available), a unique index, a unique key, or the entire row. As the cursor scrolls through the result data set, it uses the keys in this keyset to retrieve the current data values for each row. Because of this, keyset-driven cursors always detect their own updates and deletes as well as updates and deletes made by other applications. For example, suppose a keyset-driven cursor fetches a row of data from a result data set. Now suppose another application then updates that row. If the keyset-driven cursor refetches the row, it sees the changes made by the other application, because it refetched the row using its key. Figure 11–4 shows the components of a keyset-driven cursor.

When a keyset-driven cursor attempts to refetch a row that has been deleted, this row appears as a hole in the result set: The key for the row exists in the keyset but the row no longer exists in the result data set. If the key for a row is updated, the update is treated as if the original row was deleted and a new row was inserted. Thus, these rows also appear as holes in the result data set. While a keyset-driven cursor can always detect rows deleted by others, it can optionally remove the keys for rows it deletes itself from the keyset, thereby hiding its own deletes.

Rows inserted by other applications are never visible to keyset-driven cursors. That's because no keys for these rows exist in the keyset. However, a keyset-driven cursor can optionally add the keys for rows it inserts itself to the keyset. Keyset-driven cursors that do this can detect their own inserts.

Keyset-driven cursors are commonly implemented by creating a temporary table containing the keys and the row versioning information for each row in the result data set. To scroll through the original result data set, the keyset-driven cursor opens a static cursor over the temporary table. To retrieve a row in the original result data set, the keyset-driven cursor first retrieves the appropriate key from the temporary table, then it retrieves the current values for the row. If block cursors are used, the cursor must retrieve multiple keys and rows.

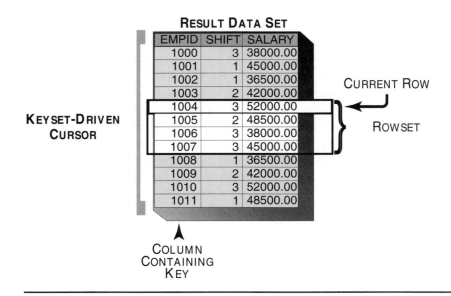

Figure 11–4 Components of a Keyset-Driven Cursor.

Mixed Cursors

A *mixed cursor* is a combination of a keyset-driven cursor and a dynamic cursor. Mixed cursors are used when the result data set is too large to reasonably save keys for. Mixed cursors are implemented by creating a keyset that is smaller than the entire result set but larger than the rowset. As long as the application scrolls within the keyset, the behavior is the same as a keyset-driven cursor. When the application scrolls outside the keyset, the behavior becomes dynamic—the cursor fetches the requested rows and creates a new keyset. After the new keyset is created, the behavior reverts to keyset-driven within that keyset.

For example, suppose a result set has 1,000 rows and uses a mixed cursor with a keyset size of 100 and a rowset size of 10. When the first rowset is fetched, the cursor creates a keyset consisting of the keys for the first 100 rows. It then returns the first 10 rows, as requested.

Now suppose another application deletes rows 11 and 101. If the cursor attempts to retrieve row 11, it encounters a hole because it has a key for this row but no row exists; this is keyset-driven behavior. If the cursor attempts to retrieve row 101, the cursor does not detect that the row is missing because it does not have a key for the row. Instead, it retrieves what was previously row 102. This is dynamic cursor behavior.

A mixed cursor is equivalent to a keyset-driven cursor when the keyset size is equal to the result data set size. A mixed cursor is equivalent to a dynamic cursor when the keyset size is equal to 1. Figure 11–5 shows the components of a mixed cursor.

Specifying the Cursor Type

An application can specify the cursor type to use before executing an SQL statement that creates a result data set. If an application does not explicitly specify a cursor type, a forward-only cursor is used by default. ODBC 1.0 applications specify cursor types by calling the **SQLSetScrollOptions()** function. ODBC 2.0 applications specify cursor types by setting the **SQL_CURSOR_TYPE** statement option to the appropriate value. ODBC 3.x applications specify cursor types by setting the **SQL_ATTR_CURSOR_TYPE** statement attribute. For keyset-driven and mixed cursors, applications can also specify the keyset size to use. ODBC 2.0 applications specify the keyset size with the **SQL_KEYSET_SIZE** statement option; ODBC 3.x applications specify the keyset size with the **SQL_ATTR_KEYSET_SIZE** statement attribute. To get a mixed cursor, an application simply specifies a keyset-driven cursor and defines a keyset size that is smaller than the actual size of the result

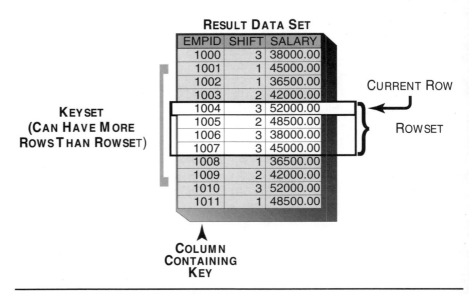

Figure 11–5   *Components of a Mixed Cursor.*

data set—if the keyset size is set to 0 (which is the default) the keyset size is set to the size of the result data set and a keyset-driven cursor is used. The keyset size can be changed any time after the cursor has been opened.

Setting Cursor Characteristics

An application can specify the characteristics of a cursor instead of specifying the cursor type. To do so, the application selects the cursor's scrollability (by setting the **SQL_ATTR_CURSOR_SCROLLABLE** statement attribute (ODBC 3.x) or the **SQL_CURSOR_SCROLLABLE** statement option (ODBC 2.0)) and sensitivity (by setting the **SQL_ATTR_CURSOR_SENSITIVITY** statement attribute (ODBC 3.x) or the **SQL_CURSOR_SENSITIVITY** statement option (ODBC 2.0)) before opening the cursor on the statement handle. The driver then chooses the cursor type that most efficiently provides the characteristics the application requested.

Whenever an application sets a statement attribute to specify either a cursor type or cursor characteristics, the driver makes any necessary changes to the other cursor control statement attributes so that their values remain consistent. Consequently, when an application specifies a cursor characteristic, the driver can change the attribute indicating cursor type to reflect the specification. Likewise, when an application specifies a cursor type, the driver can change any of the other attributes to be consistent with the characteristics of that particular cursor. The implicit setting of statement attributes is driver-defined, however, divers must follow these two rules:

■ Forward-only cursors are never scrollable.

■ Insensitive cursors are never updatable (and thus their concurrency is read-only); this is based on the definition of insensitive cursors in the ISO SQL standard.

An application that sets statement attributes to specify both a cursor type and cursor characteristics runs the risk of obtaining a cursor that is not the most efficient cursor available for meeting the application's requirements.

Scrolling and Fetching Rows

When using a scrollable cursor, applications can call **SQLFetchScroll()** (ODBC 3.x drivers) or **SQLExtendedFetch()** (ODBC 2.0 or earlier drivers) to position the cursor and fetch rows. Both of these functions support relative scrolling (next, prior, and relative n rows), absolute scrolling (first, last, and row n), and positioning by bookmark. The *FetchOrientation* and *RowNumber* parameters of both of these functions specify which rowset to fetch. An example is shown in Figure 11–6.

SQLFetchScroll() and **SQLExtendedFetch()** positions the cursor on the specified row and returns the rows in the rowset starting with that row. If the specified rowset overlaps the end of the result data set, a partial rowset is returned. If the specified rowset overlaps the start of the result set, the first rowset in the result data set is usually returned. Once a rowset has been retrieved, an application can call **SQLSetPos()** to move to a particular row within the rowset or to refresh all rows in the rowset.

In some cases, an application may want to position the cursor without retrieving any data. For example, it might want to test whether a row exists or just get the bookmark for the row without bringing other data across the network. To do this, it sets the **SQL_ATTR_RETRIEVE_DATA** statement attribute (ODBC 3.x) or the **SQL_RETRIEVE_DATA** statement option (ODBC 2.0) to **SQL_RD_OFF** before calling the **SQLFetchScroll()** or the **SQLExtendedFetch()** function. Note that the variable bound to the bookmark column (if any) is always updated, regardless of the setting of this statement attribute (option).

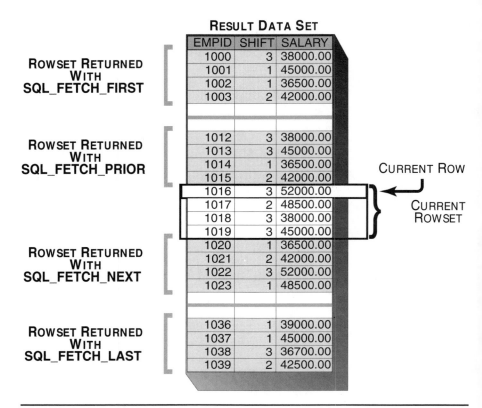

RESULT DATA SET

ROWSET RETURNED
WITH
SQL_FETCH_FIRST

EMPID	SHIFT	SALARY
1000	3	38000.00
1001	1	45000.00
1002	1	36500.00
1003	2	42000.00

ROWSET RETURNED
WITH
SQL_FETCH_PRIOR

1012	3	38000.00
1013	3	45000.00
1014	1	36500.00
1015	2	42000.00

CURRENT ROW

1016	3	52000.00
1017	2	48500.00
1018	3	38000.00
1019	3	45000.00

CURRENT
ROWSET

ROWSET RETURNED
WITH
SQL_FETCH_NEXT

1020	1	36500.00
1021	2	42000.00
1022	3	52000.00
1023	1	48500.00

ROWSET RETURNED
WITH
SQL_FETCH_LAST

1036	1	39000.00
1037	1	45000.00
1038	3	36700.00
1039	2	42500.00

Figure 11–6   *Fetching Absolute and Relative Rowsets with a Scrollable Cursor.*

The ODBC Cursor Library

Block cursors and scrollable cursors are very useful additions to many applications; however, not all drivers support them. Microsoft and other ODBC driver vendors such as Intersolv have included extended cursor functionality in their ODBC drivers. In particular, Microsoft includes a Cursor Library that implements block cursors, static cursors, positioned **UPDATE** and **DELETE** statements, and the **SQLSetPos()** function for any driver that meets the X/Open Standard CLI conformance level (the ODBC 2.0 Cursor Library only supports block cursors and static scrollable cursors). Basically, this Cursor Library is a proxy .DLL that emulates cursor support when an ODBC data source does not natively provide it. To use the ODBC cursor library, an application sets the **SQL_ATTR_ODBC_CURSORS** connection attribute (ODBC 3.x drivers) or the **SQL_ODBC_CURSORS** connection option (ODBC 2.0 drivers) before connecting to the data source.

Bookmarks

A *bookmark* is a value used to identify a row of data. The bookmark value itself is known only to the driver or data source; it can be as simple as a row number or as complex as a disk address. Bookmarks in ODBC are a bit different from bookmarks in real books. In an actual book, the reader places a bookmark at a specific page then looks for that bookmark to return to the page. In ODBC, the application requests a bookmark for a particular row, stores it, and passes it back to the cursor to return to the row. Thus, bookmarks in ODBC are similar to a reader writing down a page number, remembering it, and then looking up the page at a later point in time. Bookmarks may or may not remain valid after the cursor using them is closed. Building and maintaining bookmarks can be an expensive operation, so bookmarks should be enabled only when an application can make good use of them.

Bookmark Data Types

Bookmarks in ODBC 2.0 are 32-bit values. In ODBC 3.x drivers, all bookmarks are variable length values; 32-bit fixed-length values are supported but only for backward compatibility. This allows a primary key or a unique index associated with a table to be used as an ODBC 3.x bookmark. Before opening any cursor that is to use bookmarks, an application must set the **SQL_ATTR_USE_BOOKMARK** statement attribute (ODBC 3.x) or the **SQL_USE_BOOKMARK** statement option (ODBC 2.0) to inform the driver that bookmarks will be used. Because a variable-length bookmark can be a long value, an application should not bind to the bookmark column (column 0) unless it will use the bookmark for many of the rows in the rowset.

If an ODBC 2.0 application working with an ODBC 3.x driver uses bookmarks, variable-length bookmarks are used; however, only the first 32 bits of each variable are populated. If an ODBC 3.x application working with an ODBC 2.0 driver uses bookmarks, only 32-bit fixed-length bookmarks are used. In this case, the **SQL_ATTR_FETCH_BOOKMARK_PTR** statement attribute must point to a 32-bit value—if the bookmarks used are longer than 32-bits, such as when primary keys are used, the cursor must map the actual values to 32-bit values (it could, for example, build a hash table for them). In addition, when an ODBC 3.x application working with an ODBC 2.0 driver binds a bookmark to an application variable, the buffer length specified must always be 4.

Retrieving Bookmark Values

Bookmarks are always returned as column 0 of a result data set. An application can retrieve them in three different ways:

- Bind column 0 of the result data set containing bookmarks to an application variable/buffer. In this case, the bookmarks for each row in the rowset are returned, along with the data for other bound columns in the row, when **SQLFetch()** (ODBC 3.x only), **SQLFetchScroll()** or **SQLExtendedFetch()** is executed.

- Call **SQLSetPos()** to position the cursor on a row in the rowset, then call **SQLGetData()** for column 0. Note that if a driver supports bookmarks, it must always support the ability to call **SQLGetData()** for column 0, even if it does not allow applications to call **SQLGetData()** for other columns in the result data set that are physically located before the last bound column.

- Call **SQLBulkOperations()** with the **SQL_ADD** operation specified and column 0 bound. In this case, the cursor inserts a row and returns the bookmark for the row in the bound application variable. Because **SQLBulkOperations()** was introduced in ODBC 3.0, this method can only be used with ODBC 3.x drivers.

Scrolling By Bookmark

When using **SQLFetchScroll()** to fetch rows, an ODBC 3.x application can use a bookmark as a basis for selecting the starting row. This is a form of absolute addressing because it is not dependent on the current cursor position. To scroll to a bookmarked row, an application calls **SQLFetchScroll()** with the **SQL_FETCH_BOOKMARK** fetch orientation specified. This causes the fetch operation to use the bookmark pointed to by the **SQL_ATTR_FETCH_BOOKMARK_PTR** statement attribute; the rowset starting with the row identified by that bookmark is returned.

Comparing Bookmarks

Because bookmarks are byte-comparable, they can be compared for equality or inequality. To do so, an application treats each bookmark as an array of bytes and compares two bookmarks byte by byte. However, because bookmarks are only guaranteed to be distinct within a result data set, it makes no sense to compare bookmarks obtained from different result data sets.

Multiple Results

A result is something returned by the data source after a statement is executed. ODBC has two types of results: *result data sets* and *row counts*. You have already seen that result data sets are conceptual tables that get created when **SELECT** SQL statements are executed. Row counts are values that identify the number of rows affected by an **INSERT**, **UPDATE**, or **DELETE** SQL statement.

Whenever two or more SQL statements are executed in a batch, multiple results are produced. To process multiple results, an application must call the **SQLMoreResults()** function. This function discards the current result data set or row count value and makes the next result data set or row count value available. For example, suppose the following statements are executed as a batch:

```
SELECT * FROM Parts WHERE Price > 100.00;
UPDATE Parts SET Price = 0.9 * Price WHERE Price > 100.00
```

After these statements are executed, the application can begin fetching rows from the result data set created by the **SELECT** SQL statement because it automatically has access to it. When it is done fetching rows, it must call **SQLMoreResults()** to make the row count information about the **UPDATE SQL** statement available. If necessary, **SQLMoreResults()** discards any unfetched rows in the result data set and closes the cursor. The application can then call **SQLRowCount()** to determine how many rows were affected by the **UPDATE SQL** statement.

Whether all SQL statements in a batch are executed before any results are available is driver-specific. With some drivers, this is always the case; with other drivers, only the first SQL statement in the batch is executed—calling **SQLMoreResults()** triggers the execution of the next SQL statement in the batch.

The Advanced SQL Results Retrieval Functions

Table 11–2 lists the ODBC API functions used to perform advanced data retrieval operations on result data sets.

Each of these functions is described in detail in the remaining portion of this chapter.

Table 11–2 *The ODBC Advanced Results Retrieval Functions*

Function Name	Description
SQLFetchScroll()	Retrieves multiple rows of data (a rowset) from a result data set and returns data for all bound columns.
SQLSetScrollOptions()	Sets options that control cursor behavior.
SQLExtendedFetch()	Retrieves multiple rows of data (a rowset) from a result data set and returns data for all bound columns.
SQLMoreResults()	Determines whether there are more result data sets or row count values available and, if there are, initializes processing for them.

SQLFetchScroll

COMPATABILITY

X/OPEN 95 CLI	ISO/IEC 92 CLI	ODBC 1.0	ODBC 2.0	ODBC 3.0	ODBC 3.5
✓	✓	☐	☐	✓	✓

API CONFORMANCE LEVEL   **CORE**

Purpose   The **SQLFetchScroll()** function is used to retrieve a block containing multiple rows (a rowset) of data from a result data set.

Syntax
```
SQLRETURN    SQLFetchScroll  (SQLHSTMT        StatementHandle,
                              SQLUSMALLINT    FetchOrientation,
                              SQLINTEGER      RowNumber);
```

Parameters *StatementHandle*   An SQL statement handle that refers to a previously allocated SQL statement information storage buffer (data structure).

FetchOrientation   Specifies the direction and type of fetch the driver is to perform. This parameter must be set to one of the following values:

▪ **SQL_FETCH_FIRST**
Return the first rowset in the result data set.

▪ **SQL_FETCH_NEXT**
Return the next rowset in the result data set. If the cursor is positioned before the start of the result data set, this is equivalent to **SQL_FETCH_FIRST**.

▪ **SQL_FETCH_PRIOR**
Return the prior rowset in the result data set. If the cursor is positioned after the end of the result data set, this is equivalent to **SQL_FETCH_LAST**.

▪ **SQL_FETCH_LAST**
Return the last complete rowset in the result data set.

■ **SQL_FETCH_ABSOLUTE**
Return the rowset starting at the row number specified in the *RowNumber* parameter. If the *RowNumber* parameter is set to **0**, **SQL_NO_DATA_FOUND** is returned and the cursor is positioned before the start of the result data set.

■ **SQL_FETCH_RELATIVE**
Return the rowset *RowNumber* rows from the start of the current rowset. If the *RowNumber* parameter is set to **0**, the driver simply refreshes the current rowset. If the cursor is positioned before the start of the result data set and the *RowNumber* parameter contains a value greater than **0** or if the cursor is positioned after the end of the result data set and the *RowNumber* parameter contains a value less than **0**, this is equivalent to **SQL_FETCH_ABSOLUTE**.

■ **SQL_FETCH_BOOKMARK**
Return the rowset *RowNumber* rows from the bookmark specified by the **SQL_ATTR_FETCH_BOOKMARK_PTR** SQL statement attribute.

RowNumber
Specifies the ordinal position of the first row in the rowset to fetch (provided the *FetchOrientation* parameter is set to **SQL_FETCH_ABSOLUTE**, **SQL_FETCH_RELATIVE**, or **SQL_FETCH_BOOKMARK**).

Description
SQLFetchScroll() extends the functionality of **SQLFetch()** by retrieving multiple rows of data (a rowset) for each bound column in a result data set. **SQLFetchScroll()** returns rowset data (one or more rows) in the form of an array. The size of the rowset (number of rows) returned is specified by the **SQL_ATTR_ROWSET_SIZE** statement attribute value. Rowsets can be specified by an absolute row position, a relative row position, or by a bookmark.

When the **SQLFetchScroll()** function is called, the appropriate data transfer is performed along with any data conversion specified when the columns were bound. If the application has specified a pointer to a row status array or buffer in which to return the number of rows fetched, **SQLFetchScroll()** returns this information as well. Refer to "Block Cursors" in this chapter for more information.

NOTE: *In ODBC 3.x, this function replaces the ODBC 2.0 function* SQLExtendedFetch().

Return Codes   SQL_SUCCESS, SQL_SUCCESS_WITH_INFO, SQL_NO_DATA, SQL_STILL_EXECUTING, SQL_INVALID_HANDLE, or SQL_ERROR

SQL_SUCCESS_WITH_INFO is returned for all SQLSTATEs that can return SQL_SUCCESS_WITH_INFO or SQL_ERROR (except 01xxx SQLSTATEs), if an error occurs on one or more, but not all, rows of a multi-row operation. SQL_ERROR is returned if an error occurs on a single-row operation.

SQLSTATEs   If this function returns SQL_ERROR, one of the following SQLSTATE values may be obtained by calling the SQLGetDiagRec() function:

01000, 01004, 01S01, 01S06, 01S07, 07006, 07009, 08S01, 22001, 22002, 22003, 22007, 22012, 22015, 22018, 24000, 40001, 40003, HY000, HY001, HY008, HY010*, HY013, HY090, HY106*, HY107, HY111, HYC00, HYT01, or IM001*

*Returned by the ODBC Driver Manager.

Unless noted otherwise, each of these SQLSTATE values are returned by the data source driver. Refer to Appendix B for detailed information about each SQLSTATE value that can be returned by the ODBC Driver Manager or by a data source driver.

Comments
- SQLFetch() should be used instead of SQLFetchScroll() to fetch one row of data at a time, in a forward direction.

- An application can mix SQLFetchScroll() and SQLFetch() function calls for the same cursor. However, SQLFetchScroll() function calls cannot be mixed with SQLExtendedFetch() function calls for the same cursor.

- When working with an ODBC 2.x driver, the ODBC Driver Manager maps this function to SQLExtendedFetch().

- Before this function is called for the first time, the cursor is positioned before the start of the result data set. When called, this function positions the block cursor based on the values stored in the *FetchOrientation* and *RowNumber* parameters. After this function is executed, the current row is the first row in the rowset.

- If an application calls this function with the *FetchOrientation* parameter set to SQL_FETCH_BOOKMARK while working with an ODBC 2.x driver, the *RowNumber* parameter must be set to 0.

- Drivers are not required to support all fetch orientations; an application can call the **SQLGetInfo()** function to determine which fetch orientations are supported by the driver being used.

- The **SQL_ATTR_ROW_ARRAY_SIZE** statement attribute specifies the size (number of rows) of the rowset. If the rowset being fetched overlaps the end of the result data set, a partial rowset is returned. All remaining rows will be empty and will have a status of **SQL_ROW_NOROW**.

- **SQLFetchScroll()** and **SQLFetch()** store values in the appropriate row status array (if one exists) in a similar manner.

- **SQLFetchScroll()** and **SQLFetch()** store values in the rows fetched buffer (if one exists) in a similar manner.

- **SQLFetchScroll()** and **SQLFetch()** return error information in a similar manner.

- **SQLFetchScroll()** and **SQLFetch()** interact with descriptors in a similar manner.

- **SQLFetchScroll()** and **SQLFetch()** return data to bound columns in a similar manner. If no columns are bound, **SQLFetchScroll()** moves the cursor to the specified position without returning data.

- If the **SQL_ATTR_CURSOR_TYPE** statement attribute is set to **SQL_CURSOR_FORWARD_ONLY**, **SQL_FETCH_NEXT** must be specified in the *FetchOrientation* parameter; otherwise **SQL_ERROR** and SQLSTATE **HY**106 (Fetch type out of range) is returned.

- If the **SQL_ATTR_CONCURRENCY** statement attribute is set to **SQL_CONCUR_VALUES** or **SQL_CONCUR_ROWVER**, this function updates the optimistic concurrency values used by the data source to detect whether a row has changed. This happens each time this function fetches a new rowset, including when it refetches the current rowset (**SQLFetchScroll()** is called with the *FetchOrientation* parameter set to **SQL_FETCH_RELATIVE** and the *RowNumber* parameter set to **0**).

Prerequisites There are no prerequisites for using this function call.

Restrictions This function must be called after an SQL statement that creates a result data set is executed and before the cursor for that result data set is closed.

See Also SQLFetch(), SQLExtendedFetch()

Example   **COLUMN-WISE BINDING**   The following Visual C++ program illus-
                     trates how to use the **SQLFetchScroll()** function to retrieve multiple rows
                     of data from a result data set (in a single function call), using column-wise
                     binding.

```
/*─────────────────────────────────────────────────────────────*/
/* NAME:     CH11EX1A.CPP                                         */
/* PURPOSE: Illustrate How To Use The SQLFetchScroll() ODBC API  */
/*          Function To Retrieve Record Values And Return Them To */
/*          Arrays That Were Bound To The Columns In The Result   */
/*          Data Set Using Column-Wise Binding.                   */
/*                                                                */
/* OTHER ODBC APIs SHOWN:                                         */
/*          SQLAllocHandle()          SQLSetEnvAttr()            */
/*          SQLConnect()              SQLExecDirect()            */
/*          SQLSetStmtAttr()          SQLBindCol()               */
/*          SQLCloseCursor()          SQLDisconnect()            */
/*          SQLFreeHandle()                                       */
/*                                                                */
/*─────────────────────────────────────────────────────────────*/

// Include The Appropriate Header Files
#include <windows.h>
#include <sql.h>
#include <sqlext.h>
#include <iostream.h>

// Define The ODBC_Class Class
class ODBC_Class
{
    // Attributes
    public:
        SQLHANDLE    EnvHandle;
        SQLHANDLE    ConHandle;
        SQLHANDLE    StmtHandle;
        SQLRETURN    rc;

    // Operations
    public:
        ODBC_Class();                         // Constructor
        ~ODBC_Class();                        // Destructor
        SQLRETURN ShowResults();
};

// Define The Class Constructor
ODBC_Class::ODBC_Class()
{
    // Initialize The Return Code Variable
    rc = SQL_SUCCESS;

    // Allocate An Environment Handle
    rc = SQLAllocHandle(SQL_HANDLE_ENV, SQL_NULL_HANDLE, &EnvHandle);
```

```
    // Set The ODBC Application Version To 3.x
    if (rc == SQL_SUCCESS)
        rc = SQLSetEnvAttr(EnvHandle, SQL_ATTR_ODBC_VERSION,
                (SQLPOINTER) SQL_OV_ODBC3, SQL_IS_UINTEGER);

    // Allocate A Connection Handle
    if (rc == SQL_SUCCESS)
        rc = SQLAllocHandle(SQL_HANDLE_DBC, EnvHandle, &ConHandle);
}

// Define The Class Destructor
ODBC_Class::~ODBC_Class()
{
    // Free The Connection Handle
    if (ConHandle != NULL)
        SQLFreeHandle(SQL_HANDLE_DBC, ConHandle);

    // Free The Environment Handle
    if (EnvHandle != NULL)
        SQLFreeHandle(SQL_HANDLE_ENV, EnvHandle);
}

// Define The ShowResults() Member Function
SQLRETURN ODBC_Class::ShowResults(void)
{
    // Declare The Local Memory Variables
    SQLRETURN       rc;
    SQLUINTEGER     ArraySize = 4;
    SQLUINTEGER     SupplierIDArray[4];
    SQLINTEGER      SupplierIDLI_Array[4];
    SQLCHAR         CompanyNameArray[4][41];
    SQLINTEGER      CompanyNameLI_Array[4];
    SQLCHAR         ContactNameArray[4][31];
    SQLINTEGER      ContactNameLI_Array[4];

    SQLUSMALLINT RowStatusArray[4];
    SQLUINTEGER  NumRowsFetched;

    // Set The SQL_ATTR_ROW_BIND_TYPE Statement Attribute To Tell The
    // Driver To Use Column-Wise Binding
    rc = SQLSetStmtAttr(StmtHandle, SQL_ATTR_ROW_BIND_TYPE,
            SQL_BIND_BY_COLUMN, 0);

    // Declare The Rowset Size (By Setting The
    // SQL_ATTR_ROW_ARRAY_SIZE Statement Attribute)
    rc = SQLSetStmtAttr(StmtHandle, SQL_ATTR_ROW_ARRAY_SIZE,
            (SQLPOINTER) ArraySize, 0);

    // Store The Address Of A Row Status Array In The
    // SQL_ATTR_ROW_STATUS_PTR Statement Attribute
    rc = SQLSetStmtAttr(StmtHandle, SQL_ATTR_ROW_STATUS_PTR,
            RowStatusArray, 0);
```

```
// Store The Address Of A Rows Fetched Buffer In The
// SQL_ATTR_ROWS_FETCHED_PTR Statement Attribute
rc = SQLSetStmtAttr(StmtHandle, SQL_ATTR_ROWS_FETCHED_PTR,
        &NumRowsFetched, 0);

// Bind The Columns In The Result Data Set Returned To
// Application Arrays
rc = SQLBindCol(StmtHandle, 1, SQL_C_SLONG, SupplierIDArray, 0,
        SupplierIDLI_Array);

rc = SQLBindCol(StmtHandle, 2, SQL_C_CHAR, CompanyNameArray,
        sizeof(CompanyNameArray[0]), CompanyNameLI_Array);

rc = SQLBindCol(StmtHandle, 3, SQL_C_CHAR, ContactNameArray,
        sizeof(ContactNameArray[0]), ContactNameLI_Array);

// Display A Header
cout << "Suppliers :" << endl << endl;

// As Long As There Is Data, Retrieve Records From The Result
// Data Set And Display Them
while (rc != SQL_NO_DATA_FOUND)
{
    // Fetch Up To The Rowset Size Number Of Rows
    rc = SQLFetchScroll(StmtHandle, SQL_FETCH_NEXT, 0);

    // Check The Row Status Array And Print Only Those Rows
    // That Were Successfully Fetched
    for (unsigned int i = 0; i < NumRowsFetched; i++)
    {
        if (RowStatusArray[i] == SQL_ROW_SUCCESS ||
            RowStatusArray[i] == SQL_ROW_SUCCESS_WITH_INFO)
        {
            // Print The Supplier ID
            cout.setf(ios::left);
            cout.width(6);
            if (SupplierIDLI_Array[i] == SQL_NULL_DATA)
                cout << "<NULL>";
            else
                cout << SupplierIDArray[i];

            // Print The Company Name
            cout.setf(ios::left);
            cout.width(40);
            if (CompanyNameLI_Array[i] == SQL_NULL_DATA)
                cout << "<NULL>";
            else
                cout << CompanyNameArray[i];

            // Print The Contact Name
            cout.setf(ios::left);
            cout.width(30);
            if (ContactNameLI_Array[i] == SQL_NULL_DATA)
```

```
                    cout << "<NULL>";
                else
                    cout << ContactNameArray[i];

                cout << endl;
            }
        }
    }

    // Close the cursor
    rc = SQLCloseCursor(StmtHandle);

    // Return The ODBC API Return Code To The Calling Function
    return(rc);
}

/*———————————————————————————————————————————————————————————*/
/* The Main Function                                              */
/*———————————————————————————————————————————————————————————*/
int main()
{
    // Declare The Local Memory Variables
    SQLRETURN   rc = SQL_SUCCESS;
    SQLCHAR     DBName[10] = "Northwind";
    SQLCHAR     SQLStmt[255];

    // Create An Instance Of The ODBC_Class Class
    ODBC_Class  Example;

    // Connect To The Northwind Sample Database
    if (Example.ConHandle != NULL)
    {
        rc = SQLConnect(Example.ConHandle, DBName, SQL_NTS,
                (SQLCHAR *) "", SQL_NTS, (SQLCHAR *) "", SQL_NTS);

        // Allocate An SQL Statement Handle
        rc = SQLAllocHandle(SQL_HANDLE_STMT, Example.ConHandle,
                &Example.StmtHandle);
        if (rc == SQL_SUCCESS)
        {
            // Define A SELECT SQL Statement
            strcpy((char *) SQLStmt, "SELECT Suppliers.SupplierID,");
            strcat((char *) SQLStmt, " Suppliers.CompanyName, ");
            strcat((char *) SQLStmt, "Suppliers.ContactName ");
            strcat((char *) SQLStmt, "FROM Suppliers");

            // Prepare And Execute The SQL Statement
            rc = SQLExecDirect(Example.StmtHandle, SQLStmt, SQL_NTS);

            // Display The Results Of The SQL Query
            if (rc == SQL_SUCCESS)
                Example.ShowResults();
```

```
                // Free The SQL Statement Handle
                if (Example.StmtHandle != NULL)
                    SQLFreeHandle(SQL_HANDLE_STMT, Example.StmtHandle);
        }

            // Disconnect From The Northwind Sample Database
            rc = SQLDisconnect(Example.ConHandle);
    }

    // Return To The Operating System
    return(rc);
}
```

ROW-WISE BINDING The following Visual C++ program illustrates how to use the **SQLFetchScroll()** function to retrieve multiple rows of data from a result data set (in a single function call), using row-wise binding.

```
/*————————————————————————————————————*/
/* NAME:      CH11EX1B.CPP                                     */
/* PURPOSE: Illustrate How To Use The SQLFetchScroll() ODBC API */
/*          Function To Retrieve Record Values And  Return Them To */
/*          Arrays That Were Bound To The Columns In The Result */
/*          Data Set Using Column-Wise Binding.               */
/*                                                            */
/* OTHER ODBC APIs SHOWN:                                     */
/*          SQLAllocHandle()         SQLSetEnvAttr()          */
/*          SQLConnect()             SQLExecDirect()          */
/*          SQLSetStmtAttr()         SQLBindCol()             */
/*          SQLCloseCursor()         SQLDisconnect()          */
/*          SQLFreeHandle()                                   */
/*                                                            */
/*————————————————————————————————————*/

// Include The Appropriate Header Files
#include <windows.h>
#include <sql.h>
#include <sqlext.h>
#include <iostream.h>

// Define The ODBC_Class Class
class ODBC_Class
{
    // Attributes
    public:
        SQLHANDLE    EnvHandle;
        SQLHANDLE    ConHandle;
        SQLHANDLE    StmtHandle;
        SQLRETURN    rc;

    // Operations
    public:
        ODBC_Class();                        // Constructor
```

```
        ~ODBC_Class();                              // Destructor
        SQLRETURN ShowResults();
};

// Define The Class Constructor
ODBC_Class::ODBC_Class()
{
    // Initialize The Return Code Variable
    rc = SQL_SUCCESS;

    // Allocate An Environment Handle
    rc = SQLAllocHandle(SQL_HANDLE_ENV, SQL_NULL_HANDLE, &EnvHandle);

    // Set The ODBC Application Version To 3.x
    if (rc == SQL_SUCCESS)
        rc = SQLSetEnvAttr(EnvHandle, SQL_ATTR_ODBC_VERSION,
                    (SQLPOINTER) SQL_OV_ODBC3, SQL_IS_UINTEGER);

    // Allocate A Connection Handle
    if (rc == SQL_SUCCESS)
        rc = SQLAllocHandle(SQL_HANDLE_DBC, EnvHandle, &ConHandle);
}

// Define The Class Destructor
ODBC_Class::~ODBC_Class()
{
    // Free The Connection Handle
    if (ConHandle != NULL)
        SQLFreeHandle(SQL_HANDLE_DBC, ConHandle);

    // Free The Environment Handle
    if (EnvHandle != NULL)
        SQLFreeHandle(SQL_HANDLE_ENV, EnvHandle);
}

// Define The ShowResults() Member Function
SQLRETURN ODBC_Class::ShowResults(void)
{
    // Declare The Local Memory Variables
    SQLRETURN    rc;
    SQLUINTEGER  ArraySize = 4;

    // Define The SUPPLIER_INFO Structure And Allocate An Array
    // Of 4 Structures
    typedef struct {
        SQLUINTEGER SupplierID;
        SQLINTEGER  SupplierID_LI;
        SQLCHAR     CompanyName[41];
        SQLINTEGER  CompanyName_LI;
        SQLCHAR     ContactName[31];
        SQLINTEGER  ContactName_LI;
    } SUPPLIER_INFO;
```

```
SUPPLIER_INFO     SupplierInfoArray[4];

SQLUSMALLINT      RowStatusArray[4];
SQLUINTEGER       NumRowsFetched;

// Store The Size Of The SUPPLIER_INFO Structure In The
// SQL_ATTR_ROW_BIND_TYPE Statement Attribute - This Tells The
// Driver To Use Row-Wise Binding
rc = SQLSetStmtAttr(StmtHandle, SQL_ATTR_ROW_BIND_TYPE,
         (SQLPOINTER) sizeof(SUPPLIER_INFO), 0);

// Declare The Rowset Size (By Setting The
// SQL_ATTR_ROW_ARRAY_SIZE Statement Attribute)
rc = SQLSetStmtAttr(StmtHandle, SQL_ATTR_ROW_ARRAY_SIZE,
         (SQLPOINTER) ArraySize, 0);

// Store The Address Of A Row Status Array In The
// SQL_ATTR_ROW_STATUS_PTR Statement Attribute
rc = SQLSetStmtAttr(StmtHandle, SQL_ATTR_ROW_STATUS_PTR,
         RowStatusArray, 0);

// Store The Address Of A Rows Fetched Buffer In The
// SQL_ATTR_ROWS_FETCHED_PTR Statement Attribute
rc = SQLSetStmtAttr(StmtHandle, SQL_ATTR_ROWS_FETCHED_PTR,
         &NumRowsFetched, 0);

// Bind The Columns In The Result Data Set Returned To
// The Elements Of The SUPPLIER_INFO Structure
rc = SQLBindCol(StmtHandle, 1, SQL_C_SLONG,
         &SupplierInfoArray[0].SupplierID, 0,
         &SupplierInfoArray[0].SupplierID_LI);

rc = SQLBindCol(StmtHandle, 2, SQL_C_CHAR,
         SupplierInfoArray[0].CompanyName,
         sizeof(SupplierInfoArray[0].CompanyName),
         &SupplierInfoArray[0].CompanyName_LI);

rc = SQLBindCol(StmtHandle, 3, SQL_C_CHAR,
         SupplierInfoArray[0].ContactName,
         sizeof(SupplierInfoArray[0].ContactName),
         &SupplierInfoArray[0].ContactName_LI);

// Display A Header
cout << "Suppliers :" << endl << endl;

// As Long As There Is Data, Retrieve Records From The Result
// Data Set And Display Them
while (rc != SQL_NO_DATA_FOUND)
{
    // Fetch Up To The Rowset Size Number Of Rows
    rc = SQLFetchScroll(StmtHandle, SQL_FETCH_NEXT, 0);

    // Check The Row Status Array And Print Only Those Rows
```

```
            // That Were Successfully Fetched
            for (unsigned int i = 0; i < NumRowsFetched; i++)
            {
                if (RowStatusArray[i] == SQL_ROW_SUCCESS ||
                    RowStatusArray[i] == SQL_ROW_SUCCESS_WITH_INFO)
                {
                    // Print The Supplier ID
                    cout.setf(ios::left);
                    cout.width(6);
                    if (SupplierInfoArray[i].SupplierID_LI ==
                            SQL_NULL_DATA)
                        cout << "<NULL>";
                    else
                        cout << SupplierInfoArray[i].SupplierID;

                    // Print The Company Name
                    cout.setf(ios::left);
                    cout.width(40);
                    if (SupplierInfoArray[i].CompanyName_LI ==
                            SQL_NULL_DATA)
                        cout << "<NULL>";
                    else
                        cout << SupplierInfoArray[i].CompanyName;

                    // Print The Contact Name
                    cout.setf(ios::left);
                    cout.width(30);
                    if (SupplierInfoArray[i].ContactName_LI ==
                            SQL_NULL_DATA)
                        cout << "<NULL>";
                    else
                        cout << SupplierInfoArray[i].ContactName;

                    cout << endl;
                }
            }
        }

    // Close the cursor
    rc = SQLCloseCursor(StmtHandle);

    // Return The ODBC API Return Code To The Calling Function
    return(rc);
}

/*─────────────────────────────────────────────────────────────── */
/* The Main Function                                               */
/*─────────────────────────────────────────────────────────────── */
int main()
{
    // Declare The Local Memory Variables
    SQLRETURN   rc = SQL_SUCCESS;
```

```
SQLCHAR      DBName[10] = "Northwind";
SQLCHAR      SQLStmt[255];

// Create An Instance Of The ODBC_Class Class
ODBC_Class  Example;

// Connect To The Northwind Sample Database
if (Example.ConHandle != NULL)
{
    rc = SQLConnect(Example.ConHandle, DBName, SQL_NTS,
            (SQLCHAR *) "", SQL_NTS, (SQLCHAR *) "", SQL_NTS);

    // Allocate An SQL Statement Handle
    rc = SQLAllocHandle(SQL_HANDLE_STMT, Example.ConHandle,
            &Example.StmtHandle);
    if (rc == SQL_SUCCESS)
    {
        // Define A SELECT SQL Statement
        strcpy((char *) SQLStmt, "SELECT Suppliers.SupplierID,");
        strcat((char *) SQLStmt, " Suppliers.CompanyName, ");
        strcat((char *) SQLStmt, "Suppliers.ContactName ");
        strcat((char *) SQLStmt, " FROM Suppliers");

        // Prepare And Execute The SQL Statement
        rc = SQLExecDirect(Example.StmtHandle, SQLStmt, SQL_NTS);

        // Display The Results Of The SQL Query
        if (rc == SQL_SUCCESS)
            Example.ShowResults();

        // Free The SQL Statement Handle
        if (Example.StmtHandle != NULL)
            SQLFreeHandle(SQL_HANDLE_STMT, Example.StmtHandle);
    }

    // Disconnect From The Northwind Sample Database
    rc = SQLDisconnect(Example.ConHandle);
}

// Return To The Operating System
return(rc);
}
```

SQLSetScrollOptions

COMPATABILITY					
X/OPEN 95 CLI	ISO/IEC 92 CLI	ODBC 1.0	ODBC 2.0	ODBC 3.0	ODBC 3.5
☐	☐	✓	☐	☐	☐

API CONFORMANCE LEVEL **LEVEL 2**

Purpose The SQLSetScrollOptions() function is used to set options that control the behavior of cursors.

Syntax
```
RETCODE   SQLSetScrollOptions   (HSTMT    StatementHandle,
                                 UWORD    Concurrency,
                                 SDWORD   Keyset,
                                 UWORD    RowsetSize);
```

Parameters

StatementHandle   An SQL statement handle that refers to a previously allocated SQL statement information storage buffer (data structure).

Concurrency   Specifies the level of concurrency control that the cursor is to use. This parameter must be set to one of the following values:

▪ **SQL_CONCUR_READ_ONLY**
The cursor is to use Read-Only concurrency control (that is, it is to be a read-only cursor—no updates or deletes are allowed).

▪ **SQL_CONCUR_LOCK**
The cursor is to use the lowest level of locking to ensure that it can update or delete a row of data.

▪ **SQL_CONCUR_ROWVER**
The cursor is to use Optimistic concurrency control–comparing row versions.

▪ **SQL_CONCUR_VALUES**
The cursor is to use Optimistic concurrency control–comparing values.

KeySet   Specifies the number of rows for which to buffer keys. This parameter must be greater than or equal to the value specified in the *RowsetSize* parameter, or it must be set to one of the following values:

▨ **SQL_SCROLL_FORWARD_ONLY**
The cursor only scrolls in the forward direction.

▨ **SQL_SCROLL_STATIC**
The data in the result data set remains static (that is, the cursor does not scroll in any direction).

▨ **SQL_SCROLL_KEYSET_DRIVEN**
The driver saves and uses the keys for every row in the result data set—the cursor uses the keys to scroll in any direction.

▨ **SQL_SCROLL_DYNAMIC**
The driver is to set the value in the *KeySet* parameter to the value of the *RowsetSize* parameter.

RowsetSize   Specifies the number of rows to be fetched (retrieved from a result data set) each time the **SQLExtendedFetch()** function is called.

Description   The **SQLSetScrollOptions()** function is used to set options that control the behavior of cursors. Cursor behavior is controlled in three different areas: concurrency control, sensitivity to changes made by other transactions, and rowset size.

NOTE: *In ODBC 2.0, this function has been replaced by the* **SQLSetStmtOption()** *function. In ODBC 3.x, this function has been replaced by the* **SQLSetStmtAttr()** *function.*

Return Codes   **SQL_SUCCESS, SQL_SUCCESS_WITH_INFO, SQL_INVALID_HANDLE**, or **SQL_ERROR**

SQLSTATEs   If this function returns **SQL_SUCCESS_WITH_INFO** or **SQL_ERROR**, one of the following SQLSTATE values may be obtained by calling the **SQLError()** function:

01000, **IM**001*, **S1**000, **S1**001, **S1**010*, **S1**107*, **S1**108*, or **S1**C00

*Returned by the ODBC Driver Manager.

Unless noted otherwise, each of these SQLSTATE values are returned by the data source driver. Refer to Appendix B for detailed information about each SQLSTATE value that can be returned by the ODBC Driver Manager or by a data source driver.

Comments

■ When the ODBC Driver Manager maps **SQLSetScrollOptions()** calls for an application working with an ODBC 3.x driver that does not support **SQLSetScrollOptions()**, the Driver Manager sets the **SQL_ROWSET_SIZE** statement option, not the **SQL_ATTR_ROW_ARRAY_SIZE** statement attribute, to the value specified in the *RowsetSize* parameter. As a result, this function can only be used when fetching multiple rows with the **SQLExtendedFetch()** function.

■ ODBC 3.x and ODBC 2.0 applications should only call this function in ODBC 1.0 drivers.

■ When binding application buffers to columns in a result data set, an application must specify buffers that are large enough to hold the number of rows specified in the *RowsetSize* parameter.

■ If the application does not call this function, the default *RowsetSize* value is **1**, the default *KeySet* value is **SQL_SCROLL_FORWARD_ONLY**, and the default *Concurrency* value is **SQL_CONCUR_READ_ONLY**.

Prerequisites   There are no prerequisites for using this function call.

Restrictions   An application must call this function before it calls **SQLPrepare()** or **SQLExecDirect()** (using the same SQL statement handle) or before creating a result data set with a catalog function.

See Also   **SQLFetchScroll()**, **SQLExtendedFetch()**

Example   The following Visual C++ program illustrates how to use the **SQLSetScrollOptions()** function to specify the type of cursor to use when retrieving data from a result data set.

```
/*——————————————————————————————————————————————————————*/
/* NAME:     CH11EX2.CPP                                      */
/* PURPOSE: Illustrate How To Use The Following ODBC API Function  */
/*          In A C++ Program:                                 */
/*                                                            */
/*               SQLSetScrollOptions()                        */
/*                                                            */
/* OTHER ODBC APIs SHOWN:                                     */
/*          SQLAllocEnv()              SQLAllocConnect()       */
/*          SQLAllocStmt()             SQLConnect()            */
```

```
/*            SQLExecDirect()        SQLBindCol()                    */
/*            SQLExtendedFetch()     SQLFreeStmt()                   */
/*            SQLDisconnect()        SQLFreeEnv()                    */
/*            SQLFreeConnect()                                       */
/*                                                                  */
/*————————————————————————————————————————————————————————————————*/

// Include The Appropriate Header Files
#include <windows.h>
#include <sql.h>
#include <sqlext.h>
#include <iostream.h>

// Define The ODBC_Class Class
class ODBC_Class
{
    // Attributes
    public:
        HENV     EnvHandle;
        HDBC     ConHandle;
        HSTMT    StmtHandle;
        RETCODE  rc;

    // Operations
    public:
        ODBC_Class();                          // Constructor
        ~ODBC_Class();                         // Destructor
        RETCODE ShowResults();
};

// Define The Class Constructor
ODBC_Class::ODBC_Class()
{
    // Initialize The Return Code Variable
    rc = SQL_SUCCESS;

    // Allocate An Environment Handle
    rc = SQLAllocEnv(&EnvHandle);

    // Allocate A Connection Handle
    if (rc == SQL_SUCCESS)
        rc = SQLAllocConnect(EnvHandle, &ConHandle);
}

// Define The Class Destructor
ODBC_Class::~ODBC_Class()
{
    // Free The Connection Handle
    if (ConHandle != NULL)
        SQLFreeConnect(ConHandle);
```

```cpp
    // Free The Environment Handle
    if (EnvHandle != NULL)
        SQLFreeEnv(EnvHandle);
}

// Define The ShowResults() Member Function
SQLRETURN ODBC_Class::ShowResults(void)
{
    // Declare The Local Memory Variables
    SQLRETURN    rc;
    SQLUINTEGER  ArraySize = 4;
    SQLUINTEGER  SupplierIDArray[4];
    SQLINTEGER   SupplierIDLI_Array[4];
    SQLCHAR      CompanyNameArray[4][41];
    SQLINTEGER   CompanyNameLI_Array[4];
    SQLCHAR      ContactNameArray[4][31];
    SQLINTEGER   ContactNameLI_Array[4];

    SQLUSMALLINT RowStatusArray[4];
    SQLUINTEGER  NumRowsFetched;

    // Bind The Columns In The Result Data Set Returned To
    // Application Arrays
    rc = SQLBindCol(StmtHandle, 1, SQL_C_SLONG, SupplierIDArray, 0,
            SupplierIDLI_Array);

    rc = SQLBindCol(StmtHandle, 2, SQL_C_CHAR, CompanyNameArray,
            sizeof(CompanyNameArray[0]), CompanyNameLI_Array);

    rc = SQLBindCol(StmtHandle, 3, SQL_C_CHAR, ContactNameArray,
            sizeof(ContactNameArray[0]), ContactNameLI_Array);

    // Display A Header
    cout << "Suppliers :" << endl << endl;

    // As Long As There Is Data, Retrieve Records From The Result
    // Data Set And Display Them
    while (rc != SQL_NO_DATA_FOUND)
    {
        // Fetch Up To The Rowset Size Number Of Rows
        rc = SQLExtendedFetch(StmtHandle, SQL_FETCH_NEXT, 0,
                &NumRowsFetched, RowStatusArray);

        // Check The Row Status Array And Print Only Those Rows
        // That Were Successfully Fetched
        for (unsigned int i = 0; i < NumRowsFetched; i++)
        {
            if (RowStatusArray[i] == SQL_ROW_SUCCESS ||
                RowStatusArray[i] == SQL_ROW_SUCCESS_WITH_INFO)
            {
                // Print The Supplier ID
                cout.setf(ios::left);
                cout.width(6);
```

```
                    if (SupplierIDLI_Array[i] == SQL_NULL_DATA)
                        cout << "<NULL>";
                    else
                        cout << SupplierIDArray[i];

                    // Print The Company Name
                    cout.setf(ios::left);
                    cout.width(40);
                    if (CompanyNameLI_Array[i] == SQL_NULL_DATA)
                        cout << "<NULL>";
                    else
                        cout << CompanyNameArray[i];

                    // Print The Contact Name
                    cout.setf(ios::left);
                    cout.width(30);
                    if (ContactNameLI_Array[i] == SQL_NULL_DATA)
                        cout << "<NULL>";
                    else
                        cout << ContactNameArray[i];

                    cout << endl;
                }
            }
    }

    // Return The ODBC API Return Code To The Calling Function
    return(rc);
}

/*——————————————————————————————————————————————————————*/
/* The Main Function                                     */
/*——————————————————————————————————————————————————————*/
int main()
{
    // Declare The Local Memory Variables
    SQLRETURN    rc = SQL_SUCCESS;
    SQLCHAR      DBName[10] = "Northwind";
    SQLCHAR      SQLStmt[255];
    SQLUINTEGER  ArraySize = 4;

    // Create An Instance Of The ODBC_Class Class
    ODBC_Class  Example;

    // Connect To The Northwind Sample Database
    if (Example.ConHandle != NULL)
    {
        rc = SQLConnect(Example.ConHandle, DBName, SQL_NTS,
                (SQLCHAR *) "", SQL_NTS, (SQLCHAR *) "", SQL_NTS);

        // Allocate An SQL Statement Handle
        rc = SQLAllocStmt(Example.ConHandle, &Example.StmtHandle);
        if (rc == SQL_SUCCESS)
```

```
{
    // Define A SELECT SQL Statement
    strcpy((char *) SQLStmt, "SELECT Suppliers.SupplierID, ");
    strcat((char *) SQLStmt, "Suppliers.CompanyName, ");
    strcat((char *) SQLStmt, "Suppliers.ContactName ");
    strcat((char *) SQLStmt, "FROM Suppliers");

    // Tell The Driver To Use A Read-Only, Forward-Only Cursor
    rc = SQLSetScrollOptions(Example.StmtHandle,
            SQL_CONCUR_READ_ONLY, SQL_SCROLL_FORWARD_ONLY,
            (UWORD) ArraySize);

    // Prepare And Execute The SQL Statement
    rc = SQLExecDirect(Example.StmtHandle, SQLStmt, SQL_NTS);

    // Display The Results Of The SQL Query
    if (rc == SQL_SUCCESS)
        Example.ShowResults();

    // Free The SQL Statement Handle
    if (Example.StmtHandle != NULL)
        SQLFreeStmt(Example.StmtHandle, SQL_DROP);
}

// Disconnect From The Northwind Sample Database
rc = SQLDisconnect(Example.ConHandle);
}

// Return To The Operating System
return(rc);
}
```

SQLExtendedFetch

COMPATABILITY

X/OPEN 95 CLI	ISO/IEC 92 CLI	ODBC 1.0	ODBC 2.0	ODBC 3.0	ODBC 3.5
☐	☐	✓	✓	☐	☐

API CONFORMANCE LEVEL   **LEVEL 2**

Purpose   The **SQLExtendedFetch()** function is used to retrieve a block containing multiple rows of data (a rowset) from a result data set.

Syntax

```
RETCODE   SQLExtendedFetch    (HSTMT        StatementHandle,
                               UWORD         FetchOrientation,
                               SDWORD        RowNumber,
                               UDWORD FAR   *NumRows,
                               UWORD FAR    *RowStatus);
```

Parameters

StatementHandle

An SQL statement handle that refers to a previously allocated SQL statement information storage buffer (data structure).

FetchOrientation

Specifies the direction and type of fetch the driver is to perform. This parameter must be set to one of the following values:

▪ **SQL_FETCH_FIRST**
Return the first rowset in the result data set.

▪ **SQL_FETCH_NEXT**
Return the next rowset in the result data set. If the cursor is positioned before the start of the result data set, this is equivalent to **SQL_FETCH_FIRST**.

▪ **SQL_FETCH_PRIOR**
Return the prior rowset in the result data set. If the cursor is positioned after the end of the result data set, this is equivalent to **SQL_FETCH_LAST**.

▪ **SQL_FETCH_LAST**
Return the last complete rowset in the result data set.

▪ **SQL_FETCH_ABSOLUTE**
Return the rowset starting at the row number specified in the *RowNumber* parameter. If the *RowNumber* parameter is set to **0**, **SQL_NO_DATA_FOUND** is returned and the cursor is positioned before the start of the result data set.

▪ **SQL_FETCH_RELATIVE**
Return the rowset *RowNumber* rows from the start of the current rowset. If the *RowNumber* parameter is set to **0**, the driver simply refreshes the current rowset. If the cursor is positioned before the start of the

result data set and the *RowNumber*
parameter contains a value greater than **0,**
or if the cursor is positioned after the end of
the result data set and the *RowNumber*
parameter contains a value less than **0,** this
is equivalent to **SQL_FETCH_ABSOLUTE.**

- **SQL_FETCH_BOOKMARK**
Returns the rowset *RowNumber* rows from
the bookmark specified by the **SQL_ATTR_
FETCH_BOOKMARK_PTR** SQL statement
attribute.

- **SQL_FETCH_RESUME**
Continue returning the current rowset in
the result data set. (ODBC 1.0 only)

RowNumber   Specifies the ordinal position of the first row
in the rowset to retrieve (fetch).

NumRows   A pointer to a location in memory where this
function is to store the number of rows
actually fetched (retrieved). If an error occurs
during processing, *NumRows* points to the
ordinal position of the row (in the result data
set) preceding the row in which the error
occurred.

RowStatus   A pointer to a location in memory where this
function is to store an array of status values
that correspond to each row and that reflect
changes in status since the row was last
retrieved from the data source. Upon successful
execution of this function, each element of this
array contains one of the following values:

- **SQL_ROW_SUCCESS**
Indicates that the row was retrieved
successfully.

- **SQL_ROW_UPDATED**
Indicates that the row was updated.

- **SQL_ROW_DELETED**
Indicates that the row was deleted.

- **SQL_ROW_ADDED**
Indicates that the row was added.

- **SQL_ROW_ERROR**
Indicates that the row was unretrievable.

Description   SQLExtendedFetch() extends the functionality of SQLFetch() by retrieving multiple rows of data (a rowset) for each bound column in a result data set. SQLExtendedFetch() returns rowset data (one or more rows) in the form of an array. The size of the rowset (number of rows) returned is specified by the value of SQL_ROWSET_SIZE statement option.

When the SQLExtendedFetch() function is called, the appropriate data transfer is performed along with any data conversion specified when the columns were bound. Refer to "Block Cursors" in this chapter for more information.

NOTE: *In ODBC 3.x, this function has been replaced by the* SQLFetchScroll() *function.*

Return Codes   SQL_SUCCESS, SQL_SUCCESS_WITH_INFO, SQL_INVALID_HANDLE, SQL_STILL_EXECUTING, SQL_NO_DATA_FOUND, or SQL_ERROR

SQLSTATEs   If this function returns SQL_SUCCESS_WITH_INFO or SQL_ERROR, one of the following SQLSTATE values may be obtained by calling the SQLError() function:

01000, **01**004, **01**S01, **07**006, **08**S01, **22**003, **22**012, **24**000, **40**001, **IM**001*, **S1**000, **S1**001, **S1**002, **S1**008, **S1**010*, **S1**106*, **S1**107, **S1**111, **S1**C00, or **S1**T00,

*Returned by the ODBC Driver Manager.

Unless noted otherwise, each of these SQLSTATE values are returned by the data source driver. Refer to Appendix B for detailed information about each SQLSTATE value that can be returned by the ODBC Driver Manager or by a data source driver.

Comments   ▥ SQLFetch() should be used instead of SQLExtendedFetch() to fetch one row of data at a time in a forward direction.

▥ An application cannot mix SQLExtendedFetch() and SQLFetch() function calls for the same cursor.

▥ Before this function is called for the first time, the cursor is positioned before the start of the result data set. An application can call the SQLSetPos() function to position the cursor to a different location in the result data set.

▥ In ODBC 1.0, SQL_FETCH_RESUME could be specified in the *FetchOrientation* parameter. In later versions of ODBC, SQL_FETCH_RESUME is not supported. If the *FetchOrientation* parameter is set to SQL_FETCH_RESUME, and if the driver being used is an ODBC 2.0 or later driver, the ODBC Driver Manager returns **SQL_ERROR** and SQLSTATE **S1**C00 (Driver not capable) to the calling application.

▢ The **SQL_FETCH_BOOKMARK** fetch type was introduced in ODBC 2.0; if an application attempts to use this fetch type with an ODBC 1.0 driver, the ODBC Driver Manager returns **SQL_ERROR** and SQLSTATE **S1**106 (Fetch type out of range).

▢ If the **SQL_CURSOR_TYPE** statement option (attribute) is set to **SQL_CURSOR_FORWARD_ONLY**, **SQL_FETCH_NEXT** must be specified in the *FetchOrientation* parameter.

▢ For static cursors, *RowStatus* information is available for all rows in the rowset. For keyset, mixed, and dynamic cursors, *RowStatus* information is only available for the rows in the keyset; the driver does not save data outside the keyset and therefore has nothing to compare the newly retrieved data to.

NOTE: *Some drivers cannot detect changes to data. An application can determine whether the driver being used can detect changes to refetched rows by calling the* **SQLGetlnfo()** *with the* **SQL_ROW_UPDATES** *information type specified.*

▢ The number of elements returned to the *RowStatus* array must equal the number of rows in the rowset (as defined by the **SQL_ROWSET_SIZE** statement option). If the number of rows fetched is less than the number of elements in the status array, the driver sets remaining elements to **SQL_ROW_NOROW**.

▢ When an application calls **SQLSetPos()** with the **SQL_DELETE** or **SQL_UPDATE** option specified, **SQLSetPos()** changes the *RowStatus* array for the changed row to **SQL_ROW_DELETED** or **SQL_ROW_UPDATED**. For keyset, mixed, and dynamic cursors, if a key value is updated, the original row of data is considered to have been deleted and a new row containing the updated information has been added.

▢ **SQLExtendedFetch**, **SQLFetchScroll()**, and **SQLFetch()** return error information in a similar manner, with the following exceptions:

  ▢ When a warning occurs that applies to a particular row in a rowset, **SQLExtendedFetch()** sets the corresponding entry in the row status array to **SQL_ROW_SUCCESS**, not **SQL_ROW_SUCCESS_WITH_INFO**.

- If errors occur in every row in a rowset, **SQLExtendedFetch()** returns **SQL_SUCCESS_WITH_INFO**, not **SQL_ERROR**.

- In each group of status records that applies to an individual row, the first status record returned by **SQLExtendedFetch()** must contain SQLSTATE **01S01** (Error in row); **SQLFetchScroll()** does not return this SQLSTATE. Note that if **SQLExtendedFetch()** is unable to return additional SQLSTATEs, it must still return this SQLSTATE.

Prerequisites   An application must specify the number of rows to return in a rowset (by setting the **SQL_ROWSET_SIZE** statement option) before this function is called.

Restrictions   There are no restrictions associated with this function call.

See Also   **SQLFetch()**, **SQLFetchScroll()**, **SQLSetPos()**

Example   The following Visual C++ program illustrates how to use the **SQLExtendedFetch()** function to retrieve multiple rows of data from a result data set (in a single function call).

```
/*-----------------------------------------------------------------*/
/* NAME:      CH11EX3.CPP                                           */
/* PURPOSE: Illustrate How To Use The Following ODBC API Function   */
/*          In A C++ Program:                                       */
/*                                                                  */
/*               SQLExtendedFetch()                                 */
/*                                                                  */
/* OTHER ODBC APIs SHOWN:                                           */
/*               SQLAllocEnv()           SQLAllocConnect()          */
/*               SQLAllocStmt()          SQLConnect()               */
/*               SQLExecDirect()         SQLSetStmtOption()         */
/*               SQLBindCol()            SQLDisconnect()            */
/*               SQLFreeStmt()           SQLFreeConnect()           */
/*               SQLFreeEnv()                                       */
/*                                                                  */
/*-----------------------------------------------------------------*/

// Include The Appropriate Header Files
#include <windows.h>
#include <sql.h>
#include <sqlext.h>
#include <iostream.h>

// Define The ODBC_Class Class
class ODBC_Class
{
```

```
    // Attributes
    public:
        HENV       EnvHandle;
        HDBC       ConHandle;
        HSTMT      StmtHandle;
        RETCODE    rc;

    // Operations
    public:
        ODBC_Class();                          // Constructor
        ~ODBC_Class();                         // Destructor
        RETCODE ShowResults();
};

// Define The Class Constructor
ODBC_Class::ODBC_Class()
{
    // Initialize The Return Code Variable
    rc = SQL_SUCCESS;

    // Allocate An Environment Handle
    rc = SQLAllocEnv(&EnvHandle);

    // Allocate A Connection Handle
    if (rc == SQL_SUCCESS)
        rc = SQLAllocConnect(EnvHandle, &ConHandle);
}

// Define The Class Destructor
ODBC_Class::~ODBC_Class()
{
    // Free The Connection Handle
    if (ConHandle != NULL)
        SQLFreeConnect(ConHandle);

    // Free The Environment Handle
    if (EnvHandle != NULL)
        SQLFreeEnv(EnvHandle);
}

// Define The ShowResults() Member Function
SQLRETURN ODBC_Class::ShowResults(void)
{
    // Declare The Local Memory Variables
    SQLRETURN     rc;
    SQLUINTEGER   ArraySize = 4;
    SQLUINTEGER   SupplierIDArray[4];
    SQLINTEGER    SupplierIDLI_Array[4];
    SQLCHAR       CompanyNameArray[4][41];
    SQLINTEGER    CompanyNameLI_Array[4];
    SQLCHAR       ContactNameArray[4][31];
    SQLINTEGER    ContactNameLI_Array[4];
```

```
SQLUSMALLINT RowStatusArray[4];
SQLUINTEGER  NumRowsFetched;

// Set The SQL_BIND_TYPE Statement Option To Tell The
// Driver To Use Column-Wise Binding
rc = SQLSetStmtOption(StmtHandle, SQL_BIND_TYPE,
          SQL_BIND_BY_COLUMN);

// Declare The Rowset Size (By Setting The SQL_ROWSET_SIZE
// Statement Option
rc = SQLSetStmtOption(StmtHandle, SQL_ATTR_ROW_ARRAY_SIZE,
          (UDWORD) ArraySize);

// Bind The Columns In The Result Data Set Returned To
// Application Arrays
rc = SQLBindCol(StmtHandle, 1, SQL_C_SLONG, SupplierIDArray, 0,
          SupplierIDLI_Array);

rc = SQLBindCol(StmtHandle, 2, SQL_C_CHAR, CompanyNameArray,
          sizeof(CompanyNameArray[0]), CompanyNameLI_Array);

rc = SQLBindCol(StmtHandle, 3, SQL_C_CHAR, ContactNameArray,
          sizeof(ContactNameArray[0]), ContactNameLI_Array);

// Display A Header
cout << "Suppliers :" << endl << endl;

// As Long As There Is Data, Retrieve Records From The Result
// Data Set And Display Them
while (rc != SQL_NO_DATA_FOUND)
{
    // Fetch Up To The Rowset Size Number Of Rows
    rc = SQLExtendedFetch(StmtHandle, SQL_FETCH_NEXT, 0,
            &NumRowsFetched, RowStatusArray);

    // Check The Row Status Array And Print Only Those Rows
    // That Were Successfully Fetched
    for (unsigned int i = 0; i < NumRowsFetched; i++)
    {
        if (RowStatusArray[i] == SQL_ROW_SUCCESS ||
            RowStatusArray[i] == SQL_ROW_SUCCESS_WITH_INFO)
        {
            // Print The Supplier ID
            cout.setf(ios::left);
            cout.width(6);
            if (SupplierIDLI_Array[i] == SQL_NULL_DATA)
                cout << "<NULL>";
            else
                cout << SupplierIDArray[i];

            // Print The Company Name
            cout.setf(ios::left);
            cout.width(40);
```

```
                    if (CompanyNameLI_Array[i] == SQL_NULL_DATA)
                        cout << "<NULL>";
                    else
                        cout << CompanyNameArray[i];

                    // Print The Contact Name
                    cout.setf(ios::left);
                    cout.width(30);
                    if (ContactNameLI_Array[i] == SQL_NULL_DATA)
                        cout << "<NULL>";
                    else
                        cout << ContactNameArray[i];

                    cout << endl;
                }
            }
    }

    // Return The ODBC API Return Code To The Calling Function
    return(rc);
}

/*————————————————————————————————————————————————————————————————*/
/* The Main Function                                              */
/*————————————————————————————————————————————————————————————————*/
int main()
{
    // Declare The Local Memory Variables
    SQLRETURN   rc = SQL_SUCCESS;
    SQLCHAR     DBName[10] = "Northwind";
    SQLCHAR     SQLStmt[255];

    // Create An Instance Of The ODBC_Class Class
    ODBC_Class   Example;

    // Connect To The Northwind Sample Database
    if (Example.ConHandle != NULL)
    {
        rc = SQLConnect(Example.ConHandle, DBName, SQL_NTS,
                  (SQLCHAR *) "", SQL_NTS, (SQLCHAR *) "", SQL_NTS);

        // Allocate An SQL Statement Handle
        rc = SQLAllocStmt(Example.ConHandle, &Example.StmtHandle);
        if (rc == SQL_SUCCESS)
        {
            // Define A SELECT SQL Statement
            strcpy((char *) SQLStmt, "SELECT Suppliers.SupplierID,");
            strcat((char *) SQLStmt, " Suppliers.CompanyName, ");
            strcat((char *) SQLStmt, "Suppliers.ContactName ");
            strcat((char *) SQLStmt, " FROM Suppliers");

            // Prepare And Execute The SQL Statement
            rc = SQLExecDirect(Example.StmtHandle, SQLStmt, SQL_NTS);
```

```
        // Display The Results Of The SQL Query
        if (rc == SQL_SUCCESS)
            Example.ShowResults();

        // Free The SQL Statement Handle
        if (Example.StmtHandle != NULL)
            SQLFreeStmt(Example.StmtHandle, SQL_DROP);
    }

    // Disconnect From The Northwind Sample Database
    rc = SQLDisconnect(Example.ConHandle);
}

// Return To The Operating System
return(rc);
}
```

SQLMoreResults

COMPATABILITY

X/OPEN 95 CLI	ISO/IEC 92 CLI	ODBC 1.0	ODBC 2.0	ODBC 3.0	ODBC 3.5
☐	☐	✓	✓	✓	✓

API CONFORMANCE LEVEL   **LEVEL 1***

*IN ODBC 2.0, THIS FUNCTION WAS A LEVEL 2 API CONFORMANCE LEVEL FUNCTION

Purpose   The SQLMoreResults() function is used to determine if more result data sets or row counts are available for an SQL statement handle, and if so, to initialize processing for the next result data set or row count information available.

Syntax   SQLRETURN   SQLMoreResults   (SQLHSTMT   StatementHandle);

Parameters   *StatementHandle*   An SQL statement handle that refers to a previously allocated SQL statement information storage buffer (data structure).

Description   The SQLMoreResults() function is used to access multiple result data sets (or row count information) in a sequential manner upon the successful execution of:

■ An SQL query that was bound to one or more arrays of input parameter values.

■ Batched **SELECT**, **INSERT**, **UPDATE**, and/or **DELETE** SQL statements.

■ A stored procedure containing one or more **SELECT**, **INSERT**, **UPDATE**, and/or **DELETE** SQL statements.

After executing any of these, the application automatically has access to the first result data set or row count value created. Once the first result data set or row count value has been processed, this function can be called to determine whether another result data set or row count value is available. If another result is available, this function initializes it and makes it available for additional processing.

ROW COUNT INFORMATION AVAILABILITY   When a batch of SQL statements contains multiple consecutive row count-generating statements, it is possible that the row count information returned by these statements are rolled up into a single row count value. For example, if a batch contains five **INSERT** statements, certain data sources are capable of returning five individual row count values (one for each **INSERT** statement) while other data sources return only one row count value that represents the sum of the five individual row count values generated.

When a batch contains a combination of result data set-generating and row count-generating SQL statements, row count values may or may not be available, depending on the driver. For example, suppose a batch contains a **SELECT** statement, two **INSERT** statements and another **SELECT** statement. Depending on the driver being used, the following cases are possible:

■ The row count information for the two **INSERT** statements is not available at all. The first **SQLMoreResults()** function call makes the result data set created for the second **SELECT** statement available to the application.

■ The row count information for the two **INSERT** statements is available individually. The first **SQLMoreResults()** function call makes the row count information for the first **INSERT** statement available to the application, the second call makes the row count information for the second **INSERT** statement available to the application, and the third call makes the result data set created for the second **SELECT** statement available to the application.

■ The row count information for the two **INSERT** statements is rolled into one single row count value available to the application. The first **SQLMoreResults()** function call makes the row count information available to the application, and the second call makes the result data set created for the second **SELECT** statement available to the application.

In addition, certain drivers only make row count information available for explicit batches and not for stored procedures.

Return Codes **SQL_SUCCESS**, **SQL_SUCCESS_WITH_INFO**, **SQL_STILL_EXECUTING**, **SQL_NO_DATA**, **SQL_NO_DATA_FOUND** (ODBC 2.0 or earlier drivers), **SQL_INVALID_HANDLE**, or **SQL_ERROR**

SQLSTATEs If this function returns **SQL_SUCCESS_WITH_INFO** or **SQL_ERROR**, one of the following SQLSTATE values may be obtained by calling the **SQLGetDiagRec()** function (ODBC 3.x driver) or the **SQLError()** function (ODBC 2.0 or earlier driver):

ODBC 3.X
01000, 01S02, 08S01, 40001, 40003, **HY**000, **HY**001, **HY**008, **HY**010*, **HY**013, **HYT**01, or **IM**001*

ODBC 2.0 OR EARLIER
01000, **IM**001*, **S1**000, **S1**001, **S1**008, **S1**010*, or **S1T**00

*Returned by the ODBC Driver Manager.

Unless noted otherwise, each of these SQLSTATE values are returned by the data source driver. Refer to Appendix B for detailed information about each SQLSTATE value that can be returned by the ODBC Driver Manager or by a data source driver.

Comments ■ An application can call **SQLBindCol()**, **SQLFetch()**, **SQLFetchScroll()**, **SQLExtendedFetch()**, **SQLGetData()**, **SQLBulkOperations()**, **SQLSetPos()**, and all the metadata functions on the first or any subsequent result data sets created, just as it would if only one result data set existed.

■ If one or more row count-generating SQL statements appear between result data set-generating statements, this function can be used to step over the row count-generating statements.

■ If the current result data set contains unfetched rows when this function is called, the current result data set is discarded and the next result data set or row count value is made available.

■ If all result data sets have been processed when this function is called, **SQL_NO_DATA** (ODBC 3.x drivers) or **SQL_NO_DATA_FOUND** (ODBC 2.0 or earlier drivers) is returned.

■ For some drivers, stored procedure output parameters and return values are not available until all result data sets and row count values have been processed. For such drivers, stored procedure output parameters and return values become available only when this function returns **SQL_NO_DATA** (ODBC 3.x drivers) or **SQL_NO_DATA_FOUND** (ODBC 2.0 or earlier drivers).

■ Column bindings that were established for the previous result data set remain valid after this function is called. If the columns are different in the new result data set, an error or data truncation may occur when **SQLFetch()**, **SQLFetchScroll()**, or **SQLExtendedFetch()** is called. To prevent this, an application must explicitly rebind the columns in the new result data set as appropriate (or set the appropriate descriptor fields). Alternatively, an application can call **SQLFreeStmt()** with the **SQL_UNBIND** option specified to unbind all columns in the result data set.

■ The values of statement attributes such as cursor type, cursor concurrency, keyset size, or maximum length, may change as an application navigates through the result data sets returned by this function. If this happens, **SQL_SUCCESS_WITH_INFO** and SQLSTATE **01**S02 (Option value has changed) are returned.

■ Calling **SQLCloseCursor()** or **SQLFreeStmt()** with the **SQL_CLOSE** option specified, causes all result data sets and row counts available as a result of the execution of a batch of SQL statements to be discarded. The statement handle is returned to either the "Allocated" or "Prepared" state.

■ Calling **SQLCancel()** to cancel an asynchronously executing function when a batch of SQL statements has been executed and when the statement handle is in the "Executed," "Cursor-Positioned," or "Asynchronous" state, causes all result data sets and row counts generated by the batch to be discarded—provided the cancel operation was successful. The statement handle is returned to the "Prepared" or "Allocated" state.

■ If a batch of SQL statements or a stored procedure contains a mixture of **SELECT**, **INSERT**, **UPDATE**, and/or **DELETE** SQL statements along with other SQL statements, the other statements have no affect on this function.

■ If a searched **UPDATE** or **DELETE SQL** statement in a batch of SQL statements does not affect any rows at the data source, this function returns **SQL_SUCCESS**. This is different from when a searched **UPDATE** or **DELETE** statement that does not affect any rows at the data source is executed with **SQLExecute()**,

SQLExecDirect(), or **SQLParamData()**; these functions return **SQL_NO_DATA** (ODBC 3.x drivers) or **SQL_NO_DATA_FOUND** (ODBC 2.0 or earlier drivers).

■ If an application calls **SQLRowCount()** to retrieve row count information after a searched **UPDATE** or **DELETE** statement in a batch of SQL statements does not affect any rows in the data source, **SQL_NO_DATA** (ODBC 3.x drivers) or **SQL_NO_DATA_FOUND** (ODBC 2.0 or earlier drivers) will be returned.

■ If one of the SQL statements in a batch fails, this function returns either **SQL_ERROR** or **SQL_SUCCESS_WITH_INFO**. If the batch was aborted when the statement failed, or if the failed statement was the last statement in the batch, **SQL_ERROR** is returned. If the batch was not aborted when the statement failed, and the failed statement was not the last statement in the batch, **SQL_SUCCESS_WITH_INFO** is returned. **SQL_SUCCESS_WITH_INFO** indicates that at least one result data set or row count value was generated, and that the batch was not aborted.

Prerequisites There are no prerequisites for using this function call.

Restrictions There are no restrictions associated with this function call.

See Also **SQLParamOptions()**

Example The following Visual C++ program illustrates how to use the **SQLMoreResults()** function to move through multiple result data sets that were generated by executing a single SQL statement (using an array of parameter marker values).

```
/*-----------------------------------------------------------*/
/* NAME:     CH11EX4.CPP                                      */
/* PURPOSE: Illustrate How To Use The Following ODBC API Function */
/*          In A C++ Program:                                 */
/*                                                            */
/*             SQLMoreResults()                               */
/*                                                            */
/* OTHER ODBC APIs SHOWN:                                     */
/*          SQLAllocHandle()        SQLSetEnvAttr()           */
/*          SQLDriverConnect()      SQLSetStmtAttr()          */
/*          SQLPrepare()            SQLBindParameter()        */
/*          SQLExecute()            SQLBindCol()              */
/*          SQLFetch()              SQLDisconnect()           */
/*          SQLFreeHandle()                                   */
/*                                                            */
/*-----------------------------------------------------------*/
```

```cpp
// Include The Appropriate Header Files
#include <windows.h>
#include <sql.h>
#include <sqlext.h>
#include <iostream.h>

// Define The ODBC_Class Class
class ODBC_Class
{
    // Attributes
    public:
        SQLHANDLE   EnvHandle;
        SQLHANDLE   ConHandle;
        SQLHANDLE   StmtHandle;
        SQLRETURN   rc;

    // Operations
    public:
        ODBC_Class();                           // Constructor
        ~ODBC_Class();                          // Destructor
        SQLRETURN ShowResults();
};

// Define The Class Constructor
ODBC_Class::ODBC_Class()
{
    // Initialize The Return Code Variable
    rc = SQL_SUCCESS;

    // Allocate An Environment Handle
    rc = SQLAllocHandle(SQL_HANDLE_ENV, SQL_NULL_HANDLE, &EnvHandle);

    // Set The ODBC Application Version To 3.x
    if (rc == SQL_SUCCESS)
        rc = SQLSetEnvAttr(EnvHandle, SQL_ATTR_ODBC_VERSION,
                    (SQLPOINTER) SQL_OV_ODBC3, SQL_IS_UINTEGER);

    // Allocate A Connection Handle
    if (rc == SQL_SUCCESS)
        rc = SQLAllocHandle(SQL_HANDLE_DBC, EnvHandle, &ConHandle);
}


// Define The Class Destructor
ODBC_Class::~ODBC_Class()
{
    // Free The Connection Handle
    if (ConHandle != NULL)
        SQLFreeHandle(SQL_HANDLE_DBC, ConHandle);

    // Free The Environment Handle
    if (EnvHandle != NULL)
        SQLFreeHandle(SQL_HANDLE_ENV, EnvHandle);
}
```

```cpp
// Define The ShowResults() Member Function
SQLRETURN ODBC_Class::ShowResults(void)
{
    // Declare The Local Memory Variables
    SQLRETURN     rc2 = 0;
    SQLCHAR       SQLStmt[255];
    SQLUINTEGER   ArraySize = 3;
    SQLSMALLINT   InStock[3] = {450, 650, 1000};
    SQLCHAR       ShipTo[50];

    // Allocate An SQL Statement Handle
    rc = SQLAllocHandle(SQL_HANDLE_STMT, ConHandle, &StmtHandle);
    if (rc == SQL_SUCCESS)
    {
        // Set The SQL_ATTR_ROW_BIND_TYPE Statement Attribute To Tell
        // The Driver To Use Column-Wise Binding
        rc = SQLSetStmtAttr(StmtHandle, SQL_ATTR_PARAM_BIND_TYPE,
                SQL_PARAM_BIND_BY_COLUMN, 0);

        // Tell The Driver That There Are 3 Values For Each Parameter
        // Parameter (By Setting The SQL_ATTR_PARAMSET_SIZE
        // Statement Attribute)
        rc = SQLSetStmtAttr(StmtHandle, SQL_ATTR_PARAMSET_SIZE,
                (SQLPOINTER) ArraySize, 0);

        // Define A SELECT SQL Statement That Uses A Parameter Marker
        strcpy((char *) SQLStmt, "SELECT SHIPTO FROM ORDERS WHERE ");
        strcat((char *) SQLStmt, "LENGTH = ?");

        // Prepare The SQL Statement
        rc = SQLPrepare(StmtHandle, SQLStmt, SQL_NTS);

        // Bind The Parameter Marker In The SQL Statement To A Local
        // Application Variable
        rc = SQLBindParameter(StmtHandle, 1, SQL_PARAM_INPUT,
                SQL_C_SHORT, SQL_SMALLINT, 0, 0, (SQLPOINTER)
                InStock, 0, NULL);

        // Execute The SQL Statement
        rc = SQLExecute(StmtHandle);

        // Bind The Columns In The Result Data Set Returned To
        // Application Variables
        rc = SQLBindCol(StmtHandle, 1, SQL_C_CHAR, (SQLPOINTER)
                ShipTo, sizeof(ShipTo), NULL);

        // Display A Header
        cout << "Ship To :" << endl << endl;

        // As Long As There Is Data, Retrieve Records From The Result
        // Data Set And Display Them
        for (int i = 1; rc2 != SQL_NO_DATA; i++)
        {
            // Identify The Result Data Set
            cout << "Result Data Set : " << i << endl << endl;
```

```
            while (rc != SQL_NO_DATA)
            {
                rc = SQLFetch(StmtHandle);
                if (rc != SQL_NO_DATA)
                    cout << ShipTo << endl;
            }

            // Move To The Next Result Data Set
            cout << endl;
            rc = 0;
            rc2 = SQLMoreResults(StmtHandle);
        }

        // Free The SQL Statement Handle
        if (StmtHandle != NULL)
            SQLFreeHandle(SQL_HANDLE_STMT, StmtHandle);
    }

    // Return The ODBC API Return Code To The Calling Function
    return(rc);
}

/*-------------------------------------------------------------------*/
/* The Main Function                                                 */
/*-------------------------------------------------------------------*/
int main()
{
    // Declare The Local Memory Variables
    SQLRETURN   rc = SQL_SUCCESS;
    SQLCHAR     ConnectIn[40];

    // Create An Instance Of The ODBC_Class Class
    ODBC_Class  Example;

    // Build A Connection String
    strcpy((char *) ConnectIn,
        "DSN=SQLServer;UID=userid;PWD=password;");

    // Connect To The SQL Server Sample Database
    if (Example.ConHandle != NULL)
    {
        rc = SQLDriverConnect(Example.ConHandle, NULL, ConnectIn,
                SQL_NTS, NULL, 0, NULL, SQL_DRIVER_NOPROMPT);

        // Execute A Select SQL Statement And Show The Results
        Example.ShowResults();

        // Disconnect From The SQL Server Sample Database
        rc = SQLDisconnect(Example.ConHandle);
    }

    // Return To The Operating System
    return(rc);
}
```

12

Modifying Data

Although many ODBC applications perform most of their data manipulation operations by submitting SQL statements to a data source for execution, a couple of ODBC API functions are available to perform insert, update, and delete operations. This chapter begins by describing the three SQL statements commonly used to manipulate data: the **INSERT**, **UPDATE**, and **DELETE** statements. A discussion about positioned **UPDATE** and **DELETE** operations follows. Then, the various ways to perform positioned **UPDATE** and **DELETE** operations with the **SQLSetPos()** function are examined. Next, the various ways to insert, update, and delete data with the **SQLBulkOperations()** function are described. This is followed by a brief discussion about how data modification operations affect scrollable cursors. Finally, a detailed reference section covering each ODBC API function that can be used to perform advanced data retrieval is provided.

INSERT, UPDATE, and DELETE SQL Statements

In both embedded SQL and ODBC applications, data values can be added to, changed, or removed from a data source by executing **INSERT**, **UPDATE**, and **DELETE** SQL statements respectively. Support for each of these statements is defined in the Minimum SQL grammar conformance level and must be provided by all drivers and data sources.

The syntax for the simplest form of each of these statements is:

```
INSERT INTO [table_name] < ([column_identifier], ... ) >
query_specification | VALUES (value [, value]...)
UPDATE [table_name] SET [column] = { [value | expression |
NULL ], ... } <WHERE [where_condition] >
DELETE FROM [table_name] <WHERE [where_condition] >
```

NOTE: *The query-specification element is valid only in the Core and Extended SQL grammars; likewise, the expression and* **WHERE** *condition elements become more complex in the Core and Extended SQL grammars.*

Like other SQL statements, **INSERT**, **UPDATE**, and **DELETE** SQL statements often become more efficient when they use parameter markers in place of literal values. This efficiency can be further increased by specifying multiple values (or arrays of values) for each parameter used.

Positioned UPDATE and DELETE SQL Statements

Embedded SQL and ODBC applications can change or delete the data associated with the current row of a result data set with what is commonly referred to as a positioned **UPDATE** or **DELETE** SQL statement. In order to use a positioned **UPDATE** or **DELETE** SQL statement, an application must first create an updateable result data set by executing a **SELECT** SQL statement that contains a **FOR UPDATE** clause.

The syntax for the simplest form of a **SELECT** SQL statement with a **FOR UPDATE** clause is:

```
SELECT <ALL | DISTINCT > [item_list] FROM [table_list]
<WHERE [where_condition] > FOR UPDATE OF < [column-name],
... >
```

Once an updateable result data set has been created, the application then positions the cursor on the row to be updated or deleted by calling **SQLFetchScroll()** to retrieve a rowset containing the desired row and then calling **SQLSetPos()** to position the rowset cursor on that row. Finally, the application executes a positioned **UPDATE** or **DELETE** statement, using a statement handle that is different from the one used to create the result data set.

The syntax for the simplest form of a positioned **UPDATE** SQL statement is:

```
UPDATE [table_name] SET [column] = { [value | expression |
NULL ], ... } WHERE CURRENT OF cursor_name
```

and the syntax for the simplest form of a positioned **DELETE** SQL statement is:

```
DELETE FROM [table_name] WHERE CURRENT OF cursor_name
```

Notice that both of these statements require a cursor name. When a cursor is implicitly created by ODBC, the data source generates and assigns it a unique name. Either this cursor name or an application-defined cursor name can be used with both of these statements (Refer to Chapter 10 for more information about naming cursors).

Simulated Positioned **UPDATE** and **DELETE** Statements

Positioned **UPDATE** and **DELETE** SQL statements are supported by many, but not all, data sources. If a data source does not support positioned **UPDATE** and **DELETE** statements, the driver often simulates them. The general strategy for simulating positioned **UPDATE** and **DELETE** statements is to convert the positioned statements to corresponding searched statements. This is done by replacing the **WHERE CURRENT OF** clause with a specific **WHERE** clause that identifies the current row in the result data set. For example, suppose the CustID column uniquely identifies each row in the Customers table. The positioned **DELETE** statement:

```
DELETE FROM Customers WHERE CURRENT OF CustCursor
```

might be converted to:

```
DELETE FROM Customers WHERE (CustID = ?)
```

When replacing a **WHERE CURRENT OF** clause with a specific **WHERE** clause, a driver may use any of the following row identifiers:

■ Columns whose values serve to identify uniquely every row in the table (by calling **SQLSpecialColumns()** with **SQL_BEST_ROWID** specified, an application can see the optimal column or set of columns that could be used for this purpose).

■ Pseudo-columns, which are provided by some data sources for the purpose of uniquely identifying every row in a table (these can also be examined by calling **SQLSpecialColumns()**).

■ A unique index, if available.

■ All the columns in the result data set.

Exactly which columns a driver will use in the **WHERE** clause it constructs is driver-dependent. After the driver has replaced the **WHERE** clause, it sends the converted statement on to the data source for execution.

Depending upon the capabilities of the underlying data source, finding a unique row identifier to use can be a costly operation. However, once found, the converted statement used to simulate the positioned **UPDATE** or **DELETE** operation usually executes faster and guarantees that, at the most, only a single row will be updated or deleted.

NOTE: *Using all the columns in the result data set as the row identifier is usually much easier to set up. However, the converted statement will take longer to execute, and if the columns do not uniquely identify a row, additional rows can be unintentionally updated or deleted. This is particularly true when the select list for the result data set does not contain all the columns that exist in the underlying table. An application can remove the risk of unintentionally updating or deleting rows, by ensuring that the columns in a result data set uniquely identify each row in the underlying data source.*

Depending on which methods the driver supports for obtaining a row identifier, an application can choose the method it wants the driver to use by setting the **SQL_ATTR_SIMULATE_CURSOR** statement attribute (ODBC 3.x driver) or the **SQL_SIMULATE_CURSOR** statement option (ODBC 2.0 or earlier driver). No matter how the driver identifies rows, it usually strips the **FOR UPDATE OF** clause off the **SELECT FOR UPDATE** statement before sending it to the data source (because the **FOR UPDATE OF** clause is only used with positioned **UPDATE** and **DELETE** statements, data sources that do not support these statements generally do not support the **FOR UPDATE OF** clause).

Modifying Data with **SQLSetPos()**

In addition to using positioned **UPDATE** and **DELETE** SQL statements, ODBC applications can update or delete any row in a table (via a row in a rowset) by calling the **SQLSetPos()** function—calling **SQLSetPos()** is a convenient alternative to constructing and executing positioned **UPDATE** or **DELETE** SQL statements. **SQLSetPos()** also allows an ODBC driver to support positioned update and delete operations, even when the data source itself does not. Unfortunately, because most interaction with relational databases is done through SQL, this feature of the **SQLSetPos()** function is not widely supported.

Before **SQLSetPos()** can be used to update or delete rows in the current rowset, an application must:

1. Call **SQLExecute()** or **SQLExecDirect()** to execute an SQL statement that produces a result data set OR call a catalog function to create a result data set (refer to Chapter 10 for more information about the ODBC catalog functions).

2. Bind each column in the result data set to application variables (using **SQLBindCol()** or **SQLSetDescRec()**).

3. Call **SQLColAttribute()** (ODBC 3.x driver) or **SQLColAttributes()** (ODBC 2.0 or earlier driver) to make sure that the columns to be deleted or updated are updatable.

4. Call **SQLFetch()** (ODBC 3.x only), **SQLFetchScroll()**, or **SQLExtendedFetch()** to retrieve the data.

Updating Rows with **SQLSetPos()**

The update operation of **SQLSetPos()** updates one or more selected rows in a data source table by using data stored in application variables/buffers that have been bound to each column (unless the value in the corresponding length/indicator buffer is set to **SQL_COLUMN_IGNORE**) in a result data set. Unbound columns are not updated.

To update rows with **SQLSetPos()**, an application:

1. Places new data values in the bound variables (rowset buffers). New data values can be provided for unbound columns by calling **SQLParamData()** and **SQLPutData()**. For information on how to

send long data with **SQLSetPos()**, see the section, "Long Data, **SQLSetPos()** and **SQLBulkOperations()**," later in this chapter.

2. Stores the byte length of the data value or the appropriate indicator value (typically **SQL_NTS** or **SQL_NULL_DATA**) in the length/indicator variable of each bound column, as necessary.

3. Stores the value **SQL_COLUMN_IGNORE** in the length/indicator variable of those columns that are not to be updated. Although the application can skip this step and resend existing data, this is inefficient and risks sending values to the data source that were truncated when they were read.

4. Calls **SQLSetPos()** with the *Operation* parameter set to **SQL_UPDATE** and the *RowNumber* parameter set to the number of the row to update. If the *RowNumber* parameter is set to **0**, all rows in the rowset will be updated.

When **SQLSetPos()** returns control to the calling application, the updated row is the current row in the rowset.

When updating all rows of the rowset (**SQLSetPos()** is called with the *RowNumber* parameter set to **0**), an application can disable updating of specific rows by setting the corresponding elements of the row operation array (pointed to by the **SQL_ATTR_ROW_OPERATION_PTR** statement attribute) to **SQL_ROW_IGNORE**. The row operation array corresponds in size and number of elements to the row status array (pointed to by the **SQL_ATTR_ROW_STATUS_PTR** statement attribute).

All bound application variables/buffers should contain valid data for every row to be updated. If the application variables/buffers were populated by fetching data from a result data set and if a row status array has been maintained, the status values for each of these rows should be something other than **SQL_ROW_DELETED**, **SQL_ROW_ERROR**, or **SQL_ROW_NOROW**.

Deleting Rows Using **SQLSetPos()**

The delete operation of **SQLSetPos()** removes one or more selected rows from a table in a data source. Unbound columns are not deleted.

To delete rows with **SQLSetPos()**, an application calls **SQLSetPos()** with the *Operation* parameter set to **SQL_DELETE** and the *RowNumber* parameter set to the number of the row to delete. If the *RowNumber* parameter is set to **0**, all rows in the rowset are deleted. When **SQLSetPos()** returns control to the calling application, the deleted row is the current row in the rowset, and its row status is set to **SQL_ROW_DELETED**. Once deleted, the row (or rows) can not be used in any other positioned operation.

When deleting all rows of the rowset (**SQLSetPos()** is called with the *RowNumber* parameter set to **0**), an application can avoid deleting specific rows by setting the corresponding elements of the row operation array (pointed to by the **SQL_ATTR_ROW_OPERATION_PTR** statement attribute) to **SQL_ROW_IGNORE**.

Modifying Data Using **SQLBulkOperations()**

In addition to using **INSERT**, **UPDATE**, and **DELETE** SQL statements, ODBC applications can perform bulk insert, update, delete, or fetch operations on a data source table by calling the **SQLBulkOperations()** function—calling **SQLBulkOperations()** is a convenient alternative to constructing and executing **INSERT**, **UPDATE**, **DELETE**, and **SELECT** SQL statements. **SQLBulkOperations()** also allows an ODBC driver to support positioned updates and deletes, even when the data source itself does not. Unfortunately, because most interaction with relational databases is done through SQL, the **SQLBulkOperations()** function is not widely supported.

SQLBulkOperations() operates on the current rowset and can be used only after **SQLFetch()** or **SQLFetchScroll()** is executed. An application specifies the rows to update, delete, or refresh by caching their bookmarks. The driver retrieves the new data for rows to be updated, or the new data to be inserted into the underlying table, from application variables bound to columns in a result data set (rowset buffers). The rowset size to be used by **SQLBulkOperations()** is determined by the value stored in the **SQL_ATTR_ROW_ARRAY_SIZE** statement attribute.

Inserting Rows Using **SQLBulkOperations()**

The insert operation of **SQLBulkOperations()** inserts one or more rows of data into a table in a data source, using data stored in application variables/buffers that have been bound to each column (unless the value in the corresponding length/indicator buffer is set to **SQL_COLUMN_IGNORE**) in a result data set.

To insert rows of data with **SQLBulkOperations()**, an application:

1. Calls **SQLExecute()** or **SQLExecDirect()** to execute an SQL statement that produces a result data set OR calls a catalog function to create a result data set.

2. Sets the **SQL_ATTR_ROW_ARRAY_SIZE** statement attribute to specify the number of rows to be inserted.

3. Binds columns in the result data set to application variables (using **SQLBindCol()** or **SQLSetDescRec()**). If more than one row is to be inserted, and if column-wise binding is used, columns in the result data set must be bound to arrays; if more than one row is to be inserted, and if row-wise binding is used, columns in the result data set must be bound to an array of row structures. In either case, each array must contain one element for each row to be inserted.

4. Places new data values in each element of each bound array. New data values can be provided for unbound columns by calling **SQLParamData()** and **SQLPutData()**. For information on how to send long data with **SQLBulkOperations()**, see the section, "Long Data, **SQLSetPos()** and **SQLBulkOperations()**," later in this chapter.

5. Stores the byte length of the data value or the appropriate indicator value (typically **SQL_NTS** or **SQL_NULL_DATA**) in the length/indicator variable of each bound column, as necessary. So that each column in the new row contains a value, all bound columns with a length/indicator value set to **SQL_COLUMN_IGNORE** and all unbound columns will be set to their default values (if a default value exists) or to NULL (if no default value exists).

6. Calls **SQLBulkOperations()** with the **SQL_ADD** operation specified to perform the insert operation.

When **SQLBulkOperations()** returns control to the calling application, the current row in the rowset is unchanged. If the bookmark column (column 0) is bound to an application variable array, **SQLBulkOperations()** returns the bookmarks of the inserted rows in the array bound to that column.

Updating Rows by Bookmark Using **SQLBulkOperations()**

The update by bookmark operation of **SQLBulkOperations()** updates one or more selected rows of a data source table, using data stored in application variables/buffers that have been bound to each column (unless the value in the corresponding length/indicator buffer is set to **SQL_ COLUMN_IGNORE**) in a result data set. The rows to be updated are identified by the bookmark stored in a bound bookmark column. Unbound columns are not updated.

To update rows, by bookmark, with **SQLBulkOperations()**, an application:

1. Sets the **SQL_ATTR_USE_BOOKMARKS** statement attribute to **SQL_UB_VARIABLE**. This causes the bookmarks of all rows in a result data set to be retrieved and cached when a result data set is generated.

2. Calls **SQLExecute()** or **SQLExecDirect()** to execute an SQL statement that produces a result data set OR calls a catalog function.

3. Sets the **SQL_ATTR_ROW_ARRAY_SIZE** statement attribute to specify the number of rows to be updated.

4. Binds columns in the result data set to application variables (using **SQLBindCol()** or **SQLSetDescRec()**). If more than one row is to be updated, and if column-wise binding is used, columns in the result data set must be bound to arrays; if more than one row is to be updated, and if row-wise binding is used, columns in the result data set must be bound to an array of row structures. In either case, each array must contain one element for each row to be updated.

5. Call **SQLColAttribute()** (ODBC 3.x driver) or **SQLColAttributes()** (ODBC 2.0 or earlier driver) to make sure that the columns to be updated are updatable.

6. Copies the bookmarks for all rows to be updated into the array bound to the result data set's bookmark column (column 0).

7. Places the new data values in each element of each bound array. New data values can be provided for unbound columns by calling **SQLParamData()** and **SQLPutData()**. For information on how to send long data with **SQLBulkOperations()**, see the section, "Long Data, **SQLSetPos()** and **SQLBulkOperations()**," later in this chapter.

8. Stores the byte length of the data value or the appropriate indicator value (typically **SQL_NTS** or **SQL_NULL_DATA**) in the length/indicator variable of each bound column, as necessary.

9. Sets the value in the length/indicator buffer of those columns that are not to be updated to **SQL_COLUMN_IGNORE**. Although an

application can skip this step and resend existing data, this is inefficient and risks sending values to the data source that were truncated when they were retrieved.

10. Calls **SQLBulkOperations()** with the **SQL_UPDATE_BY_BOOKMARK** operation specified to perform the update operation.

When **SQLBulkOperations()** is executed, each element of each bound application array should contain valid data for every row to be updated. If the application arrays were populated by fetching data from a result data set, and if a row status array has been maintained, the status values for each of these rows should be something other than **SQL_ROW_DELETED**, **SQL_ROW_ERROR**, or **SQL_ROW_NOROW**.

Deleting Rows by Bookmark Using **SQLBulkOperations()**

The delete by bookmark operation of **SQLBulkOperations()** removes one or more selected rows from a data source table. The rows to be deleted are identified by the bookmark stored in a bound bookmark column.

To delete rows, by bookmark, with **SQLBulkOperations()**, an application:

1. Sets the **SQL_ATTR_USE_BOOKMARKS** statement attribute to **SQL_UB_ VARIABLE**. This causes the bookmarks of all result data set rows to be retrieved and cached when a result data set is generated.

2. Calls **SQLExecute()** or **SQLExecDirect()** to execute an SQL statement that produces a result data set OR calls a catalog function.

3. Sets the **SQL_ATTR_ROW_ARRAY_SIZE** statement attribute to specify the number of rows to be deleted.

4. Binds to an application variable (using **SQLBindCol()**) the result data set bookmark column (column 0). If more than one row is to be deleted, and if column-wise binding is used, the result data set bookmark column must be bound to an array; if more than one row is to be deleted, and if row-wise binding is used, the result data set bookmark column must be bound to an array of row structures. In either case, each array must contain one element for each row to be deleted.

5. Copies bookmarks for rows to be deleted into the array bound to the result data set bookmark column (column 0).

6. Calls **SQLBulkOperations()** with the **SQL_DELETE_BY_BOOKMARK** operation specified to perform the delete operation.

Fetching Rows by Bookmark Using **SQLBulkOperations()**

The fetch by bookmark operation of **SQLBulkOperations()** refetches one or more selected rows from a data source table and returns them in a rowset. The rows to be fetched are identified by the bookmark stored in a bound bookmark column. Columns with a length/indicator value of **SQL_COLUMN_IGNORE** are not fetched.

To fetch rows, by bookmark, with **SQLBulkOperations()**, an application:

1. Sets the **SQL_ATTR_USE_BOOKMARKS** statement attribute to **SQL_UB_VARIABLE**. This causes the bookmarks of all result data set rows to be retrieved and cached when a result data set is generated.

2. Calls **SQLExecute()** or **SQLExecDirect()** to execute an SQL statement that produces a result data set OR calls a catalog function.

3. Sets the **SQL_ATTR_ROW_ARRAY_SIZE** statement attribute to specify the number of rows to be fetched.

4. Binds columns in the result data set to application variables (using **SQLBindCol()** or **SQLSetDescRec()**). If more than one row is to be fetched, and if column-wise binding is used, columns in the result data set must be bound to arrays; if more than one row is to be fetched, and if row-wise binding is used, columns in the result data set must be bound to an array of row structures. In either case, each array must contain one element for each row to be fetched.

5. Copies into the array bound to the result data set bookmark column (column 0) the bookmarks for rows to be fetched (assuming the application has already obtained the bookmarks in a separate operation).

6. Stores the byte length of the data value or the appropriate indicator value (typically **SQL_NTS**, **SQL_NULL_DATA**) in the length/indicator variable of each bound column, as necessary.

7. Sets the value in the length/indicator buffer of those columns not to be fetched to **SQL_COLUMN_IGNORE**.

8. Calls **SQLBulkOperations()** with the **SQL_FETCH_BY_BOOKMARK** operation specified to perform the fetch operation.

There is no need for an application to use a row operation array to prevent the fetch operation from being performed on certain columns; the application selects the rows it wants to fetch by copying into the bound bookmark array only the bookmarks for those rows.

Long Data, **SQLSetPos()** and **SQLBulkOperations()**

Just as long data can be sent for bound parameters in SQL statements, it can be sent when updating rows with **SQLSetPos()** or when inserting/updating rows with **SQLBulkOperations()**. Columns for which long data is to be sent at execution time are known as *data-at-execution* columns.

Because data-at-execution columns are typically not bound, an application must bind a data-at-execution column just before calling **SQLSetPos()** or **SQLBulkOperations()** and unbind it immediately afterwards. Data-at-execution columns must be bound prior to the function call because **SQLSetPos()** and **SQLBulkOperations()** only operate on bound columns; they must be unbound after the function call so **SQLGetData()** can be used to send data to the column.

To send long data to a column at execution time, an application:

1. Stores in each bound variable a meaningful value to be used later to identify the data value to be sent in parts to the column. For example, this value might be the name or handle of a file containing data (the value stored in the bound variable is not used by the driver).

2. Stores **SQL_DATA_AT_EXEC** or the result of the **SQL_LEN_DATA_AT_EXEC(*length*)** macro in each bound length/indicator buffer. The **SQL_LEN_DATA_AT_EXEC(*length*)** macro is used when the data source that is to receive the data needs to know how many bytes of data will be sent so it can preallocate space. Both of these values indicate to the driver that the data for the column will be sent with the **SQLPutData()** function.

3. Calls the **SQLSetPos()** or the **SQLBulkOperations()** function.

When the `SQLSetPos()` or the `SQLBulkOperations()` function is called, the driver:

1. Discovers that a length/indicator buffer contains the value `SQL_DATA_AT_EXEC` or the result of the `SQL_LEN_DATA_AT_EXEC(length)` macro.

2. Returns `SQL_NEED_DATA` to the application that called the `SQLSetPos()` or the `SQLBulkOperations()` function.

When the application receives the `SQL_NEED_DATA` return code, it then:

1. Calls the `SQLParamData()` function to retrieve the address of the application variable that was bound to the data-at-execution column.

2. Calls the `SQLPutData()` function to send the column data to the driver/data source. If the data is to large to fit into a single buffer, as is usually the case with long data, the `SQLPutData()` function is called repeatedly (to send the data in parts) until all the data has been sent to the data source; it is up to the driver and data source to reassemble the data as it is received.

3. Calls the `SQLParamData()` function again to indicate that all data has been sent for the column.

When the `SQLParamData()` function is called to indicate that all data has been sent for the column, the driver:

1. Returns `SQL_NEED_DATA` and the value identifying the next column to the application that called the `SQLParamData()` function if another data-at-execution column exists. Each time `SQL_NEED_DATA` is returned to the application, the same steps are repeated to send the appropriate column data to the data source.

or

1. Returns `SQL_SUCCESS` or `SQL_SUCCESS_WITH_INFO`, along with any return value or diagnostic information that `SQLSetPos()` or `SQLBulkOperations()` can return to the function that called the `SQLParamData()` function (provided no other data-at-execution column exists).

After the `SQLSetPos()` or `SQLBulkOperations()` function returns `SQL_NEED_DATA`, and before all data has been sent for the last data-at-execution column in the result data set, the statement handle used in the `SQLSetPos()` or `SQLBulkOperations()` function call is in the "Need

Data" state and only the **SQLPutData()**, **SQLParamData()**, **SQLCancel()**, **SQLGetDiagRec()**, **SQLError()**, and **SQLGetDiagField()** functions can be called; all other functions return SQLSTATE **HY**010 (Function sequence error). If the **SQLCancel()** function is called while the statement handle is in the "Need Data" state, all processing is terminated and the statement handle is returned to its previous state.

NOTE: *An application can send any type of data value to the data source at execution time with the* **SQLPutData()** *function. However, if the data is small enough to fit in a single buffer, there is generally no reason to use the* **SQLPutData()** *function—it is much easier to bind an application variable to the column and let the driver retrieve the data from the variable when* **SQLSetPos()** *or* **SQLBulkOperations()** *is executed.*

The Effect of Added, Updated, and Deleted, Rows on Scrollable Cursor Movement

Static and keyset-driven cursors can sometimes detect when rows are added to a result data set and can sometimes remove rows when they are deleted from the result data set. However, whether a cursor provides this functionality is driver-dependant (an application can determine whether a driver provides this functionality by calling the **SQLGetInfo()** function and examining the values of the **SQL_CA2_SENSITIVITY_ADDITIONS**, **SQL_CA2_SENSITIVITY_DELETIONS**, and **SQL_CA2_SENSITIVITY_UPDATES** bitmasks). If the cursors being used can detect deleted rows but cannot remove them, addition and deletion operations have no effect on cursor movements.

On the other hand, if the cursor being used can detect when rows are added to the result data set and/or remove deleted rows from the result data set, it appears as if the cursor detects these changes only when it fetches data. This means that when **SQLFetchScroll()** is used to refetch the same rowset, additions and deletions are seen, but when **SQLSetPos()** is called with the **SQL_REFRESH** option specified they are not. That's because in the latter case, data in the rowset buffers is refreshed but not refetched; therefore, deleted rows are not removed from the result data set. Thus, when a row is inserted into or deleted from the current rowset, the cursor does not modify the rowset buffers. Instead, the cursor only detects the changes when it fetches a rowset that previously included the deleted row(s) or that now includes the inserted row(s).

When **SQLFetchScroll()** returns a rowset with a position relative to the current rowset (that is, the next rowset, the previous rowset, or a relative rowset) it does not include changes to the current rowset when calculating the starting position of the new rowset. However, it does include changes outside the current rowset—if it is capable of detecting them. On the other hand, when **SQLFetchScroll()** returns a rowset with a position that is independent of the current rowset (that is, the first rowset, the last rowset, or an absolute rowset) it includes all changes it is capable of detecting even if they are in the current rowset.

A partial rowset considered to end at the last valid row (that is, the last row for which the row status is not **SQL_ROW_NOROW**) is used to determine whether newly added rows are inside or outside the current rowset. For example, suppose the cursor is capable of detecting newly added rows and that the current rowset is a partial rowset. When the application adds new rows to the rowset, the cursor adds them to the end of the result data set. If the application then calls **SQLFetchScroll()** with the **SQL_FETCH_NEXT** fetch orientation specified, **SQLFetchScroll()** returns the rowset starting with the first newly added row.

Determining the Number of Affected Rows

After an application inserts, updates, or deletes rows, it can call the **SQLRowCount()** function to find out how many rows were actually affected by the insert, update, or delete operation. The **SQLRowCount()** function returns this information regardless of whether the insert, update, or delete operation was performed by executing an **INSERT**, **UPDATE**, or **DELETE** SQL statement, by executing a positioned **UPDATE** or **DELETE** SQL statement, by calling **SQLSetPos()**, or by calling **SQLBulkOperations()**. If a batch of **INSERT**, **UPDATE**, or **DELETE** SQL statements was executed, the number of affected rows might be a total for all SQL statements in the batch, or it might be the number for an individual statement that gets updated after each statement in the batch is executed.

In ODBC 3.x, the number of affected rows is also returned in the **SQL_DIAG_ROW_COUNT** field of the diagnostic header record associated with the statement handle used. However, the value of this field is reset after each function call (on the statement handle), whereas the value returned by **SQLRowCount()** remains the same until **SQLPrepare()**, **SQLExecute()**, **SQLExecDirect()**, **SQLSetPos()**, or **SQLBulkOperations()** is called again.

The Data Modification Functions

Table 12–1 lists the ODBC API functions used to insert, update, and/or delete records from a data source.

Each of these functions are described, in detail, in the remaining portion of this chapter.

Table 12–1 The ODBC Data Modification Functions

Function Name	Description
SQLSetPos()	Positions a cursor within a fetched block of data and allows an application to refresh data in the rowset, or update and delete data in the result data set.
SQLBulkOperations()	Performs bulk insertions and bulk bookmark operations, including **UPDATE**, **DELETE**, and **FETCH** by bookmark operations.
SQLRowCount()	Retrieves and returns the number of rows affected by the execution of an **INSERT**, **UPDATE**, or **DELETE** SQL operation.

SQLSetPos

COMPATABILITY

X/OPEN 95 CLI	ISO/IEC 92 CLI	ODBC 1.0	ODBC 2.0	ODBC 3.0	ODBC 3.5
☐	☐	✓	✓	✓	✓

API CONFORMANCE LEVEL   LEVEL 1*

*IN ODBC 2.0, THIS FUNCTION WAS A LEVEL 2 API CONFORMANCE LEVEL FUNCTION

Purpose   The `SQLSetPos()` function is used to set the cursor position in a rowset, refresh data in a rowset, or to add, update, and/or delete data in an updatable result data set.

Syntax

```
SQLRETURN  SQLSetPos  (SQLHSTMT        StatementHandle,
                       SQLUSMALLINT    RowNumber,
                       SQLUSMALLINT    Operation,
                       SQLUSMALLINT    LockType);
```

Parameters   *StatementHandle*   An SQL statement handle that refers to a previously allocated SQL statement information storage buffer (data structure).

RowNumber   Specifies the ordinal position of the row in the rowset on which to perform the operation specified in the *Operation* parameter. If this parameter is set to **0**, the operation specified is performed on every row in the rowset.

Operation   Specifies the operation to perform. This parameter must be set to one of the following values:

- **SQL_POSITION**
- **SQL_REFRESH**
- **SQL_ADD**
- **SQL_UPDATE**
- **SQL_DELETE**

LockType   Specifies how to lock the row after performing the operation specified in the *Operation* parameter. This parameter must be set to one of the following values:

▧ **SQL_LOCK_NO_CHANGE**
The driver or data source ensures that the row is in the same locked or unlocked state as it was before **SQLSetPos()** was called. This value allows data sources that do not support explicit row-level locking to use whatever locking is required by the data source to support the current concurrency and transaction isolation levels being used.

▧ **SQL_LOCK_EXCLUSIVE**
The driver or data source locks the row exclusively. A statement handle on a different connection or in a different application cannot acquire any locks on the row.

▧ **SQL_LOCK_UNLOCK**
The driver or data source unlocks the row.

Description   The **SQLSetPos()** function is used to set the cursor position in a rowset, to allow an application to refresh data in a rowset, or to add (ODBC 2.0 or earler driver), update, and/or delete data in an updatable result data set. Which operation this function actually performs is dependant on the value specified in the *Operation* parameter. Table 12–2 lists each value that can be specified for the *Operation* parameter, along with a description of the operation performed when **SQLSetPos()** is executed.

Return Codes   **SQL_SUCCESS, SQL_SUCCESS_WITH_INFO, SQL_NEED_DATA, SQL_STILL_EXECUTING, SQL_INVALID_HANDLE,** or **SQL_ERROR**

NOTE: **SQL_SUCCESS_WITH_INFO** *is returned for all SQLSTATEs that can return* **SQL_SUCCESS_WITH_INFO** *or* **SQL_ERROR** *(except **01xxx** SQLSTATEs), if an error occurs on one or more, but not all, rows of a multirow operation.* **SQL_ERROR** *is returned if an error occurs on a single-row operation.*

Table 12-2 `SQLSetPos()` Operations

Operation	Description
`SQL_POSITION`[1]	The driver positions the cursor on the row specified.
	The contents of the row status array pointed to by the `SQL_ATTR_ROW_OPERATION_PTR` statement attribute are ignored for this operation.
`SQL_REFRESH`[2]	The driver positions the cursor on the row specified and refreshes data in the rowset buffers for that row.
	This operation updates the status and content of the rows within the current fetched rowset (this includes any bookmarks used). Because the data in the buffers is refreshed, but not *refetched*, the membership in the rowset is fixed. A successful refresh does not cause added rows to appear in a rowset. This is different from the refresh operation performed by the `SQLFetchScroll()` function (with the `SQL_FETCH_RELATIVE` orientation specified), which refetches the rowset from the result data set so it can show added data and remove deleted data (if those operations are supported by the driver and the cursor being used).
	A successful refresh changes a row status value of `SQL_ROW_ADDED` to `SQL_ROW_SUCCESS` (if the row status array exists). A successful refresh changes a row status value of `SQL_ROW_UPDATED` to the row's new status (if the row status array exists).
	A successful refresh does not change rows with a row status value of `SQL_ROW_DELETED`—deleted rows within the rowset continue to be marked as deleted until the data is refetched. If the cursor supports packing (in which a subsequent `SQLFetch()`, `SQLFetchScroll()`, or `SQLExtendedFetch()` function call does not return deleted rows), deleted rows do not appear when the data is refetched.
	If an error occurs while a row is being refreshed, `SQL_ROW_ERROR` will be stored in the corresponding row status array element (if a row status arry exists).
	If a cursor is opened while the `SQL_ATTR_CONCURRENCY` statement attribute is set to `SQL_CONCUR_ROWVER` or `SQL_CONCUR_VALUES`, a successful refresh might update the optimistic concurrency values used by the data source to detect that the row has changed. If this occurs, the row versions or values used to ensure cursor concurrency are updated whenever the rowset buffers are refreshed from the server. This happens for each row that is refreshed. In this case, the contents of the row status array pointed to by the `SQL_ATTR_ROW_OPERATION_PTR` statement attribute are ignored for the `SQL_REFRESH` operation.
`SQL_ADD` (ODBC 2.0 only)	The driver adds a new row of data to the data source. Where the row is added and whether or not it becomes visible in the result data set is driver-defined. The driver retrieves the data from the variables/buffers bound to the rowset for the specified row and it retrieves the lengths of the data from the length/indicator variables bound to the rowset.
	The driver uses default values (if available) or NULL values (if default values are not available) for columns in the rowset that are not bound to application variables/buffers.
	If the specified row is less than or equal to the rowset size, the driver changes the row status array (if one exists) to `SQL_ROW_ADDED` after adding the row. At this point, the rowset variables/buffers do not match the cursor for the row. To restore the rowset variables/buffers to match the cursor, `SQLSetPos()` must be called again with the `SQL_REFRESH` option specified.

[1]This is the same as the value **FALSE** in ODBC 1.0.
[2]This is the same as the value **TRUE** in ODBC 1.0.

Table 12–2   Continued

Operation	Description
	This operation does not affect the cursor position.
SQL_UPDATE	The driver positions the cursor on the row specified and updates the underlying row of data with the values stored in the variables/buffers bound to the rowset; it retrieves the lengths of the data from the length/indicator variables bound to the rowset. If the length/indicator variable of any column is set to SQL_COLUMN_IGNORE, that column is not updated. After updating the row, the driver changes the corresponding element in the row status array to SQL_ROW_UPDATED or SQL_ROW_SUCCESS_WITH_INFO (if a row status array exists).
	It is driver-defined what the behavior is if this operation is called on a cursor that contains duplicate columns. The driver can return a driver-defined SQLSTATE, update the first column that appears in the result set, or perform other driver-defined behavior.
	The row operation array pointed to by the SQL_ATTR_ROW_OPERATION_PTR statement attribute can be used to indicate that a row in the current rowset should be ignored during a bulk update.
SQL_DELETE	The driver positions the cursor on the row specified, deletes the underlying row of data, and changes the corresponding element of the row status array to SQL_ROW_DELETED. After the row has been deleted, positioned updates and deletes, calls to SQLGetData(), and calls to SQLSetPos() to perform any operation other than the position operation (SQL_POSITION) are not valid for the row.
	For drivers that support packing, the row is deleted from the cursor when new data is retrieved from the data source. Whether or not the row remains visible is dependant upon the cursor type. For example, deleted rows are visible to static and keyset-driven cursors but invisible to dynamic cursors.
	The row operation array pointed to by the SQL_ATTR_ROW_OPERATION_PTR statement attribute can be used to indicate that a row in the current rowset should be ignored during a bulk delete.

(Adapted from table on pages 959–961 of *Microsoft ODBC 3.0 Software Development Kit & Programmer's Reference* and from the table on pages 469–470 of *Microsoft ODBC 2.0 Programmers Reference and SDK Guide*.)

SQLSTATEs   If this function returns **SQL_SUCCESS_WITH_INFO** or **SQL_ERROR**, one of the following SQLSTATE values may be obtained by calling the **SQLGetDiagRec()** function (ODBC 3.x driver) or the **SQLError()** function (ODBC 2.0 or earlier driver):

ODBC 3.X
01000, **01**001, **01**004, **01**S01, **01**S07, **07**006, **07**009, **21**S02, **22**001, **22**003, **22**007, **22**008, **22**015, **22**018, **23**000, **24**000*, **40**001, **40**003, **42**000, **44**000, **HY**000, **HY**001, **HY**008, **HY**010*, **HY**011*, **HY**013, **HY**090, **HY**092*, **HY**107, **HY**109, **HYC**00, **HYT**00, **HYT**01, or **IM**001*

ODBC 2.0 OR EARLIER
01000, **01**004, **01**S01, **01**S03, **01**S04, **21**S02, **22**003, **22**005, **22**008, **23**000, **24**000*, **42**000, **IM**001*, **S0**023, **S1**000, **S1**001, **S1**008, **S1**009*, **S1**010*, **S1**090, **S1**107, **S1**109, **S1**C00, or **S1**T00

*Returned by the ODBC Driver Manager.

Unless noted otherwise, each of these SQLSTATE values are returned by the data source driver. Refer to Appendix B for detailed information about each SQLSTATE value that can be returned by the ODBC Driver Manager or by a data source driver.

Comments

▓ In the C programming language, arrays are -based, while the *RowNumber* parameter is 1-based. This means that when a C/C++ application updates the fifth row of a rowset, it modifies the rowset buffers at array index **4** but specifies **5** in the *RowNumber* parameter.

▓ All operations position the cursor on the row the *RowNumber* parameter specified. For example, if this function is called with the *RowNumber* parameter set to **2** and the *Operation* parameter set to **SQL_DELETE**, the cursor is positioned on the second row of the rowset, and that row is deleted. The following operations require a cursor position:

 ▓ Positioned update and delete statements.

 ▓ Calls to the **SQLGetData()** function.

 ▓ Calls to the **SQLSetPos()** function with the **SQL_DELETE**, **SQL_REFRESH**, and **SQL_UPDATE** options specified.

▓ The *Operation* parameter cannot be set to **SQL_ADD** when working with ODBC 3.x drivers—in ODBC 3.x, this functionality has been replaced by the **SQLBulkOperations()** function (with the **SQL_ADD** operation specified).

▓ The *LockType* parameter is generally used only for file-based sup-port. Usually, data sources that support concurrency levels and transaction processing only support the **SQL_LOCK_NO_CHANGE** locking option.

▓ If the driver is unable to lock a row, either to perform the requested operation or to perform the locking operation specified in the *LockType* parameter, **SQL_ERROR** and SQLSTATE **42**000 (Syntax error or access violation) is returned.

▓ Although the lock type specified in the *LockType* parameter is specified for a single statement handle, the selected lock provids the same privileges to all statement handles on the connection. In partic-ular, a lock acquired by one statement handle on a connection can be unlocked by a different statement handle on the same connection.

■ A row locked by **SQLSetPos()** remains locked until **SQLSetPos()** is called again (for the same row) with the *LockType* parameter set to **SQL_LOCK_UNLOCK,** or until the statement handle used to lock the row is freed. For a driver that supports transactions, a row locked through **SQLSetPos()** is unlocked when the application commits or rolls back a transaction on the connection handle associated with the statement handle used (provided the cursor is closed when a transaction is committed or rolled back, as indicated by the **SQL_CURSOR_COMMIT_BEHAVIOR** and **SQL_CURSOR_ROLLBACK_ BEHAVIOR** information types returned by the **SQLGetInfo()** function).

■ If a driver supports the **SQL_LOCK_EXCLUSIVE** locking option, but not the **SQL_LOCK_UNLOCK** locking option, locked rows remain locked until the statement handle used to lock the row is freed.

■ In ODBC 3.x, **SQLSetPos()** can be called before **SQLFetch()** or **SQLFetchScroll()** is called.

■ The following rules apply for positioned **UPDATE** and positioned **DELETE** operations:

  ■ To guarantee that a row does not change after it is retrieved, **SQLSetPos()** should be called with the *Operation* parameter set to **SQL_REFRESH** and the *LockType* parameter set to **SQL_LOCK_ EXCLUSIVE.**

  ■ If the *LockType* parameter is set to **SQL_LOCK_NO_CHANGE,** the driver only guarantees that an **UPDATE** or **DELETE** operation will succeed if the **SQL_ATTR_CONCURRENCY** statement attribute is set to **SQL_CONCUR_LOCK.**

  ■ If the **SQL_ATTR_CONCURRENCY** statement attribute is set to **SQL_ CONCUR_ROWVER** or **SQL_CONCUR_VALUES,** the driver compares row versions or values and rejects the **UPDATE** or **DELETE** operation if the row has changed since the row was fetched.

  ■ If the **SQL_ATTR_CONCURRENCY** statement attribute is set to **SQL_CONCUR_READ_ONLY,** the driver rejects any **UPDATE** or **DELETE** operation.

Prerequisites   There are no prerequisites for using this function call.

Restrictions   There are no restrictions associated with this function call.

See Also   SQLBindCol(), SQLBulkOperations()

Examples   The following Visual C++ program illustrates how to use the **SQLSetPos()** function to position the cursor on a specific row in a rowset. This example also illustrates how to perform a positioned update.

```
/*------------------------------------------------------------*/
/* NAME:       CH12EX1A.CPP                                   */
/* PURPOSE: Illustrate How To Use The Following ODBC API Function */
/*          In A C++ Program:                                 */
/*                                                            */
/*               SQLSetPos()                                  */
/*                                                            */
/* OTHER ODBC APIs SHOWN:                                     */
/*          SQLAllocHandle()        SQLSetEnvAttr()           */
/*          SQLConnect()            SQLSetConnectAttr()       */
/*          SQLSetStmtAttr()        SQLSetCursorName()        */
/*          SQLExecDirect()         SQLBindCol()              */
/*          SQLFetchScroll()        SQLPrepare()              */
/*          SQLBindParameter()      SQLExecute()              */
/*          SQLCloseCursor()        SQLDisconnect()           */
/*          SQLFreeHandle()                                   */
/*                                                            */
/*------------------------------------------------------------*/

// Include The Appropriate Header Files
#include <windows.h>
#include <sql.h>
#include <sqlext.h>
#include <iostream.h>

// Define The ODBC_Class Class
class ODBC_Class
{
    // Attributes
    public:
        SQLHANDLE    EnvHandle;
        SQLHANDLE    ConHandle;
        SQLHANDLE    StmtHandle1;
        SQLHANDLE    StmtHandle2;
        SQLRETURN    rc;

    // Operations
    public:
        ODBC_Class();                         // Constructor
        ~ODBC_Class();                        // Destructor
        SQLRETURN UpdateRecords();
};

// Define The Class Constructor
ODBC_Class::ODBC_Class()
{
    // Initialize The Return Code Variable
    rc = SQL_SUCCESS;

    // Allocate An Environment Handle
```

```
    rc = SQLAllocHandle(SQL_HANDLE_ENV, SQL_NULL_HANDLE, &EnvHandle);

    // Set The ODBC Application Version To 3.x
    if (rc == SQL_SUCCESS)
        rc = SQLSetEnvAttr(EnvHandle, SQL_ATTR_ODBC_VERSION,
                    (SQLPOINTER) SQL_OV_ODBC3, SQL_IS_UINTEGER);

    // Allocate A Connection Handle
    if (rc == SQL_SUCCESS)
        rc = SQLAllocHandle(SQL_HANDLE_DBC, EnvHandle, &ConHandle);
}

// Define The Class Destructor
ODBC_Class::~ODBC_Class()
{
    // Free The Connection Handle
    if (ConHandle != NULL)
        SQLFreeHandle(SQL_HANDLE_DBC, ConHandle);

    // Free The Environment Handle
    if (EnvHandle != NULL)
        SQLFreeHandle(SQL_HANDLE_ENV, EnvHandle);
}

// Define The UpdateRecords() Member Function
SQLRETURN ODBC_Class::UpdateRecords(void)
{
    // Declare The Local Memory Variables
    SQLRETURN       rc;
    SQLUINTEGER     ArraySize = 12;
    SQLCHAR         ProductNameArray[12][41];
    SQLINTEGER      ProductNameLI_Array[12];
    SQLUINTEGER     UnitsOnOrderArray[12];
    SQLINTEGER      UnitsOnOrderLI_Array[12];

    SQLCHAR         SQLStmt1[255];
    SQLCHAR         SQLStmt2[255];
    SQLUSMALLINT    RowNum;
    SQLSMALLINT     NewUnitsOnOrder;

    SQLUSMALLINT    RowStatusArray[12];
    SQLUINTEGER     NumRowsFetched;

    // Declare The Concurrency Level To Use (By Setting The
    // SQL_ATTR_CONCURRENCY Statement Attribute)
    rc = SQLSetStmtAttr(StmtHandle1, SQL_ATTR_CONCURRENCY,
                (SQLPOINTER) SQL_CONCUR_ROWVER, 0);

    // Set The SQL_ATTR_CURSOR_TYPE Statement Attribute To Specify
    // That A Keyset-Driven Cursor Be Used
    rc = SQLSetStmtAttr(StmtHandle1, SQL_ATTR_CURSOR_TYPE,
                (SQLPOINTER) SQL_CURSOR_KEYSET_DRIVEN, 0);

    // Declare The Rowset Size (By Setting The
    // SQL_ATTR_ROW_ARRAY_SIZE Statement Attribute
```

```
rc = SQLSetStmtAttr(StmtHandle1, SQL_ATTR_ROW_ARRAY_SIZE,
        (SQLPOINTER) ArraySize, 0);

// Set The SQL_ATTR_ROW_STATUS_PTR Statement Attribute To Point
// To A Row Status Array
rc = SQLSetStmtAttr(StmtHandle1, SQL_ATTR_ROW_STATUS_PTR,
        RowStatusArray, 0);

// Set The SQL_ATTR_ROWS_FETCHED_PTR Statement Attribute To Point
// To A Rows Fetched Buffer
rc = SQLSetStmtAttr(StmtHandle1, SQL_ATTR_ROWS_FETCHED_PTR,
        &NumRowsFetched, 0);

// Set The Cursor Name
rc = SQLSetCursorName(StmtHandle1, (SQLCHAR *) "C1", SQL_NTS);

// Define A SELECT SQL Statement
strcpy((char *) SQLStmt1, "SELECT Products.ProductName, ");
strcat((char *) SQLStmt1, "Products.UnitsOnOrder ");
strcat((char *) SQLStmt1, "FROM Products");

// Prepare And Execute The SQL Statement
rc = SQLExecDirect(StmtHandle1, SQLStmt1, SQL_NTS);

// Bind The Columns In The Result Data Set Returned To
// Application Variables
rc = SQLBindCol(StmtHandle1, 1, SQL_C_CHAR, ProductNameArray,
        sizeof(ProductNameArray[0]), ProductNameLI_Array);

rc = SQLBindCol(StmtHandle1, 2, SQL_C_SLONG, UnitsOnOrderArray,
        0, UnitsOnOrderLI_Array);

// Display A Header
cout.setf(ios::left);
cout.width(6);
cout << "Row";
cout.setf(ios::left);
cout.width(40);
cout << "Products";
cout.setf(ios::left);
cout.width(6);
cout << "Units On Hand" << endl << endl;

// As Long As There Is Data, Retrieve Records From The Result
// Data Set And Display Them
while (rc != SQL_NO_DATA)
{
    // Fetch Up To The Rowset Size Number Of Rows
    rc = SQLFetchScroll(StmtHandle1, SQL_FETCH_NEXT, 0);

    // If No Data Was Found, Exit The Loop
    if (rc == SQL_NO_DATA)
        break;

    // Check The Row Status Array And Print Only Those Rows
```

```
// That Were Successfully Fetched
for (unsigned int i = 0; i < NumRowsFetched; i++)
{
    if (RowStatusArray[i] != SQL_ROW_DELETED)
    {
        // Print The Row Number
        cout.setf(ios::left);
        cout.width(6);
        cout << (i + 1);

        // Print The Product Name
        cout.setf(ios::left);
        cout.width(40);
        if (ProductNameLI_Array[i] == SQL_NULL_DATA)
            cout << "<NULL>";
        else
            cout << ProductNameArray[i];

        // Print The Units On Order Value
        cout.setf(ios::left);
        cout.width(6);
        if (UnitsOnOrderLI_Array[i] == SQL_NULL_DATA)
            cout << "<NULL>";
        else
            cout << UnitsOnOrderArray[i];

        cout << endl;
    }
}

// Prompt The User For Update Information
while (TRUE)
{
    // Get The Row Number To Update
    cout << endl << "Row number of row to update ? ";
    cin >> RowNum;

    // If The Row Number Entered Is Valid ...
    if (RowNum > 0 && RowNum <= NumRowsFetched)
    {
        // Get The New "Units On Order" Value
        cout << endl << "New Units On Order Value ? ";
        cin >> NewUnitsOnOrder;

        // Move The Cursor To The Correct Position
        rc = SQLSetPos(StmtHandle1, RowNum, SQL_POSITION,
                SQL_LOCK_NO_CHANGE);

        // Allocate A Second SQL Statement Handle
        rc = SQLAllocHandle(SQL_HANDLE_STMT, ConHandle,
                &StmtHandle2);
        if (rc == SQL_SUCCESS)
        {
            // Define An UPDATE WHERE CURRENT OF SQL
            // Statement
```

```
                        strcpy((char *) SQLStmt2, "UPDATE Products SET ");
                        strcat((char *) SQLStmt2, "UnitsOnOrder = ? ");
                        strcat((char *) SQLStmt2, "WHERE CURRENT OF C1");

                        // Prepare The SQL Statement
                        rc = SQLPrepare(StmtHandle2, SQLStmt2, SQL_NTS);

                        rc = SQLBindParameter(StmtHandle2, 1,
                                SQL_PARAM_INPUT, SQL_C_SHORT,
                                SQL_SMALLINT, 0, 0, (SQLPOINTER)
                                &NewUnitsOnOrder, 0, NULL);

                        // Execute The SQL Statement
                        rc = SQLExecute(StmtHandle2);

                        // Free The Second SQL Statement Handle
                        if (StmtHandle2 != NULL)
                            SQLFreeHandle(SQL_HANDLE_STMT, StmtHandle2);
                    }
                }

                // If Row 0 Was Entered, Exit The Loop
                else if (RowNum == 0)
                    break;
            }
        }

    // Close the cursor
    rc = SQLCloseCursor(StmtHandle1);

    // Return The ODBC API Return Code To The Calling Function
    return(rc);
}

/*—————————————————————————————————————————————————————————*/
/* The Main Function                                        */
/*—————————————————————————————————————————————————————————*/
int main()
{
    // Declare The Local Memory Variables
    SQLRETURN   rc = SQL_SUCCESS;
    SQLCHAR     DBName[10] = "Northwind";

    // Create An Instance Of The ODBC_Class Class
    ODBC_Class  Example;

    // If A Connection Handle Exists
    if (Example.ConHandle != NULL)
    {
        // Tell The Driver To Use The ODBC Cursor Library
        rc = SQLSetConnectAttr(Example.ConHandle,
                SQL_ATTR_ODBC_CURSORS, (SQLPOINTER)
                SQL_CUR_USE_ODBC, 0);
```

```
        // Connect To The Northwind Sample Database
        rc = SQLConnect(Example.ConHandle, DBName, SQL_NTS,
                (SQLCHAR *) "", SQL_NTS, (SQLCHAR *) "", SQL_NTS);

        // Allocate An SQL Statement Handle
        rc = SQLAllocHandle(SQL_HANDLE_STMT, Example.ConHandle,
                &Example.StmtHandle1);
        if (rc == SQL_SUCCESS)
        {
            // Prompt The User To Update Records
            if (rc == SQL_SUCCESS)
                Example.UpdateRecords();

            // Free The SQL Statement Handle
            if (Example.StmtHandle1 != NULL)
                SQLFreeHandle(SQL_HANDLE_STMT, Example.StmtHandle1);
        }

        // Disconnect From The Northwind Sample Database
        rc = SQLDisconnect(Example.ConHandle);
    }

    // Return To The Operating System
    return(rc);
}
```

The following Visual C++ program illustrates how to use the **SQLSetPos()** function to position the cursor on, and update a specific row in a rowset.

```
/*───────────────────────────────────────────────────────────── */
/* NAME:     CH12EX1B.CPP                                         */
/* PURPOSE: Illustrate How To Use SQLSetPos()ODBC API Function To */
/*          Perform A Positioned Update Operation In A C++        */
/*          Program.                                              */
/*                                                                */
/* OTHER ODBC APIs SHOWN:                                         */
/*            SQLAllocHandle()        SQLSetEnvAttr()             */
/*            SQLDriverConnect()      SQLSetStmtAttr()            */
/*            SQLSetCursorName()      SQLExecDirect()             */
/*            SQLBindCol()            SQLFetchScroll()            */
/*            SQLCloseCursor()        SQLDisconnect()             */
/*            SQLFreeHandle()                                     */
/*                                                                */
/*───────────────────────────────────────────────────────────── */

// Include The Appropriate Header Files
#include <windows.h>
#include <sql.h>
#include <sqlext.h>
#include <iostream.h>

// Define The ODBC_Class Class
```

```cpp
class ODBC_Class
{
    // Attributes
    public:
        SQLHANDLE    EnvHandle;
        SQLHANDLE    ConHandle;
        SQLHANDLE    StmtHandle;
        SQLRETURN    rc;

    // Operations
    public:
        ODBC_Class();                            // Constructor
        ~ODBC_Class();                           // Destructor
        SQLRETURN UpdateRecords();
};

// Define The Class Constructor
ODBC_Class::ODBC_Class()
{
    // Initialize The Return Code Variable
    rc = SQL_SUCCESS;

    // Allocate An Environment Handle
    rc = SQLAllocHandle(SQL_HANDLE_ENV, SQL_NULL_HANDLE, &EnvHandle);

    // Set The ODBC Application Version To 3.x
    if (rc == SQL_SUCCESS)
        rc = SQLSetEnvAttr(EnvHandle, SQL_ATTR_ODBC_VERSION,
                    (SQLPOINTER) SQL_OV_ODBC3, SQL_IS_UINTEGER);

    // Allocate A Connection Handle
    if (rc == SQL_SUCCESS)
        rc = SQLAllocHandle(SQL_HANDLE_DBC, EnvHandle, &ConHandle);
}

// Define The Class Destructor
ODBC_Class::~ODBC_Class()
{
    // Free The Connection Handle
    if (ConHandle != NULL)
        SQLFreeHandle(SQL_HANDLE_DBC, ConHandle);

    // Free The Environment Handle
    if (EnvHandle != NULL)
        SQLFreeHandle(SQL_HANDLE_ENV, EnvHandle);
}

// Define The UpdateRecords() Member Function
SQLRETURN ODBC_Class::UpdateRecords(void)
{
    // Declare The Local Memory Variables
    SQLRETURN      rc;
    SQLUINTEGER    ArraySize = 8;
```

```
SQLCHAR             LastNameArray[8][21];
SQLINTEGER          LastNameLI_Array[8];
SQLCHAR             FirstNameArray[8][16];
SQLINTEGER          FirstNameLI_Array[8];

SQLCHAR             SQLStmt[255];
SQLUSMALLINT        RowNum;

SQLUSMALLINT        RowStatusArray[12];
SQLUINTEGER         NumRowsFetched;

// Declare The Concurrency Level To Use (By Setting The
// SQL_ATTR_CONCURRENCY Statement Attribute)
rc = SQLSetStmtAttr(StmtHandle, SQL_ATTR_CONCURRENCY,
          (SQLPOINTER) SQL_CONCUR_ROWVER, 0);

// Set The SQL_ATTR_CURSOR_TYPE Statement Attribute To Specify
// That A Keyset-Driven Cursor Be Used
rc = SQLSetStmtAttr(StmtHandle, SQL_ATTR_CURSOR_TYPE,
          (SQLPOINTER) SQL_CURSOR_KEYSET_DRIVEN, 0);

// Declare The Rowset Size (By Setting The
// SQL_ATTR_ROW_ARRAY_SIZE Statement Attribute
rc = SQLSetStmtAttr(StmtHandle, SQL_ATTR_ROW_ARRAY_SIZE,
          (SQLPOINTER) ArraySize, 0);

// Set The SQL_ATTR_ROW_STATUS_PTR Statement Attribute To Point
// To A Row Status Array
rc = SQLSetStmtAttr(StmtHandle, SQL_ATTR_ROW_STATUS_PTR,
          RowStatusArray, 0);

// Set The SQL_ATTR_ROWS_FETCHED_PTR Statement Attribute To Point
// To A Rows Fetched Buffer
rc = SQLSetStmtAttr(StmtHandle, SQL_ATTR_ROWS_FETCHED_PTR,
          &NumRowsFetched, 0);

// Set The Cursor Name
rc = SQLSetCursorName(StmtHandle, (SQLCHAR *) "C1", SQL_NTS);

// Define A SELECT SQL Statement
strcpy((char *) SQLStmt, "SELECT LASTNAME, FIRSTNAME ");
strcat((char *) SQLStmt, "FROM EMPLOYEES");

// Prepare And Execute The SQL Statement
rc = SQLExecDirect(StmtHandle, SQLStmt, SQL_NTS);

// Bind The Columns In The Result Data Set Returned To
// Application Variables
rc = SQLBindCol(StmtHandle, 1, SQL_C_CHAR, LastNameArray,
          sizeof(LastNameArray[0]), LastNameLI_Array);

rc = SQLBindCol(StmtHandle, 2, SQL_C_CHAR, FirstNameArray,
          sizeof(FirstNameArray[0]), FirstNameLI_Array);
```

```cpp
// Display A Header
cout.setf(ios::left);
cout.width(6);
cout << "Row";
cout.setf(ios::left);
cout.width(25);
cout << "First Name";
cout.setf(ios::left);
cout.width(25);
cout << "Last Name" << endl << endl;

// As Long As There Is Data, Retrieve Records From The Result
// Data Set And Display Them
while (rc != SQL_NO_DATA)
{
    // Fetch Up To The Rowset Size Number Of Rows
    rc = SQLFetchScroll(StmtHandle, SQL_FETCH_NEXT, 0);

    // If No Data Was Found, Exit The Loop
    if (rc == SQL_NO_DATA)
        break;

    // Check The Row Status Array And Print Only Those Rows
    // That Were Successfully Fetched
    for (unsigned int i = 0; i < NumRowsFetched; i++)
    {
        if (RowStatusArray[i] != SQL_ROW_DELETED)
        {
            // Print The Row Number
            cout.setf(ios::left);
            cout.width(6);
            cout << (i + 1);

            // Print The First Name
            cout.setf(ios::left);
            cout.width(25);
            if (FirstNameLI_Array[i] == SQL_NULL_DATA)
                cout << "<NULL>";
            else
                cout << FirstNameArray[i];

            // Print The Last Name
            cout.setf(ios::left);
            cout.width(25);
            if (LastNameLI_Array[i] == SQL_NULL_DATA)
                cout << "<NULL>";
            else
                cout << LastNameArray[i];

            cout << endl;
        }
    }
```

```
      // Prompt The User For Update Information
      while (TRUE)
      {
          // Get The Row Number To Update
          cout << endl << "Row number of row to update ? ";
          cin >> RowNum;

          // If The Row Number Entered Is Valid ...
          if (RowNum > 0 && RowNum <= NumRowsFetched)
          {
              // Get The New "First Name" Value
              cout << endl << "New First Name ? ";
              cin >> FirstNameArray[RowNum - 1];

              // Move The Cursor To The Correct Position And
              // Update The Information In The Row
              rc = SQLSetPos(StmtHandle, RowNum, SQL_UPDATE,
                      SQL_LOCK_NO_CHANGE);
          }

          // If Row 0 Was Entered, Exit The Loop
          else if (RowNum == 0)
              break;
      }
  }

  // Close the cursor
  rc = SQLCloseCursor(StmtHandle);

  // Return The ODBC API Return Code To The Calling Function
  return(rc);
}

/*————————————————————————————————————————————————————————*/
/* The Main Function                                      */
/*————————————————————————————————————————————————————————*/
int main()
{
    // Declare The Local Memory Variables
    SQLRETURN   rc = SQL_SUCCESS;
    SQLCHAR     ConnectIn[40];

    // Create An Instance Of The ODBC_Class Class
    ODBC_Class   Example;

    // Build A Connection String
    strcpy((char *) ConnectIn,
        "DSN=SQLServer;UID=userid;PWD=password;");

    // Connect To The SQL Server Sample Database
    if (Example.ConHandle != NULL)
    {
        rc = SQLDriverConnect(Example.ConHandle, NULL, ConnectIn,
```

```
                SQL_NTS, NULL, 0, NULL, SQL_DRIVER_NOPROMPT);

    // Allocate An SQL Statement Handle
    rc = SQLAllocHandle(SQL_HANDLE_STMT, Example.ConHandle,
              &Example.StmtHandle);
    if (rc == SQL_SUCCESS)
    {
        // Prompt The User To Update Records
        if (rc == SQL_SUCCESS)
            Example.UpdateRecords();

        // Free The SQL Statement Handle
        if (Example.StmtHandle != NULL)
            SQLFreeHandle(SQL_HANDLE_STMT, Example.StmtHandle);
    }

    // Disconnect From The SQL Server Sample Database
    rc = SQLDisconnect(Example.ConHandle);
}

// Return To The Operating System
return(rc);
}
```

SQLBulkOperations

COMPATABILITY					
X/OPEN 95 CLI	ISO/IEC 92 CLI	ODBC 1.0	ODBC 2.0	ODBC 3.0	ODBC 3.5
☐	☐	☐	☐	☑	☑

API CONFORMANCE LEVEL   **LEVEL 1**

Purpose

The SQLBulkOperations() function is used to perform bulk insertions and bulk bookmark operations (including update, delete, and fetch by bookmark operations) on a specified table.

Syntax

```
SQLRETURN SQLBulkOperations (SQLHSTMT      StatementHandle,
                             SQLUSMALLINT  Operation);
```

Parameters   *StatementHandle*   An SQL statement handle that refers to a previously allocated SQL statement information storage buffer (data structure).

| *Operation* | Specifies the type of data manipulation operation to perform. This parameter must be set to one of the following values: |

 SQL_ADD
Add new rows of data.

 SQL_UPDATE_BY_BOOKMARK
Update a set of rows in which each row is identified by a bookmark.

 SQL_DELETE_BY_BOOKMARK
Delete a set of rows in which each row is identified by a bookmark.

 SQL_FETCH_BY_BOOKMARK
Retrieve (fetch) a set of rows in which each row is identified by a bookmark.

Description   The **SQLBulkOperations()** function is used to perform the following operations on the base table or view corresponding to the current query:

 Add (insert) new rows.

 Update a set of rows in which each row is identified by a bookmark.

 Delete a set of rows in which each row is identified by a bookmark.

 Retrieve (fetch) a set of rows in which each row is identified by a bookmark.

Refer to the chapter overview for detailed information on how to perform each of these operations.

Return Codes   SQL_SUCCESS, SQL_SUCCESS_WITH_INFO, SQL_NEED_DATA, SQL_STILL_EXECUTING, SQL_INVALID_HANDLE, or SQL_ERROR

NOTE: **SQL_SUCCESS_WITH_INFO** *is returned for all SQLSTATEs that can return* **SQL_SUCCESS_WITH_INFO** *or* **SQL_ERROR** *(except **01xxx** SQLSTATEs), if an error occurs on one or more, but not all, rows of a multirow operation.* **SQL_ERROR** *is returned if an error occurs on a single-row operation.*

SQLSTATEs   If this function returns **SQL_SUCCESS_WITH_INFO** or **SQL_ERROR**, one of the following SQLSTATE values may be obtained by calling the **SQLGetDiagRec()** function:

01000, **01**004, **01**S01, **01**S07, **07**006, **07**009, **21**S02, **22**001, **22**003, **22**007, **22**008, **22**015, **22**018, **23**000, **24**000, **40**001, **40**003, **42**000, **44**000,

HY000, **HY**001, **HY**008, **HY**010*, **HY**011*, **HY**013, **HY**090, **HY**092*, **HYC**00, **HYT**00, **HYT**01, or **IM**001*

*Returned by the ODBC Driver Manager.

Unless noted otherwise, each of these SQLSTATE values is returned by the data source driver. Refer to Appendix B for detailed information about each SQLSTATE value that can be returned by the ODBC Driver Manager or by a data source driver.

Comments

▓ When an ODBC 3.x application works with an ODBC 2.0 or earlier driver, the ODBC Driver Manager maps an **SQLBulkOperations()** function call with the **SQL_ADD** operation specified to a **SQLSetPos()** function call with the **SQL_ADD** operation specified.

▓ After this function is called, the block cursor position is undefined —an application must call the **SQLFetchScroll()** function to reset the cursor position. In this case, **SQLFetchScroll()** should be called with the *FetchType* parameter set to **SQL_FETCH_FIRST**, **SQL_FETCH_LAST**, **SQL_FETCH_ABSOLUTE**, or **SQL_FETCH_BOOKMARK**. Otherwise, the cursor position is undefined.

▓ If the length/indicator variable/buffer bound to a column is set to **SQL_COLUMN_IGNORE**, that column is ignored in all bulk operations performed.

▓ The **SQL_ATTR_ROW_OPERATION_PTR** statement attribute does not have to be set before this function is called.

▓ After this function is executed, the buffer pointed to by the **SQL_ATTR_ROWS_FETCHED_PTR** statement attribute contains the number of rows in the data source that were affected by the bulk operation performed.

▓ When the *Operation* parameter is set to **SQL_ADD** or **SQL_UPDATE_ BY_BOOKMARK** and the select list of the query specification associated with the cursor contains more than one reference to the same column, the driver either generates an error or it ignores the duplicated references and performs the requested operation (each driver defines how it will handle this type of situation).

▓ If bookmarks persist across cursors, there is no need for the application to call **SQLFetch()** or **SQLFetchScroll()** before performing an update by bookmark operation. If bookmarks do not persist across cursors, then the application must call **SQLFetch()** or **SQLFetchScroll()** to retrieve the bookmark values.

▓ This function can use bookmarks that have been stored by a previous cursor.

Prerequisites   There are no prerequisites for using this function call.

Restrictions   There are no restrictions associated with this function call.

See Also   `SQLBindCol()`, `SQLCancel()`, `SQLFetch()`, `SQLFetchScroll()`, `SQLSetPos()`

Example   The following Visual C++ program illustrates how to use the `SQLBulkOperations()` function to add new rows to a table that are almost duplicates of existing rows.

```
/*—————————————————————————————————————————————————————————*/
/* NAME:      CH12EX2.CPP                                       */
/* PURPOSE: Illustrate How To Use The Following ODBC API Function */
/*          In A C++ Program:                                   */
/*                                                              */
/*              SQLBulkOperations()                             */
/*                                                              */
/* OTHER ODBC APIs SHOWN:                                       */
/*          SQLAllocHandle()         SQLSetEnvAttr()            */
/*          SQLDriverConnect()       SQLSetStmtAttr()           */
/*          SQLSetCursorName()       SQLExecDirect()            */
/*          SQLBindCol()             SQLFetchScroll()           */
/*          SQLCloseCursor()         SQLDisconnect()            */
/*          SQLFreeHandle()                                     */
/*                                                              */
/*—————————————————————————————————————————————————————————*/

// Include The Appropriate Header Files
#include <windows.h>
#include <sql.h>
#include <sqlext.h>
#include <iostream.h>

// Define The ODBC_Class Class
class ODBC_Class
{
    // Attributes
    public:
        SQLHANDLE    EnvHandle;
        SQLHANDLE    ConHandle;
        SQLHANDLE    StmtHandle;
        SQLRETURN    rc;

    // Operations
    public:
        ODBC_Class();                        // Constructor
        ~ODBC_Class();                       // Destructor
        SQLRETURN AddRecords();
};

// Define The Class Constructor
```

```
ODBC_Class::ODBC_Class()
{
    // Initialize The Return Code Variable
    rc = SQL_SUCCESS;

    // Allocate An Environment Handle
    rc = SQLAllocHandle(SQL_HANDLE_ENV, SQL_NULL_HANDLE, &EnvHandle);

    // Set The ODBC Application Version To 3.x
    if (rc == SQL_SUCCESS)
        rc = SQLSetEnvAttr(EnvHandle, SQL_ATTR_ODBC_VERSION,
                (SQLPOINTER) SQL_OV_ODBC3, SQL_IS_UINTEGER);

    // Allocate A Connection Handle
    if (rc == SQL_SUCCESS)
        rc = SQLAllocHandle(SQL_HANDLE_DBC, EnvHandle, &ConHandle);
}

// Define The Class Destructor
ODBC_Class::~ODBC_Class()
{
    // Free The Connection Handle
    if (ConHandle != NULL)
        SQLFreeHandle(SQL_HANDLE_DBC, ConHandle);

    // Free The Environment Handle
    if (EnvHandle != NULL)
        SQLFreeHandle(SQL_HANDLE_ENV, EnvHandle);
}

// Define The AddRecords() Member Function
SQLRETURN ODBC_Class::AddRecords(void)
{
    // Declare The Local Memory Variables
    SQLRETURN       rc;
    SQLUINTEGER     ArraySize = 5;
    SQLCHAR         SQLStmt[255];

    // Define The ORDER_INFO Structure And Allocate An Array
    // Of 3 Structures
    typedef struct {
        SQLUINTEGER     OrderNum;
        SQLINTEGER      OrderNum_LI;
        SQLUINTEGER     StockNum;
        SQLINTEGER      StockNum_LI;
        SQLCHAR         ShipTo[7];
        SQLINTEGER      ShipTo_LI;
        SQLUINTEGER     TakenBy;
        SQLINTEGER      TakenBy_LI;
        SQLCHAR         SpecInstr[20];
        SQLINTEGER      SpecInstr_LI;
    } ORDER_INFO;

    ORDER_INFO OrderInfoArray[5];
```

```
SQLUSMALLINT    RowStatusArray[12];
SQLUINTEGER     NumRowsFetched;

// Declare The Concurrency Level To Use (By Setting The
// SQL_ATTR_CONCURRENCY Statement Attribute)
rc = SQLSetStmtAttr(StmtHandle, SQL_ATTR_CONCURRENCY,
         (SQLPOINTER) SQL_CONCUR_ROWVER, 0);

// Set The SQL_ATTR_CURSOR_TYPE Statement Attribute To Specify
// That A Keyset-Driven Cursor Be Used
rc = SQLSetStmtAttr(StmtHandle, SQL_ATTR_CURSOR_TYPE,
         (SQLPOINTER) SQL_CURSOR_KEYSET_DRIVEN, 0);

// Store The Size Of The ORDER_INFO Structure In The
// SQL_ATTR_ROW_BIND_TYPE Statement Attribute - This Tells The
// Driver To Use Row-Wise Binding.
rc = SQLSetStmtAttr(StmtHandle, SQL_ATTR_ROW_BIND_TYPE,
         (SQLPOINTER) sizeof(ORDER_INFO), 0);

// Declare The Rowset Size (By Setting The
// SQL_ATTR_ROW_ARRAY_SIZE Statement Attribute
rc = SQLSetStmtAttr(StmtHandle, SQL_ATTR_ROW_ARRAY_SIZE,
         (SQLPOINTER) ArraySize, 0);

// Set The SQL_ATTR_ROW_STATUS_PTR Statement Attribute To Point
// To A Row Status Array
rc = SQLSetStmtAttr(StmtHandle, SQL_ATTR_ROW_STATUS_PTR,
         RowStatusArray, 0);

// Set The SQL_ATTR_ROWS_FETCHED_PTR Statement Attribute To Point
// To A Rows Fetched Buffer
rc = SQLSetStmtAttr(StmtHandle, SQL_ATTR_ROWS_FETCHED_PTR,
         &NumRowsFetched, 0);

// Set The Cursor Name
rc = SQLSetCursorName(StmtHandle, (SQLCHAR *) "C1", SQL_NTS);

// Define A SELECT SQL Statement
strcpy((char *) SQLStmt, "SELECT ORDERNUM, STOCKNUM, SHIPTO, ");
strcat((char *) SQLStmt, "TAKENBY, SPECINSTR FROM ORDERS");

// Prepare And Execute The SQL Statement
rc = SQLExecDirect(StmtHandle, SQLStmt, SQL_NTS);

// Bind The Columns In The Result Data Set Returned To
// Elements Of The OrderInfoArray Array
rc = SQLBindCol(StmtHandle, 1, SQL_C_SLONG,
         &OrderInfoArray[0].OrderNum, 0,
         &OrderInfoArray[0].OrderNum_LI);

rc = SQLBindCol(StmtHandle, 2, SQL_C_SLONG,
         &OrderInfoArray[0].StockNum, 0,
         &OrderInfoArray[0].StockNum_LI);
```

```
rc = SQLBindCol(StmtHandle, 3, SQL_C_CHAR,
        OrderInfoArray[0].ShipTo,
        sizeof(OrderInfoArray[0].ShipTo),
        &OrderInfoArray[0].ShipTo_LI);

rc = SQLBindCol(StmtHandle, 4, SQL_C_SLONG,
        &OrderInfoArray[0].TakenBy, 0,
        &OrderInfoArray[0].TakenBy_LI);

rc = SQLBindCol(StmtHandle, 5, SQL_C_CHAR,
        OrderInfoArray[0].SpecInstr,
        sizeof(OrderInfoArray[0].SpecInstr),
        &OrderInfoArray[0].SpecInstr_LI);

// As Long As There Is Data, Retrieve Records From The Result
// Data Set And Display Them
while (rc != SQL_NO_DATA)
{
    // Fetch Up To The Rowset Size Number Of Rows
    rc = SQLFetchScroll(StmtHandle, SQL_FETCH_NEXT, 0);

    // If No Data Was Found, Exit The Loop
    if (rc == SQL_NO_DATA)
        break;

    // Modify The Information Retrieved
    for (unsigned int i = 0; i < NumRowsFetched; i++)
    {
        // Generate A Unique Order Number And Set Of Special
        // Instructions For The First 5 Records Retrieved
        OrderInfoArray[i].OrderNum += 100;
        strcpy((char *) OrderInfoArray[i].SpecInstr, "TEST");
        OrderInfoArray[i].SpecInstr_LI = SQL_NTS;
    }

    // Insert The Modified Records Into The Table
    rc = SQLBulkOperations(StmtHandle, SQL_ADD);

    // If The Records Were Added Successfully, Display A Success
    // Message And Exit
    if (rc == SQL_SUCCESS || rc == SQL_SUCCESS_WITH_INFO)
    {
        cout << NumRowsFetched << " new rows were added to the ";
        cout << "ORDERS table." << endl << endl;
        break;
    }
}

// Close the cursor
rc = SQLCloseCursor(StmtHandle);

// Return The ODBC API Return Code To The Calling Function
return(rc);
```

```
}

/*————————————————————————————————————————————————————*/
/* The Main Function                                                     */
/*————————————————————————————————————————————————————*/
int main()
{
    // Declare The Local Memory Variables
    SQLRETURN   rc = SQL_SUCCESS;
    SQLCHAR     ConnectIn[40];

    // Create An Instance Of The ODBC_Class Class
    ODBC_Class  Example;

    // Build A Connection String
    strcpy((char *) ConnectIn,
        "DSN=SQLServer;UID=userid;PWD=password;");

    // Connect To The SQL Server Sample Database
    if (Example.ConHandle != NULL)
    {
        rc = SQLDriverConnect(Example.ConHandle, NULL, ConnectIn,
                SQL_NTS, NULL, 0, NULL, SQL_DRIVER_NOPROMPT);

        // Allocate An SQL Statement Handle
        rc = SQLAllocHandle(SQL_HANDLE_STMT, Example.ConHandle,
                &Example.StmtHandle);
        if (rc == SQL_SUCCESS)
        {
            // Prompt The User To Update Records
            if (rc == SQL_SUCCESS)
                Example.AddRecords();

            // Free The SQL Statement Handle
            if (Example.StmtHandle != NULL)
                SQLFreeHandle(SQL_HANDLE_STMT, Example.StmtHandle);
        }

        // Disconnect From The SQL Server Sample Database
        rc = SQLDisconnect(Example.ConHandle);
    }

    // Return To The Operating System
    return(rc);
}
```

SQLRowCount

COMPATABILITY					
X/OPEN 95 CLI	ISO/IEC 92 CLI	ODBC 1.0	ODBC 2.0	ODBC 3.0	ODBC 3.5
☒	✓	✓	✓	✓	✓

API CONFORMANCE LEVEL   **CORE**

Purpose

The SQLRowCount() function is used to obtain a count of the number of rows in a table that were affected by an INSERT, UPDATE, or DELETE operation.

Syntax

```
SQLRETURN    SQLRowCount    (SQLHSTMT      StatementHandle,
                             SQLINTEGER    *RowCount);
```

Parameters

StatementHandle   An SQL statement handle that refers to a previously allocated SQL statement information storage buffer (data structure).

RowCount   A pointer to a location in memory where this function is to store a count of the actual number of rows in a table that were affected by an INSERT, UPDATE, or DELETE operation.

Description

The SQLRowCount() function is used to obtain a count of the number of rows in a table that were affected by an INSERT, UPDATE, or DELETE operation. Such an operation can be performed by executing an INSERT, UPDATE, or DELETE SQL statement, by calling the SQLSetPos() function with the SQL_ADD (ODBC 2.0 or earlier drivers only), SQL_UPDATE or SQL_DELETE operation specified, or by calling the SQLBulkOperations() function with the SQL_ADD, SQL_UPDATE_BY_BOOKMARK, or SQL_DELETE_BY_BOOKMARK operation specified.

Rows in other tables that might have been affected by an INSERT, UPDATE, or DELETE operation (for example, if cascaded deletes occurred) are not included in the row count returned by this function.

Each time SQLExecute(), SQLExecDirect(), SQLBulkOperations(), SQLSetPos(), or SQLMoreResults() is called, a count of the actual number of rows affected by an INSERT, UPDATE, or DELETE operation is stored in the **SQL_DIAG_ROW_COUNT** field of the diagnostic header record associated with the statement handle specified; this value is cached (stored) in memory in an implementation-dependent way. **SQLRowCount()** returns the cached row count value—not the value stored in the **SQL_DIAG_ROW_COUNT** diagnostic header record field. Cached row count values remain valid until the statement handle is returned to the "Prepared" or "Allocated" state, the SQL statement is re-executed, or the **SQLCloseCursor()** function is called.

NOTE: *If another ODBC API function is called after the* **SQL_DIAG_ROW_COUNT** *diagnostic header record field is set, the value returned by* **SQLRowCount()** *might be different from the actual value stored in the* **SQL_DIAG_ROW_COUNT** *field. That's because the* **SQL_DIAG_ROW_COUNT** *field is reset to* **0** *each time an ODBC API function is called.*

Return Codes

SQL_SUCCESS, **SQL_SUCCESS_WITH_INFO**, **SQL_INVALID_HANDLE**, or **SQL_ERROR**

SQLSTATEs

If this function returns **SQL_SUCCESS_WITH_INFO** or **SQL_ERROR**, one of the following SQLSTATE values may be obtained by calling the **SQLGetDiagRec()** function (ODBC 3.x driver) or the **SQLError()** function (ODBC 2.0 or earlier driver):

ODBC 3.X
01000, **HY**000, **HY**001, **HY**010*, **HY**013, **HY**T01, or **IM**001*

ODBC 2.0 OR EARLIER
01000, **IM**001*, **S1**000, **S1**001, or **S1**010*

*Returned by the ODBC Driver Manager.

Unless noted otherwise, each of these SQLSTATE values is returned by the data source driver. Refer to Appendix B for detailed information about each SQLSTATE value that can be returned by the ODBC Driver Manager or by a data source driver.

Comments

- If the number of rows affected by an **INSERT**, **UPDATE**, or **DELETE** operation can not be determined, this function returns **-1** in the *RowCount* parameter.
- If an **INSERT**, **UPDATE**, or **DELETE** operation is not performed on the statement handle specified just before this function is called, the value returned in the *RowCount* parameter is driver-defined.

■ A driver may return a value in the *RowCount* parameter for SQL statements other than **INSERT**, **UPDATE**, or **DELETE**. For example, some drivers may also return the number of rows returned by a **SELECT** SQL statement or a catalog function. However, for maximum interoperability, applications should not rely on this behavior.

Prerequisites   The **SQLExecute()** function or the **SQLExecDirect()** function should be used to execute an **INSERT**, **UPDATE**, or **DELETE** SQL statement before this function is called

or

the **SQLBulkOperations()** function should be called with the **SQL_ADD**, **SQL_UPDATE_BY_BOOKMARK**, or **SQL_DELETE_BY_BOOKMARK** operation specified before this function is called

or

the **SQLSetPos()** function should be called with the **SQL_UPDATE** or **SQL_DELETE** operation specified before this function is called.

Restrictions   There are no restrictions associated with this function call.

See Also   **SQLExecute()**, **SQLExecDirect()**, **SQLBulkOperations()**, **SQLSetPos()**

Example   The following Visual C++ program illustrates how to use the **SQLRowCount()** function to determine how many rows were affected by an **INSERT**, **UPDATE**, or **DELETE** operation.

```
/*-----------------------------------------------------------------*/
/* NAME:     CH12EX3.CPP                                           */
/* PURPOSE: Illustrate How To Use The Following ODBC API Function  */
/*          In A C++ Program:                                      */
/*                                                                 */
/*              SQLRowCount()                                      */
/*                                                                 */
/* OTHER ODBC APIs SHOWN:                                          */
/*          SQLAllocHandle()        SQLSetEnvAttr()                */
/*          SQLConnect()            SQLExecDirect()                */
/*          SQLDisconnect()         SQLFreeHandle()                */
/*                                                                 */
/*-----------------------------------------------------------------*/

// Include The Appropriate Header Files
#include <windows.h>
#include <sql.h>
#include <sqlext.h>
```

```cpp
#include <iostream.h>

// Define The ODBC_Class Class
class ODBC_Class
{
    // Attributes
    public:
        SQLHANDLE    EnvHandle;
        SQLHANDLE    ConHandle;
        SQLHANDLE    StmtHandle;
        SQLRETURN    rc;

    // Operations
    public:
        ODBC_Class();                        // Constructor
        ~ODBC_Class();                       // Destructor
};

// Define The Class Constructor
ODBC_Class::ODBC_Class()
{
    // Initialize The Return Code Variable
    rc = SQL_SUCCESS;

    // Allocate An Environment Handle
    rc = SQLAllocHandle(SQL_HANDLE_ENV, SQL_NULL_HANDLE, &EnvHandle);

    // Set The ODBC Application Version To 3.x
    if (rc == SQL_SUCCESS)
        rc = SQLSetEnvAttr(EnvHandle, SQL_ATTR_ODBC_VERSION,
                   (SQLPOINTER) SQL_OV_ODBC3, SQL_IS_UINTEGER);

    // Allocate A Connection Handle
    if (rc == SQL_SUCCESS)
        rc = SQLAllocHandle(SQL_HANDLE_DBC, EnvHandle, &ConHandle);
}

// Define The Class Destructor
ODBC_Class::~ODBC_Class()
{
    // Free The Connection Handle
    if (ConHandle != NULL)
        SQLFreeHandle(SQL_HANDLE_DBC, ConHandle);

    // Free The Environment Handle
    if (EnvHandle != NULL)
        SQLFreeHandle(SQL_HANDLE_ENV, EnvHandle);
}

/*------------------------------------------------------------------*/
/* The Main Function                                                */
/*------------------------------------------------------------------*/
int main()
{
```

```
// Declare The Local Memory Variables
SQLRETURN    rc = SQL_SUCCESS;
SQLCHAR      DBName[10] = "Northwind";
SQLCHAR      SQLStmt[255];
SQLINTEGER   RowCount;

// Create An Instance Of The ODBC_Class Class
ODBC_Class   Example;

// Connect To The Northwind Sample Database
if (Example.ConHandle != NULL)
{
    rc = SQLConnect(Example.ConHandle, DBName, SQL_NTS,
            (SQLCHAR *) "", SQL_NTS, (SQLCHAR *) "", SQL_NTS);

    // Allocate An SQL Statement Handle
    rc = SQLAllocHandle(SQL_HANDLE_STMT, Example.ConHandle,
            &Example.StmtHandle);
    if (rc == SQL_SUCCESS)
    {
        // Define An INSERT SQL Statement
        strcpy((char *) SQLStmt, "INSERT INTO Shippers ");
        strcat((char *) SQLStmt, "(CompanyName, Phone) VALUES ");
        strcat((char *) SQLStmt, "('DHL Shipping', ");
        strcat((char *) SQLStmt, "'(503) 555-1212')");

        // Prepare And Execute The SQL Statement
        rc = SQLExecDirect(Example.StmtHandle, SQLStmt, SQL_NTS);

        // Obtain And Display Information About The Number Of
        // Rows That Were Affected When The SQL Statement Was
        // Executed
        rc = SQLRowCount(Example.StmtHandle, &RowCount);
        if (rc == SQL_SUCCESS)
        {
            cout << "Number of rows affected by the INSERT ";
            cout << "SQL statement : " << RowCount << endl;
        }

        // Free The SQL Statement Handle
        if (Example.StmtHandle != NULL)
            SQLFreeHandle(SQL_HANDLE_STMT, Example.StmtHandle);
    }

    // Disconnect From The Northwind Sample Database
    rc = SQLDisconnect(Example.ConHandle);
}

// Return To The Operating System
return(rc);
}
```

13

Working
With Descriptors

In the earlier versions of ODBC, descriptors remained behind the scenes and applications had no way (or need) to
access them. With Version 3.0 of ODBC, descriptors were
brought out of hiding and some applications developers
found they could be used to help streamline several kinds
of processing. This chapter is designed to introduce you to
ODBC descriptors and to the API functions used to access
them. The first part of this chapter defines descriptors
and explains how they are used. This is followed by a discussion about the four main types of descriptors and the
basic descriptor parts. Next, the different ways descriptors can be allocated, copied, and freed is discussed. Then,
the concise functions that can be used to modify the fields
of a descriptor record are introduced. Finally, a detailed
reference section covering each ODBC API function that
can be used to control explicitly allocated descriptors is
provided.

What Are Descriptors?

Most applications that use embedded SQL to interact with a DBMS have access to a special data structure known as the *SQL Descriptor Area* (SQLDA) structure. This structure is typically used in conjunction with **PREPARE**, **DESCRIBE**, **EXECUTE**, **OPEN**, **FETCH**, and **CALL** SQL statements to pass detailed information (usually about column data) between an application and the database. In ODBC, descriptors are comparable to the SQLDA structure used with embedded SQL.

ODBC API functions that work with parameter and column data (for example, the **SQLBindCol()** and **SQLFetch()** functions) implicitly set and retrieve descriptor field information as they execute. For instance, when the **SQLBindCol()** function is used to bind column data to an application variable, it sets one or more descriptor fields to describe the complete binding assignment.

Because ODBC API functions implicitly use descriptors as needed, applications usually do not concern themselves with how descriptors are managed. In fact, there are no database operations that require an application to gain direct access to a descriptor. However, for some applications, gaining direct access to one or more descriptors helps to streamline many operations.

Types of Descriptors

Whenever an SQL statement handle is allocated, ODBC implicitly allocates the following four types of descriptors and assigns them to the statement handle:

■ An application parameter descriptor (APD)

■ An application row descriptor (ARD)

■ An implementation parameter descriptor (IPD)

■ An implementation row descriptor (IRD)

Each descriptor is used to describe one of the following:

■ A set of zero or more dynamic parameters (represented by parameter markers) in an SQL statement:

The APD contains the input parameter values as set by the application (dynamic input parameters) or the parameter values returned by a stored procedure invoked by a **CALL** SQL statement (dynamic output parameters) execution.

The IPD contains the same information as the APD after any specified data conversion is performed (dynamic input parameters), or the parameters returned, by a stored procedure invoked by a **CALL** SQL statement before any specified data conversion is performed (dynamic output parameters)

For dynamic input parameters, an application must operate on the APD before executing any SQL statement that contains dynamic parameter markers. For both dynamic input and dynamic output parameters, an application may specify different data types from those stored in the IPD to achieve data conversion.

▪ A single row of data source data:

The IRD contains the current row from the data source. (These buffers conceptually contain data as written to, or read from, the data source. However, the stored form of data source data is not specified. Therefore, the data in an IRD could have been converted from its original form.)

The ARD contains the current row of data as presented to the application after any specified data conversion has been applied.

An application operates on an ARD in any case where column data from the data source must appear in application variables. An application may specify different data types from those found in the IRD to perform data conversion of column data.

Although these four descriptors are usually used in a specific manner, each may perform a different role. For example, a row descriptor in one statement can serve as a parameter descriptor in another. For either parameter or row descriptors, if the application specifies different data types in corresponding records of the implementation and application descriptor, the driver automatically performs the necessary data conversion when it uses the descriptor.

Parts of a Descriptor

Each descriptor contains one header record and zero or more parameter or column records, depending on the descriptor type (parameter descriptor or row descriptor). The descriptor header record contains general information about the descriptor itself and each parameter/column record contains information that describes a single parameter or column. Each time a new parameter or column is associated with (bound to) an application variable, a new parameter or column record is added to the descriptor—each time a parameter or column is unbound, the corresponding parameter or column record field is removed from the descriptor. Changing a field value in the descriptor header record affects all parameters or columns associated with the descriptor; changing a field value in a parameter or column affects only the parameter or column associated with that record.

Implicitly Allocated Descriptors

It was mentioned earlier that when an SQL statement handle is allocated by an application, four descriptors are automatically allocated and assigned to the statement handle: an APD, an IPD, an ARD, and an IRD. An application can obtain handles to these implicitly allocated descriptors by calling the **SQLGetStmtAttr()** function with the appropriate attributes specified. The driver is responsible for allocating and maintaining whatever storage it needs to store the records that are or will be assigned to these four descriptors—the application does not explicitly specify the size of any of these descriptors nor does it allocate storage each time new records are added. When an SQL statement handle is freed, the driver automatically frees the four implicitly allocated descriptors that are assigned to the handle.

When an application variable is associated in some way with a SQL statement parameter marker or result data set column, several fields of the corresponding parameter/column record that is automatically added to the descriptor initially contain a NULL value. Because these field values, known as deferred fields, are not used when the record is created, the driver saves the addresses of the variables they are associated with for later use.

Once the application provides data for these deferred fields, the record is said to be bound. If the descriptor is an APD, this happens when the **SQLExecute()** or the **SQLExecDirect()** function is called. In this case, each bound record constitutes a bound parameter. For input parameters, the application must bind a parameter for each dynamic parameter marker in the SQL statement before executing the statement. For output parameters, the application is not required to bind the parameter. If the descriptor is an ARD, this happens when the **SQLFetch()**, the **SQLScrollFetch()**, or the **SQLExtendedFetch()** function is called—in this case, each bound record constitutes a bound column.

Whenever a parameter/column record in an APD, ARD, or IPD descriptor becomes bound, the driver performs a consistency check to ensure that the value of the variable and the values applicable to the deferred fields in the same record are valid and consistent. Consistency checks cannot be performed on IRD descriptors.

Explicitly Allocated Descriptors

Aside from the four implicitly allocated descriptors assigned to each SQL statement handle, an application can explicitly allocate one or more application descriptors (using the **SQLAllocHandle()** function) and assign them to a specific connection handle—but only after the application has connected to a data source. The application can then direct the driver to use that descriptor in place of a corresponding implicitly allocated application descriptor (APD and ARD descriptors) by calling the **SQLSetStmtAttr()** function with the new descriptor handle specified. Unlike implicitly allocated descriptors, explicitly allocated descriptors can be associated with more than one SQL statement handle; that is, different SQL statements can share the same explicitly allocated application descriptor. Implementation descriptors, however, cannot be explicitly allocated.

Obtaining and Setting Descriptor Information

Applications can call the **SQLGetDescRec()** or **SQLGetDescField()** function to retrieve information from a descriptor record. By calling **SQLGetDescRec()**, applications can retrieve the contents of several parameter or column record fields (which identify the data type and storage of a parameter or column) in a single function call. However, this function cannot be used to retrieve information from a descriptor header record. Applications can retrieve information from a descriptor header record by calling the **SQLGetDiagField()** function. Because many statement attributes correspond to descriptor header fields, the **SQLGetStmtAttr()** function can also be used to examine descriptor header information.

By calling the **SQLSetDescRec()** function, applications can modify the descriptor record fields that affect the data type and storage of parameters and/or columns associated with explicitly allocated descriptors. Specific fields of any explicitly allocated descriptor record can be changed or set by calling the **SQLSetDescField()** function. Again, because many statement attributes correspond to descriptor header fields, the **SQLSetStmtAttr()** function can be called in place of the **SQLSetDescField()** function to change descriptor header record information—setting an attribute through the **SQLSetStmtAttr()** function and setting the corresponding descriptor header field by calling the **SQLSetDescField()** have the same effect. Using the **SQLGetStmtAttr()** and **SQLSetStmtAttr()** functions as opposed to using the **SQLGetDescRec()** and **SQLSetDescField()** functions provides one advantage—no descriptor handle is needed.

The **SQLSetDescField()** function can also be used to define the initial (default) values used to populate record fields when an application row descriptor is first allocated. To provide a standard method for presenting database data to an application, the initial value of an explicitly allocated descriptor's **SQL_DESC_TYPE** field is always **SQL_DEFAULT**. An application may change this at any time by setting one or more fields of the descriptor record.

The concept of a default value is not valid for IRD fields. In fact, the only time an application can gain access to IRD fields is when a prepared or executed SQL statement is associated with it.

Copying Descriptors

The **SQLCopyDesc()** function can be used to copy all the record fields of one descriptor to another. Record fields can be copied from any type of descriptor; however, they can only be copied to an APD, ARD, or IPD descriptor—not to an IRD descriptor. The **SQLCopyDesc()** function does not copy the **SQL_DESC_ALLOC_TYPE** field, because a descriptor's allocation type cannot be changed. Otherwise, all record fields copied automatically overwrite any existing record fields.

Because an ARD on one statement handle can serve as the APD on another statement handle, an application can copy rows between tables without copying data at the application level. To do this, a row descriptor describing a column in a fetched row of a table is reused as a parameter descriptor for a parameter in an **INSERT** SQL statement. However, the **SQL_MAX_CONCURRENT_ACTIVITIES** information type must be greater than **1** for this operation to succeed.

Copying Rows Between Tables

Using descriptors, an application can indirectly copy data from one data source table to another. To do this, an application simply binds the same data buffers and descriptor information to two different SQL statements—one SQL statement fetches the data from a data source table; the other SQL statement inserts the data into a different data source table. The binding can be accomplished either by sharing an application descriptor (by binding an explicitly allocated descriptor as the ARD to one statement and as the APD to the other) or by using the **SQLCopyDesc()** function to copy the bindings between two different ARD and the APD descriptors associated with the SQL statements. If the SQL statements reside on two different connections, the **SQLCopyDesc()** function must be used because explicitly allocated descriptors can only be assigned to a single connection handle. The **SQLCopyDesc()** function also has to be called to copy the bindings between the IRD and the IPD descriptors of the two SQL statements.

NOTE: *In order for two SQL statements to be associated with the same connection handle, the driver being used must support multiple active statements. The driver's ability to support multiple active statements can be determined by calling the* **SQLGetInfo()** *function with the* **SQL_ACTIVE_STATEMENTS** *information type specified–the value returned must be greater than* **1.**

Freeing Descriptors

Implicitly allocated descriptors can only be freed by calling either the **SQLDisconnect()** function, which drops any statements or descriptors open on the specified connection handle, or the **SQLFreeHandle()** function with the statement handle that the descriptors are associated with specified, which frees the statement handle and all implicitly allocated descriptors associated with it. Even when freed, implicitly allocated descriptors remain valid, and the **SQLGetDescField()** function can be used to examine their contents.

Explicitly allocated descriptors can be freed either by calling the **SQLFreeHandle()** function with the descriptor handle specified (explicitly), or by calling the **SQLFreeHandle()** function with the connection handle that the descriptor is associated with specified (which implicitly frees the descriptor when the connection handle is freed). When an explicitly allocated descriptor is freed, all statement handles attached to the freed descriptor automatically revert to the descriptors that were implicitly allocated for them.

Automatic Population of the IPD

Some drivers are capable of setting an IPD descriptor's fields after a parameterized query has been prepared. When that's the case, all parameter records associated with the descriptor are automatically populated with information about the parameter, including the data type, precision, scale, and other characteristics. This information can be particularly valuable to an application when it has no other way to discover it, such as when an ad-hoc query is performed with parameters that the application does not know about.

An application can determine whether a driver supports automatic IPD population by calling the **SQLGetConnectAttr()** function with the **SQL_ATTR_AUTO_IPD** option specified. If this attribute is set to **SQL_TRUE**, the driver supports automatic IPD population and the application can enable it by setting the **SQL_ATTR_ENABLE_AUTO_IPD** statement attribute to **SQL_TRUE**.

When automatic population is supported and enabled, the driver populates the IPD fields after an SQL statement containing parameter markers has been prepared by the **SQLPrepare()** function. An application can retrieve this information by calling the **SQLGetDescField()** function, the **SQLGetDescRec()** function, or the **SQLDescribeParam()** function. The information obtained by calling any of these functions can be used to ensure that the most appropriate application variables are bound to parameters, or if not, that the appropriate data conversion is specified.

Unfortunately, automatic population of the IPD may produce a decrease in performance. If performance becomes an issue, an application can turn off automatic IPD population by setting the **SQL_ATTR_ENABLE_AUTO_IPD** statement attribute to **SQL_FALSE** (which is the default value).

Using Concise Functions to Modify Descriptors

Some ODBC API functions gain implicit access to descriptors and sometimes an application developer may find these functions more convenient to use than the **SQLSetDescField()** and **SQLGetDescField()** functions. These functions are known as concise functions because they perform a number of tasks including setting or getting descriptor field contents. Some concise functions let an application set or retrieve several related descriptor fields in a single function call.

Concise functions can be called without first obtaining a descriptor handle. That's because these functions work with the descriptor fields associated with the statement handle with which they are called. For example, the concise functions **SQLBindCol()** and **SQLBindParameter()** bind a parameter or column by setting the descriptor fields that correspond to the parameter values they receive. Both of these functions perform more tasks than simply setting descriptors—they provide a complete specification of a dynamic parameter's binding or of a specific result data set column's binding. An application can, however, change individual details of a binding specification by calling the **SQLSetDescField()** function or the **SQLSetDescRec()** function, and a binding specification for a parameter or a column can be created by making a series of suitable calls to these two functions.

The concise functions **SQLColAttribute()**, **SQLDescribeCol()**, **SQLDescribeParam()**, **SQLNumParams()**, and **SQLNumResultCols()** retrieve descriptor field values—when the **SQLColAttribute()** function is called to describe column data, it returns data stored in descriptor column record fields. In some cases, the **SQLSetStmtAttr()** and **SQLGetStmtAttr()** functions also serve as concise functions. In a sense, the **SQLGetDescRec()** and **SQLSetDescRec()** functions are also concise functions that, when called, retrieve or set the values of several descriptor fields that affect the data type and storage of parameter or column data. In fact, the **SQLSetDescRec()** function provides an effective way to change data associated with the binding information of a parameter or a column in one step.

The Descriptor Control Functions

Table 13–1 lists the ODBC API functions used to obtain information about and to modify explicitly allocated descriptors.

Table 13–1 The ODBC Descriptor Control Functions

Function Name	Description
SQLGetDescRec()	Retrieves the current values of multiple fields of a descriptor parameter/column record that describe the name, data type, and storage sizes used by the data associated with a particular parameter marker or column in a result data set.
SQLSetDescRec()	Modifies the current values of multiple fields of a descriptor parameter/column record.
SQLGetDescField()	Retrieves the current value of a field in a descriptor header or parameter/column record.
SQLSetDescField()	Changes or sets the value of a field in a descriptor header or parameter/column record
SQLCopyDesc()	Copies all records in one descriptor to another descriptor.

Each of these functions are described in detail in the remaining portion of this chapter.

SQLGetDescRec

COMPATABILITY

X/OPEN 95 CLI	ISO/IEC 92 CLI	ODBC 1.0	ODBC 2.0	ODBC 3.0	ODBC 3.5
✓	✓	☐	☐	✓	✓

API CONFORMANCE LEVEL   CORE

Purpose   The `SQLGetDescRec()` function is used to retrieve the current values of multiple fields of a descriptor parameter/column record.

Syntax

```
SQLRETURN   SQLGetDescRec   (SQLHDESC        DescriptorHandle,
                             SQLSMALLINT     RecNumber,
                             SQLCHAR         *Name,
                             SQLSMALLINT     NameMaxSize,
                             SQLSMALLINT     *NameSize,
                             SQLSMALLINT     *Type,
                             SQLSMALLINT     *SubType,
                             SQLINTEGER      *OctetLength,
                             SQLSMALLINT     *Precision,
                             SQLSMALLINT     *Scale,
                             SQLSMALLINT     *Nullable);
```

Parameters

DescriptorHandle   A descriptor handle that refers to a previously allocated descriptor information storage buffer (data structure).

RecNumber   Specifies the descriptor record from which this function is to retrieve information. Records are numbered sequentially, starting with 1 (record 0 is the bookmark record).

Name   A pointer to a location in memory where this function is to store the name of the parameter or column associated with the specified descriptor record.

NameMaxSize   The maximum size of the memory storage buffer where this function is to store the parameter or column name retrieved.

NameSize   A pointer to a location in memory where this function is to store the actual number of bytes written to the parameter/column name memory storage buffer (*DescName*).

Type	A pointer to a location in memory where this function is to store the concise SQL or C data type of the parameter or column associated with the specified descriptor record.
SubType	A pointer to a location in memory where this function is to store the interval leading precision value of the parameter or column associated with the specified descriptor record (for records whose *Type* is **SQL_DATETIME** or **SQL_INTERVAL**).
OctetLength	A pointer to a location in memory where this function is to store the length, in bytes, of the parameter or column data associated with the specified descriptor record.
Precision	A pointer to a location in memory where this function is to store the number of digits used by the data value of the parameter or column associated with the specified descriptor record (for records whose *Type* is an exact numeric data type).
Scale	A pointer to a location in memory where this function is to store the number of digits to the right of the decimal point that are used by the data value of the parameter or column associated with the specified descriptor record (for records whose *Type* is a decimal or a numeric data type).
Nullable	A pointer to a location in memory where this function is to store a value that indicates whether the parameter or column associated with the specified descriptor record can contain NULL values.

Description   The **SQLGetDescRec()** is used to retrieve the current values of multiple fields of a descriptor parameter/column record that describe the name, data type, and storage sizes used by the data associated with a particular parameter marker in an SQL statement or a column in a result data set. Unlike the **SQLGetDescField()** function, which returns a single value from one field of a descriptor record per call, the **SQLGetDescRec()** function returns several commonly used fields of a descriptor record, including the name of the of the parameter or column (**SQL_DESC_NAME** field), the concise SQL or C data type of the parameter or column (**SQL_DESC_TYPE** field), the interval leading precision value of the parameter or column (**SQL_DESC_DATETIME_INTERVAL_CODE** field), the length, in bytes of the data (**SQL_DESC_OCTET_LENGTH** field), the number of digits used by the data value (**SQL_DESC_PRECISION** field), the number of digits to the right of the decimal point (**SQL_DESC_SCALE** field), and whether the parameter or column can contain NULL values (**SQL_DESC_NULLABLE** field). Refer to the **SQLGetDescField()** function for a complete description of each field found in a descriptor record.

Return Codes   **SQL_SUCCESS**, **SQL_SUCCESS_WITH_INFO**, **SQL_NO_DATA**, **SQL_INVALID_HANDLE**, or **SQL_ERROR**

SQLSTATEs   If this function returns **SQL_SUCCESS_WITH_INFO** or **SQL_ERROR**, one of the following SQLSTATE values may be obtained by calling the **SQLGetDiagRec()** function:

01000, **01**004, **07**009*, **08**S01, **HY**000, **HY**001, **HY**007, **HY**010*, **HY**013, **HY**T01, or **IM**001*

* Returned by the ODBC Driver Manager.

Unless noted otherwise, each of these SQLSTATE values is returned by the data source driver. Refer to Appendix B for detailed information about each SQLSTATE value that can be returned by the ODBC Driver Manager or by a data source driver.

Comments   ▧ If the parameter or column name string's actual length is greater than or equal to the maximum string size value specified in the *NameMaxSize* parameter, the parameter/column name string is truncated to *NameMaxSize*–1 (the length of a NULL-termination character) characters.

▧ An application can determine the total number of parameter/column descriptor records available in a descriptor by calling the **SQLGetDescField()** function to retrieve the value of the **SQL_DESC_COUNT** field.

▧ If the value specified in the *RecNumber* parameter is less than or equal to the total number of descriptor records available, but the corresponding descriptor record does not contain data for a parameter or a column, the default values of each field are returned.

▧ If the value specified in the *RecNumber* parameter is greater than the total number of descriptor records available, **SQL_NO_DATA** is returned.

- If this function is called with an IRD descriptor handle specified in the *DescriptorHandle* parameter, and if the SQL statement associated with the IRD is in the "Prepared" or "Executed" state but there is no open cursor associated with it, **SQL_NO_DATA** is returned.

- If this function is called with a NULL pointer specified for the *Name, Type, SubType, OctetLength, Precision, Scale,* or *Nullable* parameter, no value is returned for that parameter.

- When this function is used to retrieve descriptor record field values that are undefined for a particular descriptor type, **SQL_SUCCESS** is returned, but the actual values returned are undefined. For example, if this function is called using an APD or ARD descriptor, **SQL_SUCCESS** is returned, but the values returned to the *Name* and *Nullable* parameters are undefined.

- When this function is used to retrieve descriptor record field values that are defined for a particular descriptor type, but that have no default value and that have not been set by some other ODBC API function, **SQL_SUCCESS** is returned but the actual value returned for the field is undefined.

- The values of individual descriptor fields can be retrieved by calling the **SQLGetDescField()** function.

Prerequisites   A descriptor handle must be allocated before this function is called.

Restrictions   There are no restrictions associated with this function call.

See Also   SQLSetDescRec(), SQLGetDescField(), SQLSetDescField(), SQLCopyDesc()

Example   The following Visual C++ program illustrates how to use the **SQLGetDescRec()** function to specify general information for a descriptor record.

```
/*------------------------------------------------------------*/
/* NAME:      CH13EX1.CPP                                      */
/* PURPOSE: Illustrate How To Use The Following ODBC API Function */
/*          In A C++ Program:                                  */
/*                                                             */
/*              SQLGetDescRec()                                */
/*                                                             */
/* OTHER ODBC APIs SHOWN:                                      */
/*          SQLAllocHandle()          SQLSetEnvAttr()          */
/*          SQLConnect()              SQLExecDirect()          */
/*          SQLGetStmtAttr()          SQLDisconnect()          */
/*          SQLFreeHandle()                                    */
/*                                                             */
/*------------------------------------------------------------*/
```

```
// Include The Appropriate Header Files
#include <windows.h>
#include <sql.h>
#include <sqlext.h>
#include <iostream.h>

// Define The ODBC_Class Class
class ODBC_Class
{
    // Attributes
    public:
        SQLHANDLE   EnvHandle;
        SQLHANDLE   ConHandle;
        SQLHANDLE   DescHandle;
        SQLHANDLE   StmtHandle;
        SQLRETURN   rc;

    // Operations
    public:
        ODBC_Class();                           // Constructor
        ~ODBC_Class();                          // Destructor
        SQLRETURN GetDescriptorInfo();
};

// Define The Class Constructor
ODBC_Class::ODBC_Class()
{
    // Initialize The Return Code Variable
    rc = SQL_SUCCESS;

    // Allocate An Environment Handle
    rc = SQLAllocHandle(SQL_HANDLE_ENV, SQL_NULL_HANDLE, &EnvHandle);

    // Set The ODBC Application Version To 3.x
    if (rc == SQL_SUCCESS)
        rc = SQLSetEnvAttr(EnvHandle, SQL_ATTR_ODBC_VERSION,
                (SQLPOINTER) SQL_OV_ODBC3, SQL_IS_UINTEGER);

    // Allocate A Connection Handle
    if (rc == SQL_SUCCESS)
        rc = SQLAllocHandle(SQL_HANDLE_DBC, EnvHandle, &ConHandle);
}

// Define The Class Destructor
ODBC_Class::~ODBC_Class()
{
    // Free The Connection Handle
    if (ConHandle != NULL)
        SQLFreeHandle(SQL_HANDLE_DBC, ConHandle);

    // Free The Environment Handle
    if (EnvHandle != NULL)
        SQLFreeHandle(SQL_HANDLE_ENV, EnvHandle);
}
```

```
// Define The GetDescriptorInfo() Member Function
SQLRETURN ODBC_Class::GetDescriptorInfo(void)
{
    // Declare The Local Memory Variables
    SQLINTEGER    ValueLen;
    SQLCHAR       Name[50];
    SQLSMALLINT   NameLen;
    SQLSMALLINT   Type;
    SQLSMALLINT   SubType;
    SQLINTEGER    Width;
    SQLSMALLINT   Precision;
    SQLSMALLINT   Scale;
    SQLSMALLINT   Nullable;

    // Retrieve A Handle To The Implementation Row Descriptor (IRD)
    // Associated With The SQL Statement
    rc = SQLGetStmtAttr(StmtHandle, SQL_ATTR_IMP_ROW_DESC,
             (SQLPOINTER) &DescHandle, 0, &ValueLen);

    // Obtain And Display Information About Each Column In The
    // Result Data Set
    for (int i = 1; i <= 2; i++)
    {
        rc = SQLGetDescRec(DescHandle, i, Name, sizeof(Name),
                 &NameLen, &Type, &SubType, &Width, &Precision,
                 &Scale, &Nullable);
        if (rc == SQL_SUCCESS)
        {
            cout << "Column " << i << endl << endl;
            cout << "Name      : " << Name << endl;
            cout << "Data Type : " << Type << endl;
            cout << "Sub-Type  : " << SubType << endl;
            cout << "Width     : " << Width << endl;
            cout << "Precision : " << Precision << endl;
            cout << "Scale     : " << Scale << endl;
            cout << "Nullable  : " << Nullable << endl << endl;
            cout << endl;
        }
    }

    // Return The ODBC API Return Code To The Calling Function
    return(rc);
}

/*----------------------------------------------------------------*/
/* The Main Function                                              */
/*----------------------------------------------------------------*/
int main()
{
    // Declare The Local Memory Variables
    SQLRETURN   rc = SQL_SUCCESS;
    SQLCHAR     ConnectIn[40];
    SQLCHAR     SQLStmt[255];
```

```
// Create An Instance Of The ODBC_Class Class
ODBC_Class  Example;

// Build A Connection String
strcpy((char *) ConnectIn,
    "DSN=SQLServer;UID=userid;PWD=password;");

// Connect To The SQL Server Sample Database
if (Example.ConHandle != NULL)
{
    rc = SQLDriverConnect(Example.ConHandle, NULL, ConnectIn,
            SQL_NTS, NULL, 0, NULL, SQL_DRIVER_NOPROMPT);

    // Allocate An SQL Statement Handle
    rc = SQLAllocHandle(SQL_HANDLE_STMT, Example.ConHandle,
            &Example.StmtHandle);
    if (rc == SQL_SUCCESS)
    {
        // Define A SELECT SQL Statement
        strcpy((char *) SQLStmt, "SELECT EMPID, FIRSTNAME ");
        strcat((char *) SQLStmt, "FROM EMPLOYEES");

        // Prepare And Execute The SQL Statement
        rc = SQLExecDirect(Example.StmtHandle, SQLStmt, SQL_NTS);

        // Display Information About The Implementation Row
        // Descriptor (IRD) That Is Associated With The SQL
        // Statement
        if (rc == SQL_SUCCESS)
            Example.GetDescriptorInfo();

        // Free The SQL Statement Handle
        if (Example.StmtHandle != NULL)
            SQLFreeHandle(SQL_HANDLE_STMT, Example.StmtHandle);
    }

    // Disconnect From The SQL Server Sample Database
    rc = SQLDisconnect(Example.ConHandle);
}

// Return To The Operating System
return(rc);
}
```

SQLSetDescRec

COMPATABILITY

X/OPEN 95 CLI	ISO/IEC 92 CLI	ODBC 1.0	ODBC 2.0	ODBC 3.0	ODBC 3.5
☑	☑	☐	☐	☑	☑

API CONFORMANCE LEVEL   **CORE**

Purpose   The **SQLSetDescRec()** function is used to set the values of multiple fields of a descriptor parameter/column record.

Syntax

```
SQLRETURN   SQLSetDescRec   (SQLHDESC      DescriptorHandle,
                             SQLSMALLINT   RecNumber,
                             SQLSMALLINT   Type,
                             SQLSMALLINT   SubType,
                             SQLINTEGER    OctetLength,
                             SQLSMALLINT   Precision,
                             SQLSMALLINT   Scale,
                             SQLPOINTER    Data,
                             SQLINTEGER    *StringLength,
                             SQLINTEGER    *Indicator);
```

Parameters

DescriptorHandle	A descriptor handle that refers to a previously allocated descriptor information storage buffer (data structure).
RecNumber	Specifies the descriptor record to which this function is to assign information. Records are numbered sequentially, starting with 1 (record 0 is the bookmark record).
Type	The concise SQL or C data type of the parameter or column associated with the specified descriptor record.
SubType	The interval leading precision value of the parameter or column associated with the specified descriptor record (for records whose *Type* is **SQL_DATETIME** or **SQL_INTERVAL**).
OctetLength	The length in bytes of parameter or column data associated with the specified descriptor record (for records whose *Type* is a character string or binary data type).

Precision	The number of digits used by the parameter or column data value associated with the specified descriptor record (for records whose *Type* is an exact numeric data type).
Scale	The number of digits to the right of the decimal point that are used by the data value of the parameter or column associated with the specified descriptor record (for records whose *Type* is a decimal or a numeric data type).
Data	A pointer to a location in memory where the parameter or column value associated with the specified descriptor record is stored.
StringLength	A pointer to a location in memory where the total length in bytes of the parameter or column data value associated with the specified descriptor record is stored.
Indicator	A pointer to a location in memory where an indicator value that specifies whether a NULL data value is assigned to the parameter or column associated with the specified descriptor record is stored.

Description The `SQLSetDescRec()` function is used to set multiple field values of a descriptor parameter/column record. An application can call `SQLSetDescRec()` to set the following fields of a single column or parameter descriptor record:

- `SQL_DESC_TYPE`
- `SQL_DESC_DATETIME_INTERVAL_CODE` (for records whose type is `SQL_DATETIME` or `SQL_INTERVAL`)
- `SQL_DESC_OCTET_LENGTH`
- `SQL_DESC_PRECISION`
- `SQL_DESC_SCALE`
- `SQL_DESC_DATA_PTR`
- `SQL_DESC_OCTET_LENGTH_PTR`
- `SQL_DESC_INDICATOR_PTR`

Refer to the `SQLGetDescField()` function for a complete description of each field found in a descriptor record.

Once a parameter marker in an SQL statement or a column in a result data set has been bound to an application variable, the **SQLSetDescRec()** function allows you to change multiple fields affecting the binding without having to call the **SQLBindParameter()** function or the **SQLBindCol()** function again. This function can also be used to bind a parameter marker to an application variable; however, the **SQLBindParameter()** should be used to perform the first bind operation because it sets more descriptor record field values than the **SQLSetDescRec()** function; it can set both APD and IPD descriptor record field values in one call, and it does not require the allocation of a descriptor handle.

Return Codes   SQL_SUCCESS, SQL_SUCCESS_WITH_INFO, SQL_INVALID_HANDLE, or SQL_ERROR

SQLSTATEs   If this function returns **SQL_SUCCESS_WITH_INFO** or **SQL_ERROR**, one of the following SQLSTATE values may be obtained by calling the **SQLGetDiagRec()** function:

01000, **07**009, **08**S01, **HY**000, **HY**001, **HY**010*, **HY**013, **HY**016, **HY**021, **HY**090*, **HYT**01, or **IM**001*

* Returned by the ODBC Driver Manager.

Unless noted otherwise, each of these SQLSTATE values is returned by the data source driver. Refer to Appendix B for detailed information about each SQLSTATE value that can be returned by the ODBC Driver Manager or by a data source driver.

Comments   ▨ An application can determine the total number of parameter/column descriptor records available in a descriptor by calling the **SQLGetDescField()** function to retrieve the value of the **SQL_DESC_COUNT** field.

▨ If the value specified in the *RecNumber* parameter is greater than the total number of descriptor records available, the value of the **SQL_DESC_COUNT** descriptor header record field is changed to the value specified in the *RecNumber* parameter.

▨ If an ARD descriptor handle is specified in the *DescriptorHandle* parameter, and if a NULL pointer is specified in the *Data* parameter, the parameter or column associated with the descriptor record is unbound.

▨ If a NULL pointer is specified in the *Data* parameter, the **SQL_DESC_DATA_PTR** field of the corresponding parameter/column descriptor record is set to a NULL pointer.

■ If a NULL pointer is specified in the *StringLength* parameter, the SQL_DESC_OCTET_LENGTH_PTR field of the corresponding parameter/column descriptor record is set to a NULL pointer.

■ If a NULL pointer is specified in the *Indicator* parameter, the SQL_DESC_INDICATOR_PTR field of the specified parameter/column descriptor record is set to a NULL pointer.

■ This function can be used to set the descriptor record field values of a descriptor that is not currently associated with an SQL statement.

■ While it is not mandatory, it is strongly recommended that an application sets the SQL_ATTR_USE_BOOKMARKS statement attribute before this function is used to set the values of bookmark descriptor record fields (that is, before this function is called with 0 specified in the *RecNumber* parameter).

■ When this function fails, SQL_ERROR is returned, and the contents of the fields of the descriptor record identified by the *RecNumber* parameter are undefined.

Prerequisites   A descriptor handle must be allocated before this function is called.

Restrictions   There are no restrictions associated with this function call.

See Also   SQLSetDescRec(), SQLGetDescField(), SQLSetDescField(), SQLCopyDesc()

Example   The following Visual C++ program illustrates how to use the SQLSetDescRec() function to specify general information for a descriptor record.

```
/*-------------------------------------------------------------*/
/* NAME:     CH13EX2.CPP                                        */
/* PURPOSE: Illustrate How To Use The Following ODBC API Function */
/*          In A C++ Program:                                   */
/*                                                              */
/*              SQLSetDescRec()                                 */
/*                                                              */
/* OTHER ODBC APIs SHOWN:                                       */
/*              SQLAllocHandle()      SQLSetEnvAttr()           */
/*              SQLDriverConnect()    SQLSetStmtAttr()          */
/*              SQLPrepare()          SQLGetDescRec()           */
/*              SQLExecute()          QLDisconnect()            */
/*              SQLFreeHandle()                                 */
/*                                                              */
/*-------------------------------------------------------------*/

// Include The Appropriate Header Files
#include <windows.h>
```

```cpp
#include <sql.h>
#include <sqlext.h>
#include <iostream.h>

// Define The ODBC_Class Class
class ODBC_Class
{
    // Attributes
    public:
        SQLHANDLE   EnvHandle;
        SQLHANDLE   ConHandle;
        SQLHANDLE   DescHandle;
        SQLHANDLE   StmtHandle;
        SQLRETURN   rc;

    // Operations
    public:
        ODBC_Class();                               // Constructor
        ~ODBC_Class();                              // Destructor
        SQLRETURN GetDescriptorInfo();
        SQLRETURN ShowResults();
};

// Define The Class Constructor
ODBC_Class::ODBC_Class()
{
    // Initialize The Return Code Variable
    rc = SQL_SUCCESS;

    // Allocate An Environment Handle
    rc = SQLAllocHandle(SQL_HANDLE_ENV, SQL_NULL_HANDLE, &EnvHandle);

    // Set The ODBC Application Version To 3.x
    if (rc == SQL_SUCCESS)
        rc = SQLSetEnvAttr(EnvHandle, SQL_ATTR_ODBC_VERSION,
                (SQLPOINTER) SQL_OV_ODBC3, SQL_IS_UINTEGER);

    // Allocate A Connection Handle
    if (rc == SQL_SUCCESS)
        rc = SQLAllocHandle(SQL_HANDLE_DBC, EnvHandle, &ConHandle);
}

// Define The Class Destructor
ODBC_Class::~ODBC_Class()
{
    // Free The Connection Handle
    if (ConHandle != NULL)
        SQLFreeHandle(SQL_HANDLE_DBC, ConHandle);

    // Free The Environment Handle
    if (EnvHandle != NULL)
        SQLFreeHandle(SQL_HANDLE_ENV, EnvHandle);
}

// Define The GetDescriptorInfo() Member Function
```

```
SQLRETURN ODBC_Class::GetDescriptorInfo(void)
{
    // Declare The Local Memory Variables
    SQLCHAR        Name[50];
    SQLSMALLINT    NameLen;
    SQLSMALLINT    Type;
    SQLSMALLINT    SubType;
    SQLINTEGER     Width;
    SQLSMALLINT    Precision;
    SQLSMALLINT    Scale;
    SQLSMALLINT    Nullable;

    // Obtain And Display Information About Each Column In The
    // Result Data Set
    for (int i = 1; i <= 2; i++)
    {
        rc = SQLGetDescRec(DescHandle, i, Name, sizeof(Name),
                  &NameLen, &Type, &SubType, &Width, &Precision,
                  &Scale, &Nullable);
        if (rc == SQL_SUCCESS)
        {
            cout << "Column " << i << endl << endl;
            cout << "Data Type : " << Type << endl;
            cout << "Width     : " << Width << endl << endl;
            cout << endl;
        }
    }

    // Return The ODBC API Return Code To The Calling Function
    return(rc);
}

/*-------------------------------------------------------------*/
/* The Main Function                                           */
/*-------------------------------------------------------------*/
int main()
{
    // Declare The Local Memory Variables
    SQLRETURN      rc = SQL_SUCCESS;
    SQLCHAR        ConnectIn[40];
    SQLCHAR        SQLStmt[255];
    SQLSMALLINT    Type;
    SQLINTEGER     Length;
    SQLCHAR        Data[50];
    SQLINTEGER     DataLen;

    // Create An Instance Of The ODBC_Class Class
    ODBC_Class  Example;

    // Build A Connection String
    strcpy((char *) ConnectIn,
        "DSN=SQLServer;UID=userid;PWD=password;");

    // Connect To The SQL Server Sample Database
    if (Example.ConHandle != NULL)
```

```
{
    rc = SQLDriverConnect(Example.ConHandle, NULL, ConnectIn,
            SQL_NTS, NULL, 0, NULL, SQL_DRIVER_NOPROMPT);

    // Allocate An SQL Statement Handle
    rc = SQLAllocHandle(SQL_HANDLE_STMT, Example.ConHandle,
            &Example.StmtHandle);
    if (rc == SQL_SUCCESS)
    {
        // Define A SELECT SQL Statement
        strcpy((char *) SQLStmt, "SELECT EMPID, FIRSTNAME ");
        strcat((char *) SQLStmt, "FROM EMPLOYEES");

        // Explicitly Allocate A Descriptor Handle
        rc = SQLAllocHandle(SQL_HANDLE_DESC, Example.ConHandle,
                &Example.DescHandle);

        // Assign The Descriptor Handle To The Statement Handle
        rc = SQLSetStmtAttr(Example.StmtHandle,
                SQL_ATTR_APP_ROW_DESC, (SQLPOINTER)
                Example.DescHandle, 0);

        // Prepare The SQL Statement
        rc = SQLPrepare(Example.StmtHandle, SQLStmt, SQL_NTS);

        // Modify The Information Stored In The Application Row
        // Descriptor (Which Was Populated When The SQL Statement
        // Was Prepared)
        Type = SQL_CHAR;
        Length = 50;
        rc = SQLSetDescRec(Example.DescHandle, 2, Type, 0,
                Length, 0, 0, Data, &DataLen, NULL);

        // Display The Modified Descriptor Information
        if (rc == SQL_SUCCESS)
            Example.GetDescriptorInfo();

        // Execute The SQL Statement
        rc = SQLExecute(Example.StmtHandle);

        // Free The Descriptor Handle
        if (Example.DescHandle != NULL)
            SQLFreeHandle(SQL_HANDLE_DESC, Example.DescHandle);

        // Free The SQL Statement Handle
        if (Example.StmtHandle != NULL)
            SQLFreeHandle(SQL_HANDLE_STMT, Example.StmtHandle);
    }

    // Disconnect From The SQL Server Sample Database
    rc = SQLDisconnect(Example.ConHandle);
}
```

```
// Return To The Operating System
return(rc);
}
```

SQLGetDescField

COMPATABILITY					
X/OPEN 95 CLI	ISO/IEC 92 CLI	ODBC 1.0	ODBC 2.0	ODBC 3.0	ODBC 3.5
✓	✓	☐	☐	✓	✓

API CONFORMANCE LEVEL **CORE**

Purpose

The **SQLGetDescField()** function is used to retrieve the current value of a specified descriptor record field.

Syntax

```
SQLRETURN   SQLGetDescField    (SQLHDESC       DescriptorHandle,
                                SQLSMALLINT    RecNumber,
                                SQLSMALLINT    Identifier,
                                SQLPOINTER     Value,
                                SQLINTEGER     ValueMaxSize,
                                SQLINTEGER     *StringLength);
```

Parameters

DescriptorHandle   A descriptor handle that refers to a previously allocated descriptor information storage buffer (data structure).

RecNumber   Specifies the descriptor record from which this function is to retrieve information. If any field of the descriptor header record is specified in the *Identifier* parameter, this parameter is ignored. Otherwise, this parameter should contain a number greater than or equal to **0** (Descriptor records are numbered, starting at **0**, with record number **0** being the bookmark record).

Identifier   The field of the descriptor header record or a descriptor parameter/column record whose value is to be retrieved. This parameter must be set to one of the following values:

Header Record Fields

- **SQL_DESC_ALLOC_TYPE**
- **SQL_DESC_ARRAY_SIZE**
- **SQL_DESC_ARRAY_STATUS_PTR**
- **SQL_DESC_BIND_OFFSET_PTR**
- **SQL_DESC_BIND_TYPE**
- **SQL_DESC_COUNT**
- **SQL_DESC_ROWS_PROCESSED_PTR**

Parameter/Column Record Fields

- **SQL_DESC_AUTO_UNIQUE_VALUE**
- **SQL_DESC_BASE_COLUMN_NAME**
- **SQL_DESC_BASE_TABLE_NAME**
- **SQL_DESC_CASE_SENSITIVE**
- **SQL_DESC_CATALOG_NAME**
- **SQL_DESC_CONCISE_TYPE**
- **SQL_DESC_DATA_PTR**
- **SQL_DESC_DATETIME_INTERVAL_CODE**
- **SQL_DESC_DATETIME_INTERVAL_PRECISION**
- **SQL_DESC_DISPLAY_SIZE**
- **SQL_DESC_FIXED_PREC_SCALE**
- **SQL_DESC_INDICATOR_PTR**
- **SQL_DESC_LABEL**
- **SQL_DESC_LENGTH**
- **SQL_DESC_LITERAL_PREFIX**
- **SQL_DESC_LITERAL_SUFFIX**
- **SQL_DESC_LOCAL_TYPE_NAME**
- **SQL_DESC_NAME**
- **SQL_DESC_NULLABLE**
- **SQL_DESC_NUM_PREC_RADIX**
- **SQL_DESC_OCTET_LENGTH**
- **SQL_DESC_OCTET_LENGTH_PTR**
- **SQL_DESC_PARAMETER_TYPE**
- **SQL_DESC_PRECISION**
- **SQL_DESC_ROWVER**

■ **SQL_DESC_SCALE**

■ **SQL_DESC_SCHEMA_NAME**

■ **SQL_DESC_SEARCHABLE**

■ **SQL_DESC_TABLE_NAME**

■ **SQL_DESC_TYPE**

■ **SQL_DESC_TYPE_NAME**

■ **SQL_DESC_UNNAMED**

■ **SQL_DESC_UNSIGNED**

■ **SQL_DESC_UPDATABLE**

Value	A pointer to a location in memory where this function is to store the current value of the specified descriptor record field.
ValueMaxSize	The size of the memory storage buffer where this function is to store the current value of the specified descriptor record field. If an ODBC-defined descriptor record field is to be retrieved, and if the field value is a 32-bit integer value, this parameter is ignored. If a driver-defined descriptor record field is to be retrieved, this parameter may be set as follows:

■ If the value of the specified descriptor record field is a character string, this parameter may be set to the actual length of the string or to **SQL_NTS**.

■ If the value of the specified descriptor record field is a binary string, this parameter may be set to the result of the **SQL_LEN_BINARY_ATTR**(*length*) macro. Usually, this macro places a negative value in this parameter.

■ If the value of the specified descriptor record field is anything other than a character string or binary string, this parameter may be set to **SQL_IS_POINTER**.

■ If the value of the specified descriptor record field is a fixed-length data type, this parameter may be set to **SQL_IS_INTEGER** or **SQL_IS_UINTEGER**, as appropriate.

StringLength	A pointer to a location in memory where this function is to store the actual number of bytes written to the descriptor record field value memory storage buffer (*Value*). If the descriptor record field value retrieved is not a character string value, this parameter is ignored.

Description

The `SQLGetDescField()` function is used to retrieve the current value of a specified descriptor record field. Table 13–2 lists alphabetically each value that can be specified for the *Identifier* parameter, along with a description of the information that will be returned for that value when this function is executed.

This function can be used to retrieve the value (setting) of any field in any descriptor record (regardless of the descriptor type), including header record fields, parameter/column record fields, and bookmark record fields.

Return Codes

`SQL_SUCCESS`, `SQL_SUCCESS_WITH_INFO`, `SQL_NO_DATA`, `SQL_INVALID_HANDLE`, or `SQL_ERROR`

SQLSTATEs

If this function returns `SQL_SUCCESS_WITH_INFO` or `SQL_ERROR`, one of the following SQLSTATE values may be obtained by calling the `SQLGetDiagRec()` function:

01000, **01**004, **07**009*, **08**S01, **HY**000, **HY**001, **HY**007, **HY**010*, **HY**013, **HY**021, **HY**090*, **HY**091, **HYT**01, or **IM**001*

* Returned by the ODBC Driver Manager.

Unless noted otherwise, each of these SQLSTATE values is returned by the data source driver. Refer to Appendix B for detailed information about each SQLSTATE value that can be returned by the ODBC Driver Manager or by a data source driver.

Comments

▪ An application can determine the total number of parameter/column descriptor records available in a descriptor by calling this function to retrieve the `SQL_DESC_COUNT` field value.

▪ If a descriptor header record field is specified in the *Identifier* parameter, the *RecNumber* parameter is ignored.

▪ If the value specified in the *RecNumber* parameter is less than or equal to the total number of descriptor records available, and if the corresponding descriptor record does not contain data for a parameter or column, this function returns the default value of the specified field.

Table 13–2 Descriptor Record Fields

Field Name	Data Type	Description
Header Record Fields		
SQL_DESC_ALLOC_TYPE	**SQLSMALLINT**	This field identifies how the descriptor was allocated. Valid values for this field are:
		SQL_DESC_ALLOC_AUTO: The descriptor was automatically allocated by the driver.
		SQL_DESC_ALLOC_USER: The descriptor was explicitly allocated by the application.
SQL_DESC_ARRAY_SIZE	**SQLUINTEGER**	For APD descriptors, this field contains a count of the number of values available for each parameter associated with the descriptor.
		For ARD descriptors, this field contains a count of the number of rowset rows associated with the descriptor.
		By default, the value for this field is **1**. If it contains a value greater than **1**, the **SQL_DESC_DATA_PTR**, **SQL_DESC_INDICATOR_PTR**, and **SQL_DESC_ OCTET_LENGTH_PTR** fields of each parameter/ column descriptor record contain pointers to arrays (APD or ARD descriptors only).
SQL_DESC_ARRAY_ STATUS_PTR	**SQLUSMALLINT** *	For APD descriptors, this field contains a pointer to an array of parameter operation values that can be set by the application to indicate whether a set of parameter values are to be used or ignored when **SQLExecute()** or **SQLExecDirect()** is called. Each element in this array can contain the following values:
		SQL_PARAM_PROCEED: The set of parameter values are to be used by the **SQLExecute()** or **SQLExecDirect()** function call.
		SQL_PARAM_IGNORE: The set of parameter values are not to be used by the **SQLExecute()** or **SQLExecDirect()** function call.
		If no elements in the array are set, or if this field contains a NULL pointer, all sets of parameters are used by **SQLExecute()** or **SQLExecDirect()** function calls.
		For IPD descriptors, this field contains a pointer to an array of parameter status values containing status information about each set of parameter values (after **SQLExecute()** or **SQLExecDirect()** has been executed). An application must allocate an array of **SQLUSMALLINT**s with as many elements as there

Table 13-2 Continued

Field Name	Data Type	Description
		are parameter values, and store a pointer to the array in this field. When **SQLExecute()** or **SQLExecDirect()** is called, the driver populates the specified array, unless this field contains a NULL pointer (the default), in which case no status values are generated and the array is not populated. Each element in the array can contain the following values:

SQL_PARAM_SUCCESS:
The SQL statement was successfully executed using the set of parameter values.

SQL_PARAM_SUCCESS_WITH_INFO:
The SQL statement was successfully executed using the set of parameter values; however, warning information was generated and is available in one or more diagnostic records.

SQL_PARAM_ERROR:
An error occurred while processing the SQL statement using the set of parameter values. Additional error information is available in one or more diagnostic records.

SQL_PARAM_UNUSED:
The set of parameter values was not used, possibly because some previous set of parameter values caused an error that aborted further processing, or because **SQL_PARAM_IGNORE** was set for the set of parameter values in the specified array.

SQL_PARAM_DIAG_UNAVAILABLE:
Diagnostic information is not available. An example is when the driver treats arrays of parameter values as a monolithic unit, in which case error information is not generated.

If a call to **SQLExecute()** or **SQLExecDirect()** did not return **SQL_SUCCESS** or **SQL_SUCCESS_WITH_INFO**, the contents of the array pointed to by this field are undefined.

For ARD descriptors, this field contains a pointer to an array of row operation values that can be set by the application to indicate whether the row is to be ignored by the **SQLSetPos()** function. Each element in the array can contain the following values:

SQL_ROW_PROCEED:
The row is included in the bulk operation performed by the **SQLSetPos()** function. (This setting does not guarantee that the operation will occur on the row. If the row has the

Table 13–2 *Continued*

Field Name	Data Type	Description
		status **SQL_ROW_ERROR** in the IRD row status array, the driver may not be able to perform the operation in the row.)

SQL_ROW_IGNORE:
The row is excluded from the bulk operation performed by the **SQLSetPos()** function.

If no elements in the array are set, or if this field contains a NULL pointer, all rows are included in the bulk operation performed by the **SQLSetPos()** function.

If an element in the array is set to **SQL_ROW_IGNORE**, the value in the row status array for the ignored row is not changed.

For IRD descriptors, this field contains a pointer to an array of row status values containing status information after the **SQLBulkOperations()**, **SQLFetch()**, **SQLFetchScroll()**, or **SQLSetPos()** function is called.

An application must allocate an array of **SQLUSMALLINT**s with as many elements as there are rows in the rowset, and store a pointer to the array in this field. When the **SQLBulkOperations()**, **SQLFetch()**, **SQLFetchScroll()**, or **SQLSetPos()** function is called, the driver populates the specified array, unless this field contains a NULL pointer (the default), in which case no status values are generated and the array is not populated. Each element in the array can contain the following values:

SQL_ROW_SUCCESS:
The row was successfully fetched and has not been changed since it was last fetched.

SQL_ROW_SUCCESS_WITH_INFO:
The row was successfully fetched and has not been changed since it was last fetched. However, a warning about the row was returned.

SQL_ROW_ERROR:
An error occurred while fetching the row.

SQL_ROW_UPDATED:
The row was successfully fetched and has been changed since it was last fetched. If the row is fetched again, its status will be **SQL_ROW_SUCCESS**.

Table 13–2 Continued

Field Name	Data Type	Description
		SQL_ROW_DELETED: The row has been deleted since it was last fetched.
		SQL_ROW_ADDED: The row was inserted by the **SQLBulkOperations()** function. If the row is fetched again, its status will be **SQL_ROW_SUCCESS**.
		SQL_ROW_NOROW: The rowset overlapped the end of the result data set and no row was returned that corresponded to an element of the row status array.
		If a call to **SQLBulkOperations()**, **SQLFetch()**, **SQLFetchScroll()**, or **SQLSetPos()** did not return **SQL_SUCCESS** or **SQL_SUCCESS_WITH_INFO**, the contents of the array referenced by this field are undefined.
		NOTE: If an application sets the elements of the row status array, the driver behavior is undefined.
SQL_DESC_BIND_OFFSET_PTR	**SQLINTEGER** *	For APD and ARD descriptors, this field contains a pointer to the binding offset used. By default, this field contains a NULL pointer. If this field contains a pointer to the binding offset used, instead of a NULL pointer, the driver dereferences the pointer and adds the dereferenced value to each deferred field that has a non-NULL value in the **SQL_DESC_DATA_PTR**, **SQL_DESC_INDICATOR_PTR**, and **SQL_DESC_OCTET_LENGTH_PTR** fields and uses the new pointer values when binding.
		The binding offset is always added directly to the values in the **SQL_DESC_DATA_PTR**, **SQL_DESC_INDICATOR_PTR**, and **SQL_DESC_OCTET_LENGTH_PTR** fields. If the offset is changed to a different value, the new value is still added directly to the value in each of these fields—earlier offset values are ignored.
		This field is a deferred field: It is not used at the time it is set, but is used later by the driver when it needs to determine addresses for data buffers.
SQL_DESC_BIND_TYPE	**SQLINTEGER**	In APD descriptors, this field specifies the binding orientation to use for binding dynamic parameters.
		In ARD descriptors, this field specifies the binding orientation to use when the **SQLFetch()** or **SQLFetchScroll()** function is called.

Table 13–2 Continued

Field Name	Data Type	Description
		By default, this field is set to **SQL_BIND_BY_COLUMN** and column-wise binding is used for both parameters and columns.
SQL_DESC_COUNT	**SQLSMALLINT**	This field contains the 1-based index value of the highest-numbered descriptor parameter/column record that contains data. When the driver sets the header record for the descriptor, it must set this field to show how many parameter/column records are significant. When an application allocates a descriptor handle, it does not have to specify how many descriptor records to reserve room for. Instead, as the application specifies the contents of descriptor records, the driver takes any action necessary to ensure that the descriptor handle always refers to a descriptor (data structure) of adequate size.
		This field does not contain a count of all parameters (if the descriptor is an APD or IPD descriptor) or all data columns (if the descriptor is an ARD or IRD descriptor) that are bound. Instead it contains a count of the total number of parameter/column records in the descriptor itself.
		If the highest-numbered parameter or column is unbound, the value of this field is changed to the number of the next highest-numbered parameter/column record. However, if a parameter or column with a number less than the highest-numbered parameter/column record is unbound, the value of this field is not changed.
		On the other hand, if additional parameters or columns are bound with numbers greater than the highest-numbered parameter/column record containing data, the driver automatically increases the value stored in this field.
		If the **SQLFreeStmt()** function is called with the **SQL_RESET_PARAMS** option specified, the **SQL_DESC_COUNT** fields in APD and IPD descriptors are set to **0**. If the **SQLFreeStmt()** function is called with the **SQL_UNBIND** option specified, the **SQL_DESC_COUNT** fields in ARD and IRD descriptors are set to **0**.
		An application can explicitly set the value of this field by calling the **SQLSetDescField()** function with the **SQL_DESC_COUNT** field specified. If the value stored in the **SQL_DESC_COUNT** field is explicitly

Table 13–2 Continued

Field Name	Data Type	Description
		decreased with this approach, all records with numbers greater than the new value are effectively removed. If the value is explicitly set to **0**, and the descriptor is an ARD descriptor, all data buffers except those associated with a bound bookmark column are released.
		The record count in the **SQL_DESC_COUNT** field of an ARD descriptor does not include a bound bookmark column. The only way to unbind a bound bookmark column is to store a NULL pointer in the corresponding **SQL_DESC_DATA_PTR** field.
SQL_DESC_ROWS_ PROCESSED_PTR	**SQLUINTEGER ***	In an IPD descriptor, this field contains a pointer to a buffer that contains the number of parameter value sets that have already been processed (including parameter value sets that caused an error to occur).
		In an IRD descriptor, this field contains a pointer to a buffer that contains the number of rows fetched by **SQLFetch()** or **SQLFetchScroll()**, or the number of rows affected (including rows that returned errors) by a bulk operation performed by **SQLBulkOperations()** or **SQLSetPos()**.
		If this field contains a NULL pointer, no value is returned.
		The value stored in this field is only valid if a call to **SQLExecute()**, **SQLExecDirect()**, **SQLParamData()** (IPD descriptor), **SQLFetch()**, or **SQLFetchScroll()** (IRD descriptor), returned **SQL_SUCCESS** or **SQL_SUCCESS_WITH_INFO**.
		If **SQL_SUCCESS** or **SQL_SUCCESS_WITH_INFO** was not returned, the contents of the buffer pointed to by this field are undefined, unless **SQL_NO_DATA** was returned, in which case the number **0** was also returned.
Parameter/Column Record Fields		
SQL_DESC_AUTO_ UNIQUE_VALUE	**SQLINTEGER**	For IRD descriptors, this field indicates whether a column in a result data is an auto-incrementing column. Valid values for this field are:
		SQL_TRUE: The column is an auto-incrementing column.
		SQL_FALSE: The column is not an auto-incrementing column.

Table 13–2 Continued

Field Name	Data Type	Description
SQL_DESC_BASE_ COLUMN_NAME	**SQLCHAR ***	For IRD descriptors, this field contains the name of the base column in the data source that corresponds to a column in a result data set. This field contains an empty string (" ") if a base column name does not exist (as is the case for columns that are based on expressions).
SQL_DESC_BASE_ TABLE_NAME	**SQLCHAR ***	For IRD descriptors, this field contains the name of the base table in the data source that corresponds to a column in a result data set. This field contains an empty string (" ") if a base table name does not exist or is not applicable.
SQL_DESC_CASE_ SENSITIVE	**SQLINTEGER**	For IPD and IRD descriptors, this field indicates whether a parameter or column is treated as case-sensitive for collations and comparisons. Valid values for this field are: **SQL_TRUE**: The parameter or column is treated as case-sensitive for collations and comparisons. **SQL_FALSE**: The column is not treated as case-sensitive for collations and comparisons, or the parameter or column does not contain a character value.
SQL_DESC_CATALOG_NAME	**SQLCHAR ***	For IRD descriptors, this field contains the catalog name for the base table in the data source that corresponds to a column in a result data set. This field contains an empty string (" ") if the data source does not support catalogs or if the catalog name cannot be determined. It is driver-dependant what this field contains if the column is associated with an expression or if the column is part of a view.
SQL_DESC_CONCISE_TYPE	**SQLSMALLINT**	This field specifies the concise data type for all data types, including datetime and interval data types, stored in the descriptor record (that is, that are stored in the **SQL_DESC_CONCISE_TYPE**, **SQL_DESC_TYPE**, and **SQL_DESC_DATETIME_ INTERVAL_CODE** fields). The values in the **SQL_DESC_CONCISE_TYPE**, **SQL_DESC_TYPE**, and **SQL_DESC_DATETIME_ INTERVAL_CODE** fields are interdependent—each time one field is set, the remaining fields must also be set. The **SQL_DESC_CONCISE_TYPE** field can be set by the **SQLBindParameter()**, **SQLBindCol()**, or **SQLSetDescField()** function. The **SQL_DESC_ TYPE** can be set by the **SQLSetDescField()** or **SQLSetDescRec()** function.

Table 13–2 Continued

Field Name	Data Type	Description
		If this field is set to a concise datetime or interval data type, the **SQL_DESC_TYPE** field is set to the corresponding verbose type (**SQL_DATETIME** or **SQL_INTERVAL**), and the **SQL_DESC_DATETIME_INTERVAL_CODE** field is set to the appropriate datetime or interval subcode.
		If this field is set to a concise data type other than an datatime or interval data type, the **SQL_DESC_TYPE** field is set to the same value, and the **SQL_DESC_DATETIME_INTERVAL_CODE** field is set to **0**.
SQL_DESC_DATA_PTR	**SQLPOINTER**	For APD and IPD descriptors, this field contains a pointer to an application variable that contains a parameter value.
		For ARD descriptors, this field contains a pointer to an application variable that is to receive the value of a column in a result data set. If a call to **SQLFetch()** or **SQLFetchScroll()** does not return **SQL_SUCCESS** or **SQL_SUCCESS_WITH_INFO**, the contents of the variable that is to receive the column value is undefined.
		Whenever this field is set for an APD, ARD, or IPD descriptor, the driver verifies that the **SQL_DESC_TYPE** field contains a valid ODBC or driver-specific data type, and that all other descriptor fields containing data type information are consistent. Therefore, this field should only be set in an IPD descriptor to prompt the driver to perform a consistency check.
		If an application sets the **SQL_DESC_DATA_PTR** field of an IPD descriptor and later retrieves the value of the **SQL_DESC_DATA_PTR** field, it may not receive the same value that it set.
		The column referenced by the **SQL_DESC_DATA_PTR** field of an ARD descriptor is unbound if this field is set to a NULL pointer (by calling the **SQLBindCol()**, **SQLSetDescField()** or **SQLSetDescRec()** function)—all other fields are not affected.
		This field is a deferred field: It is not used at the time it is set, but is used later by the driver when it needs to determine addresses for data buffers.

Table 13–2   Continued

Field Name	Data Type	Description
SQL_DESC_DATETIME_ INTERVAL_CODE	SQLSMALLINT	This field contains the subtype code for datetime and interval data types (both SQL and C data types).Valid values for this field are:
		SQL_CODE_DATE
		SQL_CODE_TIME
		SQL_CODE_TIMESTAMP
		SQL_CODE_DAY
		SQL_CODE_DAY_TO_HOUR
		SQL_CODE_DAY_TO_MINUTE
		SQL_CODE_DAY_TO_SECOND
		SQL_CODE_HOUR
		SQL_CODE_HOUR_TO_MINUTE
		SQL_CODE_HOUR_TO_SECOND
		SQL_CODE_MINUTE
		SQL_CODE_MINUTE_TO_SECOND
		SQL_CODE_MONTH
		SQL_CODE_SECOND
		SQL_CODE_YEAR
		SQL_CODE_YEAR_TO_MONTH
		The subcode consists of the data type name with **CODE** substituted for either **TYPE**, **C_TYPE** (for date-time data types), **INTERVAL** or **C_INTERVAL** (for interval data types).
		If the **SQL_DESC_TYPE** and **SQL_DESC_ CONCISE_TYPE** fields of an APD or ARD descriptor are set to **SQL_C_DEFAULT** and if the descriptor is not associated with an SQL statement handle, the contents of this field are undefined.
SQL_DESC_DATETIME_ INTERVAL_PRECISION	SQLINTEGER	This field contains the leading interval precision value for datetime and interval data types.
SQL_DESC_DISPLAY_SIZE	SQLINTEGER	For IRD descriptors, this field contains the maximum number of characters needed to display the data of a column in a result data set.
SQL_DESC_FIXED_ PREC_SCALE	SQLSMALLINT	For IPD and IRD descriptors, this field indicates whether a column in a result data set is an exact numeric column. Valid values for this field are:
		SQL_TRUE: The column is an exact numeric column and has a fixed precision and a non-zero scale.
		SQL_FALSE: The column is not an exact numeric column, therefore it does not have a fixed precision and scale.
SQL_DESC_INDICATOR_PTR	SQLINTEGER *	For APD and ARD descriptors, this field contains a pointer to an indicator variable.

Table 13–2 Continued

Field Name	Data Type	Description
		For APD descriptors, the indicator variable specified should be set to **SQL_NULL_DATA** if a dynamic parameter is set to NULL— if this field contains a NULL pointer, the application cannot use the descriptor record to specify NULL arguments.
		For ARD descriptors, the indicator variable specified contains **SQL_NULL_DATA** if the column in a result data set contains a NULL value—if this field contains a NULL pointer, the driver is prevented from returning information about whether the column is NULL and SQLSTATE **22**002 (Indicator variable required but not supplied) is returned by **SQLFetch()** or **SQLFetchScroll()** if the column is indeed NULL. If a call to **SQLFetch()** or **SQLFetchScroll()** does not return **SQL_SUCCESS** or **SQL_SUCCESS_WITH_INFO**, the contents of the indicator variable that this field references is undefined.
		The **SQL_DESC_INDICATOR_PTR** field determines whether the field pointed to by **SQL_DESC_OCTET_LENGTH_PTR** is set.
		If the data value for a column is NULL, the driver sets the indicator variable to **SQL_NULL_DATA** and the buffer pointed to by the **SQL_DESC_OCTET_LENGTH_PTR** field is not set. If the data value for a column is not NULL, the indicator variable this field references is set to **0**, (unless the same pointer is used in both the **SQL_DESC_INDICATOR_PTR** and **SQL_DESC_OCTET_LENGTH_PTR** fields) and the buffer pointed to by the **SQL_DESC_OCTET_LENGTH_PTR** is set to the length of the data.
		This field is a deferred field: It is not used at the time it is set, but is used later by the driver when it needs to indicate nullability (APD descriptors) or to determine nullability (ARD descriptors).
SQL_DESC_LABEL	**SQLCHAR ***	For IRD descriptors, this field contains the column label or title of a column in a result data set. If the column does not have a label, this field contains the column name. Otherwise, if the column is unlabeled and unnamed, this field contains an empty string (" ").
SQL_DESC_LENGTH	**SQLUINTEGER**	This field contains either the maximum character length for a fixed-length data type, or the actual character length of a character string (excluding the NULL-termination character) or a binary (variable-length) data type.

Table 13–2 Continued

Field Name	Data Type	Description
		For datetime and interval data types, this field contains the length, in characters, of the character string representation of the datetime or interval value. Note that this length is a count of characters, not a count of bytes.
		The value in this field may be different from the value for length as defined in ODBC 2.0.
SQL_DESC_LITERAL_ PREFIX	SQLCHAR *	For IRD descriptors, this field contains one or more characters the driver recognizes as a prefix for a literal representation of the data type. For example, a single quotation mark (') might be used for character data types, or '0x' might be used for binary data types. This field contains an empty string (" ") if a literal prefix is not applicable.
SQL_DESC_LITERAL_ SUFFIX	SQLCHAR *	For IRD descriptors, this field contains one or more characters the driver recognizes as a suffix for a literal representation of the data type. For example, a single quotation mark (') might be used for character data types. This field contains an empty string (" ") if a literal suffix is not applicable.
SQL_DESC_LOCAL_ TYPE_NAME	SQLCHAR *	For IPD and IRD descriptors, this field contains any localized (native language) name for the data type that may be different from the regular name of the data type. This field contains an empty string (" ") if no localized name has been defined.
		This field is provided for display purposes only.
SQL_DESC_NAME	SQLCHAR *	For IPD descriptors, this field contains either the name or an alias of a parameter. If the driver supports named parameters and is capable of describing parameters, the parameter name is returned in this field. If the driver does not support named parameters, this field is undefined.
		For IRD descriptors, this field contains the alias of a column in a result data set. If the column does not have an alias or if a column alias does not apply, this field contains the column name. If the column does not have an alias or name, the driver returns an empty string (" ") to this field.
		The driver sets the **SQL_DESC_UNNAMED** field to **SQL_NAMED** if it populates this field; it sets the **SQL_DESC_UNNAMED** field to **SQL_UNNAMED** if it returns an empty string (" ") to this field.

Table 13–2 Continued

Field Name	Data Type	Description
SQL_DESC_NULLABLE	**SQLSMALLINT**	For IRD descriptors, this field contains a value that indicates whether a column in a result data set can contain NULL values. Valid values for this field are: **SQL_NULLABLE**: The column can contain NULL values. **SQL_NO_NULLS**: The column can not contain NULL values. **SQL_NULLABLE_UNKNOWN**: Whether the column can contain NULL values is not known. This field pertains to a column in a result data set—not to the underlying base column. In IPD descriptors, this field is always set to **SQL_NULLABLE** (and cannot be set by an application) because dynamic parameters are always nullable.
SQL_DESC_NUM_PREC_ RADIX	**SQLINTEGER**	This field contains the radix value of the data type. For approximate numeric data types, this field contains the value **2** and the **SQL_DESC_PRECISION** field contains the number of bits allowed. For exact numeric data types, this field contains the value **10**, and the **SQL_DESC_PRECISION** field contains the number of decimal digits allowed. For numeric data types, this field can contain either **10** or **2**. For data types where radix is not applicable, this field will be set to **0**.
SQL_DESC_OCTET_LENGTH	**SQLINTEGER**	This field contains the length, in octets (bytes), of character string or binary data types. For fixed-length character types, this is the actual length in bytes. For variable-length character or binary types, this is the maximum length, in bytes. For APD and ARD descriptors, length values for character strings include the NULL-termination character. For IPD and IRD descriptors, length values for character strings do not include the NULL-termination character. This field is only defined for output or input/output parameters in APD descriptors.

Table 13–2 Continued

Field Name	Data Type	Description
SQL_DESC_OCTET_ LENGTH_PTR	SQLINTEGER *	For APD descriptors, this field contains a pointer to a variable that contains the total length, in bytes, of a dynamic argument. The value of the variable that this field references is ignored for all parameter values except character string and binary data values. If this field contains a NULL pointer, the driver assumes that character strings and binary values are NULL-terminated (binary data values should not be NULL-terminated, but should be given a length to avoid truncation); if the variable that this field references contains the value **SQL_NTS**, the dynamic parameter value must be NULL-terminated.

To indicate that a bound parameter is a *data-at-execution* parameter, an application must set this field to a variable that, at execution time, will contain the value **SQL_DATA_AT_EXEC** or the result of the **SQL_LEN_DATA_AT_EXEC()** macro. If there is more than one such field, the **SQL_DESC_DATA_PTR** field can be set to a value that uniquely identifies the parameter to help the application determine which parameter is being requested.

For ARD descriptors, this field contains a pointer to a variable that contains the total length, in bytes of a bound column value. If this field contains a NULL pointer, the driver does not return length information for the specified column in a result data set.

If a call to **SQLFetch()** or **SQLFetchScroll()** does not return **SQL_SUCCESS** or **SQL_SUCCESS_WITH_INFO**, the contents of the variable that this field references is undefined.

This field is a deferred field: It is not used at the time it is set, but is used later by the driver when it needs to determine addresses for data buffers. |
| SQL_DESC_PARAMETER_ TYPE | SQLSMALLINT | For IPD descriptors, this field indicates whether a parameter is an input, output, or input/output parameter. Valid values for this field are:

SQL_PARAM_INPUT:
The parameter is an input parameter. This is the default value for this field.

SQL_PARAM_OUTPUT:
The parameter is an output parameter.

SQL_PARAM_INPUT_OUTPUT:
The parameter is an input/output parameter. |

Table 13–2 Continued

Field Name	Data Type	Description
		For IPD descriptors, this field is set to **SQL_PARAM_ INPUT**, by default, if the IPD descriptor is not automatically populated by the driver (the **SQL_ATTR_ ENABLE_AUTO_IPD** statement attribute is **SQL_ FALSE**). An application should set this field in an IPD descriptor, for parameters that are not input parameters.
SQL_DESC_PRECISION	**SQLSMALLINT**	This field contains the maximum number of bytes needed to display the column data in character format.
		For exact data types, this field contains the number of digits in the value.
		For approximate numeric data types, this field contains the number of bits in the mantissa (binary precision).
		For **SQL_TYPE_TIME**, **SQL_TYPE_TIMESTAMP**, or **SQL_INTERVAL_SECOND** data types, this field contains the numbers of digits in the fractional seconds component of the value.
		For all other data types, this field is undefined.
		The value in this field may be different from the value for *precision* as defined in ODBC 2.0.
SQL_DESC_ROWER	**SQLSMALLINT**	For IPD and IRD descriptors, this field indicates whether a column is automatically modified by the DBMS when a row is updated. Valid values for this field are:
		SQL_TRUE: The column is a row versioning column.
		SQL_FALSE: The column is not a row versioning column.
		Setting this field is similar to calling **SQLSpecialColumns()** with the RowIdentifier parameter set to **SQL_ROWVER**.
SQL_DESC_SCALE	**SQLSMALLINT**	This field contains the scale defined for DECIMAL and NUMERIC data types.
		This field is undefined for all other data types.
		The value in this field may be different from the value for *scale* as defined in ODBC 2.0.
SQL_DESC_SCHEMA_NAME	**SQLCHAR ***	For IRD descriptors, this field contains the schema name for the base table in the data source that corresponds to a column in a result data set. This field contains an empty string if the data source does not support schemas or if the schema name cannot be determined. What this field contains if the column is associated with an expression or if the column is part of a view is driver dependent.

Table 13–2 *Continued*

Field Name	Data Type	Description
SQL_DESC_SEARCHABLE	**SQLSMALLINT**	For IRD descriptors, this field indicates how a column in a result data set can be used in an SQL **WHERE** clause. Valid values for this field are:
		SQL_SEARCHABLE: The column can be used with any comparison operator in a **WHERE** clause.
		SQL_PRED_CHAR: The column can only be used in a **WHERE** clause **LIKE** predicate. (ODBC 3.x)
		SQL_LIKE_ONLY: The column can only be used in a **WHERE** clause **LIKE** predicate. (ODBC 2.0)
		SQL_PRED_BASIC: The column can be used with all comparison operators in a **WHERE** clause except a **LIKE** predicate. (ODBC 3.x)
		SQL_ALL_EXCEPT_LIKE: The column can be used with all comparison operators in a **WHERE** clause except a **LIKE** predicate. (ODBC 2.0)
		SQL_PRED_NONE: The column cannot be used in a **WHERE** clause. (ODBC 3.x)
		SQL_UNSEARCHABLE: The column can not be used in a **WHERE** clause. (ODBC 2.0)
SQL_DESC_TABLE_NAME	**SQLCHAR ***	For IRD descriptors, this field contains the name of the base table in the data source that corresponds to a column in a result data set. This field contains an empty string (" ") if the table name cannot be determined. What this field contains if the column is associated with an expression or if the column is part of a view is driver dependent.
SQL_DESC_TYPE	**SQLSMALLINT**	This field specifies the concise SQL or C data type for all data types except datetime and interval data types. For datetime and interval data types, this field specifies the verbose data type, which is **SQL_DATETIME** or **SQL_INTERVAL**, respectively.
		The values in the **SQL_DESC_CONCISE_TYPE**, **SQL_DESC_TYPE**, and **SQL_DESC_DATETIME_INTERVAL_CODE** fields are interdependent—each time one field is set, the remaining fields must also be set. Thus, if **SQL_DESC_TYPE** is set to the verbose datetime or interval data type (**SQL_DATETIME** or **SQL_INTERVAL**), the **SQL_DESC_DATETIME_**

Table 13–2 Continued

Field Name	Data Type	Description
		INTERVAL_CODE field is set to the appropriate sub-code for the concise datatime or interval data type, and the **SQL_DESC_CONCISE TYPE** field is set to the corresponding concise data type.
		If **SQL_DESC_TYPE** is set to a concise data type other than an interval or datetime data type, the **SQL_DESC_CONCISE_TYPE** field is set to the same value, and the **SQL_DESC_DATETIME_INTERVAL_CODE** field is set to **0**.
		The **SQL_DESC_CONCISE_TYPE** field can be set by the **SQLBindParameter()**, **SQLBindCol()**, or **SQLSetDescField()** function. The **SQL_DESC_TYPE** can be set by the **SQLSetDescField()** or **SQLSetDescRec()** function.
SQL_DESC_TYPE_NAME	SQLCHAR *	For IPD and IRD descriptors, this field contains the data source-dependent data type name (for example, **CHAR**, **VARCHAR**, etc.). This field contains an empty string (" ") if the data type name is unknown.
SQL_DESC_UNNAMED	SQLSMALLINT	For an IPD descriptor, this field indicates whether a parameter has an alias or a name. In this case, valid values for this field are:
		SQL_NAMED: The **SQL_DESC_NAME** field contains a parameter alias or a parameter name.
		SQL_UNNAMED: The **SQL_DESC_NAME** field does not contain a parameter alias or a parameter name.
		For an IRD descriptor, this field indicates whether a column in a result data set has an alias or a name. In this case, valid values for this field are:
		SQL_NAMED: The **SQL_DESC_NAME** field contains a column alias, or a column name if a column alias does not apply.
		SQL_UNNAMED: The **SQL_DESC_NAME** field does not contain a column alias, or a column name.
		For both IPD and IRD descriptors, this field is set by the driver when the **SQL_DESC_NAME** field is set.
		An application can set the **SQL_DESC_UNNAMED** field of an IPD descriptor to **SQL_UNNAMED**, however SQLSTATE **HY**091 (Invalid descriptor field identifier) is returned if an application attempts to set the **SQL_DESC_UNNAMED** field to **SQL_NAMED**. The **SQL_DESC_UNNAMED** field of an IRD descriptor is read-only and cannot be set.

Table 13–2   Continued

Field Name	Data Type	Description
SQL_DESC_UNSIGNED	SQLSMALLINT	For IRD descriptors, this field indicates whether a column in a result data set's data type is signed or unsigned. Valid values for this field are:
		SQL_TRUE: The column's data type is unsigned or non-numeric.
		SQL_FALSE: The column's data type is signed.
SQL_DESC_UPDATABLE	SQLSMALLINT	For IRD descriptors, this field indicates whether a column in a result data set can be updated. Valid values for this field are:
		SQL_ATTR_READ_ONLY: The column can only be read (read-only).
		SQL_ATTR_WRITE: The column can be updated (read/write).
		SQL_ATTR_READWRITE_UNKNOWN: Whether the column can be updated is not known.
		This field describes the ability of a result data set column to be updated, not the ability of a base table column to be updated. The ability of the column to be updated in the base table on which a result data set column is based may be different from the value of this field.
		Whether a column in a result data set is updatable is based on the data type, user privileges, and the definition of the result data set itself.

■ For performance reasons, an application should not call this function for an IRD descriptor until after the SQL statement associated with the descriptor has been executed.

■ The **SQLGetStmtAttr()** function can be called to obtain the current value of any descriptor header record field that has a corresponding SQL statement attribute.

■ The **SQLColAttribute()**, **SQLDescribeCol()**, and **SQLDescribeParam()** functions can be called to obtain the current value of descriptor parameter/column or bookmark record fields.

■ If the value specified in the *RecNumber* parameter is greater than the total number of descriptor records available, **SQL_NO_DATA** is returned.

■ If this function is called with an IRD handle specified in the *DescriptorHandle* parameter, and if the SQL statement associated with the IRD is in the "Prepared" or "Executed" state but there is no open cursor associated with it, **SQL_NO_DATA** is returned.

■ When this function is used to retrieve the value of a descriptor record field that is undefined for a particular descriptor type, **SQL_SUCCESS** is returned, but the actual value returned for the field is undefined.

■ When this function is used to retrieve the value of a descriptor record field that is defined for a particular descriptor type, but has no default value and has not been set by some other ODBC API function, **SQL_SUCCESS** is returned but the actual value returned for the field is undefined.

■ The current values of descriptor record fields describing the name, data type, and storage of parameter or column data can be retrieved in a single call with the **SQLGetDescRec()** function.

■ If the value returned for the descriptor field specified in the *Identifier* parameter is a Unicode string, the *ValueMaxSize* parameter must contain an even number.

Prerequisites   A descriptor handle must be allocated before this function is called.

Restrictions   There are no restrictions associated with this function call.

See Also   SQLSetDescField(), SQLGetDescRec(), SQLSetDescRec(), SQLCopyDesc()

Example   The following Visual C++ program illustrates how to use the SQLGetDescField() function to obtain specific information from a descriptor record.

```
/*-------------------------------------------------------------*/
/* NAME:     CH13EX3.CPP                                       */
/* PURPOSE: Illustrate How To Use The Following ODBC API Function */
/*          In A C++ Program:                                  */
/*                                                             */
/*              SQLGetDescField()                              */
/*                                                             */
/* OTHER ODBC APIs SHOWN:                                      */
/*          SQLAllocHandle()          SQLSetEnvAttr()          */
/*          SQLDriverConnect()        SQLExecDirect()          */
/*          SQLGetStmtAttr()          SQLDisconnect()          */
/*          SQLFreeHandle()                                    */
/*                                                             */
/*-------------------------------------------------------------*/
```

```
// Include The Appropriate Header Files
#include <windows.h>
#include <sql.h>
#include <sqlext.h>
#include <iostream.h>

// Define The ODBC_Class Class
class ODBC_Class
{
    // Attributes
    public:
        SQLHANDLE   EnvHandle;
        SQLHANDLE   ConHandle;
        SQLHANDLE   DescHandle;
        SQLHANDLE   StmtHandle;
        SQLRETURN   rc;

    // Operations
    public:
        ODBC_Class();                           // Constructor
        ~ODBC_Class();                          // Destructor
        SQLRETURN GetDescriptorInfo();
};

// Define The Class Constructor
ODBC_Class::ODBC_Class()
{
    // Initialize The Return Code Variable
    rc = SQL_SUCCESS;

    // Allocate An Environment Handle
    rc = SQLAllocHandle(SQL_HANDLE_ENV, SQL_NULL_HANDLE, &EnvHandle);

    // Set The ODBC Application Version To 3.x
    if (rc == SQL_SUCCESS)
        rc = SQLSetEnvAttr(EnvHandle, SQL_ATTR_ODBC_VERSION,
                (SQLPOINTER) SQL_OV_ODBC3, SQL_IS_UINTEGER);

    // Allocate A Connection Handle
    if (rc == SQL_SUCCESS)
        rc = SQLAllocHandle(SQL_HANDLE_DBC, EnvHandle, &ConHandle);
}

// Define The Class Destructor
ODBC_Class::~ODBC_Class()
{
    // Free The Connection Handle
    if (ConHandle != NULL)
        SQLFreeHandle(SQL_HANDLE_DBC, ConHandle);

    // Free The Environment Handle
    if (EnvHandle != NULL)
        SQLFreeHandle(SQL_HANDLE_ENV, EnvHandle);
}
```

```
// Define The GetDescriptorInfo() Member Function
SQLRETURN ODBC_Class::GetDescriptorInfo(void)
{
    // Declare The Local Memory Variables
    SQLINTEGER    ValueLen;
    SQLCHAR       ColName[50];
    SQLINTEGER    ColNameLen;
    SQLSMALLINT   DisplaySize;

    // Retrieve A Handle To The Implementation Row Descriptor (IRD)
    // Associated With The SQL Statement
    rc = SQLGetStmtAttr(StmtHandle, SQL_ATTR_IMP_ROW_DESC,
            (SQLPOINTER) &DescHandle, 0, &ValueLen);

    // Obtain And Display Information About The First Column In The
    // Result Data Set
    rc = SQLGetDescField(DescHandle, 1, SQL_DESC_BASE_COLUMN_NAME,
            ColName, sizeof(ColName), &ColNameLen);

    rc = SQLGetDescField(DescHandle, 1, SQL_DESC_DISPLAY_SIZE,
            &DisplaySize, 0, NULL);

    if (rc == SQL_SUCCESS)
    {
        cout << "Column 1 : " << endl << endl;
        cout << "Base Column Name : " << ColName << endl;
        cout << "Display Size     : " << DisplaySize << endl;
    }

    // Return The ODBC API Return Code To The Calling Function
    return(rc);
}

/*─────────────────────────────────────────────────────────────*/
/* The Main Function                                           */
/*─────────────────────────────────────────────────────────────*/
int main()
{
    // Declare The Local Memory Variables
    SQLRETURN  rc = SQL_SUCCESS;
    SQLCHAR    ConnectIn[40];
    SQLCHAR    SQLStmt[255];

    // Create An Instance Of The ODBC_Class Class
    ODBC_Class  Example;

    // Build A Connection String
    strcpy((char *) ConnectIn,
        "DSN=SQLServer;UID=userid;PWD=password;");

    // Connect To The SQL Server Sample Database
    if (Example.ConHandle != NULL)
    {
```

```
rc = SQLDriverConnect(Example.ConHandle, NULL, ConnectIn,
        SQL_NTS, NULL, 0, NULL, SQL_DRIVER_NOPROMPT);

// Allocate An SQL Statement Handle
rc = SQLAllocHandle(SQL_HANDLE_STMT, Example.ConHandle,
        &Example.StmtHandle);
if (rc == SQL_SUCCESS)
{
    // Define A SELECT SQL Statement
    strcpy((char *) SQLStmt, "SELECT EMPID, FIRSTNAME ");
    strcat((char *) SQLStmt, "FROM EMPLOYEES");

    // Prepare And Execute The SQL Statement
    rc = SQLExecDirect(Example.StmtHandle, SQLStmt, SQL_NTS);

    // Display Information About The Implementation Row
    // Descriptor (IRD) That Is Associated With The SQL
    // Statement
    if (rc == SQL_SUCCESS)
        Example.GetDescriptorInfo();

    // Free The SQL Statement Handle
    if (Example.StmtHandle != NULL)
        SQLFreeHandle(SQL_HANDLE_STMT, Example.StmtHandle);
}

// Disconnect From The SQL Server Sample Database
rc = SQLDisconnect(Example.ConHandle);
}

// Return To The Operating System
return(rc);
}
```

SQLSetDescField

COMPATABILITY					
X/OPEN 95 CLI	ISO/IEC 92 CLI	ODBC 1.0	ODBC 2.0	ODBC 3.0	ODBC 3.5
✓	✓	☐	☐	✓	✓

API CONFORMANCE LEVEL   **CORE**

Purpose

The **SQLSetDescField()** function is used to modify the value of a specified descriptor record field.

Syntax

```
SQLRETURN    SQLSetDescField    (SQLHDESC      DescriptorHandle,
                                 SQLSMALLINT   RecNumber,
                                 SQLSMALLINT   Identifier,
                                 SQLPOINTER    Value,
                                 SQLINTEGER    ValueSize);
```

Parameters

DescriptorHandle   A descriptor handle that refers to a previously allocated descriptor information storage buffer (data structure).

RecNumber   Specifies the descriptor record that this function is to modify. If any field of the descriptor header record is specified in the *Identifier* parameter, this parameter is ignored. Otherwise, this parameter should contain a number greater than or equal to 0 (Descriptor records are numbered, starting at 0, with record number 0 being the bookmark record).

Identifier   The field of the descriptor header record or descriptor parameter/column record whose value is to be modified. This parameter must be set to one of the following values:

Header Record Fields

▨ SQL_DESC_ALLOC_TYPE

▨ SQL_DESC_ARRAY_SIZE

▨ SQL_DESC_ARRAY_STATUS_PTR

▨ SQL_DESC_BIND_OFFSET_PTR

▨ SQL_DESC_BIND_TYPE

▨ SQL_DESC_COUNT

▨ SQL_DESC_ROWS_PROCESSED_PTR

Parameter/Column Record Fields

▨ SQL_DESC_AUTO_UNIQUE_VALUE

▨ SQL_DESC_BASE_COLUMN_NAME

▨ SQL_DESC_BASE_TABLE_NAME

▨ SQL_DESC_CASE_SENSITIVE

▨ SQL_DESC_CATALOG_NAME

▨ SQL_DESC_CONCISE_TYPE

- **SQL_DESC_DATA_PTR**
- **SQL_DESC_DATETIME_INTERVAL_CODE**
- **SQL_DESC_DATETIME_INTERVAL_PRECISION**
- **SQL_DESC_DISPLAY_SIZE**
- **SQL_DESC_FIXED_PREC_SCALE**
- **SQL_DESC_INDICATOR_PTR**
- **SQL_DESC_LABEL**
- **SQL_DESC_LENGTH**
- **SQL_DESC_LITERAL_PREFIX**
- **SQL_DESC_LITERAL_SUFFIX**
- **SQL_DESC_LOCAL_TYPE_NAME**
- **SQL_DESC_NAME**
- **SQL_DESC_NULLABLE**
- **SQL_DESC_NUM_PREC_RADIX**
- **SQL_DESC_OCTET_LENGTH**
- **SQL_DESC_OCTET_LENGTH_PTR**
- **SQL_DESC_PARAMETER_TYPE**
- **SQL_DESC_PRECISION**
- **SQL_DESC_ROWVER**
- **SQL_DESC_SCALE**
- **SQL_DESC_SCHEMA_NAME**
- **SQL_DESC_SEARCHABLE**
- **SQL_DESC_TABLE_NAME**
- **SQL_DESC_TYPE**
- **SQL_DESC_TYPE_NAME**
- **SQL_DESC_UNNAMED**
- **SQL_DESC_UNSIGNED**
- **SQL_DESC_UPDATABLE**

Value	A pointer to a location in memory where the new value for the specified descriptor record field is stored.
ValueSize	The size of the new value to be stored in the specified descriptor record field (*Value*). If an

ODBC-defined descriptor record field is to be modified, and if the field value is a 32-bit integer value, this parameter is ignored. If a driver-defined descriptor record field value is to be modified, this parameter must be set as follows:

- If the new value of the specified descriptor record field is a character string, this parameter should be set to the actual length of the string or to **SQL_NTS**.
- If the new value of the specified descriptor record field is a binary string, this parameter should be set to the result of the **SQL_LEN_BINARY_ATTR**(*length*) macro. Usually, this macro places a negative value in this parameter.
- If the new value of the specified descriptor record field is anything other than a character string or binary string, this parameter should be set to **SQL_IS_POINTER**.
- If the new value of the specified descriptor record field is a fixed-length data type, this parameter should be set to **SQL_IS_INTEGER** or **SQL_IS_UINTEGER**, as appropriate.

Description

The **SQLSetDescField()** function is used to modify the value of a specified descriptor record field. Refer to the **SQLGetDescField()** function for a complete description of each field found in a descriptor record.

When descriptor record fields are set by an application, a specific sequence must be followed:

1. The **SQL_DESC_TYPE**, **SQL_DESC_CONCISE_TYPE**, or the **SQL_DESC_DATETIME_INTERVAL_CODE** field must be set.

2. After one of these fields has been set, the appropriate data type must be set—the driver sets all data type attribute fields to the appropriate default values for the data type specified. Automatic defaulting of type attribute fields ensures that the descriptor is always ready for use once a data type has been specified. Later, if an application explicitly sets a data type attribute, it is overriding the default attribute provided by the driver.

3. The `SQL_DESC_DATA_PTR` field must be set. This prompts a consistency check of all descriptor record fields. If the application changes the data type or attributes after setting the `SQL_DESC_DATA_PTR` field, the driver sets `SQL_DESC_DATA_PTR` to a NULL pointer, and the record is unbound. This forces the application to complete the proper steps in sequence, before the descriptor record is made usable.

When a descriptor record is allocated, its fields can be initialized with a specific default value, initialized without a default value, or are undefined, depending on the descriptor type the descriptor record is allocated for. Table 13–3 shows how each descriptor record field for each descriptor type (APD, IPD, ARD, and IRD) can be initialized. This table also indicates whether a field is read/write (R/W) or read-only (R).

Table 13–3 Descriptor Record Field Initialization

Field Name	Initialized With . . .	Field Characteristics
Header Record Fields		
`SQL_DESC_ALLOC_TYPE`	APD: `SQL_DESC_ALLOC_AUTO` (implicitly allocated descriptor) or `SQL_DESC_ALLOC_USER` (explicitly allocated descriptor)	APD: Read-Only
	IPD: `SQL_DESC_ALLOC_AUTO`	IPD: Read-Only
	ARD: `SQL_DESC_ALLOC_AUTO` (implicitly allocated descriptor) or `SQL_DESC_ALLOC_USER` (explicitly allocated descriptor)	ARD: Read-Only
	IRD: `SQL_DESC_ALLOC_AUTO`	IRD: Read-Only
`SQL_DESC_ARRAY_SIZE`	APD: Undefined unless the IPD is automatically populated by the driver	APD: Read/Write
	IPD: Unused	IPD: Unused
	ARD: Undefined unless the IPD is automatically populated by the driver	ARD: Read/Write
	IRD: Unused	IRD: Unused
`SQL_DESC_ARRAY_STATUS_PTR`	APD: A NULL pointer	APD: Read/Write

Table 13–3　*Continued*

Field Name	Initialized With . . .	Field Characteristics
	IPD: A NULL pointer	IPD: Read/Write
	ARD: A NULL pointer	ARD: Read/Write
	IRD: A NULL pointer	IRD: Read/Write
SQL_DESC_BIND_OFFSET_PTR	APD: A NULL pointer	APD: Read/Write
	IPD: Unused	IPD: Unused
	ARD: A NULL pointer	ARD: Read/Write
	IRD: Unused	IRD: Unused
SQL_DESC_BIND_TYPE	APD: **SQL_BIND_BY_COLUMN**	APD: Read/Write
	IPD: Unused	IPD: Unused
	ARD: **SQL_BIND_BY_COLUMN**	ARD: Read/Write
	IRD: Unused	IRD: Unused
SQL_DESC_COUNT	APD: 0	APD: Read/Write
	IPD: 0	IPD: Read/Write
	ARD: 0	ARD: Read/Write
	IRD: A driver-supplied default value	IRD: Read-Only
SQL_DESC_ROWS_ PROCESSED_PTR	APD: Unused	APD: Unused
	IPD: A NULL pointer	IPD: Read/Write
	ARD: Unused	ARD: Unused
	IRD: A NULL pointer	IRD: Read/Write
Parameter/Column Record Fields		
SQL_DESC_AUTO_UNIQUE_ VALUE	APD: Unused	APD: Unused
	IPD: Unused	IPD: Unused
	ARD: Unused	ARD: Unused
	IRD: A driver-supplied default value	IRD: Read-Only
SQL_DESC_BASE_COLUMN_NAME	APD: Unused	APD: Unused
	IPD: Unused	IPD: Unused
	ARD: Unused	ARD: Unused

Table 13–3 Continued

Field Name	Initialized With ...	Field Characteristics
	IRD: A driver-supplied default value	IRD: Read-Only
SQL_DESC_BASE_TABLE_NAME	APD: Unused	APD: Unused
	IPD: Unused	IPD: Unused
	ARD: Unused	ARD: Unused
	IRD: A driver-supplied default value	IRD: Read-Only
SQL_DESC_CASE_SENSITIVE	APD: Unused	APD: Unused
	IPD: Undefined unless the IPD is automatically populated by the driver	IPD: Read-Only
	ARD: Unused	ARD: Unused
	IRD: A driver-supplied default value	IRD: Read-Only
SQL_DESC_CATALOG_NAME	APD: Unused	APD: Unused
	IPD: Unused	IPD: Unused
	ARD: Unused	ARD: Unused
	IRD: A driver-supplied default value	IRD: Read-Only
SQL_DESC_CONCISE_TYPE	APD: **SQL_C_DEFAULT**	APD: Read/Write
	IPD: Not initialized	IPD: Read/Write
	ARD: **SQL_C_DEFAULT**	ARD: Read/Write
	IRD: A driver-supplied default value	IRD: Read-Only
SQL_DESC_DATA_PTR	APD: A NULL pointer	APD: Read/Write
	IPD: Unused [2]	IPD: Unused
	ARD: A NULL pointer	ARD: Read/Write
	IRD: Unused	IRD: Unused
SQL_DESC_DATETIME_ INTERVAL_CODE	APD: No default value	APD: Read/Write
	IPD: No default value	IPD: Read/Write
	ARD: No default value	ARD: Read/Write
	IRD: A driver-supplied default value	IRD: Read-Only
SQL_DESC_DATETIME_ INTERVAL_PRECISION	APD: No default value	APD: Read/Write

Table 13–3 *Continued*

Field Name	Initialized With . . .	Field Characteristics
	IPD: No default value	IPD: Read/Write
	ARD: No default value	ARD: Read/Write
	IRD: A driver-supplied default value	IRD: Read-Only
SQL_DESC_DISPLAY_SIZE	APD: Unused	APD: Unused
	IPD: Unused	IPD: Unused
	ARD: Unused	ARD: Unused
	IRD: A driver-supplied default value	IRD: Read-Only
SQL_DESC_FIXED_PREC_SCALE	APD: Unused	APD: Unused
	IPD: D[1]	IPD: Read-Only
	ARD: Unused	ARD: Unused
	IRD: A driver-supplied default value	IRD: Read-Only
SQL_DESC_INDICATOR_PTR	APD: A NULL pointer	APD: Read/Write
	IPD: Unused	IPD: Unused
	ARD: A NULL pointer	ARD: Read/Write
	IRD: Unused	IRD: Unused
SQL_DESC_LABEL	APD: Unused	APD: Unused
	IPD: Unused	IPD: Unused
	ARD: Unused	ARD: Unused
	IRD: A driver-supplied default value	IRD: Read-Only
SQL_DESC_LENGTH	APD: No default value	APD: Read/Write
	IPD: No default value	IPD: Read/Write
	ARD: No default value	ARD: Read/Write
	IRD: A driver-supplied default value	IRD: Read-Only
SQL_DESC_LITERAL_PREFIX	APD: Unused	APD: Unused
	IPD: Unused	IPD: Unused
	ARD: Unused	ARD: Unused
	IRD: A driver-supplied default value	IRD: Read-Only
SQL_DESC_LITERAL_SUFFIX	APD: Unused	APD: Unused

Table 13–3 Continued

Field Name	Initialized With . . .	Field Characteristics
	IPD: Unused	IPD: Unused
	ARD: Unused	ARD: Unused
	IRD: A driver-supplied default value	IRD: Read-Only
SQL_DESC_LOCAL_TYPE_NAME	APD: Unused	APD: Unused
	IPD: Default value[1]	IPD: Read-Only
	ARD: Unused	ARD: Unused
	IRD: A driver-supplied default value	IRD: Read-Only
SQL_DESC_NAME	APD: No default value	APD: Unused
	IPD: No default value	IPD: Read/Write
	ARD: No default value	ARD: Unused
	IRD: A driver-supplied default value	IRD: Read-Only
SQL_DESC_NULLABLE	APD: No default value	APD: Unused
	IPD: No default value	IPD: Read-Only
	ARD: No default value	ARD: Unused
	IRD: A driver-supplied default value	IRD: Read-Only
SQL_DESC_NUM_PREC_RADIX	APD: No default value	APD: Read/Write
	IPD: No default value	IPD: Read/Write
	ARD: No default value	ARD: Read/Write
	IRD: A driver-supplied default value	IRD: Read-Only
SQL_DESC_OCTET_LENGTH	APD: No default value	APD: Read/Write
	IPD: No default value	IPD: Read/Write
	ARD: No default value	ARD: Read/Write
	IRD: A driver-supplied default value	IRD: Read-Only
SQL_DESC_OCTET_LENGTH_PTR	APD: A NULL pointer	APD: Read/Write
	IPD: Unused	IPD: Unused
	ARD: A NULL pointer	ARD: Read/Write
	IRD: Unused	IRD: Unused
SQL_DESC_PARAMETER_TYPE	APD: Unused	APD: Unused

Table 13–3 Continued

Field Name	Initialized With . . .	Field Characteristics
	IPD: A driver-supplied default value **=SQL_PARAM_INPUT**	IPD: Read/Write
	ARD: Unused	ARD: Unused
	IRD: Unused	IRD: Unused
SQL_DESC_PRECISION	APD: No default value	APD: Read/Write
	IPD: No default value	IPD: Read/Write
	ARD: No default value	ARD: Read/Write
	IRD: A driver-supplied default value	IRD: Read-Only
SQL_DESC_ROWVER	APD: Unused	APD: Unused
	IPD: No default value	IPD: Read-Only
	ARD: Unused	ARD: Unused
	IRD: No default value	IRD: Read-Only
SQL_DESC_SCALE	ARD: No default value	ARD: Read/Write
	APD: No default value	APD: Read/Write
	IRD: A driver-supplied default value	IRD: Read-Only
	IPD: Not initialized	IPD: Read/Write
SQL_DESC_SCHEMA_NAME	APD: Unused	APD: Unused
	IPD: Unused	IPD: Unused
	ARD: Unused	ARD: Unused
	IRD: A driver-supplied default value	IRD: Read-Only
SQL_DESC_SEARCHABLE	APD: Unused	APD: Unused
	IPD: Unused	IPD: Unused
	ARD: Unused	ARD: Unused
	IRD: A driver-supplied default value	IRD: Read-Only
SQL_DESC_TABLE_NAME	APD: Unused	APD: Unused
	IPD: Unused	IPD: Unused
	ARD: Unused	ARD: Unused
	IRD: A driver-supplied default value	IRD: Read-Only
SQL_DESC_TYPE	APD: **SQL_C_DEFAULT**	APD: Read/Write

Table 13–3 Continued

Field Name	Initialized With . . .	Field Characteristics
	IPD: No default value	IPD: Read/Write
	ARD: **SQL_C_DEFAULT**	ARD: Read/Write
	IRD: A driver-supplied default value	IRD: Read-Only
SQL_DESC_TYPE_NAME	APD: Unused	APD: Unused
	IPD: Default value[1]	IPD: Read-Only
	ARD: Unused	ARD: Unused
	IRD: A driver-supplied default value	IRD: Read-Only
SQL_DESC_UNNAMED	APD: No default value	APD: Unused
	IPD: No default value	IPD: Read/Write
	ARD: No default value	ARD: Unused
	IRD: A driver-supplied default value	IRD: Read-Only
SQL_DESC_UNSIGNED	APD: Unused	APD: Unused
	IPD: A driver-s[1]	IPD: Read-Only
	ARD: Unused	ARD: Unused
	IRD: A driver-supplied default value	IRD: Read-Only
SQL_DESC_UPDATABLE	APD: Unused	APD: Unused
	IPD: Unused	IPD: Unused
	ARD: Unused	ARD: Unused
	IRD: A driver-supplied default value	IRD: Read-Only

[1]These fields are defined only when the IPD is automatically populated by the driver. If not, they are undefined. If an application attempts to set these fields, SQLSTATE **HY**091 (Invalid descriptor field identifier) is returned.

[2]The **SQL_DESC_DATA_PTR** field in the IPD can be set to force a consistency check. In a subsequent call to **SQLGetDescField()** or **SQLGetDescRec()**, the driver is not required to return the value that **SQL_DESC_DATA_PTR** was set to.

Return Codes SQL_SUCCESS, SQL_SUCCESS_WITH_INFO, SQL_INVALID_HANDLE, or SQL_ERROR

SQLSTATEs If this function returns **SQL_SUCCESS_WITH_INFO** or **SQL_ERROR**, one of the following SQLSTATE values may be obtained by calling the **SQLGetDiagRec()** function:

01000, **01**S02, **07**009*, **08**S01, **22**001, **HY**000, **HY**001, **HY**010*, **HY**013, **HY**016, **HY**021, **HY**090*, **HY**091, **HY**092, **HY**105*, **HYT**01, or **IM**001*

* Returned by the ODBC Driver Manager.

Unless noted otherwise, each of these SQLSTATE values is returned by the data source driver. Refer to Appendix B for detailed information about each SQLSTATE value that can be returned by the ODBC Driver Manager or by a data source driver.

Comments

■ An application can determine the total number of parameter/column descriptor records available in a descriptor by calling the **SQLGetDescField()** function to retrieve the value of the **SQL_DESC_COUNT** field.

■ If a descriptor header record field is specified in the *Identifier* parameter, the *RecNumber* parameter is ignored.

■ If the value specified in the *Value* parameter is a 4-byte value, either all four of the bytes are used, or just two of the bytes are used, depending on the value specified in the *Identifier* parameter.

■ This function can be used to change the binding of a parameter or column by adding an offset to the buffer pointers stored in the **SQL_DESC_DATA_PTR, SQL_DESC_INDICATOR_PTR,** or **SQL_DESC_OCTET_LENGTH_PTR** descriptor record fields. Adding offsets to these pointer values changes the binding buffers without having to calling the **SQLBindParameter()** or **SQLBindCol()** functions, which in turn allows an application to change the **SQL_DESC_DATA_PTR** field without having to change other descriptor record fields (for example, **SQL_DESC_DATA_TYPE**).

■ The **SQLSetStmtAttr()** function can be called to change the value of any descriptor header record field that has a corresponding SQL statement attribute.

■ The **SQLBindParameter(), SQLBindCol(),** and **SQLSetDescRec()** function can be used to make a complete specification for the binding of a parameter or column by setting a specific group of descriptor record fields with a single function call.

■ When this function fails, **SQL_ERROR** is returned, and the contents of the field of the descriptor record identified by the *RecNumber* and *Identifier* parameters are undefined.

■ While it is not mandatory, it is strongly recommended that an application set the **SQL_ATTR_USE_BOOKMARKS** statement attribute before this function is used to set the values of bookmark descriptor record fields (that is, before this function is called with **0** specified in the *RecNumber* parameter).

- The fields of an IRD descriptor will contain default values only after the SQL statement associated with the descriptor has been prepared or executed and the IRD has been populated, not when the statement handle or descriptor has been allocated. Any attempt to gain access to an unpopulated field of an IRD descriptor will cause **SQL_ERROR** to be returned.

- Some descriptor fields are defined for one or more, but not all, of the descriptor types (ARD, IRD, APD, or IPD). When a field is undefined for a descriptor type, it is not needed by any of the functions that use that descriptor.

- The descriptor record fields that can be accessed by the **SQLGetDescField()** function cannot necessarily be set by this function. Refer to Table 13–3 to determine which fields are read/write fields and which fields are read-only.

Prerequisites A descriptor handle must be allocated before this function is called.

Restrictions There are no restrictions associated with this function call.

See Also SQLGetDescField(), SQLGetDescRec(), SQLSetDescRec(), SQLCopyDesc()

Example The following Visual C++ program illustrates how to use the SQLSetDescField() function to specify specific information for a descriptor record.

```
/*-------------------------------------------------------------*/
/* NAME:     CH13EX4.CPP                                        */
/* PURPOSE: Illustrate How To Use The Following ODBC API Function */
/*          In A C++ Program:                                   */
/*                                                              */
/*               SQLSetDescField()                              */
/*                                                              */
/* OTHER ODBC APIs SHOWN:                                       */
/*               SQLAllocHandle()          SQLSetEnvAttr()      */
/*               SQLDriverConnect()        SQLSetStmtAttr()     */
/*               SQLPrepare()              SQLGetDescField()    */
/*               SQLExecute()              SQLDisconnect()      */
/*               SQLFreeHandle()                                */
/*                                                              */
/*-------------------------------------------------------------*/

// Include The Appropriate Header Files
#include <windows.h>
#include <sql.h>
#include <sqlext.h>
#include <iostream.h>
```

```
// Define The ODBC_Class Class
class ODBC_Class
{
    // Attributes
    public:
        SQLHANDLE    EnvHandle;
        SQLHANDLE    ConHandle;
        SQLHANDLE    DescHandle;
        SQLHANDLE    StmtHandle;
        SQLRETURN    rc;

    // Operations
    public:
        ODBC_Class();                                 // Constructor
        ~ODBC_Class();                                // Destructor
        SQLRETURN GetDescriptorInfo();
        SQLRETURN ShowResults();
};

// Define The Class Constructor
ODBC_Class::ODBC_Class()
{
    // Initialize The Return Code Variable
    rc = SQL_SUCCESS;

    // Allocate An Environment Handle
    rc = SQLAllocHandle(SQL_HANDLE_ENV, SQL_NULL_HANDLE, &EnvHandle);

    // Set The ODBC Application Version To 3.x
    if (rc == SQL_SUCCESS)
        rc = SQLSetEnvAttr(EnvHandle, SQL_ATTR_ODBC_VERSION,
                (SQLPOINTER) SQL_OV_ODBC3, SQL_IS_UINTEGER);

    // Allocate A Connection Handle
    if (rc == SQL_SUCCESS)
        rc = SQLAllocHandle(SQL_HANDLE_DBC, EnvHandle, &ConHandle);
}

// Define The Class Destructor
ODBC_Class::~ODBC_Class()
{
    // Free The Connection Handle
    if (ConHandle != NULL)
        SQLFreeHandle(SQL_HANDLE_DBC, ConHandle);

    // Free The Environment Handle
    if (EnvHandle != NULL)
        SQLFreeHandle(SQL_HANDLE_ENV, EnvHandle);
}

// Define The GetDescriptorInfo() Member Function
SQLRETURN ODBC_Class::GetDescriptorInfo(void)
{
    // Declare The Local Memory Variables
    SQLUINTEGER   Length;
```

```
        // Obtain And Display Information About The First Column In The
        // Result Data Set
        rc = SQLGetDescField(DescHandle, 2, SQL_DESC_LENGTH,
                (SQLPOINTER) &Length, SQL_IS_POINTER, NULL);

        if (rc == SQL_SUCCESS)
        {
            cout << "Column 2 : " << endl << endl;
            cout << "Length : " << Length << endl;
        }

        // Return The ODBC API Return Code To The Calling Function
        return(rc);
}

/*————————————————————————————————————————————————————————*/
/* The Main Function                                        */
/*————————————————————————————————————————————————————————*/
int main()
{
    // Declare The Local Memory Variables
    SQLRETURN       rc = SQL_SUCCESS;
    SQLCHAR         ConnectIn[40];
    SQLCHAR         SQLStmt[255];

    // Create An Instance Of The ODBC_Class Class
    ODBC_Class   Example;

    // Build A Connection String
    strcpy((char *) ConnectIn,
        "DSN=SQLServer;UID=userid;PWD=password;");

    // Connect To The SQL Server Sample Database
    if (Example.ConHandle != NULL)
    {
        rc = SQLDriverConnect(Example.ConHandle, NULL, ConnectIn,
                SQL_NTS, NULL, 0, NULL, SQL_DRIVER_NOPROMPT);

        // Allocate An SQL Statement Handle
        rc = SQLAllocHandle(SQL_HANDLE_STMT, Example.ConHandle,
                &Example.StmtHandle);
        if (rc == SQL_SUCCESS)
        {
            // Define A SELECT SQL Statement
            strcpy((char *) SQLStmt, "SELECT EMPID, FIRSTNAME ");
            strcat((char *) SQLStmt, "FROM EMPLOYEES");

            // Explicitly Allocate A Descriptor Handle
            rc = SQLAllocHandle(SQL_HANDLE_DESC, Example.ConHandle,
                    &Example.DescHandle);

            // Assign The Descriptor Handle To The Statement Handle
            rc = SQLSetStmtAttr(Example.StmtHandle,
```

```
                                              SQL_ATTR_APP_ROW_DESC, (SQLPOINTER)
                      Example.DescHandle, 0);

        // Prepare The SQL Statement
        rc = SQLPrepare(Example.StmtHandle, SQLStmt, SQL_NTS);

        // Modify The Information Stored In The Application Row
        // Descriptor (Which Was Populated When The SQL Statement
        // Was Prepared)
        rc = SQLSetDescField(Example.DescHandle, 2,
                   SQL_DESC_LENGTH, (SQLPOINTER) 20,
                   SQL_IS_UINTEGER);

        // Display The Modified Descriptor Information
        if (rc == SQL_SUCCESS)
           Example.GetDescriptorInfo();

        // Execute The SQL Statement
        rc = SQLExecute(Example.StmtHandle);

        // Free The Descriptor Handle
        if (Example.DescHandle != NULL)
           SQLFreeHandle(SQL_HANDLE_DESC, Example.DescHandle);

        // Free The SQL Statement Handle
        if (Example.StmtHandle != NULL)
           SQLFreeHandle(SQL_HANDLE_STMT, Example.StmtHandle);
    }

    // Disconnect From The SQL Server Sample Database
    rc = SQLDisconnect(Example.ConHandle);
}

// Return To The Operating System
return(rc);
}
```

SQLCopyDesc

COMPATABILITY

X/OPEN 95 CLI	ISO/IEC 92 CLI	ODBC 1.0	ODBC 2.0	ODBC 3.0	ODBC 3.5
✓	✓	☐	☐	✓	✓

API CONFORMANCE LEVEL   **CORE**

Purpose   The `SQLCopyDesc()` function is used to copy descriptor information from one descriptor handle to another.

Syntax
```
SQLRETURN   SQLCopyDesc   (SQLHDESC    SourceDescHandle,
                           SQLHDESC    TargetDescHandle);
```

Parameters   *SourceDescHandle*   The descriptor handle that refers to a previously allocated descriptor information storage buffer (data structure) that is to be copied.

TargetDescHandle   A descriptor handle that refers to a previously allocated descriptor information storage buffer (data structure) that the *source descriptor* is to be copied to.

Description   The `SQLCopyDesc()` function is used to copy descriptor information from one descriptor handle to another. When this function executes, all descriptor record fields of the source (*SourceDescHandle*) descriptor, except for the `SQL_DESC_ALLOC_TYPE` field (which specifies whether the descriptor handle was implicitly or explicitly allocated) are copied to the Destination (*TargetDescHandle*) descriptor, regardless of whether a specific field is defined for the Destination descriptor type.

Return Codes   `SQL_SUCCESS`, `SQL_SUCCESS_WITH_INFO`, `SQL_INVALID_HANDLE`, or `SQL_ERROR`

SQLSTATEs   If this function returns `SQL_SUCCESS_WITH_INFO` or `SQL_ERROR`, one of the following SQLSTATE values may be obtained by calling the `SQLGetDiagRec()` function:

01000, **08**S01, **HY**000, **HY**001, **HY**007, **HY**010*, **HY**013, **HY**016, **HY**021, **HY**092, **HYT**01, or **IM**001*

* Returned by the ODBC Driver Manager.

Unless noted otherwise, each of these SQLSTATE values is returned by the data source driver. Refer to Appendix B for detailed information about each SQLSTATE value that can be returned by the ODBC Driver Manager or by a data source driver.

Comments   ■ Descriptor record fields can be copied from any type of descriptor, however they can only be copied to an APD, ARD, or an IPD descriptor, (but not to an IRD descriptor).

■ If an IRD descriptor handle is specified in the *TargetDescHandle* parameter, `SQL_ERROR` and SQLSTATE **HY**016 (Cannot modify an implementation row descriptor) are returned.

- Fields can only be copied from an IRD descriptor if the SQL statement associated with the descriptor is in the "Prepared" or "Executed" state; otherwise, **SQL_ERROR** and SQLSTATE **HY**007 (Associated statement is not prepared) are returned.

- If an SQL statement containing dynamic parameters has been prepared, and if automatic population of IPD descriptors is supported and has been enabled, this function copies IPD descriptor field contents as they were populated by the driver (if the IPD is specified in the *SourceDescHandle* parameter). Otherwise, if the IPD is not populated by the driver, the original contents of the IPD descriptor fields are copied.

- When this function fails, **SQL_ERROR** is returned, and the contents of the fields of the descriptor specified in the *TargetDescHandle* parameter are undefined.

- All existing data in the descriptor specified in the *TargetDescHandle* parameter is overwritten when this function is executed.

- The driver copies all descriptor fields if the *SourceDescHandle* and *TargetDescHandle* arguments are associated with the same driver, even if the drivers are on two different connections or environments. If the descriptors specified in the *SourceDescHandle* and *TargetDescHandle* parameters are associated with different drivers, the ODBC Driver Manager copies all ODBC-defined descriptor record fields—driver-defined fields or fields not defined by ODBC for the descriptor type specified are ignored.

- When the **SQL_DESC_DATA_PTR** descriptor record field is copied, a consistency check is performed on the target descriptor. If the consistency check fails, **SQL_ERROR** and SQLSTATE **HY**021 (Inconsistent descriptor information) is returned and the call to **SQLCopyDesc()** is immediately aborted.

- Descriptor records can be copied across connections even if the connections are under different environments. If the ODBC Driver Manager detects that the source and destination descriptor handles do not belong to the same connection handle and that the two connection handles belong to separate drivers, it implements **SQLCopyDesc()** by performing a field-by-field copy using the **SQLGetDescField()** and **SQLSetDescField()** functions. Because, in this case, the **SQLCopyDesc()** function is implemented by calling the **SQLGetDescField()** and **SQLSetDescField()** functions repeatedly, the error queue of the descriptor handle specified in the *SourceDescHandle* parameter is cleared and SQLSTATE values that are returned by the **SQLGetDescField()** or the **SQLSetDescField()** function may be returned by this function.

■ An application may be able to associate an explicitly allocated descriptor handle with a SQL statement handle, rather than calling this function to copy fields from one descriptor to another. An explicitly allocated descriptor can be associated with another SQL statement handle on the same connection by setting the **SQL_ATTR_APP_ROW_DESC** or **SQL_ATTR_APP_PARAM_DESC** statement attribute to the handle of the explicitly allocated descriptor. In this case, this function does not have to be used to copy descriptor record field values from one descriptor to another.

Prerequisites   A descriptor handle must be allocated before this function is called.

Restrictions   There are no restrictions associated with this function call.

See Also   **SQLGetDescField()**, **SQLSetDescField()**, **SQLGetDescRec()**, **SQLSetDescRec()**

Examples   The following Visual C++ program illustrates how to use the **SQLCopyDescRec()** function to copy the information stored in an implicitly allocated descriptor to an explicitly allocated descriptor.

```
/*————————————————————————————————————————————————————— */
/* NAME:      CH13EX5.CPP                                 */
/* PURPOSE: Illustrate How To Use The Following ODBC API Function   */
/*          In A C++ Program:                             */
/*                                                        */
/*              SQLCopyDesc()                             */
/*                                                        */
/* OTHER ODBC APIs SHOWN:                                 */
/*          SQLAllocHandle()          SQLSetEnvAttr()     */
/*          SQLDriverConnect()        SQLSetStmtAttr()    */
/*          SQLPrepare()              SQLGetStmtAttr()    */
/*          SQLGetDescRec()           SQLSetDescRec()     */
/*          SQLExecute()              SQLDisconnect()     */
/*          SQLFreeHandle()                               */
/*                                                        */
/*————————————————————————————————————————————————————— */

// Include The Appropriate Header Files
#include <windows.h>
#include <sql.h>
#include <sqlext.h>
#include <iostream.h>

// Define The ODBC_Class Class
class ODBC_Class
```

```
                    {
    // Attributes
    public:
        SQLHANDLE    EnvHandle;
        SQLHANDLE    ConHandle;
        SQLHANDLE    StmtHandle;
        SQLHANDLE    DescHandle;
        SQLHANDLE    IRDDescHandle;
        SQLRETURN    rc;

    // Operations
    public:
        ODBC_Class();                                // Constructor
        ~ODBC_Class();                               // Destructor
        SQLRETURN GetDescriptorInfo(SQLHANDLE Descriptor);
};

// Define The Class Constructor
ODBC_Class::ODBC_Class()
{
    // Initialize The Return Code Variable
    rc = SQL_SUCCESS;

    // Allocate An Environment Handle
    rc = SQLAllocHandle(SQL_HANDLE_ENV, SQL_NULL_HANDLE, &EnvHandle);

    // Set The ODBC Application Version To 3.x
    if (rc == SQL_SUCCESS)
        rc = SQLSetEnvAttr(EnvHandle, SQL_ATTR_ODBC_VERSION,
                    (SQLPOINTER) SQL_OV_ODBC3, SQL_IS_UINTEGER);

    // Allocate A Connection Handle
    if (rc == SQL_SUCCESS)
        rc = SQLAllocHandle(SQL_HANDLE_DBC, EnvHandle, &ConHandle);
}

// Define The Class Destructor
ODBC_Class::~ODBC_Class()
{
    // Free The Connection Handle
    if (ConHandle != NULL)
        SQLFreeHandle(SQL_HANDLE_DBC, ConHandle);

    // Free The Environment Handle
    if (EnvHandle != NULL)
        SQLFreeHandle(SQL_HANDLE_ENV, EnvHandle);
}

// Define The GetDescriptorInfo() Member Function
SQLRETURN ODBC_Class::GetDescriptorInfo(SQLHANDLE Descriptor)
{
    // Declare The Local Memory Variables
    SQLCHAR        Name[50];
```

```
    SQLSMALLINT    NameLen;
    SQLSMALLINT    Type;
    SQLSMALLINT    SubType;
    SQLINTEGER     Width;
    SQLSMALLINT    Precision;
    SQLSMALLINT    Scale;
    SQLSMALLINT    Nullable;

    // Obtain And Display Information About The Second Column In The
    // Result Data Set
    rc = SQLGetDescRec(Descriptor, 2, Name, sizeof(Name),
              &NameLen, &Type, &SubType, &Width, &Precision,
              &Scale, &Nullable);
    if (rc == SQL_SUCCESS)
    {
        cout << "Column 2 : " << endl << endl;
        cout << "Name       : " << Name << endl;
        cout << "Data Type  : " << Type << endl;
        cout << "Sub-Type   : " << SubType << endl;
        cout << "Width      : " << Width << endl;
        cout << "Precision  : " << Precision << endl;
        cout << "Scale      : " << Scale << endl;
        cout << "Nullable   : " << Nullable << endl << endl;
        cout << endl;
    }

    // Return The ODBC API Return Code To The Calling Function
    return(rc);
}

/*------------------------------------------------------------*/
/* The Main Function                                          */
/*------------------------------------------------------------*/
int main()
{
    // Declare The Local Memory Variables
    SQLRETURN      rc = SQL_SUCCESS;
    SQLCHAR        ConnectIn[40];
    SQLCHAR        SQLStmt[255];
    SQLSMALLINT    Type;
    SQLINTEGER     Length;
    SQLCHAR        Data[50];
    SQLINTEGER     DataLen;
    SQLINTEGER     ValueLength;

    // Create An Instance Of The ODBC_Class Class
    ODBC_Class  Example;

    // Build A Connection String
    strcpy((char *) ConnectIn,
        "DSN=SQLServer;UID=userid;PWD=password;");

    // Connect To The SQL Server Sample Database
```

```
if (Example.ConHandle != NULL)
{
    rc = SQLDriverConnect(Example.ConHandle, NULL, ConnectIn,
            SQL_NTS, NULL, 0, NULL, SQL_DRIVER_NOPROMPT);

    // Allocate An SQL Statement Handle
    rc = SQLAllocHandle(SQL_HANDLE_STMT, Example.ConHandle,
            &Example.StmtHandle);
    if (rc == SQL_SUCCESS)
    {
        // Define A SELECT SQL Statement
        strcpy((char *) SQLStmt, "SELECT EMPID, FIRSTNAME ");
        strcat((char *) SQLStmt, "FROM EMPLOYEES");

        // Prepare The SQL Statement
        rc = SQLPrepare(Example.StmtHandle, SQLStmt, SQL_NTS);

        // Retrieve A Handle To The Implementation Row
        // Descriptor (IRD) Associated With The SQL Statement
        rc = SQLGetStmtAttr(Example.StmtHandle,
                SQL_ATTR_IMP_ROW_DESC, (SQLPOINTER)
                &Example.IRDDescHandle, 0,
                &ValueLength);

        // Display Descriptor Information For The Second Column
        if (rc == SQL_SUCCESS)
            Example.GetDescriptorInfo(Example.IRDDescHandle);

        // Explicitly Allocate A Descriptor Handle
        rc = SQLAllocHandle(SQL_HANDLE_DESC, Example.ConHandle,
                &Example.DescHandle);

        // Copy The Implicitly Allocated IRD Descriptor To The
        // Explicitly Allocated ARD Descriptor
        rc = SQLCopyDesc(Example.IRDDescHandle,
                Example.DescHandle);

        // Assign The Explicitly Allocated Descriptor Handle To
        // The Statement Handle
        rc = SQLSetStmtAttr(Example.StmtHandle,
                SQL_ATTR_APP_ROW_DESC, (SQLPOINTER)
                Example.DescHandle, 0);

        // Modify The Descriptor Information Associated With The
        // Second Column
        Type = SQL_CHAR;
        Length = 20;
        rc = SQLSetDescRec(Example.DescHandle, 2, Type, 0,
                Length, 0, 0, Data, &DataLen, NULL);

        // Display The Modified Descriptor Information
        if (rc == SQL_SUCCESS)
            Example.GetDescriptorInfo(Example.DescHandle);
```

```
            // Execute The SQL Statement, Using The Modified
            // Descriptor
            rc = SQLExecute(Example.StmtHandle);

            // Free The SQL Statement Handle
            if (Example.StmtHandle != NULL)
                SQLFreeHandle(SQL_HANDLE_STMT, Example.StmtHandle);
        }

        // Disconnect From The SQL Server Sample Database
        rc = SQLDisconnect(Example.ConHandle);
    }

    // Return To The Operating System
    return(rc);
}
```

14

Retrieving Status and Error Information

When an application calls an ODBC API function, it needs to know if the function call was completed successfully or if it failed. If the function was successful, the application can continue to the next step; if the function failed, the application can take corrective measures and, if necessary, call the function again. This chapter is designed to introduce you to the mechanisms used by ODBC to report the success or failure of an ODBC API function to the calling application. This chapter begins by examining the primary component ODBC uses to inform an application that a warning or error has occurred: the function return code.

This is followed by a discussion about the component used to provide specific error/warning information to an application: the diagnostic record. Next, the main components of the diagnostic record are described and both the ODBC Driver Manager's role and the driver's role in the error handling process are discussed. Then, the functions used to obtain diagnostic record information after an ODBC API function is executed are described. Finally, a detailed reference section covering each ODBC API function that can be used to obtain diagnostic record information is provided.

ODBC Return Codes

Each time an ODBC API function call is executed, a special value known as a *return code* is returned to the calling application. Unlike some functions, which are designed to return many different values and data types, the ODBC API functions are designed to return a limited number of return code values. Table 14–1 lists all possible return codes that can be generated by an ODBC API function.

The return code **SQL_INVALID_HANDLE** always indicates a programming error and should never be encountered at run time. All the other return codes provide run-time information about the overall success or failure of the function (although the **SQL_ERROR** return code can sometimes indicate a programming error).

The return code value should always be checked after an ODBC API function is called to determine whether or not the function executed successfully. If by examining the return code the application discovers that an error or warning was generated, it should then examine the diagnostic record(s) generated and process the error accordingly.

Diagnostic Records

Although the return code informs an application that an error or warning condition occurred and prevented the ODBC API function call from executing properly, it does not provide the application (or the developer, or the user) with specific information about what caused the error or warning condition to occur. Because this information is also needed, each ODBC API function generates one or more diagnostic records that provide detailed information about the success or failure of the function, along with the return code.

Table 14-1   Return Codes Generated by ODBC API Functions

Return Code	Meaning
SQL_SUCCESS	The ODBC API function completed successfully. With ODBC 3.x drivers, the application can call the **SQLGetDiagField()** function to obtain additional information from the diagnostic header record. With ODBC 2.0 or earlier drivers, no additional information is available.
SQL_SUCCESS_WITH_INFO	The ODBC API function completed successfully, however a warning or a non-fatal error was generated. The application can call the **SQLGetDiagRec()** function (ODBC 3.x), the **SQLGetDiagField()** function (ODBC 3.x), or the **SQLError()** function (ODBC 2.0 or earlier) to obtain additional information.
SQL_NO_DATA[1]	The ODBC API function completed successfully, but no relevant data was found. The application can call the **SQLGetDiagRec()** function (ODBC 3.x), the **SQLGetDiagField()** function (ODBC 3.x), or the **SQLError()** function (ODBC 2.0 or earlier) to obtain additional information.
SQL_INVALID_HANDLE	The ODBC API function failed to execute because an invalid environment, connection, statement, or descriptor handle was specified. This code is only returned when the specified handle is either a NULL pointer or the wrong handle type (for example, when a statement handle is specified for a connection handle parameter). Because this is a programming error, no additional information is available.
SQL_NEED_DATA	The application tried to execute an SQL statement, but the ODBC API function failed because data the application had indicated would be available at execution time was missing—such as when parameter data is sent at execution time or when additional connection information is needed. The application can call the **SQLGetDiagRec()** function (ODBC 3.x), the **SQLGetDiagField()** function (ODBC 3.x), or the **SQLError()** function (ODBC 2.0 or earlier) to obtain additional information.
SQL_STILL_EXECUTING	An ODBC API function that was started asynchronously is still executing. The application can call the **SQLGetDiagRec()** function (ODBC 3.x), the **SQLGetDiagField()** function (ODBC 3.x), or the **SQLError()** function (ODBC 2.0 or earlier) to obtain additional information.
SQL_ERROR	The ODBC API function failed to complete. The application can call the **SQLGetDiagRec()** function (ODBC 3.x), the **SQLGetDiagField()** function (ODBC 3.x), or the **SQLError()** function (ODBC 2.0 or earlier) to obtain additional information.

(Adapted from the table on page 258 of *Microsoft ODBC 3.0 Software Development Kit & Programmer's Reference*.)
[1]In ODBC 2.0 and earlier, this return code was **SQL_NO_DATA_FOUND**.

Diagnostic records can be used during application development to catch programming errors such as the use of invalid handles and the use of incorrect syntax in hard-coded SQL statements. Diagnostic records can be used at application run time to catch and process run-time errors and warnings such as data truncation warnings, access violations, and incorrect syntax in user-supplied SQL statements.

Two types of diagnostic records are available: one header record (record 0) and zero or more status records (records 1 and above). Both types of diagnostic records are composed of several different predefined fields. ODBC components can define their own diagnostic record fields in addition to the predefined fields. The fields in the diagnostic header record contain general information about a function's execution, including the return code, row count, number of status records, and the type of statement executed. The fields in each diagnostic status record contain information about specific errors or warnings returned by the ODBC Driver Manager, driver, or data source. Both types of diagnostic records can be thought of as data structures, however, there is no requirement for them to actually be stored as structures–the way diagnostic records are actually stored is driver-specific.

One diagnostic header record is always created each time an ODBC API function is executed (unless the return code **SQL_INVALID_HANDLE** is returned). Additionally, one or more diagnostic status records are created whenever the return code **SQL_ERROR**, **SQL_SUCCESS_WITH_INFO**, **SQL_NO_ DATA**, **SQL_NO_DATA_FOUND** (ODBC 2.0 or earlier), **SQL_NEED_DATA**, or **SQL_STILL_EXECUTING** is returned—there is no limit to the number of diagnostic status records that can be stored at any one time. Of all the information returned in a diagnostic status record, the SQLSTATE value, the native error number, and the diagnostic message text are used most often to determine exactly why a function did not perform as expected.

SQLSTATEs

Because each database product usually has its own set of product-specific diagnostic messages, the X/Open CLI and ISO/IEC 92 standards specifications define a standardized set of diagnostic message codes that are known as SQLSTATEs. By using SQLSTATEs, an application developer can use consistent error and warning message handling routines across different relational database product platforms.

SQLSTATEs are alphanumeric strings five characters (bytes) in length with the format *ccsss*, where *cc* indicates the error message class, and *sss* indicates the error message subclass. An SQLSTATE with a class of **01** is a warning; an SQLSTATE with a class of **HY** (ODBC 3.x drivers) or **Sl** (ODBC 2.0 or earlier drivers) is an error generated by either a data source or a driver, and an SQLSTATE with a class of **IM** is an error generated by the ODBC Driver Manager.

Unlike return codes, SQLSTATEs are often treated as guidelines, and drivers are not required to return them. Thus, while drivers should return the proper SQLSTATE for any error or warning they are capable of detecting, applications should not count on this always happening. The reasons for this are two-fold:

- Although ODBC (in conjunction with the X/Open CLI and ISO/IEC standards) defines a large number of errors and warnings and possible causes for those errors and warnings, it is not complete and probably never will be; driver implementations simply vary too much for this to ever occur. Any given driver probably will not return all the SQLSTATEs recognized by ODBC, and in fact, may return SQLSTATEs that ODBC does not recognize.

- Some database engines—particularly relational database engines —can return literally thousands of error and warning messages. It is unlikely that drivers for such engines map all these errors and warnings to SQLSTATE values because of the effort involved, the inexactness of the mappings, the large size of the resulting code, and the low value of the resulting code (which often returns programming errors that should never be encountered at run time). Drivers tend to map as many errors and warnings as seems reasonable and to concentrate on mapping those errors and warnings on which application logic might be based.

Because SQLSTATEs are not returned reliably, most applications just display them to the user along with their associated diagnostic message (which is often tailored to the specific error or warning that occurred) and native error code. There is rarely any loss of functionality in doing this because applications cannot base programming logic on most SQLSTATEs anyway. For example, suppose `SQLExecDirect()` returns SQLSTATE **42**000 (Syntax error or access violation). If the SQL statement that caused this error to occur is hard-coded or built by the application, this is a programming error and the code needs to be fixed. However, if the SQL statement that caused this error to occur was entered by the user, this is a user error, and the application has already done all that it can do by informing the user of the problem.

When applications do base programming logic on SQLSTATE values, they need to be able to handle situations in which the SQLSTATE value they are looking for is not returned. Exactly which SQLSTATEs are always returned can be based only on experience with numerous drivers. However, a general guideline is that SQLSTATE values for errors occurring in the driver or in the ODBC Driver Manager, as opposed to the data source, will more than likely be returned.

The following SQLSTATE values indicate run-time errors or warnings and are good candidates on which to base programming logic. However, keep in mind that there is no guarantee that all drivers will return them.

- **01**004 (Data truncated)
- **01**S02 (Option value changed)
- **HY**008 or **S1**008 (Operation canceled)
- **HY**C00 or **S1**C00 (Optional feature not implemented)
- **HY**T00 or **S1**T00 (Timeout expired)

The SQLSTATE values **HY**C00 and **S1**C00 are particularly significant because they are the only way in which an application can determine whether a driver supports a particular connection or SQL statement attribute. For a complete list of the SQLSTATEs available, refer to Appendix B, "ODBC Error Codes."

Native Error Codes

Each diagnostic status record contains a native error code if the SQLSTATE value was generated by the data source. Native error codes are data source-specific codes, therefore the information they provide is data source specific. If a diagnostic status record is generated by the ODBC Driver Manager or a driver instead of a data source, the native error code is set to −99999. Native error codes are provided so that the maximum amount of diagnostic information will be available to an application; they should never be used as a basis for programming logic.

Diagnostic Messages

A diagnostic message designed to clarify the meaning of an SQLSTATE value is often stored in a diagnostic status record, along with the SQLSTATE value. The content of this message can vary and often, a number of different diagnostic messages can be returned for the same

SQLSTATE value. For example, SQLSTATE **42**000 (Syntax error or access violation) is returned for most cases in which an error exists in SQL syntax. However, each syntax error found is likely to have its own diagnostic message.

Diagnostic messages come from both data sources and from components in an ODBC connection, such as drivers, gateways, and the ODBC Driver Manager. To help the user and support personnel determine the location and cause of a problem, component and/or data source information is usually embedded in the front of the diagnostic message text.

Typically, a data source does not directly support ODBC. Consequently, if a component in an ODBC connection receives a message from a data source, it must identify the data source as the source of the message and it must identify itself as the component that received the message. On the other hand, if a component in an ODBC connection generates an error or warning, it must identify itself as the source of the message. Therefore, the text of diagnostic messages has two different formats. For errors and warnings that do not occur in a data source, diagnostic messages have the format:

```
[vendor-identifier][ODBC-component-identifier]component-
    supplied-text
```

where:

vendor-identifier	Identifies the vendor of the component in which the error or warning occurred.
ODBC-component-identifier	Identifies the component in which the error or warning occurred.
component-supplied-text	The error or warning message text generated by the ODBC component.

For errors and warnings that occur in a data source, the diagnostic message has the format:

```
[vendor-identifier][ODBC-component-identifier][data-source-
    identifier]data-source-supplied-text
```

where:

vendor-identifier	Identifies the vendor of the component that received the error or warning directly from the data source.
ODBC-component-identifier	Identifies the component that received the error or warning directly from the data source.

data-source-identifier	Identifies the data source in which the error or warning occured. For file-based drivers, this is typically a file format, for example, dBASE, in which case the driver is acting as both the driver and the data source. For DBMS-based drivers, this is the DBMS product.
data-source-supplied-text	The error or warning message text generated by the data source.

Diagnostic Status Record Sequence

If two or more diagnostic status records are generated, they are ranked by the Driver Manager and the driver according to the following rules:

- Status records describing errors have the highest rank. Among error records, records indicating a transaction failure or possible transaction failure outrank all other records. If two or more records describe the same error condition, SQLSTATEs defined by the X/Open CLI specification (classes **03** through **HZ**) outrank SQLSTATES defined by ODBC and ODBC drivers.

- Status records describing driver-defined "No Data" values (class **02**) have the second highest rank.

- Status records describing warnings (class **01**) have the lowest rank. If two or more records describe the same warning condition, SQLSTATEs defined by the X/Open CLI specification outrank SQLSTATES defined by ODBC and ODBC drivers.

The diagnostic status record with the highest rank is always the first record in the list. If there are two or more records ranking highest, it is undefined as to which record will be first. The order of all other records is also undefined. Therefore, because warnings may appear after the first error and before other errors, all status records should be checked whenever an ODBC API function returns any code other than **SQL_ SUCCESS**.

The Driver Manager determines the final order in which to return any status records it generates. In particular, it determines which record has the highest rank and is to be returned first. Likewise, the driver is responsible for ordering any status records it generates. If status records are posted by both the Driver Manager and the driver, the Driver Manager is responsible for ordering both sets of records. The source of a record

(Driver Manager, driver, gateway, and so on) is never taken into consideration when status records are ranked.

The ODBC Driver Manager's Role in Error Checking

To prevent every driver from checking for the same errors, the ODBC Driver Manager performs as much error checking as it possibly can. At a minimum, the Driver Manager checks the following types of function parameters.

- Environment, connection, and statement handles. The Driver Manager returns **SQL_INVALID_HANDLE** when it finds a NULL or inappropriate handle.

- Required pointer parameters. The Driver Manager ensures that these parameters do not contain NULL pointers.

- Option flags that do not support driver-specific values. The Driver Manager ensures that these parameters contain legal values.

- Option flags. The Driver Manager ensures that option flags specified are supported in the version of ODBC that is supported by the driver. For example, the *InfoType* parameter of the **SQLGetInfo()** function cannot be set to **SQL_ASYNC_MODE** (introduced in ODBC 3.0) when calling an ODBC 2.0 driver.

- Column and parameter numbers. The Driver Manager ensures that these numbers are greater than **0** or greater than or equal to **0**, depending on the function. The driver is responsible for checking the upper limit of these values, based on the current result data set or SQL statement being processed.

- Length/indicator arguments and data buffer length arguments. The Driver Manager ensures that these parameters contain appropriate values.

Unless otherwise noted, the Driver Manager returns **SQL_ERROR** for all errors found in function parameter values.

The Driver Manager also ensures that the state of an environment, connection, or statement is appropriate for the function being called. For example, a connection must be in the "Allocated" state when the **SQLConnect()** function is called and a statement must be in the "Prepared" state when the **SQLExecute()** function is called. The Driver Manager returns **SQL_ERROR** for all state transition errors.

The Driver Manager also makes sure that a function being called is supported by the current driver being used. In addition, because the Driver Manager completely or partially implements a number of functions, it checks for all or some of the error and warning conditions that can occur when using those functions. Specifically:

- The Driver Manager implements the **SQLDataSources()** function and the **SQLDrivers()** function and checks for all errors and warnings in these functions.

- The Driver Manager checks whether a driver implements the **SQLGetFunctions()** function—if the driver does not implement this function, the Driver Manager implements it and checks for all errors and warnings in it.

- The Driver Manager partially implements the **SQLAllocHandle()**, **SQLAllocEnv()**, **SQLAllocConnect()**, **SQLAllocStmt()**, **SQLConnect()**, **SQLDriverConnect()**, **SQLBrowseConnect()**, **SQLFreeHandle()**, **SQLFreeEnv()**, **SQLFreeConnect()**, **SQLFreeStmt()**, **SQLGetDiagRec()**, **SQLGetDiagField()**, and **SQLError()** functions and checks for some errors in these functions. It may return the same errors as the driver for some of these functions, since both perform similar operations.

The Driver's Role in Error Checking

The driver checks for all errors and warnings that are not checked by the Driver Manager. This includes errors and warnings in data truncation, data conversion, syntax, and some state transitions. The driver may also check errors and warnings that are partially checked by the Driver Manager. For example, although the Driver Manager checks to see whether the value of the *Operation* parameter in the **SQLSetPos()** function is legal, the driver must determine whether or not it is supported.

The driver also maps native errors, or errors returned by a data source, to appropriate SQLSTATE values. Usually, driver documentation shows exactly how errors and warnings are mapped.

In addition, ODBC 3.x drivers are responsible for ordering the status records they generate (ODBC 2.0 or earlier drivers do not order status records).

Obtaining Diagnostic Information

Applications can call the **SQLGetDiagRec()** or **SQLGetDiagField()** function (ODBC 3.x driver) or the **SQLError()** function (ODBC 2.x or earlier driver) to retrieve diagnostic information. These functions accept an environment, connection, statement, or descriptor handle (ODBC 3.x only) as an input parameter and return diagnostic information about the ODBC API function that executed using the handle specified. If multiple diagnostic records were generated, the application must call one or more of these functions several times—the total number of status records available can be determined by calling the **SQLGetDiagField()** function with record number **0** (the header record number) and the **SQL_DIAG_NUMBER** option specified.

Applications can retrieve the SQLSTATE, native error code, and diagnostic message in a single call by calling **SQLGetDiagRec()** (ODBC 3.x drivers) or **SQLError()** (ODBC 2.0 or earlier drivers). However, neither of these functions can be used to retrieve information from the diagnostic header record. ODBC 3.x applications can retrieve information from the diagnostic header record by calling the **SQLGetDiagField()** function— ODBC 2.0 applications can not access diagnostic header record information— The **SQLGetDiagField()** function can also be used to obtain the values of individual diagnostic record fields. When **SQLGetDiagField()** is used in this manner, it is important to recognize that certain diagnostic fields do not have any meaning for certain types of handles.

Each of these functions are implemented by the ODBC Driver Manager and by each driver; The Driver Manager and each driver maintain diagnostic records for each environment, connection, statement, and descriptor handle. The diagnostics logged on a particular handle are automatically discarded when a new function (other than **SQLGetDiagRec()** **SQLGetDiagField()** or **SQLError()**) is executed using that handle or when the handle is freed.

Guidelines for Error Handling

At a minimum, an application should notify the user when an error or warning occurs and provide enough information so that the problem can be corrected. The following is a set of guidelines that an application should follow to correctly process warnings and errors:

■ Always check the ODBC API function return code before calling the **SQLGetDiagRec()**, **SQLGetDiagField()**, or **SQLError()** function to determine whether diagnostic information is available.

- Use the standard set of SQLSTATEs, rather than the native error codes to increase application portability.

- Only build dependencies on the subset of SQLSTATE values defined by the X/Open CLI and the ISO/IEC 92 standards specifications—return any additional SQLSTATE values as information only. (Dependencies refer to the application making logic flow decisions based on specific SQLSTATES.)

- For maximum diagnostic information, retrieve and display the diagnostic text message, the SQLSTATE value, and the native error code. If possible, include the name of the ODBC API function that returned the error in the diagnostic information displayed.

The Error/Diagnostic Message Retrieval Functions

Table 14–2 lists the ODBC API functions used to obtain diagnostic information when an ODBC API function returns a return code other than SQL_SUCCESS.

Each of these functions are described, in detail, in the remaining portion of this chapter.

Table 14–2 The ODBC Error/Diagnostic Message Retrieval Functions

Function Name	Description
SQLGetDiagRec()	Retrieves error, warning, and/or status information from the diagnostic status record generated by the last ODBC API function executed.
SQLError()	Retrieves diagnostic (error, warning, and/or status) information associated with the last ODBC API function executed (ODBC 2.0 or earlier drivers).
SQLGetDiagField()	Retrieves the current value of a field of a diagnostic header or status record that was generated by the last ODBC API function executed.

SQLGetDiagRec

COMPATABILITY

X/OPEN 95 CLI	ISO/IEC 92 CLI	ODBC 1.0	ODBC 2.0	ODBC 3.0	ODBC 3.5
✓	✓	☐	☐	✓	✓

API CONFORMANCE LEVEL   **CORE**

Purpose

The `SQLGetDiagRec()` function is used to retrieve the current values of several commonly used fields of a diagnostic status record. This record contains error, warning, and/or status information generated by the last ODBC API function executed.

Syntax

```
SQLRETURN   SQLGetDiagRec  (SQLSMALLINT    HandleType,
                            SQLHANDLE      Handle,
                            SQLSMALLINT    RecNumber,
                            SQLCHAR        *SQLSTATE,
                            SQLINTEGER     *NativeError,
                            SQLCHAR        *ErrorMsg,
                            SQLSMALLINT    ErrorMsgMaxSize,
                            SQLSMALLINT    *ErrorMsgSize);
```

Parameters

HandleType Specifies which type of handle to retrieve diagnostic information for. This parameter must be set to one of the following values:

■ **SQL_HANDLE_ENV**
Retrieve diagnostic information for an environment handle.

■ **SQL_HANDLE_DBC**
Retrieve diagnostic information for a connection handle.

■ **SQL_HANDLE_STMT**
Retrieve diagnostic information for an SQL statement handle.

■ **SQL_HANDLES_DESC**
Retrieve diagnostic information for a descriptor handle.

Handle	An environment, connection, SQL statement, or descriptor handle that refers to a previously allocated environment, connection, statement, or descriptor information storage buffer (data structure). If *HandleType* is set to **SQL_HANDLE_ENV**, this parameter can contain either a shared, or an unshared environment handle.
RecNumber	Specifies the diagnostic status record from which this function is to retrieve information. This parameter should contain a number greater than 0 (Status records are numbered, starting at 1).
SQLSTATE	A pointer to a location in memory where this function is to store the SQLSTATE value retrieved. This value is stored as a NULL-terminated 5 character string—the first two characters of this string indicate the error class and the last three characters indicate the error subclass.
NativeError	A pointer to a location in memory where this function is to store the data source-specific error code retrieved.
ErrorMsg	A pointer to a location in memory where this function is to store the error message text retrieved.
ErrorMsgMaxSize	The maximum size of the memory storage buffer where this function is to store the error message text retrieved.
ErrorMsgSize	A pointer to a location in memory where this function is to store the actual number of bytes written to the error message text memory storage buffer (*ErrorMsg*).

Description
The **SQLGetDiagRec()** function is used to retrieve the current values of several commonly used fields of a diagnostic status record. This record contains error, warning, and/or status information generated by the last ODBC API function executed. Unlike the **SQLGetDiagField()** function, which returns a single value from one field of a diagnostic record per call, the **SQLGetDiagRec()** function returns several commonly used fields of a diagnostic status record, including the SQLSTATE (**SQL_DIAG_SQLSTATE** field), the native error code (**SQL_DIAG_NATIVE** field), and the diagnostic error, warning, or status message text (**SQL_DIAG_MESSAGE_TEXT** field).

Refer to the **SQLGetDiagField()** function for a complete description of each field found in a diagnostic information record.

An application typically calls this function when a call to an ODBC API function returns something other than **SQL_SUCCESS** or **SQL_INVALID_HANDLE**. However, because any ODBC API function can post zero or more diagnostic records when it is called, an application can call this function immediately after making any ODBC API function call.

Return Codes **SQL_SUCCESS**, **SQL_SUCCESS_WITH_INFO**, **SQL_INVALID_HANDLE**, or **SQL_ERROR**

SQLSTATEs No SQLSTATE values are returned for this function because it does not generate diagnostic information for itself. Instead, this function uses the following return codes to report the outcome of its own execution:

▓ **SQL_SUCCESS**

The function successfully returned diagnostic information.

▓ **SQL_SUCCESS_WITH_INFO**

The error message buffer (*ErrorMsg*) was not large enough to hold the requested diagnostic message. No diagnostic records were generated.

▓ **SQL_NO_DATA**

The record number specified in the *RecNumber* parameter was greater than the number of diagnostic records that existed for the handle specified. This function also returns **SQL_NO_DATA** if a positive number is specified in the *RecNumber* parameter and there are no diagnostic records for the specified handle.

▓ **SQL_INVALID_HANDLE**

The handle specified in the *HandleType* and *Handle* parameters was not a valid handle.

▓ **SQL_ERROR**

One of the following occurred:

The value specified in the *RecNumber* parameter was less than or equal to **0**.

The value specified in the *ErrorMsgMaxSize* parameter was less than **0**.

Comments ▓ An application can call this function multiple times to return information from some or all the records stored in the diagnostic information data structure. ODBC imposes no limit on the number of diagnostic records that can be stored in this structure at any one time.

- This function cannot be used to retrieve information from the fields of a diagnostic header record (that is, the *RecNumber* parameter must contain a number greater than **0**). An application should call the **SQLGetDiagField()** function if it needs to obtain information from the diagnostic header record.

- If the diagnostic information generated by an ODBC API function call is not retrieved before an API function other than **SQLGetDiagRec()**, **SQLError()**, or **SQLGetDiagField()** is called using the same environment, connection, statement, or descriptor handle, that information is lost. Diagnostic information stored on a given handle is not removed as the result of a call to a function using an associated handle of a different type.

- If the error message text returned to the *ErrorMsg* parameter is a Unicode string, the *ErrorMsgValueMaxSize* parameter must contain an even number.

- An application can compare the maximum size of the memory storage buffer where this function is to store the error message text retrieved (the *ErrorMsgMaxSize* parameter) to the actual number of bytes written to the error message text memory storage buffer (the *ErrorMsgSize* parameter) to determine whether an error message was truncated.

- Multiple diagnostic messages may be generated by an ODBC API function call. When this occurs, each diagnostic message can be retrieved, one at a time, by repeatedly incrementing the value of the *RecNumber* parameter and calling this function (ODBC 3.x drivers) or by repeatedly calling the **SQLError()** function (ODBC 2.0 or earlier drivers). Calls to either function are non-destructive to the diagnostic header and diagnostic status records of the diagnostic information data structure.

- An application can determine the total number of diagnostic records available in the diagnostic information data structure by calling the **SQLGetDiagField()** function to retrieve the value of the **SQL_DIAG_NUMBER** field.

- Each type of handle (environment, connection, statement, and descriptor) can have diagnostic information associated with it. However, some diagnostic header and status record fields cannot be returned for all types of handles. The **SQLGetDiagField()** function can be used to determine which diagnostic header and status record fields are applicable for each type of handle.

- If this function is called with the *HandleType* parameter set to **SQL_HANDLE_SENV**, which denotes a shared environment handle, **SQL_INVALID_HANDLE** is returned. However, if this function is called with the *HandleType* parameter set to **SQL_HANDLE_ENV**, either a shared or an unshared environment handle can be specified in the *Handle* parameter.

Prerequisites   There are no prerequisites for using this function call.

Restrictions   There are no restrictions associated with this function call.

See Also   SQLError(), SQLGetDiagField()

Example   The following Visual C++ program illustrates how to use the SQLGetDiagRec() function to obtain general diagnostic information when an ODBC API function fails to execute properly.

```
/*———————————————————————————————————————————————————————————*/
/* NAME:      CH14EX1.CPP                                       */
/* PURPOSE: Illustrate How To Use The Following ODBC API Function */
/*          In A C++ Program:                                   */
/*                                                              */
/*                  SQLGetDiagRec()                             */
/*                                                              */
/* OTHER ODBC APIs SHOWN:                                       */
/*          SQLAllocHandle()              SQLSetEnvAttr()       */
/*          SQLDriverConnect()            Disconnect()          */
/*          SQLFreeHandle()                                     */
/*                                                              */
/*———————————————————————————————————————————————————————————*/

// Include The Appropriate Header Files
#include <windows.h>
#include <sql.h>
#include <sqlext.h>
#include <iostream.h>

// Define The ODBC_Class Class
class ODBC_Class
{
    // Attributes
    public:
        SQLHANDLE       EnvHandle;
        SQLHANDLE       ConHandle;
        SQLRETURN       rc;

    // Operations
    public:
        ODBC_Class();                           // Constructor
        ~ODBC_Class();                          // Destructor
};

// Define The Class Constructor
ODBC_Class::ODBC_Class()
{
```

```
    // Initialize The Return Code Variable
    rc = SQL_SUCCESS;

    // Allocate An Environment Handle
    rc = SQLAllocHandle(SQL_HANDLE_ENV, SQL_NULL_HANDLE, &EnvHandle);

    // Set The ODBC Application Version To 3.x
    if (rc == SQL_SUCCESS)
        rc = SQLSetEnvAttr(EnvHandle, SQL_ATTR_ODBC_VERSION,
                  (SQLPOINTER) SQL_OV_ODBC3, SQL_IS_UINTEGER);

    // Allocate A Connection Handle
    if (rc == SQL_SUCCESS)
        rc = SQLAllocHandle(SQL_HANDLE_DBC, EnvHandle, &ConHandle);
}

// Define The Class Destructor
ODBC_Class::~ODBC_Class()
{
    // Free The Connection Handle
    if (ConHandle != NULL)
        SQLFreeHandle(SQL_HANDLE_DBC, ConHandle);

    // Free The Environment Handle
    if (EnvHandle != NULL)
        SQLFreeHandle(SQL_HANDLE_ENV, EnvHandle);
}

/*─────────────────────────────────────────────────────────*/
/* The Main Function                                        */
/*─────────────────────────────────────────────────────────*/
int main()
{
    // Declare The Local Memory Variables
    SQLRETURN      rc = SQL_SUCCESS;
    SQLCHAR        ConnectIn[30];
    SQLINTEGER     NativeErr;
    SQLCHAR        SQLState[6];
    SQLCHAR        ErrMsg[255];
    SQLSMALLINT    ErrMsgLen;

    // Create An Instance Of The ODBC_Class Class
    ODBC_Class  Example;

    // Build A Connection String
    strcpy((char *) ConnectIn, "DSN=Southwind;UID=\"\";PWD=\"\";");

    // Attempt To Connect To The Southwind Sample Database (Since
    // This Database Does Not Exist, The SQLDriverConnect() Call
    // Should Fail And An Error Should Be Generated)
    if (Example.ConHandle != NULL)
    {
        rc = SQLDriverConnect(Example.ConHandle, NULL, ConnectIn,
```

```
                SQL_NTS, NULL, 0, NULL, SQL_DRIVER_NOPROMPT);

    // If The Specified Connection Was Not Established, Retrieve
    // And Display The Diagnostic Information Generated
    if (rc != SQL_SUCCESS && rc != SQL_SUCCESS_WITH_INFO)
    {
        rc = SQLGetDiagRec(SQL_HANDLE_DBC, Example.ConHandle,
                 1, SQLState, &NativeErr, ErrMsg, 255,
                 &ErrMsgLen);
        cout << "SQLSTATE : " << SQLState << endl << endl;
        cout << ErrMsg << endl;
    }

    // If The Specified Connection Was Established, Display
    // A Success Message
    else
    {
        cout << "Connected to Southwind database." << endl;

        // Disconnect From The Southwind Sample Database
        rc = SQLDisconnect(Example.ConHandle);
    }
}

// Return To The Operating System
return(rc);
}
```

SQLError

COMPATABILITY

X/OPEN 95 CLI	ISO/IEC 92 CLI	ODBC 1.0	ODBC 2.0	ODBC 3.0	ODBC 3.5
☒	☑	☑	☑	☐	☐

API CONFORMANCE LEVEL   **CORE**

Purpose   The SQLError() function is used to retrieve error, warning, and/or status information generated by the last ODBC API function executed.

Syntax

```
RETCODE  SQLError     (HENV          EnvironmentHandle,
                       HDBC          ConnectionHandle,
                       HSTMT         StatementHandle,
                       UCHAR FAR     *SQLSTATE,
                       SDWORD FAR    *NativeError,
```

```
UCHAR  FAR        *ErrorMsg,
SWORD             ErrorMsgMaxSize,
SWORD  FAR        *ErrorMsgSize);
```

Parameters

EnvironmentHandle	An environment handle that refers to a previously allocated environment information storage buffer (data structure).
ConnectionHandle	A data source connection handle that refers to a previously allocated connection information storage buffer (data structure).
StatementHandle	An SQL statement handle that refers to a previously allocated SQL statement information storage buffer (data structure).
SQLSTATE	A pointer to a location in memory where this function is to store the SQLSTATE value retrieved. This value is stored as a NULL-terminated 5 character string—the first two characters of this string indicate the error class and the last three characters indicate the error subclass.
NativeError	A pointer to a location in memory where this function is to store the data source-specific error code retrieved.
ErrorMsg	A pointer to a location in memory where this function is to store the error message text retrieved.
ErrorMsgMaxSize	The maximum size of the memory storage buffer where this function is to store the error message text retrieved.
ErrorMsgSize	A pointer to a location in memory where this function is to store the actual number of bytes written to the error message text memory storage buffer (*ErrorMsg*).

Description

The **SQLError()** function is used to retrieve diagnostic (error, warning, and/or status) information generated by the last ODBC API function executed. The diagnostic information returned consists of one or more standardized SQLSTATE values, native error codes, and corresponding text messages. This function should always be called whenever **SQL_ERROR** or **SQL_SUCCESS_WITH_INFO** is returned by an ODBC API function call.

However, because any ODBC API function can post zero or more errors when it is called, an application can call this function immediately after making any ODBC API function call.

NOTE: *Some drivers may also provide data source-specific diagnostic information whenever* **SQL_NO_DATA_FOUND** *is returned by an ODBC API function call (particularly when an SQL statement is executed).*

The ODBC Driver Manager stores error information in its own environment, connection, and SQL statement handle structures. Similarly, each driver stores error information in its environment, connection, and SQL statement handle structures. Whenever an application calls the **SQLError()** function, the Driver Manager checks to see if there are any errors in its structure for the specified handle. If it finds errors for the specified handle, it returns the first error found; otherwise, it calls the **SQLError()** function in the appropriate driver.

The Driver Manager can store up to 64 errors with an environment handle and its associated connection and SQL statement handles. When this limit is reached, the Driver Manager discards any subsequent errors posted on the Driver Manager's environment, connection, and SQL statement handle structures. The number of errors a driver can store is driver-dependent. Each time this function is called, an error is removed from the structure associated with the handle specified.

Return Codes   SQL_SUCCESS, SQL_SUCCESS_WITH_INFO, SQL_NO_DATA_FOUND, SQL_INVALID_HANDLE, or SQL_ERROR

SQLSTATEs   No SQLSTATE values are returned for this function because it does not generate diagnostic information for itself.

Comments   ▧ To obtain diagnostic information associated with an environment handle, specify a valid environment connection handle in the *EnvironmentHandle* parameter, set the *ConnectionHandle* parameter to **SQL_NULL_HDBC**, and set the *StatementHandle* parameter to **SQL_NULL_HSTMT**.

▧ To obtain diagnostic information associated with a connection handle, specify a valid connection handle in the *ConnectionHandle* parameter and set the *StatementHandle* parameter to **SQL_NULL_ HSTMT**. The *EnvironmentHandle* parameter is ignored.

▧ To obtain diagnostic information associated with an SQL statement handle, specify a valid statement handle in the

StatementHandle parameter. The *EnvironmentHandle* and *ConnectionHandle* parameters are ignored.

- If the diagnostic information generated by an ODBC API function call is not retrieved by this function before an API function other than `SQLError()`, `SQLGetDiagRec()`, or `SQLGetDiagField()` is called using the same environment, connection, or SQL statement handle, that information is lost. Diagnostic information stored on a given handle is not removed as the result of a call to a function using an associated handle of a different type.

- Multiple diagnostic messages may be generated by an ODBC API function call. When this occurs, each diagnostic message can be retrieved one at a time by repeatedly calling this function. Each time a diagnostic message is retrieved, the `SQLError()` function returns the `SQL_SUCCESS` value, and the diagnostic message is removed from the list. When there are no more SQLSTATE values to retrieve, the `SQLError()` function returns `SQL_NO_DATA_FOUND` (in which case SQLSTATE. contains **00**000, *NativeError* is undefined, *ErrorMsg* contains a single NULL termination byte character, and *ErrorMsgSize* equals **0**).

- An application can compare the maximum size of the memory storage buffer in which this function is to store the error message text retrieved (the *ErrorMsgMaxSize* parameter) to the actual number of bytes written to the error message text memory storage buffer (the *ErrorMsgSize* parameter) to determine whether an error message was truncated.

- If the memory storage buffer where this function is to store the error message text retrieved is not large enough to hold the error message text, `SQL_SUCCESS_WITH_INFO` is returned, but a corresponding SQLSTATE is not generated.

Prerequisites   There are no prerequisites for using this function call.

Restrictions   The ODBC 2.0 Driver Manager can return SQLSTATE values with a prefix of **IM**, even though these SQLSTATES are not defined by X/Open SQL CAE. Because of this, all branching logic in an application that is dependent upon SQLSTATE values should only rely on standard SQLSTATE values. Augmented SQLSTATEs should only be used for debugging purposes.

NOTE: *It may be useful to build logic dependencies on SQLSTATE class values (the first two characters of an SQLSTATE value).*

See Also

`SQLGetDiagRec()`, `SQLGetDiagField()`

Example

The following Visual C++ program illustrates how to use the **SQLError()** to obtain general diagnostic information when an ODBC API function fails to execute properly.

```
/*-------------------------------------------------------------------*/
/* NAME:     CH14EX2.CPP                                             */
/* PURPOSE: Illustrate How To Use The Following ODBC API Function    */
/*          In A C++ Program:                                        */
/*                                                                   */
/*               SQLError()                                          */
/*                                                                   */
/* OTHER ODBC APIs SHOWN:                                            */
/*          SQLAllocEnv()              SQLAllocConnect()             */
/*          SQLDriverConnect()         SQLDisconnect()               */
/*          SQLFreeConnect()           SQLFreeEnv()                  */
/*                                                                   */
/*-------------------------------------------------------------------*/

// Include The Appropriate Header Files
#include <windows.h>
#include <sql.h>
#include <sqlext.h>
#include <iostream.h>

// Define The ODBC_Class Class
class ODBC_Class
{
    // Attributes
    public:
        HENV      EnvHandle;
        HDBC      ConHandle;
        RETCODE rc;

    // Operations
    public:
        ODBC_Class();                          // Constructor
        ~ODBC_Class();                         // Destructor
};

// Define The Class Constructor
ODBC_Class::ODBC_Class()
{
    // Initialize The Return Code Variable
    rc = SQL_SUCCESS;
```

```cpp
    // Allocate An Environment Handle
    rc = SQLAllocEnv(&EnvHandle);

    // Allocate A Connection Handle
    if (rc == SQL_SUCCESS)
        rc = SQLAllocConnect(EnvHandle, &ConHandle);
}

// Define The Class Destructor
ODBC_Class::~ODBC_Class()
{
    // Free The Connection Handle
    if (ConHandle != NULL)
        SQLFreeConnect(ConHandle);

    // Free The Environment Handle
    if (EnvHandle != NULL)
        SQLFreeEnv(EnvHandle);
}

/*--------------------------------------------------------------------*/
/* The Main Function                                                  */
/*--------------------------------------------------------------------*/
int main()
{
    // Declare The Local Memory Variables
    RETCODE       rc = SQL_SUCCESS;
    SQLCHAR       ConnectIn[30];
    SQLINTEGER    NativeErr;
    SQLCHAR       SQLState[6];
    SQLCHAR       ErrMsg[255];
    SQLSMALLINT   ErrMsgLen;

    // Create An Instance Of The ODBC_Class Class
    ODBC_Class  Example;

    // Build A Connection String
    strcpy((char *) ConnectIn, "DSN=Southwind;UID=\"\";PWD=\"\";");

    // Attempt To Connect To The Southwind Sample Database (Since
    // This Database Does Not Exist, The SQLDriverConnect() Call
    // Should Fail And An Error Should Be Generated)
    if (Example.ConHandle != NULL)
    {
        rc = SQLDriverConnect(Example.ConHandle, NULL, ConnectIn,
                SQL_NTS, NULL, 0, NULL, SQL_DRIVER_NOPROMPT);

        // If The Specified Connection Was Not Established, Retrieve
        // And Display The Diagnostic Information Generated
        if (rc != SQL_SUCCESS && rc != SQL_SUCCESS_WITH_INFO)
        {
            rc = SQLError(SQL_NULL_HENV, Example.ConHandle,
                    SQL_NULL_HSTMT, SQLState, &NativeErr, ErrMsg,
                    255, &ErrMsgLen);
            cout << "SQLSTATE : " << SQLState << endl << endl;
```

```
        cout << ErrMsg << endl;
    }

    // If The Specified Connection Was Established, Display
    // A Success Message
    else
    {
        cout << "Connected to Southwind database." << endl;

        // Disconnect From The Southwind Sample Database
        rc = SQLDisconnect(Example.ConHandle);
    }
}

// Return To The Operating System
return(rc);
}
```

SQLGetDiagField

Purpose

The **SQLGetDiagField()** function is used to retrieve the current value of a field in a diagnostic header or status record (that is associated with a specific environment, connection, statement, or descriptor handle).

Syntax

```
SQLRETURN    SQLGetDiagField    (SQLSMALLINT    HandleType,
                                 SQLHANDLE      Handle,
                                 SQLSMALLINT    RecNumber,
                                 SQLSMALLINT    Identifier,
                                 SQLPOINTER     Value,
                                 SQLSMALLINT    ValueMaxSize,
                                 SQLSMALLINT    *StringLength);
```

Parameters *HandleType* Specifies which type of handle to retrieve disgnostic information for. This parameter must be set to one of the following values:

- **SQL_HANDLE_ENV**
Retrieve diagnostic information for an environment handle.

- **SQL_HANDLE_DBC**
Retrieve diagnostic information for a connection handle.

- **SQL_HANDLE_STMT**
Retrieve diagnostic information for an SQL statement handle.

- **SQL_HANDLES_DESC**
Retrieve diagnostic information for a descriptor handle.

Handle An environment, connection, SQL statement, or descriptor handle that refers to a previously allocated environment, connection, statement, or descriptor information storage buffer (data structure). If *HandleType* is set to **SQL_HANDLE_ ENV**, this parameter can contain either a shared, or an unshared environment handle.

RecNumber Specifies the diagnostic status record from which this function is to retrieve information. If any field of the diagnostic header record is specified in the *Identifier* parameter, this parameter is ignored. Otherwise, this parameter should contain a number greater than **0** (Status records are numbered, starting at **1**).

Identifier The field of the diagnostic header record or status record whose value is to be retrieved. This parameter must be set to one of the following values:

Header Record Fields

- **SQL_DIAG_CURSOR_ROW_COUNT**

- **SQL_DIAG_DYNAMIC_FUNCTION**

- **SQL_DIAG_DYNAMIC_FUNCTION_CODE**

- **SQL_DIAG_NUMBER**

- **SQL_DIAG_RETURNCODE**

- **SQL_DIAG_ROW_COUNT**

Status Record Fields

- **SQL_DIAG_CLASS_ORIGIN**
- **SQL_DIAG_COLUMN_NUMBER**
- **SQL_DIAG_CONNECTION_NAME**
- **SQL_DIAG_MESSAGE_TEXT**
- **SQL_DIAG_NATIVE**
- **SQL_DIAG_ROW_NUMBER**
- **SQL_DIAG_SERVER_NAME**
- **SQL_DIAG_SQLSTATE**
- **SQL_DIAG_SUBCLASS_ORIGIN**

Value   A pointer to a location in memory where this function is to store the current value of the specified diagnostic record field.

ValueMaxSize   The size of the memory storage buffer in which this function is to store the current value of the specified diagnostic record field. If an ODBC-defined diagnostic record field is to be retrieved, and if the field value is a 32-bit integer value, this parameter is ignored. If a driver-defined diagnostic record field is to be retrieved, this parameter may be set as follows:

- If the value of the specified diagnostic record field is a character string, this parameter may be set to the actual length of the string or to **SQL_NTS**.

- If the value of the specified diagnostic record field is a binary string, this parameter may be set to the result of the **SQL_LEN_BINARY_ATTR(*length*)** macro. Usually, this macro places a negative value in this parameter.

- If the value of the specified diagnostic record field is anything other than a character string or binary string, this parameter may be set to **SQL_IS_POINTER**.

- If the value of the specified diagnostic record field is a fixed-length data type, this

		parameter may be set to **SQL_IS_INTEGER** or **SQL_IS_UINTEGER**, as appropriate.
StringLength		A pointer to a location in memory where this function is to store the actual number of bytes written to the diagnostic record field value memory storage buffer (*Value*). If the value retrieved is not a character string value, this parameter ignored.

Description The **SQLGetDiagField()** function is used to retrieve the current value of a field in a diagnostic header or status record that is associated with a specific environment, connection, statement, or descriptor handle. A diagnostic record contains error, warning, and/or status information that is generated by the last ODBC API function executed. Table 14–3 alphabetically lists diagnostic header and status record fields, along with a description of the information returned for each field when this function is executed.

Table 14–4 describes the values of the **SQL_DYNAMIC_FUNCTION** and **SQL_DYNAMIC_FUNCTION_CODE** fields of a diagnostic header record that

Table 14–3 *Diagnostic Record Fields*

Field Name	Data Type	Description
Header Record Fields		
SQL_DIAG_CURSOR_ROW_COUNT	**SQLINTEGER**	This field contains a count of the number of rows in the current cursor. The contents of this field are only valid for SQL statement handles and then only after the **SQLExecute()**, **SQLExecDirect()**, or **SQLMoreResults()** function has been called.
SQL_DIAG_DYNAMIC_FUNCTION	**SQLCHAR ***	This field contains a string that describes the SQL statement the underlying function executed (refer to Table 14–4 for a list of valid values for this field). The contents of this field are only valid for SQL statement handles, and then only after the **SQLExecute()**, **SQLExecDirect()**, or **SQLMoreResults()** function has been called. The contents of this field is undefined before the **SQLExecute()** or the **SQLExecDirect()** function is called.

Table 14–3   *Continued*

Field Name	Data Type	Description
SQL_DIAG_DYNAMIC_FUNCTION_CODE	**SQLINTEGER**	This field contains a numeric code that describes the SQL statement executed by the underlying function (refer to Table 14–4 for a list of valid values for this field). The contents of this field are only defined for statement handles and only after a call to **SQLExecute()**, **SQLExecDirect()**, or **SQLMoreResults()**. The value of this field is undefined before a call to **SQLExecute** or **SQLExecDirect**.
SQL_DIAG_NUMBER	**SQLINTEGER**	The number of status records available for the specified handle.
SQL_DIAG_RETURNCODE	**SQLRETURN**	The return code returned by the ODBC API function. Refer to Table 14–1 for a list of valid return codes. The driver does not have to implement **SQL_DIAG_RETURNCODE**; it is always implemented by the ODBC Driver Manager. If no function has yet been called on the handle specified, **SQL_SUCCESS** is returned for **SQL_DIAG_RETURNCODE**.
SQL_DIAG_ROW_COUNT	**SQLINTEGER**	The number of rows affected by an insert, delete, or update operation performed by **SQLExecute()**, **SQLExecDirect()**, **SQLBulkOperations()**, or **SQLSetPos()**. The contents of this field are only defined for statement handles. The data in this field is also returned by **SQLRowCount()**. The data in this field is reset after every non-diagnostic function call, whereas the row count returned by **SQLRowCount()** remains the same until the statement is set back to the "Prepared" or "Allocated" state.

Status Record Fields

Field Name	Data Type	Description
SQL_DIAG_CLASS_ORIGIN	**SQLCHAR ***	A string indicating the document that defines the class portion of the SQLSTATE value in this record. Its value is "ISO 9075" for all SQLSTATEs defined by X/Open and ISO call-level interface. For ODBC-specific SQLSTATEs (all those whose SQLSTATE class is **IM**), its value is "ODBC 3.0."

Table 14–3 *Continued*

Field Name	Data Type	Description
SQL_DIAG_COLUMN_NUMBER	SQLINTEGER	If the SQL_DIAG_ROW_NUMBER field is a valid row number in a rowset or a set of parameters, this field contains the value representing the column number in the result data set or the parameter number in the set of parameters. Result data set column numbers always start at **1**; if this status record pertains to a bookmark column, the field can be **0**. Parameter numbers start at **1**. It has the value **SQL_NO_COLUMN_NUMBER** if the status record is not associated with a column number or parameter number. If the driver cannot determine the column number or parameter number this record is associated with, this field has the value **SQL_COLUMN_NUMBER_UNKNOWN**. The contents of this field are defined only for statement handles.
SQL_DIAG_CONNECTION_NAME	SQLCHAR *	A string indicating the name of the connection the diagnostic record relates to. This field is driver-defined. For diagnostic data structures associated with the environment handle and for diagnostics that do not relate to any connection, this field is a zero-length string.
SQL_DIAG_MESSAGE_TEXT	SQLCHAR *	An informational message about the error or warning. This field is formatted as described in the *Diagnostic Messages* section of this chapter. There is no maximum length to the diagnostic message text.
SQL_DIAG_NATIVE	SQLINTEGER	A driver/data source-specific native error code. If there is no native error code, the driver returns **0**.
SQL_DIAG_ROW_NUMBER	SQLINTEGER	This field contains the row number in the rowset, or the parameter number in the set of parameters, with which the status record is associated. Row numbers and parameter numbers start with **1**. This field has the value **SQL_NO_ROW_NUMBER** if this status record is not associated with a row number or parameter number. If the driver cannot determine the row number or parameter number this record is associated with, this field has the value **SQL_ROW_NUMBER_UNKNOWN**. The contents of this field are defined only for statement handles.

Table 14–3 Continued

Field Name	Data Type	Description
SQL_DIAG_SERVER_NAME	SQLCHAR *	A string indicating the server name to which the diagnostic record relates. It is the same as the value returned for a call to **SQLGetInfo()** with the **SQL_DATA_ SOURCE_NAME** *InfoType* specified. For diagnostic data structures associated with the environment handle and for diagnostics that do not relate to any server, this field is a zero-length string.
SQL_DIAG_SQLSTATE	SQLCHAR *	A five-character SQLSTATE diagnostic code.
SQL_DIAG_SUBCLASS_ORIGIN	SQLCHAR *	A string with the same format and valid values as **SQL_DIAG_CLASS_ORIGIN** that identifies the defining portion of the subclass portion of the SQLSTATE code. The ODBC-specific SQLSTATES for which "ODBC 3.0" is returned include the following: **01**S00, **01**S01, **01**S02, **01**S06, **01**S07, **07**S01, **08**S01, **21**S01, **21**S02, **25**S01, **25**S02, **25**S03, **42**S01, **42**S02, **42**S11, **42**S12, **42**S21, **42**S22, **HY**095, **HY**097, **HY**098, **HY**099, **HY**100, **HY**101, **HY**105, **HY**107, **HY**109, **HY**110, **HY**111, **HYT**00, **HYT**01, **IM**001, **IM**002, **IM**003, **IM**004, **IM**005, **IM**006, **IM**007, **IM**008, **IM**010, **IM**011, **IM**012.

(Adapted from the table on pages 728–732 of *Microsoft ODBC 3.0 Software Development Kit & Programmer's Reference*.)

apply to each type of SQL statement that can be executed with the **SQLExecute()** or **SQLExecDirect()** function.

An application typically calls this function to accomplish one of three goals:

■ To obtain specific error or warning information when an ODBC API function call has returned **SQL_SUCCESS_WITH_INFO**, **SQL_ERROR** or, in some cases, **SQL_NEED_DATA**.

■ To find out how many rows in a data source were affected when an insert, update, or delete operation was performed by calling the **SQLExecute()**, **SQLExecDirect()**, **SQLBulkOperations()**, or **SQLSetPos()** function (stored in the **SQL_DIAG_ROW_COUNT** header field), or to find out the number of rows that exist in the current open cursor, if the driver is able to provide this information (stored in the **SQL_DIAG_CURSOR_ROW_COUNT** header field).

Table 14–4 Values Returned In The **SQL_DYNAMIC_FUNCTION** And **SQL_DYNAMIC_FUNCTION_CODE** Fields Of A Diagnostic Header Record For Specific Types Of SQL Statements

Type Of SQL Statement	Value Of SQL_DIAG_ DYNAMIC_FUNCTION	Value Of SQL_DIAG_ DYNAMIC_FUNCTION_CODE
Alter Domain	"ALTER DOMAIN"	SQL_DIAG_ALTER_DOMAIN
Alter Table	"ALTER TABLE"	SQL_DIAG_ALTER_TABLE
Assertion Definition	"CREATE ASSERTION"	SQL_DIAG_CREATE_ASSERTION
Call (ODBC Procedure Extension)	"CALL"	SQL_DIAG_CALL
Character Set Definition	"CREATE CHARACTER SET"	SQL_DIAG_CREATE_CHARACTER_SET
Collation Definition	"CREATE COLLATION"	SQL_DIAG_CREATE_COLLATION
Create Index	"CREATE INDEX"	SQL_DIAG_CREATE_INDEX
Create Table	"CREATE TABLE"	SQL_DIAG_CREATE_TABLE
Create View	"CREATE VIEW"	SQL_DIAG_CREATE_VIEW
Cursor Specification	"SELECT CURSOR"	SQL_DIAG_SELECT_CURSOR
Domain Definition	"CREATE DOMAIN"	SQL_DIAG_CREATE_DOMAIN
Drop Assertion	"DROP ASSERTION"	SQL_DIAG_DROP_ASSERTION
Drop Character Set	"DROP CHARACTER SET"	SQL_DIAG_DROP_CHARACTER_SET
Drop Collation	"DROP COLLATION"	SQL_DIAG_DROP_COLLATION
Drop Domain	"DROP DOMAIN"	SQL_DIAG_DROP_DOMAIN
Drop Index	"DROP INDEX"	SQL_DIAG_DROP_INDEX
Drop Schema	"DROP SCHEMA"	SQL_DIAG_DROP_SCHEMA
Drop Table	"DROP TABLE"	SQL_DIAG_DROP_TABLE
Drop Translation	"DROP TRANSLATION"	SQL_DIAG_DROP_TRANSLATION
Drop View	"DROP VIEW"	SQL_DIAG_DROP_VIEW
Grant Authorizations	"GRANT"	SQL_DIAG_GRANT
Insert	"INSERT"	SQL_DIAG_INSERT
Positioned Delete	"DYNAMIC DELETE CURSOR"	SQL_DIAG_DYNAMIC_DELETE_CURSOR
Positioned Update	"DYNAMIC UPDATE CURSOR"	SQL_DIAG_DYNAMIC_UPDATE_CURSOR
Revoke Authorizations	"REVOKE"	SQL_DIAG_REVOKE
Schema Definition	"CREATE SCHEMA"	SQL_DIAG_CREATE_SCHEMA
Searched Delete	"DELETE WHERE"	SQL_DIAG_DELETE_WHERE
Searched Update	"UPDATE WHERE"	SQL_DIAG_UPDATE_WHERE
Translation Definition	"CREATE TRANSLATION"	SQL_DIAG_CREATE_TRANSLATION
Unknown	empty string	SQL_DIAG_UNKNOWN_STATEMENT

(Adapted from table on pages 733–734 of *Microsoft ODBC 3.0 Software Development Kit & Programmer's Reference.*)

▧ To determine which SQL operation was executed when the
SQLExecute() or the **SQLExecDirect()** function was called (stored
in the **SQL_DIAG_DYNAMIC_FUNCTION** and **SQL_DIAG_DYNAMIC_
FUNCTION_CODE** header fields).

An application typically calls this function when a previous call to an
ODBC API function has returned something other than **SQL_SUCCESS** or
SQL_INVALID_HANDLE. However, because any ODBC API function can post
zero or more diagnostic records when it is called, an application can call
this function immediately after making any ODBC API function call.

Status records are placed in a sequence that is based on row number
and the type of diagnostic information they contain. The ODBC Driver
Manager determines the final order in which to return the status records
it generates. Likewise, each driver determines the final order in which to
return the status records it generates. Refer to *Diagnostic Status Record
Sequence* in the first part of this chapter for more information about how
diagnostic status records are ordered.

If two or more status records exist, the sequence of the records is determined first by row number. The following rules apply to determining
the sequence of diagnostic record by row:

▧ Records that do not correspond to any row appear in front of
records that correspond to a particular row, because
SQL_NO_ROW_NUMBER is defined to be –1.

▧ Records for which the row number is unknown appear in front of
all other records, because **SQL_ROW_NUMBER_UNKNOWN** is defined to
be –2.

▧ All records pertaining to specific rows are sorted by the value in
the **SQL_DIAG_ROW_NUMBER** field. All errors and warnings of the
first row affected are listed, then all errors and warnings of the
next row affected, and so on.

NOTE: *The ODBC 3.x Driver Manager does not order status records in the
diagnostic queue if SQLSTATE 01S01 (Error in row) is returned by an ODBC
2.0 or earlier driver, or if SQLSTATE 01S01 (Error in row) is returned by an
ODBC 3.x driver when* **SQLExtendedFetch()** *is called or* **SQLSetPos()** *is called
on a cursor that has been positioned with* **SQLExtendedFetch()***.*

Return Codes   SQL_SUCCESS, SQL_SUCCESS_WITH_INFO, SQL_NO_DATA,
SQL_INVALID_HANDLE, or SQL_ERROR

SQLSTATEs   No SQLSTATE values are returned for this function because it does not generate diagnostic information for itself. Instead, this function uses the following return codes to report the outcome of its own execution:

▓ **SQL_SUCCESS**
The function successfully returned diagnostic information.

▓ **SQL_SUCCESS_WITH_INFO**
The error message buffer (*ErrorMsg*) was not large enough to hold the requested diagnostic field value.

▓ **SQL_NO_DATA**
The record number specified in the *RecNumber* parameter was greater than the number of diagnostic records that existed for the handle specified. This function also returns **SQL_NO_DATA** if a positive number is specified in the *RecNumber* parameter and there are no diagnostic records for the specified handle.

▓ **SQL_INVALID_HANDLE**
The handle specified by in the *HandleType* and *Handle* parameters was not a valid handle.

▓ **SQL_ERROR**
One of the following occurred:

▓ The value specified in the *Identifier* parameter was not valid.

▓ The value specified in the *Identifier* parameter was
SQL_DIAG_CURSOR_ROW_COUNT, **SQL_DIAG_DYNAMIC_FUNCTION**,
SQL_DIAG_DYNAMIC_FUNCTION_CODE, or **SQL_DIAG_ROW_COUNT** and an environment, connection, or descriptor handle was specified in the *Handle* parameter. The ODBC Driver Manager returns this error.

▓ The value specified in the *RecNumber* parameter was less than or equal to **0** and a record field was specified in the *Identifier* parameter. The *RecNumber* parameter is ignored when a header field is specified.

▓ A character string value was requested and the value specified in the *ErrorMsgMaxSize* parameter was less than **0**.

Comments   ▓ An application can call this function multiple times to return information from some or all of the records stored in the diagnostic information data structure. ODBC imposes no limit on the number of diagnostic records that can be stored in this structure at any one time.

■ If the value returned for the diagnostic record field specified in the *Identifier* parameter is a Unicode string, the *ValueMaxSize* parameter must contain an even number.

■ If the diagnostic information generated by an ODBC API function call is not retrieved before an API function other than **SQLGetDiagRec()**, **SQLError()**, or **SQLGetDiagField()** is called using the same environment, connection, statement, or descriptor handle, that information is lost. Diagnostic information stored on a given handle is not removed as the result of a call to a function using an associated handle of a different type.

■ Multiple diagnostic messages may be generated by an ODBC API function call. When this occurs, each diagnostic message can be retrieved, one at a time, by repeatedly incrementing the value of the *RecNumber* parameter and calling the **SQLGetDiagRec()** function (ODBC 3.x drivers) or by repeatedly calling the **SQLError()** function (ODBC 2.0 or earlier drivers). Calls to either function are non-destructive to diagnostic header and status record fields.

■ An application can determine the total number of diagnostic records available in the diagnostic information data structure by calling this function to retrieve the value of the **SQL_DIAG_NUMBER** field.

■ Each type of handle (environment, connection, statement, and descriptor) can have diagnostic information associated with it. However, some diagnostic header and status record fields cannot be returned for all types of handles. This function can be used to determine which diagnostic header and status record fields are applicable for each type of handle.

■ If this function is called with the *HandleType* parameter set to **SQL_HANDLE_SENV**, which denotes a shared environment handle, **SQL_INVALID_HANDLE** is returned. However, if this function is called with the *HandleType* parameter set to **SQL_HANDLE_ENV**, either a shared or an unshared environment handle can be specified in the *Handle* parameter.

■ No driver-specific header fields should be associated with an environment handle.

■ The only ODBC-specific header fields defined for a descriptor handle are **SQL_DIAG_NUMBER** and **SQL_DIAG_RETURNCODE**.

■ An application can call this function to return any diagnostic header or status record field value at any time, with the exception of the **SQL_DIAG_CURSOR_ROW_COUNT** or **SQL_DIAG_ROW_COUNT** filed, which returns **SQL_ERROR** if a statement handle is not specified. If any other diagnostic record field is undefined, this function returns **SQL_SUCCESS** (provided no other diagnostic is encountered), and an undefined value is returned for the field.

■ If the value specified for the *RecNumber* parameter is greater than or equal to **1**, the data in the specified field describes the diagnostic information returned by a function. If the value specified for the *RecNumber* parameter is equal to **0**, the field is in the diagnostic header record and contains data pertaining to the function call that returned the diagnostic information instead of the specific information.

■ Drivers can define driver-specific diagnostic header and status record fields.

■ An ODBC 3.x application working with an ODBC 2.0 or earlier driver is only able to call this function with the *Identifier* parameter set to **SQL_DIAG_CLASS_ORIGIN**, **SQL_DIAG_CLASS_SUBCLASS_ORIGIN**, **SQL_DIAG_CONNECTION_NAME**, **SQL_DIAG_MESSAGE_TEXT**, **SQL_DIAG_NATIVE**, **SQL_DIAG_NUMBER**, **SQL_DIAG_RETURNCODE**, **SQL_DIAG_SERVER_NAME**, or **SQL_DIAG_SQLSTATE**. If any other field is specified, **SQL_ERROR** is returned.

Prerequisites   There are no prerequisites for using this function call.

Restrictions   There are no restrictions associated with this function call.

See Also   SQLGetDiagRec(), SQLError()

Example   The following Visual C++ program illustrates how to use the SQLGetDiagField() to obtain specific diagnostic information when an ODBC API function fails to execute properly.

```
/*-------------------------------------------------------------*/
/* NAME:      CH14EX3.CPP                                       */
/* PURPOSE: Illustrate How To Use The Following ODBC API Function */
/*          In A C++ Program:                                   */
/*                                                              */
/*              SQLGetDiagField()                               */
/*                                                              */
/* OTHER ODBC APIs SHOWN:                                       */
/*          SQLAllocHandle()            SQLSetEnvAttr()         */
/*          SQLDriverConnect()          Disconnect()           */
/*          SQLFreeHandle()                                     */
/*                                                              */
/*-------------------------------------------------------------*/
```

```
// Include The Appropriate Header Files
#include <windows.h>
#include <sql.h>
#include <sqlext.h>
#include <iostream.h>

// Define The ODBC_Class Class
class ODBC_Class
{
    // Attributes
    public:
        SQLHANDLE      EnvHandle;
        SQLHANDLE      ConHandle;
        SQLRETURN      rc;

    // Operations
    public:
        ODBC_Class();                           // Constructor
        ~ODBC_Class();                          // Destructor
};

// Define The Class Constructor
ODBC_Class::ODBC_Class()
{
    // Initialize The Return Code Variable
    rc = SQL_SUCCESS;

    // Allocate An Environment Handle
    rc = SQLAllocHandle(SQL_HANDLE_ENV, SQL_NULL_HANDLE, &EnvHandle);

    // Set The ODBC Application Version To 3.x
    if (rc == SQL_SUCCESS)
        rc = SQLSetEnvAttr(EnvHandle, SQL_ATTR_ODBC_VERSION,
                    (SQLPOINTER) SQL_OV_ODBC3, SQL_IS_UINTEGER);

    // Allocate A Connection Handle
    if (rc == SQL_SUCCESS)
        rc = SQLAllocHandle(SQL_HANDLE_DBC, EnvHandle, &ConHandle);
}

// Define The Class Destructor
ODBC_Class::~ODBC_Class()
{
    // Free The Connection Handle
    if (ConHandle != NULL)
        SQLFreeHandle(SQL_HANDLE_DBC, ConHandle);

    // Free The Environment Handle
    if (EnvHandle != NULL)
        SQLFreeHandle(SQL_HANDLE_ENV, EnvHandle);
}
```

```
/*———————————————————————————————————*/
/* The Main Function                   */
/*———————————————————————————————————*/
int main()
{
    // Declare The Local Memory Variables
    SQLRETURN      rc = SQL_SUCCESS;
    SQLCHAR        ConnectIn[30];
    SQLCHAR        ErrMsg[255];
    SQLSMALLINT    ErrMsgLen;

    // Create An Instance Of The ODBC_Class Class
    ODBC_Class   Example;

    // Build A Connection String
    strcpy((char *) ConnectIn, "DSN=Southwind;UID=\"\";PWD=\"\";");

    // Attempt To Connect To The Southwind Sample Database (Since
    // This Database Does Not Exist, The SQLDriverConnect() Call
    // Should Fail And An Error Should Be Generated)
    if (Example.ConHandle != NULL)
    {
        rc = SQLDriverConnect(Example.ConHandle, NULL, ConnectIn,
                 SQL_NTS, NULL, 0, NULL, SQL_DRIVER_NOPROMPT);

        // If The Specified Connection Was Not Established, Retrieve
        // And Display The Error Message Generated
        if (rc != SQL_SUCCESS && rc != SQL_SUCCESS_WITH_INFO)
        {
            rc = SQLGetDiagField(SQL_HANDLE_DBC, Example.ConHandle,
                     1, SQL_DIAG_MESSAGE_TEXT, ErrMsg, 255,
                     &ErrMsgLen);
            cout << ErrMsg << endl;
        }

        // If The Specified Connection Was Established, Display
        // A Success Message
        else
        {
            cout << "Connected to Southwind database." << endl;

            // Disconnect From The Southwind Sample Database
            rc = SQLDisconnect(Example.ConHandle);
        }
    }

    // Return To The Operating System
    return(rc);
}
```

15

Querying the Data Source System Catalog

ODBC provides several API functions that are used to retrieve information from the system catalog of a specified data source. This chapter is designed to introduce you to the system catalog and to these API functions. The first part of this chapter describes the system catalog and explains how it is used. This is followed by a detailed discussion about the kinds of information returned by the ODBC catalog functions. Next, the different types of parameters used by the catalog functions are described. Then, the information available for stored procedures and the catalog functions used to obtain it is discussed. Finally, a detailed reference section covering each ODBC API catalog function is provided.

The System Catalog and the Catalog Functions

All databases have an internal structure that outlines how data is to be stored. This structure, along with information about access privileges, referential integrity, functions, and procedures is stored in a special set of system tables known as the *system catalog* (sometimes referred to as the *data dictionary*). Occasionally it becomes necessary for an ODBC application to retrieve information directly from this set of system tables. Although queries can be issued directly against the tables that comprise the system catalog, ODBC provides a set of API functions, known as the catalog functions, that are specifically designed to interact directly with a database's system catalog. By using these generic interface functions instead of custom queries, an application can avoid having to develop database product-specific or database product release-specific system catalog queries.

Data Returned by the Catalog Functions

The catalog functions are essentially a set of predefined, parameterized **SELECT** SQL statements that are either hard-coded in the driver or stored as a callable procedure within the driver's underlying data source. When called, each catalog function returns a result data set to the application via an SQL statement handle. An application can retrieve (fetch) individual rows of data from this result data set in the same manner that it would retrieve data from any other result data set.

The columns in the result data set returned by a catalog function are defined in a specific order. This is so that in future releases of ODBC, additional columns can be added without creating a problem for existing applications. Each result data set returned can contain both ODBC-specific columns and additional driver-specific columns that appear after the last ODBC-predefined column. Information about driver-specific columns, can most likely be found in the driver documentation.

Identifiers returned in the result data set produced by a catalog function are not quoted even if they contain special characters. For example, suppose the identifier quote character (which is driver-specific and can be determined by calling the **SQLGetInfo()** function) for a database is a double quotation mark (") and suppose a table in the database named Accounts Payable contains a column named Customer Name. When the

`SQLColumns()` catalog function is called using this scenario, the value returned in the **TABLE_NAME** column for this particular column is Accounts Payable, not "Accounts Payable", and the value returned in the **COLUMN_ NAME** column is Customer Name, not "Customer Name". However, a **SELECT** SQL statement designed to retrieve the names of customers in the Accounts Payable table must quote both of these names. For example:

```
SELECT "Customer Name" FROM "Accounts Payable"
```

The catalog functions are based on an SQL-like authorization model in which a connection is made based on a valid user ID (authorization name) and password, and only data for which the user has a authorization to retrieve is returned. Password protection of individual files, which does not fit into this model, is driver-defined. The result data sets returned by the catalog functions are almost never updateable and applications should not expect to be able to change the structure of a database by changing the data in these result data sets.

The execution of some catalog functions can result in the subsequent execution of fairly complex queries. Because of this, the catalog functions should only be called when needed. If the data produced by a catalog function will be used several times, an application can improve its overall performance by calling the catalog function once and saving the information returned, as opposed to making repeated function calls to obtain the same information.

Parameters (Arguments) Used in Catalog Functions

Each catalog function accepts input parameters (arguments) that are used to either identify or constrain the amount of information returned when the catalog function is executed. Catalog function input parameters fall into one of four different categories:

- Ordinary
- Pattern Value
- Identifier
- Value List

Most string parameters can be of one of two different types, depending upon the value of the **SQL_ATTR_METADATA_ID** SQL statement attribute.

Table 15–1 lists each catalog function, along with the input parameters used and the category of each parameter according to the value of the **SQL_ATTR_METADATA_ID** statement attribute (**SQL_TRUE** or **SQL_FALSE**).

Ordinary Parameters

When a catalog function input parameter (argument) is treated as an *Ordinary* parameter, it can only accept ordinary strings. If the **SQL_ATTR_METADATA_ID** statement attribute is set to **SQL_FALSE**, Ordinary parameters are treated as literal string parameters; if this attribute is set to **SQL_TRUE**, they are treated as Identifier parameters. Ordinary parameters do not accept a string search pattern or a list of values. Ordinary parameters are case-sensitive (the case of the letters in the string is significant), and quote characters in strings are taken literally. Furthermore, if an Ordinary parameter contains a NULL pointer and the parameter is a required parameter, the catalog function returns **SQL_ERROR** and SQL-STATE **HY**009 (Invalid use of NULL pointer). If an Ordinary parameter contains a NULL pointer and the parameter is not a required parameter, the catalog function's behavior is dependant on the driver.

Pattern Value Parameters

When a catalog function input parameter (argument) is treated as a *Pattern Value* parameter, it can accept both ordinary strings and strings containing one or more pre-defined search pattern characters. If the **SQL_ATTR_METADATA_ID** statement attribute is set to **SQL_FALSE**, Pattern Value parameters are treated as string parameters that accept search patterns; if this attribute is set to **SQL_TRUE**, they are treated as Identifier parameters that do not accept search patterns. The following search pattern values can be used in any Pattern Value parameter:

- The underscore character (_). Any single character can be used in place of the underscore character.
- The percent character (%). Any sequence of 0 or more characters can be used in place of the percent character.
- An escape character. A driver-specific character that is used to treat an underscore character, a percent character, and/or the escape character itself as a literal value instead of as a "wild card" value (for example, % = "%"). The driver-specific escape character can be retrieved by calling the **SQLGetInfo()** function with the

Table 15–1   The Category of Each Catalog Query Function Input Parameter as Determined by the Value of the **SQL_ATTR_METADATA_ID** Statement Attribute.

Function	Argument	Type when SQL_ATTR_ METADATA_ID= SQL_FALSE	Type when SQL_ATTR_ METADATA_ID= SQL_TRUE
SQLTables()	*CatalogName*	Pattern Value	Identifier
	SchemaName	Pattern Value	Identifier
	TableName	Pattern Value	Identifier
	TableType	Value List	Value List
SQLTablePrivileges()	*CatalogName*	Ordinary	Identifier
	SchemaName	Pattern Value	Identifier
	TableName	Pattern Value	Identifier
SQLColumns()	CatalogName	Ordinary	Identifier
	SchemaName	Pattern Value	Identifier
	TableName	Pattern Value	Identifier
	ColumnName	Pattern Value	Identifier
SQLColumnPrivileges()	*CatalogName*	Ordinary	Identifier
	SchemaName	Ordinary	Identifier
	TableName	Ordinary	Identifier
	ColumnName	Pattern Value	Identifier
SQLSpecialColumns()	*CatalogName*	Ordinary	Identifier
	SchemaName	Ordinary	Identifier
	TableName	Ordinary	Identifier
SQLStatistics()	*CatalogName*	Ordinary	Identifier
	SchemaName	Ordinary	Identifier
	TableName	Ordinary	Identifier
SQLPrimaryKeys()	*CatalogName*	Ordinary	Identifier
	SchemaName	Ordinary	Identifier
	TableName	Ordinary	Identifier
SQLForeignKeys()	*PKCatalogName*	Ordinary	Identifier
	PKSchemaName	Ordinary	Identifier
	PKTableName	Ordinary	Identifier
	FKCatalogName	Ordinary	Identifier
	FKSchemaName	Ordinary	Identifier
	FKTableName	Ordinary	Identifier
SQLProcedures()	*ProcCatalogName*	Ordinary	Identifier
	ProcSchemaName	Pattern Value	Identifier
	ProcedureName	Pattern Value	Identifier
SQLProcedureColumns	*ProcCatalogName*	Ordinary	Identifier
	ProcSchemaName	Pattern Value	Identifier
	ProcedureName	Pattern Value	Identifier
	ColumnName	Pattern Value	Identifier

(Adapted from tthe able on page 113 of *Microsoft ODBC 3.0 Software Development Kit & Programmer's Reference*.)

SQL_SEARCH_PATTERN_ESCAPE option specified. The escape character must precede any underscore, percent sign, or escape character in a Pattern Value parameter in order for that character to be treated as a literal character.

When using Pattern Value parameters, special care must be taken to escape appropriate search pattern characters. This is particularly true for the underscore character (_) which is commonly used in identifiers such as table names and column names. In fact, one mistake that's often made is to retrieve a value from one catalog function's result data set and pass it, unaltered, to a Pattern Value parameter of another catalog function. For example, suppose an application retrieves the table name **MY_TABLE** from the result data set produced by the **SQLTables()** function and passes this name to the **SQLColumns()** function to generate a list of the columns in **MY_TABLE**. Instead of getting a list of the columns defined for **MY_TABLE**, the application would get a list of the columns defined for all the tables matching the search pattern **MY_TABLE**, such as **MY_TABLE**, **MY1TABLE**, **MY2TABLE**, etc.

Another thing to keep in mind is that specifying a NULL pointer for a Pattern Value parameter does not constrain the search for that particular parameter. That's because a NULL pointer and the search pattern "%" (any characters) are treated the same. However, an empty string search pattern (that is, a valid pointer to a blank string, zero characters in length) constrains the search to match only the empty string (" ").

Identifier Parameters

When a catalog function input parameter (argument) is treated as an *Identifier* parameter, it can accept both ordinary strings and strings containing one or more pre-defined search pattern characters. If the **SQL_ATTR_METADATA_ID** statement attribute is set to **SQL_TRUE**, Identifier parameters are treated as Identifier parameters. In this case, the underscore character (_) and the percent sign (%) are treated as literal characters, not as search pattern characters. If the **SQL_ATTR_METADATA_ID** statement attribute is set to **SQL_FALSE**, Identifier parameters are treated either as Ordinary parameters or as Pattern Value parameters, depending upon the parameter value.

If an Identifier parameter contains a quoted string, the driver removes all leading and trailing blanks, and treats the string within the quotation marks literally. If the string is not quoted, the driver removes trailing blanks and converts the string to uppercase. Specifying a NULL pointer for an Identifier parameter causes all catalog functions to return **SQL_ERROR** and SQLSTATE **HY**009 (Invalid use of NULL pointer), unless the parameter specifies a catalog name for a database that does not support catalog names. Although identifiers containing special characters must be quoted in SQL statements, they must not be quoted when passed as catalog function parameters—quote characters passed to catalog functions are interpreted literally.

Keep in mind that quoted Identifier values are often used to distinguish a true column name from a pseudo-column with the same name. For example, if **ROWID** is specified in a catalog function, the function will work with the **ROWID** pseudo-column if it exists. If the pseudo-column does not exist, the function will work with the **ROWID** column. However, if **ROWID** is specified (unquoted), the function will only work with the **ROWID** column.

Value List Parameters

When a catalog function input parameter (argument) is treated as a *Value List* parameter, the parameter value consists of a list of comma-separated values that are to be used for value matching. Currently, there is only one Value List parameter used in the ODBC catalog functions: the *TableType* parameter of the **SQLTables()** function. Specifying a NULL pointer for this parameter is the same as specifying **SQL_ALL_TABLE_TYPES**, which enumerates all possible members of the value list. Value List parameters are not affected by the **SQL_ATTR_METADATA_ID** statement attribute.

Information_Schema Views

An application can also retrieve catalog information from a DBMS by using special views defined by the ANSI SQL-92 standard known as **INFORMATION_SCHEMA** views–provided the DBMS is ANSI SQL-92 compliant. If supported by the DBMS and the driver, the **INFORMATION_SCHEMA** views provide a more powerful and comprehensive means of retrieving catalog information than the ODBC catalog functions. An application can execute its own custom **SELECT** SQL statement against one of these views, join these views, or perform a union on these views. Unfortunately, **INFORMATION_SCHEMA** views are usually not supported by a DBMS. This may change as more DBMSs and drivers become ANSI SQL-92 compliant.

An application can call the **SQLGetInfo()** function with the **SQL_INFO_ SCHEMA_VIEWS** option specified to determine whether **INFORMATION_ SCHEMA** views are supported by the data source being used. To retrieve metadata from an **INFORMATION_SCHEMA** view, an application executes a **SELECT** SQL statement that specifies the schema information required.

Obtaining Information About Stored Procedures

If you recall, we saw in Chapter 2 that client/server applications are designed to run in two parts: one part executing on the client workstation and the other part executing on the server workstation where the database physically resides. The part running on the server workstation within the same transaction as the application is known as a *stored procedure*. Stored procedures are usually invoked from an ODBC application by passing the appropriate **CALL** SQL statement to the data source with either the **SQLExecDirect()** function, or with the **SQLPrepare()** function, followed by the **SQLExecute()** function. To obtain a list of stored procedures available for execution, an application can call the **SQLProcedures()** catalog function.

If a stored procedure requires information from the calling application, input parameter markers corresponding to the stored procedure's arguments must be coded in the **CALL** SQL statement. The parameter markers in the **CALL** statement are then bound to application variables with the **SQLBindParameter()** function. Before application variable binding takes place, an application can call the **SQLProcedureColumns()** catalog function to find out what kind of information a stored procedure call is expecting.

Although most stored procedure arguments can be used both for input and for output, an application should specify one type or the other when the **SQLBindParameter()** function is called. This helps avoid sending unnecessary data between the client and the server.

The ODBC Data Source Catalog Query Functions

Table 15–2 lists the ODBC API functions that are used to retrieve information from the system catalog of a specified data source.

Each of these functions are described in detail in the remaining portion of this chapter.

Table 15–2   The ODBC Error/Diagnostic Message Retrieval Functions

Function Name	Description
SQLTables()	Retrieves a list of catalog names, schema names, table names, or table types that have been defined for a data source.
SQLTablePrivileges()	Retrieves a list of table names, along with the authorization information associated with those tables, that have been defined for a data source.
SQLColumns()	Retrieves a list of column names found in one or more tables.
SQLColumnPrivileges()	Retrieves a list of column names, along with the authorization information associated with those columns, that have been defined for a specified table.
SQLSpecialColumns()	Retrieves a list of the optimal set of columns that uniquely identify a row of data in a specified table.
SQLStatistics()	Retrieves statistical information about a specified table along with a list of associated indexes for that table.
SQLPrimaryKeys()	Retrieves a list of column names that comprise the primary key of a specified table.
SQLForeignKeys()	Retrieves a list of foreign keys in a specified table or a list of foreign keys that refer to a specified table.
SQLProcedures()	Retrieves a list of stored procedure names that are stored in and that are available for a data source.
SQLProcedureColumns()	Retrieves a list of input and output parameters, the return value, and the columns in the result data set produced by a specified stored procedure.

SQLTables

COMPATABILITY

X/OPEN 95 CLI	ISO/IEC 92 CLI	ODBC 1.0	ODBC 2.0	ODBC 3.0	ODBC 3.5
✓	☐	✓	✓	✓	✓

API CONFORMANCE LEVEL   **CORE***

*IN ODBC 2.0, THIS FUNCTION WAS A LEVEL 1 API CONFORMANCE LEVEL FUNCTION

Purpose   The **SQLTables()** function is used to retrieve a list of table names (and all associated information) stored in a specified data source's system catalog.

Syntax

```
SQLRETURN   SQLTables   (SQLHSTMT      StatementHandle,
                         SQLCHAR       *CatalogName,
                         SQLSMALLINT   CatalogNameSize,
                         SQLCHAR       *SchemaName,
                         SQLSMALLINT   SchemaNameSize,
                         SQLCHAR       *TableName,
                         SQLSMALLINT   TableNameSize,
                         SQLCHAR       *TableType,
                         SQLSMALLINT   TableTypeSize);
```

Parameters

StatementHandle	An SQL statement handle that refers to a previously allocated SQL statement information storage buffer (data structure).
CatalogName	A pointer to a location in memory where either the catalog qualifier portion of a three-part table name is stored or a catalog name search pattern is stored.
CatalogNameSize	The length of the catalog qualifier name or search pattern value stored in the *CatalogName* parameter.
SchemaName	A pointer to a location in memory where a schema name search pattern is stored.
SchemaNameSize	The length of the schema name search pattern stored in the *SchemaName* parameter.

TableName	A pointer to a location in memory where a table name search pattern is stored.
TableNameSize	The length of the table name search pattern value stored in the *TableName* parameter.
TableType	A pointer to a location in memory where information about the types of tables to retrieve data for is stored. Examples of table types that might be specified include:

- "**TABLE**"
- "**VIEW**"
- "**ALIAS**"
- "**SYNONYM**"
- "**SYSTEM TABLE**"
- "**LOCAL TEMPORARY**"
- "**GLOBAL TEMPORARY**"

If a NULL pointer is specified for this parameter, all table types found will be returned.

TableTypeSize	The length of the table type value stored in the *TableType* parameter.

Description The **SQLTables()** function is used to retrieve a list of table names (and all associated information) stored in a specified data source's system catalog. The information returned by this function is placed in a result data set, which can be processed by using the same ODBC API functions used to process result data sets generated by SQL queries. Table 15–3 lists the columns in this result data set.

One or more driver-defined columns may be added to this result data set. When that is the case, applications should gain access to each driver-specific column by counting down from column 5 (**REMARKS**) of the result data set rather than by specifying an explicit ordinal position.

NOTE: *Depending on the driver being used,* **SQLTables()** *may or may not return information for all columns in the result data set. However, applications can use any valid column in the result data set, regardless of whether it contains data.*

Table 15–3   Result Data Set Returned By **SQLTables()**

Column Number	Column Name	Data Type	Description
1	**TABLE_CAT**[1] (ODBC 1.0)	VARCHAR(*128*)	The name of the catalog (qualifier) containing the **TABLE_SCHEM** value. If a data source does not support three-part table names, this column is set to NULL. If a data source supports three-part table names for a limited number of tables, this column contains an empty string (" ") for tables that do not have a catalog (qualifier) name.
2	**TABLE_SCHEM**[2] (ODBC 1.0)	VARCHAR(*128*)	The name of the schema containing the **TABLE_NAME** value. If a data source does not support three-part table names, this column is set to NULL. If a data source supports three-part table names for a limited number of tables, this column contains an empty string (" ") for tables that do not have a schema name.
3	**TABLE_NAME** (ODBC 1.0)	VARCHAR(*128*)	The name of the table, view, alias, synonym, system table, local temporary table, global temporary table, or data source-specific object.
4	**TABLE_TYPE** (ODBC 1.0)	VARCHAR(*128*)	The type of object the name in the **TABLE_NAME** column represents. Valid values for this column are: "**TABLE**" "**SYSTEM TABLE**" "**VIEW**" "**LOCAL TEMPORARY**" "**ALIAS**" "**GLOBAL TEMPORARY**" "**SYNONYM**" any other data-source specific table type identifier.
5	**REMARKS** (ODBC 1.0)	VARCHAR(*254*)	Descriptive information about the table, view, alias, synonym, system table, local temporary table, global temporary table, or data source-specific object.

(Adapted from the table on page 1024 of *Microsoft ODBC 3.0 Software Development Kit & Programmer's Reference*.)

[1]In ODBC 2.0 and earlier, this column was named **TABLE_QUALIFIER**.
[2]In ODBC 2.0 and earlier, this column was named **TABLE_OWNER**.

Return Codes   SQL_SUCCESS, SQL_SUCCESS_WITH_INFO, SQL_STILL_EXECUTING, SQL_INVALID_HANDLE, or SQL_ERROR

SQLSTATEs

If this function returns **SQL_SUCCESS_WITH_INFO** or **SQL_ERROR**, one of the following SQLSTATE values may be obtained by calling the **SQLGetDiagRec()** function (ODBC 3.x driver) or the **SQLError()** function (ODBC 2.0 or earlier driver):

ODBC 3.X
01000, **08**S01, **24**000, **40**001, **40**003, **HY**000, **HY**001, **HY**008, **HY**009*, **HY**010*, **HY**013, **HY**090*, **HY**C00, **HY**T00, **HY**T01, or **IM**001*

ODBC 2.0 OR EARLIER
01000, **08**S01, **24**000*, **IM**001*, **S1**000, **S1**001, **S1**008, **S1**010*, **S1**090*, **S1**C00, or **S1**T00

* Returned by the ODBC Driver Manager.

Unless noted otherwise, each of these SQLSTATE values is returned by the data source driver. Refer to Appendix B for detailed information about each SQLSTATE value that can be returned by the ODBC Driver Manager or by a data source driver.

Comments

- Because this function, in many cases, maps to a complex, and therefore, expensive query against a data source's system catalog tables, it should be used sparingly; if the result data set produced is to be used more than once, it should be saved, rather than be regenerated each time it is needed.

- An empty string (" ") can be stored in the memory location that the *CatalogName* parameter refers to for catalogs without names (provided the driver supports catalog names).

- An empty string (" ") can be stored in the memory location the *SchemaName* parameter refers to for schemas without names (provided the driver supports schema names).

- If the **SQL_ATTR_METADATA_ID** attribute for the statement handle specified is set to **SQL_TRUE**, the values specified for the *CatalogName*, *SchemaName*, and *TableName* parameters are treated as identifier values and their case is insignificant. However, if the **SQL_ATTR_METADATA_ID** attribute is set to **SQL_FALSE**, the values specified for the *CatalogName*, *SchemaName*, and *TableName* parameters are treated literally, and their case is significant. Refer to the "Parameters (Arguments) Used in Catalog Functions" section earlier in this chapter and to the **SQLGetStmtAttr()** function for more information.

- The values specified for the *SchemaName*, *TableName*, and *ColumnName* parameters can contain the following search pattern values:

  - The underscore character (_)
    Any single character can be used in place of the underscore character.

  - The percent character (%)
    Any sequence of 0 or more characters can be used in place of the percent character.

  - An escape character
    A driver-specific character used to treat an underscore character, a percent character, and/or the escape character itself as a literal value instead of as a wild card value (that is, % = "%").

- If the **SQL_ODBC_VERSION** environment attribute is set to **SQL_OV_ODBC3**, the value specified for the *CatalogName* parameter can contain the same search patterns that values specified for the *SchemaName*, *TableName*, and *ColumnName* parameters can contain.

- To support enumeration of catalog names, schema names, and table types, the following special semantics are defined:

  - If the value specified for the *CatalogName* parameter is **SQL_ALL_CATALOGS**, and if the values specified for the *SchemaName* and *TableName* parameters are empty strings, then the result data set produced contains a list of valid catalogs for the current data source. (All columns in the result data set except the **TABLE_CAT** column contain NULLs.)

  - If the value specified for the *SchemaName* parameter is **SQL_ALL_SCHEMAS** and if the values specified for the *CatalogName* and *TableName* parameters are empty strings, then the result data set produced contains a list of valid schemas for the current data source. (All columns in the result data set except the **TABLE_SCHEM** column contain NULLs.)

  - If the value specified for the *TableType* parameter is **SQL_ALL_TABLE_TYPES** and if the values specified for the *CatalogName*, *SchemaName*, and *TableName* parameters are empty strings, the result data set produced contains a list of valid table types for the data source. (All columns in the result data set except the **TABLE_TYPE** column contain NULLs.)

- The result data set returned by this function is ordered by **TABLE_TYPE**, **TABLE_CAT**, **TABLE_SCHEM**, and **TABLE_NAME**.

- The **SQLTablePrivileges()** function or the **SQLGetInfo()** function with the **SQL_ACCESSIBLE_TABLES** option specified can be used to determine the type of access allowed on any given table in the result data set produced by this function. If neither of these functions are used to obtain table authorization information, an application must be coded so that it can handle situations in which a user selects a table for which they have not been granted **SELECT** authorization privileges.

- If the value specified for the *TableType* parameter is not an empty string, it must contain a list of upper-case, comma-separated values specifing the table types to retrieve information for. Each value in this list can either be enclosed in single quotes, or left unquoted. For example, either " '**TABLE**', '**VIEW**' " or "**TABLE**, **VIEW**" are valid.

- If the current data source does not recognize or support a specified table type, no information is returned for that particular type of table.

- The actual amount of memory needed to store the value found in each **VARCHAR** column in the result data set produced by this function is dependent on the data source. An application can choose to set aside 128 characters (plus the NULL-terminator) for **VARCHAR** columns (to be consistent with the SQL92 standard limits), or alternatively, to allocate the actual amount of memory required by first calling the **SQLGetInfo()** function with the *InfoType* parameter set to **SQL_MAX_CATALOG_NAME_LEN**, **SQL_MAX_SCHEMA_NAME_LEN**, **SQL_MAX_TABLE_NAME_LEN**, and/or **SQL_MAX_COLUMN_NAME_LEN** to determine respectively the actual lengths of the **TABLE_CAT**, **TABLE_SCHEM**, **TABLE_NAME**, and **COLUMN_NAME** columns that are supported by the current data source.

Prerequisites

There are no prerequisites for using this function call.

Restrictions

There are no restrictions associated with this function call.

See Also

SQLTablePrivileges(), **SQLColumns()**

Example

The following Visual C++ program illustrates how to use the **SQLTables()** function to obtain information about the tables that are available in a data source.

```
/*--------------------------------------------------------------------*/
/* NAME:     CH15EX1.CPP                                              */
/* PURPOSE: Illustrate How To Use The Following ODBC API Function    */
/*          In A C++ Program:                                        */
/*                                                                   */
/*              SQLTables()                                          */
/*                                                                   */
/* OTHER ODBC APIs SHOWN:                                            */
/*          SQLAllocHandle()            SQLSetEnvAttr()              */
/*          SQLConnect()                SQLBindCol()                 */
/*          SQLFetch()                  SQLDisconnect()              */
/*          SQLFreeHandle()                                          */
/*                                                                   */
/*--------------------------------------------------------------------*/

// Include The Appropriate Header Files
#include <windows.h>
#include <sql.h>
#include <sqlext.h>
#include <iostream.h>

// Define The ODBC_Class Class
class ODBC_Class
{
    // Attributes
    public:
        SQLHANDLE    EnvHandle;
        SQLHANDLE    ConHandle;
        SQLHANDLE    StmtHandle;
        SQLRETURN    rc;

    // Operations
    public:
        ODBC_Class();                               // Constructor
        ~ODBC_Class();                              // Destructor
        SQLRETURN   ShowTableInfo();
};

// Define The Class Constructor
ODBC_Class::ODBC_Class()
{
    // Initialize The Return Code Variable
    rc = SQL_SUCCESS;

    // Allocate An Environment Handle
    rc = SQLAllocHandle(SQL_HANDLE_ENV, SQL_NULL_HANDLE, &EnvHandle);

    // Set The ODBC Application Version To 3.x
    if (rc == SQL_SUCCESS)
        rc = SQLSetEnvAttr(EnvHandle, SQL_ATTR_ODBC_VERSION,
                (SQLPOINTER) SQL_OV_ODBC3, SQL_IS_UINTEGER);

    // Allocate A Connection Handle
```

```
     if (rc == SQL_SUCCESS)
         rc = SQLAllocHandle(SQL_HANDLE_DBC, EnvHandle, &ConHandle);
}

// Define The Class Destructor
ODBC_Class::~ODBC_Class()
{
    // Free The Connection Handle
    if (ConHandle != NULL)
        SQLFreeHandle(SQL_HANDLE_DBC, ConHandle);

    // Free The Environment Handle
    if (EnvHandle != NULL)
        SQLFreeHandle(SQL_HANDLE_ENV, EnvHandle);
}

// Define The ShowTableInfo() Member Function
SQLRETURN ODBC_Class::ShowTableInfo(void)
{
    // Declare The Local Memory Variables
    SQLCHAR    TableName[129];

    // Allocate An SQL Statement Handle
    rc = SQLAllocHandle(SQL_HANDLE_STMT, ConHandle, &StmtHandle);
    if (rc == SQL_SUCCESS)
    {
        // Retrieve Information About The Tables In The Data Source
        rc = SQLTables(StmtHandle, NULL, 0, NULL, 0,
                (SQLCHAR *) "%", SQL_NTS, (SQLCHAR *) "TABLES", 6);
        if (rc == SQL_SUCCESS)
        {
            // Bind A Column In The Result Data Set Returned To
            // An Application Variable
            rc = SQLBindCol(StmtHandle, 3, SQL_C_CHAR, (SQLPOINTER)
                    &TableName, sizeof(TableName), NULL);

            // Display A Header
            cout << "Tables :" << endl << endl;

            // While There Are Records In The Result Data Set
            // Generated, Retrieve And Display Them
            while (rc != SQL_NO_DATA)
            {
                rc = SQLFetch(StmtHandle);
                if (rc != SQL_NO_DATA)
                    cout << TableName << endl;
            }
        }

        // Free The SQL Statement Handle
        if (StmtHandle != NULL)
            SQLFreeHandle(SQL_HANDLE_STMT, StmtHandle);
    }
```

```
    // Return The ODBC API Return Code To The Calling Function
    return(rc);
}

/*─────────────────────────────────────────────────────────── */
/* The Main Function                                            */
/*─────────────────────────────────────────────────────────── */
int main()
{
    // Declare The Local Memory Variables
    SQLRETURN  rc = SQL_SUCCESS;
    SQLCHAR    DBName[10] = "Northwind";

    // Create An Instance Of The ODBC_Class Class
    ODBC_Class  Example;

    // Connect To The Northwind Sample Database
    if (Example.ConHandle != NULL)
    {
        rc = SQLConnect(Example.ConHandle, DBName, SQL_NTS,
                (SQLCHAR *) "", SQL_NTS, (SQLCHAR *) "", SQL_NTS);

        // Call The ShowTableInfo() Member Function
        if (rc == SQL_SUCCESS || rc == SQL_SUCCESS_WITH_INFO)
            Example.ShowTableInfo();

        // Disconnect From The Northwind Sample Database
        rc = SQLDisconnect(Example.ConHandle);
    }

    // Return To The Operating System
    return(rc);
}
```

SQLTablePrivileges

COMPATABILITY

X/OPEN 95 CLI	ISO/IEC 92 CLI	ODBC 1.0	ODBC 2.0	ODBC 3.0	ODBC 3.5
☐	☐	☑	☑	☑	☑

API CONFORMANCE LEVEL   **LEVEL 2**

Purpose The `SQLTablePrivileges()` function is used to retrieve a list of table names stored in a specified data source's system catalog and the privileges associated with them.

Syntax

```
SQLRETURN   SQLTablePrivileges  (SQLHSTMT     StatementHandle,
                                 SQLCHAR      *CatalogName,
                                 SQLSMALLINT  CatalogNameSize,
                                 SQLCHAR      *SchemaName,
                                 SQLSMALLINT  SchemaNameSize,
                                 SQLCHAR      *TableName,
                                 SQLSMALLINT  TableNameSize);
```

Parameters

StatementHandle	An SQL statement handle that refers to a previously allocated SQL statement information storage buffer (data structure).
CatalogName	A pointer to a location in memory where the catalog qualifier portion of a three-part table name is stored.
CatalogNameSize	The length of the catalog qualifier name value stored in the *CatalogName* parameter.
SchemaName	A pointer to a location in memory where a schema name search pattern is stored.
SchemaNameSize	The length of the schema name search pattern value stored in the *SchemaName* parameter.
TableName	A pointer to a location in memory where a table name search pattern is stored.
TableNameSize	The length of the table name search pattern value stored in the *TableName* parameter.

Description The `SQLTablePrivileges()` function is used to retrieve a list of table names stored in the system catalog of a specified data source and the privileges associated with them. The information returned by this function is placed in a result data set that can be processed by using the same ODBC API functions used to process result data sets generated by SQL queries. Table 15–4 lists the columns in this result data set.

One or more driver-defined columns may be added to this result data set. When that is the case, applications should gain access to each driver-specific column by counting down from column 7 (`IS_GRANTABLE`) of the result data set rather than by specifying an explicit ordinal position.

Table 15–4   Result Data Set Returned by **SQLTablePrivileges()**

Column Number	Column Name	Data Type	Description
1	**TABLE_CAT**[1] (ODBC 1.0)	VARCHAR(*128*)	The name of the catalog (qualifier) containing the **TABLE_SCHEM** value. If a data source does not support three-part table names, this column is set to NULL. If a data source supports three-part table names for a limited number of tables, this column contains an empty string (" ") for tables that do not have a catalog (qualifier) name.
2	**TABLE_SCHEM**[2] (ODBC 1.0)	VARCHAR(*128*)	The name of the schema containing the **TABLE_NAME** value. If a data source does not support three-part table names, this column is set to NULL. If a data source supports three-part table names for a limited number of tables, this column contains an empty string (" ") for tables that do not have a schema.
3	**TABLE_NAME** (ODBC 1.0)	VARCHAR(*128*) NOT NULL	The name of the table.
4	**GRANTOR** (ODBC 1.0)	VARCHAR(*128*)	The name or authorization ID of the user granting the table privilege. If the **GRANTEE** column contains the name or authorization ID of the owner of the table identified in the **TABLE_NAME** column, this column contains "**_SYSTEM.**"
5	**GRANTEE** (ODBC 1.0)	VARCHAR(*128*) NOT NULL	The name or authorization ID of the user to whom the privilege was granted.
6	**PRIVILEGE** (ODBC 1.0)	VARCHAR(*128*) NOT NULL	The table privilege that was granted. Valid values for this column are: "**SELECT**": The **GRANTEE** is permitted to retrieve data from one or more columns of the table. "**INSERT**": The **GRANTEE** is permitted to insert new rows of data into one or more columns of the table. "**UPDATE**": The **GRANTEE** is permitted to modify the data in one or more columns of the table. "**DELETE**": The **GRANTEE** is permitted to remove rows of data from the table.

[1]In ODBC 2.0 and earlier, this column was named **TABLE_QUALIFIER**
[2]In ODBC 2.0 and earlier, this column was named **TABLE_OWNER**.

Table 15–4 Result Data Set Returned by **SQLTablePrivileges()** (Continued)

Column Number	Column Name	Data Type	Description
			"REFERENCES": The **GRANTEE** is permitted to refer to one or more columns of the table within a constraint (for example, a unique, referential, or table check constraint).
			The scope of action given to the **GRANTEE** by a specific table **PRIVILEGE** is data source-dependent. For example, one data source might permit a **GRANTEE** with the **"UPDATE"** privilege to modify the data in all columns in a table, while another data source might only permit the **GRANTEE** to modify the data in those columns for which the **GRANTOR** has the **"UPDATE"** privilege.
7	**IS_GRANTABLE**	**VARCHAR(3)**	Indicates whether the **GRANTEE** is permitted to grant the **PRIVILEGE** to other users. Valid values for this column are:
			"YES" **"NO"** **NULL**: Unknown or not applicable to the data source.
			A **PRIVILEGE** can be either grantable or not grantable, but not both.

(Adapted from the table on pages 1015–1016 of *Microsoft ODBC 3.0 Software Development Kit & Programmer's Reference*.)

NOTE: *Depending on the driver being used,* **SQLTablePrivileges()** *may or may not return information for all columns in the result data set. However, applications can use any valid column in the result data set, regardless of whether it contains data.*

Return Codes SQL_SUCCESS, SQL_SUCCESS_WITH_INFO, SQL_STILL_EXECUTING, SQL_INVALID_HANDLE, or SQL_ERROR

SQLSTATEs If this function returns **SQL_SUCCESS_WITH_INFO** or **SQL_ERROR**, one of the following SQLSTATE values may be obtained by calling the **SQLGetDiagRec()** function (ODBC 3.x driver) or the **SQLError()** function (ODBC 2.0 or earlier driver):

ODBC 3.X
01000, **08**S01, **24**000, **40**001, **40**003, **HY**000, **HY**001, **HY**008, **HY**009*,
HY010*, **HY**013, **HY**090*, **HY**C00, **HY**T00, **HY**T01, or **IM**001*

ODBC 2.0 OR EARLIER
01000, **08**S01, **24**000*, **IM**001*, **S1**000, **S1**001, **S1**008, **S1**010*, **S1**090*,
S1C00, or **S1**T00

* Returned by the ODBC Driver Manager.

Unless noted otherwise, each of these SQLSTATE values is returned
by the data source driver. Refer to Appendix B for detailed information
about each SQLSTATE value that can be returned by the ODBC Driver
Manager or by a data source driver.

Comments

▨ Because this function, in many cases, maps to a complex, and
therefore expensive, query against a data source's system catalog
tables, it should be used sparingly; if the result data set produced is
to be used more than once, it should be saved, rather than be
regenerated each time it is needed.

▨ An empty string (" ") can be stored in the memory location the
CatalogName parameter refers to for catalogs without names
(provided the driver supports catalog names).

▨ An empty string (" ") can be stored in the memory location the
SchemaName parameter refers to for schemas without names
(provided the driver supports schema names).

▨ If the **SQL_ATTR_METADATA_ID** attribute for the statement handle
specified is set to **SQL_TRUE**, the values specified for the
CatalogName, *SchemaName*, and *TableName* parameters are treated
as identifier values, and their case is insignificant. However, if the
SQL_ATTR_METADATA_ID attribute is set to **SQL_FALSE**, the values
specified for the *CatalogName*, *SchemaName*, and *TableName*
parameters are treated literally, and their case is significant. Refer to
the "Parameters (Arguments) Used in Catalog Functions" section at
the beginning of this chapter and to the **SQLGetStmtAttr()** function
for more information.

▨ The values specified for the *SchemaName* and *TableName*
parameters can contain the following search pattern values:

  ▨ The underscore character (_)
    Any single character can be used in place of the underscore
    character.

- The percent character (%)

  Any sequence of 0 or more characters can be used in place of the percent character.

- An escape character

  A driver-specific character used to treat an underscore character, a percent character, and/or the escape character itself as a literal value instead of as a wild card value (i.e. % = "%").

- The result data set returned by this function is ordered by **TABLE_CAT**, **TABLE_SCHEM**, **TABLE_NAME**, and **PRIVILEGE**.

- The actual amount of memory needed to store the value found in each **VARCHAR** column in the result data set produced by this function is dependent on the data source. An application can choose to set aside 128 characters (plus the NULL-terminator) for **VARCHAR** columns (to be consistent with the SQL92 standard limits), or alternatively, to allocate the actual amount of memory required by first calling the **SQLGetInfo()** function with the *InfoType* parameter set to **SQL_MAX_CATALOG_NAME_LEN**, **SQL_MAX_SCHEMA_NAME_LEN**, **SQL_MAX_TABLE_NAME_LEN**, and/or **SQL_MAX_COLUMN_NAME_LEN** to determine respectively the actual lengths of the **TABLE_CAT**, **TABLE_SCHEM**, **TABLE_NAME**, and **COLUMN_NAME** columns that are supported by the current data source.

Prerequisites   There are no prerequisites for using this function call.

Restrictions   There are no restrictions associated with this function call.

See Also   SQLTables(), SQLColumnPrivileges()

Example   The following Visual C++ program illustrates how to use the SQLTablePrivileges() function to obtain information about the privileges associated with the tables that are available in a data source.

```
/*------------------------------------------------------------*/
/* NAME:     CH15EX2.CPP                                      */
/* PURPOSE: Illustrate How To Use The Following ODBC API Function */
/*          In A C++ Program:                                 */
/*                                                            */
/*              SQLTablePrivileges()                          */
/*                                                            */
/* OTHER ODBC APIs SHOWN:                                     */
/*              SQLAllocHandle()          SQLSetEnvAttr()     */
/*              SQLDriverConnect()        SQLBindCol()        */
/*              SQLFetch()                SQLDisconnect()     */
```

```
/*              SQLFreeHandle()                                        */
/*                                                                     */
/*———————————————————————————————————————————————————————————————————— */

// Include The Appropriate Header Files
#include <windows.h>
#include <sql.h>
#include <sqlext.h>
#include <iostream.h>

// Define The ODBC_Class Class
class ODBC_Class
{
    // Attributes
    public:
        SQLHANDLE   EnvHandle;
        SQLHANDLE   ConHandle;
        SQLHANDLE   StmtHandle;
        SQLRETURN   rc;

    // Operations
    public:
        ODBC_Class();                               // Constructor
        ~ODBC_Class();                              // Destructor
        SQLRETURN   ShowTablePrivilegeInfo();
};

// Define The Class Constructor
ODBC_Class::ODBC_Class()
{
    // Initialize The Return Code Variable
    rc = SQL_SUCCESS;

    // Allocate An Environment Handle
    rc = SQLAllocHandle(SQL_HANDLE_ENV, SQL_NULL_HANDLE, &EnvHandle);

    // Set The ODBC Application Version To 3.x
    if (rc == SQL_SUCCESS)
        rc = SQLSetEnvAttr(EnvHandle, SQL_ATTR_ODBC_VERSION,
                (SQLPOINTER) SQL_OV_ODBC3, SQL_IS_UINTEGER);

    // Allocate A Connection Handle
    if (rc == SQL_SUCCESS)
        rc = SQLAllocHandle(SQL_HANDLE_DBC, EnvHandle, &ConHandle);
}

// Define The Class Destructor
ODBC_Class::~ODBC_Class()
{
    // Free The Connection Handle
    if (ConHandle != NULL)
        SQLFreeHandle(SQL_HANDLE_DBC, ConHandle);
```

```
        // Free The Environment Handle
        if (EnvHandle != NULL)
            SQLFreeHandle(SQL_HANDLE_ENV, EnvHandle);
}

// Define The ShowTablePrivilegeInfo() Member Function
SQLRETURN ODBC_Class::ShowTablePrivilegeInfo(void)
{
        // Declare The Local Memory Variables
        SQLCHAR   GrantorName[129];

        // Allocate An SQL Statement Handle
        rc = SQLAllocHandle(SQL_HANDLE_STMT, ConHandle, &StmtHandle);
        if (rc == SQL_SUCCESS)
        {
            // Retrieve Information About The Privileges Associated With
            // The "EMPLOYEES" Table In The Data Source
            rc = SQLTablePrivileges(StmtHandle, NULL, 0, NULL, 0,
                    (SQLCHAR *) "EMPLOYEES", SQL_NTS);
            if (rc == SQL_SUCCESS)
            {
                // Bind A Column In The Result Data Set Returned To
                // An Application Variable
                rc = SQLBindCol(StmtHandle, 4, SQL_C_CHAR, (SQLPOINTER)
                        &GrantorName, sizeof(GrantorName), NULL);

                // Display A Header
                cout << "Table Privilege Grantor :" << endl << endl;

                // While There Are Records In The Result Data Set
                // Generated, Retrieve And Display Them
                while (rc != SQL_NO_DATA)
                {
                    rc = SQLFetch(StmtHandle);
                    if (rc != SQL_NO_DATA)
                        cout << GrantorName << endl;
                }
            }

            // Free The SQL Statement Handle
            if (StmtHandle != NULL)
                SQLFreeHandle(SQL_HANDLE_STMT, StmtHandle);
        }

        // Return The ODBC API Return Code To The Calling Function
        return(rc);
}

/*-------------------------------------------------------------------------*/
/* The Main Function                                                       */
/*-------------------------------------------------------------------------*/
int main()
{
```

```
// Declare The Local Memory Variables
SQLRETURN   rc = SQL_SUCCESS;
SQLCHAR     ConnectIn[40];

// Create An Instance Of The ODBC_Class Class
ODBC_Class   Example;

// Build A Connection String
strcpy((char *) ConnectIn,
    "DSN=SQLServer;UID=userid;PWD=password;");

// Connect To The SQL Server Sample Database
if (Example.ConHandle != NULL)
{
    rc = SQLDriverConnect(Example.ConHandle, NULL, ConnectIn,
            SQL_NTS, NULL, 0, NULL, SQL_DRIVER_NOPROMPT);

    // Call The ShowTablePrivilegeInfo() Member Function
    if (rc == SQL_SUCCESS || rc == SQL_SUCCESS_WITH_INFO)
        Example.ShowTablePrivilegeInfo();

    // Disconnect From The SQL Server Sample Database
    rc = SQLDisconnect(Example.ConHandle);
}

// Return To The Operating System
return(rc);
}
```

SQLColumns

COMPATABILITY					
X/OPEN 95 CLI	ISO/IEC 92 CLI	ODBC 1.0	ODBC 2.0	ODBC 3.0	ODBC 3.5
☑	☐	☑	☑	☑	☑

API CONFORMANCE LEVEL	CORE*

*IN ODBC 2.0, THIS FUNCTION WAS A LEVEL 1 API CONFORMANCE LEVEL FUNCTION

Purpose   The **SQLColumns()** function is used to retrieve a list of column names associated with a specified table.

Syntax

```
SQLRETURN   SQLColumns   (SQLHSTMT       StatementHandle,
                          SQLCHAR        *CatalogName,
                          SQLSMALLINT    CatalogNameSize,
                          SQLCHAR        *SchemaName,
                          SQLSMALLINT    SchemaNameSize,
                          SQLCHAR        *TableName,
                          SQLSMALLINT    TableNameSize,
                          SQLCHAR        *ColumnName,
                          SQLSMALLINT    ColumnNameSize);
```

Parameters

StatementHandle	An SQL statement handle that refers to a previously allocated SQL statement information storage buffer (data structure).
CatalogName	A pointer to a location in memory where the catalog qualifier portion of a three-part table name is stored.
CatalogNameSize	The length of the catalog qualifier name value stored in the *CatalogName* parameter.
SchemaName	A pointer to a location in memory where the schema portion of a three-part table name is stored.
SchemaNameSize	The length of the schema name value stored in the *SchemaName* parameter.
TableName	A pointer to a location in memory where a table name search pattern is stored.
TableNameSize	The length of the table name search pattern value stored in the *TableName* parameter.
ColumnName	A pointer to a location in memory where a column name search pattern is stored.
ColumnNameSize	The length of the column name search pattern value stored in the *ColumnName* parameter.

Description

The **SQLColumns()** function is used to retrieve a list of columns names for a specified base table, view, system table, alias (synonym) etc. The information returned by this function is placed in a result data set that can be processed by using the same ODBC API functions used to process result data sets generated by SQL queries. Table 15–5 lists the columns in this result data set.

Table 15–5 Result Data Set Returned by **SQLColumns()**

Column Number	Column Name	Data Type	Description
1	**TABLE_CAT**[1] (ODBC 1.0)	VARCHAR(*128*)	The name of the catalog (qualifier) containing the **TABLE_SCHEM** value. If a data source does not support three-part table names, this column is set to NULL. If a data source supports three-part table names for a limited number of tables, this column contains an empty string (" ") for tables that do not have a catalog (qualifier) name.
2	**TABLE_SCHEM**[2] (ODBC 1.0)	VARCHAR(*128*)	The name of the schema containing the **TABLE_NAME** value. If a data source does not support three-part table names, this column is set to NULL. If a data source supports three-part table names for a limited number of tables, this column contains an empty string (" ") for tables that do not have a schema.
3	**TABLE_NAME** (ODBC 1.0)	VARCHAR(*128*) NOT NULL	The name of the table.
4	**COLUMN_NAME** (ODBC 1.0)	VARCHAR(*128*) NOT NULL	The name of a column in the table identified in the **TABLE_NAME** column. This column contains an empty string (" ") for columns without a name.
5	**DATA_TYPE** (ODBC 1.0)	SMALLINT NOT NULL	The ODBC or driver-specific SQL data type of the column identified in the **COLUMN_NAME** column. Valid values for this column include: SQL_CHAR, SQL_VARCHAR, SQL_LONGVARCHAR, SQL_WCHAR, SQL_WVARCHAR, SQL_WLONGVARCHAR, SQL_DECIMAL, SQL_NUMERIC, SQL_SMALLINT, SQL_INTEGER, SQL_REAL, SQL_FLOAT, SQL_DOUBLE, SQL_BIT, SQL_TINYINT, SQL_BIGINT, SQL_BINARY, SQL_VARBINARY, SQL_LONGVARBINARY, SQL_TYPE_DATE, SQL_TYPE_TIME, SQL_TYPE_TIMESTAMP, SQL_INTERVAL_MONTH, SQL_INTERVAL_YEAR, SQL_INTERVAL_YEAR_TO_MONTH, SQL_INTERVAL_DAY, SQL_INTERVAL_HOUR,

[1]In ODBC 2.0 and earlier, this column was named **TABLE_QUALIFIER**.
[2]In ODBC 2.0 and earlier, this column was named **TABLE_OWNER**.

Table 15–5   Result Data Set Returned by **SQLColumns()**   (Continued)

Column Number	Column Name	Data Type	Description
			SQL_INTERVAL_MINUTE, SQL_INTERVAL_SECOND, SQL_INTERVAL_DAY_TO_HOUR, SQL_INTERVAL_DAY_TO_MINUTE, SQL_INTERVAL_DAY_TO_SECOND, SQL_INTERVAL_HOUR_TO_MINUTE, SQL_INTERVAL_HOUR_TO_SECOND, SQL_INTERVAL_MINUTE_TO_SECOND, SQL_GUID
			For datetime and interval data types, this column contains the concise data type (such as **SQL_TYPE_DATE** or **SQL_INTERVAL_YEAR_TO_MONTH**, rather than the non-concise data type such as **SQL_DATETIME** or **SQL_INTERVAL**) (ODBC 3.x applications only).
			NOTE: SQL data types returned for ODBC 3.x, ODBC 2.0, and ODBC 1.0 applications may be different.
6	**TYPE_NAME** (ODBC1.0)	**VARCHAR(**128**)** **NOT NULL**	The data source-specific character representation of the SQL data type name identified in the **DATA_TYPE** column. Valid values for this column include:
			CHAR, VARCHAR, LONG VARCHAR, WCHAR, VARWCHAR, LONGWVARCHAR, DECIMAL, NUMERIC, SMALLINT, INTEGER, REAL, FLOAT, DOUBLE PRECISION, BIT, TINYINT, BIGINT, BINARY, VARBINARY, LONG VARBINARY, DATE, TIME, TIMESTAMP, INTERVAL MONTH, INTERVAL YEAR, INTERVAL YEAR TO MONTH, INTERVAL DAY, INTERVAL HOUR, INTERVAL MINUTE, INTERVAL SECOND, INTERVAL DAY TO HOUR, INTERVAL DAY TO MINUTE, INTERVAL DAY TO SECOND, INTERVAL HOUR TO MINUTE, INTERVAL HOUR TO SECOND, INTERVAL MINUTE TO SECOND, GUID
7	**COLUMN_SIZE**[3] (ODBC 1.0)	**INTEGER**	The maximum number of bytes needed to display the column data in character format.
			For numeric data types, this is either the total number of digits, or the total number of bits allowed in the column, depending on the value in the **NUM_PREC_RADIX** column.

[3]In ODBC 2.0 and earlier, this column was named **PRECISION**.

Table 15-5 Result Data Set Returned by **SQLColumns()** (Continued)

Column Number	Column Name	Data Type	Description
			For character or binary string data types, this is the size of the string (length), in bytes.
			For date, time, and timestamp data types, this is the total number of characters required to display the value when it is converted to a character string.
			For interval data types, this is the total number of characters in the character representation of the interval literal (as defined by the interval leading precision value).
8	BUFFER_LENGTH[4] INTEGER (ODBC 1.0)		The maximum number of bytes needed in order for the associated C application variable (buffer) to store data from this column if the value **SQL_C_DEFAULT** is specified for the *CDataType* parameter of the **SQLBindParameter() SQLBindCol()**, or **SQLGetData()** function. This length does not include the NULL-terminator character used by NULL terminated strings.
9	DECIMAL_ DIGITS[5] (ODBC 1.0)	SMALLINT	The total number of significant digits to the right of the decimal point.
			If the **DATA_TYPE** column contains **SQL_TYPE_TIME** or **SQL_TYPE_ TIMESTAMP**, this column contains the number of digits in the fractional seconds component of the time value.
			For interval data types containing a time component, this column contains the number of digits to the right of the decimal point (fractional seconds).
			For interval data types that do not contain a time component, this column contains the value zero (**0**).
			For data types where decimal digits are not applicable, this column is set to NULL.

[4]In ODBC 2.0 and earlier, this column was named **LENGTH**.
[5]In ODBC 2.0 andearlier, this column was named **SCALE**.

Table 15–5 Result Data Set Returned by **SQLColumns()** (Continued)

Column Number	Column Name	Data Type	Description
			For all other data types, this column contains the decimal digits of the column on the data source.
10	NUM_PREC_ RADIX[6] (ODBC 1.0)	SMALLINT	The radix value of the column.
			For approximate numeric data types, this column contains the value **2** and the **COLUMN_ SIZE** column contains the number of bits allowed in the column.
			For exact numeric data types, this column contains the value **10** and the **COLUMN_ SIZE** column contains the number of decimal digits allowed for the column.
			For numeric data types, this column can contain either **10** or **2**.
			For data types where radix is not applicable, this column is set to NULL.
11	NULLABLE (ODBC 1.0)	SMALLINT NOT NULL	Indicates whether the column accepts a NULL value. Valid values for this column are:
			SQL_NO_NULLS: The column does not accept NULL values.
			SQL_NULLABLE: The column accepts NULL values.
			SQL_NULLABLE_UNKNOWN: Whether the column accepts NULL values is not known.
			The value in this column is different from the value in the **IS_NULLABLE** column. The **NULLABLE** column indicates with certainty that a column can accept NULLs, but it cannot indicate with certainty that a column does not accept NULLs. The **IS_NULLABLE** column indicates with certainty that a column cannot accept NULLs, but it cannot indicate with certainty that a column accepts NULLs.
12	REMARKS (ODBC 1.0)	VARCHAR(254)	Descriptive information about the column (if any exists).
13	COLUMN_DEF (ODBC 3.0)	VARCHAR(254)	The column's default value.

[6]In ODBC 2.0 and earlier, this column was named **RADIX**.

Table 15–5 Result Data Set Returned by `SQLColumns()` (Continued)

Column Number	Column Name	Data Type	Description
			If the default value is a numeric literal, this column contains the character representation of the numeric literal with no enclosing single quotes.
			If the default value is a character string, this column contains that string enclosed in single quotes.
			If the default value is a pseudo-literal, (as is the case for **DATE**, **TIME**, and **TIMESTAMP** columns), this column contains the keyword of the pseudo-literal (for example: "CURRENT DATE") with no enclosing single quotes.
			If the default value is NULL or if no default value was specified, this column contains the word NULL with no enclosing single quotes.
			If the default value cannot be represented without truncation, this column contains the word "TRUNCATED" with no enclosing single quotes.
			The value of this column can be used in generating a new column definition, except when it contains the value "TRUNCATED".
14	SQL_DATA_ TYPE (ODBC 3.0)	SMALLINT NOT NULL	The SQL data type of the column identified in the **COLUMN_NAME** column, as it would appear in an implementation row descriptor record's **SQL_DESC_TYPE** field. This can be an ODBC SQL data type or a driver-specific SQL data type.
			This column usually contains the same value as the **DATA_TYPE** column, with the following exception:
			For datetime and interval data types, this column contains the non-concise data type (such as **SQL_DATETIME** or **SQL_INTERVAL**), rather than the concise data type (such as **SQL_TYPE_DATE** or **SQL_INTERVAL_ YEAR_TO_MONTH**). If this column contains **SQL_DATETIME** or **SQL_INTERVAL**, the specific data type can be obtained from the **SQL_DATETIME_SUB** column.

Table 15–5 Result Data Set Returned by **SQLColumns()** (Continued)

Column Number	Column Name	Data Type	Description
			NOTE: SQL data types returned for ODBC 3.x, ODBC 2.0, and ODBC 1.0 applications may be different.
15	**DATETIME_SUB** (ODBC 3.0)	**SMALLINT**	The subtype code for datetime and interval data types. For all other data types, this column is set to NULL.
16	**CHAR_OCTET_ LENGTH** (ODBC 3.0)	**INTEGER**	Contains the maximum length, in octets (bytes), for a character data type column. For single byte character sets, this column contains the same value as the **COLUMN_ SIZE** column. For all other character sets, this column is set to NULL.
17	**ORDINAL_ POSITION** (ODBC 3.0)	**INTEGER NOT NULL**	The column's sequence number in the table. The first column in the table is number 1, the second column is number 2, and so on.
18	**IS_NULLABLE** (ODBC 3.0)	**VARCHAR(***254***)**	Indicates whether the column is known to be nullable (can contain NULL values), according to the rules in the ISO SQL92 standard. Valid values for this column are:

"YES"
The column can contain NULL values.

"NO"
The column cannot contain NULL values.

(" ") (Empty string):
Whether the column can contain NULL values is not known.

An ISO SQL92-compliant DBMS cannot return an empty string.

The value returned for this column is different from the value returned for the **NULLABLE** column. (See the description of the **NULLABLE** column for details.)

(Adapted from the table on pages 544–549 of *Microsoft ODBC 3.0 Software Development Kit & Programmer's Reference.*)

One or more driver-defined columns may be added to this result data set. When that is the case, applications should gain access to each driver-specific column by counting down from column 18 (**IS_NULLABLE**) of the result data set rather than by specifying an explicit ordinal position.

> **NOTE:** *Depending on the driver being used,* `SQLColumns()` *may or may not return information for all columns in the result data set. However, applications can use any valid column in the result data set, regardless of whether it contains data.*

Return Codes   `SQL_SUCCESS`, `SQL_SUCCESS_WITH_INFO`, `SQL_STILL_EXECUTING`, `SQL_INVALID_HANDLE`, or `SQL_ERROR`

SQLSTATEs   If this function returns `SQL_SUCCESS_WITH_INFO` or `SQL_ERROR`, one of the following SQLSTATE values may be obtained by calling the `SQLGetDiagRec()` function (ODBC 3.x driver) or the `SQLError()` function (ODBC 2.0 or earlier driver):

ODBC 3.X
01000, **08**S01, **24**000, **40**001, **40**003, **HY**000, **HY**001, **HY**008, **HY**009*, **HY**010*, **HY**013, **HY**090*, **HYC**00, **HYT**00, **HYT**01, or **IM**001*

ODBC 2.0 OR EARLIER
01000, **08**S01, **24**000*, **IM**001*, **S1**000, **S1**001, **S1**008, **S1**010*, **S1**090*, **S1C**00, or **S1T**00

* Returned by the ODBC Driver Manager.

Unless noted otherwise, each of these SQLSTATE values is returned by the data source driver. Refer to Appendix B for detailed information about each SQLSTATE value that can be returned by the ODBC Driver Manager or by a data source driver.

Comments   ▨ Because this function, in many cases, maps to a complex and therefore expensive query against a data source's system catalog tables, it should be used sparingly; if the result data set produced is to be used more than once, it should be saved, rather than be regenerated each time it is needed.

▨ An empty string (" ") can be stored in the memory location the *CatalogName* parameter refers to for catalogs without names (provided the driver supports catalog names).

▨ An empty string (" ") can be stored in the memory location the *SchemaName* parameter refers to for schemas without names (provided the driver supports schema names).

▨ If the `SQL_ATTR_METADATA_ID` attribute for the statement handle specified is set to `SQL_TRUE`, the values specified for the *CatalogName*,

SchemaName, *TableName*, and *ColumnName* parameters are treated as identifier values and their case is insignificant. However, if the **SQL_ATTR_METADATA_ID** attribute is set to **SQL_FALSE**, the values specified for the *CatalogName*, *SchemaName*, *TableName*, and *ColumnName* parameters are treated literally and their case is significant. Refer to the "Parameters (Arguments) Used In Catalog Functions" section at the beginning of this chapter and to the **SQLGetStmtAttr()** function for more information.

■ The values specified for the *TableName* and *ColumnName* parameters can contain the following search pattern values:

■ The underscore character (_).
Any single character can be used in place of the underscore character.

■ The percent character (%).
Any sequence of 0 or more characters can be used in place of the percent character.

■ An escape character.
A driver-specific character used to treat an underscore character, a percent character, and/or the escape character itself as a literal value instead of as a wild card value (that is, % = "%").

■ The result data set returned by this function is ordered by **TABLE_CAT**, **TABLE_SCHEM**, **TABLE_NAME**, and **ORDINAL_POSITION**.

■ The actual amount of memory needed to store the value found in each **VARCHAR** column in the result data set produced by this function is dependent on the data source. An application can choose to set aside 128 characters (plus the NULL-terminator) for **VARCHAR** columns (to be consistent with the SQL92 standard limits), or alternatively, to allocate the actual amount of memory required by first calling the **SQLGetInfo()** function with the *InfoType* parameter set to **SQL_MAX_CATALOG_NAME_LEN**, **SQL_MAX_SCHEMA_NAME_LEN**, **SQL_MAX_TABLE_NAME_LEN**, and/or **SQL_MAX_COLUMN_NAME_LEN** to determine respectively the actual lengths of the **TABLE_CAT**, **TABLE_SCHEM**, **TABLE_NAME**, and **COLUMN_NAME** columns that are supported by the current data source.

■ When this function is executed against an ODBC 2.0 or earlier driver, the **ORDINAL_POSITION** column is not returned in the result data set produced. As a result, the order of the columns in the column list returned by this function when working with ODBC 2.0 or earlier drivers is not necessarily the same as the order of the columns returned when a **SELECT** SQL statement that retrieves all columns in the specified table is executed.

■ Some columns that may be returned by the **SQLStatistics()** function are not returned by this function. For example, this function does not return columns in an index created from an expression or filter (for example, **SALARY + BENEFITS** or **DEPT = 0012**).

Prerequisites   There are no prerequisites for using this function call.

Restrictions   There are no restrictions associated with this function call.

See Also   SQLTables(), SQLColumnPrivileges(), SQLSpecialColumns()

Example

The following Visual C++ program illustrates how to use the **SQLColumns()** function to obtain information about the columns that are available in a data source.

```
/*——————————————————————————————————————————————*/
/* NAME:      CH15EX3.CPP                                    */
/* PURPOSE: Illustrate How To Use The Following ODBC API Function */
/*          In A C++ Program:                                */
/*                                                           */
/*              SQLColumns()                                 */
/*                                                           */
/* OTHER ODBC APIs SHOWN:                                    */
/*              SQLAllocHandle()          SQLSetEnvAttr()    */
/*              SQLConnect()              SQLBindCol()       */
/*              SQLFetch()                SQLDisconnect()    */
/*              SQLFreeHandle()                              */
/*                                                           */
/*——————————————————————————————————————————————*/

// Include The Appropriate Header Files
#include <windows.h>
#include <sql.h>
#include <sqlext.h>
#include <iostream.h>

// Define The ODBC_Class Class
class ODBC_Class
{
    // Attributes
    public:
        SQLHANDLE    EnvHandle;
        SQLHANDLE    ConHandle;
        SQLHANDLE    StmtHandle;
        SQLRETURN    rc;

    // Operations
    public:
```

```cpp
        ODBC_Class();                           // Constructor
        ~ODBC_Class();                          // Destructor
        SQLRETURN  ShowColumnInfo();
};

// Define The Class Constructor
ODBC_Class::ODBC_Class()
{
    // Initialize The Return Code Variable
    rc = SQL_SUCCESS;

    // Allocate An Environment Handle
    rc = SQLAllocHandle(SQL_HANDLE_ENV, SQL_NULL_HANDLE, &EnvHandle);

    // Set The ODBC Application Version To 3.x
    if (rc == SQL_SUCCESS)
        rc = SQLSetEnvAttr(EnvHandle, SQL_ATTR_ODBC_VERSION,
                (SQLPOINTER) SQL_OV_ODBC3, SQL_IS_UINTEGER);

    // Allocate A Connection Handle
    if (rc == SQL_SUCCESS)
        rc = SQLAllocHandle(SQL_HANDLE_DBC, EnvHandle, &ConHandle);
}

// Define The Class Destructor
ODBC_Class::~ODBC_Class()
{
    // Free The Connection Handle
    if (ConHandle != NULL)
        SQLFreeHandle(SQL_HANDLE_DBC, ConHandle);

    // Free The Environment Handle
    if (EnvHandle != NULL)
        SQLFreeHandle(SQL_HANDLE_ENV, EnvHandle);
}

// Define The ShowColumnInfo() Member Function
SQLRETURN ODBC_Class::ShowColumnInfo(void)
{
    // Declare The Local Memory Variables
    SQLCHAR   ColumnName[129];

    // Allocate An SQL Statement Handle
    rc = SQLAllocHandle(SQL_HANDLE_STMT, ConHandle, &StmtHandle);
    if (rc == SQL_SUCCESS)
    {
        // Retrieve Information About The Columns Defined For The
        // "Customers" Table In The Data Source
        rc = SQLColumns(StmtHandle, NULL, 0, NULL, 0,
                (SQLCHAR *) "Customers", SQL_NTS, NULL, 0);
        if (rc == SQL_SUCCESS)
        {
            // Bind A Column In The Result Data Set Returned To
            // An Application Variable
            rc = SQLBindCol(StmtHandle, 4, SQL_C_CHAR, (SQLPOINTER)
```

```
                          &ColumnName, sizeof(ColumnName), NULL);

              // Display A Header
              cout << "Columns :" << endl << endl;

              // While There Are Records In The Result Data Set
              // Generated, Retrieve And Display Them
              while (rc != SQL_NO_DATA)
              {
                  rc = SQLFetch(StmtHandle);
                  if (rc != SQL_NO_DATA)
                      cout << ColumnName << endl;
              }
        }

        // Free The SQL Statement Handle
        if (StmtHandle != NULL)
            SQLFreeHandle(SQL_HANDLE_STMT, StmtHandle);
    }

    // Return The ODBC API Return Code To The Calling Function
    return(rc);
}


/*——————————————————————————————————————————————————————————————*/
/* The Main Function                                            */
/*——————————————————————————————————————————————————————————————*/
int main()
{
    // Declare The Local Memory Variables
    SQLRETURN   rc = SQL_SUCCESS;
    SQLCHAR     DBName[10] = "Northwind";

    // Create An Instance Of The ODBC_Class Class
    ODBC_Class   Example;

    // Connect To The Northwind Sample Database
    if (Example.ConHandle != NULL)
    {
        rc = SQLConnect(Example.ConHandle, DBName, SQL_NTS,
                  (SQLCHAR *) "", SQL_NTS, (SQLCHAR *) "", SQL_NTS);

        // Call The ShowColumnInfo() Member Function
        if (rc == SQL_SUCCESS || rc == SQL_SUCCESS_WITH_INFO)
            Example.ShowColumnInfo();

        // Disconnect From The Northwind Sample Database
        rc = SQLDisconnect(Example.ConHandle);
    }

    // Return To The Operating System
    return(rc);
}
```

SQLColumnPrivileges

COMPATABILITY

X/OPEN 95 CLI	ISO/IEC 92 CLI	ODBC 1.0	ODBC 2.0	ODBC 3.0	ODBC 3.5
☐	☐	☑	☑	☑	☑

API CONFORMANCE LEVEL   **LEVEL 2**

Purpose
The **SQLColumnPrivileges()** function is used to retrieve for a specified table a list of column names and their associated privileges.

Syntax

```
SQLRETURN   SQLColumnPrivileges (SQLHSTMT      StatementHandle,
                                 SQLCHAR       *CatalogName,
                                 SQLSMALLINT   CatalogNameSize,
                                 SQLCHAR       *SchemaName,
                                 SQLSMALLINT   SchemaNameSize,
                                 SQLCHAR       *TableName,
                                 SQLSMALLINT   TableNameSize,
                                 SQLCHAR       *ColumnName,
                                 SQLSMALLINT   ColumnNameSize);
```

Parameters

StatementHandle
An SQL statement handle that refers to a previously allocated SQL statement information storage buffer (data structure).

CatalogName
A pointer to a location in memory where the catalog qualifier portion of a three-part table name is stored.

CatalogNameSize
The length of the catalog qualifier name value stored in the *CatalogName* parameter.

SchemaName
A pointer to a location in memory where the schema portion of a three-part table name is stored.

SchemaNameSize
The length of the schema name value stored in the *SchemaName* parameter.

TableName
A pointer to a location in memory where the table name portion of a three-part table name is stored.

TableNameSize	The length of the table name value stored in the *TableName* parameter.
ColumnName	A pointer to a location in memory where a column name search pattern is stored.
ColumnNameSize	The length of the column name search pattern value stored in the *ColumnName* parameter.

Description

The `SQLColumnPrivileges()` function is used to retrieve a list of column names and the privileges associated with them for a specified table. The information returned by this function is placed in a result data set, which can be processed by using the same ODBC API functions used to process result data sets generated by SQL queries. Table 15–6 lists the columns in this result data set.

One or more driver-defined columns may be added to this result data set. When that is the case, applications should gain access to each driver-specific column by counting down from column 8 (`IS_GRANTABLE`) of the result data set rather than by specifying an explicit ordinal position.

NOTE: *Depending on the driver being used,* `SQLColumnPrivileges()` *may or may not return information for all columns in the result data set. However, applications can use any valid column in the result data set, regardless of whether it contains data.*

Return Codes

`SQL_SUCCESS`, `SQL_SUCCESS_WITH_INFO`, `SQL_STILL_EXECUTING`, `SQL_INVALID_HANDLE`, or `SQL_ERROR`

SQLSTATEs

If this function returns `SQL_SUCCESS_WITH_INFO` or `SQL_ERROR`, one of the following SQLSTATE values may be obtained by calling the `SQLGetDiagRec()` function (ODBC 3.x driver) or the `SQLError()` function (ODBC 2.0 or earlier driver):

ODBC 3.X
01000, **08**S01, **24**000, **40**001, **40**003, **HY**000, **HY**001, **HY**008, **HY**009*, **HY**010*, **HY**013, **HY**090*, **HY**C00, **HY**T00, **HY**T01, or **IM**001*

ODBC 2.0 OR EARLIER
01000, **08**S01, **24**000*, **IM**001*, **S1**000, **S1**001, **S1**008, **S1**010*, **S1**090*, **S1**C00, or **S1**T00

* Returned by the ODBC Driver Manager.

Table 15–6 Result Data Set Returned by **SQLColumnPrivileges()**

Column Number	Column Name	Data Type	Description
1	**TABLE_CAT**[1] (ODBC 1.0)	**VARCHAR(** *128* **)**	The name of the catalog (qualifier) containing the **TABLE_SCHEM** value. If a data source does not support three-part table names, this column is set to NULL. If a data source supports three-part table names for a limited number of tables, this column contains an empty string (" ") for tables that do not have a catalog (qualifier) name.
2	**TABLE_SCHEM**[2] (ODBC 1.0)	**VARCHAR(** *128* **)**	The name of the schema containing the **TABLE_NAME** value. If a data source does not support three-part table names, this column is set to NULL. If a data source supports three-part table names for a limited number of tables, this column contains an empty string (" ") for tables that do not have a schema name.
3	**TABLE_NAME** (ODBC 1.0)	**VARCHAR(** *128* **)** **NOT NULL**	The name of the table.
4	**COLUMN_NAME** (ODBC 1.0)	**VARCHAR(** *128* **)** **NOT NULL**	The name of a column in the table identified in the **TABLE_NAME** column. This column contains an empty string (" ") for columns without a name.
5	**GRANTOR** (ODBC 1.0)	**VARCHAR(** *128* **)**	The name or authorization ID of the user granting the privilege. If the **GRANTEE** column contains the name or authorization ID of the owner of the table identified in the **TABLE_NAME** column, this column contains "**_SYSTEM**." If a data source does not support column privileges, this column is set to NULL.
6	**GRANTEE** (ODBC 1.0)	**VARCHAR(** *128* **)** **NOT NULL**	The name or authorization ID of the user to whom the privilege was granted.
7	**PRIVILEGE** (ODBC 1.0)	**VARCHAR(** *128* **)** **NOT NULL**	The column privilege that was granted. Valid values for this column are: **"SELECT"** The **GRANTEE** is permitted to retrieve data from the column.

Table 15–6   Result Data Set Returned by **SQLColumnPrivileges()**   (Continued)

Column Number	Column Name	Data Type	Description
			"**INSERT**" The **GRANTEE** is permitted to provide data for the column when inserting new rows of data into the associated table.
			"**UPDATE**:" The **GRANTEE** is permitted to modify the data in the column.
			"**REFERENCES**:" The **GRANTEE** is permitted to refer to the column within a constraint (for example, a unique, referential, or table check constraint).
8	**IS_GRANTABLE**	**VARCHAR(***3***)**	Indicates whether the **GRANTEE** is permitted to grant the **PRIVILEGE** to other users. Valid values for this column are:
			"**YES**" "**NO**" **NULL:** Unknown or not applicable to the data source.
			A **PRIVILEGE** can be either grantable or not grantable, but not both.

(Adapted from the table on pages 535–536 of *Microsoft ODBC 3.0 Software Development Kit & Programmer's Reference*.)

[1]In ODBC 2.0 and earlier, this column was named **TABLE_QUALIFIER**.
[2]In ODBC 2.0 and earlier, this column was named **TABLE_OWNER**.

Unless noted otherwise, each of these SQLSTATE values is returned by the data source driver. Refer to Appendix B for detailed information about each SQLSTATE value that can be returned by the ODBC Driver Manager or by a data source driver.

Comments

■ Because this function, in many cases, maps to a complex, and therefore, expensive query against a data source's system catalog tables, it should be used sparingly; if the result data set produced is to be used more than once, it should be saved, rather than be regenerated each time it is needed.

■ An empty string (" ") can be stored in the memory location the *CatalogName* parameter refers to for catalogs without names (provided the driver supports catalog names).

■ An empty string (" ") can be stored in the memory location the *SchemaName* parameter refers to for schemas without names (provided the driver supports schema names).

■ The *TableName* parameter can not contain to a NULL pointer.

■ If the **SQL_ATTR_METADATA_ID** attribute for the SQL statement is set to **SQL_TRUE**, the values specified for the *CatalogName*, *SchemaName*, *TableName*, and *ColumnName* parameters are treated as identifier values and their case is insignificant. However, if the **SQL_ATTR_METADATA_ID** attribute is set to **SQL_FALSE**, the values specified for the *CatalogName*, *SchemaName*, *TableName*, and *ColumnName* parameters are treated literally and their case is significant. Refer to the "Parameters (Arguments) Used In Catalog Functions" section earlier in this chapter and to the **SQLGetStmtAttr()** function for more information.

■ The value specified for the *ColumnName* parameter can contain the following search pattern values:

  ■ The underscore character (_)
  Any single character can be used in place of the underscore character.

  ■ The percent character (%)
  Any sequence of 0 or more characters can be used in place of the percent character.

  ■ An escape character.
  A driver-specific character used to treat an underscore character, a percent character, and/or the escape character itself as a literal value instead of as a wild card value (that is, % = "%").

■ The result data set returned by this function is ordered by **TABLE_CAT**, **TABLE_SCHEM**, **TABLE_NAME**, **COLUMN_NAME**, and **PRIVILEGE**.

■ The actual amount of memory needed to store the value found in each **VARCHAR** column in the result data set that is produced by this function is dependent on the data source. An application can choose to set aside 128 characters (plus the NULL-terminator) for **VARCHAR** columns (to be consistent with the SQL92 standard limits), or alternatively, to allocate the actual amount of memory required by first calling the **SQLGetInfo()** function with the *InfoType* parameter set to **SQL_MAX_CATALOG_NAME_LEN**, **SQL_MAX_SCHEMA_NAME_LEN**, **SQL_MAX_TABLE_NAME_LEN**, and/or **SQL_MAX_COLUMN_NAME_LEN** to determine respectively the actual lengths of the **TABLE_CAT**, **TABLE_SCHEM**, **TABLE_NAME**, and **COLUMN_NAME** columns that are supported by the current data source.

Prerequisites   There are no prerequisites for using this function call.

Restrictions   There are no restrictions associated with this function call.

See Also   SQLColumns(), SQLTables()

Example   The following Visual C++ program illustrates how to use the QLColumnPrivileges() function to obtain information about the privileges associated with the columns that are available in a data source.

```
/*────────────────────────────────────────────────────*/
/* NAME:      CH15EX4.CPP                              */
/* PURPOSE: Illustrate How To Use The Following ODBC API Function */
/*          In A C++ Program:                          */
/*                                                     */
/*              SQLColumnPrivileges()                  */
/*                                                     */
/* OTHER ODBC APIs SHOWN:                              */
/*          SQLAllocHandle()         SQLSetEnvAttr()   */
/*          SQLDriverConnect()       SQLBindCol()      */
/*          SQLFetch()               SQLDisconnect()   */
/*          SQLFreeHandle()                            */
/*                                                     */
/*────────────────────────────────────────────────────*/

// Include The Appropriate Header Files
#include <windows.h>
#include <sql.h>
#include <sqlext.h>
#include <iostream.h>

// Define The ODBC_Class Class
class ODBC_Class
{
    // Attributes
    public:
        SQLHANDLE    EnvHandle;
        SQLHANDLE    ConHandle;
        SQLHANDLE    StmtHandle;
        SQLRETURN    rc;

    // Operations
    public:
        ODBC_Class();                       // Constructor
        ~ODBC_Class();                      // Destructor
```

```
        SQLRETURN    ShowColumnPrivilegeInfo();
};

// Define The Class Constructor
ODBC_Class::ODBC_Class()
{
    // Initialize The Return Code Variable
    rc = SQL_SUCCESS;

    // Allocate An Environment Handle
    rc = SQLAllocHandle(SQL_HANDLE_ENV, SQL_NULL_HANDLE, &EnvHandle);

    // Set The ODBC Application Version To 3.x
    if (rc == SQL_SUCCESS)
        rc = SQLSetEnvAttr(EnvHandle, SQL_ATTR_ODBC_VERSION,
                    (SQLPOINTER) SQL_OV_ODBC3, SQL_IS_UINTEGER);

    // Allocate A Connection Handle
    if (rc == SQL_SUCCESS)
        rc = SQLAllocHandle(SQL_HANDLE_DBC, EnvHandle, &ConHandle);
}

// Define The Class Destructor
ODBC_Class::~ODBC_Class()
{
    // Free The Connection Handle
    if (ConHandle != NULL)
        SQLFreeHandle(SQL_HANDLE_DBC, ConHandle);

    // Free The Environment Handle
    if (EnvHandle != NULL)
        SQLFreeHandle(SQL_HANDLE_ENV, EnvHandle);
}

// Define The ShowColumnPrivilegeInfo() Member Function
SQLRETURN ODBC_Class::ShowColumnPrivilegeInfo(void)
{
    // Declare The Local Memory Variables
    SQLCHAR   GrantorName[129];

    // Allocate An SQL Statement Handle
    rc = SQLAllocHandle(SQL_HANDLE_STMT, ConHandle, &StmtHandle);
    if (rc == SQL_SUCCESS)
    {
        // Retrieve Information About The Privileges Associated With
        // The Columns Defined For The "EMPLOYEES" Table In The Data
        // Source
        rc = SQLColumnPrivileges(StmtHandle, NULL, 0, NULL, 0,
                    (SQLCHAR *) "EMPLOYEES", SQL_NTS,
                    (SQLCHAR *) "%", SQL_NTS);
        if (rc == SQL_SUCCESS)
        {
            // Bind A Column In The Result Data Set Returned To
```

```
        // An Application Variable
        rc = SQLBindCol(StmtHandle, 5, SQL_C_CHAR, (SQLPOINTER)
                &GrantorName, sizeof(GrantorName), NULL);

        // Display A Header
        cout << "Column Privilege Grantor :" << endl << endl;

        // While There Are Records In The Result Data Set
        // Generated, Retrieve And Display Them
        while (rc != SQL_NO_DATA)
        {
            rc = SQLFetch(StmtHandle);
            if (rc != SQL_NO_DATA)
                cout << GrantorName << endl;
        }
    }

    // Free The SQL Statement Handle
    if (StmtHandle != NULL)
        SQLFreeHandle(SQL_HANDLE_STMT, StmtHandle);
}

// Return The ODBC API Return Code To The Calling Function
return(rc);
}

/*─────────────────────────────────────────────────────────────*/
/* The Main Function                                            */
/*─────────────────────────────────────────────────────────────*/
int main()
{
    // Declare The Local Memory Variables
    SQLRETURN  rc = SQL_SUCCESS;
    SQLCHAR    ConnectIn[40];

    // Create An Instance Of The ODBC_Class Class
    ODBC_Class  Example;

    // Build A Connection String
    strcpy((char *) ConnectIn,
        "DSN=SQLServer;UID=userid;PWD=password;");

    // Connect To The SQL Server Sample Database
    if (Example.ConHandle != NULL)
    {
        rc = SQLDriverConnect(Example.ConHandle, NULL, ConnectIn,
                SQL_NTS, NULL, 0, NULL, SQL_DRIVER_NOPROMPT);

        // Call The ShowColumnPrivilegeInfo() Member Function
        if (rc == SQL_SUCCESS || rc == SQL_SUCCESS_WITH_INFO)
            Example.ShowColumnPrivilegeInfo();

        // Disconnect From The SQL Server Sample Database
```

```
        rc = SQLDisconnect(Example.ConHandle);
    }

    // Return To The Operating System
    return(rc);
}
```

SQLSpecialColumns

COMPATABILITY					
X/OPEN 95 CLI	ISO/IEC 92 CLI	ODBC 1.0	ODBC 2.0	ODBC 3.0	ODBC 3.5
✓	☐	✓	✓	✓	✓

API CONFORMANCE LEVEL	CORE*

*IN ODBC 2.0, THIS FUNCTION WAS A LEVEL 1 API CONFORMANCE LEVEL FUNCTION

Purpose   The SQLSpecialColumns() function is used to retrieve unique row identifier information (that is, primary key or unique index information) for a specified table.

Syntax

```
SQLRETURN   SQLSpecialColumns  (SQLHSTMT        StatementHandle,
                                SQLUSMALLINT    RowIdentifier,
                                SQLCHAR         *CatalogName,
                                SQLSMALLINT     CatalogNameSize,
                                SQLCHAR         *SchemaName,
                                SQLSMALLINT     SchemaNameSize,
                                SQLCHAR         *TableName,
                                SQLSMALLINT     TableNameSize,
                                SQLUSMALLINT    Scope,
                                SQLUSMALLINT    Nullable);
```

Parameters

StatementHandle	An SQL statement handle that refers to a previously allocated SQL statement information storage buffer (data structure).
RowIdentifier	Specifies the type of column information to return. This parameter must be set to one of the following values:

■ **SQL_BEST_ROWID**
Indicates that the optimal column or set of
columns that can uniquely identify any row
in the specified table is to be placed in the
result data set produced by this function.

■ **SQL_ROWVER**
Indicates that the column or set of columns
which are automatically updated by the data
source when any row in the specified table is
updated by a transaction is to be placed in
the result data set produced by this
function.

CatalogName   A pointer to a location in memory where the
                       catalog qualifier portion of a three-part table
                       name is stored.

CatalogNameSize   The length of the catalog qualifier name value
                       stored in the *CatalogName* parameter.

SchemaName   A pointer to a location in memory where the
                       schema portion of a three-part table name is
                       stored.

SchemaNameSize   The length of the schema name value stored in
                       the *SchemaName* parameter.

TableName   A pointer to a location in memory where the table
                       name portion of a three-part table name is stored.

TableNameSize   The length of the table name value stored in the
                       TableName parameter.

Scope   Specifies the minimum duration for which the
                       unique row identifier will be valid. This
                       parameter must be set to one of the following
                       values:

■ **SQL_ SCOPE_CURROW**
The unique row identifier is only guaranteed
to be valid while positioned on that row.

■ **SQL_ SCOPE_TRANSACTION**
The unique row identifier is guaranteed to
be valid for the duration of the current
transaction.

■ **SQL_ SCOPE_SESSION**
The unique row identifier is guaranteed to be valid for the duration of the current connection (valid across transaction boundaries).

Nullable — Specifies whether special columns that can contain NULL values are returned by this function. This parameter must be set to one of the following values:

■ **SQL_ NO_NULLS**
Special columns that can contain NULL values should be excluded from the result data set produced by this function.

■ **SQL_ NULLABLE**
Special columns that can contain NULL values should be included in the result data set produced by this function.

Description

The **SQLSpecialColumns()** function is used to retrieve unique row identifier information (that is, primary key or unique index information) for a specified table. The information returned by this function is placed in a result data set, which can be processed by using the same ODBC API functions used to process result data sets generated by SQL queries. Table 15–7 lists the columns in this result data set.

One or more driver-defined columns may be added to this result data set. When that is the case, applications should gain access to each driver-specific column by counting down from column 8 (**PSEUDO_COLUMN**) of the result data set rather than by specifying an explicit ordinal position.

NOTE: *Depending on the driver being used,* **SQLSpecialColumns()** *may or may not return information for all columns in the result data set. However, applications can use any valid column in the result data set, regardless of whether it contains data.*

If multiple ways exist to uniquely identify any row in the specified table (for example, if there are multiple unique indexes defined for the specified table), this function retrieves the best set of row identifier column data, based on the data source's internal selection criteria.

Table 15–7 Result Data Set Returned by **SQLSpecialColumns()**

Column Number	Column Name	Data Type	Description
1	**SCOPE** (ODBC 1.0)	**SMALLINT**	The duration for which the name in **COLUMN_NAME** is guaranteed to point to the same row. Valid values for this column are: **SQL_SCOPE_CURROW:** The unique row identifier is guaranteed to be valid only while positioned on that row. **SQL_SCOPE_TRANSACTION:** The unique row identifier is guaranteed to be valid for the duration of the current transaction. **SQL_SCOPE_SESSION:** The unique row identifier is guaranteed to be valid for the duration of the current connection.
2	**COLUMN_NAME** (ODBC 1.0)	**VARCHAR(**_128_**)** **NOT NULL**	The name of the column that is either the table's primary key or part of the table's primary key. This column contains an empty string (" ") for columns without a name.
3	**DATA_TYPE** (ODBC 1.0)	**SMALLINT** **NOT NULL**	The ODBC or driver-specific SQL data type of the column identified in the **COLUMN_NAME** column. Valid values for this column include: **SQL_CHAR, SQL_VARCHAR, SQL_LONGVARCHAR, SQL_WCHAR, SQL_WVARCHAR, SQL_WLONGVARCHAR, SQL_DECIMAL, SQL_NUMERIC, SQL_SMALLINT, SQL_INTEGER, SQL_REAL, SQL_FLOAT, SQL_DOUBLE, SQL_BIT, SQL_TINYINT, SQL_BIGINT, SQL_BINARY, SQL_VARBINARY, SQL_LONGVARBINARY, SQL_TYPE_DATE, SQL_TYPE_TIME, SQL_TYPE_TIMESTAMP, SQL_INTERVAL_MONTH, SQL_INTERVAL_YEAR, SQL_INTERVAL_YEAR_TO_MONTH, SQL_INTERVAL_DAY, SQL_INTERVAL_HOUR, SQL_INTERVAL_MINUTE, SQL_INTERVAL_SECOND, SQL_INTERVAL_DAY_TO_HOUR, SQL_INTERVAL_DAY_TO_MINUTE, SQL_INTERVAL_DAY_TO_SECOND, SQL_INTERVAL_HOUR_TO_MINUTE, SQL_INTERVAL_HOUR_TO_SECOND, SQL_INTERVAL_ MINUTE_TO_SECOND, SQL_GUID**

Table 15–7 Result Data Set Returned by **SQLSpecialColumns()** (Continued)

Column Number	Column Name	Data Type	Description
			For datetime and interval data types, this column contains the concise data type (such as **SQL_TYPE_DATE** or **SQL_INTERVAL_YEAR_TO_MONTH**, rather than the non-concise data type such as **SQL_DATETIME** or **SQL_INTERVAL**) (ODBC 3.x applications only). NOTE: SQL data types returned for ODBC 3.x, ODBC 2.0, and ODBC 1.0 applications may be different.
4	**TYPE_NAME** (ODBC1.0)	**VARCHAR(128) NOT NULL**	The data source-specific character representation of the SQL data type name identified in the **DATA_TYPE** column. Valid values for this column include: **CHAR, VARCHAR, LONG VARCHAR, WCHAR, VARWCHAR, LONGWVARCHAR, DECIMAL, NUMERIC, SMALLINT, INTEGER, REAL, FLOAT, DOUBLE PRECISION, BIT, TINYINT, BIGINT, BINARY, VARBINARY, LONG VARBINARY, DATE, TIME, TIMESTAMP, INTERVAL MONTH, INTERVAL YEAR, INTERVAL YEAR TO MONTH, INTERVAL DAY, INTERVAL HOUR, INTERVAL MINUTE, INTERVAL SECOND, INTERVAL DAY TO HOUR, INTERVAL DAY TO MINUTE, INTERVAL DAY TO SECOND, INTERVAL HOUR TO MINUTE, INTERVAL HOUR TO SECOND, INTERVAL MINUTE TO SECOND, GUID**
5	**COLUMN_SIZE**[1] (ODBC 1.0)	**INTEGER**	The maximum number of bytes needed to display the column data in character form. For numeric data types, this is either the total number of digits, or the total number of bits allowed in the column. For character or binary string data types, this is the size of the string (string length), in bytes. For date, time, and timestamp data types, this is the total number of characters required to display the value when it is converted to a character string. For interval data types, this is the total number of characters in the character representation of the interval literal (as defined by the interval leading precision value).

Table 15-7   Result Data Set Returned by **SQLSpecialColumns()**   (Continued)

Column Number	Column Name	Data Type	Description
6	**BUFFER_LENGTH**[2] (ODBC 1.0)	**INTEGER**	The maximum number of bytes needed for the associated C application variable (buffer) to store data from this column if the value **SQL_C_DEFAULT** is specified for the *CDataType* parameter of the **SQLBindParameter()**, **SQLBindCol()**, or **SQLGetData()** function. This length does not include the NULL-terminator character used by NULL terminated strings.
			For numeric data, this column may contain a number different from the actual size of the data stored in the data source.
			For character or binary data, this column contains the same value as the **COLUMN_SIZE** column.
7	**DECIMAL_DIGITS**[3] (ODBC 1.0)	**SMALLINT**	The total number of significant digits to the right of the decimal point.
			If the **DATA_TYPE** column contains **SQL_TYPE_TIME** or **SQL_TYPE_ TIMESTAMP**, this column contains the number of digits in the fractional seconds component of the time value.
			For interval data types containing a time component, this column contains the number of digits to the right of the decimal point (fractional seconds).
			For interval data types that do not contain a time component, this column contains the value zero **(0)**.
			For data types in which decimal digits are not applicable, this column is set to NULL.
			For all other data types, this column contains the decimal digits of the column on the data source.
8	**PSEUDO_COLUMN** (ODBC 2.0)	**SMALLINT**	Indicates whether the column is a pseudo-column. Valid values for this column are:
			SQL_PC_PSEUDO: The column is a pseudo-column.
			SQL_PC_NOT_PSEUDO: The column is not a pseudo-column

Table 15–7 *Result Data Set Returned by* **SQLSpecialColumns()** (Continued)

Column Number	Column Name	Data Type	Description
			SQL_PC_UNKNOWN: Whether the column is a pseudo-column, is not known.
			For maximum interoperability, pseudo-columns should not be quoted with the identifier quote character returned by the **SQLGetInfo()** function.

[1]In ODBC 2.0 and earlier, this column was named **PRECISION**.
[2]In ODBC 2.0 and earlier, this column was named **LENGTH**.
[3]In ODBC 2.0 and earlier, this column was named **SCALE**.

(Adapted from the table on pages 1000–1001 of *Microsoft ODBC 3.0 Software Development Kit & Programmer's Reference*.)

The **SQLColumns()** function, which is used to return a variety of information on table columns, does not necessarily return columns that uniquely identify each row, or columns that are automatically updated when any value in the row is updated by a transaction. Therefore, some columns returned by the **SQLColumns()** function cannot be used in a select-list or **WHERE** clause. When the **SQLSpecialColumns()** function is called with the *RowIdentifier* parameter set to **SQL_BEST_ROWID**, all column(s) returned can be used in a select-list or **WHERE** clause.

Return Codes **SQL_SUCCESS, SQL_SUCCESS_WITH_INFO, SQL_STILL_EXECUTING, SQL_INVALID_HANDLE**, or **SQL_ERROR**

SQLSTATEs If this function returns **SQL_SUCCESS_WITH_INFO** or **SQL_ERROR**, one of the following SQLSTATE values may be obtained by calling the **SQLGetDiagRec()** function (ODBC 3.x driver) or the **SQLError()** function (ODBC 2.0 or earlier driver):

ODBC 3.X

01000, 08S01, 24000, 40001, 40003, HY000, HY001, HY008, HY009*, HY010*, HY013, HY090*, HY097*, HY098*, HY099*, HYC00, HYT00, HYT01, or IM001*

ODBC 2.0 OR EARLIER

01000, **08**S01, **24**000*, **IM**001*, **S**1000, **S**1001, **S**1008, **S**1010*, **S**1090*, **S**1097*, **S**1098*, **S**1099*, **S**1C00, or **S**1T00

* Returned by the ODBC Driver Manager.

Unless noted otherwise, each of these SQLSTATE values is returned by the data source driver. Refer to Appendix B for detailed information about each SQLSTATE value that can be returned by the ODBC Driver Manager or by a data source driver.

Comments

▦ Because this function, in many cases, maps to a complex and therefore expensive query against a data source's system catalog tables, it should be used sparingly; if the result data set produced is to be used more than once, it should be saved, rather than be regenerated each time it is needed.

▦ An empty string (" ") can be stored in the memory location the *CatalogName* parameter refers to for catalogs without names (provided the driver supports catalog names).

▦ An empty string (" ") can be stored in the memory location the *SchemaName* parameter refers to for schemas without names (provided the driver supports schema names).

▦ The *TableName* parameter can not contain to a NULL pointer.

▦ If the **SQL_ATTR_METADATA_ID** attribute for the statement handle specified is set to **SQL_TRUE**, the values specified for the *CatalogName*, *SchemaName*, and *TableName* parameters are treated as identifier values and their case is insignificant. However, if the **SQL_ATTR_METADATA_ID** attribute is set to **SQL_FALSE**, the values specified for the *CatalogName*, *SchemaName*, and *TableName* parameters are treated literally, and their case is significant. Refer to the "Parameters (Arguments) Used In Catalog Functions" section earlier in this chapter and to the **SQLGetStmtAttr()** function for more information.

▦ If the *RowIdentifier*, *Scope*, or *Nullable* parameters specify characteristics that are not supported by the data source, this function returns an empty result data set.

▦ If no unique row identifier information exists (that is, no primary key or unique index has been defined) for the table specified, this function returns an empty result data set.

▦ The result data set returned by this function is ordered by **SCOPE**.

- The duration for which a unique row identifier value is guaranteed to be valid is dependent on the isolation level being used by the current transaction. Refer to Chapter 3 for more information about transaction isolation levels.

- If this function is called with the *RowIdentifier* parameter set to **SQL_BEST_ROWID**, the columns returned in the result data set produced can be used by applications that need to scroll forward and backward within a result data set to retrieve the most recent data from a set of rows. This is because the column or columns of the row identifier are guaranteed not to change while the cursor is positioned on that row.

- The column or columns of a row identifier may remain valid even when the cursor is not positioned on a row; an application can determine how long a row identifier remains valid by checking the **SCOPE** column in the result data set produced by this function.

- If this function is called with the *RowIdentifier* parameter set to **SQL_BEST_ROWID**, an application can use the columns returned to reselect a row within the defined scope—a **SELECT** SQL statement is guaranteed to return either no rows or one row. If an application reselects a row based on the row identifier column or columns and the row is not found, the application can assume the row was deleted or the row identifier column(s) were modified. The opposite is not true: even if the row identifier column(s) have not been modified, other columns in the row may have changed.

- If this function is called with the *RowIdentifier* parameter set to **SQL_ROWVER**, an application can use the columns returned to determine if any columns in a given row have been updated since the row was first selected, using the row identifier. For example, after reselecting a row using a row identifier, the application can compare the previous values in the **SQL_ROWVER** columns to the ones just fetched. If the value in a **SQL_ROWVER** column differs from the previous value, the application can alert the user that data on the display has changed.

- The actual amount of memory needed to store the value found in each **VARCHAR** column in the result data set that is produced by this function is dependent on the data source. An application can choose to set aside 128 characters (plus the NULL-terminator) for **VARCHAR** columns (to be consistent with the SQL92 standard limits), or alternatively, to allocate the actual amount of memory required by first calling the **SQLGetInfo()** function with the

InfoType parameter set to **SQL_MAX_COLUMN_NAME_LEN** to determine the actual length of the **COLUMN_NAME** column that is supported by the current data source.

Prerequisites   There are no prerequisites for using this function call.

Restrictions   There are no restrictions associated with this function call.

See Also   SQLColumns(), SQLTables(), SQLStatistics()

Example   The following Visual C++ program illustrates how to use the SQLSpecialColumns() function to obtain information about the unique row identifier columns that exist in a data source.

```
/*─────────────────────────────────────────────────────────────*/
/* NAME:      CH15EX5.CPP                                        */
/* PURPOSE: Illustrate How To Use The Following ODBC API Function */
/*          In A C++ Program:                                    */
/*                                                               */
/*               SQLSpecialColumns()                             */
/*                                                               */
/* OTHER ODBC APIs SHOWN:                                        */
/*          SQLAllocHandle()            SQLSetEnvAttr()          */
/*          SQLConnect()                SQLBindCol()             */
/*          SQLFetch()                  SQLDisconnect()          */
/*          SQLFreeHandle()                                      */
/*                                                               */
/*─────────────────────────────────────────────────────────────*/

// Include The Appropriate Header Files
#include <windows.h>
#include <sql.h>
#include <sqlext.h>
#include <iostream.h>

// Define The ODBC_Class Class
class ODBC_Class
{
    // Attributes
    public:
        SQLHANDLE    EnvHandle;
        SQLHANDLE    ConHandle;
        SQLHANDLE    StmtHandle;
        SQLRETURN    rc;

    // Operations
    public:
        ODBC_Class();                            // Constructor
        ~ODBC_Class();                           // Destructor
        SQLRETURN  ShowSpecialColumnInfo();
};
```

```cpp
// Define The Class Constructor
ODBC_Class::ODBC_Class()
{
    // Initialize The Return Code Variable
    rc = SQL_SUCCESS;

    // Allocate An Environment Handle
    rc = SQLAllocHandle(SQL_HANDLE_ENV, SQL_NULL_HANDLE, &EnvHandle);

    // Set The ODBC Application Version To 3.x
    if (rc == SQL_SUCCESS)
        rc = SQLSetEnvAttr(EnvHandle, SQL_ATTR_ODBC_VERSION,
                  (SQLPOINTER) SQL_OV_ODBC3, SQL_IS_UINTEGER);

    // Allocate A Connection Handle
    if (rc == SQL_SUCCESS)
        rc = SQLAllocHandle(SQL_HANDLE_DBC, EnvHandle, &ConHandle);
}

// Define The Class Destructor
ODBC_Class::~ODBC_Class()
{
    // Free The Connection Handle
    if (ConHandle != NULL)
        SQLFreeHandle(SQL_HANDLE_DBC, ConHandle);

    // Free The Environment Handle
    if (EnvHandle != NULL)
        SQLFreeHandle(SQL_HANDLE_ENV, EnvHandle);
}

// Define The ShowSpecialColumnInfo() Member Function
SQLRETURN ODBC_Class::ShowSpecialColumnInfo(void)
{
    // Declare The Local Memory Variables
    SQLCHAR   ColumnName[129];

    // Allocate An SQL Statement Handle
    rc = SQLAllocHandle(SQL_HANDLE_STMT, ConHandle, &StmtHandle);
    if (rc == SQL_SUCCESS)
    {
        // Retrieve Information About The Special Columns Associated
        // The "Employees" Table In The Data Source
        rc = SQLSpecialColumns(StmtHandle, SQL_BEST_ROWID, NULL, 0,
                  NULL, 0, (SQLCHAR *) "Employees", SQL_NTS,
                  SQL_SCOPE_CURROW, SQL_NULLABLE);
        if (rc == SQL_SUCCESS)
        {
            // Bind A Column In The Result Data Set Returned To
            // An Application Variable
            rc = SQLBindCol(StmtHandle, 2, SQL_C_CHAR, (SQLPOINTER)
                      &ColumnName, sizeof(ColumnName), NULL);

            // Display A Header
            cout << "Special Columns For The Employees Table :";
```

```
                cout << endl << endl;

                // While There Are Records In The Result Data Set
                // Generated, Retrieve And Display Them
                while (rc != SQL_NO_DATA)
                {
                    rc = SQLFetch(StmtHandle);
                    if (rc != SQL_NO_DATA)
                        cout << ColumnName << endl;
                }
        }

        // Free The SQL Statement Handle
        if (StmtHandle != NULL)
            SQLFreeHandle(SQL_HANDLE_STMT, StmtHandle);
    }

    // Return The ODBC API Return Code To The Calling Function
    return(rc);
}

/*——————————————————————————————————————————————————————————*/
/* The Main Function                                          */
/*——————————————————————————————————————————————————————————*/
int main()
{
    // Declare The Local Memory Variables
    SQLRETURN   rc = SQL_SUCCESS;
    SQLCHAR     DBName[10] = "Northwind";

    // Create An Instance Of The ODBC_Class Class
    ODBC_Class   Example;

    // Connect To The Northwind Sample Database
    if (Example.ConHandle != NULL)
    {
        rc = SQLConnect(Example.ConHandle, DBName, SQL_NTS,
                (SQLCHAR *) "", SQL_NTS, (SQLCHAR *) "", SQL_NTS);

        // Call The ShowSpecialColumnInfo() Member Function
        if (rc == SQL_SUCCESS || rc == SQL_SUCCESS_WITH_INFO)
            Example.ShowSpecialColumnInfo();

        // Disconnect From The Northwind Sample Database
        rc = SQLDisconnect(Example.ConHandle);
    }

    // Return To The Operating System
    return(rc);
}
```

SQLStatistics

COMPATABILITY

X/OPEN 95 CLI	ISO/IEC 92 CLI	ODBC 1.0	ODBC 2.0	ODBC 3.0	ODBC 3.5
☑	☐	☑	☑	☑	☑

API CONFORMANCE LEVEL   CORE*

*IN ODBC 2.0, THIS FUNCTION WAS A LEVEL 1 API CONFORMANCE LEVEL FUNCTION

Purpose   The SQLStatistics() function is used to retrieve statistical information about a specified table and its associated indexes.

Syntax
```
SQLRETURN   SQLStatistics  (SQLHSTMT       StatementHandle,
                            SQLCHAR        *CatalogName,
                            SQLSMALLINT    CatalogNameSize,
                            SQLCHAR        *SchemaName,
                            SQLSMALLINT    SchemaNameSize,
                            SQLCHAR        *TableName,
                            SQLSMALLINT    TableNameSize,
                            SQLUSMALLINT   IndexType,
                            SQLUSMALLINT   Accuracy);
```

Parameters

StatementHandle   An SQL statement handle that refers to a previously allocated SQL statement information storage buffer (data structure).

CatalogName   A pointer to a location in memory where the catalog qualifier portion of a three-part table name is stored.

CatalogNameSize   The length of the catalog qualifier name value stored in the *CatalogName* parameter.

SchemaName   A pointer to a location in memory where the schema portion of a three-part table name is stored.

SchemaNameSize   The length of the schema name value stored in the *SchemaName* parameter.

TableName   A pointer to a location in memory where the table name portion of a three-part table name is stored.

TableNameSize	The length of the table name value stored in the *TableName* parameter.
IndexType	Specifies the type of index information that is to be returned by this function. This parameter must be set to one of the following values:

■ **SQL_INDEX_UNIQUE**
Only information pertaining to unique indexes is to be retrieved and stored in the result data set produced by this function.

■ **SQL_INDEX_ALL**
Information about all indexes is to be retrieved and stored in the result data set produced by this function.

Accuracy	Specifies whether the **CARDINALITY** and **PAGES** columns in the result data set produced by this function are to contain the most current information. This parameter must be set to one of the following values:

■ **SQL_QUICK**
Only information that is readily available at the database server is to be retrieved and stored in the result data set produced by this function.

■ **SQL_ENSURE**
The most up to date information available is to be retrieved and stored in the result data set produced by this function.

Description   The **SQLStatistics()** function is used to retrieve statistical information about a specified table and its associated indexes. When invoked, this function returns two types of information:

■ Statistical information about the table itself (if it is available), such as:

   ■ The number of rows in the table.

   ■ The number of pages used to store the table.

■ Statistical information about each index defined for the specified table, such as:

■ The number of unique values in an index.

■ The number of pages used to store the table's indexes.

The information returned by this function is placed in a result data set that can be processed by using the same ODBC API functions used to process result data sets generated by SQL queries. Table 15–8 lists the columns in this result data set.

Table 15–8 Result Data Set Returned by **SQLStatistics()**

Column Number	Column Name	Data Type	Description
1	**TABLE_CAT**[1] (ODBC 1.0)	**VARCHAR(128)**	The name of the catalog (qualifier) containing the **TABLE_SCHEM** value. If a data source does not support three-part table names, this column is set to NULL. If a data source supports three-part table names for a limited number of tables, this column contains an empty string (" ") for tables that do not have a catalog (qualifier) name.
2	**TABLE_SCHEM**[2] (ODBC 1.0)	**VARCHAR(128)**	The name of the schema containing the **TABLE_NAME** value. If a data source does not support three-part table names, this column is set to NULL. If a data source supports three-part table names for a limited number of tables, this column contains an empty string (" ") for tables that do not have a schema name.
3	**TABLE_NAME** (ODBC 1.0)	**VARCHAR(128) NOT NULL**	The name of the table to which the statistic or index applies.
4	**NON_UNIQUE** (ODBC 1.0)	**SMALLINT**	Indicates whether the index prohibits or allows duplicate values. Valid values for this column are: **SQL_TRUE**: The index allows duplicate values. **SQL_FALSE**: The index values must be unique. **NULL**: The **TYPE** column indicates that this row is an **SQL_TABLE_STAT** row (that is, it contains statistics information on the table itself).

Table 15–8   Result Data Set Returned by **SQLStatistics()** (Continued)

Column Number	Column Name	Data Type	Description
5	**INDEX_ QUALIFIER** (ODBC 1.0)	**VARCHAR(***128***)**	The character string that would be used to qualify the index name in a **DROP INDEX** SQL statement.
			If an index qualifier is not supported by the data source or if the **TYPE** column indicates that this row is an **SQL_TABLE_STAT** row (that is, it contains statistics information on the table itself), this column is set to NULL.
			If a non-NULL value is returned in this column, it must be used to qualify the index name on a **DROP INDEX** SQL statement; otherwise the value in the **TABLE_SCHEM** column should be used.
6	**INDEX_NAME** (ODBC 1.0)	**VARCHAR(***128***)**	The name of the index. If the **TYPE** column indicates that this row is an **SQL_TABLE_ STAT** row (that is, it contains statistics information on the table itself), this column is set to NULL.
7	**TYPE** (ODBC 1.0)	**SMALLINT NOT NULL**	Identifies the type of information contained in the current row of this result data set. Valid values for this column are:
			SQL_TABLE_STAT: The current row of this result data set contains statistic information on the table itself.
			SQL_INDEX_BTREE: The current row of this result data set contains information on a Binary Tree index.
			SQL_INDEX_CLUSTERED: The current row of this result data set contains information on a clustered index.
			SQL_INDEX_CONTENT: The current row of this result data set contains information on a content index.
			SQL_INDEX_HASHED: The current row of this result data set contains information on a hashed index.

Table 15–8 Result Data Set Returned by **SQLStatistics()** (Continued)

Column Number	Column Name	Data Type	Description
			SQL_INDEX_OTHER: The current row of this result data set contains information on some other type of index.
8	**ORDINAL_ POSITION**[3] (ODBC 1.0)	**SMALLINT**	The column's sequence number in the index, whose name is stored in the **INDEX_NAME** column. The first column in the index is number 1, the second column is number 2, and so on. If the **TYPE** column indicates that this row is an **SQL_TABLE_STAT** row (that is, it contains statistics information on the table itself), this column is set to NULL.
9	**COLUMN_NAME** (ODBC 1.0)	**VARCHAR(128)**	The name of the column in the index. If the **TYPE** column indicates that this row is an **SQL_TABLE_STAT** row (that is, it contains statistics information on the table itself), this column is set to NULL.
10	**ASC_OR_DESC**[4] (ODBC 1.0)	**CHAR(1)**	The sort sequence used to order the column's data. Valid values for this column are: **'A'**: The column's data is sorted in ascending order. **'D'**: The column's data is sorted in descending order. **NULL**: The **TYPE** column indicates that this row is an **SQL_TABLE_STAT** row (that is, it contains statistics information on the table itself).
11	**CARDINALITY** (ODBC 1.0)	**INTEGER**	The number of unique values in the table or index. If the **TYPE** column indicates that this row is an **SQL_TABLE_STAT** row, this column contains the number of rows in the table. Otherwise, this column contains the number of unique values in the index

Table 15–8   Result Data Set Returned by **SQLStatistics()** (Continued)

Column Number	Column Name	Data Type	Description
			If this information is not available from the data source, this column is set to NULL.
12	**PAGES** (ODBC 1.0)	**INTEGER**	The number of pages needed to store the table or index.
			If the **TYPE** column indicates that this row is an **SQL_TABLE_STAT** row, this column contains the number of pages used to store the table. Otherwise, this column contains the number of pages used to store the index.
			If this information is not available from the data source, this column is set to NULL.
13	**FILTER_ CONDITION**	**VARCHAR(***128***)**	Identifies the filter condition used if the index is a filtered index. This column contains an empty string (" ") if the filter condition cannot be determined. If the **TYPE** column indicates that this row is an **SQL_TABLE_STAT** row, if the index is not a filtered index, or if it cannot be determined whether the index is a filtered index, this column is set to NULL.

[1]In ODBC 2.0 and earlier, this column was named **TABLE_QUALIFIER**.

[2]In ODBC 2.0 and earlier, this column was named **TABLE_OWNER**.

[3]In ODBC 2.0 and earlier, this column was named **SEQ_IN_INDEX**.

[4]In ODBC 2.0 and earlier, this column was named **COLLATION**.

(Adapted from the table on pages 1008–1010 of *Microsoft ODBC 3.0 Software Development Kit & Programmer's Reference*.)

One or more driver-defined columns may be added to this result data set. When that is the case, applications should gain access to each driver-specific column by counting down from column 13 (**FILTER_CONDITION**) of the result data set rather than by specifying an explicit ordinal position.

NOTE: *Depending on the driver being used,* **SQLStatistics()** *may or may not return information for all columns in the result data set. However, applications can use any valid column in the result data set, regardless of whether it contains data.*

Return Codes   SQL_SUCCESS, SQL_SUCCESS_WITH_INFO, SQL_STILL_EXECUTING, SQL_INVALID_HANDLE, or SQL_ERROR

SQLSTATEs   If this function returns **SQL_SUCCESS_WITH_INFO** or **SQL_ERROR**, one of the following SQLSTATE values may be obtained by calling the **SQLGetDiagRec()** function (ODBC 3.x driver) or the **SQLError()** function (ODBC 2.0 or earlier driver):

ODBC 3.X

01000, 08S01, 24000, 40001, 40003, **HY000**, **HY001**, **HY008**, **HY009***, **HY010***, **HY013**, **HY090***, **HY100***, **HY101***, **HYC00**, **HYT00**, **HYT01**, or **IM001***

ODBC 2.0 OR EARLIER

01000, 08S01, 24000, **IM001**, **S1000**, **S1001**, **S1008**, **S1010***, **S1090***, **S1100***, **S1101***, **S1C00**, or **S1T00**

* Returned by the ODBC Driver Manager.

Unless noted otherwise, each of these SQLSTATE values is returned by the data source driver. Refer to Appendix B for detailed information about each SQLSTATE value that can be returned by the ODBC Driver Manager or by a data source driver.

Comments   ■ Because this function, in many cases, maps to a complex, and therefore expensive, query against a data source's system catalog tables, it should be used sparingly; if the result data set produced is to be used more than once, it should be saved, rather than be regenerated each time it is needed.

■ An empty string (" ") can be stored in the memory location to which the *CatalogName* parameter refers to for catalogs without names (provided the driver supports catalog names).

■ An empty string (" ") can be stored in the memory location to which the *SchemaName* parameter refers to for schemas without names (provided the driver supports schema names).

■ The *TableName* parameter cannot contain to a NULL pointer.

■ If the **SQL_ATTR_METADATA_ID** attribute for the statement handle specified is set to **SQL_TRUE**, the values specified for the *CatalogName*, *SchemaName*, and *TableName* parameters are treated as identifier values and their case is insignificant. However, if the **SQL_ATTR_METADATA_ID** attribute is set to **SQL_FALSE**, the values specified for the *CatalogName*, *SchemaName*, and *TableName* parameters are treated literally and their case is significant. Refer to the "Parameters (Arguments) Used in Catalog Functions" section earlier in this chapter and to the **SQLGetStmtAttr()** function for more information.

▦ The *Accuracy* parameter can not be set to **SQL_ENSURE** if the driver being used does not support ODBC extensions (i.e. it only conforms to the X/Open and/or SQL 92 standard).

▦ The result data set returned by this function is ordered by **NON_UNIQUE**, **TYPE**, **INDEX_QUALIFIER**, **INDEX_NAME**, and **ORDINAL_POSITION**.

▦ The actual amount of memory needed to store the value found in each **VARCHAR** column in the result data set produced by this function is dependent on the data source. An application can choose to set aside 128 characters (plus the NULL-terminator) for **VARCHAR** columns (to be consistent with the SQL92 standard limits), or alternatively, to allocate the actual amount of memory required by first calling the **SQLGetInfo()** function with the *InfoType* parameter set to **SQL_MAX_CATALOG_NAME_LEN**, **SQL_MAX_SCHEMA_NAME_LEN**, **SQL_MAX_TABLE_NAME_LEN**, and/or **SQL_MAX_COLUMN_NAME_LEN** to determine respectively the actual lengths of the **TABLE_CAT**, **TABLE_SCHEM**, **TABLE_NAME**, and **COLUMN_NAME** columns that are supported by the current data source.

Prerequisites   There are no prerequisites for using this function call.

Restrictions   There are no restrictions associated with this function call.

See Also   **SQLColumns()**, **SQLSpecialColumns()**

Example   The following Visual C++ program illustrates how to use the **SQLStatistics()** function to obtain information about the indexes that are available in a data source.

```
/*──────────────────────────────────────────────────────────────*/
/* NAME:      CH15EX6.CPP                                         */
/* PURPOSE: Illustrate How To Use The Following ODBC API Function */
/*          In A C++ Program:                                     */
/*                                                                */
/*               SQLStatistics()                                  */
/*                                                                */
/* OTHER ODBC APIs SHOWN:                                         */
/*          SQLAllocHandle()              SQLSetEnvAttr()         */
/*          SQLConnect()                  SQLBindCol()            */
/*          SQLFetch()                    SQLDisconnect()         */
```

```
/*              SQLFreeHandle()                                    */
/*                                                                 */
/*───────────────────────────────────────────────────────────── */

// Include The Appropriate Header Files
#include <windows.h>
#include <sql.h>
#include <sqlext.h>
#include <iostream.h>

// Define The ODBC_Class Class
class ODBC_Class
{
    // Attributes
    public:
        SQLHANDLE   EnvHandle;
        SQLHANDLE   ConHandle;
        SQLHANDLE   StmtHandle;
        SQLRETURN   rc;

    // Operations
    public:
        ODBC_Class();                           // Constructor
        ~ODBC_Class();                          // Destructor
        SQLRETURN   ShowStatisticsInfo();
};

// Define The Class Constructor
ODBC_Class::ODBC_Class()
{
    // Initialize The Return Code Variable
    rc = SQL_SUCCESS;

    // Allocate An Environment Handle
    rc = SQLAllocHandle(SQL_HANDLE_ENV, SQL_NULL_HANDLE, &EnvHandle);

    // Set The ODBC Application Version To 3.x
    if (rc == SQL_SUCCESS)
        rc = SQLSetEnvAttr(EnvHandle, SQL_ATTR_ODBC_VERSION,
                (SQLPOINTER) SQL_OV_ODBC3, SQL_IS_UINTEGER);

    // Allocate A Connection Handle
    if (rc == SQL_SUCCESS)
        rc = SQLAllocHandle(SQL_HANDLE_DBC, EnvHandle, &ConHandle);
}

// Define The Class Destructor
ODBC_Class::~ODBC_Class()
{
    // Free The Connection Handle
    if (ConHandle != NULL)
        SQLFreeHandle(SQL_HANDLE_DBC, ConHandle);

    // Free The Environment Handle
    if (EnvHandle != NULL)
```

```
        SQLFreeHandle(SQL_HANDLE_ENV, EnvHandle);
}

// Define The ShowStatisticsInfo() Member Function
SQLRETURN ODBC_Class::ShowStatisticsInfo(void)
{
    // Declare The Local Memory Variables
    SQLCHAR   IndexName[129];

    // Allocate An SQL Statement Handle
    rc = SQLAllocHandle(SQL_HANDLE_STMT, ConHandle, &StmtHandle);
    if (rc == SQL_SUCCESS)
    {
        // Retrieve Information About The Indexes Defined For The
        // "Employees" Table In The Data Source
        rc = SQLStatistics(StmtHandle, NULL, 0, NULL, 0,
                (SQLCHAR *) "Employees", SQL_NTS,
                SQL_INDEX_ALL, SQL_QUICK);
        if (rc == SQL_SUCCESS)
        {
            // Bind A Column In The Result Data Set Returned To
            // An Application Variable
            rc = SQLBindCol(StmtHandle, 6, SQL_C_CHAR, (SQLPOINTER)
                    &IndexName, sizeof(IndexName), NULL);

            // Display A Header
            cout << "Indexes For Employees Table :" << endl << endl;

            // While There Are Records In The Result Data Set
            // Generated, Retrieve And Display Them
            while (rc != SQL_NO_DATA)
            {
                rc = SQLFetch(StmtHandle);
                if (rc != SQL_NO_DATA)
                    cout << IndexName << endl;
            }
        }

        // Free The SQL Statement Handle
        if (StmtHandle != NULL)
            SQLFreeHandle(SQL_HANDLE_STMT, StmtHandle);
    }

    // Return The ODBC API Return Code To The Calling Function
    return(rc);
}

/*----------------------------------------------------------------*/
/* The Main Function                                              */
/*----------------------------------------------------------------*/
int main()
{
```

```
    // Declare The Local Memory Variables
    SQLRETURN   rc = SQL_SUCCESS;
    SQLCHAR     DBName[10] = "Northwind";

    // Create An Instance Of The ODBC_Class Class
    ODBC_Class   Example;

    // Connect To The Northwind Sample Database
    if (Example.ConHandle != NULL)
    {
        rc = SQLConnect(Example.ConHandle, DBName, SQL_NTS,
                (SQLCHAR *) "", SQL_NTS, (SQLCHAR *) "", SQL_NTS);

        // Call The ShowStatisticsInfo() Member Function
        if (rc == SQL_SUCCESS || rc == SQL_SUCCESS_WITH_INFO)
            Example.ShowStatisticsInfo();

        // Disconnect From The Northwind Sample Database
        rc = SQLDisconnect(Example.ConHandle);
    }

    // Return To The Operating System
    return(rc);
}
```

SQLPrimaryKeys

COMPATABILITY

X/OPEN 95 CLI	ISO/IEC 92 CLI	ODBC 1.0	ODBC 2.0	ODBC 3.0	ODBC 3.5
☐	☐	✓	✓	✓	✓

API CONFORMANCE LEVEL   LEVEL 1*

*IN ODBC 2.0, THIS FUNCTION WAS A LEVEL 2 API CONFORMANCE LEVEL FUNCTION

Purpose   The SQLPrimaryKeys() function is used to retrieve the list of column names that make up the primary key for a specified table.

Syntax
```
SQLRETURN   SQLPrimaryKeys (SQLHSTMT      StatementHandle,
                            SQLCHAR       *CatalogName,
                            SQLSMALLINT   CatalogNameSize,
                            SQLCHAR       *SchemaName,
                            SQLSMALLINT   SchemaNameSize,
                            SQLCHAR       *TableName,
                            SQLSMALLINT   TableNameSize);
```

Parameters	*StatementHandle*	An SQL statement handle that refers to a previously allocated SQL statement information storage buffer (data structure).
	CatalogName	A pointer to a location in memory where the catalog qualifier portion of a three-part table name is stored.
	CatalogNameSize	The length of the catalog qualifier name value stored in the *CatalogName* parameter.
	SchemaName	A pointer to a location in memory where the schema portion of a three-part table name is stored.
	SchemaNameSize	The length of the schema name value stored in the *SchemaName* parameter.
	TableName	A pointer to a location in memory where the table name portion of a three-part table name is stored.
	TableNameSize	The length of the table name value stored in the *TableName* parameter.

Description   The **SQLPrimaryKeys()** function is used to retrieve the list of column names that make up the primary key for a specified table. The information returned by this function is placed in a result data set, which can be processed by using the same ODBC API functions used to process result data sets generated by SQL queries. Table 15–9 lists the columns in this result data set.

One or more driver-defined columns may be added to this result data set. When that is the case, applications should gain access to each driver-specific column by counting down from column 6 (**PK_NAME**) of the result data set rather than by specifying an explicit ordinal position.

NOTE: *Depending on the driver being used,* **SQLPrimary keys()** *may or may not return information for all columns in the result data set. However, applications can use any valid column in the result data set, regardless of whether it contains data.*

Return Codes   SQL_SUCCESS, SQL_SUCCESS_WITH_INFO, SQL_STILL_EXECUTING, SQL_INVALID_HANDLE, or SQL_ERROR

Table 15–9   Result Data Set Returned by **SQLPrimaryKeys()**

Column Number	Column Name	Data Type	Description
1	**TABLE_CAT**[1] (ODBC 1.0)	**VARCHAR(**_128_**)**	The name of the catalog (qualifier) containing the **TABLE_SCHEM** value. If a data source does not support three-part table names, this column is set to NULL. If a data source supports three-part table names for a limited number of tables, this column contains an empty string (" ") for tables that do not have a catalog (qualifier) name.
2	**TABLE_SCHEM**[2] (ODBC 1.0)	**VARCHAR(**_128_**)**	The name of the schema containing the **TABLE_NAME** value. If a data source does not support three-part table names, this column is set to NULL. If a data source supports three-part table names for a limited number of tables, this column contains an empty string (" ") for tables wthat do not have a schema name.
3	**TABLE_NAME** (ODBC 1.0)	**VARCHAR(**_128_**) NOT NULL**	The name of the table containing the primary key.
4	**COLUMN_NAME** (ODBC 1.0)	**VARCHAR(**_128_**) NOT NULL**	The name of the primary key column in the table identified in the **TABLE_NAME** column. This column contains an empty string (" ") for columns without a name.
5	**KEY_SEQ** (ODBC 1.0)	**SMALLINT NOT NULL**	The column's sequence number in the primary key. The first column in the primary key is number 1, the second column is number 2, and so on.
6	**PK_NAME** (ODBC 2.0)	**VARCHAR(**_128_**)**	The name (identifier) of the primary key. This column is set to NULL if a primary key name is not applicable for data source.

(Adapted from the table on page 860 of _Microsoft ODBC 3.0 Software Development Kit & Programmer's Reference._)

[1]In ODBC 2.0 and earlier, this column was named **TABLE_QUALIFIER**
[2]In ODBC 2.0 and earlier, this column was named **TABLE_OWNER**.

SQLSTATEs   If this function returns **SQL_SUCCESS_WITH_INFO** or **SQL_ERROR**, one of the following SQLSTATE values may be obtained by calling the **SQLGetDiagRec()** function (ODBC 3.x driver) or the **SQLError()** function (ODBC 2.0 or earlier driver):

ODBC 3.X

01000, **08**S01, **24**000*, **40**001, **40**003, **HY**000, **HY**001, **HY**008, **HY**009*, **HY**010*, **HY**013, **HY**090*, **HY**C00, **HY**T00, **HY**T01, or **IM**001*

ODBC 2.0 OR EARLIER

01000, **08**S01, **24**000*, **IM**001*, **S1**000, **S1**001, **S1**008, **S1**010*, **S1**090*, **S1**C00, or **S1**T00

* Returned by the ODBC Driver Manager.

Unless noted otherwise, each of these SQLSTATE values is returned by the data source driver. Refer to Appendix B for detailed information about each SQLSTATE value that can be returned by the ODBC Driver Manager or by a data source driver.

Comments

▨ Because this function, in many cases, maps to a complex, and therefore expensive, query against a data source's system catalog tables, it should be used sparingly; if the result data set produced is to be used more than once, it should be saved, rather than be regenerated each time it is needed.

▨ An empty string (" ") can be stored in the memory location the *CatalogName* parameter refers to for catalogs without names (provided the driver supports catalog names).

▨ An empty string (" ") can be stored in the memory location the *SchemaName* parameter refers to for schemas without names (provided the driver supports schema names).

▨ If the **SQL_ATTR_METADATA_ID** attribute for the statement handle specified is set to **SQL_TRUE**, the values specified for the *CatalogName*, *SchemaName*, and *TableName* parameters are treated as identifier values and their case is insignificant. However, if the **SQL_ATTR_METADATA_ID** attribute is set to **SQL_FALSE**, the values specified for the *CatalogName*, *SchemaName*, and *TableName* parameters are treated literally and their case is significant. Refer to the "Parameters (Arguments) Used in Catalog Functions" section earlier in this chapter and to the **SQLGetStmtAttr()** function for more information.

▨ The *TableName* parameter can not contain a NULL pointer.

▨ The result data set returned by this function is ordered by **TABLE_CAT**, **TABLE_SCHEM**, **TABLE_NAME**, and **KEY_SEQ**.

■ The actual amount of memory needed to store the value found in each **VARCHAR** column in the result data set that is produced by this function is dependent on the data source. An application can choose to set aside 128 characters (plus the NULL-terminator) for **VARCHAR** columns (to be consistent with the SQL92 standard limits), or alternatively, to allocate the actual amount of memory required by first calling the **SQLGetInfo()** function with the *InfoType* parameter set to **SQL_MAX_CATALOG_NAME_LEN**, **SQL_MAX_SCHEMA_NAME_LEN**, **SQL_MAX_TABLE_NAME_LEN**, and/or **SQL_MAX_COLUMN_NAME_LEN** to determine respectively the actual lengths of the **TABLE_CAT**, **TABLE_SCHEM**, **TABLE_NAME**, and **COLUMN_NAME** columns that are supported by the current data source.

Prerequisites   There are no prerequisites for using this function call.

Restrictions   There are no restrictions associated with this function call.

See Also   **SQLForeignKeys()**, **SQLStatistics()**

Example   The following Visual C++ program illustrates how to use the **SQLPrimaryKeys()** function to obtain information about the columns that comprise the primary keys for a specified table.

```
/*-----------------------------------------------------------------*/
/* NAME:     CH15EX7.CPP                                           */
/* PURPOSE: Illustrate How To Use The Following ODBC API Function  */
/*          In A C++ Program:                                      */
/*                                                                 */
/*              SQLPrimaryKeys()                                   */
/*                                                                 */
/* OTHER ODBC APIs SHOWN:                                          */
/*          SQLAllocHandle()            SQLSetEnvAttr()            */
/*          SQLDriverConnect()          SQLBindCol()              */
/*          SQLFetch()                  SQLDisconnect()           */
/*          SQLFreeHandle()                                        */
/*                                                                 */
/*-----------------------------------------------------------------*/

// Include The Appropriate Header Files
#include <windows.h>
#include <sql.h>
#include <sqlext.h>
#include <iostream.h>

// Define The ODBC_Class Class
class ODBC_Class
```

```cpp
{
    // Attributes
    public:
        SQLHANDLE   EnvHandle;
        SQLHANDLE   ConHandle;
        SQLHANDLE   StmtHandle;
        SQLRETURN   rc;

    // Operations
    public:
        ODBC_Class();                                   // Constructor
        ~ODBC_Class();                                  // Destructor
        SQLRETURN   ShowPrimaryKeyInfo();
};

// Define The Class Constructor
ODBC_Class::ODBC_Class()
{
    // Initialize The Return Code Variable
    rc = SQL_SUCCESS;

    // Allocate An Environment Handle
    rc = SQLAllocHandle(SQL_HANDLE_ENV, SQL_NULL_HANDLE, &EnvHandle);

    // Set The ODBC Application Version To 3.x
    if (rc == SQL_SUCCESS)
        rc = SQLSetEnvAttr(EnvHandle, SQL_ATTR_ODBC_VERSION,
                (SQLPOINTER) SQL_OV_ODBC3, SQL_IS_UINTEGER);

    // Allocate A Connection Handle
    if (rc == SQL_SUCCESS)
        rc = SQLAllocHandle(SQL_HANDLE_DBC, EnvHandle, &ConHandle);
}

// Define The Class Destructor
ODBC_Class::~ODBC_Class()
{
    // Free The Connection Handle
    if (ConHandle != NULL)
        SQLFreeHandle(SQL_HANDLE_DBC, ConHandle);

    // Free The Environment Handle
    if (EnvHandle != NULL)
        SQLFreeHandle(SQL_HANDLE_ENV, EnvHandle);
}

// Define The ShowPrimaryKeyInfo() Member Function
SQLRETURN ODBC_Class::ShowPrimaryKeyInfo(void)
{
    // Declare The Local Memory Variables
    SQLCHAR   PKeyName[129];

    // Allocate An SQL Statement Handle
```

```
    rc = SQLAllocHandle(SQL_HANDLE_STMT, ConHandle, &StmtHandle);
    if (rc == SQL_SUCCESS)
    {
        // Retrieve Information About The Primary Keys Defined For
        // The "EMPLOYEE" Table In The Data Source
        rc = SQLPrimaryKeys(StmtHandle, NULL, 0, NULL, 0,
                (SQLCHAR *) "EMPLOYEE", SQL_NTS);
        if (rc == SQL_SUCCESS)
        {
            // Bind A Column In The Result Data Set Returned To
            // An Application Variable
            rc = SQLBindCol(StmtHandle, 6, SQL_C_CHAR, (SQLPOINTER)
                    &PKeyName, sizeof(PKeyName), NULL);

            // Display A Header
            cout << "Primary Keys :" << endl << endl;

            // While There Are Records In The Result Data Set
            // Generated, Retrieve And Display Them
            while (rc != SQL_NO_DATA)
            {
                rc = SQLFetch(StmtHandle);
                if (rc != SQL_NO_DATA)
                    cout << PKeyName << endl;
            }
        }

        // Free The SQL Statement Handle
        if (StmtHandle != NULL)
            SQLFreeHandle(SQL_HANDLE_STMT, StmtHandle);
    }

    // Return The ODBC API Return Code To The Calling Function
    return(rc);
}

/*————————————————————————————————————*/
/* The Main Function                                                   */
/*————————————————————————————————————*/
int main()
{
    // Declare The Local Memory Variables
    SQLRETURN   rc = SQL_SUCCESS;
    SQLCHAR     ConnectIn[40];

    // Create An Instance Of The ODBC_Class Class
    ODBC_Class  Example;

    // Build A Connection String
    strcpy((char *) ConnectIn,
        "DSN=SQLServer;UID=userid;PWD=password;");

    // Connect To The SQL Server Sample Database
    if (Example.ConHandle != NULL)
```

```
{
    rc = SQLDriverConnect(Example.ConHandle, NULL, ConnectIn,
            SQL_NTS, NULL, 0, NULL, SQL_DRIVER_NOPROMPT);

    // Call The ShowPrimaryKeyInfo() Member Function
    if (rc == SQL_SUCCESS || rc == SQL_SUCCESS_WITH_INFO)
        Example.ShowPrimaryKeyInfo();

    // Disconnect From The SQL Server Sample Database
    rc = SQLDisconnect(Example.ConHandle);
}

// Return To The Operating System
return(rc);
}
```

SQLForeignKeys

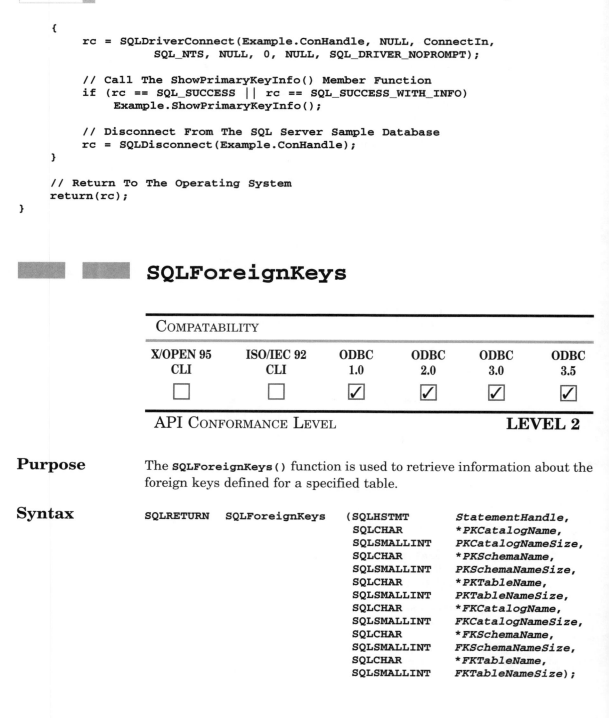

COMPATABILITY

X/OPEN 95 CLI	ISO/IEC 92 CLI	ODBC 1.0	ODBC 2.0	ODBC 3.0	ODBC 3.5
☐	☐	✓	✓	✓	✓

API CONFORMANCE LEVEL   **LEVEL 2**

Purpose The SQLForeignKeys() function is used to retrieve information about the foreign keys defined for a specified table.

Syntax

```
SQLRETURN  SQLForeignKeys  (SQLHSTMT      StatementHandle,
                            SQLCHAR       *PKCatalogName,
                            SQLSMALLINT   PKCatalogNameSize,
                            SQLCHAR       *PKSchemaName,
                            SQLSMALLINT   PKSchemaNameSize,
                            SQLCHAR       *PKTableName,
                            SQLSMALLINT   PKTableNameSize,
                            SQLCHAR       *FKCatalogName,
                            SQLSMALLINT   FKCatalogNameSize,
                            SQLCHAR       *FKSchemaName,
                            SQLSMALLINT   FKSchemaNameSize,
                            SQLCHAR       *FKTableName,
                            SQLSMALLINT   FKTableNameSize);
```

Parameters

StatementHandle	An SQL statement handle that refers to a previously allocated SQL statement information storage buffer (data structure).
PKCatalogName	A pointer to a location in memory where the catalog qualifier portion of a three-part table name of the table containing the primary key is stored.
PKCatalogNameSize	The length of the catalog qualifier name value stored in the *PKCatalogName* parameter.
PKSchemaName	A pointer to a location in memory where the schema portion of a three-part table name of the table containing the primary key is stored.
PKSchemaNameSize	The length of the schema name value stored in the *PKSchemaName* parameter.
PKTableName	A pointer to a location in memory where the table name portion of a three-part table name of the table containing the primary key is stored.
PKTableNameSize	The length of the table name value stored in the *PKTableName* parameter.
FKCatalogName	A pointer to a location in memory where the catalog qualifier portion of a three-part table name of the table containing the foreign key is stored.
FKCatalogNameSize	The length of the catalog qualifier name value stored in the *FKCatalogName* parameter.
FKSchemaName	A pointer to a location in memory where the schema portion of a three-part table name of the table containing the foreign key is stored.
FKSchemaNameSize	The length of the schema name value stored in the *FKSchemaName* parameter.
FKTableName	A pointer to a location in memory where the table name portion of a three-part table name of the table containing the foreign key is stored.
FKTableNameSize	The length of the table name value stored in the *FKTableName* parameter.

Description   The **SQLForeignKeys()** function is used to retrieve information about the foreign keys defined for a specified table. The information returned by this function is placed in a result data set, which can be processed by using the same ODBC API functions used to process result data sets generated by SQL queries. Table 15–10 lists the columns in this result data set.

Table 15–10   Result Data Set Returned by **SQLForeignKeys()**

Column Number	Column Name	Data Type	Description
1	**PKTABLE_CAT**[1] (ODBC 1.0)	VARCHAR(*128*)	The name of the catalog (qualifier) containing the **PKTABLE_SCHEM** value. If a data source does not support three-part table names, this column is set to NULL. If a data source supports three-part table names for a limited number of tables, this column contains an empty string (" ") for tables that do not have a catalog (qualifier) name.
2	**PKTABLE_ SCHEM**[2] (ODBC 1.0)	VARCHAR(*128*)	The name of the schema containing the **PKTABLE_NAME** value. If a data source does not support three-part table names, this column is set to NULL. If a data source supports three-part table names for a limited number of tables, this column contains an empty string (" ") for tables that do not have a schema name.
3	**PKTABLE_NAME** (ODBC 1.0)	VARCHAR(*128*) NOT NULL	The name of the table containing the primary key.
4	**PKCOLUMN_NAME** (ODBC 1.0)	VARCHAR(*128*) NOT NULL	The name of the primary key column in the table identified in the **PKTABLE_NAME** column. This column contains an empty string (" ") for columns without a name.
5	**FKTABLE_CAT**[3] (ODBC 1.0)	VARCHAR(*128*)	The name of the catalog (qualifier) containing the **FKTABLE_SCHEM** value. If a data source does not support three-part table names, this column is set to NULL. If a data source supports three-part table names for a limited number of tables, this column contains an empty string (" ") for tables that do not have a catalog (qualifier) name.

Table 15–10   Result Data Set Returned by **SQLForeignKeys()**   (Continued)

Column Number	Column Name	Data Type	Description
6	**FKTABLE_SCHEM**[4] (ODBC 1.0)	**VARCHAR(***128***)**	The name of the schema containing the **FKTABLE_NAME** value. If a data source does not support three-part table names, this column is set to NULL. If a data source supports three-part table names for a limited number of tables, this column contains an empty string (" ") for tables that do not have a schema name.
7	**FKTABLE_NAME** (ODBC 1.0)	**VARCHAR(***128***) NOT NULL**	The name of the table containing the foreign key.
8	**FKCOLUMN_NAME** (ODBC 1.0)	**VARCHAR(***128***) NOT NULL**	The name of the foreign key column in the table identified in the **FKTABLE_NAME** column. This column contains an empty string (" ") for columns without a name.
8	**FKCOLUMN_ NAME** (ODBC 1.0)	**VARCHAR(***128***) NOT NULL**	The name of the foreign key column.
9	**KEY_SEQ** (ODBC 1.0)	**SMALLINT NOT NULL**	The column's sequence number in the foreign key. The first column in the foreign key is number 1, the second column is number 2, and so on.
10	**UPDATE_ RULE** (ODBC 1.0)	**SMALLINT**	The action to be applied to the foreign key when an **UPDATE** SQL statement is executed. Valid values for this column are: **SQL_CASCADE**: When the primary key of the referenced table is updated, the foreign key of the referencing table is also updated. **SQL_NO_ACTION**: If updating the referenced table's primary key causes a *dangling reference* in the referencing table (that is, rows in the referencing table would have no counterparts in the referenced table), then the update is rejected. If updating the referencing table's foreign key introduces a value that does not exist as a value of the referenced table's primary key, the update is rejected. (This action is the same as the **SQL_RESTRICT** action in ODBC 2.x.)

Table 15–10 Result Data Set Returned by **SQLForeignKeys()** (Continued)

Column Number	Column Name	Data Type	Description
			SQL_RESTRICT: If updating the referenced table's primary key causes a dangling reference in the referencing table (that is, rows in the referencing table would have no counterparts in the referenced table), the update is rejected. If updating the referencing table's foreign key introduces a value that does not exist as a value of the referenced table's primary key, the update is rejected. This value is only returned by an ODBC 2.0 or earlier driver.
			SQL_SET_NULL: When one or more rows in the referenced table are updated such that one or more components of the primary key are changed, the components of the referencing table's foreign key that correspond to the changed components of the primary key are set to NULL in all matching rows of the referencing table.
			SQL_SET_DEFAULT: When one or more rows in the referenced table are updated such that one or more components of the primary key are changed, the components of the referencing table's foreign key that correspond to the changed components of the primary key are set to the applicable default values in all matching rows of the referencing table.
			If this information is not available from the data source, this column is set to NULL.
11	**DELETE_RULE** (ODBC 1.0)	**SMALLINT**	The action to be applied to the foreign key when a **DELETE** SQL statement is executed. Valid values for this column are:
			SQL_CASCADE: When the referenced table's primary key is deleted, the referencing table's foreign key is also deleted.
			SQL_NO_ACTION: If deleting a row in the referenced table causes a dangling reference in the referencing table (that is, rows in the referencing table would have no counterparts in the referenced table),

Table 15–10 Result Data Set Returned by **SQLForeignKeys()** (Continued)

Column Number	Column Name	Data Type	Description
			the delete is rejected. If deleting the referencing table's foreign key introduces a value that does not exist as a value of the referenced table's primary key, the delete is rejected. (This action is the same as the **SQL_RESTRICT** action in ODBC 2.x.)
			SQL_RESTRICT: If deleting a row in the referenced table causes a dangling reference in the referencing table (that is, rows in the referencing table would have no counterparts in the referenced table), the delete is rejected. If deleting the referencing table's foreign key introduces a value that does not exist as a value of the referenced table's primary key, the delete is rejected. This value is only returned by an ODBC 2.0 or earlier driver.
			SQL_SET_NULL: When one or more rows in the referenced table are deleted, each component of the referencing table's foreign key is set to NULL in all matching rows of the referencing table.
			SQL_SET_DEFAULT: When one or more rows in the referenced table are deleted, each component of the referencing table's foreign key is set to the applicable default in all matching rows of the referencing table.
			If this information is not available from the data source, this column is set to NULL.
12	**FK_NAME** (ODBC 2.0)	**VARCHAR(***128***)**	The name (identifier) of the foreign key. This column is set to NULL if a foreign key name is not applicable for data source.
13	**PK_NAME** (ODBC 2.0)	**VARCHAR(***128***)**	The name (identifier) of the primary key. This column is set to NULL if a primary key name is not applicable for data source.
14	**DEFERRABILITY** (ODBC 3.0)	**SMALLINT**	Indicates whether constraints are deferred or applied immediately. Valid values for this column are:
			SQL_INITIALLY_DEFERRED: Constraints are deferred initially and applied later.

Table 15–10 Result Data Set Returned by **SQLForeignKeys()** (Continued)

Column Number	Column Name	Data Type	Description
			SQL_INITIALLY_IMMEDIATE: Constraints are applied immediately.
			SQL_NOT_DEFERRABLE: Constraints cannot be deferred.

(Adapted from the table on pages 676–679 of *Microsoft ODBC 3.0 Software Development Kit & Programmer's Reference*.)

[1]In ODBC 2.0 and earlier, this column was named **PKTABLE_QUALIFIER**.
[2]In ODBC 2.0 and earlier, this column was named **PKTABLE_OWNER**.
[3]In ODBC 2.0 and earlier, this column was named **FKTABLE_QUALIFIER**.
[4]In ODBC 2.0 and earlier, this column was named **FKTABLE_OWNER**.

One or more driver-defined columns may be added to this result data set. When that is the case, applications should gain access to each driver-specific column by counting down from column 14 (**DEFERRABILITY**) of the result data set rather than by specifying an explicit ordinal position.

NOTE: *Depending on the driver being used,* **SQLForeignKeys()** *may or may not return information for all columns in the result data set. However, applications can use any valid column in the result data set, regardless of whether it contains data.*

Return Codes **SQL_SUCCESS**, **SQL_SUCCESS_WITH_INFO**, **SQL_STILL_EXECUTING**, **SQL_INVALID_HANDLE**, or **SQL_ERROR**

SQLSTATEs If this function returns **SQL_SUCCESS_WITH_INFO** or **SQL_ERROR**, one of the following SQLSTATE values may be obtained by calling the **SQLGetDiagRec()** function (ODBC 3.x driver) or the **SQLError()** function (ODBC 2.0 or earlier driver):

ODBC 3.X
01000, **08**S01, **24**000, **40**001, **40**003, **HY**000, **HY**001, **HY**008, **HY**009*, **HY**010*, **HY**013, **HY**090*, **HYC**00, **HYT**00, **HYT**01, or **IM**001*

ODBC 2.0 OR EARLIER
01000, **08**S01, **24**000*, **IM**001*, **S1**000, **S1**001, **S1**008, **S1**009*, **S1**010*, **S1**090*, **S1C**00, or **S1T**00

* Returned by the ODBC Driver Manager.

Unless noted otherwise, each of these SQLSTATE values is returned by the data source driver. Refer to Appendix B for detailed information about each SQLSTATE value that can be returned by the ODBC Driver Manager or by a data source driver.

Comments

■ Because this function, in many cases, maps to a complex, and therefore expensive, query against a data source's system catalog tables, it should be used sparingly; if the result data set produced is to be used more than once, it should be saved, rather than be regenerated each time it is needed.

■ An empty string (" ") can be stored in the memory location the *PKCatalogName* parameter refers to for catalogs without names (provided the driver supports catalog names).

■ An empty string (" ") can be stored in the memory location the *PKSchemaName* parameter refers to for schemas without names (provided the driver supports schema names).

■ An empty string (" ") can be stored in the memory location the *FKCatalogName* parameter refers to for catalogs without names (provided the driver supports catalog names).

■ An empty string (" ") can be stored in the memory location the *FKSchemaName* parameter refers to for schemas without names (provided the driver supports schema names).

■ If the **SQL_ATTR_METADATA_ID** attribute for the statement handle specified is set to **SQL_TRUE**, the values specified for the *PKCatalogName*, *PKSchemaName*, *PKTableName*, *FKCatalogName*, *FKSchemaName*, and *FKTableName* parameters are treated as identifier values and their case is insignificant. However, if the **SQL_ATTR_METADATA_ID** attribute is set to **SQL_FALSE**, the values specified for the *PKCatalogName*, *PKSchemaName*, *PKTableName*, *FKCatalogName*, *FKSchemaName*, and *FKTableName* parameters are treated literally and their case is significant. Refer to the "Parameters (Arguments) Used in Catalog Functions" section earlier in this chapter and to the **SQLGetStmtAttr()** function for more information.

■ If the *PKTableName* parameter contains a valid table name, and the *FKTableName* parameter contains an empty string (" "), this function returns a result data set containing the primary key for the specified table and all foreign keys (in other tables) that refer to it.

■ If the *FKTableName* parameter contains a valid table name, and the *PKTableName* parameter contains an empty string (" "), this function returns a result set containing all the foreign keys for the specified table and all primary keys (in other tables) to which they refer.

■ If both the *PKTableName* parameter and the *FKTableName* parameter contain valid table names, this function returns the foreign keys in the table specified in the *FKTableName* parameter that refer to the primary key of the table specified in the *PKTableName* parameter. This result data set should contain, at the most, only one key.

■ If the foreign keys associated with a primary key are requested, the result data set returned by this function is ordered by **FKTABLE_CAT**, **FKTABLE_SCHEM**, **FKTABLE_NAME**, and **KEY_SEQ**. If the primary keys associated with a foreign key are requested, the result set returned by this function is ordered by **PKTABLE_CAT**, **PKTABLE_SCHEM**, **PKTABLE_NAME**, and **KEY_SEQ**.

■ The actual amount of memory needed to store the value found in each **VARCHAR** column in the result data set that is produced by this function is dependent on the data source. An application can choose to set aside 128 characters (plus the NULL-terminator) for **VARCHAR** columns (to be consistent with the SQL92 standard limits), or alternatively, to allocate the actual amount of memory required by first calling the **SQLGetInfo()** function with the *InfoType* parameter set to **SQL_MAX_CATALOG_NAME_LEN**, **SQL_MAX_SCHEMA_NAME_LEN**, **SQL_MAX_TABLE_NAME_LEN**, and/or **SQL_MAX_COLUMN_NAME_LEN** to determine respectively the actual lengths of the **PKTABLE_CAT** and **FKTABLE_CAT** columns, the **PKTABLE_SCHEM** and **FKTABLE_SCHEM** columns, the **PKTABLE_NAME** and **FKTABLE_NAME** columns, and the **PKCOLUMN_NAME** and **FKCOLUMN_NAME** columns that are supported by the current data source.

Prerequisites   There are no prerequisites for using this function call.

Restrictions   There are no restrictions associated with this function call.

See Also   SQLPrimaryKeys(), SQLStatistics()

Example   The following Visual C++ program illustrates how to use the **SQLForeignKeys()** function to obtain information about the columns that comprise the foreign keys for a specified table.

```
/*—————————————————————————————————————————————————*/
/* NAME:     CH15EX8.CPP                                   */
/* PURPOSE: Illustrate How To Use The Following ODBC API Function */
/*          In A C++ Program:                              */
/*                                                         */
/*                  SQLForeignKeys()                       */
/*                                                         */
/* OTHER ODBC APIs SHOWN:                                  */
/*              SQLAllocHandle()        SQLSetEnvAttr()    */
/*              SQLDriverConnect()      SQLBindCol()       */
/*              SQLFetch()              SQLDisconnect()    */
/*              SQLFreeHandle()                            */
/*                                                         */
/*—————————————————————————————————————————————————*/

// Include The Appropriate Header Files
#include <windows.h>
#include <sql.h>
#include <sqlext.h>
#include <iostream.h>

// Define The ODBC_Class Class
class ODBC_Class
{
    // Attributes
    public:
        SQLHANDLE   EnvHandle;
        SQLHANDLE   ConHandle;
        SQLHANDLE   StmtHandle;
        SQLRETURN   rc;

    // Operations
    public:
        ODBC_Class();                            // Constructor
        ~ODBC_Class();                           // Destructor
        SQLRETURN   ShowForeignKeyInfo();
};

// Define The Class Constructor
ODBC_Class::ODBC_Class()
{
    // Initialize The Return Code Variable
    rc = SQL_SUCCESS;

    // Allocate An Environment Handle
    rc = SQLAllocHandle(SQL_HANDLE_ENV, SQL_NULL_HANDLE, &EnvHandle);

    // Set The ODBC Application Version To 3.x
```

```cpp
    if (rc == SQL_SUCCESS)
        rc = SQLSetEnvAttr(EnvHandle, SQL_ATTR_ODBC_VERSION,
                (SQLPOINTER) SQL_OV_ODBC3, SQL_IS_UINTEGER);

    // Allocate A Connection Handle
    if (rc == SQL_SUCCESS)
        rc = SQLAllocHandle(SQL_HANDLE_DBC, EnvHandle, &ConHandle);
}

// Define The Class Destructor
ODBC_Class::~ODBC_Class()
{
    // Free The Connection Handle
    if (ConHandle != NULL)
        SQLFreeHandle(SQL_HANDLE_DBC, ConHandle);

    // Free The Environment Handle
    if (EnvHandle != NULL)
        SQLFreeHandle(SQL_HANDLE_ENV, EnvHandle);
}

// Define The ShowForeignKeyInfo() Member Function
SQLRETURN ODBC_Class::ShowForeignKeyInfo(void)
{
    // Declare The Local Memory Variables
    SQLCHAR   FKeyName[129];

    // Allocate An SQL Statement Handle
    rc = SQLAllocHandle(SQL_HANDLE_STMT, ConHandle, &StmtHandle);
    if (rc == SQL_SUCCESS)
    {
        // Retrieve Information About The Foreign Keys Defined For
        // The "INVOICE" Table That Reference Primary Keys In Other
        // Tables In The Data Source
        rc = SQLForeignKeys(StmtHandle, NULL, 0, NULL, 0, NULL, 0,
                NULL, 0, NULL, 0, (SQLCHAR *) "INVOICE", SQL_NTS);
        if (rc == SQL_SUCCESS)
        {
            // Bind A Column In The Result Data Set Returned To
            // An Application Variable
            rc = SQLBindCol(StmtHandle, 8, SQL_C_CHAR, (SQLPOINTER)
                    &FKeyName, sizeof(FKeyName), NULL);

            // Display A Header
            cout << "Foreign Keys :" << endl << endl;

            // While There Are Records In The Result Data Set
            // Generated, Retrieve And Display Them
            while (rc != SQL_NO_DATA)
            {
                rc = SQLFetch(StmtHandle);
                if (rc != SQL_NO_DATA)
                    cout << FKeyName << endl;
```

```
                    }
            }

            // Free The SQL Statement Handle
            if (StmtHandle != NULL)
                SQLFreeHandle(SQL_HANDLE_STMT, StmtHandle);
    }

    // Return The ODBC API Return Code To The Calling Function
    return(rc);
}

/*──────────────────────────────────────────────────────────── */
/* The Main Function                                            */
/*──────────────────────────────────────────────────────────── */
int main()
{
    // Declare The Local Memory Variables
    SQLRETURN   rc = SQL_SUCCESS;
    SQLCHAR     ConnectIn[40];

    // Create An Instance Of The ODBC_Class Class
    ODBC_Class  Example;

    // Build A Connection String
    strcpy((char *) ConnectIn,
        "DSN=SQLServer;UID=userid;PWD=password;");

    // Connect To The SQL Server Sample Database
    if (Example.ConHandle != NULL)
    {
        rc = SQLDriverConnect(Example.ConHandle, NULL, ConnectIn,
                SQL_NTS, NULL, 0, NULL, SQL_DRIVER_NOPROMPT);

        // Call The ShowForeignKeyInfo() Member Function
        if (rc == SQL_SUCCESS || rc == SQL_SUCCESS_WITH_INFO)
            Example.ShowForeignKeyInfo();

        // Disconnect From The SQL Server Sample Database
        rc = SQLDisconnect(Example.ConHandle);
    }

    // Return To The Operating System
    return(rc);
}
```

SQLProcedures

COMPATABILITY

X/OPEN 95 CLI	ISO/IEC 92 CLI	ODBC 1.0	ODBC 2.0	ODBC 3.0	ODBC 3.5
☐	☐	☑	☑	☑	☑

API CONFORMANCE LEVEL   **LEVEL 1***

*IN ODBC 2.0, THIS FUNCTION WAS A LEVEL 2 API CONFORMANCE LEVEL FUNCTION

Purpose

The `SQLProcedures()` function is used to retrieve a list of stored procedure names that have been registered in a specified data source.

Syntax

```
SQLRETURN   SQLProcedures   (SQLHSTMT      StatementHandle,
                             SQLCHAR       *ProcCatalog,
                             SQLSMALLINT   ProcCatalogSize,
                             SQLCHAR       *ProcSchema,
                             SQLSMALLINT   ProcSchemaSize,
                             SQLCHAR       *ProcedureName,
                             SQLSMALLINT   ProcedureNameSize);
```

Parameters

StatementHandle

An SQL statement handle that refers to a previously allocated SQL statement information storage buffer (data structure).

ProcCatalogName

A pointer to a location in memory where the catalog qualifier portion of a three-part stored procedure name is stored.

ProcCatalogNameSize

The length of the catalog qualifier name value stored in the *ProcCatalogName* parameter.

ProcSchemaName

A pointer to a location in memory where a schema name search pattern is stored.

ProcSchemaNameSize

The length of the schema name search pattern value stored in the *ProcSchemaName* parameter.

ProcedureName

A pointer to a location in memory where a stored procedure name search pattern is stored.

ProcedureNameSize

The length of the stored procedure name search pattern value stored in the *ProcedureName* parameter.

Description   The `SQLProcedures()` function is used to retrieve a list of stored procedure names that have been registered in a specified data source and that match a specified search pattern. A procedure is a generic term used to describe an executable object, or a named entry that can be invoked using input and/or output parameters. The information returned by this function is placed in an SQL result data set, and can be processed by using the same functions used to process a result data set generated by a query. Table 15–11 lists the columns in this result data set.

One or more driver-defined columns may be added to this result data set. When that is the case, applications should gain access to each driver-specific column by counting down from column 8 (**PROCEDURE_TYPE**) of the result data set rather than by specifying an explicit ordinal position.

Table 15–11   Result Data Set Returned by **SQLProcedures()**

Column Number	Column Name	Data Type	Description
1	**PROCEDURE_ CAT**[1] (ODBC 2.0)	VARCHAR(*128*)	The name of the catalog (qualifier) containing the **PROCEDURE_SCHEM** value. If a data source does not support three-part procedure names, this column is set to NULL. If a data source supports three-part procedure names for a limited number of tables, this column contains an empty string (" ") for tables that do not have a catalog (qualifier) name.
2	**PROCEDURE_ SCHEM**[2] (ODBC 2.0)	VARCHAR(*128*)	The name of the schema containing the **PROCEDURE_NAME** value. If a data source does not support three-part procedure names, this column is set to NULL. If a data source supports three-part procedure names for a limited number of tables, this column contains an empty string (" ") for tables that do not have a schema name.
3	**PROCEDURE_ NAME** (ODBC 2.0)	VARCHAR(*128*) NOT NULL	The name of the stored procedure.
4	**NUM_INPUT_ PARAMS** (ODBC 2.0)	INTEGER NOT NULL	The number of input parameters defined for the stored procedure. At this time, applications should not rely on the data returned in this column.
5	**NUM_OUTPUT_ PARAMS** (ODBC 2.0)	INTEGER	The number of output parameters defined for the stored procedure. At this time, applications should not rely on the data returned in this column.
6	**NUM_RESULT_ SETS** (ODBC 2.0)	INTEGER NOT NULL	The number of result data sets that will be returned whenthe stored procedure is executed. At this time, applications should not rely on the data returned in this column.

Table 15–11 Result Data Set Returned by **SQLProcedures()** Continued

Column Number	Column Name	Data Type	Description
7	**REMARKS** (ODBC 2.0)	VARCHAR(254)	Descriptive information about the stored procedure (if any exists).
8	**PROCEDURE_ TYPE** (ODBC 2.0)	SMALLINT	Indicates whether the procedure is a stored procedure that does not return a value or a data source-specific function that does return a value. Valid values for this column are: **SQL_PT_PROCEDURE**: The returned object is a stored procedure; it does not return a value. **SQL_PT_FUNCTION**: The object is a function; it returns a value. **SQL_PT_UNKNOWN**: Whether the procedure returns a value or not cannot be determined.

(Adapted from table on pages 878–879 of *Microsoft ODBC 3.0 Software Development Kit & Programmer's Reference*.)

[1]In ODBC 2.0 and earlier, this column was named **PROCEDURE_QUALIFIER**.
[2]In ODBC 2.0 and earlier, this column was named **PROCEDURE_OWNER**.

NOTE: *Depending on the driver being used,* **SQLProcedures()** *may or may not return information for all stored procedures stored in the data source. However, applications can use any valid procedure, regardless of whether information about it is returned by the* **SQLProcedures()** *function.*

Return Codes SQL_SUCCESS, SQL_SUCCESS_WITH_INFO, SQL_STILL_EXECUTING, SQL_INVALID_HANDLE, or SQL_ERROR

SQLSTATEs If this function returns **SQL_SUCCESS_WITH_INFO** or **SQL_ERROR**, one of the following SQLSTATE values may be obtained by calling the **SQLGetDiagRec()** function (ODBC 3.x driver) or the **SQLError()** function (ODBC 2.0 or earlier driver):

ODBC 3.X
01000, **08**S01, **24**000, **40**001, **40**003, **HY**000, **HY**001, **HY**008, **HY**009*, **HY**010*, **HY**013, **HY**090*, **HY**C00, **HY**T00, **HY**T01, or **IM**001*

ODBC 2.0 OR EARLIER
01000, **08**S01, **24**000*, **IM**001*, **S1**000, **S1**001, **S1**008, **S1**010*, **S1**090*,
S1C00, or **S1**T00

* Returned by the ODBC Driver Manager.

Unless noted otherwise, each of these SQLSTATE values is returned by the data source driver. Refer to Appendix B for detailed information about each SQLSTATE value that can be returned by the ODBC Driver Manager or by a data source driver.

Comments

- Because this function, in many cases, maps to a complex, and therefore expensive, query against a data source's system catalog tables, it should be used sparingly; if the result data set produced is to be used more than once, it should be saved, rather than be regenerated each time it is needed.
- An empty string (" ") can be stored in the memory location the *ProcCatalogName* parameter refers to for catalogs without names (provided the driver supports catalog names).
- An empty string (" ") can be stored in the memory location the *ProcSchemaName* parameter refers to for schemas without names (provided the driver supports schema names).
- If the **SQL_ATTR_METADATA_ID** attribute for the statement handle specified is set to **SQL_TRUE**, the values specified for the *ProcCatalogName*, *ProcSchemaName*, and *ProcedureName* parameters are treated as identifier values and their case is insignificant. However, if the **SQL_ATTR_METADATA_ID** attribute is set to **SQL_FALSE**, the values specified for the *ProcCatalogName*, *ProcSchemaName*, and *ProcedureName* parameters are treated literally and their case is significant. Refer to the "Parameters (Arguments) Used in Catalog Functions" section earlier in this chapter and to the **SQLGetStmtAttr()** function for more information.
- The values specified for the *ProcSchemaName* and *ProcedureName* parameters can contain the following search pattern values:
  - The underscore character (_).
    Any single character can be used in place of the underscore character.
  - The percent character (%).
    Any sequence of 0 or more characters can be used in place of the percent character.
  - An escape character.
    A driver-specific character used to treat an underscore character, a percent character, and/or the escape character itself as a literal value instead of as a wild card value (that is, % = "%").

■ The **SQLGetInfo()** function can be called with the **SQL_ACCESSIBLE_PROCEDURES** option specified to determine whether a user has the authorization needed to execute any stored procedure found in the result data set produced by this function. If this function is not used to obtain authorization information, an application must be coded in such a way that it can handle situations in which a user attempts to execute a procedure for which they have not been granted the proper authorization privileges.

■ The result data set returned by this function is ordered by **PROCEDURE_CAT**, **PROCEDURE_SCHEM**, and **PROCEDURE_NAME**.

■ The actual amount of memory needed to store the value found in each **VARCHAR** column in the result data set produced by this function is dependent on the data source. An application can choose to set aside 128 characters (plus the NULL-terminator) for **VARCHAR** columns (to be consistent with the SQL92 standard limits), or alternatively, to allocate the actual amount of memory required by first calling the **SQLGetInfo()** function with the *InfoType* parameter set to **SQL_MAX_CATALOG_NAME_LEN, SQL_MAX_SCHEMA_NAME_LEN**, and/or **SQL_MAX_PROCEDURE_NAME_LEN** to determine respectively the actual lengths of the **PROCEDURE_CAT**, **PROCEDURE_SCHEM**, and **PROCEDURE_NAME** columns that are supported by the current data source.

Prerequisites   There are no prerequisites for using this function call.

Restrictions   There are no restrictions associated with this function call.

See Also   SQLProcedureColumns()

Example   The following Visual C++ program illustrates how to use the SQLProcedures() function to obtain information about the stored procedures that are available in a data source.

```
/*───────────────────────────────────────────────────────── */
/* NAME:     CH15EX9.CPP                                      */
/* PURPOSE: Illustrate How To Use The Following ODBC API Function */
/*          In A C++ Program:                                 */
/*                                                            */
/*              SQLProcedures()                               */
/*                                                            */
/* OTHER ODBC APIs SHOWN:                                     */
```

```
/*            SQLAllocHandle()          SQLSetEnvAttr()          */
/*            SQLConnect()              SQLBindCol()             */
/*            SQLFetch()                SQLDisconnect()          */
/*            SQLFreeHandle()                                    */
/*                                                              */
/*------------------------------------------------------------- */

// Include The Appropriate Header Files
#include <windows.h>
#include <sql.h>
#include <sqlext.h>
#include <iostream.h>

// Define The ODBC_Class Class
class ODBC_Class
{
    // Attributes
    public:
        SQLHANDLE    EnvHandle;
        SQLHANDLE    ConHandle;
        SQLHANDLE    StmtHandle;
        SQLRETURN    rc;

    // Operations
    public:
        ODBC_Class();                           // Constructor
        ~ODBC_Class();                          // Destructor
        SQLRETURN    ShowProcedureInfo();
};

// Define The Class Constructor
ODBC_Class::ODBC_Class()
{
    // Initialize The Return Code Variable
    rc = SQL_SUCCESS;

    // Allocate An Environment Handle
    rc = SQLAllocHandle(SQL_HANDLE_ENV, SQL_NULL_HANDLE, &EnvHandle);

    // Set The ODBC Application Version To 3.x
    if (rc == SQL_SUCCESS)
        rc = SQLSetEnvAttr(EnvHandle, SQL_ATTR_ODBC_VERSION,
                (SQLPOINTER) SQL_OV_ODBC3, SQL_IS_UINTEGER);

    // Allocate A Connection Handle
    if (rc == SQL_SUCCESS)
        rc = SQLAllocHandle(SQL_HANDLE_DBC, EnvHandle, &ConHandle);
}

// Define The Class Destructor
ODBC_Class::~ODBC_Class()
{
    // Free The Connection Handle
    if (ConHandle != NULL)
```

```
            SQLFreeHandle(SQL_HANDLE_DBC, ConHandle);

        // Free The Environment Handle
        if (EnvHandle != NULL)
            SQLFreeHandle(SQL_HANDLE_ENV, EnvHandle);
}

// Define The ShowProcedureInfo() Member Function
SQLRETURN ODBC_Class::ShowProcedureInfo(void)
{
        // Declare The Local Memory Variables
        SQLCHAR   ProcedureName[129];

        // Allocate An SQL Statement Handle
        rc = SQLAllocHandle(SQL_HANDLE_STMT, ConHandle, &StmtHandle);
        if (rc == SQL_SUCCESS)
        {
            // Retrieve Information About The Procedures Stored In The
            // Data Source
            rc = SQLProcedures(StmtHandle, NULL, 0, NULL, 0,
                    (SQLCHAR *) "%", SQL_NTS);
            if (rc == SQL_SUCCESS)
            {
                // Bind A Column In The Result Data Set Returned To
                // An Application Variable
                rc = SQLBindCol(StmtHandle, 3, SQL_C_CHAR, (SQLPOINTER)
                        &ProcedureName, sizeof(ProcedureName), NULL);

                // Display A Header
                cout << "Stored Procedures :" << endl << endl;

                // While There Are Records In The Result Data Set
                // Generated, Retrieve And Display Them
                while (rc != SQL_NO_DATA)
                {
                    rc = SQLFetch(StmtHandle);
                    if (rc != SQL_NO_DATA)
                        cout << ProcedureName << endl;
                }
            }

            // Free The SQL Statement Handle
            if (StmtHandle != NULL)
                SQLFreeHandle(SQL_HANDLE_STMT, StmtHandle);
        }

        // Return The ODBC API Return Code To The Calling Function
        return(rc);
}

/*————————————————————————————————————————————————————————————— */
/* The Main Function                                             */
/*————————————————————————————————————————————————————————————— */
```

```
int main()
{
    // Declare The Local Memory Variables
    SQLRETURN   rc = SQL_SUCCESS;
    SQLCHAR     DBName[10] = "Northwind";

    // Create An Instance Of The ODBC_Class Class
    ODBC_Class   Example;

    // Connect To The Northwind Sample Database
    if (Example.ConHandle != NULL)
    {
        rc = SQLConnect(Example.ConHandle, DBName, SQL_NTS,
                (SQLCHAR *) "", SQL_NTS, (SQLCHAR *) "", SQL_NTS);

        // Call The ShowProcedureInfo() Member Function
        if (rc == SQL_SUCCESS || rc == SQL_SUCCESS_WITH_INFO)
            Example.ShowProcedureInfo();

        // Disconnect From The Northwind Sample Database
        rc = SQLDisconnect(Example.ConHandle);
    }

    // Return To The Operating System
    return(rc);
}
```

SQLProcedureColumns

COMPATABILITY

X/OPEN 95 CLI	ISO/IEC 92 CLI	ODBC 1.0	ODBC 2.0	ODBC 3.0	ODBC 3.5
☐	☐	✓	✓	✓	✓

API CONFORMANCE LEVEL   **LEVEL 1***

*IN ODBC 2.0, THIS FUNCTION WAS A LEVEL 2 API CONFORMANCE LEVEL FUNCTION

Purpose   The SQLProcedureColumns() function is used to retrieve a list of input and output parameters, as well as a list of the columns that make up the result data set for a specified stored procedure.

Syntax   SQLRETURN SQLProcedureColumns (SQLHSTMT   *StatementHandle,*
                                                SQLCHAR   *ProcCatalog,*

```
SQLSMALLINT   ProcCatalogSize,
SQLCHAR       *ProcSchema,
SQLSMALLINT   ProcSchemaSize,
SQLCHAR       *ProcedureName,
SQLSMALLINT   ProcedureNameSize,
SQLCHAR       *ColumnName,
SQLSMALLINT   ColumnNameSize);
```

Parameters

StatementHandle	An SQL statement handle that refers to a previously allocated SQL statement information storage buffer (data structure).
ProcCatalogName	A pointer to a location in memory where the catalog qualifier portion of a three-part stored procedure name is stored.
ProcCatalogNameSize	The length of the catalog qualifier name value stored in the *ProcCatalogName* parameter.
ProcSchemaName	A pointer to a location in memory where a stored procedure schema name search pattern is stored.
ProcSchemaNameSize	The length of the stored procedure schema name search pattern value stored in the *ProcSchemaName* parameter.
ProcedureName	A pointer to a location in memory where a stored procedure name search pattern is stored.
ProcedureNameSize	The length of the stored procedure name search pattern value stored in the *ProcedureName* parameter.
ColumnName	A pointer to a location in memory where a column name search pattern is stored.
ColumnNameSize	The length of the column name search pattern value stored in the *ColumnName* parameter.

Description   The `SQLProcedureColumns()` function is used to retrieve a list of input and output parameters, as well as a list of the columns that make up the result data set for a specified stored procedure. This function is typically called before a stored procedure is executed so information about the parameters used by the procedure and the result data set or sets produced by the procedure is known, in advance, by the application. The information returned by this function is placed in a result data set, which can be processed by using the same ODBC API functions used to process result data sets generated by SQL queries. Table 15–12 lists the columns in this result data set.

One or more driver-defined columns may be added to this result data set. When that is the case, applications should gain access to each driver-specific column by counting down from column 19 (**IS_NULLABLE**) of the result data set rather than by specifying an explicit ordinal position.

Table 15–12   Result Data Set Returned by **SQLProcedureColumns()**

Column Number	Column Name	Data Type	Description
1	**PROCEDURE_CAT**[1] (ODBC 2.0)	**VARCHAR(***128***)**	The name of the catalog (qualifier) containing the **PROCEDURE_SCHEM** value. If a data source does not support three-part procedure names, this column is set to NULL. If a data source supports three-part procedure names for a limited number of tables, this column contains an empty string (" ") for tables that do not have a catalog (qualifier) name.
2	**PROCEDURE_ SCHEM**[2] (ODBC 2.0)	**VARCHAR(128)**	The name of the schema containing the **PROCEDURE_NAME** value. If a data source does not support three-part procedure names, this column is set to NULL. If a data source supports three-part procedure names for a limited number of tables, this column contains an empty string (" ") for tables that do not have a schema name.
3	**PROCEDURE_ NAME** (ODBC 2.0)	**VARCHAR(***128***) NOT NULL**	The name of the stored procedure.
4	**COLUMN_NAME** (ODBC 2.0)	**VARCHAR(***128***) NOT NULL**	The name of a either a parameter or a column in a result data set that is associated with the stored procedure identified in the **PROCEDURE_NAME** column. This column contains an empty string (" ") for columns without a name.
5	**COLUMN_TYPE** (ODBC 2.0)	**SMALLINT NOT NULL**	Identifies whether the name identified in the **COLUMN_NAME** column is for a parameter or for a column in a result data set associated with the stored procedure identified in the **PROCEDURE_NAME** column. Valid values for this column are:

Table 15–12 Result Data Set Returned by **SQLProcedureColumns()** (Continued)

Column Number	Column Name	Data Type	Description
			SQL_PARAM_INPUT: The name identified in the **COLUMN_NAME** column is for an input parameter.
			SQL_PARAM_OUTPUT: The name identified in the **COLUMN_NAME** column is for an output parameter.
			SQL_PARAM_INPUT_OUTPUT: The name identified in the **COLUMN_NAME** column is for an input/output parameter.
			SQL_RETURN_VALUE: The name identified in the **COLUMN_NAME** column is actually for the return value of the stored procedure.
			SQL_RESULT_COL: The name identified in the **COLUMN_NAME** column is for a column in a result data set produced by the stored procedure.
			SQL_PARAM_TYPE_UNKNOWN: Whether the name identified in the **COLUMN_NAME** column is for a parameter or for a column in a result data set cannot be determined.
6	**DATA_TYPE** (ODBC 2.0)	**SMALLINT NOT NULL**	The ODBC or driver-specific SQL data type of the parameter/column identified in the **COLUMN_NAME** column. Valid values for this column include:
			SQL_CHAR, SQL_VARCHAR, SQL_ LONGVARCHAR, SQL_WCHAR, SQL_ WVARCHAR, SQL_WLONGVARCHAR, SQL_DECIMAL, SQL_NUMERIC, SQL_SMALLINT, SQL_INTEGER, SQL_REAL, SQL_FLOAT, SQL_DOUBLE, SQL_BIT, SQL_TINYINT, SQL_BIGINT, SQL_BINARY, SQL_VARBINARY, SQL_LONGVARBINARY, SQL_TYPE_DATE, SQL_TYPE_TIME, SQL_TYPE_ TIMESTAMP, SQL_INTERVAL_MONTH, SQL_INTERVAL_YEAR, SQL_ INTERVAL_YEAR_TO_MONTH, SQL_ **INTERVAL_DAY, SQL_INTERVAL_HOUR, SQL_INTERVAL_MINUTE,** SQL_ **INTERVAL_SECOND, SQL_INTERVAL_**

Table 15-12 Result Data Set Returned by **SQLProcedureColumns()** (Continued)

Column Number	Column Name	Data Type	Description
			DAY_TO_HOUR, SQL_INTERVAL_DAY_TO_MINUTE, SQL_INTERVAL_DAY_TO_SECOND, SQL_INTERVAL_HOUR_TO_MINUTE, SQL_INTERVAL_HOUR_TO_SECOND, SQL_INTERVAL_MINUTE_TO_SECOND, SQL_GUID
			For datetime and interval data types, this column contains the concise data type (such as **SQL_TYPE_DATE** or **SQL_INTERVAL_YEAR_TO_MONTH**, rather than the nonconcise data type such as **SQL_DATETIME** or **SQL_INTERVAL**) (ODBC 3.x applications only).
			NOTE: SQL data types returned for ODBC 3.x, ODBC 2.0, and ODBC 1.0 applications may be different.
7	**TYPE_NAME** (ODBC2.0)	**VARCHAR(** *128* **) NOT NULL**	The data source-specific character representation of the SQL data type name identified in the **DATA_TYPE** column. Valid values for this column include:
			CHAR, VARCHAR, LONG VARCHAR, WCHAR, VARWCHAR, LONGWVARCHAR, DECIMAL, NUMERIC, SMALLINT, INTEGER, REAL, FLOAT, DOUBLE PRECISION, BIT, TINYINT, BIGINT, BINARY, VARBINARY, LONG VARBINARY, DATE, TIME, TIMESTAMP, INTERVAL MONTH, INTERVAL YEAR, INTERVAL YEAR TO MONTH, INTERVAL DAY, INTERVAL HOUR, INTERVAL MINUTE, INTERVAL SECOND, INTERVAL DAY TO HOUR, INTERVAL DAY TO MINUTE, INTERVAL DAY TO SECOND, INTERVAL HOUR TO MINUTE, INTERVAL HOUR TO SECOND, INTERVAL MINUTE TO SECOND, GUID
8	**COLUMN_SIZE**[3] (ODBC 2.0)	**INTEGER**	The maximum number of bytes needed to display the parameter/column data in character format.
			For numeric data types, this is either the total number of digits, or the total number of bits allowed in the parameter/column, depending on the value in the **NUM_PREC_RADIX** column.
			For character or binary string data types, this is the size of the string (string length), in bytes.

Table 15–12   Result Data Set Returned by **SQLProcedureColumns()**   (Continued)

Column Number	Column Name	Data Type	Description
			For date, time, and timestamp data types, this is the total number of characters required to display the value when it is converted to a character string.
			For interval data types, this is the total number of characters in the character representation of the interval literal (as defined by the interval leading precision value).
9	BUFFER_LENGTH[4] (ODBC 2.0)	INTEGER	The maximum number of bytes needed in order for the associated C application variable (buffer) to store data for this parameter or from this column if the value **SQL_C_DEFAULT** is specified for the *CDataType* parameter of the **SQLBindParameter()** **SQLBindCol()**, or **SQLGetData()** function. This length does not include the NULL-terminator character used by NULL terminated strings. For numeric data, this size may be different than the size of the data stored in the data source.
10	DECIMAL_DIGITS[5] (ODBC 2.0)	SMALLINT	The total number of significant digits to the right of the decimal point.
			If the **DATA_TYPE** column contains **SQL_TYPE_TIME** or **SQL_TYPE_TIMESTAMP**, this column contains the number of digits in the fractional seconds component of the time value.
			For interval data types containing a time component, this column contains the number of digits to the right of the decimal point (fractional seconds).
			For interval data types that do not contain a time component, this column contains the value zero (**0**).
			For data types where decimal digits are not applicable, this column is set to NULL.
			For all other data types, this column contains the decimal digits of the parameter/column on the data source.
11	NUM_PREC_RADIX[6] (ODBC 2.0)	SMALLINT	The radix value of the parameter/column.

Table 15–12 Result Data Set Returned by **SQLProcedureColumns()**   (Continued)

Column Number	Column Name	Data Type	Description
			For approximate numeric data types, this column contains the value **2** and the **COLUMN_SIZE** column contains the number of bits allowed for the parameter/column.
			For exact numeric data types, this column contains the value **10** and the **COLUMN_SIZE** column contains the number of decimal digits allowed for the parameter/column.
			For numeric data types, this column can contain either **10** or **2**.
			For data types where radix is not applicable, this column is set to NULL.
12	**NULLABLE** (ODBC 2.0)	**SMALLINT NOT NULL**	Indicates whether the parameter/column accepts a NULL value. Valid values for this column are:
			SQL_NO_NULLS: The parameter/column does not accept NULL values.
			SQL_NULLABLE: The parameter/column accepts NULL values.
			SQL_NULLABLE_UNKNOWN: Whether the parameter/column accepts NULL values is not known.
			The value in this column is different from the value in the **IS_NULLABLE** column. The **NULLABLE** column indicates with certainty that a parameter/column can accept NULLs, but it cannot indicate with certainty that a parameter/column does not accept NULLs. The **IS_NULLABLE** column indicates with certainty that a parameter/column cannot accept NULLs, but it cannot indicate with certainty that a parameter/column accepts NULLs.
13	**REMARKS** (ODBC 2.0)	**VARCHAR(*254*)**	Descriptive information about the parameter/column (if any exists).
14	**COLUMN_DEF** (ODBC 3.0)	**VARCHAR(*254*)**	The parameter/column's default value.
			If the default value is a numeric literal, this column contains the character representation of the numeric literal with no enclosing single quotes.

Table 15–12   Result Data Set Returned by **SQLProcedureColumns()**   (Continued)

Column Number	Column Name	Data Type	Description
			If the default value is a character string, this column contains that string enclosed in single quotes.
			If the default value is a pseudo-literal, (as is the case for **DATE**, **TIME**, and **TIMESTAMP** columns), this column contains the keyword of the pseudo-literal (for example: "CURRENT DATE") with no enclosing single quotes.
			If the default value is NULL or if no default value was specified, this column contains the word **NULL** with no enclosing single quotes.
			If the default value cannot be represented without truncation, this column contains the word **"TRUNCATED"** with no enclosing single quotes.
			The value of this column can be used in generating a new column definition, except when it contains the value **"TRUNCATED"**.
15	**SQL_DATA_TYPE** (ODBC 3.0)	**SMALLINT NOT NULL**	The SQL data type of the parameter/column identified in the **COLUMN_NAME** column as it would appear in the **SQL_DESC_TYPE** field of an implementation row descriptor record. This can be an ODBC SQL data type or a driver-specific SQL data type.
			This column usually contains the same value as the **DATA_TYPE** column, with the following exception:
			For datetime and interval data types, this column contains the non-concise data type (such as **SQL_DATETIME** or **SQL_INTERVAL**), rather than the concise data type (such as **SQL_TYPE_DATE** or **SQL_INTERVAL_ YEAR_TO_MONTH**). If this column contains **SQL_DATETIME** or **SQL_INTERVAL**, the specific data type can be obtained from the **SQL_DATETIME_SUB** column.
			NOTE: SQL data types returned for ODBC 3.x, ODBC 2.0, and ODBC 1.0 applications may be different.
16	**DATETIME_SUB** (ODBC 3.0)	**SMALLINT**	The subtype code for datetime and interval data types. For all other data types, this column is set to NULL.

Table 15–12 Result Data Set Returned by **SQLProcedureColumns()** (Continued)

Column Number	Column Name	Data Type	Description
17	CHAR_OCTET_ LENGTH (ODBC 3.0)	INTEGER	Contains the maximum length, in octets (bytes), for a character data type parameter/column. For single byte character sets, this column contains the same value as the **COLUMN_SIZE** column. For all other character sets, this column is set to NULL.
18	ORDINAL_ POSITION (ODBC 3.0)	INTEGER NOT NULL	The parameter/column's sequence number in the table. The first parameter/column is number 1, the second parameter/column is number 2, and so on.
19	IS_NULLABLE (ODBC 3.0)	VARCHAR(*254*)	Indicates whether the parameter/column is known to be nullable (can contain NULL values), according to the rules in the ISO SQL92 standard. Valid values for this column are: **"YES"**: The parameter/column can contain NULL values. **"NO"**: The parameter/column cannot contain NULL values. (" ") (Empty string): Whether the parameter/column can contain NULL values is not known. An ISO SQL92-compliant DBMS cannot return an empty string. The value returned for this column is different from the value returned for the **NULLABLE** column. (See the description of the **NULLABLE** column for details.)

(Adapted from the table on pages 867–872 of *Microsoft ODBC 3.0 Software Development Kit & Programmer's Reference.*)

[1]In ODBC 2.0 and earlier, this column was named **PROCEDURE_QUALIFIER**.
[2]In ODBC 2.0 and earlier, this column was named **PROCEDURE_OWNER**.
[3]In ODBC 2.0 and earlier, this column was named **PRECISION**.
[4]In ODBC 2.0 and earlier, this column was named **LENGTH**.
[5]In ODBC 2.0 and earlier, this column was named **SCALE**.
[6]In ODBC 2.0 and earlier, this column was named **RADIX**.

> **NOTE:** *Depending on the driver being used, `SQLProcedureColumns()` may or may not return information for all result data set columns. For example, a driver might only return information about the parameters used by a procedure and not about the columns in a result data set the procedure generates.*

This function can return information on the input parameters, the output parameters, or both the input and the output parameters associated with a stored procedure; however, it cannot return information about the descriptor information for any result data sets returned.

Return Codes   `SQL_SUCCESS`, `SQL_SUCCESS_WITH_INFO`, `SQL_STILL_EXECUTING`, `SQL_INVALID_HANDLE`, or `SQL_ERROR`

SQLSTATEs   If this function returns `SQL_SUCCESS_WITH_INFO` or `SQL_ERROR`, one of the following SQLSTATE values may be obtained by calling the `SQLGetDiagRec()` function (ODBC 3.x driver) or the `SQLError()` function (ODBC 2.0 or earlier driver):

ODBC 3.X
01000, **08**S01, **24**000, **40**001, **40**003, **HY**000, **HY**001, **HY**008, **HY**009*, **HY**010*, **HY**090*, **HYC**00, **HYT**00, **HYT**01, or **IM**001*

ODBC 2.0 OR EARLIER
01000, **08**S01, **24**000*, **IM**001*, **S1**000, **S1**001, **S1**008, **S1**010*, **S1**090*, **S1C**00, or **S1T**00

* Returned by the ODBC Driver Manager.

Unless noted otherwise, each of these SQLSTATE values is returned by the data source driver. Refer to Appendix B for detailed information about each SQLSTATE value that can be returned by the ODBC Driver Manager or by a data source driver.

Comments
- Because this function, in many cases, maps to a complex, and therefore expensive, query against a data source's system catalog tables, it should be used sparingly; if the result data set produced is to be used more than once, it should be saved, rather than be regenerated each time it is needed.
- An empty string (" ") can be stored in the memory location the *ProcCatalogName* parameter refers to for catalogs without names (provided the driver supports catalog names).

- An empty string (" ") can be stored in the memory location the *ProcSchemaName* parameter refers to for schemas without names (provided the driver supports schema names).

- If **the SQL_ATTR_METADATA_ID** attribute for the statement handle specified is set to **SQL_TRUE**, the values specified for the *ProcCatalogName*, *ProcSchemaName*, *ProcedureName*, and *ColumnName* parameters are treated as identifier values, and their case is insignificant. However, if the **SQL_ATTR_METADATA_ID** attribute is set to **SQL_FALSE**, the values specified for the *ProcCatalogName*, *ProcSchemaName*, *ProcedureName*, and *ColumnName* parameters are treated literally, and their case is significant. Refer to the "Parameters (Arguments) Used In Catalog Functions" section earlier in this chapter and to the **SQLGetStmtAttr()** function for more information.

- The values specified for the *ProcSchemaName*, *ProcedureName*, and *ColumnName* parameters can contain the following search pattern values:

  - The underscore character (_).
    Any single character can be used in place of the underscore character.

  - The percent character (%).
    Any sequence of 0 or more characters can be used in place of the percent character.

  - An escape character.
    A driver-specific character used to treat an underscore character, a percent character, and/or the escape character itself as a literal value instead of as a wild card value (that is, % = "%").

- The result data set returned by this function is ordered by **PROCEDURE_CAT**, **PROCEDURE_SCHEM**, **PROCEDURE_NAME**, and **COLUMN_TYPE**.

- The actual amount of memory needed to store the value found in each **VARCHAR** column in the result data set produced by this function is dependent on the data source. An application can choose to set aside 128 characters (plus the NULL-terminator) for **VARCHAR** columns (to be consistent with the SQL92 standard limits), or alternatively, to allocate the actual amount of memory required by first calling the **SQLGetInfo()** function with the *InfoType* parameter set to **SQL_MAX_CATALOG_NAME_LEN, SQL_MAX_SCHEMA_NAME_LEN, SQL_MAX_PROCEDURE_NAME_LEN** and/or **SQL_MAX_COLUMN_NAME_LEN** to determine respectively the actual lengths of the **PROCEDURE_CAT**, **PROCEDURE_SCHEM**, **PROCEDURE_NAME**, and **COLUMN_NAME** columns that are supported by the current data source.

Prerequisites   There are no prerequisites for using this function call.

Restrictions   This function does not return information about the attributes of result sets that may be produced when a stored procedure is executed.

See Also   SQLProcedures()

Example   The following Visual C++ program illustrates how to use the SQLProcedureColumns() function to obtain information about the columns that are associated with the stored procedures that are available in a data source.

```
/*————————————————————————————————————————————————*/
/* NAME:     CH15EX10.CPP                                       */
/* PURPOSE: Illustrate How To Use The Following ODBC API Function */
/*           In A C++ Program:                                  */
/*                                                              */
/*               SQLProcedureColumns()                          */
/*                                                              */
/* OTHER ODBC APIs SHOWN:                                       */
/*           SQLAllocHandle()            SQLSetEnvAttr()         */
/*           SQLConnect()                SQLBindCol()            */
/*           SQLFetch()                  SQLDisconnect()         */
/*           SQLFreeHandle()                                     */
/*                                                              */
/*————————————————————————————————————————————————*/

// Include The Appropriate Header Files
#include <windows.h>
#include <sql.h>
#include <sqlext.h>
#include <iostream.h>

// Define The ODBC_Class Class
class ODBC_Class
{
    // Attributes
    public:
        SQLHANDLE    EnvHandle;
        SQLHANDLE    ConHandle;
        SQLHANDLE    StmtHandle;
        SQLRETURN    rc;

    // Operations
```

```
    public:
        ODBC_Class();                               // Constructor
        ~ODBC_Class();                              // Destructor
        SQLRETURN  ShowProcedureColumnInfo();
};

// Define The Class Constructor
ODBC_Class::ODBC_Class()
{
    // Initialize The Return Code Variable
    rc = SQL_SUCCESS;

    // Allocate An Environment Handle
    rc = SQLAllocHandle(SQL_HANDLE_ENV, SQL_NULL_HANDLE, &EnvHandle);

    // Set The ODBC Application Version To 3.x
    if (rc == SQL_SUCCESS)
        rc = SQLSetEnvAttr(EnvHandle, SQL_ATTR_ODBC_VERSION,
                (SQLPOINTER) SQL_OV_ODBC3, SQL_IS_UINTEGER);

    // Allocate A Connection Handle
    if (rc == SQL_SUCCESS)
        rc = SQLAllocHandle(SQL_HANDLE_DBC, EnvHandle, &ConHandle);
}

// Define The Class Destructor
ODBC_Class::~ODBC_Class()
{
    // Free The Connection Handle
    if (ConHandle != NULL)
        SQLFreeHandle(SQL_HANDLE_DBC, ConHandle);

    // Free The Environment Handle
    if (EnvHandle != NULL)
        SQLFreeHandle(SQL_HANDLE_ENV, EnvHandle);
}

// Define The ShowProcedureColumnInfo() Member Function
SQLRETURN ODBC_Class::ShowProcedureColumnInfo(void)
{
    // Declare The Local Memory Variables
    SQLCHAR  ColumnName[129];

    // Allocate An SQL Statement Handle
    rc = SQLAllocHandle(SQL_HANDLE_STMT, ConHandle, &StmtHandle);
    if (rc == SQL_SUCCESS)
    {
        // Retrieve Information About The Columns Associated With The
        // Procedures Stored In The Data Source
        rc = SQLProcedureColumns(StmtHandle, NULL, 0, NULL, 0,
                (SQLCHAR *) "%", SQL_NTS, (SQLCHAR *) "%", SQL_NTS);
        if (rc == SQL_SUCCESS)
        {
            // Bind A Column In The Result Data Set Returned To
            // An Application Variable
```

```
        rc = SQLBindCol(StmtHandle, 4, SQL_C_CHAR, (SQLPOINTER)
                   &ColumnName, sizeof(ColumnName), NULL);

        // Display A Header
        cout << "Procedure Columns :" << endl << endl;

        // While There Are Records In The Result Data Set
        // Generated, Retrieve And Display Them
        while (rc != SQL_NO_DATA)
        {
            rc = SQLFetch(StmtHandle);
            if (rc != SQL_NO_DATA)
                cout << ColumnName << endl;
        }
    }

    // Free The SQL Statement Handle
    if (StmtHandle != NULL)
        SQLFreeHandle(SQL_HANDLE_STMT, StmtHandle);
}

// Return The ODBC API Return Code To The Calling Function
return(rc);
}


/*————————————————————————————————————————————————————————————————*/
/* The Main Function                                              */
/*————————————————————————————————————————————————————————————————*/
int main()
{
    // Declare The Local Memory Variables
    SQLRETURN   rc = SQL_SUCCESS;
    SQLCHAR     DBName[10] = "Northwind";

    // Create An Instance Of The ODBC_Class Class
    ODBC_Class  Example;

    // Connect To The Northwind Sample Database
    if (Example.ConHandle != NULL)
    {
        rc = SQLConnect(Example.ConHandle, DBName, SQL_NTS,
                   (SQLCHAR *) "", SQL_NTS, (SQLCHAR *) "", SQL_NTS);

        // Call The ShowProcedureColumnInfo() Member Function
        if (rc == SQL_SUCCESS || rc == SQL_SUCCESS_WITH_INFO)
            Example.ShowProcedureColumnInfo();

        // Disconnect From The Northwind Sample Database
        rc = SQLDisconnect(Example.ConHandle);
    }

    // Return To The Operating System
    return(rc);
```

APPENDIX A

ODBC Scalar Functions

An ODBC scalar function is an operation denoted by a function name followed by a pair of parentheses enclosing zero or more specified arguments. Because each ODBC scalar function returns a value, scalar functions can be specified in an SQL statement wherever an expression can be used.

Table A–1 describes all the scalar functions provided by ODBC. Several functions were added in ODBC 3.0 to align ODBC with the SQL-92 standards. However, it is important to note that ODBC and SQL-92 classify their scalar functions differently. ODBC classifies scalar functions by argument type; SQL-92 classifies them by return value. For example, the function **EXTRACT(***argument1* **FROM** *argument2***)** is classified as a time-date function by ODBC, because *argument1* is a datetime keyword and *argument2* is a datetime or interval expression. SQL-92, on the other hand, classifies **EXTRACT(***argument1* **FROM** *argument2***)** as a numeric scalar function, because the return value is numeric.

An application can determine which scalar functions a driver supports by calling the **SQLGetInfo()** function with the appropriate information type specified. Information types are included for both ODBC and SQL-92 classifications of scalar functions; however, because these classifications are different, a driver may only indicate whether it supports some scalar functions if an information type other than an ODBC or SQL-92 scalar function information type is specified. For example, support for **EXTRACT(***argument1* **FROM** *argument2***)** in ODBC is indicated by the **SQL_TIMEDATE_FUNCTIONS** information type; support for **EXTRACT (***argument1* **FROM** *argument2***)** in SQL-92, on the other hand, is indicated by the **SQL_SQL92_NUMERIC_VALUE_FUNCTIONS** information type.

Table A–1   ODBC Scalar Functions

Function/Syntax	Description
String Functions	
ASCII(*argument*) (ODBC 1.0)	Returns the ASCII code value of the leftmost character of **argument** as an integer.
BIT_LENGTH(*argument*) (ODBC 3.0)	Returns the length, in bits, of **argument**.
CHAR(*argument*) (ODBC 1.0)	Returns the character that has the ASCII code value specified by **argument**. The value of **argument** should be between **0** and **255**; otherwise, the value returned is data source-dependent.
CHAR_LENGTH(*argument*) (ODBC 3.0)	Returns the length, in characters, of **argument**, if **argument** is a character data type; otherwise, returns the length, in bytes, of **argument** (the smallest integer not less than the number of bits divided by 8). **CHARACTER_LENGTH** is a synonym for **CHAR_LENGTH**
CONCAT(*argument1, argument2*) (ODBC 1.0)	Returns a character string that is the result of concatenating **argument2** to **argument1**. If one of the arguments is not a character string, the result string returned is data source-dependent.
DIFFERENCE(*argument1, argument2*) (ODBC 2.0)	Returns an integer value that indicates the difference between the sounds of the words in **argument1** and **argument2**, as determined with the **SOUNDEX** function. A value of **0** indicates that the strings sound alike.
INSERT(*argument1, position, size, argument2*)) (ODBC 1.0	Returns a character string where **size** characters have been deleted from **argument1** beginning at **position**, and where **argument2** has been inserted into **argument1**, beginning at **position**.
LCASE(*argument*) (ODBC 1.0)	Returns a character string in which all uppercase characters in **argument** have been converted to lowercase.
LEFT(*argument, length*) (ODBC 1.0)	Returns a character string consisting of the leftmost **length** characters of **argument**.
LENGTH(*argument*) (ODBC 1.0)	Returns the length of **argument**, in characters, excluding trailing blanks.
LOCATE(*argument1, argument2 <, position>*) (ODBC 1.0)	Returns the starting position of the first occurrence of **argument1** within **argument2**. If a **position** is specified, it indicates the character position in **argument2** where the search is to begin. If **argument1** is not found in **argument2**, the value **0** is returned.

Table A–1 ODBC Scalar Functions (Continued)

Function/Syntax	Description
LTRIM(*argument* **)** (ODBC 1.0)	Returns the characters of **argument**, with leading blanks removed.
OCTET_LENGTH(*argument* **)** (ODBC 3.0)	Returns the length, in bytes, of **argument**. The result is the smallest integer greater than or equal to the number of bits divided by 8.
POSITION(*argument1* **IN** *argument2* **)** (ODBC 3.0)	Returns the position of **argument1** in **argument2**. The result is an exact numeric value with an implementation-defined precision and a scale of **0**.
REPEAT(*argument, count* **)** (ODBC 1.0)	Returns a character string composed of **argument** repeated **count** times.
REPLACE(*argument1, argument2, argument3* **)** (ODBC 1.0)	Returns a character string in which all occurrences of **argument2** in **argument1** have been replaced with **argument3**.
RIGHT(*argument, length* **)** (ODBC 1.0)	Returns a character string consisting of the rightmost **length** characters of **argument**.
RTRIM(*argument* **)** (ODBC 1.0)	Returns the characters of **argument**, with trailing blanks removed.
SOUNDEX(*argument* **)** (ODBC 2.0)	Returns a data source–dependent character string representing the sound of the words in **argument**. The result can be used to compare the sounds of strings.
SPACE(*argument* **)** (ODBC 2.0)	Returns a character string consisting of **argument** spaces (blanks).
SUBSTRING(*argument, position, length* **)** (ODBC 1.0)	Returns a character string that is derived from **argument**, starting at the character position specified by **position**, **length** characters in length.
UCASE(*argument* **)** (ODBC 1.0)	Returns a character string in which all lowercase characters in **argument** have been converted to uppercase.

Numeric Functions

Function/Syntax	Description
ABS(*argument* **)** (ODBC 1.0)	Returns the absolute value of **argument**.
ACOS(*argument* **)** (ODBC 1.0)	Returns the arccosine of **argument** as an angle, expressed in radians.
ASIN(*argument* **)** (ODBC 1.0)	Returns the arcsine of **argument** as an angle, expressed in radians.
ATAN(*argument* **)** (ODBC 1.0)	Returns the arctangent of **argument** as an angle, expressed in radians.

Table A–1   ODBC Scalar Functions (Continued)

Function/Syntax	Description
ATAN2(*argument1, argument2* **)** (ODBC 2.0)	Returns the arctangent of x and y coordinates, specified by **argument1** and **argument2**, respectively, as an angle, expressed in radians.
CEILING(*argument* **)** (ODBC 1.0)	Returns the smallest integer value that is greater than or equal to **argument**.
COS(*argument* **)** (ODBC 1.0)	Returns the cosine of **argument**, where **argument** is an angle expressed in radians.
COT(*argument* **)** (ODBC 1.0)	Returns the cotangent of **argument**, where **argument** is an angle expressed in radians.
DEGREES(*argument* **)** (ODBC 2.0)	Returns the number of degrees converted from **argument**, expressed in radians.
EXP(*argument* **)** (ODBC 1.0)	Returns the exponential value of **argument**.
FLOOR(*argument* **)** (ODBC 1.0)	Returns the largest integer value that is less than or equal to **argument**.
LOG(*argument* **)** (ODBC 1.0)	Returns the natural logarithm of **argument**.
LOG10(*argument* **)** (ODBC 2.0)	Returns the base-10 logarithm of **argument**.
MOD(*argument1, argument2* **)** (ODBC 1.0)	Returns the remainder (modulus) of **argument1** divided by **argument2**. If **argument1** is negative, the result is negative.
PI() (ODBC 1.0)	Returns the constant value of **pi** (π) as a floating point value.
POWER(*argument1, argument2* **)** (ODBC 2.0)	Returns the value of **argument1**, raised to the power of **argument2**.
RADIANS(*argument* **)** (ODBC 2.0)	Returns the number of radians converted from **argument**, expressed in degrees.
RAND(*<argument>* **)** (ODBC 1.0)	Returns a random floating-point value using **argument** as the optional seed value.
ROUND(*argument1, argument2* **)** (ODBC 2.0)	Returns **argument1** rounded to **argument2** places right of the decimal point. If **argument2** is negative, **argument1** is rounded to the absolute value of **argument2** places to the left of the decimal point.
SIGN(*argument* **)** (ODBC 1.0)	Returns an indicator for the sign of **argument**. If **argument** is less than zero, **−1** is returned. If **argument** equals zero, **0** is returned. If **argument** is greater than zero, **1** is returned.

Table A–1 ODBC Scalar Functions (Continued)

Function/Syntax	Description
SIN(*argument*) (ODBC 1.0)	Returns the sine of **argument**, where **argument** is an angle expressed in radians.
SQRT(*argument*) (ODBC 1.0)	Returns the square root of **argument**.
TAN(*argument*) (ODBC 1.0)	Returns the tangent of **argument**, where **argument** is an angle expressed in radians.
TRUNCATE(*argument1, argument2*) (ODBC 2.0)	Returns **argument1** truncated to **argument2** places right of the decimal point. If **argument2** is negative, **argument1** is truncated to the absolute value of **argument2** places to the left of the decimal point.

Date, Time, and Interval Functions

Function/Syntax	Description
CURRENT_DATE() (ODBC 3.0)	Returns the current date.
CURRENT_TIME(<*argument*>) (ODBC 3.0)	Returns the current local time, using **argument** as the optional seconds precision of the returned value.
CURRENT_TIMESTAMP(*argument*) (ODBC 3.0)	Returns the current local date and local time as a timestamp value, using **argument** as the optional seconds precision of the returned value.
CURDATE() (ODBC 1.0)	Returns the current date.
CURTIME() (ODBC 1.0)	Returns the current local time.
DAYNAME(*argument*) (ODBC 2.0)	Returns a mixed-case character string containing the data source–specific name of the day (for example, **Sunday–Saturday** or **Sun.–Sat.** for a data source that uses English) for the day portion of **argument**.
DAYOFMONTH(*argument*) (ODBC 1.0)	Returns the day of the month value stored in the month portion of **argument**, as an integer value in the range of **1–31**.
DAYOFWEEK(*argument*) (ODBC 1.0)	Returns the day of the week value stored in the day portion of **argument**, as an integer value in the range of **1–7** (where **1** represents Sunday for a data source that uses English).
DAYOFYEAR(*argument*) (ODBC 1.0)	Returns the day of the year value stored in the year portion of **argument**, as an integer value in the range of **1–366**.

Table A–1   ODBC Scalar Functions (Continued)

Function/Syntax	Description
EXTRACT(*argument1* **FROM** *argument2* **)** (ODBC 3.0)	Returns the *argument1* portion of *argument2* where *argument2* is a datetime or interval expression. *argument1* can be one of the following keywords: **YEAR** **MONTH** **DAY** **HOUR** **MINUTE** **SECOND** The precision of the returned value is implementation-defined. The scale is **0** unless **SECOND** is specified, in which case the scale is greater than or equal to the fractional seconds precision of *argument2*.
HOUR(*argument* **)** (ODBC 1.0)	Returns the hour value stored in the hour portion of *argument*, as an integer value in the range of **0–23**.
MINUTE(*argument* **)** (ODBC 1.0)	Returns the minute value stored in the minute portion of *argument*, as an integer value in the range of **0–59**.
MONTH(*argument* **)** (ODBC 1.0)	Returns the month value stored in the month portion of *argument*, as an integer value in the range of **1–12** (where **1** represents January for a data source that uses English)
MONTHNAME(*argument* **)** (ODBC 2.0)	Returns a character string containing the data source–specific name of the month (for example, **January–December** or **Jan.–Dec.** for a data source that uses English) for the month portion of *argument*.
NOW() (ODBC 1.0)	Returns the current date and time as a timestamp value.
QUARTER(*argument* **)** (ODBC 1.0)	Returns the quarter in *argument* as an integer value in the range of **1–4** (where **1** represents January 1 through March 31 for a data source that uses English).
SECOND(*argument* **)** (ODBC 1.0)	Returns the seconds value stored in the seconds portion of *argument*, as an integer value in the range **0–59**.
TIMESTAMPADD(*argument1, argument2, argument3* **)** (ODBC 1.0)	Returns a timestamp calculated by adding *argument2* intervals of type *argument1* to *argument3*. Valid values of *argument1* are the following keywords:

Table A–1 ODBC Scalar Functions (Continued)

Function/Syntax	Description
	`SQL_TSI_FRAC_SECOND` `SQL_TSI_SECOND` `SQL_TSI_MINUTE` `SQL_TSI_HOUR` `SQL_TSI_DAY` `SQL_TSI_WEEK` `SQL_TSI_MONTH` `SQL_TSI_QUARTER` `SQL_TSI_YEAR`
	where fractional seconds are expressed in billionths of a second.
	If **argument3** is a time value and **argument1** specifies days, weeks, months, quarters, or years, the date portion of **argument3** is set to the current date before calculating the resulting timestamp. If **argument3** is a date value and **argument1** specifies fractional seconds, seconds, minutes, or hours, the time portion of **argument3** is set to **0** before calculating the resulting timestamp.
`TIMESTAMPDIFF(argument1, argument2, argument3)` (ODBC 2.0)	Returns the integer number of intervals of type **argument1** by which **argument3** is greater than **argument2**. Valid values of **argument1** are the following keywords:
	`SQL_TSI_FRAC_SECOND` `SQL_TSI_SECOND` `SQL_TSI_MINUTE` `SQL_TSI_HOUR` `SQL_TSI_DAY` `SQL_TSI_WEEK` `SQL_TSI_MONTH` `SQL_TSI_QUARTER` `SQL_TSI_YEAR`
	where fractional seconds are expressed in billionths of a second.
	If **argument2** or **argument3** is a time value and **argument1** specifies days, weeks, months, quarters, or years, the date portion of **argument2** or **argument3** is set to the current date before calculating the difference between the timestamps. If **argument2** or **argument3** is a date value and **argument1** specifies fractional seconds, seconds, minutes, or hours, the time portion of **argument2** or **argument3** is set to **0** before calculating the difference between the timestamps.
`WEEK(argument)` (ODBC 1.0)	Returns the week value stored in the week portion of **argument**, as an integer value in the range of **1–53**.
`YEAR(argument)` (ODBC 1.0)	Returns the year value stored in the year portion of **argument**, as an integer value. The range is data source-dependent.

Table A–1   ODBC Scalar Functions (Continued)

Function/Syntax	Description
System Functions	
DATABASE() (ODBC 1.0)	Returns the name of the database corresponding to the current connection handle.
IFNULL(*argument1, argument2*) (ODBC 1.0)	Returns either ***argument1*** or ***argument2***, depending upon whether or not ***argument1*** is NULL If ***argument1*** is NULL, ***argument2*** is returned. If ***argument1*** is not NULL, ***argument1*** is returned. The possible data type of ***argument2*** must be compatible with the data type of ***argument1***.
USER() (ODBC 1.0)	Returns the user name in the DBMS. This may be different from the login name.

(Adapted from Appendix E on pages 1,251–1,261 of *Microsoft ODBC 3.0 Software Development Kit & Programmer's Reference.*)

APPENDIX B

SQLSTATE Cross-Reference

SQLGetDiagRec(), **SQLGetDiagField()**, or **SQLError()** can be called to retrieve SQLSTATE values generated when an ODBC API function returns any return code other than **SQL_NO_DATA**, **SQL_NO_DATA_FOUND** (ODBC 2.0 drivers), or **SQL_SUCCESS**. The five-character string value returned for an SQLSTATE consists of a two-character class value followed by a three-character subclass value (as defined by X/Open Data Management:Structured Query Language (SQL), Version 2 (March 1995)).

A class value of **01** indicates a warning and is accompanied by a return code of **SQL_SUCCESS_WITH_INFO**. Class values other than **01**, except for the class **IM**, indicate an error and are accompanied by a return code of **SQL_ERROR**. The class **IM** is specific to warnings and errors that derive from the implementation of ODBC itself. Class values of **HY** have been reserved by X/Open for Call Level Interfaces, which are equivalent to the ODBC 2.0 **S1** class (ODBC 3.x drivers use the **HY** class instead of the **S1** class). In any case, the subclass value 000 indicates that there is no subclass for that particular SQLSTATE.

Table B–1 contains a cross-reference listing of the SQLSTATE values that can be returned by ODBC API functions. ODBC API functions can also return driver-specific SQLSTATEs not listed in this table. Refer to the documentation for the driver/data source being used for information about additional SQLSTATE values that may be returned.

NOTE: *Although successful execution of a function is usually indicated by the return code* **SQL_SUCCESS**; *the SQLSTATE 00000 also indicates success.*

Table B–1   *SQLSTATE Cross Reference*

ODBC 3.x SQLSTATE	ODBC 2.0 SQLSTATE	Description
01000	01000	General warning. The **SQLGetDiagRec()** function (ODBC 3.x driver) or the **SQLError()** function (ODBC 2.0 or earlier driver) can be used to retrieve a driver-specific informational message (provided one is available).
01001	——	A positioned **UPDATE** or a positioned **DELETE** SQL statement was specified, and no row or more than one row was updated or deleted.
01002	01002	An error occurred while attempting to disconnect from a data source. The ODBC operation was successful; however, **SQL_SUCCESS_WITH_INFO** was returned.
01003	——	An SQL statement containing a set function (such as **AVG()**, **MAX()**, **MIN()**, etc.) other than the **COUNT()** set function was specified and **NULL** parameter values were eliminated before the set function was applied.
01004	01004	The data returned in one or more ODBC API function parameters or for one or more result data set columns was longer than the application variable/buffer or column size specified. Because of this data was truncated.
01006	01006	A **REVOKE** SQL statement was specified, and the user did not have the authorization needed to execute it.
01007	——	A **GRANT** SQL statement was specified, and the user did not have the authorization needed to execute it.
01S00	01S00	An invalid keyword or attribute value was specified in the connection string. The connect operation was successful and **SQL_SUCCESS_WITH_INFO** was returned because one of the following occurred: The unrecognized keyword was ignored. The invalid attribute value was ignored, and the default value was used.
01S01	01S01	An error occurred while retrieving (fetching) one or more rows from a result data set OR an error occurred in one or more rows while attempting to add rows in a bulk operation. The ODBC operation was successful; **SQL_SUCCESS_WITH_INFO** was returned.

Table B–1 SQLSTATE Cross Reference (Continued)

ODBC 3.x SQLSTATE	ODBC 2.0 SQLSTATE	Description
01S02	01S02	The driver did not support the value specified so it substituted a similar value. The ODBC operation was successful; **SQL_SUCCESS_WITH_INFO** was returned.
——	01S03	A positioned **UPDATE** or a positioned **DELETE** SQL statement was specified and no rows were updated or deleted.
——	01S04	A positioned **UPDATE** or a positioned **DELETE** SQL statement was specified, and more than one row was updated or deleted.
01S06	——	The requested rowset overlapped the start of the result data set or the application attempted to retrieve (fetch) data from the result data set before the first rowset was returned.
01S07	——	A bulk **FETCH_BY_BOOKMARK** operation was performed and, because the data type of the application buffer was not **SQL_C_CHAR** or **SQL_C_BINARY**, the data returned to application variables/buffers for one or more columns was truncated. (For numeric C data types, the fractional part of the number was truncated. For time, timestamp, and interval C data types containing a time component, the fractional portion of the time was truncated.)
01S08	——	The connection string specified contained a valid **FILEDSN** keyword-value pair, but the .DSN file specified was not created. The ODBC operation was successful; **SQL_SUCCESS_WITH_INFO** was returned.
01S09	——	The connection string specified contained the **SAVEFILE** keyword, but not the **DRIVER** or **FILEDSN** keyword-value pair. The ODBC operation was successful; **SQL_SUCCESS_WITH_INFO** was returned.
——	07001	The number of parameters bound to application variables was less than the number of parameter markers coded in the SQL statement specified.
07002	——	The number of parameters bound to application variables was less than the number of parameter markers coded in the SQL statement specified OR the data value provided for a bound parameter could not be converted to the data type specified.
07005	——	The SQL statement specified did not produce a result data set.

Table B–1   SQLSTATE Cross Reference (Continued)

ODBC 3.x SQLSTATE	ODBC 2.0 SQLSTATE	Description
07006	07006	The data value could not be converted in a meaningful manner to the SQL data type specified—incompatible data conversions are not allowed.
07009	——	The column number specified exceeded the maximum number of columns in the result data set.
07S01	——	An application variable whose length/indicator variable was set to **SQL_DEFAULT_PARAM** was bound to a parameter in an SQL statement, and the corresponding parameter did not have a default value.
08001	08001	The driver was unable to establish a connection with the data source specified. The connection request may have been rejected because a connection to the data source (via embedded SQL) already exists.
08002	08002	The connection handle specified has already been used to establish a connection to a data source, and that connection is still open.
08003	08003	The connection associated with the connection handle specified is not open. A connection must be established successfully (and the connection must be open) before the ODBC API function can be executed.
08004	08004	The data source rejected the attempt to establish a connection.
08007	08007	The connection to the data source failed while the ODBC API function was executing. Whether the requested **COMMIT** or **ROLLBACK** operation occurred before or after the connection failure occurred cannot be determined.
08S01	08S01	The communication link between the driver and the data source failed before the ODBC API function completed processing.
21S01	21S01	An **INSERT** SQL statement was specified and the number of values provided in the values list did not match the number of columns specified in the table column list.
21S02	21S02	A **CREATE VIEW** SQL statement was specified and the number of names provided in the table column list did not match the number of columns in the derived table defined by the query specification OR an **SQL_UPDATE_BY_BOOKMARK** bulk operation was performed and no columns were updatable because all columns were either unbound, read-only, or ignored (the value in the length/indicator variable was **SQL_COLUMN_IGNORE**).

Table B–1 SQLSTATE Cross Reference (Continued)

ODBC 3.x SQLSTATE	ODBC 2.0 SQLSTATE	Description
22001	22001	A character string assigned to a character data type column exceeded the column's maximum length and was truncated OR the length of long data was set to the data source and the actual length of the long data value sent exceeded the length specified and was truncated. The ODBC operation was successful; **SQL_SUCCESS_WITH_INFO** was returned.
22002	——-	A length/indicator variable is required (possibly to indicate that a NULL value is being sent/retrieved) but one was not supplied.
22003	22003	A numeric value assigned to a numeric data type column caused truncation of the whole part of the number, either at the time of assignment or in computing an intermediate result OR the SQL statement specified contained an arithmetic expression that caused a division by zero error to occur.
——-	22005	A value or a literal was incompatible with the data type associated with the parameter.
22007	——-	A datetime value (or the string representation of a datetime value) represented an invalid date.
22008	22008	An arithmetic operation on a date or timestamp value produced a result that was not within the valid range of date or timestamp values.
22012	22012	An arithmetic expression caused a division by zero to occur.
22015	——-	Assigning an exact numeric or interval C data type to an interval SQL data type OR assigning an exact numeric or interval SQL data type to an interval C data type caused a loss of significant digits.
22018	——-	The C data type was an exact or approximate numeric, datetime, or interval data type, the SQL data type of the column was a character data type, and the value in the column was not a valid literal of the bound C data type OR the SQL data type was an exact or approximate numeric, datetime, or interval data type, the C data type was **SQL_C_CHAR**, and the value in a column was not a valid literal of the bound SQL data type.
22019	——-	The SQL statement specified contained a **LIKE** predicate with "**ESCAPE** *escape character*" in the **WHERE** clause, and the length of the escape character following "**ESCAPE**" was not equal to 1.

Table B–1   SQLSTATE Cross Reference (Continued)

ODBC 3.x SQLSTATE	ODBC 2.0 SQLSTATE	Description
22025	——	The SQL statement specified contained "**LIKE** pattern-value **ESCAPE** escape character" in the **WHERE** clause, and the character following the escape character in the pattern value was not "**%**" or "**_.**"
22026	22026	The length of long data was set to the data source and the actual length of the long data value sent was smaller than the length specified.
23000	23000	The SQL statement specified was not executed because it would cause an integrity constraint violation to occur.
24000	24000	The SQL statement specified did not produce a result data set OR a cursor has already been opened for the specified statement handle OR the cursor associated with the specified statement handle is not positioned on a row in the result data set.
25000	25000	A transaction is in progress at the data source connection specified. As long as this transaction remains active, the connection cannot be terminated.
25S01	——	One or more connections failed to **COMMIT** or **ROLLBACK** the transaction; the outcome is unknown.
25S02	——	The driver was not able to guarantee that all work done in the global transaction could be committed or rolled back atomically; the transaction is still active.
25S03	——	The driver was not able to guarantee that all work done in the global transaction could be committed or rolled back atomically, so the transaction was rolled back.
28000	28000	The user ID and/or password specified violated restrictions defined by the data source.
34000	34000	The cursor name specified is invalid or already exists OR a positioned **UPDATE** or a positioned **DELETE** SQL statement was specified and the cursor referenced by the statement is not open.
——	37000	The SQL statement specified could not be prepared because it contained one or more syntax errors.
3C000	3C000	The cursor name specified already exists.
3D000	——	An invalid catalog name was specified.
3F000	——	An invalid schema name was specified.

Table B–1 SQLSTATE Cross Reference (Continued)

ODBC 3.x SQLSTATE	ODBC 2.0 SQLSTATE	Description
40001	**40**001	The transaction to which the SQL statement belonged was terminated (rolled back if possible) to prevent a deadlock.
40003	——	The associated connection failed before the ODBC API function completed; the state of the transaction cannot be determined.
42000	**42**000	The user does not have the necessary authorizations to execute the SQL statement specified OR the driver was unable to lock the row, as needed, to perform the requested operation.
42S01	**S0**001	A **CREATE TABLE** or a **CREATE VIEW** SQL statement was specified and the corresponding table name or view name provided already exists.
42S02	**S0**002	The SQL statement specified referenced a table name or view name that does not exist.
42S11	**S0**011	A **CREATE INDEX** SQL statement was specified and the index name provided already exists.
42S12	**S0**012	A **DROP INDEX** SQL statement was specified and the index name provided does not exist.
42S21	**S0**021	An **ALTER TABLE** SQL statement was specified and one or more column names provided in the **ADD** clause already exist in the base table.
42S22	**S0**022	The SQL statement specified referenced a non-existant column name (in a table).
44000	——	An insert or update operation was performed on a viewed table or a table derived from a viewed table that was created with the **WITH CHECK OPTION** specified (that is, one or more rows affected by an insert or update operation may no longer be present in the viewed table).
——	**70**100	The data source was unable to process the "Cancel" request.
HY000	**S1**000	A general error occurred for which there is no specific SQLSTATE and for which no specific SQLSTATE has been defined. The **SQLGetDiagRec()** function (ODBC 3.x driver) or the **SQLError()** function (ODBC 2.0 or earlier driver) can be used to describe the error and its cause.

Table B–1   *SQLSTATE Cross Reference (Continued)*

ODBC 3.x SQLSTATE	ODBC 2.0 SQLSTATE	Description
		If the **SQLDriverConnect()** function returns this error, the information specified in the connection string was insufficient for making a connect request, and an attempt to display the connection information dialog failed.
HY001	S1001	The ODBC Driver Manager was unable to allocate the memory needed to support the execution or completion of this ODBC API function.
——	S1002	The column number specified was less than 1 or greater than the maximum number of columns supported by the data source.
HY003	S1003	The C data type specified is not a valid C data type, OR the bookmark column was specified but the C data type **SQL_C_BOOKMARK** was not.
HY004	S1004	The SQL data type specified is not valid for this ODBC API function.
HY007	——	The SQL statement handle specified is not in the "Prepared" or "Executed" state.
HY008	S1008	**SQLCancel()** was called before the ODBC API function completed execution; therefore, the operation was canceled.
HY009	S1009	One or more parameter values specified contain a NULL pointer or an invalid value.
HY010	S1010	The ODBC API function was called while a data-at-execution sequence was running OR the ODBC API function was called out of sequence.
HY011	S1011	The environment, connection, or SQL statement attribute (option) specified cannot be set at this time.
HY012	S1012	The value specified was neither **SQL_ROLLBACK** nor **SQL_COMMIT**.
HY013	——	The ODBC API function call could not be processed because the underlying memory objects needed could not be accessed, possibly because of low memory conditions.
HY014	——	The driver-defined limit for the number of handles that can be allocated for the handle type specified has been reached.
HY015	S1015	No open cursor was associated with the statement handle specified and no cursor name had been set.

Table B–1 SQLSTATE Cross Reference (Continued)

ODBC 3.x SQLSTATE	ODBC 2.0 SQLSTATE	Description
HY016	——	Implementation row descriptors (IRDs) cannot be modified.
HY017	——	Invalid use of an automatically allocated descriptor handle.
HY018	——	The server declined the "Cancel" request.
HY019	——	**SQLPutData()** was called more than once for a parameter or column and it was not being used to send character or binary c data to a column with a character, binary, or data source–specific data type.
HY020	——	**SQLPutData()** was called more than once, and in one of those calls the length/indicator parameter was set to **SQL_NULL_DATA** or **SQL_DEFAULT_ PARAM**.
HY021	——	The descriptor information checked during a consistency check was not consistent.
HY024	——	An invalid environment, connection, or statement attribute (option) value was specified.
HY090	S1090	The value specified for a string or buffer parameter's size exceeds the maximum length allowed OR the value specified for a string or buffer parameter's size is less than 0 and not equal to **SQL_NTS**.
HY091	S1091	An invalid descriptor type value was specified.
HY092	S1092	The driver does not support the environment, connection, or statement attribute (option) specified.
HY093	S1093	The value specified for a ODBC API function parameter was either less than 1 or greater than the maximum number of parameters supported by the data source.
——	S1094	The scale value specified was outside the range of values supported by the data source for the SQL data type specified.
HY095	S1095	An invalid ODBC function was specified.
HY096	S1096	The information type specified was not valid for the version of ODBC supported by the driver.
HY097	S1097	An invalid column type was specified.
HY098	S1098	An invalid scope was specified.

Table B–1   *SQLSTATE Cross Reference (Continued)*

ODBC 3.x SQLSTATE	ODBC 2.0 SQLSTATE	Description
HY099	**S1**099	An invalid nullable type was specified.
HY100	**S1**100	An invalid uniqueness value was specified.
HY101	**S1**101	An invalid accuracy value was specified.
HY103	**S1**103	An invalid cursor direction was specified.
HY104	**S1**104	The precision value specified was outside the range of values supported by the data source for the SQL data type specified
HY105	**S1**105	An invalid parameter type value was specified.
HY106	**S1**106	An invalid fetch type value was specified.
HY107	**S1**107	The row value specified was less than 1.
——	**S1**108	An invalid concurrency value was specified.
HY109	**S1**109	A positioned **UPDATE** or a positioned **DELETE** SQL statement was specified and the cursor was positioned on a row that has been deleted or that could not be retrieved (fetched).
HY110	**S1**110	The driver completion value specified was invalid (that is, not **SQL_DRIVER_PROMPT**, **SQL_DRIVER_COMPLETE, SQL_DRIVER_COMPLETE_REQUIRED**, or **SQL_DRIVER_NOPROMPT**) OR connection pooling was enabled, and the driver completion value **SQL_DRIVER_NOPROMPT** was not specified.
HY111	**S1**111	An invalid bookmark value was specified.
HYC00	**S1**C00	The ODBC API function recognizes but the driver does not support one or more of the parameter or parameter values specified.
——	**S1**T00	The timeout period expired before the connection to the data source could be established; before the data source finished processing the ODBC API function; or before the data source returned the result data set generated.
HYT00	——	The login timeout period expired before the connection to the data source could be established.
HYT01	——	The connection timeout period expired before the data source responded to the request.
IM001	**IM**001	The driver/data source does not support this ODBC API function.

Table B–1 SQLSTATE Cross Reference (Continued)

ODBC 3.x SQLSTATE	ODBC 2.0 SQLSTATE	Description
IM002	**IM**002	The data source name specified was not found in the ODBC.INI file or the system registry, and no default driver has been specified OR the ODBC.INI file could not be found.
IM003	**IM**003	The driver name specified in the data source listing in the ODBC.INI file or the system registry could not be found and/or loaded OR the driver name specified with the **DRIVER** keyword could not be found and/or loaded.
IM004	**IM**004	When the ODBC Driver Manager attempted to call the driver's function for allocating an environment handle, the driver returned an error.
IM005	**IM**005	When the ODBC Driver Manager attempted to call the driver's function for allocating a connection handle, the driver returned an error.
IM006	**IM**006	When the ODBC Driver Manager attempted to call the driver's function for setting connection attributes (options), the driver returned an error.
IM007	**IM**007	No data source name or driver was specified in the connection string and the ODBC connection information dialog was not displayed.
IM008	**IM**008	The ODBC Driver Manager attempted to display the connection information dialog but failed OR the driver attempted to display its logon dialog box and failed.
IM009	**IM**009	The driver was unable to load the translation .DLL specified for the data source or the connection.
IM010	**IM**010	The data source name specified was longer than **SQL_MAX_DSN_LENGTH** characters.
IM011	**IM**011	The driver name specified was longer than 255 characters.
IM012	**IM**012	The **DRIVER** keyword-value pair specified contained a syntax error.
IM013	**IM**013	A Trace file error occurred.
IM014	——	The connection string specified contained the **FILEDSN** keyword, but the .DSN file name provided in the keyword-value pair was invalid.

Table B–1   SQLSTATE Cross Reference (Continued)

ODBC 3.x SQLSTATE	ODBC 2.0 SQLSTATE	Description
IM015	——	The connection string specified contained the **FILEDSN** keyword, but the .DSN file name provided in the keyword-value pair could not be read.
——	**S0**023	The ODBC API function attempted to add a record to a column that was not bound, that did not have a default value, and that could not be set to NULL OR the function attempted to ignore a column that did not have a default value when adding records to the data source.

APPENDIX C

Information Returned By **SQLGetInfo()**

InfoType Code	Data Type Returned	Description
SQL_ACCESSIBLE_ PROCEDURES (ODBC 1.0)	Character string	Indicates whether all ODBC API procedures returned by the **SQLProcedures()** function can be executed by the application. The following values can be returned for this *InfoType* code: **"Y"**: The application can execute all procedures returned by the **SQLProcedures()** function. **"N"**: One or more of the procedures returned by the **SQLProcedures()** function cannot be executed by the application.
SQL_ACCESSIBLE_TABLES (ODBC 1.0)	Character string	Indicates whether the current user is guaranteed **SELECT** privileges to all tables returned by the **SQLTables()** function. The following values can be returned for this *InfoType* code: **"Y"**: The user is guaranteed **SELECT** privileges to all tables returned by the **SQLTables()** function. **"N"**: One or more tables returned by the **SQLTables()** function cannot be accessed by the current user.
SQL_ACTIVE_ ENVIRONMENTS (ODBC 3.0)	SQLUSMALLINT	Identifies the maximum number of active environments the driver can support. If there is no specified limit, or if the limit is unknown, the value 0 is returned for this *InfoType* code.
SQL_AGGREGATE_ FUNCTIONS (ODBC 3.0)	SQLUINTEGER bitmask	Identifies the aggregation functions that are supported by the driver. The following values can be returned for this *InfoType* code: SQL_AF_ALL SQL_AF_AVG SQL_AF_COUNT SQL_AF_DISTINCT SQL_AF_MAX SQL_AF_MIN SQL_AF_SUM An SQL-92 Entry level–conformant driver returns all bitmasks shown.

InfoType Code	Data Type Returned	Description
SQL_ALTER_DOMAIN (ODBC 3.0)	**SQLUINTEGER** bitmask	Identifies the clauses in the **ALTER DOMAIN** SQL statement that are supported by the data source (as defined in SQL-92). The following bitmask values can be returned for this *InfoType* code:

SQL_AD_ADD_DOMAIN_CONSTRAINT: The <add domain constraint> clause is supported (Full level).

SQL_AD_ADD_DOMAIN_DEFAULT: The <alter domain> <set domain default> clause is supported (Full level).

SQL_AD_CONSTRAINT_NAME_DEFINITION: The <constraint name definition> clause is supported for naming domain constraints (Intermediate level).

SQL_AD_DROP_DOMAIN_CONSTRAINT: The <drop domain constraint> clause is supported (Full level).

SQL_AD_DROP_DOMAIN_DEFAULT: The <alter domain> <drop domain default> clause is supported (Full level).

The following bits specify the constraint attributes that are supported if the <add domain constraint> clause is supported (the **SQL_AD_ ADD_DOMAIN_ CONSTRAINT** bit is set):

SQL_AD_ADD_CONSTRAINT_DEFERRABLE (Full level)

SQL_AD_ADD_CONSTRAINT_NON_ DEFERRABLE (Full level)

SQL_AD_ADD_CONSTRAINT_ INITIALLY_DEFERRED (Full level)

SQL_AD_ADD_CONSTRAINT_ INITIALLY_IMMEDIATE (Full level)

If the **ALTER DOMAIN** statement is not supported by the data source, the value 0 is returned for this *InfoType* code.

An SQL-92 Full-level–compliant driver returns all bitmasks shown. The SQL-92 or FIPS conformance level at which this feature needs to be supported is shown in parentheses next to each bitmask.

InfoType Code	Data Type Returned	Description
SQL_ALTER_TABLE (ODBC 2.0)	**SQLUINTEGER** bitmask	Identifies the clauses in the **ALTER TABLE** SQL statement supported by the data source. The following bitmask values can be returned for this *InfoType* code:

InfoType Code	Data Type Returned	Description
		SQL_AT_ADD_COLUMN_COLLATION: The <add column> clause is supported, along with the ability to specify column collation (Full level) (ODBC 3.0).
		SQL_AT_ADD_COLUMN_DEFAULT: The <add column> clause is supported, along with the ability to specify column defaults (FIPS Transitional level) (ODBC 3.0).
		SQL_AT_ADD_COLUMN_SINGLE: The <add column> is supported (FIPS Transitional level) (ODBC 3.0).
		SQL_AT_ADD_CONSTRAINT: The <add column> clause is supported, along with the ability to specify column constraints (FIPS Transitional level) (ODBC 3.0).
		SQL_AT_ADD_TABLE_CONSTRAINT: The <add table constraint> clause is supported (FIPS Transitional level) (ODBC 3.0).
		SQL_AT_CONSTRAINT_NAME_DEFINITION: The <constraint name definition> clause is supported for naming column and table constraints (Intermediate level) (ODBC 3.0).
		SQL_AT_DROP_COLUMN_CASCADE: The <drop column> **CASCADE** clause is supported (FIPS Transitional level) (ODBC 3.0).
		SQL_AT_DROP_COLUMN_DEFAULT: The <alter column> <drop column default> clause is supported (Intermediate level) (ODBC 3.0).
		SQL_AT_DROP_COLUMN_RESTRICT: The <drop column> **RESTRICT** clause is supported (FIPS Transitional level) (ODB 3.0).
		SQL_AT_DROP_TABLE_CONSTRAINT_CASCADE The <drop constraint> **CASCADE** clause is supported (ODBC 3.0).
		SQL_AT_DROP_TABLE_CONSTRAINT_RESTRICT: The <drop column> **RESTRICT** clause is supported (FIPS Transitional level) (ODBC 3.0).
		SQL_AT_SET_COLUMN_DEFAULT: The <alter column> <set column default> clause is supported (Intermediate level) (ODBC 3.0).

InfoType Code	Data Type Returned	Description
		The following bits specify constraint attributes that are supported if specifying column or table constraints is supported (the **SQL_AT_ADD_ CONSTRAINT** bit is set):
		SQL_AT_CONSTRAINT_INITIALLY_ DEFERRED (Full level) (ODBC 3.0)
		SQL_AT_CONSTRAINT_INITIALLY_ IMMEDIATE (Full level) (ODBC 3.0)
		SQL_AT_CONSTRAINT_DEFERRABLE (Full level) (ODBC 3.0)
		SQL_AT_CONSTRAINT_NON_DEFERRABLE (Full level) (ODBC 3.0)
		The SQL-92 or FIPS conformance level at which this feature needs to be supported is shown in parentheses next to each bitmask.
SQL_ASYNC_MODE (ODBC 3.0)	**SQLUINTEGER**	Identifies the level of asynchronous support provided by the driver. The following values can be returned for this *InfoType* code:
		SQL_AM_CONNECTION: Connection level asynchronous execution is supported. Either all statement handles associated with a given connection handle execute in asynchronous mode, or all execute in synchronous mode. A statement handle on a connection handle cannot be in asynchronous mode while another statement handle on the same connection handle is in synchronous mode, and vice versa.
		SQL_AM_STATEMENT: Statement level asynchronous execution is supported. Some statement handles associated with a connection handle can be in asynchronous mode, while other statement handles on the same connection handle are in synchronous mode.
		SQL_AM_NONE: Asynchronous execution is not supported.
SQL_BATCH_ROW_ COUNT (ODBC 3.0)	**SQLUINTEGER** bitmask	Identifies how the driver computes and returns row count information. The following bitmask values can be returned for this *InfoType* code:

InfoType Code	Data Type Returned	Description
		SQL_BRC_ROLLED_UP: Row counts for consecutive **INSERT**, **UPDATE**, or **DELETE** SQL statements are rolled into one. If this bit is not set, row counts are available for each SQL statement processed.
		SQL_BRC_PROCEDURES: Row counts, if any, are available when a batch of SQL statements are executed by a stored procedure. If row counts are available, they may be rolled up, or they may be available for each SQL statement processed, depending on the **SQL_BRC_ROLLED_UP** bit.
		SQL_BRC_EXPLICIT: Row counts, if any, are available when a batch of SQL statements are executed directly by calling **SQLExecute()** or **SQLExecDirect()**. If row counts are available, they may be rolled up, or they may be available for each SQL statement processed, depending on the **SQL_BRC_ROLLED_UP** bit.
SQL_BATCH_SUPPORT (ODBC 3.0)	**SQLUINTEGER** bitmask	Identifies how batch SQL statement execution is supported by the driver. The following bitmask values can be returned for this *InfoType* code:
		SQL_BS_SELECT_EXPLICIT: The driver supports explicit batches that contain one or more result data set generating SQL statements.
		SQL_BS_ROW_COUNT_EXPLICIT: The driver supports explicit batches that contain one or more row count generating SQL statements.
		SQL_BS_SELECT_PROC: The driver supports explicit procedures that contain one or more result data set generating statements.
		SQL_BS_ROW_COUNT_PROC: The driver supports explicit procedures that contain one or more row count generating statements.
SQL_BOOKMARK_ PERSISTENCE (ODBC 2.0)	**SQLUINTEGER** bitmask	Identifies the operations through which bookmarks persist. The following bitmask values can be returned for this *InfoType* code:

InfoType Code	Data Type Returned	Description
		SQL_BP_CLOSE: Bookmarks are valid after an application calls either the **SQLFreeStmt()** function with the **SQL_CLOSE** option specified, or the **SQLCloseCursor()** function to close the cursor associated with an SQL statement handle.
		SQL_BP_DELETE: The bookmark for a row is valid after the row has been deleted.
		SQL_BP_DROP: Bookmarks are valid after their associated SQL statement handle is dropped.
		SQL_BP_TRANSACTION: Bookmarks are valid after an application commits or rolls back a transaction.
		SQL_BP_UPDATE: The bookmark for a row is valid after any column in that row has been updated, including key columns.
		SQL_BP_OTHER_HSTMT: A bookmark associated with one statement can be used with another SQL statement. However, unless **SQL_BP_CLOSE** or **SQL_BP_DROP** is returned, the cursor for the first SQL statement must be open.
SQL_CATALOG_LOCATION[1] (ODBC 2.0)	**SQLUSMALLINT**	Identifies the position of the catalog portion of a qualified table name. The following values can be returned for this *InfoType* code:
		SQL_CL_START: The catalog portion of a qualified table name is located at the beginning of the name.
		SQL_CL_END: The catalog portion of a qualified table name is located at the end of the name.
		For example, an dBASE driver returns **SQL_CL_START** because the directory (catalog) name is at the start of the table name, as in \EMPDATA\EMP.DBF. An ORACLE Server driver returns **SQL_CL_END**, because the catalog is at the end of the table name, as in ADMIN.EMP@EMPDATA.

InfoType Code	Data Type Returned	Description
		An SQL-92 Full level-conformant driver returns **SQL_CL_START** for this *InfoType* code.
		If catalogs are not supported by the data source (see the **SQL_CATALOG_NAME** *InfoType* code), the value **0** is returned for this *InfoType* code.
SQL_CATALOG_NAME (ODBC 3.0)	Character string	Indicates whether the data source supports catalog names. The following values can be returned for this *InfoType* code:
		"Y": The data source supports catalog names.
		"N": The data source does not support catalog names.
		An SQL-92 Full level-conformant driver returns **"Y"** for this *InfoType* code.
SQL_CATALOG_NAME_ SEPARATOR[2] (ODBC 1.0)	Character string	Identifies the character or characters the data source uses as a separator between a catalog name and the qualified name element that follows or precedes it.
		If catalogs are not supported by the data source (see the **SQL_CATALOG_NAME** *InfoType* code), an empty string (" ") is returned for this *InfoType* code.
		An SQL-92 Full level conformant driver returns "." for this *InfoType* code.
SQL_CATALOG_TERM[3] (ODBC 1.0)	Character string	Identifies the data source vendor's terminology (name) for a catalog. This string can be in upper, lower, or mixed case.
		If catalogs are not supported by the data source (see the **SQL_CATALOG_NAME** *InfoType* code), an empty string (" ") is returned for this *InfoType* code.
SQL_CATALOG_USAGE[4]	**SQLUINTEGER** bitmask	Identifies the SQL statement in which catalog names can be used. The following bitmask values can be returned for this *InfoType* code:
		SQL_CU_DML_STATEMENTS: Catalog names can be used in all Data Manipulation Language SQL statements: **SELECT**, **INSERT**, **UPDATE**, **DELETE**, **SELECT FOR UPDATE**, (if supported) and positioned update and delete statements.

InfoType Code	Data Type Returned	Description
		SQL_CU_PROCEDURE_ INVOCATION: Catalogs names can be used in the ODBC procedure invocation statement.
		SQL_CU_TABLE_DEFINITION: Catalog names can be used in all table definition statements: **CREATE TABLE**, **CREATE VIEW**, **ALTER TABLE**, **DROP TABLE**, and **DROP VIEW**.
		SQL_CU_INDEX_DEFINITION: Catalog names can be used in all index definition statements: **CREATE INDEX** and **DROP INDEX**.
		SQL_CU_PRIVILEGE_ DEFINITION: Catalog names can be used in all privilege definition statements: **GRANT** and **REVOKE**.
		If catalogs are not supported by the data source (see the **SQL_CATALOG_NAME** *InfoType* code), the value **0** is returned for this *InfoType* code.
		An SQL-92 Full level-compliant driver returns all bitmasks shown.
SQL_COLLATION_SEQ (ODBC 3.0)	Character string	Identifies the name of the default collation of the default character set used by the data source (for example, ISO 8859-1 or EBCDIC).
		An SQL-92 Full level compliant driver returns a non-empty string for this *InfoType* code.
SQL_COLUMN_ALIAS (ODBC 2.0)	Character string	Indicates whether the data source supports column aliases. A column alias is an alternate name that can be specified for a column in a select list by using an **AS** clause. The following values can be returned for this *InfoType* code:
		"Y": The data source supports column aliases.
		"N": The data source does not support column aliases.
		An SQL-92 Entry level-conformant driver returns **"Y"** for this *InfoType* code.
SQL_CONCAT_NULL_ BEHAVIOR (ODBC 1.0)	SQLUSMALLINT	Identifies how the data source handles the concatenation of NULL valued character data type columns with non-NULL valued character data type columns. The following values can be returned for this *InfoType* code:

InfoType Code	Data Type Returned	Description
		SQL_CB_NULL: The result of the concatenation is a NULL value.
		SQL_CB_NON_NULL: The result of the concatenation is the value of the non-NULL valued column or columns.
		An SQL-92 Entry level-compliant driver returns **SQL_CB_NULL** for this *InfoType* code.
SQL_CONVERT_BIGINT SQL_CONVERT_BINARY SQL_CONVERT_BIT SQL_CONVERT_CHAR SQL_CONVERT_DATE SQL_CONVERT_DECIMAL SQL_CONVERT_DOUBLE SQL_CONVERT_FLOAT SQL_CONVERT_INTEGER SQL_CONVERT_INTERVAL_YEAR_MONTH SQL_CONVERT_INTERVAL_DAY_TIME SQL_CONVERT_LONGVARBINARY SQL_CONVERT_LONGVARCHAR SQL_CONVERT_NUMERIC SQL_CONVERT_REAL SQL_CONVERT_SMALLINT SQL_CONVERT_TIME SQL_CONVERT_TIMESTAMP SQL_CONVERT_TINYINT SQL_CONVERT_VARBINARY SQL_CONVERT_VARCHAR (ODBC 1.0)	SQLUINTEGER bitmask	Identifies whether the specified data type conversion (named in the *InfoType* code) is supported by the data source and the **CONVERT()** scalar function. For example, to find out if a data source supports the conversion of a **SQL_INTEGER** data type to an **SQL_BIGINT** data type, an application calls **SQLGetInfo()** with the *InfoType* code **SQL_CONVERT_INTEGER** specified. The application then performs an AND operation with the returned value and **SQL_CVT_BIGINT**. If the resulting value is nonzero, the data type conversion is supported.

The following bitmask values are used to determine whether conversions are supported:

SQL_CVT_BIGINT (ODBC 1.0)
SQL_CVT_BINARY (ODBC 1.0)
SQL_CVT_BIT (ODBC 1.0)
SQL_CVT_CHAR (ODBC 1.0)
SQL_CVT_DATE (ODBC 1.0)
SQL_CVT_DECIMAL (ODBC 1.0)
SQL_CVT_DOUBLE (ODBC 1.0)
SQL_CVT_FLOAT (ODBC 1.0)
SQL_CVT_INTEGER (ODBC 1.0)
SQL_CVT_INTERVAL_YEAR_MONTH
   (ODBC 3.0)
SQL_CVT_INTERVAL_DAY_TIME
   (ODBC 3.0)
SQL_CVT_LONGVARBINARY (ODBC 1.0)
SQL_CVT_LONGVARCHAR (ODBC 1.0)
SQL_CVT_NUMERIC (ODBC 1.0)
SQL_CVT_SMALLINT (ODBC 1.0)
SQL_CVT_TIME (ODBC 1.0)
SQL_CVT_TIMESTAMP (ODBC 1.0)
SQL_CVT_TINYINT (ODBC 1.0)
SQL_CVT_VARBINARY (ODBC 1.0)
SQL_CVT_VARCHAR (ODBC 1.0)

InfoType Code	Data Type Returned	Description
		If the data source does not support any conversions for the specified data, including conversions to the same data type, the value **0** is returned for the *InfoType* code specified.
SQL_CONVERT_FUNCTIONS (ODBC 1.0)	**SQLUINTEGER** bitmask	Identifies the scalar conversion functions that are supported by the driver and its underlying data source. The following bitmask values can be returned for this *InfoType* code:
		SQL_FN_CVT_CAST: Type casting is supported.
		SQL_FN_CVT_CONVERT: Data conversion is supported.
SQL_CORRELATION_NAME (ODBC 1.0)	**SQLUSMALLINT**	Indicates whether table correlation names are supported by the data source. The following values can be returned for this *InfoType* code:
		SQL_CN_NONE: Correlation names are not supported.
		SQL_CN_DIFFERENT: Correlation names are supported, but must differ from the names of the tables they represent.
		SQL_CN_ANY: Correlation names are supported and can be any valid user-defined name.
		An SQL-92 Entry level-conformant driver returns **SQL_CN_ANY** for this *InfoType* code.
SQL_CREATE_ASSERTION (ODBC 3.0)	**SQLUINTEGER** bitmask	Identifies the clauses in the **CREATE ASSERTION** SQL statement that are supported by the data source (as defined in SQL-92). The following bitmask values can be returned for this *InfoType* code:
		SQL_CA_CREATE_ASSERTION: The **CREATE ASSERTION** SQL statement is supported by the data source.
		The following bits specify the supported constraint attribute if the ability to specify constraint attributes explicitly is supported by the data source (see the **SQL_ALTER_TABLE** and **SQL_CREATE_TABLE** *InfoType* codes):

InfoType Code	Data Type Returned	Description
		SQL_CA_CONSTRAINT_INITIALLY_ DEFERRED SQL_CA_CONSTRAINT_INITIALLY_ IMMEDIATE SQL_CA_CONSTRAINT_DEFERRABLE SQL_CA_CONSTRAINT_NON_DEFERRABLE If the **CREATE ASSERTION** statement is not supported by the data source, the value **0** is returned for this *InfoType* code. An SQL-92 Full level-compliant driver returns all bitmasks shown.
SQL_CREATE_CHARACTER_ SET (ODBC 3.0)	SQLUINTEGER bitmask	Identifies the clauses in the **CREATE CHARACTER SET** SQL statement that are supported by the data source (as defined in SQL-92). The following bitmask values can be returned for this *InfoType* code: SQL_CCS_CREATE_CHARACTER_SET SQL_CCS_COLLATE_CLAUSE SQL_CCS_LIMITED_COLLATION If the **CREATE CHARACTER SET** SQL statement is not supported by the data source, the value **0** is returned for this *InfoType* code. An SQL-92 Full level-compliant driver returns all bitmasks shown.
SQL_CREATE_COLLATION (ODBC 3.0)	SQLUINTEGER bitmask	Identifies the clauses in the **CREATE COLLATION** SQL statement that are supported by the data source (as defined in SQL-92). The following bitmask values can be returned for this *InfoType* code: SQL_CCOL_CREATE_COLLATION: The **CREATE** SQL statement is supported. If the **CREATE** SQL statement is not supported by the data source, the value **0** is returned for this *InfoType* code. An SQL-92 Full level-conformant driver returns this bitmask.
SQL_CREATE_DOMAIN (ODBC 3.0)	SQLUINTEGER bitmask	Identifies the clauses in the **CREATE DOMAIN** SQL statement that are supported by the data source (as defined in SQL-92). The following bitmask values can be returned for this *InfoType* code:

InfoType Code	Data Type Returned	Description
		SQL_CDO_CREATE_DOMAIN: The **CREATE DOMAIN** SQL statement is supported. (Intermediate level)
		SQL_CDO_CONSTRAINT_ NAME_ DEFINITION: The <constraint name definition> clause is supported for naming domain constraints (Intermediate level).
		The following bits specify the ability to create column constraints:
		SQL_CDO_DEFAULT: Specifying domain constraints is supported (Intermediate level).
		SQL_CDO_CONSTRAINT: Specifying domain defaults is supported (Intermediate level).
		SQL_CDO_COLLATION: Specifying domain collation is supported (Full level).
		The following bits specify the supported constraint attributes if specifying domain constraints is supported (**SQL_CDO_DEFAULT** is set):
		SQL_CDO_CONSTRAINT_INITIALLY_ DEFERRED (Full level)
		SQL_CDO_CONSTRAINT_INITIALLY_ IMMEDIATE (Full level)
		SQL_CDO_CONSTRAINT_DEFERRABLE (Full level)
		SQL_CDO_CONSTRAINT_NON_ DEFERRABLE (Full level)
		If the **CREATE_DOMAIN** statement is not supported by the data source, the value **0** is returned for this *InfoType* code.
SQL_CREATE_SCHEMA (ODBC 3.0)	**SQLUINTEGER** bitmask	Identifies the clauses in the **CREATE SCHEMA** SQL statement that are supported by the data source (as defined in SQL-92). The following bitmask values can be returned for this *InfoType* code:

InfoType Code	Data Type Returned	Description
		SQL_CS_CREATE_SCHEMA **SQL_CS_AUTHORIZATION** **SQL_CS_DEFAULT_CHARACTER_SET**
		An SQL-92 Intermediate level-conformant driver returns the **SQL_CS_CREATE_ SCHEMA** and the **SQL_CS_AUTHORIZATION** bitmasks. These options must also be supported at the SQL-92 Entry level, but not necessarily as SQL statements.
		An SQL-92 Full level-conformant driver returns all the bitmasks shown.
SQL_CREATE_TABLE (ODBC 3.0)	**SQLUINTEGER** bitmask	Identifies the clauses in the **CREATE TABLE** SQL statement supported by the data source (as defined in SQL-92). The following bitmask values can be returned for this *InfoType* code:
		SQL_CT_CREATE_TABLE: The **CREATE TABLE** SQL statement is supported (Entry level).
		SQL_CT_TABLE_CONSTRAINT: The specification of table constraints with the **CREATE TABLE** SQL statement is supported (FIPS Transitional level).
		SQL_CT_CONSTRAINT_NAME_DEFINITION: The <constraint name definition> clause is supported for naming column and table constraints (Intermediate level).
		The following bits specify the ability to create temporary tables:
		SQL_CT_COMMIT_PRESERVE: Deleted rows are preserved on commit (Full level).
		SQL_CT_COMMIT_DELETE: Deleted rows are deleted on commit (Full level).

InfoType Code	Data Type Returned	Description
		SQL_CT_GLOBAL_TEMPORARY: Global temporary tables can be created (Full level).
		SQL_CT_LOCAL_TEMPORARY: Local temporary tables can be created (Full level).
		The following bits specify the ability to create column constraints:
		SQL_CT_COLUMN_CONSTRAINT: Specifying column constraints is supported (FIPS Transitional level).
		SQL_CT_COLUMN_DEFAULT: Specifying column defaults is supported (FIPS Transitional level).
		SQL_CT_COLUMN_COLLATION: Specifying column collation is supported (Full level).
		The following bits specify the supported constraint attributes if specifying column or table constraints is supported:
		SQL_CT_CONSTRAINT_INITIALLY_ DEFERRED (Full level)
		SQL_CT_CONSTRAINT_INITIALLY_ IMMEDIATE (Full level)
		SQL_CT_CONSTRAINT_DEFERRABLE (Full level)
		SQL_CT_CONSTRAINT_NON_DEFERRABLE (Full level)
		The SQL-92 or FIPS conformance level at which these features are supported is shown in parentheses next to each bitmask.
SQL_CREATE_TRANSLATION (ODBC 3.0)	**SQLUINTEGER** bitmask	Identifies the clauses in the **CREATE TRANSLATION** SQL statement that are supported by the data source (as defined in SQL-92). The following bitmask values can be returned for this *InfoType* code:
		SQL_CTR_CREATE_TRANSLATION: The **CREATE TRANSLATION** SQL statement that are supported by the data source.

InfoType Code	Data Type Returned	Description
		If the **CREATE TRANSLATION** statement is not supported by the data source, the value 0 is returned for this *InfoType* code.
		An SQL-92 Full level-conformant driver returns this bitmap.
SQL_CREATE_VIEW (ODBC 3.0)	**SQLUINTEGER** bitmask	Identifies the clauses in the **CREATE VIEW** SQL statement that are supported by the data source (as defined in SQL-92). The following bitmask values can be returned for this *Info-Type* code:
		SQL_CV_CREATE_VIEW **SQL_CV_CHECK_OPTION** **SQL_CV_CASCADED** **SQL_CV_LOCAL**
		If the **CREATE VIEW** statement is not supported by the data source, the value **0** is returned for this *InfoType* code.
		An SQL-92 Entry level-conformant driver returns the **SQL_CV_CREATE_VIEW** and the **SQL_CV_CHECK_OPTION** bitmasks. An SQL-92 Full level-conformant driver returns all bitmasks shown.
SQL_CURSOR_COMMIT_ COMMIT_BEHAVIOR (ODBC 1.0)	**SQLUSMALLINT**	Indicates how a commit operation affects cursors and prepared SQL statements within the data source. The following values can be returned for this *InfoType* code:
		SQL_CB_DELETE: Cursors are destroyed and access plans for prepared SQL statements are destroyed. To use the cursor again, the application must re-prepare and re-execute the statement.
		SQL_CB_CLOSE: Cursors are destroyed, but access plans for prepared SQL statements are not destroyed. The application can call **SQLExecute()** to re-execute prepared SQL statements without having to re-prepare them.
		SQL_CB_PRESERVE: Cursors and access plans for prepared SQL statements remain as they were before the COMMIT operation was performed. The application can continue to fetch data or it can close the cursor and re-execute the SQL statement without having to re-prepare it.

InfoType Code	Data Type Returned	Description
SQL_CURSOR_ROLLBACK_ BEHAVIOR (ODBC 1.0)	**SQLUSMALLINT**	Indicates how a rollback operation affects cursors and prepared SQL statements within the data source. The following values can be returned for this *InfoType* code:

SQL_CB_DELETE:
Cursors are destroyed and access plans for prepared SQL statements are destroyed. To use the cursor again, the application must re-prepare and re-execute the statement.

SQL_CB_CLOSE:
Cursors are destroyed, but access plans for prepared SQL statements are not destroyed. The application can call **SQLExecute()** to re-execute prepared statements without having to re-prepare them.

SQL_CB_PRESERVE:
Cursors and access plans for prepared SQL statements remain as they were before the ROLLBACK operation was performed. The application can continue to fetch data or, it can close the cursor and re-execute the SQL statement without having to re-prepare it.

InfoType Code	Data Type Returned	Description
SQL_CURSOR_SENSITIVITY (ODBC 3.0)	**SQLUINTEGER**	Identifies how cursors expose changes made to a result data set. The following values can be returned for this *InfoType* code:

SQL_INSENSITIVE:
All cursors on the statement handle show the result data set without reflecting any changes made to it by any other cursor within the same transaction.

SQL_SENSITIVE:
All cursors on the statement handle show all changes made to the result data set by any other cursor within the same transaction.

SQL_UNSPECIFIED:
It is unspecified whether all cursors on the statement handle show the changes made to a result data set by another cursor within the same transaction. Cursors on the statement handle may make none, some, or all such changes made to a result data set by another cursor within the same transaction visible.

An SQL-92 Entry level-conformant driver returns **SQL_UNSPECIFIED** for this *InfoType* code. An SQL-92 Full level-conformant driver returns **SQL_INSENSITIVE** for this *InfoType* code.

InfoType Code	Data Type Returned	Description
SQL_DATA_SOURCE_NAME (ODBC 1.0)	Character string	Identifies the data source name to be used in the *DSName* parameter of the **SQLConnect()** function, or to be used with the DSN keyword in the connection string passed to the driver by the **SQLDriverConnect()** or the **SQLBrowseConnect()** function.
		If the connection string passed to the driver by the **SQLDriverConnect()** or the **SQLBrowseConnect()** function did not contain the DSN keyword (for example, if it contained the DRIVER keyword), an empty string (" ") is returned for this *InfoType* code.
SQL_DATA_SOURCE_READ_ONLY (ODBC 1.0)	Character string	Indicates whether the data source is set to READ ONLY or READ/WRITE mode. The following values can be returned for this *InfoType* code:
		"Y": The data source is set to READ ONLY mode.
		"N": The data source is set to READ/WRITE mode.
		This characteristic pertains only to the data source itself; it is not a characteristic of the driver that enables access to the data source. A driver that is read/write can be used with a data source that is read-only.
		If a driver is read-only, all its data sources must be read-only, and must return for this *InfoType* code.
SQL_DATABASE_NAME (ODBC 1.0)	Character string	Identifies the name of the current database in use if the data source defines a named object called "database."
		Note that in ODBC 3.0, the value returned for this *InfoType* code can also be returned by calling the **SQLGetConnectAttr()** function with the **SQL_ATTR_CURRENT_CATALOG** attribute specified.
SQL_DATETIME_LITERALS (ODBC 3.0)	**SQLUINTEGER** bitmask	Identifies the datetime literals that are supported by the data source (as defined in SQL-92). The following bitmask values can be returned for this *InfoType* code:
		SQL_DL_SQL92_DATE **SQL_DL_SQL92_TIME** **SQL_DL_SQL92_TIMESTAMP** **SQL_DL_SQL92_INTERVAL_YEAR** **SQL_DL_SQL92_INTERVAL_MONTH**

InfoType Code	Data Type Returned	Description
		SQL_DL_SQL92_INTERVAL_DAY
		SQL_DL_SQL92_INTERVAL_HOUR
		SQL_DL_SQL92_INTERVAL_MINUTE
		SQL_DL_SQL92_INTERVAL_SECOND
		SQL_DL_SQL92_INTERVAL_YEAR_ TO_MONTH
		SQL_DL_SQL92_INTERVAL_DAY_ TO_HOUR
		SQL_DL_SQL92_INTERVAL_DAY_ TO_MINUTE
		SQL_DL_SQL92_INTERVAL_DAY_ TO_SECOND
		SQL_DL_SQL92_INTERVAL_HOUR_ TO_MINUTE
		SQL_DL_SQL92_INTERVAL_HOUR_ TO_SECOND
		SQL_DL_SQL92_INTERVAL_MINUTE_ TO_SECOND
		Note that these are the datetime literals listed in the SQL-92 specification and are separate from the datetime literal escape clauses defined by ODBC.
		If the SQL-92 datetime literals are not supported by the data source, the value **0** is returned for this *InfoType* code.
		A FIPS Transitional level-conformant driver will indicate that a SQL-92 datetime literal is supported by providing the value **1** in the bitmask for all bits shown.
SQL_DBMS_NAME (ODBC 1.0)	Character string	Identifies the name of the DBMS product being accessed by the driver.
SQL_DBMS_VER (ODBC 1.0)	Character string	Identifies the version of the DBMS product being accessed by the driver. This information is returned in a string that has the format *mm.vv.rrrr*, where *mm* is the major version number, *vv* is the minor version number, and *rrrr* is the release version number (for example, 02.01.0000 would translate to major version 2, minor version 1, release 0). The driver must render the DBMS product version in this format, but it can also append the DBMS product-specific version as well (for example, 04.01.0000 Rdb 4.1).
SQL_DDL_INDEX (ODBC 3.0)	**SQLUINTEGER**	Identifies whether the the data source supports the creation and destruction of indexes. The following bitmask values can be returned for this *InfoType* code:

InfoType Code	Data Type Returned	Description
		SQL_DI_CREATE_INDEX: Indexes can be created.
		SQL_DI_DROP_INDEX: Indexes can be dropped.
		An SQL-92 Entry level-conformant driver returns all bitmasks shown.
SQL_DEFAULT_TXN_ ISOLATION (ODBC 1.0)	**SQLUINTEGER**	Identifies the default transaction isolation level used by the driver or data source. The following terms are used to define transaction isolation levels:
		Dirty Read: Transaction 1 changes a row. Transaction 2 reads the changed row before Transaction 1 commits the change. If Transaction 1 rolls back the change, Transaction 2 will have read a row that is considered to have never existed.
		Nonrepeatable Read: Transaction 1 reads a row. Transaction 2 updates or deletes that row and commits this change. If Transaction 1 attempts to reread the row, it will receive different row values or discover that the row has been deleted.
		Phantom: Transaction 1 reads a set of rows that satisfy some search criteria. Transaction 2 generates one or more rows (either through inserts or updates) that match the search criteria. If Transaction 1 re-executes the statement that reads the rows, it receives a different set of rows.
		If the data source supports transactions, the driver returns one of the following bitmasks:
		SQL_TXN_READ_UNCOMMITTED: Dirty reads, nonrepeatable reads, and phantoms are possible.
		SQL_TXN_READ_COMMITTED: Dirty reads are not possible. Nonrepeatable reads and phantoms are possible.
		SQL_TXN_REPEATABLE_READ: Dirty reads and nonrepeatable reads are not possible. Phantoms are possible.

InfoType Code	Data Type Returned	Description
		SQL_TXN_SERIALIZABLE: Transactions are serializable. Serializable transactions do not allow dirty reads, nonrepeatable reads, or phantoms.
		If transactions are not supported by the data source, the value **0** is returned for this *InfoType* code.
SQL_DESCRIBE_PARAMETER (ODBC 3.0)	Character string	Indicates whether the data source describes parameters. The following values can be returned for this *InfoType* code:
		"Y": Parameters can be described by the data source.
		"N": Parameters are not described by the data source.
		An SQL-92 Full level-conformant driver usually returns **"Y"** because it supports the **DESCRIBE INPUT** SQL statement. However, because this does not directly specify the underlying SQL support, describing parameters may not be supported, even in a SQL-92 Full level-conformant driver.
SQL_DM_VER (ODBC 3.0)	Character string	Identifies the version number of the ODBC Driver Manager being used. This information is returned in a string with the format *mm.vv.rrrr*, where *mm* is the major ODBC version number (as provided by the constant **SQL_SPEC_MAJOR**), *vv* is the minor ODBC version number (as provided by the constant **SQL_SPEC_MINOR**), and *rrrr* is the ODBC Driver Manager major build number (for example, 03.05.0000 would translate to major version 3, minor version 5, build number 0).
SQL_DRIVER_HENV (ODBC 1.0)	**SQLUINTEGER**	Identifies the driver's environment handle. The driver's environment handle is returned by the ODBC Driver Manager; not by the data source.
SQL_DRIVER_HDBC (ODBC 1.0)	**SQLUINTEGER**	Identifies the driver's connection handle. The driver's connection handle is returned by the ODBC Driver Manager; not by the data source.
SQL_DRIVER_HDESC (ODBC 3.0)	**SQLUINTEGER**	Identifies the driver's descriptor handle. The driver's descriptor handle is determined by the Driver Manager's descriptor handle, which must be passed as input in the *InfoValue* parameter of the **SQLGetInfo()** function. Note

InfoType Code	Data Type Returned	Description
		that in this case, the *InfoValue* parameter is both an input and output parameter. The input descriptor handle passed must have been explicitly or implicitly allocated on the connection handle being used.
		The application should make a copy of the ODBC Driver Manager's descriptor handle before specifying this *InfoType* code to ensure that the handle is not overwritten on output.
		The driver's descriptor handle is returned by the ODBC Driver Manager; not by the data source.
SQL_DRIVER_HLIB (ODBC 2.0)	**SQLUINTEGER**	Identifies the instance handle (on a Windows platform) or the equivalent (on a non-Windows platform) of the load library returned to the ODBC Driver Manager when the driver DLL was loaded. This handle is only valid for the connection handle specified in the call to **SQLGetInfo()**.
		The driver's instance handle is returned by the ODBC Driver Manager.
SQL_DRIVER_HSTMT (ODBC 1.0)	**SQLUINTEGER**	Identifies the driver's statement handle. The driver's statement handle is determined by the Driver Manager's statement handle, which must be passed as input in the *InfoValue* parameter of the **SQLGetInfo()** function. Note that in this case, the *InfoValue* parameter is both an input and output parameter. The input statement handle passed must have been allocated on the connection handle being used.
		The application should make a copy of the ODBC Driver Manager's statement handle before specifying this *InfoType* code to ensure that the handle is not overwritten on output.
		The driver's statement handle is returned by the ODBC Driver Manager; not by the data source.
SQL_DRIVER_NAME (ODBC 1.0)	Character string	Identifies file name of the driver being used to access the data source.
SQL_DRIVER_ODBC_VER (ODBC 2.0)	Character string	Identifies the version of ODBC the driver supports. This information is returned in a string with the format *mm.vv*, where *mm* is the major ODBC version number (as provided by the constant **SQL_SPEC_MAJOR**) and *vv* is

InfoType Code	Data Type Returned	Description
		the minor ODBC version number (as provided by the constant **SQL_SPEC_MINOR**) (for example, 03.05 translates to major version 3, minor version 5).
SQL_DRIVER_VER (ODBC 1.0)	Character string	Identifies the version and optionally, a description of the driver being used. This information is returned in a string that has the format *mm.vv.rrrr*, where *mm* is the major version number, *vv* is the minor version number, and *rrrr* is the release version number (for example, 02.01.0000 translates to major version 2, minor version 1, release 0). The driver must render the version in this format, but it can append a description to the version as well (for example, 04.01.0000 DB2/2 Driver).
SQL_DROP_ASSERTION (ODBC 3.0)	**SQLUINTEGER** bitmask	Identifies the clauses in the **DROP ASSERTION** SQL statement supported by the data source (as defined in SQL-92). The following bitmask values can be returned for this *InfoType* code:
		SQL_DA_DROP_ASSERTION: The **DROP ASSERTION** SQL statements supported by the data source.
		An SQL-92 Full level-conformant driver returns this bitmask.
SQL_DROP_CHARACTER_SET (ODBC 3.0)	**SQLUINTEGER** bitmask	Identifies the clauses in the **DROP CHARACTER SET** SQL statement that are supported by the data source (as defined in SQL-92). The following bitmask values can be returned for this *InfoType* code:
		SQL_DCS_DROP_CHARACTER_SET: The **DROP CHARACTER SET** SQL statement is supported by the data source.
		An SQL-92 Full level-conformant driver returns this bitmask.
SQL_DROP_COLLATION (ODBC 3.0)	**SQLUINTEGER** bitmask	Identifies the clauses in the **DROP COLLATION** SQL statement supported by the data source (as defined in SQL-92). The following bitmask values can be returned for this *InfoType* code:
		SQL_DC_DROP_COLLATION: The **DROP COLLATION** SQL statement is supported by the data source.
		An SQL-92 Full level-conformant driver returns this bitmask.

InfoType Code	Data Type Returned	Description
SQL_DROP_DOMAIN (ODBC 3.0)	**SQLUINTEGER** bitmask	Identifies the clauses in the **DROP DOMAIN** SQL statement that are supported by the data source (as defined in SQL-92). The following bitmask values can be returned for this *Info-Type* code: **SQL_DD_DROP_DOMAIN** **SQL_DD_CASCADE** **SQL_DD_RESTRICT** An SQL-92 Intermediate level-conformant driver returns all bitmasks shown.
SQL_DROP_SCHEMA (ODBC 3.0)	**SQLUINTEGER** bitmask	Identifies the clauses in the **DROP SCHEMA** SQL statement supported by the data source (as defined in SQL-92). The following bitmask values can be returned for this *InfoType* code: **SQL_DS_DROP_SCHEMA** **SQL_DS_CASCADE** **SQL_DS_RESTRICT** An SQL-92 Intermediate level-conformant driver returns all bitmasks shown.
SQL_DROP_TABLE (ODBC 3.0)	**SQLUINTEGER** bitmask	Identifies the clauses in the **DROP TABLE** SQL statement that are supported by the data source (as defined in SQL-92). The following bitmask values can be returned for this *Info-Type* code: **SQL_DT_DROP_TABLE** **SQL_DT_CASCADE** **SQL_DT_RESTRICT** An FIPS Transitional level-conformant driver returns all bitmasks shown.
SQL_DROP_TRANSLATION (ODBC 3.0)	**SQLUINTEGER** bitmask	Identifies the clauses in the **DROP TRANSLATION** SQL statement that are supported by the data source (as defined in SQL-92). The following bitmask values can be returned for this *InfoType* code: **SQL_DTR_DROP_TRANSLATION**: The **DROP TRANSLATION** SQL statement is supported by the data source. An SQL-92 Full level-conformant driver returns this bitmask.

InfoType Code	Data Type Returned	Description
SQL_DROP_VIEW (ODBC 3.0)	**SQLUINTEGER** bitmask	Identifies the clauses in the **DROP VIEW** SQL statement that are supported by the data source (as defined in SQL-92). The following bitmask values can be returned for this *InfoType* code: **SQL_DV_DROP_VIEW** **SQL_DV_CASCADE** **SQL_DV_RESTRICT** An FIPS Transitional level-conformant driver returns all bitmasks shown.
SQL_DYNAMIC_CURSOR_ ATTRIBUTES1 (ODBC 3.0)	**SQLUINTEGER** bitmask	Defines the first subset of dynamic cursor attributes that are supported by the driver (see the **SQL_DYNAMIC_CURSOR_ATTRIBUTES2** *InfoType* code for the second subset of attributes). The following bitmask values can be returned for this *InfoType* code: **SQL_CA1_NEXT**: The **SQL_FETCH_NEXT** orientation value can be specified with the **SQLFetchScroll()** function when the cursor is a dynamic cursor. **SQL_CA1_ABSOLUTE**: The **SQL_FETCH_FIRST, SQL_FETCH_ LAST**, and **SQL_FETCH_ABSOLUTE** orientation values can be specified with the **SQLFetchScroll()** function when the cursor is a dynamic cursor. (The rowset fetched is independent of the current cursor position.) **SQL_CA1_RELATIVE**: The **SQL_FETCH_PRIOR** and **SQL_FETCH_ RELATIVE** orientation values can be specified with the **SQLFetchScroll()** function when the cursor is a dynamic cursor. (The rowset fetched is dependent on the current cursor position. Note that this is separate from **SQL_ FETCH_NEXT** because in a forward-only cursor, only **SQL_FETCH_NEXT** is supported.) **SQL_CA1_BOOKMARK**: The **SQL_FETCH_BOOKMARK** orientation value can be specified with the **SQLFetchScroll()** function when the cursor is a dynamic cursor. **SQL_CA1_LOCK_EXCLUSIVE**: The **SQL_LOCK_EXCLUSIVE** lock value can be specified with the **SQLSetPos()** function when the cursor is a dynamic cursor.

InfoType Code	Data Type Returned	Description
		SQL_CA1_LOCK_NO_CHANGE: The **SQL_LOCK_NO_CHANGE** lock value can be specified with the **SQLSetPos()** function when the cursor is a dynamic cursor.
		SQL_CA1_LOCK_UNLOCK: The **SQL_LOCK_UNLOCK** lock value can be specified with the **SQLSetPos()** function when the cursor is a dynamic cursor.
		SQL_CA1_POS_POSITION: The **SQL_POSITION** operation value can be specified with the **SQLSetPos()** function when the cursor is a dynamic cursor.
		SQL_CA1_POS_UPDATE: The **SQL_UPDATE** operation value can be specified with the **SQLSetPos()** function when the cursor is a dynamic cursor.
		SQL_CA1_POS_DELETE: The **SQL_DELETE** operation value can be specified with the **SQLSetPos()** function when the cursor is a dynamic cursor.
		SQL_CA1_POS_REFRESH: The **SQL_REFRESH** operation value can be specified with the **SQLSetPos()** function when the cursor is a dynamic cursor.
		SQL_CA1_POSITIONED_UPDATE: An **UPDATE WHERE CURRENT OF** SQL statement is supported when the cursor is a dynamic cursor. (An SQL-92 Entry level-conformant driver returns this bitmask.)
		SQL_CA1_POSITIONED_DELETE: A **DELETE WHERE CURRENT OF** SQL statement is supported when the cursor is a dynamic cursor. (An SQL-92 Entry level-conformant driver returns this bitmask.)
		SQL_CA1_SELECT_FOR_UPDATE: A **SELECT FOR UPDATE** SQL statement is supported when the cursor is a dynamic cursor. (An SQL-92 Entry level-conformant driver returns this bitmask.)

InfoType Code	Data Type Returned	Description
		SQL_CA1_BULK_ADD: The **SQL_ADD** operation value can be specified with the **SQLBulkOperations()** function when the cursor is a dynamic cursor.
		SQL_CA1_BULK_UPDATE_ BY_BOOKMARK: The **SQL_UPDATE_BY_BOOKMARK** operation value can be specified with the **SQLBulkOperations()** function when the cursor is a dynamic cursor.
		SQL_CA1_BULK_DELETE _BY_BOOKMARK: The **SQL_DELETE_BY_BOOKMARK** operation value can be specified with the **SQLBulkOperations()** function when the cursor is a dynamic cursor.
		SQL_CA1_BULK_FETCH _BY_BOOKMARK: The **SQL_FETCH_BY_BOOKMARK** operation value can be specified with the **SQLBulkOperations()** function when the cursor is a dynamic cursor.
		An SQL-92 Intermediate level-conformant driver usually returns the **SQL_CA1_NEXT**, **SQL_CA1_ABSOLUTE**, and **SQL_CA1_ RELATIVE** bitmasks, because it supports scrollable cursors through the embedded **FETCH** SQL statement. Because this does not directly determine the underlying SQL support, however, scrollable cursors may not be supported, even for an SQL-92 Intermediate level-conformant driver.
SQL_DYNAMIC_CURSOR_ ATTRIBUTES2 (ODBC 3.0)	**SQLUINTEGER** bitmask	Defines the second subset of dynamic cursor attributes that are supported by the driver (see the **SQL_DYNAMIC_CURSOR _ATTRIBUTES1** *InfoType* code for the first subset of attributes). The following bitmask values can be returned for this *InfoType* code:
		SQL_CA2_READ_ONLY _CONCURRENCY: A read-only dynamic cursor in which no up-dates are allowed, is supported. (The **SQL_ ATTR_CONCURRENCY** statement attribute can be set to **SQL_CONCUR_READ_ONLY** for a dynamic cursor).
		SQL_CA2_LOCK_CONCURRENCY: A dynamic cursor that uses the lowest level of locking sufficient to ensure that the row can be updated is supported. (The **SQL_ATTR_ CONCURRENCY** statement attribute can be set to **SQL_CONCUR_LOCK** for a dynamic cursor).

InfoType Code	Data Type Returned	Description
		These locks must be consistent with the transaction isolation level set by the **SQL_ATTR_TXN_ISOLATION** connection attribute.
		SQL_CA2_OPT_ROWVER_CONCURRENCY: A dynamic cursor that uses the optimistic concurrency control by comparing row versions is supported. (The **SQL_ATTR_CONCURRENCY** statement attribute can be set to **SQL_CONCUR_ROWVER** for a dynamic cursor).
		SQL_CA2_OPT_VALUES_CONCURRENCY: A dynamic cursor that uses the optimistic concurrency control by comparing values is supported. (The **SQL_ATTR_CONCURRENCY** statement attribute can be set to **SQL_CONCUR_VALUES** for a dynamic cursor).
		SQL_CA2_SENSITIVITY_ADDITIONS: Added rows are visible to a dynamic cursor and the cursor can scroll to the added rows. (Where these rows are added to the cursor is driver-dependent.)
		SQL_CA2_SENSITIVITY_DELETIONS: Deleted rows are no longer available to a dynamic cursor, and do not leave a 'hole' in the result data set; after the dynamic cursor scrolls from a deleted row, it cannot return to that row.
		SQL_CA2_SENSITIVITY_UPDATES: Updates to rows are visible to a dynamic cursor; if the dynamic cursor scrolls from and returns to an updated row, the data returned by the cursor is the updated data, not the original data.
		SQL_CA2_MAX_ROWS_SELECT: The **SQL_ATTR_MAX_ROWS** statement attribute affects **SELECT** SQL statements when the cursor is a dynamic cursor.
		SQL_CA2_MAX_ROWS_INSERT: The **SQL_ATTR_MAX_ROWS** statement attribute affects **INSERT** SQL statements when the cursor is a dynamic cursor.
		SQL_CA2_MAX_ROWS_DELETE: The **SQL_ATTR_MAX_ROWS** statement attribute affects **DELETE** SQL statements when the cursor is a dynamic cursor.

InfoType Code	Data Type Returned	Description
		SQL_CA2_MAX_ROWS_UPDATE: The **SQL_ATTR_MAX_ROWS** statement attribute affects **UPDATE** SQL statements when the cursor is a dynamic cursor.
		SQL_CA2_MAX_ROWS_CATALOG: The **SQL_ATTR_MAX_ROWS** statement attribute affects **CATALOG** result data sets when the cursor is a dynamic cursor
		SQL_CA2_MAX_ROWS_AFFECTS_ALL: The **SQL_ATTR_MAX_ROWS** statement attribute affects **SELECT**, **INSERT**, **UPDATE**, and **DELETE** SQL statements, and **CATALOG** result data sets, when the cursor is a dynamic cursor.
		SQL_CA2_CRC_EXACT: The exact row count is available in the **SQL_DIAG_CURSOR_ROW_COUNT** diagnostic header record field when the cursor is a dynamic cursor.
		SQL_CA2_CRC_APPROXIMATE: An approximate row count is available in the **SQL_DIAG_CURSOR_ROW_COUNT** diagnostic field when the cursor is a dynamic cursor.
		SQL_CA2_SIMULATE_NON_UNIQUE: The driver does not guarantee that simulated positioned **UPDATE** or **DELETE** SQL statements will affect only one row when the cursor is a dynamic cursor. If a statement affects more than one row, **SQLExecute()** or **SQLExecDirect()** returns SQLSTATE **01**001 (Cursor operation conflict). To set this behavior, an application calls the **SQLSetStmtAttr()** function and sets the **SQL_ATTR_SIMULATE_CURSOR** statement attribute to **SQL_SC_NON_UNIQUE**.
		SQL_CA2_SIMULATE _TRY_UNIQUE: The driver attempts to guarantee that simulated positioned **UPDATE** or **DELETE** SQL statements will affect only one row when the cursor is a dynamic cursor. The driver always executes such statements, even if they might affect more than one row, such as when there is no unique key. If the driver cannot guarantee this for a given statement, **SQLExecute()** or **SQLExecDirect()** returns SQLSTATE **01**001 (Cursor operation conflict). To set this behavior, an application calls the **SQLSetStmtAttr()** function and sets the **SQL_ATTR_SIMULATE_CURSOR** statement attribute to **SQL_SC_TRY_UNIQUE**.

InfoType Code	Data Type Returned	Description
		SQL_CA2_SIMULATE_UNIQUE: The driver guarantees that simulated positioned **UPDATE** or **DELETE** SQL statements will affect only one row when the cursor is a dynamic cursor. If the driver cannot guarantee this for a given statement, **SQLExecute()** or **SQLExecDirect()** returns SQLSTATE **01**001 (Cursor operation conflict). To set this behavior, an application calls the **SQLSetStmtAttr()** function and sets the **SQL_ATTR_SIMULATE_CURSOR** statement attribute to **SQL_SC_UNIQUE**.
SQL_EXPRESSIONS_IN_ ORDERBY (ODBC 1.0)	Character string	Indicates whether the data source supports direct specification of expresions in the **ORDER BY** clause list. The following values can be returned for this *InfoType* code: **"Y"**: The data source supports expressions in the **ORDER BY** clause list. **"N"**: The data source does not support expressions in the **ORDER BY** clause list.
SQL_FILE_USAGE (ODBC 2.0)	SQLUSMALLINT	Identifies how a single-tier driver treats files in a data source. The following values can be returned for this *InfoType* code: **SQL_FILE_NOT_SUPPORTED**: The driver is not a single-tier driver, therefore files are not supported. **SQL_FILE_TABLE**: The single-tier driver treats files in a data source as tables. **SQL_FILE_CATALOG**: The single-tier driver treats files in a data source as a catalog (i.e., as a complete database). An application might use this *InfoType* code to determine how users will select data.
SQL_FETCH_DIRECTION[12] (ODBC 2.0)	SQLUINTEGER bitmask	Identifies the cursor fetch direction options supported by the driver and its underlying data source. The following bitmask values can be returned for this *InfoType* code: **SQL_FD_FETCH_NEXT** (ODBC 1.0) **SQL_FD_FETCH_FIRST** (ODBC 1.0) **SQL_FD_FETCH_LAST** (ODBC 1.0) **SQL_FD_FETCH_PRIOR** (ODBC 1.0) **SQL_FD_FETCH_ABSOLUTE** (ODBC 1.0) **SQL_FD_FETCH_RELATIVE** (ODBC 1.0) **SQL_FD_FETCH_RESUME** (ODBC 1.0) **SQL_FD_FETCH_BOOKMARK** (ODBC 2.0)

InfoType Code	Data Type Returned	Description
SQL_FORWARD_ONLY_ CURSOR_ATTRIBUTES1 (ODBC 3.0)	**SQLUINTEGER** bitmask	Defines the first subset of forward-only cursor attributes that are supported by the driver (see the **SQL_FORWARD_ONLY _CURSOR_ ATTRIBUTES2** *InfoType* code for the second subset of attributes). The following bitmask values can be returned for this *InfoType* code:

SQL_CA1_NEXT:
The **SQL_FETCH_NEXT** orientation value can be specified with the **SQLFetchScroll()** function when the cursor is a forward-only cursor.

SQL_CA1_LOCK_EXCLUSIVE:
The **SQL_LOCK_EXCLUSIVE** lock value can be specified with the **SQLSetPos()** function when the cursor is a forward-only cursor.

SQL_CA1_LOCK_NO_CHANGE:
The **SQL_LOCK_NO_CHANGE** lock value can be specified with the **SQLSetPos()** function when the cursor is a forward-only cursor.

SQL_CA1_LOCK_UNLOCK:
The **SQL_LOCK_UNLOCK** lock value can be specified with the **SQLSetPos()** function when the cursor is a forward-only cursor.

SQL_CA1_POS_POSITION:
The **SQL_POSITION** operation value can be specified with the **SQLSetPos()** function when the cursor is a forward-only cursor.

SQL_CA1_POS_UPDATE:
The **SQL_UPDATE** operation value can be specified with the **SQLSetPos()** function when the cursor is a forward-only cursor.

SQL_CA1_POS_DELETE:
The **SQL_DELETE** operation value can be specified with the **SQLSetPos()** function when the cursor is a forward-only cursor.

SQL_CA1_POS_REFRESH:
The **SQL_REFRESH** operation value can be specified with the **SQLSetPos()** function when the cursor is a forward-only cursor.

SQL_CA1_POSITIONED_UPDATE:
An **UPDATE WHERE CURRENT OF** SQL statement is supported when the cursor is a forward-only cursor. (An SQL-92 Entry level-conformant driver returns this bitmask.)

InfoType Code	Data Type Returned	Description
		SQL_CA1_POSITIONED_DELETE: A **DELETE WHERE CURRENT OF** SQL statement is supported when the cursor is a forward-only cursor. (An SQL-92 Entry level-conformant driver returns this bitmask.)
		SQL_CA1_SELECT_FOR_UPDATE: A **SELECT FOR UPDATE** SQL statement is supported when the cursor is a forward-only cursor. (An SQL-92 Entry level-conformant driver returns this bitmask.)
		SQL_CA1_BULK_ADD: The **SQL_ADD** operation value can be specified with the **SQLBulkOperations()** function when the cursor is a forward-only cursor.
		SQL_CA1_BULK_UPDATE _BY_BOOKMARK: The **SQL_UPDATE_BY_BOOKMARK** operation value can be specified with the **SQLBulkOperations()** function when the cursor is a forward-only cursor.
		SQL_CA1_BULK_DELETE_BY_BOOKMARK: The **SQL_DELETE_BY_BOOKMARK** operation value can be specified with the **SQLBulkOperations()** function when the cursor is a forward-only cursor.
		SQL_CA1_BULK_FETCH _BY_BOOKMARK: The **SQL_FETCH_BY_BOOKMARK** operation value can be specified with the **SQLBulkOperations()** function when the cursor is a forward-only cursor.
SQL_FORWARD_ONLY_ CURSOR_ATTRIBUTES2 (ODBC 3.0)	**SQLUINTEGER** bitmask	Defines the second subset of forward-only cursor attributes that are supported by the driver (see the **SQL_FORWARD_ONLY_ CURSOR_ATTRIBUTES1** *InfoType* code for the first subset of attributes). The following bitmask values can be returned for this *InfoType* code:
		SQL_CA2_READ_ONLY _CONCURRENCY: A read-only forward-only cursor, in which no updates are allowed, is supported. (The **SQL_ATTR_CONCURRENCY** statement attribute can be set to **SQL_CONCUR_READ_ ONLY** for a forward-only cursor).

InfoType Code	Data Type Returned	Description
		SQL_CA2_LOCK_CONCURRENCY: A forward-only cursor that uses the lowest level of locking sufficient to ensure that the row can be updated is supported. (The **SQL_ATTR_CONCURRENCY** statement attribute can be set to **SQL_CONCUR_LOCK** for a forward-only cursor). These locks must be consistent with the transaction isolation level set by the **SQL_ATTR_TXN_ISOLATION** connection attribute.
		SQL_CA2_OPT_ROWVER_CONCURRENCY: A forward-only cursor that uses the optimistic concurrency control by comparing row versions is supported. (The **SQL_ATTR_CONCURRENCY** statement attribute can be set to **SQL_CONCUR_ROWVER** for a forward-only cursor).
		SQL_CA2_OPT_VALUES_CONCURRENCY: A forward-only cursor that uses the optimistic concurrency control by comparing values is supported. (The **SQL_ATTR_CONCURRENCY** statement attribute can be set to **SQL_CONCUR_VALUES** for a forward-only cursor).
		SQL_CA2_SENSITIVITY_ADDITIONS: Added rows are visible to a forward-only cursor and the cursor can scroll to the added rows. (Where these rows are added to the cursor is driver-dependent.)
		SQL_CA2_SENSITIVITY_DELETIONS: Deleted rows are no longer available to a forward-only cursor, and do not leave a 'hole' in the result data set; after the forward-only cursor scrolls from a deleted row, it cannot return to that row.
		SQL_CA2_SENSITIVITY_UPDATES: Updates to rows are visible to a forward-only cursor; if the forward-only cursor scrolls from and returns to an updated row, the data returned by the cursor is the updated data, not the original data.
		SQL_CA2_MAX_ROWS_SELECT: The **SQL_ATTR_MAX_ROWS** statement attribute affects **SELECT** SQL statements when the cursor is a forward-only cursor.
		SQL_CA2_MAX_ROWS_INSERT: The **SQL_ATTR_MAX_ROWS** statement attribute affects **INSERT** SQL statements when the cursor is a forward-only cursor.

InfoType Code	Data Type Returned	Description
		SQL_CA2_MAX_ROWS_DELETE: The **SQL_ATTR_MAX_ROWS** statement attribute affects **DELETE** SQL statements when the cursor is a forward-only cursor.
		SQL_CA2_MAX_ROWS_UPDATE: The **SQL_ATTR_MAX_ROWS** statement attribute affects **UPDATE** SQL statements when the cursor is a forward-only cursor.
		SQL_CA2_MAX_ROWS_CATALOG: The **SQL_ATTR_MAX_ROWS** statement attribute affects **CATALOG** result data sets when the cursor is a forward-only cursor.
		SQL_CA2_MAX_ROWS_AFFECTS_ALL: The **SQL_ATTR_MAX_ROWS** statement attribute affects **SELECT**, **INSERT**, **UPDATE**, and **DELETE** SQL statements, and **CATALOG** result data sets, when the cursor is a forward-only cursor.
		SQL_CA2_CRC_EXACT: The exact row count is available in the **SQL_DIAG_CURSOR_ROW_COUNT** diagnostic field when the cursor is a forward-only cursor.
		SQL_CA2_CRC_APPROXIMATE: An approximate row count is available in the **SQL_DIAG_CURSOR_ROW_COUNT** diagnostic field when the cursor is a forward-only cursor.
		SQL_CA2_SIMULATE_NON_UNIQUE: The driver does not guarantee that simulated positioned **UPDATE** or **DELETE** SQL statements will affect only one row when the cursor is a forward-only cursor. If a statement affects more than one row, **SQLExecute()** or **SQLExecDirect()** returns SQLSTATE **01**001 (Cursor operation conflict). To set this behavior, an application calls the **SQLSetStmtAttr()** function and sets the **SQL_ATTR_SIMULATE_CURSOR** statement attribute to **SQL_SC_NON_UNIQUE**.
		SQL_CA2_SIMULATE_TRY_UNIQUE: The driver attempts to guarantee that simulated positioned **UPDATE** or **DELETE** SQL statements will affect only one row when the cursor is a forward-only cursor. The driver always executes such statements, even if they might affect more than one row, such as when there is no unique key. If the driver cannot guarantee

InfoType Code	Data Type Returned	Description
		this for a given statement, **SQLExecute()** or **SQLExecDirect()** returns SQLSTATE **01**001 (Cursor operation conflict). To set this behavior, an application calls the **SQLSetStmtAttr()** function and sets the **SQL_ATTR_SIMULATE_CURSOR** statement attribute to **SQL_SC_TRY_UNIQUE**.
		SQL_CA2_SIMULATE_UNIQUE: The driver guarantees that simulated positioned **UPDATE** or **DELETE** SQL statements will affect only one row when the cursor is a forward-only cursor. If the driver cannot guarantee this for a given statement, **SQLExecute()** or **SQLExecDirect()** returns SQLSTATE **01**001 (Cursor operation conflict). To set this behavior, an application calls the **SQLSetStmtAttr()** function and sets the **SQL_ATTR_SIMULATE_CURSOR** statement attribute to **SQL_SC_UNIQUE**.
SQL_GETDATA_EXTENSIONS (ODBC 2.0)	**SQLUINTEGER** bitmask	Identifies the common extensions the driver supports for the **SQLGetData()** function. The following bitmask values can be returned for this *InfoType* code:
		SQL_GD_ANY_COLUMN: The **SQLGetData()** function can be called for any unbound column, including those before the last bound column. Note that the columns must be called in order of ascending column number unless **SQL_GD_ANY_ORDER** is also returned.
		SQL_GD_ANY_ORDER: The **SQLGetData()** function can be called for unbound columns in any order. Note that **SQLGetData()** can only be called for columns after the last bound column unless **SQL_GD_ANY_COLUMN** is also returned.
		SQL_GD_BLOCK: The **SQLGetData()** function can be called for an unbound column in any row in a block of data (where the rowset size is greater than 1) after positioning to that row with **SQLSetPos()**.
		SQL_GD_BOUND: The **SQLGetData()** function can be called for bound columns as well as unbound columns. A driver cannot return this value unless it also returns **SQL_GD_ANY_COLUMN**.

InfoType Code	Data Type Returned	Description
		By default, the **SQLGetData()** function is only required to return data from unbound columns that occur after the last bound column; that are called in order of increasing column number; and that are not in a row that's in a rowset.
		If a driver supports bookmarks (either fixed- or variable-length), it must allow the **SQLGetData()** function to be called on column 0. This support is required regardless of what the driver returns for the **SQL_GETDATA_EXTENSIONS** *InfoType* code.
SQL_GROUP_BY (ODBC 2.0)	**SQLUSMALLINT**	Identifies the relationship between the columns in a **GROUP BY** clause and the non-aggregated columns in the corresponding select list. The following values can be returned for this *InfoType* code:
		SQL_GB_COLLATE: A **COLLATE** clause can be specified at the end of each grouping column. (ODBC 3.0)
		SQL_GB_NOT_SUPPORTED: **GROUP BY** clauses are not supported by the data source. (ODBC 2.0)
		SQL_GB_GROUP_BY_EQUALS_SELECT: The **GROUP BY** clause must contain all non-aggregated columns named in the corresponding select list; it cannot contain any other columns. For example, **SELECT DEPT, MAX(SALARY) FROM EMPLOYEE GROUP BY DEPT.** (ODBC 2.0)
		SQL_GB_GROUP_BY_CONTAINS_SELECT: The **GROUP BY** clause must contain all non-aggregated columns named in the corresponding select list, however, it can also contain columns not named in the select list. For example, **SELECT DEPT, MAX(SALARY) FROM EMPLOYEE GROUP BY DEPT, AGE.** (ODBC 2.0)
		SQL_GB_NO_RELATION: The columns in the **GROUP BY** clause and the columns named in the corresponding select list are not related. For example, **SELECT DEPT, SALARY FROM EMPLOYEE GROUP BY DEPT, AGE.** (ODBC 2.0)
		An SQL-92 Entry level-conformant driver returns the **SQL_GB_GROUP_BY_EQUALS_SELECT** bitmask.
		An SQL-92 Full level-conformant driver returns the **SQL_GB_COLLATE** bitmask.

InfoType Code	Data Type Returned	Description
		If none of these options is supported, the **GROUP BY** clause is not supported by the data source.
SQL_IDENTIFIER_CASE (ODBC 1.0)	**SQLUSMALLINT**	Identifies the type of case sensitivity used in object identifier names (for example, table names). The following values can be returned for this *InfoType* code:
		SQL_IC_UPPER: Identifiers in SQL are not case-sensitive and are stored in uppercase in the system catalog.
		SQL_IC_LOWER: Identifiers in SQL are not case-sensitive and are stored in lowercase in the system catalog.
		SQL_IC_SENSITIVE: Identifiers in SQL are case-sensitive and are stored in mixed case in the system catalog.
		SQL_IC_MIXED: Identifiers in SQL are not case-sensitive and are stored in mixed case in the system catalog.
		Because identifiers in SQL-92 are never case-sensitive, a driver that conforms strictly to SQL-92 (any level) never returns the **SQL_ IC_SENSITIVE** bitmask.
SQL_IDENTIFIER_QUOTE_ CHAR (ODBC 1.0)	Character string	Identifies the character that is to be used as the starting and ending delimiter of a quoted (delimited) identifier in SQL statements. (Identifiers passed in ODBC function parameters do not need to be quoted.) This character can also be used for quoting catalog function parameters when the connection attribute **SQL_ ATTR_METADATA_ID** is set to **SQL_TRUE**.
		If the data source does not support quoted identifiers, a blank string (" ") is returned for this *InfoType* code.
		An SQL-92 Full level-compliant driver returns the double quotation mark (") character for this *InfoType* code.
SQL_INDEX_KEYWORDS (ODBC 3.0)	**SQLUINTEGER** bitmask	Identifies the keywords in the **CREATE INDEX** SQL statement that are supported by the driver (as defined in SQL-92). The following bitmask values can be returned for this *InfoType* code:
		SQL_IK_NONE: None of the keywords are supported.

InfoType Code	Data Type Returned	Description
		SQL_IK_ASC: The **ASC** keyword (for ascending order) is supported.
		SQL_IK_DESC: The **DESC** keyword (for descending order) is supported.
		SQL_IK_ALL: All keywords are supported.
		If the **CREATE INDEX** statement is not supported by the data source (see the **SQL_DLL_INDEX** *InfoType* code), the value **SQL_IK_NONE** is returned for this *InfoType* code.
SQL_INFO_SCHEMA_VIEWS (ODBC 3.0)	**SQLUINTEGER** bitmask	Identifies the views (and their contents) in the **INFORMATION_SCHEMA** that are supported by the driver (as defined in SQL-92). The following bitmask values can be returned for this *InfoType* code:
		SQL_ISV_ASSERTIONS: Identifies the catalog's assertions that are owned by a given user (Full level).
		SQL_ISV_CHARACTER_SETS: Identifies the catalog's character sets that are accessible to a given user (Intermediate level).
		SQL_ISV_CHECK_CONSTRAINTS: Identifies the check constraints owned by a given user (Intermediate level).
		SQL_ISV_COLLATIONS: Identifies the catalog's character collations that are accessible to a given user (Full level).
		SQL_ISV_COLUMN_DOMAIN_USAGE: Identifies columns for the catalog that are dependent on domains defined in the catalog and that are owned by a given user. (Intermediate level).
		SQL_ISV_COLUMN_PRIVILEGES: Identifies the privileges on columns of persistent tables that are available to or granted by a given user (FIPS Transitional level).
		SQL_ISV_COLUMNS: Identifies the columns of persistent tables that are accessible to a given user. (FIPS Transitional level).

InfoType Code	Data Type Returned	Description
		SQL_ISV_CONSTRAINT_COLUMN_USAGE: Identifies the columns for the various constraints that are owned by a given user (Intermediate level).
		SQL_ISV_CONSTRAINT_TABLE_USAGE: Identifies the tables that are used by constraints (referential, unique, and assertions) and that are owned by a given user (Intermediate level).
		SQL_ISV_DOMAIN_CONSTRAINTS: Identifies the domain constraints (of the domains in the catalog) that are accessible to a given user (Intermediate level).
		SQL_ISV_DOMAINS: Identifies the domains defined in a catalog that are accessible to a given user (Intermediate level).
		SQL_ISV_KEY_COLUMN_USAGE: Identifies columns defined in the catalog that are constrained as keys by a given user. (Intermediate level).
		SQL_ISV_REFERENTIAL_CONSTRAINTS: Identifies the referential constraints owned by a given user (Intermediate level).
		SQL_ISV_SCHEMATA: Identifies the schemas owned by a given user (Intermediate level).
		SQL_ISV_SQL_LANGUAGES: Identifies the SQL conformance levels, options, and dialects supported by the SQL implementation (Intermediate level).
		SQL_ISV_TABLE_CONSTRAINTS: Identifies the table constraints owned by a given user (Intermediate level).
		SQL_ISV_TABLE_PRIVILEGES: Identifies a persistent table's privileges available to or granted by a given user (FIPS Transitional level).
		SQL_ISV_TABLES: Identifies the persistent tables defined in a catalog that are accessible to a given user (FIPS Transitional level).

InfoType Code	Data Type Returned	Description
		SQL_ISV_TRANSLATIONS: Identifies catalog character translations that are accessible to a given user (Full level).
		SQL_ISV_USAGE_PRIVILEGES: Identifies the USAGE privileges on catalog objects that are available to or owned by a given user (FIPS Transitional level).
		SQL_ISV_VIEW_COLUMN_USAGE: Identifies the columns on which the catalog's views owned by a given user are dependent (Intermediate level).
		SQL_ISV_VIEW_TABLE_USAGE: Identifies the tables on which the catalog's views owned by a given user are dependent (Intermediate level).
		SQL_ISV_VIEWS: Identifies the viewed tables defined in the catalog that are accessible to a given user (FIPS Transitional level).
		The SQL-92 or FIPS conformance level at which this feature needs to be supported is shown in parentheses next to each bitmask.
SQL_INSERT_STATEMENT (ODBC 3.0)	**SQLUINTEGER** bitmask	Identifies how the **INSERT** SQL statement is supported by the data source (as defined in SQL-92). The following bitmask values can be returned for this _InfoType_ code: **SQL_IS_INSERT_LITERALS** **SQL_IS_INSERT_SEARCHED** **SQL_IS_SELECT_INTO** An SQL-92 Entry level-conformant driver returns all bitmasks shown.
SQL_INTEGRITY[5] (ODBC 1.0)	Character string	Indicates whether the data source supports the Integrity Enhancement Facility. The following values can be returned for this _InfoType_ code: **"Y"**: The data source supports the Integrity Enhancement Facility. **"N"**: The data source does not support the Integrity Enhancement Facility.

InfoType Code	Data Type Returned	Description
SQL_KEYSET_CURSOR_ ATTRIBUTES1 (ODBC 3.0)	**SQLUINTEGER** bitmask	Defines the first subset of keyset-driven cursor attributes that are supported by the driver (see the **SQL_KEYSET_CURSOR_ATTRIBUTES2** *InfoType* code for the second subset of attributes). The following bitmask values can be returned for this *InfoType* code:

The **SQL_CA1_NEXT** orientation value can be specified with the **SQLFetchScroll()** function when the cursor is a keyset-driven cursor.

SQL_CA1_ABSOLUTE:
The **SQL_FETCH_FIRST**, **SQL_FETCH_LAST**, and **SQL_FETCH_ABSOLUTE** orientation values can be specified with the **SQLFetchScroll()** function when the cursor is a keyset-driven cursor. (The rowset fetched is independent of the current cursor position.)

SQL_CA1_RELATIVE:
The **SQL_FETCH_PRIOR** and **SQL_FETCH_RELATIVE** orientation values can be specified with the **SQLFetchScroll()** function when the cursor is a keyset-driven cursor. (The rowset fetched is dependent on the current cursor position. Note that this is separate from **SQL_FETCH_NEXT** because in a forward-only cursor, only **SQL_FETCH_NEXT** is supported.)

SQL_CA1_BOOKMARK:
The **SQL_FETCH_BOOKMARK** orientation value can be specified with the **SQLFetchScroll()** function when the cursor is a keyset-driven cursor.

SQL_CA1_LOCK_EXCLUSIVE:
The **SQL_LOCK_EXCLUSIVE** lock value can be specified with the **SQLSetPos()** function when the cursor is a keyset-driven cursor.

SQL_CA1_LOCK_NO_CHANGE:
The **SQL_LOCK_NO_CHANGE** lock value can be specified with the **SQLSetPos()** function when the cursor is a keyset-driven cursor.

SQL_CA1_LOCK_UNLOCK:
The **SQL_LOCK_UNLOCK** lock value can be specified with the **SQLSetPos()** function when the cursor is a keyset-driven cursor.

InfoType Code	Data Type Returned	Description
		SQL_CA1_POS_POSITION: The **SQL_POSITION** operation value can be specified with the **SQLSetPos()** function when the cursor is a keyset-driven cursor.
		SQL_CA1_POS_UPDATE: The **SQL_UPDATE** operation value can be specified with the **SQLSetPos()** function when the cursor is a keyset-driven cursor.
		SQL_CA1_POS_DELETE: The **SQL_DELETE** operation value can be specified with the **SQLSetPos()** function when the cursor is a keyset-driven cursor.
		SQL_CA1_POS_REFRESH: The **SQL_REFRESH** operation value can be specified with the **SQLSetPos()** function when the cursor is a keyset-driven cursor.
		SQL_CA1_POSITIONED_UPDATE: An **UPDATE WHERE CURRENT OF** SQL statement is supported when the cursor is a keyset-driven cursor. (An SQL-92 Entry level-conformant driver returns this bitmask.)
		SQL_CA1_POSITIONED_DELETE: A **DELETE WHERE CURRENT OF** SQL statement is supported when the cursor is a keyset-driven cursor. (An SQL-92 Entry level-conformant driver returns this bitmask.)
		SQL_CA1_SELECT_FOR_UPDATE: A **SELECT FOR UPDATE** SQL statement is supported when the cursor is a keyset-driven cursor. (An SQL-92 Entry level-conformant driver returns this bitmask.)
		SQL_CA1_BULK_ADD: The **SQL_ADD** operation value can be specified with the **SQLBulkOperations()** function when the cursor is a keyset-driven cursor.
		SQL_CA1_BULK_UPDATE_BY_BOOKMARK: The **SQL_UPDATE_BY_BOOKMARK** operation value can be specified with the **SQLBulkOperations()** function when the cursor is a keyset-driven cursor.

InfoType Code	Data Type Returned	Description
		SQL_CA1_BULK_DELETE_BY_BOOKMARK: The **SQL_DELETE_BY_BOOKMARK** operation value can be specified with the **SQLBulkOperations()** function when the cursor is a keyset-driven cursor.
		SQL_CA1_BULK_FETCH_BY_BOOKMARK: The **SQL_FETCH_BY_BOOKMARK** operation value can be specified with the **SQLBulkOperations()** function when the cursor is a keyset-driven cursor.
		An SQL-92 Intermediate level-conformant driver usually returns the **SQL_CA1_NEXT**, **SQL_CA1_ABSOLUTE**, and **SQL_CA1_RELATIVE** bitmasks, because it supports scrollable cursors through the embedded **FETCH** SQL statement. Because this does not directly determine the underlying SQL support, however, scrollable cursors may not be supported, even for an SQL-92 Intermediate level-conformant driver.
SQL_KEYSET_CURSOR_ATTRIBUTES2 (ODBC 3.0)	**SQLUINTEGER** bitmask	Defines the second subset of keyset-driven cursor attributes that are supported by the driver (see the **SQL_KEYSET_CURSOR_ATTRIBUTES1** *InfoType* code for the first subset of attributes). The following bitmask values can be returned for this *InfoType* code:
		SQL_CA2_READ_ONLY_CONCURRENCY: A read-only keyset-driven cursor, in which no updates are allowed, is supported. (The **SQL_ATTR_CONCURRENCY** statement attribute can be set to **SQL_CONCUR_READ_ONLY** for a keyset-driven cursor).
		SQL_CA2_LOCK_CONCURRENCY: A keyset-driven cursor using the lowest level of locking sufficient to ensure that the row can be updated is supported. (The **SQL_ATTR_CONCURRENCY** statement attribute can be set to **SQL_CONCUR_LOCK** for a keyset-driven cursor). These locks must be consistent with the transaction isolation level set by the **SQL_ATTR_TXN_ISOLATION** connection attribute.
		SQL_CA2_OPT_ROWVER_CONCURRENCY: A keyset-driven cursor that uses the optimistic concurrency control by comparing row versions

InfoType Code	Data Type Returned	Description
		is supported. (The **SQL_ATTR_ CONCURRENCY** statement attribute can be set to **SQL_CONCUR_ROWVER** for a keyset-driven cursor).
		SQL_CA2_OPT_VALUES_CONCURRENCY: A keyset-driven cursor that uses the optimistic concurrency control by comparing values is supported. (The **SQL_ATTR_CONCURRENCY** statement attribute can be set to **SQL_ CONCUR_VALUES** for a keyset-driven cursor).
		SQL_CA2_SENSITIVITY_ADDITIONS: Added rows are visible to a keyset-driven cursor and the cursor can scroll to the added rows. (Where these rows are added to the cursor is driver-dependent.)
		SQL_CA2_SENSITIVITY_DELETIONS: Deleted rows are no longer available to a keyset-driven cursor and do not leave a 'hole' in the result data set; after the keyset-driven cursor scrolls from a deleted row, it cannot return to that row.
		SQL_CA2_SENSITIVITY_UPDATES: Updates to rows are visible to a keyset-driven cursor; if the keyset-driven cursor scrolls from and returns to an updated row, the data returned by the cursor is the updated data, not the original data.
		SQL_CA2_MAX_ROWS_SELECT: The **SQL_ATTR_MAX_ROWS** statement attribute affects **SELECT** SQL statements when the cursor is a keyset-driven cursor.
		SQL_CA2_MAX_ROWS_INSERT: The **SQL_ATTR_MAX_ROWS** statement attribute affects **INSERT** SQL statements when the cursor is a keyset-driven cursor.
		SQL_CA2_MAX_ROWS_DELETE: The **SQL_ATTR_MAX_ROWS** statement attribute affects **DELETE** SQL statements when the cursor is a keyset-driven cursor.
		SQL_CA2_MAX_ROWS_UPDATE: The **SQL_ATTR_MAX_ROWS** statement attribute affects **UPDATE** SQL statements when the cursor is a keyset-driven cursor.

InfoType Code	Data Type Returned	Description
		SQL_CA2_MAX_ROWS_CATALOG: The **SQL_ATTR_MAX_ROWS** statement attribute affects **CATALOG** result data sets when the cursor is a keyset-driven cursor.
		SQL_CA2_MAX_ROWS_ AFFECTS_ALL: The **SQL_ATTR_MAX_ROWS** statement attribute affects **SELECT**, **INSERT**, **UPDATE**, and **DELETE** statements, and **CATALOG** result data sets, when the cursor is a keyset-driven cursor.
		SQL_CA2_CRC_EXACT: The exact row count is available in the **SQL_DIAG_CURSOR_ ROW_COUNT** diagnostic header record field when the cursor is a keyset-driven cursor.
		SQL_CA2_CRC_APPROXIMATE: An approximate row count is available in the **SQL_ DIAG_CURSOR_ROW_COUNT** diagnostic header record field when the cursor is a keyset-driven cursor.
		SQL_CA2_SIMULATE_NON_UNIQUE: The driver does not guarantee that simulated positioned **UPDATE** or **DELETE** SQL statements will affect only one row when the cursor is a keyset-driven cursor. If a statement affects more than one row, **SQLExecute()** or **SQLExecDirect()** will return SQLSTATE **01**001 (Cursor operation conflict). To set this behavior, an application calls the **SQLSetStmtAttr()** function and sets the **SQL_ATTR_SIMULATE_ CURSOR** statement attribute to **SQL_SC_NON_UNIQUE**.
		SQL_CA2_SIMULATE_TRY_UNIQUE: The driver attempts to guarantee that simulated positioned **UPDATE** or **DELETE** SQL statements will affect only one row when the cursor is a keyset-driven cursor. The driver always executes such statements, even if they might affect more than one row, such as when there is no unique key. If the driver cannot guarantee this for a given statement, **SQLExecute()** or **SQLExecDirect()** will return SQLSTATE **01**001 (Cursor operation conflict). To set this behavior, an application calls the **SQLSetStmtAttr()** function and sets the **SQL_ATTR_SIMULATE_CURSOR** statement attribute to **SQL_SC_TRY_ UNIQUE**.

InfoType Code	Data Type Returned	Description
		SQL_CA2_SIMULATE_UNIQUE: The driver guarantees that simulated positioned **UPDATE** or **DELETE** SQL statements will affect only one row when the cursor is a keyset-driven cursor. If the driver cannot guarantee this for a given statement, **SQLExecute()** or **SQLExecDirect()** will return SQLSTATE **01001** (Cursor operation conflict). To set this behavior, an application calls the **SQLSetStmtAttr()** function and sets the **SQL_ATTR_SIMULATE_CURSOR** statement attribute to **SQL_SC_UNIQUE**.
SQL_KEYWORDS (ODBC 2.0)	Character string	A comma-separated list of all keywords recognized by the data source. This list does not include keywords specific to ODBC or keywords used by both the data source and ODBC. Instead, this list represents all data source-specific reserved keywords.
		Interoperable applications should not use the keywords in this list to identify object names.
		The **#define** value **SQL_ODBC_KEYWORDS** contains a comma-separated list of ODBC-specific keywords.
SQL_LIKE_ESCAPE_ CLAUSE (ODBC 2.0)	Character string	Indicates whether the data data source supports an escape character for the percent character (%) and underscore character (_) in a **LIKE** predicate and the driver supports the ODBC syntax for defining a **LIKE** predicate escape character. The following values can be returned for this *InfoType* code:
		"Y": The data source supports escape characters in a **LIKE** predicate and the driver supports the ODBC syntax for defining a L**LIKE** predicate escape character.
		"N": The data source does not support escape characters in a **LIKE** predicate and/or the driver does not support the ODBC syntax for defining a **LIKE** predicate escape character.
SQL_LOCK_TYPES[12] (ODBC 2.0)	**SQLUINTEGER** bitmask	Identifies the lock types supported by the driver and its underlying data source. The following bitmask values can be returned for this *InfoType* code:
		SQL_LCK_NO_CHANGE SQL_LCK_EXCLUSIVE SQL_LCK_UNLOCK

InfoType Code	Data Type Returned	Description
SQL_MAX_ASYNC_ CONCURRENT_STATEMENTS (ODBC 3.0)	**SQLUINTEGER**	Identifies the maximum number of active concurrent SQLstatements the driver can support in asynchronous mode on a given connection.
		If there is no specific limit or if the limit is unknown, the value **0** is returned for this *InfoType* code.
SQL_MAX_BINARY_ LITERAL_LEN (ODBC 2.0)	**SQLUINTEGER**	Identifies the maximum length (number of hexadecimal characters, excluding the literal prefix and suffix returned by the **SQLGetTypeInfo()** function) that a binary literal in an SQL statement can be. For example, the binary literal 0xFFAA has a length of 4.
		If there is no maximum length or if the length is unknown, the value **0** is returned for this *InfoType* code.
SQL_MAX_CATALOG_ NAME_LEN[6] (ODBC 1.0)	**SQLUSMALLINT**	Identifies the maximum length for a catalog name in the data source.
		If there is no maximum length or if the length is unknown, the value **0** is returned for this *InfoType* code.
		An FIPS Full level-compliant driver returns at least **128** for this *InfoType* code.
SQL_MAX_CHAR_LITERAL_ LEN (ODBC 2.0)	**SQLUINTEGER**	Identifies the maximum length (number of characters, excluding the literal prefix and suffix returned by the **SQLGetTypeInfo()** function) for a character literal in an SQL statement.
		If there is no maximum length, or if the length is unknown, the value **0** is returned for this *InfoType* code.
SQL_MAX_COLUMN_NAME_ LEN (ODBC 1.0)	**SQLUSMALLINT**	Identifies the maximum length for a column name in the data source.
		If there is no maximum length, or if the length is unknown, the value **0** is returned for this *InfoType* code.
		An FIPS Entry level-compliant driver returns at least **18** for this *InfoType* code. An FIPS Intermediate level-compliant driver returns at least **128** for this *InfoType* code.
SQL_MAX_COLUMNS_IN_ GROUP_BY (ODBC 2.0)	**SQLUSMALLINT**	Identifies the maximum number of columns allowed in a **GROUP BY** clause.

InfoType Code	Data Type Returned	Description
		If there is no maximum number or if the limit is unknown, the value **0** is returned for this *InfoType* code.
		An FIPS Entry level-compliant driver returns at least **6** for this *InfoType* code. An FIPS Intermediate level-compliant driver returns at least **15** for this *InfoType* code.
SQL_MAX_COLUMNS_IN_ INDEX (ODBC 2.0)	**SQLUSMALLINT**	Identifies the maximum number of columns allowed in an index.
		If there is no maximum number, or if the limit is unknown, the value **0** is returned for this *InfoType* code.
SQL_MAX_COLUMNS_IN_ ORDER_BY (ODBC 2.0)	**SQLUSMALLINT**	Identifies the maximum number of columns allowed in an **ORDER BY** clause.
		If there is no maximum number or if the limit is unknown, the value **0** is returned for this *InfoType* code.
		An FIPS Entry level-compliant driver returns at least **6** for this *InfoType* code. An FIPS Intermediate level-compliant driver returns at least **15** for this *InfoType* code.
SQL_MAX_COLUMNS_IN_ SELECT (ODBC 2.0)	**SQLUSMALLINT**	Identifies the maximum number of columns allowed in a select list.
		If there is no maximum number, or if the limit is unknown, the value **0** is returned for this *InfoType* code.
		An FIPS Entry level-compliant driver returns at least **100** for this *InfoType* code. An FIPS Intermediate level-compliant driver returns at least **250** for this *InfoType* code.
SQL_MAX_COLUMNS_ IN_TABLE (ODBC 2.0)	**SQLUSMALLINT**	Identifies the maximum number of columns allowed in a table.
		If there is no maximum number, or if the limit is unknown, the value **0** is returned for this *InfoType* code.
		An FIPS Entry level-compliant driver returns at least **100** for this *InfoType* code. An FIPS Intermediate level-compliant driver returns at least **250** for this *InfoType* code.

InfoType Code	Data Type Returned	Description
SQL_MAX_CONCURRENT_ ACTIVITIES[7] (ODBC 1.0)	**SQLUSMALLINT**	Identifies the maximum number of active SQL statements the driver can support for a connection. A statement is defined as active if it has results pending, with the term *results* meaning rows from a **SELECT** operation or rows affected by an **INSERT**, **UPDATE**, or **DELETE** operation (such as a row count), or if it is in a "Need Data" state. This value can reflect a limitation imposed by either the driver or the data source.
		If there is no maximum number, or if the limit is unknown, the value **0** is returned for this *InfoType* code.
SQL_MAX_CURSOR_NAME_ LEN (ODBC 1.0)	**SQLUSMALLINT**	Identifies the maximum length for a cursor name in the data source.
		If there is no maximum length, or if the length is unknown, the value **0** is returned for this *InfoType* code.
		An FIPS Entry level-compliant driver returns at least **18** for this *InfoType* code. An FIPS Intermediate level-compliant driver returns at least **128** for this *InfoType* code.
SQL_MAX_DRIVER_ CONNECTIONS[8] (ODBC 1.0)	**SQLUSMALLINT**	Identifies the maximum number of active connections the driver can support for an environment. This value can reflect a limitation imposed by either the driver or the data source.
		If there is no maximum number, or if the limit is unknown, the value **0** is returned for this *InfoType* code.
SQL_MAX_IDENTIFIER_ LEN (ODBC 3.0)	**SQLUSMALLINT**	Identifies the maximum length, in characters, for a user-defined name in the data source.
		If there is no maximum length, or if the length is unknown, the value **0** is returned for this *InfoType* code.
		An FIPS Entry level-compliant driver returns at least **18** for this *InfoType* code. An FIPS Intermediate level-compliant driver returns at least **128** for this *InfoType* code.
SQL_MAX_INDEX_SIZE (ODBC 2.0)	**SQLUINTEGER**	Identifies the maximum number of bytes allowed in the combined fields of an index.
		If there is no maximum length, or if the length is unknown, the value **0** is returned for this *InfoType* code.

InfoType Code	Data Type Returned	Description
SQL_MAX_PROCEDURE_ NAME_LEN (ODBC 1.0)	**SQLUSMALLINT**	Identifies the maximum length for a procedure name in the data source.
		If there is no maximum length or if the length is unknown, the value **0** is returned for this *InfoType* code.
SQL_MAX_ROW_SIZE (ODBC 2.0)	**SQLUINTEGER**	Identifies the maximum length for a single row in a table.
		If there is no maximum length, or if the length is unknown, the value **0** is returned for this *InfoType* code.
		An FIPS Entry level-compliant driver returns at least **2,000** for this *InfoType* code. An FIPS Intermediate level-compliant driver returns at least **8,000** for this *InfoType* code.
SQL_MAX_ROW_SIZE_ INCLUDES_LONG (ODBC 3.0)	Character string	Indicates whether the maximum row size returned for the **SQL_MAX_ROW_SIZE** information type includes the length of all **SQL_LONGVARCHAR** and **SQL_LONG- VARBINARY** columns in the row. The following values can be returned for this *InfoType* code:
		"Y": The maximum row size returned for the **SQL_ MAX_ROW_SIZE** information type includes the length of all **SQL_LONGVARCHAR** and **SQL_LONGVARBINARY** columns in the row.
		"N": The maximum row size returned for the **SQL_ MAX_ROW_SIZE** information type does not in- clude the length of **SQL_LONGVARCHAR** and **SQL_LONGVARBINARY** columns in the row.
SQL_MAX_SCHEMA_NAME_ LEN[9] (ODBC 1.0)	**SQLUSMALLINT**	Identifies the maximum length for a schema name in the data source.
		If there is no maximum length, or if the length is unknown, the value **0** is returned for this *InfoType* code.
		An FIPS Entry level-compliant driver returns at least **18** for this *InfoType* code. An FIPS In- termediate level-compliant driver returns at least **128** for this *InfoType* code.
SQL_MAX_STATEMENT_ LEN (ODBC 2.0)	**SQLUINTEGER**	Identifies the maximum length (number of characters, including white space) for a SQL statement.

InfoType Code	Data Type Returned	Description
		If there is no maximum length, or if the length is unknown, the value **0** is returned for this *InfoType* code.
SQL_MAX_TABLE_NAME_ LEN (ODBC 1.0)	**SQLUSMALLINT**	Identifies the maximum length for a table name in the data source.
		If there is no maximum length, or if the length is unknown, the value **0** is returned for this *InfoType* code.
		An FIPS Entry level-compliant driver returns at least **18** for this *InfoType* code. An FIPS Intermediate level-compliant driver returns at least **128** for this *InfoType* code.
SQL_MAX_TABLES_IN_ SELECT (ODBC 2.0)	**SQLUSMALLINT**	Identifies the maximum number of tables allowed in the **FROM** clause of a **SELECT** statement.
		If there is no limit, or if the limit is unknown, the value **0** is returned for this *InfoType* code.
		An FIPS Entry level-compliant driver returns at least **15** for this *InfoType* code. An FIPS Intermediate level-compliant driver returns at least **50** for this *InfoType* code.
SQL_MAX_USER_NAME_ LEN (ODBC 2.0)	**SQLUSMALLINT**	Identifies the maximum length for a user name in the data source.
		If there is no maximum length, or if the length is unknown, the value **0** is returned for this *InfoType* code.
SQL_MULT_RESULT_ SETS (ODBC 1.0)	Character string	Indicates whether the data source supports multiple result data sets. The following values can be returned for this *InfoType* code:
		"Y": The data source supports multiple result data sets.
		"N": The data source does not support multiple result data sets.
SQL_MULTIPLE_ACTIVE_ TXN (ODBC 1.0)	Character string	Indicates whether the driver allows multiple active transactions on a single connection. The following values can be returned for this *InfoType* code:
		"Y": Multiple active transactions on a single connection are allowed.

InfoType Code	Data Type Returned	Description
		"N": Only one active transaction at a time is allowed on a connection.
SQL_NEED_LONG_DATA_ LEN (ODBC 2.0)	Character string	Indicates whether the data source needs the length of a long data value before that value is sent to it. The following values can be returned for this *InfoType* code:
		"Y": The data source needs the length of a long data value (the data type is **SQL_LONGVARCHAR**, **SQL_LONGVARBINARY**, or a long data source-specific data type) before that value is sent to it.
		"N": The data source does not need the length of a long data value before that value is sent to the it.
SQL_NON_NULLABLE_ COLUMNS (ODBC 1.0)	SQLUSMALLINT	Indicates whether the data source supports the **NOT NULL** column constraint in **CREATE TABLE** SQL statements. The following values can be returned for this *InfoType* code:
		SQL_NNC_NULL: All columns must be nullable.
		SQL_NNC_NON_NULL: Columns cannot be nullable (the data source supports the **NOT NULL** column constraint in **CREATE TABLE** statements).
		An SQL-92 Entry level-conformant driver returns **SQL_NNC_NON_NULL** for this *InfoType* code.
SQL_NULL_COLLATION (ODBC 2.0)	SQLUSMALLINT	Identifies where NULL values are sorted in a result data set. The following values can be returned for this *InfoType* code:
		SQL_NC_END: NULLs are sorted at the end of the result data set, even if the **ASC** or **DESC** keyword is specified.
		SQL_NC_HIGH: NULLs are sorted at the high end of the result data set, depending on the **ASC** or **DESC** keywords.
		SQL_NC_LOW: NULLs are sorted at the low end of the result data set, depending on the **ASC** or **DESC** keywords.
		SQL_NC_START: NULLs are sorted at the start of the result data set, even if the **ASC** or **DESC** keyword is specified.

InfoType Code	Data Type Returned	Description
SQL_NUMERIC_FUNCTIONS (ODBC 1.0)	**SQLUINTEGER** bitmask	Identifies the scalar numeric functions supported by the driver and its underlying data source. The following bitmask values can be returned for this *InfoType* code:
		SQL_FN_NUM_ABS (ODBC 1.0)
		SQL_FN_NUM_ACOS (ODBC 1.0)
		SQL_FN_NUM_ASIN (ODBC 1.0)
		SQL_FN_NUM_ATAN (ODBC 1.0)
		SQL_FN_NUM_ATAN2 (ODBC 1.0)
		SQL_FN_NUM_CEILING (ODBC 1.0)
		SQL_FN_NUM_COS (ODBC 1.0)
		SQL_FN_NUM_COT (ODBC 1.0)
		SQL_FN_NUM_DEGREES (ODBC 2.0)
		SQL_FN_NUM_EXP (ODBC 1.0)
		SQL_FN_NUM_FLOOR (ODBC 1.0)
		SQL_FN_NUM_LOG (ODBC 1.0)
		SQL_FN_NUM_LOG10 (ODBC 2.0)
		SQL_FN_NUM_MOD (ODBC 1.0)
		SQL_FN_NUM_PI (ODBC 1.0)
		SQL_FN_NUM_POWER (ODBC 2.0)
		SQL_FN_NUM_RADIANS (ODBC 2.0)
		SQL_FN_NUM_RAND (ODBC 1.0)
		SQL_FN_NUM_ROUND (ODBC 2.0)
		SQL_FN_NUM_SIGN (ODBC 1.0)
		SQL_FN_NUM_SIN (ODBC 1.0)
		SQL_FN_NUM_SQRT (ODBC 1.0)
		SQL_FN_NUM_TAN (ODBC 1.0)
		SQL_FN_NUM_TRUNCATE (ODBC 2.0)
SQL_ODBC_API_CONFORMANCE[12] (ODBC 2.0)	16-bit integer	Identifies the level of the ODBC 2.0 interface the driver conforms to. The following values can be returned for this *InfoType* code:
		SQL_OAC_NONE: The driver does not conform to any ODBC 2.0 interface level.
		SQL_OAC_LEVEL1: The driver conforms to the ODBC 2.0 Level 1 interface level.
		SQL_OAC_LEVEL2: The driver conforms to the ODBC 2.0 Level 2 interface level.

InfoType Code	Data Type Returned	Description
SQL_ODBC_INTERFACE_ CONFORMANCE (ODBC 3.0)	**SQLUINTEGER**	Identifies the level of the ODBC 3.x interface the driver conforms to. The following values can be returned for this *InfoType* code:
		SQL_OIC_CORE: The driver conforms to the ODBC 3.x Core interface level. This is the minimum level to which all ODBC drivers are expected to conform. This level includes basic interface elements such as connection functions; functions for preparing and executing SQL statements; basic result data set metadata functions; and basic catalog functions.
		SQL_OIC_LEVEL1: The driver conforms to the ODBC 3.x Level 1 interface level. This level provides all Core level functionality, plus support for scrollable cursors; bookmarks; and positioned updates and deletes.
		SQL_OIC_LEVEL2: The driver conforms to the ODBC 3.x Level 2 interface level. This level provides Core and Level 1 functionality, plus advanced features such as sensitive cursors; update, delete, and refresh by bookmarks; stored procedure support; catalog functions for primary and foreign keys and multi-catalog support.
SQL_ODBC_SQL_ CONFORMANCE[12] (ODBC 2.0)	16-bit integer	Identifies the SQL grammar level to which the driver conforms. The following values can be returned for this *InfoType* code:
		SQL_OSC_MINIMUM: The driver conforms to the Minimum SQL grammar level.
		SQL_OSC_CORE: The driver conforms to the Core SQL grammar level.
		SQL_OSC_EXTENDED: The driver conforms to the Extended SQL grammar level.

InfoType Code	Data Type Returned	Description
SQL_ODBC_VER (ODBC 1.0)	Character string	Identifies the ODBC version to which the ODBC Driver Manager conforms. This information is returned in a string with the format *mm.vv.0000*, where *mm* is the major ODBC version number (as provided by the constant **SQL_SPEC_MAJOR**) and *vv* is the minor ODBC version number (as provided by the constant **SQL_SPEC_MINOR**) (for example, 03.05 translates to major version 3, minor version 5).
		This information is returned by the ODBC Driver Manager; not by the data source.
SQL_OJ_CAPABILITIES (ODBC 2.01)	**SQLUINTEGER** bitmask	Identifies the types of outer joins that are supported by the driver and its underlying data source (as defined in SQL-92). The following bitmask values can be returned for this *InfoType* code:
		SQL_OJ_LEFT: Left outer joins are supported.
		SQL_OJ_RIGHT: Right outer joins are supported.
		SQL_OJ_FULL: Full outer joins are supported.
		SQL_OJ_NESTED: Nested outer joins are supported.
		SQL_OJ_NOT_ORDERED: The column names in the **ON** clause of the outer join do not have to be in the same order as their respective table names in the **OUTER JOIN** clause.
		SQL_OJ_INNER: The inner table (the right table in a left outer join, or the left table in a right outer join) can also be used in an inner join. This does not apply to full outer joins, which do not have an inner table.
		SQL_OJ_ALL_COMPARISON_OPS: The comparison operator in the **ON** clause of the outer join can be any of the ODBC comparison operators. If this bit is not set, only the equals (=) comparison operator can be used in outer joins.
		If the **OUTER JOIN** clause is not supported by the driver or data source, the value **0** is returned for this *InfoType* code.

InfoType Code	Data Type Returned	Description
		See the **SQL_SQL92_RELATIONAL_JOIN_ OPERATORS** *InfoType* code for more information on the support of relational join operators in a **SELECT** statement, as defined by SQL-92.
SQL_ORDER_BY_COLUMNS_ IN_SELECT (ODBC 2.0)	Character string	Indicates whether the columns in an **ORDER BY** clause must also be in the select list. The following values can be returned for this *Info-Type* code: **"Y"**: The columns in an **ORDER BY** clause must be in the select list. **"N"**: The columns in an **ORDER BY** clause do not have to be in the select list.
SQL_PARAM_ARRAY_ROW_ COUNTS (ODBC 3.0)	SQLUINTEGER	Identifies the driver's properties regarding the availability of row counts when a parameterized SQL statement is executed. The following values can be returned for this *InfoType* code: **SQL_PARC_BATCH**: Individual row counts are available for each set of parameter values provided. This is conceptually equivalent to the driver generating a batch of SQL statements, one for each parameter set in the array. Extended error information can be retrieved by using the **SQL_DESC_ARAY_ STATUS_PTR** descriptor header record field. **SQL_PARC_NO_BATCH**: There is only one row count available, which is the cumulative row count resulting from the execution of the SQL statement for the entire array of parameter values. This is conceptually equivalent to treating the SQL statement along with the entire parameter array as one atomic unit. Errors are handled the same as if a single SQL statement were executed.
SQL_PARAM_ARRAY_ SELECTS (ODBC 3.0)	SQLUINTEGER	Identifies the driver's properties regarding the availability of result data sets when a parameterized SQL statement is executed. The following values can be returned for this *InfoType* code: **SQL_PAS_BATCH**: There is one result data set available per set of parameter values provided. This is conceptually equivalent to the driver generating a batch of SQL statements, one for each parameter set in the array.

InfoType Code	Data Type Returned	Description
		SQL_PAS_NO_BATCH: There is only one result data set available, which represents the cumulative result data set resulting from the execution of the SQL statement for the entire array of parameter values. This is conceptually equivalent to treating the SQL statement along with the entire parameter array as one atomic unit.
		SQL_PAS_NO_SELECT: A driver does not allow a result data set-generating statement to be executed with an array of parameter values.
SQL_POS_OPERATIONS[12] (ODBC 2.0)	**SQLUINTEGER** bitmask	Identifies the **SQLSetPos()** function options that are supported by the driver and its underlying data source. The following bitmask values can be returned for this *InfoType* code: **SQL_POS_POSITION** **SQL_POS_REFRESH** **SQL_POS_UPDATE** **SQL_POS_DELETE** **SQL_POS_ADD**
SQL_POSITIONED_ STATEMENTS[12] (ODBC 2.0)	**SQLUINTEGER** bitmask	Identifies the positioned SQL statement options that are supported by the driver and its underlying data source. The following bitmask values can be returned for this *InfoType* code: **SQL_PS_POSITIONED_DELETE** **SQL_PS_POSITIONED_UPDATE** **SQL_PS_SELECT_FOR_UPDATE**
SQL_PROCEDURE_TERM (ODBC 1.0)	Character string	Identifies the data source vendor's name for a stored procedure (for example, "database procedure," "stored procedure," "procedure," "package," or "stored query").
SQL_PROCEDURES (ODBC 1.0)	Character string	Indicates whether the data source supports stored procedures and the driver supports procedure invocation. The following values can be returned for this *InfoType* code: **"Y"**: The data source supports procedures and the driver supports the ODBC procedure invocation syntax. **"N"**: The data source does not support procedures and/or the driver does not support the ODBC procedure invocation syntax.

InfoType Code	Data Type Returned	Description
SQL_QUOTED_IDENTIFIER_CASE (ODBC 2.0)	**SQLUSMALLINT**	Identifies the type of case sensitivity used in quoted identifiers. The following values can be returned for this *InfoType* code: **SQL_IC_UPPER**: Quoted identifiers are not case-sensitive and are stored in uppercase in the system catalog. **SQL_IC_LOWER**: Quoted identifiers are not case-sensitive and are stored in lowercase in the system catalog. **SQL_IC_SENSITIVE**: Quoted identifiers are case-sensitive and are stored in mixed case in the system catalog. **SQL_IC_MIXED**: Quoted identifiers are not case-sensitive and are stored in mixed case in the system catalog. An SQL-92 Entry level-conformant driver returns **SQL_IC_SENSITIVE** for this *InfoType* code.
SQL_ROW_UPDATES (ODBC 1.0)	Character string	Indicates whether keyset-driven or mixed cursors maintain row versions or values for all rows fetched. The following values can be returned for this *InfoType* code: **"Y"**: Keyset-driven or mixed cursors maintain row versions or values for all rows fetched; therefore, they can detect any updates made to a row since it was last fetched. (This only applies to updates, not to deletions or insertions.) The driver can return the **SQL_ROW_UPDATED** flag to the row status array when **SQLFetchScroll()** is called. **"N"**: Keyset-driven or mixed cursors do not maintain row versions or values for fetched rows.
SQL_SCHEMA_TERM[10] (ODBC 1.0)	Character string	Identifies the data source vendor's name for a schema (for example, "owner," "Authorization ID," or "Schema."). This string can be in upper, lower, or mixed case. An SQL-92 Entry level-conformant driver returns "schema" for this *InfoType* code.
SQL_SCHEMA_USAGE[11] (ODBC 2.0)	**SQLUINTEGER** bitmask	Identifies the SQL statements in which schemas can be used. The following bitmask values can be returned for this *InfoType* code:

InfoType Code	Data Type Returned	Description
		SQL_SU_DML_STATEMENTS: Schemas are supported in all Data Manipulation Language (DML) statements: **SELECT**, **INSERT**, **UPDATE**, **DELETE**, and, if supported, **SELECT FOR UPDATE** and positioned **UPDATE** and **DELETE** statements.
		SQL_SU_PROCEDURE _INVOCATION: Schemas are supported in the ODBC procedure invocation statement.
		SQL_SU_TABLE_DEFINITION: Schemas are supported in all table definition statements: **CREATE TABLE**, **CREATE VIEW**, **ALTER TABLE**, **DROP TABLE**, and **DROP VIEW**.
		SQL_SU_INDEX_DEFINITION: Schemas are supported in all index definition statements: **CREATE INDEX** and **DROP INDEX**.
		SQL_SU_PRIVILEGE _DEFINITION: Schemas are supported in all privilege definition statements: **GRANT** and **REVOKE**.
		An SQL-92 Entry level-conformant driver returns that the **SQL_SU_DML_STATEMENTS**, **SQL_SU_TABLE_DEFINITION**, and **SQL_SU_PRIVILEGE_DEFINITION** bitmasks.
SQL_SCROLL_ CONCURRENCY[12] (ODBC 2.0)	**SQLUINTEGER** bitmask	Identifies the scrollable cursor concurrency control options supported by the driver and its underlying data source. The following bitmask values can be returned for this *InfoType* code:
		SQL_SCCO_READ_ONLY: A read-only cursor, in which no updates are allowed, is supported.
		SQL_SCCO_LOCK: A cursor that uses the lowest level of locking sufficient to ensure that the row can be updated is supported.
		SQL_SCCO_OPT_ROWVER: A cursor that uses optimistic concurrency control by comparing row versions is supported.
		SQL_SCCO_OPT_VALUES: A cursor that uses optimistic concurrency control by comparing values is supported.

InfoType Code	Data Type Returned	Description
SQL_SCROLL_OPTIONS (ODBC 1.0)	**SQLUINTEGER** bitmask	Identifies the cursor scroll options that are supported by the driver. The following bitmask values can be returned for this *InfoType* code:
		SQL_SO_FORWARD_ONLY: The cursor only scrolls forward. (ODBC 1.0)
		SQL_SO_STATIC: The data in the result data set is static.(ODBC 2.0)
		SQL_SO_KEYSET_DRIVEN: The driver saves and uses the keys for every row in the result data set. (ODBC 1.0)
		SQL_SO_DYNAMIC: The driver keeps the keys for every row in the rowset (the keyset size is the same as the rowset size). (ODBC 1.0)
		SQL_SO_MIXED: The driver keeps the keys for every row in the keyset, and the keyset size is greater than the rowset size. The cursor is keyset-driven inside the keyset and dynamic outside the keyset. (ODBC 1.0)
SQL_SEARCH_PATTERN_ ESCAPE (ODBC 1.0)	Character string	Identifies the character or characters the driver uses as an escape character that permits the use of the underscore (_) and percent sign (%) pattern match metacharacters as valid characters in search patterns. This escape character is only used for those catalog function arguments that contain pattern value parameters.
		If the driver does not provide a search-pattern escape character, there is no specified limit, or if the limit is unknown, an empty string (" ") is returned for this *InfoType* code.
		Because this information type does not indicate support of an escape character in the **LIKE** predicate, SQL-92 does not include requirements for this *InfoType* code.
SQL_SERVER_NAME (ODBC 1.0)	Character string	Identifies the data source-specific server name associated with the data source.
SQL_SPECIAL_CHARACTERS (ODBC 2.0)	Character string	Identifies all special characters (that is, all characters except *a* through *z*, *A* through *Z*, *0* through *9*, and underscore) that can be used in an identifier name (for example, a table, column, or index name), on the data source. If an identifier contains one or more of these characters, the identifier must be a delimited identifier.

InfoType Code	Data Type Returned	Description
SQL_SQL_CONFORMANCE (ODBC 3.0)	**SQLUINTEGER**	Identifies the level of the SQL-92 SQL standard specification the driver conforms to. The following values can be returned for this *InfoType* code:
		SQL_SC_SQL92_ENTRY: The driver conforms to the SQL-92 Entry level.
		SQL_SC_FIPS127_2_TRANSITIONAL: The driver conforms to the FIPS 127-2 Transitional level.
		SQL_SC_SQL92_INTERMEDIATE: The driver conforms to the SQL-92 Intermediate level.
		SQL_SC_SQL92_FULL: The driver conforms to the SQL-92 Full level.
SQL_SQL92_DATETIME_ FUNCTIONS (ODBC 3.0)	**SQLUINTEGER** bitmask	Identifies the datetime scalar functions that are used by the driver and its underlying data source (as defined in SQL-92). The following bitmask values can be returned for this *Info-Type* code:
		SQL_SDF_CURRENT_DATE **SQL_SDF_CURRENT_TIME** **SQL_SDF_CURRENT_TIMESTAMP**
SQL_SQL92_FOREIGN_KEY_ DELETE_RULE (ODBC 3.0)	**SQLUINTEGER** bitmask	Identifies the rules for using a foreign key in a **DELETE** SQL statement that are supported by the data source (as defined in SQL-92). The following bitmask values can be returned for this *InfoType* code:
		SQL_SFKD_CASCADE **SQL_SFKD_NO_ACTION** **SQL_SFKD_SET_DEFAULT** **SQL_SFKD_SET_NULL**
		An FIPS Transitional level-conformant driver returns all bitmasks shown.
SQL_SQL92_FOREIGN_KEY_ UPDATE_RULE (ODBC 3.0)	**SQLUINTEGER** bitmask	Identifies the rules for using a foreign key in an **UPDATE** SQL statement that are supported by the data source (as defined in SQL-92). The following bitmask values can be returned for this *InfoType* code:
		SQL_SFKU_CASCADE **SQL_SFKU_NO_ACTION** **SQL_SFKU_SET_DEFAULT** **SQL_SFKU_SET_NULL**
		An SQL-92 Full level-conformant driver returns all bitmasks shown.

InfoType Code	Data Type Returned	Description
SQL_SQL92_GRANT (ODBC 3.0)	**SQLUINTEGER** bitmask	Identifies the clauses in the **GRANT** SQL statement that are supported by the data source (as defined in SQL-92). The following bitmask values can be returned for this *Info-Type* code: **SQL_SG_DELETE_TABLE** (Entry level) **SQL_SG_INSERT_COLUMN** (Intermediate level) **SQL_SG_INSERT_TABLE** (Entry level) **SQL_SG_REFERENCES_TABLE** (Entry level) **SQL_SG_REFERENCES_COLUMN** (Entry level) **SQL_SG_SELECT_TABLE** (Entry level) **SQL_SG_UPDATE_COLUMN** (Entry level) **SQL_SG_UPDATE_TABLE** (Entry level) **SQL_SG_USAGE_ON_DOMAIN** (FIPS Transitional level) **SQL_SG_USAGE_ON _CHARACTER_SET** (FIPS Transitional level) **SQL_SG_USAGE_ON_COLLATION** (FIPS Transitional level) **SQL_SG_USAGE_ON_TRANSLATION** (FIPS Transitional level) **SQL_SG_WITH_GRANT_OPTION** (Entry level) The SQL-92 or FIPS conformance level at which this feature needs to be supported is shown in parentheses next to each bitmask.
SQL_SQL92_NUMERIC_VALUE_ FUNCTIONS (ODBC 3.0)	**SQLUINTEGER** bitmask	Identifies the numeric value scalar functions that are supported by the driver and its underlying data source (as defined in SQL-92). The following bitmask values can be returned for this *InfoType* code: **SQL_SNVF_BIT_LENGTH** **SQL_SNVF_CHAR_LENGTH** **SQL_SNVF_CHARACTER_LENGTH** **SQL_SNVF_EXTRACT** **SQL_SNVF_OCTET_LENGTH** **SQL_SNVF_POSITION**
SQL_SQL92_PREDICATES (ODBC 3.0)	**SQLUINTEGER** bitmask	Identifies the predicates of a **SELECT** SQL statement that are supported by the data source (as defined in SQL-92). The following bitmask values can be returned for this *Info-Type* code: **SQL_SP_BETWEEN** (Entry level) **SQL_SP_COMPARISON** (Entry level) **SQL_SP_EXISTS** (Entry level)

SQL_SP_IN (Entry level)

InfoType Code	Data Type Returned	Description
		SQL_SP_ISNOTNULL (Entry level) SQL_SP_ISNULL (Entry level) SQL_SP_LIKE (Entry level) SQL_SP_MATCH_FULL (Full level) SQL_SP_MATCH_PARTIAL (Full level) SQL_SP_MATCH_UNIQUE_FULL (Full level) SQL_SP_MATCH_UNIQUE_PARTIAL (Full level) SQL_SP_OVERLAPS (FIPS Transitional level) SQL_SP_QUANTIFIED_COMPARISON (Entry level) SQL_SP_UNIQUE (Entry level) The SQL-92 or FIPS conformance level at which this feature needs to be supported is shown in parentheses next to each bitmask.
SQL_SQL92_RELATIONAL_ JOIN_OPERATORS (ODBC 3.0)	SQLUINTEGER bitmask	Identifies the relational join operators of a SELECT SQL statement that are supported by the data source (as defined in SQL-92). The following bitmask values can be returned for this InfoType code: SQL_SRJO_CORRESPONDING_CLAUSE (Intermediate level) SQL_SRJO_CROSS_JOIN (Full level) SQL_SRJO_EXCEPT_JOIN (Intermediate level) SQL_SRJO_FULL_OUTER_JOIN (Intermediate level) SQL_SRJO_INNER_JOIN (FIPS Transitional level) SQL_SRJO_INTERSECT_JOIN (Intermediate level) SQL_SRJO_LEFT_OUTER_JOIN (FIPS Transitional level) SQL_SRJO_NATURAL_JOIN (FIPS Transitional level) SQL_SRJO_RIGHT_OUTER_JOIN (FIPS Transitional level) SQL_SRJO_UNION_JOIN (Full level) The SQL-92 or FIPS conformance level at which this feature needs to be supported is shown in parentheses next to each bitmask. SQL_SRJO_INNER_JOIN indicates FIPS support for the INNER JOIN syntax, not for the inner join capability. Support for the INNER JOIN syntax is FIPS Transitional level while support for the inner join capability is FIPS Entry level.

InfoType Code	Data Type Returned	Description
SQL_SQL92_REVOKE (ODBC 3.0)	**SQLUINTEGER** bitmask	Identifies the clauses in the **REVOKE** SQL statement that are supported by the data source (as defined in SQL-92). The following bitmask values can be returned for this *InfoType* code:
		SQL_SR_CASCADE (FIPS Transitional level) **SQL_SR_DELETE_TABLE** (Entry level) **SQL_SR_GRANT_OPTION_FOR** (Intermediate level) **SQL_SR_INSERT_COLUMN** (Intermediate level) **SQL_SR_INSERT_TABLE** (Entry level) **SQL_SR_REFERENCES_COLUMN** (Entry level) **SQL_SR_REFERENCES_TABLE** (Entry level) **SQL_SR_RESTRICT** (FIPS Transitional level) **SQL_SR_SELECT_TABLE** (Entry level) **SQL_SR_UPDATE_COLUMN** (Entry level) **SQL_SR_UPDATE_TABLE** (Entry level) **SQL_SR_USAGE_ON_DOMAIN** (FIPS Transitional level) **SQL_SR_USAGE_ON _CHARACTER_SET** (FIPS Transitional level) **SQL_SR_USAGE_ON_COLLATION** (FIPS Transitional level) **SQL_SR_USAGE_ON_TRANSLATION** (FIPS Transitional level)
		The SQL-92 or FIPS conformance level at which this feature needs to be supported is shown in parentheses next to each bitmask.
SQL_SQL92_ROW_VALUE_ CONSTRUCTOR (ODBC 3.0)	**SQLUINTEGER** bitmask	Identifies the row value constructor expressions of a **SELECT** SQL statement that are supported by the data source (as defined in SQL-92). The following bitmask values can be returned for this *InfoType* code:
		SQL_SRVC_VALUE_EXPRESSION **SQL_SRVC_NULL** **SQL_SRVC_DEFAULT** **SQL_SRVC_ROW_SUBQUERY**
SQL_SQL92_STRING_ FUNCTIONS (ODBC 3.0)	**SQLUINTEGER** bitmask	Identifies the string scalar functions that are supported by the driver and its underlying data source (as defined in SQL-92). The following bitmask values can be returned for this *InfoType* code:
		SQL_SSF_CONVERT **SQL_SSF_LOWER** **SQL_SSF_UPPER** **SQL_SSF_SUBSTRING**

InfoType Code	Data Type Returned	Description
		SQL_SSF_TRANSLATE **SQL_SSF_TRIM_BOTH** **SQL_SSF_TRIM_LEADING** **SQL_SSF_TRIM_TRAILING**
SQL_SQL92_VALUE_ **EXPRESSIONS** (ODBC 3.0)	**SQLUINTEGER** bitmask	Identifies the value expressions that are supported by the data source (as defined in SQL-92). The following bitmask values can be returned for this *InfoType* code: **SQL_SVE_CASE** (Intermediate level) **SQL_SVE_CAST** (FIPS Transitional level) **SQL_SVE_COALESCE** (Intermediate level) **SQL_SVE_NULLIF** (Intermediate level) The SQL-92 or FIPS conformance level at which this feature needs to be supported is shown in parentheses next to each bitmask.
SQL_STANDARD_CLI_ **CONFORMANCE** (ODBC 3.0)	**SQLUINTEGER** bitmask	Identifies the CLI standard(s) the driver conforms to. The following bitmask values can be returned for this *InfoType* code: **SQL_SCC_XOPEN_CLI_VERSION1**: The driver conforms to the X/Open CLI Version 1 standard. **SQL_SCC_ISO92_CLI**: The driver conforms to the ISO-92 CLI standard.
SQL_STATIC_CURSOR_ **ATTRIBUTES1** (ODBC 3.0)	**SQLUINTEGER** bitmask	Defines the first subset of static cursor attributes that are supported by the driver (see the **SQL_STATIC_CURSOR_ATTRIBUTES2** *InfoType* code for the second subset of attributes). The following bitmask values can be returned for this *InfoType* code: **SQL_CA1_NEXT**: The **SQL_FETCH_NEXT** orientation value can be specified with the **SQLFetchScroll()** function when the cursor is a static cursor. **SQL_CA1_ABSOLUTE**: The **SQL_FETCH_FIRST, SQL_FETCH_LAST**, and **SQL_FETCH_ABSOLUTE** orientation values can be specified with the **SQLFetchScroll()** function when the cursor is a static cursor. (The rowset fetched is independent of the current cursor position.)

InfoType Code	Data Type Returned	Description
		SQL_CA1_RELATIVE: The **SQL_FETCH_PRIOR** and **SQL_FETCH_RELATIVE** orientation values can be specified with the **SQLFetchScroll()** function when the cursor is a static cursor. (The rowset fetched is dependent on the current cursor position. Note that this is separate from **SQL_FETCH_NEXT** because in a forward-only cursor, only **SQL_FETCH_NEXT** is supported.)
		SQL_CA1_BOOKMARK: The **SQL_FETCH_BOOKMARK** orientation value can be specified with the **SQLFetchScroll()** function when the cursor is a static cursor.
		SQL_CA1_LOCK_EXCLUSIVE: The **SQL_LOCK_EXCLUSIVE** lock value can be specified with the **SQLSetPos()** function when the cursor is a static cursor.
		SQL_CA1_LOCK_NO_CHANGE: The **SQL_LOCK_NO_CHANGE** lock value can be specified with the **SQLSetPos()** function when the cursor is a static cursor.
		SQL_CA1_LOCK_UNLOCK: The **SQL_LOCK_UNLOCK** lock value can be specified with the **SQLSetPos()** function when the cursor is a static cursor.
		SQL_CA1_POS_POSITION: The **SQL_POSITION** operation value can be specified with the **SQLSetPos()** function when the cursor is a static cursor.
		SQL_CA1_POS_UPDATE: The **SQL_UPDATE** operation value can be specified with the **SQLSetPos()** function when the cursor is a static cursor.
		SQL_CA1_POS_DELETE: The **SQL_DELETE** operation value can be specified with the **SQLSetPos()** function when the cursor is a static cursor.
		SQL_CA1_POS_REFRESH: The **SQL_REFRESH** operation value can be specified with the **SQLSetPos()** function when the cursor is a static cursor.

InfoType Code	Data Type Returned	Description
		SQL_CA1_POSITIONED_UPDATE: An **UPDATE WHERE CURRENT_OF** SQL statement is supported when the cursor is a static cursor. (An SQL-92 Entry level-conformant driver returns this bitmask.)
		SQL_CA1_POSITIONED_DELETE: A **DELETE WHERE CURRENT OF** SQL statement is supported when the cursor is a static cursor. (An SQL-92 Entry level-conformant driver returns this bitmask.)
		SQL_CA1_SELECT_FOR_UPDATE: A **SELECT FOR UPDATE** SQL statement is supported when the cursor is a static cursor. (An SQL-92 Entry level-conformant driver returns this bitmask.)
		SQL_CA1_BULK_ADD: The **SQL_ADD** operation value can be specified with the **SQLBulkOperations()** function when the cursor is a static cursor.
		SQL_CA1_BULK_UPDATE _BY_BOOKMARK: The **SQL_UPDATE_BY_BOOKMARK** operation value can be specified with the **SQLBulkOperations()** function when the cursor is a static cursor.
		SQL_CA1_BULK_DELETE _BY_BOOKMARK: The **SQL_DELETE_BY_BOOKMARK** operation value can be specified with the **SQLBulkOperations()** function when the cursor is a static cursor.
		SQL_CA1_BULK_FETCH _BY_BOOKMARK: The **SQL_FETCH_BY_BOOKMARK** operation value can be specified with the **SQLBulkOperations()** function when the cursor is a static cursor.
		An SQL-92 Intermediate level-conformant driver usually returns the **SQL_CA1_NEXT**, **SQL_CA1_ABSOLUTE**, and **SQL_CA1_REL-ATIVE** bitmask, because it supports scrollable cursors through the embedded **FETCH** SQL statement. Because this does not directly determine the underlying SQL support, however, scrollable cursors may not be supported, even for an SQL-92 Intermediate level-conformant driver.

InfoType Code	Data Type Returned	Description
SQL_STATIC_CURSOR_ ATTRIBUTES2 (ODBC 3.0)	**SQLUINTEGER** b bitmask	Defines the second subset of static cursor at tributes that are supported by the driver (see the **SQL_STATIC_CURSOR_ATTRIBUTES1** *InfoType* code for the first subset of attributes). The following bitmask values can be returned for this *InfoType* code:

SQL_CA2_READ_ONLY_CONCURRENCY: A read-only static cursor in which no updates are allowed is supported. (The **SQL_ATTR_ CONCURRENCY** statement attribute can set to **SQL_CONCUR_READ_ONLY** for a static cursor).

SQL_CA2_LOCK_CONCURRENCY: A static cursor using the lowest level of locking sufficient to ensure the row can be updated is supported. (The **SQL_ATTR_CONCURRENCY** statement attribute can be set to **SQL_ CONCUR_LOCK** for a static cursor). These locks must be consistent with the transaction isolation level set by the **SQL_ATTR_TXN_ ISOLATION** connection attribute.

SQL_CA2_OPT_ROWVER_CONCURRENCY: A static cursor that uses the optimistic concurrency control by comparing row versions is supported. (The **SQL_ATTR_CONCURRENCY** statement attribute can be set to **SQL_ CONCUR_ROWVER** for a static cursor).

SQL_CA2_OPT_VALUES_CONCURRENCY: A static cursor that uses the optimistic concurrency control by comparing values is supported. (The **SQL_ATTR_CONCURRENCY** statement attribute can be set to **SQL_ CONCUR_VALUES** for a static cursor).

SQL_CA2_SENSITIVITY_ADDITIONS: Added rows are visible to a static cursor and the cursor can scroll to the added rows. (Where these rows are added to the cursor is driver-dependent.)

SQL_CA2_SENSITIVITY_DELETIONS: Deleted rows are no longer available to a static cursor, and do not leave a 'hole' in the result data set; after the static cursor scrolls from a deleted row, it cannot return to that row.

InfoType Code	Data Type Returned	Description
		SQL_CA2_SENSITIVITY_UPDATES: Updates to rows are visible to a static cursor; if the static cursor scrolls from and returns to an updated row, the data returned by the cursor is the updated data, not the original data.
		SQL_CA2_MAX_ROWS_SELECT: The **SQL_ATTR_MAX_ROWS** statement attribute affects **SELECT** SQL statements when the cursor is a static cursor.
		SQL_CA2_MAX_ROWS_INSERT: The **SQL_ATTR_MAX_ROWS** statement attribute affects **INSERT** SQL statements when the cursor is a static cursor.
		SQL_CA2_MAX_ROWS_DELETE: The **SQL_ATTR_MAX_ROWS** statement attribute affects **DELETE** SQL statements when the cursor is a static cursor.
		SQL_CA2_MAX_ROWS_UPDATE: The **SQL_ATTR_MAX_ROWS** statement attribute affects **UPDATE** SQL statements when the cursor is a static cursor.
		SQL_CA2_MAX_ROWS_CATALOG: The **SQL_ATTR_MAX_ROWS** statement attribute affects **CATALOG** result data sets when the cursor is a static cursor.
		SQL_CA2_MAX_ROWS_AFFECTS_ALL: The **SQL_ATTR_MAX_ROWS** statement attribute affects **SELECT**, **INSERT**, **UPDATE**, and **DELETE** statements, and **CATALOG** result data sets, when the cursor is a static cursor.
		SQL_CA2_CRC_EXACT: The exact row count is available in the **SQL_DIAG_CURSOR_ROW_COUNT** diagnostic header record field when the cursor is a static cursor.
		SQL_CA2_CRC_APPROXIMATE: An approximate row count is available in the **SQL_DIAG_CURSOR_ROW_COUNT** diagnostic header record field when the cursor is a static cursor.
		SQL_CA2_SIMULATE_NON_UNIQUE: The driver does not guarantee that simulated positioned **UPDATE** or **DELETE** SQL statements will affect only one row when the cursor is a

InfoType Code	Data Type Returned	Description
		static cursor. If a statement affects more than one row, **SQLExecute()** or **SQLExecDirect()** returns SQLSTATE **01**001 (Cursor operation conflict). To set this behavior, an application calls the **SQLSetStmtAttr()** function and sets the **SQL_ATTR_SIMULATE_CURSOR** statement attribute to **SQL_SC_NON_UNIQUE**.
		SQL_CA2_SIMULATE_TRY_UNIQUE: The driver attempts to guarantee that simulated positioned **UPDATE** or **DELETE** SQL statements will affect only one row when the cursor is a static cursor. The driver always executes such statements even if they might affect more than one row, such as when there is no unique key. If the driver cannot guarantee this for a given statement, **SQLExecute()** or **SQLExecDirect()** returns SQLSTATE **01**001 (Cursor operation conflict). To set this behavior, an application calls the **SQLSetStmtAttr()** function and sets the **SQL_ATTR_SIMULATE_CURSOR** statement attribute to **SQL_SC_TRY_UNIQUE**.
		SQL_CA2_SIMULATE_UNIQUE: The driver guarantees that simulated positioned **UPDATE** or **DELETE** SQL statements will affect only one row when the cursor is a static cursor. If the driver cannot guarantee this for a given statement, **SQLExecute()** or **SQLExecDirect()** returns SQLSTATE **01**001 (Cursor operation conflict). To set this behavior, an application calls the **SQLSetStmtAttr()** function and sets the **SQL_ATTR_SIMULATE_CURSOR** statement attribute to **SQL_SC_UNIQUE**.
SQL_STATIC_SENSITIVITY[12] (ODBC 2.0)	**SQLUINTEGER** bitmask	Identifies how changes made to a static or keyset-driven cursor by the **SQLSetPos()** function or by positioned **UPDATE** or **DELETE** SQL statements are detected by an application. The following bitmask values can be returned for this *InfoType* code:
		SQL_SS_ADDITIONS: Added rows are visible to the cursor, and the cursor can scroll to the added rows. (Where these rows are added to the cursor is driver-dependent.)

InfoType Code	Data Type Returned	Description
		SQL_SS_DELETIONS: Deleted rows are no longer available to a cursor and do not leave a 'hole' in the result data set; after the cursor scrolls from a deleted row, it cannot return to that row.
		SQL_SS_UPDATES: Updates to rows are visible to a cursor; if the cursor scrolls from and returns to an updated row, the data returned by the cursor is the updated data, not the original data.
		Whether an application can detect changes made to a result data set by other cursors, including other cursors of the same application, is dependent upon the cursor type.
SQL_STRING_FUNCTIONS (ODBC 1.0)	**SQLUINTEGER** bitmask	Identifies the scalar string functions that are supported by the driver and its underlying data source (as defined in SQL-92). The following bitmask values can be returned for this *InfoType* code:

SQL_FN_STR_ASCII (ODBC 1.0)
SQL_FN_STR_BIT_LENGTH (ODBC 3.0)
SQL_FN_STR_CHAR (ODBC 1.0)
SQL_FN_STR_CHAR_LENGTH (ODBC 3.0)
SQL_FN_STR_CHARACTER_LENGTH (ODBC 3.0)
SQL_FN_STR_CONCAT (ODBC 1.0)
SQL_FN_STR_DIFFERENCE (ODBC 2.0)
SQL_FN_STR_INSERT (ODBC 1.0)
SQL_FN_STR_LCASE (ODBC 1.0)
SQL_FN_STR_LEFT (ODBC 1.0)
SQL_FN_STR_LENGTH (ODBC 1.0)
SQL_FN_STR_LOCATE (ODBC 1.0)
SQL_FN_STR_LTRIM (ODBC 1.0)
SQL_FN_STR_OCTET_LENGTH (ODBC 3.0)
SQL_FN_STR_POSITION (ODBC 3.0)
SQL_FN_STR_REPEAT (ODBC 1.0)
SQL_FN_STR_REPLACE (ODBC 1.0)
SQL_FN_STR_RIGHT (ODBC 1.0)
SQL_FN_STR_RTRIM (ODBC 1.0)
SQL_FN_STR_SOUNDEX (ODBC 2.0)
SQL_FN_STR_SPACE (ODBC 2.0)
SQL_FN_STR_SUBSTRING (ODBC 1.0)
SQL_FN_STR_UCASE (ODBC 1.0)

A driver returns the **SQL_FN_STR_LOCATE** bitmask for this *InfoType* code if an application can call the **LOCATE()** function with the **argument1**, **argument2**, and **position** arguments specified (see Appendix A).

InfoType Code	Data Type Returned	Description
		A driver returns the **SQL_FN_STR_ LOCATE_2**, bitmask for this *InfoType* code if an application can call the **LOCATE()** function with only the **argument1** and **argument2** arguments specified. A driver that fully supports the **LOCATE()** scalar function returns both the **SQL_FN_STR_LOCATE** and the **SQL_FN_STR_LOCATE_2** bitmask for this *InfoType* code.
SQL_SUBQUERIES (ODBC 2.0)	**SQLUINTEGER** bitmask	Identifies the subquery predicates in a **SELECT** SQL statement that are supported by the data source (as defined in SQL-92). The following bitmask values can be returned for this *InfoType* code:
		SQL_SQ_CORRELATED_SUBQUERIES: All predicates supporting subqueries also support correlated subqueries.
		SQL_SQ_COMPARISON **SQL_SQ_EXISTS** **SQL_SQ_IN** **SQL_SQ_QUANTIFIED**
		An SQL-92 Entry level-conformant driver returns all bitmasks shown.
SQL_SYSTEM_FUNCTIONS (ODBC 1.0)	**SQLUINTEGER** bitmask	Identifies the scalar system functions that are supported by the driver and its underlying data source (as defined in SQL-92). The following bitmask values can be returned for this *InfoType* code:
		SQL_FN_SYS_DBNAME **SQL_FN_SYS_IFNULL** **SQL_FN_SYS_USERNAME**
SQL_TABLE_TERM (ODBC 1.0)	Character string	Identifies data source vendor's name for a table (for example, "table" or "file"). This string can be in upper, lower, or mixed case.
		An SQL-92 Full level-compliant driver returns "table" for this *InfoType* code.
SQL_TIMEDATE_ADD_ INTERVALS (ODBC 2.0)	**SQLUINTEGER** bitmask	Identifies the timestamp interval values that are supported by the driver and its underlying data source for the **TIMESTAMPADD()** scalar function. The following bitmask values can be returned for this *InfoType* code:
		SQL_FN_TSI_FRAC_SECOND **SQL_FN_TSI_SECOND** **SQL_FN_TSI_MINUTE**

InfoType Code	Data Type Returned	Description
		SQL_FN_TSI_HOUR **SQL_FN_TSI_DAY** **SQL_FN_TSI_WEEK** **SQL_FN_TSI_MONTH** **SQL_FN_TSI_QUARTER** **SQL_FN_TSI_YEAR** An FIPS Transitional level-conformant driver returns all bitmasks shown.
SQL_TIMEDATE_DIFF_ **INTERVALS** (ODBC 2.0)	**SQLUINTEGER** bitmask	Identifies the timestamp interval values that are supported by the driver and its underlying data source for the **TIMESTAMPDIFF()** scalar function. The following bitmask values can be returned for this *InfoType* code: **SQL_FN_TSI_FRAC_SECOND** **SQL_FN_TSI_SECOND** **SQL_FN_TSI_MINUTE** **SQL_FN_TSI_HOUR** **SQL_FN_TSI_DAY** **SQL_FN_TSI_WEEK** **SQL_FN_TSI_MONTH** **SQL_FN_TSI_QUARTER** **SQL_FN_TSI_YEAR** An FIPS Transitional level-conformant driver returns all bitmasks shown.
SQL_TIMEDATE_ **FUNCTIONS** (ODBC 1.0)	**SQLUINTEGER** bitmask	Identifies the scalar date and time functions that are supported by the driver and its underlying data source. The following bitmask values can be returned for this *InfoType* code: **SQL_FN_TD_CURRENT_DATE** (ODBC 3.0) **SQL_FN_TD_CURRENT_TIME** (ODBC 3.0) **SQL_FN_TD_CURRENT_TIMESTAMP** (ODBC 3.0) **SQL_FN_TD_CURDATE** (ODBC 1.0) **SQL_FN_TD_CURTIME** (ODBC 1.0) **SQL_FN_TD_DAYNAME** (ODBC 2.0) **SQL_FN_TD_DAYOFMONTH** (ODBC 1.0) **SQL_FN_TD_DAYOFWEEK** (ODBC 1.0) **SQL_FN_TD_DAYOFYEAR** (ODBC 1.0) **SQL_FN_TD_EXTRACT** (ODBC 3.0) **SQL_FN_TD_HOUR** (ODBC 1.0) **SQL_FN_TD_MINUTE** (ODBC 1.0) **SQL_FN_TD_MONTH** (ODBC 1.0) **SQL_FN_TD_MONTHNAME** (ODBC 2.0) **SQL_FN_TD_NOW** (ODBC 1.0) **SQL_FN_TD_QUARTER** (ODBC 1.0) **SQL_FN_TD_SECOND** (ODBC 1.0)

InfoType Code	Data Type Returned	Description
		SQL_FN_TD_TIMESTAMPADD (ODBC 2.0) **SQL_FN_TD_TIMESTAMPDIFF** (ODBC 2.0) **SQL_FN_TD_WEEK** (ODBC 1.0) **SQL_FN_TD_YEAR** (ODBC 1.0)
SQL_TXN_CAPABLE (ODBC 1.0)	**SQLUSMALLINT**	Identifies the type of transaction support that is provided by the driver or its underlying data source. The following values can be returned for this *InfoType* code:
		SQL_TC_NONE: Transactions are not supported. (ODBC 1.0)
		SQL_TC_DML: Transactions can only contain Data Manipulation Language (DML) statements: **SELECT**, **INSERT**, **UPDATE**, **DELETE**, if supported, **SELECT FOR UPDATE**, and positioned update and delete statements. If a Data Definition Language (DDL) statement (**CREATE_TABLE**, **CREATE_VIEW**, **ALTER_TABLE**, **DROP_ TABLE**, and **DROP_VIEW**) is encountered in a transaction, an error occurs. (ODBC 1.0)
		SQL_TC_DDL_COMMIT: Transactions can only contain DML statements. If a DDL statement is encountered in a transaction, the transaction will be committed. (ODBC 2.0)
		SQL_TC_DDL_IGNORE: Transactions can only contain DML statements. If a DDL statement is encountered in a transaction, it will be ignored. (ODBC 2.0)
		SQL_TC_ALL: Transactions can contain DML statements and DDL statements, in any order. (ODBC 1.0)
		Because support of transactions is mandatory in SQL-92, an SQL-92 conformant driver (any level) never returns **SQL_TC_NONE**.
SQL_TXN_ISOLATION_ OPTION (ODBC 1.0)	**SQLUINTEGER** bitmask	Identifies the transaction isolation levels that are supported by the driver or data source. The following terms are used to define transaction isolation levels:

InfoType Code	Data Type Returned	Description
		Dirty Read: Transaction 1 changes a row. Transaction 2 reads the changed row before Transaction 1 commits the change. If Transaction 1 rolls back the change, Transaction 2 will have read a row that is considered to have never existed.
		Nonrepeatable Read: Transaction 1 reads a row. Transaction 2 updates or deletes that row and commits this change. If Transaction 1 attempts to reread the row, it receives different row values or discovers that the row has been deleted.
		Phantom: Transaction 1 reads a set of rows that satisfy some search criteria. Transaction 2 generates one or more rows (either through inserts or updates) that match the search criteria. If Transaction 1 re-executes the statement that reads the rows, it receives a different set of rows.
		If the data source supports transactions, the driver returns one of the following bitmasks:
		SQL_TXN_READ_UNCOMMITTED: Dirty reads, nonrepeatable reads, and phantoms are possible.
		SQL_TXN_READ_COMMITTED: Dirty reads are not possible. Nonrepeatable reads and phantoms are possible.
		SQL_TXN_REPEATABLE_READ: Dirty reads and nonrepeatable reads are not possible. Phantoms are possible.
		SQL_TXN_SERIALIZABLE: Transactions are serializable. Serializable transactions do not allow dirty reads, nonrepeatable reads, or phantoms.
		If transactions are not supported by the data source, the value 0 is returned for this *InfoType* code.
		An SQL-92 Entry level-conformant driver returns **SQL_TXN_SERIALIZABLE** for this *InfoType* code. A FIPS Transitional level-conformant driver returns all bitmasks shown.

InfoType Code	Data Type Returned	Description
SQL_UNION (ODBC 2.0)	**SQLUINTEGER** bitmask	Identifies how the **UNION** clause is supported by the data source. The following bitmask values can be returned for this *Info-Type* code: **SQL_U_UNION**: The data source supports the **UNION** clause. **SQL_U_UNION_ALL**: The data source supports the **ALL** keyword in the **UNION** clause. (The **SQLGetInfo()** function returns both **SQL_U_UNION** and **SQL_U_UNION_ALL** in this case.) An SQL-92 Entry level-conformant driver returns all bitmasks shown.
SQL_USER_NAME (ODBC 1.0)	Character string	Identifies the user name used in a particular database (this name can be different from the login name).
SQL_XOPEN_CLI_YEAR (ODBC 3.0)	Character string	Identifies the publication year of the X/Open standards specification that the version of the ODBC Driver Manager being used fully complies with.

(Adapted from the table on pages 759–809 of *Microsoft ODBC 3.0 Software Development Kit & Programmer's Reference*.)

[1]In ODBC 2.0 and earlier, this information type was named **SQL_QUALIFIER_LOCATION**.

[2]In ODBC 2.0 and earlier, this information type was named **SQL_QUALIFIER_NAME_SEPARATOR**.

[3]In ODBC 2.0 and earlier, this information type was named **SQL_QUALIFIER_TERM**.

[4]In ODBC 2.0 and earlier, this information type was named **SQL_QUALIFIER_USAGE**.

[5]In ODBC 2.0 and earlier, this information type was named **SQL_ODBC_SQL_OPT_IEF**.

[6]In ODBC 2.0 and earlier, this information type was named **SQL_MAX_QUALIFIER_NAME_LEN**.

[7]In ODBC 2.0 and earlier, this information type was named **SQL_ACTIVE_STATEMENTS**.

[8]In ODBC 2.0 and earlier, this information type was named **SQL_ACTIVE_CONNECTIONS**.

[9]In ODBC 2.0 and earlier, this information type was named **SQL_MAX_OWNER_NAME_LEN**.

[10]In ODBC 2.0 and earlier, this information type was named **SQL_OWNER_TERM**.

[11]In ODBC 2.0 and earlier, this information type was named **SQL_OWNER_USAGE**.

[12]This information type was supported in ODBC 2.0; it is not supported in ODBC 3.x.

APPENDIX D

How The Example Programs Were Developed

All the example programs shown in this book were developed with Visual C++ 5.0 on the Windows 95 and Windows NT 4.0 operating system. When possible, the examples were developed using the *Northwind* sample database that is automatically installed when Microsoft Access (or the Microsoft Access component of Microsoft Office) is installed. However, because the Microsoft ODBC driver for Microsoft Access does not provide support for all the ODBC API functions available, some examples were developed using Microsoft SQL Server.

Setting Up the *Northwind* Data Source

To create an ODBC User Data Source for the *Northwind* sample database, perform the following steps:

1. Invoke the *ODBC Data Source Administrator* by placing the cursor on the *32-bit ODBC* icon on the *Control Panel* and double-clicking the right mouse button. (See Figure D–1.)

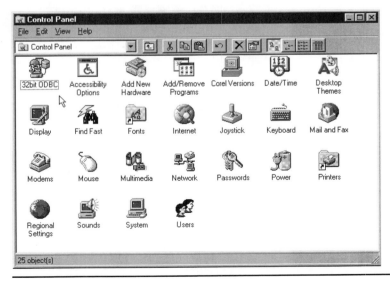

Figure D–1

2. Next, select the *MS Access 97 Database* name on the *User DSN* page of the *ODBC Data Source Administrator* and press the *Add...* push button. (See Figure D–2.)

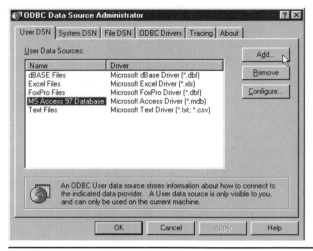

Figure D–2

3. Then, highlight the *Microsoft Access Driver (*.mdb)* driver on the *Create New Data Source* panel and press the *Finish* push button. (See Figure D–3.)

Figure D–3

4. Next, press the *Select...* push button on the *ODBC Microsoft Access 97 Setup* panel. (See Figure D–4.)

Figure D–4

5. Locate the **Northwind.mdb** database in the E:\Microsoft Office\Office\Samples directory and highlight it. Then push the OK push button. (See Figure D–5.)

Figure D–5

NOTE: *On my PC, Microsoft Office is installed on drive E:. On your PC, this may be different.*

6. After the Northwind database is selected, enter **"Northwind"** in the Data Source Name field on the ODBC Microsoft Access 97 Setup panel. Enter the description **"Northwind Sample Database"** in the Description field, and press the OK push button. (See Figure D–6.)

Figure D–6

7. Finally, when control is returned to the *User DSN* page of the *ODBC Data Source Administrator*, push the *OK* push button. (See Figure D–7.)

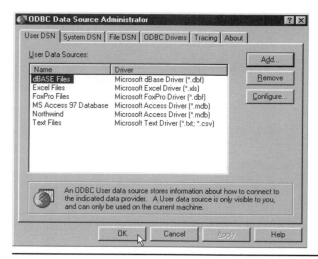

Figure D–7

How the Examples are Stored on the Diskette

To aid in application development, each of the examples shown throughout the book are provided in electronic format on the diskette provided with this book. This diskette contains the following nine directories:

Chapter_07	Chapter_10	Chapter_13
Chapter_08	Chapter_11	Chapter_14
Chapter_09	Chapter_12	Chapter_15

Each of these directories contains the examples presented in the corresponding chapters in the book. Table D–1 lists the ODBC APIs covered in each chapter, along with the corresponding example program name and the data source with which the example program works.

Table D–1   The ODBC API Example Programs

Function Name	Example Name	Data Source
Chapter 7—Initializing ODBC and Connecting to a Data Source or Driver		
SQLAllocHandle()	CH7EX1.CPP	MS Access (*Northwind*)
SQLAllocEnv()	CH7EX2.CPP	MS Access (*Northwind*)
SQLAllocConnect()	CH7EX2.CPP	MS Access (*Northwind*)
SQLConnect()	CH7EX1.CPP	MS Access (*Northwind*)
SQLDriverConnect()	CH7EX3.CPP	MS Access (*Northwind*)
SQLBrowseConnect()	CH7EX4.CPP	MS SQL Server
SQLDisconnect()	CH7EX1.CPP	MS Access (*Northwind*)
SQLFreeHandle()	CH7EX1.CPP	MS Access (*Northwind*)
SQLFreeConnect()	CH7EX2.CPP	MS Access (*Northwind*)
SQLFreeEnv()	CH7EX2.CPP	MS Access (*Northwind*)
Chapter 8—Determining and Controlling Data Source/Driver Capabilities		
SQLDataSources()	CH8EX1.CPP	MS Access (*Northwind*)
SQLDrivers()	CH8EX2.CPP	MS Access (*Northwind*)
SQLGetInfo()	CH8EX3.CPP	MS Access (*Northwind*)
SQLGetFunctions()	CH8EX4.CPP	MS Access (*Northwind*)
SQLGetTypeInfo()	CH8EX5.CPP	MS Access (*Northwind*)

Table D–1 Continued

Function Name	Example Name	Data Source
SQLGetEnvAttr()	CH8EX6.CPP	MS Access (*Northwind*)
SQLSetEnvAttr()	CH8EX6.CPP	MS Access (*Northwind*)
SQLGetConnectAttr()	CH8EX7.CPP	MS Access (*Northwind*)
SQLSetConnectAttr()	CH8EX7.CPP	MS Access (*Northwind*)
SQLGetConnectOption()	CH8EX8.CPP	MS Access (*Northwind*)
SQLSetConnectOption()	CH8EX8.CPP	MS Access (*Northwind*)
SQLGetStmtAttr()	CH8EX9.CPP	MS Access (*Northwind*)
SQLSetStmtAttr()	CH8EX9.CPP	MS Access (*Northwind*)
SQLGetStmtOption()	CH8EX10.CPP	MS Access (*Northwind*)
SQLSetStmtOption()	CH8EX10.CPP	MS Access (*Northwind*)
Chapter 9—Preparing and Executing SQL Statements		
SQLAllocStmt()	CH9EX1.CPP	MS Access (*Northwind*)
SQLPrepare()	CH9EX2.CPP	MS Access (*Northwind*)
SQLBindParameter()	CH9EX3.CPP	MS Access (*Northwind*)
SQLBindParameter() (column-wise binding)	CH9EX3A.CPP	MS SQL Server
SQLBindParameter() (row-wise binding)	CH9EX3B.CPP	MS SQL Server
SQLSetParam()	CH9EX4.CPP	MS Access (*Northwind*)
SQLParamOptions()	CH9EX5.CPP	MS SQL Server
SQLNumParams()	CH9EX6.CPP	MS Access (*Northwind*)
SQLDescribeParam()	CH9EX7.CPP	MS SQL Server
SQLExecute()	CH9EX2.CPP	MS Access (*Northwind*)
SQLExecDirect()	CH9EX8.CPP	MS Access (*Northwind*)
SQLNativeSq()	CH9EX9.CPP	MS Access (*Northwind*)
SQLParamData()	CH9EX10.CPP	MS SQL Server[1]
SQLPutData()	CH9EX10.CPP	MS SQL Server
SQLCancel()	CH9EX10.CPP	MS SQL Server

Table D–1 Continued

Function Name	Example Name	Data Source
SQLEndTran()	CH9EX11.CPP	MS Access (*Northwind*)
SQLTransact()	CH9EX12.CPP	MS Access (*Northwind*)
SQLFreeStmt()	CH9EX1.CPP	MS Access (*Northwind*)
Chapter 10—Retrieving Results (Basic)		
SQLNumResultCols()	CH10EX1.CPP	MS Access (*Northwind*)
SQLDescribeCol()	CH10EX2.CPP	MS Access (*Northwind*)
SQLColAttribute()	CH10EX3.CPP	MS Access (*Northwind*)
SQLColAttributes()	CH10EX4.CPP	MS Access (*Northwind*)
SQLBindCol()	CH10EX5.CPP	MS Access (*Northwind*)
SQLGetCursorName()	CH10EX6.CPP	MS Access (*Northwind*)
SQLSetCursorName()	CH10EX7.CPP	MS Access (*Northwind*)
SQLFetch()	CH10EX5.CPP	MS Access (*Northwind*)
SQLCloseCursor()	CH10EX8.CPP	MS Access (*Northwind*)
SQLGetData()	CH10EX9.CPP	MS Access (*Northwind*)
Chapter 11—Retrieving Results (Advanced)		
SQLFetchScroll() (column-wise binding)	CH11EX1A.CPP	MS Access (*Northwind*)
SQLFetchScroll() (row-wise binding)	CH11EX1B.CPP	MS Access (*Northwind*)
SQLSetScrollOptions()	CH11EX2.CPP	MS Access (*Northwind*)
SQLExtendedFetch()	CH11EX3.CPP	MS Access (*Northwind*)
SQLMoreResults()	CH11EX4.CPP	MS SQL Server
Chapter 12—Modifying Data		
SQLSetPos() (positioning)	CH12EX1A.CPP	MS Access (*Northwind*)
SQLSetPos() (updating)	CH12EX1B.CPP	MS Access (*Northwind*)
SQLBulkOperations()	CH12EX2.CPP	MS Access (*Northwind*)
SQLRowCount()	CH12EX3.CPP	MS Access (*Northwind*)

Table D–1   Continued

Function Name	Example Name	Data Source
Chapter 13—Working With Descriptors		
SQLGetDescRec()	**CH13EX1.CPP**	MS SQL Server
SQLSetDescRec()	**CH13EX2.CPP**	MS SQL Server
SQLGetDescField()	**CH13EX3.CPP**	MS SQL Server
SQLSetDescField()	**CH13EX4.CPP**	MS SQL Server
SQLCopyDesc()	**CH13EX5.CPP**	MS SQL Server
Chapter 14—Retrieving Status and Error Information		
SQLGetDiagRec()	**CH14EX1.CPP**	MS Access (*Northwind*)
SQLError()	**CH14EX2.CPP**	MS Access (*Northwind*)
SQLGetDiagField()	**CH14EX3.CPP**	MS Access (*Northwind*)
Chapter 15—Querying The Data Source System Catalog		
SQLTables()	**CH15EX1.CPP**	MS Access (*Northwind*)
SQLTablePrivileges()	**CH15EX2.CPP**	MS SQL Server
SQLColumns()	**CH15EX3.CPP**	MS Access (*Northwind*)
SQLColumnPrivileges()	**CH15EX4.CPP**	MS SQL Server
SQLSpecialColumns()	**CH15EX5.CPP**	MS Access (*Northwind*)
SQLStatistics()	**CH15EX6.CPP**	MS Access (*Northwind*)
SQLPrimaryKeys()	**CH15EX7.CPP**	MS SQL Server
SQLForeignKeys()	**CH15EX8.CPP**	MS SQL Server
SQLProcedures()	**CH15EX9.CPP**	MS Access (*Northwind*)
SQLProcedureColumns()	**CH15EX10.CPP**	MS Access (Northwind)

COMPILING AND EXECUTING THE EXAMPLES   You can perform following steps to recompile and execute the example programs stored on the diskette:

1. Create a directory on your hard drive and copy the example program into it.
2. Invoke the Visual C++ 5.0 Developer Studio.

3. Select New from the Visual C++ 5.0 Developer Studio File menu.

4. When the New panel is displayed, highlight *Win32 Console Application,* enter the project location (the appropriate hard drive and directory) and a project name corresponding to the directory containing the example program. Then press the *OK* push button. (See Figure D–8.)

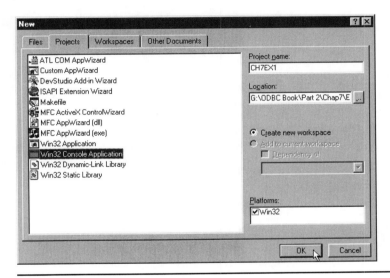

Figure D–8

5. Once the new project is created, select the *Files* tab in the right-hand window, highlight the project files entry, press the right mouse button to display the pop-up menu, and select the *Add Files To Project...* menu item. (See Figure D–9.)

6. Highlight the example file name shown in the *Insert Files into Project* window (this should be the file copied from the diskette) and press the *OK* push button. (See Figure D–10.)

7. Compile and execute the program.

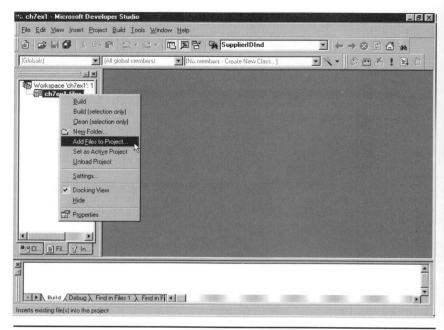

Figure D–9

Figure D–10

NOTE: *An appropriate Data Source Name, User ID, and Password must be provided in the connection string used to connect to a Microsoft SQL Server database. However, because the tables used with the Microsoft SQL Server examples are not part of a default sample database (like the* Northwind *database tables are), these examples will have to be modified (that is, the SQL statement and parameter/column bindings will have to be changed) before they can be executed.*

BIBLIOGRAPHY

Date, C.J. with Hugh Darwen. 1993. *A Guide to the SQL Standard, Third Edition*. Reading MA.: Addison-Wesley Publishing Company.

Geiger, Kyle. 1995. *Inside ODBC*. Redmond WA.: Microsoft Press.

Joint Technical Committee ISO/IEC JTC 1, and Information technology, Subcommittee SC 21. 1995. *ISO/IEC 9075-3 Information technology—Database languages—SQL—Part 3: Call-Level Interface (SQL/CLI)*, First Edition. Genéve Switzerland. ISO/IEC.

Microsoft Corporation. 1994. *Microsoft ODBC 2.0 Software Programmer's Reference and SDK Guide*. Redmond WA.: Microsoft Press.

Microsoft Corporation. 1997. *Microsoft ODBC 3.0 Software Development Kit & Programmer's Reference*. Redmond WA.: Microsoft Press.

Microsoft Corporation. 1998. *Microsoft ODBC 3.5 SDK RC3 (BETA) On-Line Help (ODBC.HLP)*. Redmond WA.: Microsoft Corporation.

Whiting, Bill, Bryan Morgan, and Jeff Perkins. 1996. *Teach Yourself ODBC Programming in 21 Days*. Indianapolis, IN.: Sams Publishing.

The X/Open Company Limited. 1995. *X/Open CAE Specification—Data Management:SQL Call Level Interface (CLI)—Document Number C451*. Reading, U.K..: X/Open Company Ltd.

Index

API Index

ABOUT THE AUTHOR

Roger Sanders is an Educational Multimedia Assets Specialist with the Secondary Education development group at SAS Institute Inc. He has been designing and programming software applications for the IBM Personal Computer for more than 15 years and specializes in system programming in C, C++, and 80×86 Assembly Language. He has written several computer magazine articles, and he is the author of *The Developer's Handbook to DB2 for Common Servers*. His background in database application design and development is extensive. It includes experience with DB2 for Common Servers, DB2 for MVS, INGRES, dBASE, and Microsoft ACCESS.